UNIX Administration

A Comprehensive Sourcebook for Effective Systems and Network Management

INTERNET and COMMUNICATIONS

This new book series presents the latest research and technological developments in the field of internet and multimedia systems and applications. We remain committed to publishing high-quality reference and technical books written by experts in the field.

If you are interested in writing, editing, or contributing to a volume in this series, or if you have suggestions for needed books, please contact Dr. Borko Furht at the following address:

Dr. Borko Furht, Director
Multimedia Laboratory
Department of Computer Science and Engineering
Florida Atlantic University
777 Glades Road
Boca Raton, FL 33431 U.S.A.

E-mail: borko@cse.fau.edu

UNIX Administration

A Comprehensive Sourcebook for Effective Systems and Network Management

Bozidar Levi

CRC PRESS

Boca Raton London New York Washington, D.C.

Library of Congress Cataloging-in-Publication Data

Levi, Bozidar.
UNIX administration : a comprehensive sourcebook for effective systems and network management / by Bozidar Levi.
p. cm. -- (Internet and data comunications series
Includes bibliographical references and index.
ISBN 0-8493-1351-1 (alk. paper)
1. Operating systems (Computers) 2.UNIX System V (Computer file) I. Title. II. Series.

QA76.76.O63 L4853 2002
005.4'82—dc21 2002017438
CIP

Direct all inquiries to CRC Press LLC, 2000 N.W. Corporate Blvd., Boca Raton, Florida 33431.

International Standard Book Number 0-8493-1351-1
Library of Congress Card Number 2002017438
Printed in the United States of America 1 2 3 4 5 6 7 8 9 0
Printed on acid-free paper

Preface

Unix Administration: A Comprehensive Sourcebook for Effective Systems and Network Management attempts to make UNIX essential and network administrative topics more accessible to a wide audience, including both academic and professional users. The selected book title fully reflects this idea: to present UNIX administration in a comprehensive way and enable effective systems and network management based on the presented text.

To achieve this goal, the book gives equal weight to UNIX systems and network concepts and their practical implementations. During the many years that I have worked as a computer hardware designer and programmer, and most recently as a UNIX administrator, I have tackled many practical UNIX and network problems. Working for different employers, I faced real-life situations in an academic environment, in the financial industry and the retail industry, and on the Internet. At the same time, while teaching at New York University and Columbia University, I met many novices in this field and learned an optimal and quick way to teach UNIX administration. This accumulated knowledge and experience have helped me to select UNIX topics that are of the utmost relevance to successful administration, and those topics served as the basis for this book. Some additional UNIX topics, significant from a historical point of view, or necessary for an overall presentation of UNIX administration, are also included. In concert, they create a logical and comprehensive text, easy to read and follow. It is impossible to say that everything existing in the UNIX administration arena is covered here — it would be impossible to put it all in a single book. However, the principal and most important UNIX administrative topics that make a complete UNIX administration environment and a sufficient base for overall UNIX management are fully explored.

UNIX was developed in two different environments: academic and industrial. Consequently, two main UNIX platforms, Berkeley UNIX (also known as Berkeley Software Distribution — BSD UNIX) and System V UNIX (also known as AT&T UNIX) have emerged. Both platforms have coexisted for many years, continuing to develop and promote UNIX. Simultaneously, many vendors started to develop their own UNIX flavors by trying to adopt the best from the two main platforms. Today we see a number of vendor-specific UNIX flavors, all based on these two main platforms. In most cases, it is even difficult to evaluate which platform is prevailing — each flavor is simply a hybrid of both platforms, often bringing something new and specific to the UNIX market. However, upon looking further at specific UNIX segments — for example, file system management, printing, accounting, etc. — one is more easily able to describe them as mostly Berkeley-like, or System V-like.

Networking, which appeared later, at a time when UNIX had already developed into quite a mature product, merged very efficiently into both UNIX platforms and virtually eliminated their differences in the network area. The TCP/IP protocols became a network standard, while UNIX provided the main underlying layer of core network services. The net effect was that UNIX network administration is more or less uniform among many existing UNIX flavors, although far from identical. Differences in kernels, available commands, and some other details do make a difference in some cases.

This book basically follows a historical UNIX path, i.e., it addresses UNIX administration with an eye to the two main UNIX platforms, Berkeley and System V. For easier conceptual understanding of administrative topics, Berkeley UNIX seems more convenient. This is probably the case, because it was primarily developed in academia. By following that pattern for each individual UNIX topic, the Berkeley platform is discussed first and afterward its System V counterpart. A practical implementation of a specific UNIX topic is accomplished through many real-life examples from different vendor-specific UNIX flavors. Now, at the start of a new millennium, Solaris, HP-UX, Linux, and AIX and SGI IRIX are the most dominant flavors, and thus, this book mainly addresses them. SunOS, as a dominant UNIX flavor for many years, is also occasionally quoted, especially because SunOS is a typical representive of Berkeley UNIX, and is still widely in use. In combination, the book is an instrumental source of the information needed to learn UNIX administration and efficiently perform the most essential and network-related UNIX administrative tasks.

This book presents a reliable UNIX administration reference book for practical UNIX implementation. However, it could be easily used for educational purposes, as a textbook, due to its education-related organization, conceptual clarifications, as well as an appropriate selection of administrative topics. Not many books of this kind are on the market that are so diverse and detailed oriented at the same time. Many practical examples and specific administrative procedures, logically connected to theoretical issues, strongly support the educational significance of this book.

UNIX Administration Sourcebook started as handouts prepared for the course "UNIX System Administration" at NYU's School of Continuous and Professional Studies and has been in full use for quite some time with very encouraging feedback from students. During this time, a number of text improvements and updates have been made, until this version was reached. UNIX is changing continually (supposedly always better) and this text presents an up-to-date version organized in a logical and comprehensive way. It can be easily used by beginners, as well as experienced administrators.

There are many books related to UNIX systems and network administration, and they all contribute to this complex arena in some way. This book contains elements that make it different from others:

- The comprehensive organization and presentation of the text
- The condensed explanation of concepts and their practical implementations
- The inclusion of both UNIX systems and network administration, in full detail
- The choice of crucial administrative topics and their full coverage
- The discussion of the most common UNIX flavors
- The text is self-sufficient for successful administration on a daily basis
- The coverage of all basic and many advanced UNIX administrative topics
- The coverage of X window system, a complex administrative topic almost always excluded from UNIX administration books
- Up-to-date text with coverage of the latest main UNIX flavors and releases
- Usefulness as a reference book as well as a textbook
- A careful selection of relevant examples based on many years of professional experience in this field
- And last but not least, many years use of the initial book text in a handout form demonstrates high usability of the text by students and professionals.

The book consists of four parts: UNIX Administration, Network Administration, Supplemental UNIX Topics, and Case Studies. A total of 82 figures fully support the existing text. Such an organization is logical, comprehensive, and easy to read.

UNIX Administration covers essential UNIX administration and contains 13 chapters. The first three chapters are an introduction to the UNIX operating system, an overview of a certain number of selected UNIX topics important for the administration, and an overview of the UNIX administration itself. The remaining chapters cover UNIX system startup and shutdown, detailed UNIX filesystem management and layout, user account management and system security, logging and printing subsystems, terminals, system backup and recovery, and time-related UNIX facilities. In combination they provide sufficient material for a successful "out-of-network" UNIX administration, which can also be called *stand-alone* UNIX administration.

Network Administration covers network-related UNIX administration and contains eight chapters. The first two chapters present an introduction to networking and, more specifically, to TCP/IP networks. Other chapters cover the main network services: domain name system (DNS), network information system (NIS), network filesystem (NFS), UNIX remote commands and secure shell, electronic mail, and the most common network applications such as telnet and ftp. Selected network topics present core network services with which each networked UNIX system has to comply.

Supplemental UNIX Topics covers several more subjects, which, by implementing certain criteria, make UNIX administration complete. These administrative topics are often handled separately, out of basic UNIX administration. Four chapters include X window system, kernel reconfiguration, modems and related UNIX facilities, and intranet technologies. X windowing, with its quite complex administration, is almost always handled separately, as well as most of the advanced intranet technologies.

Finally, Case Studies are presented in three chapters on subjects extremely important to practical UNIX implementation: UNIX installation, disk space upgrade, and several emergency situations that every UNIX administrator should expect to face at some point. Most administrators have experienced a need to bypass a "forgotten root password," and while this routine bypassing task varies among different flavors, the general hints presented can be helpful in any case.

Finally, I would like to point out that during many years of active UNIX administration, I was always thinking how nice it would be to have a single book in front of me, which together with standard UNIX online documentation (UNIX manual pages) would be sufficient for effective usual daily systems and network management. This book is a response to that idea.

Dr. Bozidar Levi
New York City
October 2001

About the Author

Dr. Bozidar Levi is an electronics engineer by education, a hardware designer and programmer by evocation, and an UNIX administration expert by profession. He received his education at the University of Belgrade, Yugoslavia, and was awarded B.S., M.S., and Ph.D. degrees in electronics and computer science. Dr. Levi joined Belgrade's Pupin Institute and had a successful career path from a junior associate to a top senior scientist, dealing with many challenging projects — mostly as a project leader. A majority of the devices and equipment he designed are still operational worldwide.

UNIX was a logical continuation of Dr. Levi's rich and extensive IT background. He has focused with enthusiasm and strength on system and network administration issues. Again, Dr. Levi made a full circle by working in academia (Hunter College of the City University of New York), in the financial industry (New York Stock Exchange), retail industry (J. Crew), and currently the Internet (Linkshare Corporation). Such a wide working range has resulted in accumulated administrative expertise and experience.

Dr. Levi has also fully exercised his educational mission: first by teaching at the University of Belgrade, and now at Columbia and New York University. His teaching has always been a rational balance between theory and practice, with strong emphasis on real-life problems. Many of his former students are employed as IT professionals in various industrial and non-industrial segments nationwide. *UNIX Administration: A Comprehensive Sourcebook for Effective Systems and Network Management* is an extended and updated version of his UNIX administration course syllabi, which are appreciated and highly rated by his students. The book merges the required theoretical background with the practical needs for a successful UNIX administration in almost any environment.

Dr. Levi has also appeared as an author or co-author in more than 60 published and presented articles and papers and has received several awards for excellence and achievement.

Contents

Section I UNIX Administration

Section III SUPPLEMENTAL UNIX TOPICS

Section IV CASE STUDIES

Section I

UNIX Administration

1

UNIX — Introductory Notes

1.1 UNIX Operating System

UNIX is a popular time-sharing operating system originally intended for program development and document preparation, but later widely accepted for a number of implementations. UNIX is today's most ubiquitous multi-user operating system, with no indication of any diminishment in the near future. Today, when a period of several years represents the lifetime of many successful IT products, UNIX is still considered the most stable and the most secure operating system on the market, three decades after its appearance. Of course, during 30 years of existence UNIX has changed a great deal, adapting to new requirements; it is hard to compare today's modern UNIX flavors with initial (now obsolete) UNIX versions. In fact, these changes and adaptations are unique to the UNIX operating system; no other operating system has so successfully evolved, time and again, to meet modern needs. The concept and basic design of UNIX deserve the credit for this remarkable longevity, as they provide the necessary flexibility for the permanent changes required to make UNIX suitable for many new applications.

UNIX, like any other operating system, is an integrated collection of programs that act as links between the computer system and its users, providing three primary functions:

1. Creating and managing a **filesystem** (sets of files stored in hierarchical-structured directories)
2. Running programs
3. Using system devices attached to the computer

UNIX was written in the C computer language, with careful isolation and confinement of machine-dependent routines, so that it might be easily ported to different computer systems. As a result, versions of UNIX were available for personal computers, workstations, minicomputers, mainframes, and supercomputers. It is somewhat curious to note that portability was not a design objective during UNIX development; rather, it came as a consequence of coding the system in a higher-level language. Upon realizing the importance of portability, the designers of UNIX confined hardware-dependent code to a few modules within the **kernel** (coded in assembler) in order to facilitate porting.

The *kernel* is the "core" of the UNIX operating system. It provides services such as a filesystem, memory management, CPU scheduling, and device I/O for programs. Typically, the kernel interacts directly with the underlying hardware; therefore, it must be adapted to the unique machine architecture. However, there were some implementations of UNIX in which the kernel interacted with another underlying system that in turn controlled the hardware. The kernel keeps track of who is logged in, as well as the locations of all files; it also accepts and enables instruction executions received from the shell as the output of interpreted commands. The kernel provides a limited number (typically between 60 and 200) of direct entry points through which an active process can obtain services from the kernel. These direct entry points are system calls (also known as *UNIX internals*). The actual machine instructions required to invoke a *system call*, along with the method used to pass arguments and results between the process and the kernel, vary from machine to machine.

The machine-dependent parts of the kernel were cleverly isolated from the main kernel code and were relatively easy to construct once their purpose had been defined. The machine-dependent parts of the kernel include:

- Low-level system initialization and bootstrap
- Fault, trap, interrupt, and exception handling
- Memory management: hardware address translation
- Low-level kernel/user mode process context switching
- I/O device drivers and device initialization code

The rest of the UNIX kernel is extremely transportable and is largely made up of the system call interface from which application programs request services.

An early implementation of the UNIX kernel consisted of some 10,000 lines of C code and approximately 1000 lines of assembler code. These figures represent some 5 to 10% of the total UNIX code. When the original assembler version was recoded in C, the size and execution time of the kernel increased by some 30%. UNIX designers reasoned that the benefits of coding the system in a higher-level language far outweighed the resulting performance drawback. These benefits included portability, higher programmer productivity, ease of maintenance, and the ability to use complex algorithms to provide more sophisticated functions. Some of these algorithms could hardly have been contemplated if they were to be coded in assembly language.

UNIX supports multiple users on suitable installations with efficient memory-management and the appropriate communication interfaces. In addition to local users, log-in access and file transfer between UNIX hosts are also granted to remote users in the network environment.

Virtually all aspects of device independence were implemented in UNIX. Files and I/O devices are treated in a uniform way, by means of the same set of applicable system calls. As a result, I/O redirection and stream-level I/O are fully supported at both the command-language and system-call levels.

The basic UNIX philosophy, to process and treat different requests and objects in a uniform and relatively simple way, is probably the key to its long life. In a fast-changing environment in which high-tech products become obsolete after a few years, UNIX is still in full operational stage, three decades after its introduction. UNIX owes much of its longevity to its integration of useful building blocks that are combinable according to current needs and preferences for the creation of more complex tools. These basic UNIX blocks are usually simple, and they are designed to accomplish a single function well. Numerous UNIX utilities, called **filters**, can be combined in remarkably flexible ways by using the facilities provided by **I/O redirection** and **pipes**. This simple, building-block approach is obviously more convenient than the alternative of providing complex utilities that are often difficult to customize, and that are frequently incompatible with other utilities.

UNIX's hierarchical filesystem helps facilitate the sharing and cooperation among users that is so desirable in program-development environment. A UNIX filesystem (or filesystem, as it has become known) spans volume boundaries, virtually eliminating the need for volume awareness among its users. This is especially convenient in time-sharing systems and in a network environment.

The major features of UNIX can be summarized as:

- Portability
- Multi-user operation
- Device independence
- Tools and tool-building utilities
- Hierarchical filesystem

1.2 User's View of UNIX

UNIX users interact with the system through a command-language interpreter called the **shell**. A shell is actually what the user sees of the system; the rest of the operating system is essentially hidden from the user's eyes. A UNIX shell (or shells, because there are different command-interpreters) is also a programming language suitable for the construction of versatile and powerful command files called **shell scripts**. The UNIX shell is written in the same way as any user process, as opposed to being built into the kernel. When a user logs into the system, a copy of the corresponding shell is invoked to handle interactions with the related user. Although the shell is the standard system interface, it is possible to invoke any user-specific process to serve in place of the shell for any specific user. This allows application-specific interfaces to coexist with the shell, and thus provide quite different views and working environments for users of the same system.

All programs invoked within the shell start out with three predefined files, specified by corresponding *file descriptors*. By default the three files are:

1. *Standard input* — normally assigned to the terminal (console) keyboard
2. *Standard output* — normally assigned to the terminal (console) display
3. *Error output* — normally assigned to the terminal (console) display

The shell fully supports:

- *Redirection* — Since I/O devices and files are treated the same way in UNIX, the shell treats the two notions as files. From the user's viewpoint, it is easy to redefine file descriptors for any program, and in that way replace attached standard input and output files; this is known as redirection.
- *Pipes* — The standard output of one program can be used as standard input in another program by means of pipes. Several programs can be connected via pipes to form a *pipeline*. Redirection and piping are used to make UNIX utilities called *filters*, which are used to perform complex compound functions.
- *Concurrent execution* of the user programs — Users may indicate their intention to invoke several programs concurrently by placing their execution in the

"background" (as opposed to the single "foreground" program that requires full control of the display). This mode of operation allows users to perform unrelated work while potentially lengthy operations are being performed in the background on their behalf.

Since UNIX was primarily intended for program development, it offers several editors, compilers, symbolic debuggers, and utilities. Other useful program development facilities of UNIX include a general-purpose macro-processor, **M4**, that is language-independent, and the **MAKE** program, which controls creation of other large programs. MAKE uses a control file (or description file) called *MAKEFILE*, which specifies source file dependencies among the constituent modules of a program. It identifies modules that are possibly out of date (by checking the last program update), recompiles them, and links them into a new executable program.

A much more elaborate system for large programming projects, called ***Source Code Control System — SCCS***, is also available under UNIX. Although SCCS was designed to assist production of complex programs, it can also be used to manage any collection of text files. SCCS basically functions as a well-managed library of major and minor revisions of program modules. It keeps track of all changes, the identity of the programmers, and other information. It provides utilities for rolling back to any previous version, displaying complete or partial history of the changes made to a module, validation of modules, and the like. A complex implementation of SCCS evolved into a simpler version named ***Revision Control System — RCS***, which is more suitable to manage text files. RCS provides most of the SCCS functionality in a simpler and more user friendly way.

Users generally have restricted access to the UNIX filesystem; however, they are fully authorized in their home directories, where they can create their own subdirectories and files. This restricted-access approach is necessary to protect the system from intended and unintended corruption, while still allowing users to have full control over their own programs.

Filesystem protection in UNIX is accomplished by assigning ownership for each file and directory that is created. At creation, the access modes for the three access classes (user-owner, group-owner, and others) are also specified. Within each access class, three separate permissions are specified: for reading, writing, and execution of the file. Since everything in UNIX is a file (or is file-like), this simple protection scheme is widely implemented throughout the whole operating system, making UNIX security and protection very efficient.

Finally, UNIX is extremely well suited for **networking**. One of the reasons for UNIX's enormous popularity and wide implementation lies in its inherent network-related characteristics. UNIX facilitates most network functions in such a way that it can appear the network has been designed expressly for the UNIX architecture. The truth is that UNIX and modern networks have been developed independently, with UNIX preceding modern network architecture by a decade. The reason UNIX handles networking so well is simple: UNIX's flexible internal organization and structure allow an almost perfect union between the UNIX and network environments.

1.3 The History of UNIX

Ken Thompson (later joined by Dennis Ritchie) wrote the first version of UNIX at Bell Labs in the late 1960s. Everything started with **MULTICS** (**MULT**iplexed **I**nformation and **C**omputing **S**ystem), at that time the joint venture project between GE, AT&T Bell Laboratories, and MIT. The next phase was the project **UNICS** (**UN**iplex **I**nformation and **C**omputing **S**ystem), which was created by some of the people from the MULTICS project (Ken Thompson, Dennis Ritchie, and Rudd Canaday). UNICS was an assembly language, single-user system for the DEC PDP-7, which at that time was the most popular minicomputer. Soon the system had been enhanced to support two users. The name UNICS was later changed to **UNIX**.

After a major rewriting in C and porting to the DEC PDP-11 family of computers, UNIX was made available to users outside of AT&T. At the time, AT&T was banned from selling computing equipment by the U.S. antitrust law, and so was forced to release UNIX practically for free. Favorable licenses for educational institutions were instrumental in the adoption of UNIX by many universities. Soon the mutual benefits for both the academic users and UNIX itself became obvious. The leader was the University of Berkeley, which adopted UNIX and tailored it significantly. UNIX also became commercially available from AT&T, together with several other variants of the system provided by other vendors. Two versions of UNIX emerged as the main UNIX platforms, with a number of "flavors" between them.

1.3.1 Berkeley Standard Distribution — BSD UNIX

BSD originated at the University of Berkeley in California and is also known as Berkeley UNIX. Since the 1970's more BSD-based UNIX releases have been derived from version 4.3 BSD, which for a long time was a dominant version in the university and engineering communities. At the same time, the even older version of 4.2 BSD UNIX is still in use in some commercial implementations. The evolution of BSD is illustrated in Figure 1.1.

Sunsoft (later Sun Microsystems) was most successful at bringing UNIX into the commercial world with its SunOS, which was originally based on SVR4 UNIX, but with many incorporated improvements of BSD. *SunOS 4.1.x* (mostly referred to only as SunOS) is actually the best-known representative of the mostly BSD UNIX. The word "mostly" indicates a number of SunOS features that did not originate in the Berkeley version of UNIX. SunOS also introduced many new features (NIS, NFS, etc) that later became overall standards in the UNIX community. In the 1990s, Sun Microsystems changed this very successful UNIX version with the next generation version *SunOS 5.x*, better known as *Solaris*. The new version presented a significant shift from BSD UNIX toward System V UNIX. SunOS continues to exist thanks to many operating commercial installations. It survived "Year 2000 syndrome" and still is supported by Sun Microsystems.

1.3.2 System V or ATT UNIX

System V was derived from an early version of System III developed at AT&T Bell Labs, which is why it is also known as ATT UNIX. For a long time, the best-known versions were Release 3 — SVR3.x and Release 4 — SVR4.x. SVR4 attempted to merge older UNIX versions (SVR3 and 4.2 BSD) into a new more powerful UNIX system; the attempt was not a complete success, although its overall contribution has been significant. Certain steps in the development of System V UNIX during this period are illustrated in Figure 1.2.

Later on, many vendors accepted System V UNIX as a base for their own, vendor-specific UNIX flavors, like: *IRIX* by Silicon Graphics Inc., *HP-UX* by Hewlett-Packard, *AIX* by IBM, or *Solaris 2.x* by Sun Microsystems. However, it is not fair to classify all of these vendor-specific UNIX flavors as the System V UNIX. Such a statement sounds quite biased. Each vendor-specific flavor includes elements from both main UNIX platforms, so we can talk about mostly BSD, or mostly ATT UNIX flavors. It is even better to talk about BSD or ATT implementations in some segments of vendor-specific UNIX flavors.

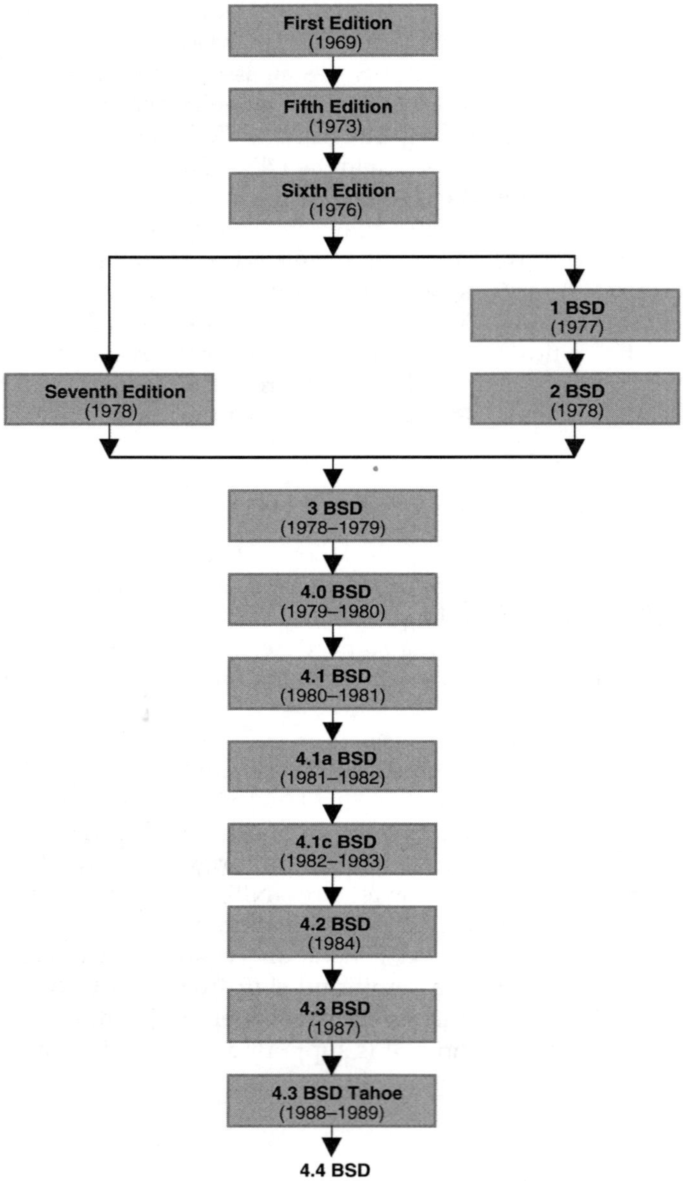

FIGURE 1.1
The development of BSD UNIX.

In the 1980s Richard Stallman started development of a C compiler for UNIX. He then started the Free Software Foundation — FSF, also known as GNU (GNU stands for "Gnu is Not Unix"). FSF just as it did when it started, manages many free pieces of UNIX-related software, such as GNU C compiler (GCC) and emacs.

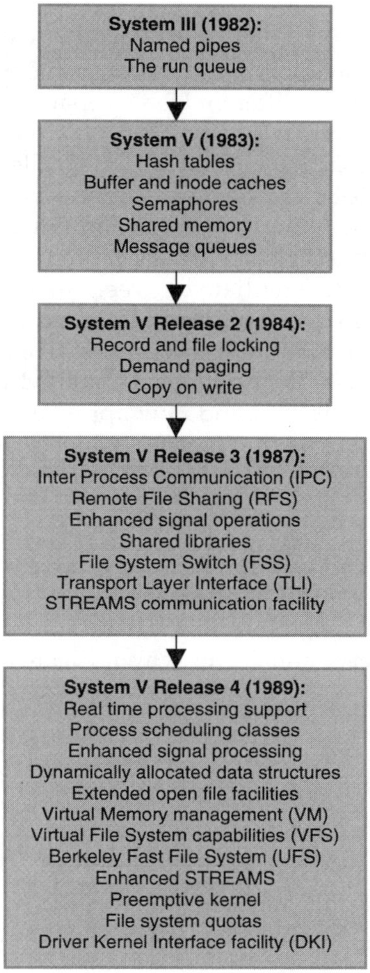

FIGURE 1.2
The development of ATT UNIX.

UNIX development in the last decade has been characterized by many vendor-specific UNIX flavors on the market. It is difficult to consider them as part of two main UNIX platforms. Each vendor tried to take the best from each of the main UNIX platforms to make a flavor better than the other vendors. In that light we can focus on, and talk about, development within individual flavors. And each of these flavors does have a certain impact on the overall trends in the UNIX development.

In its early days, UNIX was primarily run on high and mid-range computers, minicomputers, and relatively powerful workstations (by that time's standards). The appearance of microcomputers presented a new challenge for UNIX. Microsoft wrote a version of UNIX for microcomputer-based systems. Called *XENIX,* it was licensed to the Santa Cruz Operation and was closest to System V UNIX. It was later renamed *SCO UNIX;* later still it merged with *Unixware.* Other commercial versions also became available, like

Unixware, and even *Solaris for x86*. However, the main contributor in this area of microcomputer-based UNIX is *Linux*, a freeshare UNIX available to anyone who wants to try to work in the UNIX arena. Sometimes UNIX for microcomputers is classified as the third UNIX platform. We will treat different UNIX versions for minicomputers as different UNIX flavors related to one of the two main UNIX platforms.

In 1993, Linus Travalds released his version of UNIX, called Linux. Linux was a complete rewrite, originally for Intel 80386 architecture. Linux was quickly adopted and "ported" to some other architectures (including Macintosh and PowerPC); currently there are ports of LINUX for practically every single 32- and 64-bit machine available.

Today it is very difficult to differentiate between microcomputers and workstations; the boundaries between them are indistinct. Tremendous IT development has made very powerful IT resources available at low prices. This burst of activity had a very positive impact on UNIX, too — the number of installed UNIX sites rose dramatically, more people were involved in UNIX, and new application areas were conquered. The best example of this IT booming is the Internet, which primarily relies on UNIX-based servers. A thorough knowledge of UNIX has become a prerequisite for any real success in IT.

Figure 1.3 presents the main stages of the UNIX genealogy, showing mutual impacts among the different stages and within and out of the discussed UNIX platforms. For a fuller picture, this figure should continue with the list of today's available UNIX flavors presented in Figure 1.4. (Note: Figure 1.4 is only a partial list of the many UNIX flavors currently in use, and in no way indicates the extent of the individual flavor's usage.)

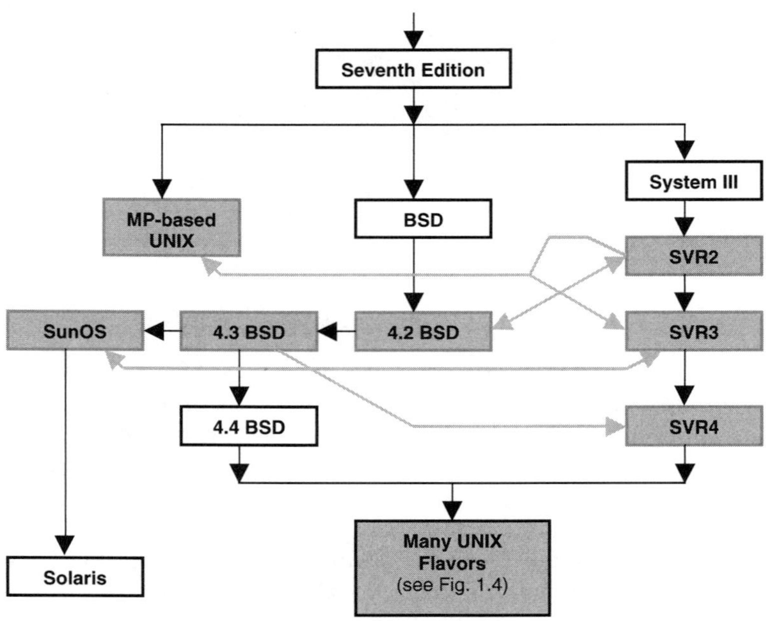

FIGURE 1.3
UNIX genealogy.

UNIX Flavor	Hardware Platform
386BSD	i386+
AIX	RS6000, PowerPC
A/UX	Macintosh
BSD	different hardware
BSD/OS	i486+
BSD/386	i386+
BSDI	x86
ConvexOS	Convex
Digital UNIX	Alpha
DGUX	Data General
DolphinOS	i486
FreeBSD	Pentium
HP-UX	HP HPPA
IRIX	SGI Indy; Mips-R8000
Linux Slackware	i486+; Sparc
Linux RedHat	i486+; Sparc; HP; IBM
Linux Suse	i486+; Sparc
Linux Turbolinux	i486+; Sparc
Linux Debian	i486+
Linux 4.0	Alpha
Linux/Mach3	Macintosh; PowerPC
Linux/m68k	Mac68k
Mach3	Mips
Mach3/Lites	i386+
Machten/m68k	Mac68k
NCR Unix	NCR S40
NetBSD	Pentium; Spark; Mac68k, Alpha
OpenBSD	x86; Mac68k
NextSTEP	Motorola
OSF/1	Alpha
Sequent	i386+
SCO Unix	i386+
SINIX	Mips R4000
Solaris	Sparc, i386+
Sony NEWS-OS	Mac68k
SunOS	Sparc, Sun3
SysV	different hardware
Ultrix	Mips
Unicos	Cray C90
Unixware	i386+

FIGURE 1.4
UNIX flavors.

1.4 UNIX System and Network Administration

Organizations that rely on computing resources to carry out their mission have always depended on systems administration and systems administrators. The dramatic increase in the number and size of distributed networks of workstations in recent years has created a tremendous demand for more, and better trained, systems administrators. Understanding of the profession of systems administration on the part of employers, however, has not kept pace with the growth in the number of systems administrators or with the growth in complexity of system administration tasks. Both at sites with a long history of using computing resources and at sites into which computers have only recently been introduced, system administrators sometimes face perception problems that present serious obstacles to their successfully carrying out their duties.

Systems administration is a widely varied task. The best systems administrators are generalists: they can wire and repair cables, install new software, repair bugs, train users, offer tips for increased productivity across areas from word processing to CAD tools, evaluate new hardware and software, automate a myriad of mundane tasks, and increase work flow at their site. In general, systems administrators enable people to exploit computers at a level that gains leverage for the entire organization.

Employers frequently fail to understand the background that systems administrators bring to their task. Because systems administration draws on knowledge from many fields, and because it has only recently begun to be taught at a few institutions of higher education, systems administrators may come from a wide range of academic backgrounds. Most get their skills through on-the-job training by apprenticing themselves to a more experienced mentor. Although the system of informal education by apprenticeship has been extremely effective in producing skilled systems administrators, it is poorly understood by employers and hiring managers, who tend to focus on credentials to the exclusion of other factors when making personnel decisions.

System administrators are the professionals that provide specific services in the system software arena. These professionals are often known by their acronym SYSADMIN. A system administrator performs various tasks while taking care of multiple, often heterogeneous, computer systems in an attempt to keep them operational. When computer systems are connected to the network, which is almost always the case today, the system administration also includes network-related duties.

UNIX administrators are part of the larger family of the system administrators. Their working platform is UNIX, and it caries many specific elements that make this job unique. UNIX is a powerful and open operating system. As with any other software system, it requires a certain level of customization (we prefer the term "configuration") and maintenance at each site where it is implemented. To configure and maintain an operating system is a serious business; in the case of UNIX it can be a tough and sometimes frustrating job. Why is UNIX so demanding? Here are some observations:

- A powerful system means there are many possibilities for setting the system configuration.
- An open system results in permanent upgrades with direct impacts on administrative issues.
- UNIX is implemented at the most mission critical points, where a downtime is not allowed.
- Networking presents a new challenge, but also a new area of potential problems.
- Different UNIX flavors bring additional system administration difficulties.

Networking in particular, with its many potential external failures, can affect a UNIX system significantly. Periodical global network degradation (too high of a load, low throughput, or even breaks in communication) can cause complex problems and bring a lot of headaches. It is easy to be misguided in tracing a problem, and to be looking for the source of troubles at the wrong place. Usually at such times everyone is looking to the UNIX people for a quick solution. The only advice is: "Be ready for such situations."

As a matter of fact, system and network administration are relatively distinct duties, and sometimes they are even treated separately. However, it is very common to look at system and network administration as two halves of the same job, with the same individuals or team responsible for both. It is fair to say that the term *network administration* is strictly related to the computer system as part of the network, and remains within the network service boundaries required for the computer functioning in the network environment. It does not cover core network elements like switches, bridges, hubs, routers, and other network-only devices. Nevertheless, the basic understanding of these topics also could make overall administration easier.

So to get to the heart of the topic, let us start with a brief discussion of the administrator's role, duties, guidelines, policies, and other topics that make up the SYSADMIN business. Most of the paragraphs that follow are not strictly UNIX related, although our focus remains on UNIX systems and network administration.

1.4.1 System Administrator's Job

Understanding system administrators' background, training, and the kind of job performance to be expected is challenging; too often, employers fall back into (mis)using the job classifications with which they are familiar. These job classification problems are exacerbated by the scarcity of job descriptions for systems administrators. One frequently used misclassification is that of programmer or software engineer. Production of code is the primary responsibility of programmers, not of the systems administrator. Thus, systems administrators classified as programmers often receive poor evaluations for not being "productive" enough. Another common misclassification is the confusion of systems administrators with operators. Especially at smaller sites, where systems administrators themselves have to perform many of the functions normally assigned to operators at larger sites, system administrators are forced to contend with the false assumption they are nonprofessional technicians. This, in turn, makes it very difficult for systems administrators to be compensated commensurate with their skill and experience.

The following text lists the main elements that describe the system administrator's job at various levels. The basic intention is to describe the core attributes of systems administrators at various levels of job performance, and to address site-specific needs or special areas of expertise that a systems administrator may have.

Generally, as for many other professions, system administrators are classified regarding their background and experience into several categories:

- ***Novices***
  - *Required background*: 2 years of college or equivalent post-high-school education or experience
  - *Desirable background*: a degree or certificate in computer science or a related field. Previous experience in customer support, computer operations, system administration, or another related area; motivated to advance in the profession
  - *Duties*: performs routine tasks under the direct supervision of a more experienced system administrator; acts as a front-line interface to users, accepting trouble reports and dispatching them to appropriate system administrators
- ***Junior***
  - *Required background*: 1 to 3 years system administration experience
  - *Desirable background*: a degree in computer science or a related field, familiarity with networked/distributed computing environment concepts (for example,

can use the route command, add a workstation to a network, and mount remote filesystems); ability to write scripts in some administrative language (Tk, Perl, a shell); programming experience in any applicable language
  - *Duties*: administers a small site alone or assists in the administration of a larger system; works under the general supervision of a system administrator or computer systems manager

- ***Intermediate/Advanced***
  - *Required background*: three to five years' systems administration experience
  - *Desirable background*: a degree in computer science or a related field; significant programming background in any applicable language
  - *Duties*: receives general instructions for new responsibilities from supervisor; administers a midsized site alone or assists in the administration of a larger site; initiates some new responsibilities and helps to plan for the future of the site/network; manages novice system administrators or operators; evaluates and/or recommends purchases; has strong influence on purchasing process
- ***Senior***
  - *Required background*: more than five years previous systems administration experience
  - *Desirable background*: a degree in computer science or a related field; extensive programming background in any applicable language; publications within the field of system administration
  - *Duties*: designs/implements complex LAN and WANs; manages a large site or network; works under general direction from senior management; establishes/recommends policies on system use and services; provides technical lead and/or supervises system administrators, system programmers, or others of equivalent seniority; has purchasing authority and responsibility for purchase justification

This is a general job classification and description for potential UNIX administrators. It can easily vary from one site to another, especially regarding official job titles. A number of other skills could also be considered:

- Interpersonal and communication skills; ability to write proposals or papers, act as a vendor liaison, make presentations to customer or client audiences or professional peers, and work closely with upper management
- Ability to solve problems quickly and completely; ability to identify tasks that require automation and automate them
- A solid understanding of a UNIX-based operating system, including paging and swapping, inter-process communication, devices and what device drivers do, filesystem concepts (inode, superblock), and use of performance analysis to tune systems
- Experience with more than one UNIX-based operating system; with sites running more than one UNIX-based operating system; with both System V and BSD-based UNIX operating systems; with non-UNIX operating systems (for example, MS-DOS, Macintosh OS, or VMS); and with internetworking UNIX and other operating systems (MS-DOS, Macintosh OS, VMS)
- Programming experience in an administrative language (shell, Perl, Tk); extensive programming experience in any applicable language

- Networking skills — a solid understanding of networking/distributed computing environment concepts, principles of routing, client/server programming, and the design of consistent networkwide filesystem layouts; experience in configuring network filesystems (for example, NFS, RFS, or AFS), in network file synchronization schemes (for example, rdist and track), and in configuring automounters, license managers, and NIS; experience with TCP/IP networking protocols (ability to debug and program at the network level), with non-TCP/IP networking protocols (for example, OSI, Chaosnet, DECnet, Appletalk, Novell Netware, Banyan Vines), with high-speed networking (for example, FDDI, ATM, or SONET), with complex TCP/IP networks (networks that contain routers), and with highly complex TCP/IP networks (networks that contain multiple routers and multiple media); experience configuring and maintaining routers and maintaining a sitewide modem pool/terminal servers; experience with X terminals and with dial-up networking (for example, SLIP, PPP, or UUCP); experience at a site that is connected to the Internet, experience installing/configuring DNS/BIND; experience installing/administering Usenet news, and experience as postmaster of a site with external connections
- Experience with network security (for example, building firewalls, deploying authentication systems, or applying cryptography to network applications); with classified computing; with multilevel classified environments; and with host security (for example, passwords, uids/gids, file permissions, filesystem integrity, use of security packages)
- Experience at sites with over 1000 computers, over 1000 users, or over a terabyte of disk space; experience with supercomputers; experience coordinating multiple independent computer facilities (for example, working for the central group at a large company or university); experience with a site with 100% uptime requirement; experience developing/implementing a site disaster recovery plan; and experience with a site requiring charge-back accounting
- Background in technical publications, documentation, or desktop publishing
- Experience using relational databases; using a database SQL language; and programming in a database query language; previous experience as a database administrator
- Experience with hardware: installing and maintaining the network cabling in use at the site, installing boards and memory into systems; setting up and installing SCSI devices; installing/configuring peripherals (for example, disks, modems, printers, or data acquisition devices); and making board-level and component-level diagnosis and repairing computer systems
- Budget responsibility, experience with writing personnel reviews and ranking processes; and experience in interviewing/hiring

Do not be afraid of this long list of additional requirements. Nobody expects UNIX systems and network administrators to be Supermen. UNIX administration is a normal job that is demanding but definitely doable.

To end this discussion, here is a joke about UNIX administrators. Consider the similarities between Santa Claus and UNIX administrators:

- Santa is bearded, corpulent, and dresses funny.
- When you ask Santa for something, the odds of receiving what you wanted are infinitesimal.

- Santa seldom answers your mail.
- When you ask Santa where he gets all the stuff he has, he says, "Elves make it for me."
- Santa does not care about your deadlines.
- Your parents ascribed supernatural powers to Santa, but did all the work themselves.
- Nobody knows who Santa has to answer to for his actions.
- Santa laughs entirely too much.
- Santa thinks nothing of breaking into your HOME.
- Only a lunatic says bad things about Santa in his presence.

1.4.2 Computing Policies

A successful system administration requires a well-defined framework. This framework is described by the corresponding computing policies within the organization where the administration is provided. There are no general computing policies; they are always site specific. Drafting computing policies, however, is often a difficult task, fraught with legal, political, and ethical questions and possibly consequences. There are a number of related issues: why a site needs computing policies; what a policy document should contain, who should draft it, and to whom it should apply. There is no a unique list of all possible rules. Each computing site is different and needs its own set of policies to suit specific needs. The goal of this section is to point out the main computing policies that directly influence the system administration. This is not possible without addressing security and overall business policies as they relate to computing facilities and their use.

Good computing policies include comprehensive coverage of computer security. However, the full scope of security, overall business, and other policies goes well beyond computer use and sometimes may be better addressed in separate documents. For example, a comprehensive security document should address employee identification systems, guards, building structure, and other such topics that have no association with computing. Computing security is a subset of overall security as well as a subset of overall computing policy. If there are separate policy documents, they should refer to each other as appropriate and should not contain excessive redundancy. Redundancy leaves room for later inconsistencies and increases the work of document maintenance.

The system administrator policy usually is not completely separated from the user policy. In practice there are few if any user policies from which a system administrator needs to be exempt. System administrators are users and should be held accountable to te same user policy as everyone else in the use of their personal computer accounts. System administrators (and any other users with "extended" system access) have additional usage responsibilities and limitations regarding that extended access, i.e., extra powers via groups or root. The additional policies should address the extended access. Further, knowledge of policies governing how staff members perform their duties (e.g. how frequently backups are done) is essential to the users. All the information on the operation of the computing facility should be documented and available to both the end users and the support staff to prevent confusion and redundancy as well as enhance communication. The policy documents should be considered as a single guide for the users and the support staff alike. We intentionally used the words "computing policies" in the plural; it is hard to talk about a unique overall policy that could cover everything needed.

System administration is a technical job. System administrators are supposed to accomplish certain tasks, to implement technical skills to enforce certain decisions based on certain rules. In other words, the system administrator should follow a specific *administrative procedure* to accomplish the needed task. A system administrator is not supposed to make nontechnical decisions, nor dictate the underlying rules. It is important to have feasible procedures, and in that sense, the administrator's opinion could be significant. But the underlying rules must be primarily based on existing business-driven computing policies.

At the end of the day, we reach the point of asking: "Will a SYSADMIN really have strictly defined procedures in the daily work that will make the administration job easier; especially, would these procedures be in written form?" The most probable answer regarding procedures will be negative. There are usually multiple ways to accomplish a certain administrative task because system configurations are changing (just think about different UNIX flavors, or new releases, or network changes). However this is not the case with computing policies; they are usually general enough to last a longer time.

We already mentioned that the computing policies are business related. They are different in academia than in industry; they are different in the financial industry than in the retail industry, or in the Internet business. They are, at least for a moment, always internal and stay in the boundaries of a college, university, or company. So they can differ by moving from one place to another. Still there are many common elements and we will try to address them.

Security policy — Definitely the most important policy, a good security policy is the best guarantee for uninterrupted business. Clear guidance in that direction is extremely important. Requests for Comments (RFCs) that present standards for new technologies also addressed this important issue. The RFC-2196 named "Site Security Handbook," a 75-page document written in 1997 by IETF (Internet Engineering Task Force), suggests the need for internal security documents as guidelines for:

- Purchasing of hardware and software
- Privacy protection
- Access to the systems
- Accountability and responsibility of all participants
- Authentication rules
- Availability of systems
- Maintenance strategy (internal vs. outsourcing)

Policy toward users — Users are main players in the ongoing business, but they must obey certain rules, and they do not have to have unrestricted access to all available resources. It is crucial to define the following user rights and responsibilities:

- Who is an eligible user
- Password policy and its enforcement
- Mutual relationship among users
- Copyright and license implementation
- Downloading of software from Internet
- Misusing e-mail
- Disrupting services
- Other illegal activities

Policy toward privileged users — The primary audience for this policy is SYSADMIN and other privileged users. These users have unrestricted access to all system resources and practically unlimited power over the systems. The policy addresses:

- Password policy and its enforcement
- Protection of user privacy
- License implementation
- Copyright implementation
- Loyalty and obedience
- Telecommuting
- Monitoring of system activities
- Highest security precaution and checkup
- Business-time and off-business-time work

Emergency and disaster policies — Good policies mean prevention and faster recoveries from disaster situations. They are essential to maintain system availability and justify spending an appropriate amount of time to protect against future disastrous scenarios. Data are priceless, and their loss could be fatal for overall business. Emergency and disaster policies include:

- Monitoring strategies
- Work in shifts
- Tools
- Planning
- Distribution of information (pager, beepers, phones)
- Personnel

Backup and recovery policy — This is a must for each system — in the middle of disastrous situations, there is no bargaining regarding the need for backup. However, the level and frequency of implemented backup vary and are business related. Generally the policy should address the following issues:

- Backup procedures
- Backup planning
- Backup organization
- Storage of backup tapes
- Retention periods
- Archiving
- Tools
- Recovery procedures

Development policy — This policy should address the need for permanent development and upgrading of the production systems. Today continual development of the IT infrastructure is essential for overall business growth; however, the development should not endanger basic production. In that light, the focus should be on:

- Development team
- Planning

- Support
- Testing
- Staging
- Cutting new releases
- Fallback

System administration will be easier if more computing policies are covered and elaborated internally and if more of the corresponding procedures are specified. It sounds strange, but less freedom in doing something usually makes the job easier. Unfortunately (or maybe fortunately) this is mostly the case only for large communities with strong IT departments that have been running for years. The majority of medium-size and small companies do not have, or have only rudimentary, specified procedure. The system administrator often does have freedom in enforcing listed policies. This freedom in action increases the administrator's responsibility, but also enhances the creativity in the work (that is why we used the word "fortunately" earlier).

1.4.3 Administration Guidelines

This section provides some additional system administration-related information.

1.4.3.1 Legal Acts

Computer network and UNIX are quite young, but they have significantly affected all spheres of human life. Today the Internet is strongly pushing ahead to replace, or at least to alter, many traditional pieces of economic infrastructures: the telecommunication industry, the entertainment industry, the publishing industry, the financial industry, postal services, and others. All kinds of middleman services, such as travel agencies, job agencies, book sellers, and music retainers, are also dramatically changing. Business-to-business (B2B) links are growing, providing an efficient mechanism to merge customers and merchants and make our online shopping easier. The full list of all affected businesses would be very, very long.

Such a huge area of human activities also opened up possibilities for misuse, fraud, theft, and other kinds of crimes. While the technological and financial capabilities have fully supported booming information technologies, legal infrastructure seems to stay far below our real needs. In many cases even when the perpetrator is caught, actual conviction is very difficult under the current laws. Recent cases involving very destructive viruses that cost businesses millions of dollars stayed in limbo even though the perpetrators were known. The case against "Napster Music Community," relating to music copyrights, was closed after a long time and was only partially successful.

At this moment we have only a few legal acts in this area, covering only several computer-crime-related topics, and sometimes those not even effectively. Definitely they do not constitute a sufficient legal framework, and further improvements and expansions are necessary.

The existing legal acts are:

- The Federal Communication Privacy Act
- The Computer Fraud and Abuse Act
- The No Electronic Theft Act
- The Digital Millenium Copyright Act

A pending problem in the implementation of the listed legal acts, as well as others that will presumably come in the future, lies in the fact that even if the corresponding laws exist in the United States, they do not exist in many other countries. Because of the global nature of the Internet and its presence in countries worldwide, it is very difficult to enforce any court decision.

1.4.3.2 Code of Ethics

The lack of general legal guidance, and often the lack of clear internal administration rules and procedures, presents new challenges in the system administrator's job. More freedom in doing the job also means more chances for wrongdoing. Under such circumstances, an extremely responsible attitude of the administrators toward all these challenges is very important. System administrators, regardless of their title and whether or not they are members of a professional organization, are relied upon to ensure proper operation, support, and protection of the computing assets (hardware, software, networking, etc.). Unlike problems with most earlier technologies, any problem with computer assets may negatively impact millions of users worldwide — thus such protection is more crucial than equivalent roles within other technologies. The ever-increasing reliance upon computers in all parts of society has led to system administrators having access to more information, particularly information of critical importance to the users, thus increasing the impact that any wrongdoing may have. It is important that all computer users and administrators understand the norms and principles to be applied to the task. At the end of the day, we come to the informal set of behavioral codes known as the code of ethics that each administrator should be aware of. A code of ethics supplies these norms and principles as canons of general concepts. Such a code must be applied by individuals, guided by their professional judgment, within the confines of the environment and situation in which they may be. The code sets forth commitments, responsibilities, and requirements of members of the system administration profession within the computing community.

The basic purposes of such a code of ethics are:

- To provide a set of codified guidelines for ethical directions that system administrators must pursue
- To act as a reference for construction of local site acceptable-use policies
- To enhance professionalism by promoting ethical behavior
- To act as an "industry standard" reference of behavior in difficult situations, as well as in common ones
- To establish a baseline for addressing more complex issues

This code is not a set of enforceable laws, or procedures, or proposed responses to possible administrative situations. It is also not related to sanctions or punishments as consequences of any wrongdoing. A partial overview of one proposal for the code of ethics follows:

Code 1: The integrity of a system administrator must be beyond reproach — System administrators must uphold the law and policies as established for the systems and networks they manage, and make all efforts to require the same adherence from the users. Where the law is not clear, or appears to be in conflict with their ethical standards, system administrators must exercise sound judgment and are also obliged to take steps to have the law upgraded or corrected as is possible within their jurisdiction.

Code 2: A system administrator shall not unnecessarily infringe upon the rights of users — System administrators will not exercise their special powers to access any private information other than when necessary to their role as system managers, and then only to the degree necessary to perform that role, while remaining within established site policies. Regardless of how it was obtained, system administrators will maintain the confidentiality of all private information.

Code 3: Communications of system administrators with all whom they may come in contact shall be kept to the highest standards of professional behavior — System administrators must keep users informed about computing matters that might affect them, such as conditions of acceptable use, sharing and availability of common resources, maintenance of security, occurrence of system monitoring, and any applicable legal obligations. It is incumbent upon the system administrator to ensure that such information is presented in a manner calculated to ensure user awareness and understanding.

Code 4: The continuance of professional education is critical to maintaining currency as a system administrator — Since technology in computing continues to make significant strides, a system administrator must take an appropriate level of action to update and enhance personal technical knowledge. Reading, study, acquiring training, and sharing knowledge and experience are requirements to maintaining currency and ensuring the customer base of the advantages and security of advances in the field.

Code 5: A system administrator must maintain an exemplary work ethic — System administrators must be tireless in their effort to maintain high levels of quality in their work. Day to day operation in the field of system administration requires significant energy and resiliency. The system administrator is placed in a position of such significant impact upon the business of the organization that the required level of trust can only be maintained by exemplary behavior.

Code 6: At all times system administrators must display professionalism in the performance of their duties — All manner of behavior must reflect highly upon the profession as a whole. Dealing with recalcitrant users, upper management, vendors, or other system administrators calls for the utmost patience and care to ensure that mutual respect is never at risk.

1.4.3.3 Organizations

There are several UNIX and system administration related organizations, support groups, and conferences. Following are just a few words about the best known ones.

1.4.3.3.1 USENIX

USENIX is the advanced computing systems association. This was originally a nonprofit membership organization for those individuals with an interest in UNIX, UNIX-related, and other modern operating systems. Since 1975 the USENIX association has brought together the community of engineers, system engineers, system administers, scientists, and technicians. All of these people have been working on the cutting edge of the computing world. The USENIX conferences have become the meeting grounds for presenting and discussing new and advanced information on developments from the computing systems. USENIX is dedicated to sharing ideas and experiences of those working with UNIX and other advanced computing systems. USENIX members are dedicated to solving problems with a practical bias, fostering research that works, communicating with both research and innovation, and providing critical thought.

USENIX supports its members' professional and technical development through a variety of ongoing activities, including:

- Member benefits
- Annual technical and system administration conferences, as well as informal, specific-topic conferences
- A highly regarded tutorial program
- Student programs that include stipends to attend conferences, low student membership fees, best paper awards, scholarships, and research grants
- Online library with proceedings from each USENIX conference
- Participation in various IEEE and Open Group standards efforts
- International programs
- Cosponsorship of conferences by foreign technical groups
- Prestigious annual awards which recognize public service and technical excellence
- Membership in the Computing Research Association and the Open Group
- SAGE, a Special Technical Group (STG) for system administrators

1.4.3.3.2 System Administrators Guild — SAGE

At the moment the System Administrators' Guild, known by its acronym SAGE, is a Special Technical Group (STG) of the USENIX Association. It is organized to help advance computer systems administration as a profession, establish standards of professional excellence and recognize those who attain them, develop guidelines for improving technical capabilities, and promote activities that advance the state of the art of the community. SAGE members are also members of USENIX.

Since its inception in 1992, SAGE has grown immensely and has matured into a stable community of system administration professionals. Organization management has been codified and stabilized. As an USENIX STG, reviews by USENIX are scheduled periodically, principally for assessing continued viability. SAGE's viability has not been an issue for some time — quite the opposite, the growth of SAGE has exceeded reasonable expectations and those of USENIX as a whole. At this point in SAGE's development, it is prudent for both SAGE and USENIX to review organizational structures, their relationships, and future developments. To that end, the SAGE executive committee reviewed the existing mission statement, its relevance for the present and the future, and the future interests and projects as they relate to that mission. While the existing SAGE Charter and Mission Statement are still relevant, the following text was adopted as a working draft that better expresses its current nature and future:

> The System Administrators Guild is an international professional organization for people involved in the practice, study, and teaching of computer and network system administration. Its principal roles are:
>
> - To always understand and satisfy the needs of system administrators so as to provide them with products and services that will help them be better system administrators
> - To empower system administrators through information, education, relationships, and resources that will enrich their professional development and careers
> - To advance the thought, application, and ethical practice of system administration

As SAGE grows, the majority of its members will be professionals who are not currently involved with SAGE. This will come as a result of the growing awareness of SAGE, different certification programs, and other future projects.

The SAGE executive committee, the USENIX board of directors, and USENIX staffs have discussed how to meet the growing needs of SAGE. At this time, there are ideas that these needs may be better met by changing SAGE from a USENIX internal STG to a sister organization established as an independent nonprofit entity. If this process continues as expected, this transition could be implemented soon. The SAGE executive committee to be elected will become the initial board of directors of SAGE. The precise legal structure and implementation details are yet to be determined.

In this plan, SAGE will continue to serve its members with the benefits with which they have become accustomed. SAGE member services and information will move to a more electronic community model. SAGE will publish its own newsletter while SAGE news will continue to be available as before. LISA will continue to be cosponsored by USENIX and SAGE. SAGE will also sponsor new conferences and programs to reach out to the broader system and network administration community. All the assets of USENIX used exclusively by SAGE will be transferred to the independent SAGE organization, including intellectual property, inventory, and current operating funds. SAGE will then operate independently from USENIX. The LISA conference will continue without change, being operated by USENIX and cosponsored by SAGE. The responsibility for all current and pending SAGE projects will also be transferred. Membership in USENIX and SAGE will be decoupled such that a person can become a member of SAGE without having to become a USENIX member. However, SAGE and USENIX will continue to provide close cooperation and mutual benefits to their members.

1.4.3.3.3 Conferences

One of the ongoing activities of USENIX and SAGE is to organize UNIX and UNIX administration-related annual and ad hoc conferences. The big events for system administrators include the general conference LISA, which is organized every year during the fall or the winter. For example, LISA '02 is scheduled for November 2002 in Philadelphia, PA. LISA stands for *Large Installation System Administration*.

LISA is more than just an exchange of technical topics. This is also the place where many system administration issues are generated, including essential ones for the sysadmin community. For example, the initial idea for an independent SAGE was born and presents the state of the discussions as of LISA 2000.

1.4.3.4 Standardization

There are no explicit standards regarding UNIX administration. There are no standards regarding system administration generally. Anyhow, administrators are obliged to follow a strict set of rules to make the system function properly. These rules were, and are, determined by the OS designers. Although they are not official standards, they have an even stronger impact on the system administration; otherwise a system will not work at all. The problem is, at least in case of the UNIX administration, different administrative rules exist for different UNIX flavors. It makes our lives more difficult, and any standardization in that way will be well received by the administrators.

In the UNIX and network arena there are significant efforts toward standardization. There are several standards bodies, both formal and informal. Each body has different rules for membership, voting, and clout. From a system administration standpoint, two significant bodies are: IETF (Internet engineering task force) and POSIX (portable operating system interfaces). Especially POSIX has contributed a lot in the area of UNIX standardization, making also a corresponding ground for its uniform and more standardized administration.

1.4.3.4.1 POSIX

The POSIX standardization effort used to run by the POSIX standards committee. During a major overhaul of the names and numbers used to refer to this project, the IEEE Portable Application Standards Committee (PASC) came into being. So currently the POSIX standards are written and maintained by PASC.

POSIX is the term for a suite of applications program interface standards to provide for the portability of source code applications where operating systems services are required. POSIX is based on the UNIX operating system (UNIX is registered trademark administrated by the Open Group), and is the basis for the Single UNIX Specification (SUS) from the Open Group. Although it is essentially based on UNIX (and the kernels services), it covers much more than just UNIX (Windows NT can be made to be POSIX compliant).

POSIX is intended to be one part of the suite of standards (a "profile") that a user might require of a complete and coherent open system. This concept is developed in IEEE Std. 1003.0–1994: Guide to the POSIX Open System Environment. The joint revision to POSIX and the Single UNIX Specification, involving the IEEE PASC committee, ISO Working Group WG15, and the Open Group (informally known as the Austin Group), is underway. More information, including draft specifications, can be found at the Austin Group Web site.

The PASC continues to develop the POSIX standards. In accordance with a synchronization plan adopted by the IEEE and ISO/IEC JTC1, many of the POSIX standards become international standards shortly after their adoption by the IEEE. Therefore, these standards are available in printed form from both IEEE and ISO, as well as from many national standards organizations. Approved standards can also be purchased from the IEEE in electronic (PDF) format. The IEEE also publishes Standards Interpretations for many of the standards (more details are available at IEEE Web site).

Cooperation among IEEE, the Open Group (X/Open), and ISO is now underway for the common UNIX/POSIX standard. Everybody can participate in the process (see the Austin Group Web site). A revision of the whole suite of UNIX and POSIX standards is going on. The plan is to make just one document, based on the UNIX 98 Single UNIX Specification, and the same document will serve as the standard in all three of the participating organizations. It is not clear, though, whether the name on the standard will be UNIX or POSIX.

POSIX System Interface standards cover those functions that are needed for applications software portability in general purpose, real time, and other applications environments. Many of the extensions and options within the POSIX system interface standards reflect the ongoing focus on more demanding applications domains such as embedded real time, etc. Interfaces that require administration privileges, or that create security risks are not included. The POSIX work consists of:

- System interface specifications for C, ADA, and FORTRAN
- Shell and utility specification
- System administration specifications for software installation, user administration, and print management
- Test methods: general methods, for system interfaces, and for shell and utilities
- Profiles documents: guide to POSIX-based profiles (concepts); supercomputing application environment, real-time application environment, multiprocessing environment, and general purpose or "traditional" environment

The POSIX shell and utility standards define tools that are available for invocation by applications software, or by a user from a keyboard. The system administration interfaces are targeted at areas where consistency of interfaces between systems is important to simplify operations for both users and systems operators. The POSIX test methods describe how to define test methods for interfaces such as those in the POSIX suite of standards. The explicit test methods for the system interface and shell and utilities standards apply the approach defined in the overview to these specific documents.

1.4.4 In This Book

This text covers related issues for both system administration and network administration on a UNIX platform. This is a challenging (but doable) task, given the many different UNIX platforms and flavors. To make the terminology simpler, we will use the term ***UNIX Administration*** to address *both* UNIX systems and network administration; the administration personnel we will call ***UNIX administrators***. This will not make UNIX administration easier, nor it will simplify our task; however, it could help to clarify some of the topics under discussion.

UNIX systems administration related issues are:

- System startup and shutdown
- User and group accounts management
- System resources management
- Filesystems
- System quotas
- System security
- Backup and restoration of the system
- Automating routine tasks
- Printing and spooling system
- Terminals and modem handling
- Accounting
- System performance tuning
- System customization — kernel reconfiguration

UNIX network administration related issues are:

- Network interface and connectivity
- Data routing
- Data multiplexing
- Network security
- Domain name service
- Network information service — NIS
- Network filesystem — NFS
- UNIX remote commands
- Network applications (telnet, FTP, etc)
- Remote printing

- Electronic mail
- UUCP
- X windowing

Despite many promises, wishes, advertisements, and attempts to standardize UNIX, the differences among existing UNIX favors are not negligible. The differences exist in UNIX implementations, but the main differences are seen in the UNIX administration. This text attempts to cover most of the UNIX administrative topics on both the BSD and System V (ATT) UNIX platforms. This is primarily achieved through brief theoretical explanations of certain topics, and the selective presentation of related examples from the different UNIX flavors. Assuming the basic knowledge of UNIX and shell programming, the presented material should be sufficient per se for a successful UNIX and network administration. To clarify certain operational details, UNIX online documentation (manual pages available on every UNIX platform) is also supposed.

2

The UNIX Model — Selected Topics

2.1 Introduction

UNIX administration presents a complex job that requires certain skills to be accomplished successfully. These skills range from a basic knowledge of computer hardware, operating systems, and programming techniques, up to ethics, psychology, and social behavior. It supposes a responsible approach to very challenging problems, and a readiness for a nonstop follow-up of everything done. An administrator usually covers many different systems (different hardware, different configurations, different software, different purposes), and each of those systems is the "baby" that requires a certain amount of attention, and the administrator must pay that attention.

Of course the level of the required skills varies; it would be wrong to expect that an UNIX administrator (especially a successful one) has to graduate in each of the listed fields to be able to respond to all administrative demands. However, it is true that some of the required skills need more than just a basic knowledge; mostly these are strictly UNIX-related skills. Nobody can fight with UNIX administrative challenges without being familiar with the UNIX operating system, the UNIX commands and how to use them. An even deeper expertise in UNIX internals could be very instrumental in an easier UNIX administration. Script programming is another fighting arena. An average UNIX administration time consists of 75 to 80% of shell programming, and only the rest is a manual administration from the keyboard.

Some selected UNIX topics are briefly discussed in this chapter to point out the most important issues for a successful UNIX administration. A certain level of knowledge of the discussed topics is still supposed — this chapter is simply trying to highlight the needed background for a comprehensive UNIX administration. The chapter should refresh the reader's memory and push ahead to consider all holes in the reader's knowledge and understanding of discussed issues. Another purpose is to present in one place most of the relevant UNIX fundamentals needed for better understanding of different administrative tasks. The reader is also advised to look into other literature for more detailed descriptions, if necessary. The terminology used is common in the UNIX community.

To help readers better understand the material, a number of examples and figures illustrate the discussed UNIX topics.

2.2 Files

In UNIX everything is **a file**, or rather, **file-like** — this makes **file issues** central to UNIX. What does this really mean? A file is a *collection of data*, or, better, a *sequence of bytes*, stored in a memory or on a disk. A file can be a program that can be executed. When such a program is running, it creates a process. Therefore, a file lies in the origin of every process. On UNIX each device is also described by a file — these are called *special device files*, but are still file-like entities. Even users on UNIX are file related, as they have associated attributes (such as what they are allowed access to) that are specified in a file-like way.

UNIX has a hierarchical tree-structured directory organization known collectively as the *filesystem* (or filesystem). The base of this tree is the ***root directory*** with the special name "/" (the slash character). In UNIX all user-available disk space is integrated into a single directory tree under /, so the physical disk unit (the disk drive itself) where a file resides is not a part of the UNIX file specification.

We already mentioned that a file is a *sequence of bytes*. Such a sequence could be a newly created user's program, written text, acquired data, or a program that is a part of the operating system itself. Many files are understandable by users, but a number of files (mostly binary executable files) are machine-interpretable only. All files, no matter what their purpose, must be stored somewhere and uniquely identified within the system. A disk is the most common medium to store files, and files are identified by ***inodes*** within accessible disk space. The kernel handles information about inodes and maintains and updates the corresponding ***inode table*** (the inode table is laid out when a filesystem is created and its size and location do not change). We will discuss those issues in more detail later.

UNIX file access is restricted and determined by file ownership and the protection settings on the file itself. A user and a group own each file; correspondingly, the file's access rights for the user and group owners, as well as for others, (those who do not belong to the owners) are explicitly specified.

2.2.1 File Ownership

Files have two owners: ***user*** and ***group***, which are decoupled and nondependent. The file's user-owner could actually be outside of the group that owns the very same file. Such flexibility enables full UNIX scalability to exclude certain members of the user-owner's group and treat them as ***others***.

Information about a file's ownership and permissions is kept in the file's **index node**, better known by its short name **inode**. UNIX does not allow direct managing of index nodes; indirect management is provided through a certain number of commands that handle specific segments of the index nodes. A brief overview of the most common of these commands follows.

The long form of the **ls** command is used to display the ownership of a file or a directory, with a slightly different meaning of options for System V and BSD UNIX:

 # ls-l System V
 # ls-lg BSD

The system response looks like:

drwx------	*2*	***bjl***	***mail***	*24*	*Mar 24 13:19*	*Mail*
-rw-rw-rw-	*1*	***bjl***	***users***	*20*	*May 2 13:26*	*modefile1*

-rw-rw-rw-	*1*	***bjl***	***users***	*20*	*May 2 13:30*	*modefile2*
-rw-rw-rw-	*1*	***bjl***	***users***	*20*	*May 2 13:30*	*modefile3*

The file ownerships are presented in the third column (for a user-owner), and fourth column (for a group-owner). In this example, all files (*modefiles 1, 2,* and *3*) are owned by the user *bjl* and the group *users*.

Ownership of a newly created file is determined in the following way:

- The user-owner is the user who has created the file
- The group-owner is:
  - Same as the group-owner for the directory where the new file was created (for BSD)
  - Same as the group to which the user who created the file belongs (for System V)

Please note that this rule only applies to newly created files; once a file is created, its ownership can be arbitrarily modified.

The **chown** command is used to change the user ownership of a file or a directory:

 # chown *newowner filename(s)*

where:

newowner A user name, or user-ID (**UID**)
filename A file name in the current directory, or a full-path file name (if multiple files are specified, they are separated by a space)

Directories are treated in the same way as files; to change the user ownership of a directory itself, type the command:

 # chown *newowner directoryname(s)*

where:

newowner A user name, or user-ID (UID)
directoryname A subdirectory name in the current directory, or a full-path directory name (if multiple directories are specified, they are separated by a space).

However, to change the user ownership of a directory *and* all subdirectories and files within it, the **chown** command should be used recursively (the option -R):

 # chown -R *newowner directoryname(s)*

(The command arguments are the same as those in the previous example.)

Who is authorized to change the user ownership?

user-owner of the file, or ***root*** (System V)
root only (BSD)

Please note that on the System V platform, if the original user-owner transfers user-ownership to another user, it can only be transferred back to the original user-owner by the new user who now owns the file, or by root. Also, such a change of ownership is restricted: some access rights cannot be transferred to the new user (we will discuss this issue in more details later).

Generally, each recursive command must be accomplished extremely carefully; the started command does not stay within the specified directory; it is propagated toward all existing subdirectories, files in these subdirectories, subsequent subdirectories, and so on, until the very end of the directory hierarchy (could be very, very deep). If implemented in the root directory, each recursive command affects every single file in the system.

Try to remember an unpleasant event when an administrator wanted to change recursively the owner for a certain directory (of course the administrator did that as the superuser). The administrator typed in the command and started to specify the full pathname of the directory; unfortunately the administrator hit unintentionally the [Enter] key too early, just after the leading "/" (slash character) of the directory path was typed. The disastrous command: ***chown -R newuser /*** was issued, causing recursive changes of many system files, and soon a collapse of the system. The only solution was to reinstall and restore the system from a backup (if such a backup is available at all).

The **chgrp** command is used to change the group ownership of a file or a directory:

 # chgrp ***newgroup filename(s)/directoryname(s)***

where:

newgroup	A group name, or a group-ID (**GID**)
filename	A file name in the current directory, or a full-path file name
directoryname	A subdirectory name in the current directory, or a full-path directory name (multiple names are separated by a space)

To change the group ownership of a directory, and all subdirectories and files within it, the **chgrp** command should be used recursively (the option -R):

 # chgrp -R ***newgroup directoryname(s)***

Who is authorized to change the group ownership?

user-owner of the file, or ***root***

Originally, the BSD UNIX allowed simultaneous changes of the file's user and group ownership, using the same **chown** command in the following way:

 # chown ***newowner.newgroup filename(s)***

 # chown -R ***newowner.newgroup directoryname***

where:

newowner	A user name, or an UID
newgroup	A group name, or a GID
filename	A file name in the current directory or a full-path file name
directoryname	A subdirectory name in the current directory, or a full-path directory name

Today, most modern UNIX flavors (whether BSD- or System V-derived) accept this useful idea and allow the same simultaneous change, with slightly different syntax:

 # chown ***newowner:newgroup filename(s)***
 # chown -R ***newowner:newgroup directoryname***

Instead of a dot (.) that was originally used as a separator between the new user and group name, now the colon (:) is introduced.

For a better understanding, a few examples follow:
Let's start with a long listing of a directory (the logged-in user is ***bjl***):

$ ls -l

drwx------	2	*bjl*	*mail*	24	*Mar 24 13:19*	*Mail*
-rw-rw-rw-	1	***bjl***	*users*	20	*May 2 13:26*	*modefile1*
-rw-rw-rw-	1	*bjl*	***users***	20	*May 2 13:30*	*modefile2*
-rw-rw-rw-	1	*bjl*	*users*	20	*May 2 13:30*	*modefile3*
-rw-rw-rw-	1	*bjl*	*users*	2106	*May 2 13:31*	*ses1.tmp*

The user can change the user and group owners for certain files:

$ chown dubey modefile1
$ chgrp other modefile2
$ ls -l

drwx------	2	*bjl*	*mail*	24	*Mar 24 13:19*	*Mail*
-rw-rw-rw-	1	***dubey***	*users*	20	*May 2 13:26*	*modefile1*
-rw-rw-rw-	1	*bjl*	***other***	20	*May 2 13:30*	*modefile2*
-rw-rw-rw-	1	*bjl*	*users*	20	*May 2 13:30*	*modefile3*
-rw-rw-rw-	1	*bjl*	*users*	2106	*May 2 13:31*	*ses1.tmp*

And then regains the group ownership of the changed file *modefile2*:

$ chgrp users modefile2

Regaining user ownership of the changed file *modefile1* is not as simple; the logged-in user ***bjl*** doesn't own this file anymore, and only the new owner or the superuser can reassign user ownership to ***bjl***. Supposing that switching to root is possible (in most cases it is not possible, only administrators know the root password that is always required to become the **superuser**):

$ su
Password: ********
 # chown bjl modefile1
 # ls -l

total 8

drwx------	2	*bjl*	*mail*	24	*Mar 24 13:19*	*Mail*
-rw-rw-rw-	1	***bjl***	*users*	20	*May 2 13:26*	*modefile1*
-rw-rw-rw-	1	*bjl*	***users***	20	*May 2 13:30*	*modefile2*
-rw-rw-rw-	1	*bjl*	*users*	20	*May 2 13:30*	*modefile3*
-rw-rw-rw-	1	*bjl*	*users*	2106	*May 2 13:31*	*ses1.tmp*

2.2.2 File Protection/File Access

First, let us introduce the terminology we will use to identify access rights to a certain file. We will use three different terms that are related to the very same issue: *file protection*, *file access*, and *file permissions*. These three terms are mutually related, and their use is primarily dependent upon the angle from which we are viewing the issue. Though file access and file permissions are directly proportional, and we often use the composite term *access permissions* (more file permissions permit wider access to the file), file access and file protection are inversely proportional (a higher file protection requires more restricted file access). Finally, they are all known as the *file mode*.

Every file has a set of permission bits that determine who has access to the file, and the type of access they have. UNIX supports three types of file access:

Access	File Meaning	Directory Meaning
Read (**r**)	View file contents	Search directory contents (***ls***)
Write (**w**)	Alter file contents	Alter directory contents (***rm***)
Execute (**x**)	Run executable file	Make it the current directory (***cd***) for a search

Notes: (x) is sometimes identified as "execute/search" access right; For a script file execution, **r** and **x** access permissions are required (each line in the script must be read to be executed).

The following table lists the permissions required to perform some of the most common UNIX commands.

Command	Minimum Access Required		Comments
	On File Itself	On Directory File *ls* in	
cd /home/username	N/A	**x**	
ls /home/username	none	**r**	
ls -s /home/username	none	**rx**	A file size determination requires a logical move to the directory itself to search the content of the inode of the specified file
cat filename	**r**	**x**	
cat >> filename	**w**	**x**	
filename	**x** (if binary)	**x**	
filename	**rx** (if script)	**x**	
rm filename	**w**	**xw**	**w** permission for a file is not a requirement (but an additional confirmation will be required); **w** permission for a directory is mandatory (removing a file means altering the directory)

Notes: It is important to understand the difference between a simple *ls* command, and any other, more elaborated *ls* command (with an option that requires a search of the file's inode). Simple listing of the directory means just to read the content of the directory; options require information from the inode of the specified file.

2.2.2.1 Access Classes

UNIX defines three basic classes of access to files, for which permissions can be specified separately:

User access (**u**) Access granted to the **user-owner** of the file

Group access (**g**) Access granted to **members** of the group that owns the file

Other access (**o**)	Access granted to **everyone else** (except root)
All classes (**a**)	Access granted to **everyone** (includes all three classes)

The access classes independently specify file modes for different categories (classes) of users. The long format (the "-l" option) of the **ls** command is used to display the file mode — see the previous example. The first column in the listing, a set of letters and hyphens, represents a file mode; the file mode includes three triplets for the three access classes **u**, **g**, and **o**. This is illustrated in the following table:

File Type		**User Access (u)**			**Group Access (g)**			**Other Access (o)**	
Position	1	2	3	4	5	6	7	8	9	10
Letter	-	r	w	x	r	w	x	r	w	x
Read access		+			+			+		
Write access			+			+			+	
Execute access				+			+			+

Note: The first letter (or hyphen) in a line (the leftmost position) represents a file type.

2.2.2.2 Setting a File Protection

We have already discussed myriad terms to refer to file protection; UNIX simply refers to a file protection as **file mode**. In UNIX parlance, to set file permissions means to change a file mode; for that purpose, the UNIX **chmod** command is used:

 # chmod access-string filename(s)

where

access-string Includes:
Access class: ***u***, ***g***, ***o***, or ***a***
Operator: +, -, or =
Permissions: ***r***, ***w***, or ***x***

filename File name in the current directory, or the full-path file name (multiple files are separated by a space).

Multiple access classes and/or permissions could be also simultaneously specified. The recursive **chmod** command is also supported, for example:

 # chmod -R go-rwx /home/username

This command will change the file mode of all files and subdirectories beneath the directory */home/username*. It will deny any kind of access for group and other, and the user access will remain unchanged.

This example specifies the file mode, using what is called *symbolic mode notation*. Alternatively, the *absolute*, or *numeric, mode notation* could be also used. The difference between the two is shown below:

user	*group*	*other*	Access classes
r w x	*r – x*	*r--*	Symbolic mode
1 1 1	*1 0 1*	*1 0 0*	Convert to binary
7	*5*	*4*	Convert to digit
	754		The corresponding absolute (numeric) mode

The command to set this particular file mode is:

 # chmod 754 *filename*

Access rights for a certain user are strictly determined by the individual permissions within the related class. It means that UNIX first determines where the user belongs – is that the *user-owner*, a member of the *group-owner*, or any other user. Once it is done, only the related file's access class is checked and accordingly a needed access to the file granted or denied. There is no a gradual top-down access class checkup in the cases when an user belongs to multiple classes (an *user-owner* could also be a member of the *group-owner*, and definitely belongs to *others*). Here is an example:

The user is ***bjl***; the long listing for the text file ***textfile*** is:

$ ls -l testfile
-rw-r--r-- 1 bjl users 15 Jul 6 20:49 textfile
With the following content:
$ cat textfile
#
 # This is just a test file
#

Let us deny read access to the user-owner ***bjl***:
$ chmod u-r testfile
$ ls -l testfile
--w-r--r -- 1 bjl users 15 Jul 6 20:49 textfile

And try to read the file again:
$ cat textfile
cat: textfile: Permission denied

However, the file can be modified
$ echo "# This is added text" >> textfile
$ echo "#" textfile

Besides the fact that user ***bjl*** is the owner of the file ***textfile*** and a member of the group ***users***, as well as that read permission is granted to the group ***users*** and to all others, the file cannot be opened for reading. The file's owner, user ***bjl***, can modify or delete the file (there is the **w** permission), but the file cannot be read. To overcome this "unusual situation," the owner has to change the file mode, and make the file readable.

$ chmod 644 testfile
$ ls –l testfile
-rw-r--r-- 1 bjl users 15 Jul 6 20:49 textfile
$ cat textfile
#
 # This is just a test file
 # This is added text
#
The same is valid for a group-owner toward group permissions.

2.2.2.3 Default File Mode

The default file mode determines file permissions for newly created files. Once a file is created, the file mode can be changed as desired. UNIX is quite flexible regarding default file mode — there is a coded system setting, and a possibility for a program setting. First of all, the usual system default file modes for directories and files are different:

- For a directory *rwxrwxrwx*, i.e., all permissions are granted
- For a file *rw-rw-rw-*, i.e., the execute permissions are initially denied

However, do not be surprised if some specific UNIX flavors or even UNIX releases behave differently.

The program setting of the default file mode is always adjusted toward a system setting, and a specified permission can only be denied (never granted); it means only a more restrictive default file mode can be dynamically created. Pay attention that this is related to the default file mode only; the **chmod** command, or renaming and copying files, are not restricted in that way.

The command **umask** is used for that purpose. Upon the command execution, all newly created files in the new environment will be automatically set according to the new default file mode. The **umask** command itself uses numeric notation to specify the default file mode, but in a slightly different way than the **chmod** command. The **umask** command sets permissions to be inhibited (masked out) when a file is created — it denies permissions. The implemented numeric notation should be an octal complement to the numeric notation of the desired file mode. Old UNIX releases supposed only the numeric notation; modern UNIX flavors allow also the use of the symbolic notation. It is highly recommended to stay familiar with the numeric notation (it works always and everywhere).

For example, to have a default file mode same as the file mode "754" in the previous example:

777 All access granted
–754 Desired access granted
023 Masked out access for default mode

The corresponding command is ***umask 023***.

2.2.2.4 Additional Access Modes

We have discussed common file permissions, which are quite self-explanatory (***read*** and ***write*** are obvious) and relatively easy to use. Some confusion is possible with respect to the ***execute*** (*x*) permission on a directory, but once we accept execution as a condition to "search the directory -> ***cd***," everything seems to be reasonable; that is why it is also known as ***execute/search*** permission. However, the three file permissions (*r*, *w*, and *x*) are far from sufficient to cover all file permission needs in UNIX, and consequently UNIX has to support additional access modes. These additional access modes are listed below:

Code	Name	Meaning
t	sticky bit	Keep executable image in memory after exit (memory resident program)
s	set UID (SUID)	Set process user ID on execution (will be discussed in greater detail)
s	set GID (SGID)	Set process group ID on execution (will be discussed in greater detail)
l	file locking	Set mandatory file locking on r/w for this file (originally System V)

When using the **ls -l** command, **SUID** and **SGID** access bits are displayed in the position of "**x** access" for the corresponding access class (SUID in the user class, SGID in the group class); the **sticky bit** is displayed in the position of **x** access for the class "others."

SUID and SGID are extremely important and are very sensitive issues from the system security standpoint. Normally, when an executable file (a program) is invoked, and the corresponding process created, the access rights to system resources of such a process (known as a process's effective IDs: EUID and EGID) are related to the user and group who started the program execution (known as the process's real IDs: RUID and RGID). However, if SUID or SGID access is set on an executable file, access to system resources is based upon the **file's user or group owner** rather than on the real user who started the program execution. This means, for example, for an executable file owned by the root, regardless of who has started its execution, the program will be executed in the same way as if the superuser had invoked it. (We will discuss this issue in more detail later by addressing process attributes.)

SUID and SGID, as well as a sticky bit, are supposed to be implemented primarily on executable files; however, they could be implemented on any file, as well as on a directory. In such a case, they have different meanings. Here is a summary:

Set Bit	File or Directory	Meaning
SUID	Executable file	Effective user ID on execution (EUID) is equal to the file user owner's ID
SUID	Nonexecutable file or directory	None
SGID	Executable file	Effective group ID on execution (EGID) is equal to the file group owner's ID
SGID	Nonexecutable file	Enable mandatory locking of the file
SGID	Directory	Opposite semantic in propagation of the group ownership; BSD behaves like System V, and vice versa
Sticky	Executable file	Memory resident program
Sticky	Nonexecutable file	Memory resident file (system's paging is skipped, as in swap files)
Sticky	Directory	Deletion of files in the directory is restricted only to the owner of the directory, or of the file itself

The aforementioned **chmod** command is used to set additional file modes. Both symbolic and absolute (numeric) notations are supported; however, on some UNIX platform only the symbolic mode notation can be used to clear an SGID bit on a directory.

The symbolic notation uses the letter *s*, together with a corresponding access class to set/clear additional access bits:

 # chmod u+s *filename* Set SUID on *filename*

 # chmod g+s *filename* Set SGID on *filename*

 # chmod o+s *filename* Set sticky bit on *filename*

Alternately, the minus sign (–) is used to clear additional access bits.

An additional, fourth triplet was introduced for the numeric notation; it corresponds to ***SUID* | *SGID* | *sticky*,** and can be presented numerically, like any other triplet. This additional triplet is the leading one, positioned in front of the other three triplets, and the leading digit in the 4-digit numeric notation identifies it. The 3-digit numeric notation is still valid; UNIX simply assumes 0 for additional access bits (there is no need for a leading zero).

The following example should make this clear; it presents the procedure to change a file mode.

The login user is ***bjl***; the current long listing of an arbitrary directory shows:

$ ls -l
drwx------ 2 bjl mail 24 Mar 24 13:19 Mail
-rw-rw-rw- 1 bjl users 20 May 2 13:26 modefile1

-rw-rw-rw-	*1*	*bjl*	*users*	*20*	*May 2 13:30*	*modefile2*
-rw-rw-rw-	*1*	*bjl*	*users*	*20*	*May 2 13:30*	*modefile3*
-rw-rw-rw-	*1*	*bjl*	*users*	*322*	*May 2 13:31*	*ses1.tmp*

The user wants to change the file mode for certain files (the symbolic notation is implemented):

$ chmod u+x modefile1
$ chmod g–w+x modefile2 modefile3
$ ls -l

drwx------	*2*	*bjl*	*mail*	*24*	*Mar 24 13:19*	*Mail*
-rwxrw-rw-	*1*	*bjl*	*users*	*20*	*May 2 13:26*	*modefile1*
-rw-r-xrw-	*1*	*bjl*	*users*	*20*	*May 2 13:30*	*modefile2*
-rw-r-xrw-	*1*	*bjl*	*users*	*20*	*May 2 13:30*	*modefile3*
-rw-rw-rw-	*1*	*bjl*	*users*	*322*	*May 2 13:31*	*ses1.tmp*

The required changes in file modes are shown in the new long listing of the directory. Now let us set SUID and SGID on certain files:

$ chmod u+s modefile1
$ chmod g+s modefile2
$ ls -l

drwx------	*2*	*bjl*	*mail*	*24*	*Mar 24 13:19*	*Mail*
-rwsrw-rw-	*1*	*bjl*	*users*	*20*	*May 2 13:26*	*modefile1*
-rw-r-srw-	*1*	*bjl*	*users*	*20*	*May 2 13:30*	*modefile2*
-rw-r-xrw-	*1*	*bjl*	*users*	*20*	*May 2 13:30*	*modefile3*
-rw-rw-rw-	*1*	*bjl*	*users*	*322*	*May 2 13:31*	*ses1.tmp*

Pay attention to the displayed position of SUID and SGID bits (they overwrite ***x*** permission). Finally, let us return to the initial file modes:

$ chmod 666 modefile1 modefile2 modefile3

drwx------	*2*	*bjl*	*mail*	*24*	*Mar 24 13:19*	*Mail*
-rw-rw-rw-	*1*	*bjl*	*users*	*20*	*May 2 13:26*	*modefile1*
-rw-rw-rw-	*1*	*bjl*	*users*	*20*	*May 2 13:30*	*modefile2*
-rw-rw-rw-	*1*	*bjl*	*users*	*20*	*May 2 13:30*	*modefile3*
-rw-rw-rw-	*1*	*bjl*	*users*	*322*	*May 2 13:39*	*ses1.tmp*

Note that SUID and SGID were cleared also; in this case (this is HP-UX flavor), implemented numeric notation works.

On the System V platform, a user-owner can change the file's ownership. Practically, it means that a user-owner can give the file to another user, also transferring owner access rights to the new owner. If the SUID or SGID bit is set on the file, such a change of file ownership could be a potential security problem. It would be very easy to create a particularly nasty scenario that would affect the new owner. Just imagine a simple script that purges the home directory of the new owner, and can be triggered by everybody (there is x permission for others). Once the script ownership was modified, and supposing the SUID is set, whoever starts the script's execution will appear as the new owner — i.e., the targeted home directory will really be purged (very unpleasant!).

Obviously System V UNIX has to protect itself from such unwelcome surprises. Let us see how in the next example:

Three test files are created by the user ***bjl***: *testfile1, testfile2,* and *testfile3.*

```
$ ls -l
-rw-r-----  1  bjl  users  0  May 27 15:07  testfile1
-rw-r-----  1  bjl  users  0  May 27 15:07  testfile2
-rw-r-----  1  bjl  users  0  May 27 15:07  testfile3
```

The SUID and SGID are set by the user-owner (numeric notation is used):

```
$ chmod 4777 testfile1
$ chmod 2777 testfile2
$ chmod 4640 testfile3
$ ls -l
-rwsrwxrwx  1  levi  users  0  May 27 15:07  testfile1
-rwxrwsrwx  1  levi  users  0  May 27 15:07  testfile2
-rwSr-----  1  levi  users  0  May 27 15:07  testfile3
```

The *"set IDs"* hide existing *"**x** access bits"* in the corresponding access classes. To make the hidden bit recognizable, the low case letter *"**s**"* is displayed if both bits *"set ID"* and *"**x** access bit"* are set, and capital letter *"**S**"* is displayed if only *"set ID"* bit is set (pay attention, not for all UNIX flavors). In this example, the file *testfile3* is not an executable file. (In that light, SUID on this file does not make a lot of sense, but it is still a good illustration of the previous point.)
The file ownership is now changed by the user-owner:

```
$ chown dubey testfile1 testfile2 testfile3
$ ls-l
-rwxrwxrwx  1  dubey  users  0  May 27 15:07  testfile1
-rwxrwxrwx  1  dubey  users  0  May 27 15:07  testfile2
-rw-r-----  1  dubey  users  0  May 27 15:07  testfile3
```

What happened? We can see that the *"set IDs"* have not been transferred to the new owner. Simply, if the file ownership was changed by the user-owner for files in which SUID and SGID were set, the file modes would also change — SUID and SGID are not transferable to another user; only the superuser can make it. (Anyhow, the superuser can make whatever it wants.)
Now, let us return everything to the initial state; since the user ***bjl*** does not own the files anymore, it will be done by the superuser. First switch to the superuser account:

```
$ su
Password: ********
# chown bjl testfile1 testfile2 testfile3
# su bjl
$ chmod 640 testfile1 testfile2
$ ls -l
-rw-r-----  1  bjl  users  0  May 27 15:07  testfile1
-rw-r-----  1  bjl  users  0  May 27 15:07  testfile2
-rw-r-----  1  bjl  users  0  May 27 15:07  testfile3
```

Note that a switch to the superuser (root) account always requires the root password, while the switch from the superuser to some other user account does not. A superuser already has full control over the system, including all user accounts.

2.2.3 Access Control Lists (ACLs)

File access permissions originate from the early days of UNIX, and they provide enough flexibility in accessing UNIX resources (objects) to meet most daily needs. This approach was made even more flexible by introducing secondary groups as desired, and by grouping individual users on a per need basis. Nevertheless, the continual development and growth in the implementation of UNIX as a platform for different applications required an even more selective approach. Modern UNIX flavors introduced ***Access Control Lists (ACLs)*** to respond to new demands.

ACLs are a key enforcement mechanism of discretionary access control (DAC), used to specify access to files by users and groups more selectively than with traditional UNIX mechanisms. ACLs permit or deny access to a list of users, groups, or combinations thereof. ACLs are supported as a superset of the UNIX operating system DAC mechanism for files, directories, and devices.

An *access control list* is a set of (***user.group, mode***) entries associated with a file that specify permissions for all possible user-ID/group-ID combinations. An entry in an ACL specifies access rights for one user and group combination. Three bits in an ACL entry represent read, write, and execute-search permissions. These permissions coexist with the traditional mode bits associated with every file in the filesystem.

An individual ACL entry could be considered *restrictive* or *permissive* depending on the context. Restrictive entries deny a user and/or group access that would otherwise be granted by less specific base or optional ACL entries. Permissive entries grant a user and/or group access that would otherwise be denied by less specific base or optional ACL entries.

The right to alter ACL entries is granted to file (object) owners and to privileged users. Privileged users are superusers and members of certain privileged groups.

For a better understanding of the relationship between ACLs and traditional file permissions, let us consider the following file and its permissions:

Permissions	User	Group	Filename
-rwxr-xr--	*bjl*	*admin*	*datafile*
The file owner is:	*bjl*		
The file's group is:	*admin*		
The name of the file is:	*datafile*		
The file owner permissions are:	*rwx*		
The file group permissions are:	*r-x*		
The file other permissions are:	*r--*		

When a file is created, three *base access control list* entries are mapped from the file's access permission bits to match the file's owner and group and its traditional permission bits. The three base ACL entries are:

1. Base ACL entry for the file's owner: (***uid.%, mode***)
2. Base ACL entry for the file's group: (***%.gid, mode***)
3. Base ACL entry for other users: (***%.%, mode***)

The basic form of an ACL entry is (***user.group, mode***). ***user*** and ***group*** can be represented by names or ID numbers; ***mode*** is represented by a letter (*r, w,* and *x* if the corresponding access is granted, or dash "- "if the access is denied). Two special symbols may also be used:

1. % symbol, representing no specific user or group
2. @ symbol, representing the current file owner or group

ACLs are superimposed on the file's traditional permissions; however, managing ACLs does not affect the traditional file mode. There is no way to change the traditional file permissions by using ACL-specific commands (the opposite is not true because base ACL entries are synchronized with the traditional file permissions). Both the traditional UNIX command ***chmod*** and ACL-specific commands may be used to change base ACL entries.

Optional ACL entries contain additional access control information, which the privileged user can set with the available ACL-specific commands to further allow or deny file access. Up to 13 additional user/group combinations may be specified. For example, the following optional ACL entries could be associated with the presented file *datafile*:

(***mhr.admin, rwx***)	Grant read, write, and execute access to user ***mhr*** in group ***admin***
(***mnm.%, ---***)	Deny any access to user ***mnm*** in no specific group (any group)

ACL entries are unique; there can only be one (*user.group, mode*) entry for any pair of *user* and *group* values; one (*user.%, mode*) entry for a given value of *user*; one (*%.group, mode*) entry for a given value of *group*; and one (*%.%, mode*) entry for each file.

There are several UNIX commands to manage ACLs, and they are all UNIX-flavor specific. Although they all have essentially the same mission, they have different command names. We will focus on Solaris-specific ACL commands.

The **getfacl** command is available on Solaris to display discretionary file information:

getfacl [-ad] ***filename(s)***

where

option **-a**	Display the filename, owner, group, and file's ACL
option **-d**	Display the filename, owner, group, and default file's ACL (if it exists)
no option	Display the filename, owner, group, file's ACL, and default file's ACL (if it exists)
filename	The filename in the current directory, or full-path filename. (multiple filenames are separated by a space; a blank line separates displayed ACLs)

A few examples (the selected file is */etc/vfstab*):

$ getfacl /etc/vfstab

# file: /etc/vfstab	***# The first three lines specify the filename, user-owner and group owner; they start with pound sign ("#").***
# owner: root	
# group: other	
user::r--	***# Permissions for user-owner (because the second field is empty).***
group::r-- #effective:r --	***# Permissions for group owner (because the second field is empty).***
mask:r--	***# Maximum permissions allowed to any user except user-owner, and to any group (including group owner); they restrict the permissions specified in other entries.***
other:r--	***# Permissions granted to others.***

In order to indicate when the group class permission bits restrict an ACL entry, an additional string "*#effective:*" specifies the actual permissions granted in the same line of the restricted entry; the string is separated by a tab character.

$ cd /etc

$ getfacl vfstab

 # file: vfstab — ***# This is the same command as in the previous example, except that the relative filename was specified.***

 # owner: root

 # group: other

user::r--

group::r--   #effective: r--

mask:r--

other:r--

$ getfacl -a vfstab

 # file: vfstab — ***# For this file, the "option –a" and "no options" display the same output because there is no default ACL.***

 # owner: root

 # group: other

user::r--

group::r--   #effective: r--

mask:r--

other::r--

$ getfacl -d vfstab

 # file: vfstab — ***# Only the first three lines are displayed because there is no default ACL.***

 # owner: root

 # group: other

The Solaris **setfacl** command is available to modify an ACL for a file or files. Two forms of the command may be used:

setfacl [-r] [-s | -m | -d] ***acl_entries filename(s)***
setfacl [-r] [-f] ***acl_file filename(s)***

where

option **-r** — Recalculates the permissions for the file's group class entry (known as the mask entry). These permissions are ignored and replaced by the maximum permissions needed for the file group class, to grant access to any additional user, owning group, and additional group entries in the ACL. The permissions for these entities remain unchanged.

option **-s** — Sets the ACL to the entries specified on the command line; all old ACL entries are removed and replaced with the newly specified ACL.

option **-m** — Adds one or more new ACL entries, and/or modifies one or more existing ACL entries; when modified, the specified permissions will replace the current permissions.

option **-d** — Deletes one or more ACL entries; the file owner, owning group, and others may not be deleted. Deleting an ACL entry does not necessarily

	have the same effect as removing all permissions from the entry by modifying the entry itself (an ACL entry superimposes on traditional file permissions).
option **-f**	Sets the ACL to the entries contained within the file named *acl_file* on the command line (see *acl_file*); the same constraints on specified entries in the *acl_file* hold as with **-s** option.
acl_entries	One or more comma-separated ACL entries of the following format (all entries are not applicable for all options): *u[ser]::operm | perm* *u[ser]:uid:operm | perm* *g[roup]::operm | perm* *g[roup]:gid:operm | perm* *m[ask]:operm | perm* *d[efault]:u[ser]::operm | perm* *d[efault]:u[ser]:uid:operm | perm* *d[efault]:g[roup]::operm | perm* *d[efault]:g[roup]:gid: operm | perm* *d[efault]:m[ask]:operm | perm* *d[efault]:o[ther]:operm | perm* Where *perm* is a permissions string composed of the letters r(read), w(write), and x(execute); the dash (-) may be specified as a place holder. *operm* is an octal representation of the above permissions, 7 -> all permissions (rwx), 0 -> no permissions (---)
uid	is a login name or user ID; for user-owner is empty
gid	is a group name or group ID; for group-owner is empty
acl_file	The file that contains ACL entries; an ACL entry is specified as a single line. Comments are permitted and they start with pound sign (#). The file can be created as an output of the **getfacl** command.

2.2.4 File Types

We mentioned earlier that in UNIX everything is a file, or is file-like. Given what we now know about file ownership and file mode, perhaps it is more appropriate to say that in UNIX everything is "dressed like a file." This means everything appears like a file, but there are still differences in the file content and the way the file is managed and processed.

These differences result in different kinds of files, or in UNIX terminology, different file types. The type of a file determines how the file will be handled.

The long listing of the **ls -l** command also displays the file type; a leading single letter, or hyphen, in the leftmost position of the first column in the listing that presents the file mode, identifies a file type. The file type is identified in the following way:

-	Plain (regular) file
d	Directory
c	Character special file
b	Block special file
l	Symbolic link
s	Socket
p	Named pipe

Here is an example:

```
$ ls-l
drwx------   2  bjl  mail   24  Mar 24 18:19  Mail
-rwxrw-rw-   1  bjl  users  20  May 2 18:26   file1
lrwxrwxrwx   1  bjl  users  20  May 2 18:28   file2 -> /usr/local/bin/file2
```

Three different file types are displayed: a regular file (-), a directory (***d***), and a symbolic link (***l***). A brief summary of file types follows.

2.2.4.1 Plain (Regular) File

A plain file is just a sequence of bytes: a data file, an ASCII file, a binary data file, executable binary program, etc. In most cases when we talk about files, we are thinking of plain files. They are identified by the hyphen (-) in the long listing of a directory they reside in.

2.2.4.2 Directory

A binary file, a directory is a list of the files within it (including any subdirectories). Entries are ***filename-inode*** pairs. In UNIX each file is identified by an ***inode*** (an official name is ***index node***). For simplicity, we will assume that an inode fully specifies the file, and that by knowing the inode, UNIX actually knows everything about the file itself (ownership, mode, type, other properties, contents, location on the disk) except its name. The directory relates the filename with the file itself; the *filename-inode* pairs that make a content of a directory itself actually establish this relationship. Although it might seem odd to a beginner, UNIX can find a filename only in the corresponding directory. If a directory is corrupted, all of its filenames can be easily lost, while the corresponding files remain unchanged and unnamed.

The special entries "." and ".." (single and double dots) refer to the directory itself and its parent directory, respectively. A directory in its long listing is identified with the letter **d**.

2.2.4.3 Special Device File

A special device file is used to describe the attached I/O device. UNIX accesses devices via their special files. In UNIX, device drivers themselves (software interfaces that control the devices) are part of the kernel, and can be accessed by using certain system calls (UNIX internals). A special device file is a kind of pointer to the corresponding device driver within the kernel; it is a very simple file that contains two pointers: major and minor numbers. The major number points to the device class, while the minor number points to the individual device within the class.

All special device files reside in the directory */dev* (and its subdirectories on System V). There are two groups of special device files: block device files and character device files.

2.2.4.3.1 Block Device File

I/O operations are provided through a group of buffers; the system maintains a buffer pool for all block devices. The block device is accessed in fixed-size blocks. Physically, the high-speed data transfer is realized using a DMA mechanism (direct memory access data transfer). The letter **b** in the long listing of a directory identifies the block device files. The following disk-related block device files are examples of block device files: */dev/disk0a* or */dev/dsk/c1d1s5*.

2.2.4.3.2 Character Device File

Nonbuffered I/O operations are provided via a character or raw device. Physically, the data transfer is performed through a registered data exchange between the device and its controller. Character devices include all devices that do not fit the block I/O transfer. The letter **c** in the long listing of a directory identifies the character device files. The following disk related raw device files are examples of character special files: */dev/rdisk0a* or */dev/rdsk/c1d1s5*.

2.2.4.4 Link

A link is a mechanism that allows multiple filenames to refer to a single file on a disk, i.e., a single inode. There are two kinds of links: hard links and symbolic links.

2.2.4.4.1 Hard Link

A hard link associates two or more filenames with an inode; each inode keeps a record of a number of linked filenames. Only when all filenames are deleted will the file itself also be deleted, and the corresponding inode released and returned as free for new file assignments. Strictly speaking, a hard link is not a separate file type; each hard link represents an already existing file with an additional filename. The only way to identify mutually hard-linked filenames is to list a directory or directories by using the "**ls -i**" command and check for identical inode numbers. The "**-i**" option displays, beside the filename, the inode number for each displayed file in the listed directory.

Hard links always remain within the same filesystem; simply, inodes cannot be shared between filesystems, and two hard links are always associated with the same inode. A hard link never creates a new file; it only attaches a new filename to the existing file. This means that a hard link only presents a new entry in a directory, a new record about a filename-inode pair.

To create a hard link use the ***ln*** command:

ln myfile hardlink

This command will create a new entry in the current directory named **hardlink** paired with the same inode number as **myfile**. There are no hard links for directories; it would be too confusing and dangerous for the system.

2.2.4.4.2 Symbolic Link

A symbolic link is a pointer file to another file elsewhere in the overall hierarchical directory tree. By creating a symbolic link, a new small file is also created; this new file contains the full-path filename of the linked file. There is no restriction on the use of symbolic links; they span filesystem boundaries independently of the origin of the linked file. Symbolic links are very common (this cannot be said for hard links); they are easy to create, easy to maintain and easy to see. The letter **l** in the long listing of a directory identifies them; a linked file is also displayed in a visually comprehensive way (see previous example for file types).

To create a symbolic link use also the ***ln*** command (with the option **-s**):

ln -s myfile symlink

This command creates another file named **symlink** in the current directory with a separate inode (since this is a completely new file) that points to the file **myfile**. Both types of links are presented in Figure 2.1. Let me explain it in more detail.

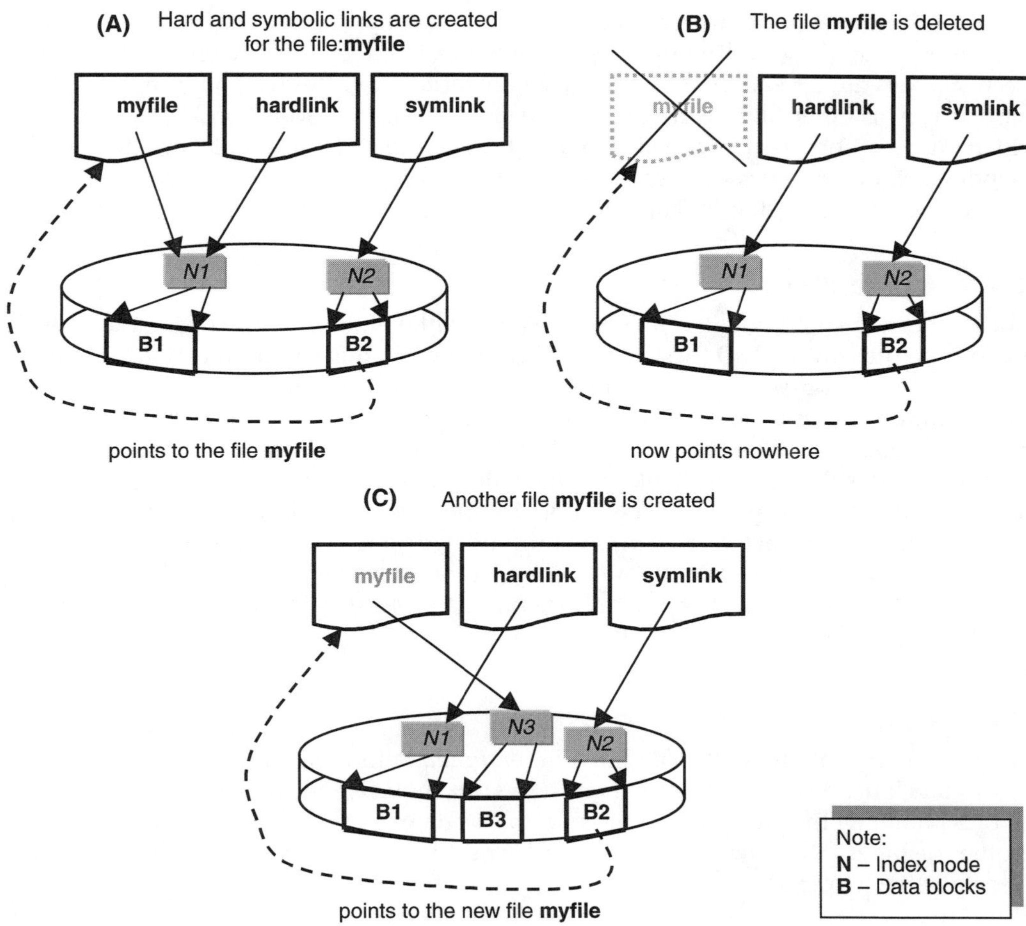

FIGURE 2.1
Hard and symbolic links.

For an existing file named **myname**, which is determined by the inode (index node) **N1**, both links are created. The hard link **hardlink** is another name for the file **myfile**, and it corresponds to the same inode **N1**. The symbolic link **symlink** represents another file determined by the inode **N2**; its contents point to the file **myfile**.

What will happen if the file **myfile** is deleted? Actually, only the filename "myfile" will be deleted; the file itself remains with its other name **hardlink** (the file content remains unchanged). The symbolic link **symlink** is now broken; it points nowhere (there is no more referenced file **myfile**).

What will happen if another file named **myfile** is created in the same directory? This is a brand new file, determined by the new index node **N3** and unrelated to the existing file **hardlink**, which continues to exist as a different file. However, the file **symlink** is now linked with the new file **myname**, and it continues to point to the newly created file **myfile**.

2.2.4.5 Socket

A special type of file used for interprocess communication on a single system or between different systems; sockets enable connection between processes. There are several kinds of sockets, and most of them are involved in network communications. UNIX domain sockets are local ones, used in local interprocess communication; they are referenced as filesystem objects. Sockets are created by the use of a special system call, *"socket"*, but can be treated in a similar way as other files (using the same system calls). However, a socket can be read or written only by processes directly involved in the connection. For example, printing systems, X windowing, or error system logging use sockets. Sockets were originally developed in BSD and later included in System V. The most probable place to find sockets is the */tmp* directory.

2.2.4.6 Named Pipe

Another mechanism, originated in System V, to facilitate interprocess communication; the named pipe presents a FIFO (first-in first-out) element in this communication. The output of one process becomes an input to another process. Named pipes are very useful when a large amount of data is involved in the interprocess communication; sometimes some application, and even OS restrictions could be bypassed by using the named pipe.

UNIX provides the command ***mknod pipename p*** to create a named pipe ***pipename***. The same command is used to create special device files and we will return to this command later. The trailing character "p" specifies the named pipe. Pay attention this is slightly different from the usual UNIX way in specifying the command option. In the long listing of a directory the leading letter **p** identifies named pipes. Again the most probable place for named pipes is the */tmp* directory.

2.2.4.7 Conclusion

Independent of a file type, the file must be ***mounted*** before it can be accessed. *Mounting* is a special UNIX process of bringing online a storage device (primarily a disk) that keeps the files, making the files accessible and their contents readable. Only mounted files become visible and can be searched, found, and processed. We will cover mounting in full details in Chapters 5 and 6.

All listed file types have different natures. They are created with file-type specific UNIX commands, but other UNIX commands are mostly applicable on all file types. The output of the same UNIX command can be different depending on the file types, but the command itself would work. For example, the command:

 # cat filename

will display the contents of the file **filename**. But if **filename** is a symbolic link, the command will display the contents of the linked file.

The common bond between all file types is the relationship of the file ownership and the file mode. This relationship is fundamental to all UNIX platforms, and this is one of the main issues that make UNIX so reliable and flexible in the constantly changing environment.

2.3 Devices and Special Device Files

A ***device*** is a dedicated piece of hardware that provides a particular function within the computer system. A device itself can be located internally or externally. Regardless of the location, devices are treated equally within their classes.

A ***device driver*** is a program that manages the system's interaction with a particular device; it presents a needed interface to translate between the hardware commands understood by the device, and the kernel. Such a system structure keeps UNIX reasonably hardware-independent.

Device drivers are parts of the kernel; they are not user processes. However, they can be accessed both from within the kernel and from the user space. User-level access is provided through ***special device files***. The kernel transforms operations on these special files into calls to the driver code.

Special device files are also called *device special files*. Independent of their naming, these files are really special and different than regular files. Their mission is special in the UNIX paradigm. We will use both names arbitrarily, or even simply *special files*.

Special device files are mapped to devices via two pointers: *major and minor device numbers*. These numbers are stored in the *inode* for a particular special file. The ***major device number*** identifies a device driver for a specific class of devices (a single driver can be used for a number of devices of the same type); the ***minor device number*** is a parameter within the specified device driver.

Each device driver has routines for performing necessary functions in its interaction with the device. These basic functions are: *probe, attach, open, close, read, reset, stop, select, strategy, dump, psize, write, timeout, interrupt processing*, and *i/o control (ioctl)*. The addresses of these functions for each driver (independent of the character and block devices) are stored in the *jump table* inside the kernel. The major device number indexes the jump tables; this is provided through another table known as *device switch table*. Briefly, the mapping is performed in the following way: the *major device number* points to the corresponding entry in the *device switch table*. The *minor device number* is passed as a parameter to the relevant function in the device driver. The device driver is free to interpret the minor number as it sees fit, although in most cases it uses it as a port number (as is the case when a single driver controls multiple devices of the same type). As soon as the kernel catches the reference, it looks up the appropriate function name in the *driver's jump table* and transfers control to it. To perform a device-specific operation that does not have a direct analog in the filesystem model (for example, ejecting a floppy disk), the *ioctl system call* is used to transfer a request directly into the driver.

This treatment of devices in a file-like way is one of the fundamental design elements that make UNIX so powerful. Just as the proven solutions for files' ownership, mode, access rights, and protection have been implemented in the case of devices, the same has been done with user commands as well. Meanwhile, existing differences in command interpretations were maintained. We will see what this all means in the following example of the **copy** command:

 # cp /path1/filename1 /path2/filename2

This command will copy the contents of the file **/path1/filename1** to the file named **/path2/filename2**, effectively overwriting the file if it already existed, or creating the file if it did not.

However, the command:

 # cp /path1/filename1 /dev/console

will copy the file **/path1/filename1** to the file **/dev/console** which is the special file for the physical console terminal. The contents of the file **/path1/filename1** will be displayed on the console screen. As we can see, special files allow I/O operations to be performed with regular interactions among UNIX files.

It is convenient to implement a device driver as an abstraction, even when there is no actual device for it to control. Such devices are known as *pseudo-devices;* for example, *pseudo-TTY* (assigned as *PTY*) is used to communicate with users over a network. From a higher-level software point of view, a pseudo-device looks like a regular device; consequently, preexisting software is transparent, allowing immediate use without the need for any modification.

2.3.1 Special File Names

By convention, special files are kept in the */dev* directory. On large systems there may be hundreds of devices, including pseudo-devices. On System V (ATT) flavors, special files are hierarchically organized, with separate subdirectories for different device types: disk, tape, terminal, pseudo-terminal, etc. On BSD platforms, */dev* is a flat directory containing all of the special files.

Special file naming is different among different UNIX flavors; however, some common rules are recognized. The following table presents the usual naming algorithms for disk-related special files:

	BSD	System V
File name	/dev/rdisk0d	/dev/rdsk/c1d0s2
Access mode	/dev/**r**disk0d	/dev/**r**dsk/c1d0s2
Device type	/dev/r**disk**0d	/dev/r**dsk**/c1d0s2
Drive	/dev/rdisk**0**d	/dev/rdsk/c1**d0**s2
Disk partition	/dev/rdisk0**d**	/dev/rdsk/c1d0**s2**
Controller		/dev/rdsk/**c1**d0s2

Unfortunately, the implemented rules are very restricted and are usually valid only for the specific flavor; naming procedures vary among flavors within the same UNIX platform.

2.3.2 Special File Creation

To create a special file, UNIX provides the **mknod** command, which has the following syntax:

mknod filename type major minor

where

filename A name of the special file to be created
type A type of the special file to be created
c — for a character (row) type special file
b — for a block type special file
p — for a named pipe (FIFO)
major A major device number (decimal or octal)
minor A minor device number (decimal or octal)

Special files are very small and simple files; they contain only two numbers (major and minor number), which are pointers to corresponding device drivers within the kernel. Only the superuser can create a special device file.

Both BSD and System V flavors often include some kind of utility program to create and install special files; usually this is a script based on **mknod** commands. One such script is ***makedev*** that originates from SunOS 4.1.x.

UNIX administrators like script utilities. First these scripts make their jobs easier. But the scripts are also very instructive. We can read them and learn precisely how the utility works and fully understand what happens behind the scenes. We can discover many of the UNIX secrets that are so useful in its daily administration.

Special files are special by nature, but they are dressed like regular files. Several years ago one student raised the questions: "Are the ownership and permissions of special files uniform over all UNIX platforms? Their purposes are the same — is there any regularity? How do you recreate a lost special device file?"

Despite the fact that these questions are very logical, there is no simple response. Ownership and mode of special files vary among different UNIX flavors, as do special file names. A very brief review of several UNIX flavors made several years ago easily proved this. Things are not changed nowadays. The ownership and mode of the */dev* directory and reviewed same-purpose special files are presented for several UNIX flavors.

SunOS
 # ls -lg / | grep dev

11 drwxr-sr-x	**2**	**bin**	**staff**	**11264**	**May 16 09:24**	**dev/**

 # ls -lg /dev
total 13

0 crw--w----	*1*	*root*	*wheel 0,*	*0*	*May 26 14:52*	*console*
0 crw-r-----	*1*	*root*	*kmem 3,*	*1*	*Mar 19 1993*	*kmem*
0 crw-r-----	*1*	*root*	*kmem 3,*	*0*	*Mar 19 1993*	*mem*
0 srwxrwxrwx	*1*	*root*	*staff 0*		*May 16 09:24*	*printer*
0 crw-rw-rw-	*1*	*root*	*staff 21,*	*16*	*Jun 11 1993*	*ptyq0*
0 crw-rw-rw-	*1*	*root*	*staff 30,*	*1*	*Mar 19 1993*	*rmt1*
0 crw-r-----	*1*	*root*	*operator 17,*	*0*	*Jan 20 14:58*	*rsd0a*
0 brw-r-----	*1*	*root*	*operator 7,*	*0*	*Sep 22 1993*	*sd0a*
	. . . . .					

ULTRIX
 # ls -lg / | grep dev

drwxr-xr-x	**4**	**root**	**system**	**12800**	**May 27 10:23**	**dev**

 # ls -lg /dev
total 46

crw--w----	*1*	*operator*	*tty 0,*	*0*	*May 27 13:01*	*console*
crw-r-----	*1*	*root*	*kmem 3,*	*1*	*May 14 15:18*	*kmem*
crw-r-----	*1*	*root*	*kmem 3,*	*0*	*Aug 7 1992*	*mem*
srwxrwxrwx	*1*	*root*	*system 0*		*May 27 10:23*	*printer*
crw-rw-rw-	*1*	*root*	*system 21,*	*16*	*May 27 13:09*	*ptyq0*
brw-------	*1*	*root*	*system 23,*	*0*	*Mar 22 1993*	*ra0a*
crw-rw-rw-	*1*	*root*	*system 36,*	*8*	*Mar 22 1993*	*rmt0h*
	. . . . .					

HP-UX

$ ls -l / | grep dev

drwxr-xr-x	**13**	**root**	**root**	**30**	**72**	**May 26 09:51**	**dev**

$ ls -l /dev

total 42

crw--w--w-	*1*	*root*	*sys*	*0*	*0x000000*	*May 26 09:51*	*console*
crw-rw-rw-	*1*	*root*	*sys*	*24*	*0x203010*	*Dec 13 16:31*	*hil1*
crw-r-----	*1*	*bin*	*sys*	*3*	*0x000001*	*Dec 13 16:31*	*kmem*
crw-r--r--	*1*	*lp*	*bin*	*11*	*0x206002*	*May 26 15:32*	*lp_panlaser*
crw-r-----	*1*	*bin*	*sys*	*3*	*0x000000*	*Dec 13 16:31*	*mem*
crw-rw-rw-	*1*	*root*	*other*	*16*	*0x000010*	*Dec 13 17:14*	*ptyq0*
crw-rw-rw-	*1*	*root*	*sys*	*23*	*0x203000*	*Dec 13 16:31*	*rhil*
	.....						

IRIX

$ ls -l / | grep dev

drwxr-xr-x	**10**	**root**	**sys**	**358**	**4**	**May 16 08:59**	**dev**

$ ls -l /dev

total 87

crw--w--w-	*3*	*root*	*sys*	*58,*	*0*	*May 25 14:33*	*console*
brw-------	*1*	*root*	*sys*	*22,*	*71*	*Mar 31 1993*	*disk2*
crw-r-----	*1*	*root*	*sys*	*1,*	*1*	*May 27 1993*	*kmem*
crw-r-----	*1*	*root*	*sys*	*1,*	*0*	*May 27 1993*	*mem*
srwx------	*1*	*root*	*lp*	*0*		*May 16 08:59*	*printer*
crw-------	*1*	*root*	*sys*	*22,*	*71*	*Sep 20 1993*	*rdisk2*
crw-rw-rw-	*3*	*root*	*sys*	*23,*	*192*	*Nov 8 1993*	*tape*
crw--w--w-	*2*	*root*	*sys*	*0,*	*1*	*Sep 10 1992*	*ttyd1*
	.....						

It is very easy to conclude that there is no uniformity among different UNIX flavors — naming, ownerships, and file modes are different. What to do if a special file is accidentally lost? Do we have to remember them all?

The only logical answer is to search for help within the same UNIX flavor. For example, to look up the same special files on another same-flavor UNIX system (if applicable). Other options are to check vendor documentation, or use other flavor-related sources (call technical support, newsgroups, Internet, etc.).

2.4 Processes

A **process** is a single program that is running in its virtual address space. The process should be distinct from a *job* or a *command*, which may be composed of many processes working together to perform a specific task. One of the main administrative tasks is to manage UNIX processes. In this section we will cover main process-related topics.

2.4.1 Process Parameters

This is a brief reminder about process parameters. We will start with the process types and main process attributes. Full understanding of process attributes is crucial for certain administrative activities, as well as for the system security. Other discussed issues are file descriptors attached to a process and process states.

2.4.1.1 Process Types

The three distinct types of processes are:

> ***Interactive processes*** — Interactive processes are initiated and controlled by a terminal session; they run in the foreground attached for the standard input STDIN (in a terminal session STDIN corresponds to the terminal) or in the background. Job control (which originated in BSD) allows a foreground process to be sent to the background and vice versa.
>
> ***Batch processes*** — Processes not associated with a terminal; these are explicitly submitted to a batch queue and executed with a lower priority in sequential order, primarily at off-peak times. Originally, batch processing was not very thoroughly developed on UNIX platforms, but third-party vendors have improved it. Batch processing is very convenient for non-urgent, long-lasting data processing such as iterative calculations and the like.
>
> ***Daemons*** — Server background processes, usually initiated at the system boot time, which continue running as long as the system is up. Daemons perform different system-related tasks; they wait in the background until some process requires their service.

2.4.1.2 Process Attributes

There are many attributes associated with UNIX processes. The following paragraphs discuss the major attributes.

> ***Process ID (PID)*** — The PID is a unique identifying number used to refer to the process. It is an integer assigned by the kernel when the process was created and cannot be changed for the lifetime of the process. Crucial for process handling, a process is always identified by its PID.
>
> ***Parent process ID (PPID)*** — The PPID is the PID of the parent process, which is the process that was directly involved in the creation of the new process. The PPID is not unique, because the same parent process could have a number of child processes. The PPID cannot be changed during the lifetime of the process.
>
> ***Real and effective user ID (RUID and EUID)*** — The real user ID (RUID) is the UID of the user who started the process; the effective user ID (EUID) is the UID used to determine the user access rights of the process to system resources (objects). The relationship between the two user ID attributes is: RUID = EUID, except if the SUID access mode was set on the program that created the process, and then EUID corresponds to the owner UID of the program (see also the *File Permissions* section of the text).
>
> ***Real and effective group ID (RGID and EGID)*** — The real group ID (RGID) is the GID of the group of the user who started the process; the effective group ID (EGID) is the GID used to determine the group access rights of the process to system resources (objects). The relationship between the two group ID attributes is: RGID = EGID, except if the SGID access mode was set on the program that created the process, and then EGID corresponds to owner GID of the program (see also the *File Permissions* section of the text).

Process group ID (PGID)—The process group ID (PGID) identifies the process group that the process belongs to; typically, multiple processes are members of the same process group and they share the same PGID. The PGID is the PID of the process group leader; this is usually the initial parent process. Unlike PID and PPID, which cannot be changed during the life of the process, PGID is under program control and can be changed by the corresponding system call (as is the case with *job control*). PGIDs are important in the processing of signals in interprocess communications. For example: the invoked shell is the process group leader for all subsequent commands that are members of the created process group; once the user logs out and terminates the shell, all currently running related processes will also terminate.

Control terminal (TTY) — The control terminal is the terminal (or pseudo-terminal) associated with the created process — the terminal that the process was started from.

Terminal group ID (TGID) — The terminal group ID (TGID) is the PID of the process group leader that opened the terminal, which is typically the login shell. The TGID identifies the control terminal (TTY) for a process group, i.e., the terminal associated with a process. The TGID is important for *job control*.

Current working directory (CWD) — The current working directory (CWD) defines the starting point for all relatively specified pathnames (filenames that do not begin with the "/" character).

Nice number — A number indicating the process priority relative to other processes. Generally, a lower nice number means a higher priority; this is true also when the nice numbers are in the range –20 to +20 (lower number in this case means more negative).

2.4.1.3 File Descriptors

File descriptors are integers used to identify files that have been attached to a process and opened for I/O. Modern UNIX systems provide more than 20 different files to be opened for a process. File descriptors 0, 1, and 2 are associated with the standard input (a keyboard), standard output (a screen), and a standard error (a screen also), respectively; they are, by default, attached to a newly created process. UNIX provides an easy method of I/O redirection by simple replacement of the input, output, and error files. In the case of *sockets*, the descriptors are called *socket descriptors*.

2.4.1.4 Process States

The existence of a process does not automatically mean it is eligible to receive and consume CPU time. There are multiple process execution states, as discussed in the following text.

Runnable — The process is ready to execute whenever there is CPU time available.

Sleeping — The process is waiting for a specific event to occur, or for some resource to become available. Interactive processes and daemons spend most of their time sleeping, waiting for terminal input or a network connection.

Stopped — The process is suspended and forbidden to run as the result of a received STOP signal; it can be restarted if it receives a CONT signal.

Zombie — The process is trying to die; another common term is ***defunct***.

Swapped — The process is removed from the system main memory to a disk (more precisely, a process image is removed). This occurs when the competition for memory is intense, a lack of available memory for new processes is obvious, and regular memory paging is unable to solve the problem efficiently. Strictly speaking, swapped is not a true process state, because a swapped process can be in one of the previously mentioned states: *sleeping*, *stopped*, or even *runnable*.

2.4.2 Process Life Cycles

Each process is living as long as the corresponding program is running. Process life cycles vary in range from "extremely short" up to "indefinitely" like for daemons (or better to say "as long as the system lives"). Process starts with its creation and lasts until terminated (program exit upon its completion) or forced to quit.

2.4.2.1 Process Creation

In UNIX a new process is created with the ***fork*** system call. An existing process, a ***parent process***, makes a copy of itself into the address space of a ***child process***. From the user's point of view, the child process is an exact duplicate of the parent process, except for two values: the PID and the parent PID. The ***fork*** system call returns the child PID to the parent process and "zero" to the child process (thus, a program can determine whether it is the parent or the child process). The ***fork*** system call involves three main steps:

1. Allocating and initializing a new structure for the child process
2. Duplicating the context of the parent process for the child process
3. Scheduling the child process to run

The memory organization and layout associated with a UNIX process contains three memory segments called:

1. *Text segment* A shared read-only segment that includes program code
2. *Data segment* A private read-write segment divided into initialized and uninitialized data parts (the uninitialized part is also known as "block started symbol" (BSS))
3. *Stack segment* A private read-write segment for system and process related data

There are two modes of the ***fork*** operation:

1. A process makes a copy of itself to handle another task; this is typical for network server daemons.
2. A process wants to execute another program. Since the only way to create a new process is through the fork operation, the process first makes a copy of itself and then the child process issues an ***exec*** system call to execute a new program.

In the later case, the ***fork*** is followed shortly thereafter by an ***exec*** system call that overlays the address space (text and data segments) of the child process with the contents of the new executable. Such a procedure is also known as ***fork-and-exec***. A new program replaces the contents of the parent process in the address space of the child process but in the same parent's environment. In this way all global environment variables, standard input/output/error, and priority are kept unchanged.

The ultimate ancestor for every process on a UNIX platform is the process with PID 1, named ***init*** and created by the system kernel during the boot procedure. The ***init*** process presents a starting point in the chain of process creations; it creates a number of other processes based on *fork-and-exec*. Among the many created processes are one or more ***getty*** processes, assigned to existing terminal lines. Their main duty is to keep the system from unauthorized login attempts; they protect the system from potential intruders, and from the damage they can cause to the system.

This is illustrated in Figure 2.2. Different stages of the creation of involved processes are presented, assuming four existing terminal lines.

Four ***getty*** processes have been *forked-and-exec* by the ***init*** process. Each ***getty*** process is taking care of one terminal line. Since a user attempts to access the system via a terminal line (more precisely via an attached terminal), ***getty*** will *exec* another program ***login*** to supply a login prompt, and to authenticate the user (it will look up the user's login and password data in the file */etc/passwd*); this is shown in the figure for the second terminal line. Upon ***login***, it checks the user's password and sets the user ID, group ID, and working directory. It will *exec* the user's ***shell*** (specified in the user's password entry in the */etc/passwd* file). In the figure this is the case with the third terminal line, and the *exec*-ed shell is Bourne shell ***sh***. In the next step, a user executes any command from the shell command line, as the presented ***ls*** command on the fourth terminal line. The shell ***sh*** *forks* its copy and then *execs* the program (command) ***ls***. All presented process IDs are generally specified; however, please note that only *fork* creates a new child process with a new process ID.

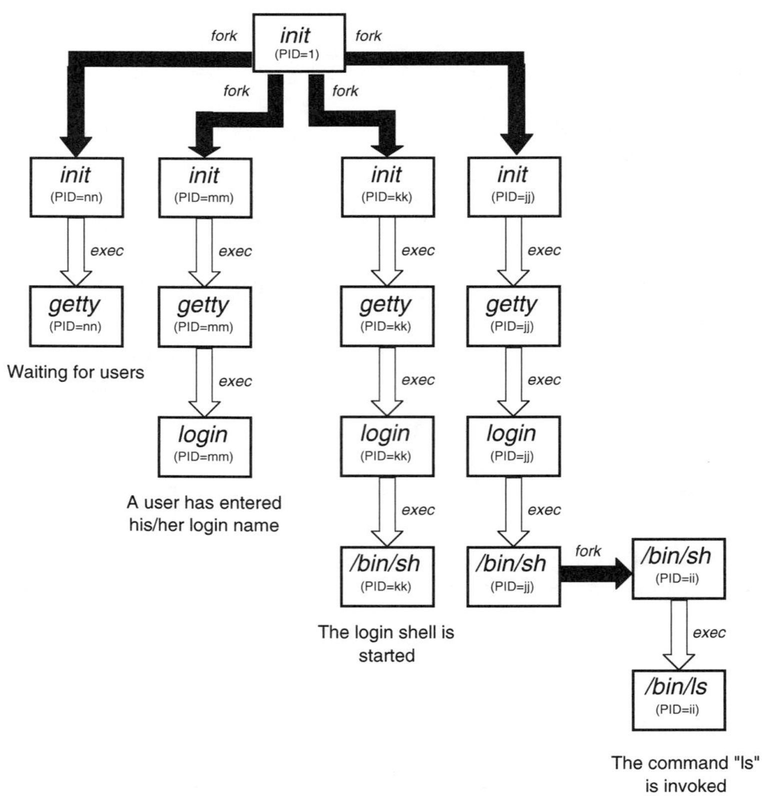

FIGURE 2.2
UNIX process creation (fork and exec).

2.4.2.2 Process Termination

A process terminates either voluntarily through an ***exit*** system call, or involuntarily as the result of a received signal. In either case, termination of a process causes a status code to be returned to its parent process. The process then cleans and closes all process-related resources:

- It cancels any pending timers.
- It releases virtual memory resources.
- It closes open descriptors.
- It handles stopped or traced child processes.

After completing those tasks the process can "die," i.e., it can be deleted from the kernel process table.

2.4.3 Process Handling

UNIX system administration involves dealing with processes on a regular basis. Monitoring a UNIX system primarily means monitoring running processes. Any change in the configuration usually requires restart of the corresponding daemons. And occasionally a certain process has to be restarted or destroyed. Handling processes is one of the main tasks in maintaining a UNIX system. Every UNIX administrator very quickly becomes familiar with these issues. This is less true for a *job control*, which is also mentioned at the end of this section. All together, the text that follows is a "good appetizer" — just for the start.

2.4.3.1 Monitoring Process Activities

Monitoring the processes running on the system is highly recommended; this is the best way to get a good sense of what normal system activity is like: what programs are run, how long they run, who runs them, and so on. In addition, when a problem on a system is encountered, the first step to figure out what the problem could be is to check the status of running processes. You can discover a lot from a simple cross-view of the status of the processes running on your system at a certain time. Such a routine procedure is also very important for system security, because any unusual system activity can be noticed and quickly stopped.

The UNIX **ps** (process status) command lists the characteristics of running processes; the format of the command is:

 # ps *[options]*

Basic options are explained in the following text. Unfortunately, there are certain differences in command options between the two main UNIX platforms, BSD and System V.

2.4.3.1.1 BSD Flavored ***ps*** *Command*

The **ps** command displays the status of currently running processes; without any options specified only the processes that are running with the effective user's ID and those that are attached to a controlling terminal are shown. Additional categories of processes can be added to the display using certain options:

- **-a** option Includes processes that are not owned by the user who issues the command itself; displays all processes attached to the control terminal

- **-x** option Includes processes without control terminals; when both **-a** and **-x** are specified, **ps** displays processes owned by anyone, with or without a control terminal
- **-r** option Restricts the list of displayed processes to the running processes: runnable processes, those in page wait, or those in short-term noninterruptible waits
- **-l** option Displays a long listing with many additional fields; gives a full picture of each displayed process
- **-u** option Displays a user-oriented listing with additional user-related fields

In its standard format, **ps** displays:

- The process ID, in the PID column
- The control terminal (if any), in the TT column
- The CPU time used by the process so far, including both user and system time, in the TIME column
- The state of the process, in the STAT column
- An indication of the COMMAND that is running

Here is an example:

```
$ ps -ax
PID    TT   STAT   TIME   COMMAND
0      ?    D      0:07   swapper
1      ?    IW     0:00   /sbin/init -
2      ?    D      0:00   pagedaemon
-----
-----
2087   p1   S      0:00   -csh (csh)
2091   p1   R      0:00   ps -ax
1996   p2   IW     0:00   -sh (csh)
```

The long listing (option **-l**) and the user-oriented (option **-u**) formats are different, as seen in the following examples (only the first six lines in the listing are displayed):

```
# ps -aux | head -6
USER  PID   %CPU  %MEM   SZ   RSS  TT  STAT  START  TIME  COMMAND
bjl   2905  30.8   3.3   228  476  p1  R     09:29  0:00  ps -aux
bjl   2906   7.7   1.4   40   200  p1  S     09:29  0:00  head -6
root     2   0.0   0.0    0     0  ?   D     May16  0:00  pagedaemon
bald  2499   0.0   0.0   36     0  co  IW    May23  6:23  telnet rs01-ch
root    85   0.0  352     0.0   0  ?   IW    May16  0:36  in.named
```

```
# ps -alx | head -6
F         UID  PID  PPID  CP  PRI  NI   SZ  RSS  WCHAN   STAT  TT  TIME  COMMAND
80003      0    0    0    0   -25  0     0   0   runout  D     ?   0:41  swapper
20088000   0    1    0    0     5  0    52   0   child   IW    ?   0:00  /sbin/init -
80003      0    2    0    0   -24  0     0   0   child   D     ?   0:00  pagedaemon
88000      0   54    1    0     1  0    68   0   select  IW    ?   0:29  portmap
88000      0   59    1    0     1  0   120   0   select  IW    ?   5:40  ypserv
```

The meaning of the columns in the listings is given below; the letters "u" and "l" indicate the options user and long; "all" stands for both.

Column	Meaning
USER (u)	The user name of the process owner
UID (l)	The user ID of the process owner
PID (all)	The process ID of the process
PPID (l)	The process ID of the parent process
%**CPU** (u)	Percentage of the CPU this process used in the previous minute
%**MEM** (u)	Percentage of real memory this process is using
PRI (l)	The priority of the process
NI (l)	NICE value; used in priority computation
RSS (all)	Resident set size (real memory size) in KB
SZ (u)	The combined size of the data and stack segment in KB
WCHAN (l)	The event for which the process is waiting or sleeping
START (u)	Starting time of the process (if created this day) or the date otherwise
TT (all)	The controlling terminal for the process
TIME (all)	The CPU time (both user and system) the process has consumed
COMMAND (all)	The command name and its arguments
STAT (all)	The state of the process given as a sequence of four letters:
First letter:	R = runnable D = short-term wait for disk S = sleeping (<20 sec) I = sleeping (>20 sec) T = stopped Z = zombie P = page wait
Second letter:	W = swapped out > = memory soft limit exceeded
Third letter:	N = reduced priority < = raised priority
Fourth letter:	Indicates some special process treatment
F (l)	Flags associated with the process and presented in hexadecimal notation (up to 8 hex. numbers). A number of flags describe the process in more detail. For a flag specification consult manual pages.

The most common format of the BSD-flavored **ps** command is:

 # ps -aux

The output of this command is an extensive listing of process-related data sufficient for most administrative needs.

*2.4.3.1.2 System V (AT&T) Flavored **ps** Command*

The **ps** command displays the status of currently running processes; without any options, only the processes associated with the current terminal are displayed. The basic options are:

- **-e** option Displays all processes
- **-f** option Produces a full listing, including the process start time
- **-l** option Displays a long listing with many additional fields

The regular output of this command is a so-called "short" listing (as opposed to the full or long listing). A short listing contains only the user and process IDs (including parent process ID), terminal identifier, start and cumulative execution time, and the command name. An example of the short listing for all processes follows:

$ ps -e

UID	*PID*	*PPID*	*C*	*STIME*	*TTY*	*TIME*	*COMMAND*
root	*0*	*0*	*0*	*Dec 31*	*?*	*0:05*	*swapper*
root	*1*	*0*	*0*	*11:23:17*	*?*	*0:00*	*init*

```
root      2     0     0  11:23:16    ?     0:00   vhand
-----
dubey  1550  1549     0  08:40:13  ttys0   0:00   -sh
bjl    1618  1591    10  09:25:59  ttys1   0:00   ps -ef
```

A full or long listing displays many additional pieces of information:

$ ps -ef | head -6

```
F S UID  PID PPID C PRI NI ADDR     SZ WCHAN    STIME   TTY TIME COMD
3 S root 0   0    0 128 20 1e0568      0        Dec 31  ?   0:06 swapper
1 S root 1   0    0 168 20 2056540  54 7ffe6000 May 16  ?   0:00 init
3 S root 2   0    0 128 20 2056480  0  1ee3d0   May 16  ?   0:01 vhand
3 S root 3   0    0 128 20 20564c0  0  1ec4d4   May 16  ?   0:00 statdaemon
3 S root 7   0    0 128 20 2056500  0  1e8dc0   May 16  ?   0:00 unhash-
                                                                 daemon
```

$ ps -l | head -5

```
F S UID  PID  PPID C PRI NI ADDR    SZ WCHAN   TTY   TIME COMD
1 S 201 9444 9443  0 158 20 2151100 52 350c1c  ttys1 0:00 sh
1 S   0 9443  106  0 154 20 2151a40 17 221728  ttys1 0:00 telnetd
1 R 201 9473 9472  7 179 20 20d7f40 17         ttys1 0:00 ps
1 S 201 9472 9444  4 154 20 2151680  6 3300e4  ttys1 0:00 head
```

The column headings and the meaning of the columns in a **ps** listing are given below; the letters "f"and "l" indicate the option (full or long) that causes the corresponding heading to appear; "all" means that the heading always appears. Note that these two options determine only which information would be displayed for a process; they do not determine the processes to be listed.

Column		Meaning
F	(l)	Flags (octal and additive) associated with the process: 0 = swapped 1 = in core 2 = system process 4 = locked in core (e.g., for I/O) 10 = traced by another process 20 = another tracing flag
S	(l)	The state of the process: 0 = nonexistent S = sleeping W = waiting R = running I = intermediate Z = terminated T = stopped X = growing
UID	(f, l)	The real user ID number of the process owner; the login name is printed under the **-f** option
PID	(all)	The process ID of the process; it is possible to kill a process if you know this datum
PPID	(f, l)	The process ID of the parent process
C	(f, l)	Processor utilization for scheduling
PRI	(l)	The priority of the process; higher numbers mean lower priority
NI	(l)	Nice value; used in priority computation
ADDR	(l)	The memory address of the process, if resident; otherwise, the disk address
SZ	(l)	The size in blocks of the core image of the process
WCHAN	(l)	The event for which the process is waiting or sleeping; if blank, the process is running
STIME	(f)	Starting time of the process. The starting date is printed instead if the elapsed time is greater than 24 hours
TTY	(all)	The controlling terminal for the process
TIME	(all)	The cumulative execution time for the process (reported in the form "min:sec")
COMD	(all)	The command name; the full command name and its arguments are printed under the **-f** option. This field is renamed **COMMAND** except when the **-l** option is specified

The most common format of the System V flavored **ps** command is:

 # ps -ef

The full listing provides all the process-related data we need for a successful administration.

2.4.3.2 Destroying Processes

The UNIX **kill** command will eliminate a process entirely:

kill [-signal] pid

where

signal Signal to be sent to the process (default: signal #15 = TERM)
pid Process identification number (PID)

A signal is optional. BSD allows the user to specify either the signal number or its symbolic name. System V requires the signal to be specified numerically.

The signal #9 (KILL) guarantees that the process will be destroyed. When a process is killed, it informs its parent process of its imminent termination (death), and waits for the parent's acknowledgment. After receiving acknowledgment, the PID of the killed process is removed from the process table.

Normally, the default **kill** command is used to terminate a process without the specified signal that corresponds to the signal #15 (TERM); such a command is also known as a *soft kill*. Upon receipt of the TERM signal, the process should exit in a normal way by closing all the resources it is using. Occasionally, a process may still exist after a soft kill command. If this occurs, another so-called hard kill has to be applied. By executing the **kill** command with the signal #9 (KILL signal), a process is forced to exit. However, this kind of process termination is not good for the system because some system resources may remain unclosed and still busy. A hard kill should be used only as a last resort in attempting to terminate a process.

Processes will not terminate (die) even after being sent the KILL signal if they fall in one of the following three categories:

1. ***Zombies*** — A process in the zombie state (presented as Z *status* or *defunct* in **ps** display) is one in which all of the process's resources have been freed, but the parent process's acknowledgment has not occurred. Zombies are always cleared when the system is booted and do not affect system performance.
2. ***Processes waiting for unavailable NFS resources*** — In such a case, a **kill** command with signal #3 (QUIT) or #2 (INT) should be used.
3. ***Processes waiting for a device to complete an operation*** — For example, waiting for a tape to finish rewinding.

Killing a process also kills all of its child processes that share the same process group. For example, killing a shell usually kills all the foreground and stopped background processes initiated from that shell, including other invoked shells. Killing a login shell is equivalent to logging the user out. It is common for children and parents to belong to the same process group, but this is not necessarily always true (see Job Control at the end of this section).

Although the name ***kill*** indicates that the command should destroy a process, its real effect depends on the selected signal that is sent to the process. Sometimes the command does not destroy a process at all, and it can even do the opposite. For example, by sending the signal CONT to a previously stopped process, the process will continue to run; you would not think a "killed" process could be "revived." In that light, a more appropriate name for the command could be ***"send signal,"*** because it better describes what the command is really doing.

The **-l** option is available to display a list of signal names:

$ kill -l (SunOS, Solaris)

HUP INT QUIT ILL TRAP ABRT EMT FPE KILL BUS SEGV SYS PIPE ALRM TERM URG STOP TSTP CONT CHLD TTIN TTOU IO XCPU XFSZ VTALRM PROF WINCH LOST USR1 USR2

$ kill -l (HP-UX)

NULL HUP INT QUIT ILL TRAP ABRT EMT FPE KILL BUS SEGV SYS PIPE ALRM TERM USR1 USR2 CHLD PWR VTALRM PROF POLL WINCH STOP TSTP CONT TTIN TTOU URG LOST DIL

As we can see, the order of listed signal names is not necessarily the same. Fortunately, the most important and most often-used signals match. The list of signals with descriptions follows.

Signal Number	Signal Symbolic Name	Signal Description
0	NULL	*No effect*
1	HUP	***Hang-up (for daemons, force a daemon to reread its configuration data)***
2	INT	***Interrupt for a process***
3	QUIT	***Quit***
	ILL	*Illegal instruction*
	TRAP	*Trace trap*
	ABRT	*ABR (IOT) trap*
	EMT	*EMT trap*
	FPE	*Arithmetic exception*
9	KILL	***Kill — destroy a process***
	BUS	*Bus error*
	SEGV	*Segmentation fault*
	SYS	*Bad argument for a system call*
	PIPE	*Broken pipe*
	ALRM	*Alarm clock*
15	TERM	***Soft termination — terminate a process***
	URG	*Socket in extremes*
	STOP	*Stop a process*
	TSTP	*Keyboard stop for a process*
	CONT	*Continue a stopped process*
	CHLD	*Status change for a child process*
	TTIN	*Invalid read*
	TTOUT	*Invalid write*
	IO	*IO possible on FD*
	XCPU	*CPU time limit up*
	XFSZ	*File size limit up*
	VTALRM	*Virtual time alarm*
	PROF	*Profiling time alarm*
	WINCH	*Window change*
	LOST	*Resource lost*
	USR1	*User-defined*
	USR2	*User-defined*

Note: An empty Signal Number field indicates that it varies among flavors. The most important signals are presented in **bold** letters.

2.4.3.3 Job Control

A ***job*** is a collection of one or more processes that share the same process group ID. ***Job control*** is a feature that allows multiple processes to start from a single terminal, and also allows some control over their execution. Job control requires support from the terminal driver, the signal mechanism, the used shell, and the underlying operating system. Job control allows the user to have multiple jobs sharing a single terminal, to move jobs from foreground to background and vice versa, to suspend and restart jobs, and to perform other miscellaneous activities. A job control-compatible shell makes each child process sent to the background a leader of its own process group. In this way, it makes a child process insensitive to signals sent to the parent shell (recall that signals have an effect on all processes within the same process group). One of the consequences is, for example, that all background processes remain alive upon the termination of the shell (when the user logs out).

There are several job-related UNIX commands, i.e., ***jobs, fg, bg,*** which are quite comprehensive and easy to use. They are primarily user oriented, although they can play a role in UNIX administration, too.

3

UNIX Administration Starters

3.1 Superuser and Users

The central entity in UNIX is a file — every activity on the system represents some kind of transaction with or between files. Consequently, administrators of UNIX systems are expected to deal with files, including the special purpose files known as configuration files. Configuring system functions, setting some system parameters, tuning a kernel, and restoring a lost file, all require the appropriate access to the needed data within the file. On the other side, system files always require privileged access. In practice, this means that the administrator has to be a superuser on the system in order to effectively administer the UNIX system.

3.1.1 Becoming a Superuser

On a UNIX platform, the ***superuser*** is a privileged user with unrestricted access to all files and commands. The name of this user account is *root*; the account is protected with a password as with any other user account.

There are two ways to become the superuser:

1. Log in directly as root. This is always possible from the system console; it is recommended that you disable the direct root log-in from other terminals as a security precaution, but this is not a requirement.
2. Switch from another user log-in account to the superuser's account by executing the **su** command.

In both cases the system will prompt for the root password. After entering the correct password, the superuser is logged into the system and has full control over all its resources. The root account is extremely sensitive; one wrong move can easily destroy important files and crash the system itself. Only knowledgeable persons should enjoy superuser status; it is very important to restrict root access only to a certain group of people who are responsible for the system itself. Obviously UNIX administrators should belong to this group.

3.1.2 Communicating with Other Users

The UNIX administrator frequently needs to communicate with other users, mostly to inform them of current administrative activities being performed on the system. Some examples include instructing all logged-in users to close their files and logout on time when a system is going to be shut down informing users when new software is installed, or passing along any other information important for regular system operations.

Several UNIX commands are available for this purpose:

- ***Sending a message to the user:***

write *username [tty]*

where

username User to whom the message is sent
[tty] Optional terminal if the user is logged in to more than one

The text of the message should be typed after the command is issued; typing Ctrl-D (^D) terminates the command. Once the message is terminated, the shell returns the command prompt. The typed text of the message will be displayed at the terminal screen of the addressed user.

- ***Sending a message to all users***

  wall (stands for "*write all*")

  The text of the message should be typed after the command was issued; typing Ctrl-D (^D) terminates the command. The typed text of the message will be displayed at the terminals of all logged-in users.

- ***Sending the message of the day***

  The *message of the day* — "***motd***" — can be used to broadcast systemwide information to all users. The file */etc/motd* keeps an arbitrary message which will be displayed during any user's log-in procedure. Log-in is probably the most convenient time to catch the user's attention, because the user is fully concentrated on the output of the log-in procedure. That makes it an ideal time to inform users about changes in the system, newly installed software, and so on.

  Any editor can be used to edit the */etc/motd* file; the default UNIX editor is "***vi***."

- ***Sending e-mail to user(s)***

  E-mail is a convenient vehicle for communicating nonurgent or lengthy messages to users. E-mail is especially convenient for informing users about automated jobs because it is very easy, for example, to send a message about the status of an executed job to the users from the script that ordered the execution.

3.1.3 The *su* Command

We already mentioned the **su** command when we discussed how to become the superuser. But the **su** commands does more; **su** allows an already logged-in user to become another user without logging out. The format of the **su** command is:

su *[-] [username [arg...]]*

where

- *(dash)*	Must be specified as the first option when the environment for the specified user is passed along unchanged, as if this user actually logged in. Otherwise, the environment is passed along with the exception of certain environment variables. Please note the differences to avoid any possible confusion regarding the new user environment.
username	Specifies the name of the new user to whom to switch; the default user name is ***root***. Without a specified user name, the command will try to switch to the superuser.
arg...	One or more optional arguments to be passed to the new shell; an ***arg*** of the form "**-c cmd_string**" executes the command string using the shell; an ***arg*** of "**-r**" gives the user a restricted shell.

The **su** command requires the user to supply the appropriate password unless a switch from the *root* to another user account is performed. If the password is correct, **su** creates a new shell process with the characteristics of the specified user (RUID, EUID, RGID, EGID, and supplementary groups). The new shell will be the shell specified in the username's *passwd entry*; otherwise the default Bourne shell **sh** will be invoked. To return to the initial user's account, type ***exit***, or *Ctrl-D* (^D) to exit the new shell. All attempts to become **su** are logged in the log file */var/adm/sulog*.

A few examples follow:

- To become user ***bjl*** while retaining the previously exported environment, execute:

  $ su bjl

- To become user ***bjl*** but also change the environment as if ***bjl*** had originally logged in, execute:

  $ su - bjl

- To execute commands with the temporary environment and permissions of user ***bjl***, type:

  $ su - bjl -c *command args*

3.2 UNIX Online Documentation

3.2.1 The *man* Command

UNIX has integrated online documentation, which is available to all users and UNIX administrators. It is very hard to imagine successful administration without the extensive online help provided by the UNIX manual pages. Every command, every option, all system calls, and many other details are fully documented and available whenever you need them, and they are always flavor-specific and accurate.

The basic online version of the UNIX reference manuals is usually located under the manual page directory */usr/man*, with possible additional topics located in the other "man" directories */dirpath/man*. The environment variable *$MANPATH* should include all "man" directories in a complete search of the selected manual page title; otherwise, the system will not be able to find and display the required manual pages.

UNIX manual pages are divided into a number of sections, each containing similar topics. The basic section organization is presented in the following table:

Contents	BSD section	System V section
User commands	1	1
System calls	2	2
C and other library routines	3	3
Special files, device drivers, hardware	4	7
Configuration files	5	4
Games	6	6 or 1 or N/A
Miscellaneous commands	7	5
Administration commands	8	1M
Maintenance commands	8	8

Note: An older organizational scheme under System V is also in use.

Modern UNIX flavors introduced new sections that were usually appended to the existing ones. It is entirely possible for the manual pages to be organized somewhat differently on your UNIX system.

Sections reside in separate subdirectories beneath the initial "man" directory. Here is an example from the Solaris 2.x platform:

$ ls -F /usr/man

```
cat-w/    man1f/   man3c/   man3r/    man4/    man7fs/   man9f/
cat./     man1m/   man3e/   man3s/    man4b/   man7i/    man9s/
man.cf    man1s/   man3g/   man3t/    man5/    man7m/    manl/
man1/     man2/    man3k/   man3x/    man6/    man7p/    mann/
man1b/    man3/    man3m/   man3xc/   man7/    man9/     windex
man1c/    man3b/   man3n/   man3xn/   man7d    man9e/
```

The UNIX **man** command is available to display specific manual pages. The command has several options, but its basic format is:

man ***man_page_title***

where

man_page_title A title we are looking for. If the specified title does not exist, or if it is spelled incorrectly, the system informs us; otherwise the required manual pages will be displayed, page by page.

The general format of the displayed manual pages includes the following paragraphs, if applicable:

NAME	A specified title with a brief description
SYNOPSIS	A format for using the specified title
DESCRIPTION	A full description of the specified title
OPTIONS	Available options for the specified title
ADDITIONAL INFO	Title-specific additional information such as like environment issues, exceptions, additional explanation, etc.
EXAMPLES	Examples for further explanation
FILES	Title-related files
SEE ALSO	Other related titles

The following example for the title ***man*** (referring to the ***man*** command) fully documents how to use the ***man*** command.

$ man ***man***

MAN(1) USER COMMANDS MAN(1) NAME

man — display reference manual pages; find reference pages by keyword

SYNOPSIS

man [-] [-t] [-M path] [-T macro-package] [[section] title ...]...
man [-M path] -k keyword...
man [-M path] -f filename...

DESCRIPTION

man displays information from the reference manuals. It can display complete manual pages that you select by title, or one-line summaries selected either by keyword (-k), or by the name of an associated file (-f).

A ***section***, when given, applies to the ***titles*** that follow it on the command line (up to the next ***section***, if any). **man** looks in the indicated section of the manual for those ***titles***. ***section*** is either a digit (perhaps followed by a single letter indicating the type of manual page), or one of the words *new, local, old,* or *public*. The abbreviations *n, l, o,* and *p* are also allowed. If ***section*** is omitted, ***man*** searches all reference sections (giving preference to commands over functions) and prints the first manual page it finds. If no manual page is located, ***man*** prints an error message.

The reference page sources are typically located in the */usr/man/man?* directories. Since these directories are optionally installed, they may not reside on your host; you may have to mount */usr/man* from a host on which they do reside. If there are preformatted, up-to-date versions in corresponding *cat?* or *fmt?* directories, **man** simply displays or prints those versions. If the preformatted version of interest is out of date or missing, **man** reformats it prior to display. If directories for the preformatted versions are not provided, **man** reformats a page whenever it is requested; it uses a temporary file to store the formatted text during display.

If the standard output is not a terminal, or if the "-" flag is given, **man** pipes its output through *cat(1V)*. Otherwise, **man** pipes its output through *more(1)* to handle paging and underlining on the screen.

OPTIONS

-t **man** arranges for the specified manual pages to be *troffed* to a suitable raster output device (see *troff*(1) or *vtroff*(1)). If both the **-** and **-t** flags are given, **man** updates the *troffed* versions of each named ***title*** (if necessary), but does not display them.

-M ***path***

Change the search path for manual pages. *path* is a colon-separated list of directories that contain manual page directory subtrees. For example, */usr/man/u_man:/usr/man/a_man makes* man search in the standard System V locations. When used with the -k or -f options, the -M option must appear first. Each directory in the *path* is assumed to contain sub-directories of the form *man[1–8l-p]*.

-T ***macro-package***

man uses ***macro-package*** rather than the standard **-man** macros defined in */usr/lib/tmac/tmac.an* for formatting manual pages.

-k ***keyword...***

man prints out one-line summaries from the *whatis* database (table of contents) that contain any of the given **keywords**. The *whatis* database is created using the *catman(8)* command with the **-w** option.

-f filename...

man attempts to locate manual pages related to any of the given **filenames**. It strips the leading pathname components from each **filename**, and then prints one-line summaries containing the resulting basename or names. This option also uses the *whatis* database.

MANUAL PAGES

Manual pages are troff(1)/nroff(1) source files prepared with the **-man** macro package. Refer to man(7), or **formatting documents** for more information.
When formatting a manual page, man examines the first line to determine whether it requires special processing.

Referring to Other Manual Pages

If the first line of the manual page is a reference to another manual page entry fitting the pattern: .so man?*/sourcefile

man processes the indicated file in place of the current one. The reference must be expressed as a pathname relative to the root of the manual page directory subtree.

When the second or any subsequent line starts with .so, **man** ignores it; *troff(1) or nroff(1)* processes the request in the usual manner.

Preprocessing Manual Pages

If the first line is a string of the form:
\"X

where ***X*** is separated from the " by a single SPACE and consists of any combination of characters in the following list, **man** pipes its input to *troff(1)* or *nroff(1)* through the corresponding preprocessors.

e *eqn(1), or neqn for nroff*
r *refer(1)*
t *tbl(1)*
v *vgrind(1)*

If *eqn* or *neqn* is invoked, it will automatically read the file */usr/pub/eqnchar* (see *eqnchar(7)*). If *nroff(1)* is invoked, *col(1V)* is automatically used.

ENVIRONMENT

MANPATH If set, its value overrides */usr/man* as the default search path. (The **-M** flag, in turn, overrides this value.)

PAGER A program to use for interactively delivering **man**'s output to the screen. If not set, '**more -s**' (see *more(1)*) is used.

TCAT The name of the program to use to display *troffed* manual pages. If not set, '**lpr–t**' (see *lpr(1)*) is used.

TROFF The name of the formatter to use when the **-t** flag is given. If not set, *troff* is used.

FILES

/usr/[share]/man	root of the standard manual page directory subtree
*/usr/[share]/man/man ?/**	unformatted manual entries
*/usr/[share]/man/cat ?/*nroffed*	manual entries
*/usr/[share]/man/fmt ?/*troffed*	manual entries
/usr/[share]/man/what is	table of contents and keyword database
/usr/[share]/lib/tma c/tmac.an	standard **-man** macro package /usr/pub/eqnchar

SEE ALSO

apropos(1), cat(1V), col(1V), eqn(1), lpr(1), more(1), nroff(1), refer(1), tbl(1), troff(1), vgrind(1), vtroff(1), whatis(1), eqnchar(7), man(7), catman(8)

NOTES

Because *troff* is not 8-bit clean, **man** has not been made 8-bit clean.
The **-f** and **-k** options use the */usr/man/whatis* database, which is created by *catman(8)*.

BUGS

The manual is supposed to be reproducible either on a photo-typesetter or on an ASCII terminal. However, on a terminal some information (indicated by font changes, for instance) is necessarily lost.

Some dumb terminals cannot process the vertical motions produced by the e (eqn(1)) preprocessing flag. To prevent garbled output on these terminals, when you use e also use **t**, to invoke col(1V) implicitly. This workaround has the disadvantage of eliminating superscripts and subscripts even on those terminals that can display them. CTRL-Q will clear a terminal that gets confused by *eqn(1)* output.

Linux provides even more; besides this, for UNIX standard online documentation, Linux also offers ***Texinfo Manual***, which presents more detailed technical descriptions of related topics. Again its use is very simple; by typing "***info topic-name***" the required information about the specified topic is displayed.

3.2.2 The *whatis* Database

The **man** command is very useful for getting information on a specific title; a title could be a command name, system call, library item, or something similar, but an existing title must always be specified. If such a title is unknown and you are searching for the manual pages related to a topic (but that topic is not the title itself), the ***whatis*** database has been provided.

UNIX allows you to build the ***whatis*** database, which is instrumental in finding information about a certain topic without knowing the relevant manual page title. The ***whatis*** database contains all of the manual page titles with a brief description of them; it primarily resides in the */usr/man/windex* file (sometimes the file name is *whatis*), but also in other additional database files in the corresponding "man" directory. The command "**man -k *topic_item***" will search through the ***whatis*** database and display all manual page titles that refer to the specified "*topic_item.*" Once the relevant title is known, the corresponding manual pages can be displayed. For a better understanding, see the **-k** option in the manual pages for the **man** command.

The ***whatis*** database must first be created locally; copying a database from another system does not work because the database must be directly linked with existing manual pages on the system where it resides. Additionally, the database should always be recreated when new manual pages are added to the system; the database must integrate the newly available titles.

The UNIX command ***catman-w*** is available to create a ***whatis*** database. It is very easy to begin to create a database, but it takes quite a while for the process to finish. It is a good idea to create a ***whatis*** database immediately upon UNIX installation.

Some UNIX flavors introduced new commands to create the ***whatis*** database. In Linux, the **whatis** and **apropos** commands are available (they have almost the same appearance as "**man -k**"), and the command ***makewhatis*** to create the ***whatis*** database.

3.3 System Information

UNIX administration means administering UNIX software or, more precisely, UNIX system software. Software requires maintenance just like any other product; but because of their complexity, software systems require a more sophisticated level of maintenance. Among the increased requirements are highly educated and skilled personnel who are capable of managing, upgrading, configuring, and fixing unpredictable and very sophisticated problems.

Software could not exist without the corresponding computer hardware. Knowledge of hardware can be very instrumental and helpful in UNIX system administration. At the very least, a UNIX administrator has to be familiar with basic system hardware configuration.

In the following text, several UNIX commands of this nature will be discussed.

3.3.1 System Status Information

To begin, let us introduce a few commands useful for checking the system status.

3.3.1.1 The uname Command

The ***uname*** command prints the basic UNIX system information to the standard output file. The displayed system data contain: hostname, operating system data, and hardware architecture data.

The format of the command is:

uname [options]

where the available options are:

- **-n** Print the hostname (the hostname may be the name by which the system is known to a communications network)
- **-s** Print the operating system name (default)
- **-r** Print the operating system release
- **-v** Print the operating system version
- **-m** Print the machine hardware name (architecture)
- **-a** Print all the above information

The output of the **uname -a** command for several UNIX flavors is presented in the following table:

ULTRIX acf4 4.3 1 RISC
HP-UX apollo A.09.03 A 9000/715 2004998919 two-user license
HP-UX baltic B.10.20 A 9000/800 1293244351 two-user license
IRIX indigo1 4.0.5 06151813 IP12
SunOS patsy 4.1.3 1 sun4c
SunOS apollo 5.3 Generic sun4m sparc
SunOS aegean 5.6 Generic_105181–17 sun4u sparc SUNW,Ultra-Enterprise
AIX rs01-ch 2 3 000187963100
Linux broome 2.2.16 #2 SMP Thu Oct 12 22:32:13 GMT 2000 i686 unknown

Supposing a default system startup, Linux offers more detailed information about OS in the file */etc/issue*. By typing:

$> cat /etc/issue
Red Hat Linux release 7.0 (Guinness)
Kernel 2.2.16 on a 4-processor i686

we will definitely learn more about our Linux installation.

3.3.1.2 The uptime Command

The ***uptime*** command displays:

- The current time
- How long the system has been up (the length of time)
- Number of users
- A rough estimate of the system load over the last estimate, every 5 and 15 minutes

Here are a few examples:

 # uptime

6:47am up 6 days, 16:38, 1 user, load average: 0.69, 0.28, 0.17	(Solaris)
9:50am up 9 days, 34 min, 3 users, load average: 0.00, 0.00, 0.00	(SunOS)
9:38am up 9 days, 27 min, 1 user, load average: 2.07, 2.03, 2.03	(HP-UX)

3.3.1.3 The dmesg Command

The ***dmesg*** command collects system diagnostic messages; it looks in a system buffer for recently generated messages when errors occur and forwards them to the standard output.

When the "-" option is used, the **dmesg** command incrementally generates messages that are new since the last time it was executed.

Sometimes, existing imperfections can stay hidden and the system appears to be working fine; in such cases the **dmesg** command could be very useful. However, the system error message buffer is of a small, finite size, so there is no guarantee that all error messages will be logged.

In the past, the **dmesg** command was also used to update the system log file (usually */usr/adm/messages*) by its periodic execution through the ***cron*** facility. A typical crontab entry:

/etc/dmesg - >> /usr/adm/messages

would update the system log file periodically. Today, such a task is obsolete, and an update of the system log file is performed by the ***syslogd*** daemon (see Chapter 9).

An example follows (from the HP-UX platform):

```
$ dmesg
May 20 16:59
Floating point coprocessor configured and enabled.
I/O System Configuration:
    Block TLB entry #8 from 0×f5000000 to 0×f5ffffff allocated.
    HPA1991AC19 Bit-Mapped Display (revision 8.02/10) in SGC slot 0
    SGC at select code 0×0
    Built-In SCSI Single-Ended Interface at select code 0×20: function number 1
    Built-In LAN controller found at select code 0×20: function number 2
    HIL interface at select code 0×20: function number 3
    Built-In RS-232C Serial Interface at select code 0×20: function number 4
    Built-In RS-232C Serial Interface at select code 0×20: function number 5
    Parallel port at select code 0×20: function number 6
    Advanced Digital Audio Interface at select code 0×20: function number 8
    System Console is on the ITE
Networking memory for fragment reassembly is restricted to 2957312 bytes
    Swap device table: (start & size given in 512-byte blocks) entry
    0 - auto-configured on root device; start = 869400, size = 152702
    Core image of 8192 pages will be saved at: block 478283 on device 0×7201600
Warning: filesystem time later than time-of-day register
Getting time from filesystem
    B2352A HP-UX (A.09.03.nodebug) #1: Mon Aug 30 21:05:26 MDT 1993
Memory Information:
    Physical: 32768 Kbytes, lockable: 26168 Kbytes, available: 27880 Kbytes
Copyright (c) 1990–1998, Rational Software Corporation.
Covered by U.S. patent no. 5,574,898.
Other U.S. and foreign patents pending.
automountd not running, retrying
automountd OK
```

3.3.2 Hardware Information

It is logical to want to upgrade your UNIX system to improve its overall performance. The first thing you need to know is the current hardware configuration of the UNIX system: how many CPUs are installed? How much memory is used? What is the size of the disk space? These simple questions are very common, and the UNIX administrator always addresses them.

A partial answer can be obtained with the UNIX command **top**. The **top** command lists the top-most CPU-consuming processes. The command is extremely instrumental in performance measurement and the tracing of potential problems. However, the command also displays basic data about the number of CPUs and memory usage, which is what we are looking for right now. An example follows:

```
# top
System: mekong                              Mon Jul 17 22:51:28 2000
Load averages: 0.91, 0.77, 0.75
199 processes: 197 sleeping, 2 running
CPU states:
CPU   LOAD    USER    NICE   SYS    IDLE   BLOCK   SWAIT   INTR   SSYS
0     0.83    1.0%    0.0%   1.4%   97.6%  0.0%    0.0%    0.0%   0.0%
1     0.99    75.2%   0.0%   24.8%  0.0%   0.0%    0.0%    0.0%   0.0%
—     —       —       —      —      —      —       —       —      —
avg   0.91    38.0%   0.0%   13.1%  48.8%  0.0%    0.0%    0.0%   0.0%
Memory: 49676K (40972K) real, 100316K (83172K) virtual, 196720K free Page# 1/19
CPU  TTY  PID    USER   PRI  NI  SIZE   RES    STATE  TIME     %WCPU  %CPU   COMMAND
                 NAME
1    q2   27047  cbw1   239  20  4740K  968K   run    173:59   99.09  98.92  udt
0    ?    398    root   154  20  108K   140K   sleep  1324:09  0.93   0.93   syncer
0    ?    7448   rpsc   168  20  4484K  696K   sleep  35:57    0.89   0.89   udt
0    p1   8405   root   178  20  1260K  340K   run    0:00     0.85   0.49   top
0    ?    6948   root   155  2   6288K  6340K  sleep  28:49    0.41   0.41   lcp
                        .....
                        .....
```

It is also a good idea to try using the available system administration tools, like the HP-UX flavored ***SAM***, or AIX flavored ***SMIT***. These always provide hardware-related information among their many other menu selections. They are very well suited to this purpose, because a search for hardware information is almost always interactive.

Otherwise, each UNIX flavor provides a different set of commands used to diagnose the installed hardware. We will discuss some of them.

3.3.2.1 The HP-UX ioscan Command

On the HP-UX platform, the special command ***ioscan*** is available for dealing with actual hardware. The command scans system hardware, usable I/O system devices, or kernel I/O system data structures, as appropriate, and lists the results. For each hardware module on the system, **ioscan** displays (by default) the hardware path to the hardware module, the class of the hardware module, and a brief description of it.

By default, the **ioscan** command scans the system and lists all reportable hardware found. The types of hardware reported include processors, memory, interface cards, and I/O devices. Entities that cannot be scanned are not listed.

The **ioscan** command recognizes the following options:

- **-C class** Restricts the output listing to those devices belonging to the specified class
- **-d driver** Restricts the output listing to those devices controlled by the specified driver
- **-f** Generates a full listing, displaying the module's class, instance number, hardware path, driver, software state, hardware type, and a brief description
- **-F** Produces a compact listing of fields separated by colons

-H hw_path Restricts the scan and output listing to those devices connected at the specified hardware path

-I instance Restricts the scan and output listing to the specified instance

-k Scans kernel I/O system data structures instead of the actual hardware and lists the results

-n Lists device file names in the output; only special files in the */dev* directory and its subdirectories are listed

-u Scans and list usable I/O system devices instead of the actual hardware. Usable I/O devices are those having a driver in the kernel and an assigned instance number.

Some of the options require additional arguments, known as *fields*, which are defined as follows:

class A device category, for example: disk, printer, or tape

instance The instance number associated with the device or card; it is a unique number assigned to a card or device within a class

hw_path A numerical string of hardware components, noted sequentially from the bus address to the device address; typically, the initial number is appended by slash ("/"), to represent a bus converter (if required by the machine), and subsequent numbers are separated by periods ("."). Each number represents the location of a hardware component on the path to the device.

driver The name of the driver that controls the hardware component

The following example shows a partial output of the **ioscan** command:

 # /usr/sbin/ioscan

H/W Path	Class	Description
	bc	
8	*bc*	*I/O Adapter*
10	*bc*	*I/O Adapter*
10/0	*ext_bus*	*GSC built-in Fast/Wide SCSI Interface*
10/0.5	*target*	
10/0.5.0	*disk*	*SEAGATE ST15150W*
10/0.6	*target*	
10/0.6.0	*disk*	*SEAGATE ST15150W*
10/0.7	*target*	
10/0.7.0	*ctl*	*Initiator*
10/4	*bc*	*Bus Converter*
10/4/0	*tty*	*MUX*
10/4/12	*ext_bus*	*HP 28696A-Wide SCSI ID = 7*
10/4/12.12	*target*	
10/4/12.12.0	*disk*	*SEAGATE ST32550W*
	....	
	....	
	....	
10/12/5.0	*target*	
10/12/5.0.0	*tape*	*HP C1533A*
10/12/5.2	*target*	
10/12/5.2.0	*disk*	*TOSHIBA CD-ROM XM-5401TA*
10/12/5.7	*target*	
10/12/5.7.0	*ctl*	*Initiator*

10/12/6	*lan*	*Built-in LAN*
10/12/7	*ps2*	*Built-in Keyboard/Mouse*
32	*processor*	*processor*
34	*processor*	*processor*
49	*memory*	*Memory*

3.3.2.2 The Solaris prtconf Command

On the Solaris platform, the ***prtconf*** command displays the system configuration information. The output includes the total amount of memory and the configuration of system peripherals formatted as a device tree.

The **prtconf** command has several options:

- **-P** Includes information about pseudo devices; by default, information regarding pseudo devices is omitted
- **-v** Specifies verbose mode
- **-F** Returns the device pathname of the console frame buffer, if one exists. If there is no frame buffer, **prtconf** returns a non-zero exit code
- **-p** Displays information derived from the device tree provided by the firmware (PROM)
- **-V** Display platform-dependent information
- **-D** For each system peripheral in the device tree, displays the name of the device driver used to manage the peripheral

The following example presents a partial output of the command running on a Sun4/65 series machine:

```
# /usr/sbin/prtconf
System configuration: Sun Microsystems sun4c
Memory size: 16 megabytes
System peripherals (software nodes):
Sun 4_65
    options, instance #0
    zs, instance #0
    zs, instance #1
    fd (driver not attached)
    audio (driver not attached)
    sbus, instance #0
    dma, instance #0
    esp, instance #0
    sd (driver not attached)
    st (driver not attached)
    sd, instance #0
    sd, instance #1 (driver not attached)
        . . . . .
        . . . . .
    le, instance #0
    cgsix (driver not attached)
    auxiliary-io (driver not attached)
    interrupt-enable (driver not attached)
    memory-error (driver not attached)
    counter-timer (driver not attached)
    eeprom (driver not attached)
    pseudo, instance #0
```

The output of the **prtconf** command is highly dependent upon the version of the PROM installed in the system. The output will be affected in potentially all circumstances.

The "driver not attached" message means that no driver is currently attached to that specific device. In general, drivers are loaded and installed (and attached to hardware instances) on demand and when needed, and may be uninstalled and unloaded when the device is not in use.

3.3.2.3 The Solaris sysdef Command

Another Solaris command that can be used for this purpose is *sysdef*. The *sysdef* command outputs the current system definition in tabular form. It lists all hardware devices, as well as pseudo devices, system devices, loadable modules, and the values of selected kernel tunable parameters. It generates the output by analyzing the named bootable operating system file (*namelist*) and extracting the configuration information from it. The default system namelist is */dev/kmem*. However, the command output is not entirely comprehensive for figuring out basic hardware information; it is more suitable for kernel-related information. This command should probably not be the first choice.

3.4 Personal Documentation

UNIX administration is a challenging job; it requires a substantial level of expertise and skills. But UNIX administration is also a routine job, in which the tasks can only be successfully accomplished by following the required procedures. To install UNIX, you must follow the vendor's instructions and recommendations; to configure an application you must strictly obey configuration rules. There is no room for improvisation; improper settings are the main causes of system instability and all related problems. Bugs in the software are a good excuse for our wrongdoings, but only rarely are they the real cause of the problems we experience.

Properly configuring a system, and ensuring all of its settings are correct, is not an easy task. Often there are plenty of small but important details that we must take care of. It is easy to forget these small issues, especially if we only deal with them occasionally. Taking notes on everything done to the system can be very instrumental for future work; such notes can be the lifesaver in some critical situations. These moments are always very stressful, and an administrator has to act quickly and accurately. There is no better advice for that time than to follow your own, already tested and proven notes.

Many administrative tasks repeat a number of times; it is common to install the same UNIX version on different machines, to configure hosts in the same network environment, to set the same application software multiple times, etc. Any notes about jobs you have done previously can be very helpful; the length of time between jobs can be large enough that you may forget many important details.

Note by note a substantial personal documentation will be built; this is your "knowledge database," and it is very important for efficient work. You will always be more familiar with your own documents than with any vendor-provided documentation. There is no need to worry about style, syntax, or language — as long as they are explicit and complete, you will always understand your own texts.

A key issue for successful UNIX administration is to be well organized. System administration is based on rules designed by others: different configuration files have different formats and syntax. Each required letter, number, dot, dash, or whatever is specified must be fully respected — there is not a great deal of freedom of choice. A UNIX administrator cannot invent another set of configuration rules, even if the existing ones do not seem very logical or convenient. It simply will not work. Past experiences can save time and make everything easier; copying a workable procedure is definitely more efficient than reinvestigating something you have already done.

In most cases, UNIX administration is also a team task. It takes a number of UNIX administrators (as well as others such as NT administrators, network administrators, helpdesk staffers, etc.) to support large company networks. One important issue, then, is how to make their collective work more efficient. One logical solution is to combine all individual documentation and then make all of this documentation available to all team members. The organization of this effort, however, is crucial.

A very efficient approach to making all system documentation available yet well organized is to put individual personal documents on the company network, creating substantial internal company site-specific documentation, and make the documentation available to all relevant associates. By posting these documents on an internal company Web site (if necessary even creating an internal Web site for this purpose), everyone will be able to obtain the necessary information about any described topic. The documentation remains open for any required update or upgrade. To prevent potential frauds, the access to documents should be restricted to administrative personnel only.

There are third-party products that provide tools to create internal knowledge databases; in most cases they offer other features, as well. However, they can be costly and sometimes too complex to work with. Creating your own internal, Web-based documentation site is simple, inexpensive, and very efficient.

3.5 Shell Script Programming

Shell programming is one of the strongest parts of the UNIX administration. This is also one of the key elements of an overall UNIX success. UNIX administrators are in love with shell programming. Where is this authoritative statement coming from? It is coming from the fact that the shell programming presents an extremely powerful tool to customize and automate your UNIX system, as well as to accomplish many manual administrative activities easier.

An intuitive and colorful graphic user interface (GUI) sounds challenging for certain complex administrative actions. However, GUI actions remain quite hidden from us. GUI is great as long as everything is going smoothly, but very frustrating once it starts to fail. And what do you do when GUI is not even running because of underlying problems? Or, how do you automate some repeated actions? Even to document needed steps in the GUI administration is not an easy task.

A good UNIX administrator tends to pack needed administrative actions into the corresponding shell scripts, and then to use the scripts instead. Well-written and tested shell scripts are always working properly, even in the most critical situations when the pressure on the UNIX administrator is always very high. There are no typos and mistyping in the shell-script implementations nor are there incorrect command options — frequent errors during manual procedures. Everything is happening correctly and in the fastest possible way. Simply, shell scripts are lifesavers.

There are also many other reasons in favor of the intensive shell programming. Time-scheduled scripts will execute successfully the same job as many times as needed, withor without provided verbose logging, e-mailing, paging, or whatever is required. We should spend the time only once, when we write the script, and only to use the script later. And always when we write a script, we should have enough time, and be doing it far from any of the pressure typical of urgent administrative actions.

Shell programming is a prerequisite for good UNIX administration. It is assumed that a UNIX administrator is familiar with shell programming. This section is not a tutorial in shell programming. Rather it points to certain aspects of shell programming that could be confusing for UNIX administrators (even if not beginners in this area). A thorough shell-programming tutorial is definitely not in the scope of this book; however, these skills are assumed throughout the pages of this book.

3.5.1 UNIX User Shell

UNIX user shell is an interface layer between the UNIX operating system and the user. It is presented in the Figure 3.1.

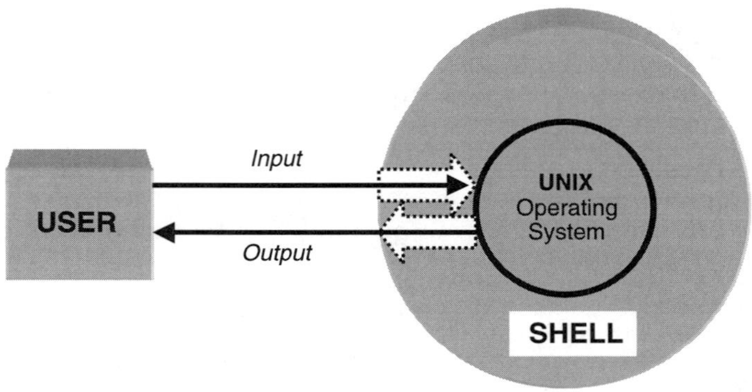

FIGURE 3.1
The user's shell layer.

There are many different UNIX shell flavors: Bourne shell ***sh***, Korn shell ***ksh***, C shell ***csh***, Bourne again shell ***bash***, enhanced C shell ***tcsh***, etc. Some shells are very similar — like ***ksh*** and ***bash***, ***sh*** is the subset of ***ksh*** — but generally they are not mutually compatible (at least in both directions). This is important to know when a shell script is invoked.

3.5.2 UNIX Shell Scripts

Shell scripts are programs that comply with the shell programming language. Shell scripts are not compiled programs; instead they are readable text files where each command line is read and processed by the shell command interpreter at the time the script is executed. Shell command interpreter processes a shell script until an erroneous command line is encountered or until it ends. A shell command line can contain:

- Any UNIX command or command sequence
- Any shell-flavored command or statement
- Any other program or shell script
- A combination of previously listed items

Each shell has a number of its own commands and statements that actually make shell programming so powerful. Make sure that they are very shell-specific in every sense: syntax and action.

3.5.2.1 Shell Script Execution

A shell script (as any other program in UNIX) can be simply invoked by its name, but the read and execute permissions for the script are required. The following example illustrates this:

sh# cat /tmpMyScript.sh (*to see content*)

```
############################
echo "Just a test of x permission"
############################
```

sh# ls -l /tmp/MyScript.sh (*to see permissions*)

```
-rw-r--r--   1 root   root   39 Aug 21 18:27/tmp/MyScript.sh
```

sh# /tmp/MyScript.sh (*to invoke shell script*)

```
sh: /tmp/test4.sh: Permission denied
```

The script can also be invoked with an explicitly specified shell. In that case the execute permission on the script is not mandatory. Some UNIX flavors will execute a shell script even without read permission granted.

sh# /bin/sh /tmp/MyScript.sh

```
Just a test of x permission
```

When invoked directly, the shell script is executed in the environment of the current user shell. The current user shell is forked, and then each command line of the shell script is processed by the shell interpreter and executed (already discussed fork-and-exec start of the program). If two shell flavors do not match (the shell script and the parent shell — for example ***bash*** script is invoked in ***csh*** environment), most probably a number of errors will be encountered for basically correct shell script.

The following examples present such situations. The arbitrary bash script named ***myscript.bash*** is invoked in the ***bash*** and ***csh*** environment:

bash# cat /tmp/myscript.bash

```
########################################
# Define variables
export TEXT1 = "This is a bash script myscript.bash"
export TEXT2="Running the script myscript.bash"
#
# Run the command
echo "$TEXT1"
echo "$TEXT2"
########################################
```

bash# /tmp/myscript.bash

```
This is a bash script myscript.bash
Running the script myscript.bash
```

bash# /bin/csh (*Switch to csh*)
csh# /tmp/myscript.bash

```
export: Command not found.
export: Command not found.
TEXT1: Undefined variable.
```

The previous problematic situation could be skipped in two ways. First, as we mentioned previously, the script can be invoked with explicitly specified shell:

bash# /bin/bash /tmp/myscript.bash *(Here shells match)*

This is a bash script myscript.bash
Running the script myscript.bash

csh# /bin/bash /tmp/myscript.bash *(Here shells don't match)*

This is a bash script myscript.bash
Running the script myscript.bash

Or the shell can be implicitly specified in the script itself. The very first line in the script of the format — ***#!/bin/shellname*** — has a special meaning. The *"/bin/shellname"* identifies the full path of the desired shell, which will be invoked first and then the script executed in this shell environment. Remember that it can be any other executable program, not necessarily the shell. However, we are assuming a shell. Here are examples:

bash# cat /tmp/myscript1.bash

```
#!/ bin/bash
#########################################
# Define variables
export TEXT1="This is a bash script myscript1.bash"
export TEXT2="Running the script myscript1.bash"
#
# Run the command
echo "$TEXT1"
echo "$TEXT2"
#########################################
```

bash# /tmp/myscript1.bash

This is a bash script myscript1.bash
Running the script myscript1.bash

csh# /tmp/myscript1.bash

This is a bash script myscript1.bash
Running the script myscript1.bash

In all the examples, the current shell spawns itself or another shell, making a "parent–child relationship" between two shells (current user's shell and the invoked shell script). However, a shell script can also be executed directly in the user's shell environment. For this purpose the shell script must be "sourced." A special shell command is used to source the script.

source myscript.sh *# for csh and csh-like shells*
. myscript.sh *# for ksh, bash, and Bourne shells*

To source a shell script means to skip the forking of the user's shell and to execute the script directly in the user's shell environment.

3.5.2.2 Shell Variables

We can define and redefine shell environment within the shell script. By invoking a new shell script, the current shell environment is transferred and the new initial shell environment created. Remember that this is a unidirectional transfer, from parent toward child shell (child inherits the parent's environment); the reverse is never possible. Regarding shell variables, only global, i.e., exported, variables could be inherited; local variables remain always within the current shell environment, and they disappear once the shell is terminated. This sometimes sounds very confusing for the novices in UNIX administration.

In this light we can better understand the need and purpose of the shell command: ***source***. If we want to define a shell environment within a single script (let us call it *environment definition script*), and then share these definitions among many other shell scripts, we must source the environment definition script. Otherwise, all definitions will last as long as the execution of the environment definition script. The following example illustrates that situation.

The user's shell is Bourne shell. Variables ***VARA*** and ***VARB*** are not defined.

```
sh# echo $VARA   # To check if $VARA is defined
sh# echo $VARB   # To check if $VARB is defined
```

The script ***/tmp/myscript2.sh*** defines the global variables VARA and VARB:

```
sh# cat /tmp/myscript2.sh
# Variable definitions
##################
VARA="VariableA"
VARB="VariableB"
Export VARA VARB
##################
```

Upon the script execution, variables ***VARA*** and ***VARB*** are still undefined in the user's shell environment. There is no way to export variables toward the parent shell environment.

```
sh# /tmpi/myscript2.sh      # Execute the script
sh# echo $VARA              # To check if $VARA is defined
sh# echo $VARB              # To check if $VARB is defined
```

Upon the sourcing of the script variables, ***VARA*** and ***VARB*** remain defined within the user's shell environment.

```
sh# . /tmp/myscript2.sh     # Source the script
sh# echo $VARA              # To check if $VARA is defined
VariableA
sh# echo $VARB              # To check if $VARB is defined
VariableB
```

The previous discussion is instrumental in understanding the user's log-in process and the initial definition of the user's shell environment, which is discussed in Chapter 7.

3.5.2.3 Double Command-Line Scanning

Shell variables are often used on the shell command-lines, as a part of UNIX or shell commands. Unfortunately, sometimes they can easily be misinterpreted. Simply, under certain conditions, shell variables could be understood literally: the variable **$VARA** from the previous example can be understood as "***$VARA***" instead of its value "***VariableA***." Just think about versatile and powerful UNIX commands (better to say UNIX utilities) like, ***awk***, ***sed***, or other commands that have their own syntax somehow different from the shell syntax. This makes a great difference and could make the use of shell variables very restricted.

The shell response to this situation is the command: ***eval***. This command allows so-called *"double command-line scanning,"* where the shell variables are first processed, developed, and then replaced for the second command-line processing. For better understanding of this command, let us see how the shell command interpreter processes a command line at all. This is presented in Figure 3.2 and explained in the following text.

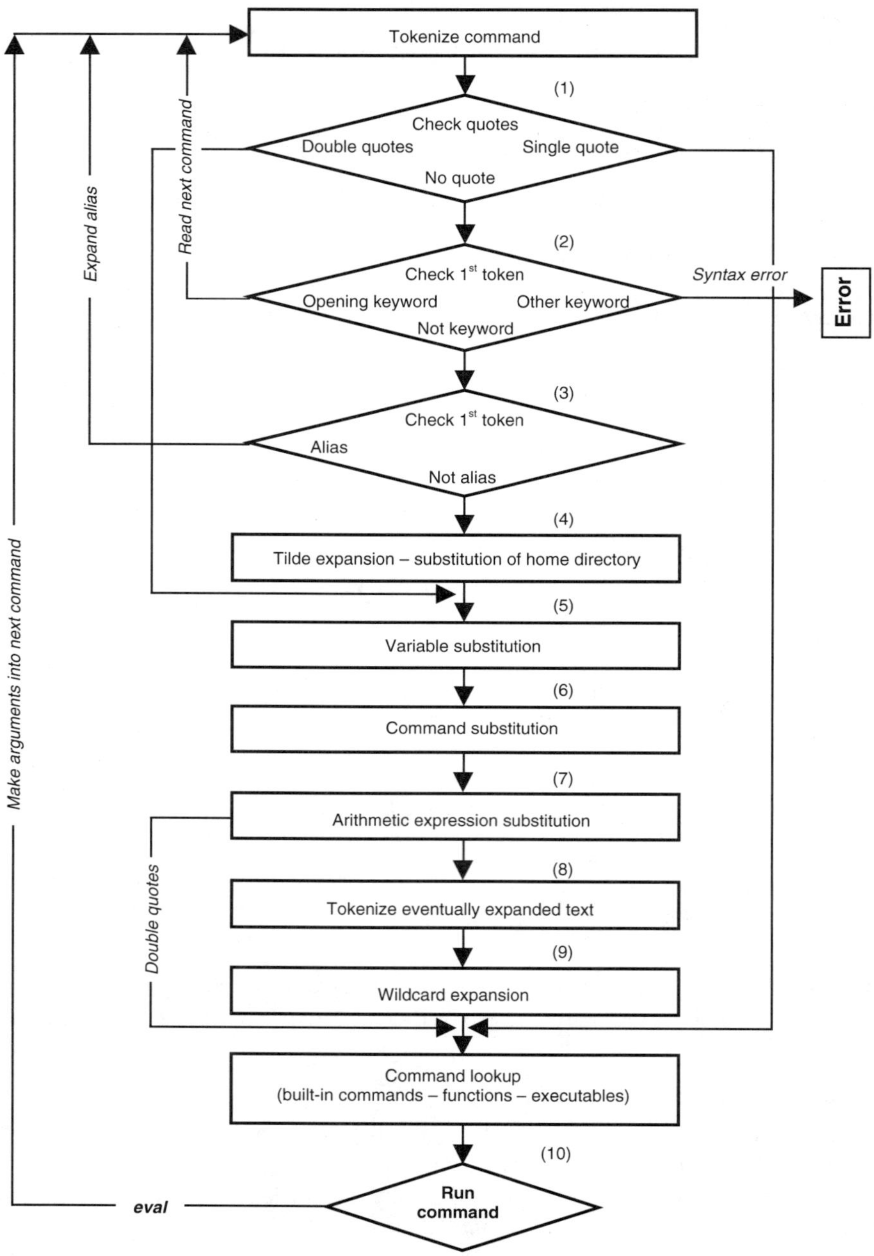

FIGURE 3.2
Shell processing of the command line.

1. The command line is "tokenized," i.e., split into its constituents: *word, keywords, IO redirectors,* and *semicolons,* according to the separating metacharacters: *space, tab, new line,), (, <, >, \, /,* and *&*.
2. The first token is tested if it is "a single-line unquoted keyword" (a keyword without quotes or continuation character). Shell statements (*if, while, until…*) and functions are treated as "opening keywords," set up internally; the processing continues with the next token.
3. The command is tested against the list of command aliases; eventual aliases are expanded and reprocessed.
4. The substitution of an eventual user's home directory.
5. The variable substitution for any expression with leading $. This is also the second processing step for double-quoted tokens (steps between are skipped).
6. The command substitution for any single back-quoted expression of the form *'expression'* or *$(expression)*. The expression is executed and substituted with the obtained result for additional processing.
7. The evaluation of the arithmetic expressions of the form $((expression)). Remember that the double-quoted expressions are processed differently from others after this step.
8. The eventual expanded text (as a result of the previous step processing) is now "tokenized" according to the shell environment internal field separators (IFS).
9. The wildcard expansion of *, ? and *[/] pairs,* and processing of regular expression operators.
10. The search for the command in all predefined command directories (according to the shell *$PATH* or *$path* variable). This is also the second, and the only, step in processing single-quoted command-line tokens.

At this point everything is ready for the command-line execution. However, if the shell command ***eval*** was specified, another round of the command processing will be performed. This is known as *double command-line scanning*.

The format of the command is: ***eval args*** where *args* includes the actual command itself and command arguments. For better understanding of this command, see the following example. The user's shell is *bash*, but it does not have any specific impact on the example (could be any other shell).

```
bash# VAR1='$VAR2'      # Define variable VAR1
bash# VAR2='Example'    # Define variable VAR2
bash# echo $VAR1        # Check the values of variables
$VAR2
bash# echo $VAR2
Example
bash# eval echo $VAR1   # Check the values of variables upon double scanning
Example
bash# eval echo $VAR2
Example
```

3.5.2.4 Here Document

An extremely powerful feature of the shell programming is its *Here Document*. The shell redirector of the form: "**<< label**" forces the input to the specified command to be the shell's standard input, which is read until the line that contains only "**label**" is reached. It means that all script command-lines within the Here Document will not be processed by the shell command interpreter. Instead they will be processed by the command specified at the start of the Here Document.

Here is an example:

```
###
myprogram << !EOF
mycommandA
mycommandB
mycommandC
!EOF
###
```

This shell script command-line sequence will start the execution and transfer the further command-line control to ***myprogram***. Command lines that follow until the terminating label ***!EOF*** are submitted to and strictly processed by ***myprogram***. The specified label can be any string, but two labels must match literally; no leading or trailing blanks on the terminating line are allowed.

Here Document enables an unattended execution of not-shell and not-UNIX commands within the shell script. It is used frequently for inception of SQL, FTP, and other command sequences into the shell environment. Unfortunately *Here Document* does not support interactive procedures — simply the next command-line is submitted as soon as the previous one is done. Generally the main disadvantage of the shell programming is its inability to act interactively if used unattended. For this purpose Espect or Perl patches are required.

Here Document makes shell script programming easier and more powerful. For more details see the FTP example in Chapter 21.

3.5.2.5 Few Tips

At the end of this brief overview of certain shell programming topics, few tips for using the shell scripts:

- A shell script inherits the caller's environment, usually the user's shell. However there are no rules for the initial environment setting. Everything defined-out-of-script is uncertain, including the search path for the implemented commands in the script. Some good advice follows:
  Define the PATH variable in the script.
  Or, use the full-path command names.
- It is very common that the fully tested shell script from the command line fails when it is run as a cron job. The reason is simple: cron environment is reduced to several default values, usually insufficient for the successful script execution.
- Always clean everything that the shell script creates temporarily. Each file is owned by its creator, and remaining temporary files could be obstacle for other script invokers.
- Pay attention to the standard and error output. The shell scripts are often running in background either.

4

System Startup and Shutdown

4.1 Introductory Notes

UNIX systems run continuously under normal circumstances. Shutting down and powering-off a UNIX system should be done rarely, usually only when a hardware upgrade is being performed or a system is being allocated, or occasionally when another action requiring a system shutdown is performed. In real life, system shutdown is more frequent, because unpredictable situations always occur.

Power-cycling a UNIX system is not the only way the system can be shut down. Rebooting is also a familiar task for any UNIX administrator; UNIX administrators know well how system rebooting can be healthy for overall system maintenance.

Nevertheless, keeping the UNIX system running is the most visible task of a system administrator. If the system crashes, everyone will complain, your phone will ring constantly, and you will find yourself anxiously trying to fix the problem and bring the system back into production. Quickly you will learn how important the system you are in charge of really is, and how many users depend on it. Even more important, you will learn how crucial a smooth, fast, proper system startup can be.

This chapter covers topics related to normal UNIX system startup and shutdown procedures. Invoking a system startup and shutdown is quite simple; the main requirement is to be the superuser on the system (an easy task for an administrator). On the other hand, making the system behave correctly, especially during startup, requires a great deal of knowledge and administrative skill. Proper system startup is supposed to customize and set the myriad of existing system configuration files that will control each portion of the UNIX system. Some of these files include system-related configuration data, but there are also site-added applications; the bottom line is that the system should be fully operational after any system startup.

Given the complexity of properly configuring the system startup, this chapter could easily be located at the end of the overall text, rather than at its beginning. However, discussing the administration of a running UNIX system without knowing how that system came to be running seems strange; it is as though we are talking about administering a nonexistent UNIX system. So this material remains in the beginning by design; it will focus on the topic of global system startup and shutdown, and we will return to individual startup and shutdown issues later, whenever it is appropriate in discussing specific UNIX topics.

From an administrative standpoint, system shutdown is the simpler procedure; at the end of the procedure a system must terminate all running processes, dismount all filesystems, and stop any other system activity. System shutdown works even if we never touch the default shutdown procedure — or perhaps it is better to say it *mostly* works, because the author of this text has witnessed a UNIX system that could not be shut down from the command line, and the only choice was to power-cycle the system. Our administrative task is to provide a graceful system shutdown. Everything must be stopped in a regular way, or the administrator will have to use the brute force method of power-cycling. System startup, on the other hand, must be done properly or the system will never come up. Obviously, more attention should be paid to system startup, and we will spend much more time discussing the startup procedure than the shutdown process.

System startup is often referred to as ***system booting***. Although "booting" specifies only one phase in the overall system startup, the two terms are commonly interchanged, as you will see in this chapter. Strictly speaking, system startup has a broader meaning than system booting.

All UNIX systems must be shut down in a regular way before any further action can be taken. You should never directly power-off UNIX systems (such as DOS-based PCs); the shutdown procedure must be implemented, otherwise disk data integrity can be corrupted (a UNIX filesystem could be damaged). The corruption can range between a relatively benign loss of data to heavy filesystem damage, which in the worst case scenario can leave a system unbootable.

The two major UNIX platforms BSD and System V have different startup and shutdown procedures, with, of course, the main differences occurring in startup. Among existing commercial UNIX flavors, the System V approach is more common; it provides more flexibility and some other administrative advantages. However, the BSD approach is somewhat easier to understand, and we will start our discussion with the BSD startup/shutdown procedure. Once the startup/shutdown concept is well understood, it will be easy to continue with the System V procedure.

4.2 System Startup

The system startup procedure is a continuous process that a UNIX system goes through, from its initial hardware-determined stage until the final production-ready stage. However, this unique system journey passes through several distinct phases, and each of these phases has its specific characteristics. The startup phases, listed in the order they occur, are:

- Bootstrap program execution
- Kernel execution
- *rc* system initialization
- Terminal line initialization

It is easier to understand the system startup procedure when the whole process is divided into several phases and each of the phases is analyzed separately, so this is the approach we will take. Although each of the listed phases is equally important for successful system startup, the ***system initialization*** phase requires the most administrative attention, so most of the following discussion will address this phase.

In each of the startup phases, the system learns enough to execute the next phase. Each phase contributes a bit to the overall system startup. At the very beginning, the system does not know very much; at the very end, the system is ready for multi-user operations.

4.2.1 The Bootstrap Program

The origin of the word *boot* (as in, "to boot the system") is *bootstrapping*, which is the process of bringing a computer system to life and ready for use. ("Bootstrapping" is actually the "nerd word" for starting up a computer.) The computer system itself is only a collection of hardware resources (registers, arithmetic/logical unit, program counter, memories, etc.) capable of executing a sequence of instructions that make a program. The program, stored in the computer's memory (any kind of memory: ROM, RAM, external magnetic memory, etc.), defines the system's activity at every moment, including its first steps during the system startup.

An initial program, the ***bootstrap program***, must be stored in the fast nonvolatile memory directly accessible by a processor, or CPU (CPU stands for central processing unit and is another term for a processor). This portion of the computer memory is known as internal read-only memory (ROM). The execution of the bootstrap program is always automatically initiated when the system is powered-on or when a system hardware reset is applied. It is also initiated when the system is rebooted from the system console. Only the initial part of the bootstrap program, the part sufficient to bring the system into a workable state to deal with other memory types, must be stored in ROM. Once this level is achieved, the bootstrap program execution can be continued from another nonvolatile media such as a hard disk, a floppy disk, a tape, or a CD-ROM, or even through the network from a boot-server (in the case of diskless workstations). For UNIX systems, regular system booting is commonly executed from a hard disk, while first-time UNIX OS installation is performed from a CD-ROM (not long ago, a tape was used).

The system has to learn enough from the ROM to be able to access a disk to continue the bootstrap program, but it still assumes a simple flat data structure on the disk. A complex disk data organization such as the UNIX filesystem data structure is still too complicated for the system at this stage; more learning is needed to deal with a filesystem. That is why the rest of the bootstrap program is stored in a special part of the disk known as the *boot partition* (sometimes also known as the *boot segment*). The main characteristic of the boot partition is its easy access and flat data structure, so the system is able to continue with the bootstrap program execution, and further learning.

The ratio of the percentage of the bootstrap program stored in the ROM versus the disk boot partition varied through time. In the early days of UNIX when only low capacity, expensive ROM was available, the first part of the bootstrap program was reduced to the bare minimum size. Today, systems include high-density ROM sufficient to store quite sophisticated bootstrap programs; this makes boot partitions less important, although they are still a part of every system startup.

Once the bootstrap program is completely executed, the system is knowledgeable enough to continue with the kernel execution.

Traditionally UNIX presents the only OS running on underlying hardware; and traditionally this is a proprietary hardware for that UNIX flavor. This fact makes a booting process unique and quite straightforward. However, once PC hardware also became common in the UNIX arena, a more flexible booting, with UNIX as one of several choices, emerged as a preferable system characteristic. Linux is an example.

On the Linux platform, the three most common booting mechanisms are:

- To boot Linux from the floppy, and leave hard drive for other OSs
- To use the ***Linux loader* (*LILO*)**, the most common case
- To run ***Loadlin***, an MS-DOS program that boots Linux from within DOS

What is exceptional with LILO is the possibility of configuring this loader in different ways to match different needs; multiple-choice booting, including a non-UNIX startup, is also possible. The configured loader should then be installed in the boot sector of the first disk, known as MBR (master boot record). When the system is started, the PC BIOS transfers control to MBR and triggers a corresponding LILO booting. Linux provides an easy LILO configuration through its */etc/lilo.conf* configuration file, and the command ***lilo*** for its installation as MBR.

4.2.2 The Kernel Execution

The bootstrap program is responsible for loading the *UNIX kernel* into the system memory. The *kernel image*, originally named ***unix*** under System V, or ***vmunix*** under BSD, is intentionally located in the *root filesystem*, because the root filesystem is the first filesystem the system mounts to access data. Mounting is a UNIX-specific procedure that makes data on the disk accessible. (We discuss this issue in great detail in following chapters.) In the past, the kernel image was located in the root directory for easier access, but today, it usually resides in a separate subdirectory. We do not refer to "mounting" the kernel; we usually just say that the kernel image was loaded into the system memory and its execution was started.

The *kernel* manages all system hardware; all hardware drivers are part of the kernel, and the only OS access to the system hardware is through the kernel. Therefore the system hardware will be available upon the completion of this phase.

Once control passes to the *kernel*, it prepares itself to run the system by initializing its internal tables and completing the hardware diagnostics that are part of the boot process. The level of diagnostics implemented varies from one UNIX flavor to another. At the very end, the kernel verifies the integrity of the root filesystem and remounts it, and starts three programs that create three basic processes. Two of them, named ***kernel processes***, function wholly within the kernel in the kernel's privileged execution mode. They are actually portions of the kernel itself, only "dressed" like processes for scheduling reasons.

On BSD systems, the two processes are:

1. ***Swapper*** (process #0), responsible for the "*swapping*" — to schedule the transfer of whole processes between the main system memory and a mandatory swap partition on the primary disk when system resources are low
2. ***Pagedeamon*** (process #2), responsible for supporting the memory-management system regarding paging — a regular transfer of data in the pages between the main system memory and the disk

On System V systems, the processes are named differently: ***sched*** for the process #0, while the process #2 is replaced with *various memory handlers*.

The third process created by the system is the ***init*** process (process #1), which performs all administrative tasks during the system startup and shutdown. The ***init*** process is an extremely important process that enables the creation of all subsequent processes (in UNIX a process can be created only by another parent process). The ***init*** process has the PID=1, and it is the ancestor of all subsequent UNIX processes and the direct parent of each user's login shell.

In the case of diskless workstations, the procedure is slightly different. Obviously, the kernel cannot be read from a nonexisting root filesystem; therefore, it must be downloaded from the network. Further kernel activities are adapted to the diskless environment.

The kernel is quite verbose and it prints messages on the console that report on the current execution status, total memory used and free, and some other information. However, the information reported varies among different UNIX flavors.

4.2.3 The Overall System Initialization

The ***init*** process does the rest of the work needed to bring the system into its final stage:

- Mounting the remaining local disk partitions
- Performing some filesystem cleanup
- Bringing on major UNIX subsystems (accounting, printing, etc.)
- Setting the system's name and time zone
- Starting the network
- Mounting remote filesystems
- Enabling user logins

4.2.3.1 rc Initialization Scripts

Most of the initialization activities are specified and carried out by means of the system ***rc initialization scripts*** stored in the */etc* directory and its subdirectories. *Rc initialization scripts* are usually named in the way that they include the acronym **rc** as part of their names (as a prefix, a suffix, or in a fullpath name). **rc** stands for **run-command** and basically explains the purpose of the scripts. These mostly ***Bourne shell programs*** are organized differently on BSD and System V platforms, although their purpose is the same. As with any other script, rc initialization scripts are readable, so we can manage them in a very comprehensive way. Besides that, rc scripts are sufficiently verbose during execution, and this is a great help if the system hangs midway through the startup, or if there are any other related problems.

Main administrative activities are related to this phase. System site-related customization means editing the rc initialization scripts. Any system upgrade means to upgrade (or to add) rc initialization scripts; any startup modification means to do something with rc initialization scripts. The rest of this section exclusively addresses these issues. Afterward, a full picture of the necessary administration in this segment should be complete.

4.2.3.2 Terminal Line Initialization

The terminal line initialization is a part of the overall system initialization; however, the implemented initialization technique is quite different than that in the *rc system initialization*, which is sufficient reason to handle this topic separately. UNIX is extremely cautious with terminal line initialization — terminal lines are "gates" to the outside world. Users access the system via terminal lines, and the essence of UNIX existence is to serve users.

Once the initialization scripts have been executed, the system is fully operational, except for the fact that no one can log in to the system. In order to provide login via a particular terminal line, there must be a corresponding controlling process listening on it (usually the ***getty*** process, but the ***ttymon*** is used on the Solaris platform). At the final initialization phase, ***init*** spawns the ***getty*** processes to all indicated terminals and the startup procedure is completed. Today, users typically log in over a network using pseudo-terminals; however, the ***getty*** program is still doing its job.

Terminal line initialization is fully covered in Chapter 11.

4.2.4 System States

Once the initialization activities are completed, the UNIX system enters the ***multi-user mode***, and users may log in to the system. But ***init*** can also place the system in ***single-user mode*** instead of completing the initialization tasks required for multi-user mode. The single-user mode corresponds to a functionally reduced UNIX system. In single-user mode, a UNIX system looks very much like a personal computer. The single-user mode is primarily dedicated to administrative and maintenance activities that require complete control over the system. The user has all superuser privileges.

In some cases, the system will automatically enter single-user mode if there are any problems in the boot process that the system cannot handle on its own (for example, filesystem problems that **fsck** cannot fix), so the system administrator must resolve the problem. The ***init*** simply spawns the Bourne shell on the system's console and waits for it to terminate before continuing with the rest of the startup sequence. Entering <CTRL-D> or the exit command from the shell prompt can terminate the spawned single-user shell. Once this is done, the system may continue into multi-user mode.

Single-user mode represents a minimal system startup with no daemons running, so many UNIX facilities are disabled. Only the root filesystem is mounted (in the most common case) and a restricted number of commands are available (commands residing in the root filesystem). Under normal circumstances, other filesystems can be mounted by hand to access other commands.

Single-user mode can be a security problem for a system, because full control over the system is granted. On older UNIX systems, no password was required, but physical access to the system was required in the single-user mode. On some systems, a front panel lock with *normal* (*secure*) vs. *maintenance* (*service*) key positions enabled multi-user vs. single-user mode; the system protection was the key, and only authorized personnel could acquire the key. Modern UNIX systems usually require a root password to enter single-user mode. None of these approaches are perfect, and all of them have some disadvantage. A request for the root password could make difficulties under different circumstances, if the root password was forgotten.

While the BSD flavored system could be in one of three possible states — *off, single-user,* and *multi-user mode* — the System V platform explicitly defines a series of system states, called *run-levels* designated by a one-character name. System V run-levels are flavor dependent; an example is listed in the following table:

Run-Level	Name and Uses
0	Power-down state => safe to power-off the system
1	Administrative state
s or S	Single-user mode (on many systems same as 1)
2	Multi-user mode for stand-alone system
3	Multi-user mode for networked system, possibly sharing disks with other systems => via RFS, TCP/IP, and NFS, or some other protocol
4	Unused => can be user defined locally
5	Firmware state => for maintenance and running diagnostics, and for booting from an alternate not-root disk
6	Shutdown and reboot state => to reboot system from some running state (s, 2, 3, or 4); the system is taken down (to run-level 0) and then rebooted back

To display the current system run-level, the following command is available:

$ who -r
. *run-level 3 Mar 14 11:14 3 0 S*

The system was taken to run-level 3, from run-level S, via run-level 0, on March 14, at 11:14. The leading dot is by default at the beginning of the line.

On the System V platform, movement between run-levels is managed by ***init***, and each run-level is controlled by its own set of initialization scripts.

4.2.5 The Outlook of a Startup Procedure

UNIX systems are configured to boot automatically when powered-on. If this is not possible, systems enter some form of the "ROM monitor mode" — a restricted ROM resident command interpreter that enables essential diagnostics, booting, and some other basic system activities. The ROM monitor mode is also the state that the system enters after being shut down; in that state, a system can be safely powered off. On some systems there is also a keystroke combination to enter this mode — for example on Sun Microsystems systems, the key (STOP-A) followed by the specific ROM monitor prompt "*OK>*."

The ROM monitor always provides the boot command, specified as "*b*" or "*boot*," among the other commands it provides. Certain options sufficient to control the system startup when problems are encountered (to boot the system from different media, into different modes, etc.) are also provided. The default booting media is the hard disk.

On old UNIX systems, manual booting from the ROM monitor was a two-stage procedure:

1. The boot command first loaded a boot program with a stand-alone shell (actually a mini-operating system).
2. A second command was then issued in a stand-alone shell to load UNIX kernel.

This two-step procedure looked like this:

>b
$$ unix

Different prompts specify two steps in the boot procedure. The technology available in the past limited the bootstrap program possibilities, which led to a more complicated startup procedure.

Today all UNIX flavors provide a relatively verbose system startup; a number of messages are directed to the console indicating the stage and status of the startup procedure. It is highly recommended that you monitor the system startup on the console. Otherwise, some trouble messages can remain undetected, which leads to a high probability for later surprises.

The startup sequences for two system user modes are presented in Figures 4.1 and 4.2. The UNIX system named "***atlas***" is running Solaris 2.x.; brief comments follow.

```
                        ----------------------- bootstrap program starts -----------------------
SUN LOGO                SPARCstation 20 (1 X 390Z50), Keyboard Present
                        ROM Rev. 2.19, 32 MB memory installed, Serial #7491530
                        Ethernet address 8:0:20:72:4f:ca, Host ID: 72724fca.

Rebooting with command:
Boot device: /iommu/sbus/espdma@f, 400000/esp@f, 800000/sd@3,0 File and args:
              ----------------------- bootstrap program ends, and kernel starts -----------------------
SunOS Release 5.4 Version generic [UNIX (R) System V Release 4.0]
Copyright (c) 1983-1984, Sun Microsystems, Inc.
              ----------------------- kernel ends, and rc initialization starts -----------------------
configuring network interfaces: le0.
Hostname: atlas
The system is coming up. Please wait.
checking ufs filesystems
/dev/rdsk/c0t2d0s6: is clean
/dev/rdsk/c0t3d0s7: is clean
/dev/rdsk/c0t2d0s0: is clean
Flushing routing table:
add net default: gateway 146.95.8.250
starting rpc services: rcpbind keyserv kerbd done.
Setting netmask of le0 to 255.255.255.0
Setting default interface for multicast: add net 244.0.0.0: gateway atlas.ph.hunter.cuny.edu
syslog service started.
Print services started.
volume management starting.
HTTP service starting.
The system is ready.
          ----------------------- rc initialization ends, and terminal line initialization starts -----------------------
atlas console login:
```

FIGURE 4.1
An illustration of a multiple-user startup sequence.

The Sun logo and first five lines are printed from the ***bootstrap*** program. These lines list basic system configuration and identification data, as well as the kind of boot device. The somewhat cryptic description of a boot device indicates an SCSI disk. The ***kernel*** prints only two identification lines that include the system version and release. Other lines are printed from initialization scripts invoked by the program ***init***. One of the lines indicates that the system was customized. The message that indicates the start of the HTTP service is not a part of a regular OS installation — obviously, this site has been customized to provide an Internet service. At the end, the login prompt is displayed upon the console initialization.

The startup procedure includes filesystem checking, one of the most important activities performed by the **fsck** utility (**fsck** is discussed in greater detail in Chapter 5). The filesystem verifications are different on BSD and System V platforms. BSD checks all filesystems on every boot; System V does not check filesystems if they were dismounted normally when the system last went down (the **fsstat** command is used for this purpose), and faster booting is enabled. Filesystem checking can result in the display of many messages depending on the current filesystem status. If more serious filesystem corruption is encountered, the system is left in single-user mode, and manual filesystem checking and repair by the administrator may be required.

A single-user startup sequence is much shorter, and it includes the *boot* and *kernel* lines. The next two lines about the network interface configuration and host's name are printed from corresponding initialization scripts involved in the system single-user startup. Finally, the console is activated and the user is informed of two possibilities:

1. Enter the system in single-user mode by entering the root password
2. Or continue with multi-user startup by entering [Ctrl-D]

If [Ctrl-D] is entered, the system continues with the multi-user startup, as in the previous case.

```
                    ----------------------- bootstrap program starts -----------------------
  SUN LOGO          SPARCstation 20 (1 X 390Z50), Keyboard Present
                    ROM Rev. 2.19, 32 MB memory installed, Serial #7491530
                    Ethernet address 8:0:20:72:4f:ca, Host ID: 72724fca.

Rebooting with command: -s
Boot device: /iommu/sbus/espdma@f, 400000/esp@f, 800000/sd@3, 0 File and args: -s
          ----------------------- bootstrap program ends, and kernel starts -----------------------
SunOS Release 5.4 Version generic [UNIX (R)  System V  Release 4.0]
Copyright (c) 1983-1984, Sun Microsystems, Inc.
          ----------------------- kernel ends, and single-user rc initialization starts -----------------------
configuring network interfaces: le0.
Hostname: atlas

INIT:  SINGLE  USER  MODE

Type Ctrl-d to proceed with normal startup,
(or give root password for system maintenance):

               >>>>>>>>>>>>>>  Since Ctrl-D is entered  <<<<<<<<<<<<<<
                    ----------------------- rc initialization continues -----------------------

INIT:  New run level:  3
The system is coming up. Please wait.
checking ufs filesystems
/dev/rdsk/c0t2d0s6:  is clean
/dev/rdsk/c0t3d0s7:  is clean
/dev/rdsk/c0t2d0s0:  is clean
Flushing routing table:
add net default:  gateway 146.95.8.250
starting rpc services:  rcpbind  keyserv  kerbd  done.
Setting netmask of le0 to 255.255.255.0
Setting default interface for multicast:  add net 244.0.0.0:  gateway atlas.ph.hunter.cuny.edu
syslog service started.
Print services started.
volume management starting.
HTTP service starting.
The system is ready.
          ----------------------- rc initialization ends, and terminal line initialization starts -----------------------
atlas console login:
```

FIGURE 4.2
An illustration of a single-user startup sequence.

4.2.6 Initialization Scripts

Once the *init* process is born, the system startup is determined by a series of rc initialization scripts which define a detailed procedure to bring the system into the multi-user mode. This is the most common case, although other system modes (run-levels) are also possible. These files control all custom-defined and site-dependent items (there are multiple rc initialization scripts), and they are executed sequentially. Generally, rc initialization scripts represent Bourne shell script files, executable at any time and on any UNIX platform. (The Bourne shell is the default shell, and it is available at the very early system stage on every UNIX platform.) The rc initialization scripts do not differ from any other shell script, except at the time of their execution. (This, by the way, is why the prefix "rc" is used in their description, as well as in the name.) However, they can also be executed from the command line at any time, and administrators can make full use of this opportunity: on System V, individual function-specific initialization scripts are often used to stop and start specific UNIX functions during regular system production. On modern UNIX platforms, sometimes Korn shell rc initialization scripts are also included (for example, on the HP-UX platform) which indicated the early availability of the Korn shell.

Understanding rc initialization scripts is a vital part of system administration — this is the place for system customization. A system administrator must be familiar with these files, their locations and, in many cases, their contents. Only then is full control over the system startup possible, and quick corrective action can follow any problem encountered during system boot time. Each modification in the initialization scripts must be done very carefully with respect for the basic administrative rule: save original script files before making any changes. If this rule is not followed, various problems can ensue.

Despite the fact that rc initialization scripts on both UNIX platforms BSD and System V serve the same purpose, the mechanisms by which they are initiated and executed are quite different. These differences require great attention, knowledge, and skills from system administrators working in a heterogeneous environment, which is very common today. Today, the System V rc approach prevails — the System V organization of the rc initialization scripts offers more flexibility and other administrative advantages. We will discuss System V initialization in greater detail after a quick survey of the BSD-style initialization.

4.3 BSD Initialization

4.3.1 The BSD *rc* Scripts

Originally, the BSD initialization was controlled only by two rc initialization scripts: ***/etc/rc*** and ***/etc/rc.local***. A general system initialization was supported by the */etc/rc* script, while the */etc/rc.local* script referred to a local site, i.e., to issues that should be customized (probably a more appropriate script name would be "*rc.site*" to avoid any possible confusion toward the logical association with a "network-local relationship"). During system booting to the multi-user mode, ***init*** executed the *rc* script, which in turn executed the *rc.local* script. If a single-user boot was performed, scripts were only partially executed; the remaining parts were executed when the single-user shell was exited.

Having only two rc initialization scripts would lead one to believe that system maintenance was easy, but in fact the reality is quite the opposite. The work required for system initialization remained the same, regardless of how many rc scripts were involved, and huge rc script files were more difficult to manage and more vulnerable to corruption during modification. It could be very difficult to find an appropriate control sequence, items were often doubled, and so on.

SunOS introduced additional script files: ***/etc/rc.boot*** and ***/etc/rc.single***. The program ***init*** invokes first *rc.boot* script and from there *rc.single* (regardless of whether the system is booting to single vs. multi-user mode); then the */etc/rc* and */etc/rc.local* files follow.

4.3.2 BSD Initialization Sequence

For a clearer picture, the block diagram of the SunOS execution sequence is presented in Figure 4.3 (it is assumed the system is booting from the local disk). The SunOS organization made a clear distinction between single and multiple-user modes; it was immediately easier to follow any problems that developed in the system booting.

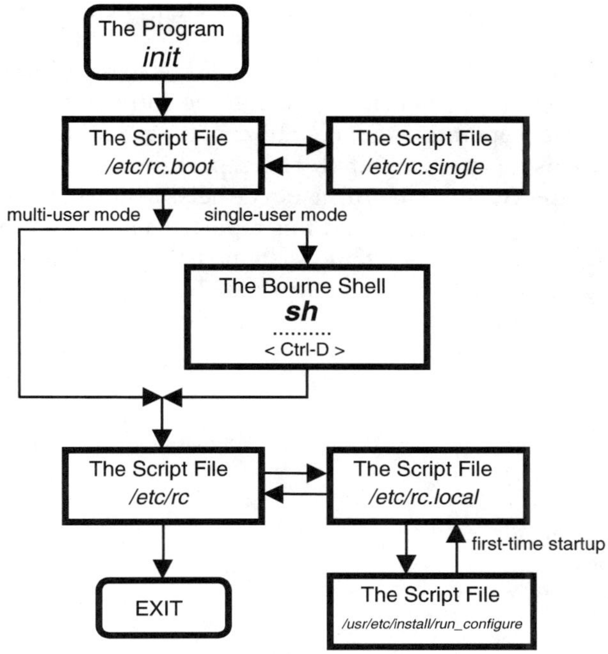

FIGURE 4.3
The execution sequence of SunOS initialization scripts.

To make system customization easier, SunOS provided a special interactive script named ***/usr/etc/install/run_configure*** that was invoked only once, the very first time the system was started upon the OS installation. Through the provided dialogue, the required parameters such as: *system name, time zone, date, time,* and *network data* were entered. The system administrator had to answer a number of questions, and new system and network data were saved for future use. The dialogue was performed via the system console. Upon successful completion, the program is never again invoked; subsequent modification can be done directly in the rc scripts.

In the single-user mode, the only way to communicate with the system is via the console; other terminals are not initialized at all. SunOS assumes that anyone who has physical access to the console is an administrator, because from the console it is easy to gain full control over the system. There is no additional system protection.

All rc files live in the */etc* directory; this is an example from SunOS 4.1.3:

$ ls -l /etc | grep rc

```
-rw-r--r--   1 root 2993   Jan 20 1996   rc
-rw-r--r--   1 root 5476   Jun 23 1996   rc.boot
-rw-r--r--   1 root  352   Jan 20 1996   rc.ip
-rw-r--r--   1 root 6169   Aug 3 1997    rc.local
-rw-r--r--   1 root 5911   Jan 20 1996   rc.local.orig
-rw-r--r--   1 root 2172   Jan 20 1996   rc.single
```

We can easily recognize all of the listed files; the file *rc.local* was modified according to the local (site) requirements, and the original file was saved. An exception is the file *rc.ip*, which is used to start up diskless systems.

All of the listed files are excellent examples of what shell scripts should look like; extremely skillful programmers write them, and it is a good idea to read them to learn the art of shell programming. However, this is out of the scope of this text.

The description of the BSD system startup should be sufficient to explain how a UNIX system is brought into an operational stage. To conclude this discussion, an additional brief report related to this topic is presented. This report is taken directly from the manual pages for ***rc*** files on the SunOS platform; nevertheless, there are some discrepancies between the actual initialization scripts and this report, even though the described scripts and manual pages belong to the very same system. This is not so unusual, and a UNIX administrator must be prepared for such surprises. The supplied online documentation simply does not always fully support all system changes and upgrades.

$ man rcfiles

NAME

rc, rc.boot, rc.local — command scripts for auto-reboot and daemons

SYNOPSIS

/etc/rc
/etc/rc.boot
/etc/rc.local

DESCRIPTION

rc and rc.boot are command scripts that are invoked by init(8) to perform filesystem housekeeping and to start system daemons. rc.local is a script for commands that are pertinent only to a specific site or client machine.

rc.boot sets the machine name and, if on SunOS 4.1.1 Rev B or later, invokes ifconfig, which uses RARP to obtain the machine's IP address from the NIS network. Then a "whoami" bootparams request is used to retrieve the system's host-name, NIS domain name, and default router. The ifconfig and hostconfig programs set the system's host-name, IP address, NIS domain name, and default router in the kernel.

If coming up multi-user, rc.boot runs fsck(8) with the -p option. This "preens" the disks of minor inconsistencies resulting from the last system shutdown and checks for serious inconsistencies caused by hardware or software failure. If fsck(8) detects a serious disk problem, it returns an error and init(8) brings the system up in single-user mode. When coming up single-user, when init(8) is invoked by fastboot(8), or when it is passed the -b flag from boot(8S), functions performed in the rc.local file, including this disk check, are skipped.

Next, rc runs. If the system came up single-user, rc runs when the single-user shell terminates (see init(8)). It mounts 4.2 filesystems and spawns a shell for /etc/rc.local, which mounts NFS filesystems, runs sysIDtool (if on SunOS 4.1.1 Rev B or later) to set the system's configuration information into local configuration files, and starts local daemons. After rc.local returns, rc starts standard daemons, preserves editor files, clears /tmp, starts system accounting (if applicable), starts the network (where applicable), and if enabled, runs savecore(8) to preserve the core image after a crash.

4.4 System V Initialization

System V organizes the initialization procedure in a more flexible, but also a more complex way using up to three levels of initialization files. During a system startup, when ***init*** takes control from the ***kernel***, it scans its configuration file ***/etc/inittab*** to learn what to do next. We should recall that System V can have multiple run-levels. The file ***/etc/inittab*** defines ***init***'s action whenever the system enters a new level; the commands to execute at each run-level are specified in the corresponding *inittab entries*. Usually, the entries are initialization script files named ***rcn*** (where "n" is a run-level number); the scripts files themselves are located in the directory ***/etc***, or sometimes in ***/sbin*** (HP-UX platform). The various ***rcn*** scripts in turn invoke other scripts that reside in the corresponding subdirectories ***rcn.d*** (again, "n" represents the specified run-level). A simplified version of the System V rebooting procedure is illustrated in Figure 4.4; the rebooting procedure first shuts down a system (the run-level 0) and then brings a system into a normal operating state (in this case the run-level 2).

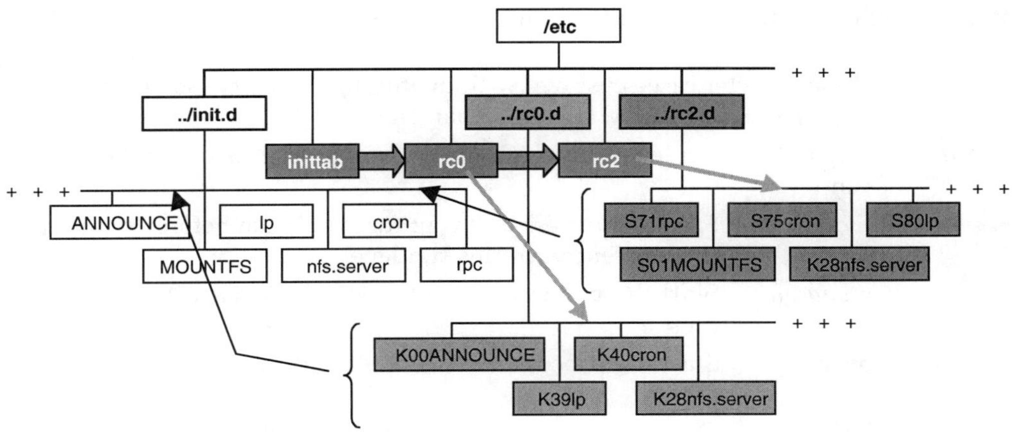

FIGURE 4.4
A graphical presentation of System V rebooting.

4.4.1 The Configuration File */etc/inittab*

We will start with ***init***'s configuration file */etc/inittab*; here is an example:

$ cat /etc/inittab (from *Red Hat Linux*, partly presented)

```
#
# inittab This file describes how the INIT process should set up
# the system in a certain run-level.
#
# Default run-level. The run-levels used by RHS are:
# 0 — halt (Do NOT set initdefault to this)
# 1 — Single user mode
# 2 — Multi-user, without NFS (The same as 3, if you do not have networking)
# 3 — Full multi-user mode
# 4 — unused
# 5 — X11
# 6 — reboot (Do NOT set initdefault to this)
#
id:2:initdefault:
# System initialization
si::sysinit:/etc/rc.d/rc.sysinit
l0:0:wait:/etc/rc.d/rc 0
l1:1:wait:/etc/rc.d/rc 1
l2:2:wait:/etc/rc.d/rc 2
```

l3:3:wait:/etc/rc.d/rc 3
l4:4:wait:/etc/rc.d/rc 4
l5:5:wait:/etc/rc.d/rc 5
l6:6:wait:/etc/rc.d/rc 6

 # Things to run in every run-level.
. . . . .
. . . . .

Each entry in the */etc/init* file is of the form:

cc:states:action:process

With the following definitions of the individual fields:

cc	Two-character case-sensitive label identifying the entry (some new implementations allow up to 14 characters)	
states	A list of the run-levels to which the entry applies; if blank, indicates all run-levels	
action	***wait***	Start the process and wait for it to finish before going on to the next entry for this run-level
	respawn	Start the process and automatically restart it when it dies
	once	Start the process if it is not already running; do not wait for it
	boot	Only execute entry at boot time and do not wait for it
	bootwait	Only execute entry at boot time and wait for it to finish
	initdefault	Specify the default run-level for system reboot
	sysinit	Use to initialize the console
	off	Kill the process if it is running
process	The command to execute	

The system scans *inittab entries* from the top down, checks that they belong to a current run-level, and executes them sequentially, respecting the contents of the entry fields. Let us analyze the previous example.

The first entry named *"id"* is not the executable one; this entry (determined as *"initdefault"*) specifies the default run-level (here it is run-level 2) to be implemented when the run-level is not explicitly specified by ***init*** itself. The following entry *"si,"* marked as *"sysinit,"* must be executed first to make the console and some other initial items operational. The specified initialization script */etc/rc.d/rc.sysinit* performs many of the "housecleaning" jobs to prepare the system for other run-level specific scripts that will come afterward. The run-level scripts for different run-levels are specified by subsequent *inittab entries* identified as l0 to l6, for the run-levels 0 to 6; this is actually the same rc initialization script named */etc/rc.d/rc,* invoked with an argument that specifies the run-level (argument 0 to 6). The script invokes other specific "stop" and "start" scripts needed for specific run-level initialization. This part of the */etc/inittab* file is crucial to our discussion; other *inittab entries* are not presented at all, and they relate to other required general initialization tasks such as power supply control, terminal line initialization, etc.

Linux has located rc initialization scripts in a separate directory */etc/rc.d* and its subdirectories, as we see in the following example:

$ ls -l /etc/rc.d

```
total 18
drwxr-xr-x   2 root   root   1024   May 13   12:24   init.d
-rwxr-xr-x   1 root   root   1871   Oct 15   1998    rc
-rwxr-xr-x   1 root   root    693   Oct 15   1998    rc.local
-rwxr-xr-x   1 root   root   7165   Oct 15   1998    rc.sysinit
drwxr-xr-x   2 root   root   1024   May 13   12:24   rc0.d
drwxr-xr-x   2 root   root   1024   May 13   12:24   rc1.d
drwxr-xr-x   2 root   root   1024   May 13   12:24   rc2.d
drwxr-xr-x   2 root   root   1024   May 13   12:24   rc3.d
drwxr-xr-x   2 root   root   1024   May 13   12:24   rc4.d
drwxr-xr-x   2 root   root   1024   May 13   12:24   rc5.d
drwxr-xr-x   2 root   root   1024   May 13   12:24   rc6.d
```

Besides the scripts *rc*, *rc.sysinit*, and *rc.local*, which are accomplishing specific tasks, other needed scripts for particular run-levels are located in the corresponding subdirectories *rc0.d* to *rc6.d*. The subdirectory *init.d* is a "depot" directory for all scripts, and it will be explained later.

The described startup procedure is almost identical on other System V platforms; the existing differences are mostly concentrated in the naming of the initialization scripts. Here is another example:

 # cat /etc/inittab (on Solaris 2.x platform)

```
ap::sysinit:/ sbin/autopush -f /etc/iu.ap
fs::sysinit:/sbin/rcS                                  >/ dev/console 2>&1 </dev/console
is:3:initdefault:
p3:s1234:powerfail:/ usr/sbin/shutdown -y -i5 -g0      >/dev/console 2>&1
s0:0:wait:/ sbin/rc0                                   >/dev/console 2>&1 </dev/console
s1:1:wait:/ usr/sbin/shutdown -y -iS -g0               >/dev/console 2>&1 </dev/console
s2:23:wait:/ sbin/rc2                                  >/dev/console 2>&1 </dev/console
s3:3:wait:/ sbin/rc3                                   >/dev/console 2>&1 </dev/console
s5:5:wait:/ sbin/rc5                                   >/dev/console 2>&1 </dev/console
s6:6:wait:/ sbin/rc6                                   >/dev/console 2>&1 </dev/console
fw:0:wait:/ sbin/uadmin 2 0                            >/dev/console 2>&1 </dev/console
of:5:wait:/ sbin/uadmin 2 6                            >/dev/console 2>&1 </dev/console
rb:6:wait:/ sbin/uadmin 2 1                            >/dev/console 2>&1 </dev/console
sc:234:respawn:/ usr/lib/saf/sac -t 300
co:234:respawn:/ usr/lib/saf/ttymon -g -h -p "'uname -n' console login: " -T sun -d /dev/console \
-l console -m ldterm,ttcompat
```

Briefly, the main differences regarding the previous example are: the default run-level is #3, the system always passes through the single-user stage (the script */etc/rcS*), and the spawned console-monitoring process is *ttymon*, instead of *getty* (this issue is discussed in greater detail in Chapter 11). Other entries are either quite similar, or they are out of the scope of this text.

4.4.2 System V *rc* Initialization Scripts

As is seen from the */etc/inittab*, an *inittab entry* points to the corresponding ***rc*** script to be directly executed by ***init*** for the specified run-level. However, what is more important is the part that stays hidden behind the scenes — this rc scripts invokes a series of additional scripts for specific system functions associated with the corresponding run-level. The invoked scripts can terminate (stop) or start a specific function, whatever is appropriate for the run-level. Sometimes the same script can be invoked twice for the same run-level: first to stop, and then to restart a specific function (so a clean function start is guaranteed).

We will start a more detailed analysis with one of the "directly invoked scripts," the script */etc/rc2* on the IRIX platform (obviously this script corresponds to run-level #2). This script is quite typically found on other System V flavors, too. For better understanding additional explanations are in bold.

$ cat /etc/rc2

```
#! /bin/sh
#Tag 0x00000f00
#ident "$Revision: 1.12 $"
#
# "Run Commands" executed when the system is changing to init state 2
# traditionally called "multi-user"
. /etc/TIMEZONE                                 Setup the time zone
                                                (source another script)
# Pickup startup packages for mounts, daemons, services, etc.
set `who -r`                                    Show run-level arguments
if [ $9 = "S" ]                                 $9 corresponds to a previous state
then                                            - was "single user mode"
echo 'The system is coming up. Please wait.'    Display the message and...
BOOT=yes                                        ...mark the system booting
elif [ $7 = "2" ]                               $7 corresponds to a required state
then                                            - is the state 2
```

This Section Invokes Individual Termination Scripts

```
  echo 'Changing to state 2.'
  if [ -d /etc/rc2.d ]
  then
    for f in /etc/rc2.d/K*                      Every termination script in the directory /etc/rc2.d
                                                is invoked with "stop" argument
    {
      if [ -s ${f} ]
      then
        /bin/sh ${f} stop
      fi
    }
  fi
fi
# handle local mounts specially, rather than as part of a generic rc2.d
# operation, so that if the some mounts fail, we can warn the user
#
if [ -f /etc/mountall ]                         Mount filesystems
then
  if /etc/mountall
  then:
  else
    echo '\07Some filesystems failed to mount; may be unable to reach multiuser state'
    sleep 5
  fi
fi
```

This Section Invokes Individual Start Scripts

```
if [ -d /etc/rc2.d ]
then
  for f in /etc/rc2.d/S*                 Every initialization script in the directory /etc/rc2
                                         is invoked with "start" argument
  {
    if [ -s ${f} ]
    then
      /bin/sh ${f} start
    fi
  }
fi
if [ "${BOOT}" = "yes" ]
then
  stty sane tab3 2>/dev/null             Set the terminal
fi
if [ "${BOOT}" = "yes" -a $7 = "2" ]
then
  echo 'The system is ready.             Display messages
elif [ $7 = "2" ]
then
  echo 'Change to state 2 has been completed.'
fi
```

Besides a number of common run-level #2 housekeeping tasks that */etc/rc2* performs, the individual start and termination scripts for all associated functions are also executed. The general mechanism for installing and executing start and termination scripts is common for all */etc/rc*n files:

> Filenames in *rcn.d* directories are of the form "***[S/K]nn[init.d filename]***" where ***S*** means start this job, ***K*** means kill (terminate) this job, and ***nn*** is the relative sequence number to terminate or start the job. When entering a state (*n* = S, 0, 2, 3, etc.), the *rcn* script executes those scripts in the */etc/rcn.d* directory that are prefixed with ***K*** followed by those scripts prefixed with ***S***. When executing each script in one of the */etc/rcn.d* directories, the *rcn* script passes a single argument. It passes the argument ***stop*** for scripts prefixed with ***K*** and the argument ***start*** for scripts prefixed with ***S***. There is no harm in applying the same sequence number to multiple scripts. In this case the order of execution is deterministic but unspecified. Guidelines for selecting sequence numbers are provided in the README files located in the directory associated with that target state (e.g.: */etc/rcn.d/README*).

For example, when changing to *init state* 2 (in this case, multi-user mode with nonexported network resources), the ***init*** process initiates *rc2*. The following steps are performed by *rc2*:

1. In the directory */etc/rc2.d* are scripts used to stop processes that should not be running in state 2. The filenames are prefixed with ***K***. Each ***K*** file in the directory is executed in alphanumeric order when the system enters *init state* 2.
2. Also in the */etc/rc2.d* directory are scripts used to start processes that should be running in state 2. As in the step above, each ***S*** file is executed.

To illustrate the above, assume the arbitrary file */etc/init.d/netdaemon* is a script that will initiate networking daemons when given the argument ***start***, and will terminate the daemons if given the argument ***stop***. It is linked to */etc/rc2.d/S68netdaemon*, and to

/etc/rc0.d/K67netdaemon. The file is executed by ***/etc/rc2.d/S68netdaemon start*** when *init state* 2 is entered and by ***/etc/rc0.d/S67netdaemon stop*** when shutting the system down (*init state 0*).

All scripts for individual system functions are written to accept the passed argument ***stop*** or ***start***, and to behave accordingly as a termination or a start script. All scripts are located in the separate "depot directory" */etc/init.d*, and they are linked to the corresponding ***K*** and ***S*** files in the */etc/rcn* subdirectories.

Let us see how this looks for the IRIX flavor:

```
# ls -l /etc/rc*
-rwxr-xr-x   1 root   sys    790  Sep 8   1992 /etc/rc0
-rwxr-xr-x   1 root   sys   1440  Sep 8   1992 /etc/rc2
-rwxr-xr-x   1 root   sys    444  Sep 8   1992 /etc/rc3
/etc/rc0.d:
total 10
l---------   1 root   sys     16  Sep 8   1992 K15cron -> /etc/init.d/cron
l---------   1 root   sys     16  Sep 8   1992 K18uucp -> /etc/init.d/uucp
l---------   1 root   sys     16  Sep 8   1992 K20mail -> /etc/init.d/mail
             .....
             .....
/etc/rc2.d:
total 19
l---------   1 root   sys     21  Sep 8   1992 S01MOUNTFSYS -> /etc/init.d
                                                 /MOUNTFSYS
l---------   1 root   sys     19  Sep 8   1992 S20sysetup -> /etc/init.d/sysetup
l---------   1 root   sys     16  Sep 8   1992 S21perf -> /etc/init.d/perf
             .....
             .....
/etc/rc3.d:
total 0
```

What can we conclude from this directory listing? The three directly invoked *rc* scripts specified in the */etc/inittab* file reside in the */etc* directory; they are scripts ***rc0***, ***rc2***, and ***rc3***. The corresponding *rcn.d* subdirectories are ***rc0.d***, ***rc2.d***, and ***rc3.d*** (although *rc3.d* is an empty subdirectory). Termination and start files in the ***/etc/rcn.d*** subdirectories are symbolic links to the scripts located in the depot directory ***/etc/init.d***. In that way, the same files appear under different names, which are more appropriate for their implementation.

The listing of the depot directory ***/etc/init.d*** is:

```
$ ls -C /etc/init.d
MOUNTFSYS    autoconfig   cron            mail       sysetup
README       bsdlpr       floppy          network    uucp
RMTMPFILES   cdromd.2     hyperchem_elm   perf       winattr
audio        configmsg    lp              savecore   xdm
```

The linked files in the */etc/rcn* directories have slightly modified names; the original filenames from the */etc/init.d* directory are preceded with the letter ***S*** or ***K***, and a two-digit number; numbers define the sequence in which the files are listed as well as executed, while the letters ***S*** and ***K*** classify files into two categories: ***start*** and ***termination scripts***, so they can be invoked differently, with the ***start*** or ***stop*** argument.

IRIX has introduced, and Linux accepted and further developed, a specific command to handle needed rc links. Many ***init*** run-levels require a careful implementation of rc start/stop scripts, i.e., the corresponding links toward *init.d* depot directory. The command

chkconfig makes this job easier. So if your system is running Linux, do not forget this possibility. If you prefer to make needed links manually, it also works.

Linux introduced one more directory level "/etc/rc.d" to confine all rc-related programs. Another Linux specific issue is that all rc scripts use functional wrappers to handle individual processes. A separate script */etc/rc.d/init.d/functions* defines a number of functions instrumental for conditional start or stoppage of programs. This script is sourced at the beginning of each individual rc script defining a very convenient environment for the system startup and shutdown, status display, and logging. Unfortunately, while such an approach works well for this purpose, in some other cases it could fail. UNIX administrators love to use rc start/stop scripts to control running daemons — it is quite common to recycle, stop, or restart daemons by executing rc scripts with an appropriate argument. Functional wrappers check for possible remaining processes and, if they exist, bypass the start of a corresponding daemon, what is correct for most situations. However, under certain circumstances remaining processes could be "legal" until they complete their task (like ***sendmail*** children during processing of the mail queue); unfortunately, a new daemon would not be started.

Basically, all listed *System V rc scripts* provide the same functions as *BSD rc scripts*. This makes sense because their task is the same: to bring the UNIX system into a workable multi-user (or any other) state. However, they are organized in very different ways, and must be administered accordingly. The System V approach prevails today.

The presented IRIX flavor is quite typical of the System V startup. Another example we will discuss is the Solaris 2.x; we will primarily emphasize the differences. The long listing of Solaris *rc* scripts shows:

 # ls -l /etc/rc*

```
lrwxrwxrwx   1 root   root   11 Apr 4 11:16   /etc/rc0 -> ../ sbin/rc0
lrwxrwxrwx   1 root   root   11 Apr 4 11:16   /etc/rc1 -> ../ sbin/rc1
lrwxrwxrwx   1 root   root   11 Apr 4 11:16   /etc/rc2 -> ../ sbin/rc2
lrwxrwxrwx   1 root   root   11 Apr 4 11:16   /etc/rc3 -> ../ sbin/rc3
lrwxrwxrwx   1 root   root   11 Apr 4 11:16   /etc/rc5 -> ../ sbin/rc5
lrwxrwxrwx   1 root   root   11 Apr 4 11:16   /etc/rc6 -> ../ sbin/rc6
lrwxrwxrwx   1 root   root   11 Apr 4 11:16   /etc/rcS -> ../ sbin/rcS
```

What specifies the Solaris ***rc*** script files? There are seven ***rc***n scripts, although not all of them are specified in the */etc/inittab* file. They actually reside in the directory */sbin* and are symbolically linked to the */etc* directory. The corresponding rc directories are:

```
/etc/rc0.d:
total 34
-rwxr--r--   3 root   sys   103   Aug 3    1994 K00ANNOUNCE
-rwxr--r--   4 root   sys   318   Jul 15   1994 K20lp
-rwxr--r--   4 root   sys   388   Aug 3    1994 K42audit
             .....
             .....
/etc/rc1.d:
total 34
-rwxr--r--   3 root   sys   103   Aug 3    1994 K00ANNOUNCE
-rwxr--r--   4 root   sys   388   Aug 3    1994 K42audit
             .....
             .....
-rwxr--r--   3 root   sys   534   Aug 3    1994 S01MOUNTFSYS
/etc/rc2.d:
total 100
-rwxr--r--   4 root   sys   318   Jul 15   1994 K20lp
```

```
                .....
-rw-r--r--      1 root    sys      1369    Aug 3      1994 README
-rwxr--r--      3 root    sys       534    Aug 3      1994 S01MOUNTFSYS
                .....
-rw-r--r--      2 root    other     547    Jun 16     12:15 S93httpsvc
                .....
/etc/rc3.d:
total 8
-rw-r--r--      1 root    sys      1708    Aug 3      1994 README
-rwxr--r--      5 root    sys      1387    Aug 3      1994 S15nfs.server
/etc/rcS.d:
total 32
-rw-r--r--      1 root    sys      2392    Aug 3      1994 README
-r-xr--r--      2 root    sys       369    Jul 16     1994 S00sxcmem
-rwxr--r--      2 root    sys      4514    Aug 3      1994 S30rootusr.sh
                .....
                .....
```

Not every ***rcn*** script has an associated *rcn.d* subdirectory (there is simply no need for all of them; do not forget that ***rcn*** scripts can be written in a different way). Finally, the existing start and termination files in the *rcn.d* subdirectories represent hard links to the function-specific scripts residing in the depot directory */etc/init.d* (this can be easily seen by using the ***ls -i*** command to check the file's inode numbers). Obviously, both types of links can be equally implemented.

4.4.3 BSD-Like Initialization

The System V initialization approach dominates today, but it is hard to judge this approach as the better one overall. Sometimes the use of a few larger script files would be more convenient, versus the implementation of a multidirectory structure with many small script files. This is probably the reason that some hybrid solutions have appeared; some System V flavors made a compromise by introducing something of the BSD initialization spirit into a System V initialization body. They avoided a more complex multilayer initialization approach, and provided one or more larger script files for any run-level, which are directly invoked from the */etc/inittab* file, or even coded in the start/stop procedures. In this way, the System V initialization reminds us very much of the BSD one, with the occasional exception as to how the scripts are invoked. A substantial level of flexibility is preserved because the */etc/inittab* file remains available. Such an approach characterized, for example, the HP-UX 9.0x, or IBM AIX 3.x platforms. Today, we can even recognize elements of such an organization in Linux.

The HP-UX 9.0x platform included only a few *rc* script files with almost the same names as on the BSD platform. Some of them were even written as Korn shell scripts, which implies the Korn shell as the default one on the system.

```
$ ls -l /etc/rc*
-r-xr--r--      1 bin     bin     15988    Apr 4    11:10   /etc/rc
-r--r--r--      1 bin     bin     21584    Mar 5    18:43   /etc/rc.utils
-rw-rw-rw-      1 root    root        0    May 4    11:23   /etc/rcflag
```

This does not necessarily mean that the presented files are the only files used in the system initialization; other files with other names can be called by these *rc* files. If we take a look into the */etc/inittab* file, we see a single *inittab entry,* named "rc" for this purpose.

$ cat /etc/inittab

```
init:4:initdefault:
stty::sysinit:stty 9600 clocal icanon echo opost onlcr ienqak ixon icrnl ignpar </dev/systty
brc1::bootwait:/ etc/bcheckrc </dev/console >/dev/console 2>&1          # fsck, etc.
slib::bootwait:/etc/recoversl </dev/console >/dev/console 2>&1          #shared libs
brc2::bootwait:/ etc/brc >/dev/console 2>&1                             # boottime commands
link::wait:/ bin/sh -c "rm -f /dev/syscon; ln /dev/systty /dev/syscon" >/dev/console 2>&1
rc ::wait:/ etc/rc </dev/console >/dev/console 2>&1                     # system initialization
powf::powerwait:/ etc/powerfail >/dev/console 2>&1                      # power fail routines
lp ::off:nohup sleep 999999999 </dev/lp & stty 9600 </dev/lp
halt:6:wait:/ usr/lib/X11/ignition/shutdown.ksh \
# NOTE: run-level 6 is reserved for system shutdown
cons:012456:respawn:/ etc/getty -h console console                      # system console
vue :34:respawn:/ etc/vuerc                                             # VUE validation and
                                                                        invocation
```

A similar situation was used by the AIX flavor with several more initialization script files:

$ ls -l /etc/rc*

```
-r-xr-xr--   1 bin    bin      1750   Feb 10 1994   /etc/rc
-r-xr-xr--   1 bin    bin      1866   Feb 10 1994   /etc/rc.bsdnet
-rw-rwxr--   1 root   system    667   Feb 10 1994   /etc/rc.ncs
-r-xr-xr--   1 bin    bin      7680   Feb 10 1994   /etc/rc.net
-rwxr-xr-x   1 root   system   2628   Jul 17 13:35  /etc/rc.nfs
-rwxr-xr-x   1 root   system   1161   Feb 12 1993   /etc/rc.pci
-rwx------   1 root   system  20832   Feb 10 1994   /etc/rc.powerfail
-rwxrwxr--   1 root   system   3950   Jul 17 13:35  /etc/rc.tcpip
```

Most of the listed ***rc*** files are invoked directly through the *inittab entries*; others are called by the invoked files, which can be seen from the */etc/inittab* file:

$ cat /etc/inittab

```
init:2:initdefault:
brc::sysinit:/ etc/brc >/dev/console 2>&1                # phase 2 of system boot
rc:2:wait:/ etc/rc > /dev/console 2>&1                   # multi-user checks
rctcpip:2:wait:/ etc/rc.tcpip >/dev/console 2>&1         # start TCP/TP daemons
rcnfs:2:wait:/ etc/rc.nfs >/dev/console 2>&1             # start NFS daemons
srcmstr:2:respawn:/ etc/srcmstr                          #system resource controller
cons::respawn:/ etc/getty /dev/console
cron:2:respawn:/ etc/cron                                #periodic (cron) daemon
qdaemon:2:once:/ bin/startsrc -sqdaemon
```

Linux implements three task-specific scripts: ***rc, rc.local,*** and ***rc.sysinit***. They are located in the rc.d directory, out of individual *rcn.d* subdirectories. In the Linux rc directory structure shown earlier, the three files have special meaning. They are presented again here.

$ ls -l /etc/rc.d

```
             .....
-rwxr-xr-x   1 root   root   1871   Oct 15 1998   rc
-rwxr-xr-x   1 root   root    693   Oct 15 1998   rc.local
-rwxr-xr-x   1 root   root   7165   Oct 15 1998   rc.sysinit
             .....
             .....
```

Their names strongly evoke "old-style" BSD rc organization, as does their purpose. Correspondingly, ***rc.local*** is assumed for a site-specific customization.

4.5 Shutdown Procedures

UNIX systems are designed to run continuously. In real life, however, from time to time it will be necessary to shut the system down (for scheduled maintenance, diagnostic purposes, relocating the system, hardware upgrades, etc.). Before the system can be powered off, a clean system shutdown is required; otherwise substantial system damage can occur. The shutdown procedure consists of several steps that should be followed:

- Notify all users that the system will be shutdown at a certain time.
- Signal all users' processes that they will be killed, allowing them time to exit gracefully.
- Place the system into single-user mode, log off all remaining users and kill all remaining processes.
- Ensure that filesystem integrity is maintained by completing all pending disk updates.

Fortunately, UNIX designers have provided the **shutdown** command and its derivatives to fulfill all the required steps smoothly. The only responsibility of a system administrator is to implement the command when the system is going to be shut down.

The **reboot** command is also supported for a majority of UNIX flavors on both platforms. It usually represents a renamed version of the **shutdown** command, although it can also have its own options. For example, on the HP-UX platform the **reboot** command behaves differently from the **shutdown -r** command (the **-r** option indicates rebooting). While the **shutdown** command terminates all processes gracefully (it sends the TERM signal to processes), the **reboot** command kills all processes unconditionally (it sends the KILL signal to processes). It is highly recommended that you check the manual pages for the availability, options, and behavior of the **reboot** command before using it on any UNIX platform.

4.5.1 The BSD *shutdown* Command

The BSD **shutdown** command has the following syntax:

shutdown ***time*** ***message***

where

time	Can have one of the three forms:	
	now	For immediate shutdown
	+m	For shutdown after *m* minutes
	hh:mm	For shutdown at this time on the 24-hour clock
message	An announcement that is sent to all users; the message is repeated with increased frequency as the shutdown time approaches	

Some BSD flavors support a nonstandard shutdown configuration file */etc/rc.shutdown*. In this case, the system administrator may place any desired command in the file, enabling its execution at shutdown. The **shutdown** command also creates the file */etc/nologin*, which automatically denies any future user attempts to log in to the system, and the contents of the file are displayed to the user. The file is deleted by the */etc/rc script* during system booting.

Several options are supported, among them:

shutdown -r Allows the system to be shut down and rebooted automatically as soon as the system enters single-user mode(or after a default time interval if not specified with command itself)

shutdown -f Allows the system to be shut down and quickly rebooted automatically as soon as the system enters single-user mode (without filesystem checking)

shutdown -h Allows the system to be shut down and halted at the point where the power may be safely turned off

shutdown -k Performs a fake shutdown with the message sent to all users, but no shutdown actually occurs

4.5.2 The System V *shutdown* Command

The System V **shutdown** command has the following syntax:

shutdown -g*n* -i*level* [-y]

where

n Number of seconds to wait for the shutdown to begin (the default value is 60 s)

level Run-level in which system should be placed:
- 0 — to turn off power
- 1 — administrative state
- S — single-user mode (default)
- 5 — firmware state
- 6 — reboot to *initdefault* state in */etc/inittab*

y Optional preanswered query for shutdown confirmation ("yes"); otherwise the command will prompt for confirmation just before the system goes down

Older System V flavors required input to the **shutdown** command from the system console. However, this could be easily bypassed by executing the command from any terminal and redirecting the standard input to the console, with the **-y** option included:

shutdown -g120 -i6 -y < /dev/console > /dev/console 2>&1

To shutdown a system immediately and reboot automatically:

shutdown -g0 -i6 -y

To shutdown and halt a system (after 60 s - default time):

shutdown -i5 -y

4.5.3 An Example

An example from the Solaris 2.x platform is presented to illustrate a system shutdown process. Even though Solaris 2.x belongs to the System V category, the **shutdown** command is more BSD-like. Once the command to halt the system is entered, a series of messages about the system's behavior appears on the console until the final halt has been reached.

$ shutdown -h now

Broadcast message from root (tty1) Thu Sep 21 10:38:59 2000...

The system is going down NOW !!

Sep 21 10:39:01 getty [61] : exiting on TERM signal

halt: sending all processes the TERM signal ....

halt: sending all processes the KILL signal ..

Unmounting filesystems .....

Done

The system is halted

5

UNIX Filesystem Management

5.1 Introduction to the UNIX Filesystem

The UNIX filesystem is the widely accepted name for UNIX's hierarchical tree-structured directory organization, which holds all files merged together, enabling equal access to them regardless of their nature or type. Any file in the UNIX filesystem can be identified by its position in the tree in two ways: by an *absolute file name*, a full-path file name that starts from the root directory (represented by "/"); or by a *relative file name*, which is relative to the current working directory. Since everything in UNIX is either a file or file-like, UNIX filesystem management is one of the most important administrative tasks. Good filesystem management is the key issue for successful UNIX administration; since most activities are related, in some way, to the filesystems, most problems are related to the filesystems, too. Sufficient knowledge and understanding of this topic is crucial for administration. The purpose of the following text is to help readers better understand UNIX filesystem issues.

The system administrator is responsible for ensuring that users have access to the files they need, as well as for keeping those files uncorrupted and secure. Basically, administering the filesystem includes the following tasks:

- Making local and remote files available to users
- Monitoring and managing file corruption, hardware failures, and user errors
- Monitoring and preventing filesystem overloading and unrestricted file growths
- Ensuring data confidentiality by limiting file and system access
- Checking for, and correcting, filesystem corruption
- Enabling a full data restore via a well-planned backup schedule
- Connecting and configuring new storage devices when needed

Some of these tasks can be performed automatically (like checking for filesystem corruption), while others are usually done manually on an as-needed basis. Some of these tasks are also discussed in greater detail in other chapters.

When discussing the UNIX filesystem, two basic issues should be made clear:

1. Filesystem visibility, i.e., how the UNIX filesystem is seen by users. The administrator's duty is to provide this visibility. We will refer to this topic as UNIX Filesystem Directory Organization, and discuss it in this chapter.

2. Filesystem layout, i.e., how the UNIX filesystem is seen by the operating system itself, and how a selected file is found, opened, modified, or stored within the available disk space. How this "jungle of files" functions at all, and how to ensure that it works well at any time. We will refer to this topic as UNIX Filesystem Layout, and discuss it in the next chapter.

As with everything in UNIX, both filesystem topics are BSD or System V colored and the main UNIX filesystem types originate from the two basic UNIX platforms. However, the differences between the two platforms are such that the corresponding filesystem types are mutually incompatible. They differ in the way directories are organized, as well as in the filesystem layout; they differ also performance-wise.

Despite differences, the filesystem layout and filesystem directory organization are relatively independent issues, and UNIX vendors are free to select the best of each filesystem type and combine and improve them, thereby making new higher-performance hybrid solutions. The Berkeley filesystem layout prevailed and today all UNIX vendors implement it. The System V filesystem layout is obsolete; however, the System V filesystem directory organization is widely implemented.

5.2 UNIX Filesystem Directory Organization

Both the BSD and the System V filesystem directory organizations will be discussed in this chapter. We will follow the usual educational approach widely implemented in this book, and we will start with the BSD filesystem. Originally there were very few differences between BSD and the System V filesystem directory organizations — BSD and SVR3 (System V Release 3) were almost the same. They are referred to as the traditional UNIX filesystem. A traditional UNIX filesystem certainly deserves to be considered first. Later on, the SVR4 (System V Release 4) introduced several significant changes in the directory organization that were accepted by many vendors, and which remain, with certain improvements, up to the present time.

Generally, any directory structure can be customized and tailored for site-specific needs. New directories can be created, and old directories can be moved or deleted. Sometimes the actual directory tree is quite different from the initial one. However, there are always plenty of elements to identify the basic flavor of the actual filesystem directory structure.

5.2.1 BSD Filesystem Directory Organization

The basic directory structure of a traditional UNIX filesystem is illustrated in Figure 5.1, which presents an idealized BSD directory tree. The directory organization of the SVR3 filesystem was quite similar, with some minor differences. Some vendors, like SunOS and AIX, followed such filesystem organization. In examining the BSD directory hierarchy, we will also address these UNIX flavors, and occasional differences will be emphasized.

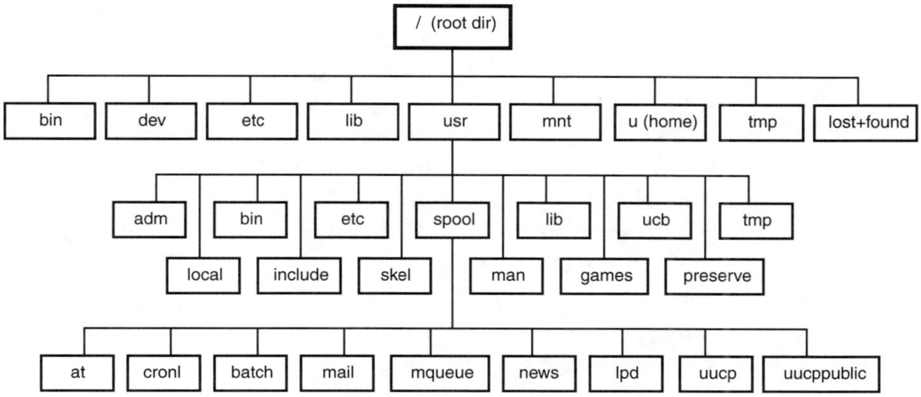

FIGURE 5.1
BSD filesystem directory organization.

A brief discussion and explanation of the directory organization presented in Figure 5.1 follows.

/ — ***The root directory*** — The base of the filesystem's tree structure. All other files and directories, regardless of their physical disk locations, are logically contained within the root directory.

/bin — ***Command binaries*** — Includes executable public programs that are part of the UNIX operating system and its utilities. Other directories with UNIX commands are ***/usr/bin***, and in some versions ***/usr/ucb***; strictly for BSD commands.

/dev — ***Device directory*** — Contains special files related to devices. In BSD this is a flat directory, while in SVR3 the directory was divided into subdirectories holding special files of a given type of devices.

/etc — ***System configuration files and executables*** — Contains most of the administration and configuration files and the executable binaries for administrative commands (including system startup scripts). Some administrative commands are stored in ***/usr/etc***.

/lib — ***Library files*** — For C and other programming languages. Some library files are also stored in ***/usr/lib***.

/mnt — ***Mount directory*** — An empty directory conventionally designed for a temporary mounting of another filesystem.

/u, /home, /users — ***User's home directory*** — Flavor-specific directory name sometimes even changed by the local site. The oldest name was ***/u***, later changed into ***/home***. Another common name for this directory is ***users***.

/tmp — ***Temporary directory*** — Scratch directory available to all users. Files in the directory should be deleted occasionally. Originally, it was supposed to clear this directory during the system startup; nowadays this is not a rule and it varies among UNIX flavors.

/lost+found — ***Lost file directory*** — Disk errors or incorrect system shutdown may cause files to be "lost." They can be fully identified and located on the disk, but they are not listed in any directory. In an attempt to repair the corrupted filesystem (by using the ***fsck*** program — will be discussed later), UNIX finds these files and puts them into this directory for later identification by users. By default the ***lost+found*** directory exists in each filesystem; this one belongs to the root filesystem.

/usr — ***This directory contains a number of subdirectories for many important parts of the UNIX system.*** A more detailed discussion about these subdirectories follows.

- ***/usr/adm*** — ***Administrative directory*** — Home directory for the special user ***adm***, dedicated to "accounting." It contains UNIX accounting files and various system log files.
- ***/usr/bin*** — ***Command binary files and shell scripts*** — Public executable programs that are part of the UNIX system (similar to ***/bin***).
- ***/usr/etc*** — ***Additional administrative commands*** — In SunOS all administrative commands are stored in this directory.
- ***/usr/lib*** — ***Library directory*** — For public library files; contains the standard C libraries for mathematics and I/O commands, and configuration files for various UNIX facilities and services, and optional software products.
- ***/usr/ucb*** — ***Original Berkeley UNIX commands*** — Developed at the University of California, Berkeley; sometimes included subdirectories for separate file types (***bin*** for binaries, ***lib*** for library, etc.).
- ***/usr/tmp*** — ***Temporary directory*** — Another depot for temporary located files.
- ***/usr/local*** — ***Local files*** — By convention, its subdirectory ***/usr/local/bin*** is reserved for any public executable programs developed on that system.
- ***/usr/includes*** — ***Include files*** — Contains C-language header files which define the C programmer's interface to standard system features and program libraries. The directory ***/usr/include/sys*** contains OS-included files.
- ***/usr/skel*** — ***Skeleton directory*** — Contains default template files to be customized and used at the site, like the users' initialization (dot) files to be copied into a user's home directory.
- ***/usr/man*** — ***Manual pages directory*** — Contains online documentation of the UNIX reference manuals, divided into subdirectories for each section of the manual. It contains several ***man#*** subdirectories holding the raw source for the manual pages in that section, and the ***cat#*** subdirectories holding the processed versions (sometimes cleared to save a space).
- ***/usr/games*** — ***UNIX game collections*** — Often removed by administrators.
- ***/usr/preserve*** — ***Preserve directory*** — Old-fashioned directory to store files.
- ***/usr/spool*** — ***Spooling directory*** — Contains subdirectories for UNIX subsystems that provide different kinds of spooling services, such as:
  ./at for time-scheduled jobs
  ./cron for batch jobs
  ./batch for batch jobs
  ./mail, and ***./mqueue*** for the email subsystem

./news for news
./lpd for the printing subsystem
./uucp, and *./uucppublic* for the UUCP subsystem

Some UNIX flavors, for example, SunOS or AIX, introduced more */usr* subdirectories (which are not presented in Figure 5.1), like:

/usr/5bin ***Executables for System V*** — In SunOS, stores executables for System V-specific commands; over time the name was changed to */usr/sbin*.

/usr/lpp ***Licensed program products*** — In AIX, optional products are stored in this directory; in particular, the subdirectory */usr/lpp/bos* holds information about the current OS release.

5.2.2 System V Filesystem Directory Organization

The UNIX filesystem directory organization described next was introduced with the SVR4 (System V Release 4). We will refer to it as the System V filesystem. The basic directory organization is presented in Figure 5.2. Today, this is the prevailing directory organization, sometimes slightly modified by UNIX vendors.

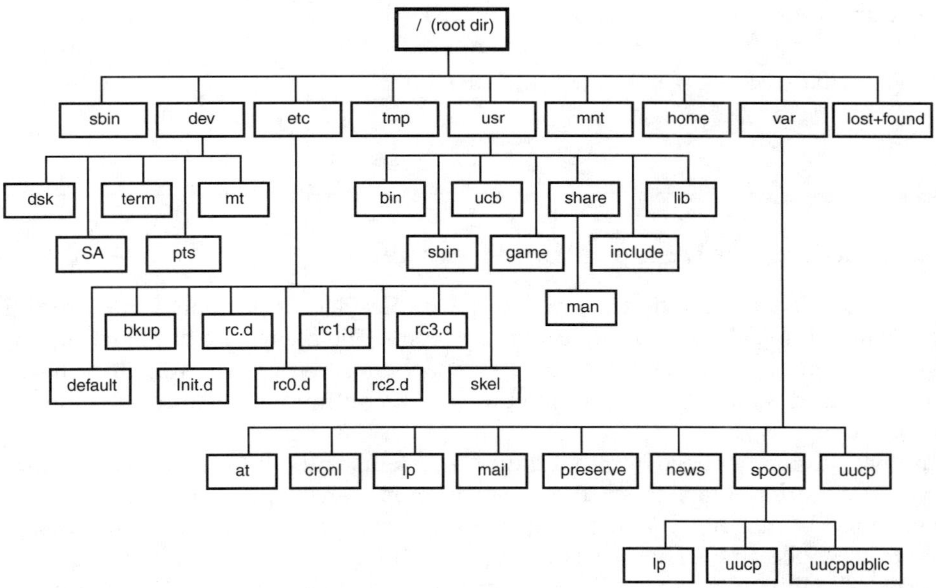

FIGURE 5.2
System V filesystem directory organization.

When comparing the directory structures presented in Figures 5.1 and 5.2, certain organizational changes can be seen. System V reorganized the traditional UNIX filesystem in several ways:

- The */dev* directory has been changed. Instead of a flat directory, a number of new subdirectories dedicated to specific devices were added: *./dsk* for disks, *./term* for terminals, *./mt* for magnetic tapes, *./pts* for pseudo-terminals, as well as *./SA* for the device-related system administration utilities.

- The new directories ***/sbin*** and ***/usr/sbin*** were introduced; the new names reflected System V binaries. Executable files were moved out of the ***/etc*** and ***/usr/etc*** directories. The contents of ***/bin*** were moved to ***/usr/bin***, and the ***/bin*** and ***/usr/etc*** ceased to exist. However, many UNIX flavors set up symbolic links toward the old locations, so the commands may seem to be in both places.
- Virtually all system configuration files were placed in the ***/etc*** directory, organized in the slightly different way. New subdirectories were created to store files in a more appropriate way (***./default*** for template configuration files, ***./bkup*** for backup configuration files, ***./skel*** for site-customized configuration files). In particular, the system rc startup files have been organized in a more flexible way: a separate depot subdirectory for start and stop scripts named ***./init.d*** and subdirectories for each system run-level, ***./rcn.d*** were introduced.
- Certain types of static data files (like manual pages, fonts, spelling data, etc.) were stored in the subdirectories under ***/usr/share***. It was supposed to share these files among a group of networked systems, eliminating the need for separate copies on each system (the name ***share*** reflected that idea).
- A new top-level directory ***/var*** was introduced to hold the volatile spooling directories, formerly placed in ***/usr/spool***. The idea was this: if ***/var*** represents a separate filesystem that keeps dynamic data, then the *root filesystem* can remain relatively static after initial system setup. This is an important step toward full support for "read-only" (RO) system disks. However, this very good idea is still far from its practical implementation. SunOS also used the ***/var*** directory.
- The ***/lib*** directory was moved into ***/usr/lib***.

5.3 Mounting and Dismounting Filesystems

At first glance, it can seem that the directories of filesystems presented in Figures 5.1 and 5.2 reside in a single place, in a single storage device. The filesystem directory organization gives no indication of disk devices or disk space boundaries. The directory tree simply continues over directories and subdirectories in a continuous fashion until the very last file in the tree.

Administrators must be aware that their filesystems could be spread over multiple disk devices. As a matter of fact, this is the most common scenario. The actual filesystem layout is determined by the filesystem configuration, and the configuration data must be well known to the operating system. The filesystem configuration data defines "break points" in the overall UNIX filesystem directory structure by establishing relationships between particular parts of the directory tree and the implemented disk space, i.e., the corresponding disk devices.

The advantages of merging all files into a single hierarchically organized overall UNIX filesystem tree structure are numerous. Identifying each file in the tree simply by its position in the tree, independently of its real physical location, makes the filesystem much easier to use. Anyone who has ever installed and reinstalled software in a different filesystem environment would appreciate such a concept very much.

A strict relationship between the filesystem directory organization and the filesystem physical layout, although hidden from the user, does exist. Otherwise, the UNIX filesystem could not work at all. In UNIX, this relationship is established in a simple and flexible way: each filesystem must be ***mounted*** before it can be used.

Mounting is the process that makes a disk's contents available to the system, merging them into an overall filesystem directory tree. ***Dismounting*** is the process that breaks established logical ties and makes the disk's contents unavailable. Both processes play important roles in the UNIX system. Mounting and dismounting are performed on the level of a filesystem that belongs to the particular disk's space, which is defined as an individual storage unit (storage entity). This could be a partition, or a whole disk, or lately even several disks together. Each such filesystem has its own hierarchical, directory-tree based file structure and all individual filesystem's attributes. We will refer to such an individual filesystem as a *partition's filesystem,* or simply as a *filesystem.* We are using the term *partition,* although another term, *volume,* would be more appropriate. The term partition has been perfectly serviceable in the past, when disks were partitioned into smaller parts, and the corresponding partitions were used as basic storage units to create filesystems. But today it is quite common to combine several disks into an equivalent storage entity known as a *volume.* Although it could sound confusing and somehow inappropriate to say that a partition consists of several disks, to keep everything simple, we will continue to use "partition" (at least until we learn more about volumes).

Mounting enables the merging of all these partitions' filesystems into a single overall UNIX filesystem. A filesystem can be arbitrarily mounted and dismounted — that is, it can be connected to any point, or disconnected from the overall UNIX filesystem at will. The only exception is the *root filesystem,* which is always mounted by the system itself in the root directory, and, while the system is up, cannot be dismounted.

5.3.1 Mounting a Filesystem

Mounting a UNIX filesystem does more than merely make its data available. Mounting eliminates all device boundaries, making the filesystem device-independent (a very important feature in software installation and implementation). Figure 5.3 illustrates the relationship between disk partitions (as basic storage units) with the associated filesystems and with the overall UNIX filesystem.

The root filesystem resides in the first partition of the root disk (the first disk — Disk #1), which is accessible via a special device file */dev/dsk/c1d0s0* (the naming of special device files can be different among different UNIX flavors). Mounting a root filesystem establishes a logical connection between the special device file */dev/dsk/c1d0s0* and a mounting point for the root filesystem in the overall UNIX hierarchical directory tree. For the root filesystem, the mounting point must be the root directory "/," and the mounting itself must be performed during the system startup (booting). A mounted root filesystem cannot be dismounted as long as the system lives.

To mount a new filesystem, the corresponding mounting point (or, as we prefer to say, mount-point) is required. A mount-point must be an accessible directory in the already mounted directory hierarchy. It explains why the mounting of the root filesystem must be done during the system startup, as well as why the root filesystem must live as long as the UNIX system itself. The mounting of the root filesystem happens when no hierarchical directory structure exists at all. Obviously it can be performed only by the system itself. In addition, dismounting of the root filesystem would be fatal for the system because the complete UNIX filesystem would be lost without chances for a recovery. A filesystem cannot be accessed if its mount-point is not accessible, and the root filesystem is the beginning of everything. However, once the root filesystem is available, a number of new mount-points can be created and designated to mount other filesystems.

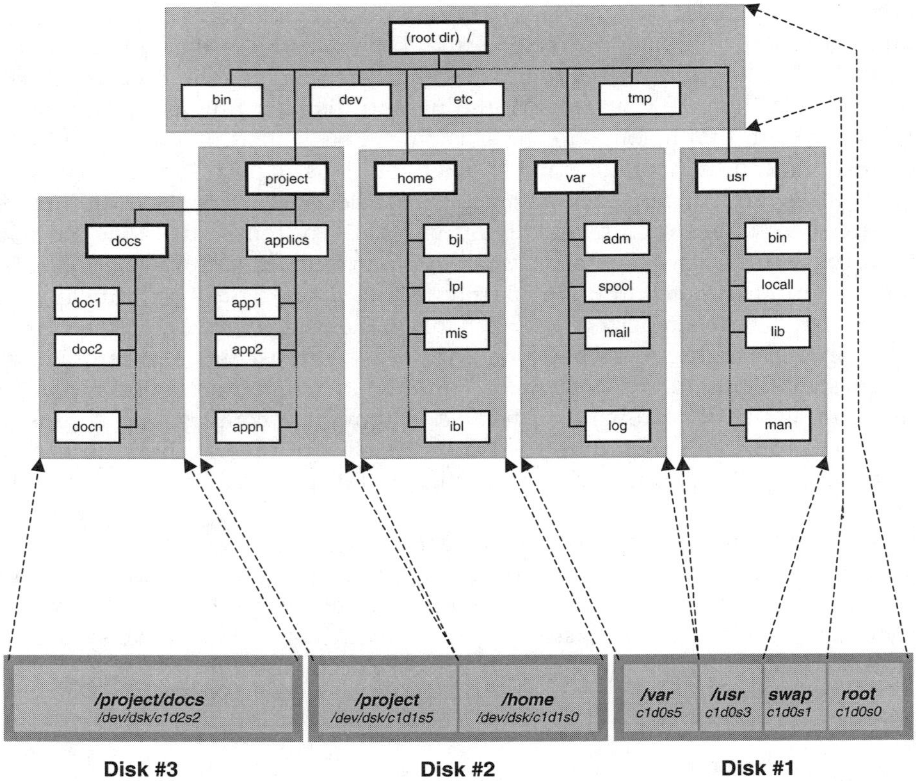

FIGURE 5.3
Mounting filesystems.

In Figure 5.3, the root filesystem contains several empty directories: ***/usr, /var, /home,*** and ***/project*** designated to merge other filesystems (any mount-points can easily be added by creating a new directory). While the first three listed filesystems are standard ones (please make clear that they are not mandatory as separate filesystems — they could be part of the root filesystem), the fourth one is very site-specific. This example illustrates a special case where two additional disk partitions (named **project** and **docs**) are dedicated to keep specific project-related data, and only the **project** filesystem is supposed to be mounted onto the root filesystem. In any case all partition sizes and mount-points are arbitrary, and they fully reflect flexibility in creating an overall UNIX filesystem. In this example, partitions' filesystems are located in disks and partitions that can be accessed via the special device files presented in Table 5.1.

An additional partition of the disk #1 (as it can be seen in the Figure 5.3), identified with */dev/dsk/c1d0s1* is dedicated to the swap partition. While the swap partition is crucial for the operating system, it is not an integral part of the UNIX filesystem and that is why it is not included in this discussion.

Four filesystems, **usr, var, home,** and **project**, are merged into the root filesystem, while the fifth one, **docs**, is merged into the **project** filesystem. This means that the **project** filesystem must be mounted before the **docs** filesystem. Additionally, the **project** filesystem contains the empty directory ***./docs*** (***/project/docs*** after the **project** filesystem is mounted) as a mount-point for the **docs** filesystem.

TABLE 5.1

Filesystem Locations and Special Device Files

Filesystem	Special Device File	Disk and Partition	Mount-Point
usr	/dev/dsk/c1d0s3	disk #1 - part. #3	*/usr*
var	/dev/dsk/c1d0s5	disk #1 - part. #5	*/var*
home	/dev/dsk/c1d1s0	disk #2 - part. #1	*/home*
project	/dev/dsk/c1d1s5	disk #2 - part. #5	*/project*
docs	/dev/dsk/c1d2s2	disk #3 - whole disk	*/project/docs*

Note: Filesystems are usually named by their mount-points; this convention is implemented here.

Please note that there is no necessary connection (even by convention) between a mount-point for a specific filesystem and a particular disk partition and its associated special device file. The collection of files in a disk partition can be mounted in any directory in an already accessible filesystem. Once the partition's filesystem is mounted, its top-level directory will take the name of its mount-point. At the same time, the top-level directory of a mounted partition's filesystem replaces the mount-point directory. As a side effect, the eventual files that could reside in the mount-point directory (if it was not empty) will disappear once the new filesystem is mounted. These data can no longer be seen and accessed, but they are not erased or overwritten. They remain unchanged but hidden for future use; they will reappear once the filesystem is dismounted. Obviously, it is highly recommended to select empty directories for the mount-points. Otherwise, disk space taken by such files will be wasted — the files cannot be accessed, nor used, but they still take up disk space.

A filesystem can only be mounted in one place at one time; that is, a special device file may only designate one mount-point in the directory tree. However, one filesystem can have another filesystem as a subtree within it.

The previous discussion was related to the local filesystems — the filesystems that reside in local disks. This is not necessarily always the case; UNIX also supports remote disks. Nevertheless, at this time we will only focus on the local filesystems, and the discussion in this chapter will primarily address these issues.

5.3.1.1 The mount Command

The ***mount*** command must be used to mount a filesystem. This is a regular UNIX command that can be invoked from the command line or a script at any time. However, the command is so crucial for the system that the security precautions require strict superuser privileges for its execution. Even the SUID bit (discussed in Section 2.2.2.2.4) doesn't work in the case of the mount command; if SUID is set, the system will simply reject execution of the command. Any security risk must be avoided, and SUID always carries a bit of it.

The generic format for the **mount** command is:

mount *[key-options] block-special-file mount-point*

The **mount** command attaches a named filesystem, identified by ***block-special-file***, to the overall filesystem hierarchy at an existing directory, identified by ***mount-point***. A number of options are available.

mount maintains a table of mounted filesystems in the filesystem status file, usually named */etc/mnttab*, or */etc/mtab*. If invoked without an argument, **mount** displays the contents of this table. If invoked with a single argument, either ***block-special-file*** or ***mount-point*** only, **mount** searches the filesystem configuration file (usually named */etc/vfstab*, or */etc/fstab*) for a matching entry, and mounts the specified filesystem in the specified directory.

The ***key-options*** can be generic ones, valid for all filesystem types, or specific for the different filesystem types. The following are the most common options:

-p	Print the list of mounted filesystems in a format suitable for use in the filesystem configuration file.
-a	Stands for all. Attempt to mount all the filesystems described in the filesystem configuration file. If a **type** argument is specified with the **-t** option, mount all file systems of that type. Some UNIX platforms have a special **mount** command for this purpose.
-f	Fake a filesystem status entry (in the filesystem status file */etc/mtab*, or */etc/mnttab*), but do not actually mount any filesystem.
-n	Mount a filesystem without making an entry in the filesystem status file.
-v	Verbose. Display messages indicating each filesystem being mounted.
-t ***type***	Specify a file system "*type*" (see the later text about filesystem types).
-r	Mount the specified file system read-only, even if the configuration entry specifies that it is to be mounted read-write. Physically write-protected and read-only filesystems should be mounted read-only. Otherwise errors occur when the system attempts to update access times, even if no write operation is attempted.
-o ***FS-specific-options***	Specify the filesystem-specific options — a comma-separated list of options valid for the corresponding filesystem type (see the text about filesystem types).

The following list shows the common options for most local UNIX filesystems.

Options	Meaning
defaults	Use all default options.
rw / ro	Read/write, or read-only; the default is *rw*.
suid / nosuid	SUID execution allowed, or not allowed; the default is *suid*.
grpid	Create files with BSD semantics for the propagation of the group ID. Under this option, files inherit the GID of the directory in which they are created, regardless of the directory's SGID bit.
noauto	Do not mount the filesystem automatically, only explicitly (ignore option -a).
remount	A filesystem mounted read-only can be remounted read-write (used in conjunction with *rw*).
intr / nointr	Allow, or do not allow, keyboard interrupts to terminate a process that is waiting for an operation on a locked filesystem; the default is *intr*.
quota / noquota	Filesystem usage limits are enforced, or are not enforced; the default is *noquota*.
rq	Read-write with quota turned on (equivalent to *rw,quota*).
largefiles / nolargefiles	Attempt to enable or disable the creation of files greater than 2GB in size; the filesystem must be created especially to support large files. The default is *nolargfiles*.

Note: It is highly recommended that you check the manual pages for the **mount** command before attempting to implement it.

A few examples of how to use the **mount** command follow; the presented situations are hypothetical.

- To mount the local filesystem */dev/xy0g* in the directory */usr*:
  # mount /dev/xy0g /usr
- To mount the hfs filesystem */dev/dsk/c1d2s0* in the directory */home*:
  #mount -t hfs /dev/dsk/c1d2s0 /home
- To fake an entry for *nd* root:
  # mount -ft 4.2 /dev/nd0 /
- To list the filesystems that are currently mounted:
  # mount
- To mount all *ufs* file systems:
  # mount -at ufs
- To save the current mount state:
  # mount -p > /etc/vfstab

5.3.2 Dismounting a Filesystem

Dismounting is the reverse process of mounting. Every mounted filesystem can be dismounted (except the root filesystem). When system shutdown is required, before the system stops entirely, all filesystems are dismounted. This is actually the only situation when the root filesystem is dismounted.

The ***umount*** command is used to dismount a filesystem. Using the command is somewhat easier than mounting; you simply type:

umount ***name***

where

name is either the name of the mounted filesystem's special file or the name of the mount-point, i.e., the directory at which the filesystem is mounted

The single argument is sufficient for full identification of the mounted filesystem. The **umount** command looks in the filesystem status file */etc/mnttab* (or, */etc/mtab*) for another argument. If a specified name cannot be found, it simply means there is no need for dismounting because the specified filesystem is not mounted at all.

umount supports the same options as the **mount** command. Online UNIX documentation often presents both commands in the same manual pages.

A few examples:

- To dismount the filesystem */dev/dsk/c1d2s0* mounted at */home*:
  umount /dev/dsk/c1d2s0 or
  umount /home
- To dismount all filesystems described in the filesystem status file */etc/mtab*:
  umount -a (Pay attention that the root filesystem can never be dismounted.)

A filesystem can be dismounted only if it is not busy. A filesystem is busy as long as any running process is requiring any resource within the filesystem. For example, when a user changes a directory within a certain filesystem (by executing the **cd** command), that filesystem becomes busy, and the superuser cannot dismount it. The only way to dismount a busy filesystem is to first make it free by destroying all related running processes. Once all processes release the filesystem, it can be dismounted. For example, to dismount the */home* filesystem (supposing it as a separate filesystem), all users must log out.

Releasing a busy filesystem is not a simple task. It is not always easy to determine which processes are associated with the filesystem. The **fuser** command could be instrumental in this case:

fuser ***[option] fsname***

where

fsname	The name of the filesystem, specified as a special device file (recommended) or a mount directory	
option	*w/o option*	Lists all involved processes, identified by their PIDs
	-u	Lists all involved processes; the login user name is added in parentheses besides the PIDs
	-k	Destroys all involved processes and makes the filesystem free

The **-k** option of the **fuser** command is dangerous, and must be used with extreme caution; for example, **"fuser -k /home"** will kick-out all logged-in users from the system.

5.3.3 Automatic Filesystem Mounting

Regardless of its form, once the filesystem configuration file is set up, mounting may take place automatically. The following commands, depending on the implemented UNIX flavor, will mount all filesystems specified in the filesystem configuration file.

# mount -a	Mostly for BSD flavors
$ mountall	Mostly for System V flavors
$ mount all	For AIX

Once the filesystem configuration file is specified properly, even the **mount** command can work with a single argument (either the mount-point or the special device file name) specified on the command line. Another argument is read and taken from the filesystem configuration file. This is a good opportunity to check newly specified filesystem configuration entries, and to avoid potential surprises once the system is rebooted.

5.3.4 Removable Media Management

Mounting and dismounting can be performed manually or automatically (in the sense that a single command can be used simultaneously for multiple filesystems). However, a command itself must always be invoked by a user or from a script. This means that each time a floppy disk or a CD-ROM is used a user must mount and/or dismount a filesystem residing on the medium. This can be frustrating for many users, but this is the way things work on many UNIX systems.

Modern UNIX versions, like Solaris 2.x, introduced a special daemon, a *media (volume) management daemon*, to manage an automatic mounting and dismounting of removable media filesystems. The daemon permanently monitors devices like floppy drives or CD-ROM drives and provides an appropriate action as soon as a medium (disk) has been inserted into a corresponding device; it also ejects a medium if requested by the user. The name for the daemon on Solaris 2.x is ***vold***:

```
$ ps -ef | grep -v grep | grep vold
  root   200   1   80   Sep 28   ?   0:01   /usr/sbin/ vold
```

The ***vold*** daemon is started during the system startup, and it lives as long as the system itself. In the presented example, the running program is */usr/sbin/vold* and the process ids are PID=200 and PPID=1 (the parent process ***init***, as for all daemons). Solaris uses the term *volume* instead of *medium*, which explains the name of the daemon.

The ***vold*** daemon takes care of all replaceable mountable devices. It automatically mounts newly inserted volumes (media), assuming a single predefined mount-point for each volume (medium) of the same device. There is no need for any additional action. Users can simply insert floppy or CD-ROM disks and use them.

The media (volume) management daemon ***vold*** is often referred to as a *volume manager*. This can be quite confusing, because the name *volume manager* is commonly used on different UNIX platforms to identify the *logical volume manager* — the suite of programs that manage logical volumes, in a new approach in the management and handling of available disk space. Instead of dealing with disk units as physical entities, they can be logically grouped and treated as logical entities. The *logical volume manager* will be discussed in greater detail later.

5.4 Filesystem Configuration

Mounting and dismounting filesystems is seldom performed manually; the **mount** command (or several **mount** commands) is executed automatically at system boot time. How does the system know which filesystems have to be mounted? Obviously, the required configuration data must be available to the system during its startup. The information about all filesystems, for use by the **mount** and other relevant commands, is stored in the ***filesystem configuration file***. The name and form of this file vary slightly between UNIX flavors. The variations originated in the traditional BSD and System V UNIX systems, and the two versions will be presented separately. Even though the BSD-type filesystem is the dominant one today, we will address both BSD and System V types of filesystem configuration files.

5.4.1 BSD Filesystem Configuration File

The BSD-style filesystem configuration file ***/etc/fstab*** was, and still is, used by many UNIX flavors: SunOS 4.1.x, HP-UX 10.20, IRIX, Linux, etc. Here is an example from SunOS:

```
$ cat /etc/fstab
/dev/sd0a          /          4.2     rw          1 1
/dev/sd0h          /home      4.2     rw          1 3
```

/dev/sd0g	***/usr***	**4.2**	***rw***	***1 2***
/dev/fd0	***/pcfs***	***pcfs***	***rw,noauto***	***0 0***
indigo1:/indigo1	*/indigo1*	*nfs*	*rw,bg,intr,hard*	*0 0*
hcprophet:/hcprophet	*/hcprophet*	*nfs*	*rw,bg,hard,intr*	*0 0*
rs01-ch:/home/2gig/rsxx-ch	*/rsxx-ch*	*nfs*	*rw,bg,hard,intr*	*0 0*

The first three entries define three local 4.2. type filesystems: ***root, usr,*** and ***home,*** in the partitions ***a, h,*** and ***g,*** of the same disk ***sd0***. This used to be a very common filesystem configuration when disk space was quite expensive. The fourth entry defines a floppy drive (***pcfs*** filesystem type). The last three lines define three NFS filesystems. To mount remote NFS filesystems, different syntax and options should be implemented; this will be discussed in another chapter.

This filesystem configuration file does not include any swap-related entry. The system obviously has used only the primary swap partition, the partition ***b*** at the disk ***sd0,*** identified by the special device file */dev/sd0b*. If it is not specified otherwise, the system by default mounts the primary swap partition. However, as we mentioned earlier, modern UNIX versions require swap configuration entries.

An example on Linux platform:

$> cat /etc/fstab

/dev/sda1	*/*	*ext2 defaults*	*1 1*
/dev/sda5	*/home*	*ext2 defaults*	*1 2*
/dev/sda8	*/log*	*ext2 defaults*	*1 2*
/dev/sda7	*/tmp*	*ext2 defaults*	*1 2*
/dev/sda2	*/usr*	*ext2 defaults*	*1 2*
/dev/sda3	*/var*	*ext2 defaults*	*1 2*
none	*/proc*	*proc defaults*	*0 0*
/dev/sda6	*swap*	*swap defaults*	*0 0*

Linux displays swap partitions, including the primary one. Most UNIX flavors today follow this approach — it is always better to see, than to guess about, the system configuration. However, the presented ***proc*** filesystem could be confusing. This configuration entry is Linux specific — ***proc*** is a quasi-filesystem which allows an easy access to handle kernel parameters by using regular UNIX commands. Although it is primarily read-only, some kernel parameters could even be modified in that way.

In the SunOS example an entry for a local filesystem has the form:

block-special-file mount-point type opts dump-freq pass-number

The fields have the following meanings:

block-special-file The name of a special block device file where the filesystem resides

mount-point The directory at which to mount the filesystem

type The filesystem type; here the implemented values are:

- *4.2* For local partitions
- *nfs* For volumes mounted remotely via NFS
- *pcfs* For DOS formatted floppy diskettes

These could also be:

- *swap* For swap partition
- *ignore* For the **mount** command to ignore this line

opts The field consists of one or more options, separated by commas. These are the usual mount options for a specified filesystem type, determined by the **type** field. For *ignore* type entries, this field is ignored. For *swap* type entries, this field should be *sw.* If the file's type is *4.2*, the options field may include the following keywords, separated by commas:

rw	Read-write filesystem
ro	Read-only filesystem
suid	The SUID access mode permitted
nosuid	The SUID access mode not permitted
quota	Quotas may be placed in effect
noquota	Quotas not in use

dump-freq A decimal number indicating the frequency with which this filesystem should be backed up. A value of 1 means every day, 2 means every other day, and so on. This field should be 0 for *swap* devices.

pass-number A decimal number indicating the order in which **fsck** should check the filesystems. The number 1 indicates that the filesystem should be checked first, 2 indicates that the filesystem should be checked second, and so on. The root filesystem must have a pass-number of 1. All other filesystems should have higher numbers. For optimal performance, two filesystems that are on the same disk drive should have different numbers; however, filesystems on different drives may have the same number, letting **fsck** check the two filesystems in parallel. The number should be 0 for a *swap* device.

5.4.2 System V Filesystem Configuration File

Since SVR4, the filesystem configuration file has been named */etc/vfstab* to reflect the newly used term *virtual*; this name is still the most common today. An example from Solaris 2.6 follows.

```
$ cat /etc/vfstab
#
# device            device                mount          FS      fsck  mount
# to mount          to fsck               point          type    pass  at boot  options
#
/proc               -                     /proc          proc    -     no       -
fd                  -                     /dev/fd        fd      -     no       -
swap                -                     /tmp           tmpfs   -     yes      -
/dev/dsk/c0t3d0s0   /dev /rdsk/c0t3d0s0   /              ufs     1     no       -
/dev/dsk/c0t3d0s6   /dev /rdsk/c0t3d0s6   /usr           ufs     1     no       -
/dev/dsk/c0t3d0s7   /dev /rdsk/c0t3d0s7   /export/home   ufs     2     yes      -
/dev/dsk/c0t3d0s1   -                     -              swap    -     no       -
/dev/dsk/c0t2d0s0   /dev /rdsk/c0t2d0s0   /applic        ufs     3     yes      -
/dev/dsk/c0t2d0s6   /dev /rdsk/c0t2d0s6   /software      ufs     4     yes      -
/dev/dsk/c0t2d0s1   -                     -              swap    -     no       -
```

Changes in the file's syntax are visible when the two main UNIX filesystem configuration files are compared, but the structure and contents of the file remain essentially identical. The configuration file on Solaris includes a header, which identifies each entry field and makes the file easier to read. Other modifications include: partitions are specified with both block and character (raw) special device files, for the filesystem mounting and checking, respectively; the entry for nonsystem-critical filesystems can be bypassed during system startup (system critical filesystems are always mounted, regardless of what is specified in the "*mount at boot*" field); and there is no more useless backup-related data.

According to the filesystem configuration file, this system contains two local disks. The first disk *c0t3d0* (this is the way Solaris identifies disks, by *controller#/target#/disk#*) with three partitions (*root*, *usr*, and *export/home*), as well as the primary *swap* partition; the second disk *c0t2d0* contains two partitions (*applic* and *software*) and the second *swap* partition. Partitions are mounted into the corresponding directories with the same names. Based on the naming scheme, the second disk seems to be added later.

Please note that the disk identification used here is not a generic one; the identification is very hardware dependent (based on the disk controller, interface, and many other factors). In the preceding example, the implemented disks are SCSI disks occupying SCSI addresses #3 and #2.

Typically, an entry in the */etc/vfstab* file has the format:

blk-spfile char-spfile mount-point type fsck-pass automount? opts

where

blk-spfile	Block special file (to be used by **mount**)
char-spfile	Character special file (to be used by **fsck**)
mount-point	Directory at which to mount the filesystem
type	Filesystem type. The possible values are: ufs (efs) — For a BSD-style filesystem *nfs* — For volumes mounted remotely via NFS *s5* — For a System V-like filesystem
fsck-pass	A decimal pass-number indicating the order in which **fsck** should check the filesystems. 1 indicates that the filesystem should be checked first, 2 if it's to be checked second, and so on. The root filesystem must have a pass-number of 1. All other filesystems should have higher numbers. Again, for optimal performance, filesystems on the same disk drive should have different numbers; however, filesystems on different drives may have the same number, allowing **fsck** to check the two filesystems in parallel.
automount?	The keyword *yes* or *no*, indicating whether the filesystem is to be automatically mounted by the **mountall** command
opts	The field consists of one or more options, separated by commas. The options field may include the following keywords: *rw* — Read-write filesystem *ro* — Read-only filesystem *rq* — Read-write filesystem with disk quotas in effect *suid* — The SUID access mode permitted *nosuid* — The SUID access mode not permitted

HP-UX 9.0x renamed the filesystem configuration file into */etc/checklist*; HP-UX 10.x named it back to */etc/fstab*, but made a corresponding link for this unusual name to keep it compatible with the previous releases. Regardless of what the file name was, its contents remained essentially the same. The next example is from HP-UX 9.0x. Starting with HP-UX 9.04, the logical volume manager (LVM) became a part of the HP-UX installation, so the logical volume can replace the partitions presented here.

$ cat /etc/checklist

```
/dev/dsk/c201d6s0     /         hfs    rw,quota     0 1     769    16409
#/dev/dsk/c201d6s0    .....     swap   end,pri= 0   0 0   16408        0
/dev/dsk/c201d5s0     /disk2    hfs    rw,suid,     0 2   16408        0
/dev/dsk/c201d5s0     .....     swap   end,pri=1    0 0   16408    31484
/dev/dsk/c201d2s0     /cdrom    cdfs   ro,suid,     0 0       0
```

Two hard disks, ***d6*** and ***d5***, containing a single partition and a swap partition and a CD-ROM disk, ***d2***, are specified; HP-UX assumes only one partition on a disk, with or without a swap partition (this is discussed in greater detail in Chapter 27). The entry for the first swap partition is commented out, but this does not affect performance, because the system always mounts the primary swap partition by default.

The next example is IRIX related. IRIX is a primarily System V flavored version of UNIX, which uses the slightly modified BSD-style */etc/fstab* file (only local filesystem entries are presented):

$ cat /etc/fstab

```
/dev/root             /         efs    rw,raw=/dev/rroot                    0 0
/dev/usr              /usr      efs    rw,raw=/dev/rusr                     0 0
/dev/dsk/dks0d2s7     /hom e    efs    rw,raw=/dev/dsk /dks0d2s7,fsc k      0 0
/dev/dsk/dks0d3s7     /dis k3   efs    rw,raw=/dev/dsk /dks0d3s7,fsc k      0 0
     . . . . .
     . . . . .
```

The implemented filesystem type is IRIX-flavored "efs."

5.4.3 AIX Filesystem Configuration File

AIX has a completely different approach to filesystem configuration (as well as to a number of other issues). AIX has introduced a journaled filesystem, ***jfs***, which is its standard filesystem type. The configuration data are specified in two filesystem configuration files: */etc/filesystems* and */etc/vfs*, both very AIX-specific. Here is an example:

$ cat /etc/filesystems

```
*  @(#)filesystems @(#)29   1.18 com/cfg/etc/filesystems, bos, bos320
*
*  This version of /etc/filesystems assumes that only the root file system
*  is created and ready. As new file systems are added, change the check,
*  mount, free, log, vol, and vfs entries for the appropriate stanza.
/:
      dev     = /dev/hd4
      vfs     = jfs
      log     = /dev/hd8
      mount = automatic
      check   = false
      type    = bootfs
      vol     = root
      free    = true
```

```
/usr:
        dev     = /dev/hd2
        vfs     = jfs
        log     = /dev/hd8
        mount   = automatic
        check   = false
        type    = bootfs
        vol     = /usr
        free    = false
        .....
        .....
/home:
        dev     = /dev/lv00
        vfs     = jfs
        log     = /dev/loglv01
        mount   = true
        check   = true
        options = rw
        account = false
        ...
        ...
```

A filesystem is confined to a logical volume. All of the information about the filesystem is centralized in the */etc/filesystems* file. Most of the filesystem maintenance commands take their defaults from this file. The file is organized into "stanzas" which are named as the filesystems are named; their contents are attribute-value pairs, which specify the characteristics of the corresponding filesystems.

The */etc/filesystems* file serves two purposes:

1. It documents the layout characteristics of the filesystems.
2. It frees the person who sets up the filesystem from having to enter and remember items such as the device where the filesystem resides, because this information is defined in the file.

Each stanza names the directory where the filesystem is normally mounted. The filesystem attributes specify all of the parameters of the filesystem. The attributes currently used are:

account Used by the **dodisk** command to determine the filesystems to be processed by the accounting system. This value can be either True or False.

boot Used by the **mkfs** command to initialize the boot block of a new filesystem. This specifies the name of the load module to be placed into the first block of the filesystem.

check Used by the **fsck** command to determine the default filesystems to be checked. The True value, enables checking while the False value disables checking. If a number, rather than the True value, is specified, the filesystem is checked in the specified pass of checking. Multiple-pass checking, described in the **fsck** command, permits filesystems on different drives to be checked in parallel.

dev Identifies, for local mounts, either the block special file where the filesystem resides or the file or directory to be mounted. System management utilities use this attribute to map filesystem names to the corresponding device names. For remote mounts, it identifies the file or directory to be mounted.

mount Used by the **mount** command to determine whether this filesystem should be mounted by default. The possible values of the *mount* attribute are:

automatic Automatically mounts a filesystem when the system is started. For example, the root filesystem line is the "mount=automatic" attribute. This means that the root filesystem mounts automatically when the system is started. The True value is not used so that **mount all** does not try to mount it, and **umount all** does not try to dismount it. Also, it is not the same as the False value because certain utilities, such as the **ncheck** command, normally avoid filesystems with a False value for the ***mount*** attribute.

False This filesystem is not mounted by default.

readonly This filesystem is mounted as read-only.

True This filesystem is mounted by the **mount all** command. It is dismounted by the **umount all** command. The **mount all** command is issued during system initialization to automatically mount all such filesystems.

nodename Used by the **mount** command to determine which node contains the remote filesystem. If this attribute is not present, the mount is a local mount. The value of the *nodename* attribute should be a valid node nickname. This value can be overridden with the **mount -n** command.

size Used by the **mkfs** command for reference and to build the filesystem. The value is the number of 512-byte blocks in the filesystem.

type Used to group related mounts. When the **mount -t string** command is issued, all of the currently dismounted filesystems with a type attribute equal to the **string** parameter are mounted.

vfs Specifies the type of mount. For example, "*vfs=nfs*" specifies that the virtual filesystem being mounted is an NFS filesystem.

vol Used by the **mkfs** command when initializing the label on a new filesystem. The value is a volume or pack label using a maximum of six characters.

log The device to which log data is written as this filesystem is modified. This is only valid for journaled filesystems.

The asterisk (*) is the comment character used in the */etc/filesystems* file. Also, the "default" stanza can be introduced to specify default attributes valid in each of the stanzas if not otherwise specified, as in the following example:

```
* Filesystem information
default:
    vol      = "AIX"
    mount    = false
    check    = false
/:
    dev      = /dev/hd4
    vol      = "root"
```

```
mount    = automatic
check    = true
log      = /dev/hd8
...etc.
```

The purpose of the second file */etc/vfs* is different. This is a generic file that defines filesystem types. Here is a self-explanatory example from the very same AIX system:

```
$ cat /etc/vfs
# @(#)vfs @(#)77   1.20 com/cfg/etc/vfs, bos, bos320
#
# this file describes the known virtual file system implementations.
# format: (the name and vfs_number should match what is in <sys/vmount.h>)
# The standard helper directory is /etc/helpers
#
# Uncomment the following line to specify the local or remote default vfs.
%defaultvfs   jfs   nfs
#
# name     vfs_number    mount_helper                  fil sys_helper
  cdrfs        5         none                          none
  jfs          3         none                          /sbin /helpers/v3fshelper
  nfs          2         /sbin/helpers /nfsmnthelp     none remote
```

5.4.4 The Filesystem Status File

The filesystem configuration file defines the configuration that the system is trying to achieve. A configuration entry does not necessarily mean that the appropriate mount attempt will be successful; there are many reasons that can cause mounting to fail. For example, for all removable media, a mount attempt will fail if a volume was not loaded into the device (floppy drive, CDROM drive, etc.), not to mention a broken disk or corrupted filesystem. Even after a successful mounting, the filesystem could be automatically or manually dismounted. Briefly, the real filesystem status does not necessarily match with the configuration requirements.

The system automatically maintains a separate table of its current filesystem status. This table is updated always when any filesystem is mounted or dismounted. The table is an ASCII readable file that can be manually modified; of course, manual modification is not recommended except as a last resort to fix an obvious error. Two file names are common for the filesystem status file: */etc/mnttab* and */etc/mtab*; both names reflect the file's purpose as a *mounted filesystem table*.

The filesystem status file contains a table of all filesystems currently mounted by the **mount** command. The **umount** command removes entries from this file. The file contains an entry (a line of information) for each mounted filesystem, which is structurally identical to the contents of the filesystem configuration file. The entry format varies slightly among UNIX flavors, just as the filesystem configuration entries do. A typical entry looks like:

fsname dir type opts freq passno

where

fsname A filesystem name
dir A mount-point directory
type A filesystem type
opts Are comma-separated filesystem options

freq A number indicating backup strategy for the filesystem
passno A number indicating the **fsck** order for the filesystem

The content of the */etc/mtab* file on SunOS is presented to illustrate the previous information:

 # cat /etc/mtab

/dev/sd0a	/	4.2	*rw,dev=0700*	1 1
/dev/sd0g	*/usr*	4.2	*rw,dev=0706*	1 2
/dev/sd0h	*/home*	4.2	*rw,dev=0707*	1 3
indigo1:/indigo1	*/indigo1*	*nfs*	*rw,bg,intr,hard,dev= 8200*	0 0
hcprophet:/hcprophet	*/hcprophet*	*nfs*	*rw,bg,hard,intr,dev= 8203*	0 0

This is the filesystem status file for the same system for which the filesystem configuration file */etc/fstab* was shown earlier. If we compare the two files, and assume the filesystems were mounted automatically during the system startup, we can conclude:

- All local filesystems are mounted.
- The floppy diskette was not inserted at the startup time, so the *pcfs* filesystem is not mounted.
- One of the *nfs* filesystems is not mounted, obviously because a connection with the remote host "rs01-ch" was not established at that time (it is a logical to speculate that the remote host was not reachable, although there could be a number of other reasons for mounting to fail).

5.5 A Few Other Filesystem Issues

For a better understanding of UNIX filesystems, let us make a brief overview of several other filesystem issues. The most intriguing issue is how many different UNIX filesystems exist. We will try to describe the actual situation in this area. We will also address another extremely important topic related to the UNIX, the topic that affects both the operating system itself and disk usage. This is swap space and its usage on a UNIX platform — this time from the angle of the UNIX filesystem organization. Finally, a more detailed description of one pseudo filesystem is presented, just to clarify mysteries around these filesystem types.

5.5.1 Filesystem Types

The filesystem type is determined by "a logical organization of the filesystem within the storage entity," or more specifically, by the filesystem layout. The filesystem layout will be elaborated in greater detail in the next chapter.

Different filesystem types are mutually incompatible. Each filesystem type has a different organization and allows a different approach to its system data and existing files. This does not mean that different filesystem types cannot coexist within the same UNIX implementation; it means that the OS has to support all of the implemented filesystem types.

The core of each filesystem is its superblock, a collection of filesystem tables, index nodes, and other system data that uniquely identify the filesystem. Creating a filesystem primarily means creating the superblock; differences in the superblocks (structure, contents, layout, etc.) literally determine the filesystem differences.

Nowadays vendor-specific UNIX filesystems are dominant. The typical System V filesystem type, known as *s5*, has practically disappeared. The superior BSD-like filesystems prevailed, with many additions and improvements introduced by different vendors. Currently, the most common local UNIX filesystem type, supported by a number of UNIX vendors, is ***ufs*** (UNIX filesystem). However, many other flavor-specific filesystem types are also in use:

- ***hfs*** On the HP-UX platform
- ***efs*** On the IRIX platform
- ***ext2*** On Linux platform
- ***jfs*** Journaled filesystem, introduced by AIX, but also implemented on other platforms. ***jfs*** has some advantages; it is more robust in the face of filesystem corruption because a journal of filesystem activities enables a rollback of incomplete transactions to maintain filesystem data consistency
- ***4.2*** An improved filesystem introduced with BSD 4.2 UNIX, and widely used on the SunOS platform (a real ancestor of the ***ufs*** filesystem)
- ***vxfs*** Veritas filesystem, an improved journaled filesystem version with a number of beneficial filesystem characteristics

Other implemented local filesystem types are:

- ***afs*** Andrew filesystem, provides some additional flexibility, especially regarding remote filesystem sharing
- ***hsfs*** High Sierra filesystem, typical for CD-ROM media
- ***cdfs*** CD-ROM filesystem
- ***pcfs*** PC filesystem (FAT filesystem), implemented for DOS-formatted floppy diskettes
- ***cachefs*** Cache filesystem, allows use of local disk space to cache frequently-used data from a CD-ROM or a remote filesystem

There are also a number of specific, pseudo filesystem types supported by different UNIX flavors:

- ***tmpfs*** Temporary filesystem, a temporary file storage in memory that swaps to bypass the overhead of writing into a disk
- ***lofs*** Loopback filesystem, a virtual filesystem to approach files using different pathnames (it is discussed in more details later in this section)
- ***tfs*** Translucent filesystem, allows mounting of a filesystem on top of existing files (mount-point does not have to be an empty directory)
- ***swapfs*** Swap filesystem, used by the kernel to manage swap space
- ***proc*** Process access filesystem, allows access to active processes and their images
- ***specfs*** Special filesystem, allows access to the special device files

Besides the listed local filesystem types, supported remote filesystem types are:

- *nfs* Network filesystem, widely used on all UNIX platforms
- *rfs* Remote file share filesystem, typical for System V and barely in use
- *autofs* Automount filesystem, an NIS-based automounted NFS filesystem

Some of the listed types are barely in use, while others are widely used. This relatively long list also is not, by any means, a complete list. In this chapter we will discuss strictly local UNIX filesystems; network filesystems will be discussed separately.

We mentioned earlier the swap partition and its crucial role on the UNIX platform. The swap partition definitely deserves more than this brief statement. A more detailed overview follows.

5.5.2 Swap Space — Paging and Swapping

UNIX systems require an appropriate **swap space** available for regular activities; otherwise, they cannot function normally and they crash immediately. The swap space is provided as a separate swap partition, and is sometimes several partitions (for primary and additional swap partitions).

UNIX systems use a virtual memory approach to access required programs and data. Virtual memory space consists of the physical memory space (known as system memory) and the corresponding disk space where programs and data actually reside. However, program execution and data processing are performed from the system memory only; therefore special techniques are required to provide the data needed from the system memory at the right time. This is the only task (but it is an extremely difficult task) of a specialized subsystem known as a *memory management system (MMS)*. This task is crucial for system performance. The system memory is continuously updated and synchronized with the disk, and programs and data are transferred in both directions. The transfer is performed in "pages," and a page is the basic unit in the data transfer.

In UNIX a part of the disk space is reserved as an extension of the system memory for temporary storage while the OS keeps track of processes that require more system memory than is available. This temporary depot is known as a swap space. When the OS recognizes the need, swap space is used for **paging** and **swapping**.

Paging is when individual memory segments, or pages, are moved to or from the swap area in an ordered way. When free memory space is low, portions of processes (primarily data segments within the process address space) are moved into the swap space to free system memory. The data segments are selected to be moved if they have not been referenced recently (different criteria can be implemented, but the most common is LRU — least recently used). When the running process tries to reference the data segment that has been transferred to the swap space, a page fault occurs and the process is suspended until the required data pages are returned into the system memory. A page fault occurs normally when a program is started for the first time; then the required pages must be brought from the disk.

The swap space is mostly organized as a flat partition, which reduces the overhead and enables faster page transfer, both in and out. This is not a necessity, but it increases the transfer efficiency. However, the existence of a swap space is a requirement; the swap space can be thought of as an extension of the system memory, and there is no operating system to operate without a system memory.

The additional *swap* partition improves system performances, but it is not mandatory. Certain UNIX versions enable the use of a *swap file* (also known as a *paging file*) within a regular filesystem, which serves the same purpose as a *swap partition*. It is important to note that the use of a *swap file* instead of a *swap partition* will not save any disk space — the required ***swapping area*** must be provided in any case, and it stays the same, independent of its "formal" organization. The main advantage of the swap file is that it can be created at any time, while the swap partition must be created in advance; its disadvantage is the time overhead in its use. To create a swap file, a special UNIX command, ***mkfile***, is available on many platforms (for example, on the SunOS platform).

Swapping occurs during a heavy workload, when memory shortage becomes critical, and the OS lacks the needed time to perform regular paging. When swapping, the kernel moves complete processes (including all associated code and data segments) to the swap area. The processes are chosen if they are not expected to run for a while. Unfortunately, it is often nearly impossible to make a perfect selection. When the process is run again it must be copied back into the system memory from the swap space. If such a transfer has to be performed repeatedly, the system performance drops sharply until the system stabilizes and continues with regular paging. The system simply spends more time doing process image and data transfer between the memory and swap areas than it spends running the same processes.

While paging represents normal system activity, swapping is an undesired event. Performance-wise, it is preferable for swapping to never occur. Unfortunately, in real life such situations are unavoidable. The best way to prevent swapping is to increase the system memory. Today, huge system memory space is quite common and the need for swapping is drastically reduced; swapping happens only occasionally, or perhaps even never.

The size of the swap space should be larger than the system memory. Theoretically, the need for swapping the complete system memory could arise. Therefore, if the system memory is upgraded, a new swap partition should also be added (unless the primary swap partition has already been sized for future memory upgrades).

The swap space is also used as a dump space. In an emergency the system could dump a complete memory image into the swap space (known as a *memory core*). This is an additional reason to have a swap space larger than the memory itself. In the case of a dump space, the requirements are even greater: the available space must be contiguous — at a dump time no overhead is allowed, and the copying of the memory into the swap partition must be simple and fast. In this case, an additional swap partition does not work; only a contiguous increase of the existing primary partition helps. Unfortunately, this demand often cannot be met; a more painful yet realistic solution is to rebuild the complete system.

Solaris 2.x went one step further by introducing the ***swapfs*** filesystem. Today, memory is not very expensive, and therefore huge system memory is not rare; new UNIX implementations frequently have GBs sized system memory. Under these circumstances, swap space can be expanded to include a part of the system memory besides the usual disk-based swap area. Then pages can be swapped from the system memory to the memory-based swap area, thereby actually staying within the system memory. The only question, then, is how the system would tell the difference between regular and swapped pages; this is the task of the ***swapfs*** filesystem. Anonymous swapped pages are named by ***swapfs*** and handled appropriately. There is no need for a literal copying of pages within memory; simply, pages stay where they were, but are marked as swapped. Swapped pages requested by the system are released for regular use. Therefore, everything happens as it would in typical swapping, except much, much faster; the system performance benefit is obvious. Please note that the phrases "a swapped page" and "to swap a page" do not necessarily refer to the swapping process; they have been also used to identify a page in the swap area and the process of transferring a page into the swap area, as a part of the regular paging procedure.

As the need for system memory increases, ***swapfs*** makes more space by backing swapped pages into the disk-based swap area (swap partition). The worst-case scenario is a well-known swap structure: physical memory is used as system memory, and the swap area is restricted to the swap partition. As soon as more room has been made in the memory, a swap space can expand in that way.

Such a flexible approach implies that all swap partitions, including the primary one, should be mounted through entries in the filesystem configuration file. Otherwise, there is no need for a default primary swap configuration entry; it is already well known to the system.

5.5.3 Loopback Virtual Filesystem

Modern UNIX versions introduced a more flexible way to merge individual filesystems into the overall UNIX hierarchical filesystem. Initially, UNIX filesystems could be handled only as complete partitions; this meant that only a complete filesystem within a partition could be merged by mounting the top-most directory from the partition's filesystem onto the mount-point (supposedly an empty directory within the overall UNIX filesystem). It also meant that to access any file within a partition, a long trip from the starting partition's point was often required. The requested long pathname could be accepted, but for a number of applications, doing so required a careful selection of the filesystem's mount-point. In some cases symbolic links could help in skipping a part of the path, thereby reaching the needed data using a corresponding shortcut. However, a real advantage would be to mount the same filesystem in different ways — such flexibility would be quite an improvement.

A new approach was introduced, known as the *loopback filesystem* (***lofs***). Once the filesystem is mounted in the usual way, ***lofs*** allows new, virtual filesystems to be created, which provide access to existing files using alternate pathnames. Once the virtual filesystem is created, other filesystems can be mounted within it without affecting the original filesystem. At the same time, filesystems that are subsequently mounted onto the original filesystem continue to be visible to the virtual filesystem. The new filesystem type ***lofs*** requires a slightly modified treatment by the OS; however, all of the filesystem's issues remain transparent.

The idea for ***lofs*** came from the network filesystem (***nfs***), which will be discussed later in Chapter 18. If something could be implemented through the network, obviously it could be implemented locally, too. Instead of a network interface, the local loopback interface should be used, and that is the origin of the filesystem's name.

An example from HP-UX 10.20 follows. The corresponding ***lofs*** entries in the filesystem configuration file */etc/fstab* are presented:

```
$ cat /etc/fstab            (partially presented, here)
    .....
/dev/vg01/lvol10            /files     vxfs   rw,suid,delaylog,datainlog   0   2
/files/export/share/ud      /usr/ud    lofs   defaults                     0   0
/files/export/home          /home      lofs   defaults                     0   0
/files/export/home          /users     lofs   defaults                     0   0
/files/tmp                  /tmp       lofs   defaults                     0   0
```

The first line defines how the initial (original) filesystem is mounted (the type, ***vxfs***, will be discussed later); the filesystem resides in the logical volume ***lvol10*** (which will also be discussed later); and it is mounted into the */files* directory. Other lines define how to remount parts of the very same filesystem (of type ***lofs***). Please note that the first column that normally identifies the logical volume, or partition, where the filesystem lives, now identifies a starting point of the part of the filesystem we want to remount. The last two columns (arguments for *fsck* and *backup*) obviously do not apply in this situation, so they are 0.

How are the systems mounted? Here is the partial report of the **mount** command:

$ mount (partially presented too)

```
.....
.....
/files on /dev/vg01/lvol10 delaylog on Sat May 16 23:30:37 1998
/usr/ud on /files/export/share/ud defaults on Sat May 16 23:31:10 1998
/users on /files/export/home defaults on Sat May 16 23:31:10 1998
/tmp on /files/tmp defaults on Sat May 16 23:31:10 1998
/home on /files/export/home defaults on Sat May 16 23:31:10 1998
```

The lines presented here correspond to those presented earlier in the filesystem configuration file */etc/fstab*. It is clear to see that the system was rebooted on Saturday, May 16, 1998.

5.6 Managing Filesystem Usage

Once a filesystem is configured and mounted properly, users can start to use files. This is the purpose of the filesystem's existence. Using filesystems also means consuming appropriate disk space. Not only users do this; the system also consumes disk space on a regular basis because a number of system log files grow continuously. Incorrect filesystem usage can also corrupt the filesystem itself, making it inaccessible. The worst-case scenario is a complete collapse and crash of the system.

Filesystems require a great deal of maintenance during their lifetimes. Primary activities are closely related to disk space usage, and we will mainly focus on that topic. To manage disk space a corresponding tool is needed; UNIX provides the necessary tools in a set of commands that are sufficient for successful management. The main commands in this group are:

- **df** To display filesystem statistics
- **du** To report on disk usage
- **quot** To report disk usage by users

The **fsck** command is used to check filesystems, and will also be discussed.

5.6.1 Display Filesystem Statistics: The *df* Command

The ***df*** command produces a report that describes the filesystems, the total capacities, and the amount of free space available, all displayed in 1kB blocks. If a filesystem, or a file, or a directory within a filesystem is specified as an argument, the report refers only to the corresponding filesystem.

The two usual flavors of the **df** command (Berkeley and System V) generate different reports. A typical BSD report displays:

 # df

```
Filesystem      Kbytes    used     avail   capacity  Mounted on
/dev/sd0a        30191    10596    16576    39%      /
/dev/sd0g       220010   173838    24171    88%      /usr
/dev/sd0h       764758   243088   445195    35%      /home
```

rs01-ch:/home/2gig/rsxx-ch	*2031616*	*1854268*	*177348*	*91%*	*/rsxx-ch*
hcprophet:/hcprophet	*18875*	*7449*	*9538*	*44%*	*/hcprophet*

This output reports the status of existing filesystems, starting with the root disk partition, and then other mounted disk partitions. Each line of the report shows:

- The filesystem name
- The total filesystem capacity in Kbytes
- The number of Kbytes in use
- The number of Kbytes available (free)
- The percentage of the filesystem's storage currently in use
- The filesystem mounting point

It sounds impossible, but the displayed percentage can be sometimes larger than 100% (the maximum value can reach 111%). How can this be? To increase transfer efficiency, 10% of the available filesystem space is sacrificed as fragmented disk space; however, the superuser can use this space if needed. So the full filesystem size is 90% of the total size (but 100% for df), and under such circumstances the filesystem can appear to be overfilled. We will return to the "10% reserved disk space" later.

This example was from SunOS 4.1.3, which supports the BSD form of the **df** command. Some UNIX flavors, like HP-UX, support both command types; to distinguish between them, the BSD type is renamed **bdf**. Here is an example from HP-UX 10.20:

$ bdf

Filesystem	*Kbytes*	*used*	*avail*	*%used*	*Mounted on*
/dev/vg00/lvol1	*91669*	*58532*	*23970*	*71%*	*/*
/dev/vg00/lvol7	*319125*	*252427*	*34785*	*88%*	*/var*
/dev/vg00/lvol6	*350997*	*294527*	*21370*	*93%*	*/usr*
/dev/vg00/lvol5	*99669*	*23060*	*66642*	*26%*	*/tmp*
/dev/vg00/lvol4	*251285*	*189044*	*37112*	*84%*	*/opt*

The logical volume manager (LVM) is a standard part of the HP-UX 10.20 and creates the needed special device files for existing logical volumes.

To get the report about index nodes (this is actually a numerical report about files), use **df -i** (the **-i** option refers to index nodes):

 # df -i

Filesystem	*iused*	*ifree*	*%iused*	*Mounted on*
/dev/sd0a	*1217*	*13887*	*8%*	*/*
/dev/sd0g	*13130*	*100150*	*12%*	*/usr*
/dev/sd0h	*10726*	*374426*	*3%*	*/home*
*rs01-ch:/home/2gig/rsxx-ch**	*	*		*/rsxx-ch*
mvaxgr:1DUB1:	*	*	*	*/mvaxgr/disku2*
hcprophet:/hcprophet	*	*	*	*/hcprophet*

The System V **df** command produces a different report. This example is from Solaris 2.6:

$ df

/	(/dev/dsk/c1t0d0s0):	1488210 blocks	290743 files
/proc	(/proc):	0 blocks	2866 files
/dev/fd	(fd):	0 blocks	0 files
/altboot	(/dev/dsk/c1t0d0 s3):	384464 blocks	98556 files

```
/tmp      (swap):                1122128 blocks    30843 files
/files    (/dev/md/dsk/d10):     1334502 blocks   344191 files
```

This example is from HP-UX 10.20:

```
$ df
/opt   (/dev/vg00/lvol4):   74224 blocks   36311 i-nodes
/tmp   (/dev/vg00/lvol5):  133284 blocks   15592 i-nodes
/usr   (/dev/vg00/lvol6):   42740 blocks   44762 i-nodes
/var   (/dev/vg00/lvol7):   69570 blocks   35897 i-nodes
/      (/dev/vg00/lvol1):   47940 blocks   11893 i-nodes
```

The report includes:

- The filesystem mount point
- The special file name
- The number of blocks (block=512 bytes)
- The number of inodes, i.e., files in use

The percentage field, with the used space represented as a percentage of the total space, is missing from the generic System V **df** report. However, this is the most used, and possibly the most valuable, piece of information generated by the BSD-type command. Some vendors, therefore, provide a special option for this purpose. On Solaris 2.x, the option **-k** in effect converts the existing **df** command into the Berkeley style one.

```
$ df -k
Filesystem           kbytes      used     avail   capacity  Mounted on
/dev/dsk/c1t0d0s0   1280786    536681    740904     43%     /
/proc                     0         0         0      0%     /proc
fd                        0         0         0      0%     /dev/fd
/dev/dsk/c1t0d0s3    192241         9    192040      1%     /altboot
swap                 565480      4416    561064      1%     /tmp
/dev/md/dsk/d10     4211882   3544631    625133     86%     /files
```

A frequent run of the **df** command is strongly recommended. This is an efficient way to prevent the filesystem from being overfilled. Typically, the administrator should be warned when 90% of the filesystem is in use. Please note that fulfilled system-critical filesystems (*root, /usr/, /var*) can be fatal for the system. It is a good idea to automate the monitoring of filesystem statistics by periodically running the **df** command. Combined with an automatically generated warning e-mail, or a paging of the administrator, this can be a very efficient early warning method and could prevent more serious system problems. Some system administrators put the **df** command in the root's login scripts to be executed as each administrator logs into the system.

5.6.2 Report on Disk Usage: The *du* Command

The **df** command is useful in detecting possible problems related to the filesystem status and size. If there are problems, appropriate action is required. The action is quite simple: the filesystem must be purged of unnecessary files to make more room. On the other hand, having a clear idea of what should be done does not mean it can be done easily. Deciding which candidates should be purged without affecting users, installed software, and in some cases the system itself is a challenge. In addition, the solution must actually provide relief: instead of deleting hundreds of small files, it is a much better idea to remove a few larger files. The ***du*** command can help with this important task.

The **du** command summarizes disk usage; it recursively reports the amount of disk space used by all files and subdirectories within a specified directory, listed on a per-subdirectory basis. Disk usage is reported in blocks (block size varies among systems); BSD uses 1KB blocks, while System V uses 512-byte blocks. Otherwise, there are no differences between the versions. A typical **du** reports look like:

Berkeley style — SunOS

```
# du /home/bjl
3753    /home/bjl/ncsa
376     /home/bjl/email
47      /home/bjl/publdoc
266     /home/bjl/ftp/drivers
        .....
        .....
11476   /home/bjl
```

System V style — HP-UX 10.x or Solaris 2.x

```
$ du /users/bjl
8       /users/bjl/current
18      /users/bjl//sessions
42      /users/bjl/.elm
2       /users/bjl/Mail
        ...
        ...
342     /users/bjl
```

Obviously there is no difference between two UNIX platforms. For each subdirectory, all of the files and subdirectories that belong are presented, as well as a separate line indicating the total amount of disk space occupied by this subdirectory. The last line presents the total usage for the specified directory. Often, this report can be inordinately long and tedious; a report with several hundred lines is obviously hard to use. By specifying the **-s** option, only the total amount of disk space that a directory and its contents occupy is displayed, while the subdirectories and files are skipped:

```
# du -s /home/bjl
11476   /home/bjl
$ du -s /users/bjl
342   /users/bjl
```

This command can be piped with others to obtain different reports, with subdirectories sorted by different criteria (size, reverse size, etc.).

An extremely convenient way to use the command is "**du -s ***;" the report will include the size of each file and the total size of each subdirectory within the current directory only. This can be very useful in tracking the change in the size of a filesystem and in determining the cause of any sudden increase in size. By starting from the mount-point directory of the oversized filesystem, we can browse through large associated subdirectories until we reach the file, or files, that caused a sudden change in the size of the filesystem.

Once the cause is detected, corrective action can be implemented. For a better understanding, just follow this example:

$ bdf /var

Filesystem	*kbytes*	*used*	*avail*	*%used*	*Mounted on*
/dev/vg00/lvol6	*524288*	*462700*	*51387*	*90%*	*/var*

The */var* filesystem has reached the critical size (supposing 90% as a critical size) and should be checked and cleared. To efficiently discover potential offenders, we have to find large subdirectories and files and check whether we can remove or resize them. We will start to browse from the filesystem mount-point, in this case */var.*

$ cd /var

$ du -s *

```
0        X11
585562   adm
2        dt
0        lost+found
36       mail
1292     opt
186746   patches
914      preserve
1886     sam
122656   spool
10       statmon
392      stm
10900    tmp
78       yp
.....
.....
```

The ***adm*** directory seems to be oversized. So, the next step is:

$ cd adm

$ du -s *

```
3038     btmp
18       cron
32254    debug
7264     diag
40       ftmp.cron.log
4        inetd.sec
1914     lp
4598     maillog
2        netstat_data
1642     nettl.LOG00
50       sulog
300892   sw
221550   syslog
52       vtdaemonlog
980      wtmp
.....
.....
```

The file *syslog* is the system log file; the OS permanently logs into the file after the system startup. It seems to be unusually large (larger than 100 MB). By checking its contents, we will quickly see many old useless log records that can be deleted from the file. Since resizing the file (preserving only those records from the last two months), the ***/var*** filesystem appears to be doing fine.

$ bdf /var

Filesystem	*kbytes*	*used*	*avail*	*%used*	*Mounted on*
/dev/vg00/lvol6	*524288*	*360000*	*154087*	*70%*	*/var*

5.6.3 Report on Disk Usage by Users: The *quot* Command

Another command related to disk usage is ***quot***, which summarizes filesystem ownership. The **quot** command reports the number of 1KB blocks used by each of the users in a specified filesystem. Only the superuser can execute this command, because it accesses the disk special files. The command syntax is:

quot *[options] block-special-file*

where

block-special-file The filesystem block special file
options The usual filesystem related options

An example:

$ quot /dev/sd0h

```
/dev/sd0h (/home):
68456    pam
29154    mindy
23693    george
11466    bjl
.....
.....
353      root
6        bin
```

5.6.4 Checking Filesystems: The *fsck* Command

A filesystem can be corrupted by any number of things: operator errors, hardware failures, etc. The **fsck** command (it stands for *filesystem check*) checks the filesystem's consistency, reports any encountered problems, and optionally tries to repair them (sometimes such repairs can cause minor data loss). The **fsck** command interactively repairs inconsistent filesystem conditions.

fsck can encounter the following filesystem problems:

- One block belonging to several files (inodes)
- Blocks marked as free but in use
- Blocks marked as used but free
- Incorrect link counts in inodes, indicating missing or excess directory entries
- Incorrect directory sizes
- Inconsistencies between inode size value and the amount of data blocks referenced in the address field

- Illegal blocks (e.g., system tables) within files
- Inconsistent data in the filesystem's tables
- Lost files (nonempty inodes that fully identify files not listed in any directory) — **fsck** places these orphaned files in the filesystem directory named *lost+found* (each filesystem has its own *lost+found* directory), so they can be recognized later by owners and reused; the name assigned to a lost file corresponds to the inode number
- Illegal or unallocated numbers in directories

On BSD, the **fsck** command is run automatically on boots and reboots. On System V, **fsck** is run at boot time on nonroot filesystems only if they have not been dismounted cleanly, i.e., if the system crashed. A manual run of the **fsck** command is needed only occasionally: at boot, when **fsck**'s automatic mode cannot fix all encountered problems, after creating a new filesystem (although it is a good idea to reboot the system upon filesystem creation, if possible), and under a few other circumstances. Nevertheless, a system administrator should understand how the **fsck** command works to be able to quickly recognize abnormal situations.

The syntax of the **fsck** command is:

fsck *[options] spec_file*

where

spec_file The name of the filesystem's special file

options Available options:

-n | -N	Answer no to all prompts, and list problems but do not repair them
-y | -Y	Answer yes to all prompts (Be careful when using this option! It repairs all damage regardless of the severity!)
-p	Preens the filesystem and performs noninteractive repairs that do not change any file's contents
-b *nn*	Use an alternate superblock located at *nn-th* block
-m	Perform a sanity check only — do not repair
-q	Quiet mode; removes nonreferenced named pipes and reconstructs the free list without comment
-f	Force filesystem checking regardless of the superblock status
-F *type*	Specify a filesystem type to be **fsck**-ed
-V	Echo, but do not execute, the command; verify and validate a command line

The **fsck** command runs faster on character special files. However, the block device must be used for the root filesystem. If the filesystem is not specified, the **fsck** command checks all filesystems listed in the filesystem configuration file (*/etc/fstab*, or */etc/vfstab*); this happens at boot time. Under AIX, the checking of filesystems is determined in the filesystem configuration file */etc/filesystems* (if the keyword *check* is *true* for a corresponding filesystem).

Normally, the **fsck** command runs with **-p** option, i.e., it silently fixes the following problems:

- Link counts in inodes too large
- Missing blocks in the free list
- Blocks in the free list and also in files

- Incorrect counts in the filesystem's table
- Nonreferenced zero-length files deleted
- Lost files placed in the filesystem's *lost+found* directory, and named by their inode number

More serious errors will be handled with a prompt for confirmation.

If **fsck** modifies any filesystem, it will display the message:

*** *FILESYSTEM WAS MODIFIED* ***

If the root filesystem is modified, an additional message also appears:

*** *REBOOT UNIX* ***

or

***** *REMOUNTING ROOT FILESYSTEM* ****

When modifications happen during a boot procedure, the reboot, or remount, is initiated automatically. If the **fsck** has been executed from the command line on the root filesystem, then the **reboot** command has to be started manually, too:

 # reboot -n

The **-n** option is very important to prevent previous execution of the **sync** command, which flushes the output buffers and might, under these circumstances, recorrupt the filesystem (the only case when the system is rebooted without **sync**-ing the disks).

An example (from the Apollo workstation and HP-UX):

```
$ fsck -y
fsck: /dev/dsk/c201d6s0: root file system
continue (y/n)? y
** /dev/dsk/c201d6s0
** Last Mounted on/
** Root file system
** Phase 1 — Check Blocks and Sizes
** Phase 2 — Check Pathnames
** Phase 3 — Check Connectivity
** Phase 4 — Check Reference Counts
FREE INODE COUNT WRONG IN SUPERBLK
FIX? yes
** Phase 5 — Check Cyl groups
SUMMARY INFORMATION (SUPER BLOCK SUMMARIES) BAD
BAD CYLINDER GROUPS
FIX? yes
** Phase 6 — Salvage Cylinder Groups
21806 files, 0 icont, 296674 used, 128312 free (1472 frags, 15855 blocks)
***** MARKING FILE SYSTEM CLEAN *****
***** FILE SYSTEM WAS MODIFIED *****
***** REBOOT HP-UX; DO NOT SYNC (USE reboot -n) *****
```

It is not the end of the world to have messages about filesystem inconsistencies during system startup. As long as the **fsck** command can fix them, sometimes even in several attempts, everything will be fine. However, it can be very upsetting if **fsck** fails; the failure usually indicates a more serious filesystem problem, frequently, a hardware-related problem that requires a more radical approach. The **fsck** command can resolve many logical inconsistencies, but it cannot repair a broken disk.

fsck is a very time-consuming command; for a large filesystem, a complete check can take a while. This is why filesystems that were cleanly dismounted during system shutdown are skipped — they will have no problems and checking them is a waste of the time. Also, the *journaled filesystem* (the ***jfs*** type) is the most robust with regards to corruption; if it is corrupted, the recovery is much faster. The price paid for such robustness is additional overhead in the filesystem use; the online journaling of filesystem transactions requires more resources and time.

6

UNIX Filesystem Layout

6.1 Introduction

In Chapter 5 we discussed the UNIX filesystem primarily from the user standpoint. UNIX users create, read, write, and purge files. And this is correct — UNIX filesystems exist to make the files accessible to users. But there is a lot of work behind the scenes to fulfill this logical requirement. This part is done by the UNIX system itself, and it is mostly hidden from the users. But UNIX administrators must be aware of this fact and should understand this process. Everybody knows that files reside on disk. They are saved somewhere, and when we need them, we get them. But how it works is more mysterious.

We use the term *filesystem layout* to explain how the files are organized within the available disk space. UNIX files cannot exist out of the UNIX filesystems. UNIX filesystem is the vehicle to organize storage resources in a usable way. The filesystem merges files in a hierarchical way and enables their physical storage, as well as access to the stored files when needed. This is always true, independent of the filesystem type and organization.

The filesystem layout is the main topic discussed in this chapter. A thorough understanding of filesystem layout is extremely important for successful filesystem management. Once this important topic is understood, many other UNIX issues will become automatically clear. Filesystem management is crucial for overall UNIX administration. This cannot be overstated. Just remember what we said earlier: *on UNIX everything is a file or file-like.* Files are in the center of UNIX. Consequently managing the files is the core of UNIX administration.

Disk space can vary in size, type, characteristics, and even location (a remote disk space can be used, just as the local one), and UNIX must respond to all possible situations. The total disk space is usually partitioned into smaller storage entities convenient for more flexible use, and a separate UNIX filesystem is created in each storage entity. To make the created filesystem visible to users, an additional step is required: it must be merged with other filesystems in an overall UNIX directory hierarchy, which we will address as "an overall UNIX filesystem." Strictly speaking the overall UNIX filesystem is not a filesystem per se, rather this is a set of merged filesystems ready for use.

UNIX filesystems are organized on two levels: physical and logical. Physical layout directly reflects the filesystem organization within a storage entity. It takes care of files' parameters and maps them into corresponding hardware parameters of the storage entity. However, the UNIX filesystem can be organized and managed in a more sophisticated way within a virtual (logical) storage space that is built around physical entities. A new level of abstraction was introduced to make filesystem organization more flexible and powerful.

Logical layouts of a storage space and its physical counterpart do not have to be necessarily the same. A logical storage can be spread over a part of a disk, over a whole disk, or as in today's modern UNIX flavors, over several disks. Nearly any combination of multiple partitions of multiple disks can be combined performance-wise in an extremely powerful way. Of course, a precise mapping of the logical storage to the physical storage counterpart is crucial. Once this bidirectional relationship is firmly established, UNIX can manage files on a logical level only.

Logical storage entities are known as ***logical volumes***, and the corresponding system software for their management is known as ***logical volume manager (LVM)***. Logical volumes appeared at the moment when the disk technology reached the point where disk size, speed, and price stopped to be issues. LVM is a relatively new UNIX topic; for most of the UNIX flavors it is still an optional piece of software. The traditional physical partitioning of disks and their usage is still dominant, but the situation is changing rapidly.

We will use the general term ***data*** to refer to the system and user data stored on the disk. User data is the real data kept in files within the filesystem; system data is the data needed to identify and manage the user data. The system data presents a necessary overhead, but from the system standpoint this data is crucial for managing the filesystem.

The data block is the smallest data unit. Each UNIX file consumes one or more blocks. If all the file's blocks are known, the file itself can be easily managed. An additional step to identify the sequence of blocks that make the file is required. This is exactly why we organize files into a filesystem. We can look to the filesystem as a kind of umbrella that covers files and provides mechanisms for their use; system data keeps information needed for their accurate identification and allocation.

6.2 Physical Filesystem Layout

In our attempt to fully understand the filesystem layout, we will follow the traditional path in managing disk space. There are a few good reasons for such an approach: it is still prevailing in use; it is always easier to start with less complex issues and then go toward more complex ones; and the strongest argument — behind any logical structure is a physical layout that can never be bypassed. At the very end, each file must be physically stored in the magnetic disk media.

Disks have cylinders: concentric circles within the disk's plates that are farther divided into tracks, or segments (we will use the term *track*). Data is always stored in blocks that are spread over the disk space; the block can be located in any track. Each track contains a well-defined number of blocks (usually 512 blocks). Each block is uniquely identified by the block number. The disk controller knows how to allocate each block specified by its number within the whole disk space. Block allocation means mapping the block number into the disk geometry (to the corresponding cylinder and track and a block in the track). Once a block is allocated, it can easily be accessed and processed.

Disks cannot be used directly from shelves; they must be prepared for data storage. In UNIX terminology, it means the physical filesystem layout must be properly defined and put in the operation. In this section we will address main issues related to the physical filesystem layout. They are grouped around:

- Disk partitions — the way to specify a storage entity for the usage
- Filesystem structures — mechanisms to manage data on the disk
- File identification and allocation — the way to identify and access files on the disk
- Performance-related issues — how to improve the performances of the filesystem

This section partially refers to Chapter 2, especially in the part about special device files.

6.2.1 Disk Partitions

For a long time the basic UNIX filesystem storage entity was a disk partition. This simply involved partitioning of the magnetic disk into several smaller pieces suitable for additional processing. You can compare this to putting filing cabinets (here partitions) within a filing closet (the disk) in an office. It is the first step to take, but still the cabinets are not prepared to store the files. Some items are still not ready; drawers and their inventories are not yet prepared. We just decided and specified the size of the storage space.

In the past, disk space was expensive. Organizing a disk into smaller pieces (partitions) benefited the system in a number of ways. The smaller partition contained a smaller filesystem that offered more flexibility in organizing the UNIX tree hierarchy. The small filesystem was more robust with regards to possible filesystem corruption. Many filesystem-related commands could run faster on a smaller filesystem (like **backup**, **fsck**, etc.). And it is easier to manage smaller filesystems.

Both UNIX platforms, BSD and System V, organized disks around fixed-size partitions (but different partitions had different sizes). UNIX treated disk partitions as independent devices; each of them was accessed as if it were a physically separate disk — consequently, the terms *partition* and *disk* could be used alternatively. One physical disk might be divided into several partitions, or be configured with only one partition. In the past disk, partitions were usually defined in advance by the OS. Thus they offered few division schemes. The number of partitions was fixed, while their size could be specified. Imagine that only a predetermined number of filing cabinets could go into the filing closet, but you could decide the size of each cabinet.

Typically each disk was divided into multiple partitions: eight partitions for BSD and ten for System V, with some overlapping of the partitions. Simple BSD disk partition schemes are presented in Figure 6.1.

Eight different partitions might be defined for a disk, named by the letters *a* to *h*; a partition could be skipped if its size was 0. The *c* partition comprised the entire disk, including the forbidden (inaccessible) area. The *g* partition overlapped with the *d*, *e*, and *f* partitions. It was not possible to use them all simultaneously, since some of them included the same disk space — for example, either partitions *d* through *f* or the partition *g* could be accessed. Actually, this disk layout offered three different ways of using the disk: divided into four partitions, or six partitions, or to use the whole disk. Each partition might hold a filesystem, or it could be used as a *swap* partition. The OS offered this flexibility — from today's point of view it was not much, but it was adequate to manage everything in a decent way.

The swap partition plays a special role in each UNIX system. UNIX memory management system (MMS) requires the dedicated disk space for normal *paging* and *swapping*. Recall the discussion of these issues from Chapter 5:

- *Paging* presents a regular exchange of data pages between the system memory and disk. Paging is an ordered process based on certain performance-related criteria.
- *Swapping* presents an emergency situation when the system encounters a significant lack of the memory space and a lack of time to do that in an ordered way. Swapping is an irregular process and performance-wise it should never happen.

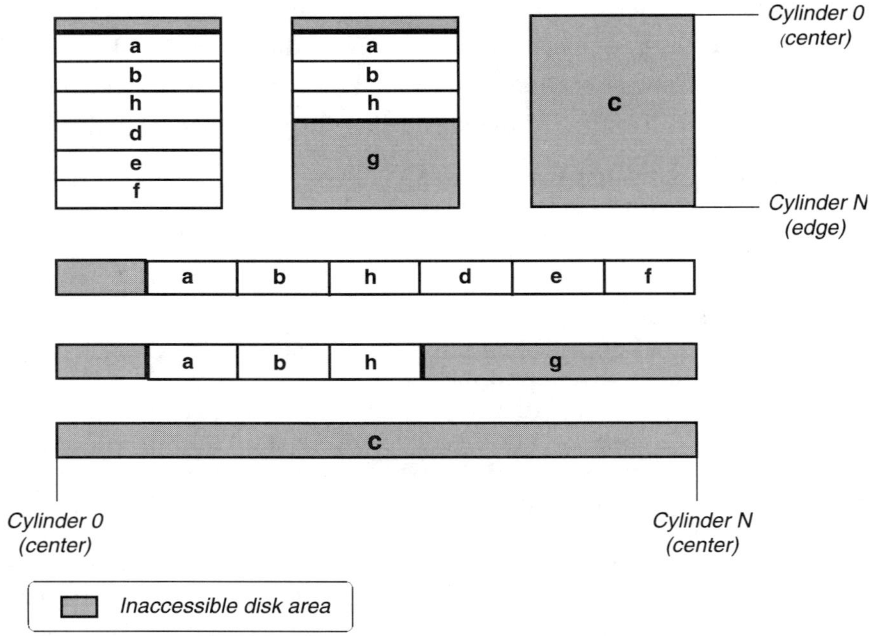

FIGURE 6.1
Simple BSD disk partitioning.

The swap partition is used as a "raw" partition. The complex filesystem structures would only make the swapping slower. Swap partition must be used in the simplest possible way and this is the "flat organization" provided by the MMS itself. Briefly, the swap partition does not know and does not care about UNIX filesystem.

A logical question arises: Why does a disk-partitioning scheme have to be defined in advance, and why in such a strict way? Why was the decision about partitioning not left to the system administrator? Supposedly the UNIX designers wanted to make this sensitive and relatively tough administrative task easier to handle; less flexibility makes things simpler. But to fully understand such an approach, perhaps a closer look into the very early stages of UNIX systems is needed.

In the early days of UNIX development, a number of disk control functions were determined on the hardware level, so the first disk controllers were quite restricted in the way they managed disk partitions; even the partition sizes were hardwired within the controller hardware. So at the time partition schemes were established, there were not a lot of choices. Since then, with the development of the technology, things have changed and most of the disk-related issues have been shifted into the software (or sometimes the firmware). To keep the new UNIX systems compatible with the old ones, the slightly modified "old partition scheme" continued to exist. The partition size can be specified arbitrarily, and in that way the number of partitions. It makes the partition scheme sufficiently flexible even for today's standards. By simply assigning its size to zero, a partition could be skipped, and any partition combination become viable. At the same time, the required special device files for the selected partitions already exist, and all needs seem to be met.

The partition scheme presented in Figure 6.1 was, and still is, implemented by Sun Microsystems. It was used by SunOS and is now used by Solaris. Despite the fact that today we can combine multiple disks (or partitions) in larger logical volumes, this partition scheme remains useful and used.

UNIX accesses any disk partition through the corresponding special device file (see Chapter 2). A special device file is a pointer to the disk driver within the kernel (in UNIX all device drivers are part of the kernel). It is essential that the kernel supports implemented disk interface; otherwise the disk cannot be used at all. You should not worry about that because UNIX fully supports all usual disk interfaces, and the kernel has been built properly during the UNIX installation.

Most UNIX flavors provide some kind of tool to create disk partitions (the ***format*** utility on Solaris and SunOS, ***SAM*** on HP-UX, ***SMIT*** on AIX, etc.). This tool automatically creates the required special device files in the */dev* directory. A special device file can be created also manually: the UNIX **mknod** command is available. Its usage is trivial, only two arguments are required: the *major* and *minor* device number. Sometimes other front-end commands, or scripts, can also be available.

6.2.2 Filesystem Structures

Disk partitioning per se will not allow you to start to use the specified disk space. UNIX files cannot be stored directly in such "raw" storage entities. UNIX files can only reside within the UNIX filesystems. Imagine again a filing closet in the office. At this point, number and sizes of cabinets are decided, but each drawer in the cabinet is still missing file holders, bars, labels, and other needed accessories. It is time now to think about these details; otherwise, we will not be able to organize the filing system for our papers.

Similarly, a UNIX filesystem has to be created in each disk partition before we can start to use it for our UNIX files. When a filesystem is built in UNIX, certain system data structures are written into the reserved system part of the partition. This system data uniquely defines the physical layout of the filesystem. Its main task is to provide correct allocation of UNIX files within this partition. Filesystems are mutually separated; each filesystem has its own independent system data structures. A single file cannot be shared between two filesystems, i.e., two partitions.

The most important filesystem data structure is the *superblock*. The *superblock* is a set of tables that contain important information about the filesystem such as its label, size, and a list of index nodes, better known by the shorter name ***inodes***. The superblock determines the filesystem type, and all incompatibilities among different filesystems (including between different UNIX filesystem types — see Chapter 5) are caused by the superblock differences. UNIX can use a specific filesystem only if knows how to read the filesystem superblock; without this understanding the disk is a compilation of senseless and useless data blocks.

A visual depiction of the BSD and System V filesystem layouts are presented in Figure 6.2. The Berkeley filesystem layout included some additional information about filesystems like the cylinder group block, while System V included certain additional dynamic information about current free space. However, the main difference was that Berkeley filesystems originally spread multiple superblock copies over the available disk space. If a *superblock* is damaged, the filesystem becomes useless. It was a good idea to keep several superblock copies separately. If one copy is damaged, the Berkeley system automatically switches to another.

Through the years, the Berkeley filesystem proved to be faster and more robust, and provided better performance. Eventually the traditional System V (known as the ***s5*** filesystem) became obsolete. System V release 4 discontinued with ***s5*** filesystem and switched to the Berkeley filesystem. Additional filesystem development continues to evolve among the specific UNIX flavors. Today all filesystems have roots in the Berkeley version; the ***s5*** filesystem disappeared. The filesystems are identified by different names: ***4.2***, ***ufs***, ***efs***, ***hfs***,

ext2, jfs, vxfs; they are mutually incompatible despite the fact that they all belong to the UNIX family of filesystems. The prevailing type in use is ***ufs***, which stands for *UNIX filesystem*. Even if the filesystem name is the same, some incompatibilities among different UNIX vendors are quite possible. Throughout this text we will steer clear of flavor-specific details and elaborate on common filesystem issues.

Another data structure, presented in Figure 6.2, is the single boot-block area reserved at the beginning of the filesystem. This area contained the bootstrap program that brings the UNIX system into operation. However, a boot block area is active only if a filesystem is bootable, i.e. if it is on the root filesystem. This filesystem structure is crucial for the system startup, but not for the rest of this chapter. That is why it is just mentioned here. We discussed booting of the system and the bootstrap program in Chapter 4.

6.2.3 Filesystem Creation

The discussed filesystem structures, including the superblock, are the result of the procedure known as to create a filesystem. In the UNIX terminology, we say to make a filesystem. UNIX provides several commands to deal with filesystems, and often additional user-friendly character-based or GUI tools. We will focus on the related UNIX commands available on all UNIX flavors. UNIX sees storage entities (at the moment we talk about disk partitions) through the corresponding special device files. Remember that storage entities are accessible through both types of special device files (character/raw and block special device files).

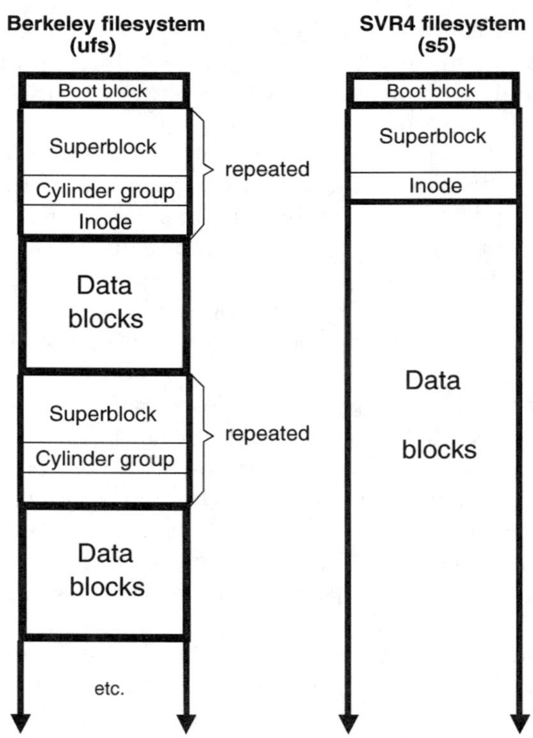

FIGURE 6.2
The filesystem layout.

6.2.3.1 The mkfs Command

This the basic UNIX command for this purpose. It offers the most flexibility; practically all filesystem parameters could be specified. For most cases, however, the default specification should be appropriate. The format of the command is:

mkfs ***[options] char-spec-file size [operands]***

where

options	Generic or filesystem type specific options
char-spec-file	The character special file for the corresponding disk partition
size	The size of filesystem in 512-byte blocks
operands	Optional arguments for a fine-tuning of the filesystem parameters such as a number of inodes to create (the default is one inode for every 2 KB of disk space), a primary block size, a fragment size, free disk space threshold, and others

The **mkfs** command is a versatile command that enables flexible creation of the filesystem; myriad of options and operands specify many details of the created filesystem. It checks for dependencies among specified parameters to prevent any wrongdoing. The command varies slightly among different vendor's flavors.

6.2.3.2 The newfs Command

Another (BSD-style) front-end command, ***newfs***, can also be used to create a filesystem. This command actually invokes the **mkfs** command but with a number of predefined filesystem parameters. It is much easier to work with this command, and the author recommends its use whenever possible. The format of the **newfs** command is:

newfs ***[options] char-spec-file***

where

options	Generic, filesystem-type specific, and **mkfs**-related options
char-spec-file	Raw (character) special file for the corresponding disk partition

Remember that most of the filesystem-related commands require character special device files to identify the storage entity (here the disk partition).

Some UNIX flavors maintain a special disk description file that facilitates the use of this command. The usual file */etc/disktab* contains description entries for each disk that can be used. Each description entry is uniquely named and fully defines a partitioned disk. Usually several entries describe the same disk with different partitioning schemes. Simply by referring to an entry, all of the necessary filesystem parameters can be obtained. This makes the use of the **newfs** command trivial:

newfs ***char-spec-file disk-name***

where

char-spec-file	Raw (character) special file for the corresponding disk partition
disk-name	The name of the entry specified in the disk description file */etc/disktab*

HP-UX (version 9) used such an approach. The main disadvantage was that required *disktab entries* could not include all available disk models. Simply, newer disk models appeared after the file installation cannot be included. This led to a frequent patching of the disk description table, which could be annoying. HP-UX (version 10) retained the disk description file for backward compatibility but switched to the new type of the **newfs** command: one that is not dependent on the disk description table.

6.2.3.3 The tunefs Command

UNIX also provides the command **tunefs** to tune (adjust) the created filesystem. The command can modify dynamically certain filesystem parameters. It is not unusual to realize after some time that the created filesystem does not optimally match your needs. The used filesystem cannot be easily recreated; in most cases it is almost impossible. This command is the UNIX response for that purpose.

Some UNIX flavors provide other filesystem specific commands, for example, a command to extend the size of a filesystem.

6.2.4 File Identification and Allocation

Another popular term for the filesystem creation is *formatting the disk* (or partition). In the PC world this is the only official term. In UNIX context, formatting literally means to create filesystem structures only, primarly the superblock. The created filesystem itself is absolutely empty — there is no single-user data in it. To compare with the filing closet and cabinets in the office: all drawers are now equipped with needed accessories; carriers and holders are there, as well as empty labels for easy identification of documents. These accessories take up some available space in the cabinets, but without them it would be very hard to file our papers.

The UNIX counterpart for the mentioned accessories is the superblock. The superblock contains the filesystem structures (system data) needed for user data management. All superblock structures are free and ready for use. The superblock consumes a certain amount of the storage space to keep its system data.

Keeping in mind the previous discussion, it becomes clear:

- Why once we reformat (create a filesystem) a disk or partition we lose all previously stored data. It does not mean that this data was purged. All stored data blocks remain unchanged, but the new superblock is now created. All system data in the old superblock was erased. UNIX does not know how to find this data.
- Why there is a difference in the size between unformatted and formatted storage space. The superblock data must also be saved in the very same storage space.

Let us see now in more detail how the UNIX filesystem identifies and allocates files within the corresponding storage space. It is worthwhile to mention that we are still staying within the physical filesystem layout boundaries.

6.2.4.1 Index Node (inode)

The most important individual entity in the filesystem superblock is the ***inode***. Inode is a shorter, more convenient, name for the ***index node***. Each file in the filesystem is completely described by its inode. An inode includes all of the file's relevant data except the file name. File names are contained in the directory where the files reside.

The content of each directory includes the file names with the references to the corresponding inodes. In this way, UNIX is able to find any file by scanning the file's directory until the file name matches. Afterward only the corresponding inode is used to access the file on the disk. A file can have several different names because several file names can be referenced to the same inode. They can appear in the same or different directories, but must remain in the same filesystem. These references are known as hard links (see Chapter 2).

An inode contains around 200 bytes, enough space to uniquely identify a file. An inode structure is presented in Figure 6.3.

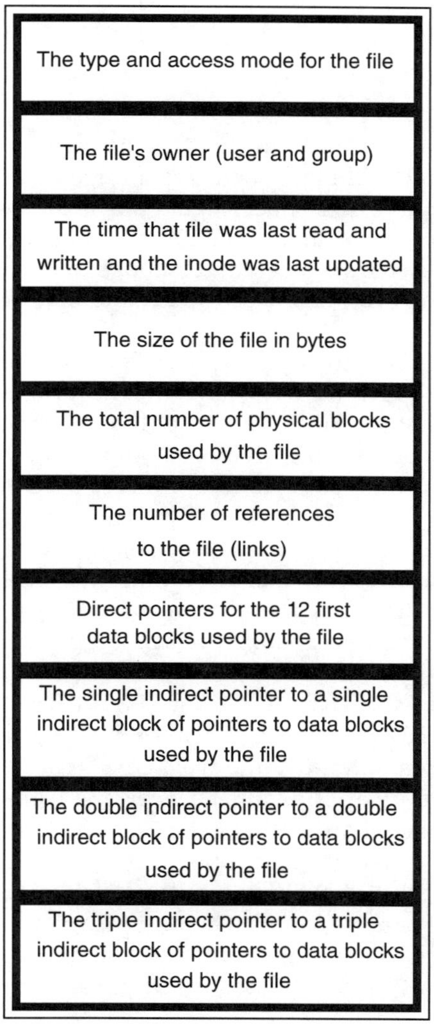

FIGURE 6.3
The inode structure.

The first part of the inode contains all information about the file. Most of the information we know from the long file listing (the ***ls -l*** command). UNIX opens and reads the inode, and learns about the file's type, ownership, and permissions. Based on this information, UNIX knows how to proceed with the file itself. Do not forget that UNIX processes different file types in a different way.

Once we are familiar with the contents of an inode, many of the already discussed issues become clear — for example, why hard links are restrained to the same filesystem, or where the system finds information for long listing of files, or how the **fsck** command can check and even fix problems in the filesystem, and many others.

The inode number, starting from one and increasing, identifies an inode. An identified inode must be allocated in the disk space before it can be used by the system. To allocate an inode is easy, because each inode is well defined within the superblock and the superblock is always stored in the reserved disk space well known to the system.

6.2.4.2 File Allocation

It is much tougher job to locate a file in the disk space. A file can contain an arbitrary number of data blocks, from a single block up to a huge number of blocks. These blocks could be spread over the whole disk space. Again this is the inode that precisely allocates the file itself. The second part of the inode contains a number of direct and indirect pointers to point to the location of each data block that belongs to this file. For most UNIX flavors the pointers are 32 bits long (4B), and we will assume that length in the discussion that follows.

An inode can directly point to as many as 12 data blocks consumed by the file. Assuming the block size of 4 KB (or 8 KB), this means a file as large as 48 KB (or 96 KB) is directly accessible. For larger files, indirect pointers must be used. A single indirect block contains additional pointers: a 4 KB block contains up to 1 K pointers, while a 8 KB block contains up to 2 K pointers. A double indirect block contains, or, better to say, points to, millions of new pointers. And finally a triple indirect pointer can be used in the case of extremely large files. If a file is very small, the file data is stored directly in the inode. Figure 6.4 illustrates how this allocation mechanism works.

A 32-bit (4 B) pointer can uniquely identify one block among as many as 4 G (4 billion) blocks. This is, simply, the address capability of a 32-bit pointer. More precisely, assuming a block size of 4 KB (or 8 KB), the maximum size of the reachable disk space (i.e., the filesystem) is, respectively, 4 G×4 KB = **16 TB** (or 4 G×8 KB = **32 TB**). Beyond that size, the block must be increased (16 KB or more) during the filesystem creation. This is one of the options of the **mkfs** command. (By the way, UNIX checks all specified options and, in the case of an inappropriate option value, cancels the command execution.) However, disk blocks could be smaller than in this example, and they would still be correct — today's disk sizes are still in the range of several dozens GB.

The presented inode structures illustrate very well a typical UNIX filesystem. It does not mean necessarily that each UNIX flavor implements the same inode structures, primarily regarding the number of direct and indirect pointers. Differences cause incompatibilities, but in general, issues discussed here are valid over all UNIX platforms.

6.2.5 Filesystem Performance Issues

Once the filesystem is in place, UNIX starts to use the same filesystem very intensively. Thus the filesystem efficiency is very important for an overall UNIX behavior. Throughout all these years, the UNIX filesystem has been developed and improved significantly. Some of the improvements have been integrated into the filesystem itself. Other optional issues have been left to UNIX administrators to be implemented on an as-needed basis. We will address a few filesystem performance issues.

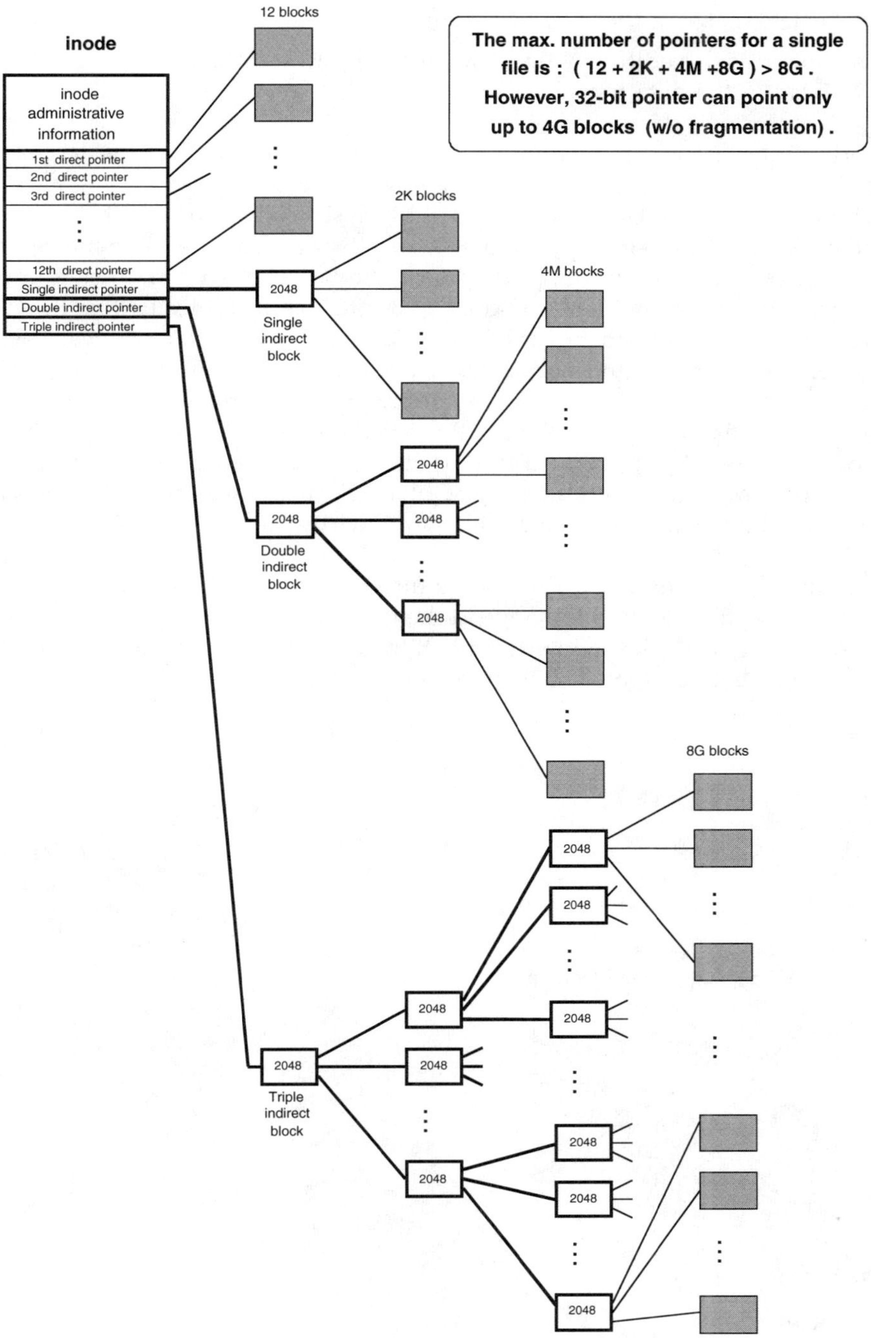

FIGURE 6.4
File layout on a disk.

6.2.5.1 File Storage vs. File Transfer

A disk block is the basic unit of data that the filesystem manages. Data are always transferred, written and read in blocks. Thus the block size determines:

- The storage efficiency — blocks cannot be used partially for data storage, regardless of the actual size of the data to be stored
- The data transfer efficiency (i.e., I/O throughput) — larger blocks cause smaller overhead in the data transfer

Two performance issues are related differently toward the block size. A large block size increases transfer efficiency, but decreases storage efficiency.

The original System V filesystem supported block sizes of 512 B and 1 KB, or sometimes 2 KB. The Berkeley filesystem supported 4, 8, 16, 32, or 64 KB. The difference in the block size was obvious. To avoid wasting disk space, the Berkeley-style filesystem introduced "block fragmentation": each block could be split into 2, 4, or typically 8 fragments. Block fragments could then be used separately to store data from different files. The transfer efficiency remained unchanged because a whole block was still used in the transfer of data. However, the storage efficiency was improved because a block, partially used by one file, could be shared with other files. At the end, each disk block is fully utilized. Of course nothing is free. The price paid for this storage improvement is the need to identify individual block fragments within a specific block. Earlier, it was enough to identify only the block; now the block fragments are also in play. The concept of block fragmentation is presented in Figure 6.5.

In this example, a hypothetical 25 KB large file was located in the three 8 KB blocks and one 1 KB block fragment. Upon a change in the file size to 51 KB, the file will consume six 8 KB blocks and three block fragments. In both cases, the remaining block fragments will be used for other files, so the wasted space is minimized.

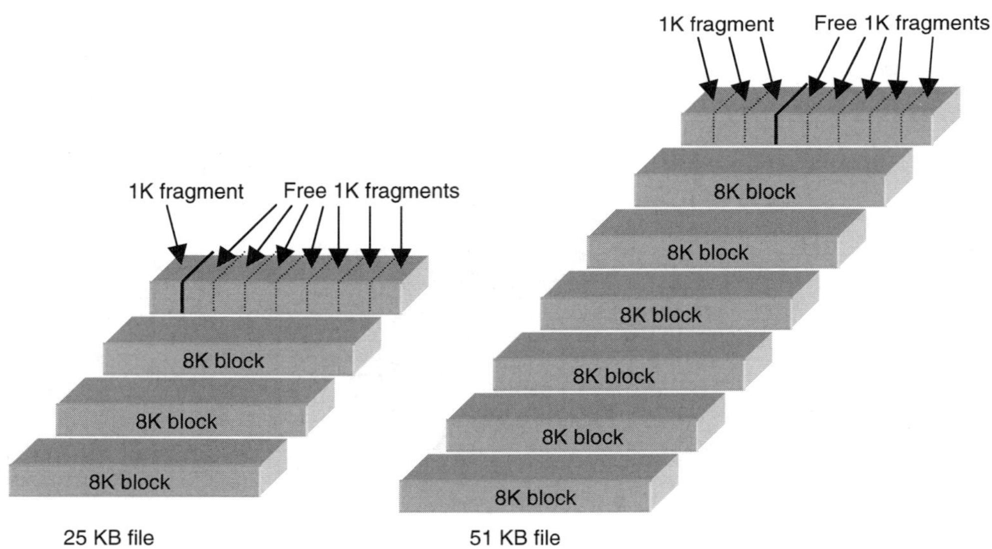

FIGURE 6.5
Berkeley-style filesystem: Blocks and fragments.

6.2.5.2 Reserved Free Space

File transfer efficiency can be improved by the introduction of the 10% filesystem free space. We briefly mentioned the 10% free space in Chapter 5 regarding the command **df**. We elaborate on this issue in more detail here.

The disk space always tends to be fragmented. The filesystem content is changing dynamically, old files are deleted and new files created. Upon the filesystem creation, the empty disk space will be quickly filled with data. Normally the filesystem tries to keep all file blocks together, so the access to the file could be faster. But the files are also deleted, and many gaps in the disk space remain after the file blocks are removed. This is known as *disk fragmentation*.

These gaps are reused, and reused, but the fragmentation of the overall disk space through time is unavoidable. Fragmented space requires more time to store and access files. Simply, the time spent in seeking and transferring chaotically allocated small chunks of the file blocks is much larger than if the blocks are allocated in larger chunks. Statistically, if 10% of the available storage space is sacrificed and not used, the performance benefits can be significant. This space is already badly fragmented and too "expensive" to be used. The remaining space offers more contiguous space for faster file allocation.

Remember that this free space is dynamically allocated and is changing through time. It always contains the most fragmented storage space in that point of time. (In addition, this 10% of space remains a forbidden zone only for users. Superuser and high-priority processes are still allowed to use that space.) The basic assumption is that these processes are beyond introduced restrictions. Those are system-related processes and should not be interrupted despite expected low-performance behavior of the system.

There is an odd consequence of this implementation. Occasionally the ***df-k*** command can report filesystem consumption larger than 100%. Although it could be quite confusing, it is still normal system behavior. Your system will not crash soon. It also does not mean that your data will spill over the edges of your disk. It simply means that 10% of reserved free space of this filesystem was also used by a superuser. A literally completely full filesystem reports 111% of space in use, and after that even a superuser identity cannot help more.

The 10% free filesystem space was introduced in the Berkeley UNIX. It has to be specified when the filesystem is created. It can be disabled at any time during the life of the filesystem. The reserved space can be returned for regular use at any time. The opposite is not possible: there is no way to introduce the 10% free space in an existing filesystem. If needed, the filesystem must be recreated, whatever it takes.

6.3 Logical Filesystem Layout

The physical approach to managing disk space is easier to understand, but it carried a number of restrictions caused by the disk hardware itself: How to overcome the finite size of a disk unit? What to do when the maximum size of the filesystem is below that needed? How to provide redundancy? And many other issues needed to improve overall system performances. The problem was especially acute in the management of large databases.

A solution was found in a different, logical approach in managing disk space. Existing physical storage entities (partitions and disks) could be combined and presented as arbitrary large logical storage entities. They then appear simply as storage entities to the operating system. The obvious benefits of such an approach are its inherent flexibility and increased capabilities.

For a better understanding of the terminology, here are a few introduction notes. Generally, the term *physical* refers to a real situation — what something physically looks like. The term *logical* refers to the way something is presented to the users. The relationship between physical and logical entities must be strictly defined and established. Once this bidirectional relationship is done, further management can be completely shifted to the logical layer. The required division of the storage space continues over the logical entities in the almost identical way we have already discussed. Of course, in real life everything is mapped back to physical entities, because they are the real providers of the needed storage space. The basic logical entity was named the *logical volume* (although this name is not used explicitly on all UNIX platforms). The most common name for the whole suite is the ***logical volume manager (LVM).***

UNIX vendors do not have a uniform approach regarding the LVM. There are several mutually incompatible versions designed by different manufacturers. We cannot even discuss BSD-like and System V-like versions; simply, the LVM appeared much later. LVM is a new, vendor-flavored product. This section briefly covers three LVM versions: AIX, HP-UX, and Solaris. It should be sufficient to help us become familiar with this important topic. However, it is fair to mention that the third-party vendor VERITAS is probably the leading designer in this field. As a matter of fact, VERITAS also contributed a great deal to all three of the versions examined.

The terminology used by the different vendors is also very vendor-specific. The same entities are named in different ways, making a complete description quite confusing. Unfortunately, issues that are already complex enough sometimes sound even more complicated due to the naming ambiguities.

6.3.1 Logical Volume Manager — AIX Flavor

AIX started early the trend toward a logical approach to disk treatment. Since AIX 3.1, *physical volumes* (correspond to the physical partition) were divided into a large number of relatively small *disk chunks* (by default their size was 4 MB). They were called *physical partitions*, but we will use the term *disk chunks* to avoid any possible confusion with physical disk partitioning. These *disk chunks* are the starting point in building other disk entities.

First, a *logical partition* (in IBM terminology) or a *logical chunk* has to be created. A logical chunk is the basic, smallest data storage unit for users. It corresponds to the single, double, or triple physical chunks. Multiple physical chunks can store the same, mirrored data. Storage of the same data on several physical locations significantly increases the reliability of the filesystem. Defined logical chunks are then used to create other logical entities. Although the logical chunks are presented continuously to the users, in reality their physical chunks could be discontinuous, expended, or replicated.

Each *physical volume* is associated and identified with the appropriate special device file. Several *physical volumes* can be combined into a single *volume group*, which is then handled as a unique logical entity. To make it clear, a *volume group* can be compared to the physical disk unit, but now not restricted to the single disk drive. In that way, an equivalent large logical disk can include several physical disks. It can now be processed as a single large unit instead of multiple smaller units. Therefore, all restrictions related to the limited size of a single disk have been overcome.

Once the *volume group* was created it could be divided (partitioned) into several smaller *logical volumes*. The new entity can be compared to the already known disk partition. But a single *logical volume* can be spread over several *physical volumes* that make the same *volume group*. It can occupy an arbitrary number of *logical chunks* (correspondingly, a number of physical chunks) on any of those *physical volumes*. This possibility of using *disk chunks* in an arbitrary way brought a new level of flexibility, and presented a big advantage over the traditional UNIX approaches. This situation is presented in Figure 6.6.

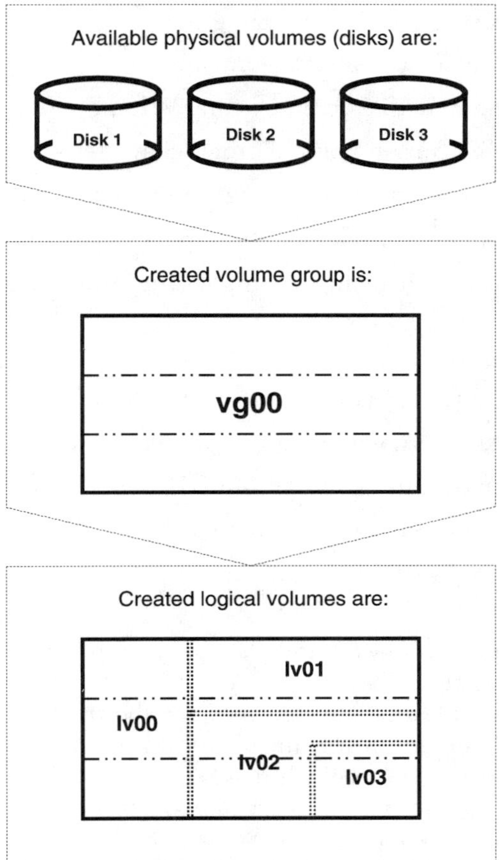

FIGURE 6.6
AIX data storage organization.

The LVM provides the necessary physical-to-logical mapping (and vice versa) and handles filesystems. Although very complex mapping and processing is going on, everything is hidden from the users. They simply use the available storage units.

For a better understanding of the new virtual entities, we will try to establish some functional relationships between AIX logical entities and the corresponding storage entities in the traditional UNIX approach:

AIX	Traditional UNIX approach
Physical volume	Disk/partition (as an accessible physical entity)
Disk chunk (partition)	None
Logical chunk (partition)	None
Volume group	Disk (as a storage space)
Logical volume	Partition

AIX introduced new commands and utilities to work with the newly introduced entities:

- For volume groups

mkvg	Create a new volume group (from one or more physical disks)
varyonvg	Activate a created volume group
varyoggvg	Deactivate a created volume group
extendvg	Add a new disk to an existing volume group
chvg	Change certain volume group characteristics
reducevg	Remove a disk from an existing volume group
importvg	Add an existing volume group to the system data base
exportvg	Remove an existing volume group from the system data base

- For logical volumes

mklv	Create a logical volume
extendlv	Increase the size of a logical volume
chlv	Change certain logical volume characteristics
lslv	List data about logical volumes
rmlv	Delete an existing logical volume

The existing AIX menu-driven *SMIT* utility (*system management interface tool*) also supports LVM in managing storage resources.

Once *logical volumes* are defined and created, we should proceed with the filesystem creation. This procedure is more or less the same as we have discussed. There is an AIX version of the well-known UNIX command ***mkfs***, as well as the AIX-specific front-end command ***crfs*** (an AIX counterpart to the usual UNIX command ***newfs***). Other UNIX commands to manage filesystems are also available.

AIX introduced a new filesystem named *journaled filesystem* (***jfs***), as its default filesystem. In the ***jfs*** each data transaction in the filesystem is temporarily recorded until its successful completion. It explains the origin of the name for the filesystem: a journaling is associated with each data transaction. If the transaction fails, old data can easily be restored from the journal. The ***jfs*** is more robust but also more expensive — an overhead in processing is related to the continuous journaling.

6.3.2 Logical Volume Manager — HP-UX Flavor

The LVM is a standard subsystem for managing disk space on the HP-UX platform. It started with HP-UX 9.04 and continues with HP-UX 10.x and HP-UX 11.x releases. With the optional support software, it offers other value-added features such as ***striping***, or ***mirroring***, or *high availability*. LVMs allow the user to consider the disks, also known as *physical volumes (PVs)*, as a pool of data storage consisting of equal-sized *physical extends* (*PEs* — the default size is 4 MB). One or more *PVs* are grouped into *volume groups (VGs)*, which then represent the basic unit of the data storage. *VGs* can be subdivided into virtual disks, called *logical volumes (LVs)*. An *LV* consists of an arbitrary number of *logical extends (LEs)* — each *LE* corresponds to one *PE* (or several *PEs*, if mirroring is implemented). An *LV* can span a number of *PVs*, or it can represent only a portion of a single *PV*. Once created, the *LVs* can be treated just like the disk partitions. *LVs* could be assigned to the filesystems, used as swap or dump devices, or used for the raw access.

In that light, a functional relationship between HP-UX LVM entities and the traditional UNIX ones is:

HP-UX	Standard UNIX approach
Physical volume	Disk/partition (as an accessible physical unit)
Physical extend	None
Logical extend	None
Volume group	Disk (as a storage space)
Logical volume	Partition

LVM provides a number of specific commands to create, display, and manage LV entities:

- To manage LVs

lvchange	Change LV characteristics
lvcreate	Create an LV in a VG
lvdisplay	Display information about LVs
lvextend	Increase space (mirrors) for LVs
lvlnboot	Prepare root, swap, and dump LV
lvrmboot	Remove an LV link to root, swap, or dump partition
lvmigrate	Migrate root filesystem from a partition to an LV
lvreduce	Decrease number of PEs allocated to LV
lvremove	Remove LVs from VG
lvmerge	Merge two LVs into one VG
lvsplit	Split mirrored LV into two LVs
lvsync	Synchronize stale mirrors in an LV

- To manage VGs

vgchange	Set VG availability
vgcreate	Create VG
vgdisplay	Display information about VGs
vgexport	Export a VG and associated LVs
vgextend	Extend a VG by adding physical volumes
vgimport	Import a VG into the system
vgreduce	Remove PV from a VG
vgremove	Remove VG from the system
vgscan	Scan PVs for VGs
vgcfgbackup	Backup the VG configuration data
vgcfgrestore	Restore the VG configuration from backed-up data
vgsync	Synchronized stale LV mirrors in VGs

- To manage PVs

pvchange	Change PV characteristics
pvcreate	Create (initialize) PVs for use in volume group
pvdisplay	Display information about PVs
pvmove	Move allocated PEs between PVs

The basic steps in using LVM include:

1. Identify the disks to be used, and create corresponding PVs — create an LVM data structure on each specified disk:

   pvcreate /dev/rdsk/c0t0d0 (a selected disk is identified by the device file *c0t0d0*)

2. Create a new VG — create a corresponding special device file and collect all PVs for the new VG (the supposed name *vg01*):

   mkdir /dev/vg01

   mknod /dev/vg01/group c 64 0x03000 (the minor number for a VG must be unique among all VGs on the system)

   vgcreate /dev/vg01 /dev/dsk/c0t0d0 (supposedly the VG includes a single PV)

   vgdisplay -v /dev/vg01 (to check the newly created VG)

3. Create LVs within the created VG:

   lvcreate -L 100 -n lvol1 /dev/vg01 (100 MB LV named ***lvol1***)

   LVM creates two special device files for each created LV: the block device file */dev/vg01/lvol1*, and the character (raw) device file */dev/vg01/rvol1*.

   lvdisplay /dev/vg01/lvol1 (to check the newly created LV)

   If there are more LVs, this step should be repeated:

   lvcreate -L 500 -n lvol2 /dev/vg01 (500 MB LV named ***lvol2***)

   lvcreate -L 200 -n lvol3 /dev/vg01 (200 MB LV named ***lvol3***)

   . . . .

4. Any operation typical for the disk partition is also allowed on the LV. To use an LV to hold a filesystem, the corresponding filesystem must be created and mounted:

   newfs /dev/vg01/rlvol1

   mkdir /mnt_dir1

   mount /dev/vg01/lvol1 /mnt_dir1

HP-UX flavored LVM is discussed in greater detail in the case study in Chapter 27.

6.3.3 Logical Volume Manager — Solaris Flavor

A powerful, versatile, and up-to-date volume manager came with Sun Enterprise Volume Manager — ***VxVM*** on the Solaris 2.x platform. The original VERITAS Volume Manager is licensed to Sun Microsystems and is delivered as either optional or standard software (depending on the system configuration). ***VxVM*** builds virtual devices called *volumes* on top of physical disks in an extraordinarily flexible way. Volumes are composed of other

VM objects that can be manipulated to make different volume configurations: to optimize performance, to provide redundancy, and to perform backup. To achieve this goal, ***VxVM*** introduced some new virtual objects.

VxVM manages the following physical and logical objects:

- *Physical disk* and *partition*, in the standard UNIX sense.
- *VM disk* — assigned to one or more *physical partitions* (or more precisely, to one or more *physical partitions* under VxVM control).
- *Disk group* — a collection of *VM disks* that share a common configuration.
- *Subdisk* — a basic logical unit to allocate disk space; a set of contiguous disk blocks. *VM disks* can be divided into one or more *subdisks* (similar to the division of physical disks into partitions).
- *Plexe* — a new logical entity that consists of one or more *subdisks*, organized in way that can provide concatenation, striping, mirroring, or RAID-5; (*plexes* are also referred to as *mirrors*).
- *Volume* — a logical disk device that appears to the filesystem as a physical partition, but does not have the physical limitations. A *volume* can consist of as many as 32 *plexes*, with one or more *subdisks*; the corresponding special device file identifies the volume. An arbitrary number of *plexes* within a *volume*, and the arbitrary way *plexes* are organized, resulted in different data storages: *volumes* handle single data copies, mirroring, striping, combined, or RAID-5.

The relationship between VxVM objects is presented in Figure 6.7.

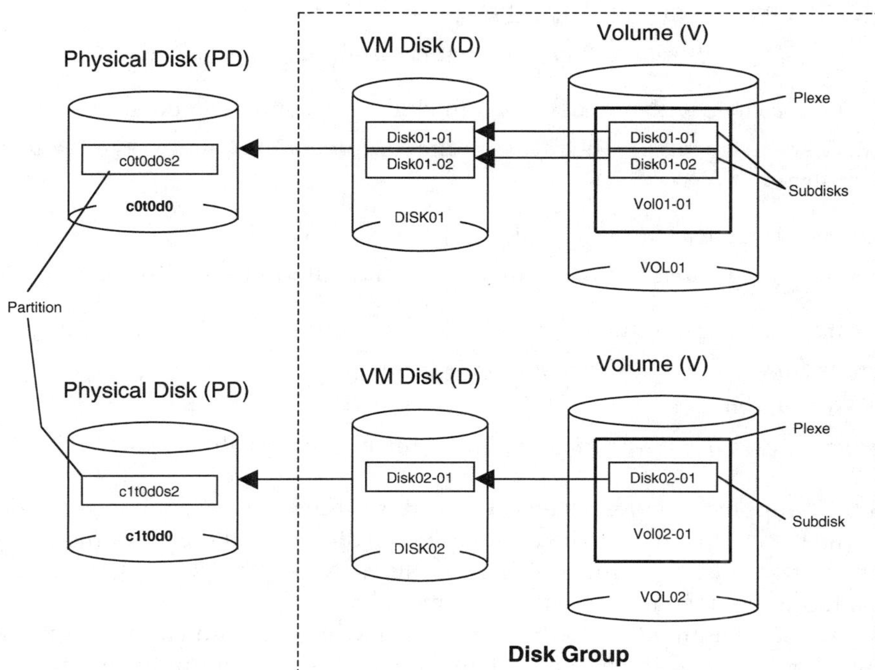

FIGURE 6.7
Relationship between VxVM objects.

Let us try to establish a functional relationship between VxVM objects and the traditional UNIX ones:

VxVM	Standard UNIX Approach
Physical disk	Disk (as an accessible physical unit)
Partition	Disk partition
VM disk	None — assigned partitions
Disk group	Disk (as a storage space)
Subdisk	None — disk blocks
Plexe	None
Volume	Partition

VxVM provides several kinds of user support tools to manage disk space. First, a suite of versatile VM commands is provided to accomplish any VM request. Second, a character-based, user friendly administration tool **vxdiskadm** enables an easy-to-use interface to manage disks. And finally, an attractive GUI visual administrator **vxva** presents a drag-and-drop tool for handling physical and logical entities.

The usual procedure to manage attached physical disks is:

1. Initialize all *physical disks* — put disks under VM control and make corresponding VM disks. For each disk:

   vxdisksetup -i *disk_device_file*

2. Create a *disk group* with the first disk in it:

   vxdg init *dg_name vmdisk_name=disk_device_file*

3. Extend a *disk group* with other disks:

   vxdg -g *dg_name adddisk vmdisk_name=disk_device_file*

4. Create a *volume* within a *disk group* (including a volume layout):

   vxassist -g *dg_name* -U *fsgen* make *volume_name* size layout=*options disk_device_file(s)*

5. Mirror a created *volume* (if requested):

   vxassist -g *dg_name* mirror *volume_name* layout=*options disk_device_file(s)*

6. Create a *filesystem* in the *volume* and mount it into a selected *directory*:

   newfs /dev/vx/rdsk/dg_*name*/*volume_name*

   mkdir /*mount_dir*

   mount /dev/vx/rdsk/dg_*name*/*volume_name* /*mount_dir*

VxVM fully supports all of the steps necessary to accomplish the requested task. At the very end, the filesystems have to be created in the volumes and then mounted to be used.

The same task can be accomplished in more steps by creating *subdisks* and *plexes* separately. This has to be done if there are some special requests.

VxVM pays special attention to the boot disk and the *root* and *swap* partitions. VxVM is coming after UNIX installation, and the initial disk configuration is based on the traditional UNIX approach. Putting blank disks under VM control is much easier than to handle preexisting filesystems, especially crucial ones like the *root* filesystem and the swap partition (also */usr* and */var,* if they were created as separate filesystems). The special procedure to put preexisting filesystems under VM control is known as ***encapsulation,*** and VxVM also fully supports its implementation.

VxVM offers needed commands to deal with introduced entities:

vxdg	Handle disks and disk groups with a number of options (subcommands)
vxassist	Handle disks with a number of options (subcommands)
vxdisksetup	Initialize physical disks
vxmake	Create VM objects
vxplex	Handle plexes
vxsd	Perform subdisk operations
vxprint	Print display VM information
vxtrace	Trace kernel VM related activities
vxrecover	Recover VM entities
vxinfo	Identify volumes
vxstat	Print volume statistics
vxvol	Handle volumes

Some of the listed commands are utilities with many options, or rather subcommands, to fulfill different VM tasks.

Solaris-flavored LVM is also discussed in greater detail in the case study in Chapter 27.

6.3.4 Redundant Array of Inexpensive Disks (RAID)

A *Redundant Array of Inexpensive Disks (RAID)* is a disk array setup, which enables the combined storage units to be used for storing duplicated (mirrored) data. The mirroring allows regeneration of the data in case of disk failures.

There are several levels of RAID:

- ***RAID-0***: Although it does not provide redundancy, *striping* is often referred to as a form of RAID, known as RAID-0. Striping is a technique of mapping data so that the data is interwoven among more physical disks. It offers a high data transfer rate and high I/O throughput, because simultaneous data access across multiple disks can be performed.
- ***RAID-1***: *Mirroring* is a form of RAID known as RAID-1. Mirroring uses equal amounts of disk capacity to store the original data and its mirror. It provides redundancy of data and offers protection against data loss in the event of physical disk failure.
- ***RAID-0+1***: Striping combined with mirroring is known as RAID-0 + 1. It merges RAID-0 and RAID-1, providing redundancy and efficient access to data.
- ***RAID-1+0***: Mirroring combined with striping is known as RAID-1 + 0. It merges RAID-1 and RAID-0, providing better redundancy and equally efficient access to data as RAID-0 + 1. Remember that for this RAID configuration mirroring is provided before striping, so multiple disk failures in different disk groups can still be handled.
- ***RAID-2***: Not widely implemented, RAID-2 uses bitwise striping across disks and uses additional disks to hold Hamming code check bits.
- ***RAID-3***: Uses a parity disk to provide redundancy. RAID-3 stripes data across all but one of the disks in the array, which is then used for the parity bit.

- *RAID-4*: Represents a modified version of RAID-3 to overcome synchronization problems when data is accessed across multiple disks. By increasing the stripe unit size, a majority of I/O operations can be located on a single disk without the need for synchronized simultaneous access to multiple disks. However, it still uses a separate parity disk to store redundant parity information. It is not widely implemented.
- *RAID-5*: Represents an improved version of RAID-4, and it is practically implemented. Instead of using a separate parity disk, the parity data are also striped across all disks; the data stripes and parity stripes could be found on all disks. In case of a disk failure, the lost data can be recovered. RAID-5 provides the performance of RAID-0 + 1, but in a more economical way.

For all the options stated here, RAID-1 + 0 is probably the superior one. This is also the most expensive one, and not supported by older volume managers and disk arrays.

6.3.5 Snapshot

LVM provides a flexible way to store and manage data. But it offers also a solution for the pending problem of the online backups. Each backup must guarantee the full consistency of the data, and a valid data recovery is possible only from the consistently backed-up data. In real life, the contents of volumes are changing permanently as long as the volumes are in use. The existing data is modified or purged, and new data is written nonstop. This is the purpose of the UNIX systems — to provide an enduring execution of application programs that always deal with data. If data is changing during the backup, which always takes a reasonable amount of time, the required data consistency cannot be achieved. At least it cannot be guaranteed. This is a big problem in the case of database backup. Inconsistently backed database files are corrupted and useless.

A solution to this problem was found in taking a data **snapshot** and then making the backup. Original data is mirrored before the start of a backup, and then backed as the "frozen" mirrored data. In the meantime, the access to the original data remains unrestricted. The online backup can then ensue.

The idea of performing a snapshot (a very quick copying) of the dynamic data is similar to the concept of taking a photograph of a moving object. Once the data is snapped, we can then make a time-consuming backup of its mirror — mirrored data is reliably consistent — it does not change. The only requirement is the prevention of any data change during the snapshot, which is easily met thanks to the short snapshot time period. LVM makes this approach feasible. There are two types of snapshots: the *volume* and the *filesystem snapshot*.

6.3.5.1 The Volume Snapshot

The volume snapshot is provided on the volume level, regardless of the upper-level data structures. The procedure is relatively simple: the *snapstart* operation creates a write-only backup in a separate volume, which gets attached to and synchronized with the original, snapped volume. Synchronized means that the original volume is mirrored to the newly attached backup volume. The synchronization takes some time, especially in the case of large volumes. However, in this period all activities on the system are continuing normally, without any restrictions. The end of the synchronization procedure is signified by a change in the snapshot mirror status, known as the *snapdone* state. Once the backup volume is synchronized with the snapped volume, it is ready to be used as a "*snapshot mirror.*"

The synchronized snapshot mirror continues to be updated until it is detached. The detachment can be schedule for any convenient time. The *snapshot volume*, an image of the *snapped volume*, will be created in that moment. The detachment itself represents the snapshot of the volume. The previous synchronization is only an unavoidable process required for a successful snapshot. The snapshot typically takes a very short time, and during this brief period the use of the system should be strictly controlled and any change of the volume content prevented. Once the detachment is done, the content of the created snapshot volume remains unchanged as long as this volume lives.

The main disadvantage of the volume snapshot is that the size of the snapshot volume must be the same or larger than the snapped volume. The same snapshot volume can be used to mirror multiple volumes at different times, but the required long-time synchronization actually restricts its multiple usage. The synchronization itself always takes a great deal of time: each volume block must be updated (mirrored) regardless of whether it was changed or not. Even the unused blocks in the volume are mirrored.

6.3.5.2 The Filesystem Snapshot

The advanced VxFS filesystem (Vx origins from VERITAS) provides a mechanism for taking a snapshot image of a mounted filesystem, which can then be used for a backup. The snapshot filesystem is an exact image of the original snapped filesystem — it is a duplicate read-only copy. The snapshot is a consistent view of the filesystem "snapped" at the point in time when the snapshot was made. Afterward all further data processing is referred to the snapshot filesystem.

The basic idea is the following: Why copy (mirror) all filesystem blocks? The majority of blocks don't change frequently. It is enough to copy only the old content of the blocks that have been changed since the snapshot was activated (started). These old contents are known as *before-images*. And a before-image has to be copied only once when the block was changed for the first time. In that way, a pool of consistent data that corresponds to the moment when the snapshot was started (we prefer to say "was taken") is preserved. It resides partially in the original (snapped) filesystem (all unchanged data blocks) and partially in the snapshot filesystem (all saved before-images). Keeping in mind the limited lifetime of a snapshot filesystem (it exists as long as the backup is going on), the expected number of modified blocks is much smaller than the total number of active blocks in the filesystem. Statistically the value of 10 to 15% seems to be sufficient during the highest level of system activity.

The benefits of the filesystem snapshot are obvious: a required snapshot filesystem (and the belonging volume) is much smaller than the original one, and there is no need for time-consuming volume synchronization. However, the implemented filesystem type has to support the filesystem snapshot. A snapshot filesystem is presented in Figure 6.8.

The snapshot filesystem contains four parts:

1. The ***superblock***, a copied, slightly modified superblock of the regular (snapped) filesystem.
2. The ***bitmap***, which contains one bit for every block of the snapped filesystem; initially, all bitmap entries are zero.
3. The ***blockmap***, which contains one entry for each block of the snapped filesystem; initially all entries are zero. When a before-image is copied from the snapped filesystem, the appropriate entry is set to the block number on the snapshot filesystem; this is the local block allocation table.
4. The ***data blocks***, which contain before-images copied from the snapped filesystem upon their first change.

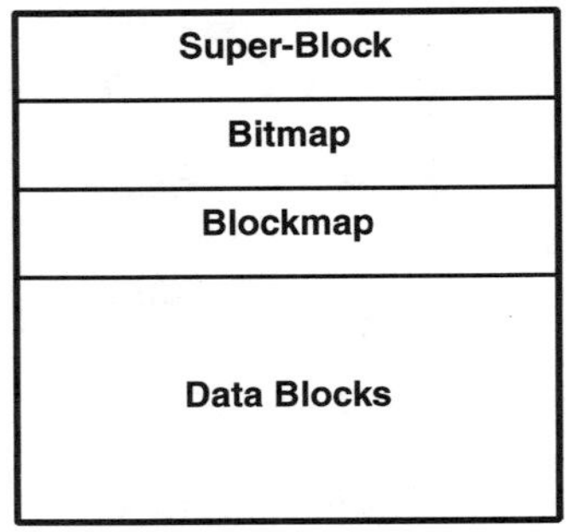

FIGURE 6.8
The snapshot filesystem structure.

The snapshot procedure starts with the mounting of an empty volume and the creation of the snapshot filesystem for the mounted snapped filesystem. As the first step, the *superblock* of the snapped filesystem is copied into the snapshot filesystem. After that, the visibility of the data in the snapped filesystem could be easily maintained through this superblock. All processes now access the snapped filesystem through the snapshot superblock rather than its own. The *bitmap* and *blockmap* are also initialized. The snapshot filesystem handles read requests by simply finding the data on the snapped filesystem and returning it to the requesting process. In the case of an inode update or a write request for any block (for example, block #N) of the snapped filesystem, the before-image of the block #N is first taken (the block is read and copied into the snapshot filesystem) and afterward the snapped filesystem is updated. The bitmap entry for the block #N is changed from its initial value 0 to 1, indicating the taken before-image of the data block #N. The blockmap entry for the block #N is also changed from its initial value 0, to the actual block number in the snapshot filesystem where the before-image was copied.

Any subsequent read request for the block #N in the snapshot filesystem will be provided after checkup of the corresponding bitmap entry, and consequently by reading data locally, from the block indicated by the blockmap entry instead of the snapped filesystem. Subsequent writes to the block #N in the snapped filesystem do not result in additional copies to the snapshot filesystem, since the before-image needs to be saved only once, the first time the block was changed.

To start a filesystem snapshot, the **mount** command is used. It is fair to say this is a modified version of this command compatible with the implemented filesystem type. It is specified by the special option "**snapof=...**" that also includes a snapshot volume. The snapshot filesystem exists as long as it is mounted, and during this period its superblock controls the snapped filesystem too. By dismounting the snapshot filesystem, the snapshot process is terminated.

For example, the following command creates a snapshot filesystem and mounts it into the */snapdir* directory:

mount -F vxfs -o snapof=/dev/volgr/fsvol /dev/volgr/snapvol /snapdir

where

-F vxfs	Defines the VxFS filesystem
-o snapof=/dev/volgr/fsvol	Defines the mounted filesystem to be snapped
/dev/volgr/snapvol	Defines the snapshot filesystem
/snapdir	Defines a mount-point for the snapshot filesystem (other options are also possible)

To terminate a snapshot, simply dismount the snapshot filesystem:

umount /snapdir

In the meantime, regular UNIX commands could be implemented on the snapshot and snapped filesystems without any restrictions. However, never forget the real nature of a snapshot filesystem — sometimes the command outputs could be very odd and confusing. For example, the ***df -k*** command implemented on the snapshot filesystem will show the size of the snapped filesystem. So, do not be confused when the snapshot filesystem is ten times larger than the actual size of the volume in which it was created. Simply, the **df** command sees the snapshot filesystem through the superblock of the snapped filesystem.

6.3.6 Virtual UNIX Filesystem

The diversity of the various UNIX filesystems and their mutual incompatibilities make their simultaneous use almost impossible. UNIX faces a challenge as to how to handle different UNIX filesystems at the same time and enables users to access their files at any time. A logical solution is to make access to files independent of their type. This would allow the users to carry out operations on a file without restrictions. It could be even extended to the not-UNIX filesystems.

Such a flexible filesystem is known as ***virtual filesystem (VFS)***, but full implementation remains in theory only. A needed flexibility is supposed to be achieved on the implementation of the filesystem independent ***vnode***. The underlying mechanism of each ***vnode*** operation is, however, always dependent upon the filesystem type associated with the file being referenced by the ***vnode***. In other words, the system must know very well how to handle the corresponding filesystem type. Thus, to perform an operation on a file, the kernel must provide mechanisms that allow the execution of a filesystem-type-dependent function to carry out an operation without knowing what that function is called or what it does. For users everything remains transparent — they can access any filesystem without knowing anything about its type. Since the kernel is independent of the filesystem type or construction, it is also flexible enough to accommodate nonUNIX filesystems such as NT, OS2, Mac, and DOS.

Despite the fact that it sounds great, the real need for VFS implementations is very questionable. Who really needs multiple UNIX filesystem types on the local drives? It sounds nice to disconnect a huge disk drive from the Solaris box, connect to the Linux box, and immediately have access to all data. But how often do we do something like that? VFS is another layer in the kernel, and another layer means more overheads in communication with the disk. No one wants that either. Cross-management of different-type files on the UNIX platform is already solved in an ordered way. Applications that deal with files on remote systems like: *ftp, rcp, scp,* and *nfs* are already fully implemented and proved. They read, write, and transfer files without any problem. Network-based backup and restore can also handle different types of files. And what is the most important, all UNIX flavors fully support filesystem types implemented on portable media like floppy and CD-ROM disks.

vnode does not have anything common with ***inode*** except that the names sound similar. These are two completely different concepts, with different purposes. ***vnode*** is mostly unknown to UNIX administrators and is not even mentioned in system administration books. There are at least two good reasons for that. The first reason was discussed earlier, while the second one is based on the assumption that VFS will not require any administration — everything should work well automatically. Despite that, VFS is briefly discussed here.

6.4 Disk Space Upgrade

Once a shortage of a disk space becomes evident on the system and all other possibilities have been exhausted, the only real solution is to add a new disk. Today, disks are cheap, and to make such a decision is easy. However, the full price of additional disk space includes other elements besides the disk price itself. In the past additional expenses have been mostly shadowed by the high disk price. Some elements worth consideration are:

- The room available for disks — internal or external
- Hardware compatibility — implemented disk interface. On the UNIX platform, SCSI interface is very common, but remember that single-ended SCSI is not compatible with the differential one, or it could be a wide SCSI, or.... Also, is there a slot available on the existing SCSI controller? And so on.
- The work on the disk installation and putting it into the operation
- Maintenance, including backup and other long-term disk-related jobs

Each of these elements has its specific price. In most cases, this price is higher than the initial price of the disk itself.

Adding a new disk is a very routine task. There is not a lot of freedom in the practical implementation, but it is good to fully understand each of the required steps. Unfortunately, almost every UNIX platform provides a different tool to implement these steps.

We have already discussed some of these steps. This time we will only list them. Steps traditionally required to add a disk, independent of the UNIX platform (even independent of the UNIX itself), may be summarized as:

- ***Disk formatting*** (also known as *low,* or *hard, formatting*) to establish the track layout onto the contiguous magnetic media of the disk plates
- ***Disk partitioning*** to establish one or more independent storage entities within the disk for further processing
- ***Filesystem creation*** (also known as *soft formatting*) to make disk partitions available for data storage.

The LVM requires a few more steps before filesystem creation. UNIX systems require some additional steps at the end to merge newly created filesystems into the overall UNIX tree hierarchical filesystem.

Today, manufacturers of disks also perform the hard formatting of the disks. There are many reasons for this first step to be performed by the manufacturers themselves; the number of tracks varies among the inner and outer disk cylinders, and an appropriate hard formatting requires the sophisticated tools. While we can skip the first step now, the other steps must be provided. Unfortunately, the required procedures vary among UNIX vendors. In Chapter 27, a few case studies about the most popular UNIX flavors are presented. Similar procedures can be implemented on other UNIX platforms.

7

User Account Management

7.1 Users and Groups

Managing user accounts is an important and unavoidable administrative duty. The overall system administration will often be evaluated by the way the user accounts are managed. Users participate in a UNIX system through their accounts: they navigate through their environment, work from their terminals, use their favorite commands, and do their jobs in their way. They want to control their resources and restrict access to them by others; however, they also want to reach all available resources. This is a profile of an average user on an UNIX system.

UNIX systems exist to be used by users; making users happy is one of the primary administrative tasks, because happy users make for a happy administrator. The advice is very simple: manage user accounts properly, be tough when necessary and flexible at other times, and pay special attention to security issues, or you could experience a lot of headache later.

From the system's standpoint, a user is not necessarily an individual. A user is any entity capable of executing programs or own files. The UNIX concepts of ownership and access privileges involve a number of system entities. These entities may be other computer systems, they may be particular system functions that run automatically, or they may be a group of people with similar functions. In most cases, however, a user is a particular individual who can log-in, edit files, run programs, and otherwise make use of the system.

Each user has a ***username*** (also known as a ***loginname***) that uniquely identifies the user. A system recognizes a user by the user's identification number (**UID**), which is assigned by the system administrator at the time the user's account is created. The administrator also assigns each new user to at least one group (a group is a collection of users who generally share similar functions). Each group has a group identification number (**GID**), which serves the same purpose as the **UID** on the user level. Together, the user's **UID** and **GID** determine the user's credentials, i.e., the access rights a user has to files and other system resources.

Basic user account information is stored in the */etc/passwd* file — this is the master user's database for all users on the system. The */etc/passwd* file is an ASCII text file, readable by everyone on the system; this general file readability is required for regular system operations. Each user is described by a single entry in the file; each entry is a single line of information. Similarly, information about groups are stored in the file */etc/group*. These two files contain comprehensive information about any user in the system, regardless of the user's origin. Both files are public information; everyone may read them, but only the superuser is allowed to modify them.

7.1.1 Creation of User Accounts

You must create a new user account to add a new user to the system. User account creation is a routine procedure that consists of several mutually related steps; most of these steps are mandatory, but a few are optional. The required procedure consists of:

- Assigning a username, a user ID number, and a primary group to the user
- Entering this data in the system user database (the */etc/passwd* file) and, if required, in any secondary password file
- Assigning a password to the new account
- Setting other user account parameters in use on the system, such as password aging, account expiration date, and other resource limits
- Creating a home directory for the user
- Placing initialization files in the home directory
- Setting the new user ownership to the home directory and initialization files
- Adding the user to any other facilities in use such as the disk quotas system
- Defining any secondary group membership for the user in the system group file, */etc/group*
- Performing any other site-specific initialization tasks
- Testing the new account

Basically, adding a new user means adding a new entry into the */etc/passwd* file. This may be done by simply editing the file using any editor (on the UNIX platform the common editor is ***vi***), or on BSD systems using the special editing command ***vipw*** (**vi** **p**ass**w**ord file). However, all UNIX systems provide some kind of utility for this purpose, a specific front-end command (sometimes a script, but usually a program) that performs efficient, accurate creations of new user accounts. On many UNIX systems, user account management is also a standard part of the existing general system administration tools (such as SAM on HP-UX platform, or SMIT on AIX platform). All of these tools/utilities create new user accounts by automatically performing the previously listed steps; of course, the administrator must supply the required personal data for the user. These utilities check the supplied data and update the system user and group databases.

Preexisting tools provide a general approach to user account creation; however, any site-specific requirements will call for additional administration. Quite often, system administrators make their own private utilities to perform site-specific functions in managing user accounts. Usually these are homemade scripts (shell, expect, perl, etc.).

Even though the use of existing utilities is highly recommended, the following text has a more basic approach. For educational purposes, the next section of the text goes through the gradual creation of a user account, step by step from the command line. First, though, let us see what the system user and group databases look like.

7.1.2 User Database — File */etc/passwd*

The master user configuration file is */etc/passwd*; every user on the system must be specified in this file. A user is identified by an entry of the following form:

name:encrypted-passwd:UID:GID:user information:home-directory:shell

The entry is a single line with multiple fields separated by colons; blank spaces are legal only in the ***user information*** field. The meanings of the fields are:

Field	Meaning
name	The username assigned to the user. Usernames are not private or secure information; they should be easy to remember; older UNIX flavors restricted the name length to a maximum of eight characters, and it is advisable to keep them within that length.
encrypted-passwd	The user's encrypted password (readable encrypted text). An empty field means no password is required to log in to the system (which is not legal and represents a security hole); an asterisk (:*:) in the field prevents anyone from logging into the system; the field cannot be edited, a password can be assigned only by using the ***passwd*** command.
UID	The user identification number. Each user must have a unique UID; it is good idea to assign UIDs sequentially starting from 100; UIDs less than 100 are conventionally used for system accounts.
GID	Determines the user's primary group membership. GID corresponds to a group identification number assigned to a group in the file */etc/group*; GIDs less than 10 are conventionally used for system groups.
user information	Usually contains the user's full name; the e-mail subsystem and commands like ***finger*** use this information; a space is a legal character in the field; other identification data, such as the address or phone number, are also common.
home-directory	The user's home directory; when a user logs into the system, this will be the initial working directory.
shell	The program that UNIX will use as a command interpreter for the user; whenever the user logs in, UNIX will automatically execute this program. The common shells are */bin/sh* (Bourne shell), */bin/csh* (C shell) or */bin/ksh* (Korn shell) – shells can be located in other directories, like */usr/bin*, or */sbin*; other shells are also legal; if the field is empty the default is the Bourne shell. Other programs can also be specified instead of a shell; often an application is automatically started once the user logs in; for example, for the user ***uucp*** the uucp program */usr/lib/uucp/uucic* is specified; another example is a "restricted user account" when a restricted shell is started.

There are no significant differences between the */etc/passwd* files on the main UNIX platforms BSD and System V. As examples, two */etc/passwd* files are presented for the SunOS and HP-UX flavors, respectively. As can be seen, their format and syntax are identical.

 # cat /etc/passwd

```
root:RolQOmj217Vrc:0:1:Operator:/:/bin/sh
daemon:*:1:1::/:
sys:*:2:2::/:/bin/csh
bin:*:3:3::/bin:
          .....
          .....
nmruser:HfeLluXTpXxnI:1200:20:NMR User:/home/nmruser:/bin/csh
fstall:1vLPSqJDArJOs:1203:20::/usr/people/fstall:/bin/csh
bjl:KVrJDBQT8fHOY:1212:20:B.J.L.:/usr/people/bjl:/bin/csh
```

$ cat /etc/passwd

```
root:PykAP9Za4p0NA:0:3::/:/bin/sh
daemon:*:1:5::/:/bin/sh
bin:*:2:2::/bin:/bin/sh
          .....
          .....
bjl:3Zd496cM81jD6:201:20:B. J. L.,Rm. 1225N,(212) 123-4567,:/users/bjl:/bin/ksh
vasili:wUjuhw6avV2P.:202:20:V. F.,Fordham University,,:/users/vasili:/bin/ksh
dhuang:d5DtupN0TE.ak:204:20:D. Huang,Wayne State University,,:/users/huang:/bin/ksh
gdubey:btRPE2WDC/S5.:206:20:G. D.,Rm. 1246N,(212) 123-7654,:/users/gdubey:/bin/ksh
```

The first part of the */etc/passwd* file specifies system entities (please note the asterisk in the password field), while the second part contains individual user login accounts. As it can be seen, encrypted passwords are readable but their contents are senseless; however, from the system security standpoint, the fact that the encrypted passwords could be read is a security risk. We will return to this issue later.

7.1.3 Group Database — File */etc/group*

The master group specification file is the file */etc/group*. The file specifies all existing groups on the system. To add a new group, you add a new one-line entry to the file. Each group on the system is specified by a single entry of the form:

group-name:*:GID:additional-users

The */etc/group* entries are similar to the */etc/passwd* entries. An entry consists of multiple fields separated by a colon (":"). The fields have following meaning:

Field	Meaning
group-name	A name identifying the group.
*	The second field is an artifact of earlier UNIX versions. It is unused and is usually filled with an asterisk.
GID	The group's identification number. By convention, standard UNIX groups have consecutive numbers beginning with 0.
additional-users	A list of users and other groups that will have access to this group's files (as a secondary group). Commas must separate users' names in the list.

An example of the */etc/group* file is presented here:

```
# cat /etc/group
root:*:0:
nogroup:*:65534:
daemon:*:1:
kmem:*:2:
    . . . . .
staff:*:10:
other:*:20:
patsyusers:*:30:
mvaxuser:*:60:root,pam,tbw,eda,shew,sweeny,varley,mindy,levi,he,\
\quigley,modest,sim,ralph,yin,baldwin,george
```

7.1.4 Creating User Home Directories

Upon adding a user entry to the */etc/passwd* file, the system administrator must create an appropriate home directory for the user. User directories are usually located in a separate filesystem, dedicated to users. Most common names for directories holding users' filesystems are: */home*, */users*, or */u*.

User home directories are named by the usernames (however, this is not a requirement). A user directory is a regular directory owned by the user, so to create a user home directory, as with any other directory, the **mkdir** command is used:

mkdir /*home*/*username*

where

home	A common starting directory for individual users' home subdirectories
username	The user's name, usually the same as the name of the user account

Even when the home directory has been created, our job is not yet complete. The directory itself has to be populated with required user-specific data, primarily related and needed for a proper user login procedure. The next paragraphs address this topic.

7.1.5 UNIX Login Initialization

Upon the creation of the user home directory, the next step is to provide the appropriate initialization data to set the user shell environment. Otherwise the whole login procedure could be compromised, and the user unable to deal with the UNIX system at all. UNIX initialization files (or better say scripts, because they are really shell scripts) define the initial individual environment for a successful start of the specified shell once the user has logged in. They are also known as *user startup files*. The login procedures follow different patterns depending on the specified user's shell in the */etc/passwd* file. Assuming the common UNIX shells, (Bourne, C, and Korn) when a user logs in to the system, the following UNIX initialization files will be executed (actually, the listed files will be sourced) after successful authentication:

User's Shell	**Sequence of Sourced Initialization Files**		
Bourne shell	*/etc/profile*	*$HOME/.profile*	
C shell	*/etc/.login*	*~ /.cshrc*	*~ /.login*
Korn shell	*/etc/profile*	*$HOME/.profile*	*$HOME/.kshrc*

Bourne Again Shell — **bash** is a default shell on the Linux platform. Basically, **bash** and **ksh** are very similar, almost identical in their implementation. So the discussion that follows related to ***ksh*** is also relevant to **bash**. However, differences in naming of initialization files exist, but the files themselves are easily recognizable. For example, a sequence of **bash** initialization files is: */etc/bash_profile*, *$HOME/.bash_profile*, and *$HOME/.bashrc*.

Please note that among the listed UNIX initialization files, some are strictly login initialization files, while others are shell initialization files. Also, the order of their execution (sourcing) varies for different shells. Most of the files are hidden files (with a leading dot in the filename), and they can be seen only if the **ls -a** command is used. The listed filenames are the common names, and some differences among UNIX flavors are possible. The three listed shells are not the only possible shells; these are only the most common shells, and they are discussed in this section. The syntax implemented to identify the user home directory corresponds to the actual shell.

The first login initialization file to be executed lives in the */etc* directory and represents a systemwide login initialization file; it is used to set a default environment for all users on the system. Only the administrator can manage these files. Other, individual (personal) initialization files reside in the user's home directory. The initialization files are shell scripts and they are sourced in the standard input stream of the specified login shell. The login initialization files *.profile* and *.login* are executed at the user's login; the shell initialization files *.cshrc* and *.kshrc* are executed every time a new shell is spawned. The files are owned by the users and may be customized by the users themselves.

7.1.5.1 Initialization Template Files

The administrator's duty is not only to manage the systemwide initialization files; the administrator must also create template initialization files for the required default personal initialization and store them in a standard location, the *skeleton* directory. Usually this is the directory */usr/skel*, or */etc/skel*, although the directories can vary among the different UNIX flavors. On most systems these "proto-files" already exist upon UNIX installation and are ready for immediate use; often only small site-specific modifications will be required. The common names for template files do not include a leading period, i.e., the names are *profile*, *login*, and *cshrc* (again, these names are not mandatory, so a number of other names are legal and used).

Therefore, to create a user's initialization files, it is sufficient to copy them from the skeleton directory into the user home directory:

$ cp /usr/skel/profile /home/username/.profile
$ cp /usr/skel/login /home/username/.login
$ cp /usr/skel/cshrc /home/username/.cshrc

Copying multiple initialization files for new accounts is recommended because it enables the use of different shells; however, if a user is restricted to using one shell exclusively, only the corresponding file/files should be copied.

To illustrate the differences between template filenames and their locations among the various UNIX platforms, a few UNIX flavors are presented:

- HP-UX 10.xx *|etc/skel/.profile*
  /etc/skel/.login
  /etc/skel/.cshrc
- HP-UX 9.0x */etc/d.profile*
  /etc/d.login
  /etc/d.cshrc
- Solaris 2.x */etc/skel/local.profile*
  /etc/skel/local.login
  /etc/skel/local.cshrc
- Linux Red Hat */etc/skel/.bash_profile* (Linux assumes a user shell: **bash**)

Depending on how the system is used, several other initialization files may also be of interest. For example, many editors have their own startup files (such as *.exrc* for the ***vi*** editor), the e-mail agent has an initialization file named *.mailrc*, the X window client utilizes several files for personal customization (*.Xdeafults*, *.dtprofile*, even the complete startup subdirectory *$HOME/.dt* exists), and other third-party software often relies on similar hidden initialization files. The C shell also supports a *.logout* file, which contains commands to be executed when the user logs out. The file is an ideal place to look if an ordered shutdown of any application is required. Under certain circumstances, all these files should also be copied when a new user account is created.

7.1.5.2 User Login Initialization Files

The user login initialization files *.login* and *.profile* perform tasks that need to be executed upon login, such as:

- Setting the search path
- Setting the default file protection (the **umask** command)

- Setting the terminal type and initializing the terminal
- Setting other environment variables
- Performing other site-specific customization functions

Login initialization files are not UNIX-platform dependent — they are shell dependent. The best way to understand the files is by analyzing several real examples. We will start with the C shell login initialization file *.login.* The content of one real user login file *.login* on the HP-UX platform is (additional comments are printed in **bold**):

 # cat /home/bjl/.login (The file lives in the user's home directory)

```
# @(#) $Revision: 64.2 $
#
# Default user .login file (/bin/csh initialization)
# Set up the default search paths:
setenv path=(/bin/usr/bin/usr/contrib/bin/usr/local/bin.)
#set up the terminal               Setting a user terminal as a "HP terminal"
eval `tset -s -Q -m ':?hp'`        (actually the user makes the decision about the terminal)
stty erase "^H" kill "^U" intr "^C" eof "^D" susp "^Z" hupcl ixon ixoff tostop
tabs
# Set up shell environment:
set noclobber                      Prevent file overwriting
set history=20                     Peep the track about 20 last commands
```

Once the user has logged in, the search command path, user terminal, and a few other environment variables are defined. Terminal initialization is an important login function; an improperly defined terminal can completely disable user interaction with the system.

Please note that the C shell login initialization file is executed after the C shell is spawned, i.e., the C shell initialization file *.cshrc* has been already executed. However, while the *.cshrc* file can be executed many more times within the same login session, the *.login* file is executed only once. This fact can be important in setting the environment (only global variables will be inherited by the newly spawned shells).

The contents of a real Korn/Bourne shell login initialization file *.profile* (again on HP-UX) follow:

$ cat /users/bjl/.profile

```
# @(#) $Revision: 66.1 $                       The systemwide profile script file has been
                                               previously executed!
#
# Default user .profile file (/bin/sh initialization).
# Set up the terminal:                         Setting a terminal
   eval `tset -s -Q -m ':?hp'`
   stty erase "^H" kill "^U" intr "^C" eof "^D"
   stty hupcl ixon ixoff
   tabs
# Set up the search paths:
   PATH=$PATH:.                                The current directory is also included
   export PATH
# Set up the shell environment:
   set -u                                      All unset variables are treated as errors
# Set up the shell variables:
   EDITOR=vi
   export EDITOR
```

We have called the file *.profile* a Korn/Bourne shell login initialization file. This is true since the script syntax matches the Bourne shell; the Bourne shell is a subset of the Korn shell, and any Bourne shell script can also be executed by the Korn shell. However, the Bourne shell cannot interpret a Korn shell-specific command, and the script execution would fail. This means that if the *.profile* file has been written as a Bourne shell script it will work for both shells; otherwise it will fail for the Bourne shell. A potential confusing point can be the way the global environment variables are exported; the Korn shell allows you to define and export a variable in a single command line, while the Bourne shell requires two command lines: one to define a variable and the other to export the defined variable. Obviously, to avoid any possible confusion, strict implementation of Bourne scripts is recommended.

In the case of the Korn shell, after the execution of the *.profile* file another K shell initialization file (usually named as *.kshrc*) can be also executed; this is a good place to locate all Korn shell-specific items, and to make the *.profile* file acceptable for both shells.

7.1.5.3 Systemwide Login Initialization Files

The systemwide login initialization files are executed before the user's personal initialization files, and they are ideal places to set the default systemwide environment for each individual user. Even though the user login and shell initialization files can later be used to modify the user environment, the execution of the systemwide files cannot be bypassed. This file sets a number of variables, such as the search path PATH, timezone TZ, e-mail file locations, and/or default file permissions; usually it also generates important messages related to all users, among others the *message of the day* — **motd**.

For Bourne and Korn shell users, the systemwide initialization file is */etc/profile*; pay attention to the file name, it is not a hidden file. An example follows (from the HP-UX platform):

```
$ cat /etc/profile
# @(#) $Revision: 70.1 $
# Default (example of) system-wide profile file (/bin/sh initialization).
# This should be kept to the bare minimum every user needs.
trap "" 1 2 3                                          # ignore HUP, INT, QUIT now.
PATH=/bin/posix:/bin:/usr/bin:/usr/contrib/bin:/usr/local/bin   # default path
MANPATH=/usr/man:/usr/contrib/man:/usr/local/man       # default path
    if [ -r /etc/src.sh ]
    then
      . /etc/src.sh                                    # set the time zone
      unset SYSTEM_NAME
    else
      TZ=MST7MDT                                       # change this for local time
      export TZ
    fi
    if [ "$TERM" = "" ]                                # if term is not set, set the
                                                       default terminal; to bemodified
                                                       later by the user
    then
      TERM=hp                                          # the default terminal type
    fi
    export PATH MANPATH TERM
# set erase to ^H
      stty erase "^H"                                  # to erase use "backspace"
# Set up the shell environment:
      trap "echo 'logout'" 0                           # on exit from the shell print
                                                       "logout"
```

```
# This is to meet legal requirements...
    cat /etc/copyright                                  # print license agreement
    if [ -r /etc/motd ]
    then
      cat /etc/motd                                     # the message of the day
    fi
    if [ -f /bin/mail ]
    then
      if mail -e                                        # notify if mail
      then
          echo "You have mail."
      fi
    fi
    if [ -f /usr/bin/news ]
    then
      news -n                                           # notify if new news
    fi
    if [-r /tmp/changetape ]                            # might wish to delete this
    then
      echo "\007\nYou are the first to log in since backup:"
      echo "Please change the backup tape.\n"
      rm -f /tmp/changetape
    fi
    trap 1 2 3                                          # leave defaults in user environment
```

The */etc/profile* file can only be managed by the administrator; users can only modify their own environment, with no impact on the other users.

For C shell users, the usual systemwide initialization file is */etc/.login*; however, on some platforms this name can be different. For example, on the HP-UX platform the systemwide initialization file is */etc/csh.login*. A real example follows:

```
$ cat /etc/csh.login
# @(#) $Revision: 74.1 $
# Default (example of) system-wide profile file (/usr/bin/csh initialization).
# This should be kept to the bare minimum every user needs.
# default path for all users.
set path=(/usr/bin /usr/ccs/bin /usr/contrib/bin)
        . . . . .
        . . . . .
set prompt="[\!] %"
# default MANPATH
setenv MANPATH /usr/share/man:/usr/contrib/man:/usr/local/man
if ( -r /etc/TIMEZONE ) then
    setenv TZ `/usr/bin/sh -c '. /etc/TIMEZONE ; echo $TZ'`     # set the TZ variable
else
    setenv TZ MST7MDT                                          # change this for local time
endif
if ( ! $?TERM ) then                                           # if TERM is not set, use the
                                                               default
    setenv TERM hp
endif
# This is to meet legal requirements...
cat /etc/copyright                                             # copyright message
# Miscellaneous shell-only actions:
if ( -f /etc/motd ) then
    cat /etc/motd                                              # message of the day
endif
if ( -f /usr/bin/mail ) then
    mail -e                                                    # notify if mail
```

```
        if ( $status == 0 ) echo "You have mail."
    endif
        if ( -f /usr/bin/news ) then
        news -n                                          # notify if new news
    endif
    if ( -r /tmp/changetape ) then                       # you might wish to delete this
        echo
        echo "You are the first to log in since backup:"
        echo "Please change the backup tape.\n"
        rm -f /tmp/changetape
    endif
```

Obviously, the presented C shell login initialization file very closely resembles the Korn/Bourne shell login initialization file */etc/profile*. This is logical, considering the two files provide the same function on the same UNIX platform for two different users' shells.

7.1.5.4 Shell Initialization Files

The C shell has introduced a special shell initialization file to set the same environment whenever a new C shell is started; a logical name for the file was selected: *.cshrc*. Following this example, other shells, including the Korn shell, have adopted a similar approach. Whenever a new shell is invoked, the shell initialization file is sourced, including the first time when a user logs into the system. Since a shell initialization file is always executed when a new shell is spawned, the local variables defined in the file behave like the global ones. However, appending new entries to an existing variable (for example, adding a new directory to the command search path) can result in an undesired multiplication of the same entry in the variable. Although this does not create a problem, such a situation should be avoided.

For the C shell, since the shell is started before the actual execution of the user *.login* file, the file *.cshrc* is executed before the *.login* file. The Korn shell follows POSIX standards and optionally executes the *.kshrc* file after the user *.profile* file; even the filename *.kshrc* is optional and can be defined arbitrarily (we will return to this later).

A new shell is always started whenever the user logs in to the system. However, an arbitrary new shell can be started at any time from the current shell from the command line, or whenever a user executes any UNIX command not built into the shell or invokes a shell script or another executable program. The primary tasks of a shell initialization file are:

- To set shell variables
- To set a prompt
- To define command aliases (alternate names for commands)

An example of a user's C shell initialization file follows (from Solaris 2.x):

```
# cat /home/bjl/.cshrc
#
# Default user .cshrc file (/bin/csh initialization).
# Usage: Copy this file to a user's home directory and edit it to
# customize it to taste. It is run by csh each time it starts up.
#
# Set up default command search path:
# (For security, this default is a minimal set.)
#    set path=( /bin /usr/bin )
```

```
# Set up C shell environment:
if ( $?prompt ) then                # shell is interactive
    set history=20                  # previous commands to remember
    set savehist=20                 # number to save across sessions
    set system=`hostname`           # name of this system
    set prompt = "$system \!:"      # command prompt
    # Sample alias:
    alias   h   history
    # More sample aliases, commented out by default:
    # alias     dir     ls
    # alias     m       more
        .....
        .....
endif
.....
.....
```

The presented *.cshrc* file defines additional environment variables, a system prompt, and command aliases and redefines the search path. There is no need to export the defined variables (the *setenv* vs. the *set* shell command); the file is executed whenever the C shell is invoked.

The Korn shell supports an optional shell initialization file, usually named *.kshrc*. This file must be defined within the user *.profile* file (although the */etc/profile* file can be also used). This is done implicitly by the variable ENV; if the variable is set to an existing readable script file (there is no need for it to be executable), the script file will be sourced whenever a new Korn shell is invoked. A possible required *.profile* sequence to set an optional Korn shell initialization file is:

```
    .....
shell = `basename $SHELL`
if [ "$shell" = "ksh" ]
then
    ENV = $HOME/.kshrc
fi
    .....
```

Obviously the ENV variable could be set to some other value, or even not set at all (then the Korn shell would behave like the Bourne shell). However, it is strongly recommended that you use the usual and expected filename *.kshrc*. Also, it is a good idea to put the previous command sequence into the systemwide login initialization file */etc/profile*, to avoid possible modification by the user.

An example of the *.kshrc* file follows (from Solaris 2.x):

```
$ cat /home/bjl/.kshrc
# @(#)kshrc
#################################################################
#
#   File: kshrc                 Version: 1.1.0
#
#   Description:                sourced by each new ksh, via ENV
#   Default location:           /etc/skell
#
#################################################################
#
```

```
# Set default file permission mode
umask 022
USER=`whoami`
OS=`uname -s`
# Set/extend the command search path
TST=`expr $PATH : ".*/usr/ucb"`
if [ "$TST" = 0 ] ; then
     PATH=$PATH:/usr/ucb
fi
unset TST
MAIL=/usr/mail/$USER
#
###============================================###

# Set prompt to user preference        # This part sets the user prompt according to the user's
                                       prompt initialization file ".prompt"
if [ -z "$PROMPTCODE" ] ; then
   if [ -r $HOME/.prompt ] ; then
      PROMPTCODE="`cat $HOME/.prompt`"
   else
      PROMPTCODE = 1
      fi
      export PROMPTCODE
fi
if [ "$USER" = "root" ] ; then
   SHELLCHR='#'
else
   SHELLCHR='$'
fi
case $PROMPTCODE in
   '0')
        PS1="$SHELLCHR"
        ;;
   '2')
        PS1="{`pwd`:!} "
        ;;
   '3')
        PS1="`whoami` $SHELLCHR"
        ;;
   '4')
        PS1="`hostname` $SHELLCHR"
        ;;
   '5')
        PS1="C:`pwd`>"
        ;;
   '6')
        PS1=${USER}@`hostname`:'${PWD}'">"
        ;;
   *)
        PS1="{$USER@`hostname`:!}"
        ;;
esac
###============================================###

#
# Remove old .history files
if [ ! -d $HOME/.history ] ; then
mkdir $HOME/.history
fi
find $HOME/.history -mtime +2-exec rm -f {} \; > /dev/null 2>&1
#
```

```
# Save history in a different file for each window
HISTFILE=$HOME/.history/sh. $$
#
# Set aliases
alias ls='ls -F'
```

The *.kshrc* file sets the individual environment for a logged-in user. Among other variables, this program sets the user's command prompt in an extremely flexible way; a user can select from seven different prompt options by setting the prompt initialization file *$HOME/.prompt*. The prompt initialization file is not so common; it is more common to set the user's prompt directly within the usual user's initialization files. However, this example illustrates the high degree of flexibility provided by UNIX to initialize the user's environment.

7.1.5.5 Setting the Proper Ownership

Finally, once the appropriate initialization files are copied to the user's home directory, the appropriate ownership for the home directory and copied files must be set for the new user, or the user's login attempt could fail. Do not forget, an administrator who possesses the superuser credentials creates a user account. This is much more than an average user would ever be able to do.

The available UNIX commands to change the directory and file ownership should be applied for this purpose. Originally, the BSD platform allows the recursive implementation of the **chown** command with a simultaneous change of the user and group ownership:

$ chown -R ***username.groupname /home/username***

Modern UNIX flavors, independently of their prevailing platform characteristics, allow a simultaneous recursive change of the user and group ownership, with the colon (:) as a separating character (e.g., Solaris 2.x, or HP-UX 10.20, or Linux):

$ chown -R ***username:groupname /home/username***

Otherwise it can be done in two steps:

$ chown -R ***username /home/username***
$ chgrp -R ***groupname /home/username***

Another possibility is to implement the **find** command (with the corresponding **-exec** option):

$ find ***/home/username*** **-exec chown** *username* {}\; **-exec chgrp** *groupname* {}\;

7.1.6 Utilities to Create User Accounts

The complete procedure to create a new user's account has been elaborated; obviously, a great deal of work is required, so it is easy to miss something. It is also obvious that the creation procedure is strictly defined and is an ideal candidate for automation. This automation has been done since the early days of UNIX.

Among the many UNIX flavors, there are (or rather, there *were*) a number of utilities (commands) for this purpose. For example, old fashioned System V flavors provided the

passmgmt command (with the needed options) to manage password files; ULTRIX provided **adduser** (as well as the **removeuser** and **addgroup** utilities); SunOS 4.1.x provides the script utility ***add_user*** (we will return to this script); AIX provides the **mkuser** command; and there are many more. The existing general UNIX administration tools, like ***SAM*** on the HP-UX platform or ***SMIT*** on the AIX platform, always include a user account management section.

Today **useradd** is the prevailing utility to administer new user accounts among existing UNIX flavors (Solaris, HP-UX, Linux, etc.); a number of options and instructions for using the utility are described in the existing manual pages. In the sense that it has options (and is described in the manual pages), this program behaves as any other UNIX command. The **useradd** utility was introduced a long time ago, with SVR4, and became a standard UNIX tool.

A list of the **useradd** options can be seen in this example from Red Hat Linux:

```
$ useradd -?
useradd: invalid option -- ?
usage:  useradd [-u uid [-o]] [-g group] [-G group,...]
                [-d home] [-s shell] [-c comment] [-m [-k template]]
                [-f inactive] [-e expire mm/dd/yy] [-p passwd] [-n] [-r] name
        useradd -D [-g group] [-b base] [-s shell] [-f inactive] [-e expire mm/dd/yy]
```

name corresponds to the user's login name, and the listed options are:

Option	Description
-D	Display default values
-u uid	Specifies the UID; **-o** option allows duplicated values
-g *group*	Specifies an existing group name or GID for the primary group
-G *group,...*	Specifies secondary groups by the group name or GID
-d *home*	Specifies the home directory
-s *shell*	Specifies the user's shell
-c *comments*	Specifies information about the user
-m	Creates a new home directory if one does not exist
-k *template*	Specifies a skeleton directory with template initialization files
-f *inactive*	Specifies a number of days for an account to be inactive
-e *mm/dd/yy*	Specifies an expiration date for an account
-p *passwd*	Specifies a password
-n	Creates a group with the same name as the user (Linux specific)
-r	Specifies a system account (Linux specific)
-b *base*	Specifies the default base home directory

Note: All listed options are not available for all UNIX flavors; password-related options, in particular, are often excluded from this utility.

The use of the **useradd** utility is well documented, self-explanatory, and easy; obviously, system administrators are encouraged to use this tool.

Unfortunately, we can only guess at what is going on behind the scenes of the execution of such a utility. The utility **useradd** is a compiled executable program, designed for a specific purpose and was never intended to be an educational example in the user account management. To get an idea of what the utility is exactly doing and how it is doing it at all, we will return to the SunOS 4.1.x platform that has provided a corresponding script program: ***user_add***. UNIX administration and script programming are complementary — as soon as we reach a script program related to an administrative issue, we have a greater chance to understand the issue itself.

The script utility ***add_user*** assumes six arguments (all arguments are self-explanatory): *username, UID, GID, "full user's name," homedirectory,* and *usershell*.

The script itself is presented in part; although the script was originally well commented, more comments (printed in **bold**) have been added for further clarity.

 # cat /usr/etc/install/add_user

```
#!/ bin/sh
# @(#)add_user 1.9 SMI
#
# add user script for use with sys-config
# arguments: uname uid gid fullname homedir shell
#
=======  This part includes general script issues  =======
                    and defines specific functions and some variables
myname=`basename $0`      #Extract the portion "add_user" from the full script
                          #name /usr/etc/add_user (the argument $0 is the
                          #script itself)
=======================================================================
# check for root                          #Only superuser is eligible to add a new
                                          user
if [ "`whoami`x" != "root"x ]; then
   echo "You must be root to do $myname!"
   exit 1
fi
# check for number of args                #The script must be invoked with six
                                          defined #arguments
if [ $# -ne 6 ]; then
   echo "${myname}: invalid number of arguments"
   echo " usage: ${myname} uname uid gid\"fullname\"homedir shell"
   exit 1
fi
# put args into named variables
uname=$1
uid=$2
gid=$3
fullname=$4
homedir=$5
shell=$6
# checks for validity of arguments
# check uid                               #First 10 uids and gids are reserved for
                                          #system entities
if test $uid -lt 10 ; then
   echo "uid: uid must be greater than 10 and less than 60000"
   exit 1
elif test $uid -gt 60000 ; then
   echo "uid: uid must be greater than 10 and less than 60000"
   exit 1
fi
# check gid
      . . . . .
      . . . . .
# check shell                             #shell must exist
if test ! -x $shell ; then
   echo "$shell: the program does not exist or is not executable"
   exit 1
fi
# check homedir                           #check for an existing home directory
```

```
# check if homedir already exists
if [ -f ${homedir} ]; then
   echo "${myname}: WARNING: a file named \"${homedir}\" already exists"
   echo "and is NOT a directory, NOT setting up user account"
   exit 1
fi
if [ -d ${homedir} ]; then
   echo "${myname}: WARNING: home directory \"${homedir}\" already exists"
   echo " no files copied, NOT setting up user account"
   exit 1
fi
# check if all but last path of homedir exits
dir=`shdirname $homedir`                          #Extract the home directory name
if test ! -d $dir ; then
   echo "$dir: does not exist or is not a directory"
   exit 1
fi
# check if $homedir is local                      #Extract a local filesystem name
                                                  (a special device file) from the output of
                                                  the df command
dfout=`df $dir | ( read aline; read aline; echo $aline)`
case $dfout in
     /dev*) ;;                                    # $dir is on local machine
     *)      echo "$dir: is not on local machine"
             exit 1;;
esac
# create a null /etc/passwd entry
# first check if one already exists               #Checking for username
if grep -s "^${uname}:" ${Passwd} ; then
   echo "${myname}: ERROR: ${uname} aleady in ${Passwd}";
   exit 1;
fi
# check if uid already exists                     #Checking for UID
if grep -s ".*:.*:${uid}:" ${Passwd} ; then
   echo "uid: ERROR: ${uid} already in ${Passwd}";
   exit 1;
fi
=>  Everything is OK!
=>  Create an entry with no password for the /etc/passwd file
=>  Emulate editor command sequence: "insert text, write to file, quit"
pwent="${uname}:: ${uid}:${gid}:${fullname}:${homedir}:${shell}"
# XXX should we use tmp file and rename it?
( echo '$' ;
  echo 'i' ;
  echo "${pwent}" ;
  echo '.' ;
  echo 'w' ;
  echo 'q' ) | ed -s ${Passwd} > /dev/null
#Check is the entry written into the /etc/passwd file
if grep -s "^${uname}:" ${Passwd} ; then
        :
else
   echo "${myname}: ERROR: password entry didn't go to ${Passwd}";
   exit 1;
fi
# make the home directory
/bin/mkdir ${homedir}
/usr/etc/chown ${uname} ${homedir}                #change user and group ownership
/bin/chgrp ${gid} ${homedir}
# add default user startup files                  #copy initialization files ...
cp /usr/lib/Cshrc ${homedir}/.cshrc
```

```
cp /usr/lib/Login ${homedir}/.login
cp /usr/lib/.sunview ${homedir}/.sunview
cp /usr/lib/.rootmenu ${homedir}/.rootmenu
/usr/etc/chown -R ${uname} ${homedir}          #change user and group ownership
/bin/chgrp -R ${gid} ${homedir}
# if ok, exit 0
exit 0
```

7.2 Maintenance of User Accounts

Once a user's account is created, the user may start using the system. The user has all rights in the user's own directory, and all privileges with regard to the user's files; for other files, a user's rights are quite restricted. A user may execute most UNIX commands and use the system in the typical way. However, a user is very limited in performing administrative tasks on the system, unless they are directly and exclusively related to the user's account. An administrator must be extremely careful in giving more privileges to a user, if such demands exist at all; otherwise, a user could compromise the system intentionally or unintentionally. When a system is corrupted, intent is not an issue; the issue is to recover the system.

The fact that a user has enough privileges to use the system in a normal way does not mean that the administrator's duties regarding the users' account are over once the account has been created. As with the system itself, user accounts also need to be managed. First, monitoring user activities is highly recommended. A number of systemwide issues can be resolved through such monitoring; sometimes troubling, even disastrous, situations can be avoided and many problems prevented in time. In some sense, such preventive monitoring and maintenance can improve the use of the system.

Another issue to contend with is the need to test and sometimes to recreate a user's environment. Although environment customization is supposed to be done by the user, sometimes it is better if the system administrator does this; often, users are not knowledgeable enough to perform this task. By using the **su - username** command (please note the hyphen character), the *superuser* can switch to a user account and create a real user environment; it is just the same as when the user logs into the system, except password verification is not required for the superuser. It is extremely useful to have the user's credentials while debugging the user's account.

The need to add a user to some other UNIX facilities in use at a specific site is also possible. Additional administrative activities can also be required in, for example, assigning disk quotas, defining mail aliases, setting print queue access, etc.

7.2.1 Restricted User Accounts

Some users are allowed only restricted use of the system. One example of a possible restriction on user access is a user who has access only to execute a single application program. Such demands are addressed by a *captive account*. In this case, the application program itself replaces the UNIX shell that usually enables full use of the system. Entries for these restricted users must be created in the */etc/passwd* file, or existing entries must be modified. Once the login process for such a user is successfully completed, the specified application program begins to execute; once the program is completed, the user will automatically be logged out.

Unfortunately, not all programs can be used in this way; if the program requires interactive use (for example, input of a variable is required) then sometimes simply using the program instead of the login shell will not work. UNIX provides a *restricted shell* to address such demands.

A restricted shell, specified as *rsh*, represents a modified version of a regular shell in which some of the "dangerous" UNIX commands are disabled (the term *dangerous* should be read considering the alternative, unrestricted use of the shell). This means that the ***cd*** (change directory) command is disabled, as are other commands designed to take the user out of the current directory. In this way, a user stays only in the home directory, has a restricted number of available UNIX commands sufficient to perform a specific job, but does not have the usual control over the system.

Another possible way to keep a user within the application is to execute the application program within the user login initialization file. Such an approach could be easier to manage (a specific user environment can be set first, and then the application started), but is more difficult to keep secure; a user could try to find a bypass during the login procedure to reach the shell.

7.2.2 Users and Secondary Groups

Assigning users to an additional group, or even several groups, is a very common task. Only the user's primary group is defined in the */etc/passwd* file; membership in additional groups, known as *secondary groups*, is specified in the group file */etc/group*. There is no difference between primary and secondary groups regarding group ownership and access permissions; the only difference between them is the way they are specified (the */etc/passwd* file versus the */etc/group* file). The BSD platform has never distinguished between primary and secondary groups (except for accounting purposes); however, the System V platform originally allowed a user to have only one active group and to switch to the other group using the **newgrp** command. The BSD approach is prevailing today.

The **groups** command can be used to display group membership:

# **groups *username***	Lists groups that ***username*** belongs to
# **groups**	Lists all user's groups

Alternatively, the **id** command that lists all of a user's identification data could also be used:

$ **id -g *username***	Lists groups that ***username*** belongs to
$ **id -g**	Lists groups that the user who invokes the command belongs to

7.2.3 Assigning User Passwords

All user accounts must have passwords; a password protects the system from intruders. It is up to the user to select the password, but some rules must be respected. It is primarily in the user's best interest to have an unbreakable password — the password maintains the user's data and privacy. No compromises regarding password issues should be allowed.

The *superuser* (*root*) may use the **passwd** command to assign an initial password for a user account. When used for this purpose, the command takes the relevant user's name as its argument:

$ **passwd *username*** Will assign a password for the user with the name ***username***; to avoid typos in specifying the new password, the system prompts for the password twice.

The same command may be used at any time to change a user's password, should this ever be necessary (for example, if a user forgets the password).

Password management and system security are very important UNIX issues, and they have been improved very much throughout the lifetime of UNIX. While in the past only some System V flavors supported the **passwd -f** option, which expires a password, forcing the user to change it at the next login, today the **passwd** command is a versatile command that supports a number of options. However, this is a topic for the section on UNIX security in Chapter 8.

A user can also change his own password. By using the **passwd** command (without any argument) the user starts the procedure for the password change. The user will first be prompted for the old password, (as a security precaution), and then twice for the new one.

7.2.4 Standard UNIX Users and Groups

All UNIX flavors predefine several standard users and groups. User names and group names are mutually independent and have no inherent relationship, even when the same name is used. Although the user and group names are arbitrary, and can vary among different UNIX platforms and flavors, there are some standard users and groups. A list of some of them, with brief descriptions, follows. This list is far from complete; these are simply a few common user and group system entities. Some discrepancies, especially regarding entry descriptions, are also possible.

The standard UNIX users are:

User	UID	Comments
root	0	The *superuser* has unrestricted access to all aspects of the system; most administrative activities must be performed by the *superuser*
daemon	1	Used to execute system server processes; only exists to own these processes and the associated files, and to guarantee that they execute with the appropriate file access permission
bin	2	Owns some executables
sys	3	Owns some system files
adm	4	Typically owns the accounting files
uucp	5	An old-fashioned UNIX-to-UNIX copy subsystem account; the user that owns the *uucp* tools and files
operator		A user with read-only access to the entire filesystem and write access as a normal user; for system operators who need to do backup, initiate system shutdown, and perform some other administrative functions
nobody	-2	Account primarily used by NFS; nowadays also by browsers; UID = -2 appears in the */etc/passwd* file as a very large integer (UIDs are presented as unsigned data type numbers)

These accounts are seldom used for login (except *root*), so their passwords are consequently disabled in the password field in the */etc/passwd* file (or in the */etc/shadow* file — to be discussed in Chapter 8).

The standard UNIX groups are:

Group	GID	Comments
root	0	In principle, a highly privileged group that own's system-related files and directories
daemon		This group exists to own spooling directories */usr/spool/** and programs responsible for transferring files. The spooling directories are temporary resting places for files that are waiting to be printed, to be transferred by *uucp*, or to be processed by some other subsystem. Owning these programs and directories provides additional security — they are not public, so no individual user can access them directly. Spooling programs use the SGID access mode, and users can only manipulate the files in these directories in ways allowed by the programs themselves
kmem	2	The BSD-like special group that owns some system programs needed to read kernel memory directly (like ***ps*** and ***pstat***)
sys		System V-like, this group is the same as the BSD-like group *kmem*
tty		This group owns special files connected to terminals; it controls access to the terminals
others		Group that may be used to own user-related resources
users		

7.2.5 Removing User Accounts

The system's users are constantly changing; new users are added, and some old users may stop using the system. There are many reasons: students are graduating and leaving college, employees are moving to other companies, a worker is no longer involved in a particular project. Administrators must therefore be ready to remove user accounts.

Removing a user account sounds very simple: remove the corresponding user entry in the */etc/passwd* file, and delete the user's home directory. It is not always so simple, though; the full removal of a user from the system can sometimes be a very tricky job and requires a careful approach.

However, disabling a user account is really very easy, and sometimes quite sufficient. It is also recommended to start the removal of a user account by first disabling it. Simply changing the user's encrypted password in the */etc/passwd* file to an asterisk will effectively deactivate a user's account. This method prevents file ownership problems that can crop up when a username is deleted.

When more drastic action is required, UNIX flavors usually offer utilities to remove users from the system, similar to the ones employed to add users to the system; some flavors even provide built-in commands for this purpose. Unfortunately, the automatic removal of a user's files from the system could be risky, so there is always a lot to be done by hand.

When removing a user from the system, a number of issues should be considered:

- Removing the user's mail files
- Removing the user from the mail aliases (the file */usr/lib/aliases)*, or redefining the alias to send mail to someone else
- Removing pending print requests
- Performing any other site-specific termination activities that may be appropriate

Users frequently interact with UNIX systems, but there are other ways a user's requests and jobs could be submitted. Time-related UNIX utilities provide this function:

cron Enables the submission of a user's jobs for periodic execution

at Enables the submission of a user's jobs for execution at specific (usually off-peak) times

batch Enables the submission of a user's jobs for execution at off-peak times, when the system is less busy

Removing a user account also includes making sure the user has not left any pending ***cron, at,*** or ***batch*** jobs in the system.

7.3 Disk Quotas

Disk space shortages are a very common problem on all systems. Often some users use the available disk space in an inappropriate way, storing and keeping everything on the system. In a multi-user environment such behavior is intolerable. The UNIX *disk quota* facility allows an administrator to limit the amount of filesystem storage that a user may consume. If quotas are enabled, the OS will maintain separate quotas for each user's disk space and the total number of files the user owns on a filesystem. Originally a BSD facility, the *disk quota* is common today in all UNIX flavors.

There are two distinct types of quotas: a *hard limit* and a *soft limit*. A user is never allowed to exceed the *hard limit*; the user will receive a message that the quota has been exceeded, and any more data storage will be refused. The *soft limit* may be exceeded only temporarily, for a limited period of time; in such cases a user will receive a warning message, but the OS grants additional storage if requested. The warning will be repeated as long as the user does not reduce the disk usage, or the limited warning period expires. If either happens, at this point the OS will react as it would in the case of a hard-limit violation.

7.3.1 Managing Disk Usage by Users

The system administrator must decide which filesystems need quotas (a ***disk quota*** is implemented on the filesystem level); usually, candidates are filesystems where users reside (/home, /users, etc.). Once the decision is made, setting the disk quota requires several steps. The first step is to modify the entry for the selected filesystem in the filesystem configuration file */etc/fstab* (or */etc/vfstab*); the option which defines the quota (usually *quota*, or *rq*) must be set, and the filesystem remounted. Next, a file named *quotas* (owned and writeable only by the superuser) must be created in the top-level directory of the filesystem for which the *disk quota* has been established, as in the following example:

$ cd /fs-top-dir	# /fs-top-dir corresponds to the to the top-most directory of the selected filesystem, i.e., the filesystem mount-point
$ touch quotas	# create an empty file "quotas" (a mandatory filename)
$ chmod 600 quotas	# make it read-write-only for the superuser

At this point, the general issues concerning disk quota are resolved; now, it is time to set the users' quota limits. This must be done individually for each user, and the limits may be determined arbitrarily among the different users. The **edquota** command is available to establish filesystem quotas (this is the only program available to edit quotas, and it invokes the standard editor — ***vi*** by default). The command can be used for a single user, or simultaneously for more users:

edquota *username(s)*

The **edquota** command will create the hard and soft limits for the specified user and the corresponding filesystem. Each user is specified by one line of the form:

fs /fsname ***blocks (soft=**10000**, hard=**12000**)*** ***inodes (soft=**0**, hard=**0**)***

The disk space (determined by blocks) and the maximum number of user's files (determined by inodes) can be limited; a *0* value indicates no limits.

The **edquota** command has several options:

-t Edit the ***time limits*** for filesystems (time limits are set on filesystems, not users); the default value is usually seven days

-p To copy quota settings between users, for example:

edquota -p *username1 username2 username3 etc.*

means copy quota settings from the user *username1* to other users: *username2*, *username3*, etc.

After all quota limits are defined, the **quotaon** command must be used to enable the ***disk quota*** facility (some systems enable quota checking automatically with filesystem mounting). Alternatively, the **quotaoff** command is used to disable quota checking.

The **quotacheck** command is available to check the consistency of the file *quotas* for the specified filesystem with the current actual disk usage. Finally, the **repquota** command is available to report the current quotas for the specified filesystem. An example follows:

repquota -av

/dev/dsk/c201d6s0 (/):

			Block limits				*File limits*		
User		*used*	*soft*	*hard*	*timeleft*	*used*	*soft*	*hard*	*timeleft*
bjl	--	*140*	*10000*	*12000*		*73*	*0*	*0*	
vasili	--	*121*	*10000*	*12000*		*63*	*0*	*0*	
ggu	--	*1025*	*10000*	*12000*		*140*	*0*	*0*	
park--	*5*	*10000*	*12000*			*5*	*0*		*0*
dubey	--	*7836*	*20000*	*23000*		*790*	*0*	*0*	
mdb	--	*77*	*10000*	*12000*		*13*	*0*	*0*	
xut	--	*837*	*10000*	*12000*		*44*	*0*	*0*	
aizin	--	*69*	*10000*	*12000*		*12*	*0*	*0*	

This report refers to the brand new HP-UX workstation, which had only a few active users at that time.

7.4 Accounting

UNIX provides versatile process accounting. The accounting subsystem records statistics about each process that is running on the system; it records process RUID (i.e., the UID of the user who started the process) and the system resource usage. It is designed primarily for tracking the system resource usage so users can be charged accordingly. However, the recorded data can also be used efficiently for other purposes, like some types of system performance and security monitoring.

The accounting subsystems on the two major platforms, BSD and System V, are different, although both are based on the very same concept. This accounting concept is simple: perform a fast recording of the necessary raw data, and later a slower processing of the recorded data. While the first part, the recording of raw data, is quite similar on the two UNIX platforms, the data processing and output methods and data formatting are very different. Besides that, on the BSD platform the accounting is enabled by default; this means the administrator must prevent the accounting if it is not desired. On the System V platform, the accounting is initially disabled and must be set by the administrator if needed. Enabling and disabling of the accounting is provided through the system rc initialization, although it can be done also from the command line.

A special system entity (a system user) ***adm*** manages accounting; all accounting-related resources (programs, directories, and files) are owned by ***adm***. When accounting is enabled, the kernel records raw process data to a binary data file that resides in the home directory of ***adm***:

For BSD and SunOS:	*/usr/adm/acct* and */var/adm/acct*
For System V and AIX:	*/var/adm/pacct* and */usr/adm/pacct*

Recorded raw data about processes include:

- Image name
- CPU time used
- Time the process started
- Associated UID and GID
- Memory usage
- Number of characters read and written
- Number of disk I/O blocks read and written
- Initiating TTY
- Various associated flags

Additional accounting data are stored in files:

- */etc/utmp* A binary log file containing data about currently logged-in users
- */usr/adm/wtmp* A binary log file that records each login and logout
- */usr/adm/lastlog* A database containing the date and time of the last login for each user

The three listed files originate in, and are a part of the accounting subsystem; however, they became standard files for almost any UNIX flavor, containing important data about login/logout activity on the system. Some UNIX commands rely on these data.

7.4.1 BSD Accounting

Accounting is enabled by default on the BSD platform; this means the appropriate startup command sequence is included in the system initialization rc script */etc/rc*:

```
if [ -f /usr/adm/acct ]; then
        accton /usr/adm/acct; echo -n 'accounting' > /dev/console
fi
```

The ***accton*** command starts (enables) accounting when an accounting file (a destination for raw data recording) is specified as its argument. If there is no argument, this command disables accounting. Obviously, the only condition to start accounting is the existence of the raw accounting file */usr/adm/acct*.

Accounting is a continuous recording of data, and the accounting file grows steadily. To control the growth of the accounting file */usr/adm/acct*, periodic file processing and resizing are required. The tool for this is the ***sa*** command (program); **sa** processes recorded raw data and merges processed data into the standard summary file */usr/adm/savacct* or the user-based summary file */usr/adm/usracct* (option **-m**).

Here is an example of how to use the **sa** command:

```
accton                          # temporarily disable accounting
cd /usr/adm                     # move to the accounting directory
mv acct acct.tmp                # rename the accounting data file
touch acct                      # recreate a zero-size accounting file
accton acct                     # re-enable accounting
sa -s acct.tmp > /dev/null      # merge data into the standard summary file "savacct" with all
                                # generated reports discarded
rm -f acct.tmp                  # delete the temporary accounting file
```

A similar script could be created and periodically executed via the ***cron*** facility (***cron*** is covered later in the Chapter 13).

The accounting data should be saved and processed before a system shutdown. The accounting shutdown procedure must be provided on time. However, in the event of a system crash, special steps must be taken: all accounting records must be manually closed, saved, and processed before accounting is restarted. The procedure essentially includes the same command sequence as in the previous example, but it must be accomplished before the system reaches a multi-user state. Practically, it means that during system booting, accounting startup has to be completed before the execution of the *rc* initialization script */etc/rc*; if the system crashed earlier, everything has been done in the single-user mode.

The aforementioned command **sa** includes a number of options; this is a versatile program that can process recorded accounting data in a number of ways. For the proper use of the **sa** command, the existing manual pages should be consulted.

Another useful tool is the ***ac*** program, which reports on user contact time. It relays data in the file */usr/adm/wtmp*, containing records on users' logins and logouts. The ***ac*** program also provides a number of options.

7.4.2 System V Accounting

The System V accounting subsystem is more powerful and versatile than the BSD one. System V uses an automated accounting system, and it includes a suite of commands, shell scripts, and C programs designed for accounting purposes; together they offer a great deal of flexibility.

We briefly describe how System V accounting works. As is common for accounting, the related directories are */usr/adm* or */var/adm*; and, as is common for System V, there is a dedicated directory hierarchy structure starting with */usr/adm/acct* (instead of the individual files typical in BSD). Three additional subdirectories are *fiscal*, *nite*, and *sum*.

The three directories provide:

/usr/adm/acct/fiscal	Keeps reports by fiscal period (usually monthly) and old binary fiscal period summary files
/usr/adm/acct/nite	Keeps daily binary summary files; daily process accounting records; raw disk accounting records; and status, error log, and lock files
/usr/adm/acct/sum	Keeps daily binary and current fiscal period cumulative summary files and daily reports

Several other files are of special interest:

/var/adm/pacct	Previously described binary data file in which the kernel writes raw data
/var/adm/acct/wtmp	Previously described binary log file that records each login and logout attempt
/var/adm/acct/nite/diskacct	A raw disk usage data file
/var/adm/fee	A file to store additional charge records specified by the administrator, using the **chargefee** command; these are extra charges for special services not covered by the accounting system

A simplified flow chart of processed data in the System V accounting subsystem is presented in Figure 7.1.

The kernel (some of the available commands could also be used) enters initial data in the raw data files; these data are then processed by a series of utilities, producing several intermediate binary summary files. At the end, there are final ASCII reports suitable for use by the system administrator. Any step in the data processing could be performed manually, but with the ***cron*** facility everything can be handled automatically. Accounting utilities and other related commands such as **runacct, acctmerg, prdaily**, and **monacct** live in the directory */usr/lib/acct*. (on HP-UX 10.xx this is the */usr/sbin/acct* directory):

$ ls -C /usr/lib/acct (Solaris 2.x)

```
acctcms    acctmerg   chargefee   monacct     ptelus.awk  utmp2wtmp
acctcon    accton     ckpacct     nulladm     remove      wtmpfix
acctcon1   acctprc    closewtmp   prctmp      runacct
acctcon2   acctprc1   dodisk      prdaily     shutacct
acctdisk   acctprc2   fwtmp       prtacct     startup
acctdusg   acctwtmp   lastlogin   ptecms.awk  turnacct
```

Daily and cumulative summary files, as well as report files, are specified by the corresponding self-explanatory names; in the case of report files, ***ddmm*** corresponds to the date (day and month).

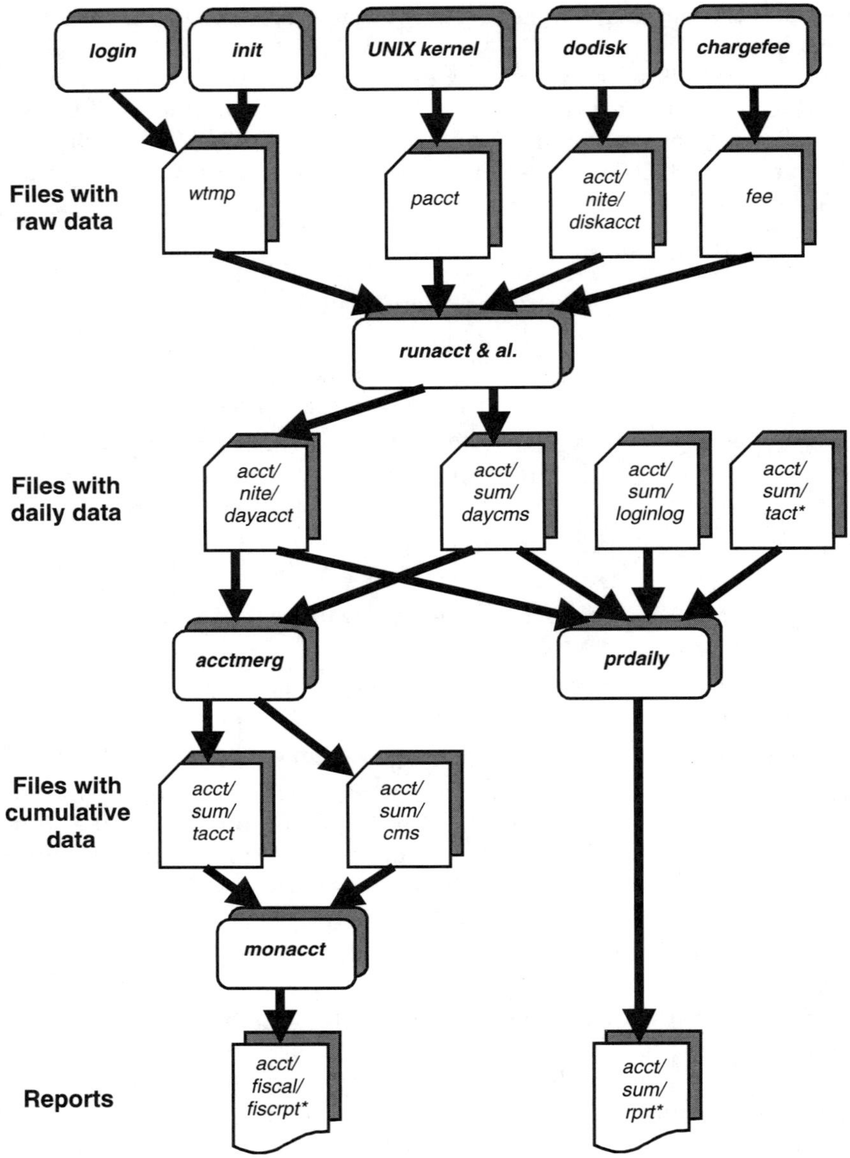

FIGURE 7.1
System V accounting subsystem.

The last step is to enable the accounting subsystem. This means the accounting should start at the system booting. The administrator performs the following steps to enable accounting (in Linux there is one more directory level */etc/rc.d*):

- Checks the rc start/stop script *acct* for the accounting subsystem in the */etc/initd.d* directory, and creates the file if it does not exist
- Creates the symbolic link in the */etc/rc2.d* directory (assuming the run level 2 corresponds to the multi-user mode): */etc/rc2.d/S22acct* -> */etc/init.d/acct*. The startup script should initiate accounting

- Creates the symbolic link in the */etc/rc0.d* directory: */etc/rc0.d/K22acct -> /etc/init.d/acct*. The stop script should invoke the **shutacct** command to shutdown accounting
- Adds the necessary *crontab entries* for various accounting utilities for the users **adm** and **root** (often, these entries already exist, and will only need to be activated)

Once these steps are completed, the accounting subsystem will start at the system booting.

For a better understanding of the start/stop procedure, the previously mentioned script files for Solaris 2.x flavor are presented here in part.

$ cat /etc/init.d/acct

```
#!/ sbin/sh
#   Copyright (c) AT&T
#   All Rights Reserved
state=$1
. . . . .
. . . . .
case $state in
'start')
            . . . . .
            . . . . .
            echo "Starting process accounting"
            /usr/lib/acct/startup
            ;;
'stop')
            echo "Stopping process accounting"
            /usr/lib/acct/shutacct
            ;;
esac
```

The main parts of the start/stop procedure are the programs: */usr/lib/acct/startup* and */usr/lib/acct/shutacct*. Both programs are scripts, as seen here:

$ cat /usr/lib/acct/startup

```
#!/ sbin/sh
#    Copyright (c) AT&T
#    All Rights Reserved
#    "startup (acct) - should be called from /etc/rc whenever system is brought up"
PATH=/usr/lib/acct:/usr/bin:/usr/sbin
acctwtmp "acctg on" /var/adm/wtmp
turnacct switch
#  "clean up yesterday's accounting files"
rm -f /var/adm/acct/sum/wtmp*
rm -f /var/adm/acct/sum/pacct*
rm -f /var/adm/acct/nite/lock*
```

Solaris provides the **turnacct** command to start or stop accounting, depending on the attached argument. This command replaces the BSD **accton** command.

The script to shutdown accounting is:

$ cat /usr/lib/acct/shutacct

```
#!/ sbin/sh
#     Copyright (c) AT&T
#     All Rights Reserved
#     "shutacct [arg] - shuts down acct, called from /usr/sbin/shutdown whenever system is taken down"
#     "arg added to /var/wtmp to record reason, defaults to shutdown"
```

```
PATH=/usr/lib/acct:/usr/bin:/usr/sbin
_reason=${1-"acctg off"}
acctwtmp "${_reason}" /var/adm/wtmp
turnacct off
```

7.4.3 AIX-Flavored Accounting

On the AIX platform, the following steps are required to set the accounting subsystem:

- As the superuser, execute the ***nulladm*** procedure (program) to ensure that each involved file has the proper access permission code 664.
- Update the file */usr/lib/acct/holidays* that contains the timetable for the accounting system.
- Turn on process accounting in the rc initialization script file */etc/rc* — activate the line */usr/etc/acc/startup*.
- Specify the filesystems covered by the accounting subsystem; in the filesystem configuration file */etc/filesystems*, check for an entry ***account=true*** in the stanza for each related filesystem.
- Enable printer usage accounting by adding the stanza ***acctfile=/usr/adm/qacct*** in the */etc/qconfig* file.
- Schedule daily and monthly accounting, and fiscal summaries for automatic execution, using the ***cron*** facility — modify the file */usr/spool/cron/crontabs/adm*.
- Set the environment variable PATH in the systemwide profile file to include ***/usr/lib/acct***.

8

UNIX System Security

8.1 UNIX Lines of Defense

System security is an extremely important issue, especially today, when computer systems are networked and directly exposed to an unknown number of intruders. UNIX designers could not anticipate such extensive development of computer technologies, but they have paid significant attention to system security and have provided a decent level of basic system protection. Standard UNIX offered two basic ways to prevent security problems:

1. Passwords were designed to prevent unauthorized users from obtaining access to the system at all.
2. File permissions were designed to allow access to the various commands, files, programs, and system resources only to designated individuals or groups of authorized users.

On a stand-alone system, which is isolated from the external world, this approach was sufficient. On a system connected to the network, however, which communicates with other known and unknown computer systems, everything is more complex and there are additional risks. For example, under some circumstances network access can bypass the regular password authentication procedures, so the system may be only as secure as the other "trusted" systems on the network.

Passwords and file permissions are certainly useful and necessary, but they should be only a part of an overall security strategy for the system itself, based upon its needs and potential threats. Various lines of defense may be set to protect the system; each of them should be seriously considered, and most of them are relatively easy to implement.

We will discuss the most common types of system defense. Although all of them are not exclusive to UNIX, they can certainly be used in UNIX systems. Some of them are part of the generic UNIX security and others are optional, but they are all widely implemented across all UNIX platforms.

The UNIX security features we will discuss here are not perfect. There are third-party add-on security packages available on the market for sites that require a higher level of security, but they are out of the scope of this text.

8.1.1 Physical Security

The first line of defense is the physical access to the UNIX system (the computer itself). From today's point of view, users do not need physical access to the system at all. They can use the system extensively without being physically near it. Visual contact between a user and the system is not a condition for successful communication (however, this is not the rule for successful system administration).

Some of the most common issues related to the physical security of the system are:

- Preventing theft and vandalism by locking the door or locking the equipment to a table or desk
- Restricting access to the system console and computer itself. To prevent the system from crashing and rebooting to the single-user mode (which is an unsecured system mode), lock the key in the secure key position (if applicable) and keep the key safe
- Controlling environmental factors such as power supply, air conditioning, and fire protection as much as possible
- Restricting (or monitoring) access to other parts of the system (terminals, modems, network facilities, and printers) to prevent vandalism on these exposed parts (which is a frequent problem)
- Restricting access to backup tapes, in particular, to protect system data

8.1.2 Passwords

If an unauthorized individual gains physical access to the system, user authentication is the next line of defense; a password keeps the system closed off, preventing unauthorized users to access the system's files (programs and data). One weakness of passwords is that if someone breaks into an account by finding out its password, the intruder has all the rights and privileges of the legitimate user.

There are a variety of methods for adding additional stumbling blocks if a password is broken, such as:

- Secondary authentication programs, which require additional input before granting access to the system
- Dialup passwords, which act as a second password when logging in via a modem
- Enhanced network authentication systems (like Kerberos) designed to protect networked systems and fileservers; some of these systems are very complex to install and maintain
- Additional authentication-based security identification devices (tokens) synchronized with the system

The system administrator must be sure that all available measures for system protection are implemented before the decision is made to upgrade a system's security. In doing this, special attention should be paid to the password-related files. It is crucial that each entry in these files includes an encrypted password or asterisk. Entries with empty password fields are extremely dangerous for the system and they represent large security holes in the system's defenses.

8.1.3 File Permissions

The next line of defense against an undesired intruder into the system is the file protection. Properly set file permissions can prevent many potential security problems. Any success in breaking into the system through the password's defense line is worthless if the protected files the intruder is interested in cannot be reached. Breaking into a user account means access is still restricted from most system resources that require high priority user's credentials. The most vulnerable aspects of file protection are the SUID and SGID access modes, because they very often enable superuser's access rights.

Some UNIX flavors provide additional ways to limit nonroot users' access to various system resources. Disk quotas, system resource limits, and printer and batch queue access restrictions protect computer subsystems from unauthorized use. A number of different attackers, which attempt to overwhelm systems by completely consuming their resources, present a permanent threat. They carry different names: *bacteria*, *rabbits*, *locusts*, *viruses*, *worms*, and *Trojan horses* but their intentions are the same.

8.1.4 Encryption

There is one hope against a complete loss of security if the root account is compromised: encryption. For some types of data files, encryption can be a fourth line of defense, providing protection against cracked root and other privileged accounts. Encryption involves a transforming of the original file (the plain or clear text) using mathematical functions or techniques. Encryption can protect data stored in the files under certain circumstances:

- Someone breaking into the system (typically as the root) and copying the data
- Someone stealing the disk, or backup tapes (or floppies), or the computer itself in an effort to get the data
- Someone acquiring the files via a network

Encryption can protect data from being read by unauthorized people, but it cannot prevent their corruption. It cannot prevent an intruder from deleting the data.

Most encryption algorithms use some sort of *key* as part of the transformation, and the same key is needed to decrypt the file later. The simplest kinds of encryption algorithms use external keys that function much like passwords; more sophisticated ones use part of the input data as a portion of the key.

UNIX provides a simple encryption program ***crypt***, using an old encryption scheme that is relatively easy to break; ***crypt*** implements a one-rotor machine designed along the lines of the *German Enigma*, but with a 256-element rotor. Methods of attack on such machines are quite well known. Encryption and decryption are based on the implemented *key* as an argument that selects a particular transformation. The overall security is based primarily on the choice of the key and its vulnerability (keep in mind, the implemented key is visible during the encryption procedure). The encryption could be made a little more secure by running the program multiple times on the same file.

Many UNIX flavors offer the *Data Encryption Standard* (DES) encryption subsystem as an optional product. DES is generally regarded as very secure, although rumors flourish about supposed built-in weaknesses. DES encrypted files are believed to be breakable, but only at great CPU-time expense.

8.1.5 Backups

Backups provide the final line of defense against some kinds of security problems and system disasters. Stolen, deleted, and corrupted data can only be recovered from the backup. A good backup scheme will almost always enable you to restore the system to something near its state at any arbitrary point in time; a worst-case scenario would be to recreate the system on entirely new hardware.

Backups provide protection against data loss and filesystem damage only in conjunction with frequent system monitoring designed to detect security problems quickly. Otherwise, a problem might not be discovered for some time. If this occurs, then backups will simply save the corrupted system state, making it necessary to go back weeks or even months to a known "clean" system state and restore by hand newer versions of files not affected by the corruption. In such a case, system recovery could be very hard work; nevertheless, system recovery is still possible.

8.2 Password Issues

Passwords play a crucial role in UNIX system protection; most UNIX systems are as secure as the implemented password policy. There are no compromises in the password policy; all available administrative tools are legal and recommended to enforce appropriate password implementation. This is an extremely sensitive administration issue, and a more detailed overview of password related issues follows.

8.2.1 Password Encryption

A password should never appear in its original form (often known as a *clear password*); the system handles only the encrypted passwords. A written clear password is an immediate security risk because a potential intruder can use it at any time. Only the users themselves should know their clear passwords. Today, the usual method of remote login to the system through the network involves a transfer of a password during user authentication; this makes the system more vulnerable to attackers, because it is possible to sniff and catch the user password on the network. Obviously, networking has introduced one more level of security risk, and we must handle this problem appropriately.

UNIX provides a decent generic password encryption that is compliant with the Data Encryption Standard (DES); it is based on a one-way hashing encryption algorithm with multiple variations intended to increase security and frustrate any use of hardware implementations of a password search. Only the first eight characters of the clear password are used; the rest are ignored. Another input argument is a *salt* (also known as a *seed*): a two-character string chosen from lower-case letters, capital letters, numbers, and dot and slash characters ("." and "/"). The *salt* is used to perturb the hashing algorithm in one of 4096 different ways, after which the password is used as the key to repeatedly encrypt a selected constant string. The final output is a unique encrypted password with its first two characters equal to the input *salt*.

The implemented one-way encryption algorithm makes decryption of the encrypted password impossible (although the salt is known from the encrypted password). The only way to break an encrypted password is to try with many guessed original passwords and by implementing the known DES encrypting algorithm to search for a matching encrypted password. This is exactly how the system performs password authentication during the login process.

UNIX provides the **passwd** command to generate an encrypted password based on the original supplied password and the time-related *salt* generated in that instant; the encrypted password is then saved in the password file (originally */etc/passwd*; today */etc/shadow*). In that way, the system knows about the *salt* to be used in future password authentication, as well as the encrypted password that should be matched.

From the security standpoint, any attempt to break a password without knowing the encrypted password is hopeless. However, by knowing the saved encrypted password (the *salt* and the encrypted password itself), breaking the password becomes more promising, although it promises to be a difficult, time-consuming job, with no guarantee of success. This is why the UNIX password encryption was characterized as "decent" at the beginning of this section: it is breakable, but it is extremely difficult to do so.

Obviously, the encrypted password should be hidden to increase system security and should be known only to the authentication subsystem. We will return to this issue later.

8.2.2 Choosing a Password

Passwords are used to prevent unauthorized people from accessing user accounts and the system in general. Even with the implemented password encryption algorithm, a password should be hard to guess. This means the first step of choosing a password is crucial from the system security standpoint. Generally, a password must be a nonobvious combination of letters and numbers, never directly related to the user. There are some rules that should be respected in choosing an appropriate password. We will start with the items that should be avoided as passwords:

- Any part of the user's name, or the name of any member of the user's extended family (even a grandmother's maiden name is much easier to find out than you might think)
- Numbers that are significant to you, or to a person significant to you: SSN, car license, phone number, birthdates, etc.
- The name of something important to you, like your favorite food, recording artist, movie, TV character, place, etc.; the same goes for people, places, and things you hate
- Any names, numbers, people, places, or other items associated with your company or institution or its products
- English words spelled correctly, especially if they appear in online dictionaries; the spell command can be used to check if a word appears in the UNIX online dictionary
- The names of famous people, places, things, fictional characters, movies, TV shows, songs, slogans, and the like
- Published password examples

Avoiding the listed items makes it harder for someone to figure out a user's password and break into the user account using a brute force trial and error method. Also, be aware that there are a number of commercial and homemade programs to break passwords. Once the encrypted password is known, the original password will be very quickly broken.

Simple modifications of any of these bad passwords, created by adding a single additional character, spelling it backward, or permuting letters, are still bad passwords and should be avoided. It does not take a password-guessing program very long to try all combinations of adding one character, reversing, and permuting.

Passwords that use two or more of the following modifications to ordinary words are usually good choices:

- Embedding one or more extra characters, especially symbol and control characters
- Misspelling it
- Concatenating two or more words or parts of words
- Interleaving two or more words

Modern UNIX flavors require passwords chosen by users to conform to certain rules, usually including being at least six characters long, including at least two alpha characters and one numeric or special character, and having at least three characters different from the previous password (when a password is changed). The superuser generally is not required to adhere to these rules.

Some general recommendations about passwords and system security are:

- The root password should be changed regularly.
- Users should be encouraged to keep their password secret and to choose passwords that are hard to guess.
- There should be no unprotected accounts on the system. This includes accounts without passwords, and still active accounts of users who have left, protected by their original passwords.
- Finally, it is a good idea to restrict the length range for the password; eight characters for the maximum length is a good choice; longer passwords could be typed in, but any extra characters are ignored.

8.2.3 Setting Password Restrictions

Breaking a password is a time-consuming job; good UNIX administration makes this job even more difficult. One of the ways to accomplish this is to force users to follow the established guidelines for safer passwords. These criteria are primarily related to the password time restrictions (known as password aging) and the password contents.

A periodic change of the password is an important step in password protection against attackers. A broken password is useless for an intruder if the password was changed after the break. However, no one likes to change passwords; once a user becomes familiar with the password it can be difficult to change it and learn a new one. Modern UNIX flavors, however, provide mechanisms whereby users can be forced to make these changes. An administrator can specify a *maximum password lifetime* (to force a user to change passwords after a certain period of time), *minimum password time* (to force a user to keep a new password for a certain period of time), *the minimum password length,* and sometimes other parameters. Setting a minimum and maximum password lifetime is referred to as specifying the *password aging*.

Old-fashioned UNIX flavors were not as concerned about password restrictions; this concept came later with other security improvements, when experiences in UNIX usage taught UNIX designers about existing real-life security challenges.

On UNIX platforms, restrictions are introduced by using the **passwd** command with various options. A few options, not necessarily supported by all UNIX flavors, are:

Option	Meaning	Example
-f	Force the user to change the password on the next login	**passwd -f *username***
-n	Specify a minimum password life time (the password cannot be changed during this time)	**passwd –n*1 username***
-x	Specify a maximum password time (the password must be changed after this time)	**passwd –x*158 username*** password aging may vary between 1 and 158 days
-l	Lock a password so the user cannot login	**passwd -l *username***

Password aging is a questionable issue. Too-frequent password changes could be counterproductive. It is easy to forget a new password, and it could be a new burden for the administrator (only the superuser can change a user's forgotten password).

The administrator should carefully consider how many of the available restrictions should be used on a specific system. Imposing too many password restrictions, sometimes pejoratively called *password fascism*, tends to be very unpopular among users and carries some hidden disadvantages. Obviously, all aspects of setting password restrictions should be seriously considered before any final decision is made. Luckily, UNIX is sufficiently flexible to meet almost any need.

8.2.4 A Shadowed Password

The */etc/passwd* file has general read permission, so the file may be read by everyone (any logged-in user, or any process). Although the password portion of the file is encrypted, it is visible at any time by anyone. This visibility of the encrypted password increases the possibility of breaking the password. To increase security, modern UNIX flavors split the data in the */etc/passwd* file into two files; all security-relevant information is removed from the */etc/passwd* file and stored in a separate file with access restricted only to the superuser and members of a selected group. This file is known as a ***shadowed password file***, and its name and entries vary from one UNIX flavor to another. The format of the file is similar to the */etc/passwd* file, but each entry includes only password-related data for a specified user (the first field in the entry specifies the username). Password-related data include the encrypted password, time of the last modification, password aging data, and other additional data (some of the existing fields are reserved for future use).

8.2.4.1 Usual Approach

Keeping password-related data hidden is a significant security improvement, and makes any potential intruder's job much more difficult and the system itself more secure. We will elaborate on the shadowed password file implementation through a few examples.

On Solaris 2.x the shadowed password file is named */etc/shadow*:

```
# ls -l /etc/passwd /etc/shadow
-rw-r--r--  1 root  sys  818  Aug 31  10:35  /etc/passwd
-r--------  1 root  sys  454  Sep 1   10:34  /etc/shadow
```

As can be seen, only the superuser can read the shadowed password file. Root access is required to find any encrypted password. If an intruder already has root access privileges, there is no need to bother with encrypted passwords at all, because the system is already defenseless.

The contents of the two files are:

```
$ cat /etc/passwd
root:x:0:1:0000-Admin(0000):/root:/sbin/sh
daemon:x:1:1:0000-Admin(0000):/:
bin:x:2:2:0000-Admin(0000):/usr/bin:
        .....
levi:x:100:1:Bozidar Levi:/home/levi:/sbin/sh
gale:x:102:1:Gale Pedowitz:/home/gale:/sbin/sh
vxs:x:105:1:Veronika Simonian:/home/vxs:/sbin/sh
        .....
        .....
```

The password field in the */etc/passwd* file is marked by "*x*", indicating to the system the need to check the shadowed password file for the encrypted password.

```
$ cat /etc/shadow
root:MhdqjkrWmdlTg:6445::::::
daemon:NP:6445::::::
bin:NP:6445::::::
        .....
levi:ALCVtjei5TBd.:9226::::::
gale:wNd1hPIAY6A1A:9399::::::
vxs:vDjsPUF7k3cwc:9384::::::
        .....
        .....
```

Each entry in the */etc/shadow* file has the form:

username:password:lastchg:min:max:warn:inactive:expire:flag

where:

username	The user's login name
password	The encrypted password (NP indicates non-login accounts)
lastchg	The date of the last change (modification), also encrypted
min	The minimum number of days between changes
max	The maximum number of days the password is valid
warn	The number of days before a user is warned
inactive	The number of days of allowed inactivity
expire	An absolute date when the login expires
flag	Reserved for a future use

Obviously, it is possible to perform very fine adjustments for each user's password. In this example, a majority of the password options have not even been implemented.

8.2.4.2 Other Approaches

The next example is from ULTRIX 4.3. This example is primarily interesting because it shows a slightly different approach to the same problem (Digital's ULTRIX 4.3 is an obsolete UNIX flavor now). In ULTRIX the name of the shadowed password file was */etc/auth*.

 # ls -lg /etc/passwd /etc/auth

-rw-r--r-- 1 root system 186340 Sep 7 13:57 /etc/passwd

-rw-r----- 1 root authread 88621 Sep 8 11:45 /etc/auth

Here a special, untypical group "*authread*" was introduced for authentication purposes. Only members of this group and the superuser had access to the shadowed file.

The password fields in the regular */etc/passwd* file were marked by the asterisk (*):

 # cat /etc/passwd | grep "lev"

levya::10694:1030:levya:/home2/math/levya:/bin/csh*

levitm::11246:1030:levitm:/home2/math/levitm:/bin/csh*

levi::11540:2020:levi:/home3/instructors/levi:/bin/csh*

An asterisk in the password field indicated that the password-related data were located in the shadowed file */etc/auth*. This could be somewhat confusing, given the earlier suggestion of how to disable login access for an active user's account; obviously for this flavor the asterisk had a different meaning.

The format of an entry in the */etc/auth* file was:

UID:password:lastchg:min:max:accmask:count:auditID:auditctrl:auditmask

where:

UID	The user's ID
password	The encrypted password
lastchg	The time of the last change (modification)
min	The minimum number of sec required between changes
max	The maximum period of time the password is valid
accmask	Special user's account parameters
count	The count of unsuccessful login attempts
auditID	The identifier used in generating audit records
auditctrl	The control in generating audit records
auditmask	The mask to determine which events will be audited

On the AIX platform, the following files contain password relevant data:

/usr/bin/passwd	The **passwd** command
/etc/passwd	Contains user IDs, user names, home directories, login shell, and finger information
/etc/security/passwd	Contains encrypted passwords and security information

The format of the */etc/passwd* file is typical, with the only difference being that an asterisk (*) in the "password field" indicates an invalid password (no one can login), while an exclamation point (!) points to the password-related data in the */etc/security/passwd* file (this is a common and normal situation).

A password must be specified in accordance with the password rules in the "pw_restrictions stanza" of the configuration file: */etc/security/login.cfg*, which includes:

min_alpha	The minimum number of alphabetic characters
min_other	The minimum number of other characters

min_diff	The minimum number of characters in the new password that are not in the old password — this is not positional; if the new password is ***abcd*** and the old password is ***edcb***, the number of different characters is 1
max_repeats	The maximum number of times a single character can be used in a password
min_age	The minimum age at which a password can be changed measured in weeks
max_age	The maximum age of a password. After this age the password must be changed. This value is measured in weeks

If a user entry in the */etc/security/passwd* file is tagged with the ***NOCHECK*** flag, the user password does not have to meet the password restrictions. If this flag is ***ADMIN***, then only the superuser can change the password. When the superuser changes a user password, the user's entry in the */etc/security/passwd* file is tagged with the ***ADMCHG*** flag, and this password must be changed the next time the user logs in.

Only 7-bit ASCII characters are supported in the passwords. Only the first 8 characters of a password are significant.

Access to the */etc/security* directory is granted only to the superuser and the group "*security.*" Besides the mentioned files ***login.cfg*** and ***passwd***, several other files reside in this directory:

- */etc/security/mkuser.default* Contains default attributes for new users
- */etc/security/group* Contains extended attributes of groups (besides the */etc/group* file)
- */etc/security/user* Contains extended attributes of users
- */etc/security/environ* Contains environment attributes of users
- */etc/security/limits* Contains process resource limits of users

Obviously, the AIX platform provides extremely versatile tools to manage users' passwords.

8.3 Secure Console and Terminals

One of the ways to protect a system is to restrict the ways a superuser logs in; if superuser access to the system is restricted to specific system peripherals, then an additional level of security is introduced, making everything more difficult for an intruder. This idea originated in the BSD platform where direct superuser login to the system is allowed only from a console and terminals that are declared *secure*. Otherwise, only regular users may login directly (the term *directly* refers to the regular authentication procedure of entering the login name); afterwards a user may switch to the superuser account, if so authorized. In this way system security is increased, because it is easy to monitor secure consoles and terminals. For other terminals, at least two passwords must be supplied to reach superuser status. In addition the use of the **su** command is always logged by the system and the information is stored in the system log file (usually */var/adm/messages*) with precise data about the time and the username of any **su** command. If necessary, it is easy to follow who became a superuser and how and when.

System V originally did not care about secure terminals; by default all terminals were secure. However, new releases introduced different mechanisms to control superuser login access; System V vendors accepted the concept of "secure terminals."

8.3.1 Traditional BSD Approach

On the BSD platform, the terminal line configuration file */etc/ttys* defines secure terminals (this file corresponds to the */etc/ttytab* file on SunOS). Both files are presented in greater detail in Chapter 11. The file lists all available system terminals. There must be an entry for every terminal port in use and arbitrary entries for unused ones. A terminal line entry has four fields:

terminal-port command terminal-type status

Each field is explained in the following table.

Field	Meaning
terminal-port	The name of the special file in */dev* that communicates with the line.
command	The command that ***init*** should execute to monitor this terminal line. *getty* For terminals and modems *none* To not create a monitoring process
terminal-type	The name of the terminal type described in */etc/termcap;* the ***TERM*** variable will be set to this value at login.
status	Zero or more keywords, separated by spaces: *on* Line is enabled *off* Line is disabled and the entry ignored *secure* Allow superuser (root) logins *window = cmd* ⇒ ***init*** should run ***cmd*** before the command specified in the field ***command***

A secure terminal is specified by the keyword ***secure*** in the ***status*** field for its entry. It is recommended to specify only the system console as secure, and never to give secure status to any modem or network terminals.

8.3.2 The Wheel Group

To become a superuser upon login on a nonsecure terminal means two passwords must be used: first the user password to login into a user account, and then the root password to switch to the superuser account. From security standpoint this is already quite an improvement. Generally, a switch to the superuser account can be accomplished from any user account.

By using the ***wheel*** group, the number of users who may execute the switch to root can be restricted to only the members of this group. Members of the *wheel* group must be specified in the */etc/group* file. In this way, the most sensitive security issue, *superuser status* (user *root*), is additionally protected; only specific users (one or more administrators) may become the superuser from any given terminal.

8.3.3 Secure Terminals — Other Approaches

HP-UX 10.x introduced the file */etc/securetty,* which defines secure terminals that allow direct superuser login. Usually, this is the console. Here is an example:

 # cat /etc/securetty

console

Solaris 2.x introduced the directory */etc/default* that includes a number of files to define the default system behavior. Among them, the file */etc/default/login* defines the login rules, including the secure terminals:

```
# ls -l /etc/default
total 26
-r--r--r--  1 bin    bin    12   Jan 8   15:08  cron
-r--r--r--  1 bin    bin    10   Jan 8   15:08  fs
-r--r--r--  1 root   sys   367   Jan 8   15:08  inetinit
-r--r--r--  1 root   sys   462   Jan 8   15:27  init
-r--r--r--  1 root   sys   678   Jan 8   15:08  kbd
-r--r--r--  1 root   sys  1251   Jan 9   17:26  login
-r--r--r--  1 root   sys    74   Jan 8   15:08  passwd
-r--r--r--  1 root   sys   819   Jan 9   17:26  su
-r--r--r--  1 root   sys   609   Oct 30  1996   sys-suspend
-r--r--r--  1 root   sys   526   Jan 8   15:08  tar
-r--r--r--  1 root   sys    16   Jan 8   15:08  utmpd
```

The contents of the file are (pay particular attention to the CONSOLE section):

```
$ cat /etc/default/login
#ident  "@(#)login.dfl  1.7  93/08/20 SMI"  /* SVr4.0 1.1.1.1  */
#
# Set the TZ environment variable of the shell.
#
#TIMEZONE = EST5EDT
# Set the HZ environment variable of the shell.
#
HZ = 100
# ULIMIT sets the file size limit for the login. Units are disk blocks.
# The default of zero means no limit.
#
#ULIMIT = 0
###################################################
# If CONSOLE is set, root can only log in on that device.
# Comment this line out to allow remote login by root.
#
CONSOLE = /dev/co nsole
###################################################
# PASSREQ determines if login requires a password.
PASSREQ = YES
# ALTSHELL determines if the SHELL environment variable should be set
ALTSHELL = YES
# PATH sets the initial shell PATH variable
PATH = /usr/dt/bin:/ usr/openwin/bin:/ usr/ucb/:/ share/local/bin
# SUPATH sets the initial shell PATH variable for root
SUPATH = /sbin:/ usr/sbin:/ usr/dt/bin:/usr/ope nwin/bin:/ usr/bin:/ usr/ucb/:/ share/local/bin
# TIMEOUT sets the number of seconds (between 0 and 900) to wait before
# abandoning a login session.
#TIMEOUT = 300
# UMASK sets the initial shell file creation mode mask. See umask(1).
#UMASK = 022
# SYSLOG determines whether the syslog(3) LOG_AUTH facility should be used
# to log all root logins at level LOG_NOTICE and multiple failed login
# attempts at LOG_CRIT.
SYSLOG = YES
```

8.4 Monitoring and Detecting Security Problems

8.4.1 Important Files for System Security

Some important files for the system security are listed in Table 8.1.

TABLE 8.1

Important Files for the System Security

Description	Files
Root account initialization files:	*/.profile, /.kshrc, /.cshrc, /.login, /.logout*
Other root initialization files:	*/.forward, /.mailrc, /.exrc, /.netrc* (see note)
Systemwide initialization files:	*/etc/profile, /etc/.login, /etc/csh.login, /etc/login*
Host equivalency related files:	*/etc/hosts.equiv, /.rhosts* (see note)
File permissions on device files:	*/dev/**
cron and ***at*** files:	*/usr/spool/cron/crontabs/*, /usr/spool/cron/at/**
All dialup related files:	*/etc/dialup, /etc/d_passwd, /etc/remote ...*
Default system settings:	*/etc/default/**
Filesystem configuration:	*/etc/fstab, /etc/vfstab, /etc/checklist* (HP-UX), */etc/filesystems (AIX)*
Exported (shared) filesystem for NFS:	*/etc/exports, /etc/dfs/share, /etc/dfs/sharetab*
User and group configuration:	*/etc/passwd, /etc/group. /etc/shadow, /etc/security/** (AIX)
Network related files:	*/etc/hosts, /etc/protocols, /etc/services, /etc/netgroup, /etc/networks*
Internet super daemon configuration:	*/etc/inetd.conf*
FTP related files:	*/etc/ftpusers, /etc/shells, $HOME/.netrc*
System logging configuration:	*/etc/syslog.conf*
System startup files:	*/etc/init.d/*, /etc/rc.config.d/*, /sbin/init.d/** (HP-UX)
System initialization (System V):	*/etc/inittab*
E-mail related files:	*/etc/mail/sendmail.cf, /etc/mail/sendmail.fc, /etc/mail/aliases, /etc/aliases*
Accounting log files:	*/usr/adm/*, /var/adm/*, etc.*
UUCP related files:	*/usr/lib/uucp/*, /etc/uucp/**
Login related raw databases:	*/var/adm/wtmp, /var/adm/utmp, /var/adm/btmp, /etc/wtmp, /etc/utmp, etc.*
All SUID and SGID files:	*wherever the files might be*

Note: Specified files are dependent on the implemented UNIX platform, flavor and release; some discrepancies are possible.

An administrator should be familiar with the correct ownership and protection of these files. Unfortunately, the correct ownership varies between BSD and System V. It is recommended to automate the monitoring and checking of these files by making a corresponding script that will be periodically (for example, daily) started by the ***cron*** facility. Many of the listed files are log files that permanently grow and have a tendency to overload the filesystems they live in; certain rotating scripts could prevent such undesired events.

The following script is presented as an example. It will check the size of specified files, prevent their uncontrolled growth, keep the last two versions of the files, and e-mail the administrator when any action is taken.

```
$ cat /usr/local/bin/check_logfiles.ksh
#!/ bin/ksh
#
# Purpose:  To monitor the current status of log files and prevent
#              their uncontrolled growth. Once a log file limit was reached
#              the log file is copied into filename.old and zero-ed.
#
```

```
#              The list of files to be monitored is given in the file ListofFiles
#              Each line specifies a file and its limit value:
#   =============================
#   Full-path filename    Limit [KB]
#
#          /var/adm/wtmp          500 KB
#          /var/adm/btmp          200 KB
#              .....
#              .....
#
# Set environment
TXT = /tmp/MFtxt                    # temp. text file
HOST = `hostname`                   # name of the host
MAILTO = sysadmin                   # email address
LBIN = /usr/local/bin               # local directory
LIST = ${LBIN}/ListofFiles          # list of files to check
BIN = /usr/bin                      # bin directory
#
# Prepare email header
${BIN}/echo "\n`${BIN}/date`:" > $TXT
${BIN}/echo "Checking the size of log files:" >> $TXT
${BIN}/echo "\n ========================================" >>$TXT
set -A LSA `cat $LIST | awk '{print $2}'`                # extract limits from the list
I = 0                                                   # reset counter
ML = "NO"                                               # reset email flag
for FILE in `cat $LIST | awk '{print $1}'`              # extract files from the list
do
   LS = ${LSA[$I]}
   FS = `${BIN}/ls -l $FILE | /bin/awk '{print $5}'`    # extract the file size in Bytes
   SZ = $LS
   LS = `expr $LS \* 1000`                              # limit size in Bytes
   if [ $FS -gt $LS ]; then                             # check the file size vs limit
      ${BIN}/cp -p ${FILE}.old ${FILE}.older            # copy *.old —> *.older
      ${BIN}/cp -p $FILE ${FILE}.old                    # copy * —> *.old
      ${BIN}/cat /dev/null $FILE                        # resetting the file to zero
      ${BIN}/echo "\nThe log file \"$FILE\" is larger than ${SZ}KB !" >> $TXT
      ${BIN}/echo "The log file \"$FILE\" copied into \"${FILE}.old\" and resized!" >> $TXT
      ${BIN}/echo "\n========================================" >> $TXT
      ML = "YES"                                        # set email flag
fi
I = `expr $I + 1`                                       # increment counter
done
# Check if anything has been done
if [ "$ML" = "YES" ]; then
   ${BIN}/mailx -s "${HOST}: Log File Check and Resize!" $MAIL TO<$TXT   # send email
fi
${BIN}/rm $TXT > /dev/null 2 > & 1                      # delete temp. text file
# < ---------------------- This is the end of the script ---------------------------------
```

8.4.2 Monitoring System Activities

Running monitoring processes on the system is another way to minimize system security risks. This should be done periodically, sometimes even several times a day. In this way, you get a good sense of what constitutes "normal" system activity (which programs are running, how long they run, and who runs them, etc.), and it makes it easier to recognize any unusual activity.

The ***ps*** command lists the characteristics of running system processes. To display all running processes in a useful form, the format of the command is:

ps	*-ax*	(BSD)
ps	*-ef*	(System V)

Note: The ***ps*** command was discussed in detail in Chapter 2.

8.4.3 Monitoring Login Attempts

Sometimes an intruder's attempts to break into the system can be detected in time if login attempts are monitored (especially unsuccessful ones). Of course, the *superuser* account is of special interest, because a break into the *superuser* account could be fatal.

8.4.3.1 The su Log File

All UNIX versions provide mechanisms for logging all attempts by users to become the superuser. Such log files can be very instrumental in tracking down potential problems caused by root actions; at least we can figure out later who the superuser was at the time. Depending on the implemented UNIX platform, the log files can be located differently (generally, log files are specified in the */etc/syslog.conf* file, which are discussed later in Chapter 9); a few examples are presented.

On the BSD platform (usually the file */usr/adm/messages*):

 # cat */usr/adm/messages*

```
            .....
            .....
May 9    09:57:53  patsy named[82]: zoneref:  Masters for secondary zone 95.146.in-addr.arpa unreachable
May 9    10:02:53  patsy named[82]: zoneref:  Masters for secondary zone hunter.cuny.edu unreachable
May 9    10:22:10  patsy su:                  'su root' succeeded for george on /dev/ttyp2
May 9    10:22:35  patsy named[82]:           reloading nameserver
May 12   15:34:24  patsy su:                  'su root' succeeded for levi on /dev/ttyp2
            .....
            .....
```

On the System V platform (usually the file */usr/adm/sulog*). On Solaris 2.x the file */etc/default/su* specifies where status messages from the ***su*** command will be stored.

$ cat */usr/adm/sulog*

```
          .....
          .....
SU 04/07  15:48 + ttyq11 baldwin-root
SU 04/11  14:41 + ttyq0 levi-root
SU 04/12  13:56 + ttyq0 root-levi
SU 04/12  14:55 + ttyq0 franck-gargiulo
      .....
SU 05/02  12:00 + console root-lp
SU 05/10  10:46 + ttyq0 baldwin-root
SU 05/12  16:15 + ttyq2 levi-root
      .....
      .....
```

8.4.3.2 History of the Root Account

A simple way to retain some information about superuser activity is to enable a root history mechanism (the C and Korn shell allow the history) through the superuser's login initialization files. For example, for the C shell:

set history = 200

set savehist = 200

A list of the last 200 commands will be saved in the file */.history*.

8.4.3.3 Tracking User Activities

Other UNIX commands are also available for tracking what users have been doing in the system. They can sometimes track down the cause of a security problem. Some of these commands are:

Command	UNIX versions	Displays information on:
last	BSD, System V, AIX	User login sessions – based on the ***wtmp*** file
lastcomm	BSD, System V, AIX	All commands executed (by user and TTY) – based on the ***pacct*** file
acctcom	System V, AIX	All commands executed (by user and TTY)
acctcms	System V, AIX	All commands executed (by time of day)

All of the commands listed find their information in the system accounting files; in the past, to use these commands, the accounting subsystem had to be running. Today, the *wtmp* file is a standard raw log file independent of the running accounting subsystem.

Generally, if accounting is activated on the system, the possibilities for tracking users and system activities are higher. This makes sense, given the basic idea of accounting, which is to collect more data on how and by whom a system is used.

9

UNIX Logging Subsystem

9.1 The Concept of System Logging

UNIX provides a flexible and configurable logging mechanism. The logging can be site-customized to fulfill a wide range of requirements with regard to the volume and level of the logging of system messages. Continuous system logging is provided primarily to enable later analysis of the system behavior when the system encounters problems. Appropriate system logging is essential on every UNIX system. A side effect of such continuous logging is the permanent growth of the number of log files, which requires attention by the system administrator.

System logging originated with BSD UNIX, and today is widely accepted on all UNIX platforms. The *system message logger* runs as a special daemon ***syslogd*** that collects messages sent by various system processes and routes them to the defined logging destinations. The **syslogd** daemon is started at boot time, and its behavior is defined by its configuration file */etc/syslog.conf*. A flexible **syslogd** configuration allows the administrator to choose from a wide range of system logging options from no logging at all to very verbose logging. The logging can also be tuned and changed throughout the lifetime of the system, enabling different levels of logging according to actual needs.

This logging flexibility is achieved by specifying three different logging issues:

1. What to log, by selecting a ***logging facility*** that indicates a subsystem (a suite of processes) that generates a log message.
2. How to log, by selecting a ***logging level*** that indicates a severity, or priority level, of the generated message to be logged.
3. Where to log, by selecting a ***logging destination*** which indicates an action to be taken to log a generated message. The generated message can be logged in a local file, forwarded to the console or users, or forwarded to a remote logging system for further processing.

The available logging facilities are:

user	User processes
kern	The kernel

mail	The mail system
daemon	System daemons, such as ***telnetd, ftpd,*** etc.
auth	The authentication (authorization) system: ***login, su, getty,*** etc.
lpr	The printer spooling system: ***lpr, lpc,*** etc.
cron	The *cron/at* facility: ***crontab, at, cron,*** etc.
local 0–7	Reserved for local use
mark	For timestamp messages produced internally by the ***syslogd*** daemon
news	Reserved for the USENET network news system
uucp	Reserved for the UUCP system
*	An asterisk indicates all facilities except for the ***mark*** facility

The defined severity (priority) levels (the highest levels are at the top) are:

emerg	For panic conditions, such as catastrophic failures
alert	For conditions that should be corrected immediately, such as a corrupted DB
crit	For warnings about critical conditions, such as hardware device errors
err	For other errors
warning	For warning messages
notice	For conditions that are not error conditions, but may require special handling
info	For informational messages
debug	For messages that are normally used only when debugging a program
none	Do not log messages; use only in combination with other levels

The listed facilities and severity levels will be discussed further when we return to the system-logging configuration.

The monitoring and detection of the listed conditions for when a corresponding message should be generated are not a part of the logging subsystem itself; rather, messages are generated within processes themselves and redirected toward the **syslogd** daemon for appropriate logging. A special device file*/dev/log* is used for the interprocess communication with the **syslogd** daemon, which is continuously listening for generated messages. Once a message is received, the **syslogd** daemon acts according to the specified configuration data related to the logging facility, the message severity level, and the logging destination.

From the system logging standpoint, the **syslogd** daemon is a core of the overall logging procedure, and it deserves to be discussed in greater detail.

9.1.1 The *syslogd* Daemon

The **syslogd** daemon logs all system messages; it reads and forwards system messages to the appropriate log files and/or users, depending upon the severity (priority) level of the message and the system facility from which the message originates. The configuration file*/etc/syslog.conf* specifies where messages are forwarded. In addition, the **syslogd** daemon periodically generates and logs mark (timestamp) messages (mark-interval is specified in minutes; the default is 20 minutes) at an "*info*" logging priority level; this facility is identified as ***mark*** in the */etc/syslog.conf* file. The presence of the *mark* messages in the log files is proof of the daemon's activity: the **syslogd** daemon is alive, active, and ready to log any received error or other message.

Only one **syslogd** daemon can be running at one point in time; an attempt to start another daemon will fail. To check for the **syslogd** process:

```
$ ps -ef | grep syslogd | grep -v grep
root   532    1   0 Apr 30 ?      0:05 /usr/sbin/syslogd
```

The **syslogd** daemon can be started with several options:

/usr/sbin/syslogd *[-d] [-D] [-f configfile] [-m markinterval] [-p path]*

where the options are:

-d	Turn on debugging. This option should only be used interactively and not in the start-up script.
-D	Prevent the kernel from directly printing its messages on the system console. In this case **syslogd** is responsible for routing all kernel messages.
-f ***configfile***	Specify an alternate configuration file.
-m ***markinterval***	Specify the interval, in minutes, between mark messages.
-p ***path***	Specify an alternative special log device file instead of */dev/log*.

The **syslogd** daemon reads its configuration file when it starts up, and again whenever it receives an HUP signal (the signal #1), at which time it also rereads the configuration file, and then opens only the log files that are listed in the file.

Typical **rc** start/stop sequences to start/stop the **syslogd** daemon are:

```
case "$1" in
'start')
   if [ -f /etc/syslog.conf -a -f /usr/sbin/syslogd ]; then
      echo "syslog service starting."
      if [ !-f /var/adm/messages ]
      then
         cp /dev/null /var/adm/messages
      fi
      /usr/sbin/syslogd 1>/dev/console 2>&1
   fi
   ;;
'stop')
      [ !-f /etc/syslog.pid ]&& exit 0
      syspid = 'cat /etc/syslog.pid'
      if [ "$syspid" -gt 0 ]; then
         echo "Stopping the syslog service."
         kill -15 $syspid 2>&1 | /usr/bin/grep -v "no such process"
      fi
      ;;
*)
      echo "Usage: /etc/init.d/syslog { start | stop }"
      ;;
esac
```

This start sequence assumes /var/adm/messages for the system log file.

As the **syslogd** daemon is started, it creates the file */etc/syslog.pid* (or */var/run/syslog.pid* on some platforms) if possible, containing its process identifier (PID). This file can be useful in handling the running **syslogd** daemon afterwards. For example, the command

$ kill -HUP `cat /etc/syslogd.pid`

will recycle the daemon, i.e., to force the **syslogd** daemon to reread its configuration file.

9.2 System Logging Configuration

Configuring the system logging means configuring the **syslogd** daemon, and to configure the **syslogd** daemon means setting the appropriate configuration file */etc/syslog.conf*. Please pay attention to the configuration file name: although the daemon name is ***syslogd***, the configuration file name is ***syslog.conf*** (there is no letter "***d***" in the filename).

9.2.1 The Configuration File */etc/syslog.conf*

The configuration file */etc/syslog.conf* contains all of the data necessary to fully specify the logging process provided by the system log daemon, **syslogd**. When started, or recycled, the **syslogd** daemon preprocesses this file through the *m4 preprocessor* to obtain the correct information for certain log files. By introducing the additional ***ifdef*** macro statement that yields one of multiple possible conditional outcomes, *m4 preprocessing* makes the configuration even more flexible. The ***syslogd*** daemon first verifies that the host is aliased as "loghost"; if the address of the loghost is the same as one of the addresses of the host system, this system is defined as the loghost. The idea of the loghost is to enable a different level of logging according to the defined logging mission of the actual system; it also enables the creation of the "logging server" and a centralized collection of logging messages from multiple hosts on the same network. The **syslogd** daemon first checks the */etc/hosts* file for the loghost address, and then it looks in DNS or NIS (discussed in Chapters 16 and 17).

The */etc/syslog.conf* file contains an arbitrary number of configuration entries needed to fully define the system logging. Blank lines are ignored, and lines for which the first nonwhite character is a "#" are treated as comments.

A logging configuration entry is composed of two TAB-separated fields:

selector ***action***

Or more specifically:

facility.level [; facility.level] [...] ***destination [, destination] [...]***

The ***selector*** field contains a semicolon-separated list of priority specifications of the form:

facility.level [; facility.level]

where

facility — the subsystem sending the message to:

user	User processes
kern	The kernel
mail	The mail system
daemon	System daemons
auth	The authentication (authorization) system
lpr	The printer spooling system
cron	The cron/at facility
local 0–7	Reserved for local use
mark	For internal timestamp messages
news	Reserved for the USENET network news system
uucp	Reserved for the UUCP system
*	All facilities except for the ***mark*** facility

Level — the severity (priority) level of the message:

emerg	For panic conditions such as catastrophic failures
alert	For conditions that should be corrected immediately
crit	For warnings about critical conditions
err	For other errors
warning	For warning messages
notice	For nonerror notices
info	For informational messages
debug	For messages during debugging (very verbose logging)
none	Do not log messages

Please note that an entry is a logging of all messages from the specified facility, with the severity (priority) level equal, or higher than the specified one. In that sense, the level ***debug*** indicates the logging of all generated messages from a specified facility. Linux introduced the characters "=" and "*!*" that, used as a prefix to the specified severity level, change its basic meaning. The character "=" indicates *this severity level only,* while "*!*" negates the entry by indicating *except this severity level and higher.* However, this enhancement remains Linux specific only.

The message logging is active only for specified entries; nonspecified facilities within the configuration file (not included in any configuration entry) are simply ignored by the **syslogd** daemon. In that sense, the level ***none*** should be combined with other facilities and severity levels for a more accurate and condensed specification of a ***logging selector***; for example:

"*.debug;mail.none"

will send all messages except mail messages to the specified destination.

The ***action*** field contains a comma-separated list of the logging destinations (where to forward the messages for logging):

destination The file, device, username, or hostname to forward messages to; values for this field can have one of four forms:

1. A filename, beginning with a leading slash, which indicates that messages specified by the ***selector*** are to be written to the specified file (the file will be opened in the append mode).
2. The name of a remote host, prefixed with an @, as in ***@hostname***, which indicates that messages specified by the ***selector*** are to be forwarded to the **syslogd** daemon on the dedicated remote system. The hostname *loghost* is an alias given to the system that is supposed to be the ***logging server***. Every system is supposed to be the loghost by default, which is defined in the local */etc/hosts* file. It is also possible to specify one system on a network to be a loghost by making the appropriate host name entries in the local */etc/hosts* files over included systems, or in DNS, or NIS. The usual way to configure the **syslogd** daemon on a loghost is: if the local machine is designated to be a loghost, then logging messages are written to the appropriate files; otherwise, they are sent to the remote loghost on the network.
3. A comma-separated list of usernames, which indicates that messages specified by the ***selector*** are to be forwarded to the specified users if they are logged in.
4. An asterisk (*), which indicates that messages specified by the ***selector*** are to be forwarded to all logged-in users.

A few examples:

- To log all mail subsystem messages except the debug ones, and all notice (or higher) messages into the file */var/log/notice*:

  ****.notice;mail.info /var/log/notice***

- To log all critical messages into the file */var/log/critical*:

  ****.crit /var/log/critical***

- To forward all kernel messages and 20-minute marks onto the system console:

  kern,mark.debug /dev/console

- To forward kernel messages of err (error) severity level, or higher, to the system named "hostname":

  kern.err @hostname

- To forward emergency messages to all users who are currently logged in to the system:

  ****.emerg ****

- To inform the users "root" and "operator" (if currently logged in) of any alert and emergency messages:

  ****.alert root,operator***

Two typical configuration files are shown next. The first example (Solaris 2.x) corresponds to a system with higher logging requirements; the configuration data are processed by the *preprocessor m4*, and depending on the actual system logging status (if the system is the loghost, or not: LOGHOST =YES or NO), the system logging configuration is defined.

$ cat /etc/syslog.conf

```
#ident      "@ (#)syslog.conf     1.4     /* Solaris 2.x */
#
# syslog configuration file.
#
# This file is processed by m4 so be careful to quote ('') names
# that match m4 reserved words. Also, within ifdef's, arguments
# containing commas must be quoted.
#
*.err;kern.notice;auth.notice                 /dev/console
*.err;kern.debug;daemon.notice;mail.crit  /var/adm/messages
*.alert; kern.err;daemon.err                 operator
*.alert                                       root
*.emerg                                       *
# if a non-loghost machine chooses to have authentication messages
# sent to the loghost machine, un-comment out the following line:
#auth.notice        ifdef('LOGHOST', /var/log/authlog, @loghost)
mail.debug          ifdef('LOGHOST', /var/log/syslog, @loghost)
#
# non-loghost machines will use the following lines to cause "user"
# log messages to be logged locally.
ifdef('LOGHOST', ,
user.err        /dev/console
user.err        /var/adm/messages
user.alert      'root, operator'
user.emerg      *
)
```

Briefly, the first section defines unconditionally:

- Forwarding to the system console all messages of a severity level equal to or higher than "err," and kernel and authentication messages greater than level "notice"
- Logging in the */var/adm/messages* file all messages of a severity level equal to or higher than "err," except for kernel, daemon, and mail messages where the threshold severity level is defined differently
- The messages to forward to the defined user operator (if defined on the system at all, and if the user is logged in at the time)
- Forwarding the alert and emergency messages to the superuser (if logged in)
- Forwarding the emergency messages to all logged-in users

The next section (entries are presented in ***bold***) defines a conditional logging configuration. The m4 macro statement:

ifdef('LOGHOST,'VAR1,VAR2)

generates the output ***VAR1***, or ***VAR2*** depending on the status of the ***LOGHOST***.
For example:

mail.debug   ifdef('LOGHOST,' /var/log/syslog, @loghost)

specifies the file */var/log/syslog* as a logging destination for all mail messages if the system is the loghost, and if it is not, forwards messages to the remote loghost.

Please note that the similar configuration entry for the authentication subsystem is commented out, and first should be activated (uncommented).

The last section, again the m4 preprocessor ***ifdef*** macro, has an output only if the local system is not the loghost; otherwise this part is ignored (an empty ***ifdef*** output). If active, user's processes are joined to all other processes specified in the first part of the configuration file (some UNIX platforms distinguish user's processes from all other processes). The bottom line in both cases is the same, because defined user processes are already covered by the first part of the configuration file (user processes are not excluded from all processes).

The second example (HP-UX 10.20) is easier to understand and still quite adequate for many implementations; however, it provides only local logging:

```
$ cat /etc/syslog.conf
# @(#) $Revision: 74.1 $
#
# syslogd configuration file.
#
# See syslogd(1M) for information about the format of this file.
#
mail.debug              /var/adm/syslog/mail.log
*.info;mail.none        /var/adm/syslog/syslog.log
*.alert                 /dev/console
*.alert                 root
*.emerg;user.none       *
```

The last entry illustrates the meaning of the ***none*** level, which defines the following: *Send system panic messages from all processes, **except from users' processes**, to **all** logged-in users!*

9.2.2 Linux Logging Enhancements

Linux has introduced few improvements into logging subsystem. Linux's logging subsystem supports sending of log messages to named pipes as well as to log files. But the main enhancements are configuration related.

In the configuration file /etc/syslog.conf few new configuration characters are introduced:

- "space" as a separating character
- "=" to prefix a priority level and indicate this priority level only (eliminates higher levels from logging)
- "!" to prefix a priority level and negate its meaning; it excludes this and higher priority levels from logging, specifying logging of only lower priority levels

To protect **syslogd** daemon from potential network intruders, new options ***-r*** and ***-h*** are introduced; they control daemon behavior toward accepting and forwarding log messages between hosts in the network. The daemon must be started appropriately if the corresponding network related logging is supposed.

Although listed logging enhancements could be disputed, under certain circumstances their implementation could be handy.

9.2.3 The *logger* Command

UNIX provides the ***logger*** command, which is an extremely useful command to deal with system logging. The **logger** command sends logging messages to the **syslogd** daemon, and consequently provokes system logging. This means we can check (from the command line at any time) the **syslogd** daemon and its configuration. The command itself can also be a part of a user program/script to generate necessary operational logging messages.

The **logger** command provides a method for adding one-line entries to the system log file from the command line. One or more message arguments can be entered with options on the command line, in which case each of them is logged immediately. If an optional message is not specified, either an optional file specified with the **-f** option or the standard input is added to the log.

The format of the command is:

logger ***[-i] [-f file] [-p priority] [-t tag] [message]...***

Where the available options and operands are:

-f *filename*	Use the contents of file *filename* as the message to log.
-i	Log the process ID of the logger process with each line.
-p *priority*	Enter the message with the specified priority (specified ***selector*** entry); the message priority can be specified numerically, or as a ***facility.level*** pair. The default priority is ***user.notice***.
-t *tag*	Mark each line added to the log with the specified tag.
message	The string arguments whose contents are concatenated together in the specified order, separated by the space (a quoted message presents a single string argument).

9.2.4 Testing System Logging

It is a good idea to test the system logging after it has been configured and the **syslogd** daemon has been recycled. The **logger** command allows efficient and detailed logging testing. Here is an example from the HP-UX 10.20 system; it is named ***black*** and has the following configuration:

```
$ cat /etc/syslog.conf
# This is the /etc/syslog.conf file
#
#
# Time marks
mark.info                         /var/log/syslog
mark.info                         /var/log/debug
# Message passing
*.info;mail.none;mail.crit        /var/log/syslog
*.debug;mail.none                 /var/log/debug
mail.info                         /var/log/maillog
# Some local screams
*.emerg                           *
# Now send everything "important" to a centralized host
mark.info                         @loghost
*.info;mail.none                  @loghost
mail.crit                         @loghost
#
```

We will test the ***mail subsystem***, or, to use the system logging terminology, the ***mail facility***. All entries in the configuration file relevant to the mail logging are printed in ***bold***. The system is configured to enable logging of all mail log messages above the *info* level in the */var/log/maillog* file; this includes everything except *debug* messages. Critical-level and above mail messages are also logged in the system log file */var/log/syslog* (besides many other system messages), and they are sent to the remote loghost, as well. Further processing and logging of the sent messages is defined by the logging configuration file */etc/syslog* at the remote system. Finally, all emergency (panic) messages are sent to all logged-in users.

The user **bjl** has issued a sequence of the **logger** command from the command line with different logging options and test messages. The **syslogd** daemon should catch all generated messages and forward them into corresponding logging files, according to the actual logging configuration.

```
$ logger -p mail.debug "Testing mail.debug"
$ logger -p mail.info "Testing mail.info"
$ logger -p mail.notice "Testing mail.notice"
$ logger -p mail.warning "Testing mail.warning"
$ logger -p mail.err "Testing mail.err"
$ logger -p mail.crit "Testing mail.crit"
$ logger -p mail.alert "Testing mail.alert"
$ logger -p mail.emerg "Testing mail.emerg"
```

Next, we check the local log files:

```
$ cat /var/log/maillog | grep Testing
May 11 16:57:38 black bjl: Testing mail.info
May 11 16:58:04 black bjl: Testing mail.notice
May 11 16:58:23 black bjl: Testing mail.warning
May 11 16:58:39 black bjl: Testing mail.err
May 11 16:58:54 black bjl: Testing mail.crit
May 11 16:59:12 black bjl: Testing mail.alert
May 11 16:59:29 black bjl: Testing mail.emerg
```

Simultaneously, the panic (emerg) message was sent to all logged-in users:

```
Message from syslogd@black at Tue May 11 16:59:29 1999...
black bjl: Testing mail.emerg
```

As expected, all test messages have been logged in the */var/log/maillog* file except the *debug* message; the emergency message was also sent, and displayed, on the terminals of all logged-in users.

```
$ cat /var/log/syslog
  .....
  .....
May 11 16:00:19 black syslogd: restart
May 11 16:03:42 black inetd[964]: Rereading configuration
May 11 16:03:42 black inetd[964]: bootps/udp: Deleted service
```

May 11 16:03:42 black inetd[964]: Configuration complete
May 11 16:14:32 black -- MARK --
May 11 16:34:32 black -- MARK --
May 11 16:45:21 black syslogd: restart
May 11 16:54:32 black -- MARK --
May 11 16:58:54 black bjl: Testing mail.crit
May 11 16:59:12 black bjl: Testing mail.alert
May 11 16:59:29 black bjl: Testing mail.emerg
May 11 17:14:32 black -- MARK --
. . . . .
. . . . .

Only the section of the interest in the huge */var/log/syslog* file is presented; the mail messages (higher than the level: *crit*) are presented in ***bold***. Pay attention to the MARK messages generated by the **syslogd** daemon, in which logging is defined by the entry:

"mark.info /var/log/syslog"

Generated mail log messages are also forwarded to the **loghost** for remote logging; this is the Solaris 2.6 system. Consequently, the loghost's */etc/syslog.conf* configuration file defines the way these messages will be locally logged. The loghost process receives remote messages in the same way as locally generated ones. The following *syslog.conf* entries at the loghost are related to the mail messages, and define their logging:

**.err;kern.debug;daemon.notic;mail.crit /var/adm/messages*
mail.debug /var/log/maillog

Checking the log files on the loghost:

$ cat /var/adm/messages | grep black | grep mail
May 11 16:58:54 black.logview.com bjl: Testing mail.crit
May 11 16:59:12 black.logview.com bjl: Testing mail.alert
May 11 16:59:29 black.logview.com bjl: Testing mail.emerg

Only mail log messages received with a level higher than *crit* are logged in the */var/adm/messages* file. However, all received mail log messages are logged in the loghost's file /var/log/maillog, because the lowest logging level is defined as *debug* (however, the debug mail message was not sent from the host **black**, because of the local logging configuration):

$ cat /var/log/maillog | grep black | grep "Testing mail"
May 11 16:57:38 black.logview.com bjl: Testing mail.info
May 11 16:58:04 black.logview.com bjl: Testing mail.notice
May 11 16:58:23 black.logview.com bjl: Testing mail.warning
May 11 16:58:39 black.logview.com bjl: Testing mail.err
May 11 16:58:54 black.logview.com bjl: Testing mail.crit
May 11 16:59:12 black.logview.com bjl: Testing mail.alert
May 11 16:59:29 black.logview.com bjl: Testing mail.emerg

9.3 Accounting Log Files

Up to now, we have discussed generic UNIX system logging. However, if the accounting subsystem is active on the system, a number of accounting-related log files provide useful logging information. The accounting is generally based on system usage statistics, and reliable statistics require continuous system monitoring and frequent data logging. The files were discussed from a system security standpoint. Here we focus strictly on their logging characteristics.

Among different accounting log files, the most significant files are */var/adm/utmp* and */var/adm/wtmp* from the system logging point of view. Accounting binary log files include raw data related to the user login/logout events: *utmp* refers to actual login sessions, while *wtmp* contains historical login/logout data; obviously, special attention should be paid to the file *wtmp*, because it grows continuously. Some platforms, like HP-UX, introduce one more file *btmp* to keep data about bad login attempts separate.

A set of UNIX commands is available to manage these binary files: ***login, who, write, last,*** etc. The ***fwtmp*** command provided on the HP-UX platform will convert a file's raw data into ASCII data, suitable for further processing. If corrupted, these files could interfere with the regular login procedure; in most cases, a simple removal and recreation of files helps. On the HP-UX platform, another command ***wtmpfix*** is also provided for this situation.

9.3.1 The *last* Command

The ***last*** command displays login and logout information about users and terminals. It looks in the */var/adm/wtmp* file (which records all logins and logouts) for information about a user, a terminal, or any group of users and terminals. The format of the command is:

last ***[-n number | -number] [-f filename] [name | tty]...***

The trailing arguments specify the names of users or terminals of interest. If multiple arguments are given, the data applicable to any of the arguments is printed. For example, the command: ***last root console*** lists all of *root*'s sessions, as well as all sessions on the console terminal. The displayed sessions of the specified users and terminals are listed starting from the most recent session first, indicating the times at which the session began, the duration of the session, and the terminal on which the session took place. The **last** command also indicates whether the session is continuing or was cut short by a reboot.

By default all logged data about sessions are displayed in the reverse order. The option **-n** ***number,*** or simply **-number** can be used (*number* corresponds to the desired number of sessions to be presented) to restrict the display to a certain number of last user's sessions.

The option **-f** ***filename*** enables the specification of log file other than the default file */var/adm/wtmp*.

The system automatically logs information about each system reboot and addresses them to the pseudo-user ***reboot***. Thus, the command:

last ***reboot***

will give an indication of the mean time between reboots.

9.3.2 Limiting the Growth of Log Files

Log files grow continuously. This is the nature of the logging process; new logging data are appended onto preexisting ones. If left unattended, the number of system log files will grow without limit, and if a verbose logging is configured, the file growth under some circumstances could be dramatic. Log files tend to consume disk space and bring a filesystem to a point that could endanger it. This is primarily a problem for the */var* filesystem — most often it is a separate filesystem and the usual location for a majority of system log files (directory */var/adm*, or */var/log*).

The significance of and the need for regular system logging is beyond question; in a critical moment, the log files could be the only source of information available to trace a problem. System logging is a requirement and has to be active on every system. However, you must monitor the growth of system log files; the system administrator is responsible for reaping any needed data from these files and keeping the files to a reasonable size.

The major offenders include:

- The various system log files in */var/adm* (or */usr/logs*), which may include *sulog*, *messages*, and other files determined in the system logging configuration file */etc/syslog.conf*, or sometimes determined in the */etc/default* directory (on some flavors, default values are defined in this directory).
- Accounting files in the directory */var/adm* (or sometimes */usr/adm*), especially files *wtmp* and *acct* (BSD) or *pacct* (System V).
- On some UNIX flavors, default subsystem log files originated from different UNIX facilities, such as *cron*, *printing subsystem*, *uucp subsystem*, etc. The usual names and locations include:

/usr/spool/lp/log	Printing log file (BSD)
/usr/spool/lp/logs/lpsched	Changes to printer status (System V)
/usr/spool/lp/logs/requests	Individual print requests (System V)
/usr/lib/cron/log	*cron* log file
/usr/sbin/cron.d/log	*cron* log file (SVR4)
/usr/spool/uucp/LOGFILE	BNU *uucp* log file
/usr/spool/uucp/SYSLOG	Version 2 *uucp* subdirectories
*/usr/spool/uucp/LOG**	(each contains multiple log files)

There are several approaches to control the growth of system log files:

- The easiest way is to truncate them by hand when they become too large. This is only possible for ASCII log files. To reduce a file to zero length, use a command like:

  $ cp /dev/null /usr/adm/sulog

  or

  $ cat /dev/null > /usr/adm/sulog

  Copying the *null* device onto the file is preferable to removing the file because in some cases the subsystem will not recreate the log file if it does not exist.
- Use the ***tail*** command to retain a small part of the current logging information (the most recent one), as in the following example:

  $ cd /usr/adm

  $ tail -100 sulog > sulog.tmp

$ cp sulog.tmp sulog

$ rm sulog.tmp

The 100 last lines of the *sulog* file will be retained.

- Keep several old versions of a log file in the system by periodically deleting the oldest one, renaming the current one, and then recreating it. The appropriate command sequence is:

  $ cd /usr/adm

  $ cp -p messages.old2 messages.old3

  $ cp -p messages.old messages.old2

  $ cp -p messages messages.old

  $ cat /dev/null > messages

The last three versions of the log file */usr/adm/messages* are preserved for the eventual need to trace some events in the past. It should to be sufficient if any problem occurs, while it also keeps disk space consumption at an acceptable level (although there is no guarantee for individual log file sizes). Such an approach is ideal for automatic periodic execution, perhaps at the beginning of each month, so the logging within the last 3 months is always available. Some UNIX flavors integrate this approach in the startup procedure, i.e., the corresponding **rc** startup script saves and resizes the system log file */usr/adm/messages* in an almost identical way. Under regular conditions, this works very well, but if there are several consecutive system boots, the complete logging from the previous periods could be lost. Other approaches are, of course, possible. One homemade solution, the *check_logfiles.ksh* script, is presented in Chapter 8.

10

UNIX Printing

10.1 UNIX Printing Subsystem

Printing is a very important issue on any UNIX platform, and is important to the job of system administration, as well. Every user on the system expects quick, reliable, high-quality printing at any time. Many users evaluate a system's performance primarily on its printing capabilities, so this is one of the most sensitive issue from the user standpoint.

As expected, UNIX offers two basic flavors of printing systems: BSD and System V. Unfortunately, the differences between these two flavors are quite significant, making them mutually incompatible. Neither flavor is more commonly used than the other; both are used widely. Some platforms even support both flavors, but the majority of UNIX systems integrate one of the two available UNIX printing subsystems.

Before we continue with a more detailed description of the two printing subsystems, let us first define the terminology used for this topic. The common term ***printing subsystem*** (or sometimes even *printing system*) identifies the entire suite of all printing related items (primarily software, but also hardware items) that effectively enable and provide printing on an arbitrary UNIX platform. Often, a printing subsystem is also identified as a *spooling subsystem* or *printer spooling subsystem*. While the first alternative name is too general (spooling is not only related to printing — it can also refer to e-mailing and other queued message subsystems), the second term seems to be quite appropriate. Nevertheless, the *spooling subsystem* in most cases refers just to the printing. In the following text, we will try to use the more comprehensive terms among the available ones.

Except for the existing differences between the BSD and System V printing subsystems, the concept of printing in both cases is quite similar. A printing subsystem consists of:

- *User commands* — Required to initiate printing. A user specifies the file to print, the print device to print it on (if there is more than one device), and other mandatory and optional details. The common terminology to identify an invoked printing is also different: on BSD they are called ***print jobs***, on System V, ***print requests***.
- *Queues* — To store and sequentially process print jobs (print requests). In its simplest form, a queue is a line of print jobs/requests waiting to use a specified print device.
- *Spooling directories* — To hold pending print jobs (print requests). On BSD, the entire file to be printed is copied in the spooling directory; on System V, by

default only a small print request file is generated, while the file to be printed is accessed in its original location at the proper time when printing actually occurs.

- *Server processes* — Printing daemons that transfer a print job (a print request) from the spooling directory to the specified printing device.
- *Administrative commands* — Print-related administrative commands to start and stop the printing subsystem or specific printers, and to manage queues and individual print jobs (print requests).

A functional diagram of a printing subsystem (with indicated differences between BSD and System V) is presented in Figure 10.1.

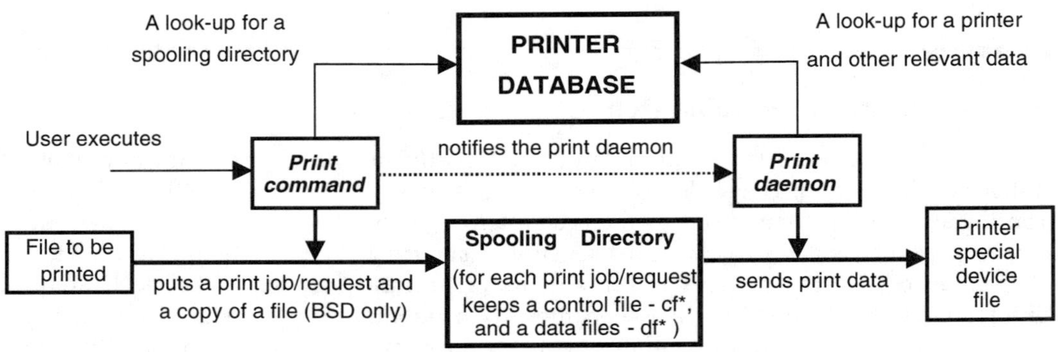

FIGURE 10.1
Functional diagram of a printing subsystem.

Once a user (or a user's process, invokes a printing, the print command performs the following:

- It looks in the printer database for necessary printing-related data such as the spooling directory and other printing arguments.
- It creates a print job (a print request for System V printing subsystem) and puts a corresponding control and data file (*cf* and *df*) in a printing queue in the corresponding spooling directory, and if it is a BSD printing subsystem, copies the file to be printed into the spooling directory.
- It notifies the print daemon about the started printing procedure.

The print daemon provides the actual printing:

- It looks in the printer database for necessary printer-related data for the started print job/request.
- It checks the status of the corresponding printer.
- It completes the printing procedure by sending the file to the printer for printing.

The start of printing and the actual printing do not necessarily coincide; a delay between the two actions is quite possible, and such delays can vary significantly, depending on the actual printer status, the volume of required printing, the queue length, and other factors. Generally, the physical printing is performed slowly, and sometimes the delays can be quite annoying.

10.1.1 BSD Printing Subsystem

The BSD UNIX system maintains multiple printers on local and/or remote sites, and multiple print queues. It can be adopted to support different types of printers. It began as a standard "line-printer spooling subsystem," but very soon it added laser printers, raster-printers, and other printing devices. Today the BSD printing subsystem represents a collection of five programs and several files:

lpr	Adds a print job to a print queue by copying the file into its spooling directory. A print job is assigned a job ID number when it is submitted, and this number is used to refer to the print job in subsequent commands. The name of the command originates from "line-printer," the most advanced printer in the early days of UNIX.
lpq	Lists jobs that are currently in the print queues.
lprm	Removes jobs from the print queues. Users may remove only their own jobs, but the superuser may remove any print job.
lpd	The printer daemon, responsible for sending data from the spooling directory to a printer (i.e., printing device).
lpc	The administrative interface to the printing subsystem.
/etc/printcap	The printer configuration file, which contains entries describing each printer on the system. The standard template version includes a number of the most common printers, which an administrator can then customize for a specific system. Usually, entries are commented-out, so the administrator should activate (remove the comment markers from) all needed entries in the file. Sometimes minor adjustments are required.

10.1.1.1 The lpr, lpq, and lprm Commands

The ***lpr*** command is available to activate the printing of a printable file:

lpr -P*printer printfile*

where

-P	Option to select a printer for this printing
printer	The name of the selected printer
printfile	The name of the file to be printed

Please note that there is no space between the **-P** option and the printer name (some UNIX platforms allow this). If the **-P** option is missing, the default printer is selected. The default printer is defined in the printer configuration file */etc/printcap*, as are all other printers.

The ***lpq*** command is available to check the current status of a print queue, i.e. to list the contents of the queue:

lpq -P*printer*

where

-P	Option to select a printer
printer	The name of the selected printer the queue belongs to

If the **-P** option is missing, the default printer is selected.

A few examples:

 # lpq –Ppp (post-script printer pp)
no entries

or

 # lpq (default local printer)
no entries

The ***lprm*** command is available to remove individual print jobs:

lprm -P*printer jobs-to-remove*

where

-P	Option to select a printer
printer	The name of the selected printer jobs to remove from
jobs-to-remove	A list of job IDs
	A list of usernames for whom to remove all jobs
	A single hyphen to remove all jobs (only if superuser)

The **lprm** command identifies print jobs by their IDs (obtained with the **lpq** command); obviously, the **lpq** command should be issued before the **lprm** command is used.

10.1.1.2 The lpd Daemon

lpd is the BSD printer spooling daemon; it sends data stored in the spooling directory to a printer to be printed. The **lpd** daemon is started by the corresponding **rc** start script during system startup. Please note that some UNIX platforms might have a commented **rc** startup sequence for the printer spooling daemon; the comment markers must be removed from the corresponding lines when the first printer is attached to the system. If they are not removed, the **lpd** daemon will not be invoked with each subsequent system booting.

The **lpd** daemon works in the logical space between users and printers; this complex task often involves unpredictable conditions that must be handled accordingly. Occasionally, the **lpd** daemon gets hung. The main symptom of this hung state is a queue filled with jobs but not printing any of them. In this case, the old daemon should be killed and a new one started. The command sequence is shown in the following example:

```
$ ps -aux | grep lpd | grep -v grep
root    208    0.0    0.2    1536    32    ?    I    0:00  /usr/lib/lpd
$ kill -9 208
$ /usr/lib/lpd
```

10.1.1.3 Managing the BSD Printing Subsystem

The "line-printer control utility," ***lpc*** is available to perform most administrative tasks connected with the BSD spooling subsystem. The **lpc** utility includes a number of internal commands (subcommands) required to handle such printer-related tasks as: shutting a printer down for maintenance, displaying a printer's status, and manipulating jobs in print queues. To invoke the **lpc** utility, simply type:

\# **lpc**
lpc>

lpc is now running and issues its own prompt. The available internal **lpc** commands are:

status *printer*	Displays the status of the line printer daemon and queue for the specified printer.
abort *printer*	Immediately terminates any printing in progress and disables all printing on the specified printer. The job stays in the queue and its printing will continue as soon as the printer is restarted (with the start command).
stop *printer*	Stops all printing on the specified printer after the current job has finished. New jobs can be added to the queue with the ***lpr*** command, but they will not be printed until the printer is started again. This command is very useful when the time comes to add or replace the printer's supplies (paper, ribbon, etc.).
start *printer*	Restarts printing on the specified printer after an abort or stop command.
disable *printer*	Prevents users (except the *superuser*) from putting new jobs into a specified printer's queue. Existing jobs continue to print, so this command is useful when a printer needs to be turned off.
enable *printer*	Allows users to spool jobs to the queue again, restoring normal operation after the ***disable*** command is issued.
down *printer*	Stops printing and disables the queue for a specified printer (its action is equal to ***disable*** plus ***stop***).
up *printer*	Enables the queue and starts printing on the specified printer (its action is equal to ***enable*** plus ***start***).

If the specified printer is *"all,"* the command itself is forwarded to every printer on the system.

10.1.2 System V Printing Subsystem

The System V spooling subsystem has the following major components:

- User commands:

  lp Initiates print requests (equivalent to ***lpr*** on BSD)
  lpstat Lists print queue contents (equivalent to ***lpq*** on BSD)
  cancel Cancels a pending print request (equivalent to ***lprm*** on BSD)

  When a user submits a print request, it is assigned a unique *request ID* that is used to identify it thereafter; *request ID*s usually consist of the printer name and a request number.

- The spooling daemon ***lpsched***, responsible for carrying out print requests by sending data to the appropriate printer.

- A suite of administrative commands (***accept, reject, enable, disable, lpadmin, lpmove, lpusers***) usually stored in the directory */usr/lib*. It is a good idea to add this directory to the root's command search path, which makes sense, because administrative printing commands require superuser privileges.
- Spooling directories in */usr/spool/lp/request* for each printer, named by the printer name. Only the print request information is stored in the corresponding directory; by default, the actual file to print is not copied. Thus, changing or deleting a file before it is printed affects the final output. The ***lp*** option **-c** can be used to force the copying of the file to the spooling area when it is submitted for printing.

10.1.2.1 The lp, lpstat, and cancel Commands

Print requests are sent to the queue for a *destination*, which can be either a specific printer (including the default one), or a *device class* (a group of the same type of printers). A *device class* provides the mechanism to group similar printing devices and declare them to be equivalent to, and substitutable for, one another. Printing is performed on the first available device in the class — for example, class ***laser*** can include all of the compatible laser printers on the system. All of the devices within a device class share a single queue.

The **lp** command places a print request into a queue, either for a specific device or a device class:

lp ***[options] file-name***

where

file-name The name of the file to be printed.

options Many options are available, but **-d *printer*** specifies the printer (queue) for printing; if this is missing the default printer is used.

The **lpstat** command will provide status information on current printing queues and devices:

lpstat ***options***

The **lpstat** command is more versatile than its BSD counterpart; there are a number of options that make this command a printing monitoring tool. The command will monitor not only the print queue status, but can handle printers themselves, as well.

The **lpstat** options are:

Option	Meaning
-a *[list]*	Display the acceptance status of the destinations for output requests for printers and classes specified in the *list*
-c *[list]*	Display the members of the classes specified in the *list*
-o *[list]*	Display print requests; the *list* may include request IDs, printer names, and class names
-p *[list]*	Display the current status of the printers specified in the *list*
-u *[list]*	Display the status of all jobs belonging to the users specified in the *list*
-v *[list]*	Display the name of printers and the pathnames of the associated devices
-s	Summary; display all classes and their members and all printers and their associated devices
-t	Display all status information (reports everything)
-d	Display the default printer destination
-r	Display the status of the printer spooling daemon

Note: "list" specifies one or more comma separated printing entities.

Here is an example: a number of printers, mostly remote ones, are defined on the HP-UX 10.20 printing-client system. The partial ***lpstat*** summary report on printers and their special device files presented below includes local printers (indicated in bold letters), and other remote printers.

$ lpstat -s

system default destination: lp26
device for lp1: /dev/null
    remote to: lp31 on ps3.printview.com
device for lp26: /dev/null
    remote to: lp26 on ps3.printview.com
device for lp29: /dev/null
    remote to: lp29 on printhost.printview.com
device for foxy: /dev/null
    remote to: LF1 on foxip.printview.com
device for poprt3: /dev/tty3 **=> *local printer***
device for poprt8: /dev/tty8 **=> *local printer***
device for wprt1: /dev/null
    remote to: LF1 on wprip.printview.com
device for xerox: /dev/null
    remote to: xerox on ps5.printview.com
    . . . . .
    . . . . .

A partial report on the printers' current status (for the same printers in the previous report) is:

$ lpstat -p

printer foxy is idle. enabled since Nov 30 11:17
  fence priority : 0
printer poprt3 disabled since Mar 12 16:46 -
  reason unknown
  fence priority : 0
printer poprt3 is idle. enabled since Mar 15 11:45
  fence priority : 0
printer wprt1 is idle. enabled since May 6 14:47
  fence priority : 0
printer xerox is idle. enabled since May 14 05:41
  fence priority : 0
printer lp26 is idle. enabled since Aug 26 12:38
  fence priority : 0
printer lp1 is idle. enabled since Jan 27 10:44
  fence priority : 0
printer lp29 is idle. enabled since Nov 24 14:12
  fence priority : 0
  . . . . .
  . . . . .

Finally, the **lpstat -t** command reports on everything. However, if there are a large number of attached printers (and especially if some remote printers are down), the command itself can take a long time to execute. In critical situations, when every second counts, it may be preferable to manually cancel pending print requests.

A system administrator may cancel any pending print request with the command:

cancel ***request-id(s)***

or

cancel ***destination***

where

request-id(s)	The ID(s) of the job/jobs to be canceled (even if they are currently printing)
destination	The name of the queue for which all jobs should be canceled

Solaris 2.x even supports the **lpr** command, this time adjusted to the System V LP environment. This means that the command is serviced by the **lpsched** daemon (there is no **lpd** daemon or **printcap** database). The **-s** option makes the command behave like the System V version: it does not copy the file to be printed into the spooling directory.

10.1.2.2 The lpsched Daemon

The printer spooling daemon ***lpsched*** is responsible for carrying out print requests by sending data to the appropriate printer/printers. It is also known as the *print service daemon*. The **lpsched** daemon under System V is actually the equivalent to the **lpd** daemon under BSD. The daemon is invoked during the system booting and is permanently running, waiting for new print requests to be stored in the spooling queues.

Each printing-related administrative action requires the **lpsched** daemon to temporarily shut down and restart. The special **lpshut** command was introduced to make this simpler; the ***lpsched*** daemon can be stopped with **lpshut** command.

10.1.2.3 Managing the System V Printing Subsystem

There is no System V equivalent to the BSD **lpc** utility; instead, a number of individual administrative printing-related commands are available. Together they form an extremely powerful and versatile suite of high-level commands to provide full control over the administration of various printing issues. The System V printing subsystem configuration also fully relies on these administrative commands. While the BSD printing subsystem requires a direct access to and interaction with printing-related configuration data/files, on System V all that is somewhat hidden from the administrator, and provided by these front-end administrative commands. We will return to these issues later.

For example, the System V printing subsystem enables the user to move a pending print request between print queues (i.e., printers) with the special command **lpmove** (there is no BSD equivalent):

lpmove ***request-id(s) new-printer***	To move some print requests
lpmove ***old-printer new-printer***	To move all print requests

where

request-id(s)	The ID(s) of the print request/requests to be moved
new-printer	The name of the new printer (queue) to move print requests
old-printer	The name of an old printer (queue) where print requests are pending

Another command pair, **accept** and **reject**, may be used to permit and inhibit spooling to a print queue; both accept a list of destinations as their argument. With the **-r** option, **reject** may specify a reason for denying requests, which will be displayed to users attempting to send new jobs to that queue.

The **enable** and **disable** commands are used to control the status of a specified printing device (printer).

The "master" printing-related administrative command is **lpadmin**. This command is so powerful that it is even more appropriate to refer to it as an *administrative tool*, a set of joined commands invoked through different **lpadmin** options. This is the "magic" command for managing all printing devices in the System V printing subsystem.

The **lpadmin** command is used to manage printers and destination classes. It defines and modifies the characteristics of printer devices and classes. All these administrative tasks are important for the printing subsystem and require full support by the **lpsched** daemon; any possible problem can be skipped with this command, but only when the **lpsched** daemon has been stopped. Once the daemon is restarted, it has learned about the new configuration.

The **lpadmin** command is a powerful tool in managing printing devices. The online manual pages contain a complete explanation of all available options for this command. Here, only some of options are listed and briefly discussed.

- To set the default destination:

lpadmin -d ***printer_name***

where

printer_name The name of the printer or device class

- To place a printer into a class (if the class does not exist it is created):

lpadmin -p ***printer_name*** **-c** ***class_name***

where

printer_name The name of the printer
class_name The name of the class

- To remove a printer from a class:

lpadmin -p ***printer_name*** **-r** ***class_name***

- To restrict (or even deny) access to destinations to specific users (by default, all users are allowed to use any destination):

lpadmin -p ***printer_name*** **-u** ***'allow:user_list'***
lpadmin -p ***printer_name*** **-u** ***'deny:user_list'***

where

user_list List of users with restricted access to printer ***print_name***; users in the list are separated by commas. Each user in the list is specified in the form: *host!username*, where *host* is the name of the host, and username indicates the user on that host (a missing host corresponds to the local system). The keyword ***all***

corresponds to all users, or all hosts. If an *allow list* exists, the access is allowed only to users in the list.

- Finally, the **lpadmin** command is used to add a new printer (local or remote) to the system, as well as to remove a printer from the system. We will discuss this important administrative task later.

It is important to remember that the proper use of the **lpadmin** command involves shutting down the ***lpsched*** daemon, and reinvoking it afterward.

10.2 Printing Subsystem Configuration

10.2.1 BSD Printer Configuration and the Printer Capability Database

The BSD and System V printing subsystems perform the same job, but in a different way. At first they seem similar, but once we reach the subject of configuring them, their differences become more apparent. While System V relies on existing front-end administrative commands (such as the **lpadmin** command), the BSD printing subsystem is mostly administered through the corresponding printer capability database using the usual UNIX tools and skills — in other words, by manual editing of the necessary configuration data. The next few paragraphs focus on these topics.

Printer configuration requires a clear understanding of the administration procedure, and there are many steps involved before the procedure is complete. System administrators, however, are quite happy with this approach, because it involves editable ASCII configuration data with full control of the configuration itself, easy scripting, and an easy multiplication of the printing configuration over multiple systems.

10.2.1.1 The /etc/printcap File

The master printer configuration database is contained in the */etc/printcap* file. This file lists all devices serviced by the BSD printer spooling subsystem. A more precise description of the file would be "printer capability database," which the name stands for. UNIX systems are usually shipped with a standard version of the */etc/printcap* file (the template file), which describes most of the printers that could be used on the system. Each printer type is described by one *printcap entry,* which consists of a sufficient number of *printcap fields* describing different printer characteristics. Upon its installation, the entries can be commented-out; the system administrator should configure */etc/printcap* by activating the proper entries for the implemented printers. Sometimes minor modifications of entries are required, though in most cases the entries match existing printers. The */etc/printcap* file includes other printer configuration data necessary for successful printing, as well as data related to the printer characteristics, making it a true ***master printer configuration file***.

The **lpd** daemon reads the printer-related data from the */etc/printcap* file on an as-needed basis. This means any configuration change will be effective immediately, and there is no need to reinvoke the daemon itself (as would be the case for the majority of daemons).

Here is an example of a */etc/printcap* file:

```
$ cat /etc/printcap
# Printer Capability Data Base
```

```
#
# Modified on Feb. 2, 1998 by the System Administrator
#
# Entry for HP LaserJet IV printer
0|lp|lj4|hplj|ljiv|ascii|HP LaserJet 4: \
   :mx#0:\
   :ms=-parity,-cstopb,-clocal,cread,ixon,ixoff,-opost:\
   :lp=/dev/ttya:sd=/usr/spool/laserjet:br#9600:\
   :fc#0777:fs#06021:sb:sh:xc#07737:x s#040:\
   :lf=/usr/adm/lpd-errs:of=/usr/lib/hplaserjet:
#
# Entry for HP plotter (for future use)
#5|HP|hp plotter|HP Plotter:\
#   :lp=/dev/ccplot:\
#   :of=/usr/spool/spff:\
#   :xn=146.95.1.3:\
#   :xp=6:\
#   :pl#0:\
#   :lf=/usr/adm/errorlog:\
#   :sh:\
#   :ff=^[.Y:fo:tr=PG;:
#
##POSTSCRIPT laser printer
pp|pp|PostScript|postscript:\
   :lp=/dev/ppplot:\
   :of=/usr/spool/spff:\
   :xn=146.95.1.3:\
   :xp=2:\
   :lf=/usr/adm/errorlog:\
   :sh:
#
# Remote printers on the microVAX computer (MVAXGR)
#
10|prvax|vx|vax|sys$print|decwriter| line printer:\
   :lp=:rm=mvaxgr:sd=/ usr/spool/lpd/vax:lf=/usr/ adm/lpd-errs:\
   :rp=sys$print:
11|lsvax|laser|sys$lspr|lsprinter| laser printer:\
   :lp=:rm=mvaxgr:sd=/usr/spool/lpd/vax:lf=/usr/ adm/lpd-errs:\
   :rp=sys$lspr:
        . . . . .
        . . . . .
#
#Remote printers on RISC computers (RS01CH and RS09CH)
#
15|exrisc|rs09ch|ex| ex printer:\
   :lp=:rm=rs09ch:sd=/usr/spool/lpd/risc:lf=/usr/adm/lpd-errs:\
   :rp=ex:
16|psrisc|rs01ch|ps|postscript| ps printer:\
   :lp=:rm=rs01ch:sd=/usr/spool/lpd/risc:lf=/usr/adm/lpd-errs:\
   :rp=ps:
         . . . . .
```

```
   .....
#
# Printer for SGI
20|lsv:\
  :lp=:rm=mvaxgr:sd=/ usr/spool/lpd/sgi:lf=/usr/ adm/lpd-errs:\
  :rp=sys$lspr:
```

The */etc/printcap* is a simplified version of the *termcap* database (discussed in Chapter 11), adapted to fully describe printers. The printer spooling subsystem accesses the *printcap* file every time it is used, allowing dynamic addition and deletion of a printer's data.

The basic rules for creating a *printcap* entry are:

- The lines beginning with # (a number sign) are comments, and are not active lines.
- Each entry can have an arbitrary number of items (fields) separated by colons (:); an entry can continue from one line to another using the usual UNIX continuation backslash character (\) at the end of a line.
- Each printer is often identified by multiple names; the names are arbitrary and are the names available to that user on the system. The first name is, by convention, a number; the second given name is the most common abbreviation for the printer, and the last name should be the long name fully identifying the printer. The second name should contain no blanks; the last name may contain blanks for readability. A vertical line (the pipe character "|") separates the printers' names, and at least one of the names should be easy to use: short, logical, and easy to remember.
- The default printer is identified by the generic name ***lp***, appended to its other names; this will be explained in greater detail later. The BSD printing commands supports a **-P *printer*** option to explicitly determine the destination printer.
- The remaining fields describe the printer's capabilities (characteristics), resources, and its use.

All ***capabilities*** in the ***printcap*** file are specified by two-character codes, and may be of three possible types:

Boolean Capabilities, which, if they appear in a field, indicate that the printer has some particular feature. Boolean capabilities are simply written in an entry's fields between the ":" characters. In the capability table that follows, they are indicated by the word "bool" in the *type* column.

Numeric Capabilities that supply information such as baud-rates, number of lines per page, etc. Numeric capabilities are specified by the word "num" in the *type* column of the capabilities table that follows. Numeric capabilities are identified by the two-character capability code with the trailing "#" character followed by the numeric value. The following example is a numeric entry stating that this printer should run at 1200 baud: "*:br#1200:*"

String Capabilities that specify a sequence that should be used to perform particular printer operations, for example, a cursor motion. String valued capabilities are specified by the word "str" in the *type* column of the capabilities table that follows. String valued capabilities are identified by the two-character capability code with the trailing "=" sign, followed by a string up to the next colon ":". For example, "*:rp=spinwriter:*" is a sample entry stating that the remote printer is named ***spinwriter***.

The table of various ***capabilities*** (in alphabetic order) follows; the most common capabilities are presented in **bold**.

Name	Type	Default	Description
af	str	NULL	**Name of accounting file**
br	num	none	If *lp* is a tty, set the baud rate
cf	str	NULL	Cifplot data filter
df	str	NULL	TeX data filter (DVI format)
du	str	0	User ID of user "daemon"
fc	num	0	If lp is a tty, clear flag bits
ff	**str**	**"\f"**	**String to send for a form feed**
fo	bool	false	Print a form feed when device is opened
fs	num	0	Like "fc" but set bits
gf	str	NULL	Graph data filter (plot(3X) format)
hl	bool	false	Print the burst header page last
ic	bool	false	Driver supports (nonstandard) ioctl to indent printout
if	**str**	**NULL**	**Name of input/communication filter (created per job)**
lf	**str**	**"/dev/console"**	**Error logging file name**
lo	str	"lock"	Name of lock file
lp	**str**	**"/dev/lp"**	**Device name to open for output**
mc	num	0	Maximum number of copies
ms	str	NULL	List of terminal modes to set or clear
mx	num	1000	Maximum file size (in BUFSIZ blocks), zero = unlimited
nd	str	NULL	Next directory for list of queues (unimplemented)
nf	str	NULL	Ditroff data filter (device independent troff)
of	**str**	**NULL**	**Name of output/banner filter (created once)**
pc	num	200	Price per foot or page in hundredths of cents
pl	num	66	Page length (in lines)
pw	num	132	Page width (in characters)
px	num	0	Page width in pixels (horizontal)
py	num	0	Page length in pixels (vertical)
rf	str	NULL	Filter for printing FORTRAN style text files
rg	str	NULL	Restricted group, only members of group allowed access
rm	**str**	**NULL**	**Machine name for remote printer**
rp	**str**	**"lp"**	**Remote printer name argument**
rs	bool	false	Restrict remote users to those with local accounts
rw	bool	false	Open printer device read/write instead of write-only
sb	bool	false	Short banner (one line only)
sc	bool	false	Suppress multiple copies
sd	**str**	**"/var/spool/lpd"**	**Spool directory**
sf	bool	false	Suppress form feeds
sh	bool	false	Suppress printing of burst page header
st	str	"status"	Status file name
tc	str	NULL	Name of similar printer; must be last
tf	str	NULL	Troff data filter (C/A/T phototypesetter)
tr	str	NULL	Trailer string to print when queue empties
vf	str	NULL	Raster image filter
xc	num	0	If lp is a tty, clear local mode bits
xs	num	0	Like "xc" but set bits

10.2.1.2 Setting the BSD Default Printer

The system default printer is defined by the generic name ***lp*** within the */etc/printcap* file. The entry for the default printer should have attached ***lp*** to one, or more of its valid names, and only one entry can have such a name. Otherwise, the default printer will not be defined properly, and the first defined default entry within the file will be interpreted as the default destination. In the past, the local printer accessed via the special file */dev/lp* was usually assumed to be the default one; however, the default printer could be any local or remote printer (***lp*** could be assigned to any entry in the file). It is not mandatory to specify a default printer at all, in fact. Obviously, none of the existing printers can be regularly named "lp"; otherwise BSD printing subsystem will assume this printer for the default one. Such a restriction does not present a real problem in the implementation.

Individual users can specify their own default printers with the ***PRINTER*** environment variable. The default printer is usually the most used printer, and the only benefit of using the default printer is the shorter printing commands (since there is no need for the **-P** option). All other printing characteristics are defined in the *printcap* file in the same way as for other printers.

10.2.1.3 Spooling Directories

The spooling directory holds files destined for a particular printer until the ***lpd*** daemon can process them for printing. Spooling directories are conventionally subdirectories located in */usr/spool* or */var/spool*. Each printer has to have a defined spooling directory; otherwise, the printing will be disabled.

The spooling directory is defined within the printer's printcap entry in the */etc/printcap* file. The field:

sd=/usr/spool/dir_name Defines the spooling directory for the corresponding printer

All spooling directories must be owned by the user ***daemon***, and the group ***daemon***, with the access mode *755* (drwxr-xr-x). Such a protection scheme gives the necessary write access to files that have been spooled, forcing users to use the printer spooling system and preventing anyone from deleting someone else's pending files, or otherwise abusing the system.

For example, to create a new spooling directory named */usr/spool/newprinter* when the new printer ***newprinter*** is added to the system, the following commands should be executed:

 # cd /usr/spool

 # mkdir newprinter

 # chown daemon.daemon newprinter (original BSD syntax)

 # chmod 755 newprinter

 # ls -ld

drwxr-xr-x 2 daemon daemon 2048 May 12 11:15 newprinter

The location of spooling directories varies among BSD UNIX flavors (for example, the common location of the spooling directory on SunOS was */var/spool*).

10.2.1.4 Filters

The UNIX "piping" ability is widely implemented in the printing subsystem. A number of filters can be inserted in sequence in print job processing; these filters match printing files with printers. This approach provides the maximum possible flexibility in printing and makes the printing subsystem independent of the implemented printers. Quite simply, all required matching and any necessary adjustment of any specific printer characteristic becomes programmable. Filters are usually shell script files, and they are specified within the printer capability database in the */etc/printcap* file. Most of the filters are correlated with the options of the print command **lpr**; a corresponding filter provides the necessary preprocessing of data to fulfill the option's requirements. However, two filters are the most common: *if* — the input filter — and *of* — the output filter. Their names often cause confusion, because the filters are used in an almost identical way: they are called by the daemon when a print job is sent to a printer (in that sense they are both output filters for the daemon, or input filters for a printing device).

When a user does not specify a filter-related option, either the *if* or *of* filter will be used. There are three cases of the corresponding *printcap* entry in the */etc/printcap* database worth examining:

1. If the field *if* occurs, but no *of* field exists, the *if* filter will be called every time any print job is sent to the print device.
2. If the field *of* occurs, but no *if* field exists, the *lpd* daemon will call the *of* filter once for all print jobs in a queue and send them en masse to the print device.
3. If both fields *if* and *of* exist, the *of* filter will be used to send the banner page, while the *if* filter will be called for every print job separately.

It is highly recommended that a system administrator use *if* filters, because they are much easier to debug; *of* filters can be very confusing.

One of the common problems related to printing is the so-called **staircase effect** in the printing. What is the staircase effect? The character pair CRLF (carriage-return/line-feed) is a common way to terminate each line of text, because old mechanical teletypes required a carriage return before shifting to a new line. UNIX continued this traditional text treatment. However, in a DOS text file, each line of text is terminated with a LF (line-feed) character only, assuming an automatic insertion of the CR (carriage-return) character. If such a file reaches the UNIX environment unchanged, from the UNIX standpoint, the file is corrupted and incomplete. Taken literally, this text file printed on an ASCII device will start each line below the end of the previous line. This is known as the staircase effect.

In today's heterogeneous system environment, transfer of files between UNIX and non-UNIX platforms is quite common (for added confusion, on the Apple/Macintosh platform each line of the text is terminated with CR character only), and situations such as the staircase effect are quite possible. The commands **unix2dos** and **dos2unix** (sometimes named **ux2dos**, and **dos2ux**) are available on the UNIX platform to correct transferred files.

This pending problem can also be fixed by providing the appropriate data filtering during printing. Some printers can be set to treat the single LF character as the (LF + CR) pair, while others cannot. In the later case, one solution is to create an appropriate input shell script filter, which will convert each line of text before printing. Below we will see two possible solutions, tested on the Linux platform. These examples are written for the *bash* shell (Bourne Again Shell) and the Panasonic KX-P4411 laser printer.

A shell script input filter that adds a CR character at the end of each line can be created:

```
#!/bin/sh
if [ "$1" = -l ];then
   cat
else
   sed -e s/$/^M
/
fi
# The "echo -ne" assumes that /bin/sh is really bash
echo -ne \\f
```

Let us name the file *crlf-if1*. The test of the first argument "$1" allows a bypass of the insertion of CR when the **lpr -l** command is used; otherwise, the CR character is inserted at the end of each line using the sequential editor ***sed*** ("^M" is a CR character, edited by ***vi*** as "*CTRL-v CTRL-m*"). At the end of the file, the "form-feed" is sent to print the last page properly.

Alternatively, the printer itself can be controlled by an external escape sequence that sets the way the printer handles LF character (it treats the LF character as two joint characters, CR+LF). For the implemented PANASONIC printer, the escape sequence is: "*ESC &k2G.*" A simple filter that uses the **echo -ne** command to send this sequence at the start of printing could be:

```
#!/bin/sh
# Filter for HP printer to treat LF as CRLF
# The "echo -ne" assumes that /bin/sh is really bash
echo -ne \\033"&k2G"
cat
echo -ne \\f
```

Let us name this file *crlf-if2*, and copy both filter files in the */usr/lib/filters* directory:

 # ls -l /usr/lib/filters/crlf-in*

```
-rwxr-xr-x   1 root   daemon   128 Dec 14 16:25 crlf-if1
-rwxr-xr-x   1 root   daemon   147 Dec 16 09:22 crlf-if2
```

Both filters are workable, but remember that the second filter is printer dependent (it can be slightly different on another printer). Finally, the */etc/printcap* file should be updated appropriately.

The corresponding entries in the */etc/printcap* file are presented:

 # cat /etc/printcap

```
# Copyright (c) 1983 Regents of the University of California.
# All rights reserved.
#   @(#)etc.printcap   5.2 (Berkeley) 5/5/88
#
# Generic printer:
# lp|Generic:\
#     :lp=/dev/lp1:sd=/usr/spool/lp1:sh:
# typical remote printer entry
#
        . . . . .
        . . . . .
#
# PANASONIC Partner jet
pan|pancrlf|panasonic|KX-P4410:\
    :lp=/dev/lp1:\
    :sd=/usr/spool/lp1:\
    :mx#0:\
    :sh:\
    :if=/usr/lib/filters/crlf-if1:\
    :lf=/usr/spool/lp1/pan-err:\
    :tr:
#
# HP Laser jet plus
ljet|hplp|hpj|HP Laserjet:\
    :lp=/dev/lp1:\
    :sd=/usr/spool/lp1:\
```

```
    :mx#0:\
    :sh:\
    :if=/usr/lib/filters/crlf-if2:\
    :lf=/usr/spool/lp1/ hp-err:
#
      .....
      .....
```

The arbitrarily named "logical" printers ("logical" because both point to the same physical printer) ***pan*** and ***ljet*** can easily use both of the above filters.

10.2.1.5 Linux Printing Subsystem

The Linux printing subsystem presents a fairly vanilla BSD implementation. There are some minor differences toward a typical BSD printing subsystem, and we will focus on them. The printer configuration database is located in the */etc/printcap* file which is empty upon the system installation. To add a printer, or printers, Linux provides the X-based graphical tool ***printtool*** which automates editing of the */etc./ printcap* file; Linux strongly recommends the use of this tool, instead of any manual modification. Basically, the usage of ***printtool*** is easy, friendly, and straightforward. The only disadvantage is a required X-server support, and relatively restricted number of printers that the tool handles. For other printers, we can always manually edit the configuration data. Several comprehensive interactive window-levels address the most common printer types, and in most cases the tool is sufficient. ***Printtool*** is illustrated in Figure 10.2.

Linux requires a defined default printer; if a default printer is not explicitly specified by the ***lp*** name, the first printer listed in the */etc/printcap* file becomes the default one. There are also some other Linux syntax-specific issues that we will talk more about in the paragraphs that follow about local and remote printers.

10.2.2 System V Printer Configuration and the Printer Capability Database

We have already mentioned that the System V printing subsystem includes the versatile and powerful administrative command **lpadmin**, which can be used to manage many printing configuration issues. The **lpadmin** command configures LP spooling systems to describe printers, classes, and devices. It is used to add and remove printing destinations, change membership in classes, change devices for printers, change printer interface programs, and change the system default destination.

However, this does not mean the **lpadmin** command is a magic solution for any printing need or problem. It is very helpful in defining and setting the printing resources, but the printing configuration must be saved after the initial setting to be available to the system when needed. It is important to understand the **lpadmin** background — what happens behind the scenes, hidden from users, and even hidden from the system administrators, for successful administration of the System V printing subsystem.

10.2.2.1 The Printer Database Directory Hierarchy on System V

The System V printer capability database is organized differently from BSDs. Instead of a huge single database file (the BSD */etc/printcap* file), in System V there is a printing-related directory hierarchy, or even hierarchies. The core of this hierarchy is the */usr/spool/lp* directory (or */var/spool/lp*, for some flavors) and the */etc/lp* (regardless of the name of the directory, the corresponding links provide uniform access to the data).

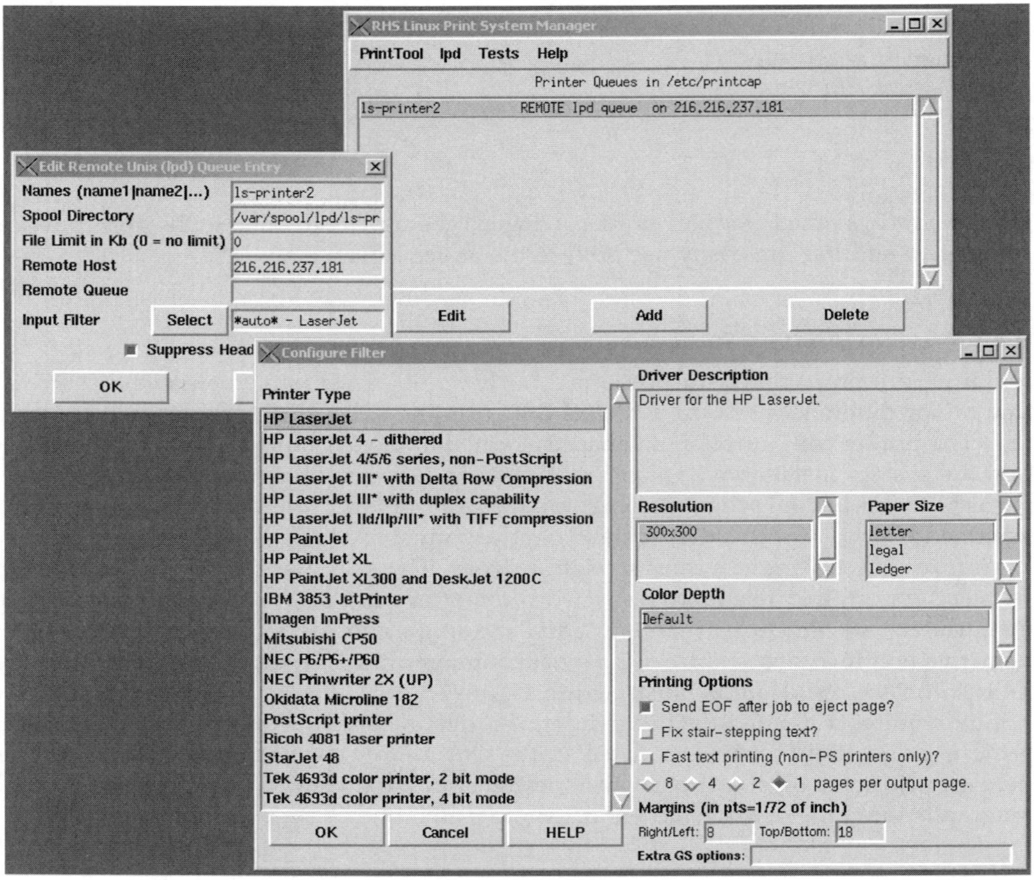

FIGURE 10.2
Linux graphical tool ***printtool***.

Let us examine the directory hierarchy. The **lpadmin** command helps the system administrator handle the printer capability database for different printer models (types). **Model interface programs** are supplied, and installed, with the LP software. These are shell procedures, C programs, or other executable programs that interface between the **lpsched** daemon and printing devices; using the BSD terminology, they are filters for printing on different printers. The standard LP software should include model programs for existing standard printers; the printer vendors should supply less-common models' files. All printer model files reside in the directory */usr/spool/lp/model*. Models should have 644 permission set if owned by ***lp*** and ***bin***, or 664 permission if owned by ***bin*** and ***bin***. Model file names must not exceed 14 characters.

Model programs are important when a new printer is added to the system; the **lpadmin** command relies on model programs (the *lpadmin -m* option) to establish an appropriate interface program for proper future printing on the new printer. Adding new printers could be quite painful without these programs, and could require advanced system administration skills. If only minor modifications are needed, one way around this quandary could be the creation of a new model program by modifying a copy of an existing model. In general, though, it is not easy to deal with model programs this way.

Model programs are scripts, i.e., readable ASCII files. Unfortunately, this is not the case with all printing related files; there are a number of binary files that can only be handled with the available LP front-end commands.

A brief trip through the */usr/spool/lp* hierarchy can provide a better understanding of the System V printing subsystem. Here is an example from the HP-UX platform:

 # ls -F /usr/spool/lp

```
FIFO          cmodel/     interface/   model/     qstatus    sinterface /
SCHEDLOCK     default     log          oldlog     receive/   smodel/
cinterface/   fonts/      lpd. log     outputq    request/
class/        info        member/      pstatus    seqfile
```

 # ls -C /usr/spool/lp/model

```
HPGL1         dumb            hp2560       hp2934a     laserjet
HPGL2         dumbplot        hp2563a      h p33440a   laserjetIIISi
HPGL2.cent    fonts           hp2564b      hp33447a    paintjet
PCL1          hp2225a         hp2565a      hp3630a     postscript
PCL2          hp2225d         hp2566b      hp7440a     quietjet
PCL3          hp2227a         hp2567b      hp7475a     rmodel
PCL4          hp2228a         hp256x.cent  hp7550a     ruggedwriter
clustermodel  hp2235a         hp2631g      hp7570a     thinkjet
colorpro      hp2276a         hp2684a      hp7595a
deskjet       hp2300–1100L    hp2686a      hp7596a
draftpro      hp2300–840L     hp2932a      hpC1208a
```

Model programs correspond to all printer models that can be attached and used on the system. This does not mean that they all are active. Only certain model files take part in creating other active files named "interface" files that reside in the directory */usr/spool/lp/interface*. Interface files are directly involved in the printing process and are important for printers currently in use. In most cases, but not all, these files are direct copies of the corresponding model files.

For example:

 # ls -l /usr/spool/lp/interface

```
total 36
-rwxr-xr-x   1 lp   lp   18416 Mar 30 14:31 panlaser
```

Only one printer is attached to this system, and it has a site-specific name ***panlaser***. The administrator named this particular printer, and the choice was quite logical since it was a Panasonic Laser Printer (please note that the choice of the printer name is arbitrary, but once the printer was installed, users must use this name). It easy to conclude from an inspection of the interface file that the file is a renamed copy of the model file *laserjet* (obviously, this Panasonic laser printer is compatible with the HP Laserjet printer).

On Solaris 2.x a majority of the LP related files reside in the */var/spool/lp* and */etc/lp* directories:

$ ls -l /var/spool/lp

```
total 18
-rw-rw-r--    1 lp     lp      0   Sep 28   09:25 SCHEDLOCK
drwxrwxr-x    2 lp     lp    512   Apr 4    1995 admins
lrwxrwxrwx    1 root   root   23   Apr 4    1995 bin -> ../../../ usr/lib/lp/bin
drwxrwxr-x    4 lp     lp    512   Sep 21   15:24 fifos
lrwxrwxrwx    1 root   root   13   Apr 4    1995 logs -> ../../ lp/logs
lrwxrwxrwx    1 root   root   25   Apr 4    1995 model -> ../../../ usr/lib/lp/model
```

```
drwxrwxr-x    3 lp     lp    512   Apr 4    1995 requests
drwxrwxr-x    2 lp     lp    512   May 9    12:20 system
lrwxrwxrwx    1 root   root   23   Apr 4    1995 temp -> /var/spool/lp/tmp/atlas
drwx--x--x    4 lp     lp    512   Apr 4    1995 tmp
```

$ ls -l /etc/lp

```
total 24
-rw-rw-r--    1 lp     lp   2141   Apr 4    1995 Systems
drwxrwxr-x    2 lp     lp    512   Apr 4    1995 alerts
drwxrwxr-x    2 lp     lp    512   Apr 4    1995 classes
drwxr-xr-x    2 lp     lp    512   Apr 4    1995 fd
drwxrwxr-x    2 lp     lp    512   Apr 4    1995 forms
drwxrwxr-x    2 lp     lp    512   May 9    13:09 interfaces
lrwxrwxrwx    1 root   root   17   Apr 4    1995 logs -> ../../ var/lp/logs
lrwxrwxrwx    1 root   root   17   Apr 4    1995 model -> /usr/lib/lp/model
drwxrwxr-x    2 lp     lp    512   May 9    13:09 printers
drwxrwxr-x    2 lp     lp    512   Apr 4    1995 pwheels
```

10.2.2.2 Setting the System V Default Printer

We should again use the mighty **lpadmin** command to set a systemwide default printer. The command:

$ lpadmin -d hplj6dp

will set the printer named *hplj6dp* as the default one. Any previously set default printer will no longer be the default, and the new default printer become active.

To check a system for the default printer, use the command:

$ lpstat -d

The default printer data is stored in the file */usr/spool/lp/default*.

10.2.3 AIX Printing Facilities

AIX has a different approach to the printing facility: printing is serviced by the spooler daemon **qdaemon**, which is the background server for handling all kinds of queues. **qdaemon** responds to the ***enq*** program, which **enqueues** print jobs and transfers all of the arguments necessary for proper printing. The front-end print commands are **lpr**, **lp,** and **qprt**, which submit print jobs to the spooler daemon via the ***enq*** program. On the other side, **qdaemon** invokes the printer backend program to manage a print job: to initialize a printer, provide filtering, generate a header, etc. Finally, the printer I/O backend **piobe** command, the print job manager, is called.

AIX introduces a bit more flexibility, and a great deal of complexity into printing, but the System Management Interface Tool (***SMIT***) provides a relatively easy-to-use and user-friendly way to administer it.

Programs that administer printing work with virtual printers — sets of attributes that define a specific software "view" of real printers. A user submitting a print job always specifies (directly or indirectly) a particular print queue for the print job. The print request can also specify a particular virtual printer; otherwise, the spooler will select the first available virtual printer associated with the print queue (in the case of multiple associated virtual printers, they are all treated as equals).

A real printer is the printer hardware attached to a serial or parallel port at a unique hardware device address. The kernel communicates with it and provides an interface with a corresponding virtual printer (however, the kernel is not aware of the concept of virtual printers). The SMIT can and should be used to add a real and a virtual printer (although the commands **mkdev** and **mkvirprt** can do the same job).

Multiple virtual printers can use the same real printer, but only one real printer (and one queue) can be associated with each virtual printer.

The attribute values used by the printer backend program reside in colon files in the *Predefined* and *Customized Databases* subdirectories: */usr/lpd/pio/predef* and */usr/lpd/pio/custom* (an AIX example):

$ ls -l /usr/lpd/pio

```
total 56
drwxrwxr-x   2 root  printq   512  Sep 22 15:48  burst
lrwxrwxrwx   1 root  system    25  Sep 22 14:31  custom -> /var/spool/lpd/pio/custom
lrwxrwxrwx   1 root  system    22  Sep 22 14:31  ddi -> /var/spool/lpd/pio/ddi
drwxrwxr-x   2 root  printq  1024  Sep 22 16:34  etc
lrwxrwxrwx   1 root  system    24  Sep 22 14:31  flags -> /var/spool/lpd/pio/flags
drwxrwxr-x   2 root  printq   512  Sep 22 16:34  fmtrs
drwxrwxr-x   2 root  printq   512  Sep 22 14:39  fonts
drwxrwxr-x   2 root  printq  2048  Sep 22 16:34  predef
```

When a new virtual printer is added, the predefined **attribute** values for the particular printer type and data stream type are copied to create a customized set of attributes for the virtual printer (they can be further customized manually). Two database directories are presented in an example from AIX:

$ ls -l /usr/lpd/pio/predef

```
total 912
-rw-rw-r--   1 root  printq  4978  Oct 18 1992   2380.asc
-rw-rw-r--   1 root  printq  5794  Jul 19 1993   2390.asc
-rw-rw-r--   1 root  printq  2598  Oct 12 1993   4019.ps
   .....
   .....
-rw-rw-r--   1 root  printq  2345  Aug 5 1993    dp2665.ps
-rw-rw-r--   1 root  printq  4500  Oct 15 1993   hplj-2.pcl
-rw-rw-r--   1 root  printq  4892  Dec 2 1993    hplj-3.pcl
-rw-rw-r--   1 root  printq  2351  Aug 5 1993    hplj-3.ps
-rw-rw-r--   1 root  printq  5182  Mar 15 1994   hplj-3si.pcl
-rw-rw-r--   1 root  printq  2595  Jul 19 1993   hplj-3si.ps
-rw-rw-r--   1 root  printq  5266  Apr 17 1994   hplj-4.pcl
-rw-rw-r--   1 root  printq  2644  Apr 17 1994   hplj-4.ps
   .....
   .....
```

$ ls -l /var/spool/lpd/pio/custom

```
total 8
-rw-rw-r--   1 root   printq   2367   Oct 2 09:45   ps:lp0
```

File names in the predefined database are of the form ***PrinterType.DataStreamType***. For instance, "***hplj-4.ps***" indicates a Hewlett Packard Laser Jet series 4 with a Post Script. File names in the customized database are of the form ***QueueName:QueueDeviceName***, given by the administrator; as in ***lp0:ps***.

All attribute values in the database colon files are character strings, regardless of whether they represent strings, integers or Boolean. An attribute value can contain embedded references to other attribute values, and can be dynamically determined.

```
$ cat /var/spool/lpd/pio/custom/ps:lp0
:056:__FLG::
:466:_1::!
:467:_2::!
    .....
:030:_L::+
:046:_X::IBM-850
:050:_Z::!
    .....
:063:_a::0
:083:_p::%?%G_2%t%{1}%e%{0}%;%?%G_z%t%{1}%e%{0}%;%+%?%{2}%=%t7%e - 10%;
:090:_s::Courier
:093:_u::1
:100:_w::80
:107:_z::0
:060:__SYS::
:321:sh::%Ide/pioburst %F[H] %Idb/H.ps | %Ide/pioformat -@%Idd/%Imm -!%Idf/piofpt %f[jJ]
    .....
:274:ia::test "$PIOTITLE" != %I@1 && BFLAG=" -b $PIOTITLE ";/usr/bin/enscript %?%CX%t%f[X]%e -
X%I_X%; -p- -q%?%G_2%t -2%;%?%G_z%t -r%;%?%G_3%t - G%;%?%G_1%t%e -B%;%?%G_L%t%e -c%;
%?%Ch%t%fbh%e%?%L_h% t -b'%I_h'%e $BFLAG %;%; -L%G_l%d -f%?%Cs%t%f!s%e%I_s%;%G_p%d -
%?%G_1%t-F%Iw7%G_p%d%;%?%G_4%t -g%;%?%G_5%t -o%;%?%L_f%t%e - %I@1%; | %Iis
    .....
:269:fn::/usr/bin/psc%is
:270:fp::/bin/pr -l%G_l%d -w%G_w%d%F[h] %I@1%ia
:331:mL::PostScript Printer
    .....
    .....
```

The customized ***ps:lp0*** file is a copy of the predefined ***hplj-4.ps*** file; in this case, the implemented post-script printer is actually the Hewlett Packard LaserJet Series 4 post-script printer.

Each attribute is specified by an entry with five fields:

msg_catalog_ID:msg_number:attribute_name::attribute_value

where:

msg_catalog_ID	Identifies the message catalog where the attribute description is stored. It can be an empty field and then the catalog is defined as the name of the colon file with the extension "*cat*."
msg_number	Identifies the message index in the catalog that contains the description of the attribute.
attribute_name	The unique name of the attribute. Alphanumeric characters and underscore (_) are permitted; longer names correspond to comments.
null-string	An empty field for future use.
attribute_value	Specifies the value of the attribute (zero to 1000 characters). Embedded references and logic for dynamically defined attribute values can be included (which generally provides an extremely powerful way to specify an attribute).

Obviously the attribute value string can be a very complex expression used in the communication between the print job manager (the **piobe** command) and the device driver interface program (the **pioout** command).

10.3 Adding New Printers

Adding a new printer onto a system is a common, unavoidable administrative task, and the system administrator must be familiar with this procedure. The following text covers printing subsystem flavors BSD and System V for both local and remote printers.

10.3.1 Adding a New Local Printer

10.3.1.1 Adding a Local BSD Printer

To add a new local printer to a BSD system, several steps must be performed:

- Physically connect a printer to the computer (parallel or serial connection).
- For serial line printers, create or modify an entry in the terminal line configuration file */etc/ttys*, or */etc/ttytab* on SunOS (this will be discussed in greater detail in Chapter 11). The entries should have status ***off***, type ***unknown***, and the keyword ***none*** in the command field.
- If this is the first printer on the system, verify that the part of the **rc** scripts to start the **lpd** daemon is active.
- Add an entry for the printer to the ***/etc/printcap*** file. If the new printer is of the same type as an existing one, the entry for the existing printer can be copied and then modified to the new values:
  - The printer name, in the name field of the entry (multiple names are allowed)
  - The special device file, in the field "***:lp= ... :***"; this field identifies the hardware connection of the local printer, which is the system address of the corresponding special device file
  - The spooling directory, in the field "***:sd= ... :***"
  - An accounting file, in the field "***:af= ... :***" if accounting is active
  - An error log file, in the field "***:lf= ... :***"
  - Other fields remain unmodified for the same type of printer
- If the new printer is the first of its type on the system, then the lines for corresponding entries in the */etc/printcap* file should be commented-out and edited. Printer vendors often provide *printcap entries* for their products.
- Create the corresponding spooling directory for the printer.
- Create the corresponding printer accounting file (if required, and given the printer name "***newprinter***"):

  # touch /usr/adm/lp_acct/newprinter

  # chown daemon /usr/adm/lp_acct/newprinter

  # chmod 755 /usr/adm/lp_acct/newprinter

Note: On some platforms (such as SunOS) the printer account directory could be */var/adm/lp_acct*.

- If the new printer should be the default printer on the system, append "*lp*" to the printer's name and remove "*lp*" from the entry of the previous default printer.
- Start the printer and its queue (given the printer name ***newprinter***):

  # lpc up newprinter

- Test the new printer by spooling a short message for printing. An effective way to do this is:

  # banner "Testing" "of" "newprinter" | lpr -Pnewprinter

  An attractive, banner-style, message should be printed.

The following example illustrates a printcap entry for a local HP LaserJet5 printer, connected to the serial port specified by the special device file */dev/ttya*; all names are arbitrary. The previously discussed fields are printed in ***bold***.

```
# Entry for HP LaserJet IV printer named newprinter
newprinter|lj5|hplj5|ljv|HP LaserJet 5: \
   :lp=/dev/ttya:sd=/usr/spool/newprinter:\
   :lf=/usr/adm/newprinter.log:\
   :ms=-parity,-cstopb,-clocal,cread,ixon,ixoff,-opost:\
   :fc#0777:fs#06021:sb:sh:xc#07737:xs#040:\
   :mx#0:br#9600:of=/usr/lib/hplaserjet:
```

10.3.1.2 Adding a Local Linux Printer

To add a Linux printer, we use the available Linux ***printtool*** utility (it is recommended, but not mandatory). In the following example we see how the */etc/printcap* file looks like after adding a local printer ***lp1*** by using this tool.

```
$ cat /etc/printcap
#
# Please don't edit this file directly unless you know what you are doing!
# Be warned that the control-panel printtool requires a very strict format!
# Look at the printcap(5) man page for more info.
#
# This file can be edited with the printtool in the control-panel.
##PRINTTOOL3## LOCAL laserjet 300×300 letter {} LaserJet Default {}
lp1|lplocal:\
        :sd=/var/spool/lpd/lp1:\
        :mx#0:\
        :sh:\
        :lp=/dev/lp1:\
        :if=/var/spool/lpd/lp1/filter:
```

From the listed printcap entry, it can be seen that the printer ***lp1*** has an alternative name ***lplocal***. It is connected to the parallel port */dev/lpl*, as well as the names of the spooling directory and input filter. Other printing parameters are related to the maximum job size and print header. The specified filter file is one among available printer-filters located in the corresponding filter depot directory. It is easy to conclude by listing the filter file itself:

$ ls -l /var/spool/lpd/lp1 | grep filter
lrwxrwxrwx 1 root root 44 Feb 5 20:10 filter -> /usr/lib/rhs/rhs-printfilters//master-filter

When a single Linux printer is specified, this printer is automatically the default one; there is no need to label this printer with the additional name ***lp***.

10.3.1.3 Adding a Local System V Printer

In System V, the administrative command ***lpadmin -v*** is used to add a new local printer. The option "**-v**" specifies a local printer and requires as argument the corresponding special device file. When a new printer is added to the system, the following information must be supplied:

lpadmin -p*newprinter* -v*special_file interface_option*

where

newprinter	The name of the new printer.
special_file	The full pathname of the special file through which the system will communicate with the new printer.
interface-options	Includes several possible options.
-m *model*	Specify a printer by the existing model type. The corresponding model program from the */usr/spool/lp/model* directory is copied into the */usr/spool/lp/interface* directory (or on some platforms, */var/spool/lp*).
-e *oldprinter*	Copy ***oldprinter***'s interface file; oldprinter must be an existing printer.
-i *interface_path*	Specify the full pathname of the printer interface file, introduced for this purpose.

The "**-e**" option is the easiest to implement when the same, already tested and proven interface from an existing printer is used for the new printer. The "**-m**" option is also easy to implement if a standard, well-known model program defines the new printer.

Creating a new custom-designed interface program (the "**-i**" option) can be a hard job; an interface program (often a script, but not necessarily a script) can be very complex. By convention, the program takes the following arguments:

$1 job ID
$2 username
$3 job title
$4 number of copies
$5 printer-specific options
$6 files to be printed

When it is invoked, the interface program standard output is redirected to the printer, and the program arguments can be processed in an arbitrary number of ways for different printing scenarios.

The simplest possible interface program is:

```
# This is the simplest LP interface
# It ignores most initial arguments, and
# prints the file as it is.
#
#!/ bin/sh
cat $6 2>&1
```

The **lpsched** daemon must be shut down during printer installation and reinvoked afterward. It is recommended that you test the new printer after installation:

$ banner "Testing" "of" "newprinter" | lp -d newprinter

10.3.2 Adding a New Remote Printer

Both printer spooling subsystems allow remote printing. A destination printer could be a part of another remote UNIX system or an individual network printer that supports UNIX-style printing (basically the TCP/IP and the corresponding type of the printing subsystem). UNIX does not differentiate between remote and network printers, it simply treats a network printer as a single printer on a remote system. This is a logical approach because a network printer is identified within the network in the same way as any other remote UNIX system.

Remote printing corresponds to the server/client model, where a client is a UNIX system in which the remote printer is defined, and where users use this printer; this is the origin of a printing request. A client requests a printing service, which is provided at another remote system, known as a print server (may not be a UNIX system).

10.3.2.1 Adding a Remote BSD Printer

The BSD printing subsystem defines remote printers, as any other printers, through its printer capability database in the */etc/printcap* file. A remote printer requires a *printcap entry* slightly different from that of a local printer. It is important to understand that:

- A number of printer characteristics are determined on the server side, where the printer is local; the client has no influence on these predefined printer characteristics, and corresponding printcap entries are meaningless and automatically outposted.
- New printcap entries, specific for remote printing, were introduced and they must be used.
- The remote destination has to be known to the system, as does the way to reach the destination. In other words, the system must be properly connected to the network.
- The print server has to support BSD printing.

In the already presented section of the */etc/printcap* file, several printcap entries refer to the remote printers. We will analyze one of them:

```
16|psrisc|rs01ch|ps|postscript| ps printer:\
  :lp=:rm=rs01ch:sd=/usr/spool/lpd/risc:lf=/usr/adm/lpd-errs:\
  :rp=ps:
```

The name of the remote printer is *psrisc* (Postscript printer on the RS6000 system); alternative names are possible.

- The empty *":lp=:"* field shows that this entry describes a remote printer (remember, for a local printer this field specifies a corresponding special device file).
- The field *":rm=rs01ch:"* indicates the destination system for remote printing (on a remote machine). It can be specified with the valid DNS name of the system (in this case, *"rs01ch"*) or its IP address (DNS and IP addressing are discussed in Chapters 15 and 16).
- The field *":rp=ps:"* holds the name of the target remote printer on the remote system (in this case, *"ps"*). This name must match the name of the corresponding local printer on the remote system.

These three fields are mandatory for the proper definition of a remote printer. It is a good idea to define several more fields that strictly define printing issues on the client side, such as:

- The field *":sd=/usr/spool/lpd/risc:"* specifies the spooling directory (in this case *"/usr/spool/lpd/risc"*). It is recommended that you use the printer name as a spooling subdirectory.
- The field *":lf=/usr/adm/lpd-errs:"* specifies the error log file. A single log file may be defined for multiple printers.

The entry does not contain any specific details about the remote printer other than its name. The needed information is specified in the */etc/printcap* file on the remote system (if the remote system is a BSD UNIX system at all), or in another appropriate way.

On the printer server side, very little administration is required. Assuming the selected remote printer already exists as a local printer there, the server's */etc/printcap* file remains unmodified. However, to allow users from a client system to access and print on the print server, the client system itself must be specified as a ***trusted system***; the hostname of the client system must be included in the server's */etc/hosts.equiv* file (this is discussed in Chapter 19), or in the server's */etc/hosts.lpd* file (the structure of this file is the same as the */etc/hosts.equiv*). Otherwise, remote print requests from the client system will be refused.

10.3.2.2 Adding a Remote Linux Printer

Although Linux is mainly BSD compliant in the printing segment, there are some odds we have to mention. Of course, use of the available ***printtool*** utility is again recommended. Supposing we are adding two more remote printers on the Linux system we have already discussed, two more */etc/printcap* entries have been specified afterward:

```
##PRINTTOOL3## REMOTE POSTSCRIPT 600×600 letter {} PostScript Default 1
lp02|testlp:\
    :sd=/var/spool/lpd/lp02:\
    :mx#0:\
    :rm=ls-printer2:\
    :rp=lp02:\
    :lpd_bounce=true:\
    :sh:\
    :if=/var/spool/lpd/lp02/filter:
```

```
##PRINTTOOL3## REMOTE lj4dith 600×600 letter {} LaserJet4dither Default {}
lp01:\
    :sd=/var/spool/lpd/lp01:\
    :mx#0:\
    :sh:\
    :rm=ls-printer1:\
    :rp=lp01:\
    :lpd_bounce=true:\
    :if=/var/spool/lpd/ lp01/filter:
```

Two added remote printers are local printers on remote machines ***ls-printer2*** and ***ls-printer1*** (actually they are network printers identified by these names); this is specified within the usual "***rm=***" fields. What is unusual is the lack of the expected BSD configuration field "***lp=;***" Linux simply assumes a remote printer except if it is not explicitly specified as the local one. Other fields are the known ones, or their variations.

10.3.2.3 Adding a Remote System V Printer

The basic concept of remote System V printing is the same as with BSD: the client/server model and the required local setting of printers on the server side remain the same. However, setting remote printers on the client side is different, and again the powerful **lpadmin** command is used. Three arguments are required to appropriately set a remote printer: a *printer name* on the client side, a print server (a *remote machine*) name, and a *remote printer* name (the name of a local printer on the server side). The **lpadmin** command provides corresponding options for these arguments. Unfortunately, the use of the command is not uniform among System V flavors — different "*lpadmin options*" are available for this purpose. We will consider two of them: Solaris 2.x and the HP-UX flavor.

10.3.2.3.1 *Setting a Remote Printer on Solaris 2.x*

lpadmin -p ***printer-name*** **-s** ***remsystem-name!remprinter-name***

where

printer-name	Name selected to designate the remote printer
remsystem-name	Name of the remote system that should provide printing (in versions up to Solaris 2.6, must be listed in the */etc/lp/Systems* file)
remprinter-name	Local name of the printer on the remote system

The */etc/lp/Systems* file contains a list (table) of all associated remote systems and printers. The ***lpsystem*** command is available to update the file. We will discuss this issue later in more detail, as a part of cross-platform printing.

10.3.2.3.2 *Setting a Remote Printer on HP-UX*

The HP-UX platform is consistent regarding this issue within releases HP-UX 9.0x, HP-UX 10.xx, and HP-UX 11.xx.

lpadmin -p*printer-name* -orm*remsystem-name* -orp*remprinter-name*

where

printer-name	Name selected to designate the remote printer
remsystem-name	Name of the remote system that should provide printing
remprinter-name	Local name of the printer on the remote system

The HP-UX approach is more flexible; it enables several printing issues besides a remote printer to be set, like specifying the commands to cancel requests to remote printers and to obtain the status of requests to remote printers. Specifying the corresponding "cancel" and "status" models provides these functions, so when the **cancel** and **lpstat** commands for remote printers are used, they refer to defined models. The template models are supplied with the LP software residing on the */usr/spool/lp/cmodel* and */usr/spool/lp/smodel* directories, and they should be sufficient for most implementations.

The corresponding **lpadmin** options to set remote cancel and status models are:

lpadmin -ocm*rcmodel* *rcmodel* is the remote cancel model
lpadmin -osm*rsmodel* *rsmodel* is the remote status model

Let us see what the template cancel and status models look like:

 # ls -l /usr/spool/lp/cmodel
total 2
-r--r--r-- 1 bin bin 107 Dec 2 1993 rcmodel

 # cat /usr/spool/lp/cmodel/rcmodel
#!/ bin/sh
 # / @(#) $Revision: 66.1 $ */*
 # This model is for remote cancel operation.
*/usr/lib/rcancel $**

 # ls -l /usr/spool/lp/smodel
total 2
-r--r--r-- 1 bin bin 107 Dec 2 1993 rsmodel

 # cat /usr/spool/lp/smodel/rsmodel
#!/ bin/sh
 # / @(#) $Revision: 66.1 $ */*
 # This model is for remote status operation.
*/usr/lib/rlpstat $**

Both models are scripts and rely on special commands (**rcancel** and **rlpstat**) provided by HP-UX to deal with remote printers. If you execute the usual printing-related commands for remote printers:

cancel -p*remprinter print-requests*

or

lpstat -p*remprinter*

instead of the expected **cancel** and **lpstat** commands, the corresponding **rcancel** and **rlpstat** commands will be executed.

10.4 UNIX Cross-Platform Printer Spooling

We have discussed BSD and System V printing subsystems in great detail; however, besides the fact that they are very different from one another, they are also mutually noncompatible. Incompatibility can be a serious obstacle in providing the unique print service on a multiplatform environment. UNIX vendors treat this problem differently (if they do at all); some UNIX flavors include both versions of printer spooling subsystems as standard parts of the UNIX distribution, while others provide specific filters, programs, commands, or utilities to bridge two subsystems. We will discuss a few cases.

10.4.1 BSD and AIX Cross-Printing

AIX supports BSD-like remote printing; the BSD-like daemon ***lpd*** is running on the system and monitoring port 515 for incoming remote print requests. In a sense, AIX supports the BSD printer spooling subsystem; the */etc/hosts.lpd* or */etc/hosts.equiv* files define trusted systems from which remote printing is allowed.

However, this is not sufficient for successful cross-printing; incoming print jobs must be additionally filtered as appropriate. Special BSD filters exist for this purpose.

ls -l /usr/lib/lpd

```
total 5504
  .....
  .....
-r-xr-x---   1 root   printq   2601   Jul 16 1994   aixlong
-r-xr-x---   1 root   printq   2797   Jul 16 1994   aixshort
-r-xr-x---   1 root   printq   3229   Jul 16 1994   aixv2long
-r-xr-x---   1 root   printq   3189   Jul 16 1994   aixv2short
-r-xr-xr-x   1 bin    bin      3394   Jul 16 1994   attlong
-r-xr-xr-x   1 bin    bin      2983   Jul 16 1994   attshort
-r-xr-x---   1 root   printq   4654   Jul 16 1994   bsdlong
-r-xr-x---   1 root   printq   3867   Jul 16 1994   bsdshort
  .....
  .....
```

Different filtering methods should be applied when remote print requests are received from other AIX systems, from System V (AT&T) systems, or from BSD systems. The corresponding administration is performed through the SMIT tool.

10.4.2 Solaris and BSD Cross-Printing

Solaris 2.x introduced the special **lpsystem** command to register remote systems with the print service; the command handles the master file for remote printing */etc/lp/Systems* and defines requested parameters to control communication with remote systems (parameters such as *type, retry* and *timeout*). The *type* parameter defines the remote system as one of two types: "s5" (System V-like, or Solaris-like, which is default), or "bsd" (BSD-like). The format of the command is:

lpsystem *[-t type] [-T timeout] [-R retry] [-y "comment"] remote_system_name*

remote_system_name is the name of the remote system from/to which print jobs can be received/sent. If it is a plus sign ("+"), then anonymous client support is enabled. If the "bsd" type is defined, then cross-platform printing is selected.

Other options of the **lpsystem** command enable the user to print out a description of the parameters associated with a specific system, to remove an entry associated with a system, and other miscellaneous functions.

The remaining steps to enable remote printing are the same as in the case of single-platform spooling, which we have already discussed.

Let us look at a practical example of remote printing setup. We want to provide remote printing on a default printer connected to the specific PC (of course, this PC is a separate host on the network, and Windows-based BSD-like remote printer and spooler daemons are running on it). The first step is to execute the command:

```
$ lpsystem -t bsd -R 1 levi
levi has been added              # this was the system response
```

The command defines BSD-like printing on the remote PC-host named ***levi***. The new entry is automatically added into the */etc/lp/Systems* file for a new remote host; although the file is an ASCII one, do not use editors to modify it. We will check the file (it is well commented, so additional explanations are not needed):

```
$ cat /etc/lp/Systems
#
#ident "@(#)Systems 1.6   93/03/19 SMI" /* SVr4.0 1.2 */
#
#  The following "#VERSION=" keyword is neccessary.
#VERSION=1
#
#  LP Spooler System Information
#
#  Format (same line separated by ":")
#
#  System-name
#     The name of the remote system.
#
#  System-password
#     The remote systems password (encrypted) for using our local LP services.
#     (Currently unused. Reserved for security version.)
#
#  Reserved
#     Must be a "-"
#
#  system-type (s5|bsd)
#     The type of the remote system.
#     s5: implies an SVR4.0 machine AND SVR4.0 lp (network independent)
#         communication protocol.
#     bsd: implies TCP/IP network communication AND BSD lpd specific communication
#         protocol. (This is used ONLY if the remote system is connected to the
#         local system via TCP/IP AND it is a BSD OS.
#
#  Reserved
#     Must be a "-"
#
#  timeout (minutes)
```

```
#       "n" == never timeout
#       "0" == do not wait for work
#       >0 == wait for work
#       Default: Never
#
#   retry (minutes)
#       "n" == do not retry if connection is dropped.
#       "0" == retry immediately if connection is dropped.
#       >0 == retry every N minutes until timeout.
#       Default: 10 minutes
#
#   Reserved
#       Must be a "-"
#
#   Reserved
#       Must be a "-"
#
#   Comment
#
#   NOTE: Unused fields must contain a dash except for the password field which should contain an "x" and the
#           comment field which can be blank.
#
#   Example:
#   Kepler:x:-:s5:-:n:10:-:-:SVR4.0 OS
#   fubar:x:-:bsd:10:n:-:-:BSD OS
#   Galileo:x:-:s5:-:30:10:-:-:
#
#   If the first field (i.e. the System Name) contains a "+", then *all* incoming connections will be established,
#   regardless of whether or not there's an entry here for the remote system! This will reduce your maintenance when
#   you have a number of clients, and you don't really care about restricting your printer. Conceivably a print
#   server could just contain a single entry of the following form for both BSD and SVR4 clients:
#   ±:x:-:s5:-:n:10:-:-:Allow all connections
#########
#
±:x:-:s5:-:n:10:-:-:Allow all connections
levi:x:-:bsd:-:n:1:-:-:Local printer on PC
```

The first entry is the default one and it allows System V remote printing from/to all hosts in the network. Sometimes it is a good idea to move out this line with the command:

```
$ lpsystem -r +
Removed "+"        # this is the system response
```

The second entry is our contribution; it defines BSD printing on the remote host "*levi*."

To list current remote printing possibilities:

```
$ lpsystem -l
System:                       +
Type:                         s5
Connection timeout:           never
Retry failed connections:     after 10 minutes
Comment:                      allow all connections
System:                       levi
Type:                         bsd
Connection timeout:           never
Retry failed connections:     after 1 minutes
Comment:                      local printer on PC
```

The next step is to define the remote printer: the name of the printer for users and a real printer's name on the remote system.

$ lpadmin -p local -s levi!default

The new printer is identified as "local" (the name is arbitrary, but once defined users must use it to identify this specific printer). The remote printer name "default" is used here to denote the default PC printer (in this case there is a single printer connected to the PC).

Two more steps are required to enable the defined printer. The following two commands should be executed at the end of the process:

$ accept local

$ enable local

Please note that starting with Solaris 2.6, the **lpsystem** command and the */etc/lp/Systems* file are becoming obsolete.

10.4.3 Third-Party Printer Spooling Systems

Generally, UNIX provides a decent printer spooling subsystem independent of the specific flavor of the given system. It works well, it is flexible enough, and it is fully supported and well documented. However, in administering it, you will soon see occasional strange printing-related behaviors, unexpected problems with printers, hangs of the printing daemon, and difficulties in maintaining printing queues. During production hours, fixing these problems can be quite painful.

These problems left a market open for third parties to develop better printer spooling software, and several solutions came into being, including third-party software (for example, EasySpooler by the Seay Systems, Inc.) and UNIX vendor-specific optional software (like HP-UX JetAdmin software). This software offers a more reliable, more stable, and easier-to-use printing environment. Of course, additional burdens are also placed on the system administrator, who must be familiar with the new software. The full benefits of the additional (or optional) software are achieved only if this software is configured and maintained appropriately.

From the user standpoint, the use of the printing subsystem must be completely transparent; users should not be aware of underlying printing software, they simply need to be able to print. From the administration standpoint, however, it is crucial to have a reliable, stable, and easy to maintain printing subsystem. Though there are no "universal formulas" to make any specific decision in creating such a subsystem, it seems that the generic UNIX printing subsystem is quite sufficient for a print client, while under some circumstances, it is worth considering third-party printer spooling software for a print server. In any case, the final decision is up to the system administrator or the administration team responsible for the actual system.

11

Terminals

11.1 Terminal Characteristics

Terminals have been common devices in the communication between users and UNIX systems for a very long time. The *modus vivendi* for each UNIX system is to provide services to users, so from the very early days of its development, UNIX has paid full attention to terminals as vehicles for users to log into the system. Evidence of this attention can be seen in many UNIX administration issues, primarily by the fact that the system guarantees an immediate respawning of the eventually killed ***getty*** process which controls each connected terminal. A terminal connection is too valuable for UNIX to allow it to be lost; a connected terminal without an attached ***getty*** process cannot function properly, so the ***getty*** process can never die. We will discuss this topic and other terminal-related issues in this Chapter.

While terminals were, in the past, the only way for the system to communicate with users, today they are used only sporadically, primarily for the system console. All major communication with users is now performed through the network. Does this mean that terminals are obsolete? Well, this statement is partially true for terminal units themselves; however, the UNIX concept of communicating with users via terminals remains. The appropriate adaptation was needed: pseudo-terminals, "logical terminals" that behave like real terminals without having a corresponding physical unit, replace the old terminals. We will also address pseudo-terminals in this Chapter.

Terminals are connected with the computer over serial lines and are accessed, like all other devices in UNIX, by the corresponding special device files. Modems are treated in almost the same way as terminals.

As with many other issues, UNIX manages terminals in two major ways; again we will address two platforms: BSD and System V (or AT&T). The two approaches are quite different; they rely on different configuration files, they are based on different terminal capability databases, and sometimes they use different administrative commands. On the other hand, they also overlap in many aspects, and through their development, some of the administrative commands have become common for both platforms.

11.1.1 BSD Terminal Subsystem

Although most of the UNIX flavors that support BSD terminal subsystem are old-fashioned platforms, sometimes even obsolete ones (or on their way to becoming obsolete), we will start with the BSD terminal subsystem. Obsolescence is generally true for terminals as input/output devices, with the exception of the console. In any case, it is difficult to discuss this topic without going back to the earlier days of UNIX, when terminals were a part of every UNIX system. However, there is no doubt about the educational benefits of discussing the BSD terminal subsystem; it explains the continuity in the UNIX development and makes it easier to understand the System V approach to terminals.

11.1.1.1 BSD Terminal Line Initialization

Terminals are connected to a system via terminal lines. To make a system available to users, the terminal lines must be initialized and put into operational mode during the system startup.

The terminal line initialization is a regular part of the startup procedure to bring the system into multi-user mode. Originally, on the BSD system, ***init***, *the process #1*, first spawns a shell during the system startup to interpret the commands in the initialization script */etc/rc*. Once the script */etc/rc* is successfully completed, ***init*** forks a copy of itself for each terminal device that is specified for use in the terminal line configuration file ***/etc/ttys***. Copies of the ***init*** program then invoke (by the *exec* system call) other system programs specified by the corresponding terminal line entries in the configuration file; usually, this was the ***/etc/getty*** program. The ***getty*** program is responsible for opening and initializing the terminal line; it sets the initial parameters for a terminal line and establishes the type of terminal attached to the line. The ***getty*** program can be directed to accept connections at a variety of baud rates. The ***getty***'s actions are driven by another configuration file ***/etc/gettytab***, known as the terminal line definition file. The whole procedure, as well as a terminal initialization, is illustrated in Figure 11.1.

A good BSD representative is *SunOS 4.1.x*, which uses a slightly modified initialization procedure; besides some changes in **rc** initialization scripts, it also renamed the terminal line configuration file into ***/etc/ttytab***. However, the purpose and initialization steps remained the same.

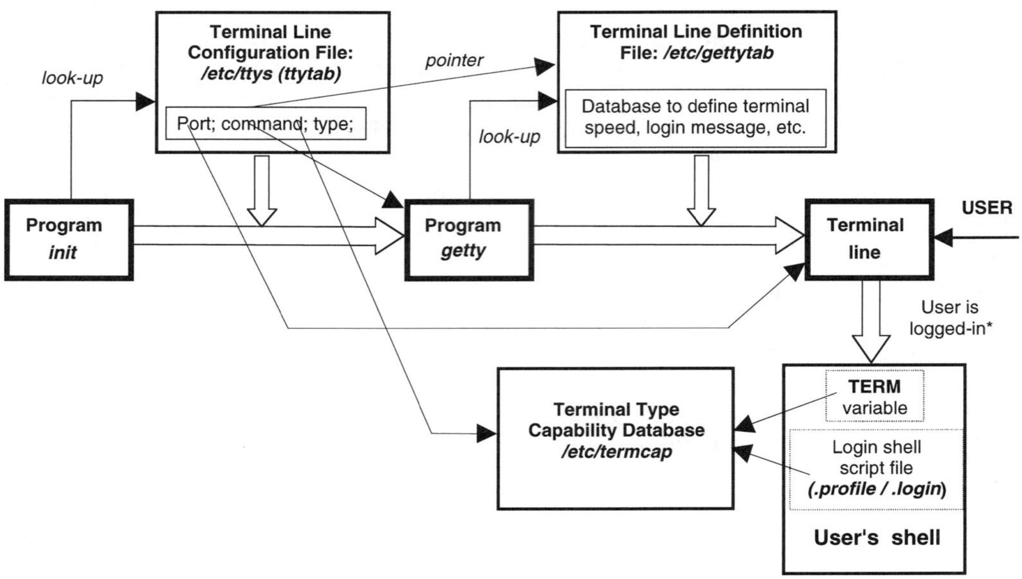

FIGURE 11.1
BSD terminal line and terminal initialization. *Note: The login procedure and password checking authentication are not presented.

The ***getty*** program waits for a user to log into the system, but the ***getty*** program invokes another authentication program ***/bin/login*** to complete the login procedure.

We will examine, in greater detail, the structures of the terminal line configuration and definition files. Both types of terminal line configuration files, */etc/ttys* and */etc/ttytab*, are presented below:

 # cat /etc/ttys

```
# @(#)ttys    6.1 (ULTRIX)
#
# name        getty                    type       status               comments
#
console    "/etc/getty std.9600"     vt100      on secure            # console terminal
tty00      "/etc/getty std.9600"     vt100      off nomodem          # direct connect tty
tty01      "/etc/getty std.9600"     vt100      off nomodem          # direct connect tty
           .....
           .....
ttyd0      "/etc/getty std.9600"     vt100      off shared secure    # modem line
ttyp0      none                                 network secure
           .....
           .....
ttyvf      none                                 network secure
```

 # cat /etc/ttytab

```
# @(#)ttytab 1.7 SMI (SunOS 4.1.3)
#
# name        getty                        type        status            comments
#
console    "/usr/etc/getty cons8"        sun         on local secure
ttya       "/usr/etc/getty std.9600"     unknown     off local
ttyb       "/usr/etc/getty std.9600"     unknown     off local
tty00      "/usr/etc/getty std.9600"     unknown     off local
.....
.....
tty0f      "/usr/etc/getty std.9600"     unknown     off local
ttyp0      none                                      network off
           .....                         .....
ttyTf      none                                      network off
```

Both configuration files list all available system terminals; both files are partially shown here. The file has to include an entry for every terminal port in use, and may have entries for unused ports. Each entry has four fields:

terminal-port command terminal-type status

where

terminal-port The name of the special device file in the */dev* directory that corresponds to the line. All serial peripherals (RS-232), such as terminals, serial printers, and modems have a port name of the form "***tty***nn," where "nn" is a two-digit hexadecimal number. Virtual terminal devices (pseudo terminals) are also listed.

command	The command that ***init*** should execute to monitor this terminal line:	
	getty	For terminals and modems
	none	Do not create a monitoring process
terminal-type	The name of a terminal type described in */etc/termcap*; the ***TERM*** variable will be set to this value at login. Alternatively, the field could contain a keyword to be used by user initialization files or the **tset** command:	
	network	Used for virtual terminal devices over the network
	unknown	Used for lines without a specific attached terminal (includes modem lines)
	dialup	Another type used for modem lines
	plugboard	Used for a board that allows different terminal cables to be swapped
status	Zero or more keywords, separated by spaces:	
	on	Line is enabled, and command will be run by ***init***
	off	Line is disabled, and the entry ignored
	secure	Allow direct ***root*** logins
	window=cmd	***init*** should run ***cmd*** before the one in the field ***command***

The files also list virtual terminals, better known as pseudo terminals; they are widely used to establish network connections to the system, which is the prevailing mechanism today for users to log in to the system. From the examples presented above, it can be seen that only the console is used locally; all other connections are provided over a network, or modem, using different terminals unknown in the time of terminal line initialization. Terminals will identify themselves once the sessions have been established.

It is interesting to note that SunOS 4.3.x, to preserve compatibility with older-style software that might still explicitly require the configuration file under the original name "*/etc/ttys*," also maintained another configuration file with that name. The file */etc/ttys* was derived from the actual terminal line configuration file */etc/ttytab* by the program ***init*** during the system startup.

This file looked like:

```
# cat /etc/ttys
12console
02ttya
02ttyb
02tty00
. . . . .
. . . . .
```

Each entry in this auxiliary configuration file described, in a condensed way, the corresponding entry in the */etc/ttytab* file. The format of an entry was:

on-flag|speed|dev-name (All fields follow one another with no space between; here the presented "|" character is only to indicate fields, and it does not exist in a real entry.)

where

on-flag Specifies the entry is active (on). On/off correspond to 1/0

speed Specifies a baud-rate of the line:
0 automatic baud-rate selection
f 1200 Baud
6 2400 Baud
2 9600 Baud
5 dial-in 1200

dev-name Specifies a special device file on the */dev* directory

Today, this file has only historical value. Let us return to the terminal line configuration file */etc/ttytab*. When reading this file, one can see that the ***getty*** program is invoked with an argument that actually points to another entry in the terminal line definition file */etc/gettytab*. Each entry in the file */etc/gettytab* describes one class of terminals. The entry is accessed every time the ***getty*** program is started.

 # cat /etc/gettytab

```
#
# @(#)gettytab 1.11 SMI; from UCB 5.7
#
# Copyright (c) 1980 Regents of the University of California.
# All rights reserved. The Berkeley software License Agreement
# specifies the terms and conditions for redistribution.
#
# Most of the table entries here are just copies of the
# old getty table, it is by no means certain, or even likely,
# that any of them are optimal for any purpose whatever.
# Nor is it likely that more than a couple are even correct
#
# The default gettytab entry, used to set defaults for all other
# entries, and in cases where getty is called with no table name
default:\
   :ap:lm=\r\n%h login\72 :sp#9600:
```

The field "*lm*" stands for login message, and it specifies the displayed prompt; here, the default login prompt is: "*hostname* login:". This field can be combined with another field "*im*" (initial message).

```
#
# This is a new entry to internationalize the console. It needs to be
# 8 bit clean so that ISO 8859 characters can be displayed without
# the window system.
cons8:\
   :p8:lm=\r\n%h login\72 :sp#9600:
#
# Fixed speed entries
#   The "std.NNN" names are known to the special case
#   portselector code in getty, however they can
#   be assigned to any table desired.
#   The "NNN-baud" names are known to the special case
#   autobaud code in getty, and likewise can
#   be assigned to any table desired (hopefully the same speed).
#
a|std.110|110-baud:\
   :nd#1:cd#1:uc:sp#110:
   . . . . .
   . . . . .
2|std.9600|9600-baud:\
   :sp#9600:
#
```

```
# Dial in rotary tables, speed selection via 'break'
d1200|Dial-1200:\
   :nx=d150:fd#1:sp#1200:
#
# Odd special case terminals
   .....
   .....
```

This file is a kind of simplified database that describes terminal lines. There is a default terminal class, ***default***, which is used to set global defaults for all classes; it is read first, and then the entries for the selected class are read and they override particular settings. The file layout and the syntax and meaning of individual fields in the file are the same as in the ***termcap*** database, a description of which follows.

11.1.1.2 The BSD termcap Database

UNIX programs are written to be independent of the characteristics of any particular kind of terminal; they call a standard manipulation library, which is then responsible for interfacing to actual terminals. Such libraries serve to map general terminal characteristics and functions to the specific character sequences required to perform them on any specific terminal.

While the actual terminals are indicated in the terminal line configuration file (*ttys*, or *ttytab*), or by users who indicate what kind of terminal they are using by setting ***TERM*** environment variable, the terminal definitions are stored in a separate database on the system. For the BSD terminal subsystem, the database is known as the ***termcap*** database (this stands for "*terminal capabilities*"), and it is contained in the huge ASCII file */etc/termcap*. The */etc/termcap* file contains a large number of entries that fully describe different terminals. It is important to notice that only terminals described in the ***termcap*** database can be implemented; otherwise the system does not know how to handle terminals that are not described.

Some third-party software, and sometimes even a part of the system software, is based on the ***termcap*** terminal capability database. This software requires an appropriate *termcap* file, even when running on the System V UNIX platforms that provide a different kind of terminal capability database known as ***terminfo***. This is sufficient reason for some System V UNIX flavors to include this file as a standard part of their installation. For example, Solaris 2.x provides the file */etc/termcap* as a link to the file */usr/share/lib/termcap*, which is an exact copy of the ***termcap*** database on SunOS 4.1.x; most of the dates in the comments are from as long as twenty years ago.

```
$ ls -l /etc | grep termcap   (Solaris)
lrwxrwxrwx   1 root   root   24 May 28 1998   termcap -> ../ usr/share/lib/termcap
```

Similarly, Linux provides an updated */etc/termcap* file; even the ***getty*** program uses this file (i.e., the ***termcap*** terminal database), while other screen-based programs use the ***terminfo*** terminal database. For example, on Red Hat Linux Rel. 5.2 (Apollo):

```
$ ls -l /etc | grep term
-rw-r--r- -   1 root   root   434898 Sep 10 1998 termcap
```

In both cases, the /etc/termcap file includes a complete parallel terminal database (both platforms, Solaris and Linux, resemble System V-flavored UNIX in this area, so the primary terminal database is ***terminfo***).

For a better idea of what the ***termcap*** database looks like, here is a part of it:

$ cat /etc/termcap

```
# ------------------------
#
# Termcap source file @(#)termcap.src 1.33 SMI; from UCB 5.28
# Please mail changes to (arpanet): termcap@berkeley
#
....
....
Mu|sun|Sun Microsystems Workstation console:\            This is a console
    :am:bs:km:mi:ms:pt:li# 34:co# 80:cl= ^L:cm=\E[%i%d;%dH:\
    :ce=\E[K:cd=\E[J:\
    :so=\E[7m:se=\E[m:us=\E[4m:ue=\E[m:rs=\E[s:\
    :md=\E[1m:mr=\E[7m:me=\E[m:\
    :al=\E[L:dl=\E[M:im=:ei=:ic=\E[@:dc=\E[P:\
    :AL=\E[%dL:DL=\E[%dM:IC=\E[%d@:DC=\E[%dP:\
    :up=\E[A:nd=\E[C:ku=\E[A:kd=\E[B:kr=\E[C:kl=\E[D:\
    :k1=\E[224z:k2=\E[225z:k3=\E[226z:k4=\E[227z:k5=\E[228z:\
    :k6=\E[229z:k7=\E[230z:k8=\E[231z:k9=\E[232z:
....
....
#
# This file describes capabilities of various terminals, as needed by
# software such as screen editors. It does not attempt to describe
# printing terminals very well, nor graphics terminals. Someday.
# See termcap(5) in the Unix Programmers Manual for documentation.
#
# Conventions: First entry is two chars, first char is manufacturer,
# second char is canonical name for model or mode.
# Third entry is the one the editor will print with "set" command.
# Last entry is verbose description.
# Others are mnemonic synonyms for the terminal.
#
# Terminal naming conventions:
# Terminal names look like <manufacturer> <model> - <modes/options>
# Certain abbreviations (e.g. c100 for concept100) are also allowed
# for upward compatibility. The part to the left of the dash, if a
# dash is present, describes the particular hardware of the terminal.
# The part to the right can be used for flags indicating special ROM's,
# extra memory, particular terminal modes, or user preferences.
# All names are always in lower case, for consistency in typing.
#
# The following are conventionally used flags:
#    rv    Terminal in reverse video mode (black on white)
#    2p    Has two pages of memory. Likewise 4p, 8p, etc.
#    w     Wide - in 132 column mode.
#    pp    Has a printer port which is used.
#    na    No arrow keys - termcap ignores arrow keys which are
#          actually there on the terminal, so the user can use
#          the arrow keys locally.
#
. . .
. . .
# Comments in this file begin with # - they cannot appear in the middle
# of a termcap entry. Individual entries are commented out by
# placing a period between the colon and the capability name.
#
# This file is to be installed with an editor script (reorder)
# that moves the most common terminals to the front of the file.
```

```
# If the source is not available, it can be constructed by sorting
# the above entries by the 2 char initial code.
# --------------------------------
....
....
# d: DEC (DIGITAL EQUIPMENT CORPORATION)          These are DEC terminals
#
# Note that xn glitch in vt100 is not quite the same as concept, since
# the cursor is left in a different position while in the weird state
# (concept at beginning of next line, vt100 at end of this line) so
# all versions of vi before 3.7 don't handle xn right on vt100.
# I assume you have smooth scroll off or are at a slow enough baud
# rate that it doesn't matter (1200? or less). Also this assumes
# that you set auto-nl to "on", if you set it off use vt100-nam below.
#
# Since there are two things here called vt100, the installer can make
# a local decision to make either one standard "vt100" by including
# it in the list of terminals in reorder, since the first vt100 in
# /etc/termcap is the one that it will find. The choice is between
# nam (no automatic margins) and am (automatic margins), as determined
# by the wrapline switch (group 3 #2). I personally recommend turning
# on the bit and using vt100-am, since having stuff hammer on the right
# margin is sort of hard to read. However, the xn glitch does not occur
# if you turn the bit off.
#
# I am unsure about the padding requirements listed here. I have heard
# a claim that the vt100 needs no padding. It's possible that it needs
# padding only if the xon/xoff switch is off. For UNIX, this switch
# should probably be on.
#
# The vt100 uses rs and rf rather than is/ct/st because the tab settings
# are in non-volatile memory and don't need to be reset upon login.
# You can type "reset" to get them set.
#
d0|vt100|vt100-am|vt100am |dec vt100:\
    :do=^J:co#80:li#24:cl=50\E[;H\E[2J:sf=5\ED:\
    :le=^H:bs:am:cm=5\E[%i%d;%dH:nd=2\E[C:up=2\E[A:\
    :ce=3\E[K:cd=50\E[J:so=2\E[7m:se=2\E[m:us=2\E[4m:ue=2\E[m:\
    :md=2\E[1m:mr=2\E[7m:mb=2\E[5m:me=2\E[m:is=\E[1;24r\E[24;1H:\
    :rf=/usr/share/lib/tabset/vt100:\
    :rs=\E>\E[?3l\E[?4l\E[?5l\E[?7h\E[?8h:ks=\E[?1h\E=:ke=\E[?1l\E>:\
    :ku=\EOA:kd=\EOB:kr=\EOC:kl=\EOD:kb=^H:\
    :ho=\E[H:k1=\EOP:k2=\EOQ:k3=\EOR:k4=\EOS:pt:sr=5\EM:vt#3:xn:\
    :sc=\E7:rc=\E8:cs=\E[%i%d;%dr:
dp|vt100-np|vt100 with no padding (for psl games):\
    :cl=\E[H\E[2J:sr=\EM:cm=\E[%i%d;%dH:nd=\E[C:up=\E[A:\
    :ce=\E[K:cd=\E[J:so=\E[7m:se=\E[m:us=\E[4m:ue=\E[m:\
    :md=\E[1m:mr=\E[7m:mb=\E[5m:me=\E[m:tc=vt100:
d1|vt100-nam|vt100nam|vt100 w/no am:\
    :am@:xn@:\
    :is=\E\E[?3l\E[?4l\E[?5l\E[?7l\E[?8h:ks=\E[?1h\E=:ke=\E[?1l\E>:\
    :tc=vt100-am:
....
....
# END OF TERMCAP
# ------------------------
```

Only part of the */etc/termcap* file is presented. We have focused on the entries for DEC VT100 type terminals, as they are very common (VT100 is presented in ***bold***). The *termcap* *entries* are very similar to the *printcap entries* which present in many cases simplified versions of *termcap* entries.

The first line in the entry is a series of names and aliases for the terminal; any of them (if they do not contain spaces) could be used as the value of the ***TERM*** environment variable. The remainder of the entry is a colon-separated series of capability codes and values. There are several kinds of capabilities:

- *Data about the terminal* — For example, the ***am*** code says that the terminal can automatically wrap long output strings onto multiple lines on the terminal screen. (Some other codes describe how many columns the terminal screen has (80), or how many lines it has (24), and so on.)
- *The sequence of characters to send to the terminal to get it to perform some action* — The codes indicate what ESCAPE sequence is required to perform some action on the terminal, for example, to move the cursor to some position (the ESCAPE character is abbreviated \E).
- *The sequence of characters emitted when a special key is pressed* — These codes hold the sequence for the special keys on the terminal (the ESCAPE character is abbreviated \E).

There are three types of capability:

1. *Boolean capabilities* — Consist of a capability name with no argument; for example, the aforementioned ***am*** for automatic wrapping
2. *Numeric capabilities* — Consist of a capability name, a sharp sign (#), and a number; for example, ***co#80*** says that the terminal has 80 columns
3. *String capabilities* — Consist of a capability name, an equal sign (=), and a string (a command sequence); for example, ***up=^K*** specifies that the sequence CTRL-K will move the cursor up one line

Once a terminal is described in the ***termcap*** database, each time a reference is made to the terminal, the system addresses the database, searches for a corresponding entry, and learns about its capabilities. The local environment variable TERMCAP can be introduced and set to the values of the terminal capabilities to make this process faster, so the repeated browsing of the ***termcap*** database can be skipped.

11.1.2 System V Terminal Subsystem

The System V approach to terminal configuration and initialization is quite different from that of the BSD terminal subsystem. The bottom line, though, is the same: to initialize terminal lines and terminals themselves. It is the details that are different: file names, their structures and layouts, and even process names. A schematic of System V terminal line and terminal initialization is presented in Figure 11.2.

11.1.2.1 System V Terminal Line Initialization

System startup on System V is partially controlled by the system run-level initialization file (table) */etc/inittab*; this is actually the configuration file for the ***init*** process which manages the system startup in the last phase, including the initialization of terminal lines.

Consequently, the configuration entries for the System V terminal line initialization are included in the */etc/inittab* file. Two examples (HP-UX and Solaris) follow:

$ cat /etc/inittab (HP-UX platform)

```
init:4:initdefault:
stty::sysinit:stty 9600 clocal icanon echo opost onlcr ienqak ixon icrnl ignpar </dev/systty
     . . . . .
     . . . . .
cons:123456:respawn:/ usr/sbin/getty console console     # system console
vue :4:respawn:/usr/vue/bin/vuerc                        # VUE invocation
# ttp1:234:respawn:/usr/sbin/getty-h tty0p1 9600
# ttp2:234:respawn:/usr/sbin/getty-h tty0p2 9600
# ttp3:234:respawn:/usr/sbin/getty-h tty0p3 9600
# ttp4:234:respawn:/usr/sbin/getty-h tty0p4 9600
# ttp5:234:respawn:/usr/sbin/getty-h tty0p5 9600
```

To activate the corresponding terminal lines, these entries should be commented-out.

$ cat /etc/inittab (Solaris 2.x platform)

```
ap::sysinit:/sbin/autopush -f/etc/iu.ap
fs::sysinit:/sbin/rcS                  >/dev/console 2>&1 </dev/console
is:3:initdefault:
s0:0:wait:/sbin/rc0 off                >/dev/console 2>&1 </dev/console
s1:1:wait:/sbin/shutdown -y -iS -g0    >/dev/console 2>&1 </dev/console
     . . . . .
co:234:respawn:/usr/lib/saf/ttymon -g -h -p "'uname -n' console login:" -T sun \
    -d/dev/console -l console -m ldterm,ttcompat
     . . . . .
```

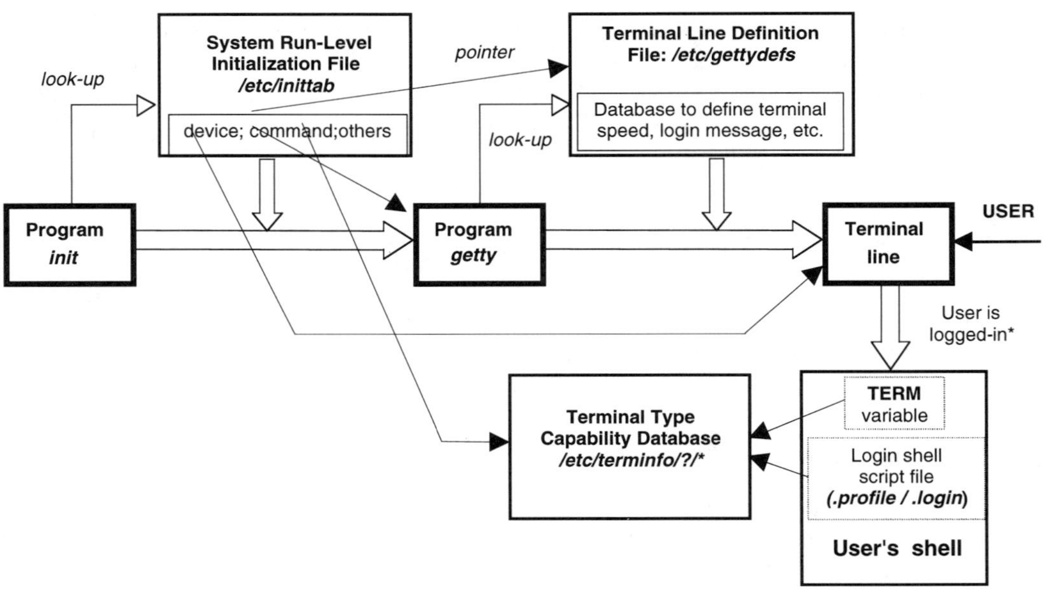

FIGURE 11.2
System V terminal line and terminal initialization. *Note: Login procedure and password checking authentication are not presented.

In both examples there are no defined terminal lines in the configuration file; literally, there are no terminals connected to the systems. The only terminal represented is the console, which is connected to the serial terminal port and included in the ***/etc/inittab*** configuration file. Any other terminal line would be defined in the same way. The console entries define the programs to be invoked to initialize terminal lines.

While the ***getty*** program exists on the HP-UX platform to initialize terminal lines, on the Solaris platform another program is renamed ***ttymon*** (to preserve compatibility with previous versions, the ***getty*** program also exists as a symbolic link to the ***ttymon*** program).

The common name for the terminal line definition file is */etc/gettydefs*, and the ***getty*** program looks there for the terminal line settings. On the Solaris platform, the file is renamed */etc/ttydefs* to match the new program name ***ttymon***.

Despite differences in file naming, the purpose of the files is the same, and the Solaris file has almost the same contents as the BSD terminal subsystem:

```
$ cat /etc/gettydefs            (HP-UX)
# @(#) $Revision: 66.2 $
# Default gettydefs file, see gettydefs(4).
#
# The entries below allow the following sequences, changing # each time a BREAK is received:
# 1200 -> 2400 -> 4800 -> 9600 -> 300 [repeats]
1200    # B1200 HUPCL IGNPAR PARENB ICRNL IXON OPOST ONLCR CS7 CREAD ISIG ICANON ECHO
              ECHOK PARENB ISTRIP IXANY TAB3
        # B1200 SANE CS7 PARENB ISTRIP IXANY TAB3 HUPCL
        #login: #2400                                   #next to try: 2400 Baud!
2400    # B2400 HUPCL IGNPAR PARENB ICRNL IXON OPOST ONLCR CS7 CREAD
              ISIG ICANON ECHO ECHOK PARENB ISTRIP IXANY TAB3
        # B2400 SANE CS7 PARENB ISTRIP IXANY TAB3 HUPCL
        #login: #4800                                   #next to try: 4800 Baud!
4800    # B4800 HUPCL IGNPAR PARENB ICRNL IXON OPOST ONLCR CS7 CREAD
              ISIG ICANON ECHO ECHOK PARENB ISTRIP IXANY TAB3
        # B4800 SANE CS7 PARENB ISTRIP IXANY TAB3 HUPCL
        #login: #9600                                   #next to try: 9600 Baud!
9600    # B9600 HUPCL IGNPAR PARENB ICRNL IXON OPOST ONLCR CS7 CREAD
              ISIG ICANON ECHO ECHOK PARENB ISTRIP IXANY TAB3
        # B9600 SANE CS7 PARENB ISTRIP IXANY TAB3 HUPCL
        #login: #300                                    #next to try: 300 Baud!
300     # B300 HUPCL IGNPAR PARENB ICRNL IXON OPOST ONLCR CS7 CREAD
              ISIG ICANON ECHO ECHOK PARENB ISTRIP IXANY TAB3
        # B300 SANE CS7 PARENB ISTRIP IXANY TAB3 HUPCL
        #login: #1200                                   #to try 1200 Baud again!
#
# This entry is for high speed modems. Most of these tend to always
# communicate to the cpu at 19200, regardless of the connection speed.
19200   # B19200 HUPCL50.0 pt IGNPAR PARENB ICRNL IXON OPOST ONLCR CS7 CREAD ISIG
              ICANON ECHO ECHOK PARENB ISTRIP IXANY TAB3
        # B19200 SANE CS7 PARENB ISTRIP IXANY TAB3 HUPCL
        #login: #19200
#
# This entry is used for the console
console # B9600 SANE CLOCAL CS8 ISTRIP IXANY TAB3 HUPCL
        # B9600 SANE CLOCAL CS8 ISTRIP IXANY TAB3 HUPCL
        #Console Login: #console
        .....
        .....
```

Each entry in the */etc/gettydefs* file has the format:

entry-label#initial-settings#final-settings#login-prompt#next-label

where

entry-label Identifies the entry; it is used in the */etc/inittab* file for reference

initial-settings Specifies the *termio I/O control codes* that ***getty*** will initialize the line

final-settings	Specifies the *termio I/O control codes* to be set before turning control over to the ***login*** program
login-prompt	Specifies the prompt that ***getty*** will display
next-label	Specifies the ***entry-label*** to be used instead, if the current attempt is broken (BREAK-key, noise, etc.). In that way, the linked list of entries can be created to enable automatic switching to other entries, for example to change the terminal line baud-rate (as is the case in the presented */etc/gettydefs* file)

The other file */etc/ttydefs* looks like:

```
$ cat /etc/ttydefs              (Solaris)
# VERSION=1
38400:38400 hupcl:38400 hupcl::19200
19200:19200 hupcl:19200 hupcl::9600
9600:9600 hupcl:9600 hupcl::4800
   . . . . .
auto:hupcl:sane hupcl:A:9600
   . . . . .
console:9600 hupcl opost onlcr:9600::console
console1:1200 hupcl opost onlcr:1200::console2
   . . . . .
contty:9600 hupcl opost onlcr:9600 sane::contty1
contty1:1200 hupcl opost onlcr:1200 sane::contty2
```

11.1.2.2 The System V terminfo Database

The ***terminfo*** database is the System V equivalent to the BSD ***termcap*** database. The basic difference between the two databases is that ***terminfo*** is a compiled database that consists of a series of binary files describing terminal capabilities. Each entry is a separate binary file in the */usr/lib/terminfo* directory hierarchy in the subdirectory named for the first letter of its name. For example, the *terminfo entry* for a **vt100** is stored in the file */usr/lib/terminfo/v/vt100*. The *terminfo entries* are compiled from source code vaguely similar to *termcap entries*. Such an approach improves efficiency, but at the price of accessibility.

The ***terminfo*** database had the advantage of being developed with the working model of the ***termcap*** database already in place. A critical analysis of the existing *termcap capabilities* made it easier to make decisions about *terminfo capability* needs, including capability improvements. Nevertheless, it is unfair to say that the ***terminfo*** database is better than the ***termcap*** database, especially because both databases continue to be developed. Simply, each database provides needed data about terminal characteristics on the corresponding UNIX platform.

The System V ***terminfo*** directory hierarchy can easily be seen with a simple listing of the basic ***terminfo*** directory: */usr/lib/terminfo*.

```
# ls -C /usr/lib/terminfo
1 3 5 7 9 C G X b d f h j l n p r t v x z
2 4 6 8 A D H a c e g i k m o q s u w y
```

All listed items are subdirectories, which can be seen from:

```
# ls -l /usr/lib/terminfo
total 100
dr-xr-xr-x    2 bin    bin    1024    Mar 5   18:28 1
dr-xr-xr-x    2 bin    bin    2048    Mar 5   18:28 2
```

```
. . .
dr-xr-xr-x    2 bin   bin   1024   Mar 5   18:28 x
dr-xr-xr-x    2 bin   bin   1024   Mar 5   18:28 y
dr-xr-xr-x    2 bin   bin   1024   Mar 5   18:28 z
```

A separate binary file defines each terminal:

 # ls -CF /usr/lib/terminfo/v

```
vc103      vc415        vi300-ss    vt100-bot-s   vt100-top -s    vt125
vc203      vi200        vi550       vt100 -nam    vt100-w         vt132
vc303      vi200-f      viewpoint   vt100-nam-w   vt100- w-am     vt220
vc303-a    vi200-ic     virtual     vt100-nav     vt100-w -nam    vt220-am
vc403a     vi200-rv     visual      vt100-nav-w   vt100-w -nav    vt320
vc404      vi200-rv-ic  vitty       vt100-np      vt100am         vt320-am
vc404-na   vi300        vk100       vt100-s       vt100nam        vt50
vc404-s    vi300-aw     vt100       vt100-s-bot   vt100s          vt50h
vc404-s-na vi300-rv     vt100-am    vt100-s-top   vt100w          vt52
```

The System V terminal subsystem provides a corresponding tool to manage binary ***terminfo*** files; several commands are available for manipulating ***terminfo*** entries:

tic Compile ***terminfo*** source

infocmp List source for a compiled ***terminfo*** entry (sometimes named the ***untic*** command)

A number of commands are also available for converting between ***terminfo*** and ***termcap*** entries:

infocmp -C List the equivalent ***termcap*** entry for a compiled ***terminfo*** entry; i.e., translate from ***terminfo*** to ***termcap***

captoinfo Translate a ***termcap*** entry into ***terminfo*** source

Please note that the conversion (translation) is never perfect, and some discrepancies are always possible.

The following example will illustrate the use of these commands. Our task is to create a new *terminfo entry* for a modified vt100 terminal; we will name this terminal "***vt100mod***." The implemented platform is Solaris 2.6.

In the first step, we will convert one of the existing vt100-related *terminfo entries* into a *termcap entry,* which then can easily be modified (*termcap entries* are ASCII, while *terminfo entries* are binary files); there is no need to create the entry from scratch. The available vt100-related entries are:

$ ls -l /usr/share/lib/terminfo/v | grep vt100

```
-rw-r--r--   2 bin   bin   1493 Jul 16 1997 vt100
-rw-r--r--   2 bin   bin   1493 Jul 16 1997 vt100-am
-rw-r--r--   2 bin   bin   1554 Jul 16 1997 vt100-bot-s
-rw-r--r--   1 bin   bin   1490 Jul 16 1997 vt100-nam
             . . . . .
             . . . . .
-rw-r--r--   1 bin   bin   1424 Jul 16 1997 vt100am
-rw-r--r--   1 bin   bin   1426 Jul 16 1997 vt100nam
-rw-r--r--   1 bin   bin   1480 Jul 16 1997 vt100s
-rw-r--r--   1 bin   bin   1416 Jul 16 1997 vt100w
```

We will pick up "vt100" and convert it into the corresponding *termcap entry*:

```
$ infocmp -C vt100 > /tmp/vt100mod
$ cat /tmp/vt100mod
#   Reconstructed via infocmp from file: /usr/share/lib/terminfo/v/vt100
vt100|vt100-am|dec vt100 (w/advanced video):\
     :am:mi:ms:xn:xo:bs:pt:\
     :co#80:li#24:\
     :DO=\E[%dB:LE=\E[%dD:RI=\E[%dC:UP=\E[%dA:ae=^O:as=^N:\
     :cd=50\E[J:ce=3\E[K:cl=50\E[H\E[J:cm=5\E[%i%d;%dH:\
     :cs=\E[%I%d;%dr:ct=\E[3g:ho=\E[H:k0=\EOy:k1=\EOP:\
     :k2=\EOQ:k3=\EOR:k4=\EOS:k5=\EOt:k6=\EOu:k7=\EOv:\
     :k8=\EOl:k9=\EOw:kb=\b:kd=\EOB:ke=\E[?1l\E:kl=\EOD:\
     :kr=\EOC:ks=\E[?1h\E=:ku=\EOA:nd=2\E[C:\
     :r2=\E>\E[?3l\E[?4l\E[?5l\E[?7h\E[?8h:rc=\E8:sc=\E7:\
     :se=2\E[m:so=2\E[1;7m:sr=5\EM:st=\EH:ue=2\E[m:\
     :up=2\E[A:us=2\E[4m:
```

The file was edited and modified, respecting the rules for *termcap entries*:

```
$ vi /tmp/vt100mod
# This terminal present the modified version of the vt100
# Was reconstructed by using "infocmp -C vt100"
#
# Reconstructed via infocmp from file: /usr/share/lib/terminfo/v/ vt100
#
vt100mod|vt100-am-mod|dec vt100 modified (w/advanced video):\
     :am:mi:ms:xn:xo:bs:pt:\
     :co#132:li#24:\
     :DO=\E[%dB:LE=\E[%dD:RI=\E[%dC:UP=\E[%dA:ae=^O:as=^N:\
     :cd=50\E[J:ce=3\E[K:cl=50\E[H\E[J:cm=5\E[%i%d;%dH:\
     :cs=\E[%i%d;%dr:ct=\E[3g:ho=\E[H:k0=\EOy:k1=\EOP:\
     :k2=\EOQ:k3=\EOR:k4=\EOS:k5=\EOt:k6=\EOu:k7=\EOv:\
     :k8=\EOl:k9=\EOw:kb=\b:kd=\EOB:ke=\E[?1l\E>:kl=\EOD:\
     :kr=\EOC:ks=\E[?1h\E=:ku=\EOA:nd=2\E[C:\
     :r2=\E>\E[?3l\E[?4l\E[?5l\E[?7h\E[?8h:rc=\E8:sc=\E7:\
     :se=2\E[m:so=2\E[1;7m:sr=5\EM:st=\EH:ue=2\E[m:\
     :up=2\E[A:us=2\E[4m:
```

Minor modifications were performed: comments, names, and column number. To make a corresponding *terminfo entry*, this modified *termcap entry* must be first converted into a *terminfo source entry* and then compiled:

```
$ captoinfo /tmp/vt100mod > /tmp/vt100.ti
captoinfo: obsolete 2 character name 'vt' removed.
synonyms are: 'vt100mod|vt100-mod|dec vt100 mod'
```

The ASCII source *terminfo entry* file */tmp/vt100mod.ti* was created in addition to the displayed message:

```
$ cat /tmp/vt100mod.ti
# This terminal present the modified version of the vt100
# Was reconstructed by using "infocmp -C vt100"
#
# Reconstructed via infocmp from file: /usr/share/lib/terminfo/v/vt100
#
```

```
vt100mod|vt100-mod|dec vt100 mod,
    am, mir, msgr, xenl, xon,
    cols#132, lines#24,
    bel=^G, clear=\E[H\E[J$<50>, cr=\r,
    csr=\E[%i%p1%d;%p2%dr, cub=\E[%p1%dD, cub1=\b,
    cud=\E[%p1%dB, cud1=\n, cuf=\E[%p1%dC, cuf1=\E[C$<2>,
    cup=\E[%i%p1%d;%p2%dH$<5>, cuu=\E[%p1%dA,
    cuu1=\E[A$<2>, ed=\E[J$<50>, el=\E[K$<3>, home=\E[H,
    ht=\t, hts=\EH, ind=\n, kbs=\b, kcub1=\EOD,
    kcud1=\EOB, kcuf1=\EOC, kcuu1=\EOA, kf0=\EOy,
    kf1=\EOP, kf2=\EOQ, kf3=\EOR, kf4=\EOS, kf5=\EOt,
    kf6=\EOu, kf7=\EOv, kf8=\EOl, kf9=\EOw, rc=\E8,
    ri=\EM$<5>, rmacs=^O, rmkx=\E[?1l\E>, rmso=\E[m$<2>,
    rmul=\E[m$<2>, rs2=\E>\E[?3l\E[?4l\E[?5l\E[?7h\E[?8h,
    sc=\E7, smacs=^N, smkx=\E[?1h\E=, smso=\E[1;7m$<2>,
    smul=\E[4m$<2>, tbc=\E[3g,
```

Pay attention to the different syntax of two entries (files). Finally, the *terminfo entry* for the modified **vt100** terminal can be compiled:

$ tic -v /tmp/vt100mod.ti
Working in /usr/share/lib/terminfo
Created v/vt100mod
Linked v/vt100-mod

The **tic** command informed us of two new terminfo entries: "*vt100mod*" and "*vt100-mod*" (although the file "*vt100-mod*" that corresponds to the alternate entry name is the link) in the */usr/share/lib/terminfo/v* directory:

$ ls -C /usr/share/lib/terminfo/v

v5410	*vi200*	*viewpoint-90*	*vt100-nam*	***vt100mod***
v90	*vi200-f*	*virtual*	*vt100-nam-w*	*vt100nam*
vanilla	*vi200-ic*	*visual*	*vt100-nav*	*vt100s*
vc103	*vi200-rv*	*visual50*	*vt100-nav-w*	*vt100w*
vc203	*vi200-rv-ic*	*vitty*	*vt100-np*	*vt102*
vc303	*vi300*	*vk100*	*vt100-s*	*vt125*
vc303-a	*vi300-aw*	*vs100*	*vt100-s-bot*	*vt132*
vc403a	*vi300-rv*	*vs100s*	*vt100-s-top*	*vt220*
vc404	*vi300-ss*	*vt-102*	*vt100-top-s*	*vt50*
vc404-na	*vi50*	*vt-61*	*vt100-w*	*vt50h*
vc404-s	*vi550*	***vt100***	*vt100-w-am*	*vt52*
vc404-s-na	*vic*	*vt100-am*	*vt100-w-nam*	*vt61*
vc415	*vic20*	*vt100-bot-s*	*vt100-w-nav*	*vt61.5*
venix	*viewpoint*	***vt100-mod***	*vt100am*	

Or, to see more details about new entries:

$ ls -l /usr/share/lib/terminfo/v | grep vt100

-rw-r--r--	***2 bin***	***bin***	***1493***	***Jul 16 1997***	***vt100***
-rw-r--r--	*2 bin*	*bin*	*1493*	*Jul 16 1997*	*vt100-am*
-rw-r--r--	*2 bin*	*bin*	*1554*	*Jul 16 1997*	*vt100-bot-s*
-rw-r--r--	***2 root***	***other***	***1267***	***May 21 17:19***	***vt100-mod***

. . . . .
. . . . .

-rw-r--r--	***2 root***	***other***	***1267***	***May 21 17:19***	***vt100mod***
-rw-r--r--	*1 bin*	*bin*	*1426*	*Jul 16 1997*	*vt100nam*
-rw-r--r--	*1 bin*	*bin*	*1480*	*Jul 16 1997*	*vt100s*
-rw-r--r--	*1 bin*	*bin*	*1416*	*Jul 16 1997*	*vt100w*

The new entries (files) have been created by the ***root***, so there is a difference in the files' ownership (it can be changed at any time, although it is not necessary); compared to the initial entry "*vt100*," there is also a difference in the size and file timestamps, which was expected.

Any modification of a *terminfo entry* must be done very carefully. The original version of an entry should be saved as a backup, and it is highly recommended that you use a slightly different name for the new entry until its testing is complete.

The method presented above is not the only way to create a new *terminfo entry*. A *terminfo*-like source ASCII entry can be directly obtained with the command ***infocmp -I***, and there is no need to deal with a *termcap*-like entry at all. However, the purpose of the previous example is to demonstrate how to perform an eventual ***termcap/terminfo*** conversion.

11.1.3 Terminal-Related Special Device Files

The special device files that correspond to the serial lines vary between UNIX flavors; they usually have names of the form ***/dev/ttyn*** (***n*** is a single or two digit number), where ***n*** refers to the line number, and starts from 0. Directly connected terminals were/are accessed via these special files. The special file ***/dev/console*** refers to the system console device. Originally, the SVR4 terminal-related special device files resided in the directory ***/dev/term***, and had names corresponding to their line numbers (for example: ***/dev/term/14***); there were often also links to the ***ttyn***-type names.

The special file ***/dev/tty*** (no suffix) serves a special purpose. It is a synonym for each process controlling TTY; it can be used to ensure output goes to the terminal, regardless of any I/O redirection.

There are also other terminal devices in */dev* that are used for indirect login sessions via a network or windowing system; these are called pseudo-terminal devices. They can also be easily recognized in the BSD terminal line configuration files */etc/ttys*, or */etc/ttytab* presented earlier; simply, the ***getty*** process is not associated with these devices. We will discuss pseudo terminals later.

11.1.4 Configuration Data Summary

The configuration and definition files relevant to terminal lines are different between the two main UNIX platforms, as well as between different UNIX flavors. Proper terminology can help somewhat in managing terminal configuration.

- On BSD platform, the following configuration files are used for terminal lines:

/etc/ttys	Terminal line configuration file
/etc/ttytab	SunOS terminal line configuration file
/etc/gettytab	Terminal line definition file
/etc/termcap	Terminal type capability database

- On System V platform, the following configuration files and directories are used for terminal lines:

/etc/inittab	System initialization configuration file
/etc/gettydefs	Terminal line definition file
/etc/ttydefs	Solaris terminal line definition file
*/usr/lib/terminfo/?/ **	Terminal type capability database

11.2 The *tset, tput,* and *stty* Commands

11.2.1 The *tset* Command

In UNIX, the type of the terminal to be used must be defined before communication with a user can commence. A terminal type can be set in several different ways. Assuming a BSD terminal approach, the type can be set through the terminal line configuration file *ttys*, or *ttytab*, or a user can set the terminal type by the ***TERM*** environment variable, or a terminal could be set with the ***tset*** command. However, only the **tset** command can be used to initialize the terminal itself.

Those two functions, setting a terminal type and initializing the terminal itself, overlap in some nonobvious ways and can be confusing for users and system administrators. Let us examine how the **tset** command works (**tset** stands for "terminal set"):

- If no arguments are specified and the environment variable ***TERM*** is already set, **tset** uses the value of ***TERM*** to determine the terminal type.
- If no arguments are specified and the environment variable ***TERM*** is not set, then **tset** uses the value specified in the */etc/ttytab* or */etc/ttys* files (BSD only).
- If a terminal type is specified as an argument, that argument is used as the terminal type, regardless of the value of the environment variable ***TERM***.
- The **-m** (*map*) *option* allows a fine degree of control in cases where the terminal type may be ambiguous: for example, if the user logs in over different types of terminal lines (sometimes on a dialup, sometimes over a network, sometimes on a hardwired line). If the **-m** option was specified, **tset** would ask the user for the currently used terminal type, and the user could respond accordingly. For example:

  $ tset -m ":?vt100"
  TERM = (vt100)

  will prompt the user for a terminal type, assuming *vt100*. If the user hits Enter, **tset** will use *vt100* as the terminal type; otherwise the user can enter any other actual terminal type, and **tset** will accept it.

To prompt for and set the ***TERM*** variable in a user's login files (*.profile* or *.login*), **tset** is often used because it accomplishes this task so well. The user can specify the ***TERM*** variable through **tset**, or generic entries can be mapped from the terminal line configuration file:

 # setenv TERM 'tset - -Q -m ":?vt100"' # *Can be implemented in the .login file;*
$ TERM='tset - -Q -m ":?vt100"'; export TERM # *Can be implemented in the .profile file.*

Given the "-" option, **tset** displays a value that it determines for the terminal type. The **-Q** (*quiet*) option causes **tset** to suppress the displaying of messages it normally sends regarding the values set for the "*Erase*" and "*Kill*" characters.

The ***TERMCAP*** environment variable can also be set with **tset**. When used this way, the entire extracted *termcap* entry corresponding to the terminal type named in the ***TERM*** variable becomes the value of the ***TERMCAP*** variable. This allows programs to start up more quickly since they do not need to search the ***termcap*** database file. The **eval** shell command is commonly used to provide this functionality, because it forces double command scanning and an appropriate variable replacement:

 # eval 'tset -sQ -m ":?vt100"'

The **-s** option causes **tset** to invoke a series of shell commands to set the ***TERM*** and ***TERMCAP*** variables accordingly (***TERMCAP*** is set to the actual contents of the appropriate *termcap* entry).

The main purpose of the **tset** command is to initialize the terminal itself. It outputs an initialization string defined in the terminal's *termcap* entry, which should set the terminal to a reasonable state. When done, it displays a message such as:

Erase is control-H
Kill is control-X

or whatever else these characters are set to. This message can be skipped with the **-Q** option.

The real effect of the initialization string that is sent to a terminal now depends only on the terminal itself. If everything is defined properly, a terminal should be initialized (reset) and ready for use.

The **tset** command originates from the BSD platform, but exists today in both versions of UNIX, BSD, and System V, albeit with slightly different executions.

11.2.2 The *tput* Command

The ***tput*** command is the System V counterpart to **tset** and is used with the ***terminfo*** capability database, but it does not have **tset**'s ability to determine the terminal type. By default, **tput** assumes that a user is using the terminal type specified by the ***TERM*** variable. To override the value of ***TERM***, another terminal type can be specified with the **-T** option, for example:

$ tput -Tvt100

However, the **tput** command can also manage terminals:

$ tput init
$ tput reset

The command issues the *initialization string*, or the *reset string*, as they are defined in the corresponding *terminfo* entries. If no *reset* entry is defined, **tput** issues the *initialization string* instead, and the command acts exactly like **tput init**.

The **tput** command enables easy control of displayed data, and it can be used within scripts to facilitate flexible and powerful data presentation. For example:

```
$ tput clear      # To clear the terminal screen
$ tput cup 0 0    # To move the cursor to the home position
$ tput cup 23 4   # To move the cursor to row 23, column 4
```

The **tput** command echoes (sends) the specified screen-control sequence compatible with the already specified terminal. The same can be done from the shell script.

Highlighting displayed text is the most popular use of the **tput** command. The so-called "stand-out mode" of the screen enables highlighting of the subsequent text in the current line on the screen, as long as the mode is on. By turning the stand-out screen mode on and off, a specified line of the text or character strings can be emphasized (highlighted) from the other text. The **tput** command:

```
$ tput smso   # Set stand-out mode on
$ tput rmso   # Reset stand-out mode (set stand-out mode off)
```

The following script illustrates this capability in greater detail:

```
$ cat /tmp/mso_example.ksh
#!/ bin/ksh
# This is the script: "/tmp/mso_example.ksh"
# This is an example how to use the screen mode "stand-out" (mso)
# Defining variables HI to set "mso", and LO to reset "mso"
HI='tput smso'
LO='tput rmso'
#
# The following line will be highlighted; pay attention to the ${HI} and ${LO}
echo "\n"
echo "${HI}This line is highlighted!${LO}"
#
# The following line illustrates how to highlight a specified parts of the line
echo "\n"
echo "This is an ${HI}example${LO} of how to highlight a specified ${HI}part of the text${LO} !"
echo "\n"
```

Upon execution, the script will display (letters printed in **bold** are highlighted):

$ *\/tmp/mso_example.ksh*
This line is highlighted!
This is an **example** of how to highlight a specified **part of the text**!
$ *<= The system prompt appears at the end of the script's execution.*

11.2.3 The *stty* Command

The *stty* command is used to specify generic terminal and terminal line characteristics. While the **tset** command performs a complete type-specific terminal initialization, **stty** sets individual terminal characteristics. The command syntax is:

stty *option [value]*

where the most common options are:

Option	Meaning	Example
n	Baud-rate	*9600*
rows n	Lines on the screen	*rows 36*
columns n	Columns on the screen	*columns 80*
erase c	Set the delete previous character to c	*erase ^h*
kill c	Set the erase command character to c	*kill ^u*
intr c	Set the interrupt character to c	*intr ^c*
eof c	Set the end-of-file character to c	*eof ^d*
susp c	Set the suspend job character to c	*susp ^z*
lnext c	Set the literal next character to c	*lnext ^v*
werase c	Set the word erase character to c	*werase ^w*
reprint c	Set the reprint line character to c	*reprint ^r*
oddp	Enable odd parity	*oddp*
evenp	Enable even parity	*evenp*
-parity	No parity is generated or detected	*-parity*
markp	Enable mark parity	*markp*
cstopb	Use two stop bits	*cstopb*
-cstopb	Use one stop bit	*-cstopb*
sane	Reset many options to reasonable settings	*sane*

Note: Not all options require a value.

The **stty** command may also be used to display the current terminal settings, for example:

```
$ stty -a
speed 9600 baud; line = 0; susp <undef>; dsusp <undef>
rows = 24; columns = 80
intr = ^C; quit = ^\; erase = ^H; kill = ^U; swtch <undef>
eof = ^D; eol = ^@; min = 4; time = 0; stop = ^S; start = ^Q
parenb -parodd cs7 -cstopb hupcl -cread -clocal -loblk -crts
-ignbrk brkint ignpar -parmrk -inpck istrip -inlcr -igncr icrnl -iuclc
ixon -ixany ixoff -rtsxoff -ctsxon -ienqak
isig icanon iexten -xcase echo echoe echok -echonl -noflsh
opost -olcuc onlcr -ocrnl -onocr -onlret -ofill -ofdel -tostop
```

On the BSD platform the same command has the format:

$ stty everything

The displayed data could be different from that specified in the ***termcap*** or ***terminfo*** databases. While the ***termcap*** and ***terminfo*** databases provide generic information about a terminal type (befitting all terminals of a given type), **stty** provides information about the current setting for a specified terminal.

The most common character to set with **stty** setting is the "*erase*" character. When logging from different places, a user can sometimes face the problem of which key to use to erase the last entered character (the most common are the "*Backspace*," "*Delete*," or "*Control-Backspace*" keys). The preferred erase character can be set from the command line on any type of terminal, simply by typing:

$ **stty erase** *[desired erase key]*

The erase character will be set appropriately and can be used in the familiar way.

The **stty** command can be used to set the erase character separately in the user's login script, *.profile*, or *.login* to avoid such surprises:

```
.....
# To set "Backspace" as the erase character
stty erase ^H
....
```

If *vi* is used to edit the login script, the sequence "***^v,^h***" (*Ctrl-v, Ctrl-h*) should be typed to specify "***^H***" (*Ctrl-H*).

11.3 Pseudo Terminals

While terminal issues are a normal part of UNIX administration, terminals as physical devices belong to the past. With the exception of the console, which is still very common at most UNIX sites, terminals are quite rare today, especially those connected to a UNIX system via serial terminal lines. Networking is a more efficient and beneficial way to communicate with a UNIX system.

The switch from serial terminal lines to networks required a corresponding UNIX adaptation to the new environment; the whole user login and authentication procedure had been based on user access via terminals. The logical approach was to preserve this concept as much as possible, and a logical consequence of this preservation was the introduction of ***pseudo terminals***.

A **pseudo terminal** is, as the name implies, a logical terminal that behaves like a regular terminal, except it does not include a physical device. Internally (within UNIX), it is seen as any other terminal; externally, it provides a needed interface (including the necessary data conversion) to the new environment.

The corresponding kernel-based driver supports a pseudo terminal, which consists of a pair of character devices: a ***master***, or ***control pseudo device***, and a ***slave pseudo device***. The slave device provides an interface to application processes identical to the one specified in the terminal database (***termcap*** or ***terminfo***). Unlike regular terminals, the slave device does not have a hardware device behind it; instead, it has another process manipulating it through the master half of the pseudo terminal. Thus anything written on the master device is given to the slave device as an input, and anything written on the slave device is presented as input on the master device, as presented in Figure 11.3.

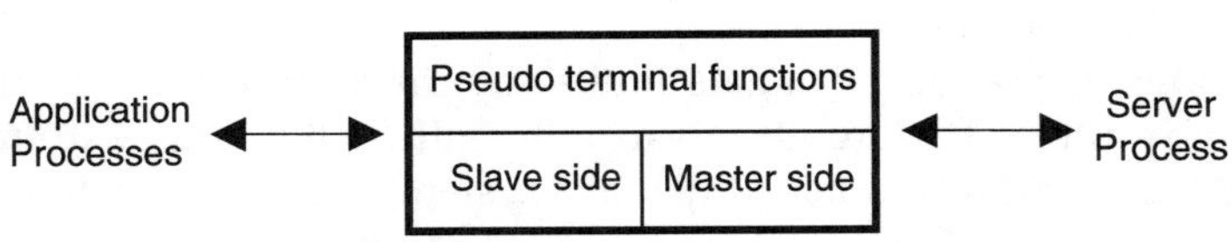

FIGURE 11.3
The pseudo terminal.

Application processes treat pseudo terminals as regular terminals, without knowing anything about what is happening behind the scenes; for ***getty, login***, and ***shell***, this is just a terminal. On the master side a network-related server process adapts the network-based data transfers into terminal-based serial data transfers. The bottom line is preestablished terminal-based communication without any real terminal involvement.

The master side of a pseudo terminal has the device name ***/dev/pty[p-s]***n. Examples include ***ptyp0***, ***ptyq3***, ***ptyr5***, or ***ptys2***. The original name on System V was (and still is) ***/dev/ptc/n***.

The slave side of a pseudo terminal (also known as a virtual terminal) has the device name ***/dev/tty[p-s]***n; for example: ***ttyp0, ttyq3, ttyr5***, or ***ttys2***. The original System V name was and is ***/dev/pts/n***, *n* is a single hexadecimal digit. The slave pseudo terminal provides a TTY-like interface to user (application) processes. The two parts work in pairs, each having the same device number *n*.

The **tty** command displays the special device file used for any login session; it always displays the slave pseudo terminal. For example, the user ***bjl*** has opened a telnet session and logged into a system named ***patsy***:

```
$ telnet patsy
SunOS UNIX (patsy)
Login: bjl
Password: ++++++++
Last login: Mon May 17 10:21:30 from atlas.ph.hunter.cuny.edu
SunOS Release 4.1.3 (PATSY) #1: Tue May 18 13:59:37 EST 1999
```

To check for the terminal through which this connection was established (in this case a pseudo terminal) use this command:

```
$ tty
/dev/ttyp2
```

The **tty** command displays the slave device of a pseudo terminal pair. This makes sense, given that the slave side is visible to the application and to user programs.

New UNIX flavors have introduced another, similar command, ***pty***, to check for the master device of a pseudo terminal pair currently in use, as seen here:

```
$ pty
/dev/ptyp2
```

Selection of a pseudo terminal to establish a user telnet session is out of the user's control. The server process picks up one of the pseudo devices available at the time and establishes the required telnet connection, i.e., session. All pseudo terminals are interchangeable, and there is no advantage or disadvantage in using any given pseudo terminal.

Pseudo terminal availability is a condition for a new user's connection (telnet or any other kind of user's session); if there is no free pseudo terminal, the UNIX system will refuse the requested user connection.

The total number of pseudo terminals limits the maximum number of simultaneous connections to the system. This number is usually sufficiently large with respect to other system characteristics, and it is more likely that a system will hit limits due to other system restrictions. Nevertheless, if the total number of pseudo terminals could cause a problem, additional pseudo terminals should be created; all UNIX flavors provide tools to create special device files, including pseudo devices.

11.4 Terminal Servers

Networks have put terminals out of business; the huge pool of existing terminals suddenly became obsolete. **Terminal servers** were introduced to prolong the use of the existing equipment in the new networked environment. A terminal server is a dedicated system that enables the connection of multiple old fashioned local terminals onto the network.

A terminal is connected to the terminal server via a serial line, in the same way terminals used to be connected directly to the computer system. The terminal server is connected to the network, and provides a mapping of each of its local serial lines into an IP address; in this way each connected terminal can appear as a networked device (IP addressing is discussed in Chapter 15). Of course, a terminal server should also convert each local serial terminal session into an appropriate telnet session with the host UNIX system. Groupings of terminals around one or more terminal servers enable more efficient connections to the host system. The benefits are obvious: idle but usable equipment can be reactivated, large lengths of cabling are not needed, and optimal locations for terminals can be selected — all thanks to relatively cheap terminal servers.

Another very useful implementation of terminal servers is somewhat unorthodox. Given a site with multiple UNIX systems and other computing facilities (a very common case, since almost every computer center can be described this way), multiple serial console lines from multiple computer systems can be connected to the terminal server. Each connected system console will be identified by an IP address, and remote access to the system consoles will be enabled. This arrangement could be extremely useful when performing regular system maintenance and administration. There is no need for physical access to the system consoles, no need to switch from one console to another, and everything can be accomplished from a single location in a more comfortable and efficient way. In fact, there is really no need even for a physical console device itself, though a single remote terminal can now emulate a number of local consoles.

12

UNIX Backup and Restore

12.1 Introduction

We live in a computer age. We use computers and they help us, but we also rely on them. And the worthiest part of any computer is the data; data is priceless, and often irreplaceable. UNIX systems are no exception to this rule. In UNIX systems, data live in files, and files live in filesystems, so discussing data means discussing files and filesystems. Readers familiar with databases know that data may also live in database spaces other than filesystems.

Users know very well the importance of their files. The files may be the results of users' hard work over several years; often, the significance of the files cannot be measured in the usual way. They are simply invaluable. On the other hand, every user knows that, sometimes, data is lost. These losses have many causes: users may delete their own files accidentally, a bug can cause a program to corrupt its data file, a hardware failure may ruin an entire disk, and so on. The damage resulting from these losses can be minor (in the best case scenario) or it can be very expensive and disastrous harm. Experience teaches us to prepare for the worst outcomes.

One of a system administrator's primary responsibilities is to plan and implement a regular backup system to protect users from such unpleasant surprises by saving all of the important files on the system. It is also the administrator's responsibility to monitor and confirm that backups are performed in a timely manner, and that backed-up files are stored safely and securely.

Files can be backed up or archived. A **backup** is the process of copying files onto another media, while **archiving** is moving files onto another media (the usual media is a tape). Data compression is used in both cases, and in both cases data can be restored if necessary. The difference is that archiving removes files from the live system as they are archived, while a backup keeps the live system unchanged. Generally, UNIX commands do not differentiate between the two procedures; this task is delegated to the backup/archive utilities. This session primarily addresses backup, except where specified otherwise.

The term *archive* is also used to identify a backup media that contains the saved data, regardless of the type of media that was implemented. This terminology can cause confusion, but it is used frequently.

Finally, archiving data raises the question of data consistency during a backup. Obviously, only consistently archived data is of any use; keeping and reusing inconsistent data is pointless and can cause many problems. Therefore, any modification of the data must be prevented during a backup; i.e., access to the files must be prohibited. This precaution led to the long-standing recommendation to backup only dismounted filesystems (so nobody can modify files), but this practice means bringing the system into single-user mode during the backup. Such a drastic limitation of the system does not work for most real-life UNIX systems, and so most system administrators ignore this recommendation. The calculated risk of backing up data from mounted filesystems is balanced by several factors:

- System activity is usually very low during a backup (backups are commonly performed at night or some other time when there are no users on the system).
- Standard filesystems have a huge number of relatively small files and any given file's backup time is a small fragment of the total filesystem's backup time. Consequently, the probability that a file could be modified in the small period of time when it is being backed up is extremely low.
- Even if a file were to be corrupted during archiving, the file could simply be excluded from that backup, and the probability that the same file would be affected during the next backup is almost nonexistent.
- Finally, in the worst-case scenario, even such a loss of a single file is not a tragedy or a disaster from the system standpoint, because the primary candidates for that kind of corruption are usually files in the spooling directory such as continually active e-mail, or something similar.

These statistically based assumptions work in many cases, especially for regular UNIX filesystems. However, once we shift into the issue of databases, data consistency becomes crucial and no chances can be taken. Database backups require stable, static conditions, which requires alternate approaches. One of these is *volume and filesystem snapshots,* which is discussed in Chapter 6.

12.1.1 Media

Magnetic tape is the most suitable media for a backup; magnetic tape was actually invented for this purpose. The nature of backing up perfectly matches the economical sequential data storage magnetic tape provides. Although magnetic tape is not the only backup media available, it is the most widely used, and is the standard backup media for almost any UNIX installation.

There are a number of different types of magnetic tapes available for backups, so selecting the most appropriate type can sometimes be a difficult task. It was simpler in the past, when 9-track tape was the only convenient media available for backing up data. Today, the situation has changed and many suitable magnetic tapes are available; backups can be performed faster and safer. A brief summary of the available choices follows:

- **9-track tape** The old (and today obsolete) medium. However, 9-track tape has been used for a very long time, and 9-track tape drives have been installed almost everywhere, so it was easy to move tapes from one system to another and from one site to another. The 9-track tape technology was quite reliable and reasonably fast, but rather expensive. Tapes were bulky, and their capacity was not too large —

roughly 150 MB at the highest density. From today's standpoint, with huge disk space common, such an extremely small tape capacity sounds odd, but it worked in the past. Unfortunately, even given the small size of old disks, unattended backup was not often possible because new tape reels had to be mounted (loaded) during the backup. A night operator's shift was almost a necessity. Today, 9-track tape drives exist (if they are used at all), primarily to restore some long-ago archived data.

- **1/4 in. cartridge tape** This tape cartridge is known as QIC. For some time it was the medium of choice for UNIX workstations. The tapes were very reliable and the tape drives were reasonably inexpensive, so they became standard equipment for most workstations. The tapes are much smaller than the 9-track ones, with almost the same capacity (150 MB cartridges are also known as QIC 150). The troubles with backing up the larger disks still persisted, but it was much easier to store and keep them.
- **8 and 4 mm tape** The new video technology has found its place in this field, revolutionizing the backup approach itself. Small in size, the tapes come in 8 mm and 4 mm, and they have an extremely large capacity: initially 2 GB, followed by 8 GB DDS-2 tapes, and today's DDS-3 tapes with an incredible capacity of 12 GB (even up to 24 GB with compression). They have become the ideal media for unattended backups for a number of implementations. Several filesystems can be backed up overnight. Today, 4 mm tapes are very common and are almost a standard device on any UNIX system. The only disadvantage is that these tapes are more sensitive to heat than other storage media.
- **DLT tape** An extremely high-density and high-capacity medium. With the capacity of 35 GB (with compression up to 70 or more GB) a DLT tape is suitable for the backup of large databases. Today, it is a very common medium for a large volume backup.
- **Robotics devices** A number of different robotics devices (tape changers, juke boxes, etc.) are widely used today. They enable flexible, unattended backups within large computer networks, with automatic mounting and dismounting of requested tapes. Equipped with bar code readers, they can fulfill various backup demands.
- **Floppy disk** A floppy disk drive is a well-known, cheap, and reliable device. However, the capacity of a floppy disk is extremely small, and it cannot be a reasonable backup option; an average filesystem backup can easily use several hundred diskettes. A floppy drive can efficiently be used to back up a few files.

12.2 Tape-Related Commands

UNIX provides a complete suite of commands designed for data archival. The commands range from those suitable to save a single file, several files, and a directory structure, up to those commands for an elaborate backup of a complete filesystem/filesystems. Of course, the reverse process is also covered: corresponding commands for data restoration/recovery are also available. All these commands are also widely implemented within the available UNIX backup/archive/restore tools, forming powerful and sophisticated vehicles for handling this unavoidable UNIX task.

Originally, all these UNIX commands were tape related, i.e., tape was assumed to be the archive media. We will discuss most of the UNIX commands of this type, which are divided into two basic groups:

1. Tape-related commands, designed to backup and restore individual files to/from a magnetic tape
2. Filesystem-related commands, designed for more elaborated archival/restoration

The UNIX commands belonging to the first group are generally available on almost all UNIX platforms; these include **tar** and **cpio**, and the **dd** command. In addition, the **mt** command is available to control the tape itself (rewinding, erasing, retention, etc.). The listed commands overlap in some respects, but each of the commands has a specific mission, unique to the command itself. There are other, flavor-specific commands as well (for example, **bar** on SunOS, or **tcio** on HP-UX) — they will not be covered in this text.

12.2.1 The *tar* Command

The ***tar*** command saves and restores files to and from archive media, usually a tape, but also any other media, such as floppy disks or others. The ***tar*** command can also be used to copy files to other files. The origin of the name ***tar*** is *tape archiving,* which obviously describes the nature of this command. It saves files, a kind of compression is applied, and a single archive file is created. When it restores files, ***tar*** decompresses them and returns them to their original forms.

The syntax of the ***tar*** command is:

tar ***key[options] [filenames]***

where

filenames The files on the specified directory, or the name of the file
key[option] Determines what action the **tar** command will take

The list of key and additional options follows:

Key	Function
r	Append ***filenames*** to an existing archive (does not work on most tapes)
x	Extract ***filenames*** from the archive; if a directory is specified, it is recursively extracted
t	Print the names of the specified files each time they occur in archive and extract them
u	Add ***filenames*** to the archive only if they are not already there or if they are modified in the meantime
c	Create a new archive and write ***filenames*** to it, destroying any existing files

Option	Function Modifier
number	Selects the tape or disk drive with the *number*; if missing, the default drive is selected
b number	Specifies the blocking factor for archive records; the default is 20 (for standard input it is always 1)
h	Forces **tar** to follow symbolic links as if they were normal files and directories, otherwise, **tar** archives only a path of the linked file or directory
v	Causes **tar** to display the name of each of the files it reads or writes
w	Displays the action to be performed on each file and waits for confirmation
f argument	Causes **tar** to use the device or file specified by the argument instead of the default one, standard input or output is specified by a hyphen (-)
l	Causes **tar** to display a message if there is a problem
m	Causes **tar** to set the current time rather than original one (when extracting)
k number	Specifies the size of archive as *number* kB (min. 250)
e	Prevents files from being split across backup volumes (tapes or floppies). If a file does not fit, **tar** prompts for a new volume; this option can only be used together with the **k** option

Note: All options can be used without the usual hyphen (-); however, most UNIX flavors allow also the use of the hyphen. The reference directory is the current directory. This is not a complete list, other options are also possible — check the manual pages.

Default values are usually defined in a separate file, such as */etc/default/archive* or */etc/default/tar.*

The **tar** command is very popular among UNIX administrators; they like this command and use it frequently. The main reasons for this popularity are:

- It is an easy to use and flexible command.
- It preserves file ownership and mode (if it is used by the superuser).
- It compresses data, creating a single archive file.
- The **tar** command can both "tar"(archive) and "untar" (extract) data.

The **tar** command is often used to transfer files or directory hierarchies from one place to another, especially in a networked environment. The selected files are first "*tar-ed,*" then transferred as a single archive file to the destination, and at the end "*untar-ed.*" Besides the fact that it is easier to handle and copy a single file, **tar** also preserves files' ownership, modes, and time stamps. **Tar** also handles symbolic links (on most UNIX platforms there is the option to copy a link or follow a link and copy a linked file).

Pay attention that un*tar*-ing is always performed in the reverse way from the original *tar*-ing. This means that archived files with absolute pathnames can be extracted only into their original locations; extracting such files to other locations requests extraordinary skills (and the use of the **chroot** command, which is definitely not recommended for novices). However, archived files with relative pathnames can be extracted into an arbitrary reference directory. The GNU flavor of the **tar** command even allows an arbitrary extraction of files archived with absolute pathnames.

In most cases the use of the **tar** command involves the following command options:

- To tar data (create an archive):

  tar -cvf ***/dev/rmt/mt_device files_to_tar***
- To list the archive (*tar*-ed data):

  tar -tvf ***/dev/rmt/mt_device***
- To untar (extract) all *tar*-ed data:

  tar -xvf ***/dev/rmt/mt_device***
- To untar (extract) selected *tar*-ed data:

  tar -xvf ***/dev/rmt/mt_device files_to_untar***

Using the **v** (verbose) option to show exactly what **tar** is doing is recommended. Sometimes, it can take quite a while for the command to terminate, and it is always good to know what happens in the meantime.

12.2.2 The *cpio* Command

The ***cpio*** command copies files into and out of archives for storage, moving, and backups. Archives can be ordinary files, directories, or backup media such as tape or floppy disks. **cpio** has several advantages over the **tar** command:

- It can back up arbitrary sets of files.
- It can back up special device files and so is suitable for full system backups on small systems.
- It packs data on tape significantly more efficiently than **tar**.
- On restore, it skips over bad spots on the tape while **tar** dies in such cases.

cpio takes its input from the standard input (i.e., keyboard), not from files specified as arguments. It waits for input (names of files typed in one line) terminated by *CTRL-D*.

The **cpio** command can be used in three different ways, defined by three different generic formats. Each format uses different *required options* that cannot be combined. There are *additional options* that can be used in all three command formats. The syntax is:

cpio -o ***[acBv]***

cpio -i ***[option] [pattern]***

cpio -p ***[option] directory***

The *required* and *additional options* have the following meaning:

Required Options	Meaning
-o *[option]*	Causes **cpio** to read a list of file names from its standard input and combine them into an archive file, which it prints as its standard output (copy out)
-i *[option] [pattern]*	Causes **cpio** to retrieve files specified by ***pattern*** (? and * are legal) from an archive created with **cpio -o**; these files are then copied to the current directory
-p *[option]* ***directory***	Causes **cpio** to read a list of ordinary files from its standard input and copy them to the specified ***directory***

Additional Options	Meaning
a	Resets access times of input files after they are copied
c	Writes the header information in ASCII characters for portability to other machines
d	Creates directories as needed; used when directories are specified to be copied
f	Copies only files not matched by pattern
l	Creates links to files in the new directories instead of copying them (if possible)
m	Does not change modification time of files when copying them
r	Allows files to be renamed as they are copied; **cpio** waits for a new name
t	List the names of the input files without copying them
u	Pushes **cpio** to overwrite files if they already exist (ordinarily, **cpio** does not copy files if they already exist)
v	Prints a list of the files being copied

The **cpio** command is usually combined (piped) with other UNIX commands to perform a requested command sequence (often within scripts). The manual use of the command (from the command line) is not very convenient, but still workable. The need to handle special device files makes this command unavoidable. Here are a few examples:

- To archive all files, starting in the current directory and continuing with subsequent subdirectories, onto the magnetic tape (identified by the tape device file *0m*):

  find . -print | cpio -o > /dev/rmt/0m
- To copy all files in the directory */dir1* into */dir2*:

  ls /dir1 | cpio -p /dir2

Although it works for any directory, the example is used primarily to copy special device files:

ls /dev/dir1 | cpio -p /dev/dir2

The **d** option is required if the directory *dir2* does not already exist.

12.2.3 The *dd* Command

The *dd* command converts and copies files with various data formats; it copies a specified input file to a specified output with possible conversions. The standard input and output are used by default. The input and output block size may be specified to take advantage of raw physical I/O.

The format of the *dd* command is:

dd *[option=value]...*

The options are:

if=*name*	Input file is taken from *name*; standard input is default
of=*name*	Output file is taken from *name*; standard output is default
ibs=*n*	Input block size *n* bytes (default is 512)
obs=*n*	Output block size *n* bytes (default is 512)
bs=*n*	Set both input and output block size, superseding **ibs** and **obs**
cbs=*n*	Conversi on buffer size
skip=*n*	Skip *n* input records before starting copy
files=*n*	Copy *n* input files before terminating (makes sense only when the input is a magnetic tape or similar device)
seek=*n*	Seek *n* records from beginning of output file before copying. This option generally only works with magnetic tapes and raw disk files and is otherwise usually useless if the explicit output file was named with the **of** option
count=n	Copy only *n* input records
conv=...	Specify a conversion (EBCDIC, ASCII, etc.)

After completion, **dd** reports the number of whole and partial input and output blocks. A few examples are:

- To read an EBCDIC tape, with blocked ten 80-byte EBCDIC card images per record, into the ASCII file filename:

  $ dd if=/dev/rmt0 of=*filename* ibs=800 cbs=80 conv=ascii, lcase

- To write the file *filename* to a 3.5-inch floppy and read from the floppy into a file *filename*, respectively:

  $ dd if=*filename* of=/dev/rfd0c bs=9k

  $ dd if=/dev/rfd0c of=*filename* bs=9k

- This command can be used to figure out the actual size of a raw disk partition or a logical volume, for example:

  $ dd if=/dev/vg00/lvol5 of=/dev/null bs=2k

  51200+0 records in

  51200+0 records out

In this example, the complete logical volume ***lvol5*** was copied into ***null*** device (nowhere); the reported number of input and output records for the defined block size of 2K determines the total raw volume size of 102.4 MB. Be careful in using this command, because a reverse selection of the input and output file would have a completely different meaning: it will erase the contents of the volume.

12.2.4 The *mt* Command

The **mt** command controls a magnetic tape drive. It can be used to position a tape at a particular place, so it is very useful when multiple filesystems/files are archived on a single tape. The command syntax is:

mt *[-t tapename] command...[count]*

Or on some UNIX platforms (like Solaris 2.x):

mt *[-f tapename] command...[count]*

If ***tapename*** is not specified, the environment variable *TAPE* is used. If *TAPE* does not exist, **mt** uses the default device (on Solaris, */dev/rmt/0*). ***tapename*** refers to a raw tape device. By default, **mt** performs the requested operation once; specify **count** to perform multiple operations. The available commands are listed below. Only as many characters as are required to uniquely identify a command need be specified.

mt supports the following internal commands:

eof Write **count** EOF marks at the current position on the tape, (**weof**).

fsf Forward space over **count** EOF marks. The tape is positioned on the first block of the file.

fsr Forward space **count** records.

bsf Back space over **count** EOF marks. The tape is positioned on the beginning-of-tape side of the EOF mark.

bsr Back space **count** records.

nbsf Back space **count** files. The tape is positioned on the first block of the file; this is equivalent to {**count**+1} **bsf**'s followed by one **fsf.**

asf Absolute space to **count** file number; this is equivalent to a rewind followed by a **fsf count**. For the **eom** commands, **count** is ignored.

eom Space to the end of recorded media on the tape. This is useful for appending files onto previously written tapes.

rewind Rewind the tape.

offline Rewind the tape and take the drive unit off-line by unloading the tape, (**rewoffl**).

status Print status information about the tape unit.

retention Rewind the cartridge tape completely, then wind it forward to the end of the reel and back to beginning-of-tape to smooth out tape tension.

erase Erase the entire tape.

12.2.5 Magnetic Tape Devices and Special Device Files

All tape-related commands deal with magnetic tape drives via corresponding special device files. The command specifies the device file, which then provides the requested operation with the tape drive. Once the operation is completed, the tape is usually rewound. To properly understand tape device files, a bit of history can be instructive. In the past, only low density and small capacity tapes were available, so it was necessary to use a number of tape volumes to backup a complete system. A multivolume backup also included the rewinding of the tape volumes once the desired transaction was completed. The easiest way to provide this unavoidable rewinding was to delegate this task to the device file; rewinding was performed automatically before the device file was closed.

The new technology brought new demands. High density and large capacity tapes enable the archival of many files, directories, and/or filesystems on a single tape, so there is no need for a multivolume backup. In fact, today the opposite exists; often, multiple filesystems must be archived on the same medium. The fact that a tape was rewound automatically when the archiving was completed became an obstacle; a new command always started from the beginning of the tape, so everything previously stored was overwritten.

That is why modified, "nonrewinding" device files have been introduced; they provide everything contained in the original device files except for the rewinding at the end, and usually they carry an additional "n" in their names (as a prefix or a suffix).

The permanent improvements in tape density were addressed in a similar way — new, modified device files handle the new higher density tapes.

Let us see what this means in practice. On Solaris 2.x (which is System V-like), all tape device files reside in the subdirectory */dev/rmt.*

```
$ ls -C /dev/rmt
0   0bn  0cb   0cn  0hb   0hn  0lb   0ln  0mb   0mn  0u   0ubn
0b  0c   0cbn  0h   0hbn  0l   0lbn  0m   0mbn  0n   0ub  0un
```

This is an example from the SunSparc20 workstation with a single 4mm DDS2 tape drive. Each device file is identified by:

/dev/rmt/ <unit number> [<density>][<BSD behavior>][norewind>]

where

<density> Is identified by the letters ***l***, ***m***, ***h***, ***u***, and ***c*** for low, medium, high, ultra, and compressed, respectively

<BSD behavior>	By the letter ***b***
<norewind>	By the letter ***n***

Tape device files can be identified in a similar way on other systems.

12.3 Backing Up a UNIX Filesystem

Filesystem-related UNIX backup/restore commands enable the handling of large, complex volume data archiving in a relatively simple way. This is especially important if a system crash occurs, when fast filesystem recovery (primarily of the root filesystem) is extremely significant. Besides the commands themselves, some UNIX platforms provide other backup/restore tools (mostly shell script based, which makes it easy to understand what they are doing and how) for the same purpose. We will discuss many of them. However, before starting with the commands/tools, a few words about planning the process of a successful data archival.

12.3.1 Planning a Backup Schedule

Performing regular backup is essential for system data security. It is a good idea to assume that the next time you use the system, all system disks will have crashed and the only available files to restore are those you had backed up previously. Keeping such a catastrophe in mind will make it obvious what needs to be backed up and how often. Backups are convenient for accidentally deleted files, but they are also essential in the event of serious hardware failures or other disasters; all hardware has a finite lifetime, and failures are always possible.

Therefore, planning is an important part of the backup process. In planning a backup schedule, several factors need to be taken into account:

- What files are critical to the users on this system?
- Where are these files located? Are they isolated in a single filesystem, for example?
- How often do these files change?
- How quickly would they need to be restored in the event of damage or loss?
- How often are the relevant filesystems available for backup? (Ideally, backups should not be performed on mounted filesystems.)
- What kinds of media are available for backups?

For example, if the system supports a large ongoing development project, it can be assumed that the files change frequently and should be backed up often. On the other hand, if the only volatile file on the system is a large database, its filesystem might need to be backed up more often than the other filesystems on the system.

In performing backups, a system administrator invests time in the present to prevent future losses. The time required for any backup schedule must be weighed against the potential losses if the files are needed but are not available.

Strictly speaking, a filesystem should be dismounted before a backup is performed (except for the root filesystem). This means that the system should be placed in single-user mode. However, this recommendation is rarely followed; in practice, backups are almost always performed on mounted filesystems. Consequently, any file modified while the backup is in progress may not be backed up correctly.

The simplest backup scheme is to copy a whole disk to a tape. This type of *full backup* is time consuming, and restoring a single filesystem from a large set of tapes is inconvenient; if the files do not change frequently, it can be a waste of time. On the other hand, if the files are changing very rapidly, then even daily *full backups* might be reasonable. In any case, a periodic *full backup* is recommended (once per month, biweekly, or once per week).

Another approach is incremental backup; in an incremental backup, a system copies only those files that have been changed since the previous backup. The concept of a backup level to distinguish different backup types is often used; each backup type has an assigned level number. By definition:

Level 0	Full backup
Level 1	Backup of all files that have changed since the last full backup
Level 2	Backup of all files that have changed since the last level 1 backup
Level 3	Backup of all files that have changed since the last level 2 backup
Level 4	Backup of all files that have changed since the last level 3 backup

and so on.

This approach and the concept of numeric backup levels are generally valid for any UNIX system, but they are only fully supported by BSD-style backup commands.

A typical backup strategy usually includes a full backup at the beginning of the determined backup period, and then several incremental backups during that period. As examples, two schemes are presented:

The Backup Period	One Week
Monday	Level 1 backup (incremental backup to the last full backup)
Tuesday	Level 1 backup (incremental backup to the last full backup)
Wednesday	Level 1 backup (incremental backup to the last full backup)
Thursday	Level 1 backup (incremental backup to the last full backup)
Friday	Level 0 backup (full backup)

The Backup Period	One Month
First Monday of each month	Level 0 backup (full backup)
All other Mondays	Level 1 backup (total incremental to the last level 0)
Tuesday	Level 2 backup (daily incremental to the previous level 1)
Wednesday	Level 2 backup (daily incremental to the previous level 1)
Thursday	Level 2 backup (daily incremental to the previous level 1)
Friday	Level 2 backup (daily incremental to the previous level 1)

The main criterion for planning a backup schedule is how the system is used. The most used portions of the filesystem may need to be backed up more often than the other parts; for example, the root filesystem with standard UNIX programs and files that rarely change does not require frequent backup. Some parts of the system, like the */tmp* directory, need never be backed up. Sometimes, additional filesystems can be created; they might need to be backed up often, or very rarely, or never at all.

The full backup should be performed whenever significant changes are made to the system, regardless of the current backup schedule. This might be one of the few times that the root filesystem gets backed up.

The worst part of doing backups is sitting around waiting for them to finish; this will often feel like wasted time. Unattended backups solve this problem for some sites. If the backup will fit on a single tape, and new technologies enable it, then the tape can be put in the drive and the backup performed during the night. In the morning the operator simply has to pick up and label the tape. However, unattended backups can be a security risk; nontrusted users with physical access to the tape drive may cause a problem.

12.4 Backup and Dump Commands

Despite the fact that system backups have always been one of the main issues in the administration of any software system, there is no uniform approach for handling this task in UNIX. Rather, the opposite is true: there are many different approaches. More specifically, there are many different utilities and commands (mostly flavor- and release-based) that address data backup and restoration. The following text is an attempt to at least briefly specify and present some of them.

12.4.1 The SVR3 and SVR4 *backup* Commands

First, a quick look into the history: backups under System V went through several phases before arriving at today's process. ***SVR3*** provided the ***backup*** command, which was really an interface to the **cpio** command. It could perform a full or an incremental backup of the filesystem, or backup a list of files, or user's home directories, to either a tape or a floppy disk. Today, the command itself is obsolete. The syntax of this **backup** command was:

backup *[options]*

The ***options*** specified the action to be performed, as seen in the following table.

Options	Meaning
-c	Complete (full) backup
-p	Partial (incremental) backup
-f *file_list*	Backup the specified files (place the list in quotes)
-u *user*	Back up all files under ***user***'s home directory
-d *spec_file*	Specify backup target device (a character special file)
-t	The specified device is a tape device (default is floppy)
-h	List the dates of the last incremental and full backup

A few examples:

$ backup -c -t -d /dev/rmt/c0s0 ***# The full backup to the first tape drive;***

$ backup -p ***# The incremental backup to the default floppy drive***
 # (/dev/rdsk/f05h);

$ backup -u ***username*** **-d /dev/rdsk/f03h** ***# Copy all files under user username's home***
 # directory to a high density 3–1/2" floppy drive.

SVR4 introduced an improved ***backup tool*** — a highly sophisticated and powerful ***backup*** utility that enabled administrators to implement and manage an arbitrarily elaborate backup plan. It enabled automation of most backup tasks (except physical mounting of tapes). On the other hand, it was more complex than absolutely necessary for some systems. Unfortunately, we cannot talk about a uniquely accepted and implemented backup utility — each System V flavor had some peculiarities. For example, on SGI IRIX even the name of the utility was abbreviated and modified into ***/usr/sbin/bru***, the *Backup and Restore Utility*, to point out its inherent restore capabilities.

A typical example of a SVR4 backup utility is the one that existed on HP-UX 9.0x. Although HP-UX 9.0x is a more-or-less obsolete UNIX flavor today, the backup utility can be used to provide an understanding of different backup/restore issues. First, it is a shell script that could be easily read and understood; second, it is based primarily on the **find** and **cpio** UNIX commands, with which administrators should be familiar.

Briefly, the backup scheduling was controlled by the configuration file */etc/archivedate* (on some UNIX systems the file was */etc/bkup/bkreg.tab*). The configuration file defined each participating filesystem in the backup, a backup schedule, destinations, and other information.

The format of the command to start a backup is:

/etc/backup [-A] [-archive] [-fsck]

The **-A** option suppressed warning messages regarding optional access control list entries. Normally, a warning message was printed for each file having optional access control list entries.

The **-archive** option caused **backup** to save all files, regardless of their modification date, and then update */etc/archivedate* using the **touch** command. **backup** sent a prompt when a new tape needed to be loaded and continued, if there was no more room on the current tape. However, the prompting did not occur if **backup** had been run from **cron**.

The **-fsck** option caused **backup** to start a filesystem consistency check (without correction) once the backup was complete. For correct results, it was important that the system had been effectively single-user while **fsck** was running (with the corresponding filesystem dismounted), especially if **-fsck** was allowed to automatically fix whatever inconsistencies it found. **backup** itself did not ensure that the system was in single-user mode.

The script ***/etc/backup*** could be customized, and several local values were available for customization:

backupdirs	Specified which directories to back up recursively (usually /, which meant all directories)
backuplog	The name of the file where start and finish times, block counts, and error messages were logged
archive	The name of the file whose date was the date of the last archive
remind	The name of the file that was checked by */etc/profile* to remind the next logged-in person to change the backup tape
outdev	Specified the output device for the backed-up files
fscklog	The name of the file where start and finish times and *fsck* output was logged

In all cases, the output from **backup** utility was a normal **cpio** archive file.

For data recovery, it is important to note that **backup** creates archive tapes with all files and directories specified relative to the root directory. Consequently, data recovery should be invoked from the root directory with recovered files' directory path names specified relative to the root directory (/).

12.4.2 The *fbackup* Command

HP-UX 10.x introduced a new flavor of the backup command, this time renamed ***fbackup***. The command itself is a powerful replacement for previous backup commands/utilities, a combination of the best characteristics of the **backup** and **dump** commands. **fbackup** enables a file/directory related backup, with an optional selection to overcome filesystem boundaries. In this way a partial backup of a single filesystem could be done, as well as a complete backup of several filesystems.

The command itself was designed to allow backups while the system is in use by providing the capability to retry an active file. However, when absolute consistency in a full backup is important, the corresponding filesystem should be dismounted, or the system placed in a single-user mode.

The **fbackup** command has the following form:

fbackup *options-arguments*

where

options-arguments A list of options with corresponding arguments

Note: Files and directories to be backed up are defined as arguments, or are a list defined as an argument.

Selected *options* are immediately followed by *corresponding arguments* (if the arguments are requested) in a comprehensive way. The most common *options* are:

Option	Meaning
c	Specifies a configuration file for the backup (an argument), unless the default configuration is used
i	Includes a filename or a directory name for the backup (an argument), and can be repeated many times
e	Excludes a filename or a directory name from the backup (an argument), and can be repeated many times
g	Specifies a "graph-file" (an argument), which is a list of included and excluded filenames/dirnames
f	Identifies the backup device to be used instead of the default */dev/rmt/0m* (an argument)
n	Cross NFS mount-points (by default **fbackup** does not cross)
l	Includes specified LOFS files and directories (by default it does not)
s	Follows symbolic links (by default it does not)
v	Verbose (otherwise **fbackup** works silently)
u	Updates the backup database
0–9	Specifies the backup level (0 is a full backup)
I	Also writes the "index" (the list of backed-up files) in the file specified as an argument (by default it is written only into the tape/volume)
V	Also writes the "volume header" in the file specified as an argument (by default it is written only into the tape/volume)
R	Continues (restarts) an interrupted backup

Note: There are more options that make **fbackup** more powerful and flexible.

The following script illustrates how the command can be used. The script provides a full backup of data defined in the graph file, a list of backed-up files is created in the index file, and the corresponding logging is provided.

$ cat /usr/local/fbackup/bin/fbackup.full

```
#!/bin/sh
#
#*****************************************************************************************
#
MT_DEVICE=/dev/rmt/0m
GRAPH_FILE=/usr/local/fbackup/graph/graph.full
INDEX_FILE=/usr/local/fbackup/index/index.full
LOG_FILE=/usr/local/fbackup/log/fbackup.log.`date +%a`
mt -t $MT_DEVICE rewind
echo "`date`: Fbackup started" > $LOG_FILE
/etc/fbackup -f $MT_DEVICE/dev/rmt/0m -0 -u -v -g $GRAPH_FILE -I $INDEX_FILE >> $LOG_FILE
echo "`date`: Fbackup finished." >> $LOG_FILE
#
#*****************************************************************************************
#
```

12.4.3 The *dump/ufsdump* Command

Originally a BSD-type command, the ***dump*** command is the most common filesystem-related UNIX backup command. Some flavor-colored variations of the command exist among different UNIX platforms, including modified command names on some System V versions: **ufsdump** or even **ufsbackup**. Despite the discrepancies in the names, the two commands **dump** and **ufsdump** behave the same (or almost the same). We will call the command ***dump/ufsdump***, just to emphasize their common functions and similar behavior.

dump/ufsdump keeps track of when it last saved each filesystem and the level at which the filesystem was saved. This information is stored in the file */etc/dumpdates*. A typical entry in this file is:

/dev/disk2e   2 Sun May 8 13:14:56 1998

This entry indicates the filesystem */dev/disk2e* was last backed up on Sunday, May 8, 1998, and it was level 2 backup. If the filesystem cannot be found in this file, it can be assumed that it was not backed up.

Here is a real example (from a still-active ULTRIX system):

$ cat /etc/dumpdates

```
/dev/rrz0a     0 Tue Sep 20 00:     38:28 1998
/dev/rrz0h     0 Tue Sep 20 00:     39:53 1998
/dev/rrz1h     0 Tue Sep 20 01:     12:35 1998
/dev/rrz2h     0 Tue Sep 20 01:     37:19 1998
/dev/rra35c    0 Tue Sep 20 02:     25:42 1998
/dev/rra34c    0 Mon Apr 19 16:     02:51 1997
/dev/rrz0a     9 Fri Sep 23 05:     48:50 1998
/dev/rrz0h     9 Fri Sep 23 05:     52:44 1998
/dev/rrz1h     9 Fri Sep 23 06:     08:55 1998
/dev/rrz2h     9 Fri Sep 23 06:     12:54 1998
/dev/rra35c    9 Fri Sep 23 06:     19:45 1998
```

The file */etc/dumpdates* must exist before the **dump/ufsdump** command is performed, and it must be owned by the user ***root*** (the best way to create the file the first time using **touch /etc/dumpdates**).

The general form of the **dump** command is:

dump ***options arguments special_file***

or, alternatively:

ufsdump ***options arguments special_file***

where

options	A list of options to be used for this backup
arguments	A list of arguments corresponding to these options; not all options require arguments
special_file	A block special file corresponding to the mounted filesystem to be backed up (on some systems a character special file is requested)

The **dump/ufsdump** command should be used carefully. Options and corresponding arguments are specified within two separate lists, but the list of arguments must strictly correspond, in order and in number, to the list of options requiring arguments. Failing to observe this rule could have disastrous effects and consequences, including destroying the filesystem. It is highly recommended that you create shell scripts that will automatically invoke **dump/ufsdump** commands with proper options and arguments to avoid human errors.

Special attention should be paid to the following two issues in using **dump/ufsdump**:

1. The filesystem to be backed up should always be **the last item on the command line**. If a tape drive specification accidentally follows the disk drive specification, the filesystem could be corrupted because **dump** will backup the tape onto the disk.
2. If the tape drive specification is missing, the backup will be performed assuming the default values. On some systems, it is necessary to select the density on the tape drive's front panel in addition to specifying the correct special device file (**dump** can unexpectedly run out of tape).

At the end the universal advice: check the manual pages for each individual command flavor, because there may be differences in their use.

The important **dump/ufsdump** options are:

Option	Meaning
0–9	The numbers **0–9** indicate the level number of the backup. Given any level ***n***, **dump** will search */etc /dumpdates* for an entry reporting the last level ***n-1*** filesystem backup (or lower). **dump** then backs up all files that have been changed since this date. If ***n*** is zero, or there is no record in */etc/dumpdates*, **dump/ufsdump** will back up the complete system. The default value for the level option is ***0*** (complete backup).
b	This option requires an argument, which specifies the blocking factor for tape writing (default is 20 blocks per write, for cartridge 126 blocks per write). A block is 512 bytes.
c	Indicates a cartridge instead of the standard half-inch reel; sets another set of default arguments.
d	This option requires an argument, which specifies the tape density in bpi (bits per inch): 1600 bpi for 1/2" tape, 1000 bpi for QIC, 54,000 bpi for 8mm tape. If the option is omitted, the default is *1600 BPI.*
f	This option requires an argument, which specifies another dump medium instead of the default tape drive (it can be a file or another device).

s	This option requires an argument, which specifies the size of the backup tape in feet The argument does not correspond literally to the tape size, so the values for different tapes must be read. If the option is omitted, the default is *2300-foot tape.*
t	This option requires an argument, which specifies the number of tracks for a cartridge tape (60MB QIC has 9 tracks; 150MB QIC has 18 tracks).
u	If **dump** finishes successfully, this option updates its history file */etc/dumpdates.*
W	This option asks **dump/ufsdump** to report which filesystems need to be backed up, without taking any action. It reads */etc/dumpdates* and */etc/fstab* to determine what filesystems need backups. If this option is present, **dump/ufsdump** will ignore all other options, except for the dump level.

Here are some argument values that produce satisfactory results on a number of typical tape drives. Note that individual options can be in any order; however, the position of each argument depends on the relative position of each option.

Tape	Command (partial)
60MB QIC	**dump** cdst 1000 425 9...
150 QIC	**dump** cdst 1000 700 18...
1/2" tape	**dump** dsb 1600 2300 126...
2GB 4mm tape	**dump** dsb 54000 6000 126...

The **dump/ufsdump** command is used in the following way:

$ dump 2usfd 2300 /dev/rmt1 6250 /dev/disk1d	*# Performs a level 2 backup on the filesystem accessed via /dev/disk1d, using a 9-track 2300 foot long* **(s)** *tape drive /dev/rmt1 at 6250 BPI density* **(d)**, *then updates the file /etc/dumpdates* **(u)**.
$ dump 3usdf 2300 6250 /dev/rmt20 /dev/disk1d	*# Performs a level 3 backup on the filesystem accessed via /dev/disk1d using the 9-track 2300 foot long* **(s)** *tape drive /dev/rmt20 at 6250 BPI density* **(d)**, *then updates the file/etc/dumpdates* **(u)**.
$ dump 1usdf 1422 /dev/rfd0a /dev/rsd0g	*# Performs a level 1 backup on the filesystem accessed via /dev/rsd0g to a floppy drive/dev/rfd0a on a Sun system, then updates the file /etc/dumpdates.*
$ dump 4Wd 6250 /dev/disk1d	*# Does not back up any filesystem. It will print a complete list of all filesystems indicating the last time each filesystem was backed up, the level at which it was backed up, and whether or not it needs to be backed up at level 4 (when the W option is specified, all other options but the level number are ignored).*

12.4.4 A Few Examples

Two real examples, one from Sun OS 4.1.x (as a BSD representative) and the other from Solaris 2.x (as a System V representative), follow. Both UNIX flavors originate from the same manufacturer, Sun Microsystems, and both examples are related to the backup of multiple filesystems on a single magnetic tape. In the first example, two filesystems are dumped to the 150 MB 1/4 inch cartridge (QIC-150). In the second example, five filesystems are dumped to the 2GB 4mm DAT tape. The BSD-like commands **dump** and **ufsdump** are used, respectively. In both cases an appropriate Bourne shell script has been created to perform the backup. In that way the possibility for any mistake was eliminated, because the scripts were tested and verified previously. The complete backup procedure has been logged in the file named *"dumpit.log."*

Here is the corresponding script, named *"backup_system,"* on Solaris 2.x:

```
$ cat /usr/local/bin/backup_system
#!/ bin/sh
#
# The sh script to dump filesystems on ATLAS
# (This is Solaris 2.6 UNIX and "ufsdump" is used).
# The filesystems on two disk drives
# (c0t3d0s3 and c0t2d0s3) are backed-up.
#
echo "Backing all filesystems on ATLAS on:" >/tmp/dumpit.log
date >> /tmp/dumpit.log
echo " " >> /tmp/dumpit.log
#
echo "Verifying the tape drive..." >> /tmp/dumpit.log
/bin/mt -f /dev/rmt/0 status >> /tmp/dumpit.log 2>&1
#
echo "Rewinding the tape..." >> /tmp/dumpit.log
/bin/mt -f /dev/rmt/0 rewind >> /tmp/dumpit.log 2>&1
echo " " >> /tmp/dumpit.log
#
echo "Starting system backup..." >> /tmp/dumpit.log
echo "Dumping root filesystem..." >> /tmp/dumpit.log
/usr/sbin/ufsdump 0ubf 96 /dev/rmt/0n /dev/rdsk/c0t3d0s0 >> /tmp/dumpit.log 2>&1
echo " " >> /tmp/dumpit.log
echo "Dumping /usr filesystem..." >> /tmp/dumpit.log
/usr/sbin/ufsdump 0ubf 96 /dev/rmt/0n /dev/rdsk/c0t3d0s6 >> /tmp/dumpit.log 2>&1
echo " " >> /tmp/dumpit.log
echo "Dumping /home filesystem..." >> /tmp/dumpit.log
/usr/sbin/ufsdump 0ubf 96 /dev/rmt/0n /dev/rdsk/c0t3d0s7 >> /tmp/dumpit.log 2>&1
echo " " >> /tmp/dumpit.log
echo "Dumping /applic filesystem..." >> /tmp/dumpit.log
/usr/sbin/ufsdump 0ubf 96 /dev/rmt/0n /dev/rdsk/c0t2d0s0 >> /tmp/dumpit.log 2>&1
echo " " >> /tmp/dumpit.log
echo "Dumping /software filesystem..." >> /tmp/dumpit.log
/usr/sbin/ufsdump 0ubf 96 /dev/rmt/0n /dev/rdsk/c0t2d0s6 >> /tmp/dumpit.log 2>&1
echo " " >> /tmp/dumpit.log
#
echo "Rewinding the tape..." >> /tmp/dumpit.log
```

```
/bin/mt -f /dev/rmt/0 rewind >> /tmp/dumpit.log 2>&1
echo " " >> /tmp/dumpit.log
#
echo "Backup is done!" >> /tmp/dumpit.log
echo "Backup is done!"
#
```

The corresponding log file */tmp/dumpit.log* is:

```
$ cat /tmp/dumpit.log
Backing all filesystems on ATLAS on:
Tue Nov 7 16:37:35 EST 1998
Verifying the tape drive...
Archive Python 4mm Helical Scan tape drive:
   sense key(0 x 0) = No Additional Sense residual=0 retries=0
   file no = 0 block no = 0
Rewinding the tape...
Starting system backup...
Dumping root filesystem...
   DUMP: Writing 48 Kilobyte records
   DUMP: Date of this level 0 dump: Tue Nov 07 16:37:36 1998
   DUMP: Date of last level 0 dump: the epoch
   DUMP: Dumping /dev/rdsk/c0t3d0s0 (atlas:/) to /dev/rmt/0n.
   DUMP: Mapping (Pass I) [regular files]
   DUMP: Mapping (Pass II) [directories]
   DUMP: Estimated 168074 blocks (82.07MB).
   DUMP: Dumping (Pass III) [directories]
   DUMP: Dumping (Pass IV) [regular files]
   DUMP: 167998 blocks (82.03MB) on 1 volume at 624 KB/sec
   DUMP: DUMP IS DONE
   DUMP: Level 0 dump on Tue Nov 07 16:37:36 1998
         . . . . .
         . . . . .
Rewinding the tape...
Backup is done!
```

The script on SunOS has an identical structure; the only difference is that the **dump** command (instead of **ufsdump**), is applied, as follows:

```
$ cat /usr/local/bin/dump_system
#!/ bin/sh
#
# The csh script to dump / and /usr filesystems
# (this is level 0 dump to the QIC 150 tape)
      . . . . .
      . . . . .
echo "Dumping root filesystem..." >> /tmp/dumpit.log
/usr/etc/dump 0cdstfu 1000 700 18 /dev/nrst0 /dev/sd0a >> /tmp/dumpit.log 2>&1
echo " " >> /tmp/dumpit.log
echo "Dumping usr filesystem..." >> /tmp/dumpit.log
/usr/etc/dump 0cdstfu 1000 700 18 /dev/nrst0 /dev/sd0g >> /tmp/dumpit.log 2>&1
```

```
echo " " >> /tmp/dumpit.log
        .....
        .....
```

The corresponding log file */tmp/dumpit.log* is:

$ cat /tmp/dumpit.log

```
Wed Nov 1 16:43:38 EST 1998
Backing root and usr filesystems
Verifying the drive...
Archive QIC-150 tape drive:
   sense key(0 x 0) = no sense   residual = 0   retries = 0
   file no = 0 block no = 0
Rewinding the tape...
Starting backup...
Dumping root filesystem...
   DUMP: Date of this level 0 dump: Wed Nov 1 16:43:42 1998
   DUMP: Date of last level 0 dump: the epoch
   DUMP: Dumping /dev/rsd0a (/) to /dev/nrst0
   DUMP: mapping (Pass I) [regular files] DUMP: mapping (Pass II) [directories]
   DUMP: estimated 13278 blocks (6.48MB) on 0.05 tape(s).
   DUMP: dumping (Pass III) [directories]
   DUMP: dumping (Pass IV) [regular files]
   DUMP: level 0 dump on Wed Nov 1 16:43:42 1998
   DUMP: Tape rewinding
   DUMP: 13262 blocks (6.48MB) on 1 volume
   DUMP: DUMP IS DONE
Dumping usr filesystem...
   DUMP: Date of this level 0 dump: Wed Nov 1 16:45:00 1998
   DUMP: Date of last level 0 dump: the epoch
   DUMP: Dumping /dev/rsd0g (/usr) to /dev/nrst0
   DUMP: mapping (Pass I) [regular files] DUMP: mapping (Pass II) [directories]
   DUMP: estimated 275898 blocks (134.72MB) on 0.96 tape(s).
   DUMP: dumping (Pass III) [directories]
   DUMP: dumping (Pass IV) [regular files]
   DUMP: 21.60% done, finished in 0:18
   DUMP: 43.98% done, finished in 0:12
   DUMP: 66.08% done, finished in 0:07
   DUMP: 87.82% done, finished in 0:02
   DUMP: level 0 dump on Wed Nov 1 16:45:00 1998
   DUMP: Tape rewinding
   DUMP: 275898 blocks (134.72MB) on 1 volume
   DUMP: DUMP IS DONE
Rewinding the tape...
Backing is done!
```

The log files */tmp/dumpit.log* on both systems report on the backup procedures, step by step — partially because of the echo lines in the scripts, and partially because of the verbose nature of the **dump** and **ufsdump** commands themselves. We will analyze them in greater detail.

Pay attention to the bold DUMP message "*Tape rewinding*" in the second log file. Although the "no-rewind" device file */dev/nrmt0* was selected, the **dump** command informs us of the tape rewinding at the end of each individual filesystem's dump. It is easy to verify, though, that this has not really happened; **dump** just misinformed us. Why?

In the search for an answer, we should recall the discussion about the tape device files. In the past, when the **dump** command was created, it was logical to assume a tape rewind at the end of a filesystem's dump. No one assumed multiple filesystem backups on the same tape. The opposite problem existed: a single filesystem dump required multiple tape volumes. Consequently, a corresponding message was a logical part of the command itself, although a device driver itself performed the rewinding independently. Today, there is no need for the tape to rewind, but this message remains, even when the "no rewind" device is used.

Checking the first log file, we see the confusing DUMP message about tape rewinding does not exist anymore. The **ufsdump** command was introduced later, and all previous bugs were fixed.

Another example illustrates the archiving of users' data, in this case the experimental nuclear magnetic resonance (NMR) data. Users keep data in a separate */data* subdirectory in their home directories; all such data should be periodically compressed and saved on a QIC-150 tape.

Again, an appropriate script file *backup_data.sh* has been created; here, the **tar** command was used for archiving data (there is no need for a complete filesystem backup). The implemented directories and file names correspond to this actual case. (The comments have been placed in **bold** type to make them more legible.)

```
$ cat /usr/CM/CMcoms/backup_data.sh
#!/ bin/sh
#
# ****************************************************
# To use type the command:
#   /usr/CM/CMcoms/backup_data
# The log file is: /home/backup_data.log
# To check the tape type: tar -tf /dev/rst0
# ****************************************************
#
# dir of accounts to be backed-up
cd /home
# Preventive initial remove of used files
rm backup_data.log 2>/dev/null
rm dirs 2>/dev/null
rm nmrusers 2>/dev/null
#
# Specify user home directories
ls > dirs
# Extracting data directories of NMR users
for dir in 'cat dirs'
do
    if [ -d $dir/data ]; then
    echo "$dir/data;" >> nmrusers
    fi
done
#
# Archiving users/data to tape
date >> /home/backup_data.log
echo "Pay attention that the tar command is using!" >> /home/backup_data.log
echo " " >> /home/backup_data.log
```

```
tar -cvf /dev/rst0 /home/nmrusers >> /home/backup_data.log
#
# Deleting temporary files
rm /home/dirs
rm /home/nmrusers
```

12.5 Restoring Files from a Backup

All the backup facilities previously discussed have corresponding file restoration facilities. Central among them is the **restore** command. Similarly to the **dump** command, **restore** also originated from the BSD UNIX, but eventually found its place on System V platforms too. Again, sometimes it has the alternate name **ufsrestore**, but it is functionally the same.

12.5.1 The *restore* Commands

Like **backup**, there are several implementations of the **restore** command; or rather the **restore** command varies among different UNIX versions and releases. A brief review follows.

12.5.1.1 The SVR3 *restore* Command

Another brief historical review: the SVR3 ***restore*** command is the complement to the described SVR3 **backup** command. It is obsolete, and the only reason to mention it here is for its educational purpose, to show the continuity in its use. The SVR3 restore command had the following format:

restore ***options file_list***

where

file_list List of files to be restored. Wildcards are allowed in quotes.
options One or more applicable options.

The options were

Option	Meaning
-c	Restore all files (a complete restoration)
-i	List contents of tape/diskette (can be used to verify backups)
-o	Overwrite existing files when restoring (by default existing files are not restored)
-d *res_dev*	Specify device *res_dev* to restore from
-t	Indicate that *res_dev* is a tape device

Here are a few examples:

 # restore -c # *Restore all files from the diskette in the default floppy drive*

 # restore -d /dev/rmt/c0s0 -t -o "/home/username/data/*.dat"

*# Restore selected files *.dat from the directory /home/username/data from a tape in the first tape drive, overwriting existing files*

12.5.1.2 The *restore/ufsrestore* Command

The BSD-style **restore** command retrieves files from backup tapes made with the BSD-style **dump** command. The command is also supported by other UNIX flavors, including some SVR4 versions (sometimes renamed **ufsrestore**). The **restore/ufsrestore** command can restore a single file, multiple files, directories, or entire filesystems. To restore an entire filesystem, the sequence of different level backups must be respected: first the most recent full dump (level 0), than level 1 backup, and so on. Therefore, to restore a filesystem as a whole, a system administrator may wish to create and mount a clean, empty filesystem, make the current working directory the directory where this filesystem is mounted, and then use the **restore/ufsrestore** command to read the backup tapes into this directory.

If the filesystem is restoring from a complete (level 0) dump, plus one or more incremental dumps, all files which have been deleted after a level 0 backup will be restored again; incremental dumps do not keep track of deleted files.

After any full restoration, the full (level 0) backup should be redone to ensure consistency between inode numbers on the disk(s) and tape(s). The **dump/ufsdump** command copies inode numbers, while the **restore/ufsrestore** command assigns inode numbers sequentially as files are restored.

The **restore/ufsrestore** command has the following form:

restore ***options arguments [files_and_dirs]***

Or, alternatively

ufsrestore ***options arguments [files_and_dirs]***

where

options	A list of options
arguments	A list of arguments corresponding to selected options
files_and_dirs	A list of files and directories to be retrieved from the tape: if omitted, the default is the entire tape

As with the **dump/ufsdump** command, the order of the *options* and *corresponding arguments* is extremely important.

The most important *options* are:

Option	Meaning
r	Read and restore the entire tape
R	Resume a partially completed restoration operation
x	Extract all files and directories listed and restore them in the current directory. Each file must have a complete path name relative to the root directory of the filesystem being restored(for example, to restore the file */a/b/c/filename* from the dump of the */a filesystem*, the file *b/c/filename* must be specified
t	Type the names of the listed files and directories on the tape
f	The corresponding argument is the name of the file or device (specified by the special file) holding the dump. If omitted, the default is the tape mounted on the default tape drive
h	If a name in the *files_and_dirs* list is a directory, only the empty directory should be restored, not the files that are within it
i	Enter interactive mode

12.5.1.3 Interactive Restore

The whole restoration procedure is much simpler once the interactive restore mode (the **restore/ufsrestore** command with the **i** option) has been entered. Once invoked, a restore menu appears, providing a user-friendly environment convenient for a comprehensive dialogue. A system administrator can scan the contents of the tape, choose files for extraction, reselect files, and perform other activities. The restore procedure is controlled by a number of designated restore commands (subcommands). The **quit** command is available to quit the interactive restore mode. The interactive restore mode is illustrated below (the example is from HP-UX 10.20).

```
$ /usr/sbin/restore -ibf 96 /dev/rmt/0mn   # Enter interactive restore mode.
restore > help                              # Display help report.
Available commands are:
   ls [arg] - list directory
   cd arg - change directory
   pwd - print current directory
   add [arg] - add 'arg' to list of files to be extracted
   delete [arg] - delete 'arg' from list of files to be extracted
   extract - extract requested files
   setmodes - set modes of requested directories
   quit - immediately exit program
   what - list dump header information
   verbose - toggle verbose flag (useful with "ls")
   help or '?' - print this list
   . . .
If no 'arg' is supplied, the current directory is used
restore > what                              # List the tape header.
Dump date: Wed Mar 10 13:36:38 1999
Dumped from: the epoch
Level 0 dump of / on apollo :/dev/vgoo/lvol1
Label: none
restore > ls                                # List the root directory (on the tape).
.:
X11/           mail/        preserve/    statmon/   yp/
adm/           ncs          rbootd/      stm/
export/        news/        run/         tmp/
log/           opt/         sam/         uucp/
lost+found/    ppl/         spool/       vue/
restore > cd adm                            # Change the current tape directory.
restore > ls                                # List the new directory (on tape).
./ adm:
.sh_history      lp/                      streams/
OLDsulog         nettl.LOG00              sulog
acct/            new._ACL                 sw/
automount.log    new._OWNER               syslog/
btmp             new._PROD_DFLT_ACL       utmp
cron/            ptydaemonlog             wtmp
diag/            rc.log                   wtmpx
dumpdates        rpc.lockd.log
eisa/            rpc.statd.log
```

```
restore > cd lp                               # Change the current tape directory.
restore > ls                                  # List the new directory (on tape).
./ adm/lp:
log              oldlog

restore >cd ..                                # Change to the previous directory (on the tape)
restore > add btmp                            # Select files to be restored; files are not
restore > add utmp                            restored until extract is entered
restore > add wtmp
restore > ls                                  # Re-list the directory (on the tape);
./adm:                                        Selected files are marked with an asterisk.
.sh_history      lp/                          streams/
OLDsulog         nettl.LOG00                  sulog
acct/            new._ACL                     sw/
automount.log    new._OWNER                   syslog/
*btmp            new._PROD_DFLT_ACL           *utmp
cron/            ptydaemonlog                 *wtm p
diag/            rc.log                       wtmpx
dumpdates        rpc.lockd.log
eisa/            rpc.statd.log

restore > add cron                            # Select a directory to be restored
restore > ls                                  # Relist the directory (on the tape)
./adm:
.sh_history      lp/                          streams/
OLDsulog         nettl.LOG00                  sulog
acct/            new._ACL                     sw/
automount.log    new._OWNER                   syslog/
*btmp            new._PROD_DFLT_ACL           *utmp
*cron/           ptydaemonlog                 *wtmp
diag/            rc.log                       wtmpx
dumpdates        rpc.lockd.log
eisa/            rpc.statd.log
restore > delete btmp                         # Cancel one of the selected files and remove the
                                              file from the extract list
restore > ls                                  # Relist the directory (on the tape)
./ adm:
.sh_history      lp/                          streams/
OLDsulog         nettl.LOG00                  sulog
acct/            new._ACL                     sw/
automount.log    new._OWNER                   syslog/
btmp             new._PROD_DFLT_ACL           *utmp
*cron/           ptydaemonlog                 *wtmp
diag/            rc.log                       wtmpx
dumpdates        rpc.lockd.log
eisa/            rpc.statd.log

restore > extract                             # Restore selected files and directory. It takes a
                                              while to restore selected data from the tape into
                                              the current directory.
restore > quit                                # Exit the interactive restore.
$
```

12.5.2 The *frecover* Command

frecover is the HP-UX 10.x restore alternative for the **fbackup** command. Even the usual name *restore* was modified. This command recovers data that have been previously "*fbacked-up.*" **frecover** selectively recovers files.

The **frecover** command has the following form:

frecover *functions-arguments options-arguments*

where

functions-arguments	A list of functions that define command activities, with corresponding arguments
options-arguments	A list of options with corresponding arguments (if requested)

Files and directories to be recovered from the tape can be specified as arguments, or can be a list specified as an argument.

Selected *functions* and *options* are immediately followed by the *corresponding arguments,* if the arguments are requested. The most common *functions* and *options* are:

Function	Meaning
r	Reads and recovers a complete *fbackup* contents to its original location (intended to recover full and incremental backups)
x	Extracts specified files and directories (recursively, unless the **h** option is implemented). Ownership, mode, and time are preserved (unless the **A** option is specified)
I	Extracts only the "index" from the tape/volume (the list of *fbackup-ed* files on the tape/volume) and writes to the file defined as an argument
V	Extracts only the "volume header" from the tape/volume and writes into the file defined as an argument
R	Continues an interrupted recovery

Option	Meaning
c	Specifies a configuration file for the recovery (an argument)
i	Includes a filename or a directory name to be extracted (an argument), could be repeated many times
e	Excludes a filename or a directory name from being extracted (an argument), could be repeated many times
g	Specifies a "graph-file" (an argument) — a list of included and excluded filenames/directory names
f	Identifies the backup device to be used instead of the default */dev/rmt/0m* (an argument)
v	Verbose — otherwise **frecover** works silently
h	Prevents a recursive extraction of selected directories
X	Recovers files relative to the current directories; normally files are recovered to their absolute path name

Note: There are additional options that make **frecover** more powerful and flexible.

The **frecover** command can be used from the command line, but the large number of options and arguments makes such an approach very difficult in practice. It is more convenient to use a homemade script that includes the **frecover** command. Here is an example; requested recover data are passed as arguments, and logging is provided out of the script.

$ cat /usr/local/frecover/bin/frecover_data

```
#!/ usr/bin/ksh
# This is the script frecover_data
# Purpose: to support frecover in background with logging
GRF=$1       # Graph file (what to recover);
MTD=$2       # Tape drive (where to recover from);
REF=$3       # Referent directory to recover data;
SFX=$4       # Type of recovery;
# frecover options:
# r - recover into original locations
# x - extract (recover) data specified by "-g"
# X - recover data relative to the current directory
# o - recover (overwrite) data irrespectively to the age
# v - verbose mode
# g - data to be recovered specified in the graph file $GRF
# f - specifies the tape drive $MTD
cd $REF
echo "`date`: frecover started..."
if [ "$SFX" = "FULL" ]; then
/etc/frecover -rov -f $MTD
else
/etc/frecover -xovX -g $GRF -f $MTD
fi
echo "`date`: frecover completed."
#
echo "`date`: tape rewinding started..."
/usr/bin/mt -t $MTD rewind
echo "`date`: tape rewinding completed."
```

12.5.3 Restoring Multiple Filesystems Archived on a Single Tape

In the case of multiple filesystems archived on a single tape, each filesystem can be restored separately by using the previously described **restore** command. Before the start of a filesystem's restoration, the tape itself must be positioned at the beginning of the corresponding filesystem's archive. This requires iterative use of the **mt** command, followed by the **restore** command, with an appropriate selection of the "rewind" and "no rewind" device files. A system administrator wrote the following README file, and it describes the restore procedure on a Solaris 2.x system for filesystems archived by the script "*backup_system*" discussed earlier (see examples for **backup** and **dump**). Solaris 2.x supports the **ufsrestore** command, which is equivalent to the ***restore*** command on other UNIX platforms. This means that the procedure presented here could be implemented on any other UNIX platform by simply replacing the **ufsrestore** with the **restore** command.

Let us see the README file:

$ cat /etc/RESTORE_SYSTEM.README

```
#
# *********************************************************************
# To restore a filesystem from a backup tape with multiple
#   filesystem's archives
# (the tape was backed-up by the script "backup_system")
# *********************************************************************
# A regular (not-Berkeley style) tape device /dev/rmt/0 is assumed
# Each individual filesystem was backed-up by the command:
#   ufsdump 0ubf 96 /dev/rmt/0n /dev/rdsk/cXtXdXsX
#
```

```
# Rewind the tape:
#   mt -f /dev/rmt/0 rewind
#
# The first filesystem on the tape is the root filesystem
# For interactive restoring type:
#   ufsrestore ibf 96 /dev/rmt/0n
# Then use the appropriate restore commands.
# Since the "quit" ufsrestore sub-command is issued, the tape is
# placed on the start of the next archived filesystem, because
# the not-Berkeley style "norewind" device /dev/rmt/0n was used.
# If the "rewind" device was used:
#   ufsrestore ibf 96 /dev/rmt/0
# the tape would automatically rewind to the begginning of the tape.
#
# To skip a filesystem on the tape, type:
#   mt -f /dev/rmt/0n fsf 1
# (you must be sure about previous tape position)
#
# To stay on the same filesystem, use the "norewind" device
# and after the "quit" ufsrestore sub-command, type:
#   mt -f /dev/rmt/0n bsf 2
#
# To reach the k-th filesystem on the tape, type:
#   mt -f /dev/rmt/0 rewind
#   mt -f /dev/rmt/0n fsf {k-1}
#
# To return (skip back) "k" filesystems on the tape, type:
#   mt -f /dev/rmt/0n bsf {k+1}
#
# For an interactive restore type:
#   ufsrestore ibf 96 /dev/rmt/0n
# then use an appropriate ufsrestore sub-commands.
#
# WARNING:  If the "rewind" device file is used, the tape will
# always rewind when the operation is completed, nevertheless
# what kind of the operation was requested; for instance,
# the command: "mt -f /dev/rmt/0 fsf 3" is senseless
#
```

12.6 Tape Control

Assuming the use of the regular (not-Berkeley style) "no rewind" device file, proper forward and backward moving of a tape still seems a little confusing. To understand this better, we should also recall that there are two types of ***mt device files***: Berkeley and regular (non-Berkeley, also known as AT&T style), and they behave differently. This means that the same set of tape-related commands would handle a tape differently depending on the type of the tape device file selected. The trailing letter "b" in the device filename identifies Berkeley-style devices, so it is very easy to distinguish between the two types of tape devices.

The system works in the following way (assuming non-Berkeley style devices):

- At the end of a recording on a tape (performed by **dump**, **tar**, or other) an EOF pointer is automatically appended after the backup record.
- Any movement of the tape is referenced by those EOF pointers.

- A tape always stops at the first block that follows a designated EOF pointer (a tape forwards just after the closest EOF pointer), whatever the direction of the previous tape movement was.
- The **mt** command, which is used to move a tape, refers to a number of EOF pointers, determined by its **count** option, to be skipped in any direction (every EOF pointer on the way is counted).

That is why the command:

mt -f /dev/rmt/0n bsf 1

does not change a tape's position.

The graphical presentation in Figure 12.1 should contribute to a better understanding of this issue.

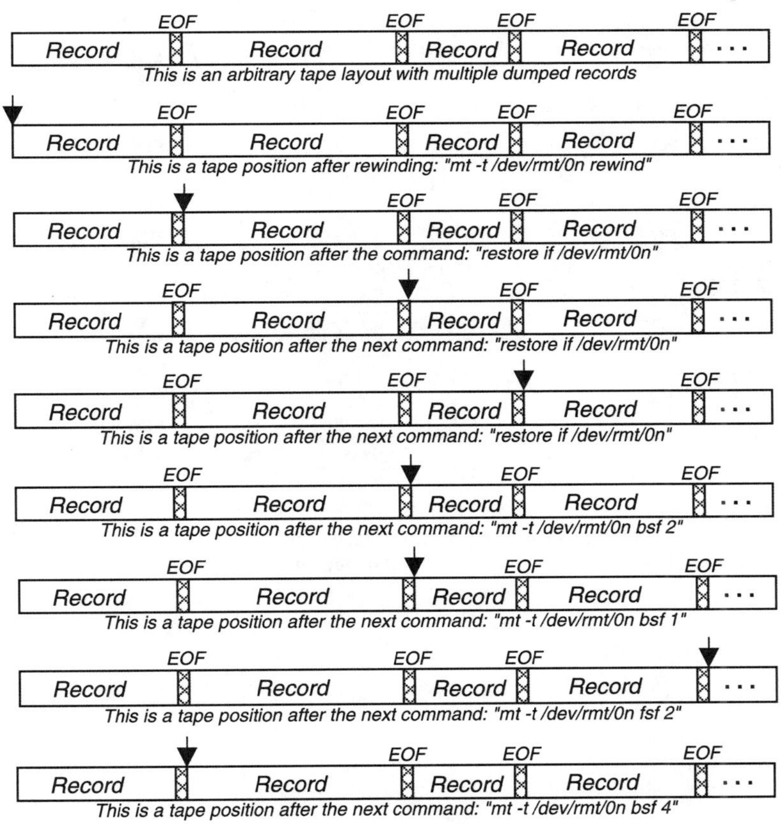

***Note:* The "no rewind" regular device file /dev/rmt/0n was used.**
On some UNIX platforms the command: "mt -f /dev/rmt/0n ..." could be used.

FIGURE 12.1
Tape control — regular (AT&T-style) tape device.

The Berkeley-style tape devices behave differently in that during tape movement, the tape remains in its actual position without forwarding to the closest EOF pointer. This small difference requires modified control of the tape during the restore procedure. This is presented in Figure 12.2.

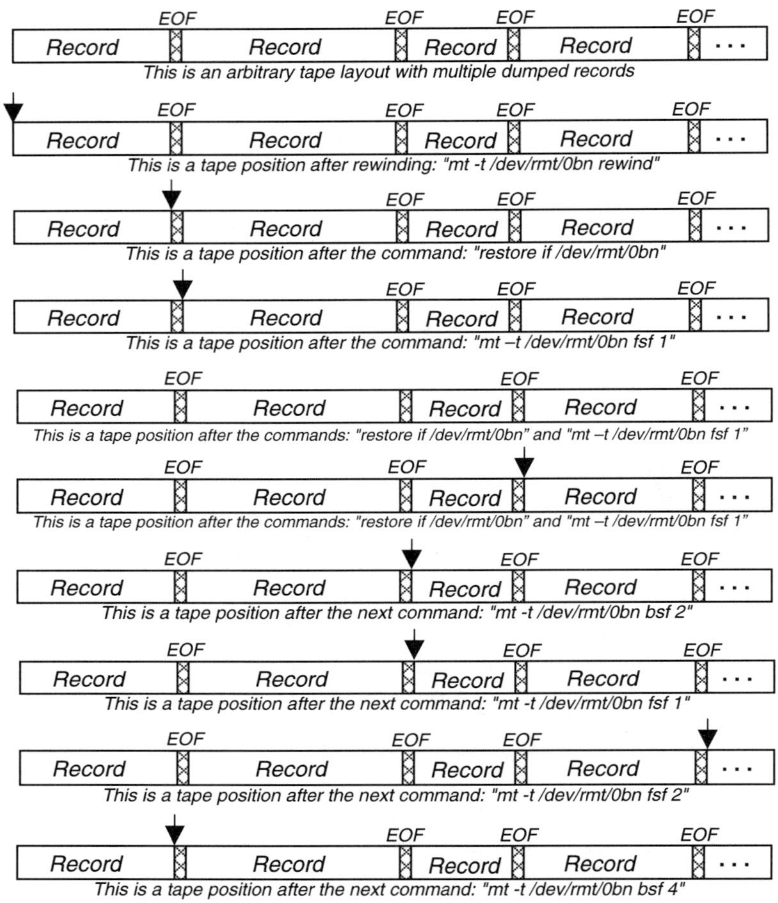

Note: The "no rewind" regular device file /dev/rmt/0bn was used.
On some UNIX platforms the command: "mt -f /dev/rmt/0bn ..." could be used.

FIGURE 12.2
Tape control — Berkeley-style tape device.

13

Time-Related UNIX Facilities

13.1 Network Time Distribution

UNIX supports the distribution of an accurate time throughout the network. This means that each host in the overall network is synchronized to a selected timeserver, or servers, which transmit a reference clock time to the time client hosts. A reference clock will generally (though not always) be a radio time code receiver that is synchronized to a source of standard time such as NIST in the U.S., or NRC in Canada. The time distribution is based on the network time protocol (NTP), currently version 4 which is fully compliant with version 3 standard, defined by Request for Comments RFC 1305, and compatible with previous versions 2 and 1, defined by RFC 1119 and RFC 1059. The computation done in the protocol is fully provided in fixed-point arithmetic, and together with the clock adjustment code, brings a high precision that maintains accuracy comparable with even the most precise external time sources.

13.1.1 The NTP Daemon

A special NTP daemon, named ***xntpd,*** is responsible for maintaining a UNIX system's time-of-day; it is also known as the *time server.* The time server provides the time service, or acts as a time client. We will use the term *the **xntpd** daemon* (or *the NTP daemon*), just to avoid any possible confusion. The ***xntpd*** daemon works in compliance with Internet standard time servers; it follows the distributed reference time. The ***xntpd*** daemon exits (collapses) if the difference in the system time and the reference time is more than 1000 sec; otherwise, it slowly brings the system time in line with the distributed reference time.

The NTP daemon reads its configuration file */etc/ntp.conf* (or */etc/inet/ntp.conf,* as on Solaris 2.x) at the startup time, and learns its duties. If any configuration change has been made, the daemon must be restarted. The daemon can be configured to act strictly as a time client by specifying appropriate configuration entries, which means it will only synchronize its own system's time, or it will act as a potential time server. The term *potential* is used to emphasize the fact that even when the local ***xntpd*** daemon is willing and ready to transfer the reference time over the network, the NTP daemons running on other hosts decide if they will use the offered service. This concept will be clearer once we explain basic configuration entries.

The ***xntpd*** daemon is not mandatory on every system. It is easy to determine if it is running on your system by executing the command (as in this example, from HP-UX 10.20):

```
$ ps -ef | grep ntp | grep -v grep
root   1284   1   0   Feb 25 ?   5:27   /usr/sbin/xntpd
```

Or, on Solaris 2.x:

```
$ ps -ef | grep ntp | grep -v grep
root   956   1   0   Mar 08 ?   0:03   /usr/lib/inet/xntpd
```

The NTP daemon is started only if the configuration file is set appropriately. Here is the partial **rc** startup sequence on Solaris 2.6 from the */etc/init.d/xntpd* rc script:

```
'start')
  # Only start if there is a config file
  if [ -r /etc/inet/ntp.conf ] ; then
    ARGS='cat /etc/inet/ntp.conf | /usr/bin/nawk '.....''
        . . . . .
        . . . . .
    If [ ! -z "$ARGS" ]
    then
        # wait until date is close before starting xntpd
        (/usr/sbin/ntpdate $ARGS ; sleep 2 ; /usr/lib/inet/xntpd)&
    else
        /usr/lib/inet/xntpd
    fi
  fi
  ;;
```

This sequence is a part of the case statement. The way the ***xntpd*** daemon is started depends on the existence and contents of the configuration file. The start script lives in the */etc/rc2.d* directory:

```
$ ls -l /etc/rc2.d | grep xntpd
203745   -rwxr--r--   4   root   sys   1266   Jul 16 1997   S74xntpd
```

It is also the hard link to the **rc** script in the */etc/init.d* depot directory:

```
$ ls -l /etc/init.d | grep xntpd
203745   -rwxr--r--   4   root   sys   1266   Jul 16 1997   xntpd
```

13.1.2 The NTP Configuration File

The configuration file determines the behavior of the ***xntpd*** daemon; we will identify it as NTP configuration file. The NTP configuration file should be administered and set correspondingly for each specific site. The existing self-explanatory template file and manual pages should be sufficient for ensuring successful time daemon setting. Four crucial configuration entries are possible to define the basic behavior of the ***xntpd*** daemon:

- ***peer*** The local time daemon operates in "symmetric active" mode. It can be synchronized to the specified remote time daemon (the time daemon on the specified remote host). In addition, the specified remote time daemon can also be synchronized by this local time daemon. Such a configuration can be implemented to prevent various failure scenarios and to provide a choice for a better time source.
- ***server*** The local time daemon operates in "client" mode. It can only be synchronized to the specified remote time daemon. This is a strictly client mode; please note that the corresponding time server is selected by the client configuration. It is assumed that the selected remote time daemon provides the time service.
- ***broadcast*** The local time daemon operates in "broadcast" mode. The local time daemon sends periodic broadcast messages to clients at a specified address, usually a broadcast address on a local network.
- ***fudge*** The support of the reference clock, used to configure reference clocks in special ways.

Configuration entries are explained in more detail within the presented template configuration file (this file is found on HP-UX platform, although NTP is not flavor-colored at all). The example configuration files that follow are also part of the template file.

$ cat /etc/ntp.conf.example

```
# Sample XNTP Configurations File
#
# Use "peer", "server" and "broadcast " statements to specify various time server to be used
# and/or time services to be provided.
#
# Peer: The peer statement specifies that the given host is to be polled in "symmetric active" mode.
#       The syntax is :
#       peer addr [ key # ] [ version # ] [ minpoll interval_in_sec ] [ prefer ]
###       peer 128.116.64.3 key 2001 version 2
#
# Server: The server statement causes polling to be done in client mode rather than symmetric
#       active. It is an alternative to the peer command above. Which you use depends on what
#       you want to achieve. The syntax is:
#       server addr [ key # ] [ version # ] [ minpoll interval_in_sec ] [ prefer ]
###       server 128.8.10.1   key 2000 minpoll 6   prefer
#
# Broadcast: The broadcast statement tells it to start broadcasting time
#       out one of its interfaces. Syntax is:
#       broadcast addr [ key # ] [ version # ] [ minpoll interval_in_sec ]
###       broadcast 128.100.49.255 # [ key n ] [ version n ]
#
# Fudge: Reference clock support which can be used to configure reference clocks
#       in special ways. The syntax is:
#       fudge 127.127.t.u [ time1 ] [ time2 ] [ stratum # ] [ refid # ] [ flag1 – flag4 ]
###       fudge 127.127.26.1 time1 -0.930        # use one "fudge" line only
###                                              # 127.127.t.u identifies a clock (see Local clock)
#
# broadcastclient: It tells the daemon whether it should attempt to sync to broadcasts or not
#       (default no)
###       broadcastclient yes # or no
#
# broadcastdelay: It configures in a default round-trip delay to use for
#       broadcast time (in seconds). The default is 0.008 second.
###       broadcastdelay 0.008
```

```
#
# Presion: The default is -6. Unless there is a good reason to do so, this
#        value should not be changed from the default value.
###         precision -6
#
# Drift file: Put this in a directory which the daemon can write to. No symbolic links
#        allowed, either.
###         driftfile /etc/ntp.drift
#
# authenticate: It configures us into strict authentication mode (or not). The default is no.
###         authenticate yes # or no.
#
# authdelay: It is the time (in seconds) it takes to do an NTP encryption on this host.
###         AUTHDELAY
#
# trustedkey: The keys defined here are used when authenticate is on. We only trust (and sync to)
#        peers who know and use these keys.
###         trustedkey 1 3 4 8
#
# keys: It specifies the file which holds the authentication keys.
###         keys /etc/ntp.keys
#
# controlkey: It indicates which key is to be used for validating mode 6 write variables commands.
#        If this isn't defined, no mode 6 write variables commands can be done on the xntpd.
###         controlkey 65534
#
# restrict: This option places restrictions on one or more systems. This is implemented as a sorted
#        address-and-mask list, with each entry including a set of flags which define what a host
#        matching the entry *can't* do. The syntax is :
#           restrict address [ mask numeric mask ] [ flag ]
#           The flags are:
#           ignore - ignore all traffic from host
#           noserve - don't give host any time (but let him make queries?)
#           notrust - give the host time, and let it queries, but don't sync to it.
#           noquery - host can have time, but can not make queries
#           nomodify - allow the host to make queries except those which are actually run-time
#                     configuration commands.
#           ntpport - Makes matches for this entry only if the source port is 123.
#
### The matching machines can be servered time, but they will be restricted to make
###       non-modifying queries
###         restrict 129.140.0.0 mask 255.255.0.0 notrust nomodify
#
### Ignore all packets from host 15.1.15.1
###         restrict 15.1.15.1 ignore
#
### Restrict 35.1.1.0 to query only
###         restrict 35.1.1.0 mask 255.255.255.0 noserve nomodify
#
### Take time from the 128.116.64.3, but don't let it query
###         restrict 128.116.64.3 noquery
#
# statdir: Indicates the full path of the directory where statistics files should be created:
###         statsdir /var/tmp/ntp
#
# statistics: Enables writing of statistics records: loopstats/peerstats.
###         statistics loopstats
###         statistics peerstats
#
# filegen: Configures the ways to generate the statistic file set. It provides a mean for handling files
# that are continously growing during the lifetime of a server. The syntax is :
```

```
#       filegen statsname [ file filename ] [ type typename ] [ link/nolink ] [ enable/disable ]
###         filegen loopstats file loopstat type week link
###         filegen peerstats file loopstat type week link
#
# Local clock: Allows the server to synchronize to its own clock.
###         server 127.127.1.1
###         fudge 127.127.1.1 stratum 10 # show poor quality
#
### Reference clocks are specified with an "invalid" ip address 127.127.t.u
### -"t" is an integer denoting the clock type
### -"u" indicates the type-specific unit number
### Spectracom Netclock/2 clocks : synchronize to netclock/2 which receives WWVB.
### server 127.127.3.x        # PSTI 1010/1020 WWV Clock
### server 127.127.4.1        # Spectracom Netclock/2 WWVB or GPS receiver /dev/wwvb1
### server 127.127.5.x        # Kinimetric Truetime 468-DC GOES receiver
### server 127.127.9.x        # MX4200 GPS receiver
### server 127.127.10.x       # Austron 2201A GPS Timing Receiver
### server 127.127.11.x       # Kinemetrics Truetime OM-DC OMEGA Receiver
### server 127.127.12.x       # KSI/Odetecs TPRO-S IRIG-B / TPRO-SAT GPS
### server 127.127.13.x       # Leitch: CSD 5300 Master Clock System Driver
### server 127/127.15.x       # TrueTime GPS/TM-TMD
### server 127.127.16.x       # Bancomm GPS/IRIG Ticktock
### server 127.127.17.x       # Datum Programmable Time System
### server 127.127.18.x       # NIST Modem Time Service
### server 127.127.23.x       # PTB Modem Time Service
### server 127.127.24.x       # USNO Modem Time Service
### server 127.127.26.1       # HP GPS receiver /dev/hpgps1
#
#
# Example configurations ==========================================
#
# NTP configuration file (ntp.conf)
# baldwin.udel.edu (128.4.1.24)
#
# This illustrates the use of an external clock with the local clock
# driver, as well as a multicast server. The prefer keyword on the
# local clock driver declares an external clock and that the time of
# this server should not be wiggled by an NTP peer, unless the
# external clock comes unstuck. Note the use of the multicast group
# ID assigned to NTP, 224.0.1.1, which identifies this as a multicast
# server rather than a broadcast one. The other NTP peers are known
# stratum-1 chimes intended as backup should the external clock croak.
#
### peer 127.127.1.0 prefer                # KSI/Odetics TPRO IRIG interface
### fudge 127.127.1.0 stratum 0 refid GPS
### broadcast 224.0.1.1 key 6 ttl 127
### peer 128.4.1.1                         # rackety.udel.edu (Sun4c/40 IPC)
### peer 128.4.1.4                         # barnstable.udel.edu (Sun4c/65 SS1 +)
### peer 128.4.1.2                         # mizbeaver.udel.edu (Bancomm bc700LAN)
### peer 128.4.1.20                        # pogo.udel.edu (Sun4c/65 SS1 +)
#
# Miscellaneous stuff
### enable auth monitor                    # enable the good stuff
### driftfile /etc/ntp.drift               # path for drift file
### statsdir /baldwin/ntpstats/            # directory for statistics files
### filegen peerstats file peerstats type day enable
### filegen loopstats file loopstats type day enable
### filegen clockstats file clockstats type day enable
#
# Authentication stuff
### keys /usr/local/bin/ntp.keys           # path for keys file
```

```
### trustedkey 3 4 5 6 14 15           # define trusted keys
### requestkey 15                      # key (7) for accessing server variables
### controlkey 15                      # key (6) for accessing server variables
### authdelay 0.000163                 # authentication delay (SPARC4c/40 IPC MD5)
#
# ==================================================================
#
# NTP configuration file (ntp.conf)
# bearegard.udel.edu (128.4.1.23)
#
### server pogo.udel.edu               # stratum 1 nearby
### server 127.127.18.1
### fudge 127.127.18.1 time1 .0035
### phone atdt913034944774 atdt913034944785 atdt913034944774
### phone atdt913034944812 atdt913034948497 atdt913034948022
#
# Miscellaneous stuff
### enable auth monitor                # enable the good stuff
### driftfile /etc/ntp.drift           # path for drift file
# statsdir /beauregard/ntpstats/       # directory for statistics files
### filegen peerstats file peerstats type day enable
### filegen loopstats file loopstats type day enable
### filegen clockstats file clockstats type day enable
#
# Authentication stuff
### keys /usr/local/etc/ntp.keys       # path for keys file
### trustedkey 3 4 5 6 14 15           # define trusted keys
### requestkey 15                      # key (7) for accessing server variables
### controlkey 15                      # key (6) for accessing server variables
### authdelay 0.000163                 # authentication delay (SPARC4c/40 IPC MD5)
#
# ==================================================================
#
#   More examples of NTP configuration files follow.
#        . . . . .
#        . . . . .
#
```

There is no need for additional comments after such an elaborate template file. However, let us see a few NTP client examples:

```
$ cat /etc/ntp.conf          (HP-UX)
## Configured using SAM by root on Thu Nov 20 15:02:29 1998
# Sample XNTP Configurations File
#
server ntphost.scps.nyu.edu version 3 prefer
####################################
```

```
$ cat /etc/inet/ntp.conf          (Solaris)
### The ntp.conf file ###
#
server tick.usno.navy.mil prefer
server tock.usno.navy.mil
#
enable auth monitor
driftfile/var/ntp/ntp.drift
statsdir/var/ntp/ntpstats/
filegen peerstats file peerstats type day enable
```

```
filegen loopstats file loopstats type day enable
filegen clockstats file clockstats type day enable
```

$ cat /etc/inet/ntp.conf (Solaris)

```
# @(#)ntp.client   1.2   99/11/09 SMI
#
# /etc/inet/ntp.client
# An example file that could be copied over to /etc/inet/ntp.conf; it
# provides a configuration for a client host that passively waits for a server to
# provide NTP packets on the ntp multicast net. A broadcast/multicast client
# can automatically discover remote servers, compute one-day delay correction
# factors and configure itself. No need for specific configuration data.
multicastclient 224.0.1.1
########################################
```

$ cat /etc/ntp.conf (Linux)

```
# @(#)ntp.client   1.2   99/11/09 SMI
#
# /etc/inet/ntp.client
# An example file that could be copied over to /etc/inet/ntp.conf; it
# provides a configuration for a client host that passively waits for a server
# to provide NTP packets on the ntp multicast net.
# multicastclient 224.0.1.1
#
# This is a ntp client configuration
# Listed ntp servers are stratum2 and located in NY
# They are open for public access
server sundial.columbia.edu prefer
server ntp1.magenet.com prefer
server ntp0.cornell.edu

# This file saves a drift calculation (it takes almost a day),
# so it makes a start of xntpd daemon faster driftfile
/var/ntp/ntp.drift
```

13.2 Periodic Program Execution

In UNIX the need for periodic program execution is a real demand. Primarily, it is a good idea to try to automate many administrative tasks, enabling their automatic periodic executions. A typical example is an unattended backup, which usually occurs at night, outside of normal business hours. Automation offers many advantages over performing the same tasks manually from the command line, such as:

- ***Greater reliability*** — Tasks are performed the same way every time. Correct and complete performance is guaranteed by the fact that the very same program has already been run a number of times without any problems.
- ***Guaranteed regularity*** — Tasks can be performed according to whatever schedule seems appropriate and need not depend on anyone's availability presence.
- ***Enhanced system efficiency*** — Time-consuming or resource-intensive tasks can be performed during off-hours.

In UNIX, automation is accomplished via ***shell scripts*** and by the ***cron*** daemon.

13.2.1 The UNIX *cron* Daemon

Periodic program execution is provided by the UNIX **cron** facility, serviced by the ***cron*** daemon (also known as the ***clock*** daemon). The **cron** daemon actually handles all jobs scheduled for time-specific, periodic executions. Periodic program executions are specified by *crontab entries,* which are stored in the system's *cron schedule files*. Programs scheduled to be executed at a specific time, or simply at any convenient time, are identified by the spooled jobs in the *cron spooling* directory. The **cron** daemon checks for time-scheduled jobs and acts accordingly.

A typical **rc** sequence to start the **cron** daemon during the system startup is:

```
#
# Checking for already running cron daemon
pid= `/usr/bin/ps -e | /usr/bin/grep cron | /usr/bin/sed -e 's/^ *//' -e 's/ .*/ /'`
case $1 in
'start')
   if [ "${pid}" = "" ]
   then
      /usr/bin/rm -f /etc/cron.d/FIFO
      if [ -x /usr/sbin/cron ]
      then
         /usr/sbin/cron
      fi
   fi
   ;;
#
# and so on ...
```

If the **cron** daemon is not already running, it will be started by a preventive housekeeping facility. The only condition is that the corresponding executable program */usr/sbin/cron* exists, which it always does.

The **cron** daemon must be configured; appropriate configuration is actually required only for jobs scheduled for periodic execution. For jobs scheduled for a single execution, there is no need for any administration; they should simply be submitted into corresponding queues for execution.

On a typical BSD platform there is a single **cron** configuration file named */usr/lib/crontab* (or sometimes, */usr/lib/crontab.local*). This is an ASCII file and may be modified by any text editor; however, superuser privileges are required. The system administrator must perform, *cron scheduling*. After modification the **cron** daemon must be reinvoked (recycled by the signal *HUP*) to activate newly created entries. It is much easier, and recommended, that you use the existing **crontab** command, which is designed for this purpose (this command will be described later).

On System V platforms (but also on SunOS), any user may add her own entries to the *cron schedule*. The entries known as *crontab entries* are stored in separate files for each of the users, in the directory */usr/spool/cron/crontabs* (or */var/spool/cron/crontabs*); users' *crontab files* are named by the user login names (including *roots*).

For example, on SunOS 4.3.1:

```
$ ls -C /var/spool/cron/crontabs
baldwin   levi   pam   root
```

On Solaris 2.6:

$ ls -C /usr/spool/cron/crontabs
espinosa informix lp oracle root sybase

On HP-UX 10.20:

$ ls -C /usr/spool/cron/crontabs
informix opgarpac root rscala

These examples show how easy it is to recognize users' personal *crontab* files.

On System V, the configuration variable ***CRONLOG*** should be set to "YES" in the */etc/default/cron* file to keep a *log* of the cron activity. From the SVR4 release on, the common location for the log file is */usr/sbin/cron.d/log* (in the past it was the file */usr/lib/cron/log*). Logging is automatic in BSD, and there is no ***CRONLOG*** variable.

A frequent way to use the ***cron*** facility for regular administrative tasks is through a series of scripts designed to run periodically: every night, once a week, or/and once a month. For example, one scenario for daily, weekly, and monthly scripts could be:

- *Daily*:
  - Remove junk files, more than three days old, from the */tmp* directory
  - Run accounting summary commands (if accounting is enabled on the system)
  - Run ***calendar***
  - Rotate log files cycled daily
  - Take a snapshot of the system with the **df** and **ps** commands
  - Perform a daily security monitoring
- *Weekly*:
  - Remove old junk files
  - Rotate log files cycled weekly
  - Rebuild the manual page database
  - Run **fsck -n** to list any disk problems
- *Monthly*:
  - List files not accessed that month
  - Produce monthly accounting reports (if accounting is enabled on the system)
  - Rotate log files cycled monthly

Additional site-dependent activities may be taken into consideration on any particular system.

The ***cron*** facility can also be used for periodic time-limited tasks. Once the desired period expires, the *crontabs entry* can be disabled or removed; the **cron** daemon must be reconfigured for a new job schedule. Unfortunately, this must be done manually, because *crontabs* entries are inclusive (multiple specified conditions work like an ***OR*** function, not an ***AND*** function).

The use of the ***cron*** facility can be restricted on a per-user basis. Two administrative files in the directory */usr/lib/cron* (on some platforms, such as Solaris 2.x, the directory is */etc/cron.d*) named *cron.allow* and *cron.deny* are available to explicitly define users who can or cannot schedule *cron-jobs*. These files function in the same way as other time-related jobs, and a detailed description can be found in the following text.

13.2.2 The *crontab* Files

A *crontab file* (the global *crontab file* on BSD, or a user's *crontab file* on System V and SunOS) contains *crontab entries*, which direct the **cron** daemon to run commands at specified intervals. Each one-line entry has the following format:

mins hrs day-of-month month weekday username cmd (BSD)
mins hrs day-of-month month weekday cmd (System V)

No spaces are allowed in the fields, except in the last ***cmd*** field. The first five fields specify the point in time when the **cron** daemon should invoke the command specified in the ***cmd*** field.

Field	Meaning	Range
mins	The minutes after the hour	0–59
hrs	The hours of the day	0–23 (0 = midnight)
day-of-month	The day within a month	1–31
month	The month of the year	1–12
weekday	The day of the week	1–7 (1 = Monday) BSD 0–6 (0 = Sunday) System V

Note: An entry in any of the fields could be a single number, a pair of numbers separated by a dash (indicating a range), a comma-separated list of numbers and ranges, or a wildcard (an asterisk).

The ***cmd*** field can be a UNIX command or a group of commands, properly separated with a semicolon, a script, or any executable program. The entire entry could be arbitrarily long, but it must be a single physical line in the file.

For example, the *crontabs entry*:

30 11 31 12 * /etc/wall%Happy New Year!%Let's make next year great!

runs the wall command at 11:30 a.m. on December 31, sending the following text to all users:

Happy New Year!
Let's make next year great!

If the command contains a percent sign (%), **cron** will use any text following this sign as standard input for ***cmd***; additional percent signs can be used to subdivide this text into lines.

Other examples:

0,15,30,45 * * * * (echo -n ''; date; echo "") >/dev/console

displays the date on the console terminal every 15 minutes (commands are grouped between parentheses in order to redirect their output as a group).

0 0 * * * find / -name "*.bak" -type f -atime + 7 -exec rm {} \;

runs the **find** command every day at midnight to remove all .bak files not accessed in the last seven days.

```
0 2 * * * /bin/sh /usr/adm/ckpwd 2>&1 | mail root
```

runs the shell script **ckpwd** every day at 2:00 a.m. and redirects standard output and standard error to mail it to the root (the shell is specified explicitly as Bourne shell).

Below is a real superuser's *crontab file* (please note the plural form of the directory name "*crontabs*" where the file lives):

```
$ cat /usr/spool/cron/crontabs/root
15   3 * * * find / -name .nfs\* -mtime+7 -exec rm -f {} \; -o -fstype nfs -prune
 5   4 * * 6 /usr/lib/newsyslog >/dev/null 2>&1
15   4 * * * find /var/preserve/ -mtime+7 -a -exec rm -f {} \;
```

The following is specified by those *crontab entries*:

- Every day at 3:15 a.m., run the **find** command to remove all *.nfs* files not modified in the last seven days, but skip the *nfs filesystem.*
- Every Sunday at 4:50 a.m., run the ***/usr/lib/newsyslog*** script (to update and store system messages for this week) with disabled standard output and error.
- Every day at 4:15 a.m., run the **find** command to remove all files not modified in the last seven days starting from the directory */var/preserve/.*

The *crontab* file could be quite complex. Here is one example (it is well-commented, so there is no need for additional explanations):

```
$ cat /usr/spool/cron/crontabs/root
# $Revision: 1.26 $
#
# The root crontab can be used to perform accounting data collection and and clean up.
# Format of lines:  #min   hour   day mo   month   daywk   cmd
#
# Remove old trash
0 5 * * * find / -local -type f '(' -name core -o -name dead.letter ')' -atime+7 -mtime+7 -exec rm -f '{}' ';'
# Remove old sendmail mail files
2 5 * * * find /usr/spool/mqueue -local -type f -mtime + 30 -exec rm -f '{}' ';'
# Remove old rwhod files
2 5 * * * find /usr/spool/rwho -local -type f -mtime + 7 -exec rm -f '{}' ';'
# Remove old vi/ex 'preserved' files
3 5 * * * find /usr/preserve -local -type f -atime + 30 -mtime + 30 -exec rm -f '{}' ';'
# Rotate the logs
1 1 * * 0 umask 033;cd /usr/lib/cron;if test -s log && test "`wc -c log`" -ge 10240; then mv -f log OLDlog;
                              touch log; killall 1 cron; fi
1 1 * * 0 umask 077;cd /usr/adm;if test -s sulog && test "`wc -c sulog`" -ge 10240; then mv -f sulog OLDsulog;
                              touch sulog; fi
1 1 * * 0 umask 033;cd /usr/adm;if test -s SYSLOG && test "`wc -c SYSLOG`" -ge 10240; then mv -f SYSLOG
                              oSYSLOG; touch SYSLOG; killall 1 syslogd; fi
2 1 * * 0 umask 033;cd /etc; if test -s wtmp && test "`wc -c wtmp`" -ge 10240; then mv -f wtmp OLDwtmp;
                              touch wtmp; if test -s xwtmp; then mv -f xwtmp OLDxwtmp; touch xwtmp; fi; fi
12 4 * * * sh /usr/spool/lp/etc/lib/log.rotate
#
# If this machine is running NIS and it's a slave server, the following
```

```
# commands keep the NIS databases up-to-date.
7 9 * * * if /etc/chkconfig yp; then find /usr/etc/yp -type f -name 'xfr.*' -mtime +1 -exec rm -f '{}' ';' ; fi
8 * * * * if test -x /usr/etc/yp/ypxfr_1ph; then /usr/etc/yp/ypxfr_1ph; fi
9 9,15 * * * if test -x /usr/etc/yp/ypxfr_2pd; then /usr/etc/yp/ypxfr_2pd; fi
10 9 * * * if test -x /usr/etc/yp/ypxfr_1pd; then /usr/etc/yp/ypxfr_1pd; fi
#
# If this machine is a NIS master, ypmake will rotate the log file
# and ensure that the databases are pushed out with some regularity.
# It is best to not build and push the databases at the same time the
# commands above on slave servers are pulling the databases.
0,17,30,45 * * * * if /etc/chkconfig ypmaster && /etc/chkconfig yp && test -x /usr/etc/yp/ypmake;
    then /usr/etc/yp/ypmake; fi
#
# dodisk does the disk accounting
0 2 * * 4 if /etc/chkconfig acct; then /usr/lib/acct/dodisk > /usr/adm/acct/nite/disklog; fi
#
# Reorganize file systems
0 3 * * 0 if test -x /usr/etc/fsr; then /usr/etc/fsr; fi
#
# This is for accounting
0 2 * * 4 /usr/lib/acct/dodisk
```

13.2.3 The *crontab* Command

The **crontab** command manages a user's *crontab* file. The command schedules jobs assigned to the individual user, to be executed automatically by ***cron***. There is no need for superuser privileges to manage users' *crontab* files; individual users can manage their own *crontab* files, including ***root***. The command always refers to the *crontab* file owned by the user who invoked its execution.

The format has two basic forms:

1. ***crontab filename*** To create or replace a *crontab* file by copying the specified file or standard input if the filename is omitted. The *crontab* file lives in the directory */usr/spool/cron/crontabs* and has the same name as the effective user name.
2. ***crontab option*** Where the option could be one of these three:
   - **-l** Display (list) the user's *crontab* file.
   - **-e** Edit the user's *crontab* file, or create an empty file if the crontab file does not exist. Once the edit is complete, the file will be copied into the *crontabs* directory as the user's *crontab* file.
   - **-r** Remove the user's *crontab* file from the *crontabs* directory.

The command is extremely useful for activating individual users' *crontab* files without needing to manage the **cron** daemon itself. However, it must be used carefully — the superuser can manage individual users' *crontab* files only by "**su**"-ing into the user's account. Be aware of the common mistake of activating a user's *crontab* entries by executing the **crontab** command as the superuser:

crontab *username*

Instead of activating the user's crontab file, the root crontab file will be overwritten by the user's crontab file (specified by "*username*") and activated; the previous root *crontab* entries will be lost (which can be a serious problem if a backup copy does not exist).

After execution of the command, the system will respond with the following message (or a similar message; this message is from the HP-UX system):

warning: commands will be executed using /usr/bin/sh

This message warns that *crontab* entries, unless they explicitly refer to other shells, should match Bourne shell "***sh***"; otherwise the execution could fail.

For small modifications of the *crontab* files, it is recommended that you use the **crontab -e** command option (as the corresponding user, of course). The command invokes the default editor (usually, the ***vi*** editor), to modify the user's *crontab* file. Once the file is modified and saved and the editor closed, the **cron** daemon will be automatically recycled; there is no need for any additional action.

13.2.4 Linux Approach

Among all UNIX flavors, Linux has improved and developed **cron** facility up the level that surpasses real administrative needs. Linux fully supports **cron** facilities that exist on the System V platform. That means everything we have already said about **cron** configuration, as well as cron-related UNIX commands, is also true of the Linux **cron** facility. However, Linux offers much more.

Linux has introduced the file */etc/crontab* which provides another scheduling table for periodic system tasks; in that way Linux has made **cron** closer to other UNIX configuration topics that do have their configuration files in the */etc* directory. Additionally Linux has even introduced a separate */etc/cron.d* subdirectory for posting of programs for periodic execution; Linux **cron** is searching for programs in this directory.

The implemented syntax for newly introduced scheduled entries corresponds to BSD format. This makes */etc/crontab* work for any user. Remember, the format of an entry in the */etc/crontab* file is:

mins hrs day-of-month month weekday username cmd

Besides the usual cron entries, Linux **cron** also understands entries that define the environment for the execution of the specified cron commands. The predefined environment makes cron entries more versatile, with a possibility of executing cron entries in an environment different from the default one.

And last but not least, Linux has introduced a number of configurable flavor-specific cron-related commands. The behavior of commands relies on their sophisticated configuration files or, in many cases, on hierarchically organized configuration directories (similar to the **rc** directory structure in the case of the system startup/shutdown).

Having all that in mind, Linux has built an extremely powerful and flexible **cron** facility, with the possibility for scheduling periodic tasks in multiple ways. Upon Linux installation, most routine periodic tasks for system maintenance are already scheduled through the */etc/crontab* file and corresponding specific commands. However, it does not demand in any way that an administrator use the */etc/crontab* file for personal needs. For users themselves, a usual System V approach is assumed.

The elaborated Linux **cron** has one disadvantage. The **cron** facility complains about errors by generating an e-mail message to the owner of the cron job. For Linux it could be quite challenging to determine where this error message is coming from. Many configuration options require many checkups, which sometimes makes this task difficult.

For a better understanding of the previous discussion, let us see a few examples.

- First, to list the *crontab* file and the *cron.d* subdirectory:

  $> ls -l /etc | grep cron

```
drwxr-xr-x  2 root   root   1024   Nov 30   17:30   cron.d
-rw-r--r--  1 root   root    385   Jan 16   20:46   crontab
```

- Then to see the contents of the */etc/crontab* file:

  $> cat /etc/crontab

```
SHELL=/bin/bash
PATH=/sbin:/bin:/usr/sbin:/usr/bin
MAILTO=root
HOME=/
# run-parts
01 * * * *  root   run-parts /etc/cron.hourly
02 4 * * *  root   run-parts /etc/cron.daily
22 4 * * 0  root   run-parts /etc/cron.weekly
42 4 1 * *  root   run-parts /etc/cron.monthly
```

The first several entries define the environment for the execution of listed commands. This is Linux specific; other flavors would complain about those lines. The second part consists of "*run-parts entries*," which are also a Linux invention. The format of the entries themselves is known, but the listed command ***run-parts*** is new — this command executes all individual programs that live in the referred subdirectories. In this case:

$> ls -l /etc/cron.*

```
/etc/cron.daily:
total 5
-rwxr-xr-x  1 root  root  276  Aug 4 2000    0anacron
-rwxr-xr-x  1 root  root   51  Aug 15 2000   logrotate
-rwxr-xr-x  1 root  root  402  Aug 23 15:56  makewhatis.cron
-rwxr-xr-x  1 root  root   99  Dec 18 17:15  slocate.cron
-rwxr-xr-x  1 root  root  221  Oct 5 20:41   tmpwatch
/etc/cron.hourly:
total 0
/etc/cron.monthly:
total 1
-rwxr-xr-x  1 root  root  278  Aug 4 2000    0anacron
/etc/cron.weekly:
total 2
-rwxr-xr-x  1 root  root  277  Aug 4 2000    0anacron
-rwxr-xr-x  1 root  root  399  Aug 23 15:56  makewhatis.cron
```

The listed programs will be executed on an hourly, daily, weekly, or monthly basis, depending on the subdirectory where they live. Some programs could be additionally configured through their configuration files, like ***logrotate*** and ***anacron***, which makes the **cron** facility even more powerful, but also more complex. Especially, ***logrotate*** has its own configuration file */etc/logrotate.conf* and additional configuration data in the subdirectory */etc/logrotate.d*, as can be seen from the following:

$> ls -l /etc/logrotate.*

```
-rw-r--r--  1 root  root  542  Aug 15 2000   /etc/logrotate.conf
/etc/logrotate.d:
```

```
total 2
-rw-r--r--  1 root  root  145  Aug 23 23:18   linuxconf
-rw-r--r--  1 root  root  763  Sep 14 18:00   syslog
```

Similarly, the program ***anacron*** has its own configuration table:

$> ls -l /etc/anacron*

```
-rw-r--r--  1 root  root  370 Aug 4 2000  /etc/anacrontab
```

Obviously Linux has gone deeper in this segment than other UNIX flavors. Whether such a sophisticated ***cron*** mechanism is really necessary is another issue. ***Cron*** is a scheduler, and all UNIX flavors support this facility. Linux does it in a more complex way — it is also fair to say, in a more powerful way.

13.3 Programs Scheduled for a Specific Time

As we mentioned earlier, the **cron** daemon also checks for jobs scheduled for execution at a specific time. These jobs are known as ***at-jobs*** — the name fully reflects the nature of the job itself. The ***at*** utility is available to schedule an *at-job* for execution; a new *at-job* can be created using the **at** utility, and submitted into the special queue (also known as the queue ***a***) for execution at the specified time.

At-jobs do not require a great deal of administration. Users can be restricted in the use of the **at** utility, i.e., their ability to schedule an *at-job* can be limited. The */usr/lib/cron/at.allow* and */usr/lib/cron/at.deny* files provide this discretion. Users can be explicitly permitted to use **at** if their names appear in the file */usr/lib/cron/at.allow*; only those users included in the file are allowed to use the utility. If the file does not exist, the file */usr/lib/cron/at.deny* is checked for explicitly denied users. If neither file exists, only a process with superuser privileges is allowed to submit a job. If only the *at.deny* file exists and is empty, global usage is permitted. Both files rely on an entry line with the user name for each of the specified users.

What does it look like on a live system? On Solaris 2.6, for example, it looks like this:

$ ls -l /usr/lib/cron

```
lrwxrwxrwx  1 root  root  16 May 28 1998  /usr/lib/cron -> ../../etc
```

Obviously, the directory */usr/lib/cron* is the link to the directory */etc/cron.d*, so the corresponding **at** allow/deny files can be reached with either path. On this system, only the *at.deny* file exists:

$ ls -l /etc/cron.d | grep "at"

```
-rw-r--r--  1 root  sys  45 May 28 1998  at.deny
```

The file has the following contents:

$ cat /etc/cron.d/at.deny

```
daemon
bin
smtp
nuucp
```

listen
nobody
noaccess

The listed users are denied the ability to use the **at** utility; these are nonindividual users, system entities, that literally cannot submit any *at-job*.

The *at-jobs* are submitted to the ***a*** queue for execution. There are two additional queues reserved for special jobs: the ***b*** queue is reserved for *batch-jobs*, and the ***c*** queue is reserved for *cron-jobs*. New queues can be created, but they must be named by lower-case letters (except the already-taken letters **a**, **b**, and **c**). This can be done by using the **-q** option of the **at** utility.

The queue characteristics are described in the */etc/lib/cron/queuedefs* file (or the */etc/cron.d/queuedefs* file). Each queue is identified by a corresponding entry of the form:

q.[njobj][nicen][nwaitw]

where

q	The name of the queue (terminated by the ".")
njob	The maximum number of jobs that can run simultaneously (terminated by the letter "j")
nice	The nice value to give to all jobs in the queue (terminated by the letter "n")
nwait	The number of seconds to wait before rescheduling a job that was deferred because more than *njob* jobs were already running (terminated by the letter "w")

By default, only the reserved queues ***a*** and ***b*** are described. Here is the *queuedefs* file on Solaris 2.6:

$ cat /etc/cron.d/queuedefs
a.4j1n
b.2j2n90w

Please note that the schedule *batch-jobs* are running with lower priority, the nice value is 2.

13.3.1 The UNIX *at* Utility

The ***at*** utility reads commands from the standard input and groups them together into an *at-job* to be executed at a later, specified time. The format of the **at** utility is:

at *[option] [operand]*
command #1
command #2
. . . . .
[Cntrl-D]

where the main options are:

-c, -k, or -s Specifies the C shell, Korn shell, or Bourne shell to be used to execute an *at-job*.

-f *file*	Specifies the path of the file to be used as the source of the *at-job*, instead of the standard input.
-l	Reports specified *at-jobs*, if any, or all *at-jobs* scheduled for the invoking user.
-m	Sends an e-mail to the invoking user upon the completion of the *at-job*. Standard output and error of the *at-job* are also e-mailed unless they are redirected elsewhere.
-q *queuename*	Specifies the queue to schedule a job for submission. Queues are identified with lowercase letters, but the reserved queues are: ***a*** for *at-jobs*, ***b*** for batch jobs, and ***c*** for *cron-jobs*.
-r *at-job-id*	Removes the *at-jobs* specified by the *at-job-id* operand.
-t *timespec*	Submits a job to be run at the time specified by the *timespec* operand.

The operands are:

at-job-id	Identifies a scheduled *at-job*
timespec	Submit the *at-job* to be run at the date and time specified. All *timespec* operands are concatenated and then interpreted.

The time can be specified as:

hours	One- or two-digit number
hours:minutes	Four-digit number (specified as AM or PM, or default as a 24-hour clock time)
midnight	Indicates the time 12:00 AM (00:00)
noon	Indicates the time 12:00 PM (12:00)
now	Indicates the current day and time, i.e., an immediate run

The date can be specified as:

date	In the form Mar 27, 2001
today	Indicates the current day
tomorrow	Indicates the day following the current day
increment	The optional increment is a number preceded by the + sign and suffixed by one of the following: minutes, hours, days, weeks, month, or years.
not specified	Today is assumed.

A few examples follow:

- To write a sorted contents of the file */home/bjl/Data.raw* into the file */home/bjl/Data.sorted* tomorrow at 10:30 am, and to send an e-mail upon completion:

  $ at -m 2030 tomorrow

  cd /home/bjl

  sort < Data.raw > Data.sorted

  [Ctrl-D]

- An *at-job* can be invoked within the same *at-job* to self-reschedule a job, although a *crontab* entry is more appropriate for such work. This "daily data processing" script named *Data.daily* will run every day:

```
#!/bin/ksh
# This is the script /usr/local/bin/Data.daily.
# It provides a needed daily data processing.
# Once it is started, the script runs every day
#
at now tomorrow < /usr/local/bin/Data.daily
# A sequence of commands for data processing
        .....
        .....
# The end of the script
```

Once the script is invoked, it schedules its immediate execution, as well as execution the next day. The next day it is repeated, and so on...

- The *"Here Document"* is very convenient for scheduling an *at-job* in a **ksh** script:

```
#!/bin/ksh
        .....
        .....
#
# To schedule the at-job for Mar. 29, this year, at 10:00 pm
at 10 pm Mar 29 << !EOF
# The sequence of commands
        .....
        .....
!EOF
# The at-job was scheduled
#
```

13.4 Batch Processing

Batch processing is a special way to run nonurgent but long-lasting and CPU-intensive programs. Such programs can run at off-peak times, when a system is not busy with the execution of other higher priority programs. Off-peak time is usually during the night, when it is not too convenient for users to start their programs. The ***batch*** utility provides a way to execute the programs submitted with a lower priority at any off-peak time, giving the system a chance to balance its CPU loading.

A job scheduled by the **batch** utility is known as a ***batch-job***; it is equivalent to an *at-job* that is submitted into the ***b*** *queue* for an immediate run with lower priority. Therefore, the **at** utility can be also used to schedule a *batch-job*:

$ at -q b -m now

However, it is more convenient to use the given **batch** utility for batch processing, and this is the usual method on the UNIX platform.

From a system standpoint, batch processing is a very useful and economical method of program execution. System administrators should encourage users to utilize it. Even though the **batch** utility is easy to use, users often do not know very much about this possibility. Sometimes they create an additional burden on the CPU at the most critical times, provoking an unnecessary substantial degradation in system performance.

Batch processing can also be an economical way to perform a number of administrative tasks.

13.4.1 The UNIX *batch* Utility

The generic form of the **batch** utility is:

```
$ batch
command #1
command #2
  . . . . .
[Ctrl-D]
```

The **batch** utility reads the standard input until the terminating EOF character [Ctrl-D] from the keyboard. It then submits the entered command sequence into the batch queue for immediate execution with a low priority. The command entered could be any UNIX command, a script, any executable program, or a combination thereof.

The *"Here Document"* is also the most convenient way to implement the **batch** utility in shell script programming, as in the following example:

```
#!/bin/ksh
        . . . . .
#
# To schedule the batch-job
batch << !EOF
# The sequence of commands
        . . . . .
!EOF
# The batch-job was scheduled
#
```

Section II

Network Administration

14

Network Fundamentals

14.1 UNIX and Networking

One of the greatest advantages of the UNIX system is its inherent network-related structure. From its very beginnings, UNIX included a number of network-based characteristics that made it quite different from other existing operating systems. At a time when network technologies were in the very early stages, UNIX already provided certain network services and powerful tools to cope with network issues between remote hosts. From a network standpoint, the concept of UNIX was so well done that it allowed an easy integration of UNIX into network technologies. It is even more appropriate to say that UNIX and networking merged, making UNIX the core operating system in the new emerging network environment. Today, even after so many years of intensive commercial use, UNIX is still far from being considered an obsolete operating system. UNIX was the first commercially successful and available network-oriented OS, and UNIX's use in networked environments was perhaps the biggest factor leading to the end of the supremacy of mainframe computers and gigantic OSs. Despite its advancing age, UNIX is still the leading OS, offering more than any other OS alone, and permanently keeping pace with newcomers.

The primary advantages of UNIX are its openness and flexibility, which make it suitable for almost any kind of upgrade. Most of these upgrades were made in the network arena, which makes sense, given the incredible advances in the field of networking. However, this flexibility and UNIX's ability to integrate so many changes only prove the sound conceptual approach that UNIX designers had while creating UNIX.

Regardless of where the credit should go, UNIX's main contribution to the overall development of computer technologies was, and still is, in networking; it is fair to say that the network-oriented UNIX concept practically enabled the tremendous growth of networking technologies.

Networks have grown so prolifically because they provide an important service: to share information among users. Computers generate and process information that is often useless unless it is shared among a group of people; the network is the vehicle that enables data to be easily shared. Once a computer has been networked, users will likely not want to return to an isolated system. Such a trend does not stop at the local level; forming a local network and cooperating with neighboring computers lead to global, worldwide networking. Today, this **global network** is known under the generic name ***Internet***, which is named after what was once the worlds largest experimental network.

Computer networking has brought new challenges and duties to system administrators. It is not enough to simply maintain the systems; the network requires a great deal of ongoing work. This issue is very important, because it affects not only a single system, but also other systems on the network. A familiarity with basic theoretical issues will make this job easier, and that is the purpose of this chapter and those following.

14.2 Computer Networks

A ***computer network*** is a communication system that connects end computers, usually referred to as ***hosts***. The hosts can range in size from small microcomputers to the largest supercomputers. From a network point of view, a host is any machine participating in network communication, independent of its basic function and configuration (single-user or multi-user, general purpose systems, dedicated servers, terminals, any kind of client, etc.).

14.2.1 Local Area Network (LAN)

A ***Local Area Network* (*LAN*)** is the network that connects hosts that are close together, typically within the same room, on the same floor, in a single building, or in a few neighboring buildings; really, any network in which the computers are no more than a few miles apart. Special modulation techniques can be implemented thanks to the small distances involved, thereby providing extremely high-speed data transmission, i.e., a high network capacity. Consequently, network throughput is also high, making possible large volume data transfer through the network.

Maintaining network traffic within a LAN with an arbitrary number of participating hosts and with a variable **network load** (the actual volume of data to be transmitted within the network) is obviously not a simple task. A number of different techniques have been developed to accomplish this, but only a few of them have led to widespread practical implementation after their experimental phase. Today, two basic types of LANs are in use: ***CSMA/CD*** and ***Token Passing*** networks.

Network configuration also varies independently of network type. Although those two issues are partially related, for the moment we will treat them separately. Two basic network topologies are common: ***bus*** and ***ring*** topologies (see Figure 14.1, a & b).

Bus structured LANs provide access to the common medium of all participating hosts simultaneously — a network configuration where each host can forward data directly to any other host, or rather, where each host can listen to any other host while it transmits data. The physical network configuration can be different: strictly bus-like; radial with a central hub; a tree structured with repeaters, bridges, amplifiers; etc. However, one condition must be fulfilled: direct bidirectional logical connection between any two hosts that share the same LAN must be provided.

Ring structured LANs integrate all participating hosts into a single physical ring in such a way that each host communicates only with two neighboring hosts — it receives data only from the preceding host, and it transmits data only to the succeeding host. To provide data transmission between two nonadjacent hosts, all hosts in between must take part in the transmission; a host in the ring retransmits data designated to the other hosts and keeps its own data. The closer distance among neighboring hosts enables faster data transmission in the ring, making them suitable for many applications. Isolated communication between adjacent hosts makes possible multiple, simultaneous, independent traffic in different parts of the ring, increasing the effective network throughput.

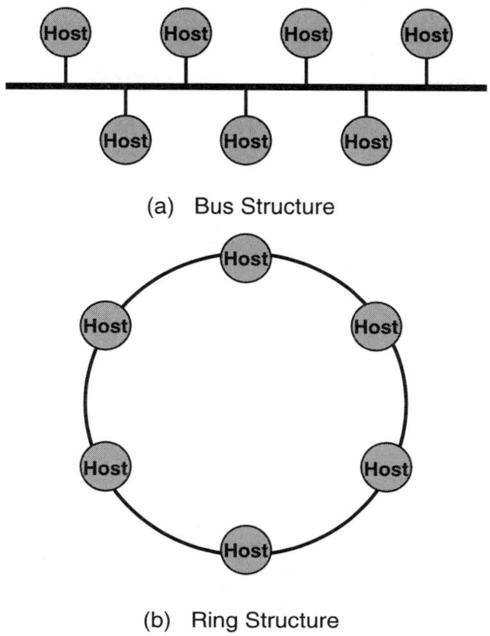

FIGURE 14.1
Bus topologies.

14.2.1.1 CSMA/CD Networks

The name stands for ***Carrier Sense Multiple Access/Collision Detect***, which actually describes the nature of the network itself. All hosts sense a modulated carrier on the network media, which means the network is busy, i.e., some of the hosts are transmitting data. When there is no carrier (the network is idle), a host can transmit its data (if such a need exists at all), making the network busy and preventing other hosts from starting their transmission. However, multiple hosts can access the network and try to start a transmission simultaneously (a host does not know anything about other hosts' needs and intentions), causing collisions on the network and corruption of transmitted data (its own, as well as other hosts' data). Each of the involved hosts recognizes a data collision easily and quickly, and stops the started transmission. Each of those hosts will retry the interrupted data transmission after a random time interval; a random delay should decrease the probability for repeated collisions among the same hosts, and increase the chances for each of them to access the idle network and transmit pending data. Of course, in the meantime, other new hosts can also try to transmit their data and enter to compete for access to the network. After some time, each of them will succeed in its attempt to reach the network, and data will be transmitted. However, this time is **stochastic**, and there is no guarantee for a deterministic response time, although practically it works very well.

CSMA/CD LANs are known as *stochastic*, or random, networks, due to their nature. They are also known as *contention* type networks, because the participating hosts compete to access the network. The best known CSMA/CD LAN, as well as the most popular and most widely used one, is the **Ethernet**; often, the whole suite of CSMA/CD networks is referred as *Ethernet-like* LANs. The basic Ethernet operates at 10 Mbps (million bits per second), so it is sometimes incorrectly identified as 10 Mbit LAN. Its successor, Fast

Ethernet, operates at 100 Mbps. The specified network speed represents the network capacity (the maximum speed at which data can be transmitted), not the effective speed at which real data are transmitted; the effective data transmission speed is always lower because of unavoidable collisions in the network. Network throughput is always lower than network capacity.

On a CSMA/CD LAN, it is typical that an increase in the network load (the total actual demands for data transmission by participating hosts) over some threshold causes a significant decrease in the network throughput. Obviously, collision time increases significantly due to the repeated attempts of multiple hosts to transmit their data. CSMA/CD networks become practically inoperable at a load over 80% of the network capacity; repeated collisions prevent data transmission at all.

CSMA/CD networks are very easy to implement. Traffic control is distributed and the implemented algorithm is very simple: each host arbitrates when a network is available and adopts its transmission to the actual situation. Adding or removing a host to/from the LAN is simple, because there is no need for any specific action. The only requirement for CSMA/CD networks is regarding their topologies; these LANs must be "bus-like" networks, i.e., each host must be able to directly reach another participating host (to listen to all other hosts).

The CSMA/CD technology is dominant today. The drawback of deterministic access to the network can easily be overcome by designing the network correspondingly: the maximum traffic load within a LAN should be kept below the network capacity. There are a number of techniques to accomplish this; primary among them are network bridging and subnetting.

14.2.1.2 Token Passing Networks

A ***Token Passing LAN*** is a local computer network in which a *uniquely defined data pattern*, called a ***token***, travels continuously through the network, passing from one host to another. Only the host that currently possesses the token has "the right" to transmit data (if the need exists at all), and its data transmission is terminated by the token, which passes the "right to talk" to another host. If there is no data to transmit, the host retransmits the token alone, preserving the continuous token circulation in the network. The token size and the time needed for a token transmission are constant; consequently, the network throughput is independent of the network load. The network response time is deterministic; the worst-case scenario determines its guaranteed value.

Control of token passing is more complex. A "logical ring" must be provided to keep up the repeated sequential token passing from one host to another, but keeping the logical ring operable is not an easy task (the token could be lost or doubled, or something else could happen). A special procedure is required to add a host to or to remove a host from the network. This is especially true in the case of the bus network structure. It is much easier to handle networks with ring topology; the token circulation is preserved by the network structure itself.

Depending on the implemented network topologies, *Token Passing* LANs are divided into *Token Bus* and *Token Ring* networks. Token Bus LANs have disappeared from the network arena due to the complexities of their control, but Token Ring LANs are widely used. Physical rings automatically provide the "logical ring" required for token passing; each host in the ring receives data from the preceding host, and transmits data to the succeeding host (each host knows and communicates with two neighboring hosts only, regardless of who they are). Inserting a new host into the ring is not a problem; removing a host means simply bypassing its previous connection. All these characteristics have contributed to the wide implementation of this type of LAN.

14.2.2 Wide Area Network (WAN)

Local area networks have revolutionized data transmission, and a number of new technologies for fast data transmission have been developed and implemented. An enormous quantity of data (unimaginable in the past) has become available through networking, promoting distributed data processing. Processing resources, and power, could be spread over the network and used more efficiently. Therefore, a distributed environment and the long-held dream of "the processors pool" that could handle incoming requests in an optimal way has become a reality.

Despite all of their advantages, LANs can only connect computers that are geographically close. How could two computers on two sides of a city communicate, or two computers in two distant cities, or states, or even continents? LAN technologies are not very useful in these cases, and more traditional and expensive telecommunication techniques must be implemented. If two distant LANs are connected with a fast link, all participating hosts "think" that they share an equivalent fast computer network, regardless of what the actual distance between those hosts is. In this fashion, we now have a ***Wide Area Network (WAN)***, as seen in Figure 14.2. In WANs there is always more traffic between neighboring hosts within the same LAN than among distant ones (because many hosts run strictly local network applications); this means that the inter-LAN link could be even slower than LANs themselves, while WAN throughput remains acceptable.

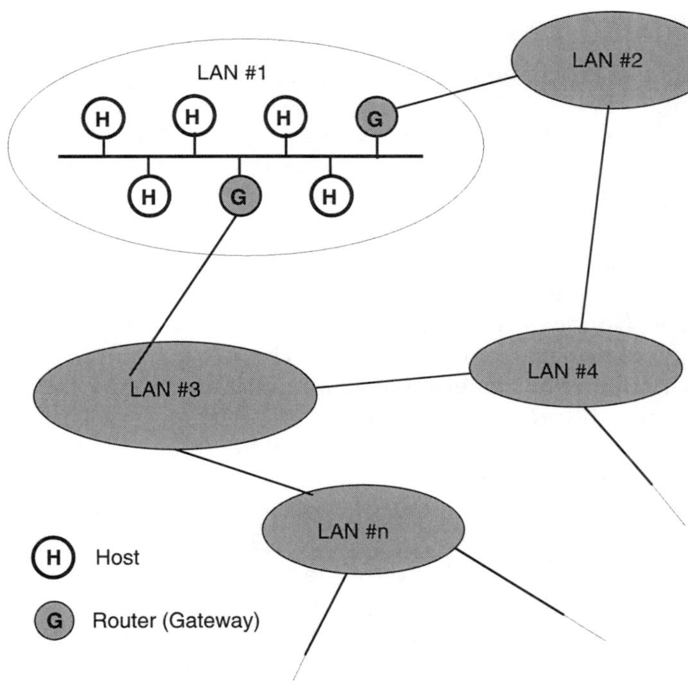

FIGURE 14.2
Wide area network.

WANs are widely used, and they are constantly evolving. Today, numerous WANs are connected into a unique worldwide WAN, a global computer network known as the ***Internet***. Multiplying LANs within WANs had two positive effects: it decreased the costs of the requested links (which became shorter and were shared among more participating LANs) and provided alternative routes to reach any host in the network.

However, the problem of reaching a distant host in a network still had to be solved. Special addressing mechanisms to uniquely identify each host in the WAN were implemented, and appropriate routing algorithms to transmit/retransmit data in the network were developed. Special, dedicated hosts, known as ***routers*** have become a part of each LAN, with their only mission to route data toward distant LANs and hosts.

There are many different LANs currently in use, and they are often mutually incompatible: different media, modulation techniques, protocols, etc. (just compare Ethernet and Token-Ring LANs for a look at the variety possible). However, such different and incompatible LANs often need to be connected together. Therefore, special devices to overcome such incompatibility must be implemented, and in the case of protocol conversion, these devices are known as ***gateways***.

The terms *gateway* and *router* are often used interchangeably, mostly because gateways also provide routing services. However, the two terms are not interchangeable — *routing* and *protocol conversions* are two independent concepts, and they are not necessarily complementary.

14.3 A TCP/IP Overview

The common thread that ties the enormous Internet community together is TCP/IP network software. The name TCP/IP refers to an entire suite of data communication protocols that define how different types of computers talk to each other. The suite gets its name from two of the protocols that belong to it: the ***transmission control protocol*** **(*TCP*)** and the ***Internet protocol*** **(*IP*)**. Although there are a number of other protocols in the suite, TCP and IP are the best known.

In 1969 the *Defense Advanced Research Projects Agency* (*DARPA*) started a research and development project to create an experimental packet switching network. This network was named ***ARPANET,*** and was built to explore techniques for providing robust, reliable, and vendor-independent data communications. The project outputs far surpassed all expectations, and a number of modern data communication techniques were developed, or at least conceptually solved. The experimental *ARPANET* was so successful that many of the organizations attached to it began to use it for their daily needs. In 1975 the *ARPANET* was converted from an experimental network to an operational one, and the responsibility for administering the network was given to the *Defense Communications Agency* (*DCA*), later renamed the *Defense Information System Agency* (*DISA*). However, the development of *ARPANET* did not stop once the network became operational; the basic TCP/IP protocols were developed after *ARPANET* was operational.

In 1983 the TCP/IP protocols were adopted as MIL standards, and all hosts (computers) connected to the network were required to convert to the new protocols. To ease this conversion, DARPA funded an expert team to implement TCP/IP in BSD UNIX, thus beginning the marriage of UNIX and TCP/IP and their triumphant, long-lasting journey. **BBN** (*Bolt, Beraneck and Newman*), was chosen to facilitate the implementation. The company, located in Boston, MA, was well known in the field of acoustics. As it was located close to MIT (the Massachusetts Institute of Technology), it attracted talented MIT graduates and very quickly gained a strong reputation in computer technologies. The project was a real success and was completed extraordinarily well. Today's Internet fully relies on the solutions introduced by BBN.

UNIX itself also contributed to the development of inter-computer communication. Besides the TCP/IP protocols used primarily to communicate throughout the local area network and more widely, UNIX also provides UUCP for communication with remote, isolated computer sites.

14.3.1 TCP/IP and the Internet

In 1983, about the same time TCP/IP was adopted as a standard, the term ***Internet*** came into common usage. *ARPANET* was divided into *MILNET*, the unclassified part of the *DDN* (Defense Data Network), and a new, smaller *ARPANET*. The term *Internet* was used to refer to the entire network. In 1990, *ARPANET* formally passed out of existence, but the Internet continued its growth, and today is greater then ever, encompassing a huge number of networks worldwide. The growth of the Internet has brought many new organizations into the network.

The name *Internet* was originally used only for the network built upon the *Internet Protocol*. Today, *Internet* is used to refer to an entire class of networks, mutually connected by a common TCP/IP protocol, making them a single worldwide logical network. The term ***internet*** (lowercase i) is also often used as a generic name to describe any collection of separate physical networks, interconnected by a common protocol.

Because TCP/IP is required for an internet connection, the large number of diverse organizations on the network became familiar with the TCP/IP suite and developed many new applications based on these protocols. In the UNIX community, the internet protocols are used for any kind of networking, even for local area networking not connected to the larger Internet. The most common (but not the only) way to use TCP/IP for the communication between neighboring sites is over a local Ethernet on the physical layer.

There is one important administrative issue related to TCP/IP. The standardization of TCP/IP resulted in only minor differences among UNIX flavors and versions, so the set of available network-related commands and tools, as well as configuration files, on both basic UNIX platforms — BSD and System V — is basically the same.

14.3.2 ISO OSI Reference Model

Network data communications require that each participant in the communication strictly respect a previously specified set of rules. This is the only way that one computer can understand another. In data communication these sets of rules are called *protocols*. The term *protocol* is not a new linguistic creation specific to data communication; it was borrowed from diplomacy, another field of human activity. Protocols are formal rules of behavior; in international relations, protocols minimize the problems caused by cultural differences when various nations work together. By agreeing to a common set of rules that are widely known and independent of any nation's customs, diplomatic protocols minimize misunderstandings; everyone knows how to act and how to interpret the actions of others. Similarly, when computers communicate, it is necessary to define a set of rules to govern their communications.

An architectural model developed by the *International Standards Organization* (***ISO***) is frequently used to describe the structure and function of data communication protocols. This architectural model, called the *Open System Interconnect (**OSI**) Reference Model*, provides a common reference for discussing communication issues. The terms defined by this model are well understood and widely used in the data communication community, and it is difficult to discuss data communications without using OSI's terminology.

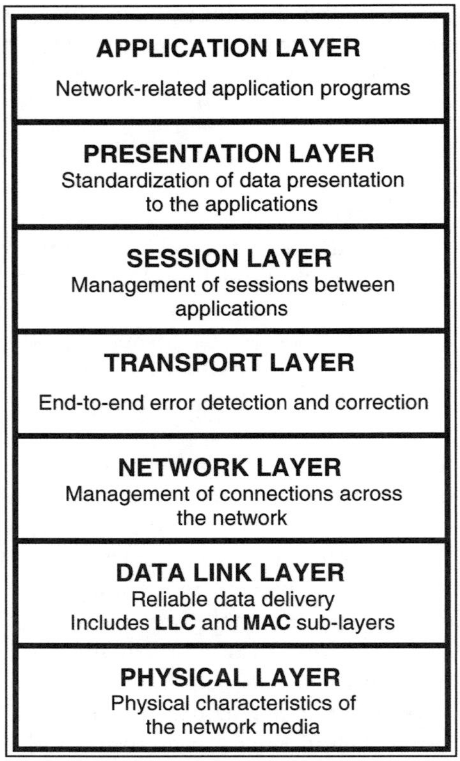

FIGURE 14.3
The ISO OSI reference model.

The ***ISO OSI Reference Model*** contains seven *layers* that define the functions of data communication subsystems. Each *layer* of the *OSI model* represents a set of functions performed when data is transferred between cooperating applications across an intervening network. The *OSI model* is presented in Figure 14.3; each *layer* is identified by its name and a short functional description. In Figure 14.3 we see that the model is like a pile of building blocks stacked one upon another; often this structure is called a *stack* or a *protocol stack*.

A layer does not define a single protocol; it defines data communication functions that may be performed by any number of protocols. Therefore, any layer may contain multiple protocols, each providing a service suitable for the functions of that layer. For example, at the *Application Layer* there are a number of network application protocols (a *file transfer protocol*, an *electronic mail protocol*, a *telnet protocol*, etc.).

Layers communicate among themselves. Every protocol (on any layer) communicates with its *peer*; a *peer* is an implementation of the same protocol in the equivalent layer on a remote system (for example, the file transfer protocol on a remote site is the *peer* of the local file transfer protocol). It is necessary for *peer* layer communications to be standardized for a successful data communication. In the abstract, each protocol is only concerned with communicating with its *peer*; it does not care about the layer above or below it. However, the *peer layers* do not communicate directly; real data flow is different from a logical one. The upper layers rely on the lower layers to transfer the data over the underlying network. Data is passed down the stack from one layer to the next, until it is transmitted over the network by the physical layer protocols (physical layer defines a way, or rather, the ways, in which data are modulated and transmitted over communication media). On the other side, at the remote end, the data is passed up the stack to the peer layer, i.e., receiving application. The individual layers do not need to know how the layers above and below them function; they only need to know how to pass data to them. This is presented in Figure 14.4.

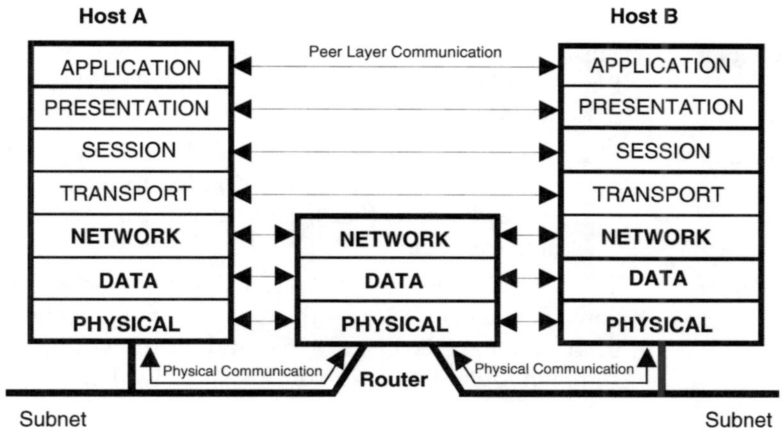

FIGURE 14.4
Data communication between OSI layers.

By splitting the data communication into a number of layers and isolating communication functions in different layers, the impact of technological changes on the entire protocol suite is minimized. It also makes the data communication system open for upgrades and extremely flexible in implementation. There are also some other advantages: it is very easy to replace an entire layer with a new (hopefully better) one without any impact on the other layers. The only disadvantage is the unavoidable overhead in data processing during the journey through the layers, but considering the benefits, this does not present a serious problem.

Figure 14.4 also shows how physical communication between two hosts on different subnets is provided (in this case Host A on one subnet, and Host B on another subnet). As we can see, the reference model for a router contains only three low-level layers; that is what the router cares about to route data in the network. Higher layers are completely ignored. A router does not check transport, session, presentation, or application data at all — they are simply routed unchanged.

A brief description of the ISO OSI model from a network data communication standpoint follows:

Application Layer This layer is the level of the protocol hierarchy where the user-accessed network processes reside. This includes all of the processes that users interact with directly, as well as other processes at this level of which users are not necessarily aware. This is actually the layer that is continuously upgraded; each new network application specifies a new application-specific protocol to be managed by this layer.

Presentation Layer	This layer provides standard data presentation routines. In the exchange of data, the cooperating applications must agree on how data is represented.
Session Layer	This layer manages the sessions (connections) between cooperating applications.
Transport Layer	This layer guarantees that the receiving site gets the data exactly as it was sent, i.e., it ensures the completeness of the data transportation.
Network Layer	This layer manages connections across the network and isolates the upper layer protocols from the details of the underlying network. It handles the addressing and delivery of data.
Data Link Layer	This layer handles a reliable delivery of data across the underling network. The layer is basically divided into two sublayers: *Logical Link Control* (*LLC*), the hardware independent sublayer *Media Access Control* (*MAC*), the hardware dependent sublayer
Physical Layer	This layer defines the characteristics of the network interface hardware needed to carry the data transmission signal. Details such as voltage levels, number and location of interface pins, signal modulation, and so on, are specified here. Ethernet stan dard IEEE 802.3 is an example.

It is not mandatory for each layer to exist in any practical implementation. Unnecessary layers can be skipped, as in the case of the router in Figure 14.4. It has the same effect as when several layers are joined together into one layer.

14.3.3 TCP/IP Protocol Architecture

The ISO OSI Reference Model presents the most common way to describe protocol architecture. The International Standard Organization established the model, and it assists in the implementation of any inter-computer communication technology. In that light, the *OSI model* could be used also to fully describe *TCP/IP protocols*. However, sometimes it is easier and more convenient to use other, simpler protocol models to describe (or rather, to understand) specific protocols; noncrucial layers for specific protocols could be ignored. For example, for an easier understanding of TCP/IP protocols, another architectural model that more closely matches the structure of TCP/IP is more appropriate. This model is known as the *Four Layer TCP/IP Architectural Model* and is presented in Figure 14.5.

The model provides a pictorial representation of the layers in the *TCP/IP protocol hierarchy*. Data is processed in the same way as in the *ISO OSI model*, except that fewer layers take part in its processing. Data is passed down or up the *protocol stack* when it is being sent to or received from a network. The flow of data is represented in Figure 14.6.

Each layer in the stack adds control information to ensure proper delivery. This control information is called a ***header***, because it is placed in front of data to be transmitted. Each layer treats all of the information it receives from the layer above as *data* and places its own *header* in front of that information. The addition of delivery information at every layer is called ***encapsulation***.

When data is received the opposite occurs. Each layer strips off its *header* and checks it before passing the data on to the layer above. Therefore each layer treats the information it receives from the lower layer as both a *header* and *data*.

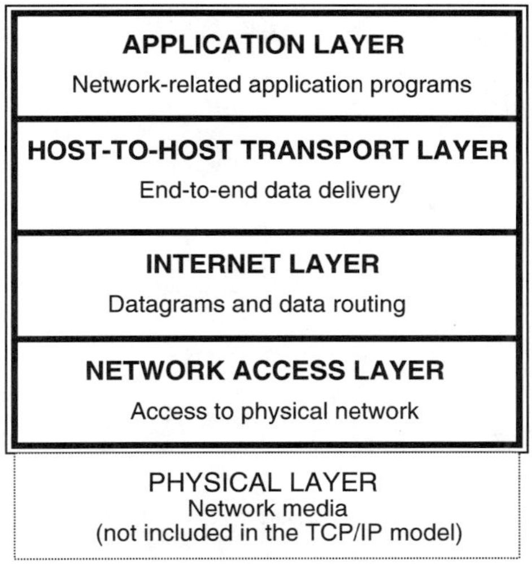

FIGURE 14.5
The four-layer TCP/IP protocol architecture.

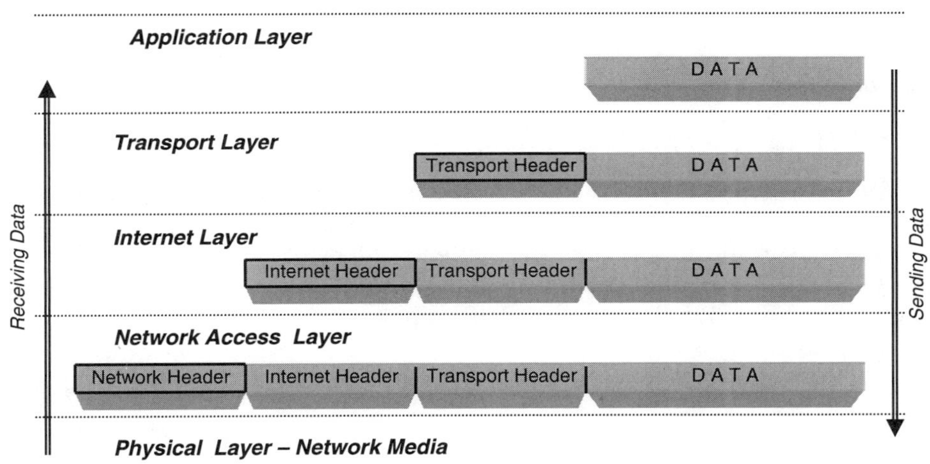

FIGURE 14.6
Data flow through the TCP/IP protocol stack.

The TCP/IP protocol stack does not include the physical layer, i.e., the stack does not treat physical network itself. However, the lowest layer depends on the implemented physical network.

Each layer has its own independent *data structures*, compatible with data structures in the neighboring layers. Conceptually this is not mandatory, but a strictly defined *interface* between layers implies such compatibility; otherwise, it would be more difficult to build the interface. Still, each layer has its own terminology to describe data structures. Figure 14.7 shows the *terms* used by different layers of TCP/IP to refer to the data being transmitted based on the two most common transport layer protocols: *TCP* and *UDP.*

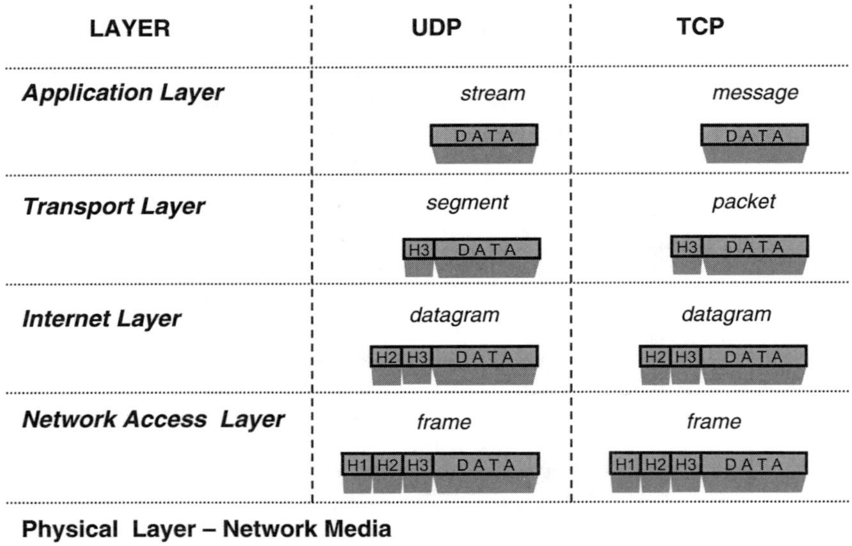

FIGURE 14.7
Data structures in the TCP/IP protocol stack.

14.4 TCP/IP Layers and Protocols

Most of the information about TCP/IP protocols is published in documents known as *Requests for Comments* (***RFC***). *RFCs* contain the latest versions of the specifications of all standard TCP/IP protocols. The style and contents of these documents are much less rigid than most standard documents of this type; *RFCs* contain a wide range of information, and they are not limited to the formal specification of data communication protocols. All *RFCs* are available on the Internet.

In the text that follows, an overview of the function of each TCP/IP layer is presented.

14.4.1 Network Access Layer

The ***network access layer*** is the lowest layer of the TCP/IP protocol hierarchy. The protocols in this layer provide data delivery to the other devices on a directly attached network. This layer defines how to use the network to transmit an ***IP datagram***. It must know the details of the underlying network (addressing scheme, packet structure, etc.) to be able to correctly format the data being sent to the network. If compared to the *ISO OSI model*, this layer encompasses the functions of its three lower layers.

The TCP/IP design hides most of the network access layer's functions from users. As new hardware technologies appear, new network access protocols must be developed so TCP/IP can use the new hardware. Consequently, there are many access protocols — one for each physical network standard.

Functions performed in this layer include *encapsulation* of *IP datagrams* into the *frames* to be transmitted by the network, and *mapping* of IP addresses to the physical addresses used by the network itself. One of TCP/IP's strengths is its addressing scheme, which uniquely identifies every host on the global network. This IP address may be converted (mapped) into whatever address is appropriate for the implemented local area network (LAN) over which the datagram is physically transmitted.

Protocols in this layer often appear as a combination of *device drivers* and related programs. The modules that are identified with network device names usually encapsulate and deliver and receive data to and from the network, while separate programs perform related functions such as address mapping.

14.4.2 Internet Layer and IP Protocol

The ***Internet layer*** is a layer above the network access layer in the protocol hierarchy. The best-known protocols in this layer are: *Internet protocol* (*IP*) and *Internet Control Message Protocol* (*ICMP*).

14.4.2.1 Internet Protocol (IP)

The most important protocol in this layer is the *Internet protocol*, better known as the *IP*. IP is the core of TCP/IP, and it provides the basic packet delivery service on which TCP/IP networks are built. All protocols in the layers above and below the Internet layer are dependent in some way on the IP to deliver data. All incoming and outgoing TCP/IP data flows deal with IP, regardless of their real destinations.

IP functions include:

- Defining the datagram, which is the basic unit of transmission in the TCP/IP network
- Defining the Internet addressing scheme
- Moving data between the layer below, the *network access layer*, and the layer above, the *host-to-host transport layer*
- Routing datagrams to remote hosts
- Performing fragmentation and reassembly of datagrams

IP is a *connectionless protocol*. This means that IP does not exchange control information, known as *handshaking*, to establish an end-to-end connection before transmitting data. Rather, the opposite is true: *connection-oriented protocols* perform handshaking with the remote system to verify that a connection is established before data transmission starts (see more details later about TCP and in Figure 14.11). IP relies on protocols in other layers to establish the connection if they require *connection-oriented* service.

IP is also an *unreliable protocol* because it contains no error detection and recovery code. Of course, this does not mean that reliable data delivery cannot be based on IP, it only means that IP does not check to ensure the data was correctly received at the remote system.

TCP/IP protocols transmit data over the network in *packets*. A *packet* contains a block of data to be transferred, as well as the full information that identifies the destination of a packet itself. Each packet travels over the network independently of any other packet. Long data structures are divided into packets for transfer over the network and reassembled at the receiving end.

The *datagram* is the packet format defined by IP, and it is presented in Figure 14.8. The first five or six 32-bit words (the sixth word is optional) form the *header*. The *header length* is specified in the field *IHL* (*Internet Header Length*). The header contains all the information necessary to identify and deliver the *datagram*. The source and destination addresses are crucial for delivery; they are the IP addresses of the source and destination hosts in the network. Two hosts in the communication mostly do not reside in the same subnet (local area network), so datagrams may travel through many network devices until they reach their destinations.

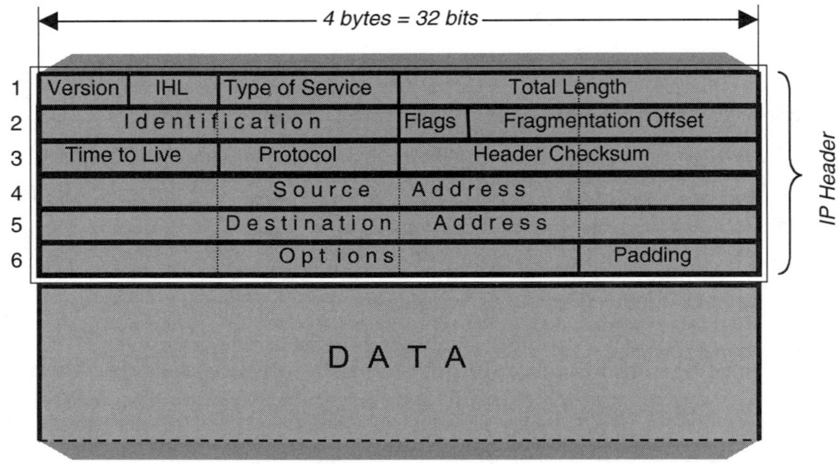

FIGURE 14.8
IP datagram format.

The *Total Length* field determines the length of a *data part* of the datagram (and should be decreased by *IHL*). Sometimes, when traveling through different networks, datagrams must be further divided into smaller packets (because of the network type they are passing through). This procedure is called *fragmentation*, and corresponding identification information is also included in the datagram header.

14.4.2.2 Internet Control Message Protocol (ICMP)

The *Internet Control Message Protocol* (*ICMP*) is an integral part of the Internet layer, and it uses the IP datagram delivery facility to send its messages. ICMP performs the following functions for TCP/IP:

- Flow control
- Detection of unreachable destinations
- Redirection of routes
- Checking of remote hosts (supports the ***ping*** command)

ICMP protocol is widely used to check connectivity with designated remote hosts. Because it resides in the Internet layer, it automatically excludes all higher layers from its communication and points to underlying layers for any possible connectivity problem. The special command ***ping*** is used for this purpose (it completely relies on ICMP) to check if the remote host is "alive," i.e., does the required connection between two hosts exist. Once a "pinging" goes in both directions, we can look for communication problems at higher layers.

14.4.3 Transport Layer and TCP and UDP Protocols

The *host-to-host transport layer* is above the *Internet layer* and is usually shortened to *transport layer.* The two most important protocols in this layer are *transmission control protocol* (*TCP*) and *user datagram protocol* (*UDP*). ***TCP*** provides reliable data delivery service with end-to-end error detection and correction. ***UDP*** provides low-overhead, connectionless datagram delivery service. Both protocols deliver data between the *application layer* and the *Internet layer.* Application programmers can choose whichever service is more appropriate for their specific applications, and both protocols are widely used. Although the whole protocol suite got the name TCP/IP, it does not mean at all that the TCP protocol is more important than the UDP protocol.

14.4.3.1 User Datagram Protocol (UDP)

UDP gives application programs direct access to a datagram delivery service (similar to IP); this allows applications to exchange messages over the network with a minimum of protocol overhead. UDP is an *unreliable, connectionless* datagram protocol. The basic UDP data block (actually for UDP the correct term should be *packet* or *message*) is presented in Figure 14.9. The *UDP header* contains only two 32-bit words. The first word includes the 16-bit *source port* and *destination port* numbers, which define applications; the second word includes the *datagram length* and a *checksum.* A very short *header* minimizes the protocol overhead.

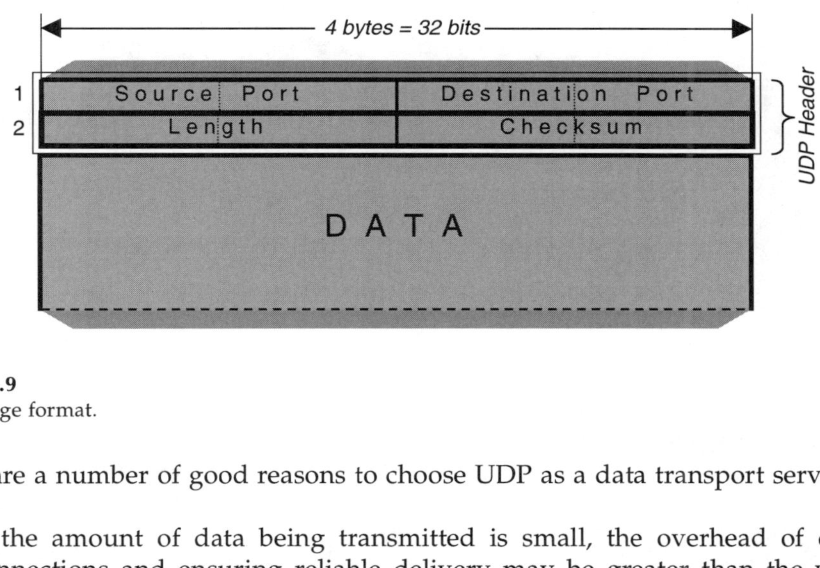

FIGURE 14.9
UDP message format.

There are a number of good reasons to choose UDP as a data transport service:

- If the amount of data being transmitted is small, the overhead of creating connections and ensuring reliable delivery may be greater than the work of retransmitting the entire data set.
- Many applications fit a *"query - response" model,* so reliable data delivery is already ensured by the applications themselves.
- Many applications provide their own techniques for reliable data delivery, so imposing another layer of acknowledgment would be redundant.

14.4.3.2 Transmission Control Protocol (TCP)

TCP is a *reliable, connection-oriented, byte-stream* protocol, where *reliability* is achieved by a mechanism called ***Positive Acknowledgment with Retransmission*** (***PAR***). Data are resent if a positive acknowledgment for already sent data is not received. A basic header for a data block (for TCP the correct term should be *segment*) is presented in Figure 14.10. Each *segment* contains a *checksum* that the recipient uses to verify that the segment is undamaged. If the transmission is OK, the recipient sends a *positive acknowledgment* back to the sender; if the segment is damaged, the recipient discards it. After an appropriate time-out period, the sender retransmits any segment for which a positive acknowledgment is missing.

Connection-oriented protocol means that TCP establishes a logical end-to-end connection between the two hosts that communicate in a procedure known as a *handshake*. The handshake is an exchange of the control information between two end points to establish a dialogue before data is transmitted. TCP indicates the control function of a segment by setting the appropriate bit in the *Flags* field in the *header* segment. TCP used a so-called *three-way handshake* in which three segments are exchanged. The handshake procedure is presented in the Figure 14.11.

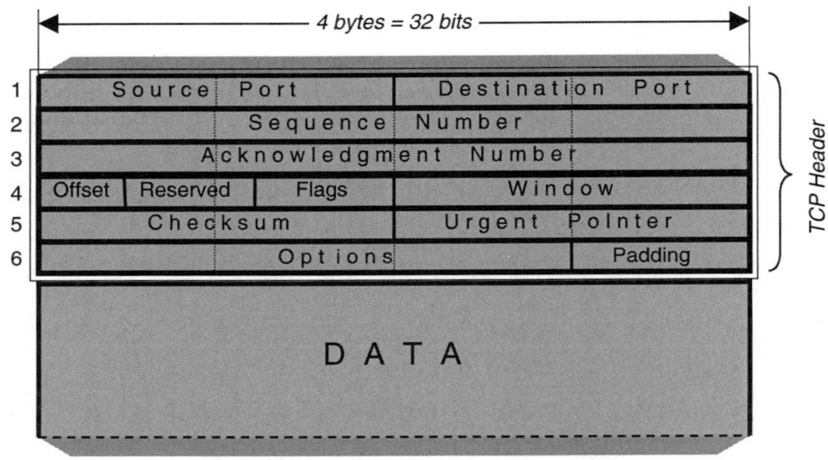

FIGURE 14.10
TCP segment format.

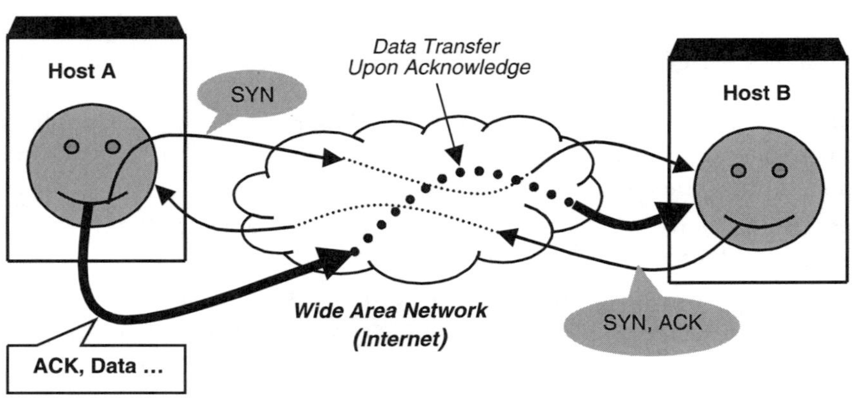

FIGURE 14.11
Three-way handshake.

Finally, a *byte-stream* protocol means that each TCP segment presents a multiple-byte data stream.

As a transport protocol, TCP is also responsible for a proper delivery of data received from the Internet layer to the correct application. A 16-bit number in the source port and destination port fields in the *header* segment identify applications. To pass data correctly to and from the *application layer* is an important part of what the *transport layer* services do.

14.4.4 Application Layer

The *application layer* is at the top of the TCP/IP protocol architecture. Everything mentioned for the ISO OSI Application Layer is also valid here. There are many different application protocols, and most of them provide user services. This is the layer under continuous upgrade, and new services are frequently added to this layer. The application layer fully relies on the three underlying layers for data delivery.

Some of the best-known application protocols are:

- *TELNET* The *network terminal protocol,* which provides remote login access over the network
- *FTP* The *file transfer protocol,* which provides interactive file transfer over the network
- *SMTP* The *simple mail transfer protocol,* which provides electronic mail delivery

The application protocols listed here are primarily user oriented. The other system-oriented applications (services) widely in use are:

- *Domain name service (DNS)* Also called *name service,* to convert (map) host names assigned to the network devices into the appropriate IP addresses and vice versa
- *Routing information protocol (RIP)* To exchange routing information
- *Network file system (NFS)* To share files between various hosts on the network
- *Network information service (NIS)* To centralize the administration over a group of hosts on the network

Some applications require user interaction, like *telnet* or *ftp,* while others run hidden from users, like *RIP, DNS, NFS,* or *NIS.* Nevertheless, UNIX administrators must know a great deal about all of them.

Figure 14.12 shows the hierarchy of TCP/IP protocols in an imaginary system. The relationship between different layer protocols is presented. It is assumed that the system is connected to the Ethernet-type network.

The main purpose of this chapter is to get a basic idea about networking. Being familiar with the TCP/IP protocol stack and basic layer functions is very instrumental in performing daily UNIX network administration. Our task will be significantly easier if we fully understand how things work in this amazing network environment known as the Internet.

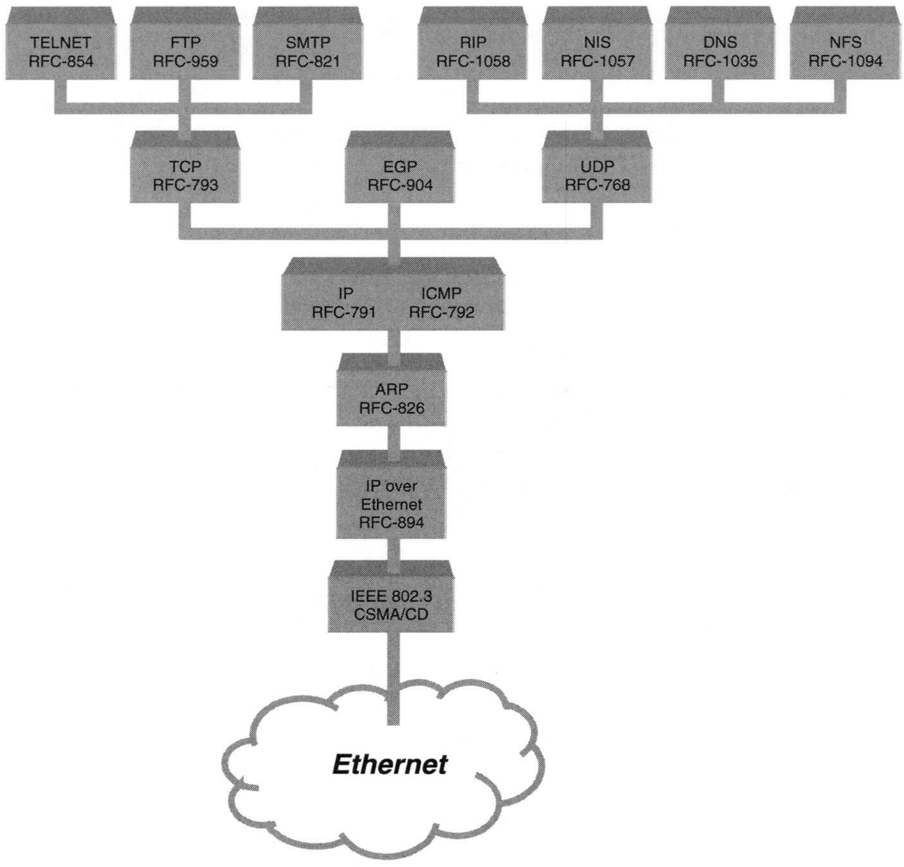

FIGURE 14.12
The hierarchy of TCP/IP protocols.

15

TCP/IP Network

15.1 Data Delivery

Two basic steps must be completed to deliver data successfully between two Internet participants. First, it is necessary to transmit the data across the network to the appropriate host. Second, the data has to be transmitted within that host to the appropriate user or process. TCP/IP uses three schemes to accomplish these tasks:

1. ***Addressing*** IP addresses uniquely identify each host on the entire internet; TCP/IP relies on IP addressing to deliver data to the correct host on the network.
2. ***Routing*** The Internet consists of many interconnected networks; different networks are connected over routers (gateways). Routing means to forward data to the correct network (or subnetwork) via an appropriate router (gateway).
3. ***Multiplexing*** Protocol numbers and port numbers identify how to deliver data to the correct software module within the host.

15.1.1 IP Address Classes

The *Internet protocol* (IP) moves data between hosts in the form of datagrams. Each datagram is delivered to the host identified by a *32-bit* ***IP address*** located in the *Destination Address* field in the datagram *header.*

An IP address contains a network part and a host part, but the format of these parts is not uniformly determined; the number of address bits used to identify the network and the number used to identify the host vary according to the class of the address. The three address classes are *class A*, *class B*, and *class C*. By examining the first few bits of an address, IP software can quickly determine the address's class and, therefore, its structure. Figure 15.1 illustrates how the address structure varies with an address class. It presents three address's classes in three arbitrary IP address examples. The rules for address classes are:

- If the first address bit is 0, this is the address of a ***class A*** network; the next seven bits identify the network itself, and the remaining 24 bits identify the host in that network. There are fewer than 128 class A network addresses and 16 million hosts' addresses available in each network (a certain number of network addresses are reserved for special purposes).

- If the first two bits are 10, this is the address of a ***class B*** network; the next 14 bits identify the network, and the remaining 16 bits identify the host in that network. There are slightly more than 16,000 class B network addresses and more than 64,000 hosts' addresses available in each network.
- If the first two bits are 11, this is the address of a ***class C*** network; the next 22 bits identify the network, and the last 8 bits identify the host in that network. There are more than 4 million class C network addresses with 256 hosts' addresses available (actually this number is lower, because the host's address 0 is reserved to identify the network itself, and the address 255 is the network broadcast address). The C class addresses that start with the first three bits 111 are reserved for special purposes, which means 2 million class C network addresses are available for general use.

IP addresses are written as four-decimal numbers separated by dots (periods). Each of the four numbers is between 0 and 255, and identified by one byte in the 32-bit address. Keeping in mind the previous division of address classes, the first decimal number fully indicates the address's class:

- Fewer than 128 — *Class A* address
- Between 128 and 191 — *Class B* address
- Greater than 191 — *Class C* address

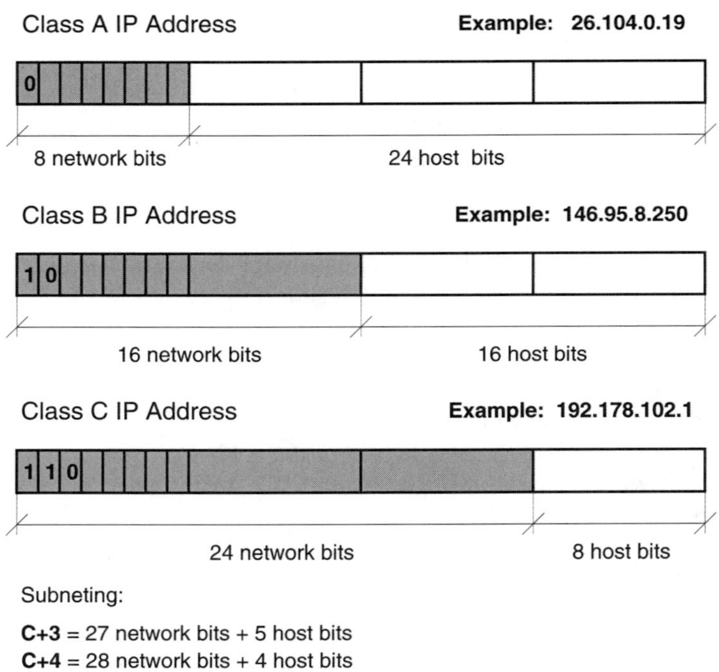

FIGURE 15.1
IP address structure.

Not all network and host addresses are available for general use. Class C addresses greater than 223 are reserved for special purposes, and certain class A addresses are also reserved, for instance,

1. *network 0* *Default route*, to simplify the routing information that IP must handle.
2. *network 127* *Loopback address*, to allow the local host to be addressed in the same manner as a remote host. This address is very important in configuring the host.

Please note that among all classes, the hosts' address 0 is reserved to identify the network itself, and the highest address within the network is reserved as a broadcast address (to propagate broadcast messages to all hosts in the network).

IP addresses are often called *hosts' addresses*. This is very common, but ***is not correct***. IP addresses are assigned to the network interfaces, not the systems themselves. Any ***router (gateway)***, is always connected to more than one network and contains more network interfaces; consequently, it has more than one IP address associated with the same system (host), and a different IP address for each of the networks it is connected to. Similarly, multihome hosts have multiple network interfaces and multiple associated IP addresses; their main task is not routing, but to improve system and network performance.

The IP addressing scheme is designed to make routing easy; it is network-oriented. The disadvantage of this approach is that many hosts' addresses among all classes are not used within the corresponding networks and have no chance to be used elsewhere, either. Given today's enormous network growth, the need for new addresses has reached the saturation point. The lack of IP addresses is obvious, and the question is how long they will be available at all. The new proposal for 132-bit IP addressing is under consideration; the main problem is how to keep the necessary compatibility with the current IP addressing system and the millions of already installed and active networks and hosts worldwide.

In the meantime, the ***intranet*** has become a workable solution. Intranets are isolated internet-type networks that use an arbitrary IP addressing scheme, so IP addresses can be repeated among different intranets. All addresses in an intranet are hidden from the Internet; they are strictly internal to the intranet, and the whole intranet appears to the Internet as a single or a few IP addresses only. Address mapping and the required isolation are provided by special systems known as ***proxy servers*** and ***firewalls***; they also protect the intranet from external intruders. The basic network services are fully provided and are transparent to intranet users; users see the system as being a part of the Internet itself (the intranet is fully discussed in Chapter 25).

It is assumed that each IP address of any class belongs to one local network; at the very least, a host understands that another host with the same network-part IP address shares the same local network. If that is literally true, then it means that the class A IP address defines a LAN with 4 million participating hosts (it is very hard to imagine the data traffic within such a network); obviously, a huge number of available host's IP addresses cannot be used in that way.

One solution to this problem is known as *subnetworking* (also referred as *subnetting*). A given IP address of a certain class can be divided into multiple IP address subclasses, each of them defining a separate subnetwork (there are no technological differences between a network and a subnetwork; the two terms are used only to identify their mutual relationship). Subnetting means expanding the network part of an IP address by some address bit of the host's address part.

While a host can easily figure out an IP address class that its own IP address belongs to, subnetting is arbitrary and the host has no information about it. For that purpose, the so-called ***netmask*** has been introduced. A netmask specifies how many address bits in an IP address correspond to the network part; by default the netmask matches the corresponding IP address class. To be operational, subnetting requires that you modify the host's netmask (actually, netmasks are, like IP addresses, associated with network interfaces, so a host could have multiple netmasks).

Netmasks are specified in a way very similar to IP addresses; a netmask is a 32-bit number that contains ***all ones*** for the network part, and ***all zeros*** for the host part. In the same way as an IP address, it is also represented by four decimal numbers separated by dots (periods); each of the four numbers is between 0 and 255 and identified by one byte in the 32-bit netmask.

The reason for subnetting is not only because too many hosts' addresses remain unused; subnetting improves network performance by making data transmission faster. Data transmission is faster because every machine on an IP network (or subnetwork) sees all of the traffic on the network. Those packets that are addressed to a specific host are received, and those that are not are bypassed. Therefore, if there are fewer actual hosts on a network (or a subnet), then each host on that network has less traffic to monitor. Subnetting decreases the network load (a smaller number of hosts compete on the same subnetwork), and separate the network traffic into local traffic within the subnetwork, and network-wide traffic; the net effect is an increase in the network throughput. The price to be paid is that for each subnetwork a new router must be added.

It is quite common to subnet class C networks, too. To describe subnets verbally, sometimes we identify them by specifying subclasses of IP addresses; for example, "C+3," or "C+4." This is shown in Figure 15.1. Keeping in mind that the class A IP address contains a *24-bit network address part*, class B IP addresses have a *16-bit network address part*, and class C IP address have an *8-bit network address part*, the meaning of the presented subnetwork identifications should be clear.

15.1.2 Internet Routing

In traditional internet structures, routing was centralized around so-called *core gateways*. This model quickly became obsolete and useless. It was replaced by the newly feasible decentralized routing model, which is based on co-equal collections of autonomous systems called ***routing domains***. *Routers* (also known as *gateways*) in different routing domains exchange routing information between themselves, do their processing for themselves, and choose the best routes.

The two terms router and gateway are widely used to identify the same routing devices. Strictly speaking, a gateway provides more functionality; besides routing, it also converts protocols among networks (for example, Ethernet to Token Ring and vice versa). In the following text the terms are used interchangeably.

Routers route data between local networks, but all devices in the network, including hosts, must make some routing decisions as well. The host itself, in fact, always makes the very first routing decision. For most hosts, the routing decision is simple:

- If the destination host is on the local network, the data is delivered directly to the destination host.
- If the destination host is on a remote network, the data is forwarded to a local router (gateway), for further delivery.

Because routing is network oriented, IP makes routing decisions based on the network portion of the IP address (determined by the corresponding netmask). By checking the network bits of the destination address, the IP module determines whether the designated host belongs to the same network, or not. This is done with simple logical operations between the *destination address, network mask,* and *host's address* (network mask has all network bits equal to 1, which is instrumental in extracting the network portion of the hosts' addresses).

After determining the destination network, the IP module looks for this network in the local ***routing table***. Datagrams are routed toward their destination as directed by the *routing table*. The routing table may be static (built during the system startup), or dynamic, continuously updated by routing protocols. However, the decision is always based on a simple table lookup.

The **netstat -[n]r** command will display the current routing table (the listed option **r** specifies the routing table, while the option **n** specifies numerical data representation; otherwise, data are represented symbolically whenever possible). Here are examples from the *SunOS/Solaris* and *HP-UX* flavors, respectively:

 # netstat -nr

Routing tables

Destination	Gateway	Flags	Refcnt	Use	Interface
127.0.0.1	*127.0.0.1*	*UH*	*1*	*730*	*lo0*
198.61.16.0	*146.95.1.15*	*UG*	*0*	*0*	*le0*
default	*146.95.1.15*	*UG*	*1*	*1575*	*le0*
198.61.17.0	*146.95.1.15*	*UG*	*0*	*0*	*le0*
. . . . .					
. . . . .					
148.84.0.0	*146.95.1.15*	*UG*	*0*	*26*	*le0*
149.4.0.0	*146.95.1.15*	*UG*	*0*	*0*	*le0*
128.228.0.0	*146.95.1.15*	*UG*	*0*	*500*	*le0*
146.95.0.0	*146.95.1.11*	*U*	*30*	*129465*	*le0*

$ netstat -nr

Routing tables

Destination	Gateway	Flags	Refs	Use	Interface
127.0.0.1	*127.0.0.1*	*UH*	*0*	*66*	*lo0*
default	*146.95.1.15*	*UG*	*0*	*4444*	*lan0*
146.95	*146.95.8.31*	*U*	*3*	*58052*	*lan0*

Obviously, the format of the *routing table* is essentially universal and independent of the UNIX flavor. Also, we can see that the first *routing table* includes too many unnecessary entries that point to the same router; three entries (as seen in the second example) are sufficient when a single router is available. Many entries in the first example are the result of the dynamic routing; the system is trying to specify optimal routes based on available routers in the network. Obviously, the only possible output must be the very same router. In other words, there is no need for dynamic routing if there is no alternative router in the network; "static routing" covers all possible routing scenarios. A larger routing table only takes more time, without any visible benefits (except some statistical data could be collected). If multiple routers are available, then dynamic routing makes a lot of sense, and should be implemented.

The routing table contains following *fields*:

Field	Meaning
Destination	The destination network or host.
Gateway	The router (gateway) to use to reach the specified destination.
Flags	The flags describe certain characteristics of this route. The possible flag values are:
	U Indicates that the route is up and operational.
	H Indicates this is the route to a specific host.
	G Indicates the route uses a gateway.
	D Indicates that this route was added because of an *ICMP* redirect.
	When a system learns of a route, it adds the route to the table.
Refcnt	Shows the number of times the route has been referenced to establish a connection.
Use	Shows the number of packets transmitted via this route.
Interface	The name of the network interface used by this route.

Most entries in the presented routing tables refer to the designated networks and are identified numerically (by their IP addresses). The entry ***127.0.0.1*** is the loopback route for the local host. The entry ***default*** is for the default route and the specified router is the default router (the default gateway). The default route is always used when there is no another entry that points to the specified designated host or network.

How does the system know about a default route? Simply, the default router must be explicitly specified and appended to the routing table. As opposed to many configuration data, where the corresponding configuration files can be edited, there is no way to edit the routing table. The special UNIX command **route** must be used for this purpose.

The **route** command can be used from the command line at any moment, and it will immediately alter the routing table; however, each manual modification will be lost upon the next system reboot. In order for the **route** command to act during normal system startup, it must be a part of a corresponding **rc** script that enables initial setting of the routing table; this is provided in different ways for different UNIX flavors.

The following example should illustrate a possible command string for this purpose:

```
        .....
# The network interface is defined using the ifconfig command
#       .....
# Initialize network routing.
# The route(1m) command manipulates the network routing tables.
        .....
        /etc/route add default 146.95.8.250 1
# adds default network destination to the routing table indicating
# a correspondence between that destination and the gateway,
# and specifying the number of hops to the gateway as 1.
        .....
```

In this example, the default router is explicitly specified within the **rc** startup script. Although it does work this way, specifying the default router within a separate file sounds more appropriate; at least future changes in the network configuration seem to be more logical. On the SunOS/Solaris platform the */etc/defaultrouter* file keeps the necessary default routing data, which is read during system startup.

15.1.2.1 The *route* Command

The ***route*** command is used to manipulate the routing table manually; root privileges are required to use it. It supports two subcommands:

add To add a route
delete To delete a route

The generic command format is:

/etc/route [-f] [-n] add [net | host] ***destination gateway [count]***
/etc/route [-f] [-n] delete [net | host] ***destination gateway [count]***

The command arguments are:

-f	Specifies the forcible deletion (flushing) of all entries in the routing table that defines the remote host for a gateway.
-n	Specifies a numerical printout of any host and network address (in "dot" notation), except for the default network address.
net or **host**	Specifies the type of destination address; could be ***net*** for "network" or ***host*** for "individual host" (this is default value if omitted).
destination	Specifies a destination system where the packet will be routed. It can be either a host name, a network name, an IP address (in "dot" notation), or the keyword ***default***, which signifies the wildcard gateway route.
gateway	Specifies the gateway (router) through which the destination is reached; can be either a host name or an IP address (in "dot" notation).
count	An integer that indicates whether the gateway is a remote host (>0) or a local host (=0; this is default value).

15.1.2.2 Dynamic Routing

The routing tables presented here correspond to the situation in which a single router is available; the host's routing decision for all out-of-network traffic is limited to the only available router. There is no choice between alternative routes to forward data, so the static routing algorithm is quite appropriate. Static routing assumes that, once defined (during the system booting), a routing table remains unchanged and valid throughout the system's lifetime.

It is recommended that you implement static routing whenever only one router exists in the local network, which is the most common case. A bit of processor time (which the system always needs) can be saved, as there is no useless routing calculation involved when the output is already known. However, many systems use dynamic routing even under such conditions (as in the first example presented). Nothing is fundamentally wrong with that; the system will work properly. But it is fair to say that no real need exists for a dynamic routing when a single router is available. The only "pro" argument is that such a system is already prepared for any eventual network upgrades (which in most cases never happen).

A single router in the local network is not acceptable in some network implementations, because a broken router completely isolates the whole network. Introducing a second router could solve this problem. The second router is not only the alternative to a broken first router; two routers can share the routing tasks, making the overall network performance better. In that case we have dynamic routing.

Dynamic routing assumes a permanent adaptation of the routing table to current network conditions; it also assumes that the optimal routing decision is always made. How can this highly desirable goal be achieved? A separate process, the ***gated*** daemon, is dedicated to this task and runs continuously. There are also other routing daemons, but **gated** is the most common, and it is a part of the UNIX distribution. The **gated** daemons running on different remote hosts communicate with one another to update information about the network status; the final output is an updated *routing table* for each individual host.

15.1.2.3 The *gated* Daemon

Gated is a routing daemon that handles the routing information protocol (RIP), border gateway protocol (BGP), exterior gateway protocol (EGP), and HELLO routing protocol. The ***gated*** process can be configured to perform all of these specified routing protocols, or any combination of them.

The generic command line is:

gated [-c] [-n] [-t *trace_option***] [-f** *config_file***] [*trace_file*]**

The daemon's arguments are:

-c	Parse the configuration file for syntax errors and then exit; related to tracing
-n	Do not modify the kernel's routing table; used for testing ***gated*** configurations
-t*trace_option*	Enable trace flags on startup; see manual pages for details
-f *config_file*	Use an alternate configuration file; by default, ***gated*** uses */etc/gated.conf*
trace_file	Trace file in which to place trace information

The **gated** daemon must be started during the system booting through a corresponding **rc** initialization script, as in the following example (this **rc** startup script is the Korn shell script):

```
if [ -x /etc/gated ]; then
   /etc/gated -f /etc/gated.conf && /bin/echo "gated daemon started"
else
   /bin/echo "Couldn't execute /etc/gated"
fi
```

The only condition required to start the **gated** daemon is the existence of the corresponding executable program; the rest is done with messages sent to console. The configuration file is ***/etc/gated.conf***, which is used to tune the daemon's behavior. Here is an example:

$ cat /etc/gated.conf

```
redirect yes;
rip quiet
static {
        default gateway 146.95.8.249 preference 150;
        };
```

This configuration file specifies:

- *redirect* ICMP (Internet control message protocol) messages, i.e., controls routing table changes based on ICMP
- *quiet* specifies that no RIP packets are to be generated
- *static* defines a static route through the second gateway (the first gateway is defined in the corresponding **rc** startup script)

This example is just to get a basic idea of what the */etc/gated.conf* file can look like. There are a number of ways to configure the **gated** daemon.

15.1.3 Multiplexing

Once data is routed through the network and delivered to a specified designated host, the remaining task is to deliver this data to the correct *user* or *process* on the host. As data moves up or down the layers of the TCP/IP protocol stack, some mechanism is needed to deliver the data to the correct protocol in each layer, step by step, and at the end the data will reach the correct application. The implemented mechanism is based on the following:

- *When sending data,* the system must be able to combine data from many applications into a few transport protocols, and from the transport protocols into the Internet protocol. Combining many sources of data into a single data stream is calling ***multiplexing***.
- *Data arriving from the network* must be ***demultiplexed,*** i.e., divided for delivery to multiple processes. To accomplish this, IP uses ***protocol numbers*** to identify transport protocols, and the transport protocols use ***port numbers*** to identify applications.

Some protocol and port numbers are reserved to identify so-called ***well-known services***. Well-known services are standard network protocols (such as *telnet* or *ftp*) that are commonly used throughout the network. The protocol and port numbers allocated to well-known services are documented in the RFCs documents. UNIX specifies protocol and port numbers in a few simple text *database files*.

15.1.3.1 Protocols, Ports, and Sockets

A protocol number is a single byte in the IP datagram header (the third word — the protocol field). The value in the field identifies the protocol in the layer above IP, the transport layer, to which the data should be passed. UNIX specifies protocol numbers in the ***/etc/protocols*** file.

After IP passes incoming data to the corresponding transport protocol, the transport protocol passes the data to the correct application process. Port numbers identify application processes, which are also called network services. A port number is a 16-bit number in the header of the UDP packet (message) or TCP segment. The *destination port number* (in the *destination port* field) identifies the application protocol that is to receive the data; the *source port number* (in the *source port* field) identifies the application protocol that sent the data. UNIX specifies port numbers in the ***/etc/services*** file.

Well-known ports are standardized port numbers that enable remote hosts to know which port to connect to for a particular network service. This simplifies the connection process because both the sender and the recipient know in advance how and where to establish connection. For example, all systems that offer *telnet* offer it on *port 23*. The data flow through the TCP/IP protocol stack in this case is presented in Figure 15.2.

However, the question is what to do when multiple users and multiple processes request the same service simultaneously. This situation can be handled only by using *dynamically allocated ports*, as seen in Figure 15.3.

The source host has requested the *telnet* service from the designated host. The source host randomly generated the source port number for the user who initiated this request (port 3408 in this case) and sent out the TCP segment with this source port number; the destination port number is 23 (the well-known service for *telnet*). The destination host has received the sent TCP segment on its port 23 and responded back to the remote host's destination port 3408. A network-wide unique connection has been established.

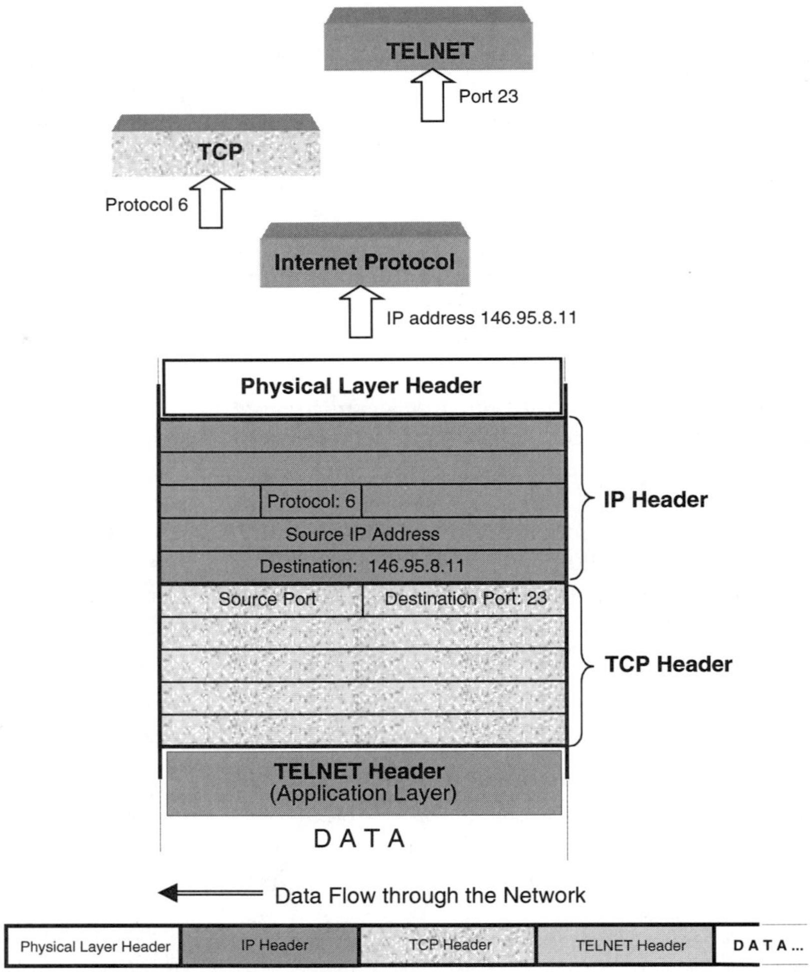

FIGURE 15.2
Protocol and port numbers.

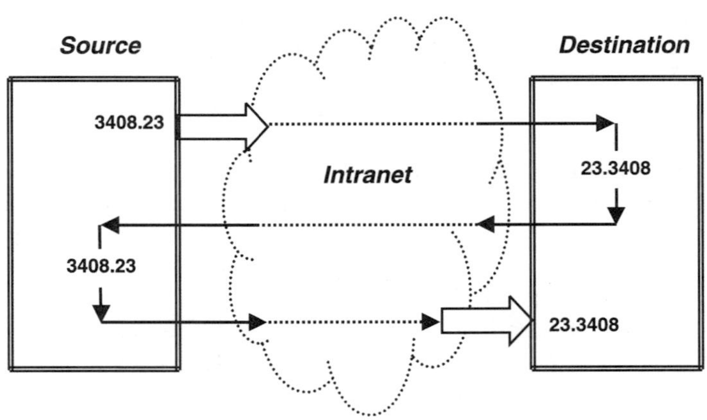

FIGURE 15.3
Dynamically allocated port numbers.

A combination of an IP address and a port number is called a ***socket***. A socket uniquely identifies a single network process throughout the entire Internet. Sometimes the terms *socket* and *port number* are used interchangeably; *well-known services* are often referred as *well-known sockets*. However, this is not correct and should be avoided.

15.1.3.2 UNIX Database Files

UNIX database files store all of the protocol and port numbers that the system needs. These files are uniform among different UNIX flavors. We will discuss them with examples from SunOS/Solaris and HP-UX.

The /etc/protocols file — The */etc/protocols* file is a simple table containing the protocol names and the protocol numbers associated with those names. The format of the table is a single entry per line; each entry consists of the *official protocol name* separated by white space from the *protocol number*; the protocol number is separated by white space from the *alias* (if any exists) for the protocol name, and *comments* begin with the # symbol.

$ cat /etc/protocols (SunOS/Solaris)

```
# @(#)protocols 1.9 90/01/03 SMI
#
# Internet (IP) protocols
# This file is never consulted when the NIS are running
#
ip      0   IP      # internet protocol, pseudo protocol number
icmp    1   ICMP    # internet control message protocol
igmp    2   IGMP    # internet group multicast protocol
ggp     3   GGP     # gateway-gateway protocol
tcp     6   TCP     # transmission control protocol
pup     12  PUP     # PARC universal packet protocol
udp     17  UDP     # user datagram protocol
```

$ **cat /etc/protocols** (HP-UX)

```
# @(#)$Header: protocols,v 1.7.109.1 91/11/21 12:02:15 kcs Exp $
# @(#)protocols5.1 (Berkeley) 4/17/89
#
# This file contains information regarding the known protocols
# used in the DARPA Internet.
#
# The form for each entry is:
# <official protocol name>  <protocol number>  <aliases>
# Note: The entries cannot be preceded by a blank space.
# Internet (IP) protocols
ip          0   IP          # internet protocol, pseudo protocol number
icmp        1   ICMP        # internet control message protocol
ggp         3   GGP         # gateway-gateway protocol
tcp         6   TCP         # transmission control protocol
egp         8   EGP         # exterior gateway protocol
pup         12  PUP         # PARC universal packet protocol
udp         17  UDP         # user datagram protocol
hmp         20  HMP         # host monitoring protocol
xns-idp     22  XNS-IDP     # Xerox NS IDP
rdp         27  RDP         # "reliable datagram" protocol
```

The /etc/services file — The other database file, */etc/services*, is very similar (in its format) to the */etc/protocols* file. Each single-line entry starts with the *official name of the service*, separated by white space from the *port number/protocol name* pair associated with that service. The port numbers are paired with transport protocol names, because different transport protocols may use the same port number. An optional list of *aliases* for the official service name may be also provided, and *comments* start with the # symbol.

$ **cat /etc/services**

```
#
# @(#)services 1.16 90/01/03 SMI
#
# Network services, Internet style
# This file is never consulted when the NIS are running
#
tcpmux          1/tcp                           # rfc-1078
echo            7/tcp
echo            7/udp
          .....
ftp             21/tcp
telnet          23/tcp
smtp            25/tcp      mail
time            37/tcp      timserver
time            37/udp      timserver
name            42/udp      nameserver
whois           43/tcp      nicname             # usually to sri-nic
domain          53/udp
domain          53/tcp
hostnames       101/tcp     hostname            # usually to sri-nic
sunrpc          111/udp
sunrpc          111/tcp
#
# Host specific functions
#
tftp            69/udp
rje             77/tcp
finger          79/tcp
          .....
pop-2           109/tcp                         # Post Office
uucp-path       117/tcp
nntp            119/tcp     usenet              # Network News Transfer
ntp             123/tcp                         # Network Time Protocol
NeWS            144/tcp     news                # Window System
#
# UNIX specific services
#
# these are NOT officially assigned
#
exec            512/tcp
login           513/tcp
shell           514/tcp  cmd                    # no passwords used
printer         515/tcp  spooler                # line printer spooler
          .....
          .....
```

15.2 Address Resolution (ARP)

The designated *IP address* and the *routing table* are the cornerstones in forwarding a datagram to a specific physical network. However, when a datagram travels across a network, it must obey the physical layer protocols used by that network. The physical layer does not understand the IP addressing scheme; it only respects its own addressing and its own rules. To make everything operational, one of the basic tasks of the network access layer of the TCP/IP stack is to map IP addresses into appropriate physical network addresses.

The most common physical local network is the *Ethernet network* (often used as a generic name for all *CSMA/CD* networks). The Ethernet network has its own addressing scheme, with *Ethernet addresses* to identify each Ethernet interface device connected to the network. An *Ethernet address* (often specified as a *MAC address*; MAC stands for the media access control sublayer in the data link layer of the ISO OSI Reference Model) should not be mistaken for an *Internet IP address*; these are two completely different addressing schemes.

Six two-digit hexadecimal numbers separated by a colon (:) specify an Ethernet address. A unique Ethernet address is assigned to each Ethernet network interface, hardwired or firmwired during its manufacture. Consequently, the Ethernet address remains hidden from users and is outside of any administrative control. However, currently some vendors put Ethernet addressing under program control, also allowing local programming of physical Ethernet addresses.

The protocol that performs IP address mapping to the physical Ethernet address is known as the *address resolution protocol (ARP)*, and it belongs to the *network access layer*. The ARP software maintains a table of IP addresses translated into Ethernet addresses. ARP itself builds the table dynamically and automatically. When ARP receives a request to translate an IP address, it first checks if the specified IP address is already in the table. If the IP address is found, ARP returns the corresponding Ethernet address to the requesting software. If the address is not found in the table, ARP broadcasts an Ethernet query to all hosts on the local Ethernet network, asking the host with the corresponding IP address to reply with its Ethernet address.

Please note that the requested IP address must be a directly reachable IP address of the host, or a router on the local network (otherwise data delivery is not possible). Note also that Ethernet addresses cannot go over the boundaries of the local network. Both the broadcasted Ethernet query and the requested IP address remain in the local network. Each host in the local network is familiar with its own IP and Ethernet addresses, and the queried host will respond with its Ethernet address.

The received response is then cached in the *ARP table*. Even though the ARP table is dynamically updated, the static entries can be also created; there is a way to specify specific Internet/Ethernet address pairs and keep them unmodified in the table (the **-s** option of the **arp** command).

All cached data are kept in the ARP table for only a certain period of time (the "time-out period," which lasts for a few seconds); once the time-out period expires, the corresponding entry is deleted. Once an entry is deleted, ARP must query for the very same data as if it had never been in the table. Permanent ARP table updating makes the ARP procedure independent of the changes in the network; otherwise, a simple replacement of a broken network card would not be possible (an Ethernet address is a part of the network interface, so by replacing the network interface card, another Ethernet address is automatically associated with the corresponding IP address).

15.2.1 The *arp* Command

The *arp* command displays and controls the contents of the IP-to-Ethernet address translation table used by the ARP protocol. Several forms of the command are available:

arp [-d] ***hostname***
arp -s ***hostname ethaddr*** **[temp] [pub] [trail]**

arp -a
arp -f ***filename***

where with no options, **arp** displays the current ARP entry for ***hostname***. The options are:

- **-a** Display all of the current ARP entries by reading the table from the kernel.
- **-d** Delete an entry for ***hostname***.
- **-s** Create an ARP entry for ***hostname*** with the Ethernet address ***ethaddr***. The entry will be permanent unless the **temp** option is given in the command. If the **pub** option is given, the entry will be published; for instance, this system will respond to ARP requests for ***hostname*** even though the hostname is not its own. The **trail** option indicates that trailer encapsulations may be sent to this host.
- **-f** Read the file named ***filename*** and set multiple entries in the ARP table; entries in the file should be of the form:

  hostname ethaddr [temp] [pub] [trail]

  with the argument meanings as given above, under the **-s** option.

Here are two examples:

 # arp -a (SunOS/Solaris)

```
hcprophet (146.95.1.2) at 8:0:20:0:9b:4d
rs01-ch (146.95.1.21) at 2:60:8c:2f:48:db
? (146.95.6.73) at 0:0:89:0:3e:4
bjl.ph.hunter.cuny.edu (146.95.8.11) at 0:0:1d:a:e5:6c
pegasus.hunter.cuny.edu (146.95.1.12) at 8:0:20:1f:39:46
denboer.ph.hunter.cuny.edu (146.95.8.12) at 0:0:1d:b:53:e2
default (146.95.1.15) at 0:0:0:0:8b:8b
indigo1.ch (146.95.6.15) at 8:0:69:6:b4:84
```

$ arp -a (HP-UX)

```
levi.ph.hunter.cuny.edu (146.95.8.11) at 0:0:1d:a:e5:6c ether
pegasus.hunter.cuny.edu (146.95.1.12) at 8:0:20:1f:39:46 ether
denboer.ph.hunter.cuny.edu (146.95.8.12) at 0:0:1d:b:53:e2 ether
hcgate1.hunter.cuny.edu (146.95.1.15) at 0:0:0:0:8b:8b ether
physpc1.ph.hunter.cuny.edu (146.95.8.28) at 0:0:1d:b:45:6a ether
```

15.3 Remote Procedure Call (RPC)

Remote Procedure Call (RPC) provides a mechanism for a host to make a procedure call that appears to be a part of the local process, while it is really executed on another, remote host in the network. The net effect is the impression that everything is executing strictly locally, although the requested resources are far apart and can be reached only through the network. Typically, the host on which the procedure call is executed has resources that are not available on the calling host. This distribution of computing services imposes a client/server relationship on the two hosts: the host owning the resource is a server for that resource, and the calling host becomes a client that needs access to the resource.

Procedure is a relatively closed program entity used in C programming, with well-defined input and output. It is very common to call a procedure from some other program to complete a certain task. Originally the calls were placed locally, and we used the term *local procedure calls* to identify them. Networking introduced a new distributed environment that offered to extend existing local applications over several remote hosts. The procedure was a logical choice for such an extension. By replacing the local procedure call with an equivalent remote procedure call, the rest of the application could remain more or less unchanged and still operational. Sun Microsystems recognized this idea, and the remote procedure call (RPC) became a standard used in networking; sometimes it is even referred to as "Sun RPC." Figure 15.4 illustrates the difference between local and remote procedure calling.

RPC uses a request-and-reply communication model; the client and the server processes communicate by means of two ***stubs***, one for the client and one for the server. A ***stub*** is the communication interface that implements the RPC protocol and specifies how messages are exchanged. Instead of executing the procedure on the local host, the RPC bundles up the arguments passed to the procedure into a network datagram. The RPC client creates a session by locating the appropriate server and sending the datagram to a process on the server that can execute the RPC. On that server, the arguments are unpacked, the server responds to the request, packages the result (if any), and sends it back to the client. On the client side, the reply is converted into a "return value" for the procedure call, and the calling application is reentered as if a local procedure is completed. This means that from an application point of view, it is not known if a local or a remote procedure call was executed.

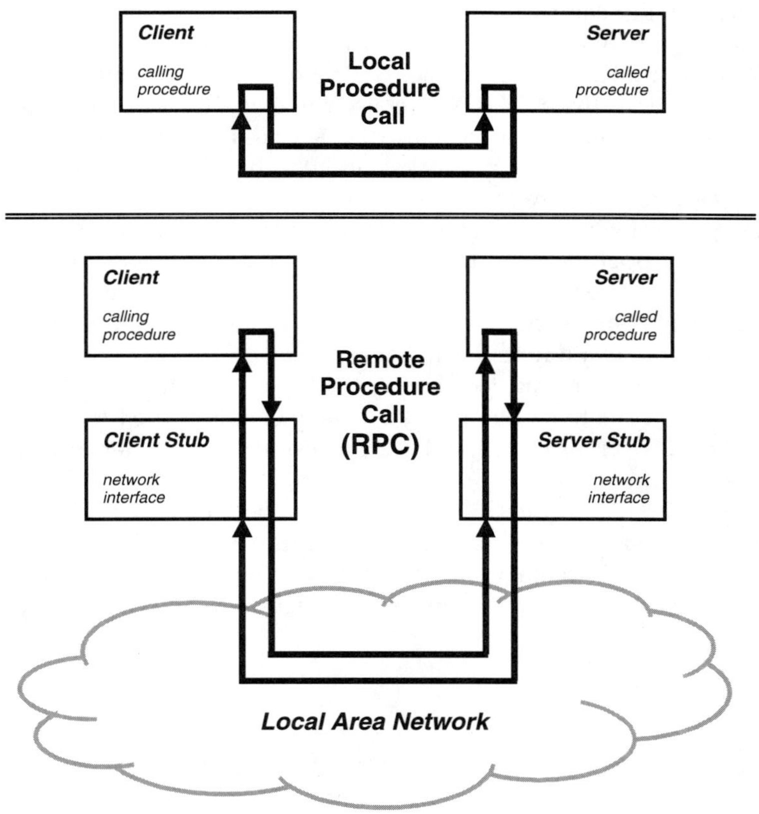

FIGURE 15.4
Local and remote procedure calling.

RPC services may be built on either TCP or UDP transport protocols, although most are UDP-oriented. The reason is because RPC services are mostly centered on short-lived requests. Using UDP forces the RPC to contain enough context information for its execution, independent of any other RPC request, since UDP packets may arrive in any order, if at all. The client may also specify a time-out period in which the remote call must be completed. Various actions can be taken if a server does not reply in the predefined time interval; the action taken depends on the application itself.

Once the concept of RCP is clear, the next logical question is: When should RCP be implemented? Does each network-based application rely on RPC, and what is a benefit of using an RPC? The following statement could help to explain these matters. A number of new network applications were created once networking become widely implemented; these applications were designed from scratch, respecting all network restrictions, specifications, and standards. These applications were run only in the distributed network environment. On another side, a number of existing local applications had to be extended and adapted to the new distributed environment. These applications were designed in a different way, they were locally oriented, and sometimes came from different host platforms; however, they had something in common: they were and are using local procedure calls in interprocess communications. The easiest way to extend them to the distributed environment and to keep full compatibility with the local environment has been to make procedures to circumvent the problem — to provide an appropriate program interface to adapt local applications to the network environment, and to keep local program characteristics intact. Thus the remote procedure call (RCP) was born.

RPC services are usually connectionless UDP-oriented services, because RPC requests do not require the creation of a long-lived network connection between the client and the server. The client communicates with the server (sends its request and receives a reply) in a connectionless fashion. However, RPC can also run over TCP, in a connection-oriented fashion. The TCP protocol may be used with RPC services whenever a large amount of data needs to be transferred (for example, NIS uses UDP, but it switches to TCP whenever it needs to transfer entire database to remote hosts).

RPC servers are generally started during system booting and run as long as the system is up. An efficient RPC operation cannot tolerate the time overhead caused by the start of a new server process when such a service is required. As a result, RPC servers are single-treated, i.e., there is one server process for the RPC service, and it executes remote requests from the client one at a time. To achieve better performance, two or more copies of the same RPC server may be started during the system startup, but each server still handles only one request at a time. There may be many clients of the RPC server, but their requests wait in the RPC server queue and are processed in the order in which they are received.

Instead of using preassigned ports, RPC service numbers designate RPC servers. The file */etc/rpc* contains a list of RPC servers and their program numbers. This approach brings the additional flexibility to implement site-specific RCP based applications; RPC service numbers can be locally customized without any impact on remote hosts.

15.3.1 The *portmapper* Daemon

An application may contain many procedures; for example, the NFS contains more than a dozen procedures, one for each filesystem operation (*"read block," "write block," "create file,"* etc.). However, RPC services still must use TCP/UDP port numbers to fit the underlying protocols. The mapping of RPC program numbers to port numbers is handled by the ***portmap*** daemon (named ***portmapper***).

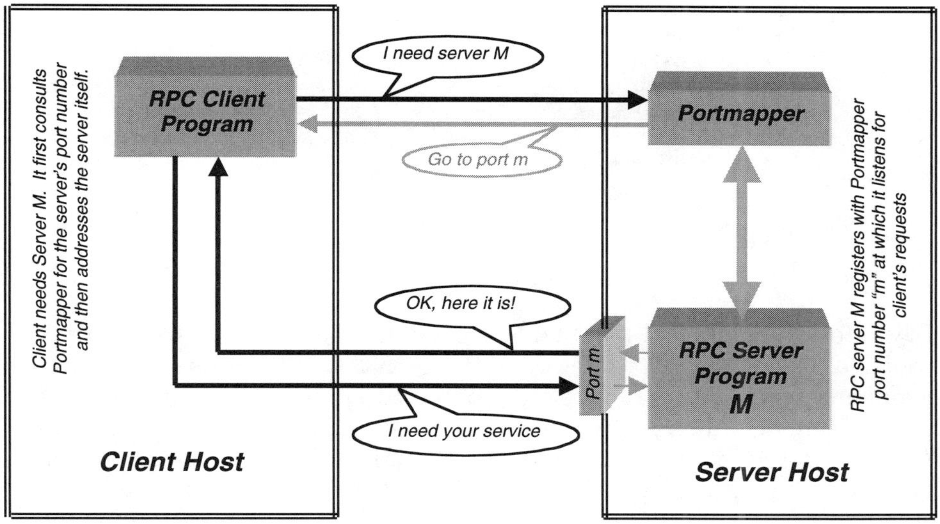

FIGURE 15.5
The RPC client/server communication.

When an RPC server is initialized, it registers its service with the **portmapper**, telling it which port it will listen on for incoming requests. An RPC client contacts the **portmapper** on the server side to learn the port number used by the RPC server; or the client may ask the **portmapper** to call the server indirectly on its behalf. This is presented in Figure 15.5. In either case, the RPC call from a client to a server must be made with the **portmapper** running. Without a running **portmapper**, all serving RPC-based applications are effectively stopped.

The port number where an RPC client can find **portmapper** is specified in the */etc/services* file:

 # cat /etc/services | grep rpc

```
portmap   111/udp      sunrpc   # SUN Remote Procedure Call
portmap   111/tcp      sunrpc   #
```

15.3.2 The */etc/rpc* File

The file */etc/rpc* contains the RPC service (program) number database; these are readable entries with the following information:

<name of server for the RPC program>   <RPC program number>   <Aliases>

Items are separated by any number of blanks and/or tab characters. A pound sign (#) indicates the beginning of a comment, and characters up to the end of the line are not interpreted by the routines that search the file.

The partial contents of the */etc/rpc* file are presented:

 # cat /etc/rpc

```
#
#  rpc 1.19 12/27
#
portmapper        100000   portmap sunrpc
```

rstatd	*100001*	*rstat rup perfmeter*
rusersd	*100002*	*rusers*
nfs	*100003*	*nfsprog*
ypserv	*100004*	*ypprog*
mountd	*100005*	*mount showmount*
ypbind	*100007*	
walld	*100008*	*rwall shutdown*
.....		
.....		
ypxfrd	*100069*	*ypxfr*
pcnfsd	*150001*	

We have already mentioned that Sun Microsystems were the first to develop the RPC; the developed version was known as *ONC RPC* (ONC stands for open network computing). Simultaneously, certain RPC-related tools and specialized commands were introduced. One of them is the **rpcinfo** command, which reports RPC information; it makes an RPC call to an RPC server and reports on its findings. The command has a number of options. The following example shows all of the RPC services registered on the local machine.

 # rpcinfo -p

program	*vers*	*proto*	*port*	
100000	*2*	*tcp*	*111*	*portmapper*
100000	*2*	*udp*	*111*	*portmapper*
100004	*2*	*udp*	*660*	*ypserv*
100004	*2*	*tcp*	*661*	*ypserv*
100004	*1*	*udp*	*660*	*ypserv*
100004	*1*	*tcp*	*661*	*ypserv*
100069	*1*	*udp*	*662*	*ypxfrd*
100069	*1*	*tcp*	*664*	*ypxfrd*
100007	*2*	*tcp*	*1024*	*ypbind*
100007	*2*	*udp*	*1027*	*ypbind*
.....				
.....				
100068	*2*	*udp*	*1044*	
100068	*3*	*udp*	*1044*	
100083	*1*	*tcp*	*1026*	

15.4 Configuring the Network Interface

An important strength of TCP/IP is its flexible use of different physical networks for the physical data transfer. Independently of the implemented physical layer, whether the host is connected to Ethernet, or Token Ring, or any other network, or even connected via a serial link, TCP/IP works the same way. Such flexibility, however, requires corresponding attention by the administrator; a single type of network interface is easier to manage than several different types. In addition, several different network interfaces can be used simultaneously, as in the case of multihome hosts connected to more than one network. In any case, independent of the type of the implemented network interface, an IP address is always assigned to each of the active network interfaces, and each network interface must be configured properly before its use. Today the prevailing network interface is Ethernet, and in the following discussion we will focus on this type of network.

Two UNIX commands are very instrumental in handling network interfaces:

1. The **ifconfig** command, to configure network interface
2. The **netstat** command, to show network-related data

15.4.1 The *ifconfig* Command

The *ifconfig* command sets, or checks, configuration values for network interfaces. It is used to set the *IP address*, the *subnet mask*, and the *broadcast address* for each interface. The format of the command is:

ifconfig *interface ipaddress netmask mask broadcast address*

The command arguments are shown in the following table:

Argument	Meaning
interface	The name of the network interface to be configured.
ipaddress	The IP address assigned to this interface. Enter an address as either an IP address (in dotted numerical form) or as a hostname; if the hostname is given, **ifconfig** must resolve the hostname - IP address. During system startup, **ifconfig** is usually executed before DNS is running, so the hostname must exist in */etc/hosts* file. SunOS/Solaris uses the */etc/hostname.ifname* file for this purpose (where *ifname* is the name of the interface).
netmask mask	The subnet mask for this interface. The ***mask*** value depends on the subnet (local network) address class (for example, 255.255.0.0 for class B, or 255.255.255.0 for class C); it could be also specified in the*/etc/netmasks* file.
broadcast address	The broadcast address for the network is defined by the ***address*** value; the default broadcast address network IP address, with all bits in the host part (determined by the netmask), is set to 1.

Each network interface must be configured before its use, and this task can be accomplished from the command line. However, to provide a proper setting during system startup, the **ifconfig** command is always included in the corresponding **rc** initialization script.

The **ifconfig** command can also be used to check already-configured network interfaces, individually or all at once. Here are a few examples:

 # ifconfig le0 (SunOS/Solaris)

le0: flags=63<UP,BROADCAST,NOTRAILERS,RUNNING>
inet 146.95.1.11 netmask ffff0000 broadcast 146.95.0.0
ether 8:0:20:8:1e:f2

 # ifconfig lo0

lo0: flags=49<UP,LOOPBACK,RUNNING>
inet 127.0.0.1 netmask ff000000

 # ifconfig -a

le0: flags=63<UP,BROADCAST,NOTRAILERS,RUNNING>
inet 146.95.1.11 netmask ffff0000 broadcast 146.95.0.0
ether 8:0:20:8:1e:f2
lo0: flags=49<UP,LOOPBACK,RUNNING>
inet 127.0.0.1 netmask ff000000

$ **ifconfig lan0** (HP-UX)

lan0: flags=63<UP,BROADCAST,NOTRAILERS,RUNNING>
inet 146.95.8.31 netmask ffff0000 broadcast 146.95.255.255

$ **ifconfig lo0**

lo0: flags=1049<UP,LOOPBACK,RUNNING>
inet 127.0.0.1 netmask ff000000

When used to check the status of an interface, the **ifconfig** command displays two output lines. The first line shows the *interface name* and the *flags* that define the interface's characteristics; the *flags* are displayed as both a *numeric value* and a set of *keywords*. The meanings of the *flag keywords* in the previous examples are:

UP	The interface is enabled for use.
BROADCAST	The interface supports broadcast, which means it is connected to the network that support broadcast (in these cases Ethernet).
NOTRAILER	The interface does not support *trailer encapsulation*. Some systems (such as SunOS) completely ignored this possibility and never used it.
RUNNING	The interface is operational.
LOOPBACK	The interface supports local loopback.

The second line of the **ifconfig** output displays information that directly relates to TCP/IP. The meanings of the *keywords* used are:

inet	Keyword *inet* is followed by the IP address assigned to this interface.
netmask	Keyword *netmask* is followed by the subnet mask written in hexadecimal format. The mask specifies valid address bits of the network (subnetwork) part of the IP address assigned to the interface.
broadcast	Keyword *broadcast* is followed by the broadcast address assigned to this interface. The system figures out the broadcast address as the maximal available IP address within the defined network (subnetwork).

15.4.2 The *netstat* Command

The ***netstat*** command displays the contents of various network-related data in a variety of formats, depending on the options specified. The command has the following syntax:

netstat *[options] [system] [core]*

where

options	One or more options preceded by a hyphen *(-)*; some options require additional arguments
system	Allows a substitute for the default, which is the kernel (such as */vmunix*)
core	Allows a substitute for the default, which is the special file */dev/kmem*

There are a number of options, some of which are shown in the following table (some options require an additional argument):

Option	Meaning
-a	Displays the state of all sockets. Without any option passive sockets used by server processes are not displayed.
-i	Displays the state of network interfaces that have been auto-configured.
-I *interface*	Displays information about the specified interface.
-g	Displays multicast information for network interfaces.
-p *protocol*	Displays statistics for the specified protocol. The recognized protocols are: tcp, udp, ip, icmp, igmp, arp, and probe.
-n	Displays network addresses numerically (as numbers). By default, hostnames are presented symbolically, if possible.
-r	Displays the routing tables. When the **s** option is also present, it displays routing statistics instead.
-v	Displays additional routing information. When **-v** is used with the **-r** option, the network masks in the route entries are also displayed; this applies only to the **-r** option.
-s	Displays statistics for all protocols.

We have already discussed the use of the **netstat** command to display hosts' routing tables; now let us see how its usage relates to the network interfaces.

The **netstat -i[n]** should be used to check the status of all available network interfaces (the optional **n** determines the way to present the addresses, numerically or symbolically). An example (SunOS/Solaris) follows:

 # netstat -in

Name	*Mtu*	*Net/Dest*	*Address*	*Ipkts*	*Ierrs*	*Opkts*	*Oerrs*	*Collis*	*Queue*
le0	*1500*	*146.95.0.0*	*146.95.1.11*	*992048*	*0*	*96835*	*0*	*389*	*0*
lo0	*1536*	*127.0.0.0*	*127.0.0.1*	*36501*	*0*	*36501*	*0*	*0*	*0*

 # netstat -i

Name	*Mtu*	*Net/Dest*	*Address*	*Ipkts*	*Ierrs*	*Opkts*	*Oerrs*	*Collis*	*Queue*
le0	*1500*	*146.95.0.0*	*patsy*	*992092*	*0*	*96851*	*0*	*389*	*0*
lo0	*1536*	*loopback*	*localhost*	*36509*	*0*	*36509*	*0*	*0*	*0*

The displayed fields have the following meanings:

Field	Meaning
Name	The name field shows the actual name assigned to this interface. This is the name that identifies an interface when the **ifconfig** command is used. An asterisk (*) in this field indicates that the interface is not enabled (is not *up*).
Mtu	The maximum transmission unit field shows the longest frame (packet) that can be transmitted by the interface without fragmentation. The *Mtu* is displayed in bytes.
Net/Dest	The network/destination field shows the network or the destination host to which this interface provides access. This field contains a network address derived from the IP address of the interface and the subnet mask. If a point-to-point link is configured, this field contains a remote host address. If the symbolical address presentation is required, this field contains the corresponding name (when the name can be resolved from the address).
Address	The address field shows the IP address or the name assigned to this interface.
Ipkts	The input packets field shows how many packets this interface has received.
Ierrs	The input errors field shows how many damaged packets this interface has received.
Opkts	The output packets field shows how many packets were sent out by this interface.
Oerrs	The output errors field shows how many of the packets caused an error condition.
Collis	The collisions field shows how many Ethernet collisions were detected by this interface. Ethernet collisions are a normal condition typical for all CSMA/CD networks and are caused by traffic contention. This field is not applicable to non-Ethernet (non-CSMA/CD) interfaces.
Queue	The packets queued field shows how many packets are in the queue, waiting to be transmitted over this interface. Normally it is zero.

The example above is typical for almost any SunOS/Solaris workstation; two network interfaces are identified: *le0* and *lo0*:

le0 A lance Ethernet interface defined by a corresponding device statement in the kernel configuration file.
lo0 The loopback interface, which every TCP/IP system has, and which is mandatory, defined in the *kernel configuration file*. On most systems this is part of the default configuration, and is configured automatically.

The next example is for the HP-UX flavor. The command output is almost the same, with different names for the network interfaces:

$ netstat -in

Name	Mtu	Network	Address	Ipkts	Ierrs	Opkts	Oerrs	Coll
ni0*	0	none	none	0	0	0	0	0
ni1*	0	none	none	0	0	0	0	0
lo0	4608	127	127.0.0.1	2221	0	2221	0	0
lan0	1500	146.95	146.95.8.31	958064	36687	62446	0	4

$ netstat -i

Name	Mtu	Network	Address	Ipkts	Ierrs	Opkts	Oerrs	Coll
ni0*	0	none	none	0	0	0	0	0
ni1*	0	none	none	0	0	0	0	0
lo0	4608	loopback	localhost	2221	0	2221	0	0
lan0	1500	146.95	apollo.ph.	958118	36687	62462	0	4

The only difference is that the *queue* field is omitted (in any case, the normal value in this field is zero). Of course, names, addresses, and numbers have different values, *ni0* and *ni1* interfaces are disabled.

The **netstat** command is also instrumental in displaying the status of sockets. The display for each socket shows the local and remote addresses, the send and receive queue sizes (in bytes), the send and receive windows (in bytes), and the internal state of the protocol.

The symbolic format normally used to display socket addresses is either *hostname.port* when the name of the host is specified, or *network.port* if a socket address specifies a network but no specific host. If the network or hostname for an address is not known (or if the **-n** option is specified), the numerical network address is shown. Unspecified, or wildcard, addresses and ports appear as "*".

The possible state values for TCP sockets are as follows:

CLOSED	Closed, the socket is not being used.
LISTEN	Listening for incoming connections.
SYN_SENT	Actively trying to establish connection.
SYN_RECEIVED	Initial synchronization of the connection is under way.
ESTABLISHED	Connection has been established.
CLOSE_WAIT	Remote shutdown, waiting for the socket to close.
FIN_WAIT_1	Socket closed, shutting down connection.
CLOSING	Closed, then remote shutdown, awaiting acknowledgment.
LAST_ACK	Remote shutdown, then closed, awaiting acknowledgment.

FIN_WAIT_2	Socket closed, waiting for shutdown from remote.
TIME_WAIT	Wait after close for remote shutdown retransmission.

The following example illustrates the use of the **netstat** command for this purpose; the host name is "**garp**." Only active sockets are presented.

$ netstat -a

Active Internet connections (including servers)

Proto	Recv-Q	Send-Q	Local Address	Foreign Address	(state)
tcp	0	0	garp.690	delft.scps.com.32771	TIME_WAIT
tcp	0	0	garp.686	delft.scps.com.32771	TIME_WAIT
tcp	0	205	garp.telnet	ink2.spcs.com.1047	ESTABLISHED
tcp	0	0	garp.nprodsoc	garp.4108	ESTABLISHED
tcp	0	0	garp.4108	garp.nprodsoc	ESTABLISHED
tcp	0	0	garp.telnet	daloia.scps.com.1095	ESTABLISHED
tcp	0	0	garp.telnet	park.scps.com.1038	ESTABLISHED
tcp	0	0	*.printer	*.*	LISTEN
tcp	0	0	garp.nprodsoc	*.*	LISTEN
tcp	0	0	*.2458	*.*	LISTEN
tcp	0	0	*.*	*.*	CLOSED
tcp	0	0	*.querix	*.*	LISTEN
			.....		
			.....		

If no options, or only the **-n** option is specified, **netstat** displays the status of active sockets only.

15.5 Super Internet Server

15.5.1 The *inetd* Daemon

A huge number of different processes run on any UNIX system. Many of them are run continuously, and we usually identify them as daemons. Some daemons are configured into the kernel and are invoked with the kernel execution; others are explicitly started during the system startup through the corresponding initialization **rc** scripts. However, UNIX also provides one special daemon with the primary task of starting other daemons, or rather, other network server processes (because the started processes run as long as their services are required). This daemon is known as the super-daemon, or the super-server; its name is ***inetd***.

The basic idea behind the **inetd** daemon was this: instead of continuously running many network server processes as daemons, with each of them listening for incoming client requests for its service, run a single daemon which will listen for incoming client requests and invoke the corresponding network server process on an as-needed basis. The super-server **inetd** is started during the system startup; when started, **inetd** reads its configuration data from the */etc/inetd.conf* file to learn about the server processes it should support. Once started, **inetd** continues to listen for configured network services as long as the system lives, or until the super-server is reconfigured.

15.5.1.1 The *inetd* Configuration

Obviously, **inetd** requires a certain level of administration, although the default configuration seems to be sufficient in most cases. The **inetd** daemon is actually very flexible and easy to configure. Occasionally, an entry could be deleted or added into the configuration file */etc/inetd.conf* to remove or add a new service.

Here is an example of the ***inetd*** configuration file:

```
$ cat /etc/inetd.conf
## Configured using SAM by root on Mon Dec 13 22:17:00
##
# @(#)$Header: inetd.conf,v 1.20.193.2 bazavan Exp $
#
# Inetd reads its configuration information from this file upon execution
# and at some later time if it is reconfigured.
#
# A line in the configuration file has the following fields separated by
# tabs and/or spaces:
#
#   service name            as in /etc/services
#   socket type             either "stream" or "dgram"
#   protocol                as in /etc/protocols
#   wait/nowait             only applies to datagram sockets, stream
#                           sockets should specify nowait
#   user                    name of user as whom the server should run
#   server program          absolute pathname for the server inetd will execute
#   server program args.    arguments server program uses as they normally are
#                           starting with argv[0] which is the name of the server.
#
# See the inetd.conf(4) manual page for more information.
##
#          ARPA/Berkeley services
ftp        stream tcp nowait root /etc/ftpd ftpd -l
telnet     stream tcp nowait root /etc/telnetd telnetd
#
# Before uncommenting the "tftp" entry below, please make sure
# that you have a "tftp" user in /etc/passwd. If you don't
# have one, please consult the tftpd(1M) manual entry for
# information about setting up this service.
# tftp       dgram udp wait root /etc/tftpd tftpd
#bootps      dgram udp wait root /etc/bootpd bootpd
#finger      stream tcp nowait bin /etc/fingerd fingerd
login        stream tcp nowait root /etc/rlogind rlogind
shell        stream tcp nowait root /etc/remshd remshd
exec         stream tcp nowait root /etc/rexecd rexecd
#
#            Other HP-UX network services
printer      stream tcp nowait root /usr/lib/rlpdaemon rlpdaemon -i
#
#   inetd internal services
daytime      stream tcp nowait root internal
daytime      dgram udp nowait root internal
time         stream tcp nowait root internal
time         dgram udp nowait root internal
                       .....
#
#   rpc services, registered by inetd with portmap
#   Do not uncomment these unless your system is running portmap!
rpc stream tcp nowait    root  /usr/etc/rpc.rexd      100017  1    rpc.rexd
rpc dgram udp wait       root  /usr/etc/rpc.rstatd    100001  1–3  rpc.rstatd
                       .....
pop     stream tcp nowait    root  /usr/local/etc/popper popper
pop2    stream tcp nowait    root  /usr/local/etc/popper popper
                       .....
```

The generic format of an *inetd.conf* entry is:

name type protocol wait-status uid server arguments

The fields in the *inetd.conf* entry are:

Field	Meaning
name	The name of a service, as listed in the */etc/services* file.
type	The type of data delivery service used, also called socket type: *stream* The TCP byte stream delivery service. *dgram* The UDP packet (datagram) delivery service. *raw* The direct IP datagram service.
protocol	The name of a protocol, as listed in the */etc/protocols* file.
wait-status	The value for this field: *wait* **inetd** waits for the daemon to release the socket, before it begins to listen for more requests *nowait* **inetd** can immediately begin to listen for more requests on that socket Generally, datagram-type daemons require "*wait*," and stream-type daemons require "*nowait.*"
uid	The user name under which the daemon runs (usually *root*).
server	The full pathname of the daemon started by **inetd**. For some small services, the value of this field can be "*internal*," because it is more efficient for **inetd** to perform such services internally than to start an external daemon.
arguments	These are any command-line arguments that should be passed to the daemon when it is started.

When an entry is added into the */etc/inetd.conf* file, special attention should be paid that all entered data are well defined. Does the executable program of the added service reside in the specified path? Is the service name listed appropriately in the */etc/services* file? ***inetd*** must know precisely the port number for where to listen for incoming requests for a new service. The protocol name must also be listed appropriately in the */etc/protocols* file, etc.

Some of the entries in the presented */etc/inetd.conf* file are commented; obviously, the corresponding services are disabled. (There is no need to delete an entry, it is sufficient simply to comment the entry out). It is common to disable services that carry any potential security risk, for example: *tftp*, or *finger*. On some systems, even very popular applications such as *telnet* and *ftp* could be disabled.

15.5.2 Further Improvements and Development

The super-server ***inetd*** is fully utilized on every UNIX platform. However, many new network client/server applications bypass the super-server and provide their own self-running daemons on the server side. The main reasons are an unavoidable time-overhead in invoking the application through the ***inetd*** daemon and the possible overload of the super-server for very busy applications. The side effect was that ***inetd*** did not grow as expected (by "grow" it means the area of its responsibility), remaining more or less the same in size since it was introduced.

Another disadvantage with the original super-server is that ***inetd*** is supporting mostly old-fashioned applications (maybe a more appropriate term is *early UNIX applications*) that existed at the time when UNIX merged with TCP/IP network. Despite the fact that these applications are very useful and still widely in use, many of them are considered insecure and not usable in an open network environment. A quick look into a common ***inetd*** configuration shows that its entries range from old-fashioned insecure applications like Trivial File Transfer Protocol (disabled by default) via remote UNIX commands that are considered security risks, to the Telnet and FTP, which use clear text in password authentication. All together many security holes exist within supported network services. Currently it is not unusual to configure super-server ***inetd*** with almost all configuration entries in the */etc/inetd.conf* file commented out, i.e., disabled. Most of today's listed ***inetd*** services have more secure replacements based on mechanisms that carry less risk in implementation. They are also mostly ***inetd*** independent, like secure shell SSH and its derivatives scp, sftp, slogin etc.). Obviously, under these circumstances ***inetd*** is not busy at all.

However, often we need a specific "discriminated" application and we are ready to accept the security risk because of its usage. Modern UNIX flavors addressed this problem by introducing an additional layer known as "access control facility for Internet services" between ***inetd*** and the application itself. Instead of invoking an application directly, ***inetd*** invokes another "wrapper program" ***tcpd*** which provides additional checkup of received request, and then starts the application itself. The basic concept is quite simple — two files are assocoated with ***tcpd*** to configure a flexible checkup of eligible requests for specific services. Files */etc/hosts.allow* and */etc/hosts.deny* enable a selective approach to each of the listed services regarding the eligible hosts that requests are coming from. By default, everything is allowed (as "old good ***inetd*** " has done), but by modifying these files, different scenarios are possible. Obviously by restricting an access to the certain application only from certain hosts, the security risks could be dramatically reduced, while a needed service is provided.

This idea originates from Linux. However, the following example is from Solaris 2.8 (also known as Solaris 8). Several new (or better, modified) *inetd.conf* entries are presented in ***bold***:

```
$ cat /etc/inetd.conf
#
#ident "@(#)inetd.conf 1.44 SMI" /* SVr4.0 1.5 */
#
# Configuration file for inetd(1M). See inetd.conf(4).
#
        .....
        .....
# IPv6 and inetd.conf
# By specifying a <proto> value of tcp6 or udp6 for a service, inetd will
# pass the given daemon an AF_INET6 socket. The following daemons have
# been modified to be able to accept AF_INET6 sockets
#   ftp telnet shell login exec tftp finger printer
# and service connection requests coming from either IPv4 or IPv6-based
# transports. Such modified services do not normally require separate
# configuration lines for tcp or udp. For documentation on how to do this
# for other services, see the Solaris System Administration Guide.
#
# You must verify that a service supports IPv6 before specifying <proto> as
# tcp6 or udp6. Also, all inetd built-in commands (time, echo, discard,
# daytime, chargen) require the specification of <proto> as tcp6 or udp6
#
# The remote shell server (shell) and the remote execution server
# (exec) must have an entry for both the "tcp" and "tcp6" <proto> values.
#
# Ftp and telnet are standard Internet services.
#
ftp      stream  tcp6    nowait  root  /usr/sbin/ tcpd     in.ftpd
telnet   stream  tcp6    nowait  root  /usr/sbin/tcpd      in.telnetd
#
# Shell, login, exec, comsat and talk are BSD protocols.
shell    stream  tcp     nowait  root  /usr/sbin/tcpd      in.rshd
shell    stream  tcp6    nowait  root  /usr/sbin/tcpd      in.rshd
```

```
login    stream   tcp6     nowait   root   /usr/sbin/tcpd          in.rlogind
exec     stream   tcp      nowait   root   /usr/sbin/ tcpd         in.rexecd
exec     stream   tcp6     nowait   root   /usr/sbin/tcpd          in.rexecd
         .....
         .....
```

Besides the introduced ***/usr/sbin/tcpd*** program, some of the presented entries relay on IPv6 ***tcp6*** protocol which will most probably replace ***tcp*** in the future. However, tcp6 is not in any way related to our previous discussion. For better understanding of tcp6 protocol, please read the comments in the presented */etc/inetd.conf* file.

The following two files are very pertinent to our discussion; files ***hosts.allow*** and ***hosts.deny*** live in the */etc* directory and specify hosts granted or denied for certain service.

```
# cd /etc
# ls -l | grep "hosts.[ad]"
-rw-r--r--   1 root   other   90   Apr  6 20:00 hosts.allow
-rw-r--r--   1 root   other    9   Jan 25 23:44 hosts.deny

# cat hosts.allow
in.ftpd: 212.35.1.51
in.rshd: 212.35.71.97
in.rexecd: 212.35.71.97
in.rlogind: 212.35.71.97

# cat hosts.deny
ALL: ALL
```

In this example, all services are denied for all hosts, except:

- *FTP* for the host "212.35.1.51"
- *remote login, remote copy,* and *remsh* for the host "212.35.71.97"

A host can be identified by its host name or IP address.

15.5.2.1 Extended Super Server xinetd

Linux (Red Hat 7.0) introduced a new, more versatile "extended super-server" named ***xinetd***. The extended super-server is a powerful replacement for **inetd** — **xinetd** performs the same functions as **inetd**, except it is doing that in a better way. Among many improvements, **xinetd** has access control mechanisms, extensive logging capabilities, and the ability to make services available based on time and can place limits on the number of servers that can be started. Having all that in mind, it is realistic to expect that other UNIX flavors would follow Linux, and that **xinetd** will become a common daemon on UNIX platform in the future.

The extended super-server is also more flexible in its implementation. While the basic concept of the super-server configuration remained preserved, everything is organized in a more efficient way, making an overall configuration even easier. Individual configuration *inetd entries* are replaced with corresponding *xinetd files* that allow more detailed configuration specification. And on the top of the configuration hierarchy is the "master" configuration file */etc/xinetd.conf*. As the name ***xinetd*** resembles the old super-server, the same concept is in place for the configuration file. The new configuration syntax is slightly different and is adapted to new requirements, but it is also self-explanatory and easy to learn. In other words it is very easy to switch from the old super-server **inetd** and administer the extended super-server **xinetd**.

We will exercise the new configuration through an example on Linux 7.0 platform. The master configuration file is:

$ cat /etc/xinetd.conf

```
#
# Simple configuration file for xinetd
#
# Some defaults, and include /etc/xinetd.d/
defaults
{
   instances        = 60
   log_type         = SYSLOG authpriv
   log_on_success= HOST PID
   log_on_failure = HOST RECORD
}
includedir /etc/xinetd.d
```

The */etc/xinetd.conf* file defines global default values that could be overwritten in each individual configuration file if needed. However, the key directive is "*includedir*" which specifies the location of configuration files for all implemented services. By commenting-out the directive, all services could be disabled, and then even the daemon **xinetd** will exit. By simple move-in/move-out of the specific configuration file toward the listed directory, the corresponding service will be enabled or disabled. And finally, each configuration file provides additional space for tuning.

Let us see the contents of the directory in this specific case:

$ ls –l /etc/xinetd.d

```
total 12
drwxr-xr-x   2  root  root  1024  Jan 9    21:44  excludedir
-rw-r--r--   1  root  root   289  Oct 17   17:13  echo
-rw-r--r--   1  root  root   303  Oct 17   17:13  echo-udp
-rw-r--r--   1  root  root   361  Mar 22   23:29  rexec
-rw-r--r--   1  root  root   361  Jul 21   20:23  rlogin
-rw-r--r--   1  root  root   414  Jul 21   20:08  rsh
-rw-r--r--   1  root  root   321  Oct 17   17:13  time
-rw-r--r--   1  root  root   308  Oct 17   17:13  time-udp
```

Only listed services, i.e., services that have listed configuration files in this directory, are supported; and they are supported if they are explicitly enabled within the files themselves. Not-listed services are definitely disabled. However, to disable or enable a certain listed service, it is easier to move the "enabled" configuration file into the subdirectory *./ excludedir* (this subdirectory was created later, and its name is arbitrary), and back if we need the service again. In this example:

$ ls –l /etc/xinetd.d/excludedir

```
total 1
-rw-r--r--   1  root  root  289  Jul 18  20:07  telnet
```

Obviously, ***telnet*** is the service that we can expect to activate later. Instead of deleting its configuration file, it is moved from the *xinetd.d directory,* and it remains ready for any future use.

Finally, here is an example of how the configuration files look:

$ cat telnet

```
# default: on
# description: The telnet server serves telnet sessions; it uses \
#   unencrypted username/password pairs for authentication.
service telnet
{
   flags           = REUSE
   socket_type     = stream
   wait            = no
   user            = root
   server          = /usr/sbin/in.telnetd
   log_on_failure += USERID
   disable         = no
}
```

The listed entries within the configuration file are very comprehensive, and they actually correspond to the already existing fields in the *inetd entries*, except for new functional extensions introduced by the extended superserver **xinetd**.

16

Domain Name System

16.1 Naming Concepts

Once a kernel is configured for TCP/IP (the current UNIX default setting), the network interface is set properly, and the routing table is established, the system is ready for a network communication. A number of extremely useful network applications and services are available so that the system may benefit from the network configuration. In the past, UNIX considered networking an option; today, networking is an integral part of any UNIX installation. Networking and network-based applications are booming today; however, it is not realistic to expect each network service to be a default part of UNIX. The UNIX philosophy is to remain open to all newcomers, and, thanks to this concept and other related issues, UNIX is supporting networking very well. UNIX is actually the main supporting platform for most network services.

The significance of different network applications and services varies; some network services are *conditio sine qua non* for other network services, while other services are optional, and are used only by a very small segment of the UNIX community. Some network applications are important from an administration point of view, and we will refer to those network services as the *core network services*.

Core network services are usually an integral part of each modern UNIX installation, and we will focus on them. Among all the core network services, perhaps the most important one is the ***name service***.

16.1.1 Host Names and Addresses

Each UNIX system on the network is uniquely identified by at least one *IP address*, and this is sufficient for systems. The machines understand these addresses very well, and they communicate among themselves without any problem. In fact, they only understand the numerical IP addresses. However, it is not very convenient for users, who are human beings, to use numerical IP addresses (four not-logically related numbers), although there are no restrictions. For example, a user wishing to telnet to the host with IP address 128.124.128.14 can do that by entering the following command:

telnet 128.122.128.14

And it will work well.

But when a user wishes to telnet to many different hosts, it would be quite hard to remember all of the required IP addresses. Users are accustomed to using another identification mechanism, *names*, to identify someone or something. The *name service*, officially named ***Domain Name Service (DNS)***, also known as ***Domain Name System*** helps in implementing this mechanism in network communications. It is much easier for a user to establish the above telnet session using the following command:

telnet acf4.nyu.edu

And it will also work well.

DNS is basically a *distributed database of host information*, which, besides host names and IP addresses, also includes some other useful information about hosts on the network. DNS makes this information available to all hosts, i.e., all users, on the network whenever they need it. By keeping data consistent and updated, the DNS database prevents any ambiguities on the network.

16.1.2 Domain Name Service (DNS)

The development of DNS followed the development of the Internet itself. In the beginning, when the network (ARPANET at that time) was a small friendly community of a few hundred hosts, a centralized host database that consisted of a single file called *HOSTS.TXT* could contain all of the required information about the hosts on the network. The file held a *name-to-address mapping* for each host existing at that time and has been maintained by the *Network Information Center*. The data were distributed from a single host named ***SRI-NIC***. Every host updated its local host database, the */etc/hosts* file, from the centralized host database, by copying all data and deleting entries not attractive for that particular site. However, the centralized host database could not support the rapid network growth, and the scheme quickly became unworkable, mostly because of the following simple reasons:

- Network traffic and processor load at the host SRI-NIC became unbearable.
- Name collisions became very frequent (SRI-NIC did not have authority over host names, only over IP addressing, so anyone could add a host with a conflicting name and break the whole scheme).
- Maintaining consistency among the increasing number of hosts became a very difficult task (just imagine the job with the millions of hosts on the network today).

Clearly, a new approach was needed. In 1984 RFCs 882 and 883 were released, defining new *naming concepts* (done by Paul Mockapetris) based on the distributed DNS database. The structure of the DNS database is very similar to the structure of a UNIX filesystem. Each unit of data in the database is indexed by a name, which is a path in a large inverted tree called the ***domain name space*** (or *DNS space*), shown in Figure 16.1.

The tree can branch any number of ways at each intersection point, called a *node*. The top-level node is called the *root domain*, and it is null labeled " " (but it is written as a single dot "."). Each node can be labeled with a label up to 63 characters long (the dot, underscore, and space characters are not allowed). The ***full domain name*** of any node in the tree is the sequence of labels on the path from that node toward the root ("*up the tree*," which is opposite to the UNIX filesystem where the direction is "*down the tree*" since the root is at the bottom in UNIX, not at the top). The labels in the *full domain name* are separated by

dots. The *trailing dot* for root can be omitted. However, the *fully qualified domain name (FQDN)*, also called the *absolute domain name*, includes this trailing dot. The root domain name is represented as a single dot.

For example:

acf4.nyu.edu	Full domain name for the host ***acf4***
acf4.nyu.edu.	Fully-qualified domain name (absolute domain name) for the host ***acf4***
.	Root domain name

At first, this seems confusing: *full names* vs. *fully-qualified names*? In some ways it is confusing, but fortunately the different forms of names have no significant influence in real implementations. Both names identify the same host (node) uniquely; applications just treat them in slightly different ways. To make the use of domain names easier, applications permit the use of shorter name versions, usually relative to a default domain, which is then automatically appended by the application itself (of course, the default domain must be predefined). If the absolute name is implemented, there is no need to append anything; the absolute name determines the node's complete domain name.

DNS requires that sibling nodes (nodes that are children of the same parent node) be named uniquely (repeated names are not allowed). This restriction guarantees a domain name uniquely defines a single node in the domain tree. This is not a real limitation, since it is implied only on the sibling nodes, not among all nodes in the tree, and the sibling nodes are supposed to be under the same administration.

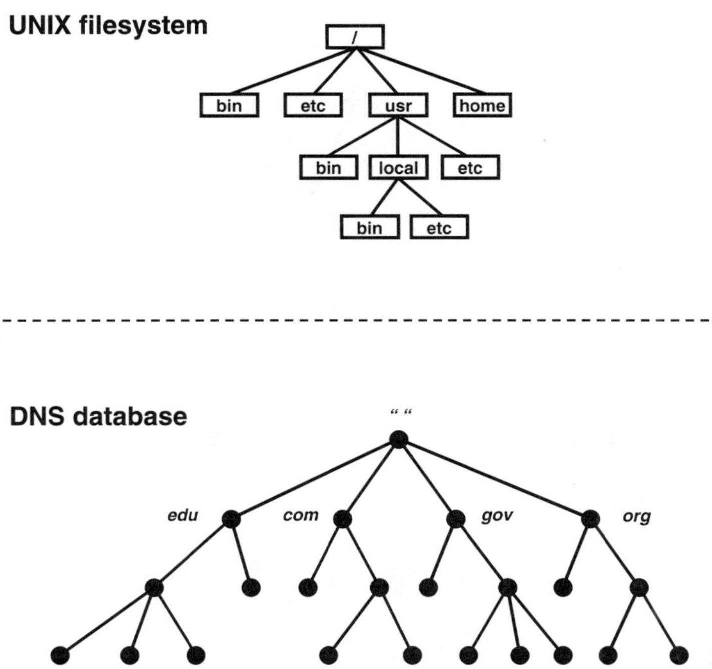

FIGURE 16.1
The structure of the DNS space.

16.1.2.1 Domains and Subdomains

A ***domain*** is simply a subtree of the domain name space. A domain's *domain name* is the same as the domain name of the starting (root) node of this subtree. This is presented in Figure 16.2. Any domain can be a part of another domain, and any domain name can be a part of another domain name, as well. Hosts are a part of the domain, too, but hosts are also domains; their domain names point to the individual hosts themselves. A domain contains all the hosts whose domain names are within this domain.

The hosts and the domain are related logically, often by organizational affiliation, and not necessarily by the location, network, or hardware type. Theoretically, hosts from the same domain can be located in different countries, or even continents; hosts' domain names are not even related to their IP addresses. In real life, though, relating the two is highly favorable and can make future administration much easier.

A domain inside the domain is often called a *subdomain*. Although a subdomain is a domain per se and can contain subdomains of its own, using this term makes it easier to explain the hierarchical structure of the domain name space (it recalls the relationship between a directory and subdirectories in the directory tree hierarchy).

The top-level domains are directly under the root domain. There are two basic types of top-level domains: *geographic* and *organizational*.

Geographic domains have been set aside for each country in the world and are identified by a two-letter code, for example:

- ***uk*** United Kingdom
- *ca* Canada
- *au* Australia
- *us* United States (this is actually rarely used for hosts within the United States)

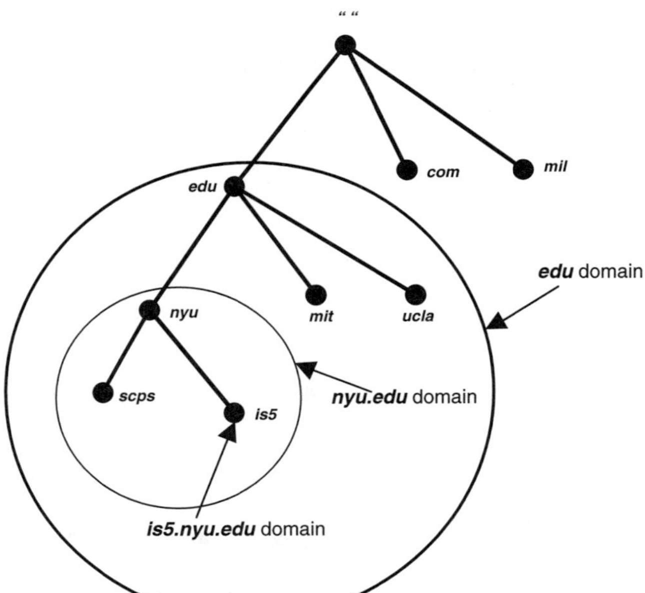

FIGURE 16.2
The domains.

The top-level domains within the United States are organizational, i.e., membership in a domain is based on the type of organization. The top-level domains belonging to this category are:

- ***com*** Commercial organizations
- ***edu*** Educational institutions
- ***gov*** Government agencies
- ***mil*** Military organizations
- ***net*** Network support organizations
- ***org*** Organizations that do not fit in any of the above, such as nonprofit organizations
- ***int*** International organizations
- ***info*** New, recently introduced top-level domain of general nature

The *Network Information Center (NIC)* had the authority to allocate domains. An official application to the NIC must be submitted to obtain a domain. The NIC's approval meant that a new domain is registered and it granted complete authority over the domain. Any *registered domain* had the authority to divide its domain into subdomains arbitrarily, without consulting the NIC. The decision to add additional subdomains is completely up to the local network administrator. Currently, NIC authority has moved to other organizations, but we will continue to refer to NIC as a central authorization body.

An address assignment is in some ways similar to a domain assignment. The NIC assigns a network address (or several addresses) corresponding to the domain, and the network administrator for the domain may assign subnet addresses and host addresses belonging to the assigned network. The NIC is the central authority that delegates power and distributes control over names and addresses to individual organizations. Once that authority has been delegated, the individual organization is responsible for managing the names and addresses it has been assigned.

The parallel between subnet and subdomain assignments is only verbal; subnets and subdomains must not be linked, although sometimes such links could make the administration easier. A subdomain may contain information about hosts from several different networks. Creating a new subnet does not require the creation of a new subdomain, and vice versa.

16.1.3 Host Database Files

The basic function of the name service is to enable the *host's domain name* to be mapped to its *IP address*, and in this way, to make inter-host communication possible. Independently of how the name service is organized for a particular site, the information must be stored somewhere, making a corresponding host database available to the host itself at any time. The corresponding *host database files* are also called ***host tables***.

16.1.3.1 The Local Host Table — */etc/hosts*

The local host table (the word *local* should be understood as internal; the data always refer to the network) is a simple text file that associates IP addresses with host names. This table is in the file */etc/hosts*. Each entry line in the host table has the following format:

ipaddress hostname aliases

where

ipaddress	IP address of the host
hostname	Domain name of the host
aliases	One or more aliases (alternative names) for this host

An example of the */etc/hosts* file is:

 # cat /etc/hosts

```
# ----------------------- /etc/hosts -----------------------
#
# Sun Host Database
#
# If the NIS is running, this file is only consulted when booting
#
127.0.0.1      localhost
146.98.1.15    default gateway
#
146.98.1.2     hcprophet
146.98.1.4     mvaxgr
146.98.1.11    patsy mailhost loghost
146.98.6.15    indigo1.ch indigo1
146.98.1.21    rs01-ch
146.98.1.22    rs02-ch
# . . .
# . . .
#
# Email relay (gateway)
128.228.1.2    cunyvm.cuny.edu ddn-gateway
#   Campus email relay
146.98.8.31    apollo.ph.myschool.scps.edu apollo.ph apollo
##
##   Other locations
146.98.2.71    everest
# . . .
# . . .
###
###   Other departments
146.98.1.111   mathsci
146.98.14.14   genectr.myschool.scps.edu genectr #rcmi smtp gateway
# . . .
# . . .
```

One entry assigns the address 127.0.0.1 to the host name *localhost*. As we already know, the class A network address 127 is reserved for the loopback network. This host address is a special address used to designate the loopback address of the local host. The special addressing convention allows the host to address itself in the same way as it addresses any remote host, using the same IP address on any host, which obviously makes the implemented software simpler. It also reduces network traffic because the local host address is associated with a loopback device that loops data back to the host before it is sent out to the network.

Although the local host table has been superseded by DNS, it is still required and used for the following reasons:

- All systems must have a small host table containing the name and address information of the host itself and sometimes of the important hosts on the local network. This table is used during the initial system startup, when DNS is not running (DNS is started in the last phase of the system startup). The */etc/hosts* file must include entries for the *host itself*, the *localhost*, the *gateways*, and depending on the implemented network services, the *servers* on the local network.

- Sites that use NIS (Network Information System) use the host table as input to the NIS host database. Even when NIS is used in conjunction with DNS, most NIS sites create a complete NIS host database that has an entry for every host on the network belonging to the NIS domain. The corresponding */etc/hosts* file must exist on the master NIS server.
- Very small sites sometimes use the host table. If there are few local hosts and there is no need to communicate with remote sites, then there is little advantage in using DNS.
- Some sites run old software that cannot use DNS; if they cannot be upgraded, these sites have to use the host table. For example, old SunOS versions did not support DNS if NIS was not running. In this case the */etc/hosts* file must be maintained.

An exception is Linux which eliminated a need for the */etc/hosts* file entirely. However, it is still recommended to maintain the file itself for a backward compatibility; Linux does not use the file */etc/hosts*, but still needs to get and keep host data somewhere; in Linux this is the file */etc/sysconfig/network*. Here is an example:

```
$> cat /etc/sysconfig/network
NETWORKING=yes
FORWARD_IPV4=false
HOSTNAME=broome
DOMAINNAME=scps.nyu.edu
GATEWAY=128.122.71.65
```

Presented domain data is related to the NIS domain (see Chapter 17 to learn about NIS); however, in this case DNS and NIS domain names match.

16.1.3.2 Aliases

Aliases provide alternate host names, alternate spellings, and shorter host names. They are painless solutions for host name changes.

They also fit well for such *generic host names*, as *loghost*, *mailhost*, *lprhost*, or *dumphost*. Some programs are written to direct their output to whichever host has been given a certain generic name. In this way, by assigning the appropriate generic host name as an alias, the output of such programs can be forwarded to any host on the network.

For example, *loghost* is a special host name used by the syslog daemon, ***syslogd***. Program **syslog** will direct its output to the host with the alias *loghost*; of course, in most cases this is the alias for the local host itself.

16.1.3.3 Maintaining the /etc/hosts File

Today, the local host database (the */etc/hosts* file) is almost obsolete. In the past, however, one of the most basic and frequently performed administrator's tasks was to maintain and update these data; it was crucial for proper network communication. The source host database provided by the NIC was, and still is, available, but before the data could be used they had to be transferred, selected, and stored appropriately, according to a very specific procedure.

16.1.3.3.1 *Handling the NIC Host Table — A Journey into the Past*

The Network Information Center (NIC) maintained a large table of Internet hosts called the *NIC host table*. The table was stored in the host **nic.ddn.mil** in the file *netinfo/hosts.txt*. Hosts included in the table are called *registered hosts*. Most of those host names are from the period when DNS was not yet implemented. Today the host table is changed only in special circumstances.

The NIC host table is no longer used for online host name IP address mapping, but some useful information about the registered hosts can still be obtained. Sometimes, especially when creating local configuration files, some of that information is sorely missed.

The NIC host table contains three types of entries: *network records*, *gateways records*, and *host records*. Each entry (i.e., each record) begins with a keyword that identifies the record type, followed by an IP address and one or more names, and some additional information. The format of the *netinfo/hosts.txt* records is shown in Figure 16.3. Some of the included information is no longer used.

The NIC *netinfo/hosts.txt* file can be retrieved interactively using FTP. However, on BSD systems the **gettable** command was specifically designed for this purpose. By using:

gettable nic.ddn.mil The large NIC host table would be transferred to the local host; this should be put in a temporary working directory (such as */tmp*).

The **htable** command should be used to convert NIC host table records into UNIX-compliant entries. Three files are then created: *hosts*, *networks*, and *gateways*. The **htable** command looked for three other files *localhosts*, *localnetworks*, and *localgateways*, which should have been previously edited to include the local data. If some of those files are missing, the **htable** command will create an empty related file. If they exist, the *NIC hosts.txt* data were appended to local data. The created files are very large and contain thousands of lines, so their practical use is questionable. Finally, the newly created files should be moved to the */etc* directory and the transferred *NIC hosts.txt* file and temporary working directory deleted.

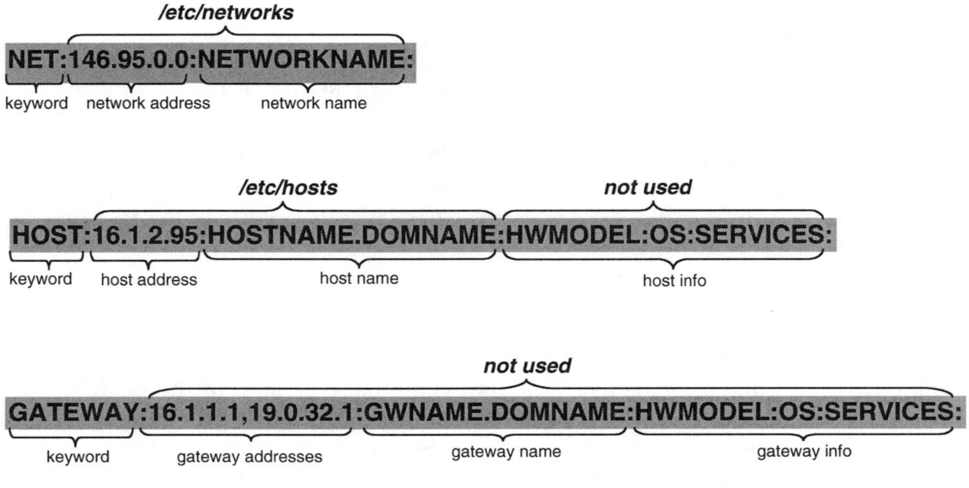

FIGURE 16.3
NIC netinfo/hosts.txt records.

The whole command sequence could be:

$ **cd /tmp**	
$ **mkdir hostsdir**	*# Create the /tmp/hostsdir directory.*
$ **cd hostdir**	*# Make /tmp/hostsdir the working directory.*
$ **vi localhosts**	*# Create local data.*
$ **vi localnetworks**	*# Create local data.*
	# The localgateways file can be ignored; the NIC hosts.txt file does not include data to update the /etc/gateways file.
$ **gettable nic.ddn.mil**	*# Transfer the NIC hosts.txt file.*
Connection to nic.ddn.mil	
Host table received	
Connection to nic.ddn.mil closed	
$ **htable hosts.txt**	*# Make the hosts and networks files, and empty the gateways file.*
Warning, no localgateways file	
$ **mv hosts /etc**	*# Move to the /etc/hosts file.*
$ **mv networks /etc**	*# Move to the /etc/networks file.*
$ **rm -R /tmp/hostsdir**	*# Delete the working directory /tmp/hostsdir.*

Most of the previously discussed issues are no longer current. The *gateway records* are ignored, and the *host records* are not needed because today DNS provides host name information. Only the *network records* still provide some kind of useful information. The */etc/networks* file is used to map network addresses to network names, so UNIX network-related commands and utilities can report in a more comprehensive and friendly way (for example, the **netstat -r** report will include network names instead of IP addresses). The file can be created from the *NIC hosts.txt* file, but this is a very time-consuming job.

NIC produced the file *netinfo/networks*.txt, which includes only *networks records*, in order to make the procedure faster. This file should be transferred via ***anonymous ftp*** from *nic.ddn.mil* into a local working directory, and then the command **htable networks.txt** should be used. The created files *hosts* and *gateways* should be discarded, and the file *networks* moved to the */etc* directory. If you ever decide to implement this painful and unnecessary procedure to transfer related data, you will learn very quickly how beneficial DNS really is.

16.2 UNIX Name Service — BIND

In UNIX, the *Berkeley Internet Name Domain (BIND)* software implements DNS. BIND is client/server software. The client side of BIND is called *resolver* — it generates the *recursive queries* for domain name information that are sent to the known *name server*. Recursive query means that the addressed name server must do everything in its power to deliver a finite answer to the resolver.

The *name server* is the program that stores information about the domain name space. In the distributed host database system, the name server generally has complete information about the part of the domain space called a *zone*. The zone is delegated to the name server, and it keeps so-called *authoritative data* about that part of the domain space. The resolver's query, however, can request data about the host outside of the server's zone. In that case the addressed name server itself must ask another server for the help. Inter-server communication continues until the positive answer is received or the time-out occurs.

Every queried server responds with *authoritative* data if they are within its zone, or with *nonauthoritative* data previously stored in its cache, or with some additional information that could lead to success more quickly.

Figure 16.4 illustrates that situation. In this example ***My resolver*** is looking for an arbitrary Internet host: ***zeus.olymp.ellada.org***. The starting point in this search presents a recursive query that ***My resolver*** is sending to known zone name server: ***ns.myschool.edu***. Obviously, it is hard to believe that the zone server, which is an authoritative name server for the resolver's zone only, would be able to respond immediately to the posted query. Nevertheless, the server will first check its cached data, and if there is no requested information cached, will continue its search by addressing one of the known root name server for help. With each step that follow, the queried server learns more, and finally it will reach an authoritative name server for the requested zone ***olymp.ellada.org*** that must respond positively to the query. A finite response doesn't always mean the host's IP address; it also could confirm that such a host doesn't exist at all.

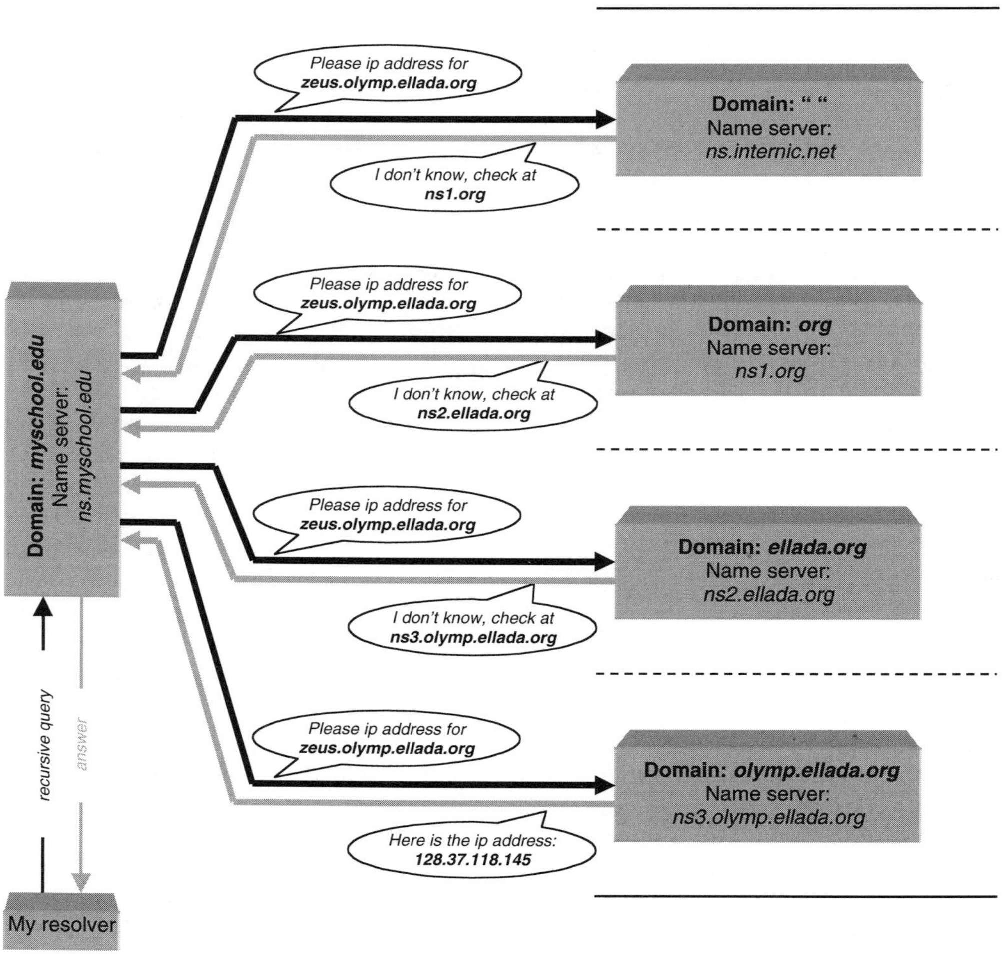

FIGURE 16.4
The sequence in the domain name resolution.

From the described procedure it is obvious that:

- A resolver must know at least one name server.
- A name server must know at least one root name server.
- A distributed host database must also include data about name servers for appropriate zones.

Data received (by a name server) about any host or name server out of its authority is stored locally (cached) for some time period (defined by the data's time-to-live argument — TTL is usually set to one day). The next time the same name resolution is queried, the appropriate cached data will be read locally almost immediately.

16.2.1 BIND Configuration

BIND can be configured to run in several different ways. The common BIND configurations are:

- Resolver-only systems
- Name servers:
  - Primary name servers
  - Secondary name servers
  - Special name servers, like caching-only servers, forwarders, etc.

16.2.2 Resolvers

A *resolver* is always present in a networked system. Locally, a resolver is responsible for domain name-to-address mapping. Any network application running on the system and requesting a name service addresses internally to the resolver. The BIND resolver is the "stub" resolver — the resolver is implemented as a library, and it is linked into the application itself.

The resolver sends a new recursive query to the name server, which means that the final answer is expected. Therefore, the resolver temporarily shifts its duty to the queried name server. The name server can be the local or external (remote) one. In principle, resolver-to-name server communication is independent of the name server's location, although local communication is much faster. If a name server is not running locally, we have the resolver-only system.

A resolver can be configured to address to several name servers (instead of only one); this is important if the name server is going down or cannot be reached by the resolver. In such cases, the resolver queries name servers sequentially until it succeeds. Once it sends a query, the resolver waits for an answer until time-out occurs. Then it retries with its query following the configured name server list.

The time-out period for each retry depends of the number of configured name servers; the basic algorithm is very simple:

- Up to four retries are provided.
- The initial time-out is 5 sec.
- For each retry, the time-out period is doubled and then divided by the number of the name servers.

In this way, the total time-out period is kept in essentially the same range and is independent of the number of name servers. An example for one, two, and three configured name servers is presented:

Retry	Name Servers Configured					
	1 Name Server	2 Name Servers		3 Name Servers		
		1st	2nd	1st	2nd	3rd
0	5s	5s	5s	5s	5s	5s
1	10s	5s	5s	3s	3s	3s
2	20s	10s	10s	6s	6s	6s
3	40s	20s	20s	13s	13s	13s
Total	*75s*	*80s*		*81s*		

16.2.2.1 Configuring a Resolver

Configuring the resolver is a relatively simple task. The resolver requires only a few parameters to be configured. The basic resolver parameters are:

- *name server IP address(es)* The *IP addresses of name servers* that resolvers may query; at least one name server must be defined. If more name servers are defined, they are queried in the order they appear in the file until the name resolution succeeds.
- *domain name* The default *domain name* which is automatically appended to the relative host domain name; in this way short host name versions inside the specified domain are allowed, and they are treated properly. Not only the specified domain name is appended, but also all derived domain name combinations (by excluding the leading subdomain, until the top-level domain is reached).

Some UNIX flavors eventually introduced other resolver parameters that made resolver configuration more powerful and flexible. Some of these parameters remained strictly flavor-specific; however, a number of them became standard in later BIND releases, supported by most UNIX flavors. They will be discussed later.

Some of the flavor specific directives are:

- *forwarder(s)* The *IP address of the forwarder(s)*, the caching-only server for the off-site host domain name service
- *hostorder* Specifies the order for the host name lookup between DNS, NIS, and the local */etc/hosts* file

There are two ways to handle resolver configuration: either use the *default configuration* or create a *custom configuration.*

The default resolver configuration involves slightly less overhead time because the resolver does not have to read a configuration file (a configuration file is read each time an application uses the resolver). However it can be used only if the name server daemon ***named*** is also running on the very same system. The default configuration assumes:

- The local host is used as the default name server.
- The default domain name is derived from the string returned by the **hostname** command, and then the leading subdomain (the part before first dot) is removed.

A *custom configuration* is mandatory if the system is not running the ***named*** daemon, or if the domain name cannot be derived from the **hostname** command. This is also the recommended resolver configuration even when previous conditions exist, because it enables every system to be configured in the optimal way.

The resolver configuration file is */etc/resolv.conf*; this is the text file, and it can be edited using any editor (for example vi). Any file modification is effective immediately, without any need for additional action. There is no corresponding resolver process (daemon); in that sense, this configuration file is processed directly each time the name service is requested. A few examples follow.

 # cat /etc/resolv.conf *for the resolver-only SunOS 4.1.3 system*

```
; ------------------------ /etc/resolv.conf --------------------------
;
domain          myschool.scps.edu
;
nameserver      146.98.1.12     ; pegasus.myschool.scps.edu
nameserver      146.98.1.17     ; orion.myschool.scps.edu
nameserver      128.228.1.10    ; acme.ucc.cuny.edu
;
```

 # cat /etc/resolv.conf *for name server SunOS 4.1.3 system*

```
; ------------------------ /etc/resolv.conf --------------------------
;
domain          myschool.scps.edu
;
nameserver      127.0.0.1       ; the host itself (localhost interface)
nameserver      146.98.1.12     ; pegasus.myschool.scps.edu
nameserver      128.228.1.10    ; acme.ucc.cuny.edu
;
```

 # cat /etc/resolv.conf *for the resolver-only IRIX system*

```
;
;Default domain to append to names
domain          myschool.scps.edu
;
;This is name server host
nameserver      146.98.1.12     ;pegasus.mys chool.scps.edu
nameserver      146.98.1.17     ;orion.mysch ool.scps.edu
nameserver      128.228.1.10    ;acme.ucc.c uny.edu
nameserver      147.225.1.2     ;nis.ans.net
;
hostresorder    local bind
```

Two universally supported entries are:

1. *nameserver* The name servers are queried in the order that they appear in the file. If the local host is one of the name servers, the generic local host address 127.0.0.1 is used.
2. *domain* The entry defines the default domain name to be appended to the relative host names (if specified without a trailing dot). The other domain name combinations are also queried.

The presented entry *hostorder* is UNIX flavor-specific, and is obsolete. In this example it defines the order of how the host names will be resolved: first by looking into the local */etc/hosts* configuration file and then using DNS (BIND). Although all new UNIX releases support this approach (name resolution among DNS, NIS, or the local host database), it is provided in a different way, by using the ***/etc/nsswitch.conf*** file (this is discussed in Chapter 17, along with other NIS issues).

Unfortunately, some BIND releases did not work properly on all UNIX platforms. For example, SunOS required that NIS be implemented, or it would ignore DNS. BIND 4.8.1 did not properly support local host address 127.0.0.1; appropriate patches were provided. Later BIND releases overcame these problems.

16.2.2.2 Other Resolver Parameters

Two basic resolver directives, *domain* and *nameserver*, are universally supported and are sufficient to fully configure the resolver. However, additional resolver parameters introduced later improved overall resolver characteristics, primarily by making it more flexible. The additional resolver parameters and the corresponding directives to specify them are:

- *search* — The list of the domain names to append to the relative host name, similar to the *domain* directive, except that it can take multiple domains as arguments; mutually exclusive with the *domain* directive (BIND 4.8.3 and later versions).
- *sortlist* — Specifies preferable resolver network numbers if multiple IP addresses are received as a response to a query. The resolver will sort received addresses appropriately, for example:

  sortlist 128.44.23.0/255.255.255.0

  specifies the subnetted class B network *128.44.23.0* (identified by the mask *255.255.255.0* separated by the slash "/"); if the whole network is specified there is no need for a mask (BIND 4.9.3 and later).
- *options ndots* — Specifies the number of dots "." an argument must have in it so that the resolver will look for it before applying the search list (BIND 4.9.3 and later).
- *options debug* — Turns on debugging output in the resolver (BIND 4.9.3 and later).
- *;* and # — Specify comment lines in the resolver configuration file; comments with # have been allowed since BIND 4.9.3.

The default search algorithm was also changed with the release of BIND 4.9.3; the domain directive specifies the default search list. The default search list originally included the default domain and each of its parent domains with two or more labels. For each relative host name (host name without a trailing dot), first a full domain is appended, then its parent domain, then the next parent domain, and so on until the last two labels. The single last label is never appended. The host name is looked up as is after the search list is applied, and then only if the host name contains at least one dot. A search is terminated as soon as a positive response to the resolver query has been obtained.

With BIND 4.9.3, the default search list includes only the default domain; in addition, the search list is applied after the host name is tried as is. Obviously, the search directive should be used for more detailed searching.

16.2.3 Name Servers

Several BIND configuration options exist for the name server software. The basic ones are discussed in the following paragraphs.

Primary name server — A *primary name server* is the authoritative source for all information about a specific domain, i.e., *zone*. It loads the domain information from locally maintained data files that are built by the network administrator. The zone file contains the most accurate information about a piece of the domain hierarchy over which this server has authority. This is the *master server* for its domain, because it can answer any related query with full authority.

Secondary name server — A *secondary name server* transfers a complete set of domain information from the *primary name server* and stores it as *local files*. This transfer is called a *zone file transfer*. This is also the *master server* for its domain; by strictly following a primary name server and keeping a complete copy of all domain information, the secondary server can answer queries about that domain with authority.

Caching-only name server — Name server software is running on the system, but no database is kept locally. It learns the answer to every name server query from some remote server and caches it locally. This means that a caching-only server only looks for external help the first time; after that it is ready to support with nonauthoritative answers. This self-learning procedure leads relatively quickly to the large local cached database. All name servers use cached information in this manner, but a *caching-only server* depends on this technique for all of its name server information.

Forwarder — The *forwarder* is a special type of caching-only server. A separate name server to resolve off-site host names can be configured to limit the off-site DNS traffic. In that case, all resolvers forward queries related to off-site hosts to this particular server, which then responds from its cached database, or continues alone to query other off-site servers. Soon a respectable off-site host database can be cached, enabling the on-site resolution of the off-site host names.

16.2.3.1 The *named* Daemon

Name server software consists of the name server daemon, ***named***, and a number of appropriate configuration files. A brief description of **named** follows:

named is the Internet domain name server. Resolver libraries use it to provide access to the Internet distributed naming database (Requests for Comments RFC 1034 and RFC 1035 are available for more details). The default configuration file is */etc/named.boot*, i.e., */etc/named.conf*. If the daemon is started with no arguments, **named** reads the default configuration file for any initial data; afterward, it continues to listen for queries on a privileged port.

The usual name for the program is *named*, though Sun systems (Solaris 2.x and SunOS 4.1.x) use the name *in.named* (which stands for *Internet name daemon*). We will discuss the name daemon **named** by primarily addressing the Solaris 2.x platform. This is a sufficiently general approach, and the possible differences among UNIX flavors are marginal.

The Solaris command to start the daemon is:

/usr/etc/in.named [-d *level*] [-p *port*] [[-b] *bootfile*]

where

-d *level*	Print debugging information; *level* is a number indicating the level of messages printed
-p *port*	Use *port* as the port number, rather than the standard port number
-b *bootfile*	Use *bootfile* as the configuration file instead of */etc/named.boot*

The main issue related to the **named** daemon is its configuration, more specifically the */etc/named.boot* file (this is the old name for the configuration file). We will talk about the **named** configuration later.

Besides the configuration file, other **named**-related files of interest are:

/etc/named.pid	The process ID
/var/tmp/named.run	Debug output
/var/tmp/named_dump.db	Dump of the name server's database

The **named** daemon is started during the system booting only if the system is configured as a name server (of any kind), i.e., it contains the basic name server configuration file */etc/named.boot*. The corresponding **rc** script sequence is:

```
if [ -f /usr/etc/in.named -a -f /etc/named.boot ]; then
        in.named;           echo -n 'named'
fi
```

Once the name server daemon is started, it writes its PID in the */etc/named.pid* file. Any later change in the name server configuration requires the daemon to be recycled. The easiest way to do that is:

 # kill -HUP 'cat /etc/named.pid'

The **named** daemon logs errors into the system log file (for SunOS/Solaris the */usr/adm/messages* file), so this file could be checked when any modification is made. Other log files can be used for debugging purposes (these were listed earlier). Once **named** is running properly, other utilities are available to make sure it is working correctly.

16.3 Configuring *named*

Configuring the **named** daemon is a complex task. The complete set of **named** configuration files contains:

/etc/named.boot

/etc/named.conf — This is the master DNS server configuration file. For a long time its name was *named.boot*, lately changed into the more appropriate name *named.conf* (since version 8). The file is crucial for **named** daemon configuration — practically everything is specified within this file. First, it specifies the name server type; then it sets **named** parameters and points to the sources of domain database information used by the server. The sources could be strictly local files (for the primary server), or transferred data from remote servers. Regardless of data origin, the names and locations of files where the data are kept are specified here.

named.hosts — The zone file that maps host names to IP addresses.

named.in-addr	The zone file for the reverse domain that maps IP addresses to host names.
named.local	The file used to locally resolve the loopback address.
named.cache	The file that points to the root domain servers.

Note: The names of the zone files could be different for some real system. They are always explicitly specified in /etc/named.boot (/etc/named.conf) file. Here listed names sound logical, but they are arbitrary and will be used in the text that follows for educational purposes only.

16.3.1 BIND Version 4.X.X

We will discuss **named** configuration by having in mind earlier BIND releases — up to version 4. Such an approach is sufficiently general, and all differences introduced by newer BIND releases (actually they start with version 8) will be completely covered in later sections.

16.3.1.1 The Configuration File /etc/named.boot

Let us start with an arbitrary example for the secondary server:

 # cat /etc/named.boot

```
;-----------------------------/etc/named.boot---------------------------
;
directory /var/named/xferd
;
;type         domain                    source host      file
;
secondary     myschool.scps.edu         146.98.1.12      named.hosts
secondary     98.146.in-addr.arpa       146.98.1.12      named.in-addr
primary       0.0.127.in-addr.arpa                       named.local
cache         .                                          named.cache
;
```

The file points the **named** daemon to all sources of DNS information. One of these sources is the remote primary name server; others are local files in the specified directory */var/named/xferd*. Some of the files, such as *named.hosts* and *named.in-addr,* should be transferred from the primary name server, while the files *named.local* and *named.cache* are the primary source of information and have to be created locally (a source host is not specified).

The possible *configuration directives* (*configuration statements*) in the configuration file *named.boot* are summarized hereafter; a number of appropriate arguments are assigned to each of the implemented configuration directives.

Directive	Function	Arguments
directory	Defines a directory for all subsequent file references	*A directory name*
primary	Declares the server as primary for the specified zone	*A domain name and a file name*
secondary	Declares the server as secondary for the specified zone	*A domain name, a primary server IP address, and a file name*
cache	Points to the cache file (root domain servers)	*"." (the root domain name) and a file name*
forwarders	Lists servers to which queries are forwarded	*A forwarder name*
slave	Forces the server to only use the forwarders	

Let us analyze the presented */etc/named.boot* file in greater detail. First, its existence ensures that the **named** daemon is invoked during the system startup, and the system is able to run the name service. The reference directory is */var/named/xferd*, and file paths in all other entries are appended to it. The specified directory name in the previous example could be an arbitrary one. However, in this example, which addresses a secondary name server, the specified name has a meaning — the directory */var/named/xferd* reminds us that the residing host database is actually transferred from the primary name server. The remaining content specifies the system as the secondary name server for the domain (zone) *myschool.scps.edu*. The host database should be transferred from the primary name server *146.98.1.12* and stored in the file */var/namedxferd/named.hosts* (as it is specified in the entries under the *secondary* and *directory* directives). It is also the secondary name server for the reverse domain *98.146.in-addr.arpa*, with the same primary server and stored data in the file */var/named/xferd/named.in-addr*. However, this server is the primary server for the *local loop zone*, and appropriate data could be found in the file */var/named/xferd/named.local*. Remember that this is the case with any name server; the primary source for local loop data is always the host itself. Finally, data about root name servers are written in the file */var/named/xferd/named.cache*.

The primary name server is configured in a similar way, but the entries under *secondary* directives are replaced with *primary* directives. The configuration file for the corresponding primary server could be:

 # cat /etc/named.boot

```
;----------------------------/etc/named.boot---------------------------
;
directory /var/named/zone
;
; type       domain                   source host     file
;
primary      myschoolrscps.edu                        named.hosts
primary      98.146.in-addr.arpa                      named.in-addr
primary      0.0.127.in-addr.arpa                     named.local
cache        .                                        named.cache
;
```

Even the names of the data files are the same; however, the referenced source directory is slightly renamed to reflect better the server's mission (again this is an arbitrary move). However, the appropriate data files *named.hosts* and *named.in-addr* for this zone must be created from scratch — simply they are the primary and the only authoritative source of information for these zones.

The same system can be the primary name server for certain zones, and the secondary name server for others (in some ways every secondary server works like this — it is the primary server for the reverse local loop domain). Obviously only one primary name server can exist for a zone, but there can be a number of secondary servers. The secondary name servers for the same zone communicate with the corresponding primary name server, keeping their databases updated. All communication issues are defined by the primary server for a zone and written in the header of the appropriate data file. A data file is automatically transferred to all secondary servers at the beginning, and when it has been modified (this is known as a zone-transfer).

16.3.1.2 Standard Resource Records

The previously discussed *named.boot* file is the configuration file for the **named** daemon. All other referred data files (*named.hosts, named.in-addr, named.local*, and *named.cache*) store domain name database information. They all have the same basic format and use the same type of records; those records are known as standard *resource records* (*RR*). BIND defines, in RFC 1033, the following RR types:

RR Text Name	RR Type	Function
Start of authority	SOA	Marks the beginning of a zone's data and defines parameters that affect the entire zone
Name server	NS	Identifies a domain's name server
Address	A	Converts a host name to an IP address
Pointer	PTR	Converts an IP address to a host name
Mail exchange	MX	Identifies where to deliver e-mail for a given host's domain name
Canonical name	CNAME	Defines an alias host name
Host information	HINFO	Describes a host's hardware and OS
Well-known services	WKS	Advertises host's network services

The format of a resource record is:

name ttl IN type data

where

name The name of DNS object the RR references; it can be an individual host, or an entire domain. The name is relative to the current domain unless it ends with a dot; if a name is omitted, the RR applies to the last named object.

ttl Time-to-live defines the length of time, in seconds, that the information in this RR should be kept in the cache. Usually it is omitted and the default minimal value set for the entire zone is applied.

IN An Internet class of the RR

type Identifies the RR type (according to the previous table)

data The information specific to the RR type:

SOA	A list of appropriate parameters for the zone
NS	A name server domain name
A	An IP address
PTR	A host domain name
CNAME	An alias host name
MX	A mail exchange host name
HINFO	Abbreviated hardware and OS descriptions
WKS	A list of implemented network services, etc.

16.3.1.3 The Resource Record Files

Individual RR files are discussed in more detail in this section.

16.3.1.3.1 The *named.hosts* File

The *named.hosts* file contains most of the domain information. This file converts host names to IP addresses. Obviously A records are prevailing, but the file also contains NS, MX, CNAME, and other records. This file only exists on the primary name server. All other servers get this information from the primary server.

The **named** configuration file points to this file, together with the domain for which the file contains authoritative data. The file *named.hosts* is presented in the following example:

```
# cat /var/named/named.hosts
; /var/named/named.hosts
;
; (for last update see the serial of the SOA record)
; ==================================================
; NAME        TTL     CLASS     TYPE      RDATA
; ==================================================
;
@                     IN        SOA       pegasus.myschool.scps.edu.sajhc.myschool. scps.edu. (
                      9906091             ; Serial - corresponds to update date
                      3600                ; Refresh every 1 hour
                      600                 ; Retry every 10 minutes
                      2419200             ; Expire after 4 weeks
                      86400 )             ; Default min. TTL value of 1 day
;
                      IN        NS        pegasus.myscool.scps.edu.
                      IN        NS        orion.myschool.scps.edu.
                      IN        NS        acme.ucc.cuny.edu.
                      IN        NS        nis.ans.net.
                      IN        NS        ns.ans.net.
                      IN        NS        cunixd.cc.columbia.edu.
;
; loopback
loopback              IN        A         127.0.0.1
localhost             IN        CNAME     loopback
;
; ***************************************
; ***************************************
; **          MY SCHOOL                **
; ***************************************
; ***************************************
;
$ORIGIN myschool.scps.edu.
pegasus     IN    A        146.98.1.12
            IN    HINFO    "Sun" "SunOS"
            IN    MX       10 pegasus
patsy       IN    A        146.98.1.11
            IN    HINFO    "Sparc1" "SunOS"
            IN    MX       10 patsy
mvaxgr      IN    A        146.98.1.4
            IN    HINFO    "VAX" "VMS"
            IN    MX       10 mvaxgr.myschool.scps.edu.
hcgate1     IN    A        146.98.1.15
            IN    HINFO    "CISCO" "MGS"
;       .....
;       .....
$ORIGIN ph.myschool.scps.edu.
; Physics and Astronomy
;
bjl         IN   A        146.98.8.11
            IN   HINFO    "PC" "DOS"
bjlnote     IN   A        146.98.8.22
            IN   HINFO    "ZNOTE" "DOS"
;       .....
        .....
```

The *named.hosts* file begins with an SOA record. The @ sign refers to the last previously defined domain (here, in the *named.boot* file), which is still the actual one. A few NS records follow, defining name servers for this domain. The rest are A records (predominantly), HINFO records, and MX records; other records could also be included.

The SOA record defines very important file parameters:

- *Serial number* of the file — every time the file is updated the serial should be increased
- *Refresh time* — the time period in seconds that secondary servers must query the primary server for possible changes (update) of the file
- *Retry time* — the time period in seconds that the secondary server must retry its query if the previous one did not succeed
- *Expire time* — the time period in seconds that the database is considered as the actual one after the primary name server has stopped running and does not respond to any query
- *Minimum TTL* — default time-to-live of records stored in the cache

It is extremely important to increase the serial number after any update of the *named.hosts* file. For secondary name servers, this is the only sign that the file has been updated. When querying the primary server, a secondary server actually checks the current serial of the file; after comparing this value with the serial of the file's copy that it already keeps, the decision about the file's transfer is made. Obviously any file update without a serial number increase is useless, because it will not be spread toward secondary servers.

It can be useful to implement the current date as the serial number for a current file update, in order to continue the increasing order of the sequence of serials. A serial is a 32-bit number (up to 4 billion), so even the full date is acceptable. An example is presented for the update done on May 23, 2000:

2000052302 (The last two digits are a daily version — the second version for this day)

16.3.1.3.2 The named.local File

The only purpose of the *named.local* file is to convert the IP address 127.0.0.1 (the loopback address) into the generic name *localhost*. This is the zone file for the reverse domain 0.0.127.in-addr.arpa. Because all systems use the same loopback address, this file is identical on every server. Also, every server has authority over its loopback address; every server is the primary server for its loopback address.

The *named.local* file is shown below:

 # cat /var/named/named.local

```
; ------------------------------ /var/named/named.local ------------------------------
;
@    IN    SOA    patsy.myschool.scps.edu.    sajhc.cunyvm.myschool.scps.edu. (
                  9704065      ; serial
                    10800      ; refresh every 3 hours
                     3600      ; retry every 1 hour
                  1209600      ; expire after 2 weeks
                    86400 )    ; default min. TTL value of 1 day
;
     IN    NS     pegasus.myschool.scps.edu.
1    IN    PTR    localhost.
;
```

16.3.1.3.3 The *named.cache* file

This is the cache initialization file for every server that maintains a cache of domain data; it contains the information needed to begin building such a domain when the name server starts. The *named.cache* file contains the names and addresses of the root servers. An example of *named.cache* file is presented:

 # cat /var/named/named.cache

```
; ------------------------------ /var/named/named.cache ------------------------------
;
; @(#)root.cache   1.15   (Berkeley)   89/09/18
;
.    99999999    IN    NS    NS.NIC.DDN.MIL.
     99999999    IN    NS    NS.NASA.GOV.
     99999999    IN    NS    TERP.UMD.EDU.
     99999999    IN    NS    KAVA.NISC.SRI.COM.
     99999999    IN    NS    AOS.ARL.ARMY.MIL.
     99999999    IN    NS    NIC.NORDU.NET.
     99999999    IN    NS    C.NYSER.NET.
     99999999    IN    NS    NS.INTERNIC.NET.
;
;
;
;
; Root domain servers adresses
;
NS.NIC.DDN.MIL.      99999999   IN   A   192.112.36.4
NS.NASA.GOV.         99999999   IN   A   128.102.16.10
                     99999999   IN   A   192.52.195.10
TERP.UMD.EDU.        99999999   IN   A   128.8.10.90
KAVA.NISC.SRI.COM.   99999999   IN   A   192.33.33.24
AOS.ARL.ARMY.MIL.    99999999   IN   A   128.63.4.82
                     99999999   IN   A   192.5.25.82
NIC.NORDU.NET.       99999999   IN   A   192.36.148.17
C.NYSER.NET.         99999999   IN   A   192.33.4.12
NS.INTERNIC.NET.     99999999   IN   A   198.41.0.4
;
```

The file contains only NS and A records. The root domain is indicated by a single dot. First, a set of NS records identifies the name servers for the root domain, and then a set of A records defines the IP addresses for those root name servers. Traditionally, TTL is set to the largest possible value 99999999 (the root servers are never removed from the cache).

Although the root name servers do not change often, it is recommended that you periodically check the accuracy of these data. An accurate list of root servers is available via *anonymous ftp* from NIC.DDN.MIL host, in the file *netinfo/root-servers.txt*.

16.3.1.3.4 The Reverse Domain File: *named.in-addr*

The *named.in-addr* file is very similar in structure to the *named.local* file. Both files translate IP addresses into host names, so both include PTR records. However, while *named.local* translates only one address, the loopback address, the *named.in-addr* file contains authoritative data for the entire zone. First, let us see what a reverse domain really is.

The **reverse domain** maps numeric IP addresses into host domain names; this is the reverse of the normal process, which converts domain names to IP addresses, so this is the origin of the name itself. To keep the same hierarchical naming concept, which is down-to-up, i.e., from the host name via the subnetwork and network to the top-level domain name, each host's IP address should be reversed. The only problem is that the reversed IP address of one host could be the IP address of another host. To ensure proper interpretation of the reversed IP address, the suffix IN-ADDR.ARPA is introduced. In this way a new top-level domain IN-ADDR.APRA is created, and this is the reverse domain. Any "IP address-like" domain name that belongs to the reverse domain (with the trailing ***in-addr.arpa*** name) represents the reverse IP address of a unique host. It can be uniquely translated only to the appropriate host domain name.

Here is an example of the reverse domain file *named.in-addr*:

 # cat /var/named/named.in-addr

```
;
; /var/named/named.in-addr
;
; (for last update see the serial of the SOA record)
; =========================================
; NAME      TTL     CLASS       TYPE      RDATA
; =========================================
;
@                   IN          SOA       pegasu s.myschool.scps.edu.sajhc.cunyvm.cuny.edu. (
                    9906191               ; Serial — correspons to update date
                    3600                  ; Refresh every 1 hour
                    600                   ; Retry every 10 minutes
                    2419200               ; Expire after 4 weeks
                    86400 )               ; Default min. TTL value of 1 day
;
                    IN          NS        pegasus.myschool.scps.edu.
                    IN          NS        orion.myschool.scps.edu.
                    IN          NS        acme.ucc.cuny.edu.
                    IN          NS        nis.ans.net.
                    IN          NS        ns.ans.net.
                    IN          NS        cunixd.cc.columbia.edu.
;
$ORIGIN 1.98.146.in-addr.arpa.
4                   IN          PTR       mvaxgr.myschool.scps.edu.
11                  IN          PTR       patsy.myschool.scps.edu.
12                  IN          PTR       pegasus.myschool.scps.edu.
15                  IN          PTR       hcgate1.school.scps.edu.
;        .....
;        .....
$ORIGIN 2.98.146.in-addr.arpa.
71                  IN          PTR       everest.school.scps.edu.
73                  IN          PTR       kilimanjaro.school.scps.edu.
;        .....
;        .....
$ORIGIN 8.98.146.in-addr.arpa.
11                  IN          PTR       bjl.ph.school.scps.edu.
22                  IN          PTR       bjlnote.ph.school.scps.edu.
;        .....
;        .....
```

The *named.in-addr* file in this example is the zone file for the *98.146.in-addr.arpa* domain. This file is created only on the primary name server (the same as for the *named.hosts* file) and then transferred to all secondary name servers. Like all zone files, it starts with the SOA record, with the @ sign in the named field as the reference to the current domain defined in the *named.boot* file, which points to this file as the zone file. The SOA record was explained when we discussed the *named.hosts* file.

The NS records follow the SOA record, just as in the *named.hosts* file. Other records are different; these are PTR records. The PTR records provide IP address-to-host name conversions.

16.3.2 BIND Version 8.X.X

In the previous text we discussed a number of DNS issues, keeping in mind earlier (but still prevailing) versions of BIND up to BIND 4.9.X; these versions we simply call BIND 4.X.X. However, the permanent development of network technologies has had an impact on DNS, too. The new 8.1.2 version of BIND has brought a number of significant changes in the DNS configuration (in some ways, the huge shift in the version number also reflected the level of the newly introduced changes).

First, the DNS configuration file */etc/named.boot* is renamed */etc/named.conf* — a logical change to follow the usual UNIX naming pattern for configuration files. The main change, though, was in the configuration file syntax, and we will briefly elaborate on these changes. It is also important to note that all changes are related only to the contents of the configuration file */etc/named.conf*; the corresponding DNS database files remain, at least for the moment, unchanged.

In BIND 4.X.X, comments in the configuration file were the same as in the database files — they started with a semicolon and finished at the end of the line. For example:

; This line is the comment

In BIND 8.X.X, three types of comments are applicable:

/ This line is the comment */*	C-style comments
// This line is the comment	C++-style comments
# This line is the comment	Shell-style comments

The old style comment (from BIND 4.X.X) that starts with a semicolon is no longer allowed; the meaning of the semicolon is completely different, as it is now used to end a configuration statement.

Now knowing how to distinguish comments from the configuration data, the BIND 8.X.X *named.conf* files for the already presented name servers (see the corresponding BIND 4.X.X *named.boot* files on the previous pages), now have the following contents.

For the secondary name server:

```
# cat /etc/named.conf
// ----------------------------/etc/named.conf---------------------------
// The BIND 4.X.X entry "directory /var/named/xferd" becomes
options {
   directory "/var/named/xferd";
   // Additional options could be placed here
};
// BIND 4.X.X entries of the type: "type   domain   source host   file"
// are specified with the following BIND 8.X.X entries
// The entry "secondary   myschool.scps.edu   146.98.1.12   named.hosts"
zone "myschool.scps.edu" in {
   type slave;
   file "named.hosts";
   masters { 146.98.1.12; };
};
```

```
// The entry "secondary   98.146.in-addr.arpa   146.98.1.12   named.in-addr"
zone "98.146.in-addr.arpa" in {
   type slave;
   file "named.in-addr";
   masters { 146.98.1.12; };
};
// The entry "primary   0.0.127.in-addr.arpa   named.local"
zone "0.0.127.in-addr.arpa" in {
   type master;
   file "named.local";
};
// The entry "cache   .   named.cache"
zone "." in {
   type hint;
   file "named.cache";
};
```

For the primary name server:

```
# cat /etc/named.conf
// ------------------------------/etc/named.conf----------------------------
// The BIND 4.X.X entry "directory /var/named/zone" becomes
options {
   directory "/var/named/zone";
   // Additional options could be placed here
};
// BIND 4.X.X entries of the type: "type   domain   source host   file"
// are specified with the following BIND 8.X.X entries
// The entry "primary   myschool.scps.edu   named.hosts"
zone "myschool.scps.edu" in {
   type master;
   file "named.hosts";
};
// The entry "primary   98.146.in-addr.arpa   named.in-addr"
zone "98.146.in-addr.arpa" in {
   type master;
   file "named.in-addr";
};
// The entry "primary   0.0.127.in-addr.arpa   named.local"
zone "0.0.127.in-addr.arpa" in {
   type master;
   file "named.local";
};
// The entry "cache   .   named.cache"
zone "." in {
   type hint;
   file "named.cache";
};
```

These two examples show how the previously specified BIND 4.X.X configuration entries are converted into new BIND 8.X.X configuration data. At the same time, full compatibility is preserved and all database files remain unchanged. However, BIND 8.X.X offers much more than a simple data syntax conversion; it has introduced a number of new configuration data that are making DNS more powerful and flexible in implementation. We will briefly list all BIND 8.X.X features; some of them are inherited from BIND 4.X.X.

BIND 8.X.X	Description
acl	Creates a named "address-match-list" that could be used in specifying options
include	Inserts the specified file at the point that the include statement is encountered
key	Defines a key ID which can be used in a server statement to associate an authentication method
logging	Defines the logging behavior
options	Sets up global options as:
directory pathname	To specify a referent starting location for other configuration data
named-xfer pathname	To specify a location of the transferred DNS database
dump-file pathname	To specify a file to dump data
pid-file pathname	To specify a file to store the PID of the **named** daemon
statistics-file pathname	To specify a file to dump statistics
auth-nxdomain yes/no	To control the authentication method
fake-iquery yes/no	To allow a fake name resolution
fetch-glue yes/no	To control a cache build-up
multiple-cnames yes/no	To allow an alias to be specified multiple times
notify yes/no	To control an automatic notifying of secondary name servers upon DNS database changes
recursion yes/no	To specify recursive or nonrecursive name server
forward only/first	To specify a forwarder-only name server
forwarders ip-addr; ip-addr;...	To forward off-site DNS queries to specified server/servers
check-names	To control the way a check of valid hostnames is provided: *(master/slave/response) (warn/fail/ignore)*
allow-query address-match-list	To restrict queries to certain IPaddress zones
allow-transfer address-match-list	To prevent unauthorized zone transfer
listen-on port address-match-list	To support "two name servers in one"
query-source address	To control the source of incoming queries: *(ip-addr/*) (port/*)*
max-transfer-time-in number	To limit the duration of a zone transfer
transfer-format	To control the format of zone transfers to improve efficiency: *(one-answer/many-answers)*
transfers-in number	To limit the total number of initiated zone transfers
transfer-per-ns number	To limit the number of zone transfers initiated per name server
coresize size-spec	To change the core size limit
datasize size-spec	To change the data segment size limit for the **named** daemon
files size-spec	To change the open files limit
stacksize size-spec	To change the stack segment limit for the **named** daemon
cleaning-interval number	To change the cleaning interval of staled entries (default 60 min)
interface-interval number	To change the interval of scanning internal host's network interfaces (default 60 min)
statistics-interval number	To change the frequency to dump statistics into the statistics file
topology address-match-list	To favor specified name servers on certain networks over others
server	Defines the characteristics to be associated with this name server (it overrides the options statement):
bogus yes/no	To prevent querying of a specific server
transfers number	To limit the total number of initiated zone transfers
transfer-format	To control the format of zone transfers to improve efficiency *(one-answer/many-answers)*
zone	Defines the zones maintained by the name server (it overrides the options statement):
domain-name	To specify a domain type: *(in/hs/hesoid/chaos), in* -> internet
type	To specify a zone authority: *(master/slave/stub/hint), master* -> primary, *slave* -> secondary, *hint* -> root zone "."
file pathname	To specify the name of the database file
masters (ip-addr; ip-addr; ...)	To specify the primary server/servers for the zone
check-names (warn/fail/ignore)	To control the way the check of valid host names is provided
allow-update address-match-list	To prevent unauthorized zone update

allow-transfer address-match-list	To prevent unauthorized zone transfer
max-transfer-time-in number	To limit the duration of a zone transfer
notify yes/no	To control the automatic notification of secondary name servers upon DNS database changes
also-notify (ip-addr; ip-addr;...)	To control the automatic notification of specified name servers upon DNS database changes

Some of the listed BIND 8.X.X features also existed in the BIND 4.X.X version; their configuration format is now changed. However, a majority of them are new and were introduced in the BIND 8.X.X version.

16.3.2.1 Subdomains and Parenting

Once a domain reaches a certain size, the need to distribute the management of parts of the domain to various organizational units can become a reality. This need could also exist for other, nontechnical requirements, primarily for business-related reasons. In that case, the domain would be divided into a certain number of "child" subdomains, and this procedure is known as *parenting*.

Good parenting involves a sensible delegation of the new subdomains to create new zones. A corresponding relationship between the name servers for the parent and child zones is also assumed. Simply put, each child zone must be advertised within the parent zone; otherwise, nobody will know there is a new child zone. The parent-child zone relationship is actually the core of DNS, and we already pointed to this requirement for a successful name service; everything starts from the root name servers that are the top-parents within DNS space.

This process is slightly easier to administer if the same administration team handles both the parent and child zones. However, if different organizations are involved, a certain level of coordination among them is required; otherwise parenting will fail.

We already know that there are basically two different types of zones: one for a hostname-to-IP address lookup, and one for a reverse IP address-to-hostname lookup (these are known as ***in-addr.arpa* zones**). The administration of the two zone types is independent. As a matter of fact, DNS will even function for most applications even if the *in-addr.arpa* zone is not set properly (many applications do not check hostnames for reverse IP addresses).

Generally, it is easier to administer the first zone type; there are no serious restrictions in handling them:

- There is no explicit limit in the number of participating hosts.
- The subdomain and host name rules are so flexible that it is easy to adapt to current parenting needs.
- Participating hosts can belong to different subnetworks (IP subdomains).

This is not the case with the second zone type, where:

- A restricted number of hosts could belong to the zone. For example, the *in-addr.arpa* zone for each Class C IP address can have up to 254 hosts (the address 0 identifies the network, and 255 is the broadcast address).
- There is not a lot of freedom in *in-addr.arpa* naming; practically everything is predefined.

- The hosts within certain *in-addr.arpa* zones can be split among different domains that belong to different organizations, and are administered by different people. It is very common today to assign only a portion of the available IP addresses within the network to a certain customer — this is basically how ISP organizations (Internet service providers) work.

While the same team usually administers the parenting and delegation of hostnames (which always means an easier coordination of required activities), it is almost a rule that someone else manages the parent *in-addr.arpa* zone (today this is usually your ISP). The consequence is that in real life, the hostnames-to-IP address administration is usually done satisfactorily, while the *in-addr.arpa* administration is trickier and can be more difficult. In the following text, we will focus on parenting from the standpoint of the *in-addr.arpa* administration and try to make this topic more clear through corresponding examples.

Originally, each *in-addr.arpa* zone covered one Class IP address; this also meant that the size and subnetting possibilities varied among the Class A, B, and C IP zones. Obviously, larger *in-addr.arpa* zones offer more possibilities for subnetting; they can be subnetted on an "octet" or "non-octet" boundary. Class C networks can be subnetted only on a non-octet boundary.

To subnet a Class B network on an octet boundary means to create Class C sized subnetworks, with a network mask 255.255.255.0, i.e., 24 network bits and 8 host bits. For example, the Class B network 146.98.0.0 (also identified as 146.95/16; the network IP address is left of the slash character, and the number of network bits is to the right) can be subnetted between the third and fourth octet of the IP address. Newly created subnetworks can be assigned to a different organizational unit (division, or department, or etc.). For example, one such subnetwork is 146.98.8.0 (alternatively identified as 146.98.8/8) and could be delegated to another DNS administration team for maintenance.

Subnetting on an octet boundary is easier to administer, because the corresponding *in-addr.arpa* zone can be uniquely identified in a condensed way; in the previous example, the zone "8.98.146.in-addr.arpa" uniquely identified all hosts within that subdomain. It is enough to advertise the new name server in the parent zone "98.146.in-addr.arpa" to delegate this zone to the new name server. The following entries in the parent zone specify new name servers ***ns1.ph.school.scps.edu***, and ***ns2.ph.school.scps.edu***:

8.98.146.in-addr.arpa 86400 IN NS ns1.ph.myschool.scps.edu.
8.98.146.in-addr.arpa 86400 IN NS ns2.ph.myschool.scps.edu.

This means that the authoritative answers for this zone can be obtained from the new name servers, and not from the name servers that handle the parent zone "98.146.in-addr.arpa." Of course, the new name servers must be set as a primary and a secondary server for the new zone; this situation assumes the appropriate setup of the configuration file *named.boot* (BIND 4.X.X), or *named.conf* (BIND 8.X.X) and the corresponding database file.

Subnetting on a non-octal boundary requires more administrative work, simply because we cannot specify all subnetted hosts within a single standard *in-addr.arpa* entry; subnetted hosts are now split among multiple *in-addr.arpa* zones and maintained by different name servers. The issue is how to extract certain hosts from the standard *in-addr.arpa* zone, put them into the new nonstandard *in-addr.arpa* zone, and delegate the DNS administration to the new name servers.

Let us suppose a Class C network 193.95.110.0 (alternately, 193.95.110/24) is subnetted in such a way that IP addresses in the range of 193.95.110.16 to 193.95.110.47 form a separate zone. The problem is that we cannot put these hosts in any widely known and understandable standard *in-addr.arpa* zone that will uniquely identify just those hosts, and then handle such a zone; the smallest *in-addr.arpa* zone corresponds to the Class C network, and we need only a portion of that. How do we provide an appropriate name service that will reflect the naming and maintenance by those who own and use the hosts in that address range?

Basically, there are three ways to solve this problem:

1. The first way is to leave the DNS administration within the parent zone and coordinate the subdomain DNS policy with the parent zone administration team; in practice this could be quite annoying, especially if frequent DNS changes are expected.
2. The second way is to delegate each *in-addr.arpa* name within this range in the parent zone to the new name servers. This works, but sometimes it can be a very time-consuming job. It means, in our example, to specify the following entries in the parent zone "*110.95.193.in-addr.arpa*":

   16.110.95.193.in-addr.arpa. 86400 IN NS ns1.unixadm.com.
   16.110.95.193.in-addr.arpa. 86400 IN NS ns2.unixadm.com.
   17.110.95.193.in-addr.arpa. 86400 IN NS ns1.unixadm.com.
   17.110.95.193.in-addr.arpa. 86400 IN NS ns2.unixadm.com.

   And so on for other *in-addr.arpa* names in the specified range until the last one…

   47.110.95.193.in-addr.arpa. 86400 IN NS ns1.unixadm.com.
   47.110.95.193.in-addr.arpa. 86400 IN NS ns2.unixadm.com.

   Besides that, the new name servers ***ns1.unixadm.com*** and ***ns2.unixadm.com*** must be set, and configured for each individual IP address listed in the parent zone.
3. The third way is the recommended one. The only way to group specified *in-addr.arpa* names into a new nonstandard *in-addr.arpa* zone is to make them aliases to the new *in-addr.arpa* names that belong to the new nonstandard *in-addr.arpa* zone. To accomplish this, the new *in-addr.arpa* names should be attached as canonical names to the existing ones. Once this is done, we can treat the new nonstandard *in-addr.arpa* zone as any other standard *in-addr.arpa* zone; the new zone can then be delegated to the new name servers.

In our example, we will introduce the new nonstandard *in-addr.arpa* zone "*16-47.110.95.193.in-addr.arpa*" and delegate to the new name servers ***ns1.unixadm.com.*** and ***ns2.unixadm.com.***:

16-47.110.95.193.in-addr.arpa. 86400 IN NS ns1.unixadm.com.
16-47.110.95.193.in-addr.arpa. 86400 IN NS ns2.unixadm.com.

Also, the new *in-addr.arpa* names that are parts of the newly introduced *in-addr.arpa* zone should be attached as canonical names:

16.110.95.193.in-addr.arpa. IN CNAME 16.16-47.110.95.193.in-addr.arpa.
17.110.95.193.in-addr.arpa. IN CNAME 17.16-47.110.95.193.in-addr.arpa.
18.110.95.193.in-addr.arpa. IN CNAME 18.16-47.110.95.193.in-addr.arpa.

.....

.....

47.110.95.193.in-addr.arpa. IN CNAME 47.16-47.110.95.193.in-addr.arpa.

The new name servers ***ns1.unixadm.com*** and ***ns2.unixadm.com*** must also be set; however, their configuration is quite standard, and the newly introduced zone *"16-47.110.95.193.in-addr.arpa"* is treated as any other standard *in-addr.arpa* zone.

The selected name for the new *in-addr.arpa* zone is arbitrary; it is recommended that it be a logical one, but this is not a requirement. However, the same name must be used in the parent zone and the new name servers.

16.4 Using *nslookup*

nslookup is a debugging tool provided as part of the BIND software package. It allows anyone to directly query name servers and retrieve any of the information known to the DNS. It is very helpful for determining if the servers are running correctly. A brief review of ***nslookup*** follows.

nslookup is a program to query Internet domain name servers. If a name server is not configured, ***nslookup*** uses NIS (if NIS is configured). Otherwise the local host table, **/etc/hosts**, is used.

nslookup has two modes: interactive and noninteractive. Interactive mode allows the user to query a name server for information about various hosts and domains, or to print a list of hosts in the domain. Noninteractive mode is used to query a name server for information about one host or domain.

The format of the ***nslookup*** command is:

nslookup *[-option ...] [-[server]]*

Interactive mode is entered in the following cases:

- No arguments are given
- The first argument is a hyphen (-). The optional second argument is a host name or Internet address of a name server.

Noninteractive mode is used when the name of the host to be looked up is given as the first argument. The optional second argument is a host name or Internet address of a name server.

Unfortunately, ***nslookup*** uses its own libraries, which are different from resolver libraries. This means that under some circumstances, a name resolution output could be different when using ***nslookup*** from the result when resolver is used. In other words, a testing of DNS could be successful, while the name service does not work properly.

16.4.1 The *nslookup* Interactive Mode

A number of ***nslookup*** subcommands are available in the interactive mode. When entering into the interactive mode, ***nslookup*** responds with information about the current default server and with the prompt (>). Subcommands can be interrupted at any time by using the interrupt character. To exit, type *Ctrl-D* (EOF) or type **exit**. To treat a built-in command as a host name, precede it with an escape character (\). An unrecognized subcommand is interpreted as a host name.

The most important subcommands are:

host** [server]* Look up information for ***host using the current default server or using *server* if specified. If ***host*** is an Internet address and the query type is A or PTR, the name of the host is returned. If ***host*** is a name and does not have a trailing period, one or more domains are appended to the name. Answers from a name server's cache are labeled "nonauthoritative."

server** domain* or ***lserver** domain* Change the default server to *domain*. ***lserver uses the initial server to look up information about *domain* while ***server*** uses the current default server.

root Changes the default server to the server for the root of the domain name space. The name of the root server can be changed with the **set root** command.

ls [*option*] domain [> *filename*] or ***ls*** [*option*] domain [>> *filename*] List the information available for *domain*, optionally creating or appending to *filename*. The default output contains host names and their Internet addresses. *option* can be one of the following:

Option	Meaning	
-t *querytype*	Lists all records of the specified type.	
-a	Lists aliases of hosts in the domain.	
-d	Lists all records for the domain.	
-h	Lists CPU and operating system information for the domain.	
-s	Lists well-known services of hosts in the domain.	
help or ***?***	Prints a brief summary of commands.	
exit	Exits the program.	
***set** keyword [= value]*	This command is used to change state information that affects the ***nslookups***. Valid keywords are:	
all	Prints the current values of the various options to **set**. Information about the current default server and host is also printed.	
class=value	Change the query class to one of:	
	IN	The Internet class (default)
	CHAOS	The Chaos class
	HESIOD	The MIT Athena, Hesiod class
	ANY	Wildcard (any of the above)
nodebug	Turn debugging mode on. More information is printed	
debug	about the packet sent to the server and the resulting answer (default = *nodebug*).	
nod2	Turn exhaustive debugging mode on. Essentially all fields	
d2	of every packet are printed (default = *nod2*).	
nodefname	If set, append the default domain name to a single-	
defname	component ***nslookup*** request (default = *defname*).	
domain=name	Change the default domain name to ***name***. The default domain name is appended to an ***nslookup*** request. (Default = value from hostname, */etc/resolv.conf* or *LOCALDOMAIN*).	
noignore	Ignore truncation errors (default = *noignore*).	
ignore		
type=value	Change the type of information returned from a query to:	
querytype=value	**A**	Host's Internet address
	CNAME	Canonical name for an alias
	HINFO	Host CPU and operating system type
	MX	Mail exchanger
	NS	Name server for the named zone
	PTR	Host name if the query is an Internet address, otherwise the pointer to other information
	SOA	Start of authority record
	TXT	Text information
	WKS	Well-known service description
	ANY	All types of data

port=value	Change the default TCP/UDP name server port to *value* (default = *53*).
norecurse *recurse*	Tell the name server to query other servers if it does not have the information (default = *recurse*).
retry=number	Set the number of retries to *number*. When a reply to a request is not received within a certain amount of time (which can be changed with **set timeout**), the timeout period is doubled and the request is re-sent. The retry value controls how many times a request is re-sent before giving up (default = *4*).
root=host	Change the name of the root server to *host*. This affects the **root** command (default = *ns.nic.ddn.mil*).
nosearch *search*	If the ***nslookup*** request contains at least one period but does not end with a trailing period, append the domain names in the domain search list to the request until an answer is received (default = *search*).
srchlist=name1/name2/	Change the default domain name to *name1* and the *do-main search list* to *name1*, *name2*, etc. A maximum of six names separated by slashes (/) can be specified.
timeout=number	Change the initial timeout interval for waiting for a reply to *number* seconds. Each retry doubles the timeout period (default = *5 seconds*).

If the lookup request was not successful, an error message is printed. Possible errors are:

Time-out	The server did not respond to a request after a certain amount of time.
No response from server	No name server is running on the server machine.
No records	The server does not have resource records of the current query type for the host, although the host name is valid.
Nonexistent domain	The host or domain name does not exist.
Connection refused	Connection was refused.
Network is unreachable	The connection to the name server could not be made at the present time.
Server failure	The name server found an internal inconsistency in its database and could not return a valid answer.
Refused	The name server refused to service the request.
Format error	The name server found that the request packet was not in the proper format.

16.4.2 A Few Examples of *nslookup* Usage

Let us see a few examples. The default domain is ***myschool.scps.edu*** and it is determined by the */etc/resolve.conf* file on the host that provided the lookup. The first name server defined in this very same file is ***pegasus.myschool.scps.edu***, which is the primary name server for this domain.

$ **nslookup**

Default Name Server: pegasus.myschool.scps.edu ***# The default data type is A.***

Address: 146.98.1.12

> **patsy** ***# Look up the host's address.***

Name Server: pegasus.myschool.scps.edu

Address: 146.98.1.12

Name: patsy.myschool.scps.edu

Address: 146.98.1.11

```
> apollo.ph                                    # Look up the host's address.
Name Server:   pegasus.myschool.scps.edu
Address:   146.98.1.12
Name:   apollo.ph.myschool.scps.edu
Address:   146.98.8.31
> apollo.ph.                                   # Look up the host's address.
Name Server:   pegasus.myschool.scps.edu       # (absolute host's name)
Address:   146.98.1.12
*** pegasus.myschool.scps.edu can't find apollo.ph.: Non-existent domain
>set type=ptr                                  # Shift to another data type (PTR).
> 146.98.8.31                                  # Look up the host's name.
Name Server:   pegasus.myschool.scps.edu
Address:   146.98.1.12
31.8.98.146.in-addr.arpa    name = apollo.ph.myschool.scps.edu
>set type=ns                                   # Shift to another data type (NS).
>myschool                                      # Look up the domain name servers.
Name Server:   pegasus.myschool.scps.edu
Address:   146.98.1.12
myschool.scps.edu           nameserver = pegasus.myschool.scps.edu
myschool.scps.edu           nameserver = orion.myschool.scps.edu
myschool.scps.edu           nameserver = acme.ucc.cuny.edu
myschool.scps.edu           nameserver = nis.ans.net
myschool.scps.edu           nameserver = ns.ans.net
myschool.scps.edu           nameserver = cunixd.cc.columbia.edu
pegasus.myschool.scps.edu   internet address = 146.98.1.12
orion.myschool.scps.edu     internet address = 146.98.1.17
acme.ucc.cuny.edu           internet address = 128.228.1.10
nis.ans.net                 internet address = 147.225.1.10
ns.ans.net                  internet address = 192.103.63.100
cunixd.cc.columbia.edu      internet address = 128.59.40.142
>set type=soa                                  # Shift to another data type (SOA).
>myschool                                      # Look up the zone SOA record.
Name Server:   pegasus.myschool.scps.edu
Address:146.98.1.12
myschool.scps.edu
   origin = pegasus.myschool.scps.edu
   mail addr = sajhc.cunyvm.cuny.edu
   serial = 9406091
   refresh = 3600 (1 hour)
   retry = 600 (10 min)
   expire = 2419200 (28 days)
```

```
   minimum ttl = 86400 (1 day)
>server orion                               # Shift to another name server.
Name Server:   orion.myschool.scps.edu      # The data type is SOA.
Address:   146.98.1.17
> myschool                                  # Look up the zone SOA record.
Name Server:   orion.myschool.scps.edu
Address:   146.98.1.17
myschool.scps.edu
   origin = pegasus.myschool.scps.edu
   mail addr = sajhc.cunyvm.cuny.edu
   serial = 9406091
   refresh = 3600 (1 hour)
   retry = 600 (10 min)
   expire = 2419200 (28 days)
   minimum ttl = 86400 (1 day)
>exit   (or Ctrl-D)
$
```

A great deal of very useful information can be obtained with the ***nslookup*** utility, such as hosts' names, IP addresses, a list of name servers for domains, etc. The last two lookups of the zone SOA records for ***myschool.scps.edu*** domain are especially interesting. The host ***pegasus.myschool.scps.edu*** is declared the primary name server for this domain, and the host ***orion.myschool.scps.edu*** the secondary name server. Identical serial numbers in both SOA records indicate that the host databases in the name servers are equals, i.e., the secondary name server ***orion*** follows the primary name server ***pegasus***.

nslookup can be used in many other ways to look up DNS data, as well as to perform very sophisticated debugging.

17

Network Information Service (NIS)

17.1 Purpose and Concepts

Networking has led to the introduction of an enormous number of different network applications, which in turn has brought new qualities to computer use. The single host environment has been replaced by multiple hosts, which offer their resources to users and create an almost unrestricted working environment. However to make and maintain such a working environment, a certain level of administration is required; otherwise, everything becomes useless.

Multiple hosts in the network present multiple administrative points and require more attention and work to be provided. Can you imagine the network with several hundred computers in it and a new user account to be opened on each of them; or maybe a deletion or modification?

The ***Network Information Service** (or **System**) - **NIS***, initially known as the *Yellow Pages*, is an administrative database that enables a central control over a group of hosts (computers) that belong to the same, so-called ***NIS domain***. NIS converts important administrative files into a database that can be queried over the network. This ensures that all hosts in the NIS domain have access to the very same administrative databases, which can then be centrally maintained. In NIS terminology, the databases are called ***NIS maps***; they are all created at the single host, the ***NIS master server***, and made accessible through the network to all hosts in the NIS domain — the ***NIS clients***. Any modification of an administrative file at the NIS master server can be easily transferred to an NIS map, and immediately made transparent to all other hosts. Since the number of NIS hosts could be very large, the benefit of a centralized administration is obvious: instead of repeating the same administrative task dozens, or even hundreds, of times, everything has to be done only once. The consistency of the data is guaranteed and achieved in an optimal way. In addition, a sufficient flexibility in administering individual hosts is preserved; NIS enables a selective approach to all administrative issues.

NIS is Sun Microsystems' "baby," and it was a very successful product, first implemented on the SunOS platform. Despite some inherent security problems, other UNIX vendors quickly adopted NIS. Today NIS is a standard part of any UNIX installation. Sun Microsystems later released a new version of the Network Information System, known as ***NIS+***. This was a new product for the same purpose, but definitely a different software package. The basic idea has been to improve the older product with the preserved compatibility. Unfortunately things do not always happen as expected. The new product has not been so successful, and Solaris is practically the only UNIX flavor that implemented it. Neither of the main UNIX players followed this path. Chances for some future comeback of NIS+ are also cumbersome. Today it seems that another product, ***LDAP***, is the most serious candidate to replace NIS.

LDAP stands for *Lightweight Directory Access Protocol* and presents a project to provide global directory services over the Internet in an easier way. The idea is to obtain different types of information from distributed databases spread all over the Internet (like e-mail addresses, phone numbers, etc.). Each "individual" LDAP server would manage its own database about its own community. Individual servers will then be hierarchically merged, making needed information accessible worldwide. The concept of LDAP is quite close to the DNS concept; this is not strange, bearing in mind their similarities and the fact that DNS has been going on so successfully for quite a long time. LDAP was specified in the RFC-1777. LDAP mechanisms could also be used to distribute administrative data, of course in a slightly more restrictive way. The existing RFC-2307 with the title "*An Approach for Using LDAP as a Network Information Service*" indicates such a tendency.

This chapter will focus strictly on NIS. An NIS domain contains a selected number of hosts, and it is built on the ***client-server model***. An NIS server is a host that contains NIS maps; NIS clients are hosts that query information from these maps. Servers are further divided into ***master*** and ***slave*** servers. The master server is the true single owner of the databases, and the only one responsible for their modification and distribution to the slave servers — this process is known as *pushing NIS maps*. Slave servers are optional. All NIS servers, master and slave, are equal in providing NIS service to individual NIS clients. They keep the same administrative data, and a client simply addresses the closest server, whatever this server is, with a query for the needed data (an NIS map).

The client-server model does not mean a strict division of hosts to the exclusive client-hosts versus server-hosts. The model is intended to separate client and server processes that could communicate through the network, but also locally; the client and a server process can run on the same host. This is a usual pattern for almost all network services, including NIS. Although the server-only NIS host is possible, it happens very rarely; usually the NIS client process is also running on the same host. However, NIS client-only hosts are very common and they represent a majority of the hosts in an NIS domain.

Each individual NIS host must be configured appropriately for the NIS service; once this is done, all future centralized administration is performed through the NIS master server. The needed flexibility in NIS can be achieved at the client side by a selective adjustment of the client-specific exceptions. The local administrative data on each NIS client could be fully replaced with the NIS maps, but the maps can also be appended to the local data. In that case, a client first looks up local data and then queries an NIS server for the information.

With the distinction between NIS servers and clients firmly established, each UNIX system fits into the NIS scheme in one of the following ways:

- *Client only* — Generally the most common NIS configuration, typical for any UNIX hosts whether it is a desktop workstation or a powerful server of any kind. An NIS client queries an NIS server for needed information and correspondingly receives queried information.
- *Server only* — The host that handles client NIS queries, but it does not use NIS for its own operations. It can be useful when a server has to provide global information (like password data or similar) to a number of NIS clients, but

security concerns prohibit the server from using these same data. Server-only configuration is extremely rare and it is not recommended.

- *Client and server* — The same host functions as an NIS server and as an NIS client; its management is streamlined with that of other client-only hosts.

An NIS domain is presented in Figure 17.1.

NIS provides the concept of ***domain*** to allow an administrator to set different policies for different UNIX hosts. Actually a domain is a set of NIS maps, and the maps enforce a certain administrative policy. In principle, a client can belong to several different domains and refer toward any map from any of those domains. However in real life this is not a frequent case — mostly a host looks up data from one set of NIS maps, i.e., UNIX host is assigned to a single "default NIS domain."

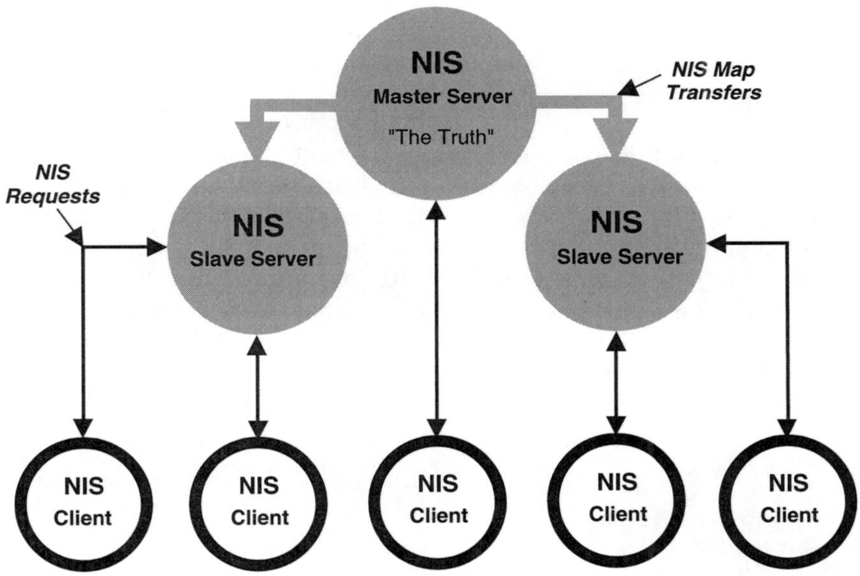

FIGURE 17.1
An NIS domain: NIS master, slaves, and clients. Note: The Network Information Service (NIS) was formerly known as *Sun Yellow Pages* (*YP*). The functionality of the two remains the same; only the name has changed. The name *Yellow Pages* is a registered trademark in the United Kingdom of British Telecommunications plc, and may not be used without permission.

17.2 NIS Paradigm

This section will address the main aspects of NIS: processes that make NIS operational, main NIS players (servers and clients), and NIS domain and databases. NIS is extremely useful and helpful in UNIX administration. For UNIX users it is completely transparent and invisible.

17.2.1 *yp* Processes

Let us see how to put an NIS host into motion. Basic NIS management involves setting NIS on the servers and enabling NIS on the client hosts. Enabling is always an easy job, while setting requires more skills. The server setting includes three main steps:

1. Set a new NIS environment and identify the master and slave servers.
2. Start the ***ypserv*** daemon, which makes a system act as an NIS server.
3. Add new slave servers when the growth of the NIS domain reaches a point of needing more server bandwidth.

Enabling an NIS client requires two main steps:

1. Adapt the client's administrative files to the NIS environment so the client can benefit from NIS.
2. Start the ***ypbind*** daemon, which allows the client to make NIS queries from the "chosen" server. The algorithm to choose a server is trivial: the client sends a broadcast query for available servers and bind to the first one that has responded to the query. The established relationship remains valid as long as the NIS communication between two hosts exists.

Two basic ***yp*** *daemons* define NIS activities on the host (the prefix ***yp*** originates from the initial name for the service *yellow pages*, which was later changed to NIS). The ***ypserv*** daemon runs on an NIS server, the ***ypbind*** daemon runs on an NIS client, and both daemons run on an NIS server-and-client host. The daemons must be started during the system startup (booting) if other required conditions are fulfilled. They can be invoked manually from the command line also, but the manual start is supposed only the first time upon the NIS installation and during the testing.

A typical **rc** startup sequence for the NIS looks like:

```
   .....
dname = `domainname`
if ["$dname" -a -d /var/yp ]; then
   echo "NIS domainname is $dname"
   echo -n "starting NIS services:"
   if [ -f /usr/etc/ypserv -a -d /var/yp/$dname ]; then
       ypserv;   echo -n 'ypserv'
       # Master NIS server runs the XFR daemon
       # otherwise should be commented-out
       ypxfrd;   echo -n 'ypxfrd'
   fi
   .....
   # NIS client runs the YPBIND daemon (most common case)
   # otherwise should be commented-out (very rare case)
   ypbind; echo -n 'ypbind'
   .....
fi
```

What are the requirements to start the **yp** daemons? First, this is the defined NIS domain, which is easily tested in the first line; the command ***domainname*** will return the name of the NIS domain and set the variable *$dname* appropriately. The following *if statement* provides the rest if the host belongs to the NIS domain. The daemons **ypserv** and **ypxfrd** will be invoked only if the NIS-related directory */var/yp/$dname* exists —

this is the directory where the NIS database is kept (the existence of NIS database indicates the role of the host as an NIS server). Otherwise, the host is NIS client-only and the client daemon ***ypbind*** is started. By commenting certain lines in the **rc** script, it is possible to adjust the startup sequence for the master server, as well as a server-only host.

The **ypserv** is the NIS server daemon and it is running on every server-host; the **ypxfrd** daemon enables a push of NIS maps from the master server to slave servers and it runs on the master server. NIS maps should be pushed from the master server to slave servers always when changes occur; otherwise changes will not be properly propagated through NIS domain. A periodic pushing could also be scheduled through the ***cron*** facility independently of the actual map changes. However, to overcome any possible gap between two scheduled map transfers and changes of those maps, it is a good idea to push updated NIS maps from master to slave servers immediately upon their modification. NIS software supports such an approach and provides the needed tool for that purpose; it is based on the standard UNIX ***make*** utility and the provided description file */var/yp/Makefile* that could be easily customized for specific server's needs. We will return to this topic later.

17.2.2 To Create an NIS Server

The presented *rc* startup procedure assumes the NIS domain was already set, independently of the nature of the host itself. However, the procedure to set NIS for the first time is slightly different. An NIS master server should be created first, then NIS slave servers, and finally NIS clients. Pay attention that only one master server for the NIS domain can exist. So let us start with the NIS master server. We will follow the creation procedure performed from the command line:

17.2.2.1 Set the NIS domain

Execute the **domainname** command, with the name of the NIS domain as its argument:

domainname ***NISdomain***

where

NISdomain should be an actual name of the NIS domain.

17.2.2.2 Set the Master Server

Execute the command:

/full-pathname/ypinit -m

The **ypinit** command is not in the usual command search path (for the obvious reason of preventing its accidental execution), so the full command pathname must be specified. Depending on the UNIX flavor, the common directories where the command lives are */usr/etc/yp* or */usr/sbin*. The command interactively creates the domain subdirectory */var/yp/NISdomain* and then builds a complete set of NIS maps based on the local *"/etc files."* Keep in mind that */etc files* on the master server fully define the NIS maps and in that way fully determine NIS policies. An example of how to create the NIS master server follows (the host is named ***NISmaster*** and everything happens on the Solaris 2.x platform — the procedure is interactive and the entered responses are presented in ***bold-italic***):

$ /usr/sbin/ypinit -m

In order for NIS to operate successfully, we have to construct a list of the NIS servers. Please continue to add the names for YP servers in order of preference, one per line. When you are done with the list, type a <control D> or a return on a line by itself.

next host to add: NISmaster
next host to add: ***NISslave***
next host to add: ***[Enter another hostname]***
next host to add: ***[Enter another hostname]***
next host to add: ***[Hit Enter key]***
The current list of yp servers looks like this:
NISmaster
NISslave
another slave server name
another slave server name
Is this correct? [y/n: y] ***y***
Installing the YP database will require that you answer a few questions.
Questions will all be asked at the beginning of the procedure.
Do you want this procedure to quit on non-fatal errors? [y/n: n] ***n***
OK, please remember to go back and redo manually whatever fails. If you don't, some part of the system (perhaps the yp itself) won't work.
The yp domain directory is /var/yp/NISdomain
Can we destroy the existing /var/yp/NISdomain and its contents? [y/n: n] ***y*** *There will be no further questions.*
The remainder of the procedure should take 5 to 10 minutes.
Building /var/yp/NISdomain/ypservers…
Running /var/yp /Makefile…
updated passwd
updated group
updated hosts
updated ethers
updated networks
updated rpc
updated services
updated protocols
updated netgroup
updated bootparams
updated aliases
updated publickey
updated netid
updated netmasks
updated timezone
updated auto.master
updated auto.home
updated auto.direct
updated auto.share
updated locale
NISmaster has been set up as a yp master server without any errors.
If there are running slave yp servers, run yppush now for any data bases which have been changed. If there are no running slaves, run ypinit on those hosts which are to be slave servers.

The first created map is "*ypservers*," which includes the names of all NIS servers for this NIS domain, based on the host names entered by the administrator during the master server creation. This map is crucial for an update of the NIS databases on the slave servers, because it contains a list of the registered slave servers. It is assumed that at this moment the specified slave servers are not yet running NIS; if they are, it is a good idea to recreate them as the slave servers. Also, **ypinit** does not check for other possible master servers in the same NIS domain, it is up to the administrator to ensure that multiple master servers are not created.

Once **ypinit -m** finishes, the NIS service should be started manually by issuing the **ypserv** command; the **rc** startup script can also be used, everything needed for the proper script execution should be there).

17.2.2.3 Set the Slave Server

Execute the command:

/full-pathname/ypinit -s NISmaster

where ***NISmaster*** is the name of the master server.

Here is an example (the host is named ***NISslave*** and the implemented platform is again Solaris 2.x; the entered responses are presented in ***bold-italic***):

$ /usr/sbin/ypinit -s NISmaster

Installing the YP database will require that you answer a few questions.
Questions will all be asked at the beginning of the procedure.
Do you want this procedure to quit on non-fatal errors? [y/n: n] ***n***
OK, please remember to go back and redo manually whatever fails. If you don't, some part of the system (perhaps the yp itself) won't work.
The yp domain directory is /var/yp/NISdomain
Can we destroy the existing /var/yp/NISdomain and its contents? [y/n: n] ***y***
There will be no further questions. The remainder of the procedure should take a few minutes, to copy the data bases from NISmaster.
Transferring locale.byname...
Transferring auto.share...
Transferring auto.direct...
Transferring auto.home...
Transferring auto.master...
Transferring timezone.byname...
Transferring netmasks.byaddr...
Transferring netid.byname...
Transferring publickey.byname...
Transferring mail.byaddr...
Transferring mail.aliases...
Transferring bootparams...
Transferring netgroup.byhost...
Transferring netgroup.byuser...
Transferring protocols.byname...
Transferring services.byservicename...
Transferring services.byname...
Transferring rpc.bynumber...
Transferring networks.byaddr...
Transferring networks.byname...
Transferring ethers.byname...
Transferring netgroup...
Transferring ethers.byaddr...
Transferring hosts.byaddr...
Transferring hosts.byname...
Transferring group.bygid...
Transferring group.byname...
Transferring passwd.byuid...
Transferring protocols.bynumber...
Transferring ypservers...
Transferring passwd.byname...
NISslave's nis data base has been set up without any errors.

The newly created slave server will pull NIS data from the master server and store its own copies of the maps; the slave server must be included in the *ypservers* map, otherwise the master server will reject the transfer of maps. If a new slave server is not included in the map (it is realistic situation, because the new slave server could be added later), the *ypservers* map on the master server must be re-edited. How can an NIS map be re-edited?

The *ypservers* map cannot be re-edited literally. NIS maps are not ASCII files and their contents are odd and noncomprehensive; they are in the *ndbm* format that is not readable at all, but is very convenient for fast machine searching. Each NIS map is built (for better understanding, we can say compiled) from a corresponding source ASCII file. Re-editing an NIS map means to re-edit its source file and then recompile the map itself. For the most part, the source files are usually configuration */etc files* on the master server. However, in the case of the NIS map *ypservers*, there is no corresponding source file at all; this map has been built based on the supplied data during the master server creation. Consequently to re-edit this map is a tricky business. One possible approach is:

First, the old contents of the *ypservers* map must be dumped into an arbitrary temporary file:

$ ypcat -k ypservers > /tmp/ypservers

Keep in mind that the **ypcat** command dispalys the map contents in a comprehensive ASCII format. Then, edit the ASCII file */tmp/ypservers* and add a new slave server:

$ vi /tmp/ypservers

Finally, make the new *ypservers* map based on the re-edited */tmp/ypservers* file (the implemented UNIX utility *makedbm* provides the needed map compilation):

$ cat /tmp/ypservers | /usr/sbin/makedbm - /var/yp/\`domainname\`/ypservers

The new slave server is now included into the *ypservers* map, and the master server will treat it correspondingly. The master server uses the *ypservers* map to identify registered slave servers for NIS databases pushing. NIS clients do not base their binding to the slave servers on this map; clients do not check servers for eligibility, they simply trust servers. This means that even if this map is not propagated after an update, it will not affect overall NIS behavior. But this also means, that a not-registered slave server could be accepted by clients as the eligible one, which is a security risk.

The **ypcat** command is used to read the contents of the NIS maps; its **-k** option (which prints each value with the preceding associated key) is required in the case of the *ypservers* map.

17.2.2.4 Start NIS Service

Finally, when **ypinit -s** finishes, the NIS service should be started manually by initiating the ***ypserv*** daemon (simply by issuing the **ypserv** command, or **ypstart** command, or even the corresponding ***rc*** start script for NIS).

17.2.3 To Create an NIS Client

The procedure presented here is the traditional, and still the prevailing, approach for the majority of UNIX flavors in creating an NIS client; some modern UNIX flavors could require a slightly different procedure to accomplish the same task. Both approaches are addressed within the presented steps.

1. Make sure that local */etc files* on the client host (primarily */etc/passwd* and */etc/group*) include the NIS marker "+" as the last entry. The "+" marker indicates that the NIS map should be appended to the local configuration file; otherwise, the local configuration data will be ignored. Remember that modern UNIX flavors could handle this request differently, primarily through the */etc/nsswitch.conf* file (we will discuss this issue later).
2. Afterward, execute the **domainname** command to set the NIS domain name:

   domainname *NISdomain*.

   where ***NISdomain*** is the name of the NIS domain.
3. Finally, start the **ypbind** daemon, which is responsible for locating the closest NIS server and maintaining the binding with the chosen server (the NIS ***rc*** startup script can be used instead).

17.2.4 NIS Domain Name

We see that a host understands that it belongs to a certain NIS domain if it can locally extract the name of the NIS domain, that is, if the NIS domain is set on this host. There is no list of valid or invalid domain names, so any extracted name is accepted as valid; an NIS domain could simply be set (with any extracted name) or unset (there is no extracted name). The host will accept that name and look up the corresponding NIS server/servers. The **NIS domain name** is an arbitrary name, but it is a good idea to use some logical names (not because of the NIS hosts — for machines there are no senseless names; mostly because of us, to understand NIS organization more easily). There was an opinion in the past that some advantages exist if this name matches the DNS domain name. I have never figured-out any advantage of that kind, except that in the past some network applications could be confused if these names were different; but those times are far behind us. In most cases it is not even possible do match NIS and DNS domain names.

The NIS domain name is set by the **domainname** command, and it is usually saved in the file */etc/defaultdomain*). For example, to set the name of the NIS domain to ***NISdomain***, and then check out later, the following command sequence can be used:

$ domainname NISdomain

$ domainname

NISdomain

$ cat /etc/defaultdomain (on Solaris, HP-UX, SunOS ...)

NISdomain

Bear in mind that this is not the case for every UNIX flavor. Sometimes the specified NIS name is not even saved in any file — rather it is kept in the memory. For the permanent NIS setting, another supposed file must be manually edited, and by reading that file during the startup, the system learns about NIS and keeps it in the memory. This is the case on Linux, and the mention file is */etc/sysconfig/network* — entry *DOMAINNAME*.

Unfortunately, these files or entries are misinterpreted as the DNS domain name; sometimes administrators make the mistake and even try to set DNS in that way. It only confuses the system, which now recognizes itself as an NIS client in a not-existing NIS domain. Remember, in DNS there is no an explicit location for the DNS domain name; this is indirectly specified within the */etc/resolv.conf* file (directive *domain* or *search*).

17.2.5 Databases/NIS Maps

The NIS maps are the central issues of the Network Information Service; they are propagated through the network and accessed by each host in the NIS domain. NIS maps contain administrative data generated on the single place (master server) but spread over the network and used by all clients. Clients use these maps exclusively or combined with their own local administrative data; NIS maps can replace (local data are completely ignored) or be appended to the local data. Basically the client's search for needed data is terminated once the match is accomplished. Originally, when maps were appended, local data had priority over maps. Modern UNIX flavors could reverse this default search; they allow users to customize the search pattern within the */etc/nsswitch.conf* file. We will discuss this approach later; for the moment, we will follow the traditional approach.

The following table lists NIS maps with brief explanations about their nature:

NIS Map	Source	Integration	Description
ypservers	NIS servers names	Replace	The list of NIS servers
bootparams	*/etc/bootparams*	Append	Boot server names for diskless nodes
ethers.byname	*/etc/ehters*	Replace	Used by RARP
ethers.byaddr	*/etc/ehters*	Replace	Used by RARP
group.byname	*/etc/group*	Append	Groups in the NIS domain
group.bygid	*/etc/group*	Append	Groups in the NIS domain
hosts.byname	*/etc/hosts*	Replace	Host database
hosts.byaddr	*/etc/hosts*	Replace	Host database
mail.aliases	*/etc/aliases*	Append	E-mail aliases
mail.byaddr	*/etc/aliases*	Append	E-mail aliases
netgroup.byhost	*/etc/netgroup*	Replace	Groups of hosts and users
netgroup.byuser	*/etc/netgroup*	Replace	Groups of hosts and users
netid.byname	UID & GID info	Derived	Data derived from group, password, and hosts files; includes user-group data
netmasks.byaddr	*/etc/netmasks*	Replace	Networks and netmasks data
networks.byaddr	*/etc/natworks*	Replace	Network names and IP addresses
networks.byname	*/etc/natworks*	Replace	Network names and IP addresses
passwd.byname	*/etc/passwd*	Append	User login data
passwd.byuid	*/etc/passwd*	Append	User login data
protocols.bynumber	*/etc/protocols*	Replace	Protocol names and numbers
protocols.byname	*/etc/protocols*	Replace	Protocol names and numbers
rpc.bynumber	*/etc/rpc*	Replace	RPC numbers
services.byname	*/etc/services*	Replace	Service names

Note: Two NIS maps, **ypservers** and **netgroup**, are strictly NIS related; for netgroup the corresponding source files must be created. Other custom-made maps can be also created.

The **NIS map** column lists existing NIS maps. Occasionally there are two maps for the same administrative purpose; the two maps contain the same data sorted in different ways, appropriate for a fast data search based on the corresponding search-key.

The **Source** column lists the source data files for the corresponding NIS maps. These are mostly well-known administrative (configuration) */etc* files.

The **Integration** column specifies whether an NIS map fully replaces the corresponding source file (the data in the file are ignored), or if it is appended to the file (first the file is read, and then the NIS map if the data was not found).

The **Description** column gives a brief description of the corresponding NIS map.

The NIS maps live only on NIS servers; for the supposed NIS domain named ***NISdomain*** they are located in the directory */var/yp/NISdomain*. Here is an example (Solaris 2.x):

$ ls -C /var/yp/'domainname'

```
auto.direct.dir          netgroup.dir
auto.direct.pag          netgroup.pag
auto.home.dir            netid.byname.dir
auto.home.pag            netid.byname.pag
auto.master.dir          netmasks.byaddr.dir
auto.master.pag          netmasks.byaddr.pag
auto.share.dir           networks.byaddr.dir
auto.share.pag           networks.byaddr.pag
bootparams.dir           networks.byname.dir
bootparams.pag           networks.byname.pag
ethers.byaddr.dir        passwd.byname.dir
ethers.byaddr.pag        passwd.byname.pag
ethers.byname.dir        passwd.byuid.dir
ethers.byname.pag        passwd.byuid.pag
group.bygid.dir          printers.conf.byname.dir
group.bygid.pag          printers.conf.byname.pag
group.byname.dir         protocols.byname.dir
group.byname.pag         protocols.byname.pag
hosts.byaddr.dir         protocols.bynumber.dir
hosts.byaddr.pag         protocols.bynumber.pag
hosts.byname.dir         publickey.byname.dir
hosts.byname.pag         publickey.byname.pag
locale.byname.dir        rpc.bynumber.dir
locale.byname.pag        rpc.bynumber.pag
mail.aliases.dir         services.byname.dir
mail.aliases.pag         services.byname.pag
mail.byaddr.dir          services.byservicename.dir
mail.byaddr.pag          services.byservicename.pag
netgroup.byhost.dir      timezone.byname.dir
netgroup.byhost.pag      timezone.byname.pag
netgroup.byuser.dir      ypservers.dir
netgroup.byuser.pag      ypservers.pag
```

The format of NIS maps is known as ***ndbm***; the *ndbm* format is suitable for fast machine searching, but it is not readable; NIS maps are adopted to machines, not to human beings. Each NIS map actually includes two files identified with the extensions "*dir*" and "*pag*." We will return to the *ndbm* format later.

Once NIS is running, references to the local administrative files are handled in two fundamentally different ways:

1. The NIS maps replace files; local files are ignored. These include the following files: ***ethers***, ***netmasks***, ***networks***, ***protocols***, ***rpc***, ***services***, and ***netgroup*** (the last one is a special case).
2. NIS maps append to some files; the files are read first, and only if the appropriate entry is not found will the NIS maps be queried. These include the following files: ***passwd***, ***bootparams***, ***group***, and ***aliases***.

Traditionally to append an NIS map, the corresponding file had to include an "NIS marker" entry as the last configuration line. This is a special entry that starts with the plus sign (+), followed by the colon separator to make it fit the syntax of the file. The plus sign indicates that more data can be found in the corresponding NIS map. Even for modern UNIX flavors that handle this differently, the plus sign does no harm.

By appending an NIS map to the file, it is possible to specify local configuration data applicable only to the specific client-host and make it different from other NIS hosts. In this case, centralized NIS databases include global data, while needed exceptions could easily be realized through the local data. For example, certain users could be authenticated only locally and have access only to certain hosts, not to each host in the NIS domain.

Make sure that the superuser authentication is always provided locally, independently of the NIS settings. The root password is too sensitive an issue to be uniform all over the network. If it were, the root password from the master server would be valid everywhere; it would be too much!

17.2.5.1 The */etc/netgroup* File

One of the first network-specific issues that NIS addressed was the so-called *network group*. In the network environment, there is a real need to group and uniquely identify users from different hosts and different parts of the network because they share something in common; they could be involved in the same project, or share the same information space, or whatever). NIS offered a solution in the form of the **netgroup**.

The NIS map *netgroup* was introduced, as well as the new source configuration file for that purpose */etc/netgroup*. Obviously this file has a sense only if NIS is running, and more precisely, the file has to exist only on the master NIS server. The file specifies groups of hosts and users that can be referenced with a single pointer — users on different hosts, even different NIS domains, can form a **netgroup** and be treated together. Basically, *netgroup entries* are similar to *group entries* on a stand-alone system, except that they are not restricted to the single host. However, *netgroup* entries do not imply any owner/permission relationship — they act strictly as pointers.

The basic format of an entry in the */etc/netgroup* file is:

groupname member [member] ...

where

groupname Any name assigned to a netgroup.

member An item included in the group, which can be:
- Another *netgroup*
- *Individual item* defined by the triple: (***hostname, username, domainname***)

An omitted argument in the *domainname* field indicates the netgroup is valid in the current NIS domain; a hyphen (-) in the *hostname* and *username* fields means that no value is included.

17.3 NIS Management

Once NIS is set, it works quite well, hidden from users and in some ways even hidden from administrators. However, as everything else, NIS also requires maintenance — checking the NIS status and modifying and updating the NIS database are regular administrative duties. NIS is an extremely useful network service, but sometimes NIS can cause a lot of headaches. Usual UNIX commands cannot be efficiently used; that is why NIS has introduced a number of new commands to handle NIS processes and maps in order to make this management easier. Today these commands are mostly standard on every UNIX platform. A brief survey of some useful NIS-specific commands follows.

17.3.1 *yp* Commands

The NIS-specific commands (we will call them **yp**-related commands) live in several directories, most often */bin*, */usr/sbin*, and */usr/lib/netsvc/yp*. It is very easy to recognize these commands; they start with the prefix **yp**. The following table briefly describes the commands (the command layout is from Solaris 2.x; some differences are possible on other UNIX flavors):

yp Command	Description
/bin/ypcat	Prints all values in an NIS map; the **-k** option is required for the *ypservers* map: **ypcat -k ypservers**
/bin/ypmatch	Prints values of selected keys in an NIS map, for example to display password data for the user "bjl": **ypmatch bjl passwd**
/bin/yppasswd	Changes the login password in the NIS database without affecting local data. It behaves very much like the regular **passwd** command.
/bin/ypwhich	Lists which host is a current NIS server and supplies NIS services for the host; very useful command to check the current binding of an NIS client toward available NIS servers.
/usr/sbin/ypalias	Changes aliases in the NIS database.
/usr/sbin/ypinit	Builds and installs NIS databases on a master or slave NIS server (already discussed).
/usr/sbin/yppoll	Queries a specified NIS server (the default is the bound server) for information about a specific NIS map. The information includes the time (in seconds) when the map was built, and a master server for the map. For example, to get information about the *group* map: **/usr/sbin/yppoll -h NISslave group** or **/usr/sbin/yppoll group**
/usr/sbin/ypset	Binds the client to a particular NIS server. It is useful for binding an NIS client that is not on a broadcast network, since broadcasting is a method by which the **ypbind** process (a client) locates an NIS server. If **ypbind** is already bound to a **ypserv** process, this command can have an effect only if **ypbind** was started with the **-ypset** option that allowed a change in the current binding (this is specific to Solaris).
/usr/lib/netsvc/yp/ypbind	The NIS client process (already discussed).
/usr/lib/netsvc/yp/yppush	Forces a propagation of the specified NIS map (database) from the master server toward slave servers.
/usr/lib/netsvc/yp/ypserv	The NIS server process (already discussed).
/usr/lib/netsvc/yp/ypstart */usr/lib/netsvc/yp/ypstop*	Starts and stops NIS services, ***ypstart*** automatically determines the NIS configuration status of the system and starts the appropriate daemons, and ***ypstop*** stops the NIS daemons.
/usr/lib/netsvc/yp/ypxfr	Starts the transfer of an NIS map (database) from an NIS server. The ***cron*** facility should be used for periodic execution of the command command to keep the NIS database synchronized.
/usr/lib/netsvc/yp/ypxfr_1p erday */usr/lib/netsvc/yp/ypxfr_1p erhour* */usr/lib/netsvc/yp/ypxfr_2p erday*	Template scripts for a periodic start of an NIS maps (database) transfer: once daily, once per hour, and twice daily.
/usr/lib/netsvc/yp/ypxfrd	The NIS database transfer daemon (already discussed).

17.3.2 Updating NIS Maps

The NIS maps update is the most frequent activity in NIS management. Each change in configuration requires the map update and propagation; for example, when a new user is added or when a new group is created, the corresponding NIS maps must be updated and pushed toward all slave servers. This is a routine procedure, and often some front-end tool is provided (sometimes even self-made) to make this routine job even easier. We will forget about possible tools, and suppose that everything must be done from the command line. First, any changes and map updates are always performed on the NIS master server; once the source /etc file is modified, it is necessary to rebuild the corresponding NIS map (the map update actually means to rebuild the map). Afterward the map is ready to be pushed to slave servers; in that way databases on the master and slave servers remain synchronized.

Behind the scenes the routine procedure to update and push an updated NIS map is quite complex and requires a number of sequential steps to be executed. Each of those individual steps could essentially be accomplished from the command line, but it will be a real nightmare to follow the required algorithm thoroughly. However, UNIX provides efficient engineering tool for such scenarios: this is the UNIX ***make*** command (or rather, the ***make*** utility) that can simplify the execution of very complex algorithms to the point of issuing only a single command, the **make** command itself.

It is out of the scope of this text to elaborate the **make** utility/command. Just to mention briefly that **make** reads the description file (by default **make** is looking for the description file named *Makefile* located in the current directory) and follows its instructions. The format and syntax of the description file *Makefile* is specific but well known to the **make** command itself. Each entry in the file describes (specifies) several individual steps to accomplish a certain action; all entries together accomplish the task.

UNIX NIS software provides the needed *Makefile* to build NIS databases/maps; this is the description file ***/var/yp/Makefile*** suitable for most NIS implementation. If some domain-specific customization is required, it is not a big deal to modify this file; its content is readable and quite comprehensive even for novices. Customization mostly means to choose among several options, or rename or add some new NIS map.

17.3.2.1 The *make* Utility and NIS

With no arguments, ***make*** will try to create *dbm databases* for all NIS maps that are out-of-date, and then execute ***yppush*** to notify the slave servers that there have been changes. Keep in mind that the implemented algorithm (described by */var/yp/Makefile*) includes the comparison of timestamps of the source files and current maps to determine if the maps are out-of-date; otherwise, it skips the map creation. The trick to force a map update is just to modify the timestamp on the corresponding source */etc* file without modifying its content; the UNIX ***touch*** command does that.

If a map is supplied as an argument on the command line, **make** will update that map alone. By typing **make passwd**, the *password map* will be created and pushed. Likewise, **make hosts** and **make networks** will create and push the host and network maps, based on the contents of the */etc/hosts* and */etc/networks* source files.

make uses three special variables: *DIR*, which gives the directory of the source files; *NOPUSH*, which, when non-null, inhibits doing a ***yppush*** of the new database maps; and *DOM*, used to construct a domain other than the master's default domain. The default for *DIR* is */etc*, and the default for *NOPUSH* is the *null string*.

The ***/usr/sbin/makedbm*** command is used to create the NIS maps in the required *ndbm* format; this command is invoked by the ***make*** utility. The command **makedbm** takes *infile* and converts it to a pair of files in *ndbm format*, namely *outfile.pag* and *outfile.dir*. Each line of the input file is converted to a single *dbm record*. All characters up to the first TAB or SPACE form the key, and the rest of the line is the data. The command understands the continuation character "\" at the end of the line, but does not treat "#" as a comment character. *infile* can be "-," in which case the standard input is read. It also generates a special entry with the key *yp_last_modified*, which is the date of *infile* (or the current time, if *infile* is "-").

The common options for the **makedbm** command are:

-l	Lowercase; convert the keys of the given map to lower case, so that host name matches, for example, can work independently of upper or lower case distinctions.
-s	Secure map; accept connections from secure NIS networks only.
-i *yp input file*	Create a special entry with the key *yp input file*.
-o *yp output name*	Create a special entry with the key *yp output name*.
-d *yp domain name*	Create a special entry with the key *yp domain name*.
-m *yp master name*	Create a special entry with the key *yp master name*. If no master host name is specified, *yp master name* will be set to the local host name.
-u *dbmfilename*	Undo a *dbm* file; that is, print out a *dbm* file one entry per line, with a single space separating keys from values.

makedbm requests a special "key value form" of the input file, which is different from the existing "*/etc* source files." It is very easy to write shell scripts to convert standard source files (such as */etc/passwd*) to the required key value form; a simple *awk* script can make this efficiently:

```
#!/ bin/awk -f
BEGIN { FS = ":"; OFS = "\t"; }
{ print $1, $0 }
```

When implemented on the */etc/passwd* file, the script will take the */etc/passwd* file and convert it to a form that can be read by **makedbm** to make the NIS file *passwd.byname*. In that case the key is a *username* (the first field in the *passwd* entry), and the value is the remaining line in the */etc/passwd* file.

Similarly, the *awk* script implemented on the */etc/passwd* file will take the */etc/passwd* file and convert it to a form that can be read by **makedbm** to make the NIS file *passwd.byuid*.

```
#!/ bin/awk -f
BEGIN { FS = ":"; OFS = "\t"; }
{ printf ("%-10d", $3); print $0 }
```

That is, the key is a *userID* (the third field in the *passwd* entry), and the value is the rest of the line in the */etc/passwd* file.

This is exactly what the **make** utility is doing before the **makedbm** command is implemented.

Once a corresponding NIS map is generated, it is pushed to NIS slave servers. The **Makefile** defines each step in the execution of the **make** command/utility. An example from Solaris/SunOS platform follows (the file is only partially presented):

 # cat /var/yp/Makefile

```
#
#     @(#)make.s cript 1.36 SMI
#
# This file should reside in both /var/yp/Makefile and /usr/lib/NIS.Makefile.
# It should only be executed from /var/yp.
#
# ========================================================
# Set the following variable to "-b" to have NIS servers use the domain name
# resolver for hosts not in the current domain.
B=-b
#B=   Will be discussed later!
# ========================================================
DIR =/etc
DOM = `domainname`
NOPUSH = ""
ALIASES = /etc/aliases
YPDIR=/usr/etc/yp
YPDBDIR=/var/yp
YPPUSH=$(YPDIR)/yppush
MAKEDBM=$(YPDIR)/makedbm
        . . . . .
        . . . . .
MKALIAS=$(YPDIR)/mkalias
CHKPIPE= || ( echo "NIS make terminated:" $@ 1>&2; kill -TERM 0 )
k:
        @if [ ! $(NOPUSH) ]; then $(MAKE) $(MFLAGS) -k all; \
        else $(MAKE) $(MFLAGS) -k all NOPUSH=$(NOPUSH);fi
all:    passwd group hosts ethers networks rpc services protocols \
        netgroup bootparams aliases publickey netid netmasks c2secure \
        timezone auto.master auto.home auto_share
        . . . . .
        . . . . .
passwd.time: $(DIR)/passwd
@(awk 'BEGIN { FS=":"; OFS="\t"; }/^[a-zA-Z0-9_]/{ print $$1, $$0 }' $(DIR)/ passwd
$(CHKPIPE))\ | $(MAKEDBM) - $(YPDBDIR)/ $(DOM)/ passwd.byname;
@(awk 'BEGIN { FS=":"; OFS="\t"; } /^[a-zA-Z0-9_]/{ printf("%-10d ", $$3); print $$0 }'
$(DIR)/passwd\
$(CHKPIPE))| $(MAKEDBM) - $(YPDBDIR)/$(DOM)/passwd.byuid;
@touch passwd.time;
@echo "updated passwd";
@if [ ! $(NOPUSH) ]; then $(YPPUSH) -d $(DOM) passwd.byname; fi
@if [ ! $(NOPUSH) ]; then $(YPPUSH) -d $(DOM) passwd.byuid; fi
@if [ ! $(NOPUSH) ]; then echo "pushed passwd"; fi
group.time: $(DIR)/group
        . . . . .
        . . . . .
hosts.time: $(DIR)/hosts
        @(sed -e "/^#/ d" -e s/#.*$$/ /$(DIR)/hosts $(CHKPIPE)) | \
        ($(STDHOSTS) $(CHKPIPE)) | \
        (awk '{for (i = 2; i = NF; i++) print $$i, $$0}' $(CHKPIPE))| \
        $(MAKEDBM) $(B) -l - $(YPDBDIR)/ $(DOM)/ hosts.byname
        @($(STDHOSTS) $(DIR)/ hosts $(CHKPIPE))| \
        (awk 'BEGIN { OFS="\t"; } $$1 !~ /^#/ { print $$1, $$0 }' $(CHKPIPE)) | \
        $(MAKEDBM) $(B) - $(YPDBDIR)/ $(DOM)/ hosts.byaddr;
        @touch hosts.time;
```

```
        @echo "updated hosts";
        @if [ ! $(NOPUSH) ]; then $(YPPUSH) -d $(DOM) hosts.byname; fi
        @if [ ! $(NOPUSH) ]; then $(YPPUSH) -d $(DOM) hosts.byaddr; fi
        @if [ ! $(NOPUSH) ]; then echo "pushed hosts"; fi
ethers.time: $(DIR)/ ethers
        . . . . .
networks.time: $(DIR)/ networks
        . . . . .
services.time: $(DIR)/ services
        . . . . .
rpc.time: $(DIR)/ rpc
        . . . . .
protocols.time: $(DIR)/ protocols
        . . . . .
netgroup.time: $(DIR)/ netgroup
        . . . . .
bootparams.time: $(DIR)/ bootparams
        . . . . .
aliases.time: $(ALIASES)
        . . . . .
netmasks.time: $(DIR)/ netmasks
        . . . . .
passwd: passwd.time
group: group.time
      . . . . .
      . . . . .
auto.share: auto.share.time
$(DIR)/ netid:
$(DIR)/ timezone:
```

As could be seen from this example, there are a number of references to files named *filename.time*. These files are only used as references to the point in time when corresponding maps were last updated. This means only source files modified after that time will be processed; otherwise, there is no need for an update — the latest version of the map already exists. The only interesting parts of the *filename.time* files are the associated timestamps; the files themselves are zero-sized, which can be seen in the following long listing of these files:

```
$ ls -l /var/yp/*.time
-rw-r--r--   1 root   other   0 Jul 21 11:36 ../ aliases.time
-rw-r--r--   1 root   other   0 Jun 24 09:51 ../ auto.direct.time
                . . . .
                . . . .
-rw-r--r--   1 root   other   0 Jul 21 11:37 ../ passwd.time
-rw-r--r--   1 root   other   0 Jun 24 09:51 ../ protocols.time
-rw-r--r--   1 root   other   0 Jun 24 09:51 ../ publickey.time
-rw-r--r--   1 root   other   0 Jun 24 09:51 ../ rpc.time
-rw-r--r--   1 root   other   0 Jun 24 12:04 ../ services.time
-rw-r--r--   1 root   other   0 Jun 24 09:51 ../ timezone.time
```

17.3.3 Troubleshooting

From an administrative standpoint, NIS is a great network service; it makes overall administration faster, easier, and most important, consistent over the whole network. Unfortunately, in real life everything is not so smooth. Occasionally NIS can experience unexpected problems and complications: temporary breaks in network communication can cause unexpected behavior in the ***yp*** processes, and consequently NIS can respond in a very strange way. Some tips on checking NIS for possible problems are listed in the text that follows.

- Use the **ypcat** command to check the contents of an NIS map. For example, if a user cannot login, first check to see if the user is an eligible NIS user at all; use the command:

  # ypcat passwd | grep bjl

  bjl:TsVN4O2C6IFGM:1215:1001:B.J.L.:/home/bjl:/bin/ksh

  It will present all password data for the specified user "*bjl*." The **ypmatch** command can also be instrumental in such situations. Make sure that the names of the maps do not include the extensions we normally see in a listing of the directory */var/yp/`domainname`*.
- Occasionally you might need to find out which NIS server is bound to a certain client-host; knowing the bound NIS server makes it much easier to trace any NIS related problem. Use the **ypwhich** command; inappropriately bound NIS servers can cause a lot of trouble. For example, by logging into the NIS client and typing:

  # ypwhich

  NISServerName

  the currently bound NIS server will be shown. Is this the server you were expecting? Is it the closest server, or is it strange that this server is bound at all? These are questions that may arise.
- Suppose you want to switch the client toward another NIS server, or in the NIS terminology to bind with another server. This is not an easy task. Binding is a negotiated session between the client and the server that first responded to the client broadcast call; a bind remains active as long as the server provides NIS services, i.e., responds to the client's queries. To accomplish this task, you have to do the following:

  The first step might be to stop and restart the ***ypbind*** process — the client will probably now bind another server that we expect to be free. Let us figure out the process ID:

  # ps -ef | grep ypbind | grep -v grep

  root 14228 1 0 Apr 13 ? 0:05 /usr/lib/netsvc/yp/ypbind

  Then stop the daemon:

  kill 14228

  And finally restart the daemon:

  # /usr/lib/netsvc/yp/ypbind
- If the result is not the one expected and the same server remains stubbornly bound, then more drastic action is required. For example, you might temporarily stop the ***ypserv*** daemon at the NIS server itself; obviously the client will then be forced to bind to another server. Afterward, the ***ypserv*** daemon can be restarted. The commands **/usr/lib/netsvc/yp/ypstop** and **/usr/lib/netsvc/yp/ypstart** are available if you ever decide on such an action. However, this could be too drastic; do not forget that even a short stoppage of the ***ypserv*** daemon at the NIS server will affect other clients, too.

- NIS actually provides a command to set NIS binding arbitrarily; this is the **ypset** command. Unfortunately, some UNIX flavors (like Solaris) restrict the use of the command — by default the **ypset** command is disabled. The ***ypbind*** daemon must be started with the **-ypset** option to enable the command. This makes everything more difficult in the real life, but this possibility is worth remembering.
- The worst-case scenario is the need to rebuild a complete NIS domain, to rebuild a master server and all slave servers with the same or a changed configuration. Although it sounds dramatic, an NIS rebuild is a very fast procedure and can often be accomplished without affecting current production.
- Occasionally, you will need to force a rebuild and push of some of the NIS maps. The simplest way is to change the timestamp of the corresponding source file (there is no need to modify the file itself), and then to follow the usual procedure for a map update. Of course, everything happens at the master server, for example:

  # touch /etc/passwd

  # cd /var/yp

  # make passwd

17.3.4 Security Issues

NIS is an extremely helpful network service and is widely used and supported by all UNIX flavors. However, it is also fair to say that NIS does have some inherent security holes that make it more vulnerable to potential intruders. The NIS security drawback is so acute that sometimes NIS is not even allowed to be considered as an option. This is the case with networks where security is the most important issue and has the highest priority.

There is no magic formula to define the security boundaries for the safe NIS usage. This decision remains to the designers and administrators of each individual subnetwork; there is always a tradeoff between NIS advantages and disadvantages. The following text points to the two major NIS-related security issues.

The first disadvantage is that NIS makes all encrypted passwords visible. Even though NIS servers and clients hide local encrypted passwords in the */etc/shadow* file, making them invisible to potential intruders, NIS advertise them on the network. NIS uses encrypted passwords for the authentication of NIS users, and they are transferred over the network within the NIS *passwd* map — first when it is pushed to slave servers, but also whenever an NIS client queries for the password to authenticate a specific user.

The fact that the *passwd* map includes encrypted passwords also means that any user can read the map and get this data. For example:

 # ypcat passwd

```
tthacker:aQ0mpUfu7OuGs:2889:1034:Tom Thacker:/home/tthacker:/bin/ksh
selliott:eDZUQCN5X3ylY:2873:1034:Sam Elliott:/home/selliott:/bin/ksh
lcreasey:BcJdCeqYm7O8U:2530:1034:Lean Creasey:/home/lcreasey:/bin/ksh
jjohnsto:RNJtQ/4wiaBBs:3036:1019:John Johnston:/home/jjohnsto:/bin/ksh
     .....
     .....
root:J.WEn2PxKhlbg:0:1:Operator:/:/bin/ksh
     .....
     .....
```

This command will display all data about all NIS users, including the encrypted passwords; even the *superuser* data at the master server will be posted. For an intruder, this is a good starting point to try to break a password.

The second disadvantage is less feasible, but is still a pending security problem. We have already mentioned that NIS binding does not include any security checkup; the *ypservers* map is not even checked as a part of this procedure. An NIS client sends a broadcast query and simply trusts to the NIS server that has first responded and identified itself as a server for this NIS domain. The very same server continues to supply the client host with all administrative data, including user login names and passwords; obviously such a server has full control over this client.

Let us suppose an intruder has built a fake NIS server in your network. This server is not in the *ypservers* map, but this map only restricts pushing of the data from the master server toward slave servers. The fake server has fake maps, sufficient to break into the client host. Once the intruder gains control of the real client host, the rest of the job becomes much easier.

It should not be easy to build a fake server in the network that you administer. Regular checkups should prevent such attempts. But to prevent something you must first be aware of such a possibility, and that was the purpose of this text.

17.3.5 A Few NIS Stories

17.3.5.1 Too Large an NIS Group

NIS domains cover several dozen UNIX servers and more than a thousand users. Each user has login access to each host, but the access to certain data, i.e., certain files, is restricted and based on the file's group ownership. Users belong to multiple secondary groups and accordingly can use the needed data. The master NIS server is Solaris 2.6 box, and NIS load is properly spread over several slave servers. The problem appeared when the size of certain secondary groups hit NIS limits.

Each secondary group is specified as a single line in the */etc/group* file on the master server (in the usual UNIX way). However, NIS cannot swallow the lines longer than 1K characters; once the group hits the limit, the conversion into ndbm format fails. The addition of new users into the groups and the growth of the group entries soon caused the problem — the system could not create a group map properly. How is this inherent NIS restriction overcome?

- The first idea was to make smaller secondary groups and then merge them into one larger group. However, UNIX does not allow specifying a group as a member of another group; only users can be members of the group. So this idea did not work.
- Another idea was to decrease the size of the secondary groups by changing the user's primary group in a way to match our needs. This worked, but only for a while. Despite the required tedious work to modify two configuration files — */etc/passwd* and */etc/group* — this painful situation soon became unmanageable. We had to look for another solution.
- Could we try with ***netgroup***? At least we could combine multiple groups together without restriction. But the ***netgroup*** is just a pointer, it does not own any resource. It can work for some other situation, but not in this case.
- It seems that the only workable solution is to create multiple smaller secondary groups with the same GID (group ID number). UNIX does not care about group name, it looks only for GIDs. So users that belong to groups with different group names can access the same files that are owned by the same GID; obviously it works.

The author is not delighted with this solution, but it seems to be the only one that works. In UNIX multiple names associated with the same ID number (whether these are groups or users) are technically feasible, but this is not a healthy approach. Under certain conditions it could be quite confusing when data are displayed.

17.3.5.2 Invalid Slave Server

The NIS domain was in production for quite some time. In the meantime, several slave servers had been added and removed from NIS. Everything appeared to be properly done. Suddenly, users started complaining that they could not log in to one of the most important production hosts. The funny side of this story is that some other users could log in to the same host, and they could do their jobs without any problem. What has caused the problem?

After some investigation on the host, the administrator realized that the bound slave NIS server was one of the obsolete machines that used to be a slave server in the past, but had been removed from NIS a long time ago. What happened suddenly and why was NIS service only partially provided now?

The happy ending of this story is quite simple. When this obsolete slave server was removed from NIS, the cleaning job was not properly and completely done. The NIS server daemon ***ypserv*** had been stopped and the machine really ceased to provide NIS service. The server map *ypservers* was also properly cleaned from the old slave server entry, so everything seemed to be OK. This machine continued to be an NIS client. However, the NIS database in the directory *"/var/yp/`domainname`"* had never been removed; database contents corresponded to the time when the slave server was stopped and had not been updated afterward.

Everything was OK up to the next machine booting. Once the machine was rebooted it recognized itself as the slave server in this NIS domain (to understand why please check the **rc** startup script) and started to provide NIS service from its obsolete database. At that moment, our host found this machine to be the most convenient NIS server and started to use its data to, among other things, authenticate users that tried to log in. Old users that had not changed their authentication data in the meantime did not have any problem; new users and users that had changed passwords could not log in to the host.

So the mystery was solved — every job, including the shutdown of the NIS server, must be completely done; otherwise…

17.3.5.3 Change of the NIS Domain Name

NIS administration is not an area of great expertise for many UNIX administrators, especially managing many of its confusing and controversial issues. This is why it is often an interview topic when UNIX administrators apply for jobs. For example, what will be your response to the question: "Your task is to change the NIS domain name for the production NIS domain with, let us say, five servers and 100 clients. How will you make this? Of course any downtime is not allowed."

Think about the following scenario:

- Shut down master server and one of the slave servers. The remaining three slave servers should be sufficient to continue to provide NIS services. If this is not the case, a temporary slave server could be added, of course before the master server has gone down (it is assumed that the procedure to add the new slave server is known — do not forget to modify ***ypservers*** map).

- Recreate master server with the new domain name and old NIS database (local /etc files remained the same). Recreate the downed slave server for the new domain name. This step is actually equivalent to the procedure when servers are created the first time — simply, we are creating the new NIS domain besides the existing one. It does not affect current clients and slave servers that are not yet part of the new NIS domain.
- Switch a number of clients (30–40%) to the new domain; change the domain name (the command ***domainname***), and recycle ***ypbind*** daemon on each of the clients.
- Shut down one more slave server and recreate for the new NIS domain.
- Switch another 20% of clients to the new NIS domain.
- Repeat the procedure for remaining slave servers and clients.

At the end, the old domain name is purged and the new domain name activated.

17.4 NIS vs. DNS

The domain name system (DNS) is the dedicated global service that spans the entire Internet with only one goal — to provide information about hosts worldwide; to be more specific, to provide host names and IP addresses. DNS is fully discussed in Chapter 16. The Network Information Service (NIS) is a dedicated service to provide various administrative data for a certain number of hosts contained within the specified NIS domain; these data also include host names and IP addresses. Obviously DNS and NIS overlap in this sphere — host names and IP addresses for the related hosts could be managed from both places.

The logical question is, can NIS and DNS coexist peacefully? The answer is definitely yes, but it requires additional administration. Having in mind that the local */etc/hosts* files provide also the data about host names and IP addresses, we come to the three independent sources for the same data. Who has priority? How is data synchronized? What do you do if the same data are inconsistent? These are only few of the potential problems that we have to handle.

17.4.1 The */etc/nsswitch.conf* File

Modern UNIX flavors, like Solaris, HP-UX, or Linux, provide a special name-service-switch configuration file */etc/nsswitch.conf*, which specifies the lookup policy used to define the order and the conditions under which various sources are queried to obtain the desired information. The lookup policy is defined by an *nsswitch-entry* specified by the system administrator; this is a text line with an understandable syntax. The following sources (databases) are allowed to be used in the specified policy: ***dns*** (domain name system), ***nis*** (Network Information Service), and ***files*** (local configuration files).

An ***nsswitch-entry*** must be on a single line, and includes:

info-class : src [criteria src [criteria src]]

where

info-class Refers to the class of information being queried: for example, ***hosts*** for the host name service resolution.

src Refers to a source (network database) to be queried, as stated earlier (***dns***, ***nis***, and ***files***).

criteria Optional field containing ***status=action*** pairs enclosed in square brackets, which represent the criteria when, and how, to query the following source. The valid ***status*** strings are: ***SUCCESS***, ***NOTFOUND***, ***TRYAGAIN***, and ***UNAVAIL***. The valid ***action*** strings are: ***continue*** and ***return*** — to continue query with the next source on the line if the associated status for this action has occurred, or to terminate the search and return any result of the last query. Default actions are:
For ***SUCCESS=return***
For ***NOTFOUND=return***
For ***UNAVAIL=continue***
for ***TRYAGAIN=return***
The only exception is that all the actions associated with the last source in the entry are always set to ***return*** and cannot be overridden.

The following example from HP-UX 10.20 illustrates the different policies for querying hostname resolution:

```
$ cat /etc/nsswitch.conf
#
# This file contains different configurations to query hostname resolution.
# Comment and comment-out corresponding entries that match the required policy.
#
# To use DNS first then /etc/hosts, if DNS is either not up and running, or does
# not contain any answer in its database
hosts: dns [NOTFOUND=continue] files
#
# To use /etc/hosts first then DNS, if /etc/hosts does not contain any answer
# in its database
# hosts: files [NOTFOUND=continue] dns
#
# To use NIS first then /etc/hosts, if NIS is either not up and running, or does
# not contain any answer in its database
# hosts: nis [NOTFOUND=continue] files
#
# See the Administering Internet Services Manual and the switch(4) man page
# for more information on the name service switch.
#
```

The origin name of this file is related to the host name resolution; thus the "ns" prefix in the file name stands for the name service. However, only one *nsswitch-entry* in the file strictly addresses this issue; other entries are related to other network services and arbitrate between NIS and local databases for the corresponding service, like in the following example on the Linux platform:

```
$ cat /etc/nsswitch.conf
# /etc/nsswitch.conf
#
# An example Name Service Switch config file. This file shoul be sorted with the most-used
# services at the beginning.
#
# The entry '[NOTFOUND=return]' means that the search for an entry should stop if the search
# in the previous entry turned up nothing. Note that if the search failed due to some other reason
# (like no NIS server responding) then the search continues with the next entry.
```

```
#
# Legal entries are:
# nisplus or nis+          Use NIS+ (NIS version 3)
# nis or yp                Use NIS (NIS version 2), also called YP
# dns                      Use DNS (Domain Name Service)
# files                    Use the local files
# [NOTFOUND=return]        Stop searching if not found so far
#
# Example – obey only what nisplus tells us...
# services:                nisplus [NOTFOUND=return] files
# networks:                nisplus [NOTFOUND=return] files
# protocols:               nisplus [NOTFOUND=return] files
#
#passwd:                   files nis
shadow:                    files nis
group:                     files nis
#
hosts:                     files dns
#
bootparams:                files
ethers:                    files
netmasks:                  files
networks:                  files
protocols:                 files
rpc:                       files
services:                  files
automount:                 files
aliases:                   files
#
netgroup:                  nis
```

Obviously this host is an NIS client. However NIS is not used for host name resolution. The presented configuration is very common for NIS clients and it includes a number of other configuration data.

17.4.2 Once upon a Time

It was some time before the */etc/nsswitch.conf* file became the final solution to this "search-among-many" issue. In the past, UNIX flavors handled this issue differently. There were essentially three ways to integrate NIS with DNS:

1. Run NIS without DNS, which was the default procedure. Even if DNS was running, routines that used NIS ignored DNS unless the necessary changes had been made.
2. Use the NIS maps first, then go to DNS for host names that were not managed by NIS.
3. Ignore NIS for host names and use only DNS. Using DNS without NIS required a rebuilding of the library routines that looked up host names so they no longer made NIS library calls.

Besides these, other specific approaches floated around. For example, in DEC's ULTRIX OS, the order in which the local */etc/hosts* file, the NIS map, and the DNS name servers were queried for host information was specified in the */etc/svc.conf* file. SGI IRIX 4.X included the nonstandard directive ***hostorder*** in the */etc/resolv.conf* file to specify the sequence in which the hostname/IP address data would be searched.

SunOS 4.1.x required an additional intervention in the */var/yp/Makefile*. For DNS to have an effect, the entries with so-called *magic cookies* had to be modified from their default values:

# *B* =-*b*	became ***B* = -*b***
***B*=**	became **# *B* =**

Unfortunately, SunOS 4.1.x also carried another surprise: if NIS was not running on the host, then DNS would not operate properly, despite the fact that the */etc/resolv.conf* file and other local DNS related data were set up correctly. The corresponding patch was released to overcome this problem. There were rumors at that time that this was an intentional bug; just to favor NIS over DNS — NIS was SunOS's invention. I never determined if it was an intentional or unintentional bug, but I remember very well it was quite painful to put everything in operation.

18

Network File System (NFS)

18.1 NFS Overview

The ***Network File System (NFS)*** is one of the network services that have quickly gained a leading role in the emerging networked environment. NFS allows directories and files to be shared across a network. It is supported by virtually all UNIX flavors and many non-UNIX platforms. Through NFS, users and programs can access files residing at remote systems as if they were local files. In an ideal NFS environment, users neither know nor care where files are actually located. The benefits of such an approach are obvious:

- NFS reduces local disk storage requirements because a network can store a single copy of a directory accessible by everyone on the network.
- NFS simplifies common support tasks, because files can be updated centrally (at the single site) and yet be available through the network.
- NFS allows users to use familiar UNIX commands to manipulate remote files instead of learning new ones; from the user standpoint everything is fully transparent.

NFS is built on the *RPC protocol* (remote procedure call) and imposes a client-server relationship on the hosts that use NFS. An NFS server is a host that owns one or more filesystems and makes them available on the network; an NFS client mounts remote filesystems from one or more servers, and uses them in a way equivalent to local filesystems.

There are two aspects related to system administration when using NFS: choosing a filesystem naming and mounting scheme, and then configuring the servers and clients to adhere to this scheme. Users themselves do not know a lot about NFS, they simply benefit from using it.

Certain actions are required on both the server and client sides to configure NFS. NFS has introduced new terminology to identify the required steps in the procedure itself. On the server side, to advertise and make a filesystem available on the network is known as *to export a filesystem*, or *to share a filesystem* (as in Solaris 2.x); on the client side, to implement an exported filesystem is known as *to mount a remote filesystem*. The two actions are complementary: nonexported filesystems cannot be mounted, and non-mounted exported filesystems cannot be used. We will discuss these issues in greater detail later.

18.1.1 NFS Daemons

NFS requires the full support of several daemons, which perform basic server and client NFS-related functions. Based on the RPC model and protocol, NFS includes a number of processes involved on both sides. The NFS related daemons are:

nfsd *[option]* The ***NFS server daemon,*** which runs on the server side. The daemon services the client's NFS requests. The *option* specifies how many daemons should be started; the common value is eight.

biod *[option]* The ***NFS block I/O daemon*** handles the client side of the NFS I/O. The *option* specifies the number of daemons to be started; the common value is eight.

rpc.lockd The ***NFS lock daemon,*** which handles file lock requests on both sides; a client requests file locks and a server grants them.

rpc.statd The ***NFS status monitor daemon,*** which provides monitoring services requested by the ***rpc.lockd*** daemon. More specifically, this daemon allows locks to be reset properly after a crash. The daemon runs on both sides: client and server.

rpc.mountd The ***NFS mount daemon*** runs on the server side and processes the client mount requests.

The NFS-related daemons are started during the system booting, within the corresponding initialization script files. A typical startup sequence consists of several *if* statements and appropriate commands, mostly like the one presented here:

```
          .....
          .....
if [ -f /usr/etc/biod ]; then
   biod 4;                        echo -n ' biod'
fi
echo '.'
          .....
          .....
#
# if the /etc/exports file exists it becomes the nfs server
#
if [ -f /etc/exports ]; then
    >/etc/xtab
    exportfs -a
    nfsd 8 &                      echo -n 'nfsd'
    .....
    rpc.mountd -n
    .....
fi
    .....
    .....
#
# start up status monitor and locking daemon if present
#
if [ -f /usr/etc/rpc.statd ]; then
    rpc.statd &                       echo -n 'statd'
fi
```

```
if [ -f /usr/etc/rpc.lockd ]; then
    rpc.lockd &                    echo -n 'lockd'
fi
.....
.....
```

In order to start any of the NFS daemons, a very logical condition must be fulfilled: a corresponding program must exist. However, for an NFS server, an additional condition is required: the existence of the file */etc/exports*, which actually represents the NFS configuration file and contains information about all directories the server is exporting to its NFS clients; otherwise the ***nfsd*** daemon will not start. If the file exists, the command **exportfs** is executed; this command reads the */etc/exports* file and exports specified directories. The command also lists current information in the */etc/xtab* file, which is later used by the ***rpc.mountd*** daemon. This sequence is different on Solaris because of the existing differences in file naming and locations.

18.2 Exporting and Mounting Remote Filesystems

18.2.1 Exporting a Filesystem

To avoid any confusion in the text that follows, we will try to make things clear at the very beginning. Two terms are used to describe an NFS server advertising and making a filesystem available networkwide:

1. ***export*** — used by most UNIX flavors
2. ***share*** — used by Solaris 2.x

Unfortunately, this dual terminology has also had an impact on the naming of the corresponding NFS-related files; different names are in use for files and data with the same purpose.

We will use the term ***export***, which has been the only term actually used for a long time. The term ***share*** may better explain the nature of the action, but still sounds strange to the majority of UNIX administrators. Both types of files will be simultaneously presented.

The first step in configuring an NFS server is to determine which filesystems are to be exported and the restrictions that will be placed on their export. Only filesystems that can be beneficial to clients should be exported. Once selected, they have to be specified in the */etc/exports* file or, in the case of Solaris 2.x, in the */etc/dfs/dfstab* file (unfortunately the format and syntax of these files are different).

Exporting a filesystem means making the filesystem available to remote hosts. However, the server still has full control over the exported filesystem (at least, the filesystem physically belongs to the server and resides in its local disk space), permitting access to remote clients only in predefined ways.

It is not mandatory for an exported filesystem to match the complete server's local filesystem; only a part of the local filesystem can be exported. When the server exports a filesystem, it actually refers to an arbitrary starting directory within the local filesystem, and exports everything beneath that directory. This is presented in Figure 18.1.

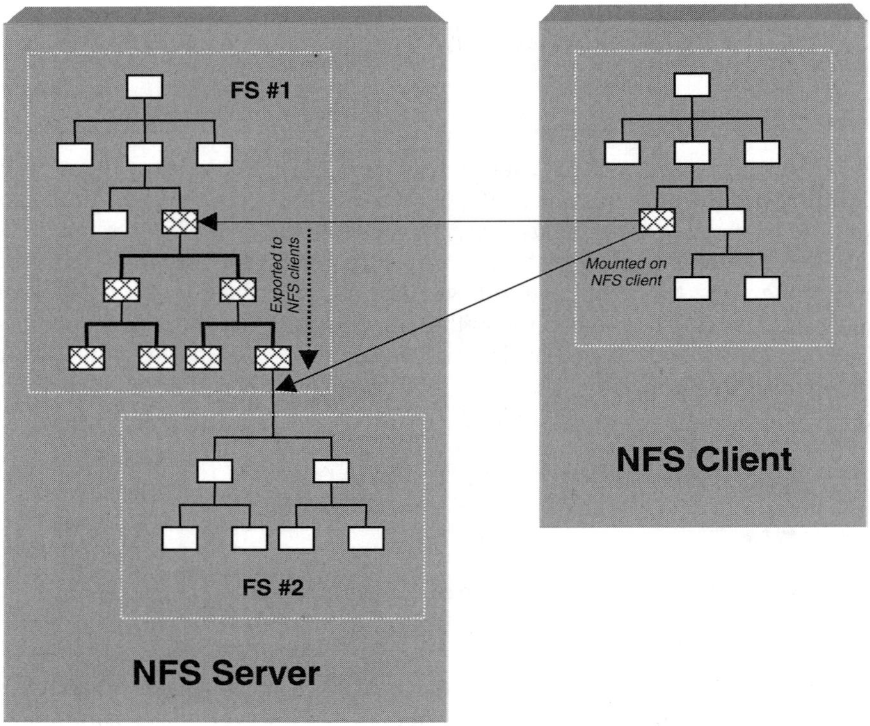

FIGURE 18.1
Exporting NFS.

A filesystem exporting is performed by the UNIX command ***/usr/sbin/exportfs*** (on some flavors, also ***/usr/etc/exportfs***); on Solaris 2.x the equivalent command is ***/usr/sbin/share***. A brief description of the **exportfs** command follows. Although the **share** command (on Solaris 2.x) does the same job, please note that some noncrucial differences among the two commands are possible.

18.2.1.1 The exportfs and share Commands

The **exportfs** command makes a local directory or a filename available for mounting over the network by NFS clients. It is normally invoked at boot time within the corresponding **rc** startup script and uses information contained in the */etc/exports* file to export specified directories (which must be specified as full pathnames). The command can also be invoked from the command line at any time to alter the list or characteristics of exported directories and filenames (superuser privileges are required). Directories and files that are currently exported are listed in the file */etc/xtab* (on Solaris 2.x this is the file */etc/dfs/sharetab*).

The format of the **exportfs** command is:

/usr/sbin/exportfs [***-options*** **] [** ***pathname*** **]**

With no options or arguments, **exportfs** prints out the list of directories and filenames currently exported.

The options are:

Option	Meaning
-a	All. Export all pathnames listed in */etc/exports*.
-i	Ignore the options in */etc/exports*. Normally, **exportfs** will consult */etc/exports* for the options associated with the exported pathname.
-u	Un-export the indicated pathnames (Solaris 2.x introduced the **unshare** command for this purpose).
-v	Verbose. Print each directory or filename as it is exported or un-exported.
-o *arguments*	Specify a comma-separated list of optional characteristics for the pathname being exported. *args* can be selected from among:
ro	Export the pathname read-only. If not specified, the pathname is exported read-write.
rw=hostname[:hostname]...	Export the pathname read-mostly. Read-mostly means exported read-only to most machines, but read-write to those specified. If not specified, the pathname is exported read-write to all.
anon=uid	If a request comes from an unknown user, use UID as the effective user ID. Root users (UID 0) are always considered "unknown" by the NFS server unless they are included in the "root option" below. If the client is a UNIX system, only root users are considered "unknown." All other users are recognized, even if they are not in */etc/passwd;* the default value for UID is the user ID of the user "nobody." If user "nobody" does not exist, the value "–2" is used. Setting the value of *anon* to "–1" disables anonymous access.
root=hostname[:hostname]...	Give root access only to the root users from a specified *hostname.* The default is for no hosts to be granted root access. This is an essential security precaution to prevent superuser privileges over exported filesystems by clients' root users.
access=client[:client]...	Give mount access to each *client* listed. A *client* can either be a host name or a netgroup. Each *client* in the list is first looked for in the */etc/hosts* database, and then in the */etc/netgroup* database. The default value allows any machine to mount the given directory.
secure	Require clients to use a more secure protocol when accessing the directory.

Once a filesystem has been exported, a new directory cannot be exported if it is either a parent or a subdirectory of one that is currently exported and within the same local filesystem. It would be illegal, for example, to export both */usr* and */usr/local* if both directories resided in the same disk partition. In other words, already exported filesystems cannot be extended toward a parent directory; if necessary, the filesystem must be un-exported first, and then re-exported by referring to the parent directory instead. Exporting a child directory at a later time does not make sense either, because all child directories within the same local filesystem are already exported.

The following are a few examples of the use of the command (for both the **exportfs** and **share** commands):

- **exportfs** without any options lists the currently exported directories and files:

  # exportfs

- To export entries specified in the */etc/exports* file:

  # exportfs -a

- To un-export all exported files and directories:

  # exportfs -ua

- To un-export all exported files and directories and print each directory or file name as it is un-exported:

  # exportfs -uav

- To export */usr* to the world, ignoring options in */etc/exports*:

  # exportfs -i /usr

- To export */usr/bin* and */var/adm* read-only to the world:

  # exportfs -i -o ro /usr/bin /var/adm

- To export */usr/bin* read-write only to systems ***black*** and ***white***:

  # exportfs -i -o rw=black:white /usr/bin

- To export root access on */var/adm* only to the system named ***red***, and mount access to both ***red*** and ***blue***:

  # exportfs -i -o root=red, access=red:blue /var/adm

- To export (share) the */export/disk* filesystem read-only:

  # share -F nfs -o ro /export/disk

- If **share** commands are invoked multiple times on the same filesystem, the last **share** invocation supersedes the previous one (the options set by the last **share** command replace the old options). For example, if read-write permission was given to ***userA*** on */usr/fs1*, then to give read-write permission also to ***userB*** on the same filesystem */usr/fs1* you would do the following:

  # share -F nfs -o rw=userA:userB /usr/fs1

18.2.1.2 The Export Configuration File

The export configuration file */etc/exports* is actually the NFS server configuration file. The basic purpose of the file is to specify exported file systems during the startup of the NFS service (primarily during the system booting). On Solaris 2.x, the corresponding file is */etc/dfs/dfstab*. Both files control which files and directories will be exported, which hosts may access them, and what kind of access is allowed.

Here is an example:

 # cat /etc/exports

```
/patsy      -access=hcprophet:indigo1:indigo2:mvaxgr:rs01ch:rs02ch:rs03ch
/usr/man
/etc        -ro,access=gatorchem
/home       -access=gatorchem
```

Each entry in the file has the format:

directory [-option][,option]...

where

directory Defines a filesystem (a directory structure) specified by the reference starting directory (it can be even a single file) available for export.

option Each option specifies a condition for the export of that directory:

- ***ro*** Read-only prevents clients from writing to this directory.
- ***rw*** Read-write permits clients to read and write to this directory; a *sign* = with a list of clients

separated by the colons can also be included. If the list is omitted all clients are granted read-write access.

access=hostlist Permits the mounting of this directory only to hosts specified in the *hostlist* (the list of clients separated by colons); this is necessary, otherwise all hosts on the Internet are allowed to mount this directory.

Another example is from the Solaris 2.x platform:

$ cat /etc/dfs/dfstab

```
/usr/sbin/share   -F nfs   -o rw /var/mail
/usr/sbin/share   -F nfs   -o ro /usr/share/man
/usr/sbin/share   -F nfs   -o ro,anon=0 /files/os
/usr/sbin/share   -F nfs   -o rw,root=delft:aegean   /files/export
/usr/sbin/share   -F nfs   -o rw,root=delft:aegean   /files1/export
/usr/sbin/share   -F nfs   -o rw,root=delft:aegean   /files2/export
/usr/sbin/share   -F nfs   -o ro /cdrom
```

This file contains a list of **share** commands to be executed during the NFS startup; it is a part of the corresponding **rc** initialization script. Each entry in the list is a full command string, just like when the command is executed from the command line.

18.2.1.3 The Export Status File

The export configuration files specify how to configure our NFS server. If everything is set up properly, the specified configuration should also be established upon system startup. However, there is not an absolute guarantee that this will always happen. A hardware failure can prevent the export of the broken disk, locally nonmounted file-systems cannot be exported, an exported filesystem can later be manually un-exported, and so on.

The **exportfs** command, as well as its Solaris counterpart the **share** command, maintains another file that reflects at every moment the current status of exported filesystems. This is the */etc/xtab* file, which is a system file that contains a list of currently exported directories and files. To ensure that this file is always synchronous with current system data structures, do not attempt to edit */etc/xtab* by hand. On Solaris 2.x the file is named */etc/dfs/sharetab*. It is helpful to remember that whenever the **exportfs** or **share** command is executed without any specified options, it reads the contents of the export status file.

The nature and format of the both files is the same. Here is an example on the Solaris 2.x platform that corresponds to the previously presented */etc/dfs/dfstab* NFS configuration file.

 # cat /etc/dfs/sharetab

```
/var/mail          -   nfs   rw
/usr/share/man     -   nfs   ro
/files/export      -   nfs   rw,root=delft:aegean
/files/os          -   nfs   ro,anon =0
/files1/export     -   nfs   rw,root=delft:aegean
/files2/export     -   nfs   rw,root=delft:aegean
```

If we carefully compare the two files, the export configuration file */etc/dfs/dfstab* and this export status file */etc/dfs/sharetab*, we see that all of the specified filesystems are exported except the */cdrom* filesystem. In this case, the discrepancy is easy to explain: if a CD-ROM disk is not inserted into the CD-ROM drive, the */cdrom* filesystem cannot be exported at all.

18.2.2 Mounting Remote Filesystems

An exported filesystem cannot be used before it is mounted on the client side; mounting an exported system means to mount and later access a remote filesystem through the network. That is the whole idea of NFS. Technically, mounting a remote filesystem is quite different from mounting a local one; from an administrative standpoint the differences are minor, but from the user standpoint there is no difference at all.

18.2.2.1 The *showmount* Command

Before we start mounting a remote filesystem, we must decide which NFS server to use, and which filesystems are to be exported and available from the server. Any necessary information about the filesystems to be exported can be obtained with the **showmount** command and a reference to the corresponding server. For example:

 # showmount -e patsy (***patsy*** *is the NFS server and it belongs to the same domain*)

export list for patsy:
/patsy hcprophet,indigo1,indigo2,mvaxgr,rs01ch,rs02ch,rs03ch
/usr/share/man (everyone)
/etc gatorchem
/home gatorchem

The export list shows the NFS directories (filesystems) exported by the server ***patsy,*** as well as their properties. In this case the list matches the previously presented export configuration file */etc/exports*. Regardless of what the list looks like, it is up to us to decide how to mount the available remote filesystem. As in the case of local filesystems, there is no a magic formula for this; the decision depends on many other factors.

18.2.2.2 The *mount* Command and the Filesystem Configuration File

Mounting a remote filesystem means attaching it to the client's UNIX overall hierarchical directory structure. The mounted remote filesystems are integrated into an overall directory tree. The same **mount** command that mounts local filesystems is used for this purpose. The differences are in the way the remote filesystems are identified, and some specific filesystem properties.

We have already described the **mount** command in great detail. Here, only the issues related to remote filesystems will be discussed. The format of the **mount** command applicable to remote filesystems is:

mount ***server-name:remote-directory local-directory [-o options]***

where

server-name Identifies an NFS server

remote-directory Identifies all or part of a directory exported by that server, and must be an absolute pathname (starting with a leading/)

local-directory Identifies the *mount-point*, the client's directory where the *remote-directory* will be attached to the client's filesystem. It must be an absolute pathname, *local-directory* must be created before **mount** is executed, and it is very common to use *server-name* for the last level name in the *local-directory*

options	One or more options applicable for NFS (though some of them are only applicable to NFS) such as:	
	bg/fg	If the first attempt fails, retry in background or foreground
	retry=n	The number of times to retry
	timeo=n	Set the time-out to *n* tenths of second
	intr	Allows keyboard interrupt
	soft/hard	Return an error if the server does not respond or continue to retry until the server responds

The **umount** command is used to dismount a mounted remote filesystem. There is no difference in using the **umount** command for locally or remotely mounted filesystems.

Generally speaking, remote filesystems are treated just like any local filesystem. The differences are in the type of the filesystem (in this case it is the *nfs* type), and in some options specific to the filesystem type. Consequently, NFS filesystems could, and should, be mounted automatically during the system startup. This means the necessary information for mounting remote filesystems should be appended in the client's filesystem configuration file (usually the file */etc/fstab*, or */etc/vfstab*).

An example follows:

```
# cat /etc/fstab | grep nfs
.....
hcprophet:/hcprophet      /hcprophet         nfs   rw,hard,bg,intr   0  0
patsy:/patsy              /patsy             nfs   rw,hard,bg,intr   0  0
rs01ch:/home/2gig/rs      / rs               nfs   rw,hard,bg,intr   0  0
mvaxgr:/export/DUB1       /mvaxgr/disku2     nfs   rw,soft,bg,intr   0  0
mvaxgr:/export/DUB2       /mvaxgr/disku3     nfs   rw,soft,bg,intr   0  0
```

Please note that only NFS-related entries are presented. The very same names in different columns do have different meanings; for example, the first column "*patsy:/patsy*" identifies the NFS server ***patsy*** and the exported directory ***/patsy***, while the second column ***/patsy*** identifies mount-point, which is the directory ***/patsy***. All specified options are NFS-specific. The last two columns "0 0" do not make a lot of sense, because filesystem checkup and backup are always provided at the server's side (this is the filesystem configuration file on the client's side).

A corresponding entry in the filesystem status file (*/etc/mtab* or */etc/mnttab*) is automatically created for each successfully mounted remote filesystem, just as it would be for any mounted local filesystem.

18.3 Automounter

The ***automounter***, better known as the ***automount***, is a tool that automatically mounts NFS filesystems when they are referenced, and dismounts them when they are no longer needed. Maintaining remote filesystems that are permanently mounted also keeps processor resources permanently busy, with an unavoidable impact on the system's overall performance. It is a good idea to mount a remote filesystem only when its data are needed; otherwise a remote filesystem remains dismounted and the required processor resources are released for other tasks. The price we must pay for this benefit is additional automount-related administration. Using data for the first time takes slightly longer because the corresponding remote filesystem must be automounted. Once mounted, the remote filesystem remains mounted as long as it is used; after a certain time of inactivity (the usual time-out is a few minutes) the remote filesystem is automatically dismounted.

Another benefit of using the automounter is the fact that there is no longer any need to keep filesystem configuration data (the file */etc/fstab* or */etc/vfstab*) up to date by hand. The information required for a mounting, including the NFS server, filesystem pathnames on the server, local mount points and mount options, are now part of the automount configuration data, which are usually maintained as NIS maps. In that way, the NIS management can also be implemented on the NFS configuration data, so a single NIS map can be handled and spread through the network to all NFS clients.

The automounter was, and is, an integral part of the majority of UNIX flavors. A public domain version called ***amd*** is also available; it is kernel independent and can be used on almost any UNIX system.

There are many motivations for using the automounter:

- The filesystem configuration data (*/etc/fstab* and */etc/vfstab* files) on every host becomes much less complex.
- The automount maps may be maintained using NIS, thereby streamlining the administration of mount tables for all hosts in the network the same way NIS streamlines other information.
- The exposure to the risk of hanging a process when an NFS server crashes is greatly reduced; the automounter dismounts all filesystems that are not in use, removing dependencies on file servers that are not currently referenced by the client.
- The automounter can extend the basic NFS mount protocol to find the *nearest server* for replicated, read-only filesystems; in this case that server will handle the mount requests, reducing the load on the more heavily used network hardware.

An automounter is a daemon (usually named ***automountd***) that automatically and transparently mounts NFS filesystems as needed. It monitors attempts to access directories that are associated with an ***automount map***, as well as all subdirectories and files beneath these directories. For example, on Solaris 2.x platform:

```
# ps -ef | grep auto | grep -v grep
root 890   1   0   May 09 ?   1312:29   /usr/lib/autofs/automountd
```

The daemon is usually quite busy; in this example we see that the daemon at this machine has consumed a huge chunk of CPU time.

When a corresponding directory or file is referenced (referenced to be accessed, or for another reason), the daemon mounts the appropriate remote filesystem associated with the referenced point. All relevant data for a successful mounting must be defined in direct or indirect automount maps, and the corresponding remote filesystem must be exported at the NFS server for this specific client. The bottom line is that, instead of being permanently mounted, the exported NFS filesystem is mounted only when it is used.

The automounter interacts with the kernel in the following ways:

- It uses the automount map to locate an appropriate NFS server, the exported filesystem, and the mount data.
- It then mounts the filesystem in a temporary location and replaces the associated referenced mount point (the entry for the directory) with a symbolic link to the temporary location.
- Afterward, if the filesystem is not accessed within an appropriate interval (by default, 5 minutes), it dismounts the filesystem and removes the symbolic link.
- If the referenced mount-point (specified directory) does not already exist, the automounter creates it, and then removes it upon exiting.

18.3.1 The Automount Maps

The automount maps include all necessary data required for a successful automount operation, and they can be specified as local files or NIS maps. Regarding their nature, automount maps are divided into:

- ***Direct maps*** — Contain mapping for any number of nonrelated directories. Each entry in the map lists a directory that is automatically mounted as needed. The direct map as a whole is not associated with any single directory.
- ***Indirect maps*** — Specify mapping for the subdirectories to be mounted under the directory indicated in the entry. The indirect map as a whole is associated with the directory in the entry, providing more data related to the belonging subdirectories.
- ***Included maps*** — The contents of another map can be included within the map; it simply replaces a complete entry in the map. The included map is identified by the leading "+" sign.
- ***Special maps*** — These are special cases; currently there are three such maps: "-hosts," "-passwd," and "-null."

The file */etc/auto_master* is known as the master map for the automounter; it is actually the *automount configuration file*, and it specifies the locations of all other automount maps. Here is an example:

```
$ cat /etc/auto_master
# Master map for automounter for this host
# The map reflects the site configuration
#
# Mount-point      Map            Mount-opt ions
/-                 auto_direct    -ro
/net               -hosts         -rw,soft
/home              auto_home      -rw
/share             auto_share     -rw
#
# This configuration is slightly different than the common one
# for other clients; other clients simply includes the NIS auto_master map
# (which is here commented-out)
# +auto_master
```

The automounter reads each of the entries to learn how to behave. Each entry defines the relationship between a directory and a corresponding NFS filesystem, in a direct or an indirect way. The entry "/-" defines direct mappings; it points to the */etc/auto_direct* file for the actual direct mappings. Often, the NIS map is used instead of presented entries. The ***+auto_master*** refers to the NIS map "*auto_master,*" which spreads a unique configuration all over the network. However, for this host this is not the case; obviously this host is the NIS master server.

The main candidates for the automount are the ***home*** and ***share*** filesystems — the first one to provide the same user's access to any machine in the network, the second one because of its purpose (to be shared among all machines). They are fully determined indirectly through the */etc/auto_home* and */etc/auto_share* files. Please note that any exported filesystem can be controlled by an automounter; this is simply an administrative decision. Also, the naming of the corresponding indirect automount map is not mandatory; the map itself is specified within the *auto_master* configuration file. It is logical for the map's name to match the name of the exported remote filesystem, but it is not necessary, and an arbitrary name for the map could be used instead.

18.3.1.1 An Example

An example of the *auto_home* and *auto_share* maps follows. The contents of two configuration files are:

```
$ cat /etc/auto_home
# Home directory map for automounter
#       for nis clients
# The map reflects site configuration
#
+auto_home
```

As we can see, the */etc/auto_home* file includes a single line: the NIS map ***auto_home*** replaces all individual users' entries, and this could be a very long list (hundreds, even thousands of users), which should be defined only at a single host — the NIS master server. A home directory must be defined in the usual NFS way (*hostname:pathname*) for each user.

```
$ ypcat -k auto_home
rmargoli    aegean:/files1/export/home/rmargoli
nrosenbl    aegean:/files1/export/home/nrosenbl
lchristi    aegean:/files1/export/home/lchristi
fhomolka    aegean:/files1/export/home/fhomolka
dandjeli    aegean:/files1/export/home/dandjeli
      ...
      ...
ktung       aegean:/files1/export/ home/ktung
cteti       aegean:/files1/export/home/cteti
ssze        aegean:/files1/export/home/ssze
mlee        aegean:/files1/export/home/mlee
bbae        aegean:/files1/export/home/bbae
kwu         aegean:/files1/export/home/kwu
cko         aegean:/files1/export/home/cko
```

Similarly, for the */etc/auto_share* file:

$ cat /etc/auto_share

```
# Shared directory map for automounter
#       for nis clients
# The map reflects a site configuration
+auto_share
```

And the NIS *auto_share* map:

$ ypcat -k auto_share

```
suitespot    aegean:/files1/export/share/suitespot
totalnet     hunter:/files/export/share/totalnet
catalog      aegean:/files1/export/share/catalog
sybase       peri:/files/export/share/sybase
public       aegean:/files1/export/share/public
     .....
     .....
openv        mekong:/files/export/share/openv
batch        aegean:/files1/export/share/batch
mail         admin:/var/mail
http         peri:/files/export/share/http
man          aegean:/usr/man
doc          aegean:/files1/export/share/doc
```

When any subdirectory in the directory ***/share*** is referenced, (or any of subdirectories or files beneath) the corresponding NFS filesystem specified in the automount ***auto_share*** map (i.e., the */etc/auto_share* file or the subsequent NIS map) is temporarily mounted. This is done automatically and is transparent to users and processes; they do not know anything about the huge job that is accomplished before getting the required data. The same happens if the directory ***/home*** is referenced, except that the file ***/etc/auto_home*** and the subsequent NIS map ***auto_home*** are used instead.

The hierarchical structure of the automount configuration data provides a flexible way to join data from different systems into a unified network-based collection of data. In that way, each user can log in to any system, and access the same data in the same home directory that actually resides on some other system. Simply, users are always "at home," regardless of where they started their login process.

A simple mapping entry takes the form:

key [-mount-options] location ...

where

key — The full pathname of the directory to mount when used in a direct map, or the simple name of a directory in an indirect map

mount-options — A comma-separated list of mount options

location — Specifies a filesystem from which the directory/subdirectory may be mounted. In the case of a simple NFS mount, location takes the form: *host:pathname*, where:

- *host* — The name of the host from which to mount the filesystem (if omitted, the pathname refers to the local device)
- *pathname* — The pathname of the directory to mount

We have talked about indirect automount maps. Let us see how the */etc/auto_direct* file looks:

$ cat /etc/auto_direct

```
# Direct map for automounter for nis client
# The map reflects a site configuration
#
+auto_direct
```

Let us see the NIS *auto_direct* map:

$ ypcat -k auto_direct

In this case the *auto_direct* map is empty. Otherwise, the very same rules are implemented as with the *auto_home* and *auto_share* maps, except that the NIS *auto_direct* map is empty. Please note that the map exists, but it is empty — there is simply no need for direct mappings at this site.

The entry:

net -host

has a special meaning; "-host" is a special map used to mount all exported filesystems from any host that the automounter can mount (the assumed key is the host name of an NFS server). In other words, the directory */net* includes subdirectories named by the host names of NFS servers that have exported their filesystems to this machine. Obviously, subdirectories below are exported directories. Here is an example:

$ cd /net

$ ls -l

```
total 10
lrwxrwxrwx  1 root  root  26 Jun 8 15:01  admin -> /tmp_mnt/net/admin
lrwxrwxrwx  1 root  root  29 Jun 8 15:02  aegean -> /tmp_mnt/net/aegean
lrwxrwxrwx  1 root  root  38 Jun 8 15:02  baltic -> /tmp_mnt/net/baltic
lrwxrwxrwx  1 root  root  33 Jun 8 15:02  delft -> /tmp_mnt/net/delft
lrwxrwxrwx  1 root  root  33 Jun 8 15:01  hunter -> /tmp_mnt/net/hunter
```

$ cd admin

$ ls -l

```
total 4
drwxrwxr-x   11 root   sys    512 Jun 5 13:30    export
dr-xr-xr-x   3 root    root   96 Jun 8 15:01     files2
dr-xr-xr-x   3 root    root   96 Nov 12 1997     usr
dr-xr-xr-x   2 root    root   96 Jun 8 15:01     var
```

Since we have mentioned most of the advantages of the automounter, it is fair to also mention some of its disadvantages. When the host (where the home directories reside) is down, users will still be able to login to other hosts, but they will not be able to reach their home directories and data; this situation takes some time to correct. Also, don't be surprised when you list a directory that is a mount point for automounter, and you don't see the expected subdirectory; don't forget that the automounter mounts only referenced directories — once you reference a previously unseen directory (for example, "cd" to the subdirectory and back), it will appear in the directory list, until it is dismounted again.

Today, the automount is widely in use — it improves network performance, makes maintenance easier, and makes the network behave as an equivalent large system. It integrates all of the advantages of NFS and NIS, bringing them together for users' benefits.

18.4 NFS — Security Issues

NFS and NIS are two independent services in the network environment. Their missions are quite different: NFS is the user-oriented service, enabling the use of remote filesystem resources locally, and NIS helps UNIX administrators accomplish the system administration through the network in a uniform and well-organized way. Obviously, the two services can exist separately.

However, NFS requires, in some ways, that NIS also be implemented. This is not a "must", but is highly recommended to keep the user administrative database uniform and consistent on all NFS clients. What is the reason for this statement?

NFS identifies users by their UID; this is not unusual on UNIX systems, but in this specific case NFS users are coming from different client-hosts. If it happens that two different users at two different NFS client hosts have equal UIDs (this is a very probable situation), NFS recognizes them as the same, single user. It also means that all NFS resources (directories, files, etc.) would be accessible, in an unrestricted way, to both users. And this is a problem, a main drawback of NFS, and a security hole that simply eliminates the possible use of NFS in some highly secure network environments. This situation can easily be prevented by using NIS to administer NFS clients, and by providing conditions for safe NFS implementation, i.e., each user has a single UID networkwide.

19

UNIX Remote Commands

19.1 UNIX *r* Commands

This is a topic that illustrates in greater detail why UNIX is so suitable for network implementations. UNIX designers realized long ago the significance of tightening multiple hosts into a unique working environment, where a whole network of connected hosts appears as an "equiva-lent host." Such an equivalency, based on mutual trusting relationships among all participating hosts, eliminates the need for individual user authentication and enables easy and powerful local and remote processing.

If you ever had the task of handling a dozen hosts in a network, you would understand this very well. How do you execute the same (or a similar) program efficiently on a dozen hosts? And just imagine if you should run them every day, or every hour, or even more frequently. What do you do if it is not a dozen hosts, but a hundred, or maybe five hundred, or a thousand?

It is hard to imagine the efficient maintenance of hosts in a network environment without UNIX remote commands. UNIX remote commands are the vehicles that make each host in the network accessible in an extremely comfortable and efficient way. We will call them ***UNIX r commands***, according to the implemented prefix "*r*" in their names.

What are the *UNIX r-commands*? Among all available commands, UNIX also provides a set of remote commands:

rlogin Remote login provides interactive access to remote hosts. A user can reach a remote host through the network, log in, and perform all activities regularly provided by the host.

rcp Remote copy allows files to be copied from or to remote systems. Its syntax is similar to the regular copy (***cp***) command, except that the file path includes the name of a remote host. It moves the files between hosts on the network using a simple command-line interface.

rsh (remsh) Remote shell passes a command to a remote host for execution. Standard output and standard error from the remote execution are returned to the local host.

The third command listed is not a single command at all; here we talk about a UNIX shell that includes all UNIX commands. This is an extremely powerful and versatile way to execute any UNIX command (or set of commands) on a remote host, with full control over their execution, just as if everything is happening locally.

Some UNIX flavors, like HP-UX, use ***remsh*** for "remote shell"-ing (even the verb "remshing" is widely implemented), because ***rsh*** (also in use) could be misinterpreted for a "restricted shell." Although both terms are correct, the command name **remsh** will be used in the text that follows.

The main advantages of using *UNIX r-commands* is the fact that they are used in very familiar ways, just like any other, local UNIX command is used. However, an efficient remshing is supposed to bypass the authentication on a remote host, and it could affect some security issues. Bypassing the authentication is always a challenge for potential intruders; this means everything must be set up very carefully to avoid possible security problems. This is accomplished by establishing a so-called trusted relationship between hosts involved in remote command execution.

Trusted hosts (another term used is *equivalent hosts*) establish a special mutual relationship where a certain number of users, known as ***trusted users*** receive special treatment. Once authenticated, trusted users at one host are assumed to be allowed without any additional authentication into another trusted host. Trusted users have direct access to remote hosts and play a central role in implementing UNIX r-commands. We will come back to this issue later. First, a brief description of *UNIX r-commands* follows.

For some UNIX r-commands (more precisely, for the ***rlogin*** command) an equivalency (trusted relationship) among the involved hosts is not mandatory — the host equivalency only makes the command execution more efficient. If there is no equivalency, additional authentication is required. However, a majority of UNIX r-commands will fail without provided host equivalency.

19.1.1 The *rlogin* Command

A remote login session from one host to the remote host named *hostname* is established by ***rlogin***. The format of the command is:

rlogin *[-option] [-l username] hostname*

Hostnames are listed in the *hosts database*, which may be contained in the local */etc/hosts* file, the NIS database, DNS database, or a combination of these. Either official hostnames or nicknames (aliases) may be specified in *hostname* (however, a host equivalency can be implemented only when official hostnames are used).

Each remote host may have a file named */etc/hosts.equiv* containing a list of trusted hostnames with which it shares usernames. Users with the same username on both the local and remote host may ***rlogin*** from the host listed in the remote host's */etc/hosts.equiv* file without supplying a password.

Individual users may set up a similar private equivalence list with the file *.rhosts* in their home directories. Each line in this file contains two names, a *hostname* and a *username*, separated by a space. An entry in a remote user's *.rhosts* file permits the user named *username* who is logged into *hostname* to ***rlogin*** to the remote host as the remote user without supplying a password.

If the name of the local host is not found in the */etc/hosts.equiv* file on the remote host, and the local username and hostname are not found in the remote user's *.rhosts* file, then the remote host will prompt for a password. Hostnames listed in */etc/hosts.equiv* and *.rhosts* files must be the official hostnames listed in the hosts database; nicknames (aliases) may not be used in either of these files.

19.1.2 The *rcp* Command

The remote file copy command to copy files between hosts is ***rcp***. The format of the command is:

rcp *[-p]* ***filename1 filename2***
rcp *[-pr]* ***filename...directory***

Each *filename* or *directory* argument is either a remote file name of the form *hostname:path*, or a local file name. If a *filename* is not a full path name, it is interpreted relative to the home directory on *hostname.*

rcp does not prompt for passwords; the user who executes ***rcp*** must be the trusted user on *hostname* before remote command execution is allowed. ***rcp*** also handles third-party copies, where neither source nor target files are on the local host (copying from one to another remote host).

Hostnames may also take the form *username@hostname:filename* to use *username* rather than your current local user name as the username on the remote host. ***rcp*** also supports Internet domain addressing of the remote host, so that *username@host.domain:filename* specifies the username to be used, the hostname, and the domain in which that host resides. Filenames that are not full path names will be interpreted relative to the home directory of the user named *username* on the remote host.

The options are:

-p Attempt to give each copy the same modification times, access times, and modes as the original file

-r Recursively, copy each subtree rooted at *filename;* in this case the destination must be a directory

19.1.3 The *remsh (rsh)* Command

The remote shell command, ***remsh (rsh)***, has the following format:

remsh *[-l* ***username*** *] [-n]* ***hostname*** *[* ***command*** *]*
rsh *[-l* ***username*** *] [-n]* ***hostname*** *[* ***command*** *]*

remsh connects to the specified *hostname* and executes the specified *command.* ***remsh*** copies its standard input to the remote command, the standard output of the remote command to its standard output, and the standard error of the remote command to its standard error. Interrupt, quit, and terminate signals are propagated to the remote command; ***remsh*** normally terminates when the remote command does.

If the *command* is omitted, instead of executing a single command, ***remsh*** logs you in on the remote host using ***rlogin***.

Shell metacharacters that are not quoted are interpreted on the local host, while quoted metacharacters are interpreted on the remote host.

Hostnames are given in the *hosts database*, which may be contained in the local */etc/hosts* file, the NIS database, the DNS database, or some combination of the three.

Each remote host may have a file named */etc/hosts.equiv,* containing a list of trusted hostnames with which it shares usernames. Users with the same username on both the local and remote hosts may ***remsh*** from the hosts listed in the remote host's */etc/hosts.equiv* file.

Individual users may set up a similar private equivalence list with the file *.rhosts* in their home directories. Each line in this file contains two names, a hostname and a username, separated by a space. The entry permits the user named *username* who is logged into *hostname* to use ***remsh*** to access the remote host as the remote user.

remsh will not prompt for a password if access is denied on the remote host (it simply fails) unless the *command* argument is omitted (it is equivalent then to ***rlogin***).

The options are:

-l *username* Use *username* as the remote username instead of the local username. In the absence of this option, the remote username is the same as the local username.

-n Redirect the input of ***remsh*** to */dev/null*. This option is sometimes needed to avoid unfortunate interactions between ***remsh*** and the ***shell*** that invokes it.

A few examples:

- The following command appends the remote file *FileonHost2.there* from the host called *Host2* to the file called *FileonHost2.here* on the host called *Host1*:

  Host1: remsh Host2 cat FileonHost2.there >> FileonHost2.here

- The next example appends the file *FileonHost2.there* on the host called *Host2* to the file *FileonHost2.there.again*, which also resides on the host called *Host2*:

  Host1: remsh Host2 cat FileonHost2.there ">>" FileonHost2.there.again

The quoting of the >> sign changes the redirection of the standard output to another file on the remote host. There is a more comprehensive way to specify this very same command:

Host1: remsh Host2 "cat FileonHost2.there >> FileonHost2.there.again"

It is clear now that the "remshing" is completely executing at the remote host.

19.2 Securing the UNIX *r* Commands

The ***r commands*** bypass the usual user authentication and password verification for logins, and that can create some security problems. That means that the setting of trusted users and trusted hosts must be carefully performed; otherwise, it could compromise the system security. In networks isolated from the Internet, with a relatively restricted number of users who essentially belong to the same category of users (within the same department, the same division, the same company, etc.), this configuration may not seem so critical. However, never forget that improperly configured ***r commands*** can open access to the system resources to virtually anyone in the world.

On some sites, the ***r commands*** are completely eliminated (because of security concerns); this can be done by simply disabling (commenting out) the corresponding entries, the */etc/inetd.conf* file. Another possibility is to retain the ***r commands*** and to force them to request passwords from all users; in this case, you would delete the */etc/hosts.equiv* file, and make sure that users do not create personal *.rhosts* files in their home directories. This is a less drastic solution, the ***rlogin*** command (and some parts of the ***remsh*** command) will still work, and the regular authentication login procedure will secure the access to the system. The only drawback is that everything that makes the ***r commands*** great will fail.

Most sites, however, like the convenience and power of the ***r commands*** and the password-free access. In such cases, correctly setting the configuration files */etc/hosts.equiv* and *$HOME/.rhosts* is very important (here the *sh* specification for the users' home directory $HOME is used). Free access to the system must be allowed only to the trusted users. Basically, the users' authentication is delegated to the remote trusted hosts; if a user is already logged-in to the remote trusted host, then the same user is also allowed on the local system. The system assumes that, given two identical usernames on two hosts, the same person owns both accounts. Trusted hosts are also called *equivalent hosts*, and this is the origin of the name of the *hosts.equiv* file.

The implemented authentication mechanism requires databases that define the trusted hosts and the trusted users:

- */etc/hosts.equiv* Defines the trusted hosts and users for the entire system
- *$HOME/.rhosts* Defines the trusted hosts and users for an individual user account

19.2.1 The */etc/hosts.equiv* File

The */etc/hosts.equiv* file defines the hosts and users that are granted *r command access* to the system. But this file can also define hosts and users that are explicitly denied trusted access. Not having the trusted access does not mean that a user does not have access to the system at all, it just means that the user is required to supply a password.

The basic format of entries in the */etc/hosts.equiv* file is:

[+ | -][hostname][username]

where

hostname The name of the "trusted" host, optionally preceded by a plus (+) sign; a + sign used alone means "*any* host." If a *hostname* is preceded by a minus (-) sign, it explicitly means that the host is not an equivalent (trusted) system, and all users from this host must always supply a password.

username The name of the "super-trusted" user on the "trusted" host who is granted access to all user accounts without being required to provide a password (the root account is not included). If a *username* is preceded by a minus (-) sign, it means that the user is not trusted (regardless of what may be true about the host), and must always supply a password.

Some of the specified entries are not recommended! For example, the *standalone + sign* in place of a host name, which allows access from any host anywhere, is strongly discouraged. Also, the entry **+ *somename*** will open your system to the user *somename* from any host worldwide, with full rights over all user accounts. An intruder who can create the account *somename* on any host can gain complete control over all user accounts on your system.

Generally the leading + sign for *hostname* should be avoided, because a simple typographical error could give a standalone plus sign (an extraneous space between + and *hostname* will have this effect). Also, the */etc/hosts.equiv* file should not begin with the - sign as the first character, because it confuses some systems, though it is legal.

The selection of trusted hosts is up to the system administrator, but considerable attention should be paid to this issue.

19.2.2 The *$HOME/.rhosts* File

The *.rhosts* file grants or denies password-free *r command access* to a specific user's account. It is placed in the user's home directory and contains entries that define the trusted hosts and users in exactly the same way as */etc/hosts.equiv* file, but only for a single user account.

This file can be useful to establish equivalence among the different account names that a user can have on different systems. It is not always possible for a user to open accounts under the same login name everywhere. This file enables users to skip this obstacle. By putting all *hostname-username* pairs in the user's *.rhosts* file, the user can use ***commands*** from those hosts without being queried for a password (despite the differences of the *usernames* on those hosts).

However, the *.rhosts* file cannot override the *hosts.equiv* file. The two files are processed in the following way: the *hosts.equiv* file is searched first, followed by the user's *.rhosts* file, if it exists. The first explicit match determines whether or not password-free access is allowed. If the *hosts.equiv* file does not exist, however, then the *.rhosts* file alone determines password-free access to the corresponding account. A system administrator should pay attention to that fact.

When a root user attempts to access a system via ***r commands***, the *hosts.equiv* file is skipped, and only the */.rhosts* file is consulted (supposing "/" as a superuser's home directory). This allows root access to be more tightly controlled and separated from other users who can then be configured collectively by the *hosts.equiv* file.

19.2.3 Using UNIX *r*-Commands — An Example

To better understand the advantages of using UNIX ***r commands*** in a network environment, let us suppose the following arbitrary, but realistic, situation. Our task is to check the status of a number of processes running on a number of hosts and to generate a corresponding report. Let us suppose a list of hosts is given in the file */usr/local/index/HostList* (each line includes a single hostname); a list of processes in the file */usr/local/index/ProcessList* (each line includes a process name); and the report is written in the file */usr/local/logs/Report*. Upon successful completion, the report should be printed or e-mailed.

The *ksh* script named ***check_processes***, owned by the user ***chk_oper***, and executed from the host ***CentralHost*** is supposed to do this job efficiently. The script remotely checks the status of the listed processes on each of the listed hosts (this could be hundreds of hosts, and hundreds of processes), and locally displays the related status messages and writes them into the ***Report*** file. The only requirement for successful script execution is to provide the equivalency between ***CentralHost*** and all checked hosts for the user ***chk_oper***, who executes the script (this can be done through the */etc/hosts.equiv* file or the *.rhost* file in the home directory for the user ***chk_oper***). The script is presented below:

$ cat /usr/local/bin/check_processes

```
#!/bin/ksh
  # This is the script "check_processes"
  # Purpose:    To check the status of listed processes at listed hosts
  # Input:      Listed processes in the file "/usr/local/index/ProcessList";
  #             Listed hosts in the file "/usr/local/index/HostList".
  # Output:     generated report at standard output and in the file "/usr/local/logs/Report".
  #             could be printed on default printer and/or email to the user
  #
```

```
# First specify variables - it is easier to work with them
PROCESSES=/usr/local/index/ProcessList
HOSTS=/usr/local/index/HostList
REPORT=/usr/local/logs/Report
ALIAS=chk_oper

# The starting timestamp
echo "\n\nThe script check_processes started on `date`\n" | tee $REPORT

# A single loop for all listed processes at all listed hosts
for Host in `cat $HOSTS`
do
  for Process in `cat $PROCESSES`
  do
    echo "****************************************" | tee -a $REPORT
    echo "Checking the host \"$Host\":" | tee -a $REPORT
    remsh $Host /bin/ps -ef | eval grep "$Process" > /dev/null 2>&1
    if [ $? -eq 0 ]
    then
    echo "The process \"${Process}\" is running." | tee -a $REPORT
    else
    echo "The process \"${Process}\" is missing." | tee -a $REPORT
    fi
  done
  echo "\n****************************************" | tee -a $REPORT
done
# The ending timestamp
echo "\n\nThe script \"check_processes\" completed on `date`\n\n" | tee -a $REPORT
#
# To print the report (uncomment the line)
# lp $REPORT
#
# To email the report (uncomment the line)
# mailx -s "Process Status Report" $ALIAS < $REPORT
#
# To delete the report (uncomment the line)
# rm $REPORT
#
```

This is just an example to illustrate the strength of "remshing." The rest of the example shows how to generate a comprehensive and effective report; of course, there are a number of other ways to do this.

19.3 Secure Shell (SSH)

There is no doubt about the benefits of using UNIX ***r commands***. However, even with all of the precautions in configuring host equivalencies, remshing is considered insecure. The reason is very simple: UNIX ***r commands*** use a clear text in communication, including the transfer of user passwords, and it is very difficult to protect such communication from any kind of tinkering in the network. Obviously, remsh-ing lacks additional encryption in the communication between remote hosts that would make it fully secure.

UNIX ***r commands*** are very suitable for protected networked environments, where cracking into the system is not the main issue. In a network behind a firewall, dedicated to internal users and protected from external intruders, remshing is an irreplaceable tool for many applications. Such networks are known as "secure," and there is no need for an additional level of implemented security.

A third-party product known as ***Secure Shell* (*SSH*)** is intended to replace UNIX ***r commands*** in a nonsecure networked environment; it provides secure encrypted communications between two hosts over a nonsecure network. ***SSH*** is based on the client/server model, and consists of the secure shell client ***ssh*** and the secure shell daemon ***sshd*** on the server side. The two programs communicate mutually and provide basically the same service as the UNIX ***r commands***.

A sufficient level of security is achieved by using one of the several supported encryption algorithms to encrypt data in the communication between the two sides, client and server. The encryption is based on the corresponding RSA keys, known only to the two sides in such a communication; the keys are completely hidden and they never appear on the network. Without knowing the keys, the data decryption is practically impossible.

SSH quickly get a substantial attention in a nonsecure network environment, and has found a wide practical implementation. It becomes a kind of standard on UNIX platform, and an unavoidable administrative topic. It also continues to develop and improve making its daily usage more secure, reliable and convenient.

19.3.1 SSH Concept

SSH is based on the encryption of the messages in the network communication between two participants. The implemented encryption algorithm is known as RSA authentication, which is accomplished by the corresponding processes running on the participating hosts.

19.3.1.1 RSA Authentication

RSA authentication is based on public key cryptography. The idea is to implement two encryption keys, one for encryption and another for decryption. It is not possible (on a human time scale) to derive the decryption key from the encryption key. The encryption key is called the public key, because it can be given to anyone and it is not secret. The decryption key, on the other hand, is secret, and is called the private key.

RSA authentication is based on the impossibility of deriving the private key from the public key. The public key is stored on the server side in the user's *$HOME/.ssh/authorized_keys* file. The private key is only kept on the user's side (local machine, laptop, or other secure storage). When a user tries to log in, the client tells the server the public key that the user wishes to use for authentication (it does not send the key itself, it simply points to the desired public key that already exists on the server side). The server then checks if this public key is admissible. If so, it generates a 256-bit random number, encrypts it with the public key, and sends the value to the client. The client then decrypts the number with its private key, computes a 128-bit MD5 checksum from the resulting data, and sends the checksum back to the server (only the checksum is sent to prevent chosen-plaintext attacks against RSA).

The server computes a checksum from the correct data (the generated random number is known only to the server) and compares the two checksums. Authentication is accepted if the checksums match (theoretically this indicates that the client alone knows the correct key, but for all practical purposes there is no doubt).

The RSA private key can be protected with a **passphrase**. The passphrase can be any string; it is hashed with MD5 to produce an encryption key for 3DES, which is used to encrypt the private part of the key file. With passphrase, authorization requires access to the key file and the passphrase. Without passphrase, authorization depends only on possession of the key file.

RSA authentication is the most secure form of authentication supported by this software. It does not rely on the network, routers, domain name servers, or the client machine. The only thing that matters is access to the private key.

All this, of course, depends on the security of the RSA algorithm itself. RSA has been widely known since about 1978, and no effective methods for breaking it are known if it is used properly. Care has been taken to avoid the well-known encryption pitfalls. Breaking RSA is widely believed to be equivalent to factoring, which is a very difficult mathematical problem that has received considerable public research. So far, no effective methods are known for numbers bigger than about 512 bits. However, as computer speeds and factoring methods are increasing, 512 bits can no longer be considered secure. The factoring work is exponential, so 768 or 1024 bits are widely considered to be secure in the near future.

19.3.1.2 The ssh Client

The client ***ssh*** connects and logs into the specified remote host. The user must prove the identity to the remote host by using one of several available methods. Initially SSH supported the following authentication methods:

- The first method presents the host equivalency, which is basically the same as for the UNIX ***r-commands*** (based on the */etc/hosts.equiv* and *$HOME/.rhosts* files), with two newly introduced alternate files */etc/shost.equiv* and *$HOME/.shosts*. Although the two additional *shosts* files have the same function as the already existing *rhosts* files, they are known only to ***ssh***; this means that they immediately eliminate ***rlogin/remsh*** connections. This method is not normally allowed because it is not secure; it bypasses all of the additional encryption that makes SSH secure.
- The second method consists of the authentication method based on the host equivalency combined with RSA-based host authentication. This means that if the login would be permitted by the files *.rhosts, .shosts, /etc/hosts.equiv,* or */etc/shosts.equiv*, and additionally if it can verify the client's host key, then login is permitted. This authentication method closes security holes due to IP spoofing, DNS spoofing, and routing spoofing. It also assumes that *rlogin/remshing* is disabled, because the corresponding host-equivalency related files could be in place.
- As a third authentication method, ***ssh*** supports RSA-based challenge-response authentication, also known as pure RSA authentication. The scheme is based on previously discussed public-key cryptography: the encryption and decryption are done using separate keys (known only to the client and server), and it is not possible to derive the decryption key from the encryption key.
- The fourth authentication method that ***ssh*** supports is authentication through a TIS authentication server; the idea is to ask a separate TIS authentication server ***authsrv*** for the user authentication data.
- Finally, the default authentication method is password-based; if other methods fail, i.e., they are not set, the SSH server will request the user's password to allow user login. However, the password is always transferred encrypted (never as a plain text).

Additional authentication methods have been introduced, and more are expected in the future. Some of them are discussed later in this text.

The core of the SSH is the implemented RSA authentication protocol. Each user creates a *public/private* key pair for authentication purposes. The server side knows the public key, and only the user knows the private key. The file *$HOME/.ssh/authorized_keys* (in the user's home directory on both sides) contains the public keys that are permitted for logging in. During the login procedure, the ***ssh*** program indicates to the server which key pair it would like to use for authentication. The server checks if the key is permitted, and if so, responds with a challenge, a random number, encrypted by the indicated public key. The challenge can only be decrypted using the proper private key. The client then decrypts the challenge using the private key, proving that this is an eligible user to login, but without disclosing it to the server.

When the server has accepted the user's identity, it either executes the given command or allows the user to log into the host and gives a normal shell on the remote host. All communication with the remote command or shell will be automatically encrypted.

SSH provides a number of scripts and programs that makes its installation and setting easier. Running the *ssh-keygen* program creates the RSA key pairs; other programs help in automatically creating the file *authorized_keys* in the user's home directory.

ssh is a secure full replacement for ***remsh*** (***rsh***), but ***ssh*** is not the only SSH-related client program; two other programs that belong to the same group are:

1. ***scp***, which copies files between hosts — a secure equivalent to the UNIX ***rcp***. It uses ***ssh*** for transfer and uses the same authentication and provides the same security as ***ssh***. Unlike ***rcp***, ***scp*** will not fail but ask for a password if it is required. Files to be transferred are specified in the same way as for ***rcp***.
2. ***slogin***, which is secure remote login — a secure equivalent to the UNIX ***rlogin***. It behaves the same as ***ssh*** without the specified command option and actually is a symbolic link to the ***ssh*** program.

It is also fair to mention ***sftp*** — the secure FTP — which is a secure equivalent to the regular file transfer FTP.

19.3.1.3 The sshd Daemon

The ***sshd*** daemon listens at the SSH server side for connections from ***ssh*** clients. It is normally started at boot time within the corresponding **rc** startup script created during the SSH installation. It forks a new daemon for each incoming connection. The forked daemons handle key exchange, encryption, authentication, command execution, and data exchange.

The following example is from the Solaris 2.x platform:

```
# ps -ef | grep ssh | grep -v grep
root   1434   1   0   May 09 ?   46:28   /share/local/bin/sshd
```

Each host has a host-specific RSA key (normally 1024 bits long). Additionally, when the ***sshd*** daemon starts, it generates a server-specific RSA key (normally 768 bits long); this key is regenerated every hour if it has been used and is never stored on a disk.

Whenever a client connects to the server, the ***sshd*** daemon sends its host and server public keys to the client. The client compares the host key against its own database to verify that it has not changed. In return, the client then generates a 256-bit random number; it encrypts this random number using both keys, the host and the server ones, and sends the encrypted generated number to the server. Both sides then start to use this random number as a "session encryption key" for all further communication in the session; it is the client who selects among several supported encryption algorithms (the default algorithm is IDEA). Afterward an authentication dialog follows. The client tries to authenticate itself by using one of the supported authentication methods.

Upon the successful client's authentication, a dialog for preparing the session is entered. Once the session is established, the client requests a shell or execution of a command. The exchange of encrypted data continues until the user program terminates and all connections are closed. The server then sends the command exit status to the client and both sides exit.

The ***sshd*** daemon can be configured using command-line options or a configuration file; command-line options override values specified in the configuration file. If the configuration data are changed, the ***sshd*** daemon must be recycled (forced to reread its configuration data by sending HUP signal to the daemon).

19.3.2 SSH Configuration

SSH offers many options in its use; obviously, an appropriate configuration is required. Both sides, server and client, must be configured properly. Even the default configuration (which is, by the way, sufficient for most sites) involves setting the configuration file supplied during the SSH installation.

The server configuration file is */etc/sshd_config*; the file contains keyword-value pairs, one per line. Lines starting with "#" and empty lines are treated as comments and ignored. There are many configuration lines, and only some of them, which are included in the following example, will be discussed.

$ cat /etc/sshd_config

```
##########################################################################
#
#  File:  sshd_config
#
#  Purpose:  sshd configuration file.
#
#  Description:  Controls the behavior of the sshd server
#
#  Used by:  sshd
##########################################################################
#
# Port 22
ListenAddress 0.0.0.0
HostKey /etc/ssh_host_key
RandomSeed /etc/ssh_random_seed
ServerKeyBits 768
LoginGraceTime 600
KeyRegenerationInterval 3600
PermitRootLogin nopwd
StrictModes yes
QuietMode no
X11Forwarding yes
PrintMotd no
KeepAlive yes
SyslogFacility DAEMON
RhostsAuthentication no
RhostsRSAAuthentication no
RSAAuthentication yes
PasswordAuthentication no
PermitEmptyPasswords no
UseLogin no
FascistLogging yes
IdleTimeout 15m
CheckMail no
```

```
IgnoreRhosts yes
Umask 022
#
###########################################################################
```

Most of the configuration entries are self-explanatory; nevertheless we will briefly describe them in the order of their appearance.

Configuration Entry	Meaning
• *Port*	Specifies the port number that ***sshd*** listens on (default is 22).
• *ListenAddress*	Specifies the IP address of the interface where the ***sshd*** server socket is bound (0.0.0.0 means any IP address).
• *HostKey*	Specifies the file containing the private host key (the default is */etc/ssh_host_key*).
• *RandomSeed*	Specifies the file containing the random seed for the server. The file is updated regularly (the default is */etc/ssh_random_seed*).
• *ServerKeyBits*	Defines the number of bits in the server key (the minimum value is 512, the default is 768).
• *LoginGraceTime*	After this time in seconds the server disconnects if the user has not successfully logged in (0 means indefinitely, the default is 600).
• *KeyRegenerationInterval*	If the server key has been used, it is automatically regenerated after this time period in seconds (0 means never, the default is 3600).
• *PermitRootLogin*	Specifies whether the root can login using ***ssh***; *yes* allows login with the password authentication, while *no* or *nopwd* disables password authentication for root (the default is *yes*).
• *StrictModes*	Specifies whether ***ssh*** should check file mode and ownership of the user's home directory and *.rhosts* file before accepting login (the default is *yes*).
• *QuietMode*	Specifies if the logging in the system log is required (the default is *no*).
• *X11Forwarding*	Specifies whether X11 forwarding is permitted, i.e., X session forwarded through the encrypted channel (the default is *yes*).
• *PrintMotd*	Specifies whether ***sshd*** should print message of day from the */etc/motd* file (the default is *yes*).
• *KeepAlive*	Specifies whether "keepalive" messages should be sent to another side, and is instrumental in maintaining the connection properly (the default is *yes*).
• *SyslogFacility*	Specifies the "facility" entry in the system log file for ***sshd*** logging (the default is DAEMON).
• *RhostsAuthentication*	Specifies whether authentication using the *rhosts* or */etc/hosts.equiv* files is sufficient (the default is *no*).
• *RhostsRSAAuthentication*	Specifies whether *rhosts* and */etc/hosts.equiv* authentication combined with RSA host authentication is allowed (the default is *yes*).
• *RSAAuthentication*	Specifies whether pure RSA authentication (challenge-response) is allowed (the default is *yes*).
• *PasswordAuthentication*	Specifies whether password authentication is allowed (the default is *yes*).
• *PermitEmptyPasswords*	If password authentication is allowed, it specifies whether the server allows login to accounts with empty password fields (the default is *yes*).
• *FascistLogging*	Specifies if verbose logging is used, which violates users' privacy (the default is *no*).
• *IdleTimeout*	Sets idle timeout limit (s, m, h, d, or w) to terminate an idle child ***sshd*** process.
• *CheckMail*	Specifies whether ***sshd*** should print information about new e-mail when a user logs in (the default is *yes*).

• *IgnoreRhosts*	Specifies that *rhosts* and *shosts* files will not be used in authentication, while */etc/hosts.equiv* and */etc/shosts.equiv* are still in use (the default is *no*).
• *Umask*	Sets default umask for **sshd** and its children — must be an octal number (the default is 000).

The client configuration file is */etc/ssh_config*. The file structure is the same as for the server configuration. Here is an example:

$ cat /etc/ssh_config

```
##########################################################################
#
#          File:   ssh_config
#       Purpose:   ssh client configuration file.
#   Description:   Provides defaults for users, and the values
#                  could be changed in per-user configuration files
#                  or on the command line.
#    Directions:   Configuration data is parsed as follows:
#                  1. command line options
#                  2. user-specific file
#                  3. system-wide file
#                  Any configuration value is only changed the first
#                  time it is set. Thus, host-specific definitions
#                  should be at the beginning of the configuration
#                  file, and defaults at the end.
#       Used by:   ssh, scp, slogin, sdist
#
##########################################################################
#
Compression yes
CompressionLevel 9
ConnectionAttempts 3
FallBackToRsh no
ForwardAgent yes
ForwardX11 yes
GlobalKnownHostsFile /etc/ssh_known_hosts
UserKnownHostsFile /etc/ssh_known_hosts
KeepAlive yes
RhostsAuthentication no
RhostsRSAAuthentication no
RSAAuthentication yes
TISAuthentication no
PasswordAuthentication yes
UseRsh no StrictHostKeyChecking no
BatchMode no
StrictHostKeyChecking no
IdentityFile ~ /.ssh/identity
```

Some of the listed configuration entries are identical to those in the previously presented server configuration file. Others are quite self-explanatory, so we will not elaborate on them separately.

19.3.3 SSH Installation and User Access Setup

Both the server and client software components need to be installed on hosts where SSH is supposed to be used. In addition, users must each generate their own keys (private and public) and place the public key on the remote hosts to have access to them. SSH software installation is platform specific, and more details and basic instructions can be found in the files README and INSTALL located in the SSH package directory. A set of installation programs and Makefiles are also available.

19.3.3.1 Setup of the ssh Client

The *ssh* client program should be placed in any directory included in the $PATH variable (the directories */usr/local/bin* or */share/local/bin* are good choices; symbolic links are also allowed). SSH version 1 requires two other files to work properly: */etc/ssh_config* and */etc/ssh_known_hosts* (SSH version 2 substitutes the second file with the corresponding subdirectory).

```
# ls -l /etc | grep ssh | grep -v grep
-rw-r--r--  1  root  other  1647  Aug 28  1999  ssh_config
-rw-r--r--  1  root  other  7167  Sep 15  1999  ssh_known_hosts
                    .....
                    .....
```

We have already discussed the client configuration file */etc/ssh_config*; now we will focus on the file */etc/ssh_known_hosts*. It is necessary for the target host to be listed in this file; the public key of each target host (specified in the host's */etc/ssh_host_key.pub*) should be added to the file. Each entry is modified by prepending the host name and removing the trailing *user@host*; the Perl program ***make-ssh-known-hosts*** is available for this purpose. To illustrate what it means, here is an SSH version 1 example:

```
# cat /etc/ssh_known_hosts
red 1024 37 3407288340532312154575772332552 .............................. 3300931358351036817979597
blue 1024 35 16598146735277155628901488556055 ........................... 814526930376266985504229
green 1024 33 13292087958394603763415136614608 .......................... 148812837934617969703913
```

Each public key is specified by a single line that starts with the host's name (here ***red***, ***blue***,..., ***green***, etc.) and ends with a 1024-digit key (here only partially presented). Once copied, the file should be owned by root, with permissions: "rw- r-- r—".

After SSH installation, the ssh access for each individual user (including the superuser) must be set separately. Once a user's access is activated, the user continues to use ***ssh*** in the same way as the UNIX ***r-commands***.

19.3.3.2 Root Access

Assuming "/" as the superuser home directory, root on the originating host must first generate a key that is kept in the hidden subdirectory "*/.ssh*". As root, run the command:

ssh-keygen *-f /.ssh/identity -N ""*

The **-N** option specifies the passphrase; if omitted no passphrase is implemented. This process will produce three files (file names vary among SSH versions):

1. The private key: */.ssh/identity*
2. The public key: */.ssh/identity.pub*
3. The random seed: */.ssh/random_seed*

Target hosts to whom the superuser wishes to connect must have the active ***sshd*** daemon and the originating root's public key added to the file */.ssh/authorized_keys*. In addition, the directories and files "*/*", "*/.rhosts*", "*/.shosts*", and "*/.ssh*" must not be writable by anyone else. Although keys could be copied from one host to another, different root keys on each target host increase the security.

The process produces private keys with/without passphrase to protect them. A passphrase increases security, but it must be typed in each time, and correspondingly must be a part of all related scripts.

19.3.3.3 Individual User Access

Basically the procedure is more or less the same as for the superuser. Each individual user of ***ssh*** (or ***scp***, or ***slogin***) must first generate needed keys that are kept in the user home directory on the originating host (the ***ssh*** client host). To generate keys the user should execute:

ssh-keygen *-f $HOME/.ssh/identity -N ""*

Again the passphrase is optional. The process will produce three files in the user's home directory (again file names could be different):

1. The private key: *$HOME/.ssh/identity*
2. The public key: *$HOME/.ssh/identity.pub*
3. The random seed: *$HOME/.ssh/random_seed*

The target hosts that the user wishes to connect to must have the user's public key (*identity.pub*) added to its file *$HOME/.ssh/authorized_keys*. Please note that the file *identity.pub* was created at the client host, and should be appended to the file *authorized_keys* at each targeted server host. Assuming secure root access between two hosts has been already established, the following script could be very instrumental in setting individual users' access:

```
#!/ bin/ksh
##########################################################################
#
#   File:           UserKey
#   Purpose:        Create a ssh key for user and add public key to the ssh server host
#   Directions:     UserKey [-n] username hostname (-n option generates a new key)
#   Invoked by:     root
#
##########################################################################

if [ "$1" = "-n" ]; then
   NKEY=YES
   USER=$2
   SHOST=$3
else
   NKEY=NO
   USER=$1
   SHOST=$2
fi
# Assumed user home directory
HOME=/home/$USER
# First create remote user ssh directory
echo "\nCreate user ssh directory on $SHOST"
ssh $SHOST chmod 755 /$HOME
ssh $SHOST rm -f /$HOME/.rhosts
ssh $SHOST mkdir -p /$HOME/.ssh
ssh $SHOST chown $USER /$HOME/.ssh
ssh $SHOST chmod 755 /$HOME/.ssh
```

```
# Generate local and remote ssh keys (if required)
if [ "$NKEY" = "YES" ]; then
   echo "\nGenerating local key for $USER"
   su - $USER -c /usr/pkg/ssh/bin/ssh-keygen -f $HOME/.ssh/identity -N ""
   echo "Generating key for $USER on $SHOST"
   ssh $SHOST su - $USER -c /usr/pkg/ssh/bin/ssh-keygen -f $HOME/.ssh/identity -N ""
fi
# Create the remote file authorized_keys
echo "Adding public key to $SHOST"
scp ${SHOST}:/$HOME/.ssh/identity.pub ${SHOST}:/$HOME/.ssh/authorized_keys
cat /$HOME/.ssh/identity.pub | ssh $SHOST "cat >> /$HOME/.ssh/authorized_keys"
ssh $SHOST chown $USER /$HOME/.ssh/authorized_keys
ssh $SHOST chmod 644 /$HOME/.ssh/authorized_keys
########################################################################
```

Such a script makes a setting of a user access to the target host very easy. The script itself can be improved in many ways, as well.

19.3.4 SSH — Version 2

Secure shell protocol and supporting software continue to develop and improve. The previous text, especially the part that addresses SSH configuration and access setup, primarily refers to the initial SSH version, known as Version 1. At the moment, the latest SSH version is Version 2, which provides a set of radical improvements over Version 1. To make a difference between versions they are identified as SSH1 and SSH2 respectively; the same is implemented on binaries and configuration data, they have a corresponding suffix within their names.

SSH2 was totally rewritten and it provides:

- Better-understood and more secure protocol
- New design and new cryptography and mathematics algorithms
- An integrated secure file transfer
- Support for multiple public key algorithms, including Diffie-Hellman key exchange
- New authentication methods like Pluggable Authentication Modules (PAM), integration with Kerberos, and usage of SecureID

New design and coding of SSH2 has also had some disadvantages; unfortunately SSH1 and SSH2 protocols are not compatible with each other. Many implemented security and performance enhancements would not have been possible if protocol-level compatibility with SSH1 had been retained. However, to continue to work with already installed SSH1 clients, SSH2 daemon could be configured to recognize their appearance and automatically to invoke the SSH1 daemon to provide the requested service in the SSH1 way. Such a solution requires both SSH installations on the same host (at the server side) and should work well. Nevertheless, sometimes it could be even easier to upgrade all SSH1 clients to SSH2. The new version offers much more, and it is worth it to make such a move. Even when we talk about SSH2, we are mostly thinking of late SSH2 releases (SSH 2.3.x and up) which provide more stable and secure connections. Otherwise, to configure everything and make it work smoothly could be quite a hard job.

SSH2 provides an easier configuration and much better understanding between client and server during the connection. The first time such a connection is established, client and server exchange necessary public keys automatically and prepare everything for future sessions. There is no more need for an explicit manual transfer of the public key to enable the communication between hosts at all; this is accomplished in an elegant way during the first user's attempt to access a target host. Afterward the authentication and data transfer is accomplished in the secure way, even in a nonsecure network environment.

This is illustrated in the example that follows. User ***bjl*** on the host **pink** (originating host, i.e., SSH2 client host) is trying to access the host **red** (target host, i.e., SSH2 server host) for the first time. Two pieces of SSH2 software on two hosts establish the following "first-time SSH2 handshake" dialogue:

```
[bjl@pink /home/bjl]# ssh -l bjl red
Host key not found from database.
Key fingerprint:
xubis-fygos-fumon-bakyc-sogeh-gopap-hopub-bymov-ni zig-samus-huxyx
You can get a public key's fingerprint by running
% ssh-keygen -F publickey.pub
on the keyfile.
Are you sure you want to continue connecting (yes/no)? yes
Host key saved to /home/bjl/.ssh2/hostkeys/key_22_red .pub
host key for red, accepted by bjl Sun May 06 2001 14:20:15
bjl's password:
```

User's actions are presented in ***bold italic***. The user initiates the SSH connection, and confirms continued connecting. For a successful secure remote login, at the end a user's password on the target host **red** must be entered. Such a dialogue happens only the first time; once the user's key is saved on the originating host **pink**, each succeeding connection will simply require the password only. Obviously it is much easier than transferring needed keys manually in advance for every user, and it is equally secure.

Each transferred key is saved as a separate file in the user's home directory "./.ssh2/keyhosts", instead of as an entry in the single file (the case with SSH version 1). It makes handling of this data easier and flexible. Here is an example:

```
# ls –l /home/bjl/.ssh2/hostkeys
total 54
-rw-------  1 bjl  20  737  Sep 13  2000  key_22_red.pub
-rw-------  1 bjl  20  737  Aug 30  2000  key_22_blue.pub
-rw-------  1 bjl  20  737  Sep 13  2000  key_22_gray.pub
                .....
                .....
-rw-------  1 bjl  20  737  Aug 30  2000  key_22_green.pub
```

Each file contains a public key for the specified host.

Another significant SSH2 improvement is in the authentication area. Authentication itself could be configured in many different ways, and the default one is password-based. However, in the following text the procedure to set SSH2 "host-based authentication" will be described. The reasons to choose this authentication method over others are very simple. First, there are many situations when we have to escape default password authentication between certain hosts and for specific users, as in the case of centralized monitoring, remote scripts, etc. Second, this authentication method works very well for SSH2 (what we cannot say for Version 1, and even for some early SSH2 releases).

For an easier understanding of the described procedure we will suppose the following:

- ***SSHSERVER*** is the name of the host with running ***sshd2*** daemon, to which we are trying to connect; the name could be full canonical host name, or short host name if two hosts share the same DNS domain and DNS is properly set.
- ***ServerUser*** is the user name on the host ***SSHSERVER*** into which we would like to login.

- ***SSHCLIENT*** is the name of the host with running ***ssh2*** client, where we invoke the connection; the name could be full canonical host name, or short host name if two hosts share the same DNS domain and DNS is properly set.
- ***ClientUser*** is the user name on the host ***SSHCLIENT*** that should be allowed to log in to ***ServerUser*** on the host ***SSHSERVER***.
- The needed SSH2 software is installed on both hosts ***SSHSERVER*** and ***SSHCLIENT*** and individual host keys are generated on both machines (SSH2 automatically generates keys upon its installation).

The procedure consists of several steps:

1. Copy the public key ***hostkey.pub*** on ***SSHCLIENT*** into ***SSHSERVER*** and rename into "*ssh-dss.pub*" for this host. Execute on ***SSHCLIENT***:

   scp */etc/ssh2/hostkey.pub SSHSERVER:/etc/ssh2/knownhosts/SSHCLIENT.ssh-dss.pub*. Upon password authentication the file with the public key will be copied.
2. To avoid a possible confusion regarding implemented host names (full canonical names vs. short host names), SSH2 could be set to use only full host names. The entry in the ***sshd2*** configuration file */etc/ssh2/ssh2d_config*:

   DefaultDomain <this dns domain name>

   will force the use of full canonical host name. Obviously, we then have to also use full host names.
3. On the host ***SSHSERVER***, create or update the hidden file *.shosts* in the home directory for the user ***ServerUser***. The contents of this file have to include the full host name and the name of the user allowed to log in to this account (in this case ***SSCLIENT*** and ***ClientUser***):

   SSCLIENT ClientUser
4. On the host ***SSHSERVER***, the ***sshd2*** configuration must include host-based authentication, as well as ***ssh2*** configuration on the client side on the host ***SSHCLIENT***. Both configuration files *SSHSERVER:/etc/ssh2/sshd2_config* and *SSHCLIENT:/ etc/ssh2/ssh2_config* have to have ***hostbased*** keyword in the authentication entry:

   AllowedAuthentication hostbased, passwd,...

   Other authentication methods could be listed in the entry, but the "***hostbased***" keyword has to be the first in the line. Also, the "***rhosts***" authentication should be prevented; the default entry:

   IgnoreRhosts no

   should not be changed.
5. Each change in the ***sshd2*** daemon configuration requires recycling of the daemon itself:

   kill -HUP 'cat /var/run/sshd2.pid'

   This example supposes the process ID - PID of the running ***sshd2*** daemon is kept in the file */var/run/sshd2.pid*, which is not a must and is flavor specific. Probably it is easier to check for the actually running daemon by executing:

   ps –ef | grep sshd2

   and determining the PID of the leading ***sshd2*** daemon (keep in mind that multiple ***sshd2*** daemons can run simultaneously, and we are looking for the leading one).

20

Electronic Mail

20.1 E-mail Fundamentals

E-mail is probably the most attractive topic for users. Almost every user on the network uses electronic mail (known by its acronym ***e-mail***). Users do not know very much about UNIX, but they like to use, and they benefit from using, e-mail. Usually this is a love-hate relationship between users and e-mail; users love having an e-mail system, but they hate it when it does not work. This relationship is exacerbated by the fact that only a few of them have any idea how e-mail actually works and really understand e-mail processes. The most common misunderstanding is to confuse **e-mail** with other popular network applications, like ***telnet*** or ***ftp.*** And when the DNS issue arises during a discussion of e-mail, the confusion is complete.

It is not so easy to explain the principles of **e-mail** in a few words. For starters, e-mail can be compared to regular ground mail service, or snail mail; this is the most helpful description that we have. If we use this analogy, though, we should also point out other services analogous to the common network applications: *telnet* corresponds to the *phone service, ftp* to *fax service,* and *DNS* is an *operator* to help to resolve name/address/phone number relationships.

E-mail is based on several supporting programs and protocols that enable local and networkwide e-mail service. The programs accomplish different tasks sequentially in the e-mail generation, e-mail transfer (transportation), and e-mail delivery; the protocols define rules for the interprogram communications.

There are two categories of e-mail programs: "mail user agents," or ***MUA* programs,** and "mail transport agents," or ***MTA* programs.** An *MUA* agent is any number of programs that users run to read, reply to, compose, and dispose of e-mail. These include, for example, the original UNIX mail program ***/bin/mail,*** the Berkeley ***mail*** or its System V equivalent ***mailx,*** and freely available programs like ***mush, elm, pine,*** and ***mh,*** as well as other commercial programs.

An *MTA* agent is a program that handles mail delivery for many users and forwards e-mail between machines. The central mail transport program, the one most used today, is ***sendmail.*** On UNIX this is the default MTA program. Other mail programs are implemented around ***sendmail. sendmail*** determines and invokes other delivery agents called ***Mailers*** to deliver e-mail and to further transfer e-mail. This is shown in Figure 20.1. ***Mailers*** are sometimes considered the third category of e-mail programs and named "delivery agents," or ***MDA programs.*** In this text mailers are treated as a part of the MTA program.

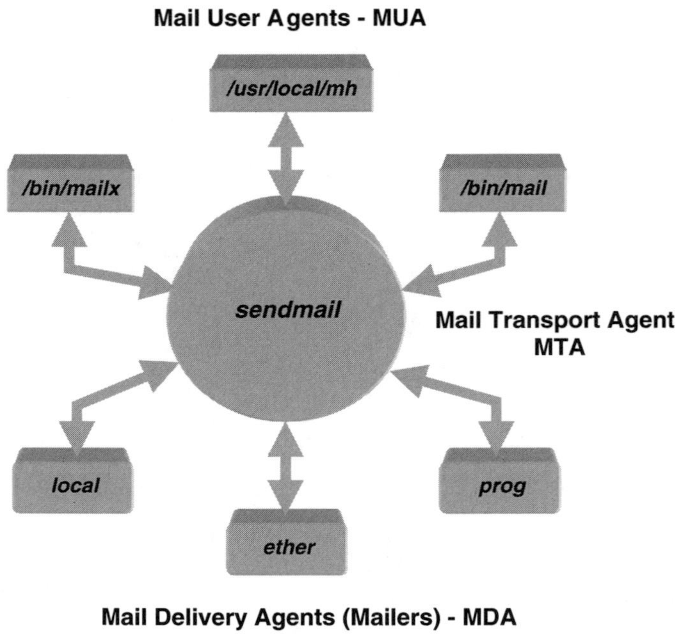

FIGURE 20.1
The flow of e-mail through the system.

When an e-mail sent to a user arrives at its destination, it will be placed in the user's **mailbox.** A mailbox is a file, or sometimes a directory of files, where incoming e-mail is stored. On UNIX this is a file named with the username, and by default located in the */var/mail* directory; once the received e-mail is read by the user it is transferred into another mailbox located in the user's home directory.

sendmail is the core of e-mail and the central administration issue for successful e-mailing. Two ***sendmail*** programs (with the help of an appropriate ***mailer***) provide the transfer of e-mail from one machine to another over the network. The protocol used in the exchange of messages is known as the ***SMTP*** protocol — ***simple mail transport protocol. MUA programs*** make an interface between e-mail users and ***sendmail.*** From the user's point of view, they are the most important links in the chain — they make e-mail user-friendly, and they are also what seem "broken" when e-mail is not working. However, the impact of MUA programs on overall e-mail is marginal, and their significance exists mostly within a local environment. Nevertheless, an administrator is not freed from the duty of maintaining ***MUA programs,*** but the main administration concern is definitely focused on ***sendmail.*** The text that follows reflects these facts.

Each e-mail message (just as in regular mail) has an *envelope* with the recipient's and sender's addresses, and a message content that consists of a *header* and a *body.* A recipient's address is the *address* to which the message should be delivered. ***sendmail* parses** and analyzes the e-mail addresses, learns of the destination, and decides where and how to deliver it. It might not be delivered immediately to the final recipient; the "where" of the delivery could be any host on the network able to continue with the e-mail transport. If this is the case, ***sendmail*** does not deliver the e-mail to the host; it forwards the e-mail to a specialized host called a ***mailhost,*** which knows how to handle e-mail very well. This means that the generated e-mail message could be delivered directly to the recipient's host, but it could also be sent via a number of mailhosts. The route depends primarily on the e-mail recipient's address, but sometimes is affected by the current network conditions.

The message content is not touched by ***sendmail,*** although the format of the **header** is set within the ***sendmail*** configuration. The header contains information about who authored the e-mail message, the intended recipient, the time of creation, the subject of the message, delivery stamps, etc. The body is separated from the header by a blank line, and contains the information the sender is trying to communicate (most users see a message body as the message itself).

For many years, e-mail messages were plain ASCII text without any need for a specific structure for message bodies. The implemented SMTP protocol was a 7-bit protocol based on the US-ASCII character set, which limited bytes of data sent to using only low-order 7 bits; the 8th bit has been always treated as zero. This was suitable for plain English text, but many foreign languages (especially Asian ones), as well as binary multimedia data (graphics, programs, audio, video, etc.) require a valid 8th bit. To transfer this data without loss, the message must first be encoded into 7-bit data. A solution was found in the ***MIME*** *(multipurpose Internet mail extensions, specified in RFC 2045/2046)* encapsulation. MIME specifies how to encode data when necessary, but it is still the responsibility of the recipient's MUA program to use this information appropriately and to display the message in a form understandable to the user.

The explosion of multimedia messages brought on the need for "real 8-bit message transfer." It is possible to encode messages into 7-bit transfer, but it is cumbersome and the resulting encoded message is significantly (typically 33%) larger than the original one. SMTP protocol has been extended to allow 8-bit transfer to meet this need; the general extension mechanism to SMTP known as ***ESMTP*** is specified in RFC 1869, while the specific extension to allow 8-bit transfer called ***8BITMIME*** is specified in RFC 1652. If an MTA program cannot negotiate the proper transfer of 8-bit data, it has either to encode the message into 7-bit data using MIME, or return the message to the sender indicating the reason for return. MIME and ESMTP have common goals; they were developed in conjunction with each other toward the same end. ***sendmail*** versions 8.6 and newer support ESMTP; versions 8.7 and newer support the 8BITMIME extension.

E-mail deliveries are generally very fast. They are measured in seconds, minutes, or hours. Nevertheless, delivery time is not a deterministic value — there is no way to predict the exact delivery time, because it depends on a number of issues, especially if many mailhosts are involved in the e-mail transportation. Sometimes it can even be measured in days (if hosts in the chain of the e-mail delivery crash, or overload, or have network problems, etc.); an e-mail message can even be lost (fortunately, this happens only occasionally). In that sense, the e-mail really does resemble regular ground mail.

The central ***sendmail*** issue is "where and how" to send e-mail; ***sendmail*** parses the e-mail recipient's address and makes such decisions based on the rules (algorithms) specified in its configuration file. There is no standardized algorithm, mandatory for each e-mail site, for e-mail address parsing. It is left to the ***sendmail*** administrator to implement the most appropriate algorithm. Several template ***sendmail*** configuration files are available as part of any UNIX implementation to make this job easier. In fact, most of today's UNIX flavors provide advanced ***sendmail*** configuration templates, prepared for comprehensive customization, which require the administrator to supply only site-specific information. However, it is also fair to say that in some nonstandard cases such templates could be insufficient, and a more elaborative administration could be required. We will return to this issue once we learn about the contents of the ***sendmail*** configuration file.

Among the many decisions that ***sendmail*** makes, one is to reject an e-mail message because of an ambiguous recipient's or sender's address. The most common reasons for such action is a misspelled recipient's address which really should be rejected, but in some rare situations even a correct address could be returned as a result of an improper ***sendmail*** configuration (because the specified address type is not covered by the implemented ***sendmail*** parsing algorithm) or another temporary ***sendmail***-related problem. Do not be surprised when an e-mail address that works when used from one host, does not work from another. Fortunately, this does not happen often, and it can be overcome with an appropriate sendmail configuration setting.

20.1.1 Simple Mail Transport Protocol (SMTP)

SMTP is the basic e-mail protocol. SMTP stands for ***simple mail transfer protocol,*** and it is based on the TCP/IP suite. This is the language that ***sendmail*** understands well, and peer communication between two involved ***sendmail*** programs is actually an exchange of SMTP messages.

A simplified presentation of such a communication (or rather, a conversation) between two arbitrary hosts, identified as ***ms1.mydomain*** and ***ms3.yourdomain,*** is shown in Figure 20.2. The two hosts communicate directly. The local ***sendmail*** is delivering an e-mail from the local user ***me*** to the remote user ***you;*** it literally talks to the remote host's ***sendmail*** about having an e-mail message from the user ***me*** on the local host sent to the user ***you*** on the remote host (the e-mail address is ***you@ms3.yourdomain***). The local ***sendmail*** conveys the sender and recipient information before it transmits the e-mail message; the address information constitutes the *envelope,* and it is conveyed separately from the message header. Only one recipient may be listed in the envelope, although the same e-mail could be addressed to more recipients simultaneously. Any division of a "multiple-addressed" e-mail into multiple "single-addressed" envelopes must be performed before the address parsing; SMTP assumes a single recipient only.

To get a better look at the SMTP protocol, another example using ***sendmail*** in verbose mode follows. The verbose mode lists the complete dialogue between the two ***sendmail*** programs on the sender's and recipient's hosts. In this example the e-mail message is sent by the sender ***bjl@patsy.myschool.scps.edu*** to the recipient ***mis@apollo.ph.myschool.scps.edu;*** the text for the e-mail is in the file named "*indata.mail*". Again, the two hosts communicate directly (there are no relay *mailhosts* in the e-mail delivery).

```
# /usr/lib/sendmail -v mis@apollo.ph.myschool.scps.edu < indata.mail
mis@apollo.ph.myschool.scps.edu... Connecting to apollo.ph.myschool.scps.edu via ether...
Trying 146.98.8.31... connected.
220 apollo.ph.myschool.scps.edu HP Sendmail (1.38.193.4/16.2) ready at Tue, 5 Jul 1998 17:06:13 -0400
>>> HELO patsy.myschool.scps.edu
250 apollo.ph.myschool.scps.edu Hello patsy.myschool.scps.edu, pleased to meet you
>>> MAIL From:<bjl@patsy>
250 <bjl@patsy>... Sender ok
>>> RCPT To:<mis@apollo.ph.myschool.scps.edu>
250 <mis@apollo.ph.myschool.scps.edu>... Recipient ok
>>> DATA
354 Enter mail, end with "." on a line by itself
>>>.
250 Ok
>>> QUIT
221 apollo.ph.myschool.scps.edu closing connection
mis@apollo.ph.myschool.scps.edu... Sent
```

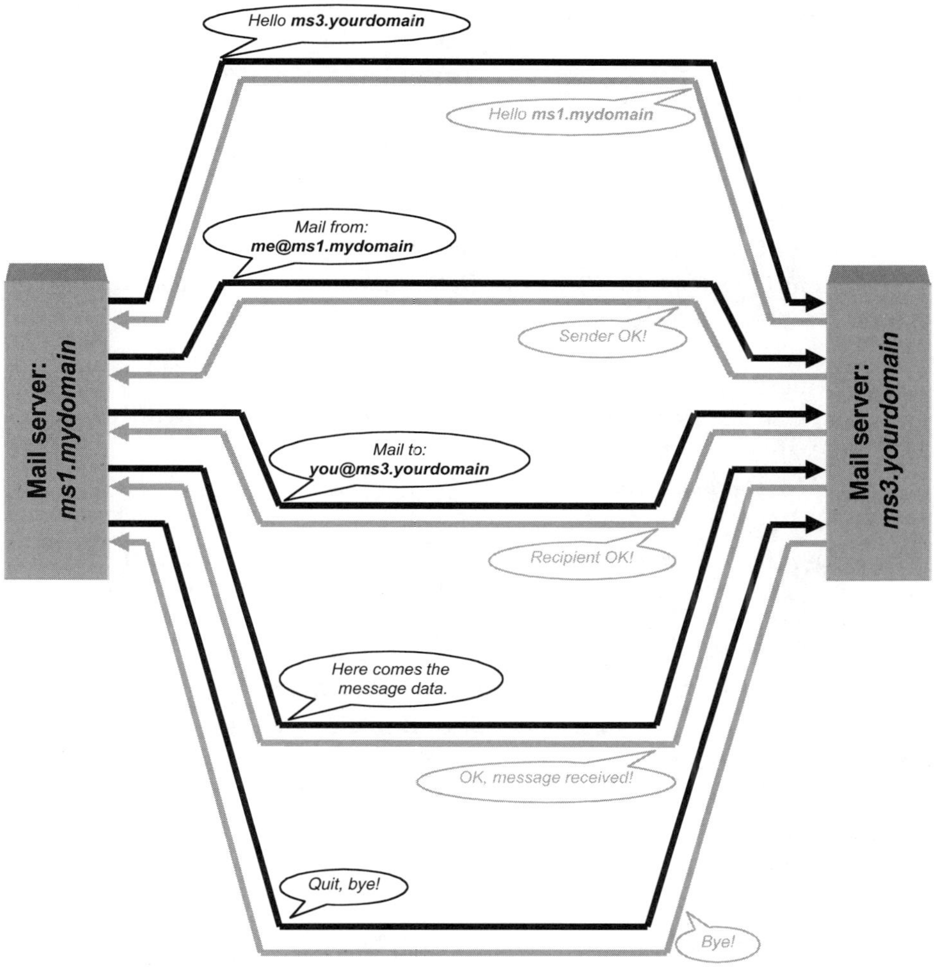

FIGURE 20.2
A simplified presentation of SMTP.

The lines that begin with ***numbers*** and the lines that begin with >>> characters constitute the SMTP conversation. The lines starting with >>> characters display what the sender's host was saying; the replies from the recipient's host are displayed with leading numbers.

- The first two lines are messages at the sender's host, describing what ***sendmail*** is doing:

  mis@apollo.ph.myschool.scps.edu... Connecting to apollo.ph.myschool.scps.edu via ether... Trying 146.98.8.31... connected.

  The first line shows to whom the e-mail is addressed and that the host *apollo.ph.myschool.scps.edu* is on the network. The second line shows the IP address of the recipient's host (in this case the IP address was obtained by DNS).
- Once the sender's ***sendmail*** has connected to the recipient's host, it waits for the other side to initiate further conversation. The recipient says it is ready by sending the number ***220*** followed by its domain name (this is the only required information);

the program name (usually, but not always, *sendmail*); and the version of that program. It also states that it is ready and gives its local date and time.

220 apollo.ph.myschool.scps.edu HP Sendmail (1.38.193.4/16.2) ready at Tue, 5 Jul 1998 17:06:13 -0400

- Next, the sender's ***sendmail*** sends the hello message ***HELO*** (this is not a typo); the recipient replies with ***250*** and the acknowledgment that the sender's hostname is acceptable:

  >>> HELO patsy.myschool.scps.edu

  250 apollo.ph.myschool.scps.edu Hello patsy.myschool.scps.edu, pleased to meet you

- If all has gone well so far, the sender's ***sendmail*** sends the name of the e-mail sender (the user on that host) from the envelope of the e-mail message; the recipient's ***sendmail*** accepts the sender's name and replies with the message starting with the number ***250:***

  >>> MAIL From:<bjl@patsy>

  250 <bjl@patsy>... Sender ok

- Next, the sender's ***sendmail*** sends the name of the e-mail recipient (the user on the remote host) from the envelope of the e-mail message; the recipient's ***sendmail*** accepts (in this case) or rejects this name (then it would reply with an error "User unknown"). The reply starts with the number ***250:***

  >>> RCPT To:<mis@apollo.ph.myschool.scps.edu>

  250 <mis@apollo.ph.myschool.scps.edu>... Recipient ok

- After the envelope information has been sent, the sender's ***sendmail*** attempts to send the e-mail data (header and body combined):

  >>> DATA

  354 Enter mail, end with "." on a line by itself

  >>>.

  The DATA message essentially tells the recipient to get ready for a data receipt; the sent data is not displayed, and only a single dot on a line by itself is used to mark the end of a mail message — this is a convention of the SMTP protocol. To prevent misinterpretation of any lines in the e-mail body that could contain a single dot, the sender's ***sendmail*** inserts an extra dot at the beginning of any line that begins with a dot; the recipient's ***sendmail*** removes those extra dots.

- After the e-mail message has been successfully sent, it is confirmed by the recipient's ***sendmail.*** The sender's ***sendmail*** sends QUIT to say all is done, and the recipient's ***sendmail*** acknowledges that it is closing the connection:

  250 Ok

  >>> QUIT

  221 apollo.ph.myschool.scps.edu closing connection

- The last line simply confirms that the e-mail message was successfully delivered:

  mis@apollo.ph.myschool.scps.edu... Sent

20.1.2 The MTA Program *sendmail*

The central point of a UNIX e-mail system is the MTA program ***sendmail;*** consequently a major part of the overall text is related to ***sendmail,*** and more specifically to the ***sendmail*** administration.

20.1.2.1 The *sendmail* Daemon

The ***sendmail*** daemon runs nonstop on each host that is intended to fully support e-mail. The ***sendmail*** daemon listens on port 25 and processes incoming e-mail. The daemon is invoked during system startup from an **rc** initialization script file, usually executing the following, or a similar command sequence:

```
if [ -f /usr/lib/sendmail -a -f /etc/sendmail.cf ]; then
   (cd /var/spool/mqueue; rm -f nf* lf*)
   /usr/lib/sendmail -bd -q1h; echo -n " sendmail"
fi
```

The **rc** script first checks for the existence of the ***sendmail*** program and its configuration file */etc/sendmail.cf.* If both are found, the mail queue directory is checked and cleared of any possible remained *nfs* or locked file found there; it is possible that the system went down while the mail queue was being processed, so unprocessed files may have been inadvertently left behind. They must be removed during system booting to make a place for their reprocessing, as well as for new files.

Next, the script starts ***sendmail*** with two command line options. The option **-bd** tells ***sendmail*** to run as a daemon, causing ***sendmail*** to listen nonstop to port 25 for incoming e-mail. The **-q** option determines how often the mail queue is processed; for most systems a setting of ***1h*** (one hour) is a good choice. For larger mailhosts (mail servers) more frequent mail queue processing could be more appropriate; 30 minutes (**-q30m**) or even 15 minutes (**-q15m**) could be better choices. This time relates only to the mail queue processing; an e-mail received on port 25 is processed immediately, and only if it fails to be delivered is the e-mail put in the mail queue for later reprocessing.

The ***sendmail*** daemon runs as long as the system is alive. However, once it becomes too busy, the ***sendmail*** daemon will spawn another daemon/daemons to help in e-mail processing. Child daemons will exit upon completing their tasks, but the parent daemon continues to run even if it is idle.

20.1.2.2 The *sendmail* Command

sendmail is actually a versatile and powerful UNIX command that can be executed from the command line at any time. The "*daemon option* **-bd**" is only one of many possible options. ***sendmail*** can also be invoked to complete a single job, as with any other UNIX command; this is often done during ***sendmail*** testing and debugging.

For a better understanding of ***sendmail,*** the main program characteristics are summarized below:

- ***sendmail*** sends a message to one or more people, routing the message over networks as needed. ***sendmail*** does internetwork forwarding as necessary to deliver the message to the correct place.
- ***sendmail*** is not intended as a user interface routine; other MUA programs provide user-friendly front ends. ***sendmail*** is used only to deliver preformatted messages. With no flags, ***sendmail*** reads its standard input up to an EOF or a line with a single dot, and sends a copy of the letter (message) found there to the address listed. It determines the way to send the message based on the syntax and contents of the addresses.
- On the sender's side, the recipient's address is looked up in the *local aliases file* (or by using NIS), and **aliased** appropriately. In addition, if there is a *.forward*

file in the recipient's home directory, ***sendmail*** forwards a copy of each message to the list of recipients that the file contains. Preceding the address with a backslash can prevent aliasing. Normally, the sender is not included in alias expansions (for example, if *john* sends to *group*, and *group* includes *john* in the expansion, then the e-mail will not be forwarded to *john*).

- ***sendmail*** can route mail directly to other known hosts in a network. The list of hosts to which mail is directly sent depends on the ***sendmail*** configuration, but could also be maintained by certain related files.
- The format of the sendmail command is:

/usr/lib/sendmail [option]

Where some of the options are:

Option	Action
-bd	Run as a daemon, waiting for incoming SMTP connections.
-bi	Initialize the alias database.
-bm	Deliver mail in the usual way (default).
-bp	Print a summary of the mail queue and list all mails currently in the queue.
-bt	Run in address test mode. This mode reads addresses and shows the steps in parsing, and it is used for debugging configuration address parsing rules.
-bv	Verify names only — do not try to collect or deliver a message. Verify mode is normally used for validating users or mailing lists.
-bz	Create the configuration freeze file.
-n	Do not do aliasing.
-h*N*	Set the hop count to *N*. The hop count is incremented every time the mail is processed; when it reaches a limit, the mail is returned with an error message.
-q [*time*]	Process saved messages in the queue at given intervals. If *time* is omitted, process the queue once. *time* is given as a tagged number, where ***s*** is seconds, ***m*** is minutes, ***h*** is hours, ***d*** is days, and ***w*** is weeks. For example, **-q1h30m** or **-q90m** would both set the timeout to one hour thirty minutes.
-t	Read message for recipients. "To:"', "Cc:", and "Bcc:" lines will be scanned for people to send to, the "Bcc:" line will be deleted before transmission, and any address in the argument list will be suppressed.
-v	Verbose mode, alias expansions will be announced; SMTP dialogue presented, etc.

- ***sendmail*** is supported by the following files, which means ***sendmail*** looks for and uses the following files:

/etc/aliases	ASCII data for alias names (alternatively */etc/mail/aliases*)
/etc/sendmail.cf	The configuration file
/etc/sendmail.fc	The frozen configuration file v
/etc/sendmail.st	Collected statistics
/usr/lib/mailhosts	A list of hosts to which e-mail can be sent directly
/usr/lib/sendmail.hf	The help file
/var/spool/mqueue/*	Temporary files and queued mail
$HOME/.forward	A list of recipients for forwarding messages (user based)
/usr/bin/mail	To deliver local mail
/usr/sbin/mailx	To deliver local mail (alternatively)

Note: Except for */etc/sendmail.cf*, the actual pathnames are all specified in */etc/sendmail.cf*; the pathnames presented here are only approximations. For new sendmail releases, the configuration file is moved into */etc/mail/sendmail.cf*.

sendmail's processing of an incoming e-mail (regardless of whether it is coming from a local MUA program or a remote ***sendmail***) is based on the listed files. The significance of the files varies, but certainly the most important file is the ***sendmail*** configuration file */etc/sendmail.cf* — this file will be discussed in greater detail later. However, some other files, such as the global mail aliases file, personal mail forwarding files, the frozen sendmail configuration file, as well as delivery programs, ***mailers***, deserve some attention too. Let us start with them.

20.1.2.3 Other *sendmail* Constituents

To fully respond to such a demanding task, ***sendmail*** relies on other related programs and files, which are briefly summarized in the following material.

20.1.2.3.1 Global Mail Aliases

The global mail aliases file */etc/aliases* (sometimes linked to */etc/mail/aliases*) provides, on the system level:

- Alternate names (nicknames) for individual local users
- Forwarding of mail to other hosts
- Mailing lists

The basic format of an entry in the */etc/aliases* file is:

alias: recipient[, recipient, ...]

where

alias The name to which the e-mail is addressed

recipient Another local user name, the name of another alias, or a full e-mail address containing both a user name and a host name (this enables forwarding to a remote host); additionally, it could be multiple recipients for a single alias, which enables the use of a mailing list

Aliases are widely used to specify individual users as nicknames for special names like *postmaster, hostmaster,* or *root,* and to deliver e-mail to the real users who do these jobs. They can also be used to implement simplified e-mail addressing. Without them, the concept of ***sendmail*** would definitely not be so powerful; they play a central role in e-mail delivery within today's Intranet networks.

An example of the *aliases* file follows; there is no need for additional comments.

```
$ cat /etc/aliases
##
# Aliases can have any mix of upper and lower case on the left-hand side,
#     but the right-hand side should be proper case (usually lower)
#
#     >>>>>>>>>>      The program "newaliases" will need to be run after
#     >> NOTE >>      this file is updated for any changes to
#     >>>>>>>>>>      show through to sendmail.
#
#     @(#)aliases 2.30 SMI
##

# Following alias is required by the mail protocol, RFC 822
# Set it to the address of a HUMAN who deals with this system's mail problems.
Postmaster: root
```

```
# Alias for mailer daemon; returned messages from our MAILER-DAEMON
# should be routed to our local Postmaster.
MAILER-DAEMON: postmaster

# Aliases to handle mail to programs or files, eg news or vacation
# decode: "|/usr/bin/uudecode"
nobody: /dev/null

# Sample aliases:
# Alias for distribution list, members specified here:
#staff:wnj,mosher,sam,ecc,mckusick,sklower,olson,rwh@ernie
# Alias for distribution list, members specified elsewhere:
#keyboards: :include:/usr/jfarrell/keyboards.list
# Alias for a person, so they can receive mail by several names:
#epa:eric
#######################################################################################
# Local aliases below #
#######################################################################################
# The list of local aliases follows
bjl blevi
     . . .
     . . .
```

It is important to pay attention to the fact that ***sendmail*** does not use the */etc/aliases* file directly. This is an ASCII file used to edit the raw aliases data, but the modified file must first be processed by the **newaliases** command (which is equivalent to the **sendmail -bi** command) to create the ***dbm*** aliases files (*aliases.dir* and *aliases.pag*) used by ***sendmail.*** In that way, a search through the aliases database is much faster.

20.1.2.3.2 Personal Mail Forwarding Files

In addition to the global e-mail forwarding provided by the */etc/aliases* file, ***sendmail*** allows individual users to define their own personal forwarding in the *.forward* file in their home directories. ***sendmail*** checks for this file after using the */etc/aliases* file and before making a final mail delivery to the user. If a personal *.forward* file exists, ***sendmail*** respects its directives. The format of the directives in the personal *.forward* file is equivalent to the format of the */etc/aliases* entries.

20.1.2.3.3 Mail Delivery Programs — Mailers

sendmail is the MTA program and it does not handle the mail delivery itself; one exception is when the mail should be delivered over a TCP/IP network to another remote host. Instead, ***sendmail*** invokes other programs that perform the mail delivery; these programs are known as *delivery agents,* or simply *Mailers.* This is illustrated in Figure 20.3.

Mailers' definitions are included in the ***sendmail*** configuration file. However, the criteria for the selection of a *mailer* is not a part of the *mailer'*s definition; ***sendmail*** simply decides when a *mailer* will be used, and supplies it with the necessary delivery data.

On the other side, the *mailer'*s definition supplies ***sendmail*** with the information it needs to know how to invoke the *mailer.* The initial information ***sendmail*** needs includes the name and location of the delivery program, but the complete information contains some additional arguments. Generally, the syntax of the ***sendmail*** configuration data is quite different from other UNIX configuration data, and we will discuss it in greater detail later. At the moment, let us focus on the *mailer'*s definition specified by the *"**M** configuration entry"* in the ***sendmail*** configuration file. Its generic form is:

M=mailer-name P=mailer-path F=mailer-flags S=send-rules R=receive-rules A=mailer-arguments

where:

- ***M*=** Identifies a *mailer*'s definition configuration entry with a symbolic name under which ***sendmail*** recognizes the corresponding delivery agent. The symbolic name follows the ***M*** with no intervening space.
- ***P*=** Specifies the full pathname of the *mailer* program that performs the mail delivery. This field should be [TCP] or [IPC] for e-mail forwarding over the TCP/IP network performed by ***sendmail*** itself.
- ***F*=** Specifies certain flags that tell ***sendmail*** more about the *mailer* definition. Each flag is a single letter and is Boolean — being set or not set by being correspondingly present or absent.
- ***S*=** Specifies which rule set to use when rewriting the sender's address (this will be explained later).
- ***R*=** Specifies which rule set to use when rewriting the recipient's address (this will be explained later).
- ***A*=** Specifies the command-line arguments to be supplied to each corresponding *mailer* program.

There is no limitation regarding the number of specified *mailers;* names of defined *mailers* are also arbitrary. However, two *mailers* are mandatory: the ***local*** and ***prog.*** These *mailers* must be always defined, regardless of whether they are needed or used. They enable e-mail delivery to local users (*mailer* ***local***) or to local programs (*mailer* ***prog***). If they do not exist, ***sendmail*** will not start, and it will print a corresponding error message. Obviously, other *mailers* should also be defined for ***sendmail*** to function properly, but the ***sendmail*** program itself does not strictly require them.

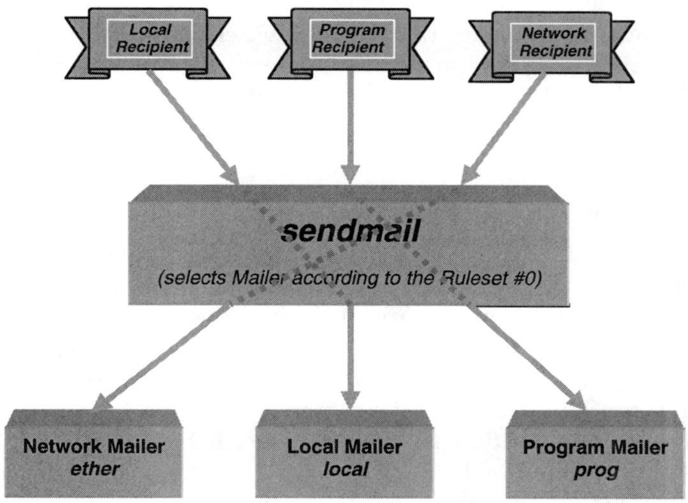

FIGURE 20.3
Sendmail vs. mailers relations.

20.1.2.3.4 *The* sendmail *Configuration File*

This is the central ***sendmail*** issue; the configuration file fully defines ***sendmail***'s behavior — everything is specified within this file. The ***sendmail*** configuration file is */etc/sendmail.cf* (sometimes */usr/lib/sendmail.cf* and lately */etc/mail/sendmail.cf*). The *sendmail.cf* file has three main functions:

1. It defines the ***sendmail*** environment.
2. It rewrites addresses into the appropriate syntax for further e-mail processing.
3. It maps addresses into the instructions necessary to deliver the e-mail.

Many different configuration entries in the configuration file are required to perform all of these functions:

- **Macro** definitions and **option** entries define the environment.
- **Rewrite rules** transform e-mail addresses from one format to another.
- **Mailer** definitions specify the programs necessary to deliver e-mail.

The syntax of these entries is terse and complex. It makes most system administrators reluctant to even read a *sendmail.cf* file; only a few feel comfortable with modifying the configuration. At the start time, ***sendmail*** reads the configuration file and learns how to behave; for this reason, the syntax is designed to match the program needs, which is not necessarily easy for humans to read. All configuration commands, specifications, options, and variables are similar in that each one is only one character long, and hard to recognize and remember. It is easy to confuse a single character command with a single character variable. Despite that difficulty, the ***sendmail*** configuration file must be fully understood for a successful administration.

20.1.2.3.5 The Frozen **sendmail** *Configuration File*

sendmail always reads the configuration data when it is started. A converted *dbm* image of the ASCII configuration file */etc/sendmail.cf* can be created to make this reading faster. This file is called a frozen configuration file */etc/sendmail.fc* (or sometimes */usr/lib/sendmail.fc*). The following command must be executed to create a frozen configuration file:

/usr/lib/sendmail -bz

Only freezing the previously modified ASCII sendmail.cf file can change the frozen configuration file. The advantage of the frozen configuration is that ***sendmail*** will start up faster; the disadvantage is that an additional step is needed to change the ***sendmail*** configuration. It is easy to forget this step, but any change in the file */etc/sendmail.cf* does not impact the frozen configuration until the command **sendmail -bz** is executed.

The frozen ***sendmail*** configuration is frequently used, but it is not a requirement. ***sendmail*** simply checks for the file. If the */etc/sendmail.fc* frozen configuration file exists, it is parsed; otherwise, the */etc/sendmail.fc* configuration file is read.

20.2 *Sendmail* Configuration

Many ***sendmail*** configuration files have the same or similar structure. Most of them are descendants of a few original template files. They are never written from scratch; several versions of templates are always included in any UNIX implementation, and new versions can be downloaded if needed. Everything is designed to make the job easier. Usually, the closest *sendmail.cf* template should be selected for the desired implementation, and then customized. Most of the template ***sendmail*** configuration files require minor modification to be practically implemented.

20.2.1 The *sendmail.cf* File

The overview of the *sendmail.cf* structure that follows describes several sections that specify certain ***sendmail*** configuration entities and include functionally similar entries. The discussed sections are taken from one of the real-life sendmail configuration files. An already well-commented configuration file will be elaborated in greater details in an attempt to make odd configuration entries more friendly and comprehensive. The idea is to get a better feeling for the ***sendmail*** configuration syntax, for the sections that should be customized, for how much administrative work needs to be done, and especially to understand ***sendmail*** parsing algorithms and decision making mechanisms.

The ***sendmail*** configuration file presented here is for a host that is known as a *subsidiary machine,* i.e., the host that fully supports e-mail, but does not belong to the group of main mail servers. The reason for such a selection is very logical; first, it is less complex, so it is easier to understand the configuration entries, and second, a majority of systems belong to this category. Let us begin!

```
$ cat /etc/sendmail.cf
##############################################################################
#  SENDMAIL CONFIGURATION FILE FOR SUBSIDIARY MACHINES
#
#  You should install this file as /etc/sendmail.cf
#  if your machine is a subsidiary machine (that is, some
#  other machine in your domain is the main mail-relaying
#  machine). Then edit the file to customize it for your
#  network configuration.
#
#  See the manual "System Administration for the Sun Workstation."
#  Look at "Setting Up The Mail Routing System" in the chapter on
#  Communications. The Sendmail references in the back of the
#  manual are also very useful.
#
#  @(#)subsidiary.mc 1.11 SMI; from UCB arpa.mc 3.25
#
---------------------------------------- to be continued ----------------------------------------
```

These self-explanatory introductory comments describe the file mission. Each comment line starts with the "#" character, and it is ignored by the ***sendmail*** program itself. Before continuing, a few more remarks on syntax:

- Each line (except comments) in the configuration file is a configuration entry.
- The very first character (a single uppercase letter) defines the type of the entry.
- The format of a configuration entry is type-dependent, but the majority of entries are a contiguous string, in which a character's position has a specific meaning.

- ***sendmail*** reads entries sequentially, from the beginning to the end of the file; this is important in the case of mutually related entries such as rewrite rule entries.
- Generally, all configuration entries can be modified (assuming adequate knowledge and skill), but only a few must be customized.

Now, since we are ready to properly read the configuration entries, let us continue with the configuration file:

```
-------------------------------- /etc/sendmail.cf continued --------------------------------
# local UUCP connections -- not forwarded to mailhost
CV
# my official hostname
Dj$w.$m
# major relay mailer
DMether
# major relay host
DRapollo.ph.myschool.scps.edu
# CRmailhost

####################################################################################
#
#   General configuration information
#
# local domain names
#
# These can now be determined from the domainname system call.
# The first component of the NIS domain name is stripped off unless
# it begins with a dot or a plus sign.
# If your NIS domain is not inside the domain name you would like to have
# appear in your mail headers, add a "Dm" line to define your domain name.
# The Dm value is what is used in outgoing mail. The Cm values are
# accepted in incoming mail. By default Cm is set from Dm, but you might
# want to have more than one Cm line to recognize more than one domain
# name on incoming mail during a transition.
# Example:
# DmCS.Podunk.EDU
# Cm cs cs.Podunk.EDU
#
# known hosts in this domain are obtained from gethostbyname() call
Dmph.myschool.scps.edu
---------------------------------------- to be continued ----------------------------------------
```

The sections presented above are:

Local information — Generally, local information is site-dependent and it should be modified to correspond to the specific implementation. Some of the local data can be generated automatically by the system itself, such as the host and domain names, but others must be specified explicitly in the configuration file, and then the corresponding macro and class definitions are used.

General macros and classes — General macros and classes are used to define general names and aliases. They include different domains and relays. Usually the lines with generic names are already included in the configuration file, but they should be customized correspondingly for the site.

20.2.1.1 Macro and Class Definitions

For a better understanding of the presented entries, as well as others that follow, a brief explanation of the macro and class definitions follows.

20.2.1.1.1 The Define Macro Command

The define macro command — **D** — defines a macro and stores a value in it. Once the macro is defined, it can be used to provide the stored value to other *sendmail.cf* commands or directly to ***sendmail*** itself (defined macros are specified by their names and the leading "$" character. This allows ***sendmail*** configurations to be shared by many systems, simply by modifying a few system-specific macros.

A macro name can be any single ASCII character. Lowercase letters are reserved for ***sendmail***'s own internal macros; user-created macros use uppercase letters as names.

sendmail's internal macros are:

Name	Function
a	Origination date in RFC 822 format
b	Current date in RFC 822 format
c	Hop count
d	Date in UNIX (ctime) format
e	SMTP entry message
f	Sender "from" address
g	Sender address relative to the recipient
h	Recipient host
i	Queue ID
j	"Official" domain name for this site
l	Format of the UNIX *from* line
n	Name of the daemon (for error messages)
o	Set of "operators" in addresses
p	***sendmail***'s PID
q	Default format of sender address
r	Protocol used
s	Sender's host name
t	Numeric representation of the current time
u	Recipient user
v	Version number of ***sendmail***
w	Hostname of this site
x	Full name of the sender
z	Home directory of the recipient

Some of ***sendmail***'s internal macros must be defined within the *sendmail.cf* file:

Name	Value Assigned This Macro	Example
e	SMTP entry message	De$j Sendmail $v ready at $b
j	Site's official domain name	***Dj$w.$D***
l	Format of the UNIX from line	***DlFrom $g $d***
n	Name used in error messages	***DnMAILER-DAEMON***
o	Set of operators in addresses	***Do.:%\@!^=/***
q	Default sender address format	Dqg?x ($x)$.

Note: All of the listed macros must be specified in a configuration file, but only the value assigned to macro ***j*** is usually modified. The macro ***$D*** is user-defined.

The definition of "macro **q**" contains a conditional: ***$?x ($x)$.***. It tests whether "macro **x**" has a value set, and if the "macro **x**" has been set, whether the text following the conditional is interpreted. The constructs "**$?**" and "**$.**" specify the beginning and the end of the conditional. This means that **q** is assigned the value of "macro **g**", and the value of "macro **x**" in the parentheses if the "macro **x**" is set. The conditional can be used with an "else" construct, which is "**$|**". An example explaining the full syntax of the conditional is:

$?x *text1* $| *text2* $.

Which is interpreted as:

if	x is set	(construct **$?**)
	use ***text1***	
else		(construct **$|**)
	use ***text2***	
fi		(construct **$.**)

Although user-defined macros can be identified by an arbitrary capital letter, it is common to identify certain macros by the following letters:

Macro	Description
B	Bitnet relay
C	DECnet relay
D	The local domain — usually not needed
E	Reserved for X.400 relay
F	Fax relay
H	Mail hub (for mail clusters)
L	Luser relay
M	Masquerade (who I claim to be)
R	Relay (for unqualified names)
S	Smart host
U	My UUCP name (if I have a UUCP connection)
V	UUCP relay (class V hosts) v
W	UUCP relay (class W hosts)
X	UUCP relay (class X hosts)
Y	UUCP relay (all other hosts)
Z	Version number

20.2.1.1.2 The Define Class Command

Two commands, **C** and **F**, define ***sendmail*** classes. A ***class*** is an array of values. They are used when multiple values are handled in the same way; for example, multiple names for the local host, or a list of *uucp* names. Classes allow ***sendmail*** to compare against a list of values, instead of multiple comparisons against single values. Special pattern matching symbols are introduced for this purpose: the "**$=**" symbol matches any value in a class, and the "**$~**" symbol matches any value not in a class.

Classes have single character names, and user-created classes use uppercase letters for names. Class values can be defined on a single line, on multiple lines, or loaded from a file.

The **C** command is used to assign the class from a single or multiple lines, for example:

CV*host1 host2 host3*

or

CV*host1 host2*

CV*host3*

Each new line with values in the class definition is appended to previously defined class values.

The **F** command is used to load the class values from a file, for example:

Fw*/etc/sendmail.cw* will define the class "w" as the contents of the file */etc/sendmail.cw*

A few class definitions may need to be modified in the ***sendmail*** configuration file. These are classes related to the alias host names, to special domains for mail routing, or some other site-dependent data.

Similarly as with macros, some of the letters are used as usual names for specific classes; they are presented in the following table:

Class	Description
B	Domains that are candidates for best MX lookup
E	Addresses that should not seem to come from macro $M
F	Hosts to forward for
G	Domains that should be looked up in generic table
L	Addresses that should not be forwarded to macro $R
M	Domains that should be mapped to macro $M
O	Operators that indicate network operations (cannot be in local names)
P	Top level pseudo-domains: BITNET, DECNET, FAX, UUCP, etc.
R	Domains we are willing to relay (pass anti-spam filters)
U	My UUCP name (if I have a UUCP connection)
V	UUCP hosts connected to relay macro $V
W	UUCP hosts connected to relay macro $W
X	UUCP hosts connected to relay macro $X
Y	Locally connected smart UUCP hosts
Z	Locally connected domain-ized UUCP hosts
.	The class containing only a dot
[	The class containing only a left bracketv

The configuration file continues with the ***Version number.***

```
------------------------------- /etc/sendmail.cf continued -------------------------------
# Version number of configuration file
DVSMI-4.1
------------------------------------- to be continued -------------------------------------
```

The ***version number*** is the macro **V**, and is defined as any other macro. It usually does not require modification, but it can be a good idea to keep track of the changes made to the ***sendmail*** configuration. The version number is the place to do it. Each time the configuration is changed, the ***version number*** can be modified.

Afterward, the ***Standard macros*** (sometimes also known as ***Special macros***) are specified:

```
------------------------------- /etc/sendmail.cf continued -------------------------------
### Standard macros
# name used for error messages
DnMailer-Daemon
```

```
# UNIX header format
DlFrom $g $d
# delimiter (operator) characters
Do.:%@!^=/ []
# format of a total name
Dq$g$?x ($x)$.
# SMTP login message
De$j Sendmail $v/$V ready at $b
---------------------------------------- to be continued -----------------------------------------
```

The ***Standard (special) macro*** section includes some special macros used by ***sendmail.*** For example, the name that ***sendmail*** uses to identify itself when it returns error messages, or the message that ***sendmail*** displays during an SMTP login. All macros are defined in the usual way. There is no need for any modification of this section.

The ***Options*** section follows:

```
-------------------------------- /etc/sendmail.cf continued --------------------------------
### Options
# Remote mode - send through server if mailbox directory is mounted
OR
# location of alias file
OA/etc/aliases
# default delivery mode (deliver in background)
Odbackground
# rebuild the alias file automagically
OD
# temporary file mode -- 0600 for secure mail, 0644 for permissive
OF0600
# default GID
Og1
# location of help file
OH/usr/lib/sendmail.hf
# log level
OL9
# default messages to old style
Oo
# Cc my postmaster on error replies I generate
OPPostmaster
# queue directory
OQ/usr/spool/mqueue
# read timeout for SMTP protocols
Or15m
# status file -- none
OS/etc/sendmail.s
# queue up everything before starting transmission, for safety
Os
# return queued mail after this long
OT3d
# default UID
Ou1
---------------------------------------- to be continued -----------------------------------------
```

The ***Options*** section specifies all of the implemented ***sendmail*** options. A leading uppercase letter "O" identifies each option entry; the second letter is the option name. Occasionally, some of the options can be modified if an already defined (or default) option does not correspond to the real situation. When options define pathnames for needed files and directories, it is highly recommended to keep their standard locations.

Besides the options defined for this specific configuration, other options are also available:

Option	Meaning
aN	Wait N min. for @:@, than rebuild the alias file
Bc	Define the blank substitution character
c	Queue mail for an expensive mailer
di	Deliver interactively
dq	Deliver during the next queue run
ee	Mail error messages and return 0 status
em	Mail back error messages
ep	Print error messages
eq	Return exit status; no error messages
ew	Write back error messages
f	Retain UNIX-style "From" lines
I	Use the BIND (DNS) to resolve host names
i	Ignore dots in incoming messages
Mxval	Set macro **x** to val
m	Send to me, too
Nnet	Define the name of the home network as "net"
qn	Define factor *n* used to decide when to queue jobs
v	Run in verbose mode
Wpass	Define password "pass" used for the remote debug
Xl	Refuse SMTP connections if load average exceeds "l"
xl	Queue messages if load average exceeds "l"
Y	Deliver each queued job in separate job
yn	Lower priority of a job by "n" for each recipient v
Zn	Decrease a job's priority by "n" each time it is run
zn	Factor used with precedence to determine message priority

An option could be a string, an integer, a Boolean, or a time interval. There are no user created options; the meaning of each option is hard-coded within the ***sendmail*** program. For options missing from the configuration file, the default values are supposed.

The configuration continues with the sections: ***Message precedences*** and ***Trusted users***.

```
------------------------------- /etc/sendmail.cf continued -------------------------------
### Message precedences
Pfirst-class=0
Pspecial-delivery=100
Pjunk=–100

### Trusted users
T root daemon uucp
--------------------------------------- to be continued ---------------------------------------
```

- ***Message precedences*** Assigns priority to messages entering its queue (it is known as "message precedence;" the higher the precedence number, the greater the precedence of the message (the default is 0). There is no need to modify this section.
- ***Trusted users*** Defines a list of users who are trusted to override the sender address using the *mailer* flag **-f;** could be a security problem, so it is better not to modify it.

The ***Headers*** section defines the format of headers that ***sendmail*** inserts into e-mail.

```
-------------------------------- /etc/sendmail.cf continued --------------------------------
### Format of headers
H?P?Return-Path: <$g>
HReceived: $?sfrom $s $.by $j ($v/$V)  id $i; $b
H?D?Resent-Date: $a
H?D?Date: $a
H?F?Resent-From: $q
H?F?From: $q
H?x?Full-Name: $x
HSubject:
H?M?Resent-Message-Id: <$t.$i@$j>
H?M?Message-Id: <$t.$i@$j>
HErrors-To:
############################
---------------------------------------- to be continued ----------------------------------------
```

Macros defined within the ***headers*** are expanded before the header is inserted; it is unlikely to need to change the headers. For a better understanding of the header's entries, reread the paragraph on how the macros are defined.

The remaining sendmail configuration lines are related to ***Rulesets*** and ***Rewrite Rules.*** This is the section that defines ***sendmail*** parsing algorithms and decision-making mechanisms. This is the most important part of the configuration file. We will return to this section later.

Mailers are a separate section inserted between ***rulesets;*** *mailers* are defined by the **M** command. We have already discussed this topic earlier, so let us see what real mailer's entries look like.

```
-------------------------------- /etc/sendmail.cf continued --------------------------------
# Local and Program Mailer specification (mandatory)
Mlocal, P=/bin/mail, F=rlsDFMmnP, S=10, R=20, A=mail -d $u
Mprog, P=/bin/sh, F=lsDFMeuP, S=10, R=20, A=sh -c $u
##############################################################
#####
##### Ethernet Mailer specification
#####
##### Messages processed by this configuration are assumed to remain
##### in the same domain. This really has nothing particular to do
##### with Ethernet - the name is historical.
Mether, P=[TCP], F=msDFMuCX, S=11, R=21, A=TCP $h
# UUCP Mailer specification
Muucp, P=/usr/bin/uux, F=msDFMhuU, S=13, R=23, A=uux - -r -a$f $h!rmail ($u)
---------------------------------------- to be continued ----------------------------------------
```

Two *mailers,* ***local*** and ***prog,*** are mandatory for every ***sendmail*** configuration file. In this case these are the program/ *bin/mail* and Bourne shell */bin/sh.* Two other defined *mailers* are: ***ether*** for ***sendmail*** communication through the network (specified by [TCP]), and ***uucp*** (program */usr/bin/uux*) for UUCP delivery via phone line.

20.2.2 Rulesets and Rewrite Rules

Rulesets define rules for how to transform e-mail addresses into the format suitable for e-mail delivery. A leading uppercase letter "S" and the ruleset number identify them. Newer ***sendmail*** versions also allow the textual identification of a ruleset; this could make it easier to determine the purpose of the ruleset (the name usually describes the basic function of the ruleset).

A ***ruleset*** includes one or more ***rewriting rules,*** which are individual lines (entries) that define a specific address transformation; an empty ruleset is also allowed. A leading uppercase letter "**R**" identifies rewriting rule entries. The end of a ruleset is defined by the beginning of the next ruleset, or any other configuration entry (except a rewrite rule entry). An input to the ruleset is an address to be parsed, and the output is the parsed input address. A ruleset is called by ***sendmail*** directly, or by another ruleset. Rewriting rule entries within a ruleset are processed sequentially. When empty (a ruleset without any rewriting rule entry), it preserves an address unchanged (the input and output addresses are equal).

Let us see what rulesets look like:

```
-------------------------------- /etc/sendmail.cf continued --------------------------------
###########################
### Rewriting rules ###
###########################

# Sender Field Pre-rewriting
S1                              # an empty ruleset
# None needed.

# Recipient Field Pre-rewriting
S2                              # an empty ruleset
# None needed.
# Name Canonicalization
# Internal format of names within the rewriting rules is:
#               anything<@host.domain.domain...> anything
# We try to get every kind of name into this format, except for local
# names, which have no host part. The reason for the "<>" stuff is
# that the relevant host name could be on the front of the name (for
# source routing), or on the back (normal form). We enclose the one that
# we want to route on in the <>'s to make it easy to find.
#

### = = = = = = = = = =  # here is the beginning of Ruleset #3


S3
# handle "from:<>" special case
R$*<>$*             $@@                     turn into magic token

# basic textual canonicalization
R$*<$+> $*          $2                      basic RFC822 parsing

# make sure <@a,@b,@c:user@d>               syntax is easy to parse -- undone later
R@$+,$+:$+          @$1:$2:$3               change all "," to ":"
R@$+:$+             $@$>6<@$1>:$2           src route canonical

R$+:$*;@$+          $@$1:$2;@$3             list syntax
R$+@$+              $:$1<@$2>               focus on domain
R$+<$+@$+>          $1$2<@$3>               move gaze right
R$+<@$+>            $@$>6$1<@$2>            already canonical

# convert old-style names to domain-based names
# All old-style names parse from left to right, without precedence.
R$-!$+              $@$>6$2<@$1.uucp>       uucphost!user
```

```
R$-.$+!$+           $@$>6$3<@$1.$2>     host.domain!user
R$+%$+              $@$>3$1@$2          user%host

### = = = = = = = = = =  # here is the end of Ruleset #3

# Final Output Post-rewriting
S4
R$+<@$+.uucp>  $2!$1                    u@h.uucp => h!u
R$+                 $: $>9 $1           Clean up addr
R$*<$+> $*          $1$2$3              defocus

############################
# Rewriting rules
#
#######  A number of rewrite rules follow, but they are not presented here.
#######
---------------------------------------- to be continued ----------------------------------------
```

The specified rulesets and rewrite rules are the only ones that ***sendmail*** knows about and follows. They must be sufficient for a complete and correct e-mail processing. It is not very common to modify this part, although a deeper ***sendmail*** customization is usually related to this section. This is also the most probable place to look if problems in the e-mail delivery are encountered. If a modification in this section is unavoidable, it must be done extremely carefully.

20.2.2.1 The Ruleset Sequence

We already mentioned that a ruleset could be invoked from another ruleset, or by ***sendmail*** directly. A direct ruleset invocation is the result of the coded ruleset sequence in the ***sendmail*** program. By default all e-mail addresses follow the same ruleset path during their parsing. At the beginning, this path was uniform for all e-mail addresses. However, based on the accumulated experience of the long-time usage of ***sendmail*** and increased security demands, the default ruleset sequence has been modified and improved lately. Since the ***sendmail*** version 8, separate default ruleset paths have been introduced in parsing envelope and header e-mail addresses. Simply, the envelope and header addresses could be processed in the different ways depending of the implemented delivery procedure, i.e., mailer for the processed e-mail.

This is presented in Figure 20.4. Depending of the implemented ***sendmail*** version, the flow of the addresses through the default rulesets called directly by ***sendmail*** corresponds to one of the two ruleset patterns.

- *Each box marked by a number* defines the numeric name of the corresponding ruleset.
- *S = box* stands for a ruleset whose numeric name is defined by the **S** field in the *mailer* definition. Each *mailer* may specify its own ruleset for *mailer*-specific cleanup of the sender address before the message is delivered.
- *R = box* stands for a ruleset whose numeric name is defined by the R field in the *mailer* definition. Each *mailer* may specify its own ruleset for *mailer*-specific cleanup of the recipient address before the message is delivered.
- Lower case letters ***e*** and ***h*** correspond to *envelope* and *header* addresses respectively.

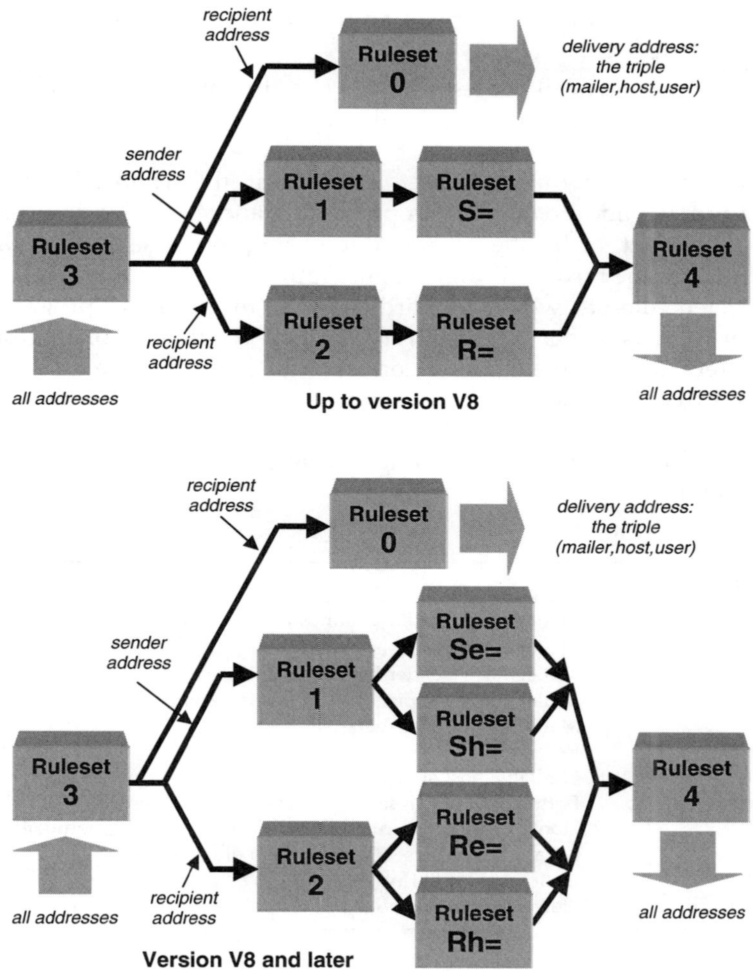

FIGURE 20.4
Sequence of rulesets.

Rulesets can be thought of as subroutines, or functions, designed to process e-mail addresses. They are called from *mailer* definitions, from individual ***rewrite rules***, or directly by ***sendmail.*** Five rulesets built in ***sendmail*** have special functions:

1. ***Ruleset 3*** is the first ruleset to be applied to addresses. It converts an address to the canonical form: ***local-part@host.domain***. Do not forget that for quite a time the Internet e-mail addressing concept (which is completely prevailing nowadays) has been only one of the implemented e-mail addressing mechanisms. In such a diverse addressing environment, it was extremely important to find some common ground.
2. ***Ruleset 0*** is applied to the addresses used to deliver the e-mail. It is applied after ***ruleset 3***, and only to the recipient addresses, which are actually used for e-mail delivery. It resolves the recipient address to the triple ***mailer-host-user.*** This is presented in Figure 20.5.
3. ***Ruleset 1*** is applied to all sender addresses in the message. Nowadays it is usually an empty ruleset.

4. ***Ruleset 2*** is applied to all recipient addresses in the message. Nowadays it is usually an empty ruleset.
5. ***Ruleset 4*** is applied to all addresses and is used to translate back internal address formats into the initial external address formats.

There are, of course, many other rulesets specified in the ***sendmail*** configuration file. These rulesets provide additional address processing and are called by existing rulesets using the ***$>n*** construct, or by the ***sendmail*** according to the selected ***mailer*** upon the ***ruleset 0*** completion: the boxes "S" and "R" in Figure 20.4.

Besides the listed rulesets, which are hard-coded in the ***sendmail*** program, the identification of other rulesets seems to be arbitrary. A ruleset could be named arbitrarily (with numbers, or letters, or combined), and a corresponding rewrite rule modified to call the newly identified ruleset. However, there are some conventions in naming a ruleset, and it is highly recommended to stay within them.

The following table lists the usual naming of rulesets for certain purposes (other than those hard-coded in ***sendmail***):

Rulset #	Purpose
1x	Mailer rules (sender qualification)
2x	Mailer rules (recipient qualification)
3x	Mailer rules (sender header qualification)
4x	Mailer rules (recipient header qualification)
5x, 6x, 7x	Mailer subroutines (general)
8x	Reserved
90	Mailtable host stripping
96	Bottom half of ruleset 3 (ruleset 6 in old sendmail)
97	Hook for recursive ruleset 0 call (ruleset 7 in old sendmail)
98	Local part of ruleset 0 (ruleset 8 in old sendmail)
99	Guaranteed null (for debugging)
Text	New ***sendmail*** versions use textual ruleset naming either

20.2.2.2 The Ruleset 0

A special section in the ***sendmail*** configuration file is dedicated to the ***ruleset 0***; this is the core ruleset for e-mail delivery. It parses the e-mail address and makes the crucial decision of "***where and how to deliver e-mail.***" To make such a decision, ***sendmail*** always applied ***ruleset 0*** over the recipient's e-mail address; the output must be either a decision about the destination and the corresponding *mailer,* or an error.

There is even special rewrite rule syntax for ***ruleset 0. Ruleset 0*** defines the triple (*mailer, host, user*) that specifies the mail delivery program, the recipient host, and the user-recipient. This is presented in Figure 20.5.

The special transformation syntax in ***ruleset 0*** is:

$#mailer$@host$:user

where:

mailer	Mailer name defined by the M command in the *sendmail.cf* file
host	Hostname of the host to deliver email (could be different than the recipient host)
user	Username of the recipient user on the recipient host
$#, $@,*** and ***$:	Leading constructs for these three parts respectively

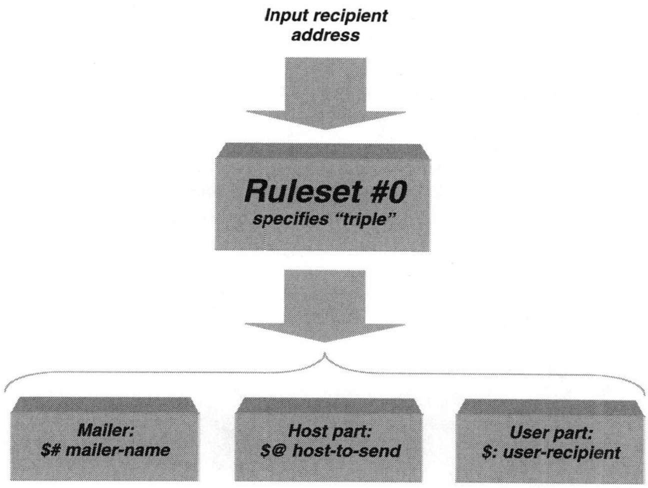

FIGURE 20.5
Ruleset 0 resolves a triple: {*mailer, host, user*}.

There is one special variant of this syntax, also used only in ***ruleset 0,*** that passes an error message to the user:

$#error$:*message*

where
message Arbitrary text of the error message returned to the user.

Ruleset 0 is usually located at the end of the ***sendmail*** configuration file (although the order of rulesets is arbitrary). We will complete the presentation of the */etc/sendmail.cf* file with this ruleset.

*Note: All final decision-making rewrite rules are printed in "**bold-italic**".*

```
-------------------------------- /etc/sendmail.cf continued --------------------------------
##### RULESET ZERO PREAMBLE

# Ruleset 30 just calls rulesets 3 then 0.
S30
R$*                        $: $>3 $1                  First canonicalize

R$*                        $@ $>0 $1                  Then rerun ruleset 0

S0
# On entry, the address has been canonicalized and focused by ruleset 3.
# Handle special cases.....
R@                         $#local $:$n               handle <> form
# Earlier releases special-cased the [x.y.z.a] format, but SunOS 4.1 or later
# should handle these properly on input.
# now delete redundant local info
R$*<$*$=w.LOCAL>$*         $1<$2>$4                   thishost.LOCAL
R$*<@LOCAL>$*              $1<@$m>$2                  host == domain gateway
R$*<$*$=w.uucp>$*          $1<$2>$4                   thishost.uucp
R$*<$*$=w>$*               $1<$2>$4                   thishost
```

```
# arrange for local names to be fully qualified
R$*<@$%y>$*                 $1<@$2.LOCAL>$3               user@etherhost

# For numeric spec, you can't pass spec on to receiver, since old rcvr's
# were not smart enough to know that [x.y.z.a] is their own name.
R<@[$+]>:$*                 $:$>9 <@[$1]>:$2              Clean it up, then...
R<@[$+]>:$*                 $#ether $@[$1] $:$2           numeric internet spec
R<@[$+]>,$*                 $#ether $@[$1] $:$2           numeric internet spec
R$*<@[$+]>                  $#ether $@[$2] $:$1           numeric internet spec

R$*<$*.> $*                 $1<$2>$3                      drop trailing dot
R<@>:$*                     $@$>30$1                      retry after route strip
R$*<@>                      $@$>30$1                      strip null trash & retry

##################################################
### Machine dependent part of ruleset zero ###
##################################################

# resolve names we can handle locally
R<@$=V.uucp>:$+             $:$>9 $1                      First clean up, then...
R<@$=V.uucp>:$+             $#uucp $@$1 $:$2              @host.uucp:...
R$+<@$=V.uucp>              $#uucp $@$2 $:$1              user@host.uucp

# optimize names of known ethernet hosts
R$*<@$%y.LOCAL>$*           $#ether $@$2 $:$1<@$2>$3      user@host.here

# other non-local names will be kicked upstairs
R$+                         $:$>9 $1                      Clean up, keep <>
R$*<@$+> $*                 $#$M $@$R $:$1<@$2>$3         user@some.where
R$*@$*                      $#$M $@$R $:$1<@$2>           strangeness with @

# Local names with % are really not local!
R$+%$+                      $@$>30$1@$2                   turn % => @, retry

# everything else is a local name
R$+                         $#local $:$1                  local names
------------------------------- the end of /etc/sendmail.cf -------------------------------
```

20.2.3 Creating the *sendmail.cf* File

All UNIX implementations provide ***sendmail*** configuration template files for several of the most common situations; other templates can be found on the network. Usually the appropriate *sendmail.cf* file can be placed in operation by copying a corresponding template file and performing minimal site-specific customization. Two templates, for main and subsidiary mailhosts, are essential. The main mailhost is supposed to be a knowledgeable mail server dedicated to this business, and a subsidiary mailhost is the prevailing ***sendmail*** configuration that relies on another main mail server. Customizing a system as a subsidiary mailhost is very easy. Usually it is enough to specify only the hostname of a known main mailhost (main mail server) where external e-mail would be forward for further processing and delivery. Sometimes it can even be done out of the *sendmail.cf* file itself: by appending the alias name "mailhost" with the real hostname of the mail server (could be done in DNS, or NIS or even */etc/hosts* file). Of course, it works only if the *sendmail.cf* file points to the generic entity "mailhost."

More sophisticated configuration changes require more knowledge and skills. A manual modification of the *sendmail.cf* file is always possible and doable, and it is even quite common. However, an alternative approach to generate site-specific ***sendmail*** configuration files in an easier and more comprehensive way also exists. It compiles the needed *sendmail.cf* file based on the specified site-specific information. All rulesets and rewrite rules that make a dominant part of the file are automatically created. The input site-specific data are specified in the files that terminate with the *mc* extension; again, a number of *template mc files* are available. What makes this approach different is the fact that these template files are small comprehensive files, and easy to modify if necessary. We will briefly discuss the required procedure.

Template mc files are contained in the ***sendmail*** installation subdirectory *cf,* with an obvious suffix *.mc.* They must be run through the ***m4 macro processor*** to produce a corresponding *cf* configuration file. The other requirement is a preloaded description file *cf.m4.* Once all of the required files are in place, the following command should be executed:

m4 ${CFDIR}/m4/cf.m4 config.mc > config.cf

where

$CFDIR	is the root of the *cf* directory
config.mc	is the name of the template *mc* file
config.cf	is the name of the ***sendmail*** configuration file

To make everything even easier a front-end *Build script* that specifies all needed compilation steps is also available. Simply by typing:

Build config.cf

The corresponding ***sendmail*** configuration file *config.cf* will be created based on the *config.mc* file. The file name is arbitrary, but the existence of a same-name **mc** file is required.

Let us examine a typical *mc* file:

$ cat generic-solaris2.mc

```
divert(-1)
#
# Copyright (c) 1998 Sendmail, Inc. All rights reserved.
# Copyright (c) 1983 Eric P. Allman. All rights reserved.
# Copyright (c) 1988, 1993
# The Regents of the University of California. All rights reserved.
#
# By using this file, you agree to the terms and conditions set
# forth in the LICENSE file which can be found at the top level of
# the sendmail distribution.
#
# This is a generic configuration file for SunOS 5.x (a.k.a. Solaris 2.x)
# It has support for local and SMTP mail only. If you want to
# customize it, copy it to a name appropriate for your environment
# and do the modifications there.
#
divert(0)dnl
VERSIONID('@(#)generic-solaris2.mc   8.8 (Berkeley) 5/19/1998')
OSTYPE(solaris2)dnl
DOMAIN(generic)dnl
MAILER(local)dnl
MAILER(smtp)dnl
```

sendmail uses the M4 macro processor to compile the configuration files. The most important thing to know is that M4 is stream-based, that is, it does not understand lines.

For this reason, in some places you may see the word *dnl,* which stands for *delete through newline;* essentially, it deletes all characters starting at the *dnl* up to and including the next newline character. In most cases ***sendmail*** uses this only to avoid lots of unnecessary blank lines in the output. It could be also used to comment-out an **mc** entry.

Other important directives are *define(A, B)* which defines the macro *"A"* to have the value *"B"*. Macros are expanded as they are read, so one normally quotes both values to prevent expansion, for example:

define('SMART_HOST', 'smart.school.edu')

Please note that M4 macros are expanded even in lines that appear to be comments, for example:

 # See FEATURE(foo) above

This will not do what you expect, because the FEATURE(foo) will be expanded. This also applies to:

 # And then define the $X macro to be the return address

because "define" is an M4 keyword. If you want to use these words, surround them with single quotes, 'like this'.

The following partial listing of the ***sendmail*** *cf* subdirectory shows few of *template mc files,* and the corresponding ***sendmail*** configuration *cf* files (pay attention to their sizes):

$ ls -l /opt/sendmail/cf/cf

```
total 1548
-r-xr-xr-x   1 root   other     535   Dec 29 1998   Build
-r--r--r--   1 root   other    4163   Dec 29 1998   Makefile
-r--r--r--   1 root   other   29824   Oct 21 1999   cs-solaris2.cf
-r--r--r--   1 root   other     989   Dec 29 1998   cs-solaris2.mc
-r--r--r--   1 root   other   28785   Feb 5 1999    generic-hpux10.cf
-r--r--r--   1 root   other     763   Dec 29 1998   generic-hpux10.mc
-r--r--r--   1 root   other   28787   Feb 5 1999    generic-solaris2.cf
-r--r--r--   1 root   other     787   Dec 29 1998   generic-solaris2.mc
      .....
      .....
-r--r--r--   1 root   other   29641   Oct 21 1999   mail.cs.cf
-r--r--r--   1 root   other    1250   Dec 29 1998   mail.cs.mc
```

Though the existing tools will help in managing ***sendmail*** configuration, a thorough understanding and knowledge of the contents of the *sendmail.cf* file is crucial for a successful ***sendmail*** administration.

20.3 The Parsing of E-mail Addresses

Rewrite rules are the core of the *sendmail.cf* file. ***Rulesets*** are groups of associated rewrite rules that can be referenced by a number, or lately any alphanumeric combination. In the **S*n*** command syntax, ***n*** is the number that identifies the ruleset. Normally, numbers in the range of 0 to 99 are used, but there are no restrictions on ruleset numbering. Among all rulesets, ***ruleset 0*** is the most important. However, each ruleset contributes to a successful address parsing and helps ***sendmail*** accomplish its basic task: to deliver e-mail.

20.3.1 Rewriting an E-mail Address

A thorough knowledge of rewrite rules is required for a full understanding of how an address parsing is accomplished; the following text should help with this topic.

Each rewrite rule is defined by the **R** command. The syntax of the **R** command is:

R*lhs*   *rhs*   *comment*

where

lhs Left-hand side, specifies the ***pattern*** to match the input address against. If the matching occurs, the specified ***rhs*** over the input address is performed.

rhs Right-hand side, specifies the ***transformation*** (the rules to transform) input address if pattern matching occurs (if ***lhs*** is true).

comment This field contains comments referring to this entry; it is ignored by ***sendmail,*** but good comments are very important for understanding what is happening in the line.

20.3.2 Pattern Matching

The ***lhs*** matches the input address against the pattern, and if a match is found, rewrites the address in a new format using the rules defined in the ***rhs.*** A rule may process the same address several times because, after being rewritten, the address is again compared against the pattern. If it still matches, it is rewritten again. This cycle of pattern matching and rewriting continues until the address no longer matches the pattern.

Macros, classes, literals, and special metasymbols provide the pattern matching. The macros, classes, and literals provide the values against which the input is compared, while the **metasymbols** define the rules used in matching the pattern. Some metasymbols used for pattern matching are:

Metasymbol	Meaning
$*	Match zero or more tokens
$+	Match one or more tokens
$-	Match exactly one token
$=x	Match any token in class **x**
$~x	Match any token not in class **x**
$x	Match all tokens in macro **x**
$%x	Match any token in the NIS map named in macro **x**
$!x	Match any token not in the NIS map named in macro **x**
$%y	Match any token in the NIS *hosts.byname* map

We see that all metasymbols request a match for some number of ***tokens.*** What is the token itself? A token is a string of characters in an e-mail address delimited by an ***operator;*** and the operators are the characters defined in the macro "**o**" in the *sendmail.cf* file. Operators are also counted as tokens when an e-mail address is parsed.

Let us examine an e-mail address and its parsing. ***sendmail*** first tokenizes the address; for example:

bjl@patsy.myschool.scps.edu => ***bjl , @ , patsy , . , myschool , . , scps , . , edu***

This e-mail address contains nine tokens and they are stored internally in a buffer called *workspace.* When the ***lhs*** of a rule is evaluated, a corresponding *pattern* is also tokenized, and then those tokens are compared to the tokens in the workspace. If both the workspace and the ***lhs*** contain the same tokens, a match is found, and the ***lhs*** comparison is true.

Assume the pattern "**$-@$+**" in the ***lhs;*** after tokenizing it:

$-@$+ => ***$- , @ , $+***

The previous address matches the pattern because:

- It has exactly one token before the @ literal, so it matches the requirement of the **$-** metasymbol.
- It has an @ symbol that matches the pattern's literal @.
- It has one or more tokens after the @ literal, so it matches the requirement of the **$+** metasymbol.

When an address matches a pattern, the corresponding strings from the address that match the metasymbols are assigned to indefinite tokens (because they may contain more than one token value). The indefinite tokens are identified numerically according to their relative position in the pattern of the metasymbol that they matched. This means that the indefinite token produced by the match of the first metasymbol is called **$1**; the match of the second metasymbol is called **$2**; the third is **$3**, and so on. The indefinite tokens created by the pattern matching can then be referenced by their new names: **$1**, **$2**, **$3**, etc.

From the previous example:

$1 => ***bjl***

$2 => ***patsy.myschool.scps.edu*** (It contains seven tokens.)

20.3.3 Address Transformation

The ***rhs*** of a rewrite rule specifies the format to use for rewriting the address, i.e., the appropriate transformation algorithm. It is defined using the same values as for ***lhs***: literals, macros, and special metasymbols. Literals in the ***rhs*** are written into the new address exactly as they appear. Macros are expanded and then written. The metasymbols perform special functions in the transformation. Some metasymbols and their functions are:

Metasymbol	Meaning
$n	Substitute indefinite token **n**
$[name$]	Substitute canonical name
$>n	Call ruleset **n**
$@	Terminate ruleset
$:	Terminate rewrite rule
$#...	Special syntax (explained later)

The following example demonstrates how indefinite tokens are used:

- Assume the old-fashioned input address (but very illustrative one for this purpose) ***bjl@bithost.bitnet*** has been preliminarily processed and now is:

  bjl<@bithost.bitnet>
- Assume the current rewrite rule is:

  R$+<@$+.bitnet> $1%$2<@$B> Use the BITNET relay
- Assume that the macro **B,** which is the BITNET relay, is previously defined as *cunyvm.cuny.edu.*

The complete transformation process is presented in Figure 20.6.
A brief explanation of each step in the address transformation follows:

- The address matches the pattern because it contains one or more tokens before the literals **<@** (the token **bjl**), and one or more tokens between literals **<@,** and **.bitnet>** (the token **bithost).**
- The pattern match produces two indefinite tokens, **$1** (with the value ***bjl***) and **$2** (with the value ***bithost***) that are used in further address transformation.
- The transformation contains the indefinite token **$1,** a literal **%,** the indefinite token **$2,** a literal **<@,** the macro **B,** and a literal **>.**
- Keeping in mind values for the indefinite tokens **$1** and **$2** and the macro **B,** the input address can be rewritten as:

  bjl%bithost<@cunyvm.cuny.edu>

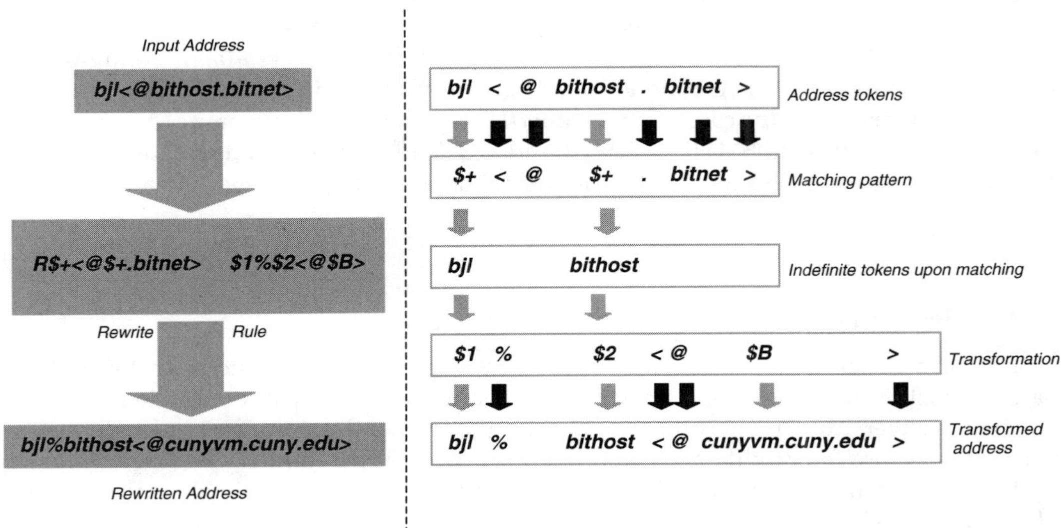

FIGURE 20.6
Rewriting an address. *Note: BITNET relay host **$B** is **"cunyvm.cuny.edu"***

This example explains the implementation of the metasymbol **$n**, and the substitution of the indefinite tokens. However, there are also other metasymbols that could be used in the rule's ***rhs***:

- The **$[*name*$]** metasymbol is based on the DNS and converts a host's nickname or its IP address to its canonical name by passing the value name to the Name Server for resolution.
- The **$>n** metasymbol calls a ruleset **n** and passes the address defined by the remainder of the transformation to the ruleset **n** for processing, for example:
  - **$>9$1%$2** This transformation calls ruleset 9 (metasymbol $>9), and passes the contents of $1, a literal %, and the contents of $2 to ruleset 9 for processing. When ruleset 9 finishes processing, it returns a rewritten address to the calling rule. The return transformed address is then compared again to the pattern in the calling rule. If it still matches, ruleset 9 is called again.
- The recursion built into rewrite rules creates the possibility for infinite loops. The **$@** and **$:** metasymbols are used to control processing; the **$@** terminates the entire ruleset and the remainder of the transformation is the value returned by the ruleset; the **$:** controls the execution of the individual rewrite rule only once. So these two metasymbols could be used to prevent recursion and looping.

20.4 Testing *sendmail* Configuration

sendmail provides powerful tools for configuration testing and debugging. These tools are invoked from the command line using some of the many ***sendmail*** command-line arguments (options). Testing is highly recommended after each ***sendmail*** configuration change to verify what has been done, and to gain confidence in the new configuration.

We already discussed the case when ***sendmail*** is invoked in verbose mode (**-v** argument); it displays the complete SMTP exchange and we can observe communication between source and destination hosts. A few more useful options are presented hereafter.

20.4.1 Testing Rewrite Rules

Problems in e-mail delivery could be caused by implemented rewrite rules for address parsing. Testing the rewrite rules can prevent many problems with e-mail delivery (and not only delivery, but many other problems, too). Generally, testing should always be performed before the modified configuration is put into operation.

The new frozen configuration file *sendmail.fc* must be created (if this file is used at all), after testing has been performed successfully and the ***sendmail*** daemon has been recycled or reinvoked. If reinvoked, the ***sendmail*** daemon should be restarted with the same arguments as during system startup (the necessary command can be found in the corresponding **rc** initialization file).

20.4.2 The *sendmail -bt* Command

We run the ***sendmail -bt*** command from the command line to get more information about rewrite rules. Once it is started, ***sendmail*** prompts for input using the *greater than* symbol (>). At the prompt, enter a ruleset number and the e-mail address you want to test. The address is easy to select; you can start with the most common addresses, and finish with specific, strange, but applicable ones. Among many rulesets, *ruleset 0* is an obvious candidate for the test. In this way you can cover nearly all of the possible cases and be sure that your system is running properly.

Ruleset 3 is the first ruleset applied to all addresses (see Figure 20.4), and many ***sendmail*** versions assume the same in the address test mode. No matter which ruleset is specified, the address is first processed by *ruleset 3* and then by the selected ruleset. This is not the case with all ***sendmail*** versions. Usually, ***sendmail*** informs you whether *ruleset 3* is included by default or not before the address processing starts.

To find out which *mailer* is delivering the test e-mail, process a recipient address through *ruleset 0* (remember *ruleset 3* could be, but might not be, called by default). It is relatively easy to determine if everything is working correctly or not by following the messages that ***sendmail*** displays at the start and the exit from each ruleset about the input and the output address. It is more difficult to figure out the reason for incorrect address parsing if something goes wrong (the syntax of rewrite rules is not very friendly), but at least an incorrect ruleset can be identified.

In the presented example *ruleset 0* was tested for three e-mail addresses, with supposedly three different outputs for *mailers.* The testing was performed on the host *patsy.myschool.scps.edu;* the first address is the local one, the second address belongs to the same domain so it can be delivered directly to the final destination, and the third one is out of the domain and its delivery is performed over a mail relay (in this case the mailhost: *mail1.scps.edu*).

```
# /usr/lib/sendmail -bt
ADDRESS TEST MODE
Enter <ruleset> <address>

> 0 bjl@patsy.myschool.scps.edu
rewrite:  ruleset 3   input:    "bjl" "@" "patsy" "." "myschool" "." "scps" "." "edu"
rewrite:  ruleset 6   input:    "bjl" "<" "@" "patsy" "." "myschool" "." "scps" "." "edu" ">"
rewrite:  ruleset 6   returns:  "bjl" "<" "@" "patsy" "." "LOCAL" ">"
rewrite:  ruleset 3   returns:  "bjl" "<" "@" "patsy" "." "LOCAL" ">"
rewrite:  ruleset 0   input:    "bjl" "<" "@" "patsy" "." "LOCAL" ">"
rewrite:  ruleset 30  input:    "bjl"
rewrite:  ruleset 3   input:    "bjl"
rewrite:  ruleset 3   returns:  "bjl"
rewrite:  ruleset 0   input:    "bjl"
rewrite:  ruleset 9   input:    "bjl"
rewrite:  ruleset 9   returns:  "bjl"
rewrite:  ruleset 0   returns:  $# "local" $:"bjl"
rewrite:  ruleset 30  returns:  $# "local" $:"bjl"
rewrite:  ruleset 0   returns:  $# "local" $:"bjl"

> 0 bjl@apollo.ph.myschool.scps.edu
rewrite:  ruleset 3   input:    "bjl" "@" "apollo" "." "ph" "." "myschool" "." "scps" "." "edu"
rewrite:  ruleset 6   input:    "bjl" "<" "@" "apollo" "." "ph" "." "myschool" "." "scps" "." "edu" ">"
rewrite:  ruleset 6   returns:  "bjl" "<" "@" "apollo" "." "ph" "." "LOCAL" ">"
rewrite:  ruleset 3   returns:  "bjl" "<" "@" "apollo" "." "ph" "." "LOCAL" ">"
```

rewrite: ruleset 0 input: "bjl" "<" "@" "apollo" "." "ph" "." "LOCAL" ">"
rewrite: ruleset 0 returns: $# "ether" $@ "apollo" "." "ph" "." "myschool" "." "scps" "." "edu"
$: "bjl" "<" "@" "apollo" "." "ph" "." "myschool" "." "scps" "." "edu" ">"

> 0 bjl@acf4.yourschool.edu

rewrite: ruleset 3 input: "bjl" "@" "acf4" "." "yourschool" "." "edu"
rewrite: ruleset 6 input: "bjl" "<" "@" "acf4" "." "yourschool" "." "edu" ">"
rewrite: ruleset 6 returns: "bjl" "<" "@" "acf4" "." "yourschool" "." "edu" ">"
rewrite: ruleset 3 returns: "bjl" "<" "@" "acf4" "." "yourschool" "." "edu" ">"
rewrite: ruleset 0 input: "bjl" "<" "@" "acf4" "." "yourschool" "." "edu" ">"
rewrite: ruleset 9 input: "bjl" "<" "@" "acf4" "." "yourschool" "." "edu" ">"
rewrite: ruleset 9 returns: "bjl" "<" "@" "acf4" "." "yourschool" "." "edu" ">"
rewrite: ruleset 0 returns: $# "ddn" $@ "mail1" "." "scps" "." "edu" $: "bjl" "<" "@" "acf4" "." "yourschool" "." "edu" ">"
> **^D**

The same test procedure can be implemented for other rulesets and addresses.

20.4.3 The Debugging Level

The level of information that ***sendmail*** displays during the testing can be arbitrary selected; the ***sendmail*** command with the **-d** option is used for this purpose:

sendmail -d*level*

where *level* corresponds to the selected debugging level.

Numbers identify the debugging levels. Larger numbers correspond to higher debugging levels with more detailed displayed information. Selecting a higher debugging level does not always make it easier to determine the source of an error. The displayed data could contain too much useless information, while the important piece becomes hidden between all of the unimportant data.

Once selected, a debugging level remains active until the next new level (higher or lower) is selected again.

20.4.4 Checking the Mail Queue

sendmail is also a very powerful tool for checking the mail queue. As we know, all unprocessed e-mail requests are temporarily stored in the mail queue for later processing. ***sendmail*** periodically reprocesses the mail queue for a certain period (the default is 5 days) before it returns an error message to the sender about undelivered e-mail; the queued e-mail is then removed from the queue.

The command **sendmail -bp** displays the status of the mail queue. It is recommended that you run this command occasionally to check for possible problems in mail queuing. Too many pending e-mail requests are usually a sign of some ***sendmail***-related problems. Too many queued e-mail requests could keep ***sendmail*** daemons so busy that e-mail starts to work improperly.

The mail queue is located in the */var/spool/mqueue* directory by simply listing the directory and counting the listed files:

ls /var/spool/mqueue | wc -l

We can also conclude something about queued e-mail requests. Please note that two files represent each e-mail request: control and a data file. A lock file is also temporarily created during the request processing.

The command **sendamil**.**-qv** is very instrumental in forcing e-mail queue processing (the **q** option), and provides a verbose display of all steps in the processing (the **v** option).

A great deal of information about pending e-mail requests can be obtained by combining these two commands, and this may help point out eventual problems in the ***sendmail*** configuration.

20.5 Mail User Agents

sendmail plays the central role in the e-mail show, but it is fair to say a few words about MUA programs, too. From the user point of view these programs are the most important for e-mail use. We will briefly present the generic UNIX MUA program ***mail*** (the BSD flavor, also known as ***Mail***), later named ***mailx*** (BSD flavor */usr/ucb/mailx*); its System V counterpart ***mailx*** was almost identical. The very same program is also used as ***sendmail***'s local *mailer* for local e-mail deliveries. Obviously, using the same program as a MUA and as a local *mailer* sounds very logical.

20.5.1 The *Mail* Program and *.mailrc* File

In the following text, the generic names ***mail*** and *.mailrc* are used to identify the most common UNIX BSD flavored MUA program and its configuration file; some differences in naming on some UNIX platforms are possible. ***mail*** was the first comfortable (today, this statement is quite disputable, but in the past it was true), flexible, interactive tool for composing, sending, and receiving e-mail messages; it included a number of mail subcommands for this purpose. While reading e-mail messages, ***mail*** provides a user with commands to browse, display, save, delete, and respond to the messages. While sending e-mail, ***mail*** allows editing and reviewing of messages being composed, and the inclusion of text from files or other messages.

The incoming e-mail is stored in the **system mailbox** for each user; it is appended to the current file contents. This is a file named after the user name in the directory */var/spool/mail*. ***mail*** normally looks in this file for incoming messages, but the environment variable MAIL can be set to overwrite the default value, and to specify a different file. When a user reads a message it is marked to be moved to a secondary file for storage. This secondary file, called the **mbox,** is normally the file *mbox* in the user's home directory. Setting the MBOX environment variable can change this location. Messages remain in the **mbox** file as read e-mail until the user deliberately removes them.

20.5.1.1 Starting *mail*

Once started, ***mail*** reads commands from a systemwide mail startup file (*/usr/lib/Mail.rc*) to initialize certain systemwide variables; then it reads from a private mail startup file called the *.mailrc* file (it is normally the file *.mailrc* in the user's home directory, but this can be changed by setting the MAILRC environment variable) for personal commands and variable settings. Most of the ***mail*** subcommands are legal inside the mail startup files. The most common use of the files is to set up initial display options and alias lists. Any errors in the mail startup file cause the remaining lines in that file to be ignored.

A user can invoke ***mail*** from the command line to send a message directly to a recipient if the recipient e-mail address is included as an argument on the command line. When no recipients appear on the ***mail*** command line, ***mail*** enters the *command mode,* from which the user can read received messages. If there are no received messages, ***mail*** prints: *No mail for username* and exits.

When in *command mode* (i.e., while reading messages), the user still can send e-mail messages with the ***mail*** subcommands.

20.5.1.2 Sending E-mail Messages

mail is in *"input mode"* while a user is composing an e-mail message to send. If no subject was specified as an argument to the ***mail*** command, a prompt for the subject is printed. After typing in the subject line, ***mail*** enters *"input mode"* to accept the text of the user's message to be sent.

As the user types in the message, ***mail*** stores it in a temporary file. The user can enter the appropriate *tilde escape commands* at the beginning of an input line to review or modify the message. The user types a single dot (or EOF character, normally Ctrl-D) on a line by itself to indicate that the message is ready to send. ***mail*** submits the message to ***sendmail*** for delivery to each specified recipient.

Recipients can be local users identified by their usernames, e-mail addresses of the form *name@domain, uucp* addresses of the form *[host!...host!]host!username,* files for which the user has write permission, or alias groups.

20.5.1.3 Reading E-mail Messages

When the user enters *command mode* to read e-mail messages, ***mail*** displays a header summary of the first several messages, followed by a prompt for one of the mail subcommands listed below. The default prompt is the "&" (ampersand) character.

Messages are listed and referred to by numbers. At any time, the current message is marked by the ">" (greater than) character in the header summary; this is the default message for ***mail*** subcommands that require an optional list of messages (if a message number, as an argument, is omitted).

20.5.1.4 *Mail* Subcommands

While in the *command mode,* the default subcommand is "print" (if the user terminates an empty command line with *Return,* or *Enter* only). The help menu is available (the "?" subcommand) for a complete list of ***mail*** subcommands. A partial list of mail subcommands follows:

mail Subcommand	Meaning
?	Print a summary of commands.
alias alias name *group alias name*	Declare an *alias* for the specified *names.* The *names* are substituted when *alias* is used as a recipient. This is useful in the *.mailrc* file.
delete [message-list]	Delete specified messages from the **system mailbox.** If the variable "autoprint" is set, print the message following the last message deleted.
headers [message]	Print the page of headers which includes the specified *message.* The "screen" variable sets the number of headers per page.
list	Print all commands available. No explanation is given.
mail recipient...	Mail a message to the specified *recipients.*

print [message-list] *type [message-list]*	Print the specified messages. If the *crt* variable is set, messages longer than the number of lines it indicates are paged through with the command specified by the PAGER variable. The default paging command is "more."
reply [message-list] *respond [message-list]*	Send a response to the author of each message in the *message-list.* The subject line is taken from the first message. If record is set to a filename, a copy of the reply is added to that file. If the "replyall" variable is set, the actions of reply/respond are reversed. The reply-sender command is not affected by the "replyall" variable, but sends each reply only to the sender of each message.
exit	Exit from ***mail*** without changing the **system mailbox.** No messages are saved in the **mbox.**
quit	Exit from ***mail,*** storing messages that were read in the **mbox** file and unread messages in the **system mailbox.** Messages that have been explicitly saved in a file are deleted unless the variable "keepsave" is set.
save [message-list] [filename]	Save the specified messages in the named file. The file is created if it does not exist. If no *filename* is specified, the file named in the MBOX variable is used, or **mbox** in the user's home directory, by default. Each saved message is deleted from the **system mailbox** when ***mail*** terminates unless the "keepsave" variable is set.

Note: ***mail*** will accept a sufficient number of leading letters of a command that uniquely identify the command itself.

20.5.1.5 Forwarding E-mail Messages

The subcommands ***-f*** and ***-m*** with a message number as an argument are available to forward a specific message to another user (these ***mail*** subcommands are also known as *tilde-escape commands*). To forward e-mail messages automatically, add a comma-separated list of addresses for additional recipients into the *.forward* file in the user's home directory (we already discussed this possibility earlier). Please note that the forwarding addresses must be correctly specified and valid, or the forwarded e-mail message could "bounce."

20.5.1.6 Variables

The behavior of ***mail*** is governed by predefined variables that are set and cleared using the **set** and **unset** commands.

Environment variables — Values for the following variables are inherited from the shell and read in automatically from the environment; they cannot be altered from within ***mail***:

HOME => *directory*	The user's home directory.
MAIL => *filename*	The name of the initial mailbox file to read (instead of the standard system mailbox). The default is */var/spool/mail/username.*
MAILRC => *filename*	The name of the personal startup file. The default is *$HOME/.mailrc.*

Mail variables — The variables can also be initialized within the *.mailrc* file, or set and altered interactively using the **set** command. They can also be imported from the environment (in which case their values cannot be changed within ***mail***). The **unset** command clears variables. The **set** command could also be used to clear a variable by prefixing the word *no* to the name of the variable to be cleared.

20.5.2 POP and IMAP

There are several different approaches to building a distributed e-mail infrastructure, such as shared filesystem strategies, proprietary LAN-based protocols, the X.400 P7 protocol, and the Internet-based protocols. Among the Internet-based protocols, the best known and most used are ***Post Office Protocol (POP)*** and ***Internet Message Access Protocol (IMAP)***. POP is the older and still better known protocol; IMAP offers a superset of POP, and also provides good support for certain additional e-mail processing.

Three basic modes of remote mailbox access are in use: *offline, online,* and *disconnected;* they are described in the RFC-1733. In the *offline paradigm,* e-mail is delivered to a mail server, and a PC or MAC user periodically invokes a mail client program that connects to the mail server and downloads all of the pending e-mail to the user's own machine. Thereafter, all e-mail processing is local to the client machine. Offline access mode is a kind of store-and-forward service, intended to transfer e-mail on demand from the mail server (the drop point for incoming e-mail) to a single destination machine. Once transferred, e-mail messages are deleted from the mail server.

In the *online paradigm,* e-mail is also delivered to a mail server, but the mail client does not copy it all at once and then delete it from the mail server. It is an interactive client-server model, in which the client can ask the server for headers, or bodies of specified e-mail messages, or to set certain criteria for e-mail searching, or to set certain e-mail message flags (like "deleted" or "answered"). E-mail messages remain on the mail server until the user explicitly removes them. A user may save messages directly on the client machine, or save them on the server, or be given the choice of doing either.

The two paradigms reflect different requirements and styles of use, and they do not mix very well. Offline is intended for the people who use a single client machine all the time. It is not well suited for accessing one's inbox of recent e-mail, or for saved-message folders from different client machines at different times; the offline download-and-delete mail access tends to scatter e-mail across different client computers. On the other hand, the main advantage of offline access is that it minimizes the use of server resources and connect time when implemented via dialup.

POP and IMAP can be seen as representatives of the two mentioned paradigms. The two protocols are described in greater detail in the text that follows.

20.5.2.1 Post Office Protocol (POP)

Post Office Protocol (POP) is ""the language" that mail clients (predominantly PC and Macintosh workstations) use in communication with an appropriate mail server (usually a UNIX system). POP primarily supports offline e-mail processing. Although the limitations of offline access have triggered interest in using POP in online mode, POP simply does not have some of the functionality needed for a high-quality online (or disconnect) operation. Nevertheless, POP also provides a "pseudo online" mode of operation, wherein client programs can leave e-mail on the mail server; however, its use is often dependent on the pervasive availability of the remote filesystem protocol.

On the server side, POP is supported by the POP daemon that is waiting for requests from surrounding clients. Actually, the super server ***inetd*** listens for incoming clients' requests and invokes the POP daemon. The usual name for the POP daemon program is ***popper,*** although other names are also in use (for example, on the Solaris platform the name for the POP3 daemon is ***ipop3d***). One logical and expected name, ***popd,*** is a regular UNIX command and cannot be used for this purpose. In the following text the daemon's name ***popper*** is used.

There are two versions of POP protocols: ***POP-2*** and ***POP-3*** (enhanced version); they are defined in RFC 1081, 1082, and 1939. The description of the POP-3 daemon follows.

20.5.2.1.1 The **popper** *Daemon*

Popper is an implementation of the POP server that runs on a variety of UNIX systems to manage e-mail for Macintosh and PC clients. The program was originally developed at the University of California at Berkeley.

The format of the command to launch the program is:

/usr/etc/popper [-d] [-t *tracefile*]

The **-d** option sets the socket to debugging and turns debugging on. All debugging information is saved using ***syslog***. The **-t *tracefile*** option turns debugging on and saves the trace information in *tracefile* (see Debugging Mode).

The POP program is available on the network: via *anonymous ftp* from ***ftp.cc.berkeley.edu;*** two files in the *pub* directory (a compressed tar file ***popper.tar.Z*** for PC and a Macintosh StuffIt archive in BinHex format called ***MacPOP.sit.hqx***).

20.5.2.1.2 POP *Transactions*

popper is the program that is launched by ***inetd*** when it gets a service request on port 110 (the official POP port numbers are 110 for POP3 and 109 for POP2); consequently the term *POP server* is more appropriate than POP daemon. The ***popper*** server initializes and verifies that the peer client IP address is valid, and logs a corresponding warning message otherwise. The server enters the authorization state, during which the client must correctly identify itself by providing a valid UNIX UID and password on the server's host machine. No other exchanges are allowed during this state (other than a request to quit). If authentication fails, a warning message is logged and the session ends. Once the user is identified, ***popper*** changes its own user and group IDs to match that of the user and enters the transaction state; it also makes a temporary copy of the user's maildrop (ordinarily in */usr/spool/mail*), which is used for all subsequent transactions. These include the bulk of POP commands to retrieve mail, delete mail, undelete mail, and so forth. A Berkeley software extension also allows the user to submit an e-mail message (parcel) to be mailed using the ***sendmail*** program (this extension is supported in the HyperMail client distributed with the server). When the client quits, ***popper*** enters the final update state during which the network connection is terminated and the user's maildrop is updated with the (possibly) modified temporary maildrop.

Logging — ***popper*** uses *syslog* to keep a record of its activities; by default, it uses logging priority "notice" for all messages except debugging, which is logged at priority "debug." The default log file is */usr/spool/mqueue/POPlog,* or */usr/spool/mqueue/syslog* (this can be changed, if desired).

Debugging — ***popper*** will log debugging information when the **-d** parameter is specified after its invocation in the *inetd.conf* file. Care should be exercised in using this option since it generates considerable output in the *syslog* file. Alternatively, the **-t *tracefile*** option will place debugging information into file "*tracefile*" using *fprintf* instead of *syslog.*

Telnet to port 110 (or 109 if you set it up that way) to check if the POP server ***popper*** is running on an UNIX system; for example, on a BSD UNIX host:

%> telnet bsdhost 110

Trying...
Connected to bsdhost.domain.edu.
Escape character is '^]'.
+OK UCB Pop server (version 1.6) at bsdhost starting.
%> quit
Connection closed by foreign host.

Or, on a Solaris platform:

```
%> telnet sunhost 110
Trying...
Connected to sunhost.
Escape character is '^]'.
+OK sunhost Solstice (tm) Internet Mail Server (tm) POP3 2.0 at Sun, 3 Jan 1999 19:19:41 -0500 (EST)
%> quit
+OK BYE
Connection closed by foreign host.
```

Limitations — ***popper*** copies the user's entire maildrop to the temporary directory */tmp* and then operates on that copy. If the maildrop is particularly large, or if inadequate space is available in */tmp*, then the daemon will refuse to continue and will terminate the connection. This is important to keep in mind if huge e-mail messages are expected.

20.5.2.2 Internet Message Access Protocol (IMAP)

Internet Message Access Protocol (IMAP) is another "language" that mail clients (predominantly PC and Macintosh workstations) use, this time in an interactive communication with an appropriate mail server (usually an UNIX system). It is a method of accessing e-mail or bulletin board messages that are kept on a mail server. IMAP was designed to include POP capabilities and adds support for online and disconnect modes of remote mailbox access. IMAP version 4 is defined in RFC 1730.

IMAP can also do offline mail processing, but its main functionality is in the online and disconnect modes of operation. Essentially, IMAP was designed to permit manipulation of remote mailboxes as if they were local to the user. Depending on the mail client's implementation of IMAP and the mail server administration, the user may either save messages onto the client machine, or save them on the mail server.

IMAP is a more complex protocol to implement than POP; however, IMAP has several advantages over POP. Key goals for IMAP include:

- Be fully compatible with Internet messaging standards, e.g., MIME.
- Allow message access and management from more than one computer.
- Allow access without reliance on less efficient file access protocols.
- Provide support for online, offline, and disconnected access modes.
- Support concurrent access to shared mailboxes.
- Client software needs no knowledge about the server's file store format.

IMAP includes operations for creating, deleting, and renaming mailboxes; checking for new messages; permanently removing messages; setting and clearing flags; MIME parsing (so clients do not need to) and searching; and selective fetching of message attributes, texts, and portions thereof for efficiency.

More specifically, IMAP allows:

- Manipulation of persistent message status flags, such as "Seen," "Deleted," "Answered," as well as user-defined flags
- Storage of messages as well as fetching them; a message from an incoming message folder can be appended to an archive folder, or vice versa

- Concurrent updates and access to shared mailboxes, which is useful when multiple users are processing messages coming into a common inbox because changes in mailbox states could be propagated to all concurrently active clients
- Processing of non-e-mail data, like NetNews or documents; this is very handy for uniformly accessing different classes of information
- Offline access mode for minimum connect time and server resources; useful in situations where the only access to the mail server is via expensive dialup connections, and multiplatform access to the mailboxes is not needed
- Permits online performance optimization, especially over low-speed links

IMAP was originally developed in 1986 at Stanford University. However, it garnered wide attention almost a decade later, and today IMAP is implemented in more and more software products. It is still not as well-known as earlier-released and less-capable alternatives such as POP.

There is a companion protocol to IMAP, called Internet message support protocol (IMSP), defined for user configuration management. IMSP permits the same location-independent (multiplatform) access to personal configuration data such as address books, bookmark lists, etc. that IMAP offers for mailboxes.

20.5.2.3 Comparing POP vs. IMAP

The basic characteristics of IMAP and POP reflect the characteristics of the online and offline access paradigms; their differences also determine the main differences between the two protocols. The summarized differences between the two paradigms are:

- Two distinct modes of use:
  - offline = On-demand retrieval to a single client machine
  - online = Interactive access to multiple mailboxes from multiple clients
- Offline paradigm advantages:
  - Minimum use of connect time
  - Minimum use of server resources
- Online paradigm advantages:
  - Ability to use different computers at different times
  - Ability to use "dataless" client machines, as in labs
  - Platform-independent access to multiple mailboxes
  - Tossibility of concurrent access to shared mailboxes

A brief comparison of POP and IMAP shows:

- Characteristics common to both POP and IMAP:
  - Both can support offline operation
  - E-mail is delivered to a shared active mail server
  - New e-mail is accessible from a variety of client platform types
  - New mail is accessible from anywhere in network
  - Both protocols are open
  - Both implementations are freely available (including source)

    - Clients available for PCs, MACs, and UNIX
    - Commercial implementations available
    - Internet oriented; no need for a SMTP gateway
    - Both protocols deal with access only; both rely on SMTP to send
    - Both protocols support persistent message IDs (for disconnected operation)
- POP protocol advantages:
    - A simpler protocol; easier to implement
    - More client software currently available
- IMAP protocol advantages:
    - Manipulates persistent message status flags
    - Stores messages as well as fetches them
    - Can access and manage multiple mailboxes
    - Supports concurrent updates and access to shared mailboxes
    - Suitable for accessing non-e-mail data; e.g. NetNews or documents
    - Can also use offline paradigm for minimum connect time and disk use
    - Companion protocol defined for user configuration management (IMSP)
    - Constructs to permit online performance optimization, especially over low-speed links

In summary, IMAP offers advantages over POP in three areas: richer functionality in manipulating the user's inbox, the ability to manage mail folders other than the user's inbox, and primitives to allow optimization of online performance, especially when dealing with large MIME messages.

Because there are freely available IMAP development libraries, its additional complexity over POP should not be a significant obstacle to use. Therefore, a reasonable conclusion is that the only advantage of POP over IMAP is that there is currently more POP software available. However, this is changing rapidly, and IMAP's functional advantages over POP are nothing less than overwhelming.

21

UNIX Network Support

21.1 Common UNIX Network Applications

The majority of network applications are not strictly required for the network to operate, but they provide user services that are central to the network's implementation; without them, the network serves no real purpose. Many of these applications require no special configuration. Once the UNIX system is configured properly and the network is set up (including the setup of the Internet super daemon ***inetd***), a number of network applications can be used immediately; other network applications require some administration. Among the most common network applications, we will briefly discuss three:

1. ***telnet*** The network terminal protocol, which provides remote login over the network
2. ***ftp*** The file transfer protocol, which is used for file transfers over the network
3. ***finger*** Provides information about remote users

These applications are instrumental in daily UNIX administration. Because of their inherent interactive nature, they are primarily used from the command line, but they can also be a part of shell scripts and other programs.

All three applications are based on the client/server model. On the client side, the corresponding application program is supposed to be started (from the command line, script, or any other program) on an as-needed basis. The server side is handled by the corresponding daemons (***telnetd, ftpd,*** and ***fingerd***) that are invoked by the Internet super server (the ***inetd*** daemon) once a client request is received at the corresponding port.

None of the three applications require a lot of work to be properly set; they just need to be enabled or disabled on the server side. These actions are provided through the ***inetd*** configuration file */etc/inetd.conf*. Since the ***inetd*** daemon and the */etc/inetd.conf* file were covered in Chapter 15, only the */etc/inetd.conf entries* related to these applications are presented in the following example:

```
$ cat /etc/inetd.conf
        .....
        .....
#  ARPA/Berkeley services
```

ftp	*stream*	*tcp*	*nowait*	*root*	*/etc/ftpd*	*ftpd -l*
telnet	*stream*	*tcp*	*nowait*	*root*	*/etc/telnetd*	*telnetd*
# finger	*stream*	*tcp*	*nowait*	*bin*	*/etc/fingerd*	*fingerd*
	. . . . .					

In this example, ***ftp*** and ***telnet*** are enabled, while ***finger*** is disabled (the entry is commented-out and deactivated).

21.1.1 Telnet

Telnet provides a user interface to a remote system using the TELNET protocol. If ***telnet*** is invoked without arguments, it enters command mode, indicated by its own prompt (*telnet*). In this mode, it accepts and executes the "*telnet commands*" (these will be listed later). When invoked with arguments, it performs an open command with those arguments. The format of the command is:

telnet ***[hostname [port]]***

where

hostname Is the name of the remote host

port Is the port number of the network service (application) — the default is 23 for ***telnet***

Once a connection has been opened, ***telnet*** enters input mode. In this mode, typed text is sent to the remote host. The input mode entered will be either "character at a time" or "line by line," depending on what the remote system supports. In character-at-a-time mode, most text typed in is immediately sent to the remote host for processing. In line-by-line mode, all text is echoed locally, and (usually) only completed lines are sent to the remote host. The "local echo character" (initially "^E") may be used to turn off and on the local echo (this would mostly be used to enter passwords without the password being echoed).

While connected to a remote host, telnet command mode may be entered by typing the telnet "escape character" (by default "^]", which is "Ctrl-Right Bracket"). The normal terminal editing conventions are available when in the command mode.

21.1.1.1 Telnet Commands

A number of commands are available. The command can be typed partially (only enough letters of each command to uniquely identify it need be typed). The most frequently used commands are:

Telnet Commands	Meaning
open host [port]	Open a connection to the named host. If no port number is specified, ***telnet*** will attempt to contact a TELNET server at the default port. The host specification may be either a host name or an IP address specified in the "dot notation."
close	Close a TELNET session and return to command mode.
quit	Close any open TELNET session and exit ***telnet***. An EOF (in command mode) will also close a session and exit.
mode type	*type* is either *line* (for line-by-line mode) or *character* (for character-at-a-time mode). The remote host is asked for permission to go into the requested mode. If the remote host is capable of entering that mode, the requested mode will be entered.

status	Show the current status of ***telnet***. This includes the peer one is connected to, as well as the current mode.
display [*argument…*]	Display all, or some, of the set values.
? [*command*]	Get help. With no arguments, ***telnet*** prints a help summary. If a *command* is specified, ***telnet*** will print the help information only for that command.
send arguments	Send one or more special character sequences to the remote host (more than one *argument* may be specified at a time).
set argument value	Set any one of a number of *telnet variables* to a specific value. The special value "off" turns off the function associated with the variable. The values of variables may be interrogated with the display command.

It is very common to use ***telnet*** for a login to a remote host for the purpose of doing UNIX administration on the host. Please note that ***telnet*** uses a clear-text in communications, including the transfer of the password, which could be a significant disadvantage in a nonsecure environment; otherwise, it is very easy to use.

Telnet allows you to specify a port other than the default one for a TELNET session. In that way ***telnet*** can be instrumental in checking that a port is active, i.e., whether or not the daemon is running behind and listening on that port. There is no chance to establish a session (***telnet*** understands only TELNET protocol), but the daemon will respond if it is alive. For checking purposes, that is quite sufficient.

Telnet is not suitable for shell script programming at all, because of its strictly interactive nature including the interactive login procedure.

21.1.2 FTP

ftp is the user interface to the standard file transfer protocol (FTP). ***ftp*** transfers files to and from a remote host (network site). On the client side, the remote host with which ***ftp*** is to communicate may be specified on the command line. If this is done, ***ftp*** immediately attempts to establish a connection to an FTP daemon on that host; otherwise, ***ftp*** enters its command interpreter and waits for ***ftp*** *commands* from the user (these will be listed later); it also displays the prompt *ftp>*.

The format of the ***ftp*** command is:

ftp *[-options] [hostname]*

where options may be specified at the command line, or to the command interpreter:

-d	Enable debuggin.
-g	Disable filename globbing.
-i	Turn off interactive prompting during multiple file transfers.
-n	Do not attempt "auto-login" upon initial connection. If auto-login is enabled, ***ftp*** checks the *.netrc* file in the user's home directory for an entry describing an account on the remote machine. If no entry exists, ***ftp*** will prompt for the login name of the account on the remote machine (the default is the login name on the local machine), and, if necessary, prompts for a password and an account with which to login.
-v	Show all responses from the remote server, and report on data transfer statistics. This is turned on by default if ***ftp*** is running interactively with its input coming from the user's terminal.
hostname	The name of the remote host.

21.1.2.1 FTP Commands

The most used *"ftp command interpreter commands"* are:

FTP Commands	Meaning
! [*command*]	Run *command* as a shell command on the local machine. If no command is given, invoke an interactive shell.
ascii	Set the "representation type" to "network ASCII." This is the default type.
bell	Sound a bell after each file transfer command is completed.
binary	Set the "representation type" to "image."
bye	Terminate the FTP session with the remote server and exit ***ftp***. An EOF will also terminate the session and exit.
case	Toggle remote computer file name case mapping during **mget** commands. When case is on (the default is off), remote computer file names with all uppercase letters are written in the local directory with the letters mapped to lower case.
cd *remote-directory*	Change the working directory on the remote machine to *remote-directory.*
close	Terminate the FTP session with the remote server and return to the command interpreter. Any defined macros are erased.
delete *remote-file*	Delete the file *remote-file* on the remote machine.
debug [*debug-value*]	Toggle debugging mode. If an optional *debug-value* is specified, it is used to set the debugging level. When debugging is on, ***ftp*** prints each command sent to the remote machine, preceded by the string "-->."
dir [*remote-directory*] [*local-file*]	Print a listing of the directory contents in the directory named *remote-directory* and, optionally, place the output in *local-file*. If no directory is specified, the current working directory on the remote machine is used. Output is sent to the terminal if no local file is specified, or if *local-file* is "-."
disconnect	A synonym for (is the same as) **close**.
get *remote-file* [*local-file*]	Retrieve the *remote-file* and store it on the local machine. If the local file name is not specified, it is given the same name it has on the remote machine.
help [*command*]	Print an informative message about the meaning of *command*. If no argument is given, ***ftp*** prints a list of the known commands.
lcd [*directory*]	Change the working directory on the local machine. If no *directory* is specified, the user's home directory is used.
ls [*remote-directory*] [*local-file*]	Print an abbreviated listing of the contents of a directory on the remote machine. If *remote-directory* is left unspecified, the current working directory is used. The output is sent to the terminal if no local file is specified, or if *local-file* is "-."
mdelete [*remote-files*]	Delete the *remote-files* on the remote machine.
mdir *rote-files local-file*	Like **dir**, except multiple remote files may be specified. If interactive prompting is on, ***ftp*** will prompt the user to verify that the last argument is indeed the target local file for receiving **mdir** output.
mget *remote-files*	Expand the *remote-files* on the remote machine and do a **get** for each file name thus produced.
mkdir *directory-name*	Make a directory on the remote machine.
mls *remote-files local-file*	Like **ls**, except multiple remote files may be specified. If interactive prompting is on, ***ftp*** will prompt the user to verify that the last argument is indeed the target local file for receiving **mls** output.
mode [*mode-name*]	Set the "transfer mode" to *mode-name*. The only valid *mode-name* is *stream*, which corresponds to the default "stream" mode.
mput *local-files*	Expand wild cards in the list of local files given as arguments and do a **put** for each file in the resulting list.
open *host* [*port*]	Establish a connection to the specified *host* FTP server. An optional port number may be supplied, in which case ***ftp*** will attempt to contact an FTP server at that port. If the *auto-login* option is on (default), ***ftp*** will also attempt to automatically log the user in to the FTP server.
prompt	Toggle interactive prompting. Interactive prompting occurs during multiple file transfers to allow the user to selectively retrieve or store files. By default, prompting is turned on. If prompting is turned off, any **mget** or **mput** will transfer all files, and any **mdelete** will delete all files.

put *local-file* [*remote-file*]	Store a local file on the remote machine. If *remotefile* is left unspecified, the local file name is used after processing according to any *ntrans* or *nmap* settings in naming the remote file. File transfer uses the current settings for "representation type," "file structure," and "transfer mode."
pwd	Print the name of the current working directory on the remote machine.
quit	A synonym for (is the same as) **bye**.
recv *remote-file* [*local-file*]	A synonym for (is the same as) **get**.
remotehelp [*command-name*]	Request help from the remote FTP server. If a *command-name* is specified it is supplied to the server as well.
rename *from to*	Rename the file *from* on the remote machine as the name *to*.
reset	Clear reply queue. This command resynchronizes command/reply sequencing with the remote FTP server. Resynchronization may be necessary following a violation of the FTP protocol by the remote server.
rmdir *directory-name*	Delete a directory on the remote machine.
send *local-file* [*remote-file*]	A synonym for (is the same as) **put**.
sendport	Toggle the use of PORT commands. By default, ***ftp*** will attempt to use a PORT command when establishing a connection for each data transfer. The use of PORT commands can prevent delays when performing multiple file transfers. If the PORT command fails, ***ftp*** will use the default data port. When the use of PORT commands is disabled, no attempt will be made to use PORT commands for each data transfer. This is useful when connected to certain FTP implementations that ignore PORT commands but incorrectly indicate they have been accepted.
status	Show the current status of ***ftp***.
type [*type-name*]	Iet the "representation type" to *type-name*. The valid *type-names* are *ascii* for "network ASCII", and *binary* or *image* for "image." If no type is specified, the current type is printed. The default type is "network ASCII."
user	*user-name* [*password*] [*account*] Identify yourself to the remote FTP server. If the password is not specified and the server requires it, ***ftp*** will prompt the user for it (after disabling local echo). If an account field is not specified and the FTP server requires it, the user will be prompted for it. If an account field is specified, an account command will be relayed to the remote server after the login sequence is completed if the remote server did not require it for logging in. Unless ***ftp*** is invoked with "auto-login" disabled, this process is done automatically on initial connection to the FTP server.
verbose	Toggle verbose mode. In verbose mode, all responses from the FTP server are displayed to the user. In addition, if verbose mode is on, statistics regarding the efficiency of the transfer are reported when a file transfer completes. By default, verbose mode is on if ***ftp***'s commands are coming from a terminal, and off otherwise.
? [*command*]	A synonym for (is the same as) **help**.

Command arguments with embedded spaces may be quoted with quote (") marks. If any command argument that is not indicated as being optional is not specified, ***ftp*** will prompt for that argument. Use the terminal interrupt key (usually Ctrl-C) to abort a file transfer. Any submitted transfers will immediately be halted.

The listed set of ***ftp*** *commands* is only a partial list of the most common commands; obviously, ***ftp*** provides a quite powerful set of its own commands (please note those are not UNIX commands, although many of them share the same command name).

ftp is basically an interactive network application; however, ***ftp*** supports an "auto-login" procedure upon initial host connection, i.e., under certain conditions the authentication can be automatically provided. That makes ***ftp*** more suitable for shell script programming, and it is frequently used to transfer files between remote hosts.

Another useful feature is that ***ftp*** allows *"anonymous access,"* an ***ftp*** account for global read-only access. Both features will be briefly discussed.

21.1.2.2 FTP Auto-Login

ftp uses login data from the hidden file *.netrc* located in the user's home directory. The file must be owned by the user and read/write only by the user; it contains data too sensitive (like the ***ftp*** clear-text password) to be compromised by any other user. An entry in the *.netrc* file fully describes one ***ftp*** login session for a specified host. ***ftp*** always consults the file for the corresponding login data when establishing an initial contact with a host. If there is no appropriate entry, a regular login procedure is implemented and the user is fully authenticated; otherwise, the specified username and password are automatically submitted.

Here is an example:

```
$ cd /home/bjl
$ cat .netrc
machine hostname1 login username1 password letmein1
machine hostname2.domain2.com login username2 password letusin2
machine 208.208.25.153 login username3 password passme3
```

Three entries are presented for three hosts identified in different ways. Each entry contains three fields, and each field consists of two subfields:

- Field #1: The directive "*machine*" and the hostname are specified as relative, or with the absolute (full canonical) hostname, or numerically as its IP address.
- Field #2: The directive "*login*" and the *loginname* used to log into the ***ftp*** host (this name is independent of the username of the owner of the *.netrc* file).
- Field #3: The directive "*password*" and the actual clear-text password used to log into the ***ftp*** host.

Once the login procedure is provided automatically, ***ftp*** becomes quite suitable for shell scripting. In the following example the Korn shell "Here document" is used for the FTP session to exchange certain ASCII files between two hosts. The rest of the script is not shown, and it could be used for different purposes, primarily for the FTP data preprocessing and post-processing.

```
$ cat /home/username1/ftpscript.ksh
#!/bin/ksh
#
# Prepare FTP related variables
FTPSITE = hostname2
LOCDIR = /share/local_dir
REMDIR = /pub/remote_dir
FILETOPUT = filename1
FILETOGET = filename2
LOG = /tmp/ftpscript.log
          .....
          .....
cd $LOCDIR
ftp $FTPSITE <<EOF 1>>$LOG 2>&1
cd $REMDIR
ascii
put $FILETOPUT
get $FILETOGET
bye
EOF
          .....
          .....
```

The *Here* document starts with the ***ftp*** command and terminates with the specified termination character sequence, in this case "EOF." The whole FTP session is recorded (logged) in the specified log file (standard output and error are redirected into the log file). Once the *Here* document is started, the Korn shell transfers control to the "***ftp command interpreter;***" all lines within the *Here* document are strictly ***ftp*** *commands* and they are executed sequentially, one after another. At the end, control is transferred back to the Korn shell again.

As we can see, the *Here* document establishes an FTP session, the user authentication is automatic (there is an entry for this session in the *.netrc* file), and two files are exchanged in ASCII mode. At the end, the FTP session is closed.

Each ***ftp*** *command* line is executed upon the completion of the previous line, independent of the command exit status. In this example, only by checking the log file we can determine the status of each individual specified command.

21.1.2.3 Anonymous FTP

Anonymous ***ftp*** is an FTP session in which a user logs into the remote server using the user name *anonymous* and, by convention, the real user name or e-mail address as the password. The purpose of anonymous ***ftp*** is to enable the retrieval of publicly available files and programs from *FTP servers* on the Internet. With anonymous ***ftp***, anyone can login without having an account on an *FTP server*. Of course, access to the server's directories is assumed to be restricted to the read-only mode.

Using the anonymous ***ftp*** service offered by a remote server is very simple. However, setting up an anonymous ***ftp*** service on a system is more complicated. In the text that follows, the basic steps required to build an anonymous FTP site are briefly described.

1. Add user **ftp** to the */etc/passwd* file:

   New entry: *ftp:*:UID:GID:Anonymous ftp:/usr/ftp*

2. Add group **anonymous** to the */etc/group* file:

   New entry: *anonymous:*:GID*

3. Create an *ftp home directory* owned by **ftp** that cannot be written to by anyone:

   mkdir /usr/ftp

   chown ftp /usr/ftp

   chgrp anonymous /usr/ftp

   chmod 555 /usr/ftp

4. Create a *bin directory* under the *ftp home directory* that is owned by **root** and that cannot be written to by anyone. The **ls** program should be placed in this directory and changed to execute-only mode (111):

   mkdir /usr/ftp/bin *# It is already owned by root!*

   chmod 555 /usr/ftp/bin

   cp /bin/ls /usr/ftp/bin

   chmod 111 /usr/ftp/bin/ls

5. Create an *etc directory* under the *ftp home directory* that is owned by **root**, and that cannot be written to by anyone. Create special *passwd* and *group* files in this directory with a single entry equal to the entry added to */etc/passwd* and */etc/group* files, and change the mode of both files to read-only mode (444):

   mkdir /usr/ftp/etc *# It is already owned by root!*

   chmod 555 /usr/ftp/etc

cat /etc/passwd | grep ftp: >/usr/ftp/etc/passwd

cat /etc/group | grep anonymous: >/usr/ftp/etc/group

chmod 444 /usr/ftp/etc/passwd /usr/ftp/etc/group

6. Create a *pub directory* under the *ftp home directory* that is owned by **ftp** and that is corresponding in mode, depending on which rights will be granted to anonymous users. Here, the read-only mode (444) is assumed:

   mkdir /usr/ftp/pub

   chown ftp /usr/ftp/pub

   chgrp anonymous /usr/ftp/pub

   chmod 444 /usr/ftp/pub

7. Check the ownership, mode, and contents of all newly created directories and files.

For most UNIX systems, the installation is complete upon completion of the listed steps, but some UNIX flavors might require some additional procedures. Once the system is ready, files for public use can be copied into the */usr/ftp/pub* directory. They should not be owned by **ftp** to prevent overwriting of the files by remote anonymous users, and their mode must be set to 644 (or 444).

At the end, a thorough test of the installed anonymous ***ftp*** service is recommended to ensure that the *ftp server* provides the desired service without providing additional undesired ones. Anonymous ***ftp*** is a potential security risk, and it should be installed carefully and properly.

21.1.3 Finger

By default, ***finger*** displays information about each logged-in user, including login name, full name, terminal name, idle time, login time, and location (*tty* for users logged in locally, *hostname* for users logged in remotely), if known. Idle time is in minutes if it is a single integer, hours and minutes if a ":" is present, or days and hours if a *d* is present. The format of the ***finger*** command is:

finger [*options*] *name...*

where the available options are:

- **-m** Match arguments only on user name (not first or last name)
- **-l** Force long output format
- **-s** Force short output format
- **-q** Force quick output format, which is similar to short format except that only the login name, terminal, and login time are printed
- **-i** Force "idle" output format, which is similar to short format except that only the login name, terminal, login time, and idle time are printed
- **-b** Suppress printing the user's home directory and shell in a long format printout
- **-f** Suppress printing the header that is normally printed in a non-long format printout
- **-w** Suppress printing the full name in a short format printout
- **-h** Suppress printing of the *.project* file in a long format printout
- **-p** Suppress printing of the *.plan* file in a long format printout

When one or more *name* arguments are given, more detailed information is given for each *name* specified, whether they are logged in or not. A *name* may be a first or last name or an account name. Information is presented in a multiline format, and includes (in addition to the information mentioned above):

- The user's home directory and login shell
- The time they logged in if they are currently logged in, or the time they last logged in if they are not, as well as the terminal or host from which they logged in and, if a terminal, the comment field in */etc/ttytab* for that terminal
- The last time they received mail, and the last time they read their mail
- Any plan contained in the file *.plan* in the user's home directory
- Any project on which they are working described in the file *.project* (also in that directory)

If a *name* argument contains an at-sign, "@," then a connection is attempted to the machine named after the at-sign, and the remote *finger daemon* is queried. The data returned by that daemon is printed.

The main drawback, and the reason that ***finger*** is often disabled, is the security risk it carries. Why expose information about users on your system to potential intruders? Users' accounts are main targets for every intruder, who will first try to catch a user account, and then work on switching to some high privileged user (to **root**, if possible).

There is one special situation when the use of ***finger*** could be extremely valuable. When user dial-in access is provided, as with PPP, an IP address is dynamically assigned to the user's machine; the same user's machine can be identified by a different IP address at a different time. On the other side, some applications are strictly based on the known IP address of the session participants; for example, X windowing requires the IP address of the X server to launch a specified application properly. Obviously, for the application to succeed, the IP address assigned to the logged-in user must be known.

finger could help in this case. When a user logs into the host, the dynamically assigned IP address identifies the user's originated logical machine (please note that this logical machine is mapped through the dial-in connection into the real machine). By ***finger***-ing a specified user, the information about the assigned IP address will be displayed, and this is what an application needs for successful completion. A relatively simple script could be made and used for the purpose of extracting the dynamically assigned IP address and passing this address to the application for its use. This should be made clear in the following example.

The user ***bjl*** dialed in and logged into the specific host with the intent of launching an X-based application on the user's PC that emulates an X terminal. The user was authenticated by the remote access server **rashost**, which dynamically assigns one of the 16 available IP addresses to the authenticated dial-in connection; the IP address is in the range: *rashost01 - rashost16*, with an appropriate DNS record.

The ***finger*** command on the host shows (only the relevant lines are presented):

```
$ finger
Login   Name      TTY      Idle   When        Where
bjl     B. J. L.  pts/10   3      Sat 14:29   rashost08.example.net
        . . . . .
```

Keeping this command output in mind, the following script will extract the assigned DNS record (it is equivalent to an IP address) of the established dial-in connection, and launch the desired X-based application "***xnb***" on the user's PC.

$ cat xnb2pc

```
#!/bin/ksh -p
#
# This script starts XNB session at the user PC
# Once the user connects via modem, and upon a
# successful authentication, an ip address is assigned
# to the established dial-in connection (this address varies
# among different connections). To launch an XNB session
# the DISPLAY variable must be defined appropriately.
# The other requirement is a running Xterminal client on PC
# (for example Exceed)
#
# This line extracts corresponding DNS record; it cleans everything in the line in front
# of the DNS record, as well as all trailling spaces
CONN='finger | grep rashost | grep bjl | sed -n 1p | sed 's/^..*rashost/rashost/g ' | sed 's/ *$//g''
export DISPLAY="${CONN}:0.0"
# The DISPLAY variable is specified
# Everything seems to be ready for the XNB launch
/usr/xnbpath/bin/xnb -display $DISPLAY&
```

21.2 Host Connectivity

In a network, the essential condition is that the connectivity between hosts must be provided. It is obvious that without full host connectivity, none of the network applications can be accomplished. A break in the host connectivity is a very common cause for network application failure. Checking the host connectivity is also the most frequent, and usually the first step, in tracing problems related with network applications.

UNIX provides a certain number of applicable commands for this purpose; two of them are ***ping*** and ***traceroute***.

21.2.1 The *ping* Command

The ***ping*** command tests whether a remote host can be reached from the system where **ping** was activated. This simple function is extremely useful for testing network connections, and in determining whether further testing should be done. If **ping** shows that packets can travel to the remote host and back, the problem you seek to identify might be in the upper protocol layers; if packets cannot make the round-trip, lower protocol layers are probably at fault.

The basic format of the **ping** command (some variations are possible on different flavors) is:

ping *hostname [packetsize] [count]*

where

- ***hostname*** The hostname or IP address of the remote host being tested.
- ***packetsize*** Defines the size in bytes of the test packets. The default is 56 bytes.
- ***count*** The number of packets to be sent in the test. Otherwise, **ping** continues to send test packets until you interrupt it (usually with Ctrl-C); in most cases five packets should be sufficient for a test.

Here is an example, **ping**-ing the host ***acf4.nyu.edu*** (at the NYU campus) from the host ***patsy.hunter.cuny.edu*** (at the Hunter College campus):

 # ping -s acf4.nyu.edu 56 5

PING acf4.nyu.edu: 56 data bytes
64 bytes from ACF4.NYU.EDU (128.122.128.14): icmp_seq = 0. time = 73. ms
64 bytes from ACF4.NYU.EDU (128.122.128.14): icmp_seq = 1. time = 61. ms
64 bytes from ACF4.NYU.EDU (128.122.128.14): icmp_seq = 2. time = 79. ms
64 bytes from ACF4.NYU.EDU (128.122.128.14): icmp_seq = 3. time = 89. ms
64 bytes from ACF4.NYU.EDU (128.122.128.14): icmp_seq = 4. time = 70. ms
----ACF4.NYU.EDU PING Statistics----
5 packets transmitted, 5 packets received, 0% packet loss
round-trip (ms) min/avg/max = 61/74/89

The **-s** option is included for the SunOS/Solaris flavors to display packet-by-packet statistics. Other **ping** implementations do that by default.

If the packet loss is high, or the response time is very slow, or packets are arriving out of order, then there could be a network problem. If this happens on a wide area network, there is nothing to worry about. TCP/IP is designed for unreliable networks, and some wide area networks suffer a lot of packet loss. On a local area network, however, that indicates some trouble.

In a high throughput local network, or a network with few routing steps (also known as "hops"), the round-trip time should be near zero; there should be no or small packet loss, and the packet should arrive in order. If these parameters are not met, there is a problem with the network resources. The most frequent problems are: improper cable termination, a bad cable segment, or a bad piece of "active" hardware such as repeater, bridge, hub, switch, or transceiver. If this is a case, further testing and searching for problem could be directed to those areas.

When the **ping** testing completely fails, **ping** displays an error message, such as:

-unknown host	The remote host cannot be resolved by name service; try to **ping** with a host's IP address to locate the problem.
-network unreachable	The local system does not have a route to the remote system; try again and after that, look at the routing table and default gateway.

Ping-ing takes some time, especially if a designated host is not reachable; **ping** retries multiple times with the host, waiting for a response until timeout occurs. This is why some flavors also includes a "fast-ping" command ***/etc/fping***, which tries only once and generates a corresponding response.

The main advantage of the **ping** command is that it relies on lower ISO OSI model layers (physical, data link, and network), and in that way could make a sharp distinction between the host connectivity and problems on higher layers (transport, session, presentation, or application). ***ping*** is using ***ICMP*** protocol (*Internet control message protocol*), and it makes it completely independent of the TCP/IP stack so typical for all network applications. Briefly, ***ping*** can only address a host, and check the connectivity with the specified host; there is no way to check an application by using ***ping***. Sometimes you could witness a discussion about "*ping-ing a port*" with an idea to check the application itself; such a discussion is completely senseless — ***ping*** does not know anything about a port, it simply does not know anything about higher OSI model leyers where the port is located.

21.2.2 The *traceroute* Command

The ***traceroute*** command is available to track routing-related problems in the network. As the command name says, it displays the route of the probe packets sent toward the destination host.

Tracking the route that packets follow (or finding the miscreant gateway that's discarding the packets) can be difficult. **traceroute** utilizes the IP protocol TTL field ("time-to-live") and attempts to elicit an ICMP response from each gateway along the path to the destination host.

traceroute attempts to trace the route an IP packet would follow to the destination host by launching UDP probe packets with a small TTL (time-to-live), and then listening for an ICMP "time exceeded" reply from a gateway. It starts the probes with a TTL of one ("1") and increases by one until it gets an ICMP "port unreachable" (which means it reached the "host") or hits a max (the default is 30 hops). Three probes are sent at each TTL setting and a line is displayed showing the TTL, IP address of the gateway, and round trip time of each probe. If the probe answers come from different gateways, the address of each responding system will be displayed. If there is no response within a 5 second timeout interval, an asterisk ("*") is displayed for that probe. To prevent the destination host from processing the UDP probe packets, the destination port is set to an unlikely value.

traceroute has the format:

traceroute [*options*] *hostname* [*packetlength*]

where the only mandatory parameter is the name of the destination host ***hostname***; other parameters are optional. The default packet length is 40 bytes. A partial list of options includes:

Option	Meaning
-f *first_ttl*	Set the initial time-to-live used in the first outgoing probe packet.
-g *gateway*	Specify a loose source route gateway (8 maximum).
-i *interface*	Specify a network interface to obtain the source IP address for outgoing probe packets. This is normally only useful on a multihomed host.
-m *max_ttl*	Set the maximum time-to-live (maximum number of hops) used in outgoing probe packets. The default is 30 hops (the same default used for TCP connections).
-p *port*	Set the base UDP port number used in probes (default is 33434). It is assumed that nothing is listening on the UDP ports ranging from base to (base + *n*hops – 1) at the destination host (so an "ICMP PORT_UNREACHABLE" message will be returned to terminate the route tracing). If something is listening on a port in the default range, this option can be used to pick an unused port range.
-s *src_addr*	Use the following IP address (usually given as an IP address, not a hostname) as the source address in outgoing probe packets. On multihomed hosts (with multiple interfaces), this option can be used to force the source address to be something other than the IP address of the interface the probe packet is sent on. If the IP address is not one of this machine's interface addresses, an error is returned and nothing is sent.
-t *tos*	Set the "type-of-service" (TOS) in probe packets to the following value (the default is zero). The value must be a decimal integer between 0 and 255. This option can be used to see if different TOSs result in different paths. Not all values of TOS are legal or meaningful — see the IP spec. for definitions. Useful values are probably "-t 16" (low delay) and "-t 8" (high throughput).
-w *waittime*	Set the time (in seconds) to wait for a response to a probe (the default is 5 seconds).
-d	Enable socket level debugging.
-i	Use ICMP ECHO instead of UDP datagrams.
-n	Display hop addresses numerically.
-r	Bypass the normal routing tables and send directly to a host on an attached network. If the host is not on a directly attached network, an error is returned.
-v	Verbose output, ensures that all received ICMP packets are listed.
-x	Toggle checksums. Normally, this prevents **traceroute** from calculating checksums.

An example follows:

$ traceroute allspice.lcs.mit.edu.

```
traceroute to allspice.lcs.mit.edu (18.26.0.115), 30 hops max
1 helios.ee.lbl.gov (128.3.112.1) 0 ms 0 ms 0 ms
2 lilac-dmc.Berkeley.EDU (128.32.216.1) 19 ms 19 ms 19 ms
3 lilac-dmc.Berkeley.EDU (128.32.216.1) 39 ms 19 ms 19 ms
4 ccngw-ner-cc.Berkeley.EDU (128.32.136.23) 19 ms 39 ms 39 ms
5 ccn-nerif22.Berkeley.EDU (128.32.168.22) 20 ms 39 ms 39 ms
6 128.32.197.4 (128.32.197.4) 59 ms 119 ms 39 ms
7 131.119.2.5 (131.119.2.5) 59 ms 59 ms 39 ms
8 129.140.70.13 (129.140.70.13) 80 ms 79 ms 99 ms
9 129.140.71.6 (129.140.71.6) 139 ms 139 ms 159 ms
10 129.140.81.7 (129.140.81.7) 199 ms 180 ms 300 ms
11 129.140.72.17 (129.140.72.17) 300 ms 239 ms 239 ms
12 * * *
13 128.121.54.72 (128.121.54.72) 259 ms 499 ms 279 ms
14 * * *
15 * * *
16 * * *
17 * * *
18 ALLSPICE.LCS.MIT.EDU (18.26.0.115) 339 ms 279 ms 279 ms
```

Note that gateways 12, 14, 15, 16, and 17 have reached timeout limits, and either do not send ICMP "time exceeded" messages or send them with a TTL too small to reach the originated host. There could be many different reasons for this; in this specific case it is known that gateways 14–17 are running the MIT C Gateway code that does not send "time exceeded" messages.

Section III

Supplemental UNIX Topics

22

X Window System

22.1 An Introduction to the X Window System

X Window System is a network-based software package that provides the user's friendly graphical interface. We will refer to X Window System shortly as X, or X11. X is based on the *client/server model,* in which the X client (application program) does not directly access the display; instead it communicates with the X server (the corresponding display program) with the single task to control displaying. X was developed at MIT and is maintained by a not-for-profit consortium of vendors and universities, first known as MIT X Consortium, succeeded by X Consortium from 1993. It is a relatively highly standardized package that runs on almost every platform; X appeared relatively late, so it presents a compromise between needs of many vendors. The best known release is X11R6, although version X11R5 is also widely in use. All efforts to standardize X11 culminated in the introduction of Common Desktop Environment (CDE), which had offered the best of X11. Today, CDE is the standard part of most UNIX installations, usually accompanied by a vendor-specific flavor of X11. CDE related X components are easy to recognize, they always do have "dt" prefix in their names (stands for DeskTop).

X11 presents a highly flexible and configurable package; correspondingly, an adequate administrative effort must be made to optimize X11 for the local site. Nevertheless, X11 can run with its default settings, which is sufficient for most of the implementations. We will discuss those issues in the first part of this Chapter. Although, every client/server model does have two sides, studying X11 practically means to study the client side; X configuration and customization is always provided on the client host.

Today, users are very familiar with the windows environment; almost every PC provides some version of the Microsoft Windows system. Although, MS Windows does not belong to X11, the similarities in the use are obvious; however, the rest is quite different. Nevertheless, credit for a broader introduction of windows as a graphic, user-friendly interface and environment actually should go to Macintosh for its contribution in this arena in the early 1970s.

22.1.1 The Design of X11

We mentioned already that X is based on the client/server model. One important feature of the client/server model is that client and server programs can communicate remotely, although, they can also reside at the very same system. An X client and an X server communicate using the ***X Protocol***, which is supported by domain sockets internally and TCP/IP externally. Many implementations consist of X servers and X clients running on independent remote machines, mutually connected by fast links. Links could be any kind of distant connections within a wide area network (WAN), or mid-speed modem, or, what is the most common, a local area network (LAN). This fact makes X ideal in a distributed computing environment — users can open a number of windows on a number of server machines, dealing simultaneously with a number of tasks running on a number of remote client machines.

When an X client and an X server are running on distant machines, each of them provides its part of the common task. The X server is a part of the user's local display machine; this machine could be very simple, even a single-tasking DOS-based PC. A complex part of the common task is happening at the client side, which is usually, a powerfull, multi-user system capable of running sophistiacted graphic applications. This feature has led to an intensive development of low-cost ***X terminals***, designed especially for running X server. Using X terminals, multiple users can run graphics-intensive programs without a need to possess their own expensive powerful machines.

The client-server terminology confuses novices in the X arena. Since the *X server* runs on a local display system on the user's desk, it is often incorrectly thought that the display system is running an X client program. It is common to think of a server as something that is accessed across the network (a comparison with the file servers, print servers, or other kinds of, usually, remote servers, is almost inevitable). However, in the case of X11, a system in front of us includes a display and a keyboard, made available to X client application programs running on distant hosts (machines). The X server is a "display server" — it provides the "display service" to the remote applications (clients). This is presented in the Figure 22.1.

An *X server* can run any sort of bitmap graphic displays. A graphic display consists of at least one monitor (screen), a pointing device, and a keyboard. They differ regarding:

- *Monitors* different screen sizes, resolutions, color support, etc.
- *Pointing devices* a mouse, a trackball, a touchscreen, a lightpen, etc.
- *Keyboards* a keyboard layout, control sequences

The *X server* insulates X clients from low-level differences; it means that the *X server* mediates between clients and graphic display's hardware characteristics; it provides mapping between physical resources and corresponding logical identifiers.

Unfortunately, the requirement for a "configurability" could not miss the X application itself. An X application (an *X client*) is generally running on a multi-user system, and basically could display on any connected *X server* on the network. Consequently, there are always dependencies and preferences that the user needs to be able to express. Two or more users can run the same X application simultaneously from totally different *X servers;* therefore, *X clients* need to be configurable by each individual user. This is not an odd idea — character-based UNIX programs do the same, using appropriate "dot" files in the user's home directory: *.mailrc, .exrc, .newsrc* (even *.profile, .login,* and *.cshrc* files could belong to this category). Different X servers may also require their own preferences, so *X clients* need to be configured versus the server, also. Finally, X client executables can run on different system platforms, system-specific defaults are also required. Obviously, X applications should be configurable at each of the mentioned levels (they are configured primarily via "*resources variables*"); we will discuss these issues in more detail.

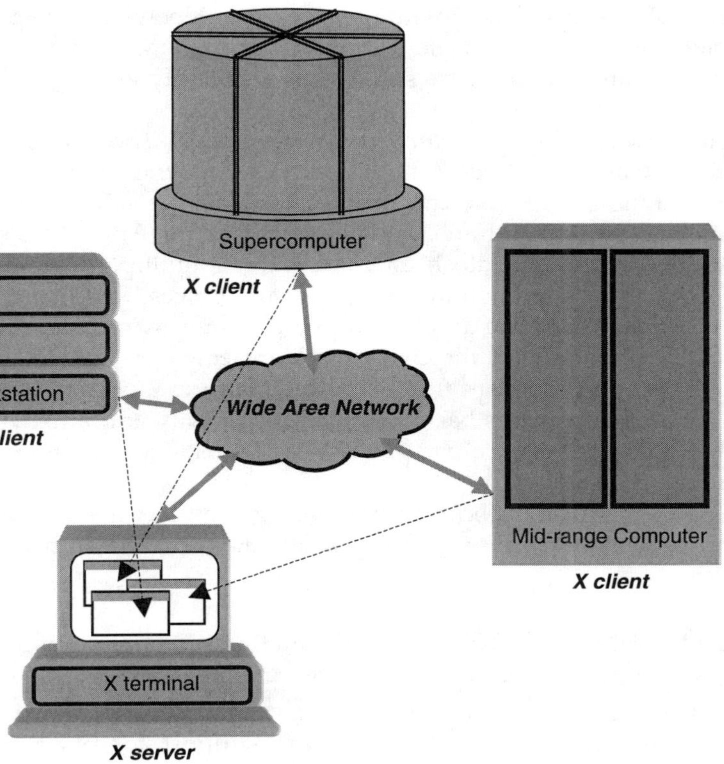

FIGURE 22.1
An X server with multiple X clients.

We have mentioned an application as an *X client;* however, beside the application itself, other X clients also take part actively in an X display session (briefly, an *X session*). First, the *X session* must be started similarly to any other character-based session (for example, *login session* is started by ***init, getty,*** and ***login*** programs involved — recall the login procedure). In the early days of X11, an X session was started by a specific X startup program, like the program ***xinit***. Later, this task was delegated to the ***X display manager*** — the program that enables the start of an X *session* by executing an appropriate user-configurable program. For X11, the first real ***X display manager*** was the ***xdm*** program (alternatively, an *X session* could be also started by the ***xinit*** command). We will return to both issues later.

Another client program is an ***X window manager*** which provides the basic framework for moving, resizing, and managing windows. This is the only ***window manager***'s task, but the crucial one for the entire X session. While in a traditional character-based world, a session is defined by the lifetime of a *user's login shell,* here it is usually the lifetime of the ***window manager*** (in X environment, a user's login process does not necessarily have a terminal-like interface to connect with). The ***window manager*** is in charge of performing the flexible and usable concept of windowing, i.e., opening a number of independent windows on a single display, which appears to user, and behaving, as multiple parallel independent displays. Having in mind the restricted display resources (the screen dimensions, etc.), additional features such as window moving, resizing, overlapping, iconizing, and other had to also be provided.

What will be presented in a window does not depend on the ***window manager***; it depends only on the associated client application program, invoked through this window. The ***window managers*** could be started independently, or together with the X client application.

Finally, a few words about ***graphic user interface*** (***GUI***). The concept for a ***GUI*** originated in the mid-1970s at Xerox's Palo Alto Research Center, where the basic GUI elements such as windows, a mouse, and the "point-and-click" style of software were developed. The first commercially successful product was offered on the Apple Macintosh platform. The "look and feel" of the Macintosh interface features multiple windows, use of a mouse device, pop-up and pull-down menus, object and process icons, and dialogue boxes, all of which have come to define user-friendly computing environments. Interest in GUIs has grown steadily, especially in the UNIX marketplace where the ***GUI*** is running under X Windows — ***X11*** — and makes the computing platform more accessible to a wider range of users. While ***X11*** supplies basic graphic functionality and a networkable windowing system, the ***GUI*** implements a particular style of interaction, a *look and feel* within the X11 environment.

On the UNIX platform, *X clients* are built using a number of programming libraries that make X implementation easier — they insulate the programmer from the very details of the *X protocol:*

- The lowest layer is ***Xlib***, which is actually used only in cases where the direct control of the dialogue with the X server is required.
- On top of ***Xlib***, the *X Toolkit Instrinsics,* known as ***Xt***, are built; they simplify a graphic user interface by creating support for objects called ***widgets***. *Widgets* are basic prototypes for common GUI elements, such as *scrollbars, menus,* etc., as well as other *glue objects* that enable complete window implementation.
- On top of the *Xt* additional GUI libraries are layered, and they actually, together with a *window manager,* make a full GUI support.

The three most common GUIs were provided by the ***Athena widgets***, the ***OSF/Motif***, and the ***OPEN LOOK*** specifications. Each of those specifications also included the corresponding *window manager;* fortunately, a set of conventions provides interoperability of *clients* and *window managers* from different *X-based GUIs.*

Supposing that the X design is more clear now, let us summarize briefly how everything works. *X clients* and *X servers* communicate mutually using the *X protocol* they understand very well. This communication could be local (both the X client and X server live on the same machine) or remote through the network. *X protocol* relates to the *GUI objects* that are well known to both sides in the communication. Instead of transferring large descriptions of the wanted graphic presentations, short messages that refer to appropriate GUI elements are used. We still have the full flexibility with preserved fast communication between a client and a server. In the worst case, when a wanted graphic presentation is not covered by the GUI objects, a full graphic image could be transferred; however, it happens only occasionally. Of course, the price that must be paid is both sides in such a communication, an X client and an X server, should support X protocol.

Benefits in using X windowing are numerous. X enables a flexible distribution of resources within the network. The execution of an application and the interaction with the very same application are divided, and could be arbitrary located, optimizing the efficient use of available resources. A number of users could access simultaneously a number of applications, by making an optimal balance between processing and displaying resources. In the distributed computer environment, X makes a step closer to the dream of having a whole network that appears as *"a single equivalent powerful processing (computer) system."*

22.1.2 The X Administration Philosophy

The basic philosophy that X is built on is that X provides "a mechanism, not a policy." This is a good approach if you have in mind future development and improvements. However, from an administrative standpoint it makes maintenance more difficult. The lack of strict rules and standards left vendors free to create their own rules, and X administrators without much guidance. There are many different flavors of X: the "standard" X11 distribution maintained by the X Consortium; then various vendor-configured versions that are derived from MIT X11 but configured for a vendor's operating system and proprietary look and feel. There are Open Windows, which runs on Sun platform; DECWindows, which runs on DEC platform; AIXWindows, which runs on IBM AIX platform; VUE (Visual User Environment), which runs on HP-UX platform; and more. ***Common Desktop Environment*** (***CDE***) seems to be a successful attempt to bring a common X platform as a standard; as far it was accepted by most of the vendors and combined with vendor-specific X packages.

This means that X could behave differently on different UNIX platforms. An administrator can easily realize that the system reacts differently than expected. The fact that the X Consortium provides only the mechanism and relies on vendors to decide how to use it, made some holes and gaps in the implementation. An administrator must be aware of what is hidden "under the hood," before using that. This is one of the most difficult issues in X administration. Despite that X is supported by relatively ample documentation (the word here is about online documentation — manual pages), to reach a right topic, sometimes could be quite a hard job.

Nevertheless, to come out with the issue of a *philosophy of X administration,* it would be that X is made to fit the needs of its users. The administrator has the responsibility to determine the user's need and configure X accordingly. X is installed in all sorts of environments, from academia, via industry, to home offices with a single standalone machine. For that reason, almost everything in X is configurable at multiple levels. The X Display Manager can be configured in several different places, to meet practically any need. Even the source code to X is available for those who want to create their own workarounds. The fundamental idea is that if you do not like the way something is working, change it.

We will continue our discussion about X having in mind the standard X distribution, especially its CDE release. However, to copy with the CDE, an appropriate knowledge of older X releases is required. Finally, through a number of examples we will also touch some vendor-specific flavors (mostly HP VUE). The full understanding of the standard X distribution is a giant step in maintaining other vendor-specific X flavors.

22.1.3 Window Managers

From the previous discussion it is obvious that ***window managers*** play a special role among all X programs. A few relatively simple tasks in managing a window — open, move, resize, close, pop-up, and pop-down menus — create a formidable working space that fundamentally changed the man-machine interface. Today, the window environment (not necessarily X windows) is a common working environment for almost every user.

The original MIT *window manager* was the ***twm*** — ***T**ab **W**indow **M**anager.* (It was the only *window manager* provided in the MIT X distribution.) There are also many other *window managers* distributed by vendors. One of the most popular *window managers* is ***mwm***, the ***M**otif **W**indow **M**anager* which implements the *OSF/Motif* look and feel (*OSF* stands for *open system foundation); OSF/Motif* also includes a complete graphic user interface. Another popular *window manager* was ***olwm***, a *window manager* for *OPEN LOOK.* Other *window managers* were: ***swm*** - the ***S**olbourne **W**indow **M**anager* — which can simulate both *olwm* and *mwm* in separate modes; ***gwm***, a public domain *window manager* that can simulate *mwm;* and ***tvwm*** and ***olvwm***, which present versions of *twm* and *olwm* respectively, but they support a virtual root window. (A root window is larger than the portion visible on the display, and it can be scrolled around to bring different sections into view.) Today, the *CDE **D**esktop **W**indow **M**anager* (***dtwm***) is probably the most attractive; it was based on the *OSF/Motif* ***mwm***, version 1.2.4.

Although, the administration is more or less similar for different window managers, some discrepancies are possible. Consulting the corresponding vendor's documentation is always recommended. We will discuss this issue regarding the ***mwm***, ***dtwm***, and occasionally, ***twm***. Most of the examples are ***mwm/dtwm*** related.

A *window manager* is normally invoked through the user's startup script when an X session is started. However, the window manager could be also started from the command line, as any other UNIX program. For example:

 # *dtwm &* will invoke *CDE DT Window Manager* in the background

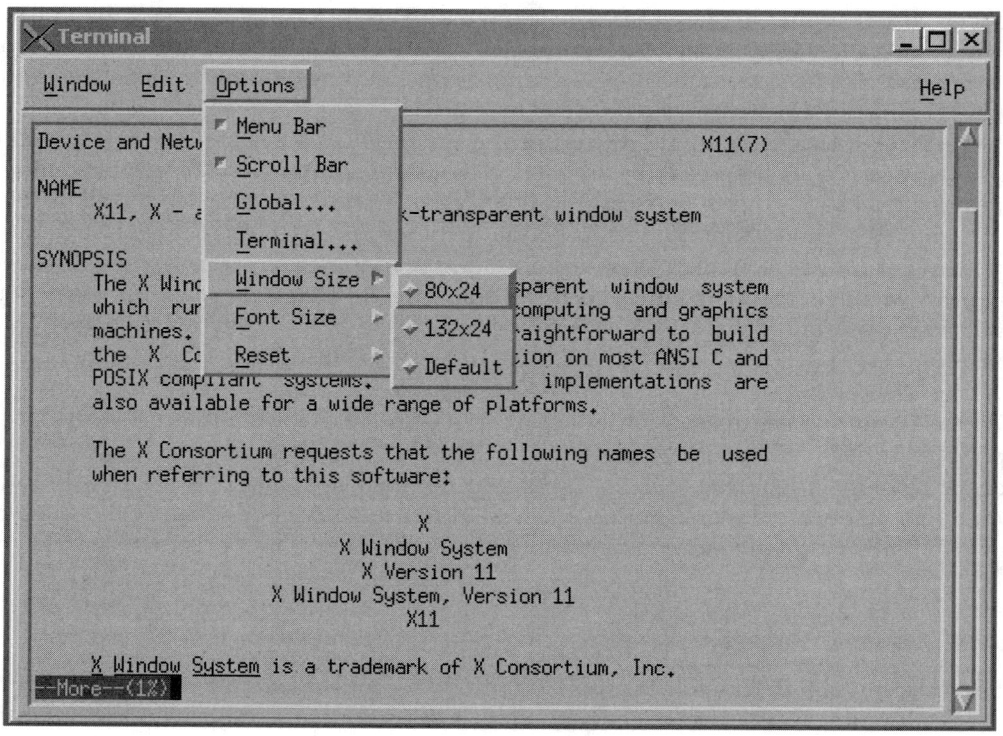

FIGURE 22.2
The CDE terminal emulator *dtterm* supported by *dtwm*.

The *window manager* gives each window its own borders and titlebar. As an example, the ***dtterm*** window launched on the Solaris 2.6 platform (***dtterm*** presents the client program for the CDE-based terminal emulation) is presented in the Figure 22.2.

By moving the cursor (pointer) into the window's titlebar, and holding down the left mouse button, the window could be moved. By pressing small icons at the upper right corner of the titlebar, the window could be resized or iconified. Pop-down menus are also available to handle window, select options, and others.

Different X flavors do have different X-based terminal emulators; they are functionally similar, but the contiguous esthetic, and sometimes functional, improvements are evident. An older version of the X-based terminal, ***xterm***, (launched on SunOS 4.1.3 platform) is presented in the Figure 22.3.

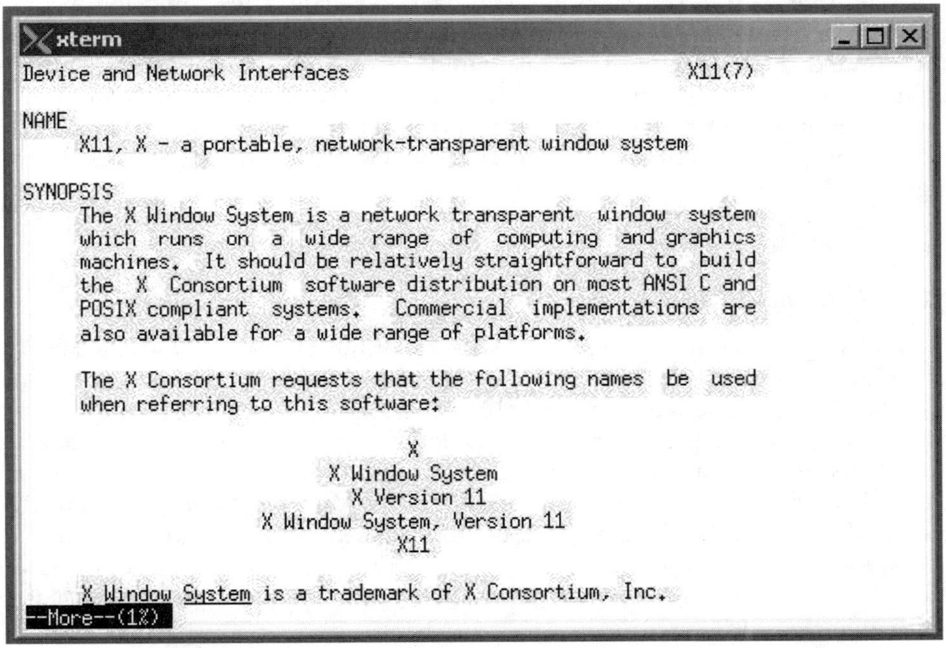

FIGURE 22.3
The X terminal emulator *xterm* supported by *twm*.

The behavior of a *window manager* could be configured by editing its configuration files in several ways; one of the ways is to manage the configuration file in an individual user's directory (for ***mwm*** the local configuration file is *.mwmrc;* correspondingly, for ***tdwm*** is the *.dtwmrc* file, for ***twm*** the *.twmrc,* etc. The default behavior of the window manager at the system level could be configured via the *system.mwmrc* file (for ***mwm***), and correspondingly: *system.dtwmrc,* or *system.twmrc.* We will discuss in more detail the *window manager*'s configuration administration later in the text.

22.2 The X Display Managers

The first real ***X Display Manager*** (***xdm***) has been in use for quite a long time. During this period it experienced several major changes; the last one was the introduction of the ***CDE***

Login Service Manager* (*dtlogin*)**, that, de facto, replaced ***xdm. Although there are many conceptual, and not only conceptual, similarities between ***xdm*** and ***dtlogin***, they present two different programs to provide the same basic task. Understanding one of them practically means to understand the other one as well. We will try to cover both programs; the ***xdm*** definitely deserves such an approach. First, ***xdm*** is not yet obsolete and is still widely in the use, and second, from an educational point of view it could be easier to understand X topics through the ***xdm*** description. We will refer to both programs as: "***xdm/ dtlog***"; please be aware that the purpose of the two programs is the same, and they are not running simultaneously.

xdm/dtlogin runs as a daemon on a host machine (the host machine is the system where an X application lives). The program provides a way for users to log in and start initial clients, regardless of what X server they use; this is the most common way. There was also another way to control X session; users on many sites could log in the usual way through a login session, and then start the X server and any clients by issuing the ***xinit*** command. However, ***xinit*** is considered obsolete by the X Consortium, and all necessary functionality was built into ***xdm*** (later inherited by ***dtlogin***). ***xdm/dtlogin*** is also an essential tool for providing an access through the network to/from X terminals. Both programs include systemwide configuration facilities, enabling the desired default settings.

22.2.1 *xdm/dtlogin* Concepts

The ***xdm/dtlogin*** program is simply an X client program, or a set of client programs, responsible for the first and last points of the connection, control, and coordination of the user session. For a network-connected X server, the ***xdm/dtlogin*** is working functionally in the way similar to the ***init***, ***getty*** and ***login*** programs for connected ASCII terminals.

xdm/dtlogin manages a collection of X displays, both local and remote. The emergence of X terminals guided the redesign of several parts of this system (including the ***xdm*** program), along with the development of the X Consortium standard *XDMCP* (the *X Display Manager Control Protocol*). It was designed to provide services necessary to run a "session" (similar to that provided on character terminals), prompting for login/password, and authenticating the user.

Since a user logs in, in the most general case, the X session could be started, usually, invoking an X terminal emulation such as *xterm*, *dtterm*, or similar, and the user's shell spawned. As a matter of fact, everything resembles the character-based terminal environment, except the X-based session is graphically superior, and more user friendly. However, the X terminal emulator is not a must, any X-based application could also be started, and then the real benefits of X11 become obvious: unlimited possibilities of graphic presentation. Such an application could be launched from any host machine in the network, not necessarily the one where the user has logged in. Having in mind the powerful UNIX remote command executions, "remsh-ing" (recall Chapter 19), this is a routine task, proven in many practical implementations. The whole network appears as a powerful multihost system, with optimally distributed functions among available resources, but, from the user's point of view, fully integrated into a single system.

Today, in high processing intensive networks, with a huge number of users, X windows plays an important role. Users log in to dedicated "login servers," launch applications from dedicated application servers, access large database servers, and interact with the applications via the X servers, i.e., low cost X terminals. The overall effect is: users have the feeling that everything happens in front of them — "It is amazing that such a small X terminal can so efficiently handle such a difficult job!!!"

xdm/dtlogin keeps the track of which X servers are allowed to be connected, and negotiates and establishes such a connection (of course, the connection is the logical one). After resetting the X server, ***xdm/dtlogin*** starts the *Xsetup* script to assist in setting up the X server's screen the user sees; it sends a graphic login widget (login box) to the X server display, or displays. To simplify, let us suppose an X server with a single display, i.e., an X terminal (X terminals run the X server program, and they understand very well the X protocol). This is how, and why, a graphic login widget appears at the X terminal screen.

Since a user logs in, i.e., enters a name and password, the user is authenticated using the same mechanism as the ***login*** program. Then ***xdm/dtlogin*** runs a series of shell scripts; the simplified execution flow charts for two programs are presented, respectively, in the Figures 22.4a and b.

The ***xdm*** first invokes the *Xstartup* script as the root, followed by the *Xsession* script as the user. The starting scripts normally start all desired X clients, including one or more terminal emulators, each of which will contain an interactive shell. Executed scripts call other scripts to complete all necessary initial tasks.

When the session is terminated, ***xdm*** resets the X server and (optionally) restarts the whole process. More precisely, when a user logs out (or when the "controlling" process of the X session has been terminated), ***xdm*** runs the *Xreset* script to close all connections, clean up, and resets the X terminal to a *ready for log on* state, displaying again the login widget, ready for another user session.

The ***dtlogin*** manages an X session in a very similar way; existing differences will be discussed later with other ***dtlogin*** configuration issues.

xdm/dtlog is a very ambitious program. It can be configured in a number of ways, controlling logins on multiple X servers, creating customized X sessions, offering some basic network security features, and so on. A more detailed description follows.

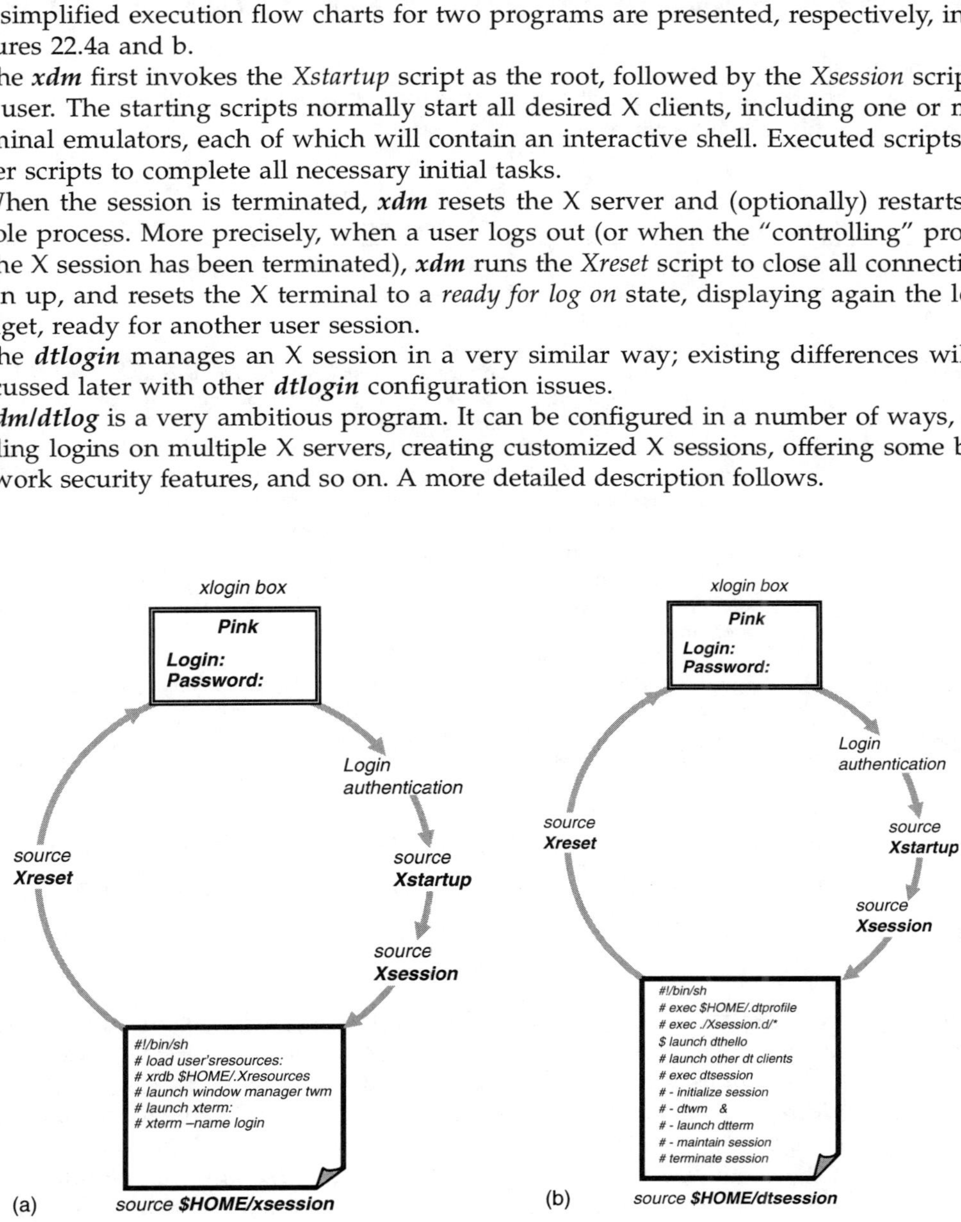

FIGURE 22.4
(a) The *xdm* execution flow chart; (b) The *dtlogin* execution flow chart.

Because the programs provide the first interface that users would see, they are designed to be simple to use and easy to customize to the needs of a particular site. Both programs could be started in a number of ways, i.e., they have a number of identical options.

To start the program from the command line, the format of the command is:

xdm *[options]* for the ***xdm***

or

dtlogin *[options]* for the ***dtlogin***

where the possible *options* are listed.

Note that all of the options, except *-config,* specify values which could also be specified in the configuration file as resources.

Option	Description
-config *configuration_file*	Specifies a resource file which specifies the remaining configuration parameters. This replaces the default configuration file: for ***xdm*** */usr/lib/X11/xdm/xdm-config* for ***dtlogin*** */usr/dt/config/Xconfig*
-daemon	Specifies "true" as the value for the *daemonMode resource.* This makes ***xdm/dtlogin*** close all file descriptors, disassociate the controlling terminal, and put itself in the background when it first starts up. It is the default behavior.
-debug *debug_level*	Specifies the numeric value for the *debugLevel re*source. A non-zero value causes ***xdm/dtlogin*** to print piles of debugging statements to the terminal; it also disables the "*daemonMode*" resource, forcing ***xdm/dtlogin*** to run synchronously. (To interpret these debugging messages, a copy of the source code for the program is almost a necessity — it is very hard to use.)
-error *error_log_file*	Specifies the value for the "*errorLogFile*" resource. This file contains errors from ***xdm/dtlogin*** as well as anything written to the "stderr" by the various scripts and programs run during the progress of the session.
-nodaemon	Specifies "false" for the *daemonMode* resource value.
-resources *resource_file*	Specifies the value for the "*resources*" resource. This file is loaded to specify configuration parameters for the authentication widget.
-server *server_entry*	Specifies the value for the "*servers*" resource.
-udpPort *port_number*	Specifies the value for the "*requestPort*" resource. This sets the port number to be monitored for XDMCP requests. XDMCP uses the registered well-known udp port 177.
-session *session_ program*	Specifies the value for the "*session*" resource. This indicates the program to run when the user has logged in as the session.
-xrm *resource_specification*	This allows an arbitrary resource to be specified, just as most toolkit applications (only for ***xdm***).

xdm/dtlogin was designed to operate in a wide variety of environments, and to determine its "typical usage" is probably a misnomer. Nevertheless, this section focuses on configuring ***xdm/dtlogin*** for a quite "typical" environment.

First, the ***xdm/dtlogin*** configuration file should be set up. For ***xdm***, the master configuration file, named *xdm-config* contains references to all other files. A good idea is to locate all these files in the same directory; usually, this is */usr/lib/X11/xdm* which would contain all of the relevant files. For ***dtlogin***, the master configuration file, named *Xconfig,* also contains references to all other files. Its default location is in the directory */usr/dt/config;* however, it could take several other locations.

xdm was introduced with X11R3 and had a serious problem related to X terminals that are turned off and on again during an active X session. The problem was solved with X11R4, introducing the *XDM Control Protocol* (*XDMCP*). XDMCP changed the concept of a static X11 configuration into the dynamic one, where X servers and ***xdm*** are negotiating the connection, and exchanging status messages during the session. ***dtlogin*** knows only the concept of dynamic configuration.

xdm/dtlogin could be executed from the command line at any time; however, it was mostly running as the daemon at the client host. The start of ***xdm/dtlogin*** became a regular part of the **rc** initialization script files, and it is activated as a daemon during the system startup.

While the concept, and the descriptions of two programs, ***xdm*** and ***dtlogin***, match, their configuration is slightly different. The differences are in the names of the configuration files, their locations, as well as their contents. How to configure two programs is discussed and presented separately.

22.2.2 *xdm* Configuration Files

xdm is configured through a set of editable ASCII files; the files reside usually in the */usr/lib/X11/xdm* directory and the user's home directory. A simplified graphic presentation of the ***xdm*** configuration is given in the Figure 22.5. Keep in mind that the listed names are usual, but they could be renamed in the master configuration file *xdm-config*.

Let us check the existing *xdm files* on Solaris 2.6. platform (although, on this platform the ***CDE*** is the primary X support):

$ ls /usr/openwin/lib/X11/xdm

```
GiveConsole      TakeConsole    Xaccess    Xresources    Xservers
Xsession         Xsetup_0       chooser    xdm-config    libXdmGreet.so
libXdmGreet.so.1.0
```

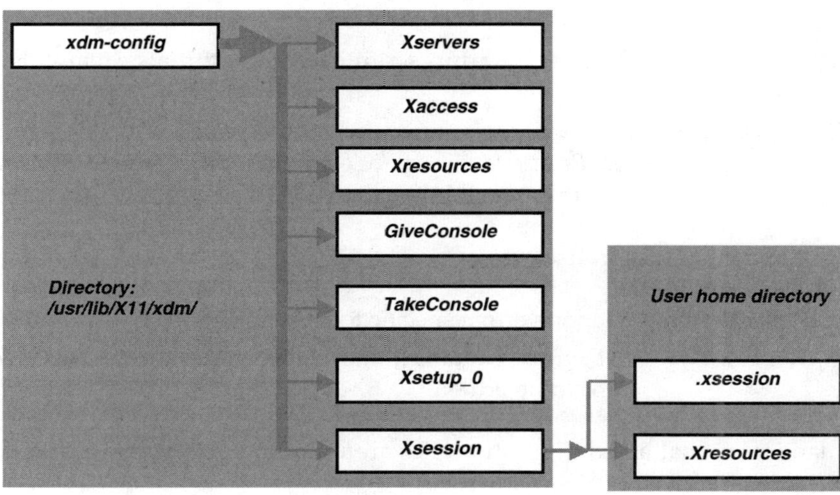

FIGURE 22.5
The *xdm* configuration files.

Most of the files link to the corresponding files in */usr/openwin/lib/xdm:*

$ ls /usr/openwin/lib/xdm

GiveConsole	*Reset*	*StartOW*	*Startup*	*TakeConsole*
Xaccess	*Xresources*	*Xservers*	*Xsession*	*Xsetup_0*
chooser	*xdm-config*			

The configuration files of the interest are:

xdm-config The master configuration file; it specifies all configuration files for ***xdm***.

Xservers A list of X servers to be explicitly managed by ***xdm***. The local display server usually needs to be listed also.

Xaccess Configures an access control for XDMCP, specifying different behavior according to the sort of query used (will be discussed later, with security issues).

Xresources Resources to be loaded via ***xrdb*** (the client that loads resources directly into the X server) by servers managed by ***xdm***.

GiveConsole A shell script that changes the ownership of the console to the user.

TakeConsole A shell script that changes the ownership of the console back to the root.

Xsetup_0 A shell script used for display set up specific to the local console server.

Xsession The initial startup script used by each individual X session. The script itself invokes other individual "dot" script files from the user's home directory: *.xsession* and *.Xresources.*

Xsetup A shell script to assist in setting up the login screen the user sees, along with the *xlogin widget.*

Xstartup A shell script executed since the user logs in.

Xreset A shell script executed at the end of the session to clean up and reset X server.

In the user's home directory, the following files are used by ***xdm*** in its default configuration:

$HOME/.xsession User-specific startup script executed by the systemwide *Xsession* script.

$HOME/.Xresources User-specific resources read by the systemwide *Xsession* script if *$HOME/.xsession* does not exist (otherwise, the *$HOME/.xsession* script is responsible for their loading).

Additional individual files in use are:

$HOME/.xsession-errors Reports errors specific to a user's X session — not to be edited.

$HOME/.Xauthority Machine-readable authorization codes for the user's server — not to be edited.

It is not mandatory that all configuration files are used and exist; the existing configuration files are specified in the *xdm-config* file.

Here is an old, but workable, example from an Xhost running ***xdm***; SunOS 4.1.x has supported only ***xdm***.

 # cat /usr/lib/X11/xdm/xdm-config

DisplayManager.servers:	*/usr/lib/X11/xdm/Xservers*
DisplayManager.errorLogFile:	*/usr/ lib/X11/xdm/xdm-errors*
DisplayManager.pidFile:	*/usr/lib/X11/xdm/xdm-pid*
*DisplayManager*resources:*	*/usr/lib/X11/xdm/Xresources*
*DisplayManager*session:*	*/usr/lib/X11/xdm/Xsession*
DisplayManager._0.authorize:	*true*
*DisplayManager*authorize:*	*false*

All listed files reside in the directory /usr/lib/X11/xdm; this is recommended, but not mandatory. The next example presents the listing of this directory (the example is from SunOS 4.1.3 which supported only ***xdm***):

 # ls /usr/lib/X11/xdm

Xresources *Xservers* *Xsession* *xdm-config* *xdm-errors* *xdm-pid*

Another example includes several files more (Silicon Graphics, Inc., IRIX 4.x — also supported only ***xdm***):

$ ls /usr/lib/X11/xdm

Xlogin	*Xservers*	*Xstartup*	*xdm-errors*	*Xreset*
Xsession	*Xstartup-remote*	*xdm-pid*	*Xresources*	*Xsession-remote*
xdm-config				

Additional files are supposed to support the start of a remote session, as well as the way to log in and to reset the session; *xdm-errors* is the ***xdm*** error-log file, while *xdm-pid* contains the ***xdm*** process ID.

22.2.2.1 Customizing xdm

Having in mind the general idea of ***xdm*** and how to get it going on, we will discuss in more detail the way to customize ***xdm***. These skills are transparent in the CDE environment. To be able to customize ***xdm*** means first to understand basic configuration files.

22.2.2.1.1 The xdm-config *File*

Let us start with the master configuration file *xdm-config*. The master configuration file for the ***xdm*** client program, it specifies esential configuration data, i.e., all other important files. Its syntax follows standard resource specification syntax. The keyword *DisplayManager* is starting each resource entry in the file. In particular, resource specification follows one of the three forms:

DisplayManager.variable: *value* — This is a resource that makes sense only when applied to ***xdm*** proper; for example, the entry:

DisplayManager.servers: /path/filename

specifies which file should be used for listing the X servers to be managed by ***xdm***.

DisplayManager.DISPLAY.variable: *value* — This is a resource that applies only to a single display server, specified by DISPLAY; for example, the entry:

DisplayManager._0.authorize: true

enables access control on the local server.

*DisplayManager*variable:*	*value*	This is a generalization of the previous form. By putting an asterisk instead of display name (dots are also omitted), all servers not specifically defined otherwise are specified. Here is an example: *DisplayManager*authorize: false* *DisplayManager._0.authorize:true* identifies only the local server that will use access control.

Here is another example — the configuration file *xdm-config* on IRIX platform (an old, but illustrative example):

$ cat /usr/lib/X11/xdm/xdm-config

```
#== === === === === === === === === === === === ===
DisplayManager.servers:           /usr/lib/X11/xdm/Xservers
DisplayManager.errorLogFile:      /usr/lib/X11/xdm/xdm-errors
DisplayManager.pidFile:           /usr/lib/X11/xdm/xdm-pid
#== === === === === === === === === === === === ===
DisplayManager*resources:         /usr/lib/X11/xdm/Xresources
DisplayManager*reset:             /usr/lib/X11/xdm/Xreset
DisplayManager*authorize:         off
DisplayManager*startup:           /usr/lib/X11/xdm/Xstartup-remote
DisplayManager*session:           /usr/lib/X11/xdm/Xsession-remote
#== === === === === === === === === === === === ===
DisplayManager._0.startup:        /usr/lib/X11/xdm/Xstartup
DisplayManager._1.startup:        /usr/lib/X11/xdm/Xstartup
DisplayManager._0.session:        /usr/lib/X11/xdm/Xsession
DisplayManager._1.session:        /usr/lib/X11/xdm/Xsession
#== === === === === === === === === === === === ===
DisplayManager._0.openTimeout:    90
DisplayManager._0.startAttempts:  1
DisplayManager._0.authFile:       /usr/lib/X11/xdm/xdm-auth
DisplayManager._0.loginProgram:   /usr/lib/X11/xdm/Xlogin
#== === === === === === === === === === === === ===
```

In this example recognize all entry formats, including the general way to start remote X sessions. Most entries are self-explanatory (for more detailed explanations, the manual pages are always available). We will briefly discuss some of them.

The first three entries point to the files that define X servers (i.e., X server programs), to the log-file, and to the ***xdm*** PID file. Then, a list of entries with the asterisk following, identifying other configuration files and data we are already familiar with.

The entries:

DisplayManager._0.startup: /usr/lib/X11/xdm/Xstartup
DisplayManager._0.session: /usr/lib/X11/xdm/Xsession

specify the program which is executed (as root) after the authentication process succeeds. The conventional name for the script used is *Xstartup* (by default there is no a startup program), and the script to be executed (as the user) to start an X session is conventionally named *Xsession* (by default, the X terminal emulator ***/usr/bin/X11/xterm*** is supposed). Both entries refer to the first local X server (#0). However, two local servers are foreseen, #0 and #1; two other entries refer to the local X server #1. Other X servers are supposed to be remote, and they are identified by the previous entries with an asterisk.

The remaining entries refer also to the local X server #0, specifying additional configuration data; for example, the entries

DisplayManager._0.authFile: */usr/lib/X11/xdm/xdm-auth*
DisplayManager._0.loginProgram: */usr/lib/X11/xdm/Xlogin*

specify the file that is used for authentication, and the corresponding login program.

Other entries specify numeric resources that control ***xdm*** behavior when attempting to open X server, the timeout period, and how many times the attempting process should be repeated.

Watch for the possible appearance of the resource entry (not existing in this example)

DisplayManager.autoRescan: *false*

that disables the ***xdm*** to reread the configuration file on its own. By default, this entry is "true" and the ***xdm*** is configured to reread the configuration file after the session terminates and the files have been changed. If this entry exists after any modification of configuration files, ***xdm*** must be recycled (re-invoked).

22.2.2.1.2 The Xservers *File*

The *Xservers* file was designed in X11R3, to define the X11 configuration staticly; it listed all X servers to be managed by ***xdm***. It meant that each X server had to have an appropriate entry in the file; ***xdm*** has read the file at the startup and has learned about all existing X servers. Since the XDMCP was introduced, the X servers (X terminals) became responsible for querying the host for an *xdm connection;* the *xdm connection* became negotiable between an eligible X server and ***xdm*** (eligible X servers are defined in the other configuration file *Xaccess*). The consequence was that previously required data were no longer needed. Nevertheless, the *Xservers* file is not obsolete; it is still used to start the X session on the local console display which does not normally support XDMCP, as well as for old-fashioned pre-X11R4 remote X servers that do not know about XDMCP (today it is very unlikely to find such X servers; however…).

Here is an example:

```
# cat /usr/lib/X11/xdm/Xservers
:0   local   /usr/bin/X11/X
```

The only entry tells the ***xdm*** that the console display name *:0* is on the local machine, and that the command */usr/lib/X11/X* should be used to start the corresponding X server; the command is executed when ***xdm*** is started up. Usually, /usr/lib/X11/X is a symbolic link to the actual server program (a server program is machine dependent; for example, "*Xsun*" could be the corresponding program on the Sun platform). Here is an example from Solaris 2.6, where the X server program lives in the other directory */usr/openwin/bin*:

```
$ ls -l /usr/openwin/bin | grep "^X"
lrwxrwxrwx  1 root  root       6  May 28 1998  X -> ./Xsun
-rwxr-sr-x  1 root  root  903512  Jul 7 1997   Xsun
```

For X servers that run on other XDMCP noncompliant machines, the entries are of the form:

xthostname:0 foreign Old Pre-X11R4 XTerminal

where, "*xthostname:0*" specifies the machine and display where the X server is running, and "*foreign*" identifies the X server as the remote (not local) one. Other fields are ignored, i.e., treated as comments.

A logical question is: "How does an X client application know, during an X session, how to address the appropriate X server among many eligible X servers?". Here, X11 relies on the UNIX environment variable DISPLAY. In a similar way as the variable TERM identifies a character-based terminal, the DISPLAY variable identifies the X server for the invoked X clients. If this variable is not defined (or wrongly defined), the started X client will display an error message: *Can't open display.*

Another way to identify the X server (and, indirectly to define the DISPLAY variable) is by starting an X client program with "-display" option and specified X server.

This is, probably, the right moment to elaborate how an X server is specified; an X server is identified by:

Hostname:DisplayNumber.ScreenNumber

where

Hostname	Presents the name of the machine that provides X service (could also be IP address), followed by colon ":"
DisplayNumber	Numerically identifies a corresponding display server running on the server machine (could be more displays), followed by dot "."
ScreenNumber	Numerically identifies a screen of the specified display (a display with multiple screen is possible)

In real life, the most common X servers are X terminals, with a single running display server, and a single screen. Consequently, the most common X server identification is: *hostname:0.0.* Later in the text, we will return to this issue.

22.2.2.1.3 The Xresources *File*

The *Xresources* file is loaded into each individual X server as it is connected to ***xdm***. In that way, the X server learns about client's resource needs and becomes ready to provide an appropriate X service. The most important function of the *Xresources* file is to set resources for clients or widgets that are run before the user actually logs in. At least, it is necessary to load the *xlogin widget* (the *xlogin box*) since it is run before the user logs in at all (if you are not happy about the login box appearance, this is the place to look for a modification). The resources specified in the *Xresources* file are loaded by the server via another client, the ***xrdb*** client. Here is an example:

```
# cat /usr/lib/X11/xdm/Xresources
xlogin*login.translations: #override\
    <Key>F1: set-session-argument(failsafe) finish-field()\n\
    <Key>Return: set-session-argument() finish-field()
xlogin*greeting: CLIENTHOST
xlogin*borderWidth: 3
#ifdef COLOR
xlogin*greetColor: #f63
xlogin*failColor: red
```

*xlogin*Foreground: black*
*xlogin*Background: #fdc*
#else
*xlogin*Foreground: black*
*xlogin*Background: white*
#endif

The resources starting with the string *xlogin* (practically all here-included resources) are used by the *xlogin box*. ***xlogin*** sends the box to the display, prompting the user for a name and password. The box also displays the actual client hostname (specified here as "CLIENTHOST"); this could be replaced by any arbitrary greeting message string. By editing the resource:

*xlogin*greeting: "Welcome to CLIENTHOST"*

the greeting message will become friendlier than just the hostname, as it used to be.

The syntax of the Xresources file is slightly different from other configuration files. The reason is that the ***xrdb*** runs the resource file through a C preprocessor (*cpp* by default). It gives extra flexibility, because the appropriate cpp commands like *#ifdef*, *#else*, and *#endif* could be used; (the pound character "#" is reserved for this purpose and cannot be used for comment lines). For comments, the bang character, "!" is used as the leading character in the comment lines.

In the presented example, the first entry (resource) for ***xlogin*** is a translation table, used to define how special keystrokes might be used within the client (pay attention, the entry contains several lines terminating with the back-slash "\" which indicates that the resource specification continues). This entry defines the *F1 key* as the "failsafe key;" by pressing F1, the so-called *failsafe X session* is performed. In such a case, the execution of the individual *.xsession* script is skipped, which could be very important when the script is corrupted. Instead, only a single *xterm* window is defined (enough to make necessary corrections). The *Return key* indicates the end of the password and the start of the user's session.

The various colors specified here are more or less reasonable for most of the displays; otherwise, they can be tuned. COLOR is one of the variables that is predefined in ***xrdb***, as well as CLIENTHOST. Colors themselves can be specified by their commonly used names (red, black, white, etc.), or "RGB values" directly (those color resources start with "#" character and number following it). The server translates these names into appropriate screen color using a RGB color database (usually can be found in */usr/lib/X11/rgb.txt*). The RGB values are expressed as hexadecimal numbers, with one, two, three, or four digits for each field (R, G, and B). Fields that have fewer than four digits are padded out with zero's following each digit. The hexadecimal numbers indicate how much *red* (R), *green* (G), or *blue* (B) should be displayed (*zero* being none, and *"ffff"* being on full)

22.2.2.1.4 *The* Xsession *File*

The *Xsession* file is the script executed since a user logs in. This is a systemwide script, and each modification on the file must be performed extremely carefully. To customize an individual user's session, the *$HOME/.xsession* file is available. The file is pointed by the session resource for that display in the master configuration file. We will return to this file later, when we talk about user-specific X environment.

22.2.2.1.5 *The* Xreset *File*

The *Xreset* file is a script that is executed after the session terminates. This script is not a must, so most often none is provided. Sometimes, it is provided as an empty script, ready to be customized if necessary, as in the next example:

```
$ cat /usr/lib/X11/xdm/Xreset
#!/bin/sh
#
# Xreset
#
# This program is run as root after the session terminates but
# before the display is closed
#
```

22.2.3 *CDE* Configuration Files

At this point we have an idea how X works in the user's area, and what the basic X configuration really means. We discussed old-fashioned, but existing, and still very present X environment, based on ***xdm***. This knowledge is definitely transparent toward newer X releases, like the ***CDE*** is. It will be an easy job for us to understand the CDE configuration, and what to do to provide a desired workable cde-based X environment. Practically, all we need is a very brief review about CDE configuration.

Let us start with the fact that during the system startup, the program ***dtlogin*** is started as the daemon, instead of ***xdm***. Here is an example from Solaris 2.6:

```
$ ps -ef | grep "/usr/dt" | grep -v "grep"
root 1111  1    0    Jan 06 ?    0:00 /usr/dt/bin/dtlogin -daemon
```

and HP-UX 10.20:

```
$ ps -ef | grep "/usr/dt" | grep -v "grep"
root   1401   1381  0    Jan 5 ?   0:00 /usr/dt/bin/dtlogin
root   1381      1  0    Jan 5 ?   0:00 /usr/dt/bin/dtrc /usr/dt/bin/dtrc
```

The ***dtlogin*** daemon was started within the *dtrc* script.

CDE configuration files live in the directory */usr/dt/config* (the configuration directory could also be */etc/dt/config* — by default *CDT configuration files* are first checked in this directory, and then in */usr/dt/config*). The master configuration file is renamed *"Xconfig"* (quite a logical choice).

```
$ ls -F /usr/dt/config
C/             Xreset*          cmsd.conf      en_US.UTF-8/    sessionexit*
Xaccess        Xservers         cz/            hu/             svc/
Xconfig        Xsession.d/      dtlogin.rc*    images/         sys.dtprofile*
Xfailsafe*     Xsession.ow*     dtspcdenv      pl/             tr/
Xinitrc.ow     Xsession.ow2*    dtterm.tc      ru/             xfonts/
Xpasswd*       Xsetup*          dtterm.ti      sdtdict/
Xpasswd2*      Xstartup*        el/            sessionetc*
```

The more significant files for the discussion that follows are presented in ***bold***. Pay attention that files were listed with "-F" option; consequently, "*" is appended for executable files and "/" for directories.

The *CDE configuration files* are similar to the ***xdm*** configuration files; we will discuss a few of them, so we could get the full picture about X11. Most of them are so well commented that additional explanations are almost not needed. The presented platform is Solaris 2.6, although the files are more or less same for all UNIX flavors. Comments in **bold** are added for better understanding of scripts.

The ***dtlogin daemon*** is started during the system startup, by the *dtlogin.rc* scripts:

$ cat /usr/dt/config/dtlogin.rc

```
#!/ bin/sh
#
# "@(#)dtlogin.rc.src 1.4 94/08/11
#
# This version of the dtlogin.rc script can be used on the Solaris(TM)
# operating system to initiate CDE tasks such as starting the dtlogin
# process.
#
# Common Desktop Environment
#
# (c) Copyright 1993, 1994 Hewlett-Packard Company
# (c) Copyright 1993, 1994 International Business Machines Corp.
# (c) Copyright 1993, 1994 Sun Microsystems, Inc.
# (c) Copyright 1993, 1994 Novell, Inc.
#
# When placed in the /etc/rc2.d directory and named appropriately, such as
# "S99dtlogin", this script will automatically start the dtlogin window
# after the Solaris(TM) system boots to its multi-user level.
#
# This script is also called indirectly by the CDE dtconfig command.
mode=$1      # The argumant "start" and "stop" are used during the system startup and
             # shutdown, and are of the interest here; the argument "reset" is used to
             # recycle the dtlogin daemon, while the argument "update_printer" is used
             # to update printers
#
usage_error() {
echo " $0 start                 (start dtlogin process)"
echo " $0 stop                  (stop dtlogin process)"
echo " $0 reset                 (reset dtlogin process)"
echo " $0 update_printers       (update print actions)"
echo " "
}
      . . . . .
      . . . . .
# The definition of the functions "update_printers" and "login_server_pid" are skipped
case "$mode" in
'start')
   update_printers                           # execute the function to update printers
   if [ -x /usr/dt/bin/dtlogin ] ; then
      /usr/dt/bin/dtlogin -daemon&           # start dtlogin as a daemon
   fi
   ;;
'stop')
#   get dtlogin pid
    dtlogin_pid='login_server_pid'           # get the PID of the dtlogin daemon
#   kill dtlogin process
       if [ "$dtlogin_pid" != "" ] ; then
          /usr/bin/kill $dtlogin_pid         # stop the dtlogin daemon (kill the process)
       fi
       ;;
'reset')
```

```
#   get dtlogin pid
        dtlogin_pid='login_server_pid'          # get the PID of the dtlogin daemon
#   reset dtlogin process
        if [ "$dtlogin_pid" != "" ] ; then
           /usr/bin/kill -HUP $dtlogin_pid      # Recycle the dtlogin daemon
                                                # (send the HUP signal)
        fi
        ;;
'update_printers')
    update_printers                             # execute the function to update printers
    ;;
*)
    usage_error                                 # otherwise excute the function
                                                "usage_error"
    exit 1                                      # (how to use the script)
    ;;
esac
exit 0
# ==================================================================
```

CDE master configuration file is renamed *Xconfig;* however, its purpose stays the same, while its content reflects introduced changes versus ***xdm***. In the Figure 22.6 a simplified graphic presentation of the dtlogin configuration is given. Some of the presented files are not necessarily listed in the *Xconfig* file; however, they are used by programs invoked through this file.

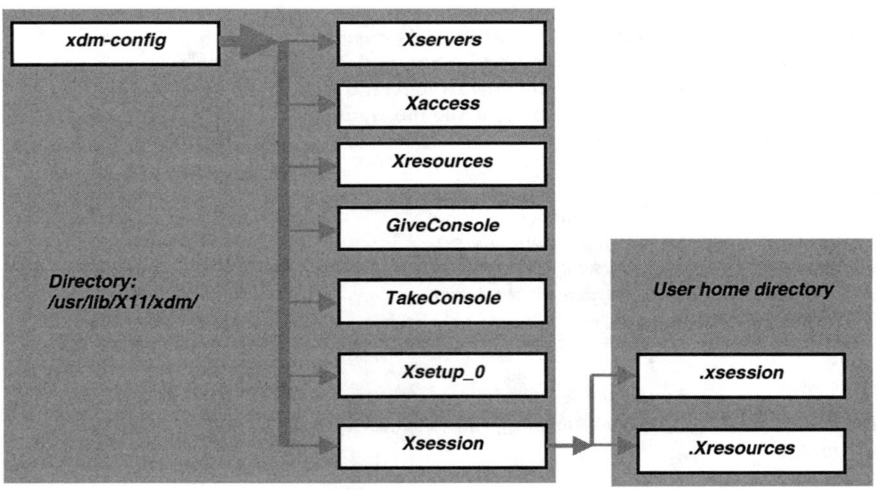

FIGURE 22.6
The CDE configuration files.

Here is a real configuration file:

$ cat /usr/dt/config/Xconfig

```
##############################################################################
#
# Xconfig
#
# Common Desktop Environment (CDE)
```

```
# Configuration file for the Login Manager
#
# $XConsortium: Xconfig.src /main/cde1_maint/5 1995/11/30 21:58:42 montyb $
#
# ************** DO NOT EDIT THIS FILE **************
#
# /usr/dt/config/Xconfig is a factory-default file and will be unconditionally overwritten upon
# subsequent installation. Before making changes to the file, copy it to the configuration directory,
# /etc/dt/config.
#
# This file contains behaviour resources for the CDE DT Login Manager. It also specifies the
# location of other configuration files used by the Login Manager.
#
# Appearance resources for the login screen are contained in the file
# specified by the "*resources" resource below.
#
# Most resources can be limited to a single display by including the display name in the resource.
# If the display name is not included, the resource will apply to all displays managed by the Login
# Manager. When specifying the display name, replace the ":" character in the name with an
# underscore "_". If the name is fully qualified, also replace dot "." characters with underscores.
#
# Example:
# Dtlogin*machine_domain_name_0*startup: /etc/dt/config/Xstartup.aa
#
# For more information see the man page, Dtlogin(1X).
#
###################################################################################
Dtlogin.errorLogFile:      /var/dt/Xerrors
Dtlogin.pidFile:           /var/dt/Xpid
###################################################################################
# Note: If you do not specify a full path beginning with a "/"
#         dtlogin will first search for the following files in
#         /etc/dt/config then in /usr/dt/config.
#
###################################################################################
Dtlogin.accessFile:        Xaccess
Dtlogin.servers:           Xservers
Dtlogin*resources:         %L/Xresources
Dtlogin*startup:           Xstartup
Dtlogin*reset:             Xreset
Dtlogin*setup:             Xsetup
Dtlogin*failsafeClient:    Xfailsafe
   . . . . .
   . . . . .
# Other resource entries follow
```

The brief description of the CDE configuration files listed in the master configuration file *Xconfig* follows; we are already more or less familiar with them.

Xservers	List of displays for ***dtlogin*** to explicitely manage
Xresources	Resource definitions specifying the appearance of the login screen
Xsetup	Script executed as "root" prior to display of the login screen
Xstartup	Script executed as "root" after a user has successfully authenticated
Xsession	Script executed as the authenticated user has started the user's session
Xfailsafe	Script executed as the authenticated user has started a failsafe session
Xreset	Script executed as "root" after the user's session has exited

Most of the listed *CDE configuration files* are like the corresponding ***xdm*** configuration files; they are better commented, and occasionally, some improvements have been made. Following the previous discussion related to ***xdm***, the CDE configuration files *Xservers* and *Xresources* are presented. While the file *Xservers* stayed unchanged, with the single line that specifies the local X server (this file became almost obsolete since the introduction of X11R4, without need for any improvement, except to be better commented), the file Xresources got new configuration sections for more precise X tuning. Both files are originally so well commented, that there is no need for additional explanations.

$ cat /usr/dt/config/Xservers

```
##########################################################################
#
# Xservers
#
# Common Desktop Environment
#
# Configuration file for all Xservers started or managed by the Login Manager
# BEST TO NOT EDIT /usr/dt/config/Xservers directly.
#
# /usr/dt/config/Xservers is a factory-default file and will
# be unconditionally overwritten upon subsequent installation.
# Before making changes to the file, should copy it to the configuration
# directory, /etc/dt/config.
#
# @(#)Xservers.src 1.16 96/07/21
#
##########################################################################
#
# This file should contain an entry to start the X window server on the
# local workstation's display.
#
# If the local display has an associated character device, it should also
# be specified in the line. An example is the "console" device in the
# example line below. This allows Dtlogin to correctly monitor that device
# when [Command Line Login] mode is selected from the login screen.
#
# <HostName>:0 <class> local@console /usr/openwin/bin/X :0 <options>
#
# If no character device is associated directly with the display, then
# "none" should be specified.
#
# <HostName>:0 <class> local@none    /usr/openwin/bin /X :0 <options>
#
# By default, the ":0" display is associated with the "/dev/console"
# character device. If the true console on the system is not the same
# as the ":0" graphics display, then the appropriate device or "none"
# should be specified for the ":0" display.
#
# An example need of "none" here would be a Sun system that had been
# configured to direct console I/O thru a tty port instead of using
# the workstation's display.
#
# If you want multiple-displays running dtlogin then make sure the
# connection number matches the display name, for example.
#
# <HostName>:1 local@none /usr/openwin/bin/X :1 <options>
#
# This means the X-server is started on connection number "1" and the
# display is connecting to the X-server on "1" through display name
```

```
# "LocalHost:1".
#
# If you have some X terminals connected which do not support XDMCP,
# you can add them here as well. Using XDMCP is recommended over
# entries in this file and should be used whenever possible.
#
# Example Syntax, the items between "< >" are optional:
#
# <HostName>:0 <class> local@console        /usr/openwin/ bin/X :0 <options>
# <HostName>:1 <class> local@none           /usr/openwin/bin /X :1 <options>
# XTermName:0 <class> foreign
#
# A "*" in the first field of the entry for a local server
# will be expanded to "<hostname>:0" by Dtlogin. This
# syntax is valid only within this file.
#
# * Local local@console /usr/openwin/bin/Xsun :0
#
# If the display type of "local_uid" is used, a user name such as "root"
# must follow in next field. In this example, by placing "root" here,
# Login will start a local Xserver under the user id of "root". On Sun
# system's this will give Xserver the ability to raise interactive
# scheduling priority of a client with mouse/keyboard focus to increase
# performance of the application.
#
# :0 Local local_uid@console root /usr/openwin/bin/Xsun :0
#
# In limited situations, the Xserver should not be run under a "root" id
# for security reasons. Examples are usually specific to Xserver
# extensions.
#
# On Sun Xservers one example involves the Display Postscript extension.
# If the DPS extension is granted access (via Xserver option line) to read
# and write Unix files via the "-dpsfileops" option (see Xsun man page) it
# should not be run under a "root" user id. For increaseced security,
# could instead run it as the "nobody" user.
#
# :0 Local local_uid@console nobody /usr/openwin/bin/Xsun :0 -dpsfileops
#
# Another example of interest here for Sun's Xserver is how to start on
# two or more screens. A two screen example follows.
#
# :0 Local local_uid@console root /usr/openwin/bin/X -dev /dev/fb0 -dev /dev/fb1
# See the Xsun.1 and Xserver.1 man pages for additional options of
# interest.
#
##############################################################################

:0 Local local_uid@console root /usr/openwin/bin/Xsun :0 -nobanner
```

The file *Xresources* is shown partially, with a few fully presented sections; for others only headers are listed, while the list of contents skipped. Be aware that this file has a different syntax; commented lines start with "!".

```
$ cat /usr/dt/config/Xresources
!!###########################################################################
!!
!! Xresources
!!
!! Common Desktop Environment
```

```
!! Configuration file for the Login Manager
!!
!! ************** DO NOT EDIT THIS FILE **************
!!
!! /usr/dt/config/Xresources is a factory-default file and will
!! be unconditionally overwritten upon subsequent installation.
!! Before making changes to the file, copy it to the configuration
!! directory, /etc/dt/config. You must also update the resources
!! resource in /etc/dt/config/Xconfig.
!!
!! $XConsortium: Xresources.src /main/cde1_maint/6 1995/12/01 14:04:59 rcs $
!!
!!#######################################################################
!!
!! This file contains appearance and behaviour resources for the Dtlogin
!! login screen. These are designed to be read into the root window
!! property via the 'xrdb' program. Dtlogin will do this automatically
!! after the server is reset and will remove them before the session
!! starts.
!!
!! Dtlogin contains internal default values for all resources. To
!! override a default value, uncomment the appropriate line below and
!! supply the desired value.
!!
!! Customization hints are included at the end of this file.
!!
!!#######################################################################
!! Motif visuals
     .....
     .....
!!#######################################################################
!!#   translations for the text field widget
     .....
     .....
!!#######################################################################
!! COLORS
     .....
     .....
!!#######################################################################
!! FONTS
!! labelFont                   button and label text
!! textFont                    help and error dialog text
#if WIDTH < 1024
Dtlogin*labelFont:             -dt-interface system-medium-r-normal-s*-*-*-*-*-*-*-*-*:
Dtlogin*textFont:              -dt-interface user-medium-r-normal-s* -*-*-*-*-*-*-*-*:
Dtlogin*greeting.fontList:     -dt-interface system-medium-r-normal-xl*-*-*-*-*-*-*-*-*:
#else
Dtlogin*labelFont:             -dt-interface system-medium-r-normal-l*-*-*-*-*-*-*-*-*:
Dtlogin*textFont:              -dt-interface user-medium-r-normal-l* -*-*-*-*-*-*-*-*:
Dtlogin*greeting.fontList:     -dt-interface system-medium-r-normal-xxl*-*-*-*-*-*-*-*-*:
#endif
!!
!!#######################################################################
!! CURSOR
     .....
     .....
!!#######################################################################
!! GREETING
Dtlogin*greeting.foreground:         black
Dtlogin*greeting.background:         #a8a8a8
Dtlogin*greeting.labelString:        Welcome to %LocalHost%
```

```
Dtlogin*greeting.persLabelString:      Welcome %s
Dtlogin*greeting.alignment:            ALIGNMENT_CENTER
!!##########################################################################
!! Size of Text Input Area
      .....
      .....
!!##########################################################################
!! MISC
      .....
      .....
!!##########################################################################
!! LANGUAGE MENU NAME MAPPINGS
      .....
      .....
!!##########################################################################
!! Session MENU NAME MAPPINGS
!! Number of desktop's defined here for session menu
      .....
      .....
!!##########################################################################
!! CHOOSER
      .....
      .....
!!##########################################################################
!!
!! To disable options in dtgreet window, uncomment the appropriate
!! line below.
      .....
      .....
!!*************************************************************************
!!                         CUSTOMIZATION HINTS
!!
!! The login screen was designed to be easy to customize for a variety of
!! attributes. These include...
!!
!!     1. custom logo bitmap
!!     2. custom greeting message
!!     3. colors
!!     4. fonts
!!
!! Users may replace the default logo with a custom one of their choice.
!! Colors and fonts can be changed using the standard Motif resources for
!! the appropriate widget and/or class.
!!
!!*************************************************************************
```

22.2.4 Vendor-Specific X Flavors — a Configuration Example

All vendor-specific flavors of X do have a quite similar approach regarding their configuration. It is logical, bearing in mind their common starting base in X11R4; they all are only flavored versions of the same X11. The similarity is even higher if we talk about ***CDE***. Historically, ***CDE*** appeared after vendor-specific X flavors, and it integrated the best of all of them. Maybe it is fair to say that ***CDE*** resembles them, rather than the opposite.

Talking about vendor-specific flavors of X, we will mostly refer to Hewlett-Packard *Visual User Interface (VUE).* Although some discrepancies are possible between vendors' X flavors, such a generalization is quite acceptable, and correct. We will briefly check the VUE configuration (implemented platform is HP-UX 10.20).

The basic VUE configuration seems to be very similar to the CDE, even regarding file names. The VUE configuration file is named *Xconfig* (as in CDE) and it configures VUE quite deep; almost all VUE resources are defined by the file itself. The configuration files live in the directory */usr/vue/config;* its listing is presented. Some of the files are named differently, but are still recognizable. The directory also includes systemwide configuration files for other clients and the *VUE Window Manager* – ***vuewm***.

$ ls /usr/vue/config

Xaccess	***Xconfig***	*Xconfig.orig*	***Xerrors***	***Xfailsafe***
Xpid	***Xreset***	***Xresources***	*Xservers*	***Xsession***
Xsession.test	***Xstartup***	*def-actions*	*dialogs*	*import*
panels	*sys.font*	*sys.res.lite*	*sys.resources*	*sys.ses.lite*
sys.session	*sys.vueprofile*	***sys.vuewmrc***	*types*	

VUE is started, during the system startup by the special "inittab entry" in the */etc/inittab* file:

$ cat /etc/inittab | grep "vue"

vue :4:respawn:/ usr/vue/bin/vuerc # VUE invocation

The started program is running as a daemon:

$ ps -ef | grep "vue" | grep -v "grep"

root 1441 10 Jan 5 ? 0:00 /usr/vue/bin/vuerc /usr/vue/bin/vuerc

The structure of the configuration file Xconfig is very much like the CDE configuration file; however, there are differences in the contents. The file is partially presented:

$ cat /usr/vue/config/Xconfig

```
##########################################################################
###
### Xconfig
###
### Configuration file for the Login Manager.
###
### @(#)Hewlett-Packard Visual User Environment, Version 3.0
### Copyright (c) Hewlett-Packard Company
###
### ______________________________
###
### This file contains behaviour resources for the HP VUE Login Manager.
### It also specifies the location of other configuration files used by
### the Login Manager.
###
### Appearance resources for the login screen are contained in the file
### specified by the "*resources" resource below.
###
### Most resources can be limited to a single display by including the
### display name in the resource. If the display name is not included, the
### resource will apply to all displays managed by the Login Manager. When
### specifying the display name, replace the ":" character in the name
### with an underscore "_". If the name is fully qualified, also replace
### dot "." characters with underscores.
###
```

```
### Example:
###
### Vuelogin*hpaaa_cv_hp_com_0*startup: /etc/vue/config/Xstartup.aa
###
### For more information see the man page, Vuelogin(1X).
###
##########################################################################
Vuelogin.errorLogFile:       /var/vue/Xerrors
Vuelogin.pidFile:            /var/vue/Xpid
Vuelogin.accessFile:         /etc/vue/config/Xaccess
Vuelogin.servers:            /etc/vue/config/Xservers
Vuelogin*resources:          /etc/vue/config/Xresources
Vuelogin*startup:            /etc/vue/config/Xstartup
Vuelogin*session:            /etc/vue/config/Xsession
Vuelogin*reset:              /etc/vue/config/Xreset
Vuelogin*failsafeClient:     /etc/vue/config/Xfailsafe
##########################################################################
## Other well commented "configuration sections" follow
     .....
     .....
```

Administering vendor-specific X flavors recalls our previous discussion. The concept is the same, and configuration rules are the same, data organization is the same, and configuration files are almost the same. Differences are primarily in the naming of programs and configuration files; even the names are recognizable. All X-related administrative skills are fully transparent.

22.3 Access Control and Security of X11

22.3.1 XDMCP Queries

X is running in a network environment; it means the client host can be hypothetically accessed by any host on the network; sometimes, with "naughty" intentions. The only requirement for a potential intruder is to declare as an X server. Obviously, security issues are of a special interest from an administrative standpoint.

First, let us see how a client host could be accessed at all. There are three types of queries defined in XDMCP (X Display Manager Control Protocol) to access a client host: ***direct***, ***indirect***, and ***broadcast***. The queries originate from a remote X server (to be more clear, in the text that follows, we will refer to a "remote X server" as an "X terminal"). The three types of queries are presented in the Figure 22.7.

A ***direct query*** means addressing a particular client host and asking for a connection; the running X daemon (again, we will refer to an X daemon keeping in mind both ***xdm*** or ***dtlogin***) could accept or deny such a request. If it accepts, the login screen is launched on the corresponding X terminal.

An ***indirect query*** allows the X daemon on the addressed client host to decide what to do with the query; it could respond directly to the X terminal query forward the query to another client host, or offer a user at the X terminal a choice between multiple client hosts. All this could be configured accordingly.

A ***broadcast query*** presents a general query throughout the network for any client host running X daemon to respond. The first client host that responds to the query positively makes the connection with the corresponding X terminal.

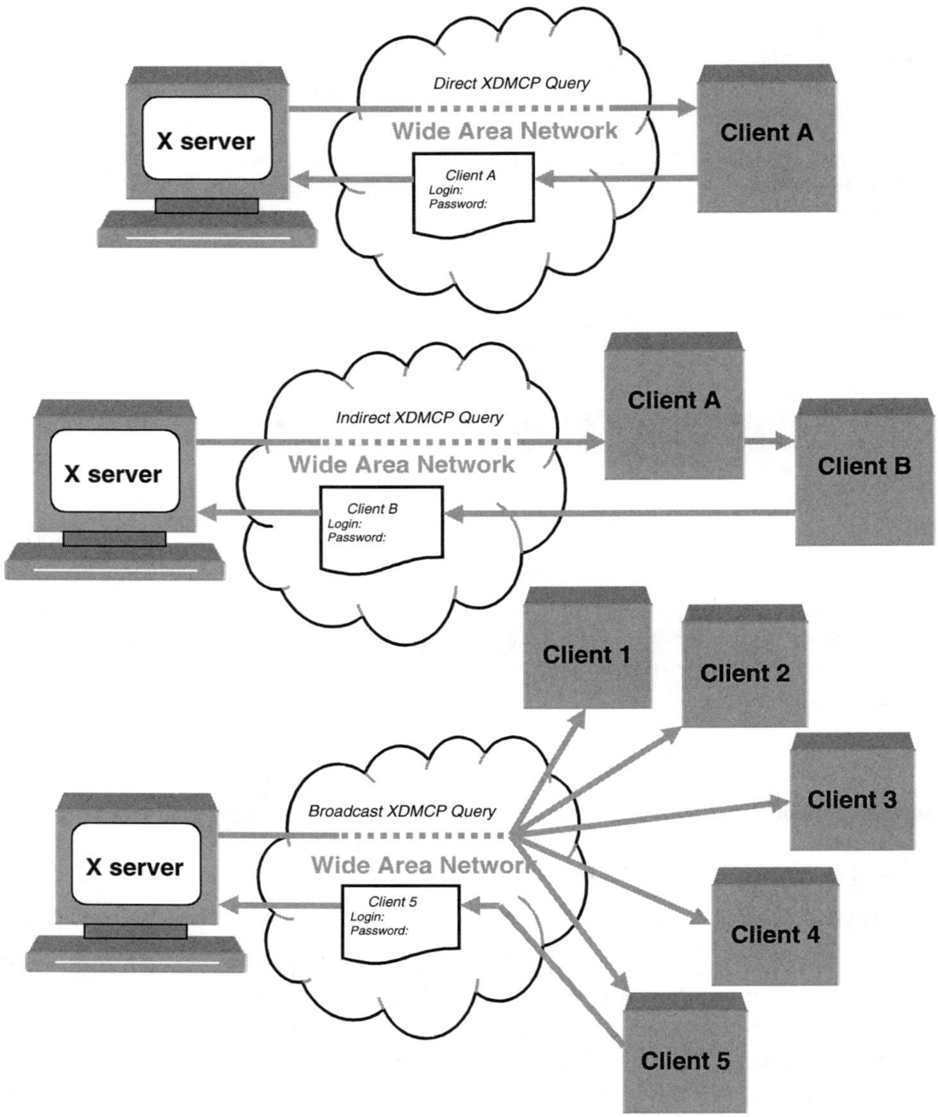

FIGURE 22.7
Direct, indirect, and broadcast queries.

22.3.2 The *Xaccess* File

The special file, named *Xaccess*, was introduced with X11R5 to allow administrators to control how the X daemon responds to different types of queries. This file (the opposite of its name) is not related to the host access control; all that this file controls is the eligibility of a particular X terminal to get a login window; users still need to supply their user names and passwords to log in to the host.

Eligible X terminals are simply listed in the *Xaccess* file; queries from unlisted, or explicitly denied, X terminals are simply ignored by the X daemon, without possibility of establishing an X connection. By default, in its MIT-distributed form, the *Xaccess* file is configured to allow direct and broadcast connections from any X terminal.

Here is an example; pay attention, this is the CDE configuration file, so all references in the file are toward the ***dtlogin*** daemon:

$ cat /usr/dt/config/Xaccess

```
##############################################################################
#
# Xaccess
# Common Desktop Environment
#
# ************** DO NOT EDIT THIS FILE **************
#
# /usr/dt/config/Xaccess is a factory-default file and will
# be unconditionally overwritten upon subsequent installation.
# Before making changes to the file, copy it to the configuration
# directory, /etc/dt/config. You must also update the accessFile
# resource in /etc/dt/config/Xconfig.
#
# $XConsortium: Xaccess.src /main/cde1_maint/2 1995/08/30 16:21:28 gtsang $
#
##############################################################################
#
# This file contains a list of host names which are allowed or
# denied XDMCP connection access to this machine. When a remote
# display (typically an X-termimal) requests login service, Dtlogin
# will consult this file to determine if service should be granted
# or denied.
#
# # Access control file for XDMCP connections
#
# To control Direct and Broadcast access:
#   pattern
#
# To control Indirect queries:
#   pattern    list of hostnames and/or macros ...
#
# To use the chooser:
#   pattern    CHOOSER BROADCAST
# or
#   pattern    CHOOSER list of hostnames and/or macros ...
#
# To define macros:
#   %name    list of hosts ...
#
# The first form tells dtlogin which displays to respond to itself.
# The second form tells dtlogin to forward indirect queries from hosts
# matching the specified pattern to the indicated list of hosts.
# The third form tells dtlogin to handle indirect queries using the
# chooser; the chooser is directed to send its own queries out via the
# broadcast address and display the results on the terminal.
# The fourth form is similar to the third, except instead of using the
# broadcast address, it sends DirectQuerys to each of the hosts in the list
#
# In all cases, dtlogin uses the first entry which matches the terminal;
# for IndirectQuery messages only entries with right hand sides can
# match, for Direct and Broadcast Query messages, only entries without
# right hand sides can match.
#
# Information regarding the format of entries in this file is
```

```
# included at the end of the file.
###########################################################################
#
# Entries...
*                                     # grant service to all remote displays
# The nicest way to run the chooser is to just ask it to broadcast
# requests to the network – that way new hosts show up automatically.
# Sometimes, however, the chooser can't figure out how to broadcast,
# so this may not work in all environments.
*   CHOOSER BROADCAST   #any indirect host can get a chooser
#
# If you'd prefer to configure the set of hosts each terminal sees,
# then just uncomment these lines (and comment the CHOOSER line above)
# and edit the %hostlist line as appropriate
#
#%hostlist                            host-a host-b
#*   CHOOSER %hostlist                #
###########################################################################
#
#                                ENTRY FORMAT
#
# An entry in this file is either a host name or a pattern. A
# pattern may contain one or more meta characters ('*' matches any
# sequence of 0 or more characters, and '?' matches any single
# character) which are compared against the host name of the remote
# device requesting service.
#
# If the entry is a host name, all comparisons are done using
# network addresses, so any name which converts to the correct
# network address may be used. For patterns, only canonical host
# names are used in the comparison, so do not attempt to match
# aliases.
#
# Preceding either a host name or a pattern with a '!' character
# causes hosts which match that entry to be excluded.
#
# When checking access for a particular display host, each entry is
# scanned in turn and the first matching entry determines the
# response.
#
# Blank lines are ignored, '#' is treated as a comment delimiter
# causing the rest of that line to be ignored,
# ex.
#       !xtra.lcs.mit.edu     # disallow direct/broadcast service for xtra
#       bambi.ogi.edu         # allow access from this particular display
#       *.lcs.mit.edu         # allow access from any display in LCS
#
```

While the *direct* and *broadcast* queries are easy to understand and administer, the *indirect* query, especially its *chooser* option, could be a little confusing. The *Xaccess* file gives an opportunity to the administrator to configure the X daemon for a transfer of an *indirect* query from an arbitrary X terminal, or a group of X terminals, to the other, specified, client host. The *chooser* is presented in the Figure 22.8.

For example, the *Xaccess* entry:

```
*.scps.nyu.edu          clientname.scps.nyu.edu
```

will forward an *Indirect* query from any X terminal in the *scps.nyu.edu* domain directly to the client host *clientname.scps.nyu.edu.*

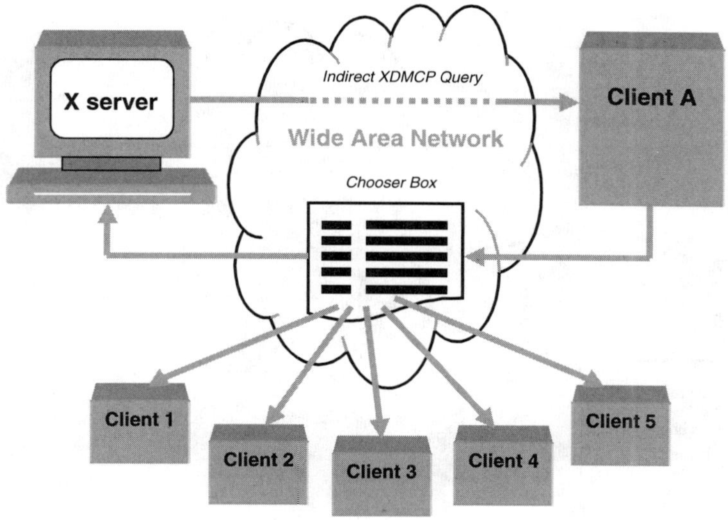

FIGURE 22.8
The chooser.

Alternatively, to set the X daemon to respond to an *indirect* query with the *Chooser Box* on the X terminal screen, offers a user the chance to choose between several displayed client hosts. The *Xaccess* entry:

.scps.nyu.edu CHOOSER client1.scps.nyu.edu client2.scps.nyu.edu client3.scps.nyu.edu

will allow the user on any X terminal in the *scps.nyu.edu* domain to choose the client host between *client1, client2,* and *client3.*

Instead of a list of client hosts to choose from, the Xaccess entry:

.scps.nyu.edu CHOOSER BROADCAST

allows the user on the X terminal to choose among all client hosts that respond to the ***chooser*** broadcast query.

Chooser is the compiled client program; the opposite of other client programs that are scripts, this program cannot be read; however, it could be configured via the *Xresources* file.

22.3.3 Other Access Control Mechanisms

The described X terminal eligibility checking, provided by the *Xaccess* file, is not the only available access control; there are several other host-based and user-based access control mechanisms. The host-based scheme involves a system file */etc/X**n**.hosts* and can be controlled using the ***xhost*** client program. The user-based schemes involve authorization capabilities provided by the ***xauth*** program and XDMCP protocol.

The */etc/X**n**.hosts* file contains a list of hosts that are allowed to access local X server ***n*** (this file resides on the X server side). In most cases, a single local X server is running on a particular system, so the */etc/X0.hosts* file is the only important one. This file is not included in any default configurations of X11, and it must be edited by a system administrator. This file lists all client hosts that X server can communicate with. How it works is presented in Figure 22.9a.

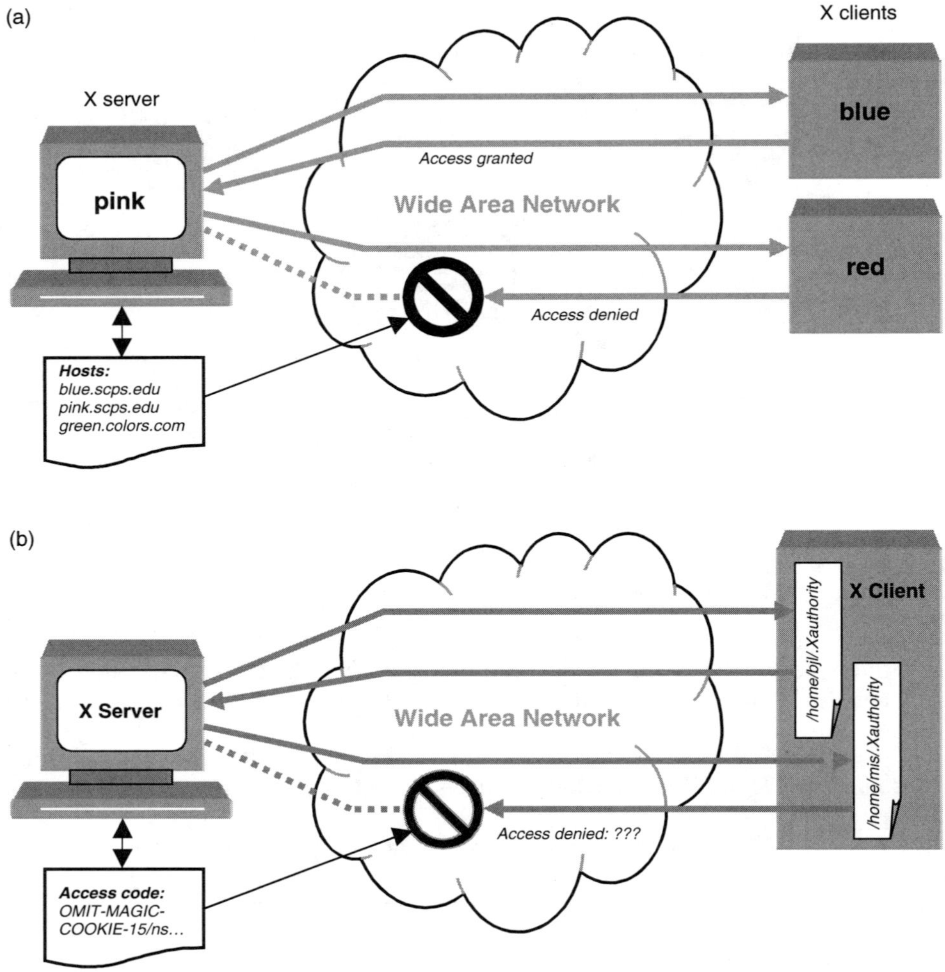

FIGURE 22.9
(a) Host-based access control; (b) User-based access control.

In this hypothetical example, the local X server **pink:0.0** could be accessed by the host **blue.scps.edu** (hosts in the same domain do not require the domain name suffix, but it is recommended to use it), while the access is denied to the host **red.scps.edu**. Additional acceptable hosts are also **pink.scps.edu** (the host where the X server is running), and **green.colors.com**; all these hosts are specified in the */etc/X0.hosts* file at the host **pink.scps.edu**.

The ***xhost*** command could be used, interactively, to grant or deny access to the X server, i.e., to modify the */etc/X0.hosts* file. This could be done only since a login session was established with the X server we want to change access to. Otherwise, such an attempt would be rejected, and an error message displayed.

The host-based access control is insufficient for true security; it has some conceptual drawbacks. For example, it is overridden by NIS, and any user included in the NIS password map is granted access regardless of the host's status. Because of that, starting with X11R4, a user-based access control mechanism was introduced to supplement, or actually, to replace the host-based one. A user-based access control is built into the XDMCP, but it can be used also independently. The most common method is known under the name: *MIT-MAGIC-COOKIE-1,* and will be briefly discussed. Other user-based access control mechanisms, as *XDM-AUTHORIZATION-1,* or *SUN-DES-1,* will not be elaborated on.

The *MIT-MAGIC-COOKIE-1,* presented in Figure 22.9b, is the most common method, although it is not the most secure one. If both the client host and the X server are configured to use this method, then when a user logs in using an X daemon, a machine readable code is put in a file called *.Xauthority* in the user's home directory. This code, called a *magic cookie,* is also transferred to the X server. Practically, the *magic cookie* presents some kind of a "passcode" known only to a particular X server, and a particular user on a particular host (do not read it literally — as a matter of fact, all that is hidden from the real user).

Once the *magic cookie* is established for that X session, each client program must present the passcode before it is allowed to connect to the X server. The only way for a client to get the passcode is by reading the *.Xauthority* file in the user's home directory. The existing permissions for this file are "write and read" only for its user-owner, and it means that only client programs started by the same user can read the *magic cookie.* Obviously this type of access control is based entirely on UNIX file permissions, and it is as secure as the user's account (protected by a password). Here is a real example:

```
# ls -l /home/sam/.Xautority
-rw ----------- 1 sam 99 Dec 12 16:29 /home/sam/.Xauthority

# cat /home/sam/.Xauthority
OMIT-MAGIC-COOKIE-15/nsO6ZzEasP1/7vcmx370MIT-MAGIC-COOKIE-15/nsO6ZzEasP1/7v
```

The displayed passcode does not make a lot of sense, especially because it contains nonprinting characters that could not even be displayed.

The access control is activated through the corresponding, master configuration file, by the authorization resource entry:

DisplayManager.DISPLAY.authorize: true

The concept of the ***MIT-MAGIC-COOKIE-1*** supposes that all client programs have access to the *magic cookie* in the *.Xauthority* file. This is OK, as long as the client programs are local at the host where the user's home directory, with the *.Xauthority* file, is located. However, in the distributed processing environment, it is not a must. The solution was found with the program ***xauth,*** which is used to propagate the magic cookie from one client host to another. ***xauth*** extracts a user's authorization information for the current display, copies it to another machine, and merges it into the *$HOME/.Xauthority* file on the remote machine.

In the hierarchy of access controls, the user-based access control is overridden by the host-based access control. For that reason, it is important that no host is being listed in the host-based access list at the X server side; for any listed client host, the user-based access control will be automatically bypassed. To check from the command line for any client host listed, type:

```
# xhost
access control enabled, only authorized client can connect
```

If a bunch of hosts are also listed afterward, they should be removed, or their users will have access granted regardless of user-based access control (use the command "***xhost -***" to remove all hosts).

From an administrative point of view, user-based access control does not require any attention; the individual *.Xauthority* file lives in the user's home directory, together with other "dot" files. The only concern is the fact that host-based access control could override the user-based one.

22.4 The User X Environment

Up to now, we have mostly discussed X systemwide issues. Although, a good systemwide X setting could be sufficient for relatively satisfactory X windowing, to customize an individual user's X environment, other configuration files are of importance. These files are usually located in the user's home directory and have an influence only on the individual X sessions.

The user X environment is made up of many components; possibilities to manage it are numerous. However, it is too complex to leave everything to a user, although it can be treated as a personal issue. The administrator is still responsible for this segment of X, and an approach to create a useful default environment is recommended. This is particularly done through system-wide configuration data; however, there is a lot of space also in the user-related arena.

The user X environment is crucial for a successful X11 implementation. Users do not know very much about a good X11 concept; they do not know about X11 flexibility and versatily; they simply do not care about that. They know what they see in front of them, and how they could use it. Their own look and feel is the only issue in their evaluation of X. That is why an administrator must pay considerable attention to setting a user X environment. The first step is to understand how X works in this area.

22.4.1 Components of the *xdm*-Based User X Environment

The user X session starts with the execution of the *Xsession* script, when the user logs in successfully; the script is executed with the user's credentials. *Xsession* checks for user's specific session settings in the user's home directory (it looks for the script *.xsession*) and sources them. However, if the individual *.xsession* script does not exist, *Xsession* sets a decent systemwide default user's X environment. This is a fair approach that gives a chance to an administrator/user to set an arbitrary user X environment, if such a wish exists at all. *Xsession* also provides the way to escape into *failsafe mode* (providing a single **xterm** window sufficient to fix the problem) if the configuration is corrupted in any way.

The Xsession is actually very simple script, presented here:

$ cat /usr/lib/X11/xdm/Xsession

```
#!/ bin/sh
case $# in
1)
    case $1 in
    failsafe)
                  exec xterm -C -fn 9×15bold -geometry 80×24+50+50
                  ;;
    esac
esac
startup=$HOME/.xsession
```

```
resources=$HOME/.Xresources
if [ -f $startup ]; then
      if [ -x $startup ]; then
              exec $startup
      else
              exec /bin/sh $startup
      fi
else
      if [ -f $resources ]; then
              xrdb -load $resources
      fi
      mwm &
      xrefresh
      exec xterm -fg white -bg black -fn 9x15bold -sb -C -geometry 107x24+25+501 -ls
fi
```

This script recognizes the eventually required failsafe mode (defined by the translation resource entries in the *Xresources* file) to provide an escape from the ordinary session. In that case a single *xterm* window is sent to the display and the script exits. Otherwise, the script looks for the script file *.xsession* in the user's home directory, and if it exists, executes it. If the *.xsession* does not exist, this script creates a workable X session by, first loading individual resources by the ***xrdb*** (if the file *.Xresources* exists in the user's home directory), and then invokes the ***mwm*** window manager in the background, followed by an *xterm* window.

At this point, an X session is established, and the user could continue interaction with the X client host, with all the benefits that an X11 environment offers. Instead of X terminal emulator, any other X-based application could be started.

Assuming the need to create an individual user X environment, there are up to three X configuration files in the user's home directory to be set (in addition to the standard UNIX shell startup dot files): *.xsession, .Xresources,* and corresponding window manager *rc* file. We already mentioned them, but now we will look at them in more detail. While the *.Xresources* file could be seen as an extension of the already existing systemwide *Xresources* file, the *.xsession* file works more as a replacement than as an extension (if the file exists, it is the only one executed for a user X session).

The *$HOME/.xsession* file is the shell script that actually starts each of the applications in a user's startup environment. Here is an example for an arbitrary user "sam:"

```
# cat /home/sam/.xsession
#!/ bin/sh
# Add /usr/local/bin to the path for this script:
PATH=$PATH:/usr/loca/bin
export PATH
#
# Set up a pattern for the root window:
xsetroot -bitmap /usr/include/X11/bitmaps/pattern1
#
# Merge in user resources:
xrdb -merge $HOME/.Xresources
#
# Start some applications:
xterm -title FirstWindow -g 75x35+1+1 &
xterm -title SecondWindow -g -1-1 &
    .....
    .....
```

Besides others, two ***xterm*** windows are set up, one of the size 75×35, starting from the upper left corner, and the second of the default size, starting from the lower right corner.

The *$HOME/.Xresources* file contains user-specific resource definitions. These resources define user's client preferences: for user's ***xterm*** windows, a user's favorite font, a scroll bar, etc. Here is an example:

```
# cat /home/sam/.Xresources
! Resource definition file.
!
! XTerm definitions:
XTerm*font:-misc-fixed-bold -r-normal--15-140-75-75-c-90-iso8859-1
XTerm*scrollBar:true
XTerm*saveLines:200
     .....
     .....
```

An appropriate font is set up instead of the default one, as well as a scroll bar with up to 200 saved lines to be scrolled.

22.4.2 Components of the CDE User X Environment

The way to start an user's session in ***CDE*** is slightly different, but more powerful and flexible. ***CDE*** also uses the *Xsession* script file to initialize a user's session; but a real job is done by the desktop session manager, which is invoked from the *.Xsession* script. The default file is */usr/dt/bin/Xsession,* and could be copied into */etc/dt/config/Xsession* and customized for the systemwide user setting (correspondingly, the *Xsession entry* in the CDE master configuration file *Xconfig* should be modified also). The *CDE Xsession* script:

- sources the user's *$HOME/.dtprofile* file, and enables an individual user's setting
- sources any existing script in the directory */etc/dt/config/Xsession.d*
- sources any existing script in the directory */usr/dt/config/Xsession.d*
- launches the desktop welcome client, *dthello*
- sources the setup script to search applications, *dtsearchpath*
- launches the help client, *dthelpgen*
- launches the application manager directory setup client, *dtappgather*
- executes the desktop session manager, *dtsession*

Obviously, there is a number of invoked programs, and a number of places where a general or an individual user session could be tuned. The *Xsession* script is a systemwide file, used for all users; the individual user setting could be provided through the individual *.dtprofile* file, the individual *.Xdefaults* file (used by the session manager *dtsession*), and the individual window manager configuration file. A similar approach has been implemented in the past by some vendor-specific X flavors, and CDE adopted that for its own needs.

Let us see what the Xsession script looks like. Although it appears long, the script is only partially presented.

```
$ cat /usr/dt/bin/Xsession
#!/ bin/ksh
##############################################################################
#
```

```
# Xsession
#
# Common Desktop Environment (CDE)
# Configuration script for the Login Manager
#
# ************** DO NOT EDIT THIS FILE **************
#
# /usr/dt/bin/Xsession is a factory-default file and will
# be unconditionally overwritten upon subsequent installation.
# Modification is discouraged.
#
# $XConsortium: Xsession.src /main/cde1_maint/7 1995/11/17 14:43:10 gtsang $
#
#
# This script starts the user's session. It searches for one of three
# types of startup mechanisms, in the following order:
#
# DT       existence of CDE DT Session Manager on the system
# XDM      "$HOME/.xsession" (executable)
# xinit    "$HOME/.x11start" (executable)
#
# If none of these startup mechanisms exist, a default window manager
# and terminal emulator client are started.
#
##############################################################################
#
# Initialize session startup logging
#
exec >/dev/null 2>/dev/null
LOGDIR=$HOME/.dt
LOGFILENAME=$LOGDIR/startlog
      . . . . .
      . . . . .
##############################################################################
#
# Global environment section
#
# DT pre-sets the following environment variables for each user.
#
# (internal)
# DISPLAY       set to the value of the first field in the Xservers file.
# HOME          set to the user's home directory (from /etc/passwd)
# LANG          set to the display's current NLS language (if any)
# LC_ALL        set to the value of $LANG
# LOGNAME       set to the user name
# PATH          set to the value of the Dtlogin "userPath" resource
# USER          set to the user name
# SHELL         set to the user's default shell (from /etc/passwd)
# TZ            set to the value of the Dtlogin "timeZone" resource
#
# (Xsession)
# TERM          set to xterm
# EDITOR        set to the default editor
# KBD_LANG      set to the value of $LANG for certain languages
# MAIL          set to "/var/mail/$USER"
#
# Three methods are available to modify or add to this list depending
# on the desired scope of the resulting environment variable.
#
# 1. X server and/or all users on a display     (Xconfig file)
# 2. all users on a display                     (Xsession file)
```

```
# 3. individual users                    (.dtprofile file)
#
#
###########################################################################
TERM=dtterm
SESSION_SVR='hostname'
DISPLAY_HOLD=$DISPLAY
     . . . . .
     . . . . .
###########################################################################
#
# Default desktop component configuration variable settings
#
# This section sets the default value for variables controlling
# some desktop components.
#
     . . . . .
     . . . . .
     . . . . .
###########################################################################
#
# Append desktop font aliases to font path
#
     . . . . .
     . . . . .
###########################################################################
#
# Source user's desktop profile
#
# This section determines if the user has a desktop profile in their
# home directory. If not, the desktop default profile is copied to
# the home directory. The desktop profile is then sourced. The purpose
# is to incorporate any per-user/per-session environment customizations
# and thereby propagate them to applications and desktop components.
#
DTSYSPROFILE=sys.dtprofile
DTPROFILE=.dtprofile
     . . . . .
     . . . . .
# load system default resources
     . . . . .
     . . . . .
#
# source the .dtprofile.
if [ -f $HOME/$DTPROFILE ]; then
  Log "sourcing $HOME/$DTPROFILE..."
. $HOME/$DTPROFILE
fi
#
# envirornment vars that must not be changed by dtprofile
DISPLAY=$DISPLAY_HOLD
# Safety checks for .dtprofile setting important env variables
# to non-existent or incorrect values. If so, reset to default values.
     . . . . .
     . . . . .
###########################################################################
#
# External Xsession processing section
#
# This section searches the Xsession.d subdirectory and sources
# the files contained therein. The purpose is to set up any
```

```
# per-user/per-session environment customizations and thereby propagate
# them to applications and desktop components.
#
DT_XSESSION_DIR=Xsession.d
for i in $DT_CONFIG_PATH
do
  if [[ -d $i/$DT_XSESSION_DIR ]]; then
    # Run custom Xsession scripts for this session.
    for SCRIPT in $(ls $i/$DT_XSESSION_DIR); do
      if [ -x $i/$DT_XSESSION_DIR/$SCRIPT -a \
        \( ! -d $i/$DT_XSESSION_DIR/$SCRIPT \) ]; then
        Log "sourcing $i/$DT_XSESSION_DIR/$SCRIPT..."
        .$i/$DT_XSESSION_DIR/$SCRIPT
      fi
    done
  fi
  done
##############################################################################
#
# Startup section.
#
# Note: The ksh syntax ${parameter%% *} is used when appropriate to
#         remove any command line options that may have been included
#         in the definition of a DT executable below.
#
##############################################################################
#
# Prepare for session startup #
      .....
      .....
#
# Start the session for different user's shells
Log "session log file is $dtstart_sessionlogfile"
      .....
      .....
case ${SHELL##*/} in
csh )     .....
          .....
  (set path = ( $DT_BINPATH \$path /usr/openwin/bin ); $tooltalk ); \
  $startup >>&! $dtstart_sessionlogfile" ;;
tcsh).
          .....
          .....
  (set path = ( $DT_BINPATH \$path /usr/openwin/bin ); $tooltalk ); \
  $startup >>&! $dtstart_sessionlogfile" ;;
*)
          .....
          .....
  PATH=/usr/dt/bin:\ $PATH:/usr/openwin/bin $tooltalk; \
  $startup >> $dtstart_sessionlogfile 2>&1" ;;
esac
          .....
          .....
###################### eof ################################
```

CDE does not support an individual *.Xresources* file; there is no such file in the user's home directory. ***CDE*** provides the common *Xresources* file that contains the resource definitions specifying the appearance of the login screen. This file could be customized, but not on a per-user basis; the login widget is common for all users. The default *Xresources* file is */usr/dt/config/Xresources.* For a customization, the file should be copied into */etc/dt/config/Xresources*, and then modified. ***CDE*** first searches for the *Xresources* in the directory */etc/dt/config*, and then in */usr/dt/config*.

For an individual user X environment setting, the *$HOME/.dtprofile* file is available. This file is used to set anything specific for a user; otherwise the default setting is applied. The *.dtprofile* file coexists together with well-known UNIX user login script files, *.profile* or *.login*, depending on the user's login shell. We will talk more about this file later in the paragraph treating the shell environment.

However, there is another ***CDE client***, unknown in earlier X versions, important in managing a user session; this is the CDE session manager ***dtsession***. The ***dtsession*** client manages a user session from login to logout. It supports per-user basis:

- To initialize a session
- To launch a window manager by default ***dtwm***
- To restore a home (default) or current session
- To lock a session
- To launch a screen saver on command or timeout
- To act as a color server for other DT clients
- To save home (default) or current session
- To display and handle a dialog at logout
- To terminate a session

dtsession relies on the following files:

- The customized file */etc/dt/config/en_US/sys.session* , or the default file */usr/dt/config/en_US/sys.session* that specifies a set of applications for the user's initial session. It searches first for the customized file.
- The customized file */etc/dt/config/en_US/sys.resources*, or the default file */usr/dt/config/en_US/sys.resources* that specifies desktop resources. It searches first for the customized file.
- The file *.Xdefault* in the user's home directory that specifies user specified resources
- The file */usr/dt/app-defaults/en_US/Dtsession* that specifies the default *dtsession* resources.

Actually, the correct paths for all files listed here include the subdirectory identified by the environment variable $LANG, in this case specified by *en_US*.

Here is an example, the user's . *Xdefault* file on Solaris 2.6 platform. It is easy to recognize the Sun X flavor named OpenWindows:

```
$ cat /home/bjl/.Xdefaults
OpenWindows.WorkspaceColor:        #40a0c0
OpenWindows.IconLocation:          top
OpenWindows.MultiClickTimeout:     4
OpenWindows.SelectDisplaysMenu:    False
OpenWindows.WindowColor:           #b7e5e5
OpenWindows.DragRightDistance:     100
OpenWindows.Beep:                  always
OpenWindows.SetInput:              followmouse
OpenWindows.ScrollbarPlacement:    right
OpenWindows.PopupJumpCursor:       True
# ======================================
```

Up to now, we have mentioned a number of script files, or programs, that are invoking by *Xsession,* or *dtsession,* or whatever. All these programs could be customized on a systemwide basis, and many of them on a user-specific basis. ***CDE*** includes a default systemwide setting in the directory */usr/dt/app-defaults/en_US* . By using the precise CDE terminology, these files are resource description files for different CDE applications; practically, they are configuration files that enable application customizations. It is easy to recognize these files; they usually start with the prefix "*Dt*" (pay attention to the capital "D"). We already mentioned one of them: "*Dtsession,*" when we talked about the *dtsession* script. For an individual user-based customization, the corresponding resource file could be copied into the user home directory and modified accordingly.

Some default resource files are shown in the following list of existing files on Solaris 2.6 (the "en_US" subdirectory is the link to "C"):

$ ls -C /usr/dt/app-defaults/C

```
Dt          Dtfile        Dtksh         Dtsession   Sdtfontadm
Dtbuilder   Dthello       Dtmail        Dtstyle     Sdtfprop
Dtcalc      Dthelpprint   Dtpad         Dtterm      Sdtimage
Dtcm        Dthelpview    Dtprintinfo   Dtwm        Solregis
Dtcreate    Dticon        Dtscreen      Sdtaudio    UNIXbindings
```

22.4.3 Window Manager Customizations

Window managers are launched by the *Xsession* script, directly or indirectly (as for CDE by the invoked *dtsession* script). Their customization is crucial for the user overall look and feel of X; a window manager configuration is defined by its startup **rc** file. We will discuss the two currently most used window managers: Motif Window Manager (***mwm***) and its configuration file *.mwmrc,* and CDE (or DT) Window Manager (***dtwm***) and its configuration file *.dtwmrc.*

22.4.3.1 Motif Window Manager (mwm)

Let us start with the older window manager, ***mwm***. We already mentioned a systemwide ***mwm*** configuration file *system.mwmrc;* however, a more appropriate term for this file could be a default window manager configuration file. X works in the following way: it searches for a configuration file in several possible locations, starting from the user's home directory and ending with the systemwide default configuration file; the first file found will be used to configure window manager. A user has a chance to set his/her own X configuration; otherwise, the default file always exists and defines a decent and reasonable X environment. It is recommended to copy the default configuration into the user's home directories, i.e., *system.mwmrc* into *.mwmrc* (this is the task of the administrator), and give users an opportunity to modify them. Otherwise, X would use the default configuration file (in this case, the file *system.mwmrc* found in some of the assumed locations; at the end in the */usr/lib/X11* directory), without any individual customization. As a matter of fact, in most cases, it is too much for users to modify their individual configurations, so the systemwide default setting is actually used.

Here is an example. Comments in **bold** are not a part of the file; they are added for better understanding of the file:

$ cat /usr/lib/X11/system.mwmrc

```
#
# DEFAULT mwm RESOURCE DESCRIPTION FILE (system.mwmrc and .mwmrc)
```

```
#
# menu pane descriptions
# Root Menu Description          =>
```

The "Root Menu" is invoked by clicking in the root window (see the Button Bindings description). The "Root Menu" is the pop-down menu with the here specified fields. By clicking on the field, the corresponding function is started.

```
Menu RootMenu
{
"Root Menu"          f.title
"New Window"         f.exec "xterm &"
"Shuffle Up"         f.circle_up
"Shuffle Down"       f.circle_down
"Refresh"            f.refresh
no-label             f.separator
"Restart..."         f.restart
}
# Default Window Menu Description          =>
```

This is the default window menu; it can be started (function *f.post_wmenu*) using an appropriate key or button (defined by Key or Button Bindings)

```
Menu Default Window Menu
{
Restore      _R     Alt<Key>F5      f.normalize
Move         _M     Alt<Key>F7      f.move
Size         _S     Alt<Key>F8      f.resize
Minimize     _n     Alt<Key>F9      f.minimize
Maximize     _x     Alt<Key>F10     f.maximize
Lower        _L     Alt<Key>F3      f.lower
no-label                            f.separator
Close        _C     Alt<Key>F4      f.kill
}
#
# key binding descriptions         =>
```

This resource is a set of key bindings that are used to configure window manager behavior; a function defined as "*f.function_name*" is started when a key is pressed within the indicated context.

```
Keys DefaultKeyBindings
{
Shift<Key>Escape                 window/icon            f.post_wmenu
Meta<Key>space                   window/icon            f.post_wmenu
Meta<Key>Tab                     root/icon/window       f.next_key
Meta Shift<Key>Tab               root/icon/window       f.prev_key
Meta<Key>Escape                  root/icon/ window      f.next_key
Meta Shift<Key>Escape            root/icon/window       f.prev_key
Meta Shift Ctrl<Key>exclam       root/con/window        f.set_behavior
Meta<Key>F6                      window                 f. next_key transient
Meta Shift<Key>F6                window                 f.prev_key transient
<Key>F4                          icon                   f.post_wmenu
}
#
# button binding descriptions         =>
```

This resource is a set of button bindings that are used to configure window manager behavior; a function defined as "*f.function_name*" is started when a button press occurs with the pointer over a framed client window, an icon, or the root window.

```
Buttons DefaultButtonBindings
{
<Btn1Down>      icon/frame     f.raise
<Btn3Down>      icon           f.post_wmenu
<Btn1Down>      root           f.menu RootMenu
}
Buttons ExplicitButtonBindings
```

```
{
.....
.....
}
Buttons PointerButtonBindings
{
.....
.....
}
#
# END OF mwm RESOURCE DESCRIPTION FILE
```

A full explanation of available functions specified as *f.function_name* can be found in the manual pages for the ***mwm*** window manager.

22.4.3.2 CDE Window Manager (dtwm)

The same approach is implemented in the *CDE environment;* the only differences are in the locations of files and their names. The default CDE window manager configuration file (sometimes also called the *window manager resource description file*) *sys.dtwmrc* lives in the directory */usr/dt/config*. The manager searches for the following files (using the Bourne/Korn shell notation for the user's home directory):

```
$HOME/.dt/en_US/dtwmrc              <- the "en_US" is linked to the "C" subdirectory
$HOME/.dt/dtwmrc
/etc/dt/config/en_US/sys.dtwmrc
/etc/dt/config/sys.dtwmrc
/usr/dt/config/en_US/sys.dtwmrc
/usr/dt/config/sys.dtwmrc           <- this is the default file
```

Again, the first file found is the first used; at the end, the default settings must be found.

```
$ cat /usr/dt/config/sys.dtwmrc
################################################################################
#
# Original copy: /usr/dt/config/C/sys.dtwmrc
#
# The Resource Description File for the CDE Window Manager dtwm
#
# (c) Copyright 1993, 1994 Hewlett-Packard Company.
# (c) Copyright 1993, 1994 International Business Machines Corp.
# (c) Copyright 1993, 1994 Sun Microsystems, Inc.
# (c) Copyright 1993, 1994 Unix System Labs, Inc., a subsidiary
# of Novell, Inc.
#
# $XConsortium: sys.dtwmrc.src /main/cde1_maint/3 1995/10/30 17:23:26 drk $
#
################################################################################
###
#
# Please make a COPY of this file before editing it.
#
# Personalized copies typically exist as:
#
# $HOME/.dt/dtwmrc
```

```
#
###
###
#
# Root Menu Description
#
###
Menu DtRootMenu      =>  The "Root Menu" is invoked by clicking in the root window; it is
                         the pop-down menu with the here specified fields. By clicking on
                         the field, the corresponding function is started.
{
   "Workspace Menu"                  f.title
   "Programs"                        f.menu ProgramsMenu
   no-label                          f.separator
   "Shuffle Up"                      f.circle_up
   "Shuffle Down"                    f.circle_down
   "Refresh"                         f.refresh
   "Minimize/Restore Front Panel"    f.toggle_frontpanel
   no-label                          f.separator
   "Restart Workspace Manager..."    f.restart
   no-label                          f.separator
   "Log out..."                      f.action ExitSession
}
Menu ProgramsMenu      =>  This is the submenu in the "Root Menu".
{
"Programs"                 f.title
"File Manager..."          f.action DtfileHome
"Text Editor..."           f.action TextEditor
"Mailer..."                f.action Dtmail
"Calendar..."              f.action Dtcm
no-label                   f.separator
"Terminal..."              f.action Terminal
"Console..."               f.action DttermConsole
no-label                   f.separator
"Clock..."                 f.action OWclock
"Calculator..."            f.action Dtcalc
"Performance Meter..."     f.action OWperfmeter
"Printer Manager..."       f.action DtPrintManager
"Audio Tool..."            f.action OWaudiotool
no-label                   f.separator
"Image Viewer..."          f.action SDTimage
"Snapshot..."              f.action SDTsnapshot
"Icon Editor..."           f.action Dticon
no-label                   f.separator
"Style Manager..."         f.action Dtstyle
"App Manager..."           f.action Dtappmgr
"Help..."                  f.action Dthelpview
"AnswerBook..."            f.action OWanswerbook
}
       .....
       .....
###
#
# Key Bindings Description
#
###
       .....
       .....
###
#
# Mouse Button Bindings Description
```

```
#
###
        .....
        .....
###
#
# Defaults: Window menus, key bindings, and mouse button bindings
#
###
        .....
        .....
###
#
# User Customization: $HOME/.dt/user.dtwmrc (if it exists)      => This is an alternate way to append
#                                                                  user-specific settings to the system-
                                                                   wide ones
###
INCLUDE
{
$HOME/.dt/user.dtwmrc
}
################# End of the dtwmrc file ####################
```

22.4.4 The Shell Environment

How does the X environment relate to the UNIX shell? Although the shell is external to the X environment, X clients running on UNIX systems necessarily depend on the shell being set properly — more specifically, on properly defined environment variables and the command search path.

The most important shell environment variable for an X client is DISPLAY. The DISPLAY environment variable is used by all X clients to determine what X server to display on. Since any X client can connect to any X server that allows it, all X clients need to know what display to connect to upon startup. If DISPLAY is not properly set, the client cannot execute.

The DISPLAY variable can be simply checked, for example:

 # echo $DISPLAY

:0.0

Earlier X11 releases could also display *unix:0.0.*

A good time to define the DISPLAY variable is probably when a user logs into the system (same as when we are specifying a terminal for the character-based sessions). For example, the DISPLAY variable could be defined as a global one in the user's *.login,* or *.profile* file, depending on the user's shell:

setenv DISPLAY hostname:0.0

DISPLAY=hostname:0.0 ; export DISPLAY

Obviously *hostname* is the X terminal name, known to DNS, NIS, or local host database (could also be an IP address). There are also opinions that the DISPLAY variable should not be a part of login script, because it restricts a user to a specific X terminal.

The value of DISPLAY variable can be overridden from the command line by using:

 # xterm -display hostname:0.0 &

This command invokes the ***xterm*** program to run in background; ***xterm*** is a terminal emulator for the X window system; it provides DEC VT102 and Tektronix 4014 compatible terminals for programs that cannot use the window system directly. The *-display* option specifies the X server to contact, in this case the host ***hostname***. The host name is followed by the colon and the string 0.0 which specifies the *display_number* and the *screen_number.* For better understanding of the syntax of the DISPLAY variable, please refer to the previous discussion about the *Xservers* file in Section 22.2.2.1.2.

In the case of a local console display, both names: "***:0.0***" and "***hostname:0.0***" are acceptable and they work; however, they imply different ways of connecting to the X server. The first one specifies that the client should connect using UNIX domain sockets (IPC), while the other one specifies that the client should connect using Internet domain sockets (TCP/IP).

Another important issue concerning shell environment is the search path. The search path needs to include the directories containing X executables. Assuming that the X executables are in the */usr/bin/X11* and */usr/local/bin/X11* directories, the corresponding user's startup shell script *.profile* and *.cshrc* should be modified by extended PATH entries, respectively:

```
PATH=/usr/ucb:/ bin:/ usr/bin:/ usr/bin/X11:/ usr/local/bin/X11:.
export PATH
```

and

```
set path = (/usr/ucb /bin /usr/bin /usr/bin/X11 /usr/local/bin/X11)
```

Note that this is only an example, and that other directories can also be included or omitted; it can also be realized in different ways.

The *.xsession* startup script, typical of older X releases, had redefined the search path, unless specified otherwise. It assumed the standard locations for X client programs. If clients resided in different directories, an appropriate modification had been required.

The CDE counterpart, the *.dtprofile* script, coexists with the *.profile* file (supposing the user Bourne or Korn shell environment; the same is true also for *.login* and the C shell). Simply, the usual character-based login script *.profile* could be sourced by the *.dtprofile,* or ignored, i.e., replaced. This idea was inherited from other vendor-specific X flavors and has been proved to be the very effective one. This is quite obvious from the following example; the whole file is actually a long discussion about the file purpose and how to implement it; please, read it carefully.

```
$ cat /home/bjl/.dtprofile
#############################################################################
###
### .dtprofile
###
### user personal environment variables
###
### Common Desktop Environment (CDE)
###
###
### $Revision: 1.7 $
###
#############################################################################
###
### Your $HOME/.dtprofile is read each time you login to the Common Desktop
```

```
### Enviroment (CDE) and is the place to set or override desktop
### environment variables for your session. Environment variables set in
### $HOME/.dtprofile are made available to all applications on the desktop.
### The desktop will accept either sh or ksh syntax for the commands in
### $HOME/.dtprofile.
###
### By default, the desktop does not read your standard $HOME/.profile
### or $HOME/.login files. This can be changed by uncommenting the
### DTSOURCEPROFILE variable assignment at the end of this file. The
### desktop reads .profile if your $SHELL is "sh" or "ksh", or .login
### if your $SHELL is "csh".
###
### The desktop reads the .dtprofile and .profile/.login without an
### associated terminal emulator such as xterm or dtterm. This means
### there is no available command line for interaction with the user.
### This being the case, these scripts must avoid using commands that
### depend on having an associated terminal emulator or that interact
### with the user. Any messages printed in these scripts will not be
### seen when you log in and any prompts such as by the 'read' command
### will return an empty string to the script. Commands that set a
### terminal state, such as "tset" or "stty" should be avoided.
###
### With minor editing, it is possible to adapt your .profile or .login
### for use both with and without the desktop. Group the statements not
### appropriate for your desktop session into one section and enclose them
### with an "if" statement that checks for the setting of the "DT"
### environment variable. When the desktop reads your .profile or .login
### file, it will set "DT" to a non-empty value for which your .profile or
### .login can test.
###
### example for sh/ksh
###
###   if [ ! "$DT" ]; then
###      #
###      #commands and environment variables not appropriate for desktop
###      #
###      stty ...
###         tset ...
###         DISPLAY=mydisplay:0
###         ...
###   fi
###
###   # environment variables common to both desktop and non-desktop
###   #
###   PATH=$H OME/bin:$PATH
###   MYVAR=value
###   export MYVAR
###   ...
###
### example for csh
###
###   if ( ! ${?DT} ) then
###      #
###      # commands and environment variables not appropriate for desktop
###      #
###      stty...
###      tset...
###      setenv DISPLAY mydisplay:0
###      ...
###   endif
###
```

```
###  #environment variables common to both desktop and non-desktop
###  #
###  setenv PATH $HOME/bin:$PATH
###  setenv MYVAR value
###  ...
###
### Errors in .dtprofile or .profile (.login) may prevent a successful
### login. If after you login, your session startup terminates and you
### are presented with the login screen, this might be the cause. If this
### happens, select the Options->Sessions->Failsafe Session item on the
### login screen, login and correct the error. The $HOME/.dt/startlog and
### $HOME/.dt/errorlog files may be helpful in identifying errors.
###
# If $HOME/.profile (.login) has been edited as described above, uncomment
# the following line.
#
DTSOURCEPROFILE=true
#
```

The preceding example, and this is the most common *dtprofile* configuration, fully includes the *.profile,* or *.login* file, depending on user's shell; consequently, the previous shell environment setting stays valid. However, it requires a slightly modified *.profile* file, as it could be read in the comments of the presented file.

The idea to integrate the existing character-based environment and new graphic environment has already been a part of other vendor-specific X flavors. ***CDE*** brought that as a standard approach, enabling both options, to include, or exclude *.profile* (or alternatively, *.login*) file when a user logs in to the system (of course, in an X environment).

To illustrate that, the *.vueprofile* script is presented. *Visual User Environment* (***VUE***) is the HP-specific X flavor, implemented on all HP-UX platforms: from HP-UX 9.0x, via HP-UX 10.x, and also preserved on HP-UX 11.x. New HP-UX releases support both ***VUE*** and ***CDE***. The *.vuelogin* is the VUE counterpart for the *.dtlogin* file; actually, it is fair to say the opposite, the file *.vuelogin* existed earlier. The file is well commented, so an additional explanation is not needed.

$ cat /users/bjl/.vueprofile

```
#!/ bin/sh
##########################################################################
###
### .vueprofile
### user personal environment variables
### Hewlett-Packard Visual User Environment, Version 3.0
###
##########################################################################
###
### VUE pre-sets the following environment variables for each user.
###
###  DISPLAY               set to the value of the first field in the Xservers file
###  EDITOR                set to the HP VUE default editor
###  ENV                   set to "$HOME/.kshrc"
###  HOME                  set to the user's home directory (from /etc/passwd)
###  KBD_LANG              set to the value of $LANG for some languages (see Xsession)
###  LANG                  set to the display's current NLS language (if any)
###  LC_ALL, LC_MESSAGES   set to the value of $LANG
###  LOGNAME               set to the user name
###  MAIL                  set to "/usr/mail/$USER"
###  PATH                  set to the value of the Vuelogin "userPath" resource
###  USER                  set to the user name
###  SHELL                 set to the user's default shell (from /etc/passwd)
```

```
### TERM                          set to xterm
### TZ                            set to the value of the Vuelogin "timeZone" resource
###
### Three methods are available to modify or add to this list depending
### on the desired scope of the resulting environment variable.
###
### 1. X server and/or all users on a display     (Xconfig file)
### 2. all users on a display                     (Xsession file)
### 3. individual users                           (.vueprofile file)
###
###
### Personal environment variables can be set in the script file
### "$HOME/.vueprofile". The files /etc/profile and $HOME/.profile are
### not read by VUE as they may contain terminal I/O based commands
### inappropriate for a graphical interface. Users should set up
### ".vueprofile" with personal environment variables for their VUE
### session.
###
### VUE will accept either sh, ksh, or csh syntax for the commands in this
### file. The commands should only be those that set environment
### variables, not any that perform terminal I/O, ex. "tset" or "stty".
### If the first line of ".vueprofile" is #!/bin/sh, #!/bin/ksh, or
### #!/bin/csh, VUE will use the appropriate shell to parse the commands.
### Otherwise the user's default shell ($SHELL) will be used.
###
### With minor editing, it is possible to adapt $HOME/.profile (.login)
### for use both with and without HP VUE. Group the statements not
### allowed for VUE into one section and enclose them with an "if"
### statement that checks for the setting of the "VUE" environment
### variable. Then set the "VUE" environment variable at the bottom of
### this script (.vueprofile) and log in again. From then on changes
### need only be made to $HOME/.profile (.login).
###
### example for sh/ksh
### #
#### commands and environment variables used when logging in without VUE
### #
### if [ ! "$VUE" ]; then
###     stty...
###       tset...
###       DISPLAY=mydisplay:0
###       MAIL=/usr/mail/$USER
###       EDITOR=/bin/vi
###       ...
### fi
###
### #
### # environment variables common to both VUE and non-VUE
### #
### PATH=$HOME/bin:$PATH
###       ...
###
### Errors in .vueprofile or .profile (.login) may prevent a successful
### login. If so, log in via the Fail-safe session and correct the error.
###
##########################################################################
#
# if $HOME/.profile (.login) has been edited as described above, uncomment
# one of the two following lines, depending on your default shell.
#
VUE=true; export VUE; . $HOME/.profile; unset VUE          # sh, ksh
```

```
# setenv VUE true; source $HOME/.login;          unsetenv VUE # csh
#
# @(#) $Revision: 66.1 $
```

The resemblance between *.vueprofile* and *.dtprofile* files is obvious; although, the *.dtprofile* file is an improved version. The *.vueprofile* also requires a corresponding modification of the user's *.profile* file (or *.login*). What it means can be seen in the following example:

```
$ cat /users/bjl/.profile
# User .profile file (/bin/sh initialization).
#
# Testing VUE environment
if [ ! "$VUE" ]; then
   # Set up the terminal:        <----    this part is active only if VUE is not implemented!
   TERM=vt100
   export TERM
   tset -Q
   stty erase "^?" kill "^U" intr "^C" eof "^D"
   stty hupcl ixon ixoff
   tabs
   echo " Your terminal is $TERM"
   echo ""
   # Set up the shell environment:
   set -u
   trap "echo 'logout'" 0
   # Set up the shell variables:
   EDITOR=vi
   export EDITOR
fi                               <----    the end of the part
# Set up the search paths:
        PATH=$PATH:/usr/local/TeX/bin:.
        export PATH
#
```

22.5 Miscellaneous

22.5.1 Other Startup Methods

X display manager, ***xdm*** (still widely in use), and the newer CDE related ***dtlogin*** are the methods of choice for starting X. This is a very elegant way of starting an X session on an X server (usually, an X terminal), remotely, or locally. We have already elaborated on these programs, as well as other X programs and configuration files around; therefore, we are more or less familiar with this startup procedure. The ***xdm***, or ***dtlogin***, are typically started during the system booting, they run as daemons through the whole system life and take care of keeping the X service running and getting users logged in. After the startup, a window with the login widget appears, welcoming users and asking for user name and password. After a user has successfully logged in, they start up the user's X environment and everything needed for an X session.

However, for the sites that support more than one window system, this is not the best choice. Such sites might choose to use the ***xinit*** program instead for starting X manually. A user logs-in in a conventional way and then executes the ***xinit*** command. The command simply invokes a user-specified program to start the server, invokes another user-specified program to start any desired client, and then waits for either to finish. When the X client exits, the ***xinit*** will kill the X server, and then terminate. Since either, or both, of the user-specified programs may be shell scripts, this gives substantial flexibility at the expense of nice interface (for this reason, ***xinit*** is not intended for end users).

The ***xinit*** is an obsolete program, and it is slowly being pushed out. It is supposed (and it is also announced by many vendors) that new X releases will no longer support ***xinit***.

Strictly speaking, the ***xinit*** is the core program for starting X; however, it is not the only one. The ***startx*** script is a front-end to the ***xinit*** that provides a somewhat nicer user interface; some X flavors use the ***x11start*** script instead. For the brief discussion that follows, this is not of special interest, so all references will be made to the ***xinit***.

Supposing the local display is being used and the ***xinit*** was activated from the command line, the starting procedure consists of:

- The ***xinit*** first starts up the X server for the local display; by default, it starts the generic program called */usr/bin/X11/X* (which is usually a link to the real server program); however, the default value can be overridden by entering another command in the user's file *$HOME/.xserverrc.*
- Since the X server was started, the ***xinit*** looks for a shell script called *$HOME/.xinitrc;* if the file does not exist, ***xinit*** uses the default systemwide file */usr/lib/X11/xinit/xinitrc.*
- If both files are missing, the ***xinit*** starts a default ***xterm*** session:

  xterm -geometry +1+1 -n login -display :0

  and sends a single ***xterm*** window to the local display to get a user started.

Here is an obsolete, but illustrative, example of the ***xinit*** systemwide configuration file *xinitrc*:

$ cat /usr/lib/X11/xinit/xinitrc

```
#!/bin/sh
userresources=$HOME/.Xresources
usermodmap=$HOME/.Xmodmap
sysresources=/usr/lib/X11/xinit/.Xresources
sysmodmap=/usr/lib/X11/xinit/.Xmodmap
# merge in defaults and keymaps
if [ -f $sysresources ]; then
xrdb -merge $sysresources
fi
if [ -f $sysmodmap ]; then
   xmodmap $sysmodmap
fi
if [ -f $userresources ]; then
   xrdb -merge $userresources
fi
if [ -f $usermodmap ]; then
   xmodmap $usermodmap
fi
# start some nice programs
twm&
xclock -geometry 50×50-1+1 &
xterm -geometry 80×50+494 +51 &
xterm -geometry 80×20+494 -0 &
```

The configuration file supposes the start of the ***tab window manager (twm)*** in the background and launches the ***clock*** and two ***xterm*** windows.

All of the rules related to the *.xsession* file could be applied to the *.xinitrc* file; this is why, quite often, the *.xinitrc* file was simply linked to the *.xsession*. However, before linking two files, there are three points to be considered:

1. The *.xsession* file is generally a shell script, but it can actually be any executable file. The *.xinitrc* file must be a Bourne shell script.
2. The *.xsession* file must be an executable file. The *.xinitrc* file does not have to be executable.
3. The *.xsession* script does not inherit the user's login shell environment. The *.xinitrc* script inherits the environment of the shell from which the ***xinit*** was started.

22.5.2 A Permanent X11 Installation

An X11 package (today, this is primarily the CDE package) is mostly a standard part of a UNIX installation. It means, upon the UNIX installation, X11 is more or less ready for use; of course, site-dependent X11 setting is always assumed, although default X setting works in most cases. For some UNIX platforms, the installation of the X11 package itself could even be skipped, especially if the platform supports the vendor-specific X flavor (although, today, it is quite common to have a CDE package installed together with a vendor-specific X flavor, or customized in the vendor-specific way). For others, the X11 could still be treated as optional software. Nevertheless, an installation approach with the X11 is the same as any other software package, and must be configured appropriately for future system rebootings; it means a certain tribute should be paid to the X11 **rc** startup initialization.

In the past, an X11 **rc** setting was a must; X11 used to be an optional software to be added later, tested, and then integrated into the overall UNIX system. The integration assumed a permanent X11 installation and a corresponding **rc** startup setting.

X11 is started during the system startup through the corresponding **rc** initialization scripts, as is common for all UNIX daemons. On a typical BSD platform this is the */etc/rc.local* file, while on a System V platform even the */etc/inittab* table could be used. A brief survey of different UNIX flavors follows:

- On ***Solaris 2.x*** platform the **rc** start/stop script *dtlogin* is used; the corresponding ***S-start***, and ***K-stop*** scripts are hard linked to this file:

  $ ls -li /etc/init.d | grep "dtlogin"
  203657 -rwxr--r-- 4 root sys 2613 Jun 26 1998 dtlogin

  $ ls -li /etc/rc2.d | grep "dtlogin"
  203657 -rwxr--r-- 4 root sys 2613 Jun 26 1998 S99dtlogin

  $ ls -li /etc/rc0.d | grep "dtlogin"
  203657 -rwxr--r-- 4 root sys 2613 Jun 26 1998 K10dtlogin

- On ***HP-UX*** platform (9.0x, 10.10, 10.20, 10.30 ...) the start procedure is the same, except the other file name and locations are used, and symbolic links are implemented:

$ ls -l /sbin/init.d | grep dtlogin
-r-xr-xr-x 1 bin bin 3002 May 30 1998 dtlogin.rc
$ ls -l /sbin/rc3.d | grep dtlogin
lrwxr-xr-x 1 root sys 23 Jun 10 1998 S990dtlogin.rc -> /sbin/init.d/dtlogin.rc
$ ls -l /sbin/rc2.d | grep dtlogin
lrwxr-xr-x 1 root sys 23 Jun 10 1998 K100dtlogin.rc -> /sbin/init.d/dtlogin.rc

- The HP flavor of X, ***VUE***, is started through the */etc/inittab* file:
  vue:34:respawn:/usr/vue/bin/vuerc
- On ***SunOS 4.1.x*** the */etc/rc.local* script is used; a typical sequence to start the ***xdm*** was:
  if [-f /usr/bin/X11/wdm]; then
  * /usr/bin/X11/xdm; echo -n "XDM"*
  fi
- On ***IRIX*** platform */etc/inittab* is used; here is an example with the ***xdm***:
  xw:23:respawn:/usr/bin/X11/xdm -nodaemon
- On ***AIX*** platform the */etc/rc.tcpip* script is used; for example, an entry to start the ***xdm*** looked like:
  start /usr/bin/X11/xdm "$src_running"

22.5.3 A Few X-Related Commands

X is an extremely rich environment, that offers users a lot. Once users become familiar with X, it is hard to believe they would be eager to return to the character-based world. Advantages and benefits of using X are enormous, and this session should encourage administrators to bring X to life on their systems. Programmers and developers should seriously consider the X environment for their new projects; everybody could only benefit from an X implementation.

Besides a nice and friendly environment, X also brought many new, powerful, and versatile utilities (commands) that could be efficiently used, especially for script programming, to make scripts more powerful and productive. We will list a few X-related commands; readers are encouraged to browse the manual pages for more information, as well as for other X commands.

xwd The utility to dump an image of an X window. It allows storage of window images in a specially formatted dump file that could later be read by other X utilities for redisplay, printing, editing, formatting, archiving, image processing, etc.

xwud The X image displayer. The utility undumps and displays in a window an image saved in a specially formatted dump file (produced by ***xwd***).

xpr The utility to print an X window dump. It takes as input a window dump file produced by ***xwd*** and formats it for output on PostScript and some other PCL compatible printers.

The ***xwud*** is a complementary utility to the ***xwd***. The two utilities could be combined in a very attractive way. For example, we can use ***xwd*** to dump (save) an X image at an X display into a file, and then launch the saved X image by the ***xwud*** to another X display.

In that way, it is possible to monitor X users by scanning (dumping) their screens and display the dumped images at the administrator's screen. By involving ***xpr,*** printouts are also possible.

By presenting these X utilities, we will close our session dedicated to X11. After quite a long discussion, and many real-life examples, we should be ready to enter successfully into the X administration arena.

23

Kernel Reconfiguration

23.1 Introduction to Kernel Reconfiguration

The ***UNIX kernel*** is the part of the UNIX operating system that manages the system hardware. Kernel presents control software between OS and the underlying hardware, merging all system devices into a functional OS controllable system. Kernel remains memory resident while the system is up; otherwise a system would behave very poorly. We have already talked about the kernel in Chapter 4 when we discussed system startup. Then we learned that the executable image of the kernel is invoked after a bootstrap program execution and it continues to run at all times. Now, we return to this topic to elaborate the duties of the system administrator regarding the kernel.

The *kernel* is a site-dependent, memory resident executable program; this means the *kernel* must be appropriately configured for a particular UNIX system implementation. Each installed UNIX system also has a configured kernel; this is usually a generic kernel compliant for most system implementations. However, site-specific conditions and a special system mission could require different, more appropriate kernel configuration. Then we have to change an existing kernel, and we talk about ***kernel reconfiguration.*** Generally, reconfiguring the *kernel* means to create, or to modify, an appropriate *kernel configuration file,* which defines the kernel correspondingly. In most cases it also means to compile a reconfigured kernel afterward. All changes in a kernel become effective upon rebooting the system, because the newly configured kernel could be invoked only at the next system startup; there is no way to change an actual memory resident kernel image.

As a matter of fact, a kernel reconfiguration presents a routine procedure defined by UNIX designers that an administrator should strictly follow. There is not a lot of freedom in implementing this procedure; the existing rules must be fully respected, or our kernel reconfiguration will fail. A failed kernel also means a "sick" UNIX system, sometimes even a not-bootable one. An administrator must know how to handle such situations; a full understanding of this procedure is very instrumental in doing this successfully. It raises a crucial question, how to bring the system back from a "bad" kernel to the previously "workable" one. We must always be prepared for the worst-case scenario.

BSD and System V have very different kernel configuration files and reconfiguration procedures. Also, within each of these two UNIX platforms, significant variations exist among different vendors. That is why it is probably more appropriate to talk about vendor-flavored kernel reconfiguration. Nevertheless, we will try to keep continuity with earlier chapters — partially by following this topic historically, and partially by elaborating on the dominant modern UNIX flavors.

The nature of a kernel makes it almost impossible to create a "universal kernel" applicable to any situation. Different hardware configurations require different kernel configurations, and some trade-off must be found. Some systems are shipped with a *minimal kernel*, so changes may be needed when new hardware or software is added. Usually when new software is installed, the kernel changes, if required, are performed automatically by the installation procedure. This is also the case when OS patches are implemented if the patches are kernel related. In both cases, to become effective, a system reboot is required after implementation.

23.2 Kernel Configuration Database

Both UNIX platforms, BSD and System V, use the ***kernel configuration files*** to specify and keep configuration data. Traditionally the configuration data had to be compiled into the kernel binary for later loading into the system memory and its effective usage. This is still the prevailing concept. For compilation purposes, usually some kind of front-end **config** command is used (sometimes this program has a different name, but always the same purpose) to build the kernel. A general approach assumes the UNIX kernel as a C program to be compiled and installed by using available UNIX utilities, primarily the **make** command. The front-end **config** command reads the *kernel configuration file* and generates the corresponding kernel binary. This procedure is not so straightforward and it is mostly realized in several steps. During this procedure, other UNIX commands are invoked (by the ***make*** utility) and other files are needed to compile and link the kernel. Generally, the kernel is built offline, and its execution started during the next system startup. Solaris has a slightly different approach — certain parts of the kernel are fully built online during the system startup.

Specifying an entry in the kernel configuration database does not mean that the system must possess the corresponding hardware device or peripheral. It means that the kernel will be ready to support such device or peripheral if it is attached to the system. In other words, specifying an entry in the kernel configuration file will enable the appropriate system's function. The system checks its current hardware configuration during its startup and initializes (activates) all existing devices and peripherals. However, if the entry for an existing device is missing in the kernel configuration file, the system cannot support this device at all.

One might think that a kernel configuration file should contain all possible entries, so we can be sure that any system hardware configuration will be supported. This is a nice idea, but such an approach will create a large, memory-consuming, slow-to-execute kernel image (do not forget that the kernel is a memory-resident program). Nevertheless, this is a trend among modern versions of UNIX. On the other hand, the approach of stripping a kernel configuration down to the existing system's exact hardware configuration can result in a restrictive kernel, inflexible for future system upgrades. Like everything in life, a satisfactory compromise should be achieved.

It is important to make a strict distinction between a *kernel configuration file* and the *kernel* itself. A kernel configuration file is an ASCII file that defines all kernel nondefault data and arguments. A kernel (or rather, a kernel image) is an image of the built kernel, a memory-resident executable that provides the interface between system hardware and the operating system. Modifying the kernel configuration file does not mean modifying the kernel itself; one more step is required: to compile, i.e., to rebuild, the kernel (Solaris is an exception because it rebuilds the kernel online).

23.3 BSD-Like Kernel Configuration Approach

In addition to the fact that each UNIX flavor has its own kernel configuration procedure independent of its prevailing UNIX platform affiliation, we will start here with SunOS flavor. For many years, SunOS was a main player in the UNIX arena and its kernel reconfiguration has been a number 1 issue. Today SunOS does not play the same role, but its educational value is still significant: SunOS is a good representative of BSD UNIX, with a comprehensive configuration structure important for an easier understanding of needed kernel administration. Keeping all that in mind, we are specifying its kernel configuration as BSD-like.

On a BSD platform, the kernel configuration file is usually located in the directory */usr/sys/conf*. On SunOS the directory is */usr/share/sys/sun4c/conf*. There is no standard name for the kernel configuration file, and it is common to name it after the name of the machine on which it is installed (however, it is not mandatory — a generic kernel works as well as the named one). A large kernel configuration file named ***GENERIC*** is a part of the UNIX installation, and it configures all of the standard devices for the system, including the network devices. No modifications are necessary for the generic kernel configuration file to run basic local and network services.

We will address several aspects of the kernel configuration. First, let us see the basic kernel configuration entries. Then we will talk about the kernel configuration procedure, and finally, about the available UNIX command for this purpose. At the end, we should have a full picture of how everything works on the BSD platform.

23.3.1 Basic Configuration Entries

The kernel contains an identifying string that is helpful in discovering the name of the configuration file itself. Assuming the usual kernel binary name *vmunix*:

$ strings /vmunix | grep SunOS
SunOS Release 4.1.3 (PATSY) #1: Fri Feb 25 13:59:37 EST 1996

The string enclosed in parentheses is the name of the configuration file. In this example, the name of the kernel configuration file is ***patsy***, while the kernel binary (kernel image) name is ***vmunix***. It is important to make a difference between kernel configuration data saved in the ASCII kernel configuration file, and the corresponding compiled kernel executable invoked during the system startup.

The configuration file contains a sequence of one-line entries specifying different aspects of the kernel's configuration. Basically, there are 12 different types of configuration lines, which are briefly described here:

1. ***machine*** — Identifies the system's architecture. This entry should not be changed.
2. ***cpu*** — Identifies the particular model, or often several models. It is not recommended that you change it, but building a kernel that only runs on one type of system reduces the kernel size.
3. ***ident*** — An identifier for the kernel. This should be the same as the name of the configuration file and the build directory. It is not the kernel's image file name, which is usually *vmunix*.

4. ***maxusers*** This is the most important configuration parameter, as it controls the size of the most important kernel tables. It is an estimate of the number of users the system will be able to service simultaneously and comfortably (count one user for each timesharing user, one for each window that is typically in use, and one for each diskless client served). It is not a limit on the maximum number of users for the system. Reducing ***maxusers*** is one way to increase the amount of available memory. However, many other system parameters are also decreased: the number of users that the system supports effectively, the number of processes that can run simultaneously, the number of files that can be open, etc. Generally, modifying ***maxusers*** will affect the system's performance significantly, so an appropriate tradeoff must be performed.

5. ***timezone*** The time zone in which the system is running. Its setting has become very complex to take into account all kinds of international timekeeping rules.

6. ***config*** There may be more *config lines*; they specify the actual name of the kernel executable, the location of the boot partition, and the location of the swapping and dump partitions. Usually, all those parameters are specified within the single *config line* with more arguments. If some of the arguments are missing, the kernel uses the default values.

7. ***options*** There may be a number of different options that the kernel supports. They often define certain optional system features. It is not enough, per se, to configure only the kernel; the appropriate hardware and software support must also exist on a system.

8. ***pseudo-device*** There may be a number of *pseudo-device lines.* Each line tells the kernel to include a certain software option that is technically a device driver but does not correspond to a physical device. Most of them are related to the networking and windowing systems. Although it seems that many of them could be eliminated and some space saved, in practice that is not the case. Networking and windowing are so basic to modern systems that it is almost inconceivable to operate without them.

The four remaining types of configuration lines involve ***Device Specification***; this is by far the most system-dependent part of the kernel configuration. It is possible to reduce the kernel's memory requirements by leaving out devices that you do not need. However, this can be tricky; many systems have hidden devices that you do not know about, but you need all the same. So, be extremely careful with removing devices from the kernel.

9. ***device-driver*** Sometimes specified only as ***device.*** These lines describe all devices except disk and tape controllers, disk and tape drives, and bus interfaces (i.e., controllers that connect one bus to another).

10. ***controller*** These lines describe disk controllers, tape controllers, and bus interfaces (i.e., controllers that connect one bus to another). Today, the most common controllers are the SCSI controllers.

11. *disk* These lines describe disk drives; a *controller line* by itself is not sufficient, because most disk controllers can handle two or more disk drives. That means a *disk line* is needed for every disk drive that exists. Today, disks are most often connected to a SCSI controller.

12. *tape* These lines describe tape drives. The same remarks for the *disk lines* are also valid for tapes.

Let us see what the *GENERIC* configuration file looks like on SunOS 4.1.3. The file itself is relatively well-commented; nevertheless, additional comments, printed in ***bold***, are included for a better understanding of the various entries.

```
$ cat /usr/share/sys/sun4c/conf/GENERIC
#
# @(#) GENERIC from master 1.28 90/09/21 SMI
#
# This config file describes a generic Sun-4c kernel, including all
# possible standard devices and software options.
#
# The following lines include support for all Sun-4c CPU types.
# There is little to be gained by removing support for particular
# CPUs, so you might as well leave them all in.
#
machine   "sun4c"              # Identifies the system's architecture and model
cpu       "SUN4C_60"           # Sun-4/60 (it's really for all the Sun-4c's)
#
# Name this kernel GENERIC.
#
ident     "GENERIC"            # To rename kernel, modify this name. If "GENERIC"
                               is used, the kernel name corresponds to the name
                               of the kernel configuration file.

# This kernel supports about 8 users. Count one user for each
# timesharing user, one for each window that you typically use, and one
# for each diskless client you serve. This is only an approximation used
# to control the size of various kernel data structures, not a hard limit.
#

maxusers  8                    #The most important parameter that controls the
                               size of the most important kernel tables, it is an
                               estimated value of the users that system will serve
                               without a decrease in the system performance
                               (taking into account additional load, as NFS, etc).
                               This is not a hard limit!
#
# Include all possible software options.  #There may be any number of options lines, which
                               request certain optional system features.

# The INET option is not really optional; every kernel must include it.
options INET          # basic networking support — mandatory
#
# The following options are all filesystem related. You only need
# QUOTA if you have UFS. You only need UFS if you have a disk.
# Diskless machines can remove QUOTA, UFS, and NFSSERVER. LOFS and TFS
```

```
# are only needed if you're using the Sun Network Software Environment.
# HSFS is only needed if you have a CD-ROM drive and want to access
# ISO-9660 or High Sierra format CD discs.
options QUOTA        # disk quotas for local disks
options UFS          # filesystem code for local disks
options NFSCLIENT    # NFS client side code
options NFSSERVER    # NFS server side code
options LOFS         # loopback filesystem — needed by NSE
options TFS          # translucent filesystem — needed by NSE
options TMPFS        # tmp (anonymous memory) filesystem
options HSFS         # High Sierra (ISO 9660) CD-ROM filesystem
options PCFS         # Unix access to MS-DOS filesystem
#
                     .....
                     .....
#
# Build one kernel based on this basic configuration.
# It will use the generic swap code so that you can have
# your root filesystem and swap space on any supported device.
# Put the kernel configured this way in a file named "vmunix".
Config vmunix swap generic
```

 # Specifies the actual name of the kernel executable, the location of the boot partition, and the locations of the swapping partitions (by default, those are the "a" partition on the first disk for the root, and the "b" partition for the primary swapping partition).

```
#
# Include support for all possible pseudo-devices.
```

#Pseudo-device lines tell the kernel to include certain software drivers that don't correspond to physical (hardware) devices.

```
#
# The first few are mostly concerned with networking.
# You should probably always leave these in.
pseudo-device  pty      # pseudo-tty's, also needed for SunView
pseudo-device  ether    # basic Ethernet support
pseudo-device  loop     # loopback network – mandatory
#
       .....
       .....
#
# The following section describes which standard
```

 # These lines spell out the configuration of the system's peripherals in more detail.

```
# device drivers this kernel supports.
#
device-driver  sbus       # 'driver' for sbus interface
device-driver  sbwtwo     # monochrome frame buffer
device-driver  gthree     # 8-bit color frame buffer
device-driver  cgsix      # 8-bit accelerated color frame buffer
device-driver  cgtwelve   # 24-bit accelerated color frame buffer
device-driver  dma        # 'driver' for dma engine on sbus interface
##################
device-driver  esp        # Emulex SCSI interface
##################
device-driver  fd         # Floppy disk
device-driver  audioamd   # AMD79C30A sound chip
```

```
device-driver   le          # LANCE ethernet
device-driver   zs          # UARTs
#
# The following section describes SCSI device unit assignments.
scsibus0 at esp                        # declare first scsi bus
disk sd0 at scsibus0 target 3 lun 0  # first hard SCSI disk
disk sd1 at scsibus0 target 1 lun 0  # second hard SCSI disk
disk sd2 at scsibus0 target 2 lun 0  # third hard SCSI disk
disk sd3 at scsibus0 target 0 lun 0  # fourth hard SCSI disk
tape st0 at scsibus0 target 4 lun 0  # first SCSI tape
tape st1 at scsibus0 target 5 lun 0  # second SCSI tape
disk sr0 at scsibus0 target 6 lun 0  # CD-ROM device
#
scsibus1 at esp                        # declare second scsi bus
        . . . . .
scsibus2 at esp                        # declare third scsi bus
        . . . . .
scsibus3 at esp                        # declare fourth scsi bus
        . . . . .
        . . . . .
```

23.3.2 The BSD-Like Kernel Configuration Procedure

The *README* file, which resides in the same directory as the *GENERIC* file, includes a detailed description of the kernel configuration procedure. This file is fully presented, with additional comments in ***bold:***

$ cat /usr/share/sys/sun4c/conf/README
CONFIGURING THE KERNEL
1. Choose a name for your configuration of the system; here, PICKLE.

2. Create the config file by making a writable copy of GENERIC:
cp GENERIC PICKLE; chmod +w PICKLE ***# Copy and rename the configuation file and make it writeable.***

3. Edit PICKLE to reflect your system, e.g., delete devices that will never be present on your system. ***# Modify and create a new configuration file.***

4. Run config:
/etc/config PICKLE
(the directory ../ PICKLE will be made if it doesn't exist and a "make depend" will be done unless you specify a "-n" flag)

5. Make the new system:
cd ../ PICKLE
make

6. Typically the running kernel should be "/vmunix" because programs like 'ps' and 'w' expect "/vmunix" to be the running kernel.
Save the original kernel, install the new one in /vmunix, and try it out:
mv /vmunix /vmunix.old ***# Rename the old kernel.***
cp vmunix /vmunix ***# Copy a new kernel.***

/etc/halt	***# Halt the system.***
b vmunix	***# Boot the system (with the new kernel).***

7. If the system does not appear to work, boot and restore the original kernel, then fix the new kernel:

/etc/halt	***# Halt the system.***
b vmunix.old -s	***# Boot the system single-user with the old kernel.***
mv /vmunix.old /vmunix	***# Replace the kernel with the old kernel.***
^D [Ctrl-D]	***# Brings the system up multi-user.***

CONFIGURING AN OBJECT-ONLY DISTRIBUTION ***# What is mandatory?***

The following lines from the GENERIC config file must be in every config file for object-only configurations:

```
machine        "sunN"   # where 'N' is 2 or 3 or 4
options        INET
pseudo-device  loop
```

Failing to include these lines in a config file will probably result in undefined routines during the making of the kernel, but may just silently cause the resulting kernel to blow up.

Except for drivers which supply the source for sizing data structures (e.g., xy_conf.c, sc_conf.c, xd_conf.c), you may not configure in more devices of a particular type than is allowed by the distributed object code in ../OBJ. Attempting to do so will not be detected and may cause the kernel to appear to work but have only occasional failures. Double check the .h files in ../OBJ if you change the number of devices configured for any standard drivers.

ADDING A DEVICE DRIVER ***# How to upgrade a configuration file.***

New device drivers require entries in ../../sun/conf.c, files, and possibly ../../sun/swapgeneric.c and devices. They are included by mentioning the device name in the config file.

The described BSD-like approach consists of three main steps:

1. Modify the kernel configuration file — items 1, 2, and 3
2. Compile and build the new kernel image based on new configuration data, and replace the old kernel with the new one — items 4, 5, and 6
3. Implement the new kernel — item 7

From an administrative standpoint, item 7 is extremely important; it describes a "fall-back" procedure if something goes wrong with the newly built kernel. A good system administrator must always be ready if something goes wrong — a fallback scenario is a must even for much smaller system changes; in the case of kernel reconfiguration, it is probably the major issue.

Another important issue is the kernel image name. Although we have used the term *usual name* for the default kernel name ***vmunix***, it is extremely important to preserve this name. Some important UNIX commands (for example the ***ps*** command) suppose the default kernel name and do not work properly if the kernel is renamed. That is the reason why the fallback procedure first boots the system into the single-user mode, overwrites the "bad new" kernel with the "good old" one, and then continues with multi-user mode (presented in item 7), instead of booting the system directly into multi-user mode with the old renamed kernel.

23.3.3 The *config* Command

The **config** command is used to configure the system's kernel and is sometimes named **autoconfig,** or something else that denotes its autonomous nature. Here, the BSD-type SunOS **config** command is briefly described

The syntax of the command is:

/usr/etc/config ***[-fgnp] [-o obj dir] config_file***

config builds system configuration files. It performs the preparation necessary for building a new system kernel. The *config_file* named on the command line describes the kernel to be made in terms of options desired in the system, table sizes, and device drivers to be included. Running **config,** requires several input files located in the current directory (typically the *conf* subdirectory of the system source including your *config_file*). If the directory named *../config_file* does not exist, **config** will create one. One of **config**'s output files is a *makefile*, which is used with **make** to build the kernel.

config must be run from the *conf* subdirectory of the system source (in a typical Sun environment, from */usr/share/sys/sun{2,3,3x,4,4c }/conf*).

Watch for errors while **config** is running. Never use a kernel that **config** has complained about; the results are unpredictable. If **config** completes successfully, the directory can be changed to the *../config_file* directory, where it has placed the new *makefile*, and **make** can be used to build a kernel.

The output files placed in this directory include *ioconf.c*, which contains a description of I/O devices attached to the system; *mbglue.s*, which contains short assembly language routines used for vectored interrupts; a *makefile*, which is used by **make** to build the system; a set of header files (*device_name.h*) which contain a number of various devices that may be compiled into the kernel, and a set of swap configuration files which contain definitions for the disk areas to be used for the root filesystem, swapping, and system dumps.

The available options are:

-f Set up the *makefile* for fast builds, which is accomplished by building a *vmunix.o* file that includes all the *.o* files that have no source. This reduces the number of files that have to be stated during a system build. Prelinking all the files for which no source exists into another file, which is then linked in place of all of these files when the kernel is made, performs the reduction. This *makefile* is faster because it does not state the object files during the build.

-g Get the current version of a missing source file from its SCCS history, if possible.

-n Do not do the "make depend." Normally, **config** will do the "make depend" automatically. If this option is used, **config** will print "Don't forget to do a 'make depend'" before completing, as a reminder.

-p Configure the system for profiling. This option is only available for systems with full source releases.

-o *obj_dir* Use *../obj_dir* instead of *../OBJ* as the directory to find the object files when the corresponding source file is not present, in order to generate the files necessary to compile and link your kernel.

Note that there are differences among kernel configuration commands of different UNIX flavors and types; always consult the available documentation!

23.4 Other Flavored Kernel Reconfigurations

This part of the chapter presents several other kernel configuration procedures. The presented UNIX flavors are mostly System V-like, so conditionally we can say they represent System V kernel configuration procedures. Unfortunately there is not a lot in common among them, and the title used for this part is definitely more appropriate than strictly System V-related title.

Generally, each implementation of System V had its own kernel configuration procedure. There were major differences between SVR2, SVR3, and SVR4. Because of all of the difficulties in practical implementation, System V vendors have done much to automate the process. Therefore, if a new software package should be added, the system administrator can run a system configuration program to install the package and automatically make the necessary kernel changes. The System V approach is not a single kernel configuration file; instead, it includes a number of so-called *master files* that contain configuration information used to create a kernel; this means that the kernel configuration database is a collection of files. The files reside in the *master directory* that has a different name for different flavors.

We will discuss this topic with the HP-UX, Solaris, and Linux UNIX flavors in mind. Even though this review should provide sufficient expertise to understand other implementations, it is recommended that you see vendors' documentation and manuals for each specific case, as well as the system's online manual pages. Even within the same vendor flavors, completely different approaches between succeeding releases are possible, as is the case with HP-UX 9.0x and HP-UX 10.x.

23.4.1 HP-UX 10.x Kernel Configuration

In HP-UX 10.x the kernel binary is created offline, and the newly created kernel binary will be executed upon the next system reboot. The front-end HP-UX flavored command **config** is used to configure device drivers, swap and dump devices, and tunable system parameters. The **config** command reads a user-provided system description in the file */stand/system*, as well as the provided master kernel configuration tables (files), and generates the following:

- A C program source file that defines the system configuration
- A *makefile* file used to compile the C program and relink the newly configured system (the ***make*** utility is used for this purpose)

The **config** command performs these steps automatically, so the new kernel binary is the end result of its execution. Correspondingly, our task is to appropriately modify the kernel description file */stand/system*, and execute the **config** command.

The default kernel values, as well as the permitted ranges of kernel parameters, are defined within master files in the directory */usr/conf/master.d*:

```
# ls -l /usr/conf/master.d
total 146
-r--r--r--  1 bin  bin  17122  Mar 18  21:47  core-hpux
-r--r--r--  1 bin  bin   3950  Jun 10   1996  dfs
-r--r--r--  1 bin  bin   1170  Jun 10   1996  dskless
-r--r--r--  1 bin  bin   5474  Apr 3   13:45  flkmgr
-r--r--r--  1 bin  bin   4086  Jun 10   1996  lan
-r--r--r--  1 bin  bin   3716  Aug 26   1996  lan100bt_hppb
-r--r--r--  1 bin  bin   4309  Jun 10   1996  lvm
-r--r--r--  1 bin  bin   5069  Jun 10   1996  net
-r--r--r--  1 bin  bin   4001  Jun 10   1996  proc-resrc-mgr
-r--r--r--  1 bin  bin   4115  Mar 20   1997  spt
-r--r--r--  1 bin  bin   6358  Jun 10   1996  streams
-r--r--r--  1 bin  bin   4748  Jun 10   1996  streams-tio
-r--r--r--  1 bin  bin   4279  Jun 10   1996  vxfs
```

Not all of the master files presented here reside on every system; their presence depends on the installed hardware and software. However, some of them always exist, for example, the master file ***core-hpux.*** This file defines all tunable kernel parameters. Do not forget that kernel reconfiguration mostly involves tuning kernel parameters. To add a new driver is only required if new hardware is added, and swap and dump devices rarely change. Also, if drivers are specified in the kernel description file, it does not mean they must be active; drivers are always hardware dependent, and can be active only if the appropriate hardware exists.

Let us see what a kernel description file looks like:

```
# cat /stand/system
* Drivers and Subsystems
asp
btlan1
ccio
cdfs
clone
core
diag0
   . . .
   . . .
pts
sad
sc
scsi1
sdisk
sio
stape
tpiso
uipc
vxbase
wsio
* Kernel Device info
vxadv
diag2
```

dmem	
dev_config	
dump lvol	
** Tunable parameters*	
maxfiles	*75*
maxfiles_lim	*1275*
maxswapchunks	*1031*
maxuprc	*175*
maxusers	*350*
msgmax	*32768*
msgmnb	*32768*
msgmni	*100*
msgseg	*7168*
msgtql	*256*
nfile	*15364*
npty	*250*
nstrpty	*250*
semmnu	*1170*
msgssz	*8*

Rebuilding the kernel could be a risky business; any failure in the kernel could be catastrophic for the system itself. The old "workable" kernel image */stand/vmunix* must always be saved for a possible fallback. By default, the **config** command creates the new kernel image */stand/build/vmunix* (*vmunix_test* if SAM was used); the new kernel must be moved (copied) into the */stand* directory, where the system looks for the kernel "vmunix," during startup. If something goes wrong with the new kernel, the fallback procedure must be implemented:

- Halt or reboot the system (if possible; you must be logged in as ***root*** to do this). The worst-case scenario is to power-cycle the system.
- Follow messages on the console and discontinue the system booting. HP-UX allows you to interrupt the booting by pressing any key within the announced 10 second interval.
- Continue with the booting; at the *menu* prompt, type:

  boot
- Accept to *Interact with IPL*; type *y*.
- Bring the system into single-user mode using the old kernel. Assuming the old kernel was saved as */stand/vmunix.fbk*, at the "*ISL*" prompt, type:

  hpux -is /stand/vmunix.fbk
- While the system is in single-user mode, fallback to the old kernel:

  mv /stand/vmunix.fbk /stand/vmunix
- Reboot the system into multi-user mode:

  shutdown -r 0

23.4.2 Solaris 2.x Kernel Configuration

A Solaris kernel resembles to a generic SunOS kernel. During system startup, a machine looks for attached devices and initializes the appropriate drivers. However, unlike a SunOS BSD-like kernel, which leaves all drivers resident in the memory, Solaris kernel loads only drivers for devices that are detected as active on the system (this can be changed only by explicitly forcing a system to do it differently).

Consequently, a Solaris kernel is a collection of software modules that includes the core image file */kernel/unix* and all of the modules loaded into the system memory — the so-called loadable modules. Solaris is also searching for kernel data in several other platform-specific directories, if it fails to find them in the directory */kernel.* The core image file */kernel/unix* is a system executable file, which contains basic operating system services. It is loaded first, during system booting (whether you are booting from a disk, a CD-ROM, or over a network); loadable modules are also loaded during the system startup, although they could be loaded at any time later (even from the command line). To be more precise, Solaris first looks for the kernel image file named *unix*, but if it does not find this file, it then looks for an alternate name *genunix*.

The kernel configuration can be controlled using the system specification file */etc/system*, also known as the system configuration information file. This file contains commands that are read by the kernel and used to customize the system; commands are useful in modifying the system's treatment of its loadable modules.

The syntax of the */etc/system* file consists of a list of keyword/value pairs, which are recognized by the system as valid commands. Commands that modify the system's operation with respect to loadable kernel modules require you to specify the module type by listing the module's namespace. The following namespaces are currently supported:

drv Modules in this namespace are device drivers.

exec Modules in this namespace are execution format modules. The following exec modules are currently provided for a SPARC system: *aoutexec*, *elfexec*, *intpexec*; and for a x86 system: *coffexec*, *elfexec*, *intpexec.*

fs These modules are filesystems.

sched These modules implement a process scheduling algorithm.

strmod These modules are STREAMS modules.

sys These modules implement loadable system-call modules.

misc These modules do not fit into any of the above categories, so are considered "miscellaneous" modules.

All of those modules reside in the appropriate subdirectories in the */kernel* directory:

```
$ ls -l /kernel
total 2112
drwsrwsrwt  2 root  sys     2048  Nov 15  14:26  drv
drwxr-xr-x  2 root  sys      512  Apr 4    1995  exec
drwxr-xr-x  2 root  sys      512  Apr 4    1995  fs
drwxr-xr-x  2 root  sys      512  Apr 4    1995  misc
drwxr-xr-x  2 root  sys      512  Apr 4    1995  sched
drwxr-xr-x  2 root  sys      512  Apr 4    1995  strmod
drwxr-xr-x  2 root  sys      512  Apr 4    1995  sys
-rwxr-xr-x  1 root  sys  1058400  Jul 15   1994  unix
```

Except for the kernel executable image (named *unix*), all of the listed items are namespaces' subdirectories. A slightly deeper view into a namespace's subdirectory (the most representative is the driver's subdirectory) shows:

```
$ ls /kernel/drv
   arp         gt          mcp.conf     rootnex sy
   arp.conf    icmp        mcpp         rtvc          sy.conf
   be          icmp.conf   mcpp.conf    sad           tcp
   bpp         id          mcpzsa       sad.conf      tcp.conf
```

bwtwo	*id.conf*	*mcpzsa.conf*	*sbus*	*tcx*
cgeight	*iommu*	*mm*	*sbusmem*	*tl*
cgfourteen	*ip*	*mm.conf*	*sbu smem.conf*	*tl.conf*
cgsix	*ip.conf*	*obio*	*sd*	*udp*
cgthree	*ipi3sc*	*openeepr*	*sd.conf*	*udp.conf*
cgtwelve	*isp*	*openeepr.conf*	*soc*	*vme*
clone	*iwscn*	*options*	*sp*	*vmemem*
clone.conf	*iwscn.conf*	*options.conf*	*sp.conf*	*vmemem.conf*
cn	*le*	*pln*	*ssd*	*wc*
cn.conf	*lebuffer*	*pln.conf*	*ssd.conf*	*wc.conf*
conskbd	*ledma*	*pn*	*st*	*xbox*
conskbd.conf	*leo*	*profile*	*st.conf*	*zs*
consms	*llc1*	*profile.conf*	*stc*	*zsh*
consms.conf	*llc1.conf*	*pseudo*	*stc.conf*	*zsh.conf*
dma	*log*	*pseudo.conf*	*sx*	
esp	*log.conf*	*qe*	*sx_cmem*	
fd	*mcp*	*qec*	*sx_cmem.conf*	

As we can see, their configuration files can configure most drivers. The supported commands (or directives) are described in the */etc/system* file itself.

```
$ cat /etc/system
*ident  "@(# )system  1.15  92/11/14 SMI" /* SVR4 1.5 */
*
* SYSTEM SPECIFICATION FILE
*
* moddir:
*   Set the search path for modules. This has a format similar to the
*   csh path variable. If the module isn't found in the first directory
*   it tries the second and so on. The default is /kernel /usr/kernel
*   Example:
*     moddir: /kernel /usr/kernel /other/modules

* root device and root filesystem configuration:
*   The following may be used to override the defaults provided by
*   the boot program:
*   rootfs:    Set the filesystem type of the root.
*   rootdev:   Set the root device. This should be a fully
*              expanded physical pathname. The default is the
*              physical pathname of the device where the boot
*              program resides. The physical pathname is
*              highly platform and configuration dependent.
*   Example:
*     rootfs:ufs
*     rootdev:/sbus@1,f80 00000/esp@0,800000/sd@3,0:a
*   (Swap device configuration should be specified in /etc/vfstab.)

* exclude:
*   Modules appearing in the moddir path which are NOT to be loaded,
*   even if referenced. Note that 'exclude' accepts either a module name,
*   or a filename which includes the directory.
*   Examples:
*     exclude: win
*     exclude: sys/shmsys

* forceload:
*   Cause these modules to be loaded at boot time, (just before mounting
*   the root filesystem) rather than at first reference. Note that
*   forceload expects a filename which includes the directory. Also
*   note that loading a module does not necessarily imply that it will
```

```
*   be installed.
*   Example:
*     forceload: drv/foo

* set:
*   Set an integer variable in the kernel or a module to a new value.
*   This facility should be used with caution. See system(4).
*   Examples:
*   To set variables in 'unix':
*     set nautopush = 32
*     set maxusers = 40
*   To set a variable named 'debug' in the module named 'test_module'
*     set test_module:debug = 0x13
```

A single supported command is missing here: the *include* directive, which includes the listed loadable modules. The command itself is pointless, because the system will, by default, include all requested modules, so there is no need to use this command at all.

In an ideal world, Solaris would correctly identify the system hardware environment and automatically configure and build an appropriate kernel. In the real world, unfortunately, flaky, nonstandard, or just buggy hardware (or sometimes software drivers themselves) can cause unexpected problems. That is why Solaris does not check by default for a possible new hardware configuration when the system is rebooted; it is too expensive and unnecessary. Testing to detect new hardware takes time, and changes in hardware configuration are infrequent. And when they happen, we can explicitly require the system to accomplish this task. This is indicated by the boot-argument **"-r"** which is passed to the kernel to force hardware configuration checkup in such situations. By booting the system from "ok" prompt:

ok boot -r

or, rebooting the system from the command prompt:

 # reboot-- -r (pay attention to doubled dash character, because the flag "-r" is passed to the ***boot*** command as a boot-argument)

Correspondingly the startup procedure will include the search for its hardware configuration and all attached devices. Commands *drvconfig* and *disks* accomplish the same task from the command line, each of them in its own area.

Solaris also provides several tools to display a current machine's configuration — commands like *prtconf*, *sysdef*, or *modinfo*:

- The ***prtconf*** command displays the machine's general configuration, including machine type, model number, amount of memory, and hardware information about configured devices.
- The ***sysinfo*** command includes also pseudo-device drivers, tunable kernel parameters, and filenames of loaded modules.
- The ***modinfo*** command displays information about dynamically loaded modules.

To conclude, Solaris does not build the kernel image offline. All changes in the kernel configuration implemented through the system specification file ***/etc/system*** will take effect upon the next system booting, when all modified parameters will be loaded into the memory and the new kernel memory resident image will, assuming everything was properly done, continue to run. However, there are not many "visible" indicators that the configuration changes became really effective. The kernel image file ***/kernel/unix*** remains unchanged, as well as other kernel module executables. Changes are loaded into memory, and in some way hidden from a direct checkup; we can only indirectly come to conclusions about changes through system behavior.

Stubborn administrators, who want to check new kernel configuration online, must take a look into kernel memory resident data; the available tool is Solaris general-purpose debugger ***adb***. The following example describes how to check actual kernel parameters for semaphores, shared memory, and message queue on Solaris 2.7 (64-bit version).

Become a superuser and execute the following command sequence (# presents a command prompt; additional comments are in ***bold***):

```
# uname –a                                     # just to check system data
SunOS atlas 5.7 Generic sun4u sparc SUNW,Ultra-80
#
# cd/
# modload /kernel/sys/shmsys                   # force loads shm module
# modload /kernel/sys/semsys                   # force loads sem module
# modload /kernel/sys/msgsys                   # force loads msg module
# adb -k /dev/ksyms /dev/mem                   # use adb to look at kernel
physmem 7cf0e

shminfo/2E2D                                   # dumps the shm parameters (2 in unsigned
                                               # decimal format, and 2 in long decimal format)
shminfo:
shminfo:          1048576        1      100      6

seminfo/10D                                    # dumps 10 sem parameters in long decimal format
seminfo:
seminfo:               10       10       60     30
                       25       10       10    104
                    32767    16384
msginfo/6D1u                                   # dumps msg parameters (6 in long decimal
                                               # format and 1 in unsigned decimal format)
msginfo:
msginfo:              100    65535    65535     50
                       16       40     8192

$q                                             # quits adb
#                                              # back to the command prompt
```

How do we understand displayed kernel parameter values? And how do we specify an appropriate number of parameters and a display format? These data could be found in the corresponding header files in the */usr/include/sys* directory (files *shm.h, sem.h* and *msg.h*).

For *shared memory* parameters:

 # cat /usr/include/sys/shm.h

```
  .....
/*
* IPC Shared Memory Facility.
*/
  .....
  .....
/*
* Shared memory information structure
*/
```

```
struct    shminfo {
          size_t    shmmax,    /* max shared memory segment size */
                    shmmin;    /* min shared memory segment size */
          int       shmmni,    /* # of shared memory identifiers */
                    shmseg;    /* max attached shared memory */
                               /* segments per process */
};
  .....
  .....
```

Each displayed value corresponds to a tunable "shared memory" parameter:

```
1048576  =>  shmmax
      1  =>  shmmin
    100  =>  shmmni
      6  =>  shmseg
```

For *semaphore* parameters:

 # cat /usr/include/sys/sem.h

```
  .....
/*
* IPC Semaphore Facility.
*/
  .....
  .....
/*
* Semaphore information structure
*/
struct   seminfo {
         int   semmap;    /* # of entries in semaphore map */
         int   semmni;    /* # of semaphore identifiers */
         int   semmns;    /* # of semaphores in system */
         int   semmnu;    /* # of undo structures in system */
         int   semmsl;    /* max # of semaphores per id */
         int   semopm;    /* max # of operations per semop call */
         int   semume;    /* max # of undo entries per process */
         int   semusz;    /* size in bytes of undo structure */
         int   semvmx;    /* semaphore maximum value */
         int   semaem;    /* adjust on exit max value */
};
  .....
  .....
```

Each displayed value corresponds to a tunable "semaphore" parameter:

```
100  =>  semmap
 10  =>  semmni
 60  =>  semmns
 30  =>  semmnu
 25  =>  semmsl
 10  =>  semopm
 10  =>  semume
104  =>  semusz
```

32767 => semvmx
16384 => semaem

In this example, the displayed parameter values present default kernel parameters for shared memory and semaphore; it means this very kernel has not been tuned in this segment.

For *"message"* parameters:

 # cat /usr/include/sys/msg.h

```
      .....
/*
* IPC Message Facility.
*/
      .....
      .....
/*
* Message information structure.
*/
struct  msginfo {
        int         msgmap;    /* # of entries in msg map */
        int         msgmax;    /* max message size */
        int         msgmnb;    /* max # bytes on queue */
        int         msgmni;    /* # of message queue identifiers */
        int         msgssz;    /* msg segment size (should be word size multiple) */
        int         msgtql;    /* # of system message headers */
        ushort_t    msgseg;    /* # of msg segments (MUST BE < 32768) */
};
      .....
      .....
```

Correspondingly, displayed "message queue" values are:

10 => msgmap
65535 => msgmax
65535 => msgmnb
50 => msgmni
16 => msgssz
40 => msgtgl
8192 => msgseg

Finally, what is a Solaris fallback scenario if something really goes wrong with kernel reconfiguration, so the system cannot boot properly. The approach is very similar to SunOS, which is quite understandable keeping in mind the same vendor behind both products. We should boot the system into single-user mode, replace kernel or kernel configuration file, with "old good" data, and reboot the system into multi-user mode; afterward we can continue our reconfiguration activities.

Once we halt the system and get the OK prompt (by typing the "halt" command, or by sending "break" signal to the console <Stop-A>), we can boot the system into single-user mode with the additional optional flag "-a" to be asked about kernel execution:

ok boot –as Will ask for kernel configuration data, such as where to find the system file, where to mount root, and even override the name of the kernel itself. Default responses will be contained in square brackets, and may simply be confirmed by hitting the RETURN key.

However, do not forget to save kernel core image and */etc/system* file before any kernel modification.

23.4.3 Linux Kernel Configuration

The official Linux kernel configuration file is the hidden file ***/usr/src/linux/.config.*** This file specifies almost all kernel configuration data. We say "almost" because the tuning kernel parameters (parameters that we are dealing mostly with) unfortunately are not a part of this file; Linux handles them differently, and we will address them later. For a moment we will focus on this file and the way to configure a new kernel.

The file ***/usr/src/linux/.config*** contains unusually huge numbers of kernel-related data, allowing a detailed kernel specification regarding selected devices to be added, or compiled as a loadable module. To avoid possible mistakes, Linux recommends not editing this file directly, but rather using any of several tools available as "***make***" targets that make more friendly user-interfaces for that purpose. Change the directory to */usr/src/linux* and type:

- ***make xconfig*** — to bring up an X-based GUI
- ***make menuconfig*** — to invoke a cursor-based menu
- ***make config*** — to start a character based query-response dialogue
- ***make oldconfig*** — to carry the existing configuration to a new version with minimal work

Obviously the presented sequence of available interfaces is directly related to how easy the kernel configuration process will be; correspondingly GUI is the most comfortable, but it requires a workable X environment, sometimes not available.

Nevertheless, whichever interface was implemented, the bottom line is a modified kernel configuration file *.config*. The following example shows only a small piece of the content of an actual configuration file for Linux kernel v.2.4.2. The idea is just to get a feel for implemented configuration entries. The full listing of the file would probably take more than 10 pages.

```
# cat /usr/src/linux/.config
#
# Automatically generated by make xconfig: don't edit
#
CONFIG_X86 = y
CONFIG_ISA = y
     .....
     .....
#
# Processor type and features
# CONFIG_M386 is not set
CONFIG_M686 = y
     .....
     .....
#
# General setup
CONFIG_NET = y
CONFIG_PCI = y
```

```
     .....
     .....
     .....
#
# ARCnet devices
CONFIG_DUMMY = m
     .....
     .....
     .....
#
# Filesystems
# CONFIG_QUOTA is not set
CONFIG_AUTOFS4_FS = y
CONFIG_VFAT_FS = m
     .....
     .....
     .....
#
# Kernel hacking
# CONFIG_MAGIC_SYSRQ is not set
```

The configuration file covers more than 40 different aspects of the kernel configuration, and most of these aspects could be specified with multiple configuration entries — sometimes even a few dozen entries. Each entry could be set (specified as "y"), or "not set" (commented-out), or realized as a loadable module (specified by "m"). Together they all make a whole configuration scenario quite confusing. Fortunately, a default setting and available tools, especially GUI with a decently verbose online help, make this task affordable. GUI is presented in Figure 23.1. Also our task is to reconfigure the existing kernel, and usually it comes at the end to handle a limited number of configuration entries.

Following are a few notes about kernel configuration/reconfiguration:

- Having unnecessary drivers will make the kernel bigger, and can under some circumstances lead to problems; a nonexistent controller card may confuse other controllers.
- Compiling the kernel with a higher "processor type" could result in a not-workable kernel.
- A kernel with math-emulation compiled in will still use the coprocessor if one is present: the math emulation will just never get used in that case. The kernel will be slightly larger but will work on different machines regardless of whether they have a math coprocessor or not.
- The "kernel hacking" configuration details usually result in a bigger or slower kernel (or both), and can even make the kernel less stable.

Once we are happy with implemented changes and the *.config* file is modified appropriately, we have to rebuild the kernel to make those changes effective. This is the routine multistep procedure that we can summarize in the following way:

1. Run ***make depend***, or the shorter version ***make dep***, to set up all the dependencies correctly.
2. Run ***make clean*** to make a clean build environment, although this step is not mandatory.
3. Run ***make bzImage*** to create a compressed kernel image. To make a boot disk (without root filesystem or LILO), insert a floppy disk and run ***make bzdisk***.

4. If any part of the kernel is specified as *module*, run ***make modules*** followed by ***make modules_install***.
5. Keep a backup kernel saved in case something goes wrong. Make sure to keep a backup of the modules corresponding to that kernel, as well.
6. In order to boot a new kernel, the new kernel image ***/usr/src/linux/arch/i386/boot/bzImage*** (obtained after compilation in step 3) should be copied to the place where the regular bootable kernel is located, in most cases to be copied into ***/boot/vmlinuz.*** Do not forget to save the old kernel image for a potential fallback if it is overridden by the new one. However, it is not mandatory because the new kernel could be named differently (both kernel images, the bootable kernel and fallback kernel, are specified within the ***/etc/lilo.conf*** file).
7. Edit the ***/etc/lilo.conf*** file to reflect kernel configuration changes; specify the new and fallback kernel images and reinstall boot loader LILO. Reinstalling of LILO is accomplished by running the ***/sbin/lilo*** command.
8. After reinstalling LILO, the kernel configuration process is completed. To make changes effective, system must be rebooted.

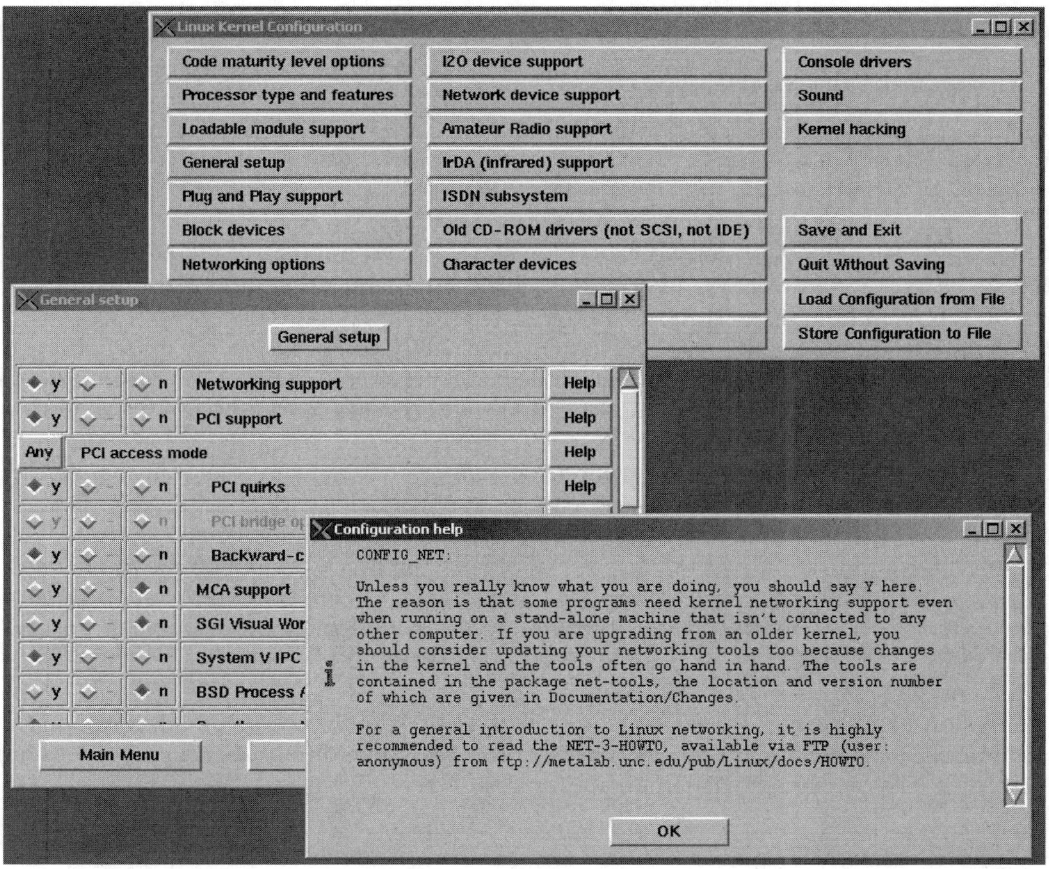

FIGURE 23.1
The GUI tool to configure the Linux kernel.

An important step in kernel reconfiguration is an appropriate processing of the boot loader LILO, which strictly speaking is not a part of the kernel at all. However, if the usual kernel naming is preserved and both kernel images (the new and the old kernel image) are copied over existing bootable and fallback kernels which are already specified in the existing ***/etc/lilo.conf*** file, step 7 could be skipped.

The following example shows an actual LILO configuration file:

$ cat /etc/lilo.conf

```
boot = /dev/sda
map = /boot/map
install = /boot/boot.b
prompt
timeout = 30
linear
compact
image = /boot/vmlinuz-2.4.2
   label = l-2.4.2
   initrd = /boot/initrd-2. 4.2.img
   read-only
   root = /dev/md0
image = /boot/vmlinuz-2.2.14 –5.0smp
   label = linux
   initrd = /boot/initrd-2. 2.14–5.0smp.img
   read-only
   root = /dev/md0
image = /boot/vmlinuz-2.2.14 –5.0
   label = linux-up
   initrd = /boot/initrd-2. 2.14–5.0.img
   read-only
   root = /dev/md0
```

As can be seen above, a configuration file starts with a number of global options (the top seven lines), followed by descriptions of the options for the various kernel images. An option in an image description will override a global option. This file specifies kernel images by using nonstandard kernel names. The newly compiled bootable kernel image is ***/boot/vmlinuz-2.4.2***, while two fallback kernel images are specified as ***/boot/vmlinuz-2.2.14–5.0smp*** and ***/boot/vmlinuz-2.2.14–5.0.*** We will discuss later how to implement the specified fallback kernel images.

Unfortunately, the kernel configuration file ***.config*** does not provide a mechanism for tuning kernel parameters. Or maybe a more appropriate word is *fortunately,* because requirements for the tuning of kernel parameters are more frequent, and the relatively complex reconfiguration of the kernel is avoided. For this purpose Linux provides an extensive kernel-to-user interface through "virtual files" in the ***/proc*** filesystem, or more specifically, in the ***/proc/sys/kernel*** directory. Even more than that, to avoid a possible confusion around existing /proc files (are they read-only or read-write), the handy front-end command ***/sbin/sysctl*** is available.

The command ***sysctl*** is used to read and modify kernel parameters at runtime; the parameters available are those listed under */proc/sys/*, while tuning kernel parameters are located in */proc/sys/kernel/.* The command options are:

sysctl [-n] variable	to read the specified parameter, for example: ***sysctl kernel.ostype*** *kernel.ostype = Linux*

	use the *-n* option to disable printing of the key name when printing values: ***sysctl -n kernel.ostype*** *Linux*
sysctl [-n] variable = value	to set an individual variable online; it remains effective until the next reboot, for example: ***sysctl kernel.ostype = RedHat***
sysctl –w variable = value	to change a setting in the */etc/sysctl.conf* file, for example: ***sysctl -w kernel.ostype = RadHat***
sysctl –p /etc/sysctl.conf or, simply: ***sysctl -p***	to load and make effective content of the specified sysctl configuration file (by default it is */etc/sysctl.conf*); this command option is applied during the system startup
sysctl –a	to list all system configuration parameters and, among them, also kernel parameters

The following example presents the output of the ***sysctl –a*** command; only kernel parameters are fully listed (for other system parameters only one line is shown):

```
$ /sbin/sysctl -a
sunrpc.nlm_debug = 0
  . . . . .
dev.raid.speed_limit_max = 100 000
  . . . . .
fs.binfmt_misc.status = enabled
  . . . . .
net.unix.max_dgram_qlen = 10
  . . . . .
vm.page-cluster = 4
  . . . . .
kernel.overflowgid = 65534
kernel.overflowuid = 65534
kernel.random.uuid = 2c396920 -8db7-4d2a-8dde-ed9fd456a0fe
kernel.random.boot_id = bc469e 92-1bc6-424d-9f81-abb2469eb495
kernel.random.write_wakeup_threshold = 128
kernel.random.read_wakeup_threshold = 8
kernel.random.entropy_avail = 0
kernel.random.poolsize = 512
kernel.threads-max = 131070
kernel.sem = 250    32000    32    128
kernel.msgmnb = 16384
kernel.msgmni = 16
kernel.msgmax = 8192
kernel.shmmni = 4096
kernel.shmall = 2097152
kernel.shmmax = 524288000
kernel.rtsig-max = 10 24
kernel.rtsig-nr = 0
kernel.modprobe = /sbin /modprobe
kernel.printk = 64    1    7
kernel.ctrl-alt-del = 0
kernel.real-root-dev = 2304
kernel.cap-bound = –257
kernel.panic = 60
kernel.domainname =
```

kernel.hostname = atlas.scps.nyu.edu
kernel.version = #2 SMP Fri Feb 23 18:38:55 GMT 2001
kernel.osrelease = 2.4.2
kernel.ostype = Linux

Note: The same data could be seen by reading individual files in */proc/sys* or, more specific to the kernel, in */proc/sys/kernel* directory.

Once we are familiar with the ***sysctl*** command, it becomes easy to tune the kernel parameter. At the end the ***/etc/sysctl.conf*** file also should be modified to keep the tuned changes permanent.

Finally, an actual */etc/sysctl.conf* file is presented here:

$ cat /etc/sysctl.conf

```
#net.ipv4.ip_local_port_range = 32768–61000
#net.ipv4.ip_forward = 0
#net.ipv4.tcp_syncookies = 0
#net.ipv4.tcp_keepalive_probes = 1
#net.ipv4.ip_default_ttl = 64
#net.ipv4.tcp_keepalive_probes = 3
#net.ipv4.tcp_keepalive_time = 360
#net.ipv4.tcp_max_ka_probes = 5
#net.core.netdev_max_backlog = 1000
#net.core.rmem_default = 32768
#net.core.wmem_default = 131072
#net.core.rmem_max = 32768
#net.core.wmem_max = 131072
#net.core.optmem_max = 40960
fs.file-max = 16384
#fs.inode-nr = 65536
#net.ipv4.tcp_window_scaling = 0
kernel.shmmax = 524288000
kernel.panic = 60
```

Obviously, in this specific case most of the kernel parameters have their default values. By the way, they are listed in the previously presented ***sysctl –a*** output.

And last but not least is the question of what to do if something goes wrong with the newly reconfigured kernel. How do we accomplish the required fallback?

Assuming an appropriate LILO configuration, where the bootable and one or more fallback kernel images are properly specified, the fallback becomes trivial. When booting, the boot loader will wait by default for four seconds (40 deciseconds, 1decisecond is 1/10 of a second), or whatever is specified in the LILO configuration file, for us to press Shift. If we do not, then the first specified kernel image (in our example ***/boot/vmlinuz-2.4.2***, that was probably installed just a few minutes ago) will be booted. If we do, the boot loader will ask which image to boot. In case we forgot the possible choices, we can press [TAB] or [?], and a corresponding menu with available kernel images will be presented. We now have the choice of booting this brand new kernel, or an old trusted fallback kernel ***/boot/vmlinuz-2.2.14-5.0smp***, or a third specified kernel ***/boot/vmlinuz-2.2.14-5.0***, or whatever. There can be up to 16 kernel images specified in the */etc/lilo.conf* file.

24

Modems and UUCP

24.1 Introduction to Modems

A modem is a telecommunication device that provides long-distance data transfer over a transmission line to reach another remote device. Long-distance data transfer is based on the fact that the data stream is modulated into the robust carrier suitable for remote transmission, which is then demodulated on the receiving end. Basically, data are inserted into some of the carrier parameters, to be later extracted and retrieved. Modulation techniques could be different, i.e., different carrier parameters could be affected: amplitude, frequency, phase, or other, and they identify the type of a modem. Each modem consists of two parts:

- Transmitter, or modulator, which provides a modulation of input data into the carrier suitable for remote data transfer.
- Receiver, or demodulator, which provides demodulation of received carrier and extraction of transferred data.

The name ***modem*** presents an acronym for ***MO****dulator*-***DEM****odulator* and identifies a single bidirectional transmission device. The transmission is performed *serially, asynchronously,* or *synchronously,* in the *half-duplex* mode where a data transmit and receive are performed at different times, or in the *full-duplex* mode where a data transmit and receive are performed simultaneously. The implemented modulation techniques and the transmission speeds could be different, but two modems involved in the communication at two ends of a transmission line must be mutually compatible.

By attaching modems to computers, two remote computers can interchange data. Historically, modems were used a long time before LANs appeared, and for quite a time they presented the only devices suitable for remote computer communication. UNIX designers had in mind modems to connect distant computer systems when they introduced UUCP. Remote terminals also used modems to connect to a computer system, and this is partially covered in Chapter 11 about terminals. Today modems are primarily used to connect home computer systems to ISP servers that provide an access to the Internet. Physically, modems are attached to the computer serial ports, the same ones that could be used to attach any other terminal. That fact is important for the discussion that follows.

In the past modems presented "dumb" devices that only provided a conversion of serial data signals into the form suitable for remote transmission, and vice versa. Only a few control signals have been used between DCE (data communication equipment) like a computer's serial interface, and DTE (data terminal equipment), i.e., the modem itself. Signals like request to send (RTS), clear to send (CTS), and data carrier detect (DCD), played the main role (besides DSR — data set ready — and DTR — data terminal ready signals). New technologies brought many improvements into the modem arena; modems became "smart" devices and opened new horizons for their implementations. Probably the main change was a possibility for an independent modem configuration in an extremely flexible way. A new ASCII-based protocol, known as AT commands, has been introduced for that purpose; by issuing a sequence of AT commands from the computer, a modem can be configured in different ways to match different needs.

Short and cryptic AT commands are always prefaced by the letters "AT," which stand for "attention — expect a command to follow." Several AT commands could be combined behind the same AT prefix, making the command syntax more condensed. While AT commands are quite cryptic for us, they are very comprehensive for a modem itself, and set the modem appropriately. A flexible modem configuration improves modem efficiency, making data transmission easier for the computer itself. Modems are independent in establishing mutual connection; the initial communication sequence between two distant modems (known as *modem handshake*) checks for the actual quality of interconnecting media and adjusts for optimal modem speed and modulation parameters. This modem adaptability guarantees an optimal data transmission.

AT commands are beyond the scope of this text; we will strictly address UNIX modem-related issues. However, AT commands are parts of communication programs which support data transmission, and familiarity with AT commands is always instrumental in fully understanding how modems work.

Once a modem is put in operation, the central issue becomes how to efficiently transfer data over such a low-speed device (for many years even 300 bps modems have been rare). In other words, how to optimally organize data transfer keeping in mind all the frustrating modem characteristics. Many file transfer protocols have been introduced, and some of them remained in use till nowadays:

- Xmodem is one of the most used file transfer protocols. Originally it used 128B packets and simple checksum method of error detection. Later enhancements, Xmodem-CRC and Xmodem-1K, present improved versions of the original Xmodem protocol.
- Ymodem is essentially the Xmodem-1K protocol that allows multiple batch file transfer. Its improved variant is Ymodem-g that supports error-control modems.
- Zmodem is generally the best protocol that has two significant features: it is more efficient and it provides crash recovery. If a Zmodem transfer is interrupted for any reason, the transfer can be resurrected later and already transferred data need not be re-sent.

Listed protocols are supported by following send/receive programs: sx and rx, sy and ry, and sz and rz, respectively, which are available also on UNIX platform.

24.1.1 UNIX and Modems

To clarify the relationship between UNIX and modems, we must keep in mind that for a long time, a modem has been treated primarily as a part of the transmission line and not the computer system itself. The modem, as a terminating part of the transmission line, was connected to a serial interface, and correspondingly UNIX has focused on how to control the serial interface. So modem control actually refers to controlling serial lines that traditionally have been dedicated to connect user terminals.

A long-standing deficiency of most UNIX implementations was the inability for the same modem to be used to *dial in* and *dial out* simultaneously, in a full-duplex mode. The two main reasons for this were:

1. The driver that controls the serial port was designed for another purpose — to control data flow between a terminal and the system. So, the driver monitors for the specific signal that identifies the presence of data on the line, the data carrier detect signal (*DCD*), to start any communication with the attached terminal.
2. And, when a *DCD* signal is detected, a ***getty*** program is invoked to start a *login process,* i.e., to put the *login prompt* on the line.

This is quite OK when an attached terminal dials in, even if it is done over a modem. However, what happens if the system itself should initialize the communication over the modem? Obviously, when the system dials out, the DCD signal is missing. Another obstacle presents the **getty** program itself. If a remote system attempts to start a communication, **getty** may respond to the dialed remote system with a *login prompt;* and if the remote system reacts in the very same way, sending its own *login prompt,* the connection can never be established. Two systems send repeated *login* and *password* messages at each other, leaving the connection in a kind of *deadly embrace.*

It is also fair to say that modems have never been a real UNIX concern. Once networking boomed, and UNIX so successfully merged with networking, modems were pushed even more to the side. UNIX focused on providing basic network services, and a network connection became an integral part of each UNIX system. Modems are more attractive for the desktop side where UNIX never dominated. It does not mean that UNIX has completely ignored modem topics; each UNIX flavor provides some kind of modem control. It also gave a chance to third-party developers to fill the existing gap, providing needed software widely implemented on all UNIX platforms.

24.2 UNIX Modem Control

The lack of a general UNIX approach to control modems resulted in many different, flavor-specific solutions. In an early UNIX phase, solutions were based on flexible UNIX organization and existing functions of a similar nature and purpose; later, each flavor introduced some kind of modem-related commands and sometimes modem control relays on the third-party UNIX upgrade. We briefly discuss all three listed approaches.

24.2.1 Terminal Lines and Modem Control

This approach probably belongs to history, but it is illustrative to understand a conflicting situation in attaching a general-purpose bidirectional modem to a dedicated serial terminal line. It is important to understand that the obstacle is not the used serial port (the implemented hardware itself allows bidirectional serial communication), but rather the existing control software, primarily the invoked **getty** program on the terminal line at system startup.

UNIX provided different flavor-colored solutions for this problem. SunOS has a mechanism that allows a serial port to be used in both directions; the driver supports two entry points, one for each direction. For each terminal line identified by the device *tty0–tty127*, the existing driver is monitoring for DCD (data carrier detect) signal and puts up a **getty** program. Devices with minor numbers 128–255 (by convention named *cu0–cu127*) refer to the same physical devices but allow the device to be opened even when DCD is not present. The net effect is that a modem can be attached to a terminal line ***tty***n (by convention usually renamed to ***ttyd***n) and used for dial-in, but also used for dial-out when referred to by the name ***cua***n.

The administrator should create two different special files for the terminal line to which the modem is attached; for dial-in — ***/dev/ttyd***n (n = modem line number) and for corresponding dial-out — ***/dev/cua***n. The dial-in device ***/dev/ttyd***n would be entered as a normal entry in the terminal line configuration file */etc/ttytab.*

The two special files differ only in their *minor device numbers* (subtype within device class), with an offset of 128 (could be seen by the ***ls -l*** command). To create these special files, the ***mknod*** command is used, as for any other device. Here is an example:

```
# mknod  /dev/ttyd1  c  12  1
# mknod  /dev/cua1   c  12  129
```

Two character special files for the class 12 (terminal lines) are created. The corresponding entries for terminal lines in the */etc/ttytab* should be replaced with:

```
# The following entries represent the same physical modem
ttyd1  "/usr/etc/getty d2400"  unknown on   # dialin entry (enabled)
cua1   none                    unknown off  # dialout entry (disabled)
```

Finally, the "software carrier detect" for the dial-out version of the port should be disabled:

```
# ttysoftcar n /dev/cua1
```

Once it is done, the use of special files ***/etc/ttyd1*** and ***/etc/cua1*** is possible.

For more detailed explanations and complete installation, SunOS provides the manual page named ***zs.***

System V UNIX flavors specify the terminal line, i.e., serial port initialization, through the */etc/inittab* file. When a modem is attached to the system, the appropriate port must be enabled for duplex communication. It can be done by replacing the **getty** program in the corresponding *inittab-entry* with another, more sophisticated program that supports both, **getty** and duplex communication (such programs exist on the System V, for example the program ***uugetty***). An *inittab-entry* could be:

```
27:2:respawn:/usr/lib/uucp/uugetty -r tty12 2400
```

Another approach is also possible; to invoke the ***init*** program to reinitialize the terminal line for dial-in and dial-out, using different *init-run-levels* (for example, 2 and 3). Then, invoking

```
# init 2
```

will initialize the terminal line for dial-in, including the **getty** program (the corresponding *inittab-entry* with the **getty** must exist for run-level #2). By invoking

 # init 3,

the terminal line will be enabled for dial-out (the previous *inittab-entry* with the **getty** must be excluded from the run-level #3).

24.2.2 Modem-Related UNIX Commands

There is no uniform UNIX set of modem-related commands; they are always flavor specific. Most UNIX flavors point to the command ***uugetty,*** but this command was primarily designed for a different purpose; more about this command and its implementation can be found in the section on UUCP. Several other commands will be briefly described, or sometimes even only listed in the following text.

24.2.2.1 The *cu* Command

cu calls up another UNIX system, a terminal, or possibly a non-UNIX system. The command exists, for example, on Solaris and HP-UX flavors. It manages an interactive conversation with possible transfers of files. It is convenient to think of ***cu*** as operating in two phases:

1. The connection phase in which the connection is established
2. The conversation phase

The format of the command is:

cu options { telno /systemname }

cu accepts many options. The *-c, -l,* and *-s* options play a part in selecting the medium; the remaining options are used in configuring the line. The command is directly related to UUCP, and it uses some UUCP configuration data. Some of the options are listed.

Option	Meaning
-c device	Force ***cu*** to use configuration entries in the UUCP file */etc/uucp/Devices* that match the user specified device.
-s speed	Specify the transmission speed; the default value is "Any" speed that depends on the */etc/uucp/Devices file.*
-l line	Specify a device name to use as the communication line. Combined with other options could also depend on the UUCP configuration files. The most common case is that a specified device is a directly connected asynchronous line (for instance, /dev/term/a) required. However the specified device need not be in the /dev directory. If the specified device is associated with an auto dialer, a telephone number must be provided.
-b bits	Specifies the number of bits processed on the line (either 7 or 8). This allows connection between systems with different character sizes. By default, the character size of the line is set to the same as the current local terminal.
telno	When using an automatic dialer, specifies the telephone number; the equal sign "=" identifies secondary dial tone, while the minus sign "-" placed appropriately, a delay of 4 seconds.
systemname	Specifies a system name, which can be used rather than a telephone number. In this case, ***cu*** will obtain an appropriate direct line or telephone number from a UUCP system file.

For example:

- To dial a system whose telephone number is 9-1-212-567-1234 using 2400 baud (where dial tone is expected after the 9):

  # cu -s 2400 9=12125671234
- To log in to a system connected by a direct line:

  # cu -l /dev/term/b
- To dial a system with a specific line and speed:

  # cu -s 1200 -l term/b
- To use a system name:

  # cu systemname

24.2.2.2 The *tip* Command

The ***tip*** command (or utility) connects to the remote system and establishes a full-duplex terminal connection. Once the connection is established, a remote session using ***tip*** behaves like an interactive session on a local terminal. The command is Solaris flavored.

The format of the command is:

tip [-v] [-speed-entry] { hostname | phone-number | device }

The remote file contains entries describing remote systems and line speeds used by ***tip.*** Each host has a default baud rate for the connection, or the speed is specified in the speed-entry option.

When phone number is specified, ***tip*** looks for an entry in the remote file of the form: *tip -speed-entry* to set the connection speed accordingly.

When device is specified, ***tip*** attempts to open that device, but will do so using the access privileges of the user (the user must have read/write access to the device). ***tip*** interprets any character string beginning with the slash character (/) as a device name.

When establishing the connection, ***tip*** sends a *connection message* to the remote system. The default value for this message can be found in the remote file.

When ***tip*** starts up, it reads commands from the file *.tiprc* in the user's home directory.

Some other UNIX commands that belong to this category are, for example, the Solaris-flavored commands ***ttymon*** and ***ttyadm*** for control of the serial lines, or the same purpose Linux-flavored commands ***mgetty*** or ***agetty.***

24.3 Third-Party Communication Software

The existing "gap" in the full UNIX control of modems is partially filled with the third-party software. Most of this software is available across different UNIX flavors, sometimes free for an implementaion, and sometimes even distributed with the operating system itself. Popular programs of this type are, for example, ***minicom, C-kermit, ecu, pcomm/ procomm,*** or ***xcomm.*** We will briefly present the ***C-kermit*** program.

24.3.1 C-Kermit

Kermit is a family of file transfer, management, and communication software programs from Columbia University available for most computers and operating systems (known as ***C-kermit***). The version of Kermit for UNIX supports both serial connections (direct or dialed) and TCP/IP connections. ***C-Kermit*** can be thought of as a user-friendly and powerful alternative to ***cu, tip, uucp, ftp,*** and ***telnet;*** a single package for both network and serial communications, offering automation, convenience, and language features not found in the other packages. It fully supports modem dialing, file transfer and management, terminal connection, character-set translation, and script programming. Together, ***C-Kermit, Kermit 95, MS-DOS Kermit,*** and ***IBM Mainframe Kermit*** offer a consistent and nearly universal approach to inter-computer communications.

C-Kermit is Copyright (C) 1985, 1996 by the Trustees of Columbia University in the City of New York. The copyright notice must not be removed, altered, or obscured.

C-Kermit is thoroughly documented in the book by Frank da Cruz and Christine M. Gianone, *Digital Press,* Second Edition, 1997. For serious users of C-Kermit, particularly those who plan to write C-Kermit script programs, this book is highly recommended. Book sales are the primary source of funding for the nonprofit Kermit Project. New features added since the most recent edition of the book was published are documented in the online file *ckcker.upd.* Hints, tips, limitations, and restrictions are listed in *ckcker.bwr* (general C-Kermit) and *ckuker.bwr* (UNIX-specific); http link is *www.columbia. edu/kermit/.*

C-Kermit can be used in two modes:

1. Remote mode when C-Kermit establishes a connection to another computer by direct serial connection, by dialing a modem, or by making a network connection.
2. Local mode when C-Kermit gives a terminal connection to the remote computer, using an actual terminal, emulator, or UNIX workstation terminal window or console driver for specific terminal emulation.

C-Kermit also has two types of commands:

1. The familiar UNIX-style command-line options.
2. An interactive dialog with a prompt that provides a small but useful subset of C-Kermit's features for terminal connection and file transfer, plus the ability to pipe files into or out of C-Kermit for transfer. It also provides an access to dialing, script programming, character-set translation, and in general, detailed control and display of all C-Kermit's features. Interactive commands can also be collected into command files or macros.

The format of the command to start ***C-Kermit*** is:

kermit *[command-file] [options...]*

Among the options there is a group of so-called action options that require certain actions to be accomplished. If there are no action options on the command line, C-Kermit starts in interactive command mode: a greeting message and then the "C-Kermit>" prompt. If the action options are specified on the command line, C-Kermit takes the indicated actions and then exits directly back to UNIX. Either way, C-Kermit executes the commands in its initialization file *ckermit.ini* (usually located in the directory */usr/share/lib/kermit*), before it executes any other commands. An exception is when an alternative initialization is explicitly requested.

C-Kermit is an extremely powerful and versatile program with many C-Kermit commands for:

- Program management
- Connection establishment and release
- Terminal connection
- File transfer
- File management
- Client/server operation
- Script programming

Each of the listed command groups contain a decent number of C-Kermit commands; all together it enables the most sophisticated tasks to be successfully completed. It is common to specify C-Kermit commands with capital letters, and we will follow this convention.

A large number of existing options can also be divided into:

- Action options of the type connect, send/receive files, enter/terminate server mode and similar
- Setting options that specify in more detail different kermit parameters involved in the file transfer, connection procedure, and similar
- Other options of the type skip/alternate initialization, foreground, background, forced stay, explicit interactive, remote, or debug mode, etc.

For a better understanding of how C-Kermit works, let's see the most common scenario for C-Kermit file transfer between two directly connected computers, identified here as local and remote computer. The file transfer is slightly different over the network. Although other methods are also possible, this basic method should work in all cases, and it consists of:

- Start C-Kermit on the local computer and establish a connection to the remote computer. Use the sequence:

  SET MODEM TYPE modem-name

  SET LINE device-name

  SET SPEED bits-per-second

  DIAL phone-number if you are dialing.

  (SET NETWORK network-type and SET HOST host-name-or-address for network connections).
- Set any other necessary communication parameters, such as PARITY, DUPLEX, and FLOW-CONTROL.
- Give the CONNECT command.
- Log in to the remote computer.
- Start C-Kermit on the remote computer, give any desired SET commands for the file, communication, or protocol-related parameters. If a transfer of binary files is supposed, on the transmitting side SET FILE TYPE BINARY to the C-Kermit program.

- To transfer a file or file group, give the local C-Kermit a SEND command, followed by a filename or "wildcard" file specification, for example:

  send filename.txt # (send one file)

  send filename.* # (send a group of files)
- To receive a file or files, give the remote C-Kermit a RECEIVE command. The sending and receiving C-Kermit will exchange name and other attributes of each file.
- Escape back to the C-Kermit program on the local computer to get a local Kermit program's prompt.
- To transfer binary files, give the command SET FILE TYPE BINARY to the Kermit program that is sending the files.
- To receive files, tell the local C-Kermit program to RECEIVE; to transfer files tell the local C-Kermit program to SEND, specifying a filename or wildcard file specification. In other words, tell the C-Kermit program what to do first, SEND or RECEIVE, then escape back to the local C-Kermit and give it the opposite command, RECEIVE or SEND.
- When the transfer is complete, give a CONNECT command to talk to C-Kermit on the remote computer again. Type EXIT to get back to the command prompt on the remote computer. When everything is done, log out and then (if necessary) escape back to Kermit on the local computer. Then another connection could be made, or EXIT from the local C-Kermit program.

C-Kermit's file transfer protocol defaults are deliberately conservative, resulting in file transfer that almost always works, but might be somewhat slow. To increase file transfer performance on computers and connections that permit it, use:

SET RECEIVE PACKET-LENGTH to increase the packet length

SET WINDOW to increase the packet window size

SET PREFIXING to reduce the overhead of control-character prefixing

Alternatively, it is worth it to try the FAST command to enable all these performance options at once. Also on serial connections, use hardware flow control (SET FLOW RTS/CTS) if available, rather than software (XON/XOFF) flow control.

Obviously, there are quite a number of steps that should be properly done for a successful output. It sounds like a good idea to script a quite complex scenario and make everything much simpler.

Two examples how to use ***C-Kermit*:**

- Remote-mode example (C-Kermit is on the far end) — send the file "filename.bin" in the binary mode (option -i) using a window size of 4 (option -v 4):

  kermit -v 4 -i -s filename.bin
- Local-mode example (C-Kermit makes the connection):

  kermit -l /dev/tty0p0 -b 19200 -c -r -n

  This command takes following actions:

  Makes a 19200-bps direct connection through the device */dev/tty0p0*

  Connects (option -c) to login

  Presumably starts a remote C-Kermit program and tells it to send a file

  Receives the file (option -r)

  Then connects back (option -n) to finish up and log out

For dialing out, specify a modem type, and use a different device name:

kermit -m hayes -l /dev/cul0p0 -b 2400 -c -r –n

At the end let's see one quite complex real-life example. The task is to transfer data on a regular daily basis from a UNIX system to the bulletin-board site. The available resources are: 16-line modem pool (modem server) on the local area network and used by many users, and public telephone network. The UNIX system accesses the modem pool through the local area network. The solution presented here supposes:

- Data to be transferred are ready and saved in the file "FileToGo."
- A dynamic creation of the "take-file" that will reflect the actual environment and status of modem lines.
- Invoke the C-Kermit program (the file "take-file" is used for its initialization).
- A file transfer from UNIX system to the bulletin-board site with a verbose message displaying.

The following script named "bbkermit.ksh" fully accomplishes this task. The command syntax is:

*/share/local/ckermit/bin/**bbkermit.ksh** /share/local/ckermit/etc/**bbkermit.ini***

Assuming specified paths and filenames (filenames are presented in ***bold***), the script dynamically specifies the so-called ***take-file*** and then invokes ***C-Kermit*** program, which uses the so created take-file for its own initialization. The created take-file consists of two parts:

1. Dynamic modem-pool-related portion created in the script
2. Static bulletin-board-specific portion specified in the passed file ***bbkermit.init***

The presented script ***bbkermit.ksh,*** as well as ***bbkermit.ini*** file, corresponds to a specific C-Kermit implementation; however, they can be easily used as templates for many other similar implementations. Both are well commented and quite comprehensive. Please read them for more detailed information.

$ cat bbkermit.ksh

```
#!/bin/ksh
#
# This script modifies kermit take-file, and accomplishes the transfer of the file
# FileToGo to the bulletin-board site via 24-port modem-pool. The modified
# kermit take-file consists of two major part: modem-pool specific part dynamically
# specified within this script, and static site specific part specified in the file "bbsite.ini",
# and passed as an argument to this script. To fully understand this script a basic
# knowledge of C-Kermit is supposed. All path and file names are arbitrary

# Define global variables
CKERMIT=/share/local/c-kermit/bin/kermit      # C-Kermit executable
ZMDIR=/share/local/zmodem/bin                 # zmodem executables directory
mpool=mpoolhost                               # actual modem-pool host name
user=modpool                                  # actual modem-pool user ID
password=abc48fgh                             # actual modem-pool password
min_port= 2000                                # starting modem-pool port number
max_port= 2024                                # ending modem-pool port number
```

```
# Define a usage statement function
function show_usage {
   echo "Usage: bbkermit.ksh <takefile>"
}

# Check usage
if [ $# -lt 1 ]; then
   show_usage
fi
takefile=$1

# Check specified file
if [ ! -f "$takefile" ]; then
        echo "Error: Cannot read file '$takefile'"
        exit 1
fi

# Create a temporary file that can only be read by the current user
# This file will keep final kermit take-file data
TMPFILE=/tmp/bbkermit.$$
touch $TMPFILE
chmod 600 $TMPFILE

# Create the final 'take' file for kermit dynamically
# The "here document" specifies a sequence of C-Kermit
# commands for the final kermit take-file

cat << !EOF > $TMPFILE

########### Start of the here document ##############

# Setup the paths and macros for the zmodem executables
# All zmodem executables named sz, sb, sx, csz, csb and csx,
# as well as rz, rb, rx, crz, crb and crx reside in this directory
define \%t $ZMDIR

# Setup send macro definitions
define sz if = \v(argc) 1 end 1 {sz what file(s)?}, -
redirect \%t/csz \%1 \%2 \%3 \%4 \%5 \%6 \%7 \%8 \%9
define sb if = \v(argc) 1 end 1 {sb what file(s)?}, -
redirect \%t/csb \%1 \%2 \%3 \%4 \%5 \%6 \%7 \%8 \%9
define sx if = \v(argc) 1 end 1 {sx what file?}, -
redirect \%t/csx \%1 \%2 \%3 \%4 \%5 \%6 \%7

# Setup receive macro definitions
define rz redirect \%t/crz
define rb redirect \%t/crb
define rx if = \v(argc) 1 end 1 {rx what file?}, -
redirect \%t/crx \%1

# Define the starting modem-pool port number
define \%p $min_port

# This is the reference starting point to acquire a free modem-pool port
:ACQUIRE_MODEM

# Clear the line (Only needed for multiple passes through this loop)
hangup

# Increment the port (\%p) by one (The real starting port is 2001)
assign \%p \Feval(\%p + 1)

# If we've tried all the ports and can't get in, then just exit
if > \%p $max_port exit 1

# Attempt to connect to the specified port
echo Attempting to connect on port \%p
telnet $mpool \%p
```

```
# If port is in use, then jump back up to :ACQUIRE_MODEM and try the next port
if failure goto ACQUIRE_MODEM

# Log into modem-pool
input 5 sername:
if failure goto ACQUIRE_MODEM

# Enter userid and password
output $user\13
input 5 assword:
if failure goto ACQUIRE_MODEM
# To prevent the appearance of the clear password in the take-file
# the password itself is previously saved in the kermit variable "\%w"
output \%w\13
sleep 3

# Check that modem is responding
output AT\13
input 5 OK if failure goto ACQUIRE_MODEM

!EOF
########### End of the here document ##############

# Add the user specified take-file onto the end of the temporary file
cat $takefile >> $TMPFILE
if [ $? -ne 0 ]; then
        rm $TMPFILE
        exit 1
fi
# Run kermit using TMPFILE as a final take-file. The password is
# define here, so that it won't show up in the temporary file.

$CKERMIT << !EOF
define \%w $password
take $TMPFILE
!EOF

# Remove tempfile
rm -f $TMPFILE
```

The kermit initialization file follows:

$ cat bbsite.ini

```
# This file presents the second portion of the kermit initialization sequence
# that is dynamically created before the C-Kermit invocation and saved in the
# then created kermit take-file. It contains bulletin-board site specific data,
# cannot be copied as it is. The displayed syntax is C-Kermit specific.
# Phone number to dial
output ATDT12125671234\13

# The following sequence depends on the actual dialogue between
# this host and the bulletin-board site. Each input entry specifies the
# time to wait and the expected "pattern" to be received

input 70 CONNECT
if failure goto ACQUIRE_MODEM

input 20 logon id:
if failure goto ACQUIRE_MODEM
# Login ID – for zmodem TP002324
output TP002324\13

input 20 password:
if failure goto ACQUIRE_MODEM
# No password on this account
output \13
```

```
input 20 cmd>
if failure exit 1
# zmodem production= 1224, test= 1299
output $$ADD ID=TP002324 BID='TESTING'\13

input 20 seconds
if failure exit 1
# Change directory for file to send named FileToGo
cd /share/bulletin-board/data

# Send the file with periodic (fake) key insertion
# Program "sz" to transmit the file is dynamically set
sz -w16384 FileToGo
if failure exit 2

input 50 cmd>
if failure exit 1
output LOGOFF\13
input 30 LOGOFF completed
```

24.4 Introduction to UUCP

UUCP stands for "**U**NIX to **U**NIX **C**o**p**y" and represents a collection of programs designed to provide communication between different UNIX systems. UUCP performs: a transfer of files between UNIX systems; a command execution on a remote UNIX system; and mailing to users on a remote UNIX system. Basically, UUCP uses standard serial connections and a telephone service, but could also run on local networks. Each connection is established on a user-request basis, creating a corresponding dial-up link. Each UNIX system involved in an UUCP connection has files that describe the other systems directly linked to it, including the type of the available links. To create these files is the task of the system administrator; generally, UUCP requires minimal supervision and overall administration.

UUCP is an old-fashioned UNIX subsystem; nowadays, many will say an obsolete topic. However, a more accurate description could be: UUCP appeared relatively early, but it is still going on and is trying to keep pace with other, more-advanced communication technologies; in other words UUCP is still in use — not very often, but sufficiently often to find its place among other overall UNIX administration topics. The UUCP skills could also be useful in managing some other UNIX issues, especially in the modem-related area. Finally, thanks to the UUCP, the author of this text has been able to stay in daily touch with friends in one besieged city, during one senseless war; UUCP deserves, at least, to be a part of this text.

UUCP also supports *Usenet,* a bulletin-board network that uses the public domain Netnews software to exchange news about a wide variety of topics.

24.4.1 How Does UUCP Work?

Using UUCP basically means dealing with three main programs:

1. ***uucp,*** for a file transfer to or from a remote machine (similar to the *cp* program; however, with extended addressing capabilities)
2. ***uux,*** for a command execution on a remote machine (usually restricted in some way because of security reasons)

3. ***mail,*** a version of a mail program that is compatible with UUCP (this is */bin/mail;* it should not be confused with */usr/ucb/mail* that is an e-mail user agent that was discussed in the Chapter 20)

The listed programs are user related, i.e., they are primarily used from the command line. However, it happens much more in the background; two running UUCP daemons, ***uucico*** and ***uuxqt,*** invisible to users actually do most of the work. ***uucico*** is involved in transferring files and remote execution requests between UNIX systems, and ***uuxqt*** in their processing on a remote UNIX system.

UUCP is a "store-and-forward" subsystem: requests for transfer and remote processing are not executed immediately; instead they are spooled for later execution. UUCP daemons take care of spooled requests and process them once the connection between remote UNIX systems has been established. A more detailed description of what happens is:

- When ***uucp*** or ***uux*** programs are invoked, a "work file" containing information about the source and destination files, the program options, and the type of requests is created in the directory */usr/spool/uucp.* If a file transfer was required, a file to be transferred is also copied.
- The ***uucico*** daemon is involved to make the transfer; it scans the spool directory for work files and attempts to contact specified remote UNIX systems and execute the instructions in the work files. In the *BNU UUCP* version, an intermediate process called ***uusched*** does the scan and calls ***uucico*** when the needed conditions are met.
- The work files contain only a part of the information ***uucico*** needs to know: ***what to do,*** but not ***when*** or ***how to do it.*** This information is contained in a set of the UUCP configuration files in the directory */usr/lib/uucp,* and this is a duty of the system administrator to set up in advance.

24.4.2 UUCP Versions

The first UUCP system was built in 1976 at AT&T Bell Laboratories, and this version was known as *Version 2 UUCP.* It was distributed with UNIX Version 7 in 1977. Updated versions were already incorporated in the SVR1 and SVR2 platforms.

Soon, UUCP was included in BSD 4x UNIX platform, as well as in other vendor-specific UNIX flavors: Sun Microsystems SunOS and DEC's Ultrix. The version shipped with BSD 4.2 was known as *Truscott UUCP.* All those UUCP versions were based on the updates made at Duke University (known as *Duke UUCP,* which is no longer in use).

With SVR3, a new upgraded version known as *BNU* (an acronym for *basic network utility*) began to be distributed. This version was/is also known as *HoneyDanBer UUCP.* Further UUCP improvement and update continued on both major UNIX platforms. The *BSD 4.3's UUCP* presented another significant update, merging some BNU features while retaining more continuity with other Version 2 UUCP implementations. The trend has continued up to the present time. Typically, as for all of UNIX, different UUCP flavors and versions have much in common, and they provide the very same tasks. A kind of generalization could be to say that the BSD-like UNIX platforms were primarily oriented toward the *Version 2 UUCP,* while the System V-like UNIX platforms were *BNU UUCP* oriented. We will discuss this topic bearing in mind both major UUCP versions, underlying specific differences as they appear.

How can we be sure about a running UUCP version? By listing the */usr/lib/uucp* directory and searching for some typical files, we can conclude something; if the file *L.sys* is there, this is *Version 2 UUCP;* otherwise, the file *Systems* belongs to *BNU UUCP.* The "UUCP home directory" has been changed; for example on SunOS, the file */etc/uucp/L.sys* existed. Nowadays, Solaris, HP-UX and other modern UNIX flavors, keep UUCP configuration files in the */etc/uucp* directory.

24.4.3 UUCP Chat-Transfer Session

Assuming the basic idea of how UUCP works, let us analyze in more detail a UUCP session. Let's suppose a hypothetical case:

- Two remote UNIX hosts: ***red*** and ***blue*** have all the facilities to communicate over the telephone network.
- A UUCP file transfer from the host ***red*** for the host ***blue*** is initiated.
- Both hosts are set up appropriately.

The last line saying: "set up appropriately" is the crucial one; the way the hosts would communicate absolutely depends on the way the UUCP subsystems are configured. Everything is written in the UUCP configuration file: on a *BNU UUCP* subsystem the */etc/uucp/Systems* file (earlier */usr/lib/uucp/Systems*), or on a *Version 2 UUCP* subsystem the */etc/uucp/L.sys* file (or */usr/lib/uucp/L.sys*).

A corresponding configuration entry at the host ***red*** would look like:

blue   Any   ACU   19200   3217654   ogin: iamred   ssword: passme

This entry defines that the system ***red*** can call the system ***blue:***

- At ***any*** time
- Over a modem connected to a telephone line (**ACU** = Automatic Calling Unit)
- At a speed of ***19200*** bps
- Using the telephone number ***3217654***
- Logging in with login name: ***iamred***
- Identifying with password: ***passme***

A UUCP session for the supposed configuration data starts with a user's command at the host ***red*** and continues until the remote system daemon at the host ***blue*** verifies the transfer.

If there are multiple ways to reach a remote host, it could be multiple entries for that host in the configuration file. However, the configuration file (*Systems* or *L.sys*) only includes a designation for the specified connection; it does not describe the implemented hardware. Another file, *Devices* in BNU (or *L-devices* in Version 2), contains one-to-one mapping between the designated connection and what device name the daemon ***uucico*** should use to access the actual device (for example, the serial line to use). If a device is a modem, additional needed information how to dial could be found in the file *acucap*, or *Dialers* in BNU (or *modemcap* in Version 2). In the early days of UUCP, some UUCP versions even had dialing instructions hardcored into the ***uucp*** program.

There are several reasons why the file transfer may not occur immediately. First, the transfer can be restricted to a particular time (through the configuration file itself); second, the telephone line can be busy at that very moment. In that case, ***uucico*** will leave the corresponding status file and try again the next time it is invoked. The procedure will repeat until successful transfer is performed, or the minimum retry period has elapsed (by default, 55 or 60 minutes).

The file transfer is performed between two ***uucico*** daemons, on the source and the destination host. The ***uucico*** on the source (calling) system is playing "master role" — it controls the link; the ***uucico*** on the destination (receiving) system plays "slave role" — it checks local permissions to authorize the transfer. Two daemons communicate (chat) between themselves; when nothing is left to be transferred in either direction, they agree to hang up. At that point, another daemon ***uuxqt*** is invoked to scan the spool directory for any outstanding execution request from the remote system. If such a request exists, ***uuxqt*** forks a command to do what the user asked for.

We will return to the UUCP configuration files later.

24.5 UUCP Commands, Daemons, and Related Issues

We already mentioned major UUCP commands and daemons. Now, we will discuss them in more detail.

24.5.1 The Major UUCP Commands

UUCP related commands are located in the */usr/bin* directory:

```
$ ls -l /usr/bin | grep uucp          (HP-UX 10.20)
-r-sr-xr-x  1 uucp  bin  45056  May 30  1996  uucp
-r-sr-xr-x  1 uucp  bin  24576  May 30  1996  uuls
-r-sr-xr-x  1 uucp  bin  12288  May 30  1996  uuname
-r-sr-xr-x  1 uucp  bin  16384  May 30  1996  uusnap
-r-sr-xr-x  1 uucp  bin  36864  May 30  1996  uustat
-r-sr-xr-x  1 uucp  bin  49152  May 30  1996  uux
```

Among them, two commands present core UUCP commands that existed through all UUCP flavors and releases; they are ***uucp*** and ***uux***.

24.5.1.1 The *uucp* Command

The ***uucp*** command copies each *source-file* to the named *destination-file.* A filename may be a fullpath name on the local system (host), or may have the form:

system-name!pathname

where

system-name Specifies a remote system (host). The *system-name* may also be a list of names such as:
system-name!system-name!...!system-name!pathname

in which case an attempt is made to send the file via the specified route to the destination. The shell metacharacters *?*, *, and *[ ]* appearing in the pathname part will be expanded on the appropriate system.

pathname Specifies the fullpath of the designated file.

The ***uucp*** preserves execute permissions across the transmission and grants read and write permissions to everybody (file mode 666).

The format of the ***uucp*** command is:

uucp -options source-file destination-file

where

source-file Specify a source file to be copied
destination-file Specify a designated copied file

and the options are:

Option	Meaning
-c	Use the source file when copying out rather than copying the file to the spool directory. This is the default.
-C	Make a copy of outgoing files in the UUCP spool directory, rather than copying the source file directly to the target system. This lets you remove the source file after issuing the ***uucp*** command.
-d	Make all necessary directories for the file copy. This is the default.
-f	Do not make intermediate directories for the file copy.
-j	Output the job identification ASCII string on the standard output. This job identification can be used by ***uustat*** to obtain the status or terminate a job.
-m	Send mail to the requester when the copy is complete.
-r	Do not start the ***uucico*** daemon, just queue the job.
-ggrade	*grade* is a single letter or number, from 0 to 9, A to Z, or a to z; 0 is the highest grade, and z is the lowest grade. Lower grades will cause the job to be transmitted earlier during a particular conversation. The default *grade* is n. By way of comparison, ***uux*** defaults to A; ***mail*** is usually sent at grade C.
-nusername	Notify *username* at the remote system (that is, send *username* mail) that a file was sent.
-xdebug-level	Produce debugging output on the standard output. A *debug-level* is a number between 0 and 9; higher numbers give more detailed information. The 5, 7, and 9 are good numbers to try; they give increasing amounts of detail.

24.5.1.2 The *uux* Command

The ***uux*** will gather files from various systems, execute a command on a specified system and send the standard output to a file on a specified system.

For security reasons, most installations limit the list of commands executable on behalf of an incoming request from ***uux,*** permitting only the receipt of mail. Remote execution permissions are defined in the corresponding configuration file.

The ***command-string*** is made up of one or more arguments that look like a shell command line, except that the command and file names may be prefixed by ***system-name***!; a null ***system-name*** is interpreted as the local system. The format of the uux command is:

uux -options command-string

The "-" option sends the standard input to the ***uux*** command as the standard input to the ***command-string.*** Other options are:

Option	Meaning
-b	Return whatever standard input was provided to the ***uux*** command if the job fails (that is, returns a non-zero exit status).
-c	Use the source file when copying out rather than copying the file to the spool directory. This is the default.
-C	Force the copy of local files to the spool directory for transfer.
-n	Do not return any indication by mail of success or failure of the job.
-p	Same as "-": the standard input to ***uux*** is made the standard input to the ***command-string.***
-r	Do not start the ***uucico*** daemon, just queue the job.
-z	Return an indication by mail even if the job succeeds (that is, returns a zero exit status).
-aname	Use *name* as the user identification replacing the initiator user ID. Notification will be returned to the user.
-ggrade	*grade* is a single letter or number, from 0 to 9, A to Z, or a to z; 0 is the highest grade, and z is the lowest grade. Lower grades will cause the job to be transmitted earlier during a particular conversation. The default *grade* is A.
-xdebug-level	Produce debugging output on the standard output. A *debug-level* is a number between 0 and 9; higher numbers give more detailed information. The 5, 7, and 9 are good numbers to try; they give increasing amounts of detail.

The ***uux*** will attempt to get all files to the execution system. For files that are output files, the file name must be escaped using parentheses. For example, the command:

uux ahost!cut -f1 bhost!/usr/file \(chost!/usr/file\)

gets the file */usr/file* from the system ***bhost*** and sends it to the system ***ahost,*** performs the ***cut*** command on that file, and sends the result of the ***cut*** command to the file */usr/file* on the system ***chost*** (pay attention also to the escape backslash characters in front of parentheses).

The ***uux*** command would notify if the requested command on the remote system was disallowed, or if the command fails (returns a non-zero exit status). This notification could be turned off by the ***-n*** option. The response comes by remote mail from the remote system (machine). For example the command:

uux "!diff ahost!/example/file1 bhost!/busr/example/file2 > !~/example/file.diff"

will get the *file1* and *file2* files from the systems ***ahost*** and ***bhost,*** execute the ***diff*** command, and put the results in the file *file.diff* in the local *PUBDIR/example* directory.

24.5.2 The UUCP Daemons

UUCP daemons present server programs involved in the execution of different UUCP jobs — they provide some of the required UUCP-related services. They are started on an as-needed basis, or by other programs. Most of the UUCP daemons live in the */usr/lib/uucp* directory:

$ ls -C /usr/lib/uucp (Solaris 2.x)

Uutry	***uucico***	*uudemon.crontab*	***uuxqt***
bnuconvert	*uucleanup*	*uudemon.hour*	
remote.unknown	*uudemon.admin*	*uudemon.poll*	
uucheck	*uudemon.cleanup*	***uusched***	

We will discuss in more detail the following UUCP daemons: ***uucico, uuxqt, uusched,*** and ***uucpd.***

24.5.2.1 The *uucico* Daemon

uucico is the file transport daemon involved in transfers of UUCP work files; both discussed UUCP commands, ***uux*** and ***uucp,*** only spool jobs into the queue that should be transferred by this daemon. Depending on the UUCP version, this daemon could be started by the other daemon-scheduler, ***uusched,*** or manually — primarily for debugging purposes.

The format of the command to start the daemon is:

/usr/lib/uucp/uucico -options

with the major options:

- ***-d****spool-directory* Define the directory *spool-directory* that contains UUCP work files to be transferred; the default directory is */usr/spool/uucp.*
- ***-i****interface* Define the interface used with ***uucico.*** This interface only affects slave mode. Known interfaces are UNIX (default).
- ***-r****role-number* Specify the role that ***uucico*** should perform. A *role-number* is the digit 1 for a master mode, or 0 for a slave mode (default). The master mode should be specified when ***uucico*** is started by another program or ***cron.***
- ***-s****system-name* Specify the remote system *system-name* to try to contact; it is required when the role is master.
- ***-x****debug-level* Produce debugging output on the standard output. A *debug-level* is a number between 0 and 9; higher numbers give more detailed information. The 5, 7, and 9 are good numbers to try; they give increasing amounts of details.

24.5.2.2 The *uuxqt* Daemon

uuxqt is the daemon involved in executing remote job requests from remote systems generated by the use of the ***uux*** command on remote hosts (the ***mail*** program also uses ***uux*** for remote mail requests). The ***uuxqt*** daemon searches the spool directories looking for "X." files. For each "X." file, ***uuxqt*** checks to see if all required data files are available and accessible, and if the specified commands are permitted for the specified system. A corresponding configuration file is used to validate file accessibility and command execution permission (primarily the file *Permissions*).

The format of the command is:

/usr/lib/uucp/uuxqt [-ssystem-name] [-xdebug-level]

where the option:

- ***-s****system-name* Specifies the remote system name *system-name.*
- ***-x****debug-level* Produces debugging output on the standard output. A *debug-level* is a number between 0 and 9; higher numbers give more detailed information. The 5, 7, and 9 are good numbers to try; they give increasing amounts of detail.

There are two environment variables that must be set before the ***uuxqt*** command is executed:

UU_MACHINE	Machine that sends the job
UU_USER	User that sends the job

The variables could be specified within the program that invokes the ***uuxqt*** daemon, or any other way.

24.5.2.3 The *uusched* Daemon

The ***uusched*** daemon is the UUCP file transport scheduler; it is usually started indirectly by the ***cron*** facility (literally it is started by another UUCP program ***uudemon.hour,*** that sets a needed environment for a successful execution of this daemon, and which is actually started by the ***cron***).

The format of the command is:

/usr/lib/uucp/uusched *[-**u**debug-level] [-**x**debug-level]*

where the available options are only for debugging purposes; a *debug-level* is a number between 0 and 9; higher numbers give more detailed information:

*-**u**debug-level*	Specifies the debug level to be passed to the ***uucico*** program
*-**x**debug-level*	Specifies the debug level for internal output messages

An example of the needed ***cron*** entry on the Solaris platform, to start indirectly the ***uusched*** daemon is:

15,45 * * * * /etc/uucp/uucp/uudemon.hour

Every half hour the program ***uudemon.hour*** is started; that invokes the ***uusched*** daemon.

24.5.2.4 The *uucpd* Daemon

The ***uucpd*** daemon supports a UUCP connection over the network. This daemon was developed and introduced later; originally, UUCP was based on the connections other than over the network. Obviously, UUCP had to be adapted to the emerging networking that has become a common way to communicate between computer systems. Sometimes, the daemon is named ***in.uucpd,*** like on the Solaris platform.

uucpd is invoked by the super server ***inetd,*** when a UUCP connection is established (via the corresponding well-known UUCP port). The corresponding ***inetd*** configuration entry (HP-UX 10.20):

$ cat /etc/inetd.conf | grep uucp
uucp stream tcp nowait root /usr/sbin/uucpd uucpd

This entry is usually commented out; to activate the ***uucpd*** daemon the line must be uncommented and the ***inetd*** server recycled.

The corresponding UUCP-related port is:

$ cat /etc/servisces | grep uucp
uucp 540/tcp uucpd # uucp daemon

Once invoked, the ***uucpd*** daemon prompts for login, requesting the ***uucico*** process at the other end (the daemon at the remote host that started connection) to supply a username and password.

24.5.3 The UUCP Spool Directories and Files

A discussion on UUCP files and directories very quickly focuses on the UUCP spool directory. Despite the fact that UUCP configuration files are located in the */etc/uucp* directory, and UUCP related programs in the */usr/lib/uucp* directory, to maintain and administer UUCP properly, understanding of the spool directory is the most important.

The contents of the spool directory are constantly changing. In addition to log files, which are always added when a transfer occurs, there are a large number of work files that are dynamically created and deleted during the UUCP communication between UNIX systems. A work file contains the instructions for ***uucico*** such as the name of the file to be copied (transferred), ownership and permissions, destination, and so on. A work file is created under the name:

C.dest_unameAjob_ID

where

C	Stands for a *control file,* to distinguish from a *data file* (***D***)
dest_uname	A remote system name, truncated to seven characters
A	A letter indicating the file processing order (letters A to Z, and a to z, or some specific letters depending of the UUCP version)
job_ID	A job identification 6-digit number

Each work file can contain up to 20 requests for the file transfer or execution for a given system.

For files that are copied to the spool directory (***uucp -C*** option), the corresponding data files use the same name with the prefix "***D.***" When a remote command execution is requested, an execute file is created with the prefix "***X;***" temporary files have the prefix "***TM,***" lock files "***LCK,***" and status files "***STST.***"

One of the major improvements of *BNU UUCP* was the introduction of the better organized *spool* directory:

/usr/spool/uucp/	
.Admin	Administrative files
.Corrupt	Corrupt files that could not be processed
.Log	Log files
.Old	Old log files
.Sequence	System sequence numbers
.Status	System status file
.Workspace	UUCP temporary workspace area
.Xqtdir	Remote executions
.system_name1	Files to/from the specific systems
.system_name2	"
.system_name3	"
/usr/spool/uucp/.Log/	
uucp/	Directory of ***uucp*** request logs
uucico/	Directory of ***uucico*** execution logs
uux/	Directory of ***uux*** request logs
uuxqt/	Directory of ***uuxqt*** request logs or remote command executions on the local system

Probably the biggest administrative problem concerning UUCP is the spool directory cleanup to clean out jobs that have been spooled but not completed successfully. In most UUCP implementations, there are automatic shell scripts to do this cleanup; the only elements to adjust are the frequency those scripts should be running and the lifetime of UUCP work files.

24.6 Configuring a UUCP Link

A brief description of an UUCP chat-transfer session at the beginning of this chapter shed light on some of the configuration files. However, to configure an UUCP link properly, it is not enough to configure those files only; there are several steps more that must be performed:

- Establish a communication link between the two UNIX hosts in question; usually, a modem based dial-out link.
- Give a name to the UNIX system that identifies the system uniquely.
- Create entries in the *Systems* (or *L.sys*) file that describes when and how to reach other UNIX systems.
- Create entries in the *Devices* (or *L-devices*) file that describes communication devices (hardware issues).
- For modems unknown to the system, create dialing instructions.
- Apply security mechanisms.

Some systems provide menu-driven installation utilities that make the task easier. However, the discussion that follows assumes managing from the command line.

24.6.1 Serial Line-Related Issues

The baseline of the UUCP network is a physical communication link; a proper communication link is a basic requirement for UUCP to work at all. Until the link has been established, nothing else matters.

There are three types of communication links:

1. Direct (hardwired RS-232 link)
2. A modem (used via telephone line)
3. A network (TCP/IP)

When a direct or a modem communication link is in question, they both relate to the system's serial lines; from the UNIX standpoint, they target the serial ports. UNIX addresses serial ports, as any other device, via the corresponding special device files (special device files point further to the corresponding drivers that are parts of the kernel). For the serial ports, these are terminal-related device files, specified as */dev/ttynn* (where *nn* identifies the port's number). Basically, it was supposed to use serial ports to connect the system's terminals, to provide regular user's communication with the system. The ***getty*** program has monitored the serial lines and started a login process as soon as it detected any activity on the line. When it happened, the ***getty*** program would immediately send back the login prompt and exec the ***login*** program to continue the login process.

Such an approach seems to be OK if only a terminal could be at the other side of the serial line, and the only possible sender is a user who wants to log in to the system. However, for another kind of communication which is not "login related," the ***gettys*** behavior seems to be an obstacle. Actually, it is appropriate for ***getty*** to monitor dial-in lines; but for dial-out lines, ***getty*** should be disabled.

This is the "well-known" problem with serial lines monitored by the ***getty*** program, when they are not used for an exclusive login into the UNIX system. However, to realize a different bidirectional serial communication, the alternatives are:

- Use two ports (one for "in" and the other for "out")
- Use a single port in two ways

In both cases, additional administrative work must be done.

UUCP assumes the second approach. *BNU UUCP* provides a bidirectional program called ***uugetty*** (an improved version of the ***getty*** program) that could be used instead of ***getty.*** The ***uugetty*** program is wise enough not to respond with a "login prompt" when the line is in use for outgoing calls; instead it continues with an appropriate dialogue.

To enable the start of the ***uugetty*** program on the System V platform during the system startup, the */etc/inittab* table should include a corresponding UUCP entry like this one:

uu:2:respawn:/usr/lib/uucp/uugetty -r tty07 19200

where

r	option tells ***uugetty*** to wait to read for a character before putting up a login prompt
tty07	is the supposed serial port (terminal line)
19200	is a modem's speed

uugetty is a common replacement for the ***getty*** program to enable the bidirectional communication required by UUCP over the corresponding serial line. However, this is not a must; on Solaris 2.x the regular terminal line monitoring program ***ttymon*** is smart enough to know how to handle the UUCP related bidirectional communication. Solaris 2.x does not even provide the program ***uugetty.***

24.6.2 UUCP Configuration Files

Once a serial link has been set, a number of other configuration and description data must also be provided. These data define the UUCP behavior on the system and are located in the several UUCP configuration files. Two examples follow.

$ ls -C /etc/uucp (HP-UX 10.20)

Devices	*Dialers*	*Maxuuxqts*	*Poll*
Dialcodes	*Maxuuscheds*	*Permissions*	***Systems***

$ ls -C /etc/uucp (Solaris 2.x)

Config	*Dialcodes*	*Limits*	*Sysfiles*
Devconfig	*Dialers*	*Permissions*	***Systems***
Devices	*Grades*	*Poll*	*remote.unknown*

24.6.2.1 The UUCP Systems Data

First, the appropriate configuration data about assumed remote systems (hosts) should be provided:

- A remote system name
- Convenient time to call
- Phone number of attached remote modem
- UUCP login name on the remote system
- UUCP password on the remote system

Both sides in a UUCP communication need these data, and they always relate to the remote system on the other side. If we recall the example from the beginning of this section, we can easily recognize these configuration data.

The data are placed into the *UUCP systems* configuration file: *Systems* on *BNU UUCP* or *L.sys* on *Version 2 UUCP.* An entry in the file describes one link; multiple links with the same system are described with multiple entries. The generic format of an entry is:

sys_name schedule device_type speed phone_number chat_script

where

sys_name The name of the remote system (the DNS hostname could be used).

schedule The time schedule when the local system can call the remote one:
- ***Any*** the system can call on any day
- ***Never*** the system should never call but should just wait to be called
- ***Wk*** any weekday (any weekday could be also specified: ***Su, Mo, Tu, We, Th, Fr,*** and ***Sa***); the time subfield is specified by two 24-hour clock times separated by a dash: ***1900–2300*** specifies time between 7 and 11 p.m

device_type The type of a device to be used for the call:
- ***ACU*** for Automatic Call Unit
- ***ttynn*** for direct links (*ttynn* is the name of a special device file in the */dev* directory
- ***TCP*** for TCP/IP connection (the port for ***uucp*** service is specified in the */etc/services* file)

speed The speed in "bps" for a device (some systems also allow the speed range).

phone_number The dialer sequence to be used by the modem to call the remote system.

chat_script A string describing the initial conversation between two systems. More details follow.

The ***chat_script*** presents a text string of the remainder of the entry, after the ***phone_number.*** It consists of *expect-send* pairs, separated by spaces, with optional "*subexpect-subsend*" pairs separated by hyphens, as in the following example:

```
ogin:   BREAK-ogin:   myuuname   ssword:   myuupass
  ↑       ↑    ↑         ↑          ↑          ↑
expect    |    |        send      expect      send
       subsend subexpect
```

The *expect* and *subexpect* fields specify literally what the system expects to receive from the remote system. This is the reason why login/password *expect* fields are specified as ***ogin:*** and ***ssword:***. These words are sufficient for unique login/password identification and also cover a number of possible "Login:" and "Password:" prompting from the remote system; they even allow the additional leading text. By the way, the *subsend* field BREAK enables adjustment of the modem speed between two systems (of course if the device supports it — see Chapter 11, Terminals).

When ***uucico*** is invoked, it scans the *UUCP systems* configuration file for the name of the system to call, as well as for a valid time to call. If it is a time to call, it checks the device type and speed fields, and other device-related configuration data. The next step is to check for locked files for that device type in the spool directory; if locked files exist, it means this device type is already in use. Then, ***uucico*** checks if there is another device of the requested type and speed to use it. If no device is available, ***uucico*** returns to the UUCP system configuration file to see if there is another configuration entry for the same system. If not, the call is terminated and postponed until later.

24.6.2.2 The UUCP Devices Data

The third field in each entry in the *UUCP systems* configuration file gives the name of a device type to be used when calling the remote system. If the direct link is in question, this is a special device file for the corresponding serial port; otherwise, additional information about the device of the specified type is needed. The specified device type is actually a pointer to an entry in another configuration file, the *UUCP devices* configuration file *Devices* on BNU UUCP, or *L-devices* on Version 2 UUCP. The contents of the *UUCP devices* configuration files for two UUCP versions are different, and the files will be discussed separately.

In *BNU UUCP*, the */etc/uucp/Devices* file contains information for direct links, automatic call units, and network connections. The strict file syntax rules require that each entry must begin in the first column; otherwise the entry is ignored. Each entry contains five fields and has the following format:

type dataport dialer_port speed dialer_token_pairs

where

type	The type of link: ***Direct*** for a line to a computer, modem, or LAN switch to be used by the program ***cu*** (test utility) ***ACU*** for a modem connection ***network*** for TCP/IP connection ***sys-name*** for direct links to a particular system ***sys-name***
dataport	The device name of the port used for making the connection. For direct serial links and modems this is the name of the special file in the */dev* directory that corresponds to the serial port used for the UUCP link.
dialer_port	An optional field that is used for special type of ***ACU,*** and which specifies the dialer; otherwise it is ignored, the field has a dummy value: "-."
speed	The "baud rate" of the device for modems and direct links; it can be also "***Any***" to match any speed requested in the *Systems* file.
dialer_token_pairs	The remainder of the line contains pairs of dialer names and tokens (each pair represents a dialer and an argument to pass to that dialer defined in another file *Dialcode*).

In the *Version 2 UUCP*, each port connected to a modem or direct cable to another system should be described in the *L-devices* file. An entry contains four fields and has the following format:

type device call_unit speed

where

type The type of link:
- ***DIR*** for a direct link
- ***ACU*** for a modem connection
- ***TCP*** for TCP/IP connection

device The name of the special file in the */dev* directory that corresponds to the serial port used for the UUCP link.

call_unit If a system uses a true ACU, two separate devices could be used to place the call: the dialer itself (referred to as *cua*) and the data line (referred to as *cul*); for a smart modem with built-in dialer, this field has a dummy value: "-"or "0."

speed The "baud rate" of the port for modems and direct links or the port number to use for local area network connections.

24.6.2.3 Other Configuration Data

The UUCP systems and devices configuration files always exist, and they are essential for the UUCP configuration. Other configuration files sometimes depend on the UUCP flavor and implemented modems; sometimes they are even optional. The differences among existing UUCP configuration files could also be seen in the earlier presented listings of the */etc/uucp* directories for two similar BNU UUCP flavors on HP-UX and Solaris platforms. We will focus on the way the maximum number of simultaneous UUCP daemons is restricted.

While on HP-UX platform files: *Maxuuxqts* and *Muxuuscheds* specify separately limits for the corresponding UUCP daemons, Solaris has introduced a single file, named *Limits,* for that purpose. This file is presented hereafter; the file is so well commented that additional explanations are not needed.

$ cat /etc/uucp/Limits

```
#ident   "@(# )Limits  1.2   SMI"    /* from SVR4 bnu:Limits 1.1 */
#
#        Limits provides a means of specifying the maximum number of
#        simultaneous uucicos, uuxqts, and uuscheds that are permitted.
#        5 uucicos, 2 uuxqts, and 2 uuscheds are reasonable.
#
#        FORMAT:
#                 service=<service name> max=<number>
#        where
#                 <service name> is "uucico" or "uuxqt" or "uusched",
#                 <number> is the limit that is permitted for that service.
#        The fields are order insensitive, case sensitive, and the first match in the file wins.
#
#        If the Limits file does not exist or it is unreadable or <number is> not a positive number,
#        then there will no overall limit for that service.
#
service=uucico max= 5
service=uuxqt max= 2
service=uusched max= 2
```

Some of the UUCP programs are periodically activated through the system ***cron*** facility. Although ***cron*** presents an independent UNIX facility, it is fair to emphasize dependencies between ***cron*** and ***UUCP***; a proper ***UUCP*** configuration always requests a proper ***cron*** configuration as well. The UUCP-related crontab entries live in the */usr/spool/cron/crontabs/uucp* file.

24.7 UUCP Access and Security Consideration

UUCP implies a remote access to the local system. A remote access always raises issues of system security. If left unprotected, the UUCP system could allow any remote user to copy in or out files, or execute commands locally. There is no need to emphasize how it could be an opportunity and challenge for intruders, and how it could be dangerous for the system itself. Fortunately, there are quite a lot of security measures already in place, as well as the possibility for additional ones.

UUCP appears in front of a system as a user-entity; the UUCP-related user account named ***uucp*** exists on any system as a system-related account. As for all other users' accounts, UUCP must first log in to the system, and it must pass the whole login/password procedure. Upon a successful login, UUCP does not receive a regular shell; instead it has restricted access and invokes a copy of the local ***uucico*** program. And besides that, there are a few more mechanisms available to increase the level of security of the local site, as:

- Creating additional *passwd* file entries to grant individual access to separate calling systems
- Restricting local file access by remote system, or requiring a call-back for certain system logins
- Controlling the remotely executed commands
- Controlling the forwarding of files from and for other systems
- Assigning appropriate file access modes and ownership to protect the UUCP files (with sensitive data) from outside users

We will pass quickly through most of these issues.

On most systems, the */etc/passwd* file includes the ***uucp*** entry which specifies needed administrative data (UUCP user and group ID, and indirectly the ownership of all UUCP directories and files) and working environment upon login (working directory and, instead of the usual shell, the spawned initial program ***uucico***). On some systems two separate user entries exist for the same purpose. Here is an extracted ***uucp*** user entry:

$ cat /etc/passwd | grep uucp

uucp:x:5:3::/usr/spool/uucppublic:/usr/lib/uucp/uucico

As can be seen from the entry, the UUCP working directory is the spool directory */usr/spool/uucppublic,* and the started program is *uucico.* The UUCP password entry is the regular part of any user authentication; however, the account is closed by default and must be activated.

Often multiple UUCP accounts are provided, as in this example from HP-UX 10.20:

$ cat /etc/passwd | grep uucp

uucp::5:3::/var/spool/uucppublic:/usr/lbin/uucp/uucico*

nuucp::11:9::/var/spool/uucppublic:/usr/lbin/uucp/uucico*

Multiple UUCP accounts give more flexibility; it is possible to provide different access to the system for different remote systems, based on the corresponding UUCP login name. However, in this example, both accounts are closed (pay attention to the asterisk in the password field — it means UUCP is not activated on this system).

24.7.1 Additional Security in BNU UUCP

BNU UUCP provides additional protection, based on *login IDs,* and a fine control over remote system logins, based on the introduced file named *Permissions.* In addition, there is also the file named *remote.unknown* that controls whether or not an "unknown system" (one not listed in the *Systems* file) could log in.

The *Permissions* file has two types of entries:

1. *LOGNAME* entries gain specific permissions for individual login IDs that are used when remote systems call this system, i.e., this system accesses remote systems.
2. *MACHINE* entries gain specific permissions for individual systems when this system calls them; i.e., remote systems access this system.

To have full access control, the administrator must create separate login IDs and write combined *MACHINE* and *LOGNAME* entries.

Both entries in the *Permissions* file consist of an arbitrary number of option/value pairs of the format:

option=value (no spaces around "=" sign)

Available options are listed in the following table. A class code "M" or "L" designates whether an option could be used with a *MACHINE* or a *LOGNAME* entry.

Option	Class	Description
LOGNAME	L	Specifies the login IDs to be used by remote systems
MACHINE	M	Specifies systems that the local system can call
REQUEST	M, L	Specifies whether the remote system can request to set up file transfer from this computer (default is "no")
SENDFILES	L	Specifies whether the called system can execute locally queued requests during a session
READ	M, L	Specifies the directories that uucico can use for requesting files (default is *uucppublic*)
WRITE	M, L	Specifies the directories that uucico can use for depositing files (default is *uucppublic*)
NOREAD	M, L	Exceptions to READ option or default
NOWRITE	M, L	Exceptions to WRITE option or default
CALLBACK	L	Specifies whether or not the local system must call back before transaction occurs (default is "no")
COMMANDS	M	Commands that the remote system can execute locally (the keyword ALL grants access to all commands)
VALIDATE	L	Used to verify calling system's identity
MYNAME	M	Used to link another system name to the local system
PUBDIR	M,L	Specifies the directory for local access

The *Permissions* file could sound quite confusing, and the best way to explain how it works is by an example. This is presented here, through the presentation of the *Permissions* files on three arbitrary UUCP systems: ***blue, red*** and ***black.***

$ cat /etc/uucp/Permissions

```
#ident    "@(# )Permissions   1.6   SMI"    /* from SVR4 bnu:Permissions 2.2 */ #
#
# per-machine and per-login permissions, e.g.,
# LOGNAME=Usun MACHINE=sun VALIDATE=sun COMMANDS=rmail \
# REQUEST=yes SENDFILES=yes
#
# See the System and Network Administration Manual for more information.
#
#        ----------------------------------------------------------------------------------------------------
#
# To configure the machine "blue":
# "red" logs in to "blue" as "Ured", and can request and send files regardless of who started
# the call. "red" can read and write to all directories on "blue" except the /blue/only directory,
# and can execute any command; other machines are not allowed.
#
# -->  Uncomment following lines on the host "blue"
# LOGNAME=Ured MACHINE=red READ=/ WRITE=/ COMMANDS=ALL NOREAD=/#blue/only \
# SENDFILES=yes REQUEST=yes
#
#        ----------------------------------------------------------------------------------------------------
#
# To configure the machine "red":
# "blue" logs in to "red" as "Ublue", and can request and send files regardless of who started
# the call. "blue" can read and write to all directories on "red" except the /red/only directory,
# and can execute any command. Any other machine logs in to "red" as "nuucp", and can
# request files regardless of who started the call, but will send files only when it calls. Other
# machines can read and write only from the public directory (the default), and can execute only
# the default list of commands.
#
# --> Uncomment following lines on the host "red"
# LOGNAME=Ublue MACHINE=blue READ=/ WRITE=/ COMMANDS=ALL NOREAD=/#red/only \
# SENDFILES=yes REQUEST=yes
#
# LOGNAME=nuucp MACHINE=OTHER SENDFILES=yes REQUEST=yes
#
#        ----------------------------------------------------------------------------------------------------
#
# To configure the machine "black":
# "red" logs in to "black" as "Ured", and can request and send files regardless of who started
# the call. "red" can read and write to all directories on "black" except the /black/only directory,
# and can execute any command; other machines are not allowed.
#
# --> Uncomment following lines on the host "black"
# LOGNAME=Ured MACHINE=red READ=/ WRITE=/ COMMANDS=ALL NOREAD=/#black/only \
# SENDFILES=yes REQUEST=yes
#
#        ----------------------------------------------------------------------------------------------------
#
```

24.7.2 Additional Security in Version 2 UUCP

Version 2 UUCP provides five files for controlling remote system access.

- ***/usr/lib/uucp/USERFILE*** — This file controls local access of files and directories. This is the text file with entries that specify four constraints on file transfer:

  1. Which file can be accessed by a local user
  2. Which file can be accessed by a remote system
  3. The login name that a remote system must use to talk to the local system
  4. Whether a remote system must be called back by the local system to confirm its identity

  The entry format is:

  user_name,system_name [c] path_name(s)

  where

user_name	The login name for a remote user or the name of a local user
system_name	The name of a remote system
c	An optional call-back flag; if exists, the local ***uucico*** must call back the remote system in order to establish its identity before the next conversation can occur
path_name(s)	A list of absolute paths separated by blanks; a blank field indicates open access to any file

  The use of the *USERFILE* is probably the most complicated part of UUCP. Every UUCP version treats it differently, and the use of file is different depending on who is using it: ***uucp, uux, uucico*** in master or slave role, etc.). Besides that, the effect of its use is very ambiguous.

- ***/usr/lib/uucp/L.cmds*** — This file specifies commands that could be executed locally by a remote system (alternatively, the name of the file is *L-cmds,* and *uuxqtcmds*). A typical *L.cmds* file might contain the following list of commands:

  rmail

  rnews

  lp

  who

  Special attention should be paid if new commands are added; some sufficiently general commands like ***cat*** can override the security restrictions.

- ***/usr/lib/uucp/SQFILE*** — This file is an optional file that keeps a record of the conversation counts and date/time of the last conversation for a particular system. The file contains an entry for each system that the conversation count check is performed. The remote system must also have a corresponding entry for this system in its *SQFILE.*

- ***/usr/lib/uucp/FWDFILE*** — This file controls the ability of remote systems to forward files through the system to other connected remote systems.

- ***/usr/lib/uucp/ORIGFILE*** — This file is also available on some UUCP implementations with the same function as the *FWDFILE.*

25

Intranet

25.1 Introduction to Intranet

The enormous growth of the Internet has continued since its introduction. Everybody realized very quickly the benefits of being connected to the Internet. The first Internet consumers were recruited from the academic environment. Businesses followed. Home users joined the race. Soon the Internet became overcrowded. Two main problems emerged:

1. Security concerns — Each networked computer was accessible and exposed to potential attackers and intruders. The business systems were the most vulnerable, and they had to be better protected.
2. The Internet address capacity was saturated — Each computer in the network consumes at least one IP address, and the IP addressing mechanism was quite limited in providing needed addresses.

The solution was found in the intranet. An intranet presents a private network with an arbitrary number of participating hosts that is connected to the Internet at a single point (or more precisely a few points). It means that the whole intranet appears in front of Internet as a single participant. It requires only a single, or a few, IP addresses at the Internet side, while internally it can provide all Internet services to an arbitrary numbers of hosts. In the intranet any IP address can be used, because this IP address never appears outside of the intranet. Intranets are only for internal use, so the same IP addresses can be repeated in many intranet networks. Traditionally the class A IP address 10.0.0.0 is reserved for intranet purposes. However, it is not mandatory to use just this address. Of course the implemented intranet IP addresses, whatever they are, must remain within the intranet itself. This is shown in the Figure 25.1.

Intranet and Internet have a single connection point. This is a bidirectional link that provides a required flow of data in and out of the intranet. But this is also the point that separates intranet from Internet. This is very important because:

- It allows the full control of the data flow.
- It protects the intranet from an unauthorized access from the Internet.
- It redirects traffic.
- It is relatively easy to implement at the single place, while the rest of the network remains unchanged.

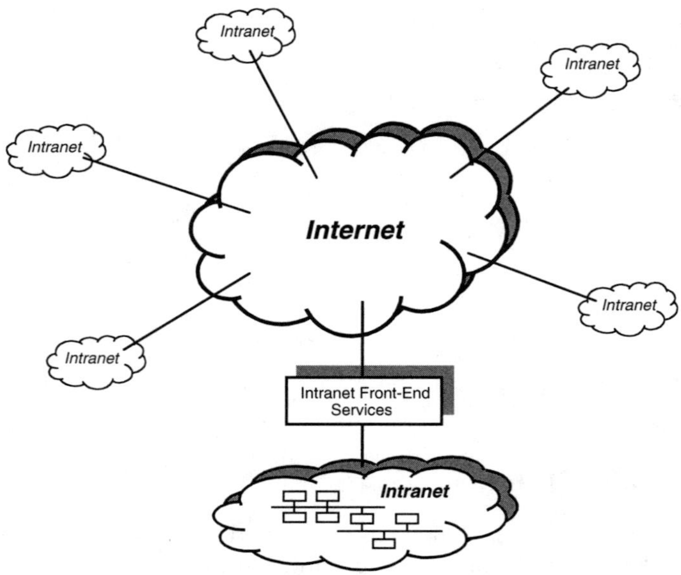

FIGURE 25.1
Intranet.

An intranet provides all Internet services to the local hosts. From the standpoint of the local users, an intranet is fully transparent toward the Internet. Converting intranet addresses to Internet addresses provides the required transparency and vice versa, whenever it is needed. This is known as *address mapping*. Thanks to that we can say the intranet remains part of the Internet, and every local host remains a participant in the Internet. Frankly, it would be more appropriate to say "every local host has a feeling that it remains a participant in the Internet."

To accomplish transparency, several intranet technologies have been developed. These are primarily specialized network applications (services). Once again UNIX has proved to be a dominant OS platform to run these applications. The specialized equipment also has been developed — the specialized hardware always improves performance.

25.1.1 Intranet vs. Internet

An intranet has many elements in common with the Internet. But the intranet also differs from its "big brother." The intranet and Internet implement basically the same technologies, but their basic missions are different. Intranet and Internet are merging together, but they are also very cautious and susceptible at the connection points. Simply, we must be aware of their differences and similarities.

Intranet is a world in itself. It is sufficiently separated from the Internet to introduce its own more restricted local rules of behavior, but also sufficiently merged to the Internet to benefit from its globalization and worldwide access. We can name this relationship as a marriage driven by interests. There is not "too much love" in the intranet-Internet relationship.

For a better understanding of this relationship, let us try to summarize the main aspects of both; afterward it will be easier to understand the administrative duties in this area.

The basic Internet characteristics are:

- This is a global, worldwide network.
- Its basic mission is globalization.
- It is open and eager to accommodate new participants.
- It consists of a huge number of mutually connected subnetworks and an enormous number of participating hosts (computers).
- It provides different network services.
- Different network technologies are implemented.
- Different hardware and software platforms are used.
- Network control is distributed.
- Databases are distributed.
- Costs are distributed.

Despite many different and distributed issues, the Internet works, and it works very well. We are all witnesses of the enormous success of the Internet.

The basic intranet characteristics are:

- This is a private, dedicated network.
- It is basically business oriented.
- Its growth is strictly controlled.
- The concept is Internet-like.
- Access to and from the out-of-Intranet world is restricted.
- There is full control over the network.
- Mostly the same network technologies are implemented throughout an intranet.
- Mostly the same hardware and software platforms are used.
- It is a part of Internet.
- It overrides some Internet restrictions.

In some ways, we can say that an intranet is a "small Internet" where we have even more control and influence. Such a statement is mostly true, but it does not make our job "smaller."

Finally, what can we conclude about an intranet as a part of the Internet?

- The same technologies are implemented.
- The concept is almost the same.
- Security issues are different.
- Ownership is different.
- Special concerns exist regarding connections with the Internet.

From an administrative standpoint, there are no significant differences between administering a UNIX host in an intranet or on the Internet. This is logical since UNIX administration is primarily focused on configuring a UNIX host in the local network (LAN where the UNIX host belongs). This administration is independent of the wider network layout regarding whether this LAN belongs to an intranet or the Internet. UNIX administrative responsibilities terminate with routers in the LAN. Afterward other administrative skills are required.

25.1.2 Intranet Design Approach

Today an intranet is a common thing. Thousands and thousands of different size Intranets are running and blooming around. You can even order an intranet as a package, to choose among several packet solutions. Everything will be delivered and put in operation for a certain price. Whether it really matches your needs is another question.

Of course an intranet has its price, and you have to doublecheck whether your budget can cover these costs. Before you decide to go ahead with the intranet, the following are worth considering:

- *Do you expect to save money?* Typically, intranet technologies are used at the beginning for such things as telephone directories, data sheets, material safety sheets, surveys, human resources materials, travel policies, and job postings. Even when used in such a limited way, the intranet return on investment is quite significant for companies adopting the technology.
- *Do you expect to spend money and to need outside help?* Making your Internet and intranet look and behave correctly will probably involve bringing in outside help. This help should always include knowledge transfer. Transferring knowledge on how to design a site and make programming interfaces in the existing systems and managing employee-added content would pay back later. Your employees can manage this infrastructure once the experts have left.
- *Do you expect things to happen more quickly?* Company manuals can be placed on your intranet the instant they are completed. Likewise, changes can be made instantly and be instantly available. Expect that your corporate data will be made available more quickly. And there is no more listening to why a software program has to be installed on hundreds or even thousands of machines before it is fully applicable.
- *Do you expect to have to manage employee involvement on your site?* As the intranet site grows, you will have to look at controlling the appearance of documents, managing how your employees can navigate your site, and making security arrangements.
- *Do you expect to have to address Internet technology at some point?* Many believe that Internet technologies are replacing the PC as the engine for information technology market growth. How much did your company spend last year on PC and related technologies? Now shift some of this money over to the Internet and reconsider the costs.

Funding for the intranet can be based on different criteria. Some companies consider it a cost of doing business while others fund it on a value-based allocation. Remember that there will be ongoing operating expenses that could be even greater than the initial expense of setting up the intranet.

Security is extremely important. An intranet extends a company's reach, but it also increases its vulnerability and exposure. Security policies must be in place to dictate who has access to what information, when they can get the information, and how much information they can get. Firewall software provides the needed security mechanisms, but the security policies have to be written down, maintained, communicated, enforced, and constantly monitored. All of this is necessary to ensure the livelihood of the company is not threatened.

Return on investment can be quite substantial. Conservative figures place the payback at a low of 23% to a high of 88%, over one to two years. Costs of paper dissemination and printing will be reduced, but the greatest benefits realized will relate to information flow.

It is also very important to decide who will control the intranet. Often the IT department is given control of the intranet, and this is usually a mistake. IT is very good at handling hardware and software but not as good at knowledge management. Intranet management requires skills in professional research and information gathering. Strict cooperation with IT is needed to efficiently disseminate high-quality information via the intranet, but the control to the content of the intranet should remain with the company management, or maybe within the HR department. Departments within the organization may be allowed to maintain their own Web pages and publish their own documents, but the core information for the company should remain under the control of a single management body.

Having intranet control centralized has other benefits in addition to ensuring the quality of the data. It allows for better maintenance of the site and can simplify startup and ongoing use. It can provide consistent navigation for all users if all the links are established on the main page. It also allows uniform customization of links for various users, based on an individual department's information needs.

Here are fundamental principles for designing an intranet. Starting with an appropriate solution is very important.

1. Define business needs — do not underestimate your real needs, but also do not exaggerate!
2. Choose technology wisely — cheap initial solutions usually are not the cheapest ones. If reliability and stability are your concern, the choice of UNIX for the server platforms sounds quite logical.
3. Opt for function over glitz — the functionality always has priority over entertainment.
4. Make room for growth — the business will grow, think about an easy upgrade.
5. Include a site map for navigation — the graphic presentation of the intranet structure is important. It always saves time and prevents problems.
6. Do not get carried away with fonts and colors — good visual appearance on the intranet site is important, but do not exaggerate (there are many other issues to complete).
7. Test the usability of the interface — be realistic in choosing resources involving the Internet.
8. Check the network security — security is always an issue, for some businesses the most important one.
9. Obey the law — it is internal, but rules still exist.
10. Stay focused — always remember the mission of your intranet.

25.2 Intranet Front-End Services

The intranet was followed by a number of applications to support it. Sometimes it is even hard to say who was first on the market: did the intranet provoke some applications, or did the applications pave the route for the intranet introduction. This is the classic story about "the chicken and the egg." These applications primarily address intranet-Internet relationships. We will call them "intranet front-end services" based on the fact that the front-end of the intranet is placed toward the Internet.

These front-end services also require administration, often quite complex. Strictly speaking the administration of the applications of that kind is out of the scope of the usual UNIX administration. However, it does not mean that UNIX administrators never face problems caused by these services. At least they are also running on the UNIX platform. There is no doubt about the need to have a certain level of knowledge regarding these applications.

The most common intranet front-end applications are briefly discussed in this section. You will notice a lack of detailed information on administration, but this is intentionally done. Details of this kind are outside the scope of this book. However the issues that are discussed should make a solid background for further improvements, if needed.

25.2.1 Firewalls

A firewall is a structure intended to keep a fire from spreading. Buildings have firewalls made of brick walls that completely divide sections of the building. In a car, a firewall is the metal shield separating the engine and passenger compartments. This is the origin of the term *firewall* we use when a private network (the intranet) is separated from the public network (the Internet). Intranet firewalls are intended to keep the flames of Internet hell out of the intranet itself — or to keep the intranet community pure and chaste by denying them access to the evil Internet temptations.

A firewall protects networked computers from intentional hostile intrusion that could compromise confidentiality or result in data corruption or denial of service. It may be a hardware device (usually part of a router) or a software program running on a secure host computer. We will consider the second one, presented in the Figure 25.2. In either case, it must have at least two network interfaces, one for the network it is intended to protect, and one for the network it is exposed to. A firewall sits at the junction point between the two networks, a private network (intranet) and a public network (Internet). The earliest firewalls were simply routers.

A firewall examines all traffic routed between the two networks to see if it meets certain criteria. If it does, the traffic is routed between the networks; otherwise it is stopped. A firewall filters both inbound and outbound traffic. It can also manage public access to private networked resources such as host applications. It can be used to log all attempts to enter the private network and trigger alarms when hostile or unauthorized entry is attempted.

Firewalls can filter packets based on:

- The source and destination addresses and port numbers — known as *address filtering*.
- The specific types of network traffic — also known as *protocol filtering* because the decision to forward or reject traffic is dependant upon the protocol used, for example HTTP, ftp, or telnet.
- The packet attribute or state.

There are two access denial methodologies used by firewalls (see Figure 25.3):

1. A firewall may allow all traffic through unless it meets certain criteria.
2. A firewall may deny all traffic unless it meets certain criteria.

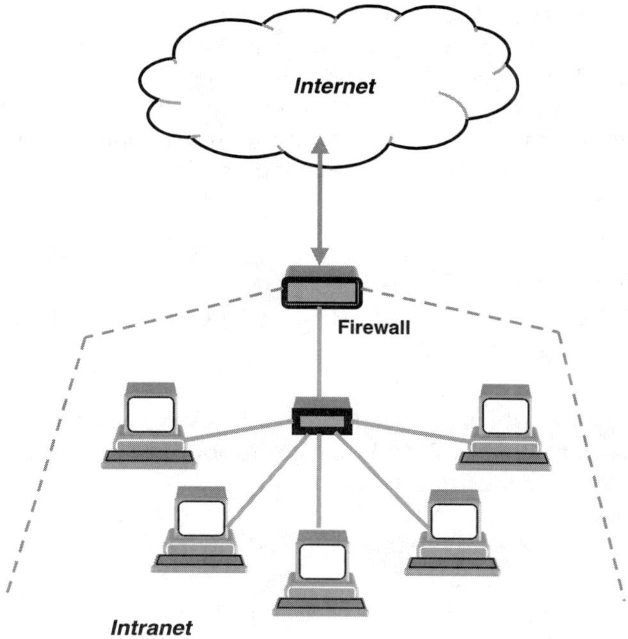

FIGURE 25.2
Firewall.

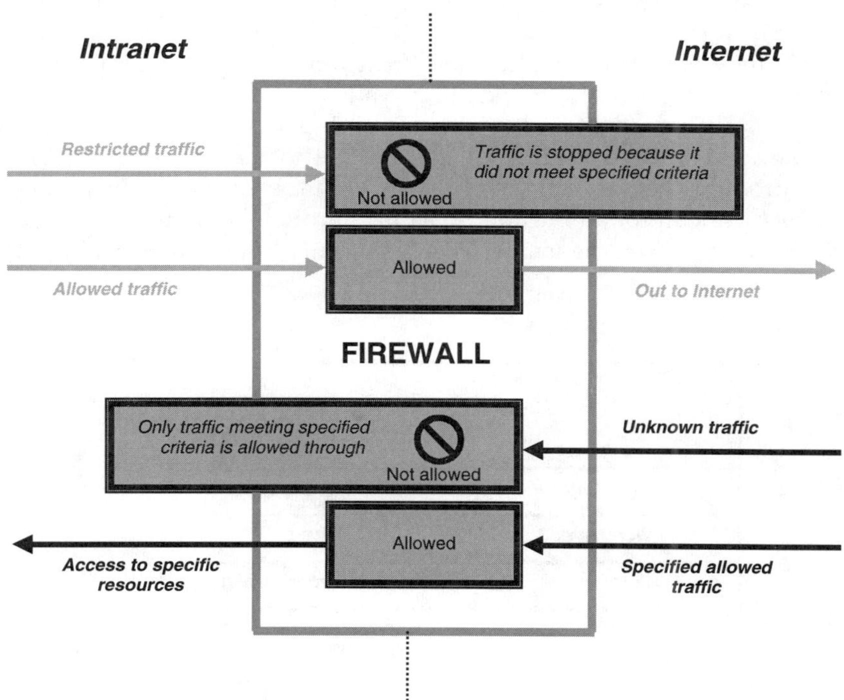

FIGURE 25.3
Basic firewall operation.

The type of criteria used to determine whether traffic should be allowed through varies from one type of firewall to another. Firewalls may be concerned with the type of traffic, or with source or destination addresses and ports. They may also use complex rule bases that analyze the application data to determine if the traffic should be allowed through. How a firewall determines what traffic to let through depends on which network layer it is operating. A discussion on network layers and architecture follows.

25.2.1.1 Firewall Techniques

Referring to the ISO OSI model or TCP/IP stack, firewalls operate at different layers to use different criteria to restrict traffic:

- The lowest layer at which a firewall can work is layer three in the ISO OSI model. This is the *network layer.* In TCP/IP the corresponding layer is the *internet protocol layer.* This layer is concerned with routing packets to their destination. At this layer a firewall can determine whether a packet is from a trusted source, but cannot be concerned with what it contains or what other packets it is associated with.
- Firewalls that operate at the *transport layer* know a little more about a packet and are able to grant or deny access depending on more sophisticated criteria.
- At the *application layer,* firewalls know a great deal about what is going on and can be very selective in granting access.

It would appear then that firewalls functioning at a higher layer in the stack must be superior in every respect. This is not necessarily the case. The lower in the stack the packet is intercepted, the more secure the firewall. If the intruder cannot get past level three, it is impossible to gain control of the operating system.

Professional firewall products catch each network packet before the operating system does; thus, there is no direct path from the Internet to the operating system's TCP/IP stack. They introduce their own IP layer that is very robust toward incoming attacks. It is therefore very difficult for an intruder to gain control of the firewall host computer and then "open the doors" from the inside. This is presented in the Figure 25.4.

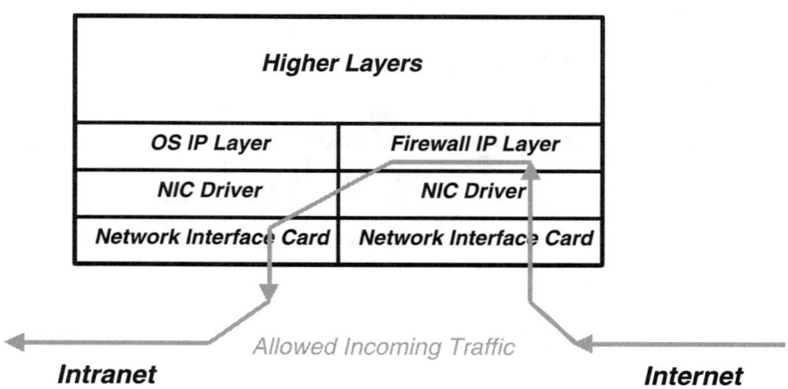

FIGURE 25.4
Firewall IP layer.

Firewalls examine the source IP addresses of packets to determine if they are legitimate. A firewall may be instructed to allow traffic through if it comes from a specific trusted host. A malicious cracker would then try to gain entry by "spoofing" the source IP address of packets sent to the firewall. If the firewall thought that the packets originated from a trusted host, it might let them through unless other criteria were not met. Of course the cracker would need to know a good deal about the firewall's rule base to exploit this kind of weakness. This reinforces the principle that technology alone will not solve all security problems. Responsible management of information is essential. There are management solutions to technical problems, but no technical solutions to management problems.

An effective measure against IP spoofing is the use of a virtual private network (VPN) protocol such as *IPSec*. This methodology involves encryption of the data in the packet as well as the source address. The VPN software or firmware decrypts the packet and the source address and performs a checksum. If either the data or the source address have been tampered with, the packet will be dropped. Without access to the encryption keys, a potential intruder would be unable to penetrate the firewall.

25.2.1.2 Firewall Types

Firewalls fall into four broad categories: packet filters, circuit level gateways, application level gateways, and stateful multilayer inspection firewalls.

Packet filtering firewalls — Packet filtering firewalls work at the network level of the ISO OSI model or the IP layer of TCP/IP (see Figure 25.5a). They are usually part of a router. In a packet filtering firewall, each packet is compared to a set of criteria before it is forwarded. Depending on the packet and the criteria, the firewall can drop the packet, forward it, or send a message to the originator. Rules can include source and destination IP address, source and destination port number, and protocol used, however this firewall does not support sophisticated rule-based models. The advantage of packet filtering firewalls is their low cost and low impact on network performance. Most routers support packet filtering. Even if other firewalls are used, implementing packet filtering at the router level affords an initial degree of security. Network address translation (NAT) routers offer the advantages of packet filtering firewalls but can also hide the IP addresses of computers behind the firewall and offer a level of circuit-based filtering.

Circuit level gateways — Circuit level gateways work at the session layer of the ISO OSI model or the TCP layer of TCP/IP. They monitor TCP handshaking between packets to determine whether a requested session is legitimate. Information passed to a remote computer through a circuit level gateway appears to have originated from the gateway. This is useful for hiding information about protected networks. Circuit level gateways are relatively inexpensive and have the advantage of hiding information about the private network they protect. On the other hand, they do not filter individual packets (see Figure 25.5b).

Application layer gateways — Application layer gateways, also called *proxy firewalls*, are similar to circuit-level gateways except that they are application specific. They can filter packets at the application layer of the ISO OSI model or TCP/IP stack (see Figure 25.5.c). Incoming or outgoing packets cannot access services for which there is no proxy. In plain terms, an application level gateway that is configured to be a web proxy will not allow any ftp, telnet or other traffic through. Because they examine packets at application layer, they can filter individual application specific commands. This cannot be accomplished with either packet filtering firewalls or circuit level neither of which knows anything about the application level information. Application layer gateways can also be used to log user activity and logins. They offer a high level of security, but have a significant impact on network performance. This is because of the context switches that slow down network access dramatically. They are not transparent to end-users because they require manual configuration of each client computer.

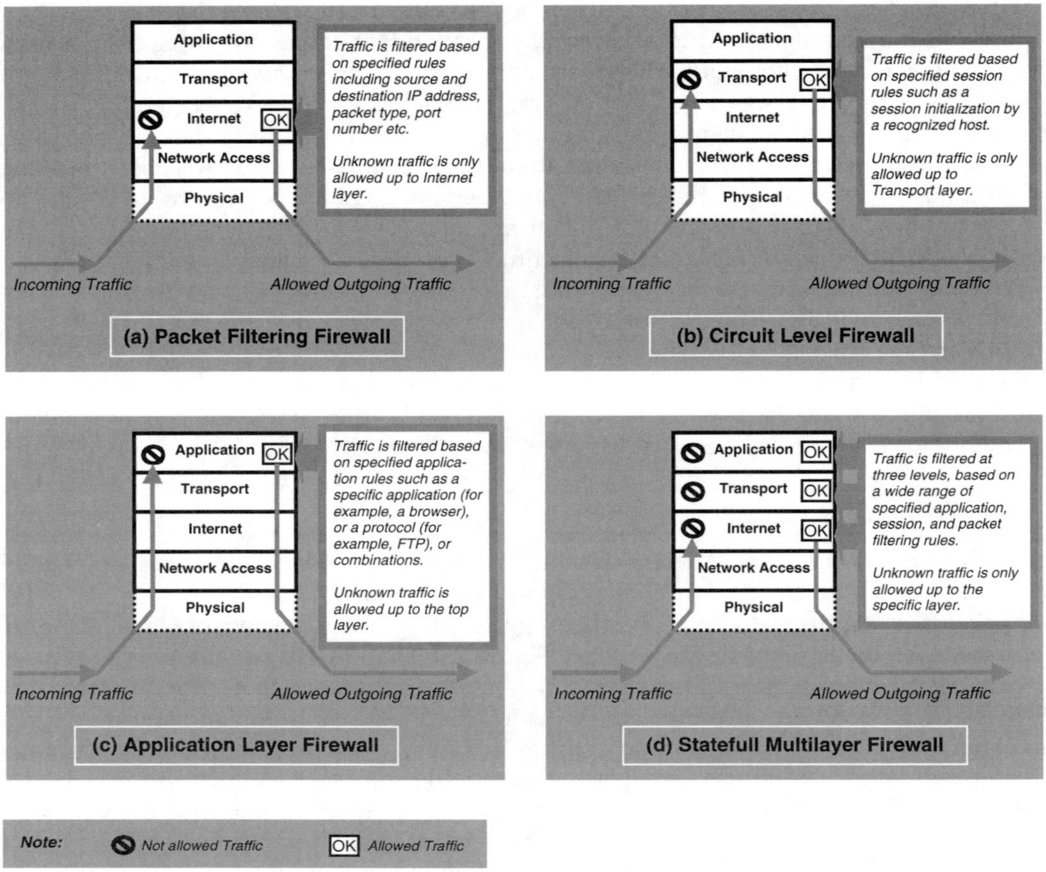

FIGURE 25.5
Basic firewall types.

Stateful multilayer firewalls — Stateful multilayer firewalls, or more specifically *stateful multilayer inspection firewalls*, combine the aspects of the other three types of firewalls (presented in Figure 25.5d). They filter packets at the network layer, determine whether session packets are legitimate and evaluate contents of packets at the application layer. They allow direct connection between client and host, alleviating the problem caused by the lack of transparency of application level gateways. They rely on algorithms to recognize and process application layer data instead of running application specific proxies. Stateful multilayer firewalls offer a high level of security, good performance, and transparency to end users. They are expensive, however, and, due to their complexity, are potentially less secure than simpler types of firewalls if not administered properly.

25.2.1.3 Firewall Implementation

At the end of the day we have to decide about the firewall we want to implement in our intranet. In most cases this is not an easy decision. There are several issues to consider when implementing a firewall in the intranet:

1. **Determine the access denial methodology to use** — It is recommended to begin with the methodology that denies all access by default. In other words, to start

with a firewall that routes no traffic and is effectively a brick wall with no doors in it.

2. **Determine inbound access policy** — If all of the internet traffic originates in the intranet, a straightforward NAT router sounds quite sufficient. It will block all inbound traffic that is not in response to requests originating from within the LAN. The true IP addresses of intranet hosts behind the firewall are never revealed to the outside world, making intrusion extremely difficult. Indeed, intranet host IP addresses are nonpublic addresses, making it impossible to route traffic to them from the Internet. Packets coming in from the Internet in response to requests from local hosts are addressed to dynamically allocated port numbers on the public side of the NAT router. These change rapidly, making it difficult or impossible for an intruder to make assumptions about which port numbers to use. If the requirements involve secure access to intranet-based services from Internet-based hosts, then it is needed to determine the criteria to be used in deciding when a packet originating from the Internet may be allowed into the intranet. The stricter the criteria, the more secure your network will be. Ideally the Internet IP addresses that may originate inbound traffic should be known and specified. By limiting inbound traffic to packets originating from these hosts, the likelihood of hostile intrusion is reduced. The inbound traffic could also be limited to certain protocol sets such as ftp or http. All of these techniques can be achieved with packet filtering on a NAT router. If the Internet IP addresses cannot be known in advance, and also the protocol filtering cannot be used, then a more complex rule-based model must be used. This can lead to a stateful multilayer inspection firewall.
3. **Determine outbound access policy** — If intranet users only need access to the Internet Web sites, a proxy firewall may give a high level of security with access granted selectively to appropriate users. This type of firewall requires manual configuration of each Web browser on each intranet machine. Outbound protocol filtering can also be transparently achieved with packet filtering and no sacrifice in security. If a NAT router with no inbound mapping of traffic originating from the Internet is also used, then intranet users can freely access all services on the Internet with no security compromise. The risk of intranet users behaving irresponsibly with e-mail or with external hosts remains, but this is more a management issue and must be dealt with as such.
4. **Determine if dial-in or dial-out access is required** — Dial-in access bypasses the router and as such it requires a secure remote access PPP server that should be placed outside the firewall. Dial-out access must be made secure in such a way that hostile access to the intranet through the dial-out connection becomes impossible. The safest way is to physically isolate the computer from the intranet. Alternatively, personal firewall software may be used to isolate the intranet network interface from the external access interface.
5. **Decide whether to buy a complete firewall product, have one implemented by a systems integrator, or implement one yourself.**

Once the above issues have been settled, the appropriate firewall can be implemented. The decision will depend as much on the availability of in-house expertise as on the complexity of the need. A satisfactory firewall may be built with little expertise if the requirements are straightforward. However, complex requirements will not necessarily entail recourse to external resources if the system administrator has sufficient grasp of the elements. Indeed, as the complexity of the security model increases, so does the need for in-house expertise and autonomy.

25.2.1.4 Problems and Benefits

The firewall is an integral part of any security program, but it is not a security program in and of itself. An overall security program involves data integrity, service or application integrity, data confidentiality, and authentication. Firewalls only address the issues of data integrity, confidentiality, and authentication of data that is behind the firewall. Any data that transits outside the firewall is subject to factors out of the control of the firewall. It is therefore necessary for an organization to have a well-planned and strictly implemented security program that includes, but is not limited to, firewall protection.

Firewalls also introduce problems of their own. Information security involves constraints, and users do not like this. Firewalls restrict access to certain services. Firewalls can also constitute a traffic bottleneck. They concentrate security in one spot, aggravating the single point of failure phenomenon. The alternatives however are either no Internet access or no security, neither of which is acceptable in most organizations.

Firewalls protect the intranet networks from hostile intrusion from the Internet. Consequently, thanks to the firewalls, many intranets are now connected to the Internet where Internet connectivity would otherwise have been too great a risk.

Firewalls allow network administrators to offer access to specific types of Internet services to selected intranet users. This selectivity is an essential part of any information management program and involves not only protecting private information assets, but also knowing who has access to what. Privileges can be granted according to job description and need rather than on an all-or-nothing basis.

At the moment, among the best-ranked firewall hardware is Nokia, while very respected firewall software is made by CheckPoint.

25.2.2 Viruswalls

VirusWall is the name of an antivirus product by Trend Micro. This is the scanning package against network malicious codes to support the application gateway firewalls. It seems that this name is quite appropriate for the text that follows. First, it fully explains its purpose: to fight the viruses and other attackers to the intranet; and second, it suggests its location in the intranet, parallel with the firewall.

25.2.2.1 Computer Viruses and Other Malicious Codes

There are many "nasty" offenders traveling through the Internet with their only wish being to harm "naïve" hosts ready to offer them a hand. The most tragic part of this story is that, in most cases, they are doing it just for fun. These are different malicious programs (sometimes very simple programs) looking for holes in your defense, ready to attack and often damage your system. Among them, viruses are the best known, and the most dangerous.

A computer virus is a program — a piece of executable code — that has the unique ability to replicate. Like biological viruses, computer viruses can spread quickly and are often difficult to eradicate. They can attach themselves to just about any type of file and are spread as files that are copied and sent from individual to individual.

Besides replication, some computer viruses have something else in common: a damage routine that can deliver the virus payload. While payloads may sometimes only display messages or images, they can also destroy files, reformat your hard drive, or cause other kinds of damage. If the virus does not contain a damage routine, it can still cause trouble by taking up storage space and memory, and downgrading the overall performance of your computer.

In the past, most viruses spread primarily via floppy disk, but the Internet has introduced new virus distribution mechanisms. With e-mail now used as an important business communication tool, viruses are spreading faster than ever. Viruses attached to e-mail messages can infect an entire intranet in a matter of minutes, costing companies millions of dollars annually in productivity loss and clean-up expenses.

Viruses will not go away any time soon. More than 10,000 have been identified, and 200 new ones are created every month, according to the International Computer Security Association. With numbers like those, it is safe to say that most organizations will deal regularly with virus outbreaks. No one who uses computers is immune to viruses.

25.2.2.1.1 *Life Cycle of a Virus*

Computer viruses have a life cycle that starts when they are created and ends when they are completely eradicated. The following outline describes each stage.

- Creation — Certain programming knowledge and skills are required to create a virus.
- Replication — Viruses replicate by nature. A well-designed virus will replicate for a long time before it activates, which allows it plenty of time to spread.
- Activation — Viruses that have damage routines will activate when certain conditions are met, for example, on a certain date or when a particular action is taken by the user. Viruses without damage routines do not activate, instead they cause damage by stealing storage space.
- Discovery — This phase does not always come after activation, but it usually does. When a virus is detected and isolated, data is sent to the International Computer Security Association ICSA to be documented and distributed to antivirus developers. Discovery usually takes place on time before the virus becomes a real threat to the computing community.
- Assimilation — At this point, antivirus developers modify their software so that it can detect the new virus. This can take anywhere from one day to six months, depending on the developer and the virus type.
- Eradication — If enough users install up-to-date virus protection software, any virus can be wiped out. So far no viruses have disappeared completely, but some have long ceased to be a major threat.

25.2.2.1.2 *Virus Types*

The majority of viruses fall into four main classes:

Boot sector viruses — Until the mid-1990s, boot sector viruses were the most prevalent virus type, spreading primarily in the 16-bit DOS world via floppy disk. Boot sector viruses infect the boot sector on a floppy disk and spread to a user's hard disk and can also infect the master boot record (MBR) on a user's hard drive. Once the MBR or boot sector on the hard drive is infected, the virus attempts to infect the boot sector of every floppy disk that is inserted into the computer and accessed.

Boot sector viruses work like this: by hiding on the first sector of a disk, the virus is loaded into memory before the system files are loaded. This allows it to gain complete control of DOS interrupts so that it can spread and cause damage.

These viruses often replace the original contents of the MBR or DOS boot sector with their own contents and move the sector to another area on the disk. Cleaning up a boot sector virus can be performed by booting the machine from an uninfected floppy system disk rather than from the hard drive, or by finding the original boot sector and replacing it in the correct location on the disk.

File-infecting viruses — File infectors, also known as *parasitic viruses*, operate in memory and usually infect executable files with the following extensions: *.COM, *.EXE, *.DRV, *.DLL, *.BIN, *.OVL, *.SYS. They activate every time the infected file is executed by copying themselves into other executable files and can remain in memory long after the virus has activated.

Thousands of different file-infecting viruses exist, but similar to boot sector viruses, the vast majority operate in a DOS 16-bit environment. Some, however, have successfully infected Microsoft Windows, IBM OS/2, and Apple Computer Macintosh environments.

Multipartite viruses — Multipartite viruses have characteristics of both boot sector viruses and file-infecting viruses.

Macro viruses — Macro viruses currently account for about 80 percent of all viruses, according to the International Computer Security Association, and are the fastest growing viruses in computer history. Unlike other virus types, macro viruses are not specific to an operating system and spread with ease via e-mail attachments, floppy disks, Web downloads, file transfers, and cooperative applications.

Macro viruses are, however, application-specific. They infect macro utilities that accompany such applications as Microsoft Word and Excel, which means a Word macro virus cannot infect an Excel document and vice versa. Instead, macro viruses travel between data files in the application and can eventually infect hundreds of files if undeterred. Macro viruses are written in "every man's programming language" — Visual Basic — and are relatively easy to create. They can infect at different points during a file's use, for example, when it is opened, saved, closed, or deleted.

25.2.2.1.3 Some Other Malicious Codes

It is fair to list two more intruders:

Trojan horses — A Trojan horse is a program that performs some unexpected or unauthorized, usually malicious, action such as displaying messages, erasing files, or formating a whole disk. A Trojan horse is not infective, i.e., it does not infect other host files. Once its action is terminated (if we survive), there is no need for additional cleaning. To get rid of the Trojan horse, deleting the program is sufficient.

Worms — A computer worm is a self-contained program (or set of programs) that is able to spread functional copies of itself or its segments to other computer systems. The propagation usually takes place via network connections or e-mail attachments. To get rid of the worm, the program has to be deleted.

25.2.2.2 The Viruswall Implementation

A viruswall responsibility is to protect the intranet from viruses and other malicious codes that travel through the Internet and attack all network participants. Most of the malicious codes are doing that unselectively; as soon as they realize any possibility for an action, they act. And they are produced on a daily basis worldwide. This is an unfortunate challenge that we face, and we must respond appropriately. The viruswall is a solution.

The viruswall duties could be divided into two categories: *basic* and *extended*. Basic duties are a must for a safer intranet (the term *safer* is used intentionally — there is no guarantee for 100% safety); extended duties are optional and they improve intranet performance and safety.

Basic duties include:

- Real-time virus detection in the inbound traffic (outbound traffic can be also included):
  - SMTP protection complements intranet mail server to scan received e-mails for the viruses.
  - HTTP protection keeps infected files from being downloaded and allows setting of uniform, intranet security standards for Java and other HTTP-related applications.
  - FTP protection works transparently to ensure that infected files are not downloaded from the Internet.
- Blocking the entering of other malicious codes
- Virus pattern file update (new viruses must be known to be fight successfully):
  - Automatic periodic updates
  - On demand

Extended duties include:

- Blocking of spam and other unwanted e-mail traffic:
  - Full spam filtering
  - Automatic spam source and keyword-list update
  - Customizable
- Control distribution of sensitive e-mail contents:
  - Prevention of confidential or inappropriate material leaving the intranet
  - Customized profile-based filtering
- Manage the delivery of large messages to optimize the network bandwidth:
  - Monitoring of the e-mail traffic patterns
  - Postponement of the delivery of e-mail based on customizable criteria
- Monitoring of ongoing Internet traffic (sudden unusual increase in the external traffic usually signifies virus attacks):
  - Prediction of virus attacks based on the traffic statistic
  - Prevention of inbound traffic under suspicious Internet traffic circumstances

The viruswall can run on the firewall machine. Assuming sufficient processing hardware power of the implemented machine, such an approach is quite feasible. But it is also quite vulnerable — a single failure in the machine can shut down the intranet completely. Firewall-viruswall is the crucial Intranet front-end service and the need for a redundancy is obvious, including on the hardware level. And if two machines are already in place, than it is also good idea to provide these two services under normal circumstances on two different machines. If one machine happens to be down, then the corresponding service could be switched to another machine. This is presented in the Figure 25.6.

The regular configuration supposes that the firewall and viruswall software are installed on both machines, but only one application is activated on each machine (firewall or viruswall). Full communication between the firewall and viruswall machines is provided all the time. The inbound traffic is directed to the firewall. Firewall forwards messages to the viruswall for their antivirus scanning. Scanned messages are then allowed into the intranet. If a virus or some other malicious code is detected in the message, the message itself is stopped and erased. Optionally the message sender and recipient are informed about detected problem.

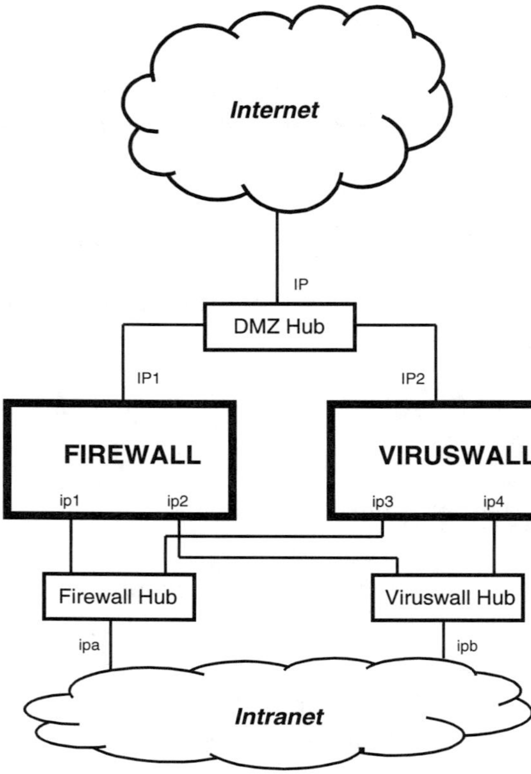

FIGURE 25.6
Firewall-viruswall configuration.

All internal IP addresses are programmable to allow an easy automatic reconfiguration. If one machine fails, the failed application should be started on another machine, and the internal network interfaces reconfigured appropriately. Relatively simple start/stop shell scripts could accomplished this task efficiently.

An additional benefit of such a firewall-viruswall solution is that less demanding hardware can be implemented. Regularly this task is divided between two machines; in emergency situations a certain decrease in the speed and the performance is tolerable.

25.2.3 Proxy Servers

Proxy servers are store-and-forward caches that separate the intranet community from the external Internet world. An intranet application configured to use the proxy server never leaves the intranet boundaries. Instead, it always connects to the proxy server and asks it to proceed with the application requests.

How does it work? A proxy server receives a request for an Internet service (let us assume retrieving a Web page) from an intranet user. If the request passes filtering requirements, the proxy server looks it up in its local cache of previously downloaded Web pages. If it finds the requested page, it returns the page to the user without needing to forward the request outside to the Internet. If the requested page is not in the cache, the proxy server, acting as a client on behalf of the user, uses one of its own IP addresses to request the page from the Web server. When the page is returned, the proxy server relates it to the original request and forwards it on to the user.

During this transaction, the proxy server remains invisible to the intranet user. All requests and returned responses appear to deal directly with the addressed Internet server. As a matter of fact, the proxy server is not completely invisible. Its address must be known to, and specified as a configuration parameter to, the user's browser or other protocol programs.

Proxy servers usually have the ability to cache documents that they retrieve on behalf of the clients. But this is not mandatory; proxy servers can also function without document caching. If caching is part of the process, they are known as the *caching proxy servers*. A caching proxy server is presented in Figure 25.7.

The squared numbers in the figure indicate the order of events. The client requests a certain document (1), which is handled by the proxy server (2). The retrieved document (3) is cached in the proxy's cache (4) and also returned to the client (5). When another client requests the same document (6), it can be fulfilled from the cache (7) and returned to the other client (8).

Caching has several beneficial effects:

- Faster response — A proxy server that is closer or on a faster link can supply a cached document faster than the remote master server.
- Reduced load — If a document can be retrieved from a cache, then the network traffic is reduced.
- Lower cost — The reduced traffic means a lower cost. Caching proxy servers could be used to compensate expansive or slow network traffic at any place in the inner or outer network.

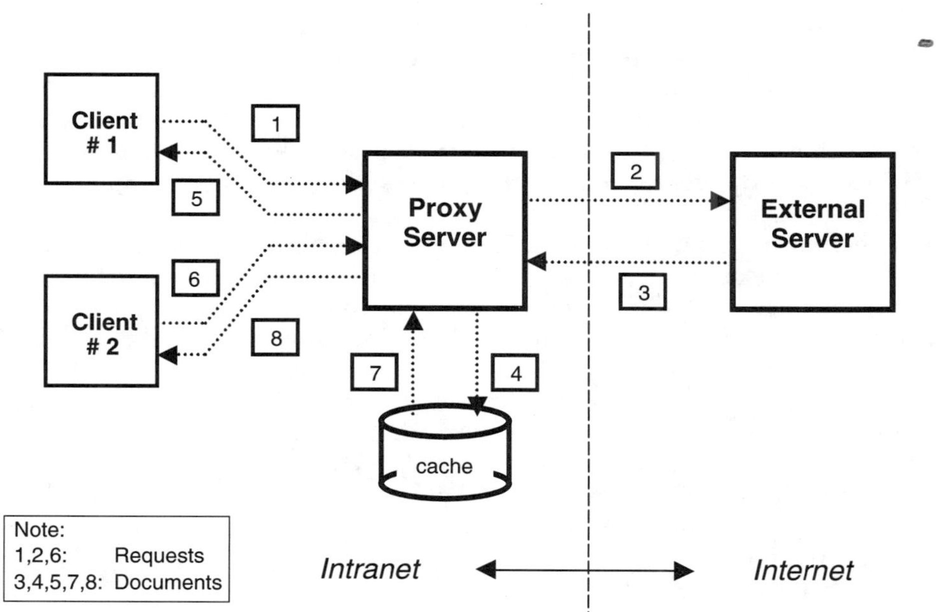

FIGURE 25.7
Caching proxy server.

A main difficulty with implementing caching is determining when a cached document is out of date. Cached documents are not updated, and they can differ from the original ones. The extreme case of this occurs for virtual documents. Virtual documents are created on request and they are practically immediately out of date. Caching proxy servers take three steps to address the problem of obsolete documents:

1. Virtual documents are not cached at all.
2. Retrieved documents are marked with an expiration time, and their cached copies are used only until this time. Afterward, upon the next client's request, a new copy of the document is retrieved from the master server.
3. A creation time is assigned with each cached document. If the document has not changed on the master server then the master server will reply with a new expiration time rather than the whole document.

The needed cache space is another issue related to the caching proxy server. How much cache space should be reserved to obtain relatively good results? Typically the optimal size is quite modest and actually does not present a real issue. A few GB of disk space seems to be sufficient to keep the effectiveness of the caching proxy server quite high. In most cases for Web documents, the hit rate remains in the range of 40 to 50%. This is the percentage of Web clients' requests that are serviced from the cache, when no external network traffic is required. To return the ball to our courtyard, we can say that one half of Web requests will not leave the intranet boundaries at all.

Proxy servers can also filter data and act similarly to a firewall. But a proxy server is less restrictive than a real firewall. From the security standpoint it is always better to opt for a real than a quasi firewall for that purpose. Some Internet service providers (IPSs) make all their users use a proxy server and block sites with unsuitable material. This is very common in some countries. Without elaborating the political correctness of such an approach, from the proxy's standpoint this is quite feasible.

The functions of proxy, filtering (firewall), and caching can be separated among several server programs or combined in a single package. Different server programs can run on different machines, so these functions can even be physically separated. Even caching can be provided on a different box from the proxy server. Any other combination is also possible.

Proxy servers are intranet oriented. They act on behalf of intranet clients for outside services. But proxy servers can play the opposite role. They can help the users coming from the outside to get some internal services. Today this is quite common in the academic environment. Library resources should be available to students and faculties at any time, while they are on campus, as well as when they are off campus. When off-campus users want to access the library, they actually reach a proxy server that first authenticates them. Afterward the communication continues between the users and the proxy server that on behalf of them accesses the library resources for the needed data. The provided service is identical as if it is was performed on campus. The only requirement for users is to configure their off-campus PCs appropriately to use the proxy server.

There are two basic types of proxy servers:

1. Application proxies — perform work for users
2. SOCKS proxies — cross-wire ports between clients and targeted servers

25.2.3.1 *Application Proxies*

This is the proxy type we have already discussed. It automates the process of connecting an intranet client to the outside world, i.e., an Internet server. Everything happens via an application proxy server, which also performs needed logging and optional filtering. Application proxy servers can also authenticate users. Before the connection is made, the proxy server can ask the user to log in first. To a Web user this would make each site look like it required a login.

25.2.3.2 *SOCKS Proxies*

SOCKS proxies cross-wire users' internal connection to another outside connection. They simply act as a switchboard for the incoming and outgoing connections.

SOCKS is a generic proxy protocol for TCP/IP-based networking applications. It includes two more components in the connection picture: the SOCKS server and the SOCKS client. This is presened in Figure 25.8.

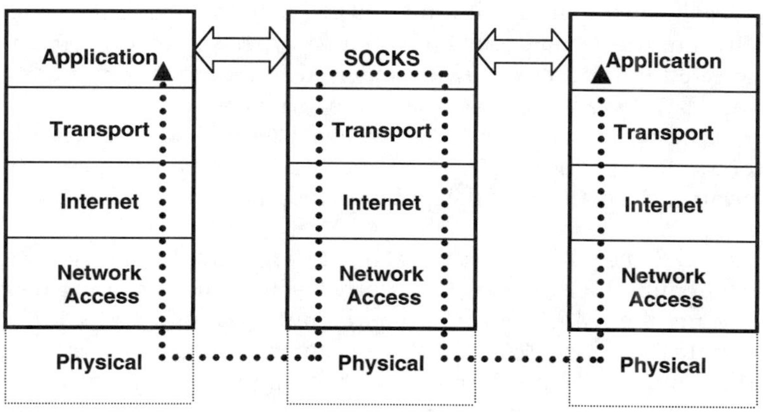

FIGURE 25.8
SOCKS proxy protocol.

When an application client needs to connect to an application server, the client connects to a SOCKS proxy server. The SOCKS proxy server connects to the application server on behalf of the client and relays data between the application client and the application server. For the application server, the SOCKS proxy server is the client.

The SOCKS protocol performs multiple functions:

- Makes connection requests
- Sets up proxy circuit
- Relays application data
- Optionally authenticates the users

SOCKS was originally intended as a network firewall. Because of its simplicity and flexibility, SOCKS has been used as a generic application proxy, in virtual private networks (VPNs), and for extranet applications. SOCKS offers unique features and benefits:

- Application-independent protection — as soon as new applications appears, SOCKS can protect them without need for any additional development.

- Flexible protection through a variety of access control policies based on user, application, and time criteria, in addition to source and destination addresses.
- Bidirectional proxy support — SOCKS identifies communication target through domain names, overriding the restriction of using the private IP addresses. SOCKS can use domain names to establish bidirectional communication between separate LANS with overlapping IP addresses.

Other IP-layer based proxy mechanisms, like the network address translation (NAT), support only unidirectional connections, from the private network (the intranet) toward the external network (the Internet). For some applications, like multimedia applications, it simply cannot work; these applications request the return data channel.

25.2.4 Web Services

We have discussed in this section primarily intranet-related services. Without these services, or at least some of them, intranet cannot function at all. The services themselves are functionally unidirectional, and their main purpose is to protect an intranet and provide the selected transparency toward external Internet services. Just recall firewalls or proxy servers. But there is another side of the intranet-Internet story: do we want also to present our intranet community to the external world? In most cases the answer is positive. Intranet owners, whoever they are — companies, organizations, colleges — wish to publish certain information to the public. And they can find the audience on the Internet.

Web services make this wish become a reality. As an example let us look at a company's intranet. The company's Web page on the Internet is its public face and presents the image the company wants the world to see. It may be built glamorously, with many graphics and special features to attract Web visitors — potential patrons and customers — and catch their attention. While the intranet is the company's private face, hidden from external viewers, that makes a working environment for its employees, the purpose of Web services is the opposite — advertise the company to as many people as possible. And both use almost the same hardware and software for the two very different purposes. A Web service can exist without an intranet (there are many Web sites without intranet backings), while the opposite is extremely rare. Everybody tends to want to be recognizable worldwide.

There are many variations on the name *Web services*: World Wide Web (WWW), Web Hosting, Information Superhighway, and sometimes even simply *intranet*. Without elaborating the correctness of certain names, we will primarily use the name Web service/services.

Web services are self-contained, modular applications that could be described, published, located, and invoked over a network:

- A Web service needs to be created, and its interfaces and invocation methods must be defined.
- A Web service needs to be published to one or more network repositories for potential users to locate them.
- A Web service needs to be located for being invoked by potential users.
- A Web service needs to be invoked to be of any benefit.
- A Web service may need to be unpublished when it is no longer available or needed.

These "academic definitions" of Web services could be expressed in other, more comprehensive ways:

- Web services are HTML/XML-based information exchange systems that use a network for direct application-to-application interaction. These systems can include programs, objects, messages, and/or documents.
- Web services provide data-independent mechanisms to programmatically expose business services on the network using HTML/XML protocols and formats.
- Web services could be accessed by using browsers (Web clients), but do not requires the use of either browsers or HTML/XML.

The foundation of the Web services is the hyper-text transfer protocol (HTTP) a simple TCP/IP-based application protocol (default port number is 80). The HTTP protocol is used to format, transmit, and link documents of different type (text, graphics, sounds, animation, and video). Web-based information comes in a standardized format known as hyper-text markup language (HTML). Hyper-text in the name means that the text contains "hot links" which, when activated, refer directly to another body of information. Markup language means documents are prepared in a generic way that will allow them to be displayed on any client's video display. HTML documents are generally referred to as *web pages*. An improved version of HTML is known as extensible markup language (XML). XML is already in wide use today, and it will probably completely replace HTML in the future.

The JavaTM 2 Platform, Enterprise Edition (J2EE) technology provides a component-based approach to the design, development, assembly, and deployment of Web services. The J2EE platform provides a multitiered distributed application model, the ability to reuse components, a unified security model, and flexible transaction control. By intent, Web services are not implemented in a monolithic way, but rather represent a collection of several related technologies. At a bare minimum, any Web service entails a connection between two applications — in programmers' parlance, a remote procedure call (RPC) — in which queries and responses are exchanged in XML over HTTP. The more generally accepted definition, however, implies implementation of a stack of specific, complementary standards, as presented in the Figure 25.9.

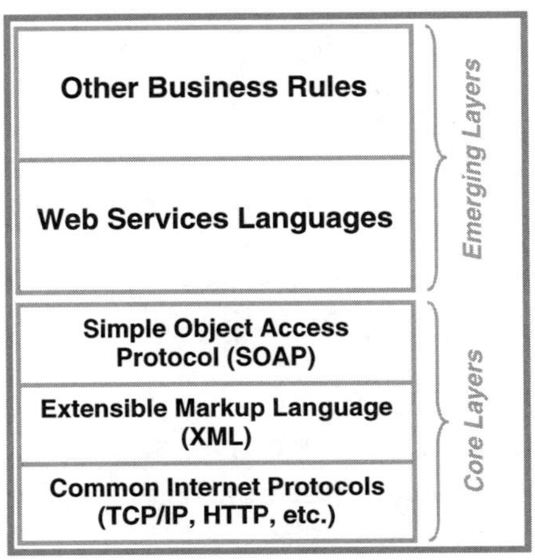

FIGURE 25.9
The Web services technology stack.

Today, the core layers that define basic Web services communication have been widely accepted and likely will be implemented quite uniformly. Higher-level layers that define strategic aspects of business processes remain an open question, however, and it is possible that divergent approaches will emerge. The development of generally open and accepted standards is a key strength of the coalitions that have been building Web services infrastructure. At the same time, these efforts have resulted in a dizzying array of jargon and acronyms. We will focus on the core layers; higher layers are business-related, and they are beyond the scope of this text.

Core layers of the Web services stack are:

- *Common Internet Protocols*. Although not specifically tied to any transport protocol, Web services build on ubiquitous Internet connectivity and infrastructure to ensure nearly universal reach and support. In particular, Web services will take advantage of HTTP, the same connection protocol used by Web servers and browsers.
- *Extensible Markup Language (XML)*. XML is a widely accepted format for exchanging data and its corresponding semantics. It is a fundamental building block for nearly every other layer in the Web services stack.
- *Simple Object Access Protocol (SOAP)*. SOAP is a protocol for messaging and RPC-style communication between applications. It is based on XML and uses common Internet transport protocols like HTTP to carry its data. SOAP has been submitted to the World Wide Web Consortium (W3C) standards body and will emerge soon as "XML Protocol (XP)."

Web services, as they are described here, make a framework for further development and implementations in the area of e-businesses. In that light they are more appropriate for future events than the current state of the art. However, the origins of Web services are in the today's WWW, and WWW is currently the main player on the Internet.

WWW is built as a server/client application. At the server side is the Web server, which hosts Web sites, provides support for HTTP and other implemented protocols, and executes server-side programs that perform certain functions. Such programs are CGI scripts or servlets (CGI stands for *common gateway interface*) that provide dynamic creation of Web pages. Web server provides services to one or more Web containers. A Web container presents a ubiquitous, accessible, and consistent platform that provides a first-class environment for deploying and running of the Web service.

Web browsers are at the client side. The browser is a program that reads Web-based information in the standardized HTML/XML format. It contacts a remote Web server and places requests on behalf of users. The requested documents are then transferred and displayed on the user's video display. Currently, the two most popular browsers are Netscape Navigator and Microsoft Internet Explorer.

The browser follows the specified pointer to look for certain objects or service. This pointer is known as the ***uniform resource locator (URL)*** and contains five basic components:

1. *Protocol* or *application* identified by:
   - http:// HTTP protocol to access Web pages
   - https:// secure HTTP protocol based on HTTP/SSL
   - ftp:// FTP protocol to transfer files
   - mailto: Send e-mail to the designated address
   - news: Access Usenet newsgroups

- telnet:// TELNET protocol for remote login
- ldap:// Access LDAP directory services
- file:// Access a local file on the browser's machine

2. *Hostname* Domain host name of the Web server.
3. *TCP port* Optional; otherwise the default port is assumed (80 for HTTP).
4. *Directory* Optional; otherwise the document directory configured at Web server is assumed.
5. *Filename* Optional; otherwise the default filename "index.html" is assumed. The filename is case sensitive.

As an example, the following URL:

http://www.scps.nyu.edu/demo/example.html

specifies Web page *example.html* on the Web server *www.scps.nyu.edu* in the subdirectory *demo* (the subdirectory is referred to the configured document home directory for the server).

The WWW includes more than just Web page browsing. This is a suite of many well-known network services. The implemented URL identifies the requested network service (the first URL component).

A Web server is a daemon, usually named ***httpd***, which is listening for incoming HTTP requests at the configured port (default port number is 80). The Web server configuration is an OS-independent procedure characterized by a separate set of configuration rules. Generally Web server configuration files are well-commented, with logical and comprehensive syntax and an intuitive content. They are definitely very different from old-fashioned condensed and unfriendly UNIX configuration files, which were designed a long time ago to be primarily machine oriented. Unfortunately, it does not mean that the configuration of a Web server is an easy task. There are many configuration details, enough for quite a tick book.

Today the most popular and the most implemented Web server is Apache (more than 70% of all server installations worldwide). This is not unusual, bearing in mind the quality of this freeware product. The following example presents a piece of the Apache configuration file. The only purpose is to illustrate the format and syntax of the configuration data without any detailed elaboration.

$ cat /usr/local/apache/conf/httpd.conf (presented only partially)

```
    .....
    .....
#
### Section 3: Virtual Hosts
#
# VirtualHost: If you want to maintain multiple domains/hostnames on your
# machine you can setup VirtualHost containers for them.
# Please see the documentation at <URL:http:/ /www.apache.org/docs/vhosts/>
# for further details before you try to setup virtual hosts.
# You may use the command line option '-S' to verify your virtual host
# configuration.
#
# If you want to use name-based virtual hosts you need to define at
# least one IP address (and port number) for them.

# < VirtualHost 146.25.91.112 >
DocumentRoot /usr/local/myserver/www/
ServerName myserver.scps.nyu.edu
< Directory "/usr/local/myserver/www/">
AllowOverride AuthConfig
```

```
    Options FollowSymLinks
    Order allow,deny
    Allow from all
    SetHandler server-parsed
    </Directory>
    ScriptAlias /cgi-bin/ "/usr/local/myserver/cgi-bin/"
    ScriptAlias /admin/ "/usr/local/myserver/admin/ "
    ScriptAlias /gifs/ "/usr/local/myserver/www/gi fs/"
    <Directory "/usr/local/myserver/cgi-bin/">
      AllowOverride None
      Options FollowSymLinks
      Order allow,deny
      Allow from all
    </Directory>
  </VirtualHost>
          .....
          .....
```

To respond to incoming requests for Web pages, multiple Web server daemons are running simultaneously, and new daemons could be spawned on an as needed basis. The number of daemons, both initial and maximum, is configurable. These configuration parameters should reflect real needs and processing power of the implemented Web server's hardware. Here is an example:

```
$ ps -ef | grep http | grep -v grep
root    470    1  0  12:43 ?  00:00:03 /usr/local/apache/bin/httpd
nobody  473  470  0  12:43 ?  00:00:01 /usr/local/apache/bin/httpd
nobody  474  470  0  12:43 ?  00:00:00 /usr/local/apache/bin/httpd
nobody  475  470  0  12:43 ?  00:00:00 /usr/local/apache/bin/httpd
nobody  476  470  0  12:43 ?  00:00:00 /usr/local/apache/bin/httpd
nobody  477  470  0  12:43 ?  00:00:01 /usr/local/apache/bin/httpd
nobody  478  470  0  12:43 ?  00:00:00 /usr/local/apache/bin/httpd
nobody  479  470  0  12:43 ?  00:00:01 /usr/local/apache/bin/httpd
nobody  480  470  0  12:43 ?  00:00:01 /usr/local/apache/bin/httpd
nobody  481  470  0  12:43 ?  00:00:00 /usr/local/apache/bin/httpd
nobody  482  470  0  12:43 ?  00:00:00 /usr/local/apache/bin/httpd
```

Pay attention to the RUID of the daemons. The very first daemon is invoked during the system startup by the process ***init*** (the daemon's PPID=1) and it has superuser RUID. Ten more daemons are then spawned, but they have RUID "nobody" (user's entity "nobody" owns Web stuff). The number of spawned daemons is specified in the Apache configuration file */usr/local/apache/conf/httpd.conf*. More daemons will be invoked online if needed.

Web pages require permanent maintenance and update. Otherwise they soon become obsolete and nonattractive. A good Web page has to be well organized, clear, simple, and intuitive to follow, readable and comprehensive. An overcrowded page could be counterproductive because users are eager to browse quickly through presented material. It is better to put the existing material in several linked pages instead of a single page. Finally, an appropriate balance between textual and graphic presentation is a key for a successful Web page.

It is very difficult to predict an exact number of hits to a newly designed Web server. But an increase in the load over the time is expected. The scalability and the availability of the Web services are very important. A possible solution can include multiple Web servers behind a special front-end device known as the *load director*. All servers provide the same service, and the load director controls a load balance among all available servers. If an individual server fails, the load is distributed between other active servers.

A need for Web services is primarily business driven. But it would be naïve to expect that all business problems will be solved if you provide a technically good WWW site. Following are some tips on what not to expect from a Web presence:

- *Do not expect a WWW site to produce miracles*. Placing a Web page up on the Internet is no longer enough. If you want people to visit, you must drive them there. The Internet must be a part of a total marketing mix in order to be effective. It must be a reason for customers to place an order, or anything else for that matter. The reason could be anything from greater and easier access to information, up to saving money by placing an order over the Internet.
- *Do not think of the Web as a place for outsiders only*. The Web can also be inside the company's intranet for information like employee manuals, questionnaires, employees' 401 K plans, as well as core business functions like placing orders, workflow applications, etc.
- *Do not expect to have to throw away the existing hardware and software*. The company has made substantial investments in the core business systems over time. As a general principal, needed information should be accessible on the Internet/intranet site.
- *Do not expect to be dependent on one hardware/software company ever again*. A properly done Internet/intranet site (including any custom programming that has to be done) should be able to run on any platform. If IT personnel have chosen a Solaris operating system, a properly done site should be able to run on a Hewlett-Packard, IBM, or DEC box, too.
- *Do not ignore this technology*. The only thing that is certain is that competitors are not ignoring the Web. This technology (if properly implemented) will allow closer communications with customers, with suppliers and even between employees in the company. In this millennium, information will be the most valuable commodity of most companies, and the Web allows for information to move quickly in a format that is accessible to vast numbers of people. In turn, this information will allow businesses to move more quickly and to save money.

25.2.5 Other External Services

This title refers to the services that are offered to the out-of-intranet users. We will address them as external or Internet users, and the offered services as the external services. External users are also regular intranet users at the off-business time. Once the employees step out of the company offices and continue to work from homes, they appear in front of the intranet the same as the other external users. External services are generally business driven. Besides Web server, which is today a common service, other external services are always questionable. As much as we open our intranet for external access, proportionally we increase a risk to be attacked by potential intruders. Of course it does not mean that additional external services are not allowed. It only means that everything should be done carefully to prevent unpleasant surprises.

The main candidate for other external services is the FTP service. If our business supposes downloading, or even uploading of data by external users, then an Internet-oriented FTP server sounds reasonable. If the FTP access should be granted to an unspecified number of external users, then an anonymous FTP site should be built. We addressed this topic in Chapter 21. In any case we have to administer and maintain the FTP site internally, i.e., from the intranet.

The FTP site could be realized in different ways. One approach is to build the FTP server with its own external network interface and spend one more external IP address for this purpose. In this case it is important to prevent any attempt to penetrate from the Internet through the FTP site into the intranet. Even if the FTP site is compromised, it should remain within its own boundaries.

Another approach is to leave the FTP site behind the firewall and access the FTP server through the firewall. The firewall will redirect external ftp traffic based on the intranet IP address and the FTP port number. At the same time, the firewall combined with the viruswall can scan the ftp traffic and protect the FTP server itself. This approach sounds more secure, and probably easier to realize.

An external access to the intranet e-mail service also sounds very convenient. Intranet users have to have access to their e-mail from home, during the trips, or whatever. Why restrict the use of e-mail strictly to the business time?. Especially when the e-mail service itself is not restricted to the intranet at all. Again several approaches are possible. We can allow access to the intranet e-mail server from the external POP and IMAP clients (as it is done internally). But the external POP or IMAP clients require the installed client software and corresponding setting and configuration. When the user moves to another PC, everything must be redone. Another issue is security. Again we must open tunnels through the firewall for new services and effectively decrease overall intranet security.

There is another approach to allow Web e-mail access. It does not request anything special on the client side — the standard browser is sufficient to access and log in to the server, and browse the e-mail. At the server side there is more work to do to provide Web service and support e-mail handling. But it is worth doing it — this is a safer and more flexible and robust solution.

One more example of an external access to the intranet data we already discussed in Section 25.2.3 by talking about proxy servers. The example addressed the problem of how to allow the students and faculty to access the campus library from the Internet.

The list of possible external services is not finished with those examples. Under certain circumstances, other services can also require external access. How everything will be realized depends on our wishes, business needs, and technical possibilities. In most cases nontechnical issues prevail in making certain decisions.

However, there is only one "most important issue" and that is the security of the intranet. Never forget that by opening our intranet to the external world, we always accept a certain risk to be compromised.

25.3 Inside the Intranet

This section presents intranet as an insider anticipates it. It is focused on the major technical topics related to the intranet. The idea is to discuss the main intranet components and issues, without going too deeply in to details. The title "Inside the intranet" should emphasize the fact that the intranet itself, as a self-sufficient network, is a point of interest.

This section addresses both intranet aspects: hardware and software, as some other intranet-specific issues.

25.3.1 Network Infrastructure and Desktops

An intranet presents a size-restricted network, usually contained within several rooms, a floor, several floors or a building. Intranet users belong to the same company, organization, department, division, or some other organizational entity, but always within the same administrative control. An intranet connects users' workstations, better known as desktops (desktop computers) with intranet servers, providing a workable environment to run the business more efficiently. A restricted area covered by an intranet makes a ground for an economical implementation of the high-tech technologies in a number of various ways. An intranet could be even realized as a single local area network (LAN). However, it is always better, performance-wise, to organize an intranet as a hierarchical network instead of a flat one. Subnetting is always beneficial regarding the network throughput and speed. An intranet realized as a wide area network (WAN) also has other advantages. For LAN and WAN see Chapter 14.

A direct consequence is that the Intranet implements the same technologies used on the Internet. All hardware and software pieces of an intranet are "déjà vu" from the Internet. The basic intranet infrastructure includes the same kind of twisted-pair, fiber optic, and even wireless transmission links, bridges, hubs, switches, routers, and gateways, already seen and known from the Internet. The most common LAN technologies are Ethernet, Fast Ethernet, Gigabit Ethernet, ARCnet, as well as Token Ring. Sometimes ISDN and dial-in connections are also in use.

A client/server model is the main characteristic of the intranet. The clients are desktop computers that are connected by high-speed links into the intranet network. The server is a powerful, high-speed computer with a larger disk capacity. It provides a specific service to the desktop clients. Both servers and desktops contain the network support software that is required to run the network and carry out the certain service. An example of the network service is the Web service; a firewall is another example.

Web software allows the server to support HTTP so it can exchange information with the clients. Firewall software will provide the security needed to protect internal information from the outside world. Browser software allows the use of hyperlinks to go from one place to another in a document, or to go to a completely different document. These three pieces of software are basic for an intranet today, but other network software already in use on the Internet can be added to provide other useful functions.

Intranet is not only a hardware-software tale. A successful intranet primarily depends on the staff that is running this intranet. As always, the human factor is again crucial for a success. An intranet often involves new staffing, and consultants may be needed to get the project started. After the intranet is in place, a Web developer and an information designer will be needed. People will also be needed to train employees in using the intranet.

Desktop computers (we will address them simply as "desktops") constitute the largest group of participants of the intranet. They are attached to each individual user, and they are the main vehicles in using the Intranet. In most cases desktops are personal computers (PCs), and sometimes Macintosh workstations (Macs), or UNIX workstations (primarily Linux). It means that the desktops primarily run on the Microsoft Windows platforms (all flavors). At the same time, intranet servers are mostly UNIX or NT based. Obviously an intranet presents a mixture of the different platforms on the operating system level too. A rough division on that level could be that desktops are Windows dominated, while the server side is UNIX dominated. There are exceptions to this, but we like to say: "exceptions only prove the rule."

The needed glue to make an intranet operational, despite all existing differences, is the implemented network software. TCP/IP is the dominant network protocol implemented in the intranet, although some other network protocols are also used, like Novel Netware IPX or Microsoft NetBIOS. This is slightly different from the Internet where TCP/IP is the almost exclusive protocol in use.

At the end, what can we conclude? In general, the intranet infrastructure matches the Internet in both areas: hardware and software. The same hardware and software (or at least very similar ones) means that all Internet-based skills could be fully implemented on the intranet. This statement is also valid for UNIX administration skills.

25.3.2 Internal Services

We can look to the intranet as an extension of the Internet. Especially from the user standpoint, the intranet is only the vehicle to join the larger family of Internet users. In that light, it is fair to conclude that Web browsing, e-mail, and a few of the other best-known Internet services are the ones expected by the intranet users. Users hate restrictions on using the Internet, and intranet firewalls could restrict this usage significantly. By using the intranet terminology, users are looking for full transparency toward Internet. In most cases they do not care and do not know about the intranet, but they complain if they cannot fulfill their Internet wishes.

Making external Internet services available internally greatly depends on the implemented intranet policy: What do the intranet users need, and what should be given to them? And, primarily, the intranet users are treated as clients (one exception is X windowing, where the intranet is on the server side). Technically it always means how to configure and tune the intranet firewall.

Besides the extension of Internet services within the intranet, there is also another group of internal network services that are strictly intranet oriented. We mentioned that the concept of the intranet is the same as Internet. We even said that the intranet is the "small Internet." This means that the network services available on the Internet could be directly implemented on the intranet. They range from X windowing, via DNS, to the WWW and DHCP. Some of them are even mandatory.

A list of such services is (or rather could be):

- DNS is the mandatory service. Intranet hosts are invisible outside of the intranet and nobody can replace this service. Internal host name resolution must be covered by the internal DNS service. DNS requests for external (Internet) hosts should be forwarded to some external DNS server. For more details about DNS see Chapter 16.
- Print service is definitely needed; users always print something (the paperless office still does not fully exist). The print service can be organized around print servers with multiple local printers, or around individual network printers directly connected to the intranet (they directly provide the print service). Today the latter is more common. For more details about printing, see Chapter 10.
- NIS is preferable for administering the UNIX part of the intranet. The intranet environment is almost ideal for centralized administration. The whole intranet is usually under the same administrative jurisdiction, protected from external interferences, and it is very easy to define administrative domains. For more details about NIS see Chapter 17.
- NFS is highly suitable for intranet file service. It provides data consistency intranet-wide, and makes the data backup and restore easier. For not-UNIX

clients (DOS, NT, Mac), a number of emulation software products is available, like free Samba or other professional packages (Xinet, Totalnet, etc.). For more details about NFS see Chapter 18.

- Intranet is ideal for networked backup implementations, like free Amanda, or professional products as Legato Networker or Veritas NetBackup.
- E-mail is certainly needed within the intranet, as well as with external Internet users. There is no difference between the two; e-mail traffic must be routed through the firewall. The inbound e-mail traffic has to be scanned for viruses and other malicious codes. Today e-mail is the main "transporter" of nasty offenders, and the intranet must be protected accordingly. This is efficiently provided by the intranet viruswall. For more details about e-mail see Chapter 20.
- Intranet community consists of trusted hosts. So internal remote login and other remote commands (including "remshing") should be quite safe, as well as telnet, ftp, and other "insecure" network services.

  Despite internal intranet safety, the secure remote commands and secure "shelling" (SSH) are recommended even within the intranet. Today SSH should be standard on every computer, especially on the UNIX platform.
- Intranet actually means the small Internet confined within a company or organization. This also means that internal Web services are also very useful within the intranet. All internal information could be published on the internal Web site, and they will be available companywide. But everything remains among the intranet users. Technically, internal Web service is the same as the external one. The difference is only that the audience is restricted strictly to the intranet community.
- Most other Internet services are also possible within the intranet. The only issue is what are the benefits of their implementations. Each new service has a price, and it is not worth it to support senseless network services.
- Among all mandatory, recommended, possible, and senseless network services, there is one that sounds like it was invented for the intranet environment. This is the dynamic host configuration protocol (DHCP). We will elaborate on this service in more detail.

25.3.2.1 Dynamic Host Configuration Protocol (DHCP)

DHCP (dynamic host configuration protocol) is a protocol that allows the centralized and automatic assignment of IP configurations on a computer network. Each participant in the network communication requires a unique IP address. Up to now we have assumed a manual IP address assignment, and we learned about the corresponding UNIX configuration behind it. A manually assigned IP address is known as a "static IP address" and it is almost standard on the UNIX platform. UNIX hosts are assumed to run primarily as network servers and they need in most cases a static IP address.

But intranet is not exclusively UNIX based. Desktop computers are the most numerous participants in the Intranet, and mostly they are not UNIX hosts at all. Although the manual IP configuration always can be implemented, the ability to assign IP client configurations automatically can alleviate the painful process of intranet IP address management. Network administrators have quickly appreciated the importance, flexibility, and ease-of-use offered in DHCP.

DHCP was introduced by the Internet Engineering Task Force (IETF), and it is specified in RFC documents. DHCP lets a network administrator supervise and distribute IP addresses from a central point. The purpose of DHCP is to provide the automatic (dynamic) allocation of IP client configurations for a specific time period (called a *lease period*) and to eliminate the work necessary to administer a large IP network.

For every computer to be online, a unique IP address is required. What makes an intranet unique is the fact that the majority of computers should not be online continuously. The truth is that they spend more time offline or inactive. Also, when mobile computer users travel between sites, they have had to relive this process for each different site from which they connected to a network. So there are many reasons to automate the process of adding machines to a network and assigning unique IP addresses.

How does DHCP work? When a client needs to start up TCP/IP operations, it broadcasts a request for address information. The DHCP server receives the request, assigns a new address for a specific time period (called a lease period), and sends it to the client together with the other required configuration information. This information is acknowledged by the client and used to set up its configuration. The DHCP server will not reallocate the address during the lease period and will attempt to return the same address every time the client requests an address. The client may extend its lease with subsequent requests, and may send a message to the server before the lease expires telling it that it no longer needs the address so it can be released and assigned to another client on the network.

The use of DHCP in the intranet is extremely useful and efficient. Manual configuration requires the careful input of a unique IP address, subnet mask, default router address, and a DNS server address. In an ideal world, manually assigning client addresses should be relatively straightforward and error free. Unfortunately, we do not live in an ideal world; computers are frequently moved and new machines get added to a network. Also if other intranet resources such as routers change, this could mean changing many system configurations. For an administrator, this process can be time-consuming, tedious, and error prone. DHCP has several major advantages over manual configurations. Each intranet computer gets its configuration from a pool of available IP addreses automatically for a specific leasing period, meaning no wasted IP numbers. When a computer has finished with the address, it is released for another computer to use. Configuration information can be administered from a single point. And major network resource changes require only the DHCP server to be updated with the new information, rather than each computer in the intranet.

The benefits of dynamic addressing are especially helpful in mobile computing environments where users frequently change locations. New mobile users in the intranet simply plug in their laptop to the network, and receive their required configuration automatically. When moving to a different network using another DHCP server, then that network's server will supply the configuration. No manual reconfiguration is required at all.

At the same time, DHCP servers are easy to administer and can be set up in just a few minutes. The DHCP servers have to run continuously as they must be available at all times when clients need IP access.

Some machines in the intranet need to be at fixed addresses. For example, all servers, routers, printers, and similar devices that have to be accessible by all clients. The changes in their IP addresses would disable the corresponding services. The DHCP server should be capable of assigning pre-allocated IP addresses to these specific machines.

To avoid conflicts between addresses assigned by the DHCP server and those assigned manually, intranet users should be discouraged, or preferably prevented, from reconfiguring their own IP addresses. Also some older operating systems do not support DHCP.

25.3.3 Virtual Private Network (VPN)

Intranet seems to be a magic solution for many companies and organizations. All intranet users (company employees) are grouped together in a safe environment with all needed Internet services available for their efficient work. However, an intranet is a space-restricted network, contained within relatively limited geographical area.

How can a remote company branch office be included in the company intranet? How do retail organizations with hundreds of stores nationwide provide each store with the access to the intranet servers and databases that they desperately need?

Today ***virtual private network (VPN)*** sounds like a solution for this problem. VPN technology allows us to build a low cost *virtual intranet* that incorporates all remote participants, by using the existing Internet infrastructure. There is no need for a significant investment, while the needed network privacy is preserved over the large geographical area. VPN supplies network connectivity over a possibly long physical distance. In this respect, VPN is a form of wide area network (WAN). The key feature of a VPN, however, is its ability to use public networks like the Internet rather than rely on private leased lines. VPN technologies implement restricted-access networks that use the Internet resources without sacrificing features and basic security.

Traditionally a company or an organization that wanted to build a WAN needed to procure expensive, dedicated lines to connect their offices together. Typically a leased-line WAN supported a long-distance intranet. Besides file sharing and e-mail, the long-distance intranet provided access to intranet Web sites and videoconferencing systems. In addition, the intranet was open selectively to partners to provide their services, known as extranet services.

A VPN can support the same intranet/extranet services as in a traditional long-distance intranet. But VPN has also grown in popularity for its ability to support *remote access service*. In recent years, many companies have increased the mobility of their users by allowing more employees to telecommute. Employees also continue to travel and face an increasing need to stay "plugged in" to the company intranet. Companies that do not use VPNs must resort to implementing specialized secure dial-up services. To log in to an intranet, a remote user must call into a intranet's dial-in access server (using either a 1–800 number or a local number). The overhead of maintaining such a system internally, coupled with the possibility of high long distance charges incurred by travelers, make VPNs an appealing option here.

VPN remote access architecture is presented in the Figure 25.10. A remote node (client) wanting to log in to the company intranet calls into a local Internet service provider (ISP). Once on the Internet, the VPN client establishes a connection to the intranet VPN server maintained at the company site. Once the connection has been established, the remote client can communicate within the intranet just as securely over the Internet as if it resided on the internal network itself.

A simple extension of the VPN remote access architecture shown in Figure 25.10 allows Internetworking: an entire remote network (rather than just a single remote client) joins the local network. Rather than a client-server connection, a server-server VPN connection joins two networks to form an extended intranet, known as extranet.

VPNs do not offer any network services that are not already offered through alternative mechanisms. However, a VPN does use a unique mix of technologies that promises to improve on the traditional approaches.

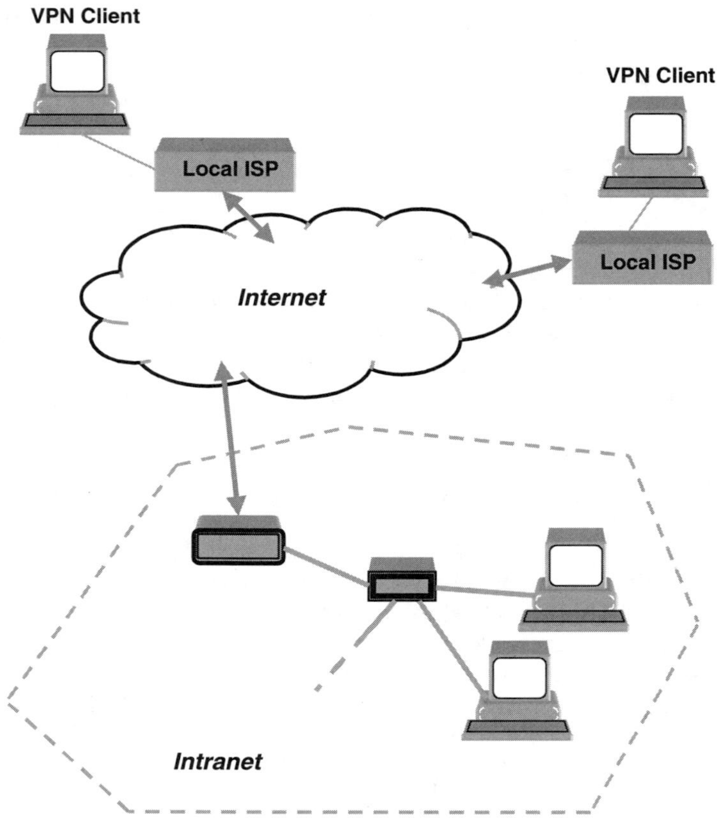

FIGURE 25.10
Virtual private network (VPN).

VPN promises two main advantages over competing approaches:

1. Cost savings – There is no more need for expensive long-distance leased lines. With VPNs, only a relatively short dedicated connection to the ISP provider is required. This connection could be a local leased line (much less expensive than a long-distance one), or it could be a local broadband connection such as DSL, cable modem, or ISDN service. Another way VPN reduces costs is by lessening the need for long-distance telephone charges for remote access. A third, more subtle way that VPN may lower costs is through the offloading of the support burden. With a VPN, the ISP rather than the company intranet must support dial-up access. ISP can in theory charge much less for their support than it costs a company internally because the public ISP cost is shared among potentially thousands of customers.
2. Scalability – As a company grows and more remote hosts must be added to the intranet, the cost of the traditional approach with leased lines increases dramatically. Four branch offices require six lines for full connectivity, five offices require ten lines, and so on. This phenomenon is known as a *combinatorial explosion*, and in a traditional WAN this explosion limits the flexibility for growth. VPN that uses the Internet avoids this problem by simply tapping into the geographically distributed access already available.

Main VPN disadvantages are:

1. VPNs require an in-depth understanding of public network security issues and proper deployment of precautions.
2. The availability and performance of an organization's wide-area intranet with the implemented VPN over the Internet, depends on factors largely outside of its own control.
3. VPN technologies from different vendors may not work well together due to immature standards.
4. VPN needs to accommodate protocols other than IP and existing ("legacy") internal network technology.

Generally speaking, these four factors constitute the "hidden costs" of a VPN solution. Whereas VPN advocates emphasize cost savings as the primary advantage of this technology, detractors cite hidden costs as the primary disadvantage of VPNs.

VPN works hard to ensure the data remains secure, but even its security mechanisms can be breached. Particularly on the Internet, sophisticated hackers with ample amounts of free time will work equally hard to "steal" VPN data if they believe it contains valuable information. Most VPN technologies implement strong encryption so that data cannot be directly viewed using network sniffers. VPN may be more susceptible to "man in the middle" attacks, however, that intercept the session and impersonate either the client or server. In addition, some private data may not be encrypted by the VPN before it is transmitted on the Internet. IP headers, for example, will contain the IP addresses of both the client and the server. Hackers may capture these addresses and choose to target these devices for future attacks.

VPN technology is based on a *tunneling* strategy. Tunneling involves encapsulating packets constructed in a base protocol format within some other protocol. In the case of VPNs run over the Internet, packets in one of several VPN protocol formats are encapsulated within IP packets.

Several network protocols have been implemented for use with VPNs. These protocols emphasize *authentication* and *encryption* in VPNs and attempt to close some of the security holes inherent in VPNs. Authentication allows VPN clients and servers to correctly establish the identity of people when accessing the intranet. Encryption allows potentially sensitive data to be hidden from the general Internet public.

Point-to-point tunneling protocol (PPTP) — PPTP is a protocol specification developed by several companies. People generally associate PPTP with Microsoft because nearly all flavors of Windows include built-in support for the protocol. The initial releases of PPTP for Windows by Microsoft contained security features that some experts claimed were too weak for serious use. Microsoft continues to improve its PPTP support, though. PPTP's primary strength is its ability to support non-IP protocols. The primary drawback of PPTP is its failure to choose a single standard for encryption and authentication. Two products that both fully comply with the PPTP specification may be totally incompatible with each other if, for example, they encrypt data differently.

Layer two tunneling protocol (L2TP) — The original competitor to PPTP in VPN solutions was L2F — a protocol implemented primarily in Cisco products. In an attempt to improve on L2F, the best features of it and PPTP were combined to create a new standard called L2TP. L2TP exists at the data link layer (layer two) in the ISO OSI model — thus the origin of its name. Like PPTP, L2TP supports non-IP clients, but it also fails to define an encryption standard. However, L2TP supports non-Internet based VPNs including frame relay, ATM, and SONET.

Internet protocol security (IPsec) — IPsec is actually a collection of multiple related protocols. It can be used as a complete VPN protocol solution, or it can be used simply as the encryption scheme within L2TP or PPTP. IPsec exists at the network layer (layer three) in the ISO OSI model. IPsec extends standard IP for the purpose of supporting more secure Internet-based services (including, but not limited to, VPNs). IPsec specifically protects against "man in the middle attacks" by hiding IP addresses that would otherwise appear on the wire.

SOCKS network security protocol — The SOCKS system provides a unique alternative to other protocols for VPNs. SOCKS functions at the session layer (layer five) in the ISO OSI model, compared to all of the other VPN protocols that work at layer two or three. This implementation offers advantages and disadvantages over the other protocol choices. Functioning at this higher level, SOCKS allows administrators to limit VPN traffic to certain applications. To use SOCKS, however, administrators must configure SOCKS proxy servers within the client environments as well as SOCKS software on the clients themselves (see the section about proxies).

A number of vendors offer VPN-related products. These products sometimes do not work with each other because of the choice of incompatible protocols (as described above) or simply because of lack of standardized testing. Some VPN products are hardware devices. Most VPN devices are effectively routers that integrate encryption functionality. Other types of VPN products are software packages. VPN software installs on top of a host operating system and can require significant customization for the local environment. Many vendor solutions comprise both server-side hardware and client-side software designed for use with the hardware.

VPN technology can also be used within the intranet itself to control access to individual subnets on the private network. In this mode, VPN clients connect to a VPN server that acts as a gateway to computers behind it on the subnet. Note that this type of VPN implementation does not involve Internet resources because everything happens within the intranet. However, it does take advantage of the security features and convenience of VPN technology.

An amazing amount of development effort has been invested in VPN technologies. Yet the task of choosing and deploying a VPN solution remains far from simple. It may prove helpful to train workers in at least the basics of VPN clients to help them migrate to new VPN deployments. They have to be aware of the traffic congestion and router failures on the Internet that can adversely impact the performance of the implemented VPN. It is also important when building a VPN to choose a high-quality ISP.

25.3.4 UNIX and Not-UNIX Platform Integration

An intranet is heterogeneous in many aspects, on different implementation levels, including the OS level. Same network services could be accomplished on multiple OS platforms, and the implemented OS platform is completely hidden from the users. All differences are mostly invisible. However, this is not the case regarding the needed administration for provided intranet services. Simply, sometime things are not going so smoothly, and we cannot ignore underlying differences. They can have a substantial impact to the overall intranet behavior and performances.

Basically, desktops belong to MS Windows (W95, W98, NT, W2000, etc.). Not necessarily everywhere, and not exclusively, but definitely Windows dominate. We will address it as NT platform. Main intranet servers are mostly UNIX-based (again this is not the rule, rather the most frequent situation). UNIX appears as a more stable and reliable platform for the crucial network services. Such division could be considered as the biased one (at least this book is about UNIX), but this is a fact at the beginning of this millennium. The end of the millennium will probably belong to platforms other than UNIX.

Intranet users simply use the network resources (hardware and software) and complain if something does not work, or works slowly. A typical working scenario is that a user logs in via a desktop, checks e-mail, and continues to work in the intranet environment. NT clients access UNIX servers, request certain services on behalf of users, and return requested data to users. On the surface, this working intranet environment looks uniform and contiguous. In reality there are certain discontinuities in its implementation.

Generally, the intranet benefit of using multiple OS platforms is that each platform is implemented on those places in the intranet where its advantages lead to better overall performance. But there are also some disadvantages of mixed OS implementations. A certain level of the intranet customization can help to diminish these disadvantages. This customization is primarily related to a unified intranet administration and management. To accomplish this task, a larger integration of implemented OS platforms is needed to avoid existing differences in their administrations. The following text is an attempt to point to the main issues related to the integration of the UNIX and NT platforms to make the intranet a technically better place to work.

1. A uniform administration of individual user accounts — Users have to have the same login name, user ID, primary group, home directory, as well as authentication data (password). This is not trivial in the heterogeneous environment. UNIX supports NIS for centralized system administration (see Chapter 17). But NIS is unknown to NT. Centralized NT administration is provided via one or more primary domain controllers (PDC). The two approaches are mutually incompatible, and the need for their integration is obvious. More specifically it means that the UNIX Master NIS Server and NT Primary Domain Controller have to share the same administrative data and push them all over the intranet. In that way UNIX NIS clients and desktops will see the same user administrative data.

   There is third-party software that delivers the same. But we advocate a homemade solution. First we have to proclaim the master NIS server for the central administrative resource for the whole intranet. Simultaneously UNIX part of the Intranet will be fully covered. Then we have to force that each action on the NIS master is automatically transferred and remotely invoked on the NT PDC. That will cover the NT part of the network. Afterward every user will be identified identically anywhere on the intranet.

   A homemade program (even a script) can handle the needed synchronization between NIS master and PDC. This presents a cost-effective and efficient solution.

2. A uniform administration of groups — unique groups over the whole intranet are very important for a secure intranet operation. The groups have to be the same and users should belong to the same groups. Access to the data is usually based on the file's mode, and they are shared only among members of the same group. Unfortunately, the required uniqueness is not possible for certain system groups that are too specific in UNIX and NT. These system groups remain, as they are, each in its own platform without any impact on the wider intranet behavior.

   The same approach from the previous paragraph can be implemented: NIS master vs. PDC integration. The same homemade program can handle group data in the same way as the user data.

3. A uniform administration of authentication data — More specifically, the same password should be valid all over the Intranet. Users hate multiple passwords: one password to login, another for e-mail, a third for... And how to handle needed password changes? Again NIS master seems as the most appropriate for the password maintenance, which will then be pushed toward PDC and NT community.
4. An integrated intranet file service — Users have to have unrestricted access to the same data. Especially users' home directories should be unique. A kind of unified intranet file service (UIFS) has to be provided. UNIX network filesystems — NFS (see Chapter 18) are incompatible with NT Common Internet Filesystem (CIFS). Neither side can provide UIFS for both UNIX and NT parts of an intranet.

   The most appropriate solution could be a UNIX NFS file server with the CIFS emulation software on it. UNIX file servers are stable and robust in their implementations. UNIX nfs clients approach the file server normally, while at the same time the CIFS emulation software accommodates NT clients. There are several commercial CIFS emulation products, as well as the freeware Samba package.

   User home directories could and should be located on the UIFS file server/servers. UIFS and unique home directories relax other network applications also. Especially, it is easier to enforce the required backup policy. Simply, important data to be backed up are grouped together on one or several UIFS servers. There is no need to worry about desktop data.
5. A unified print service is much easier to accomplish. Network printers are compatible with both UNIX and NT clients. If a printing center organized around a print server with multiple local printers is needed, NT print server is probably a better choice.
6. A unified e-mail service is also easy to accomplish; a UNIX e-mail server seems to be appropriate. Sendmail (see Chapter 20) is a mature and reliable e-mail product proven through all years of its wide use. The compatibility of the intranet e-mail server with UNIX and NT clients is based, however, on the implementation of POP and IMAP protocols, which are independent of sendmail and transparent over both platforms.
7. Most other intranet services can run on any OS platform independently, like firewall, viruswall, or proxy. The only criterion for the implemented OS platform is overall service performance.

Section IV

Case Studies

26

UNIX Installation

26.1 Introductory Notes

The first step in dealing with an UNIX system is to install the operating system itself. On a UNIX platform, delivered systems with the OS preinstalled is more an exception than the rule. In any case, among the administrative duties are the UNIX installation (when we say "UNIX installation" we are thinking "UNIX OS installation") and the initial configuration of the installed UNIX system that will allow access for further upgrades.

UNIX installation per se should not be a problem. There are two main reasons why:

1. The installation procedure is usually well documented; the provided documentation usually covers all possible installation scenarios, as well as potential troubleshooting.
2. The system is not in an operational stage, and we are relaxed during the installation. It is easy to repeat an installation procedure if something is going wrong, we have started everything from scratch, so we can do the same again.

Nevertheless, any real installation example is always welcome and helpful. Different installation scenarios and options, and a general installation approach in the provided documentation can sometimes be confusing. Existing dilemmas can be quickly resolved if we have an appropriate installation case in front of us. This is the purpose of this chapter. A few installation examples for the currently most common UNIX flavors — Solaris, HP-UX, and Linux — could be very helpful in a number of real installation cases, and also very educational for the readers.

OS installation is the first step in making a UNIX system workable. However, this is not the only step in accomplishing this task, as well as keeping a UNIX system compliant with unavoidable upgrades, updates, and patches. The second part of this chapter addresses these issues. For both parts it is assumed that we have workable hardware in front of us, that we have access to the system console, and that the CD drive is available.

26.2 UNIX Installation Procedures

In this part, the installation procedure examples for a few common UNIX flavors are documented. Despite the fact that they are sufficiently general and applicable for listed

UNIX flavors, they are also site-specific. Please keep in mind that some differences in the installation procedures caused by different system hardware configurations and/or operating system versions and releases are always possible. This is the reason why, in each of the examples that follow, the relevant initial information is always provided.

26.2.1 HP-UX Installation

The following text describes in detail steps performed in installing HP-UX 10.20 operating system on the Series 800 HP system — model E35; the host is named "blue" in this example. The described installation procedure also includes a mirroring of the root filesystem, which is realized as a single filesystem that also includes /usr and /var.

1. Power-on the system.
2. Insert the "HP-UX 10.20 Install and Core OS" CD into the CD drive.
3. Follow messages on the console. Pay attention to the message:
   "To discontinue press any key within 10 seconds! ..."
   and ***hit any key.***
4. Respond to questions:
   Boot from primary boot path (Y or N)? > ***n***
   Boot from alternate boot path (Y or N)? > ***n***
   Enter boot path, command, or ?> ***boot 56/52.2*** (or corresponding CD hardware path)
   Since the CD was selected (hardware path 56/52.2), respond to the question:
   Interact with IPL (Y or N)?> ***n***
5. The Install Program on the CD is started, and the ***Welcome Screen*** appears.
   Select ***Install HP-UX*** and continue dialogue.
   Would you like to enable networking now? > ***y***
6. The screen: ***HP-UX Install Utility — Network Configuration***

hostname:	***blue***	
ip address:	***XX.XX.XX.XX***	(enter corresponding IP address)
router:	***XX.XX.XX.XX***	(enter corresponding IP address)
netmask:	***255.255.255.0***	(or another netmask)

   Select ***OK***.
7. The screen: ***HP-UX Install Utility — Select System Root disk***
   Select ***56/52.6.0*** for the primary boot disk (or corresponding disk hardware path).
8. The screen: ***HP-UX Install Utility — Select Whole System Configuration***
   Select ***LVM Configuration with VxFS (Journaled file system).***
   Select ***OK***.
9. The screen: ***HP-UX Install Utility — View/Modify Basic Configuration***

Primary swap size	(for example ***1200***, or accept offered value)
Secondary swap size	***none***
Software selection	***CDE Runtime Environment***
Software language	***English***
Locale setting	***default***
FS file name length	***Long***
/home Configuration	***none***
How many disks in root group ***one***	
Make volatile dirs separate	***true***
Create /export volume	***false***

   Select ***OK***.
10. The screen: ***HP-UX Install Utility — Configure File System***

mount directory	*size (MB)*	*volume usage*	*disk group*
/	1420	*VxFS*	*vg00*
/stand	48	*HFS*	*vg00*
(swap)	560	*swap*	*vg00*

    Select ***OK***.
11. Since configuration was done, continue installation by using ***swinstall*** utility in the noninteractive mode.

The screen: ***HP-UX Install Utility — Enter SD-UX swinstall information***
Do you want to interact with SD-UX swinstall? > ***No***
Select ***OK***.

12. The ***swinstall*** procedure continues; it takes almost one hour. Once it is completed, log in to the system as "root" and set the password.

Once the HP-UX OS is installed, the system itself should be appropriately configured for its mission. The following text describes the most common needed administrative steps to customize the installed system. Of course, the described steps are not mandatory — they are very much site-dependent; please read them as appropriate. Also, HP-UX provides a menu-based tool, **system administration manager (SAM)**, to help in the system administration — it is available upon OS installation. In some of the following steps, **SAM** is used to accomplish specific tasks.

13. Log in as ***root***.
14. Using "vi" modify the file */etc/issue* to reflect the host's name ***blue***.
    blue [HP Release B.10.20]
15. Create/prepare configuration files for ***Automounter*** if needed. This step is site-specific and probably could be skipped in most installations. In this example Automounter is used to mount home and share filesystems exported by the NFS server; and NIS maps specify the configuration data.
    /etc/auto_direct:
    +auto_direct
    /etc/auto_master:

/-	*auto_direct*	*-ro*
/net	*-hosts*	*-rw*
/home	*auto_home*	*-rw*
/share	*auto_share*	*-rw*

    /etc/auto_home:
    +auto_home
    /etc/auto_share:
    +auto_share
16. Modify/prepare the following files for NIS:
    /etc/passwd
    /etc/group
    Add NIS marker "+" as the last line in the file; it will be in effect until the */etc/nsswitch.conf* file is created. Again this step probably could be skipped; in this example NIS is implemented.
17. For most of the network-related services that follow, it is easier to use the ***SAM*** tool than to modify configuration files from the command line. However, such an approach is also acceptable. Enter ***sam*** to start ***SAM*** from the command line.
18. Select ***Networking and Communications***.
    Select ***Name Service Switch***.
    For each displayed entry, select *Action/Configure Name Service Switch* and provide the necessary data. The default values could be OK for most of implementations Select ***Network Information Service***.
    Select *Action/Set Domain Name* and set to ***domain-name*** (enter the name for your NIS domain if applicable at all).
    Select ***Networked File System***.
    Select *Mounted Remote File Systems*.
    Select *Action/Enable Automounter*.
    Note: If there are problems, please check the **rc** configuration file */etc/rc.config.d/namesvrs* (it includes configuration data for NIS) and */etc/rc.config.d/nfsconf* (for NFS client and Automounter).
19. Return to the ***SAM Main Menu*** and select ***Time***.
    Select ***NTP Network Time Resources***.
    Select *Action/Add Remote Server or Peer…*
    Enter Host Name: ***ntphost*** (or the name of the time server).
    Select *Action/Start NTP*.
20. Return to the ***SAM Main Menu*** and select ***Printer and Plotters***.
    Select ***LP Spooler***.
    Select *Printer and Plotters*.

Select *Action/Add Remote Printer/Plotter.*
Printer name: ***printer-name***
Remote system: ***system-name***
Remote printer name: ***remote-name*** (for network printer ***LF1***)
Make the printer default one; select *Action/Set as Default Destination.*
Return to the ***SAM Main Menu*** and exit.

21. Create/prepare the file */etc/shells* to include all shells that FTP users could use. Otherwise, the FTP access to the system would be restricted.
22. Modify the system-wide file */etc/profile* to reflect your login needs.
23. Build the ***whatis database***.
    Execute ***catman -w*** — it takes a while.

At this point the basic system configuration is set and the system is ready for use.

26.2.2 Solaris Installation

Solaris installation procedure is presented in the following text. Solaris 2.6 (SunOS 5.6) is installed on Sun Enterprise 3000 server with disk arrays, named ***red***. Enterprise Volume Manager 2.5 and Veritas Filesystem are also installed. The system has multiple network interfaces.

1. Power-on system.
2. Set NVRAM
   ok> ***set-defaults***
   ok> ***setenv boot-device disk***
   ok> ***setenv local-mac-address? true***
3. Put Solaris 2.6 Software CD in drive.
   ok> ***boot cdrom***
4. Select a Locale.
   USA — English (ASCII only)
   . . . . .
   . . . . .
   Type a number and press Return or Enter [0]: ***0***
5. What type of terminal are you using?
   1) ANSI Standard CRT
   2) DEC VT52
   3) DEC VT100
   Type the number of your choice and press Return: **3**
6. The Solaris Installation Program
   Select *F2_Continue*

   Note: At this point if function keys do not work, press <Esc> and then <Esc-2> instead of <F2>, and <Esc-6> instead <F6>).
7. Identify This System
   Select *F2_Continue*
8. Host Name
   Host name: ***red***
   Select *F2_Continue*
9. Network Connectivity
   Networked
   ----
   *[**X**] Yes*
   [ ] No
   Select *F2_Continue*
10. IP Address
    IP address: **XX.XX.XX.XX** (corresponding IP address)
    Select *F2_Continue*
11. Confirm Information
    Select *F2_Continue*

12. Name Service
    Name service
    [ ] NIS+
    [ ] NIS (formerly yp)
    [X] Other (to set DNS appropriately)
    [ ] None
    Select *F2_Continue*
13. Confirm Information
    Select *F2_Continue*
14. Subnets
    System part of a subnet
    [X] Yes
    [ ] No
    Select *F2_Continue*
15. Netmask
    Netmask: 255.255.255.0 (or whatever)
    Select *F2_Continue*
16. Time Zone
    [X] United States
    Select *F2_Continue*
    [X] Eastern
    Select *F2_Continue*
17. Date and Time
    Set date and time
    Select *F2_Continue*
18. Confirm Information
    Select *F2_Continue*
19. Solaris Interactive Installation
    Select *F4_Initial* Select *F2_Continue*
20. Allocate Client Services?
    Select *F4_Allocate*
21. Select Platforms
    [X] sparc.sun4u
    [X] sparc.sun4m
    [X] sparc.sun4c
    [ ] sparc.sun4d
    Select *F2_Continue*
22. Allocate Client Services

Type	# of Clients	X	Size Per = Total Size	Mount Point
ROOT	*5*	*X*	*25 = 125*	*/export/root*
SWAP	*5*	*X*	*32 = 160*	/export/swap

    Select *F2_Continue*
23. Select Software
    [ ] Entire Distribution plus OEM support .. *1196.00 MB*
    [X] Entire Distribution .... *1189.00 MB*
    [ ] Developer System Support .... *1124.00 MB*
    [ ] End User System Support .... *864.00 MB*
    [ ] Core System Support .... *665.00 MB*
    Select *F2_Continue*
24. Select Disks

Disk	Device (Size)	Available Space
[X]	*c0t0d0 (8633 MB) boot disk*	*8633 MB*
Total Selected:	*8633 MB*	
Suggested Minimum:	*844 MB*	

    Select *F2_Continue*

25. *Preserve Data?*
    Select *F2_Continue*
26. *Automatically Lay Out File Systems?*
    Select *F2_Auto_Layout*

File Systems for Auto-layout
[X] /
[ ] /export
[ ] /export/root
[ ] /export/swap
[ ] /opt
[ ] /usr
[ ] /usr/openwin
[ ] /var
[X] swap

    Select *F2_Continue*
27. File System and Disk Layout
    Select *F4_Customize*
    Customize Disk: ***c0t0d0***
    Boot Device: ***c0t0d0s0***
    Entry: swap *Recommended: 258 MB* *Minimum: 0 MB*

Slice	Mount Point	Size (MB)
0	*/*	*1779*
1	*swap*	*6452*
2	*overlap*	*8633*
3	*/altboot*	*401*
4		*0*
5		*0*
6		*0*
7		*0*

Capacity:	*8633 MB*
Allocated:	*8633 MB*
Free:	*0 MB*

    Select *F2_OK*

File System/Mount Point	Disk/Slice	Size
/	*c0t0d0s0*	*1779 MB*
swap	*c0t0d0s1*	*6452 MB*
overlap	*c0t0d0s2*	*8633 MB*
/altboot	*c0t0d0s3*	*401 MB*

    Select *F2_Continue*
28. Mount Remote File Systems?
    Select *F2_Continue*
29. Profile
    Select *F2_Continue*
30. Reboot After Installation?
    [X] Auto Reboot
    [ ] Manual Reboot
    Select *F2_Begin Installation*

At this point the installation is started, and it takes awhile. Once the OS is installed, the basic system administration should be provided. It is described here:

31. Log in to host and set the root password.
32. Set terminal:
    TERM = vt100
    export TERM
    stty rows 24 columns 80
33. Modify */etc/inittab*
    cp -p /etc/inittab /etc/inittab.fb
    modify the entry for "console": instead of "sun" => "unknown"
    You can modify */etc/default/login* file to allow the direct root login from the network; comment-out the line:
    CONSOLE = /dev/null
    This should be allowed only temporarily, during the software installation.
    Also copy and modify the root login file */.profile* for an easier work.
    cp /etc/skel/login.profile/.profile
34. Install QFE Drivers (this example assumes Quad FastEthernet network interface) Put Sun Quad FastEthernet drivers CD in drive.
    cd /cdrom/sun_quadfast_2_1/Sol_2.6
    pkgadd -d . SUNWqfed SUNWqfedu
    Respond "yes" to the question about executing scripts with "root" credentials.
    Switch the network interface to "qfe0"
    mv /etc/hostname.hme0 /etc/hostname.qfe0
    Define the router
    echo "XX.XX.XX.XX" > /etc/defaultrouter (corresponding IP address)
    reboot -- -r
35. Installation of supplemental software (in this example) of packages for:
    Hardware testing

SUNWvts	Online Validation Test Suite
SUNWvtsmn	Online Validation Test Suite Man Pages
SyMON	Monitor system hardware status and OS performance
SUNWsyc	Solstice SyMON Server's standalone configd program
SUNWsye	Solstice SyMON Event Manager/Generator/Handler
SUNWsym	Solstice SyMON Man Pages
SUNWsyrt	Solstice SyMON Runtime Library and Tcl Scripts
SUNWsys	Solstice SyMON Server's Commands and Data
SUNWsyu	Solstice SyMON System Monitor System Commands and GUI
SUNWsyua	Solstice SyMON Images for UE servers
SUNWodu	Online Diagnostic Utilities
INTERSOLV's	ODBC Driver manager
ISLIodbc	ODBC (Open DataBase Connectivity) Driver Manager
ISLIodbcD	Demo ODBC (Open DataBase Connectivity)
Mutli-Dialect	dBASE Driver

    Put SMCC Software Supplement for Solaris 2.6 CD in drive.
    cd /cdrom/supp_sol_2_6_smcc/Product
    *pkgadd -d . SUNWvts SUNWvtsmn SUNWsyc SUNWsye SUNWsym *
    *SUNWsyrt SUNWsys SUNWsyu SUNWsyua SUNWodu *
    ISLIodbc ISLIodbcD
    Respond "yes" to all questions, accept defaults for ODBC directories
36. Installation of Patches
    It is a time to install patches, if required. The installation procedure is described later.
37. Installation of Volume Manager
    Volume Manager is the optional software and its installation is not a must. Nevertheless, it is described later in the paragraph Installation of Additional Software. This procedure mirrors the root disk and creates the additional disk group ***dg01*** with two volumes — ***vol01*** ands ***vol02***.
38. Installation of Veritas Filesystem VxFS
    Veritas Filesystem (VxFS) is the implemented filesystem in this example. The installation procedure is described later.
39. Create and mount filesystems:
    Supposing two additional filesystems with mount-points */files1* and */files2*, and two created volumes ***vol01*** and ***vol02*** in the disk group ***dg01***

Create mount points:
mkdir /files1 /files2
Make filesystems:
mkfs -F vxfs -o largefiles,bsize = 8192,logsize = 2048 /dev/vx/rdsk/dg01/vol01
mkfs -F vxfs -o largefiles,bsize = 8192,logsize = 2048 /dev/vx/rdsk/dg01/vol02
Add following to /etc/vfstab:
/dev/vx/dsk/dg01/vol0 1 /dev/vx/rdsk/dg01/vol01 /files1 vxfs 1 yes -
/dev/vx/dsk/dg01/vol0 2 /dev/vx/rdsk/dg01/vol02 /files2 vxfs 1 yes -
Mount filesystem:
mount /files1
mount /files2

40. Set NVRAM
In step 38 the root disk was mirrored. For a proper system booting from the mirrored root volume, the NVRAM must be modified in the following way:
To force the definition of alias devices:
/usr/sbin/eeprom use-nvramc? = true
To specify boot devices: root disk and mirrored disk rd501 (if the mirrored root disk is different than rd501 specify correspondingly; for example: vx-rd002):
/usr/sbin/eeprom boot-device = "disk vx-rd501"
/usr/sbin/eeprom diag-device = "disk vx-rd501"
To specify alias devices for alternate booting vx-rd501, and alternatively vx-rd002 (pay attention the following is valid only when rd501 = c2t64d0 and rd002 = c1t64d0):
/usr/sbin/eeprom nvramrc =
"devalias vx-rd501 /sbus@2,0/SUNW,socal@d,10000/ sf@1,0/ssd
@w2100002037160238,0:a
devalias vx-rd002 /sbus@2,0/SUNW,socal@d,10000/ sf@0,0/ssd
@w2100002037160b1f,0:a"

41. Set the printer/printers:
lpadmin -p printer-name -s system-name!remote-name
or for the network printer
lpadmin -p printer-name -s system-name!LF1

42. Configure additional network interfaces, for example:
/usr/sbin/ifconfig qfe0:1 inet 10.2.110.249 netmask 255.255.255.0 up
/usr/sbin/ifconfig qfe1 plumb
/usr/sbin/ifconfig qfe1 inet 10.2.120.249 netmask 255.255.255.0 up
/usr/sbin/ifconfig qfe1:1 inet 10.2.130.249 netmask 255.255.255.0 up
/usr/sbin/ifconfig qfe2 plumb
/usr/sbin/ifconfig qfe2 inet 10.2.140.249 netmask 255.255.255.0 up
/usr/sbin/ifconfig qfe2:1 inet 10.2.150.249 netmask 255.255.255.0 up

43. Setup network services
DNS, i.e., */etc/resolv.conf* file
SSH (if required)
NIS (if implemented)
Sendmail (if applicable)
NTP (if needed)
Other (if applicable)

44. Backup/dump the configured system data (root filesystem)
shutdown -yi s -g 0 (single-user mode)
ufsdump 0cfu /dev/rmt/0 /dev/vx/dsk/rootvol

26.2.3 Linux Installation

Linux installation resembles other UNIX installations. It is quite logical; Linux is only one of many UNIX flavors, and the bottom line is the same: to bring a system into a workable state. On the other hand, Linux is specific in some aspects, especially regarding the implemented hardware platform which is not the proprietary one; just the opposite — Linux is implemented on hardware originally dedicated to other operating systems. This is exactly what makes Linux so attractive — it is successfully running on relatively cheap and familiar hardware. We will try to emphasize those issues specific to Linux installation.

The following text describes a complete Linux installation on Intel PC architecture. It is supposed that the available hardware includes a CD-ROM drive and sufficient memory and hard drive space. It is also supposed that there is no other OS preinstalled on the system itself.

1. Select the installation method and media between:
   a. Bootable Linux floppy disk (known as *local boot disk*)
   b. Bootable Linux CD-ROM disk
2. Power-on the system and enter in the system's BIOS setup mode (usually by pressing on time ***[TAB]*** or ***[F1]*** key).
3. Prepare for booting the installation program (this program will provide Linux installation later).
   a. If the bootable CD-ROM is a choice, the system must be set to boot from CD-ROM disk — set correspondingly the system's BIOS; instead of the usual booting sequence: "floppy disk A and then hard disk C," set "CDROM disk" (probably D or E).
   b. If local boot disk is a choice, boot the system and then select CD-ROM as the installation media. Actually, in both cases CD-ROM is the selected media, and Linux installation is provided from the CD-ROM disk.
4. Beginning the Installation
   We recommend "text installation mode"; on "boot" prompt type:
   boot: ***text***
5. Language Selection
   Select *English*
6. Keyboard Configuration
   Select *Generic, US,* or whatever is appropriate
7. This step depends on the previously selected installation method:
   a. if local boot disk was the choice, a media selection screen for Linux installation is displayed (CD-ROM is not the only possibility, although we are discussing this case):
      Select *CD-ROM*
   b. if Bootable CD-ROM was the choice, a Welcome screen is displayed
   From this step we continue Linux installation from the CD-ROM disk
8. Welcome Screen
   Select *OK*
9. Installation Type
   Select *Workstation, Server,* or another choice
10. Partitioning
    Linux provides an automatic partitioning (sometimes could be satisfactory), or manual partitioning with Disk Druid, which is probably more appropriate.

    -------------------------------- Current Disk Partitions --

Mount Point	*Device*	*Requested*	*Actual*	*Type*
	hda1	*512M*	*512M*	*Linux native*
	hda5	*2048M*	*2048M*	*Linux native*
	hda6	*620M*	*620M*	*Linux swap*
	hda7	*2048M*	*2048M*	*Linux native*
	hda8	*1024M*	*1024M*	*Linux native*

Drive Summaries

Drive	*Geom [C/H/S]*	*Total*	*Used*	*Free*
	hda	. . . .		

    Edit partitions and at the end select *OK*
11. Formatting Partitions
    Choose all newly created partitions and select *OK* to format them
12. Hostname Configuration
    Enter a fully qualified domain name for the system, for example:
    Hostname ***green.myschool.spcs.edu***
13. Network Configuration
    Enter network-related data, for example:

Use bootp/dhcp:	*no*
IP address:	*146.28.123.18*
Netmask:	*255.255.255.0*

Default gateway (IP) *146.28.123.1*
Primary nameserver: *146.28.123.31*
Select *OK*

14. Mouse Configuration
Choose the appropriate mouse type, for example:
Generic - 2 Button Mouse (PS/2)
Select *OK*
15. Time Zone
Choose the appropriate time zone, for example:
America/New_York
Select *OK*
16. Root Password
Specify root password
Password: *xxxxxxxxxx*
Pasword (again) *xxxxxxxxxx*
Select *OK*
17. Creating User Accounts
An optional step — consequently you can skip this.
18. Individual Package Selection
A list of common software packages is offered. Upon selection, the system checks for a video card and later the selected packages are installed. Among packages are possible dependencies, and they must be resolved. A package is properly installed only if all other required packages are also installed.
19. Video Card Confirmation
Detected video card is displayed; if system cannot detect a video card, a list of available video cards is displayed. Choose the video card and confirm.
Select *OK*
20. Package Installation
Installation dialog screens are displayed:
    a. To begin dialog
    b. Package installation status dialog
21. Create Boot Disk
Creating a boot floppy disk is recommended; insert a blank floppy and
Select *OK*
22. X Window Configuration
The ***Xconfigurator*** utility provides an easy X window configuration. It allows a choice of standard or custom monitor, video memory, clockchip, video mode, and finally testing of the X configuration.
23. Congratulation Screen
At this point Linux installation is complete, and the system should be available for use.

26.3 Supplemental Installations

OS installation presents a basic step in preparing a UNIX system for its final mission. However, by installing OS and providing needed system administration for its normal operation, we just "open the door" of the system for its further usage. There are more things to do afterward, and system administrators have a long-term responsibility for the installed OS. Installation is a one-time job, but maintenance is forever. By saying that, we are strictly thinking of UNIX OS as a general-purpose vehicle to provide successful implementations of different application software. To administer the application software is a separate topic, and it is beyond the scope of this text.

Each UNIX flavor provides some tolls and commands that should make this job easier. Graphic or character-based tools like HP-UX's ***SAM***, or AIX's ***SMIT***, or Linux's ***Linuxconfig*** present relatively user-friendly, partially intuitive, and definitely big helpers in handling many administrative jobs, especially when we are performing infrequent tasks. Their usage is strongly recommended, but it is always a good idea to understand what happens behind their friendly appearance.

What should we expect upon an OS installation? First to install supplemental system software that makes our OS better and our work easier; this term, *supplemental system software*, is so broad that we can put everything underneath. However, one issue is especially critical, and that is permanent OS upgrade and improvement, mostly through a number of released patches. The following text describes several installation procedures for different UNIX flavors.

26.3.1 Supplemental System Software

26.3.1.1 Installation of Sun Enterprise (Veritas) Volume Manager 2.5

1. Included packages are:

SUNWvmdev	Sun Enterprise Volume Manager (header files)
SUNWvmman	Sun Enterprise Volume Manager (manual pages)
SUNWvxva	Sun Enterprise Volume Manager Visual Admin
SUNWvxvm	Sun Enterprise Volume Manager

2. Put Sun Enterprise Volume Manager 2.5 CD in drive and type:
   cd /cdrom/sun_sevm_2_5_sparc/Product
   pkgadd -d. SUNWvmdev SUNWvmman SUNWvxva SUNWvxvm
   Respond yes to all questions
3. Connect all external drives and reboot the system
   reboot -- -r (pay attention to doubled hyphen characters)
4. Start the installation:
   vxinstall
5. Interactive installation procedure continues
   Volume Manager Installation Options
   Menu: VolumeManager/Install
   1 Quick Installation
   2 Custom Installation
   ? Display help about menu
   ?? Display help about the menuing system
   q Exit from menus
   Select an operation to perform: **2**
   Encapsulate Boot Disk [y,n,q,?] (default: n) **y**
   Enter disk name for [<name>,q,?] (default: rootdisk) **root01**
   The Volume Manager has detected the following disks on controller c1:
   c1t0d0 c1t16d0 c1t17d0 c1t18d0 c1t19d0 c1t1d0 c1t2d0 c1t20d0
   Select an operation to perform: **4 (Leave these disks alone.)**
   The Volume Manager has detected the following disks on controller c2:
   c2t100d0 c2t101d0 c2t102d0 c2t112d0 c2t113d0 c2t114d0
   Select an operation to perform: **4 (Leave these disks alone.)**
   The following is a summary of your choices.
   c0t0d0 Encapsulate
   Is this correct [y,n,q,?] (default: y) **y**
   Shutdown and reboot now [y,n,q,?] (default: n) **n**

The Volume Manager installation is completed. Volume Manager has detected 14 additional disks. Disk *c0t0d0* is supposed for a mirror of the root disk (remember that we are dealing here with additional disks only — Solaris OS is already installed on the boot disk that we have referred to as "root disk"); remaining 13 disks are left for later Volume Manager configuration.

26.3.1.2 Installation of Veritas Filesystem 3.X

1. Put Veritas Foundation Suite CD in drive.
   /usr/sbin/pkgadd -d /cdrom/vrts_9803/Solaris_2_6/pkgs VRTSvxfs VRTSfsdoc

*Do you want to install these conflicting files [y,n,?,q] **y***
*Do you want to install these as setuid/setgid files [y,n,?,q] **y***
*Do you want to continue with installation of <VRTSvxfs> [y,n,?] **y***

2. Enter license key
   /usr/sbin/vxfsserial -c
   Please enter your key:
   Once you enter the license key of the form: "4959 4803 5362 2285 3667 7868 1623 9" the installation process continues until completed.

26.3.1.3 Two Pseudo-Installation Scripts

The following two scripts could be used in handling some volume manager and veritas filesystem issues. In some ways they are also a part of the installation procedure, and that is why they are presented here. The first script creates a disk group named ***mydg*** that includes 12 + 1 disks (one disk is supposed to be a spare for online disk replacement), and a volume named ***myvol*** within this disk group. The volume ***myvol*** consists of six striped and mirror disks — RAID 0 + 1. The script named ***make_mydg.csh*** illustrates nicely the required procedure to accomplish this task, and could be easily used as a guide for similar actions from the command line.

$ cat /usr/local/bin/make_mydg.csh

```
#!/ bin/csh
#==========================================================================
# The script:     make_mydg.csh
#
# Purpose:        to create a disk group named mydg with a single volume named myvol over six
#                 striped and mirrored disks (RAID 0+1) over the whole available disk space
#
# Note:           disk layout is specified within the script
#
# disk group mydg
set MYDG = (      c1t1d0.md01  c1t2d0.md02  c1t3d0.md03 \
                  c1t4d0.md04  c1t5d0.md05  c1t6d0. md06 \
                  c2t1d0.md11  c2t2d0.md12  c2t3d0. md13 \
                  c2t4d0.md14  c2t5d0.md15  c2t6d0. md16 \
                  c2t16d0.mdsp   )
#
# mydg disk group, plex 1
set MYDGP1 = (md01 md02 md03 md04 md05 md06)
#
# mydg disk group, plex 2
set MYDGP2 = (md11 md12 md13 md14 md15 md16)

#
# Initialize each disk – put under VM control
foreach DISK ($MYDG[*])
   set NAME = $DISK:e
   set DEV = $DISK:r
   echo "Initializing $DEV"
   /etc/vx/bin/vxdisksetup -i $DEV
end

#
# Create mydg disk groups
set NAME = $MYDG[1]:e
set DEV = $MYDG[1]:r
echo "Initializing mydg disk group with $NAME"
vxdg init mydg $NAME = $DEV
```

```
foreach DISK ($MYDG[2-])
   set NAME = $DISK:e
   set DEV = $DISK:r
   echo "Adding $NAME to mydg disk group"
   vxdg -g mydg adddisk $NAME=$DEV
end

vxedit set spare=on mdsp

#
# Create the mydg volume myvol over all available disk space (dedicated for a filesystem)
# The size of volume is maximum available, striped over 6 disks and mirrored (RAID 0 + 1)
#

set MAX='vxassist -g mydg -U fsgen -p maxsize layout=stripe,nolog nstripe=$#MYDGP1 stripeunit=128 $MYDGP1'

echo "Initializing myvol to a size of $MAX"
/usr/sbin/vxassist -g mydg -U fsgen make myvol01 $MAX \
layout = stripe,nolog nstripe = $#MYDGP1 stripeunit = 128 $MYDGP1

echo "Synchronizing mirror of myvol"
batch << EOF
/usr/sbin/vxassist -g mydg mirror myvol layout = stripe $MYDGP2
EOF

#
# End of script
#=======================================================================
```

The second script, ***make_myvol.csh***, presents a kind of continuation of the first script; here the disk group named ***mydg*** is already created, and this script could be used to create a new volume of an arbitrary name, size, and type.

$ cat /usr/local/bin/make_myvol.csh

```
#!/ bin/csh
#=======================================================================
#
# Purpose:  to create an arbitrary volume of the arbitrary size and type within the predefined disk
#           group mydg; new volume is striped and mirrored (RAID 0+1) over the available disk
#           space
#
# Note:     volume name, size and type are passing script arguments #1, #2 and #3

if (${#argv} != 3) then
echo " "
echo "Usage: /usr/local/bin/make_myvol name size type"
echo " "
exit (1)
endif

set myvol='echo ${argv[1]}'
set size = 'echo ${argv[2]}'
set type = 'echo ${argv[3]}'

if ( $type !~gen ) then
set type = fsgen
endif

echo " "
echo "The volume name is: $myvol - the size is: $size – the type is: $type"
echo "If it is correct hit <Enter> key - otherwise type <Cntrl>C"
echo " "
read
```

```
# the disk group mydg exists - this is its layout
set MYDG=( c1t1d0.md01  c1t2d0.md02  c1t3d0.md03 \
           c1t4d0.md04  c1t5d0.md05  c1t6d0. md06 \
           c2t1d0.md11  c2t2d0.md12  c2t3d0. md13 \
           c2t4d0.md14  c2t5d0.md15  c2t6d0. md16 \
           c2t16d0.mdsp  )

# mydg disk group, plex 1
set MYDGP1=(md01 md02 md03 md04 md05 md06)

# mydg disk group, plex 2
set MYDGP2=(md11 md12 md13 md14 md15 md16)

#
# Create the mydg volume $myvol (the name is specified as the argument #1)
# The size of volume is $size, striped over 6 disks, and mirrored (RAID 0+1)
# (the size is specified as the argument #2). The type (fsgen or gen) is specified
# as the argument #3.

echo "Initializing $myvol of a type $type and a size of $size"
/usr/sbin/vxassist -g mydg -U $type make $myvol $size \
layout=stripe,nolog nstripe=$#MYDGP1 stripeunit=128 $MYDGP1

echo "Syncronizing mirror of $myvol"
batch << EOF
/usr/sbin/vxassist -g mydg mirror $myvol layout=stripe $MYDGP2
EOF

#
# End of script
#=================================================================
```

26.3.1.4 Installation of Optional HP-UX Software

Procedures for a few common optional software packages are presented.

HP-UX MirrorDisk/UX Software

1. Insert CD "HP-UX Applications, disk 1 of 3"
   Log in as ***"root"***
   Mount CD: ***mount /dev/dsk/c2t2d0 /SD_CDROM***
   Enter: ***swinstall***
2. Install "MirrorDisk/UX software"
   Select ***OK*** for:
   Source depot type: "Local CD"
   Source host name: "blue"
   Source depot path: "/SD_CDROM"
3. From "***Action***" pop-down menu select: "***Add new codeword***"
   Enter ***Customer ID*** and ***Codeword***
4. Select/mark [*m*] "***MirrorDisk/UX***" software
   From "***Action***" pop-down menu select "***Install (analysis)***"
   Follow the procedure, select "***Logfile***"
   Since the analysis is completed, select ***OK***
   Start the installation, select ***YES***
   Follow the procedure, select "***Logfile***"
   Since the installation was completed, select ***OK*** and then ***DONE***
   At the end, the system would be rebooted

We can now implement the installed optional software to mirror root disk. Steps that follow describe the required procedure.

5. Log in as ***root***
6. To mirror Root Filesystem and Primary Swap (must be done manually from the command line):
   Create a bootable physical volume from the second disk:
   pvcreate -B /dev/rdsk/c2t5d0 (use the ***-f*** option if it is denied)

Add the physical volume to the root volume group vg00:
vgextend /dev/vg00 /dev/dsk/c2t5d0

Place boot utilities in the second disk boot area (make the disk bootable):
mkboot /dev/rdsk/c2t5d0

Add the AUTO file in the second disk boot LIF area:
mkboot -a "hpux (52.5.0;0)/ stand/vmunix" /dev/rdsk/c2t5d0

Mirror logical volumes and swap:
lvextend -m 1 /dev/vg00/lvol1 /dev/dsk/c2t5d0
lvextend -m 1 /dev/vg00/lvol2 /dev/dsk/c2t5d0
lvextend -m 1 /dev/vg00/lvol3 /dev/dsk/c2t5d0

Verify the boot information:
lvlnboot -v

Optionally, the system could be rebooted to check if it appears OK.

HP-UX OnLine Journaled Filesystem

1. Insert the tape ***OnLine Journaled FS*** into the tape drive
   Login as ***root***
   Enter: ***swinstall***
2. The screen: "***Specify Source***"
   Source depot type: "*Local Tape*"
   Source host name: "*scarlet*"
   Source depot path: /
   Software filter: *none*
   Select ***OK***.
3. Enter / mark [*m*] the bundle ***AdvJornalFS*** to install
   Select ***Action/Install (analysis)***
   Follow instructions to complete.

   Select/enter/read ***Logfile***.
   Since the analysis was completed, select ***OK*** to install.

   Select/enter/read ***Logfile***.
   Since the installation was completed, select ***DONE***.

   At the end, the system would be rebooted.
4. To list (check) installed journaled FS software
   Login as "***root***"
   swlist -l product * | grep VxFS

HP JetAdmin for UNIX Utility Software

1. Insert CD "HP-UX Applications, disk 3 of 3"
   Log in as ***root***
   Mount CD: ***mount /dev/dsk/c2t2d0 /SD_CDROM***
   Enter: ***swinstall***
2. To install HP JetAdmin software:
   Select ***OK*** for:
   Source depot type: "*Local CD*"
   Source host name: "*blue*"
   Source depot path: "*/SD_CDROM*"
3. From ***Action*** pop-down menu select: ***Add new codeword***
   Enter ***Customer ID*** and ***Codeword***
4. Select/mark [*m*] ***HP JetAdmin for UNIX Utility*** software
   From ***Action*** pop-down menu select ***Install (analysis)***.
   Follow the procedure, select ***Logfile***.
   Since the analysis is completed, select ***OK***.

Start the installation, select ***YES***.
Follow the procedure, select ***Logfile***.
Since the installation was completed, select ***OK*** and then ***DONE***.

5. Exit ***swinstall*** and dismount CD
   umount /SD_CDROM

26.3.2 Patches

26.3.2.1 Solaris Patch Installation

1. Download needed patches and put in the */patches* directory
   mkdir /patches
   ftp $HOST (where $HOST is machine with patches, or obtain from "***sunsolve.sun.com,***" or "***sunsolve1.sun.com***")
2. Ftp-ed files are of the form: "PatchID.tar.Z," where "PatchID" corresponds to the listed files. Once patches are downloaded uncompress them:
   cd /patches
   uncompress *
3. Untar each patch:
   tar -xvf PatchID.tar
   The corresponding subdirectories with needed files are created.
4. Continue with individual patch installation.
   A few examples of individual patch installations follow:

   OS Patches
   cd /patches/2.6_Recommended
   ./ install_cluster
   Are you ready to continue with install? [y/n]: ***y***

   Volume Manager
   cd /patches/105463–04
   patchadd.

   Flashprom Patches (updates):
   cd /patches/103346–11
   ./ flash-update-11
   Do you wish to flash update your firmware? y/[n] : ***y***
   Are you sure you wish to continue? y/[n] : ***y***
   halt
   ok> setenv auto-boot? false

   Power-cycle machine
   ok> power-off

   Power-on machine
   ok> setenv auto-boot? true
5. Optionally remove downloaded patches:
   rm -R /patches

26.3.2.2 HP-UX Patch Installation

Three different installation procedures are presented, for a single patch, multiple patches, and a set of patches provided on CD.

HP-UX Individual Patches

1. Download individual patches from the HP Web site: ***http:/ /us-support.external. hp.com.*** You can register at any time as a new user (you must be registered to use the site). Alternatively, patches could be ftp-ed from the HP ftp site:
   i3107ffs.external.hp.com/hp-ux_patches/s800/10.X

To ftp, follow the procedure:

```
mkdir /tmp/PATCHES
cd /tmp/PATCHES
ftp HP_ftp_site_name
cd /hp-ux_patches/s800/10.X
ls
get whatever_patch_name
```

Select and download a patch.

2. Become "root" at the target HP-UX host.
3. Copy a patch (for example: ***PHKL_xxxxx***) to the temporary directory (for example: */tmp/PATCHES*) if not already there.
4. Change the directory and unshar the patch:
   ```
   cd /tmp/PATCHES
   sh PHKL_xxxxx
   ```
   Two files will be created: ***PHKL_xxxxx.depot*** and ***PHKL_xxxxx.text***
   You can read the text file to learn more about the patch (including how to install it).
5. Run ***swinstall*** to install the patch:
   ```
   swinstall -x autoreboot = true -x match_target = true \
   -s /tmp/PATCHES/PHKL_xxxxx.depot
   ```
   The selected patch will be installed. If the installation requests rebooting it will be automatically done (option autoreboot = true).
6. To check if the patch is installed:
   a. If the patch was installed individually:
   ```
   swlist | grep PHKL_xxxxx
   ```
   b. If the patch was installed within a fileset:
   ```
   swlist -l fileset | grep PHKL_xxxxx
   ```
   This is recommended; it also includes the first case (the opposite is not true).
   c. For patches that affect the kernel (PHKL and PHNE), to check:
   ```
   what /stand/vmunix | grep PHKL_xxxxx
   ```

HP-UX Multiple Patches — For multiple individual patches, creating a single jumbo patch to be installed at once is recommended. A sequential installation of multiple patches sometimes does not work because of existing dependencies among the patches. This example describes how to create a single jumbo patch that includes multiple patches, to be installed at one time.

1. Make a list of required patches. For example a new model of 19 GB disk, unknown at the time of the OS installation, has to be added to the system. The list of required patches is (information could be obtained from HP-UX Technical Support Center, Web site, or other):

Status Catalog	Text (Nine Patches)
PHCO_16591	*fsck_vxfs(1M) cumulative patch*
PHKL_16751	*SIG_IGN/SIGCLD,LVM,JFS,PCI/SCSI cumulative patch*
PHKL_16957	*Physical dump devices configuration patch*
PHKL_17858	*Fix for mount/access of disc sections*
PHKL_18522	*LOFS cumulative patch*
PHCO_18563	*LVM commands cumulative patch*
PHKL_19159	*Correct process hangs on ufs inodes*
PHKL_19540	*VxFS (JFS) mount,fsck cumulative changes*
PHNE_19936	*cumulative ARPA Transport patch*

2. Be sure to have all of the required patches unsharred and in one directory; for example /source/ is the path to patches, and /target/ is the new depot (do not mkdir).
   ```
   swcopy -x enforce_dependencies=false -s /source/ \* @ /target
   ```
   Here is an example, assuming the .depot files are in the /tmp dir:
   ```
   swcopy -x enforce_dependencies=false -s /tmp/PHKL_16751.depot \*
   @/tmp/hp_patch
   ```
   You must run this command for each patch.

3. When you are done, start the "swinstall" menu:
   swinstall -s /tmp/hp_patch
   Select "options" and make sure that the top five options are checked (marked):
   select all the patches
   mark for install
   install analysis

HP-UX Set of Patches on CD

1. Insert CD "HP-UX Recommended Patches Extension Software" (last available version). Log in as "root" and mount the CD:
   mount /dev/dsk/c2t2d0 /SD_CDROM
2. Enter ***swinstall***, to start swinstall menu-driven utility:

The screen: "Specify Source"	
Source depot type:	*"Local CDROM"*
Source host name:	*"scarlet"*
Source depot path:	*/SD_CDROM/10.x/800/10.20/XSW800HWCR1020*
Software filter:	*none*

   Select ***OK***.
3. Select ***Action/Match What Target Has*** and follow messages.
4. Select ***Action/Install (analysis)*** and follow instructions to complete:
   Select/enter/read ***Logfile***.
   Since the analysis was completed, select ***OK*** to start installation; it takes about one hour.
   Select/enter/read ***Logfile***.
   Since the installation was completed, select ***DONE***.
   At the end, the system would be rebooted.
5. Log in as "root" and mount CD:
   mount /dev/dsk/c2t2d0 /SD_CDROM
6. Enter ***swinstall*** to start swinstall menu-driven utility.

The screen: Specify Source	
Source depot type:	*"Local CDROM"*
Source host name:	*"scarlet"*
Source depot path:	*/SD_CDROM/10.x/800/10.20 /XSW800GR1020*
Software filter:	*none*

   Select ***OK***.
7. Select ***Action/Match What Target Has*** and follow messages.
8. Select ***Action/Install (analysis)*** and follow instructions to complete:
   Select/enter/read ***Logfile***.
   Since the analysis was completed, select ***OK*** to install; it takes about one hour.
   Select/enter/read ***Logfile***.
   Since the installation was completed, select ***DONE***.
   At the end, the system would be rebooted.

27

Upgrade Disk Space

27.1 Adding a Disk

Adding a disk is a routine task, and to accomplish this task, the procedure specific to the particular UNIX flavor must be fully respected and followed. To add a new disk does not mean simply to connect a disk — there are several more steps that must be accomplished:

- To partition a disk, and prepare one or more independent disk partitions
- To create a filesystem, and make disk partitions available for data storage
- To mount created filesystem, and make accessible for data storage

If logical volume manager (LVM) is used, a few more steps are required before a filesystem creation, to create a logical volume for further processing.

27.1.1 New Disk on the Solaris Platform

Solaris 2.x (as well as the earlier Sun Microsystems UNIX version, SunOS 4.1.x) provides the disk utility **format** to partition a disk. Once it is invoked (from the command line by typing **format**), an interactive, menu-driven, user-friendly program offers a number of useful disk-related commands. At the very start, all attached and detected disks are displayed. Solaris requires the system to be rebooted with the **-r** option for new disk/disks to be detected. Solaris does not check the system for new hardware every time it is booted; hardware checking takes additional time, so normally it is assumed there are no changes in the system hardware configuration. In the rare situations when the system is being upgraded, Solaris needs an explicit action by the administrator:

```
$ reboot -- -r
```

or

```
$ halt
OK > boot -r
```

The **OK>** prompt specifies the *system monitor mode* (the low-level system ROM resident program that enables a number of monitoring functions, primarily checking the hardware and booting the system). It is actually recommended to first check that the disk is connected properly:

```
OK>  probe-scsi
     .....
     .....
```

And then boot the system:

```
OK> boot -r
```

Assuming everything is done properly, the system should recognize and display the new disk (as well as the preexisting disks). Since a new disk was selected, the FORMAT MENU is displayed:

```
FORMAT MENU:
disk        -    select a disk
type        -    select (define) a disk type
partition   -    select (define) a partition table
current     -    describe the current disk
format      -    format and analyze the disk
repair      -    repair a defective sector
show        -    translate a disk address
label       -    write label to disk
analyze     -    surface analysis
defect      -    defect list management
backup      -    search for backup labels
quit    .
format> partition                              # select the partition command
PARTITION MENU:
a       -   change 'a' partition
b       -   change 'b' partition
c       -   change 'c' partition
d       -   change 'd' partition
e       -   change 'e' partition
f       -   change 'f' partition
g       -   change 'g' partition
h       -   change 'h' partition
select  -   select a predefined label
name    -   name the current label
print   -   display the current label
label   -   write partition map and label to the disk
quit
partition> x                                   # select the partition to be defined
                                               (by a corresponding letter)
partition x          -     starting cyl        0,   # blocks    0 (0 / 0 / 0)
Enter new starting cyl [0]: 0
Enter new # blocks [ 0, 0 /0 /0 ]:             XXXX
partition> y                                   # repeat for all partitions to be defined
  .....
  .....
partition> quit                                # return to the FORMAT MENU
FORMAT MENU:
  .....
  .....
  .....
```

quit
format> **quit** *# exit from the format utility*
$ *# UNIX prompt*

At this point one or more disk partitions are created; each partition represents an independent entity identified by a corresponding special device file. Now a filesystem can be created in each of the new partitions. Supposing default values for the filesystem parameters:

$ **newfs -v /dev/rdsk/c#d#t#s#** *c#d#t#s# identifies the partition*

Finally, new filesystems should be mounted and merged into the overall UNIX hierarchical filesystem. The corresponding mount-points (new directories) for new filesystems must be previously defined:

$ mkdir ***/new-mount-point*** *# create directory for filesystem mounting*

$ mount /dev/dsk/c#d#t#s# ***/new-mount-point*** *# mount the filesystem*

Once the procedure is complete and the new disk is added to the system, it is recommended that you perform disk checking (with the **df** command) to see if everything was done properly.

The filesystem mounting above was performed manually, and everything is ready except for the very next system booting. To ensure automatic mounting at system start-up, the filesystem configuration file */etc/vfstab* must be modified to include entries for the new filesystems; the file can be edited manually or with the **mount -p** command.

This procedure is required if the LVM is not used; otherwise, as soon as the system recognizes a new disk, the LVM takes full control over the whole disk, and everything needed afterward is provided by the LVM itself.

27.1.2 New Disk on the SunOS Platform

The procedure and available utilities on SunOS 4.1.x are almost the same as those for Solaris 2.x. Since SunOS 4.1.x does not deliver any significant advantages and will most likely become obsolete soon, the many existing installations will produce a major need for disk upgrades. If we are familiar with upgrading disks on Solaris 2.x, then we know how to handle SunOS 4.1x upgrades, too.

There are, however, small differences in the procedure. SunOS does not recognize the boot option **-r**; it always checks for newly attached hardware, which actually makes the procedure easier. Given that slight difference, the procedure described above for Solaris can be copied here: the same *format utility*, the same partitioning scheme, etc. The only remaining difference is in the specification of the corresponding special device files:

$ newfs -v /dev/rsdxx *# xx identifies the partition*

And the mounting of the new filesystem:

$ mkdir ***/new-mount-point*** *# create directory for filesystem mounting*

$ mount /dev/sdxx ***/new-mount-point*** *# mount the filesystem*

After the mount is complete, the filesystem configuration file */etc/fstab* should be modified. The entry format is also slightly different than that of the Solaris platform.

27.1.3 New Disk on the HP-UX Platform

Since the release of HP-UX 9.04, the LVM is a standard part of the HP-UX installation; the HP-UX specific System Administration Management tool (SAM) enables relatively comfortable disk integration into the system. However, we will discuss a disk upgrade on a lower level using the available UNIX commands; correspondingly, we will also refer to some "old" HP-UX issues, among others the disk description file */etc/disktab*. The basic idea is that an example such as this is a good illustration for similar procedures on other UNIX platforms.

On the HP-UX platform, a disk can be divided into one active partition (referred to as a *section*), with or without an additional *swap* partition; actually, all available disk space not included in the created filesystem is automatically designated as the *swap* area. It is up to the system administrator to decide the size of these two available partitions; in most cases a whole disk will be used as a single active partition.

In the case of a new SCSI disk, special attention should be paid to the SCSI bus termination and the selection of an appropriate SCSI address. Once a disk is physically connected and the system has recognized its presence at boottime (HP-UX provides a useful command, **ioscan**, to check the existing system peripherals), a check for the required special device file is recommended:

$ ls -l /dev/dsk

```
brw-r-----  1 root  sys  7 0x201000 Dec 13 1993 c201d0s0
brw-r-----  1 root  sys  7 0x201100 Dec 13 1993 c201d1s0
brw-r-----  1 root  sys  7 0x201200 Apr 19 11:52 c201d2s0
brw-r-----  1 root  sys  7 0x201300 Dec 13 1993 c201d3s0
brw-r-----  1 root  sys  7 0x201400 Dec 13 1993 c201d4s0
brw-r-----  1 root  sys  7 0x201500 Dec 13 1993 c201d5s0
brw-r-----  1 root  sys  7 0x201600 May 12 17:58 c201d6s0
```

$ ls -l /dev/rdsk

```
crw-r-----  1 root  sys  47 0x201000 Dec 13 1993 c201d0s0
crw-r-----  1 root  sys  47 0x201100 Dec 13 1993 c201d1s0
crw-r-----  1 root  sys  47 0x201200 Apr 19 11:52 c201d2s0
crw-r-----  1 root  sys  47 0x201300 Dec 13 1993 c201d3s0
crw-r-----  1 root  sys  47 0x201400 Dec 13 1993 c201d4s0
crw-r-----  1 root  sys  47 0x201500 Dec 13 1993 c201d5s0
crw-r-----  1 root  sys  47 0x201600 Dec 13 1993 c201d6s0
```

Generally, the corresponding special device file will be there; the system creates all special device files related to the recognized SCSI controller (in this case seven devices can be connected to the SCSI controller at SCSI addresses 0–6, and the address 7 identifies the controller itself). If by any chance this is not the case, the special device file must be created in the usual way with the **mknod** command.

The disk partitioning and filesystem creation can be performed simultaneously with the **mkfs** command (the SCSI-ID = 5 is assumed):

$ **mkfs /dev/rdsk/c201d5s0** ***s0 ns nt b0 f0 ncpg minfree rps nbpi***

where

s0 Size of the partition "sector" in KB => ***s0*** **=** ***ns*** × ***nt*** × ***nc*** (***nc*** = number of cylinders/disk) — the size of the filesystem ***s0*** indirectly determines the swap partition also

ns	Number of sectors/track
nt	Number of tracks/cylinder
b0	Block size in bytes
f0	Fragment size in bytes
ncpg	Number of cylinders per group (default is 16)
minfree	Minimum percentage of free disk space allowed (default is 10%)
rps	Number of disk revolutions per second
npbi	Number of user file spaces per inode (the default value is 2 KB/inode)

The simpler method is to use the friendlier front-end command **newfs**. The command looks into the disk description file */etc/disktab* for the type of the disk a filesystem is being created in, calculates the appropriate parameters, and then invokes the **mkfs** command. The */etc/disktab* file describes all disks being used by the system. If we are using an already-supported disk, the use of the **newfs** command is trivial:

$ newfs /dev/rdsk/c201d5s0 ***disk_name***

Regardless of which one of the previously mentioned commands was used to partition and create the filesystem, UNIX versions that rely on the disk description file */etc/disktab* (as the HP-UX 9.0x did), require an appropriate description entry in the file for the specified disk, or the command fails.

It is quite possible that an entry for new disk models could be missing from the file; then the description file must be patched (patches can be obtained from the vendor's Internet site). As a last resort, the administrator can edit the file, following the pattern of existing entries in the file, and using obtained technical data about the disk.

The */etc/disktab* file describes the ways in which a disk can be partitioned (for each disk multiple entries are defined), and a correspondent filesystem created. The ***disk_name*** identifies the entry in the file; actually, several names identify the same disk with different partitioning schemes. The file is very well commented and self-explanatory. Here, the disk description file from HP-UX 10.20 is partly presented; please note the initial remarks in the file header, which are HP-UX-specific.

```
$ cat /etc/disktab
# @(#) $Revision: 72.15 $
##########################################################################
#    disktab: Data Base and Informational File                             #
#    for both HP-IB (CS/80, Amigo) and SCSI discs                          #
#                                                                          #
#    This file is provided for backward compatibility with previous releases #
#    of HP-UX. Its use is discouraged. The newfs command can provide       #
#    defaults for the parameters defined by this file.                     #
#                                                                          #
##########################################################################
#    PRELIMINARY:                                                          #
#      All discs, including fixed (hard) discs and all                     #
#      removable media, must be formatted before they can                  #
#      be used. Formatting is the process of preparing                     #
#      a new disc to receive information and assuring                      #
#      media integrity.                                                    #
#                                                                          #
#      To format an HP-UX disc, use the HP-UX command:                     #
#            % mediainit                                                   #
#                                                                          #
```

```
#     IMPORTANT: Some discs require an interleave different          #
#        than one (1). This file contains information to             #
#        help you make the correct choice. An improper               #
#        performance.                                                #
#                                                                    #
#                                                                    #
#     GENERAL: Disktab is a simple database which describes disc     #
#        geometries and disc section characteristics.                #
#        Entries consist of a number of fields, separated            #
#        by ':'. The first entry for each disc gives the             #
#        name(s) which are known for the disc, separated             #
#        and is unused by newfs. Sectors are of size                 #
#        DEV_BSIZE = 1024 bytes.                                     #
#                                                                    #
######################################################################
#     DISK GEOMETRY AND PARTITION LAYOUT TABLES.                     #
#     Key:                                                           #
#     (Leading field is name -- can be any string)                   #
#        ty    Information about the disk (informational only)       #
#        ns    number of 1k sectors/track                            #
#        nt    number of tracks/cylinder                             #
#        nc    number of cylinders/disk                              #
#        s0    size of file system in 1k blocks                      #
#        b0    block size in bytes                                   #
#                 (only 8192 or 4096 supported)                      #
#        f0    fragment sizes in bytes                               #
#                 (1K, 2K, or 4K are supported)                      #
#        se    #bytes/physical sector (informational only)           #
#        rm    rpm (rotational speed of platters)                    #
######################################################################
#     EXPLANATION:                                                   #
#        s0 = ns * nt * nc                                           #
#        Sectors not allocated to the file system will be            #
#        used in the swap area. If no swap is required, s0           #
#        represents the actual amount of disc space available        #
#        on the disc. In general, any space reserved for swap        #
#        must be in increments of 2 megabytes i.e. swap will         #
#        be utilized in multiples of:                                #
#           2 * 1024 * 1024 (= 2,097,152 bytes)                      #
#                          . . . . .                                 #
#                          . . . . .                                 #
#                                                                    #
######################################################################
#     GENERAL GUIDELINES (and HINTS) for CREATING NEW ENTRIES:       #
#        - How much swap is required                                 #
#        - Swap must be reserved in multiples of 2 megabytes         #
#        - The O/S needs some swap to run                            #
#        - An attempt to make ns a multiple of b0 will               #
#          enhance performance. At a minimum, attempt to             #
#          make it a multiple of the fragment size (f0).             #
#        - diskinfo(1m) is a useful utility for determining          #
#          the parameters necessary to make disctab entries.         #
#                                                                    #
#        An entry should have a unique name, and conform             #
#        approximately to the following skeleton:                    #
#                                                                    #
#        vendor_model:\                                              #
#           :comment (how much swap):ns#X:nt#X:nc#X:\                #
#           :s0#X:b0#8192:f0#1024 :\                                 #
#           :se#X:rm#X:                                              #
#                                                                    #
```

```
#                    .....                                          #
#                    .....                                          #
#                                                                   #
#####################################################################
.....
.....
# SEAGATE ST11200N
# Set rotdelay = 0 ms for optimal file system perf (see tunefs(1M))
#
SEAGATE_ST11200N_noswap|SEAGATE_ST11200N_noreserve:\
  :No swap or boot:ns#38:nt#13:nc#2075:\
  :s0#1025050:b0#8192:f0#1024:\
  :se#512:rm#5400:
#
SEAGATE_ST11200N_200MB:\
  :200 MB reserved for swap & boot:ns#38:nt#13:nc#1661:\
  :s0#820534:b0#8192:f0#1024:\
  :se#512:rm#5400:
  .....
  .....
```

An example follows for the manually edited entry for a new 2GB SEAGATE disk (obviously, its information was not included in the table at that time):

```
#######################################################
# SEAGATE ST12400N
# Edited by the System Administrator
#######################################################
SEAGATE_ST12400N_noswap|SEAGATE_ST12400N_noreserve:\
  :No swap or boot:ns#41:nt#19:nc#2621:\
  :s0#2041759:b0#8192:f0#1024:\
  :se#512:rm#5400:
SEAGATE_ST12400N_swap|SEAGATE_ST12400N_150MB:\
  :150 MB reserved for swap & boot:ns#41:nt#19:nc#2423:\
  :s0#1887517:b0#8192:f0#1024:\
  :se#512:rm#5400:
#######################################################
    .....
    .....
```

Once disk partitioning and filesystem creation are performed, the filesystem must be mounted. For future system booting, the filesystem configuration file (*/etc/vfstab, /etc/fstab,* or on HP-UX 9.0x as */etc/checklist*) should also be updated to add the new entries. In this specific case, on HP-UX 9.0x, the configuration file before the update was:

$ cat /etc/checklist

```
/dev/dsk/c201d6s0     / hfs         rw,quota    0  1  0
/dev/dsk/c201d2s0     /cdrom cdfs   ro,suid,    0  0  0
/dev/dsk/c201d6s0     ..... swap    pri = 0     0  0  0
```

... and after the update:

$ cat /etc/checklist

```
/dev/dsk/c201d6s0   / hfs         rw,quota     0  1  0
/dev/dsk/c201d2s0   /cdrom cdfs   ro,suid,     0  0  0
/dev/dsk/c201d6s0   ..... swap    pri = 0      0  0  0
/dev/dsk/c201d5s0   /disk 2 hfs   rw,suid,     0  2  0
/dev/dsk/c201d5s0   ..... swap    end,pri = 1  0  0  0
```

27.2 Logical Volume Manager Case Study

Case description: The system includes 12 disk units divided between two SCSI controllers. The operating system and the logical volume manager are installed on the root volume/disk (the first disk of the dozen). Our task is to mirror the root and swap volumes and to create new mirrored volume/volumes among the remaining disks. The RAID0+1 is preferable.

We will show the procedure for two UNIX flavors: HP-UX 10.20 and Solaris 2.6. In both cases, the procedure will be managed from the command line. Both flavors, however, include higher-level administration tools: HP-UX SAM and Solaris GUI Volume Administrator *V×VA*.

Notice: All included data about special device files, volume and group names, and sizes, are system dependent.

27.2.1 LVM on the HP-UX Platform

LVM is a standard part of the OS distribution for HP-UX 9.04, HP-UX 10.x, and future releases. The regular installation procedure implements LVM, and the OS is installed on volumes. Let us suppose the following OS layout upon the installation (this is, by the way, default):

Volume	Volume Group	Mount Directory	Description
lvol1	*vg00*	*/stand*	*kernel*
lvol2	*vg00*		*swap*
lvol3	*vg00*	/	*root FS*

To mirror the root disk to the second disk (identified by /dev/dsk/c2t5d0 and /dev/rdsk/c2t5d0):

- Create a bootable physical volume:
  pvcreate -B ***/dev/rdsk/c2t5d0***
- Add the physical volume to the root volume group vg00:
  vgextend ***/dev/vg00 /dev/dsk/c2t5d0***
- Place the boot utilities into the disk boot area (make the disk bootable):
  mkboot ***/dev/rdsk/c2t5d0***
- Add the AUTO file into the disk boot LIF area:
  mkboot -a ***"hpux (52.5.0;0)/ stand/vmunix" /dev/rdsk/c2t5d0***
- Mirror logical volumes (incl. swap):
  lvextend -m ***1 /dev/vg00/lvol1 /dev/dsk/c2t5d0***
  lvextend -m ***1 /dev/vg00/lvol2 /dev/dsk/c2t5d0***
  lvextend -m ***1 /dev/vg00/lvol3 /dev/dsk/c2t5d0***
- Verify the boot information:
  lvboot -v

The ten remaining disks will be placed into the *volume group* ***vg01***, and new *logical volumes* will be created. Please note that HP-UX LVM supports RAID0 (striping) or RAID1 (mirroring) only. RAID0+1 is not supported; however, there is a tricky way to accomplish RAID0 + 1 (which is not recommended). The implementation of striping and mirroring separately follows:

- Create (initialize) physical volume for each of the ten disks:
  pvcreate ***/dev/rdsk/c0t1d0***
  pvcreate ***/dev/rdsk/c0t2d0***
  . . .
  pvcreate ***/dev/rdsk/c1t4d0***
  pvcreate ***/dev/rdsk/c1t5d0***
- Create the special device file for the volume group ***vg01***:
  mkdir ***/dev/vg01***
  chmod ***755 /dev/vg01***
  mknod ***/dev/vg01/group c 64 0×010000***
  chmod ***640 /dev/vg01/group***
- Create the volume group ***vg01***:
  vgcreate ***/dev/vg01 /dev/dsk/c0t1d0***
  vgextend ***/dev/vg01 /dev/dsk/c0t2d0***
  . . .
  vgextend ***/dev/vg01 /dev/dsk/c1t4d0***
  vgextend ***/dev/vg01 /dev/dsk/c1t5d0***
- Check the created volume group:
  vgdisplay -v ***/dev/vg01***

To make the 3.8 GB mirrored logical volume lvol4 (supposing 2 GB disks):

- Create the 1.9 GB logical volume ***lvol4*** on the first available disk ***/dev/dsk/c0t0d0***:
  lvcreate -n ***lvol4*** **-M** ***n*** **-C** ***y*** **-L** ***1900 /dev/vg01***
- Increase the logical volume size of the next disk ***/dev/dsk/c0t2d0***:
  lvextend -L ***3800 /dev/vg01/lvol4 /dev/dsk/c0t2d0***
- Mirror to disks ***/dev/dsk/c1t1d0*** and ***/dev/dsk/c1t2d0***:
  lvextend -m ***1 /dev/vg01/lvol4 /dev/dsk/c1t1d0 /dev/dsk/c1t2d0***
- Check physical volume layout:
  pvdisplay -v ***/dev/dsk/c0t1d0***
  pvdisplay -v ***/dev/dsk/c0t2d0***
  pvdisplay -v ***/dev/dsk/c1t1d0***
  pvdisplay -v ***/dev/dsk/c1t2d0***

To make a journaled (VxFS) filesystem:

- Create VxFS filesystem:
  newfs -F vxfs ***/dev/vg01/rvol4***

- Mount the new filesystem:

  mkdir ***/mntvol4***

  mount ***/dev/vg01/lvol4 /mntvol4***

- Modify the */etc/fstab* file; add the entry:

  /dev/vg01/lvol4 /mntvol4 vxfs delaylog, datainlog,rw,suid 0 2

To make 4 GB striped logical volume lvol5 across the six remaining disks:

- Create the logical volume (LVM will select all disks):

  lvcreate -n lvol5 -i 6 -I ***4 /dev/vg01***

- Check physical volume layout:

  pvdisplay -v ***/dev/dsk/c0t3d0***

  pvdisplay -v ***/dev/dsk/c0t4d0***

  pvdisplay -v ***/dev/dsk/c0t5d0***

  pvdisplay -v ***/dev/dsk/c1t3d0***

  pvdisplay -v ***/dev/dsk/c1t4d0***

  pvdisplay -v ***/dev/dsk/c1t5d0***

- Create VxFS filesystem:

  newfs -F vxfs /dev/vg01/rvol5

- Mount the new filesystem:

  mkdir ***/mntvol5***

  mount ***/dev/vg01/lvol5 /mntvol5***

- Modify the */etc/fstab* file; add the entry:

  /dev/vg01/lvol5 /mntvol5 vxfs delaylog, datainlog,rw,suid 0 3

The remaining disk space can be managed in a similar way.

27.2.2 LVM on the Solaris Platform

For Solaris, VxVM is optional software; the standard OS installation uses disk partitions. Let us suppose that the OS was installed on two disk partitions (this is one of the possible outputs of the installation program):

Partition	Mount Directory	Description
c0t0d0s0	/	*kernel*
c0t0d0s1		*swap*

To prepare the root and swap mirrored volumes:

- Encapsulate the existing root and swap disk and create the mandatory default *disk group "**rootdg**"* and the *root* and *swap* volumes:

  vxencap -g rootdg -c ***btd01=c0t0d0***

- Initialize and add a new disk into the *disk group "**rootdg**"*:

  vxdisksetup -i *c1t0d0*

  vxdg -g *rootdg adddisk btd02=c1t0d0*

- Mirror the *root* and *swap* volumes:

  vxrootmir *btd02*

  vxassist mirror swapvol layout *=contig,diskalign btd02*

- or alternatively:

  vxassist mirror rootvol layout *=contig,diskalign btd02*

  vxbootsetup *$V_opt btd02*

  vxassist mirror swapvol layout *=contig,diskalign btd02*

- Modify *EEPROM variables* to make the system bootable from the alternate disk:

  eeprom use-nvramrc *?=true*

  eeprom nvramrc *="devalias vx-btd02 hwpath_for_c1t0d0"*

  eeprom boot-device *="disk vx-btd02"*

The ten remaining disks will be placed into the disk group *"appldg"* and the new RAID0+1 volume will be created. VxVM supports RAID0+1.

- Initialize remaining disks:

  vxdisksetup -i *c0t1d0*

  vxdisksetup -i *c0t2d0*

  . . . . .

  vxdisksetup -i *c1t4d0*

  vxdisksetup -i *c1t5d0*

- Create a new disk group with the first disk:

  vxdg init *appldg apd01=c0t1d0*

- Add the other disks into the group:

  vxdg -g *appldg adddisk apd02=c0t2do*

  vxdg -g *appldg adddisk apd03=c0t3do*

  . . . . .

  vxdg -g *appldg adddisk apd09=c1t4do*

  vxdg -g *appldg adddisk apd10=c1t5do*

- Create the striped volume ***applvol*** of the maximum size (RAID0), across five VM disks (supposing Bourne or Korn shell):

  *MAX = '**vxassist -g** appldg **-U fsgen -p maxsize layout=** stripe,nolog,nstripe=5 \
  stripeunit= 128 apd01 apd02 apd03 apd04 apd05'*

  ***vxassist -g** appldg **-U fsgen make** applvol $MAX **layout=** stripe,nolog,nstripe=5 \
  stripeunit= 128 apd01 apd02 apd03 apd04 apd05*

- Mirror the created volume ***applvol*** (RAID0), across five remaining VM disks (RAID 0 + 1):

  ***vxassist -g** appldg **mirror** applvol **layout=** stripe apd06 apd07 apd08 apd09 apd10*

28

UNIX Emergency Situations

28.1 Introductory Notes

UNIX systems run and behave very stably, especially if they are properly configured for their missions. Unfortunately, unpredicted and unwanted situations occur. A UNIX system, as any other computer system, can experience different problems giving quite a hard time to UNIX administrators. It is very important to be ready to handle such events.

This chapter describes several procedures to overcome certain emergency situations. It is very instructive in the sense of what to do if something similar happens. Although the illustrated examples are related to Solaris and HP-UX flavors, they could also provide hints on how to approach the same problems on other UNIX platforms. In the first part, the problem of forgotten root password is addressed; more or less every UNIX administrator faces the same problem during the professional carrier. The second part describes some other cases when a recovery action is required, or at least preparedness for such an action is supposed.

All presented examples are fully documented.

28.2 Lost Root Password

Almost all UNIX administrators during their professional careers face the problem of a "lost root password;" occasionally a root password for some of the existing UNIX systems drops out of our control, and we are no longer able to administer that system. In a network with several hundred UNIX boxes, administered by dozens of UNIX administrators, it is not so unusual to find a "forgotten" system that nobody has taken care of lately. How it happened, and why it has happened, is another issue; the fact is that a superuser access to this very system is not possible, and we desperately need it.

UNIX predicts such situations, and each UNIX flavor does have a procedure to solve them. The forgotten password can never be recreated — it can only be replaced with a new password. However, UNIX allows the change of a password only if the old password is previously submitted as a proof of an authorized password replacement. Obviously, at the moment we are not able to fulfill this requirement. So the solution is to purge the encrypted root password in the */etc/passwd* file or */etc/shadow* file, where encrypted passwords are normally kept. For this action the UNIX system has to be brought in the single-user mode. Two examples follow.

28.2.1 Solaris and Lost Root Password

This paragraph describes the emergency procedure to change the root password on Solaris 2.X platform if the root password was lost (forgotten). When root access to the system is not possible, the usual procedures to change a password by using the command ***passwd,*** or to bring the system into "single-user" mode cannot be implemented. The emergency procedure requires the Solaris 2.X OS Installation CD disk.

1. Start Solaris 2.X from CD in single-user mode. Put Solaris 2.6 Software CD in the CD drive.
   ok> ***boot cdrom -s***
   At this point the Mini OS — single-user mode — from CD is loaded into memory.
2. Mount root filesystem to /a mount point — this directory already exists for this purpose, although another mount point could also be created:
   mount /dev/dsk/c0t3d0s0 /a (this is an example — here the corresponding device file for the root partition must be used)
3. Set a terminal for easy editing:
   TERM = vt100
   export TERM
4. Purge encrypted root password from "shadow" file:
   $ cd /a/etc
   $ vi shadow (delete encrypted password from the root password entry — leave the field blank)
   At this point, the old lost root password is removed and the root access to the system is possible; there is no password at all, and the system should be disconnected from the network to prevent potential intruders.
5. Reboot the system:
   $ reboot
6. Set/change the root password:
   $ passwd
   . . . . .
   . . . . .
7. This step may be used if there is some booting problem with the boot disk. Upon booting to single-user mode from CD, run fsck on the root partition.
   $ fsck /dev/rdsk/c0t3d0s0 (use the corresponding device file for the root partition)

28.2.2 HP-UX and Lost Root Password

To change a lost (forgotten) root password, the system must be brought into the single-user mode. Since a system reboot requires the root password, the only possible way is to power-off the system (a system halt also requires the root password), with an unavoidable risk for a filesystem corruption. Once it is down, the procedure is:

1. Power-on the system.
2. Follow messages on the console. Pay attention to the message:
   "To discontinue press any key within 10 seconds...," hit any key.
3. At main menu prompt enter:
   Main Menu: Enter command or menu > ***boot***
   Respond to the question:
   Interact with IPL (Y or N)? > y
   booting...
   At ISL prompt enter:
   ISL > ***hpux -is***
4. The system continues booting and enters the SINGLE USER mode. Purge the encrypted root password from /etc/shadow file.
5. Reboot the system into the multi-user mode:
   $ shutdown -r 0
6. Change the root password:
   $ passwd
   . . . . .
   . . . . .

28.3 Some Special Administrative Situations

A few practical examples of how to handle system emergency situations are described here. They illustrate very important and difficult administrative tasks related to potential system disasters and their later recovery. The good system administrator should be prepared to respond appropriately to the worst-case system scenarios.

28.3.1 Solaris Procedure to Create an Alternate Boot Partition

The purpose of an alternate boot partition is to enable the system booting in case the OS on the primary partition is corrupt. Booting from an alternate partition provides a minimal core OS configuration; however, it should be sufficient to fix the primary root filesystem.

The primary root filesystem is mounted in *"/ root"* directory, or if it is mirrored in */boot1* and */boot2* directories (two root partitions from two disks that are mirrored.)

To boot the system from an alternate partition, the alternate partition must be specified in the system's NVRAM for an easy booting (otherwise a hardware path should be specified). Supposed names are: "altboot", or "altboot1" and "altboot2" for multiple alternate boot partitions.

To boot from an alternate partition (for example *"altboot"*) type:

ok > ***boot altboot***

To reboot the system with an alternate boot partition, type:

***reboot -- altboot***

The detailed procedure to install Solaris 2.6 into an alternate partition follows:

1. Put Solaris 2.6 Software CD in the drive.
   ok > ***boot cdrom***
   At this point Mini OS from the CD is loaded into memory and minimal required root filesystem mounted in /tmp.
2. Select a Locale
   0) USA - English (ASCII only)
   Type a number and press Return or Enter [0]: ***0***
3. What type of terminal are you using?
   1) ANSI Standard CRT
   2) DEC VT52
   3) DEC VT100
   Type the number of your choice and press Return: 3
4. The Solaris Installation Program
   Select ***F2_Continue***
   At this point if function keys do not work, press *<Esc>*, and then *<Esc-2>* instead of *<F2>* and (*<Esc-6>* instead *<F6>*)
5. Identify This System
   Select ***F2_Continue***
6. Host Name
   Enter a corresponding hostname
   Select ***F2_Continue***
7. Network Connectivity
   Networked

   [X] Yes
   [ ] No
   Select ***F2_Continue***
8. IP Address
   Enter a corresponding IP address (permanent or temporary)
   Select ***F2_Continue***

9. Primary Network Interface
   If there are multiple network interfaces, you will be asked for:
   Select network interface ***hme*** (or whatever...)
   [X] hme0
   [ ] kme 1
   Select ***F2_Continue***
10. Confirm Information
    Select ***F2_Continue***
11. Name Service
    [ ] NIS+
    [ ] NIS (formerly yp)
    [X] Other
    [ ] None
    Select ***F2_Continue***
12. Subnets
    System part of a subnet
    [X] Yes
    [ ] No
    Select ***F2_Continue***
13. Netmask
    Netmask: **255.255.255.0**
    Select ***F2_Continue***
14. Time Zone
    [X] United States
    Select ***F2_Continue***
    [X] Eastern
    Select ***F2_Continue***
15. Date and Time
    Set date and time
    Select ***F2_Continue***
16. Confirm Information Select ***F2_Continue***

At this point, system identification is completed, and the Solaris Installation Program is started.

17. Solaris Interactive Installation
    Select ***F4_Initial***
    Select ***F2_Continue***
18. Allocate Client Services?
    Select ***F2_Continue***
19. Select Software
    Note: Select ***"Core System Support"***
    [ ] Entire Distribution plus OEM support.. *838.00 MB*
    [ ] Entire Distribution .... *831.00 MB*
    [ ] Developer System Support .... *764.00 MB*
    [ ] End User System Support .... *504.00 MB*
    [X] Core System Support .... *309.00 MB*
    Select ***F2_Continue***
20. Select Disks
    Note: Select a corresponding disk where an alternate boot partition resides (for example).

Disk Device (Size)	Available Space
[ ] c0t0d0 (8633 MB)	*8633 MB*
[ ] c2t0d0 (4092 MB)	*4092 MB*
[ ] c2t1d0 (8633 MB)	*8633 MB*
[ ] c2t2d0 (8633 MB)	*8633 MB*
[X] c3t0d0 (4092 MB) boot disk	*4092 MB*
[ ] c3t1d0 (8633 MB)	*8633 MB*
[ ] c3t2d0 (8633 MB)	*8633 MB*
Total Selected:	*4092 MB*
Suggested Minimum:	*838 MB*

Select ***F2_Continue***

21. Preserve Data?
    This is the crucial step! Root partition must be preserved; to preserve the partition it must be renamed from "/" to "/ *root*" (or "/ *root1*"). /*altboot* partition should be renamed to "/" to install OS in it.
    Mark (set X) "/root" and "swap" to be preserved (although swap is not important); "overlap" (whole disk) is already marked!
    Select ***F2_Continue***
22. Automatically Layout File Systems?
    Select ***F4_Manual Layout***
23. File System and Disk Layout
    At this point a disk layout is displayed.
    Pay attention that /root partition must be preserved!
    Select ***F2_Continue***
24. Mount Remote File Systems?
    Select ***F2_Continue***
25. Profile
    At this point an installation profile is displayed!
    Select ***F2_Continue***
    A warning message about remaining free disk space could be ignored!
26. Reboot After Installation?
    [X] Auto Reboot
    [ ] Manual Reboot
    Select ***F2_Begin Installation***

The installation of the OS core is relatively quick. You will be informed about the installation status during this time. Do not set the root password when asked for (upon the automatic reboot) — just hit *Return* twice.

NOTE: Do not assume that the system modifies NVRAM to boot from this partition permanently! All required modifications will be done manually.

27. Log in to the system and set a workable environment.
28. Set NVRAM
    For the proper system booting from the alternate boot partition the NVRAM must be modified in the following way:
    Check the contents of following NVRAM locations: "*use-nvramrc?*" and "*nvramrc.*"
    Type: "***eeprom***"
    If needed, modify:
    eeprom use-nvramc? = true
    eeprom nvramrc = "*...whatever was written...*
    devalias altboot hw_path_for_this_disk:d"
    where "*hw_path_for_this_disk*" must be properly specified!
29. Test everything by rebooting the system with the primary and the alternate boot partition.

For primary partition type:	***reboot***
or:	***halt***
	ok > ***boot***
For alternate partition type:	***reboot -- altboot***
or:	***halt***
	ok > ***boot altboot***

28.3.2 Solaris Recovery of the Failed Mirrored Boot Disk

The following procedure refers to the Solaris system recovery when one of the mirrored boot disks fails, and the implemented Disk Manager is "***DiskSuite 4.1.***" The procedure itself is sufficiently general for many different hardware configurations.

The tested configuration consisted of two SCSI disks:

c0t3do -> prime boot disk
c0t1d0 -> mirrored disk

The test included removal of the prime boot disk, and the system power recycling. Afterward, the disk was returned into the system.

root (/)	mirror d10 -> d11 (c0t3d0s0) & d12	(c0t1d0s0)
swap	mirror d20 -> d21 (c0t3d0s1) & d22	(c0t1d0s1)
/altboot (ufs)	mirror d30 -> d31 (c0t3d0s3) & d32	(c0t1d0s3)
dedicated partitions (slices) c0t3d0s7 and c0t1d0s7 are used for metadevice database replicas (each for three replicas)		

The system was shut down, and the prime boot disk taken out. The system was rebooted again with a single disk (mirrored boot disk). A number of warning and error messages were displayed during the system startup (mostly related to the "read-only or missing files"). The system has required maintenance -> single-user mode!

The System Recovery

1. Bring the system into the single-user mode, enter the root password.
2. Remove metadevice db replicas from the "broken" disk (the quotes are used because the disk was not really broken!):
   cd /usr/opt/SUNWmd/sbin
   Check the current status — should be six replicas:
   ./ metadb
   Remove replicas:
   ./ metadb -d c0t3dos7
   Check again — should be three replicas:
   ./ metadb
3. Unmirror (detach) all mirrors — must be done forcibly:
   $> metadetach -f d10 d11
   d10: Submirror d11 is detached
   $> metadetach -f d20 d21
   d20: Submirror d21 is detached
   $> metadetach -f d30 d31
   d30: Submirror d31 is detached
   Keep in mind that concats/submirrors d11, d21, and d31 belong to the "broken" disk — prime root disk (c0t3d0); otherwise should be d12, d22, and d32. Reboot the system, type: ***reboot.***
4. The system should boot into multiuser mode with a single disk; everything appears to be correct. Log in as root. To check the status:
   metastat The concats/submirrors from the broken disk (in this case d11, d21, and d31) need maintenance
5. Reinstall the disk.
   Power-off the system.
   $> poweroff
   or
   $> halt
   ok power-off
   Return (reinstall) the disk and power-on the system.
6. Recreate database replicas.
   Log in as root.
   Check the current status — should be three replicas:
   metadb
   Add three more replicas for the returned disk:
   metadb -a -c 3 c0t3dos7
   Check again — should be six replicas:
   metadb
   Check the status of metadevices:
   metastat
   Reboot the system:
   reboot -- disk1

7. Remirror disks.
   Check the status of db replicas:
   metadb
   Mirror (reattach) concats/submirrors:
   $> metattach d10 d11
   d10: Submirror d11 is attached
   $> metattach d20 d21
   d20: Submirror d21 is attached
   $> metattach d30 d31
   d30: Submirror d31 is attached
8. Check for completion of mirroring (recycling). To check the status of mirroring (recycling) type:
   metastat
9. Reboot the system when recycling is complete:
   reboot

Disk Replacement — If the mirrored disk is broken, this disk must be replaced (this is the most probable case), and the new empty disk must be prepared for mirroring. Supposing three partitions with root filesystem *"/"*, ***swap,*** and additional filesystem ***/altboot,*** the procedure to replace and remirror the disk is:

1. Partition the disk *c0t3d0* to match the boot disk *c0t1d0.* Use ***format*** utility.
2. Type: ***format***
   Select the boot disk: ***c0t1d0***
   Type: ***partition*** *("p" is sufficient)*
   Type: ***print*** *("p" is sufficient)* — *to see current root partitioning*
   Type: ***quit*** *("q" is sufficient)*
   Type: ***disk*** — *to select the new disk "c0t3d0"*
   Type: ***partition***
   Create all partitions as on the root disk
   Type: ***label*** — *to save a new partitioning table into the disk*
   Ready to label disk, continue? ***y***
3. Create "state database replicas" in a new disk (pay attention to identify the partition/slice "s7"):
   metadb -a -c 3 c0t3d0s7
   Three additional db replicas will be created in a dedicated slice "s7" of the new disk. To check created db replicas:
   metadb
4. Reboot the system — type: ***reboot.***
5. Mirror root filesystem.
   Create the *concat/submirror d11:*
   $> ***metainit -f d11 1 1 c0t3d0s0***
   d11: Concat/Stripe is setup
   Attach *concat/submirror "d11"* to the mirror *d10:*
   $> ***metattach d10 d11***
   d10: Submirror d11 is attached
   Mirroring itself will take awhile!
6. Mirror swap.
   Create the *concat/submirror d21:*
   $> ***metainit -f d21 1 1 c0t3d0s1***
   d21: Concat/Stripe is setup
   Attach *concat/submirror d21* to the mirror *d20:*
   $> ***metattach d20 d21***
   d20: Submirror d21 is attached
   Mirroring itself will take awhile!
7. Mirror /altboot.
   Create the *concat/submirror d31:*
   $> ***metainit -f d31 1 1 c0t3d0s3***
   d31: Concat/Stripe is setup
   Attach *concat/submirror "d31"* to the mirror *d30:*
   $> ***metattach d30 d31***
   d30: Submirror d31 is attached
   Mirroring itself will take awhile!

8. Check for completion of mirroring (recycling). To check the status of mirroring (recycling) type:
   metastat
9. Reboot the system when recycling is complete:
   reboot

28.3.3 HP-UX Support Disk Usage

HP-UX allows system startup from the support CD disk, which can be very convenient for some emergency situations.

1. Insert CD "HP-UX Support Disk" into CD drive.
2. Power-on the system.
3. At main menu prompt enter:
   Main Menu: Enter command or menu > ***boot 56/52.2.0*** (an example for CD HW path)
   Respond to the question:
   Interact with IPL (Y or N)? > ***y***
   booting...
   At ISL prompt enter:
   ISL > 800 Support
4. The system continues booting from the Support CD disk (although some messages refer to Support Tape)
   ...
   Boot
   :disk (56/52.2.0:0); ERECOVERY
   ...
   ...
   Welcome to the HP-UX recovery process!
   [Run a Recovery Shell]
   [Cancel and Reboot]
   [Help]
   Select and enter: ***Run a Recovery Shell***
5. Respond to the question:
   Would you like to startup networking at this time? [n] ***n*** (or just Enter)
6. Following messages are displayed:
   HP-UX SUPPORT MEDIA
   WARNING: YOU ARE SUPERUSER !!
   NOTE: Commands residing in the RAM-based file system are unsupported 'mini' commands. These commands are only intended for recovery purposes.
   Loading commands needed for recovery!
   WARNING: If ANYTHING is changed on a root (/) that is mirrored a "maintenance mode" (HPUX -lm) boot MUST be done in order to force the mirrored disk to be updated.
7. At the end, the support main menu is displayed:
   SUPPORT MEDIA MAIN MENU
   s Search for a file
   b Reboot
   l Load a file
   r Recover an unbootable HP-UX system
   x Exit to shell
   c Instructions on chrooting to lvm /(root)
8. Enter "***c***" to see "chroot" instuctions:
   Exit to the shell and run '***chroot_lvmdisk***'
9. Follow these instructions; enter "***x***"
   Support# ***chroot_lvmdisk***
   Enter the hardware path associated with the '/' (ROOT) file system (example: 56/52.6.0)
   *Enter "**56/52.6.0**" or "**56/52.5.0**", depending on selected boot disk.*
   The selected root FS is checked...
   ...
   Mounting c2t6d0s1lvm to the Support Tape's /ROOT directory...
   ...
   Finally the system root FS is mounted onto "/ROOT"

10. To remount the system's root filesystem, and start Bourne shell, enter:
    cd /ROOT ; chroot /ROOT /sbin/sh
    The system's root filesystem is mounted onto "/" (the "*/stand*" filesystem is also mounted). Other filesystems could be mounted manually, as well as any UNIX command executed (including a filesystem check) from the command line.
11. To return to *Support shell*, enter ***exit***.
12. To return to *SUPPORT MEDIA MAIN MENU*, enter ***exit***.
13. To reboot the system, in the *SUPPORT MEDIA MAIN MENU*, enter ***b***.
    NOTE: System rebooting...
    ...
    ...
    Regular rebooting process continues...

28.3.4 HP-UX Procedure to Synchronize a Mirrored Logical Volume

The data in a mirrored copy, or copies, of a logical volume could become "out of sync" or "stale" (for example as a result of disk power failure, or a replacement of a disk). In such cases, to reestablish identical data, synchronization must occur. This procedure refers to HP9000 Series 700/800 computer systems.

Automatic Synchronization — When a nonactive volume group is activated, either automatically at boot time or later with the ***vgchange*** command, LVM automatically synchronizes the mirrored copies of all logical volumes within the volume group, replacing data in physical extents marked as "*stale*" with data from "*nonstale*" extents. Otherwise, no automatic synchronization occurs and manual synchronization is necessary.

LVM also automatically synchronizes mirrored data in the following cases:

- When a disk comes back online after experiencing a power failure
- When a logical volume is extended by increasing the number of mirror copies; then the newly added physical extents will be synchronized

Manual Synchronization

1. Check the status of a logical volume, to see if it contains any stale data:
   lvdisplay -v /dev/vg02/lvol3
   Identify which disk contains the stale physical extents.
2. To synchronize manually the data in one or more logical volumes (an example):
   lvsync /dev/vg02/lvol3
3. To synchronize manually the data in all logical volumes in one or more volume groups (an example):
   vgsync /dev/vg02

Disk Replacement

1. Save the volume group configuration data (an example):
   vgcfgbackup /dev/vg02
   By default the configuration data are saved in */etc/lvmconf/vg02.conf*.
2. Remove the broken disk from the volume group by using (an example):
   vgreduce /dev/vg02 /dev/dsk/c1t3d0
3. Physically disconnect and replace the broken disk.

4. Restore saved LVM configuration data to the replaced disk (an example):

   vgchange -a n /dev/vg02

   vgcfgrestore -n /dev/vg02 /dev/dsk/c1t3d0

   The volume group must be first deactivated, and then configuration data restored from the default backed-up file */etc/vmconf/vg02.conf.*

5. Reactivate the volume group (an example):

   vgchange -a y /dev/vg02

6. Manually synchronize all the extents in the volume group (an example):

   vgsync /dev/vg02

28.3.5 HP-UX Support Tape and Recovery of Root Disk

HP-UX provides a powerful way for recovery of a corrupted or broken root disk. A special procedure allows a transfer of the content of the root disk onto the tape, and a creation of the bootable support tape. In the critical situations when the root disk is broken or corrupted, the system could be started from the support tape and its content now transferred back to the disk. There is no need for OS reinstallation and later root recovery, a previously copied root disk is simply recreated.

This procedure is described in the following text. Pay attention to the specified hardware paths for the root disk and the tape specific to this example. The HP-UX specific Support Media Tool COPYUTIL is used. The first part describes the procedure to create the support tape, while the second one describes disk recovery. The support tape could be a good replacement for mirroring of the root disk.

Part One — How to Create a Support Tape — The ***COPYUTIL*** utility could be found on the SUPPORT CD. The system must be booted from the SUPPORT CD to use the ***COPYUTIL.***

1. Booting the system from the SUPPORT CD:
   Log in as ***root***
   Reboot the system
     shutdown -r -y 0
   Follow messages on the console, until the system displays:
       .....
     To override, press any key within 10 seconds.
   Hit any key!
   After the message: "*Boot terminated,*" the main menu will be displayed:
     Insert SUPPORT CD into CD Drive
     At the main menu prompt, type:
       Main Menu: Enter command or menu > ***boot 10/12/5.2.0*** [hardware path for CD Drive]
     Follow messages and enter corresponding responses:
       Interact with IPL (Y or N)? > ***y***
       Booting...
       ISL > ***ode***
       ODE > ***ls***   *to list available utilities*
       ODE > ***copyutil***
2. Since ***COPYUTIL*** checked for available devices, a list of all devices found will be displayed. Depending on the system hardware configuration, it could be done in two steps: first, the SCSI busses only, and then devices (upon the selection [all]). In this example:

T 0	*10/12/5.0.0*	*HPC1533A/C1 530B tape drive (internal)*
D 1	*10/0.6.0*	*SEAGATE ST15150W disk drive (root disk)*
D 2	*10/0.5.0*	*SEAGATE ST15150W disk drive (another disk)*
		.....
		.....
T 11	*10/4/16.3.0*	*HPC1533A/C 1530B tape drive (external)*

3. *COPYUTIL > **backup***
   *Enter the Disk index ([q]/?): **1*** root disk
   *Enter the Tape index ([q]/?): **0*** internal tape drive
   or, you can use the external tape drive: index 11
   Depending on the existing tape drive, an additional question could be displayed:
   *Use data compression? (y/[n]? **n*** do not use compression
   ** Please Load into Tape Drive, Tape Volume 0 for Backup.*
   If you have to, you may safely remove the SUPPORT MEDIA now.
   At this point, eject the SUPPORT CD from the CD drive
4. Continue the procedure:
   *Ready to continue ([y]/n/q/?): **y***
   Checking for the beginning of tape: DONE
   ....10% completed
   ....20% completed
   ....30% completed
   ....40% completed
   ....50% completed
   ....60% completed
   ....70% completed
   ....80% completed
   ....90% completed
   ....100% completed
   End of BACKUP
   Please wait while I rewind the tape
   Depending on the size of the disk tape capacity, a single tape might not be sufficient. The system asks for another tape by repeating the menu. It is easy to figure out when 100% is completed.
   *COPYUTIL > **exit***
   Replace the SUPPORT MEDIA now, if you removed it earlier.
   At this point, close the CD drive with the SUPPORT CD.
5. Exit
   *ODE > **exit*** to return ISL prompt
   ISL >
   Note: The system was booted from the SUPPORT CD; at this point we can power-cycle (power off and on) the system, or continue with bringing the system into the recovery mode (recommended):
   *ISL > **800SUPPORT***
6. Once the system reaches the recovery menu (it takes some time) select:
   [Cancel and Reboot]
   NOTE: System rebooting
   The full test of the system is performed, so it takes awhile!
7. The regular system startup continues.
8. Labeling the support tape
   The COPYUTIL tape/tapes of the root disk are ready. They could be used for the recovery (restore) of the root disk, if necessary. Label them as: *"Hostname: COPYUTIL# of Root Disk."*

Part Two — How to Recover (Restore) the Root Disk from the "COPYUTIL Tape"

9. The system recovery procedure is similar to the preparation of the support tape.
   The differences are:
   Now the source media is a tape.
   Now the destination media is a disk.
   The ***COPYUTIL*** utility could be found only on the SUPPORT CD. The system must be booted from the SUPPORT CD to use the ***COPYUTIL.***
10. Booting the system from the SUPPORT CD:
    Power-on (reset) the system
    Follow messages on the console, until the system displays:
    . . . . .
    To override, press any key within 10 seconds.
    Hit any key.
    After the message: "Boot terminated," the main menu will be displayed:
    Insert SUPPORT CD into CD Drive.

At the main menu prompt, type:

Main Menu: Enter command or menu > ***boot 10/12/5.2.0*** *[hardware path for CD Drive]*

Follow messages and enter corresponding responses:

Interact with IPL (Y or N)? > ***y***
Booting…
ISL> ***ode***
ODE> ***ls*** to list available utilities
ODE> ***copyutil***

Because ***COPYUTIL*** checked for available devices, a list of all found devices will be displayed. This can be done in two steps, first, the SCSI busses only, and then the devices.

T 0 10/12/5.0.0 HPC1533A/C1 530B tape drive (internal
D 1 10/0.6.0 SEAGATE ST15150W disk drive (root disk)
D 2 10/0.5.0 SEAGATE ST15150W disk drive (another disk)
. . . . .
. . . . .
T 11 10/4/16.3.0 HPC1533A/C1530B tape drive (external)

11. *COPYUTIL >* ***restore:***
    Enter the Tape index ([q]/?): 0 internal tape drive
    Enter the Disk index ([q]/?): 1 root disk

    or, you can use the external tape drive: index 11.

    Depending on the existing tape drive, an additional question could be displayed:

    Use data compression? (y/[n]?) ***n*** do not use compression
    ** Please Load into Tape Drive, Tape Volume 0 (or the Desired Tape).*
    If you have to, you may safely remove the SUPPORT MEDIA now.

    At this point, eject the SUPPORT CD from the CD drive.
12. Continue procedure:
    Ready to continue ([y]/n/q/?): ***y***
    Checking for the beginning of tape: DONE
    ……….10% completed
    ……….20% completed
    ……….30% completed
    ……….40% completed
    ……….50% completed
    ……….60% completed
    ……….70% completed
    ……….80% completed
    ……….90% completed
    ……….100% completed
    Restored Successful.
    COPYUTIL> ***exit***
    Replace the SUPPORT MEDIA now, if you removed it earlier.

    At this point, close the CD drive with the SUPPORT CD.
13. Exit.
    ODE> ***exit*** to return ISL prompt
    ISL> ***800SUPPORT***

    Note: The system was booted from the SUPPORT CD; at this point it can be power-cycled (power off and on), or brought into the recovery mode in this way!

    Once the system reaches the Recovery Menu (it takes some time) select:

    [Cancel and Reboot]
    NOTE: System rebooting

    The full test of the system is performed, so it takes awhile!
14. The regular system startup continues.

Recommended Reading

UNIX — General, Shells, Programming

Abrahams, Paul W. *UNIX for the Impatient* (2nd ed.). Reading, MA: Addison-Wesley, 1996.
Anderson, Gail et al. *The UNIX C Shell Field Guide*. Englewood Cliffs, NJ: Prentice Hall, 1986.
Black-Elderman, David N. *Perl for System Administration*. Sebastopol, CA: O'Reilly & Associates, 2000.
Cameron, Debra et al. *Learning GNU Emacs* (2nd ed.). Sebastopol, CA: O'Reilly & Associates, 1996.
Christiansen, Tom et al. *Perl Cookbook*. Sebastopol, CA: O'Reilly & Associates, 1999.
Cutler, Ellie et al. *SCO UNIX in a Nutshell*. Sebastopol, CA: O'Reilly & Associates, 1994.
Dougherty, Dale et al. *sed & awk* (2nd ed.). Sebastopol, CA: O'Reilly & Associates, 1997.
Dubois, Paul. *Using csh and tcsh*. Sebastopol, CA: O'Reilly & Associates, 1995.
Gilly, Daniel et al. *UNIX in a Nutshell*. Sebastopol, CA: O'Reilly & Associates, 1992.
Guelich, Scott et al. *CGI Programming with Perl* (2nd ed.). Sebastopol, CA: O'Reilly & Associates, 2000.
Gunter, David et al. *Windows NT & UNIX Integration Guide*. Berkeley, CA: Osborne/McGraw-Hill, 1997.
Kochan, Stephen G. et al. UNIX Shell Programming (Rev. ed.). Carmel, IN: Hayden Books, 1990.
Lamb, Linda et al. *Learning the vi Editor* (6th ed.). Sebastopol, CA: O'Reilly & Associates, 1998.
Lowell, Jay Arthur. *UNIX Shell Programming* (2nd ed.). New York, NY: John Wiley & Sons, Inc., 1990.
Newham, Cameron et al. *Learning the bash* (2nd ed.). Sebastopol, CA: O'Reilly & Associates, 1998.
Pearce, Eric. *Windows NT & UNIX Integration — from a UNIX Perspective*. Sebastopol, CA: O'Reilly & Associates, 1998.
Peek, Jerry et al. *Learning the UNIX Operating System* (4th ed.). Sebastopol, CA: O'Reilly & Associates, 1997.
Robbins, Arnold. *UNIX in a Nutshell; System V* (3rd ed.). Sebastopol, CA: O'Reilly & Associates, 1999.
Rosenblatt, Bill. *Learning the Korn Shell*. Sebastopol, CA: O'Reilly & Associates, 1994.
Schwartz, Randal L. et al. *learning Perl* (2nd ed.). Sebastopol, CA: O'Reilly & Associates, 1997.
Siever, Ellen et al. *Linux in a Nutshell* (3rd ed.). Sebastopol, CA: O'Reilly & Associates, 2000.
Sobel, Mark G. *SunOS and BSD: A Practical Guide to the UNIX System* (3rd ed.). Redwood City, CA: The Benjamin/Cummings Publishing Company, 1995.
Wall, Larry et al. *Programming Perl* (2nd ed.). Sebastopol, CA: O'Reilly & Associates, 1996.
Wilson, James. *Berkley UNIX: A Simple and Comprehensive Guide*. New York, NY: John Wiley & Sons, Inc., 1991.

UNIX — Basic Administration

Barrett, Daniel J. et al. *SSH, The Secure Shell: The Definitive Guide*. Sebastopol, CA: O'Reilly & Associates, 2001.
Eckstein, Robert. *Using Samba*. Sebastopol, CA: O'Reilly & Associates, 1999.
Frish, Aeleen. *Essential System Administration* (2nd ed.). Sebastopol, CA: O'Reilly & Associates, 1995.

Garfinkel, Simson et al. *Practical UNIX Security* (2nd ed.). Sebastopol, CA: O'Reilly & Associates, 1996.
Gast, Matthew et al. *Network Printing*. Sebastopol, CA: O'Reilly & Associates, 2000.
Kaplenk, Joe. *UNIX System Administrator's Interactive Workbook.* Upper Saddle River, NJ: Prentice Hall PTR, 1999.
Lehey, Greg. *Porting UNIX Software — From Download to Debug*. Sebastopol, CA: O'Reilly & Associates, 1995.
Nemet, Evi et al. *UNIX System Administration Handbook* (3rd ed.). Upper Saddle River, NJ: Prentice Hall PTR, 2001.
Oram, Andrew et al. *Managing Projects with make* (2nd ed.). Sebastopol, CA: O'Reilly & Associates, 1991.
Preston, Curtis W. *UNIX Backup and Recovery.* Sebastopol, CA: O'Reilly & Associates, 1999.
Peek, Jerry et al. *UNIX Power Tools* (2nd ed.). Sebastopol, CA: O'Reilly & Associates, 1997.
Strang, John et al. *termcap & terminfo* (3rd ed.). Sebastopol, CA: O'Reilly & Associates, 1988.
Welsh, Matt et al. *Running Linux* (3rd ed.). Sebastopol, CA: O'Reilly & Associates, 1999.

UNIX — Networking

Albitz, Paul et al. *DNS and BIND* (4th ed.). Sebastopol, CA: O'Reilly & Associates, 2001.
Alcott, Neall. *DHCP for Windows 2000*. Sebastopol, CA: O'Reilly & Associates, 2001.
Charlie, Scott et al. *Virtual Private Networks* (2nd ed.). Sebastopol, CA: O'Reilly & Associates, 1998.
Checkwick, William R. et al. *Firewalls and Internet Security* (2nd ed.). Reading, MA: Addison-Wesley, 2000.
Comer, Douglas E. et al. *Internetworking with TCP/IP* (3rd ed.). Upper Saddle River, NJ: Prentice Hall, 1999.
Costales, Bryan et al. *sendmail* (2nd ed.). Sebastopol, CA: O'Reilly & Associates, 1997.
Cutler, Ellie et al. *The X Window System in a Nutshell*. Sebastopol, CA: O'Reilly & Associates, 1992.
Hall, Eric. *Internet Core Protocols: The Definitive Guide*. Sebastopol, CA: O'Reilly & Associates, 2000.
Hunt, Craig. *TCP/IP Network Administration* (2nd ed.). Sebastopol, CA: O'Reilly & Associates, 1998.
Hunt, Craig et al. *Windows NT TCP/IP Network Administration*. Sebastopol, CA: O'Reilly & Associates, 1998.
Kirch, Olaf et al. *Linux Network Administrator's Guide* (2nd ed.). Sebastopol, CA: O'Reilly & Associates, 2000.
Larson, Matt et al. *DNS on Windows 2000* (2nd ed.). Sebastopol, CA: O'Reilly & Associates, 2001.
Laurie, Ben et al. *Apache: The Definitive Guide* (2nd ed.). Sebastopol, CA: O'Reilly & Associates, 1999.
Mui, Linda et al. *X Window System Administrator's Guide*. Sebastopol, CA: O'Reilly & Associates, 1993.
Peek, Jerry. *MH & xmh — E-mail for Users & Programmers*. Sebastopol, CA: O'Reilly & Associates, 1993.
Stern, Hal et al. *Managing NFS and NIS* (2nd ed.). Sebastopol, CA: O'Reilly & Associates, 2001.
Stevens, Richard W. *TCP/IP Illustrated, Volume 1: The Protocols*. Reading, MA: Addison-Wesley, 1994.
Stevens, Richard W. *UNIX Network Programming*. Englewood Cliffs, NJ: Prentice Hall, 1990.
Tanenbaum, Andrew. *Computer Network* (3rd ed.). Upper Saddle River, NJ: Prentice Hall, 1996.
Zwicky, Elizabeth D. et al. *Building Internet Firewalls* (2nd ed.). Sebastopol, CA: O'Reilly & Associates, 2000.

UNIX — Kernel, Performances, Internals, Advanced

Beck, Michael et al. *Linux Kernel Internals.* Reading, MA: Addison-Wesley, 1997.
Bloomer, John. *Power Programming with RPC.* Sebastopol, CA: O'Reilly & Associates, 1992.

Bovet, Daniel P. et al. *Understanding the Linux Kernel.* Sebastopol, CA: O'Reilly & Associates, 2000.

Cockroft, Adrian et al. *Sun Performance and Tuning: Java and the Internet.* Upper Saddle River, NJ: Prentice Hall, 1998.

Curry, David A. *Using C on the UNIX System.* Sebastopol, CA: O'Reilly & Associates, 1991.

Curry, David A. *UNIX System Programming for SVR4.* Sebastopol, CA: O'Reilly & Associates, 1996.

Goodheart, Berny et al. *The Magic Garden Explained: The Internal of UNIX SVR4.* Prentice Hall of Australia, 1994.

Loukides, Mike. *System Performance Tuning.* Sebastopol, CA: O'Reilly & Associates, 1990.

McKusick, Marshal Kirk et al. *The Design and Implementation of the 4.4BSD Operating System.* Reading, MA: Addison-Wesley, 1996.

Pate, Steve D. *UNIX Internals: A Practical Approach.* Harlow, England: Addison-Wesley Longman, 1996.

Rubini, Alessandro et al. *Linux Device Drivers* (2nd ed.). Sebastopol, CA: O'Reilly & Associates, 2001.

Stevens, Richard W. *Advanced Programming in the UNIX Environment.* Reading, MA: Addison-Wesley, 1993.

Wong, Brian L. *Configuration and Capacity Planning for Solaris Servers.* Mountain View, CA: Sun Microsystems Press, 1997.

Index

E

F

G

H

I

J

K

L

M

N

O

P

Q

R

T

U

V

W

X

Y

Z